Western Europe

Ireland p386
Britain p108
The Netherlands p502
Germany p260
Belgium & Luxembourg p72
France p180
Switzerland p638
Austria p38
Italy p420
Portugal p528
Spain p564
Greece p336

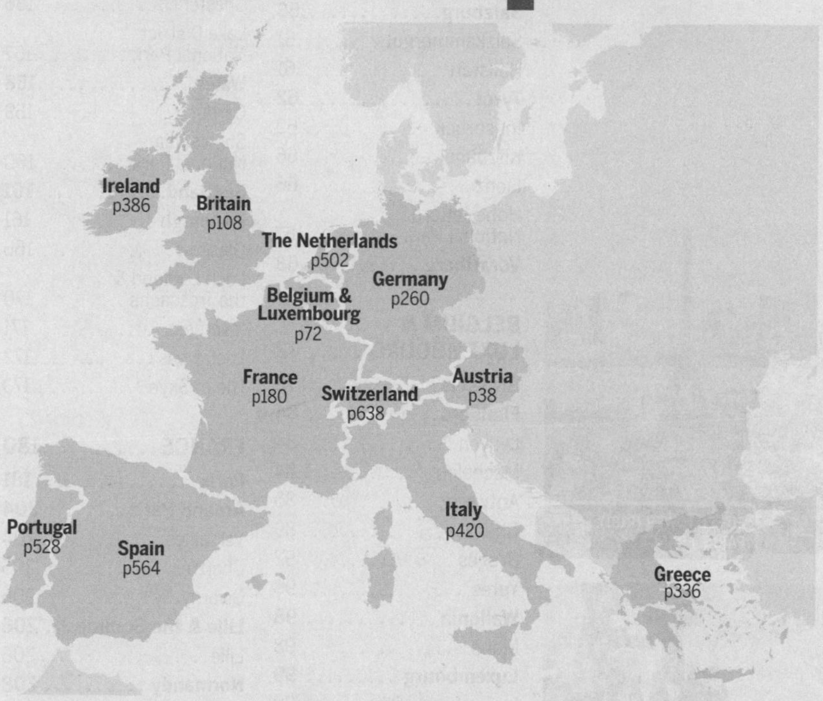

Oliver Berry, Gregor Clark, Marc Di Duca, Duncan Garwood, Catherine Le Nevez … Andy Sym… …nan

PLAN YOUR TRIP

EIFFEL TOWER (P181), PARIS, FRANCE

ALXPIN / GETTY IMAGES ©

BAGPIPE PLAYER, EDINBURGH (P161), SCOTLAND

BRENDAN HOWARD / SHUTTERSTOCK ©

ON THE ROAD

Contents

ON THE ROAD

SANTORINI (P360), GREECE

Contents

SURVIVAL GUIDE

Welcome to Western Europe

Interlocking countries and cultures create a jigsaw of history, art, architecture and cuisines, along with time-honoured traditions and inspired new trends.

Living History

In Western Europe, history is all around you: in prehistoric Cro-Magnon caves, in otherworldly passage tombs and stone circles, in the tumbledown remains of Greek temples and Roman bathhouses, in ostentatious chateaux and palaces where power was wielded and geopolitical boundaries were shaped and reshaped, in the winding streets and broad boulevards of the many stately cities, and at poignant sites including the D-Day beaches and the remnants of the Berlin Wall. Understanding Europe's history is a vital part of figuring out what makes these countries what they are today, both individually and as part of a greater whole.

Extraordinary Art & Architecture

An architectural heritage spanning seven millenniums has given rise to iconic, instantly recognisable landmarks, from Rome's Colosseum to Cologne's cathedral, London's Big Ben and Paris' Eiffel Tower, along with sky-scraping contemporary additions. This expressive environment is inextricably tied to Western Europe's artistic legacy. The home turf of virtuosos from Michelangelo to Monet, Botticelli to Banksy continues to inspire boundary-pushing new artists.

Thriving Culture

Distinct cultures, defined by their language, customs, specialities, idiosyncrasies, sense of style and way of life, make Western Europe an endlessly fascinating place to travel. Along country borders in particular, you can see where cultures intertwine and overlap. You'll also see subtle cultural shifts between each country's own regions, and the influence of trade and immigration over the centuries. Wherever you travel, allow time to soak up local life in public squares, parks and gardens, vibrant festivals, and in neighbourhood pubs and cafes where you can watch the world go by.

Celebrated Food & Drink

Eating and drinking is celebrated with gusto in Western Europe. Every country has its own unique flavours, incorporating olive oils and sun-ripened vegetables in the hot south, rich cream and butter in cooler areas, fresh-off-the-boat seafood along the coast, delicate river and lake fish, and meat from fertile mountains and pastures. Each country has its own tipples too, spanning renowned wines, beers, stouts and ciders, and feistier firewater including aperitifs and digestifs. One of the best ways to whet your appetite is to browse vibrant street markets laden with seasonal produce.

Why I Love Western Europe

By Catherine Le Nevez, Writer

I love that you only have to travel a short distance in Western Europe to find yourself in a completely different environment. From the language, streetscapes, street food, music and fashion to the climate, topography and spectacular landscapes, as well as the rhythm of daily life, there's an astonishing diversity in this compact area that's easily accessible thanks to its fantastic transport network. What I love most, though, isn't the countries' differences but the similarities that unite them – above all, a passion for the quality of life here and a community spirit that transcends individual borders.

For more about our writers, see p704

Above: Colosseum (p422), Rome, Italy

Western Europe

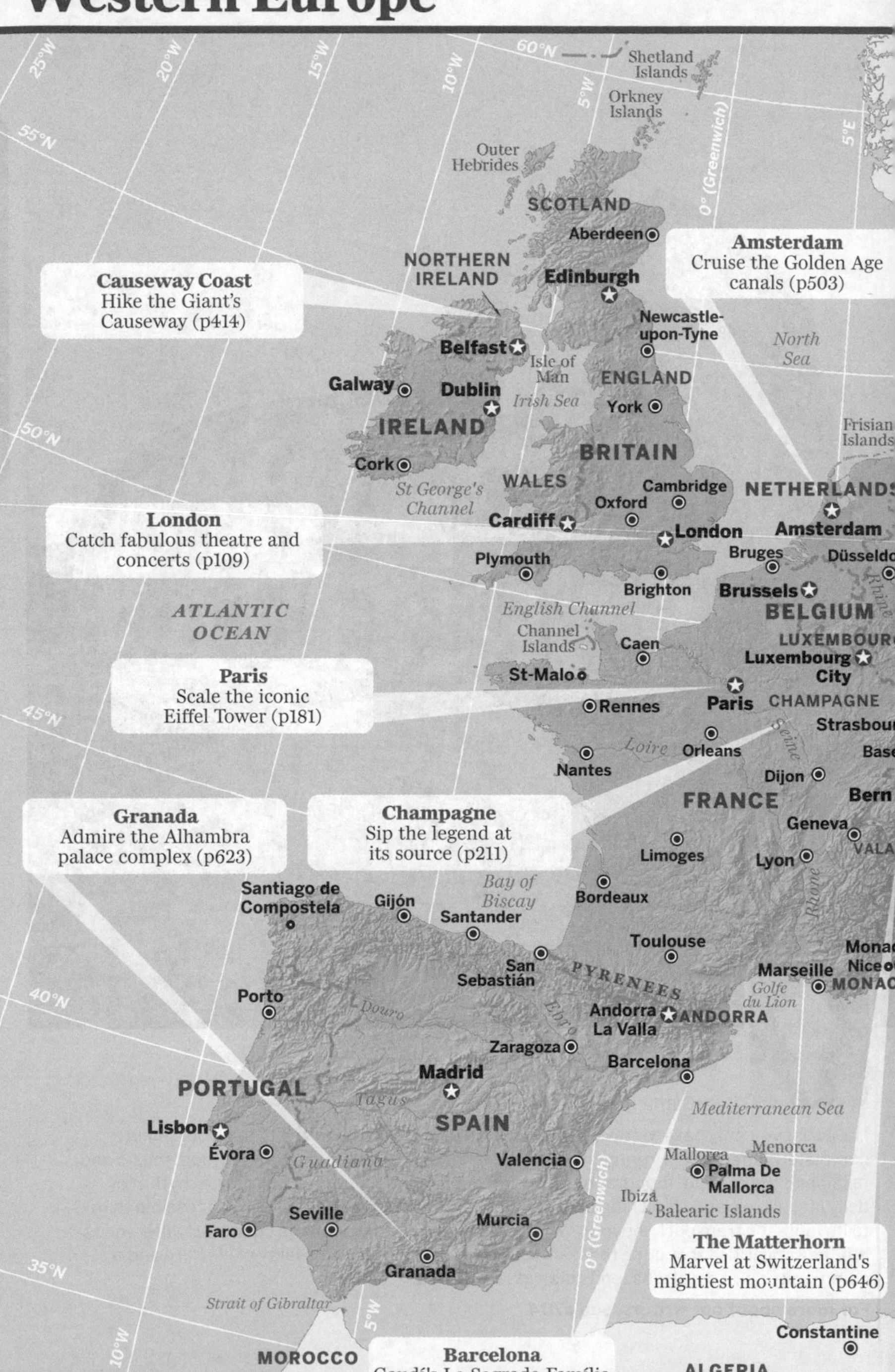

0
1,000 km
0
500 miles
Berlin
Learn about the infamous Wall (p261)
Munich
Beer halls and beer gardens (p285)
Vienna
Imperial Vienna's architectural legacy dazzles (p39)
Venice
Romantic waterways and exceptional art (p453)
Rome
Survey the Palatino's evocative ruins (p422)
Tuscany
Vineyards bathed in golden light (p464)
Santorini
Whitewashed island with spectacular sunsets (p360)
FINLAND
Helsinki
St Petersburg
Åland
60°N
Tallinn
Oslo
Stockholm
ESTONIA
Saaremaa
Moscow
LATVIA
SWEDEN
Gotland
Rīga
RUSSIA
Baltic Sea
Öland
DENMARK
LITHUANIA
BELARUS
Copenhagen
Vilnius
RUSSIA
Zealand
Bornholm
Kaliningrad
Minsk
Stralsund
POLAND
Schwerin
Odra
Elbe
Berlin
Warsaw
UKRAINE
Kiev
Dnieper
Dresden
Erfurt
Frankfurt-am-Main
Prague
CZECH REPUBLIC
SLOVAKIA
CARPATHIAN MOUNTAINS
MOLDOVA
Chişinău
Stuttgart
Bratislava
Munich
Vienna
Budapest
Salzburg
LIECHTENSTEIN
HUNGARY
45°N
Vaduz
AUSTRIA
Black Sea
SLOVENIA
Ljubljana
CROATIA
ROMANIA
Bucharest
Zagreb
Venice
Milan
Po
BOSNIA & HERCEGOVINA
ITALY
Bologna
San Marino
SAN MARINO
Sarajevo
SERBIA
BULGARIA
Pisa
TUSCANY
Perugia
MONTENEGRO
KOSOVO
Priština
Sofiya
İstanbul
Podgorica
Skopje
Sea of Marmara
Elba
Adriatic Sea
MACEDONIA
Ajaccio
Rome
Tirana
APPENINES
Bari
Thessaloniki
ALBANIA
Sassari
Naples
Salerno
Tyrrhenian Sea
Aegean Sea
Lesvos
TURKEY
Ioannina
Corfu
Evia
Cagliari
Aeolian Islands
Ionian Sea
Ionian Islands
Athens
Palermo
Tripoli
GREECE
Cyclades Islands
Sicily
Dodecanese Islands
Tunis
Pantelleria
Syracuse
TUNISIA
MALTA
Valletta
Crete

Western Europe's Top 26

1

Eiffel Tower, Paris

1 Initially designed as a temporary exhibit for the 1889 Exposition Universelle (World Fair), the elegant, webbed-metal art-nouveau design of Paris' Eiffel Tower (p181) has become the defining fixture of the French capital's skyline. Its 1st floor incorporates two glitzy glass pavilions housing interactive history exhibits; outside them, peer d-o-w-n through glass flooring to the ground below. Visit at dusk for the best day and night views of the glittering City of Light, and toast making it to the top at the sparkling Champagne Bar.

Live Music, London

2 Music lovers will hear London calling – from the city's famed theatres, concert halls, nightclubs, pubs and even tube stations, where on any given night countless performers take to the stage. Find your own iconic London experience, whether it's the Proms at the Royal Albert Hall (pictured; p135), an East End singalong around a pub piano, a classic musical in the West End, a superstar-DJ set at one of the city's hottest clubs, or an up-and-coming guitar band at a local boozer.

JAN-OTTO / GETTY IMAGES ©

2

JUSTIN TALLIS / STRINGER / GETTY IMAGES ©

3

4

Ancient Rome

3 Rome's famous 'seven hills' (there are actually nine) offer superb vantage points. The Palatino (pictured; p422) is a gorgeous green expanse of evocative ruins, towering pines and unforgettable views over the Roman Forum, containing the remains of temples, basilicas and public spaces. This was the social, political and commercial hub of the Roman empire, where Romulus supposedly founded the city and where ancient Roman emperors lived in unimaginable luxury. As you walk the cobbled paths you can almost sense the ghosts in the air.

Venice

4 There's something especially atmospheric about Venice on a sunny winter's day. With far fewer tourists around and the light sharp and clear, it's the perfect time to lap up the magical atmosphere of the romantic waterways. Wander Dorsoduro's shadowy back lanes while imagining secret assignations and whispered conspiracies at every turn. Then linger in one of Venice's top galleries, the Peggy Guggenheim Collection (p455), which houses works by many of the giants of 20th-century art in her palatial canalside former home, Palazzo Venier dei Leoni.

Imperial Vienna

5 Imagine what you could do with unlimited riches and Austria's top architects at your disposal and you have the Vienna of the Habsburgs. The monumentally graceful Hofburg (pictured; p39) whisks you back to the age of empires as you marvel at the treasury's imperial crowns, the equine ballet of the Spanish Riding School and the chandelier-lit apartments fit for an empress. The palace is rivalled in grandeur only by the 1441-room Schloss Schönbrunn, a Unesco World Heritage site, and the baroque Schloss Belvedere, both set in exquisite landscaped gardens.

Remembering the Berlin Wall

6 Even after nearly three decades, it's hard to comprehend how the Berlin Wall separated the city for 28 years. The best way to examine its role and ramifications is to make your way – on foot or by bike – along the Berlin Wall Trail. Passing the Brandenburg Gate and analysing graffiti at the East Side Gallery (pictured; p268), the world's largest open-air mural collection, the path brings it all into context. It's heartbreaking and hopeful and sombre, but integral to understanding Germany's capital today.

Tuscany

7 Battalions of books, postcards and TV shows try to capture the essence of the enchanting Italian region of Tuscany, but nothing can match experiencing it for yourself. Here, monumental art cities and picture-perfect towns, including its magnificent capital Florence (pictured; p465), as well as tower-famed Pisa and medieval Siena, are filled with Renaissance treasures. They vie for visitors' attention with medieval monasteries and rolling hills ribboned by ancient vineyards bathed in golden light. Also vying for attention is some of Italy's finest food and wine.

Barcelona's La Sagrada Família

8 The brainchild of Antoni Gaudí remains a work in progress close to a century after the architect's death. Wildly fanciful and deeply profound, inspired by nature and barely restrained by a Gothic style, Barcelona's La Sagrada Família (p589) climbs skyward; when completed, the highest tower will be more than half as high as today's. The improbable angles and radical departures from architectural convention confound, but the decorative detail of the Passion and Nativity Facades are worth studying for hours.

7

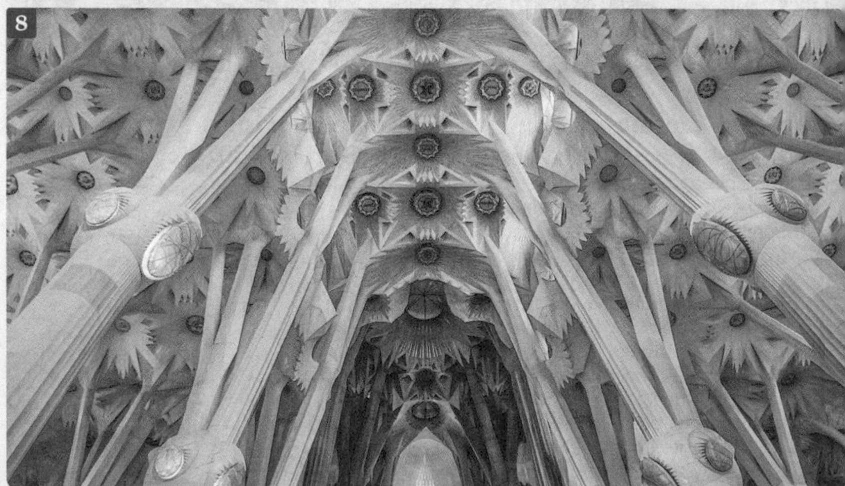
8

9

MARQUES / SHUTTERSTOCK ©

10

11

NIKADA / GETTY IMAGES ©

The Matterhorn

9 It graces Toblerone packages and evokes stereotypical 'Heidi' scenes, but nothing prepares you for the impact of seeing the Matterhorn for yourself. When you arrive at the timber-chalet-filled village of Zermatt (p646), Switzerland's mightiest mountain soars above you, mesmerising you with its chiselled, majestic peak. Gaze at it from a tranquil cafe terrace, hike in its shadow along the tangle of alpine paths above town with cowbells clinking in the distance, or pause on a ski slope to contemplate its sheer size.

Alhambra, Granada

10 In Spain's sultry southern Andalucía region, in the city of Granada, is the Alhambra (p623). The world's most refined example of Islamic art, this palatial World Heritage–listed site is the enduring symbol of 800 years of the Moorish rule of Al-Andalus. The Alhambra's red fortress towers dominate the Granada skyline against the Sierra Nevada's snowcapped peaks, while its geometric Generalife gardens complement the exquisite detail of the Palacio Nazariés, where Arabic inscriptions proliferate in the stucco-work. Put simply, this is Spain's most beautiful monument.

Beer-Drinking in Munich

11 The southern German state of Bavaria is synonymous with brewing and its capital, Munich (the country's third-largest city), has an astounding variety of places to drink. There's the rollicking Oktoberfest festival, of course, and then there are the famous beer halls, from the huge and infamous, such as Hofbräuhaus (p291), complete with oompah bands, to the traditional and wonderful, such as Augustiner Bräustuben, inside the Augustiner brewery, as well as sprawling, high-spirited beer gardens like Chinesischer Turm where you can enjoy a frothy, refreshing stein.

Navigating Amsterdam's Canals

12 The Dutch capital is a watery wonderland. Amsterdam (p503) made its fortune in maritime trade, and its Canal Ring was constructed during the city's Golden Age. Stroll alongside the canals and check out its narrow, gabled houses and houseboats, or relax on a canalside cafe terrace. Or, better still, go for a ride. From boat level you'll see a whole new set of architectural details, such as the ornamentation bedecking the bridges and, come nightfall, glowing lights reflecting in the ripples.

Causeway Coast, Northern Ireland

13 Hiking the Causeway Coast takes you through some of Northern Ireland's most inspiring coastal scenery. Its grand geological centrepiece is the Giant's Causeway, a World Heritage–listed natural wonder incorporating 40,000 hexagonal basalt columns, built by mythical giant Finn McCool to fight his rival Benandonner in Scotland (or, more prosaically, formed by cooling lava 60 million years ago). Another highlight is the Carrick-a-Rede rope bridge (pictured; p414) swaying above the water.

WESTEND61 / GETTY IMAGES ©

SAIKO3P / SHUTTERSTOCK ©

Santorini, Greek Islands

14 On first view, startling Santorini (Thira; p360) grabs your attention and doesn't let go. The submerged caldera, surrounded by lava-layered cliffs topped by villages that look like a sprinkling of icing sugar, is one of nature's great wonders, best experienced by a walk along the clifftops from the main town of Fira to the northern village of Oia. The precariousness and impermanence of the place is breathtaking. Recover from your efforts with Santorini's ice-cold Yellow Donkey beer in Oia as you wait for its famed picture-perfect sunset.

Luxembourg

15 Beyond the gleaming glass banks and high-powered financial centres that help make Luxembourg Europe's wealthiest country, the diminutive Grand Duchy is a picturesque patchwork of undulating fields, thickly wooded hills and deep-cut river valleys. Take in Luxembourg City's extraordinary fortifications along 'Europe's most beautiful balcony', the pedestrian promenade Chemin de la Corniche (p100), which winds along the 17th-century city ramparts. Further afield, Luxembourg's bucolic countryside is strewn with impressive castle ruins.

Greek Antiquity

16 Follow the path of history across Greece's dramatic Mediterranean landscape. From Athens' renowned Acropolis (pictured; p338) to the monastery-crowned rock spires of Meteora, Greece is home to some of Europe's most impressive historical sights, including the oracular Ancient Delphi, perched above the Gulf of Corinth; Olympia, home to the first Olympic Games; Epidavros' acoustically perfect theatre; and the mystical Sanctuary of Asclepius, an ancient healing centre. Olive and orange groves surround the vast ruins of Mystras, once part of the Byzantine Empire.

17

DANYL / SHUTTERSTOCK ©

18

19

Belgium's Beer & Chocolate

17 Belgium has a brew for all seasons, and then some. The range of Belgian beer styles is exceptional, each served in its own special glass. You can sip a selection in timeless cafes, hidden in the atmospheric cores of Belgium's great art cities – Ghent, Bruges, Antwerp and Brussels – with their unique blends of medieval and art nouveau architecture; try Au Bon Vieux Temps (p81) in Brussels. Belgium also has an unparalleled range of chocolate shops selling melt-in-the-mouth pralines incorporating classic and intriguing new flavour combinations.

Slow-Boating the Rhine

18 A boat ride through the romantic Rhine Valley (p310) between Koblenz and Mainz is one of Germany's most memorable experiences. As you sit back on deck, glorious scenery drifts slowly past like a magic lantern: vineyard-clad hills, idyllic riverside towns and, every now and then, a mighty medieval castle. Stop off for a hearty meal, sample a few of the local wines and spend an hour or two wandering around a half-timbered village – the Rhine is a highlight of any Western Europe trip.

Alfama, Lisbon

19 With its labyrinthine alleyways, hidden courtyards and curving, shadow-filled lanes, the Alfama (p530) is a magical place to lose all sense of direction and delve into the soul of the Portuguese capital. On the journey, you'll pass bread-box-sized grocers, brilliantly tiled buildings and cosy taverns filled with easygoing chatter, with the aroma of chargrilled sardines and the mournful rhythms of fado drifting in the breeze. Then you round a bend and catch sight of steeply pitched rooftops leading down to the glittering river, the Tejo.

The Netherlands by Bike

20 The nation (p502) where everyone rides bikes to commute, to shop, to socialise or just for the sheer enjoyment is perfectly designed for cyclists. Much of the landscape is famously below sea level and pancake-flat; you can glide alongside canals, tulip fields and windmills; there are more than 32,000km of dedicated bike paths; rental outlets are everywhere; and except for motorways there's virtually nowhere bicycles can't go. Even if you just take the occasional spin, it will be a highlight of your travels.

Bath

21 Britain has many beautiful cities, but Bath (p142) is the belle of the ball. The Romans built a health resort to take advantage of the steaming-hot water bubbling to the surface here; the springs were rediscovered in the 18th century and Bath became the place to see and be seen in British high society. Today, Bath's Georgian architecture of sweeping crescents, grand town houses, and Palladian mansions (not to mention Roman remains, a beautiful abbey and a 21st-century spa) make the former hometown of novelist Jane Austen a must.

20

21

Chamonix

22 Skiing, mountaineering, trekking, canyoning, rafting, you name it, French mountaineering mecca Chamonix (p226), in the glaciated Mont Blanc massif, has it all and more. Afterwards, toast your triumphs at Chamonix' chic après-ski bars before getting up the next day to tackle the area's outdoor challenges all over again. And even if you're not an adrenalin junkie, year-round you can take the vertiginous Téléphérique de l'Aiguille du Midi cable car from Chamonix to the top of Aiguille du Midi and marvel at the unfolding Alpine scenery.

Champagne, France

23 Name-brand Champagne (p211) houses such as Mumm, Mercier and Moët & Chandon, in the main towns of Reims and Épernay, are known the world over. But what's less well known is that much of Champagne's best liquid gold is made by thousands of small-scale *vignerons* (winemakers) in hundreds of villages. Dozens welcome visitors for a taste and the chance to shop at producers' prices, making the region's scenic driving routes the best way to sample fine bubbly amid rolling vineyards and gorgeous villages.

22

23

THOOM / SHUTTERSTOCK ©

CANADASTOCK / SHUTTERSTOCK ©

Dublin

24 Ireland's capital city contains all the attractions and distractions of an international metropolis, but manages to retain the intimacy and atmosphere of a small town. Whether you're strolling stately St Stephen's Green, viewing prehistoric treasures and Celtic art at the superb National Museum of Ireland – Archaeology, or learning about Ireland's hard-fought path to independence at Kilmainham Gaol (pictured; p389), you're never far from a friendly pub where the craic is flowing. And, of course, you can sink a pint of the black stuff at the original Guinness brewery.

Edinburgh

25 Renowned for its exuberant festivals and especially lively in the summer, Scotland's atmospheric capital, Edinburgh, is also well worth visiting out of season, to see Edinburgh Castle (pictured; p161) silhouetted against the blue spring sky with yellow daffodils gracing the slopes below; to see its graceful gardens strewn with autumnal leaves; or witness fog cloaking the spires of the Old Town, with rain on the cobblestones and a warm glow beckoning from the window of a pub on a chilly winter's day.

Salzburg

26 Salzburg is storybook Austria. A Unesco World Heritage Site with 17th-century cobbled streets, its baroque *Altstadt* (Old Town) looks much as it did when Mozart lived here (his birth house is now a museum, as is his one-time residence), both from ground level and from the 900-year-old Festung Hohensalzburg (pictured; p57) cliff-top fortress high above. For many, this is first and foremost *Sound of Music* country, where you can be whisked into the gorgeous steep hills that are alive with visitors year-round.

Need to Know

For more information, see Survival Guide (p667)

Currency

Euro (€) Austria, Belgium, France, Germany, Greece, Republic of Ireland, Italy, Luxembourg, the Netherlands, Portugal, Spain

Pound (£; also called 'pound sterling') Britain, Northern Ireland

Swiss franc (CHF, also Sfr) Switzerland

Visas

Generally not required for stays of up to 90 days for citizens of most Western countries.

Money

ATMs are widespread. Credit-card use varies by country; Visa and MasterCard are the most widely accepted.

Time

Greenwich Mean Time/UTC Britain, Ireland, Portugal, Canary Islands (Spain)

Central European Time (GMT/UTC plus one hour) Austria, Belgium, France, Germany, Italy, Luxembourg, the Netherlands, Spain (except Canary Islands), Switzerland

Eastern European Time (GMT/UTC plus two hours) Greece

When to Go

High Season (Jun–Aug)

➡ Visitors arrive and Europeans hit the road; prices peak.

➡ Beautiful weather means that everybody is outside at cafes.

➡ Businesses in major cities often have seasonal closures around August.

Shoulder (Apr, May, Sep & Oct)

➡ Moderate weather with frequent bright, clear days.

➡ Almost everything is open.

➡ Considered high season in some places such as Italy's big art cites (Rome, Florence, Venice).

Low Season (Nov–Mar)

➡ Apart from ski resorts and Christmas markets, much is closed in regional areas.

➡ Perfect for enjoying major cities where indoor attractions and venues stay open.

➡ Prices often plummet.

Useful Websites

Lonely Planet (www.lonelyplanet.com/europe) Destination info, hotel bookings, traveller forums and more.

The Man in Seat 61 (www.seat61.com) Comprehensive information about travelling Europe by train.

Ferrylines (www.ferrylines.com) Excellent portal for researching ferry routes and operators throughout Europe.

Michelin (www.viamichelin.com) Calculates the best driving routes and estimates toll and fuel costs.

BBC News (www.bbc.co.uk/news) Find out what's happening before you arrive.

Europa (http://europa.eu) Official website of the EU.

Important Numbers

EU-wide general emergency	☎112
UK general emergency	☎999

Tipping

Adding another 5% to 10% to a bill at a restaurant or cafe for good service is common across Western Europe, although tipping is never expected.

Daily Costs

Budget: Less than €100

- Dorm bed: €20–50
- Double room in budget property per person: €40–65
- Excellent markets; restaurant main under €12
- Local bus/train tickets: €5–10

Midrange: €100–250

- Double room in midrange hotel per person: €65–125
- Restaurant main €12–25
- Museum admission: free–€15
- Short taxi trip: €10–20

Top End: More than €250

- Iconic hotel per person: from €125
- Destination restaurant three-course meal with wine per person: from €65
- Prime tickets to a performance in a grand opera house per person: from €60

What to Take

Phrasebook for rewarding experiences interacting with locals

Earplugs to sleep peacefully in the heart of boisterous culture

Travel plug (adaptor)

Pocket knife with corkscrew as corked wine bottles are the norm; screw caps are rare (just remember to pack it in your checked-in luggage)

Arriving in Western Europe

Major gateway airports in Western Europe include the following:

Schiphol Airport (Amsterdam; p526) Trains (20 minutes) to the centre.

Heathrow Airport (London; p176) Trains (15 minutes) and tube (one hour) to the centre.

Aéroport de Charles de Gaulle (Paris; p202) Many buses (one hour) and trains (30 minutes) to the centre.

Frankfurt Airport (Frankfurt; p309) Trains (15 minutes) to the centre.

Leonardo da Vinci Airport (Fiumicino, Rome; p439) Buses (one hour) and trains (30 minutes) to the centre.

Getting Around

Air Cheap airfares make it easy to fly from one end of the continent to the other.

Bicycle From coasting along the flat Netherlands landscape alongside canals to tackling mountainous trails in Italy, Western Europe is ideal for cycling. Bike-rental outlets abound.

Boat Relax at sea on board ferries between Ireland and Britain, Britain and the continent, Spain and Italy, Italy and Greece.

Car In Britain and Ireland, drive on the left; in continental Europe, drive on the right. Car hire is readily available throughout Western Europe. Non-EU citizens might consider leasing a vehicle, which can work out cheaper.

Train Trains go almost everywhere; they're often fast and usually frequent.

For much more on **getting around**, see p676

If You Like...

Castles & Palaces

Strategically designed castles and vast royal palaces surrounded by extravagant grounds continue to astound visitors.

Château de Versailles Opulence abounds in the palace's shimmering Hall of Mirrors and sumptuous fountained gardens. (p204)

Schloss Neuschwanstein In the heart of the Bavarian Alps, this is everyone's (including Disney's) castle fantasy. (p295)

Conwy Castle With eight defensive towers, this Welsh fortress is what a serious castle should look like. (p160)

Hofburg An imperial spectacle, Vienna's Hofburg exemplifies royal excess. (p39)

Alhambra Spain's exquisite Islamic palace complex in Granada is a World Heritage–listed marvel. (p623)

Gravensteen The counts of Flanders' turreted stone castle looms over the medieval Belgian city of Ghent. (p89)

Kilkenny Castle Majestic riverside castle in the delightful Irish town of Kilkenny. (p397)

Château de Bourscheid Luxembourg's most evocative medieval ruined castle. (p103)

Historic Sites

Western Europe is layered in millennia upon millennia of history that you can explore today.

Stonehenge Britain's most iconic – and mysterious – archaeological site, dating back some 5000 years. (p142)

Pompeii Wander the streets and alleys of this great ancient city, buried by a volcanic eruption. (p485)

Athens Ancient Greek wonders include the Acropolis, Ancient Agora, Temple of Olympian Zeus and more. (p337)

Amsterdam's Canal Ring Stroll the Dutch capital's Golden Age canals lined with gabled buildings. (p503)

Bruges Beautiful Renaissance town in Belgium with gables, canals, bell towers and a beguiling overall harmony. (p92)

Dachau Germany's first Nazi concentration camp is a harrowing introduction to WWII's horrors. (p292)

West Belfast Falls and Shankill Rds are emblazoned with murals expressing local political and religious passions. (p410)

Cultural Cuisine

Every country in Western Europe has its own unique delicacies; these are just a taster.

Spanish tapas Small dishes of every description; cured Iberian ham or a perfect stuffed olive... (p634)

Greek mezedhes Shortened to *meze*, these tasting dishes include *dolmadhes* (stuffed vine leaves) and *oktapodi* (octopus). (p382)

British fish and chips Cod expertly battered, fried and served with chips and quality vinegar is sublime. (p177)

German Wurst Germany has hundreds of varieties of sausages – often the source of great local pride. (p333)

Austrian Wiener schnitzel Made with veal, this tender, breadcrumbed dish is the real deal. (p70)

French bread *Boulangeries* (bakeries) in France turn out still-warm, crusty baguettes and richer treats like buttery croissants.

Dutch cheese The tastiest hard, rich *oud* (old) Gouda varieties have strong, complex flavours. (p526)

Belgian chocolate Buy a box of velvety, extravagant confections.

Top: Spanish tapas

Bottom: Gravensteen castle (p89), Ghent, Belgium

Italian pizza The best are wood-fired, whether Roman (thin crispy base) or Neapolitan (higher, doughier base). (p496)

Portuguese custard tarts Portugal's *pastel de nata* is a must-taste. (p556)

Swiss fondue Dip bread into a bubbling pot of melted Emmental and Gruyère cheese and white wine. (p662)

Beer & Wine

Europe packs a large variety of beer and wine into a small space: virtually every region has at least one signature tipple.

Belgian beer Belgium is famed for its lagers, white beers, abbey beers and monastery-brewed 'Trappist beers'. (p106)

Bordeaux wines Tour the vineyards where some of France's finest reds are produced. (p255)

Champagne Visit century-old cellars to sip France's feted bubbles. (p255)

Portuguese port Enjoy port-wine tastings across the Rio Douro from Porto at Vila Nova da Gaia. (p556)

English ales Served at room temperature, so the flavours – from fruity to bitter – come through. (p177)

Tuscan Chianti The warm burnt-umber colours of the iconic Italian region are palpable in every glass. (p464)

German Riesling This classic white wine is renowned for its quality.

Scotch whisky Have a dram of Scotland's signature distilled spirit aged in oak barrels for three-plus years. (p177)

Cafes & Bars

Whether it's a coffee savoured for an hour or a pint with a roomful of new friends, you'll find plenty of places to imbibe like a local.

Vienna's coffee houses Unchanged in decades and redolent with an air of refinement. (p48)

Irish pubs Guinness' iconic stout tastes best on home turf, expertly hand-pulled in a traditional pub. (p394)

Brussels' bars Historic treasures hidden in alleys around the Bourse serve Belgian beer including spontaneously fermented lambic. (p81)

Parisian cafes Opening on to wicker-chair-strewn terraces, Paris' cafes are the city's communal lounge rooms. (p196)

Dutch brown cafes Cosy, candlelit havens named for the former tobacco stains on the walls. (p510)

Greek tavernas Sip anise-flavoured ouzo in Greece's rustic tavernas. (p343)

Outdoor Fun

Don't just stare at the beautiful scenery, dive right into it, no matter the season.

Strolling the English countryside England's entire countryside seems tailor-made for beautiful, memorable walking. (p174)

Cycling the Netherlands Pedal past the creaking windmills and shimmering canals of the gloriously flat, tulip-filled Dutch countryside. (p517)

Skiing year-round Head to the glaciers near Austria's alpine city Innsbruck for downhill action. (p62)

Windsurfing the Mediterranean The wind is always howling in Tarifa, Spain, the windsurfing capital of Europe. (p632)

Hillwalking in Ireland The starkly beautiful Connemara region is prime hillwalking country with wild, remote terrain. (p417)

Hiking the Swiss Alps Hundreds of kilometres of trails web Switzerland's Jungfrau region, with jaw-dropping views. (p652)

Beaches

From blindingly white Mediterranean sand lapped by cobalt-blue waters to pounding Atlantic surf, beaches abound in Western Europe.

St-Tropez Plage de Pampelonne is studded with the French Riviera's most glamorous drinking and dining haunts. (p549)

Lefkada Cliffs drop to broad swaths of white sand and turquoise waters on this untrammelled Greek island. (p380)

Menorca Beaches are tucked away in little coves like pearls in oysters on this Spanish Balearic island. (p613)

Baleal Pumpin' Portuguese surf beach. (p547)

Nightlife

Throbbing nightclubs, historic theatres and intimate venues are all part of the scene after dark.

Berlin Countless cutting-edge clubs, where DJs experiment with the sounds of tomorrow. (p261)

London Dozens of theatre productions, from crowd-pleasing musicals to serious drama, take to London's stages nightly. (p109)

Paris Romantic strolls amid the lit-up splendour can end in jazz clubs, cafes, cabarets and more. (p181)

Madrid Night-time energy never abates in a city where life is lived on the streets 24/7. (p565)

Art

From ancient artefacts to creations that defy comprehension, Europe's art is continually evolving.

Musée de Louvre Paris' pièce de résistance is one of the world's largest and most diverse museums. (p185)

Tate Modern London's modern-art museum fills a huge old power station on the banks of the Thames. (p116)

Galleria degli Uffizi Florence's crowning glory contains the world's greatest collection of Italian Renaissance art. (p468)

Rijksmuseum The Netherlands' premier art trove is packed with old masters. (p505)

Museo del Prado This extraordinary museum forms part of Madrid's golden mile – one of Europe's richest art concentrations. (p565)

Centre Belge de la Bande Dessinée Brussels' comic museum occupies an art nouveau building. (p82)

Architecture

The architecture in Western Europe spans the centuries and is as diverse as the continent itself.

Cathédrale Notre Dame de Paris Paris' gargoyled cathedral is a Gothic wonder. (p185)

Meteora Late 14th-century monasteries perch dramatically atop enormous rocky pinnacles in Meteora, Greece. (p351)

Lefkada (p380), Greece

La Sagrada Família Gaudí's singular work in progress, Barcelona's cathedral boggles the mind. (p589)

Pantheon Commissioned during Augustus' reign, the portico of Rome's Pantheon is graced by Corinthian columns. (p423)

Grand Place Brussels' showpiece central square is ringed by gilded guild houses. (p73)

Overblaak Development This late 20th-century Rotterdam complex incorporates a 'forest' of 45-degree-tilted cube-shaped apartments. (p518)

Shard London's dramatic splinter-like building is a contemporary icon. (p117)

Music

Classical music of royalty, soulful songs of the masses, pop culture that changed the world and much more.

Staatsoper Vienna's state opera is the premier venue in a city synonymous with classical music. (p49)

Teatro alla Scala Italian opera is soul-stirring in the crimson-and-gilt splendour of Milan's opera house. (p449)

Galway The Emerald Isle hums with traditional Irish-music pubs; Galway on the west coast has a cornucopia. (p405)

Alfama Lisbon's atmospheric Alfama district is one of the most evocative places to hear the melancholy, nostalgic songs of Portuguese fado. (p530)

Scenic Journeys

There are beautiful journeys aplenty in Europe, from the Highlands of Scotland to the soaring, snow-covered peaks of the Swiss Alps.

Scottish Highlands The Inverness–Kyle of Lochalsh route is one of Britain's great scenic train journeys. (p171)

Cinque Terre Five picture-perfect Italian villages linked by a trail along beaches, vineyards and olive groves. (p443)

Romantic Rhine Valley Storybook German river cruise past forested hillsides, craggy cliffs, terraced vineyards and idyllic half-timbered villages. (p310)

Bernina Express The Unesco-recognised train route between Tirano and St Moritz is one of Switzerland's most spectacular. (p647)

Month by Month

TOP EVENTS

Christmas Markets December

Oktoberfest, Munich September

Carnevale, Venice February

Edinburgh International Festival August

Notting Hill Carnival, London August

January

Chilly and in some places snowy, the first month of the year isn't Western Europe's most festive. But museum queues are nonexistent, cosy cafes have crackling fireplaces and it's a great time to ski.

Hogmanay

An enormous, raucous Edinburgh street party, Hogmanay, sees in the new year in Scotland. It's replicated Europe-wide as main squares resonate with champagne corks and fireworks.

Vienna Ball Season

If you've dreamed of waltzing at Vienna's grand balls, you won't want to miss the Austrian capital's ball season, when 300 or so balls are held in January and February. The most famous is the lavish Opernball (Opera Ball).

February

Carnival in all its manic glory sweeps through Catholic regions of continental Europe – cold temperatures are forgotten amid masquerades, street festivals and general bacchanalia. Couples descend on romantic destinations such as Paris for Valentine's Day.

Carnaval

Pre-Lent is celebrated with greater vigour in Maastricht than anywhere else in northern Europe. While the rest of the Netherlands hopes the canals will freeze for ice-skating, this Dutch corner cuts loose with a celebration that would have done its former Roman residents proud.

Carnevale

In the pre-Lent period before Ash Wednesday (14 February 2018; 6 March 2019), Venice goes mad for masks. Costume balls, many with traditions centuries old, enliven the social calendar in this storied old city like no other event. Even those without a coveted invite are swept up in the pageantry. (p458)

Karneval/Fasching

Germany doesn't leave the pre-Lent season solely to its neighbours. Karneval (Fasching) is celebrated with abandon in the traditional Catholic regions of the country including Cologne, much of Bavaria, along the Rhine and deep in the Black Forest.

March

Leaves start greening city avenues and festivities begin to flourish. And days get longer – the last Sunday morning of the month ushers in daylight saving time.

St Patrick's Day

Parades and celebrations are held on 17 March in Irish towns big, such as Dublin, and small to honour St Patrick. While elsewhere the day is a commercialised romp of green beer, in his home country it's a time to celebrate with friends and family.

April

Spring arrives with a burst of colour, from the glorious bulb fields of the Netherlands to the blossoming orchards of Spain. On the southernmost beaches it's time to shake the sand out of the umbrellas.

Semana Santa

Procession of penitents and holy icons in Spain, notably in Seville, during Easter week (from 25 March 2018; 14 April 2019). Throughout the week thousands parade in traditional garb. (p618)

Settimana Santa

Italy celebrates Holy Week with processions and passion plays. By Holy Thursday (29 March 2018; 18 April 2019), Rome is thronged with the faithful and even nonbelievers are swept up in the emotion and piety of hundreds of thousands of faithful flocking to the Vatican and St Peter's Basilica. (p425)

Greek Easter

The most important festival in the Greek Orthodox calendar. The emphasis is on the Resurrection so it's a celebratory event – the most significant part is midnight on Easter Saturday (7 April 2018; 28 April 2019) when fireworks explode. The night before, candlelit processions hit the streets.

Feria de Abril

The southern Spanish city of Seville's beautiful old squares come alive during this week-long party held in late April to counterbalance the religious peak of Easter. (p619)

Koningsdag (King's Day)

On 27 April (26 April if the 27th is a Sunday) the Netherlands celebrates Koningsdag (King's Day), the birthday of King Willem-Alexander. There are events nationwide but especially in Amsterdam, where – uproarious partying, music and outrageous orange get-ups aside – there's a giant flea market.

May

Outdoor activities and cafe terraces come into their own. The weather is especially pleasant in the south throughout the Mediterranean regions. Yachts ply the harbours while beautiful people take to the sun loungers.

Brussels Jazz Marathon

Brussels swings to around-the-clock jazz performances for three days over the second-last weekend in May during the Brussels Jazz Marathon (www.brusselsjazzmarathon.be). Free performances are everywhere from open stages in city squares to tight-packed cafes and pubs, and encompass everything from zydeco to boogie-blues.

Cannes Film Festival

Celebrities, would-be celebrities and plenty of starstruck spectators hit the French Riviera's glitziest seafront, La Croisette, during Cannes' famous film festival, held over two weeks in May.

Queima das Fitas

Fado fills the air in the Portuguese town of Coimbra, whose annual highlight is this boozy festival of traditional music and revelry during the first week in May, when students celebrate the end of the academic year.

Karneval der Kulturen

This joyous street carnival celebrates Berlin's multicultural tapestry with parties, global nosh and a fun parade of flamboyantly costumed dancers, DJs, artists and musicians over four days in mid-May.

June

The huge summer travel season hasn't started yet but the sun has burst through the clouds, the weather is gorgeous, and long daylight hours peak during the summer solstice (between 20 and 22 June).

Festa de Santo António

In Portugal's capital, the Festa de Santo António (Festival of Saint Anthony), from 12 June to 13 June, wraps up the three-week Festas de Lisboa (www.festasdelisboa.com), with processions and dozens of street parties; it's liveliest in the Alfama.

Festa de São João

Live music on Porto's plazas and merrymaking take place in Portugal's second city. Squeaky plastic hammers (available for sale everywhere) come out for the unusual custom of whacking one another. Everyone is fair game – don't expect mercy. (p555)

Glastonbury Festival

One of England's favourite outdoor events is Glastonbury's long, muddy weekend of music, theatre and New Age shenanigans. Tickets usually go on sale in autumn, and always sell out within minutes. (p147)

Luxembourg National Day

Held on 23 June, Luxembourg National Day is the Grand Duchy's biggest event – a celebration of the birth of the Grand Duke (though it has never actually fallen on a Grand Ducal birthday).

Gay Pride

European Gay Pride celebrations take place on a summer weekend usually in late June but at times as late as August. Amsterdam hosts the world's only waterborne pride parade.

July

Visitors have arrived from around the world, and outdoor cafes, beer gardens and beach clubs are hopping. Expect beautiful – even scorching – weather anywhere you go.

Palio

Siena's great annual event is the Palio (2 July and 16 August), a pageant culminating in a bareback horse race round Il Campo. The city is divided into 17 *contrade* (districts), of which 10 compete for the *palio* (silk banner). (p476)

Sanfermines ('Running of the Bulls')

From 6 to 14 July, Pamplona, Spain, hosts the famous Sanfermines festival (aka Encierro or 'Running of the Bulls'), when the city is overrun with thrill-seekers, curious onlookers and, yes, bulls. (p605)

Bastille Day

Fireworks and military processions mark France's national day, 14 July. It's celebrated in every French town and city, with the biggest festivities in Paris, where the storming of the Bastille prison kick-started the French Revolution.

Festival d'Avignon

In France's lavender-scented Provence region, hundreds of artists take to the stage and streets of Avignon during July's world-famous Festival d'Avignon. The fringe Festival Off (www.avignonleoff.com) runs from early July to early August. (p242)

Montreux Jazz Festival

It's not just jazz: big-name rock acts also hit the shores of Lake Geneva during the first two weeks of July. The cheaper music festival Paleo (http://yeah.paleo.ch) takes place in Nyon, between Geneva and Lausanne, in the second half of July. (p645)

Gentse Feesten

The charming Belgian city of Ghent is transformed into a 10-day party of music and theatre; a highlight is a vast techno celebration. (p89)

August

Everybody's on the move as major European city businesses shut down and residents head off to enjoy the traditional month of holiday. If it's near the beach, from Germany's Baltic to Spain's Balearic, it's mobbed.

Edinburgh International Festival

Three weeks of innovative drama, comedy, dance, music and more, held in Edinburgh. Two weeks overlap with the celebrated 3½-week Fringe Festival (www.edfringe.com), which draws innovative acts from around the globe. Catch cutting-edge comedy, drama and productions that defy description. (p163)

Notting Hill Carnival

For three days during the last weekend of August, London's Notting Hill echoes to the beats of calypso, ska, reggae and soca at London's most vibrant outdoor carnival, where the local Caribbean community shows the city how to party. (p125)

Salzburg Festival

Austria's renowned Salzburger Festspiele attracts international stars from late July to the end of August when it stages some 200 productions spanning theatre, classical music and opera. (p59)

Street Parade

In Switzerland, it's Zürich's turn to let its hair down with an enormous techno parade. All thoughts of numbered accounts are forgotten as bankers and everybody else parties to deep-base thump, thump, thump.

September

It's cooling off in every sense, from the northern countries to the romance started on an Ibiza dance floor. But it's often the best time to visit, with sparkling days and reduced crowds.

Venice International Film Festival

The Mostra del Cinema di Venezia is Italy's top film festival and one of the world's top indie film fests. Judging is seen as an indication of what to look for at the next year's Oscars. (p458)

Festes de la Mercè

Barcelona knows how to party until dawn and it outdoes itself around 24 September for the Festes de la Mercè: four days of concerts, dancing, *castellers* (human-castle builders), fireworks and *correfocs* – a parade of firework-spitting dragons and devils. (p592)

Oktoberfest

Germany's legendary beer-swilling party originates from the marriage celebrations of Crown Prince Ludwig in 1810. Munich's Oktoberfest runs for the 15 days before the first Sunday in October. Millions descend for whopping 1L steins of beer and carousing that has no equal. (p289)

Galway Oyster Festival

Oyster-opening championships are just the start of this spirited seafood festival in Ireland's colourful west-coast city of Galway, which also has tastings, talks, cooking demonstrations and plenty of live music and merrymaking. (p405)

October

October heralds an autumnal kaleidoscope, along with bright, crisp days, cool, clear nights and excellent cultural offerings, with prices and visitor numbers way down. Daylight saving ends on the last Sunday morning of the month.

Belfast International Arts Festival

Belfast hosts the UK's second-biggest arts festival over two weeks in late October/early November in and around the city's Queen's University. (p411)

November

Leaves have fallen and snow is about to in much of Europe. Even in the temperate zones around the Mediterranean it can get chilly, rainy and blustery. Most seasonal attractions have closed for the year.

Guy Fawkes Night

Bonfires and fireworks flare up across Britain on 5 November recalling the failed antigovernment 'gunpowder plot' from 1605 to blow up parliament (Fawkes was in charge of the explosives). Go to high ground in London to see glowing explosions erupt everywhere.

December

Twinkling lights, brightly decorated Christmas trees and shop windows, and outdoor ice-skating rinks make December an enchanting month to be in Western Europe, where every region has its own traditions.

Christmas Markets

Christmas markets are held across many European counties, particularly Germany and Austria. Germany's best is Nuremberg's Christkindlesmarkt. Warm your hands through your mittens holding a hot mug of mulled wine and find that special present.

Natale

Italian churches set up an intricate crib or *presepe* (nativity scene) in the lead-up to celebrating Christmas. Some are quite famous, most are works of art and many date back hundreds of years and are venerated for their spiritual ties.)

Itineraries

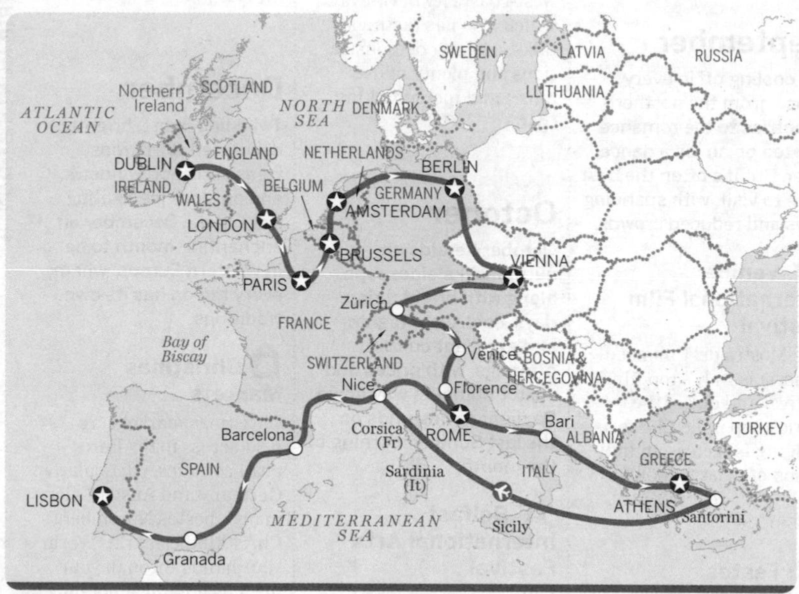

Ultimate Europe

Have limited time but want to see a bit of everything? Hit the highlights on this trip.

Start in **Dublin**, soaking up its vibrant pubs and rich literary history. From Ireland, fly to **London** for great theatre. Then catch the Eurostar train through the English Channel tunnel to beautiful **Paris**.

Travel north to **Brussels** for amazing beer and chocolate, then further north to free-spirited **Amsterdam**, making time to cruise its canals. Go east, stopping for a cruise on the Rhine, and spend a few days exploring (and surviving) the legendary nightlife in **Berlin**. Next, visit **Vienna** for architectural and classical-music riches. Zip west to **Zürich** and the Swiss Alps for awe-inspiring ski slopes and vistas.

Head to canal-laced **Venice**, art-filled **Florence** and historic **Rome**. Train it to **Bari** and take a ferry to **Athens**, then explore island beaches, starting with the stunning **Santorini**. Connect by air or go by ferry and train to the French Riviera (aka the Côte d'Azur) to check out quintessential Mediterranean destinations such as **Nice**. Continue to **Barcelona**, then the Moorish towns of southern Spain like **Granada**. End your trip in the hilly quarters of **Lisbon**, toasting your grand journey with Portugal's port wine.

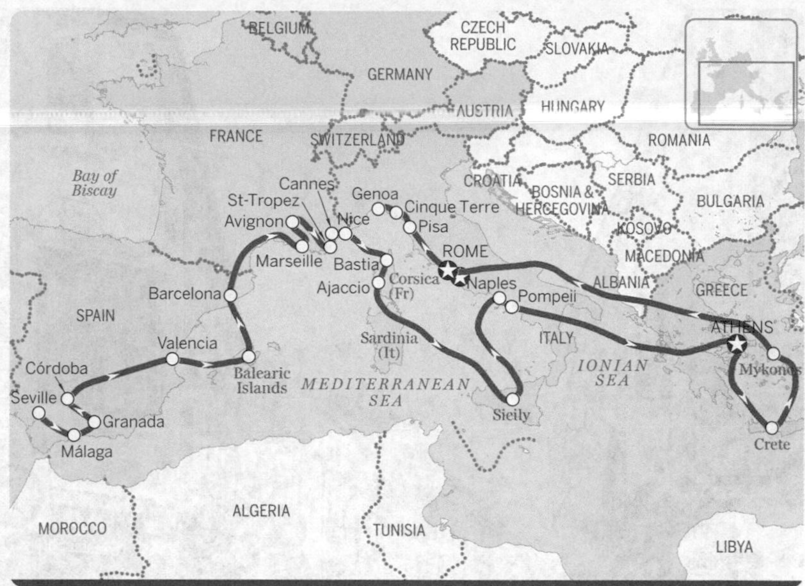

Mediterranean Europe

Beautiful weather and breathtaking scenery are the draws of this comprehensive tour that takes in famous towns and cities from antiquity to the present.

Start in southern Spain in orange-blossom-scented **Seville** and soak up the architecture, sunshine and party atmosphere. Make your way up the eastern coast past the Moorish town of **Málaga** and on to **Granada** and **Córdoba**. Then it's back to the coast at **Valencia**, home of Spain's famous rice-dish paella, for a ferry-hop to the parties and beaches of the **Balearic Islands**.

Back on the mainland, **Barcelona** brims with the architecture of Gaudí. From here, head into France's fabled Provence region, where in **Marseille** you can see the fortress that was inspiration for the novel *The Count of Monte Cristo*. Then leave the sea for Provence's lush hills and lavender-scented towns around the rampart-hooped city of **Avignon**. On to the **French Riviera** and its playground for the rich and famous, **St-Tropez**. The charming seaside city **Nice** is a perfect jumping-off point for other nearby coastal hot spots such as glamorous **Cannes**.

Cruise by ferry to Corsica and experience the traditional lifestyle of quiet fishing villages. Hit the bustling old port of **Bastia**, Napoléon Bonaparte's home town **Ajaccio**, then the glittering harbour of Bonifacio to hop on a ferry south to Sardinia and on to **Sicily** to visit its colossal temples and famous volcano, Mt Etna.

Catch a ferry to **Naples**, on the Italian mainland, and take a trip to **Pompeii**. Move east to Brindisi for a ferry to Greece that passes rocky coasts seen by mariners for millennia, landing in Patra. Head to **Athens** to wonder at the Greek capital's ancient treasures before boarding a plane or ferry to magical islands such as **Crete** and **Mykonos**. Return to Italy, taking time to wander amid the ruins and piazzas of **Rome**. Continue north through Tuscany, stopping at **Pisa** to see its famous 'leaning tower'. Finish up along the Ligurian coast, travelling via the brightly coloured coastal villages making up the **Cinque Terre**, strung between plunging cliffs and vine-covered hills, to the port city of **Genoa**.

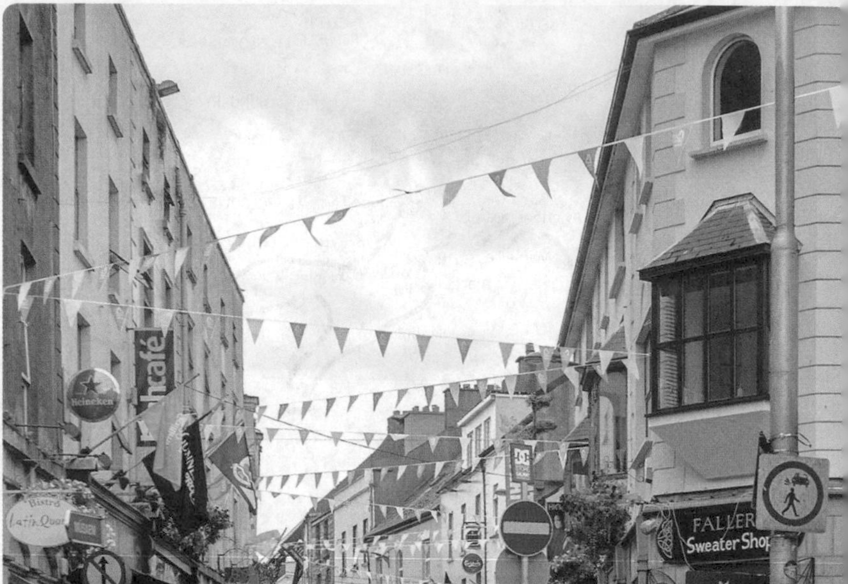

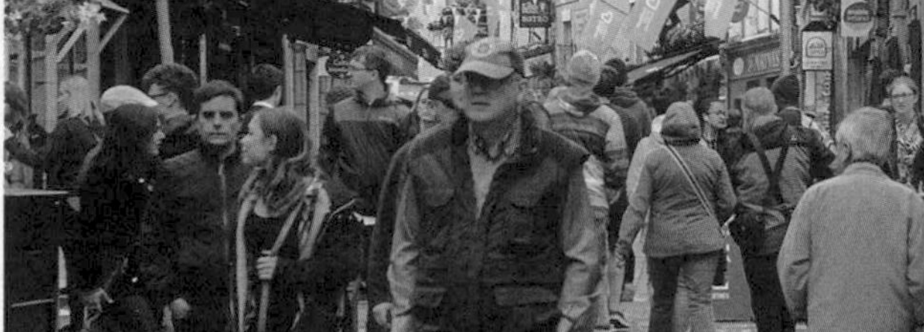

HIT1912 / SHUTTERSTOCK ©

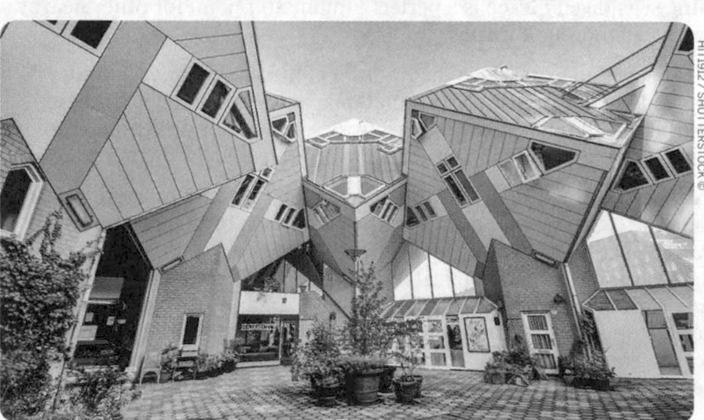

Top: Galway (p405), Ireland

Left: Cube Houses or *Kubuswoningen* in Rotterdam (p518), by architect Piet Blom

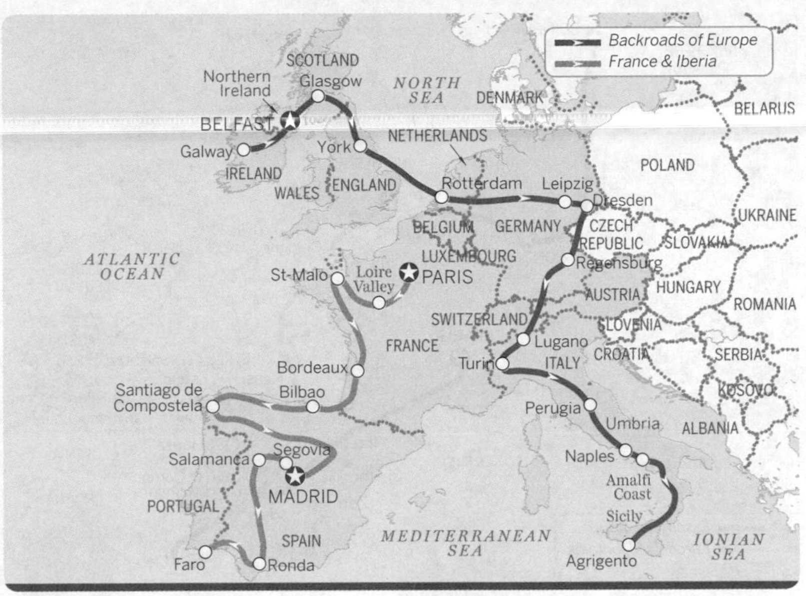

Backroads of Europe

Already visited the major capitals? Start discovering the rest of Europe.

The far west of Ireland is rugged and uncrowded; start in bohemian **Galway**. Then travel to Northern Ireland – **Belfast** From here, it's also easy to strike out to awe-inspiring natural sights such as the Giant's Causeway. Catch a ferry to reach the dynamic Scottish city of **Glasgow**. Swing south to the atmospheric walled English city of **York**. Hop across to the Netherlands, where buzzing **Rotterdam** is a veritable open-air gallery of modern and cutting-edge architecture.

Travel to the dynamic eastern German cities of **Leipzig**, and **Dresden**, whose historic core has been restored to its 18th-century glory. Turn south via the stunning Bavarian student hub of **Regensburg**, to the Swiss town of on the shores of its sparkling namesake lake. Cross into Italy and stop at the cultured city of **Turin**, followed by **Perugia**. In Italy's south, explore frenetic **Naples** and the winding **Amalfi Coast**. Scoot over to **Sicily** to experience its rugged landscapes as well as its ancient and colourful culture. Marvel at the Grecian Valley of the Temples in **Agrigento**, which rivals anything in Greece itself.

2 WEEKS

France & Iberia

Get a feel for three of Europe's most diverse countries on this relatively compact jaunt.

Start in **Paris**, discovering the magnificent monuments and hidden backstreet bistros of the City of Light. Visit the chateaux of the **Loire Valley**, then take the fast TGV train to Brittany. Walk the 17th-century ramparts encircling **St-Malo** and sample authentic Breton cider. Track south along the Atlantic coast, where red wine reaches its pinnacle around **Bordeaux**. Cross the border to the Basque city of **Bilbao**, best known for the magnificent Guggenheim Museum, before continuing to the pilgrimage shrine of **Santiago de Compostela**.

Spain's art-rich capital, **Madrid**, is prime for night owls: an evening of tapas and drinks in tiny bars can postpone dinner until midnight. Spend a day exploring beautiful **Segovia**. And don't skip the sandstone splendour of lively **Salamanca**. Plan on using a car to explore the many hill towns of Andalucía. Narrow, winding roads traverse sunburnt landscapes and olive orchards before reaching the whitewashed buildings of **Ronda**. Finally, go west via Seville to Portugal's pretty Algarve region, finishing in **Faro**.

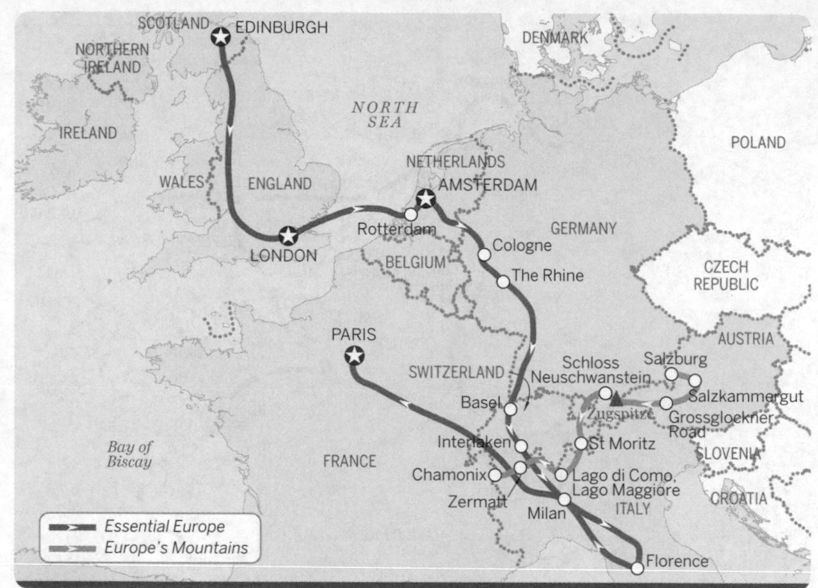

2 WEEKS Essential Europe

Watching Europe from the window of a train or gazing at the sea rolling past the handrail of a ferry is the way generations of travellers have explored the continent, and it's still as idyllic today.

Start in the engaging Scottish capital **Edinburgh**, then take the train to pulsating **London** and on to Harwich for a ferry crossing to Hoek van Holland. From here, trains connect to the dynamic city of **Rotterdam** and the gabled Golden Age canalscapes of **Amsterdam**.

Take a fast train to cathedral-crowned **Cologne** and then relax on a river cruise down the vineyard-ribboned **Rhine**. Alight at Mainz and connect by train through **Basel** to picturesque **Interlaken** for the slow-moving local trains and trams that wend through the majestic Alps. Then take a train past soaring mountain scenery to stylish **Milan**, home to da Vinci's refectory fresco *The Last Supper*. From Milan, fast trains zip to Tuscany's resplendent capital, **Florence**, a veritable Renaissance time capsule. Connect in Milan to snuggle up on the night train to **Paris**, feeling the romance in the rhythm of the rails.

2 WEEKS Europe's Mountains

Buckle up for an exhilarating road trip through some of Europe's most majestic peaks.

From the storybook Austrian city of **Salzburg**, head east to the mountain-ringed, jewel-like lakes of the **Salzkammergut** region. To the south is the heart-in-mouth **Grossglockner Road**, with 36 switchbacks over 48km as it traverses Austria's highest peak, Grossglockner.

Northwest, on the Austrian–German border, lies the 2962m-high **Zugspitze**. From here it's a short jaunt to Füssen, crowned by King Ludwig II's fairy-tale castle **Schloss Neuschwanstein**.

Swing southwest to one of Switzerland's ritziest ski resorts, **St Moritz**. Continue southwest into Italy to the sparkling lakes of **Lago di Como** and **Lago Maggiore** beneath the towering peaks.

Zigzag back into Switzerland to **Zermatt**, with views of the 4478m-high Matterhorn. Then make your way southwest to mighty Mont Blanc – Western Europe's highest peak and its feted ski resort **Chamonix** across the border in France, by the Mer de Glace glacier.

On the Road

Austria

Includes ➡

Best Places to Eat

- ➡ Lingenhel (p48)
- ➡ Griechenbeisl (p48)
- ➡ Punks (p48)
- ➡ Magazin (p60)
- ➡ Die Wilderin (p64)

Best Places to Stay

- ➡ Grand Ferdinand Hotel (p47)
- ➡ Magdas (p47)
- ➡ Hotel am Brillantengrund (p47)
- ➡ Haus Ballwein (p59)
- ➡ Hotel Weisses Kreuz (p64)

Why Go?

For such a small country, Austria is ridiculously large on inspiration. This is the land where Mozart was born, Strauss taught the world to waltz and Julie Andrews grabbed the spotlight with her twirling entrance in *The Sound of Music*. It's where the Habsburgs ruled over their spectacular, sprawling 600-year empire.

These past glories still shine in the resplendent baroque palaces and chandelier-lit coffee houses of Vienna, Innsbruck and Salzburg, but beyond its storybook cities, Austria's allure is one of natural beauty and outdoors adventure. Whether you're schussing down the legendary slopes of Kitzbühel, climbing high in the Alps of Tyrol or cycling the banks of the mighty Danube, you'll find the kind of landscapes that no well-orchestrated symphony or singing nun could ever quite do justice.

When to Go

Vienna

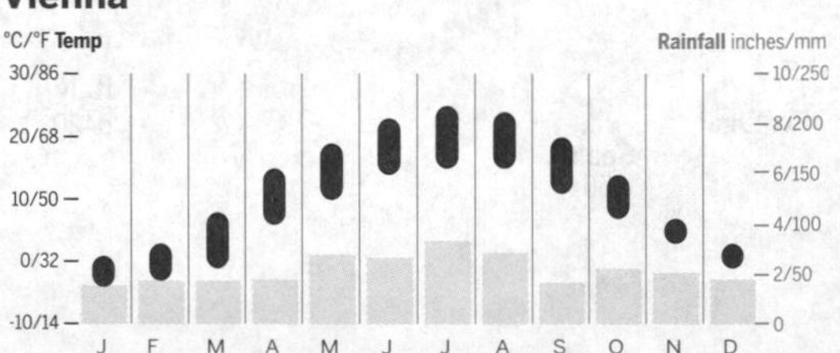

Jul–Aug Alpine hiking in Tyrol, lake swimming in Salzkammergut and lots of summer festivals.

Sep–Oct New wine in vineyards near Vienna, golden forest strolls and few crowds.

Dec–Jan Christmas markets, skiing in the Alps and Vienna waltzing into the New Year.

VIENNA

01 / POP 1,766,750

Few cities in the world waltz so effortlessly between the present and the past like Vienna. Its splendid historical face is easily recognised: grand imperial palaces and bombastic baroque interiors, revered opera houses and magnificent squares. But Vienna is also one of Europe's most dynamic urban spaces. A stone's throw from Hofburg (the Imperial Palace), the MuseumsQuartier houses provocative and high-profile contemporary art behind a striking basalt facade. In the Innere Stadt (Inner City), up-to-the-minute design stores sidle up to old-world confectioners, and Austro-Asian fusion restaurants stand alongside traditional *Beisl* (small taverns).

Sights

Vienna's magnificent series of boulevards, the Ringstrasse, encircles the Innere Stadt, with many of the city's most famous sights situated on or within it, including the monumental Hofburg palace complex. Just outside the Ringstrasse are exceptional museums including the Kunsthistorisches Museum and the ensemble making up the MuseumsQuartier, while attractions further afield include the sumptuous palaces Schloss Schönbrunn and Schloss Belvedere.

★Hofburg PALACE

(Imperial Palace; www.hofburg-wien.at; 01, Michaelerkuppel; 1A, 2A Michaelerplatz, D, 1, 2, 46, 49, 71 Burgring, U Herrengasse) FREE Nothing symbolises Austria's resplendent cultural heritage more than its Hofburg, home base of the Habsburgs from 1273 to 1918. The oldest section is the 13th-century **Schweizerhof** (Swiss Courtyard), named after the Swiss guards who used to protect its precincts. The Renaissance **Swiss gate** dates from 1553. The courtyard adjoins a larger courtyard, **In der Burg**, with a monument to Emperor Franz II adorning its centre. The palace now houses the Austrian president's offices and a raft of museums.

★Kaiserappartements PALACE

(Imperial Apartments; www.hofburg-wien.at; 01, Michaelerplatz; adult/child €12.90/7.70, incl guided tour €15.90/9.20; 9am-6pm Jul & Aug, to 5.30pm Sep-Jun; U Herrengasse) The Kaiserappartements (Imperial Apartments), once the official living quarters of Franz Josef I and Empress Elisabeth, are dazzling in their chandelier-lit opulence. The highlight is the **Sisi Museum** (01-533 75 70; 01, Michaelerkuppel; adult/child €12.90/7.70, incl guided tour €15.90/9.20; 9am-6pm Jul & Aug, to 5.30pm Sep-Jun), devoted to Austria's most beloved empress, which has a strong focus on the clothing and jewellery of Austria's monarch. Multilingual audio guides are included in the admission price. Guided tours take in the Kaiserappartements, the Sisi Museum and the **Silberkammer** (Silver Depot; 01, Michaelerkuppel; adult/child €12.90/7.70, incl guided tour €15.90/9.20; 9am-6pm Jul & Aug, to 5.30pm Sep-Jun), whose largest silver service caters to 140 dinner guests.

★Kaiserliche Schatzkammer MUSEUM

(Imperial Treasury; www.kaiserliche-schatzkammer.at; 01, Schweizerhof; adult/child €12/free; 9am-5.30pm Wed-Mon; U Herrengasse) The Kaiserliche Schatzkammer contains secular and ecclesiastical treasures, including devotional images and altars, particularly from the baroque era, of priceless value and splendour – the sheer wealth of this collection of crown jewels is staggering. As you walk through the rooms you see magnificent treasures such as a golden rose, diamond-studded Turkish sabres, a 2680-carat Colombian emerald and, the highlight of the treasury, the imperial crown.

ITINERARIES

Two Days

Make the most of **Vienna**, spending your first day visiting the Habsburg palaces and Stephansdom before cosying up in a *Kaffeehäus* (coffee house). At night, check out the pumping bar scene.

One Week

Plan for two long and lovely days in Vienna, plus another day exploring the **Wachau** (Danube Valley) **wine region**, a day each in **Salzburg** and **Innsbruck**, a day in St Anton am Arlberg or Kitzbühel **hiking** or **skiing** and then a final day exploring the **Salzkammergut** lakes.

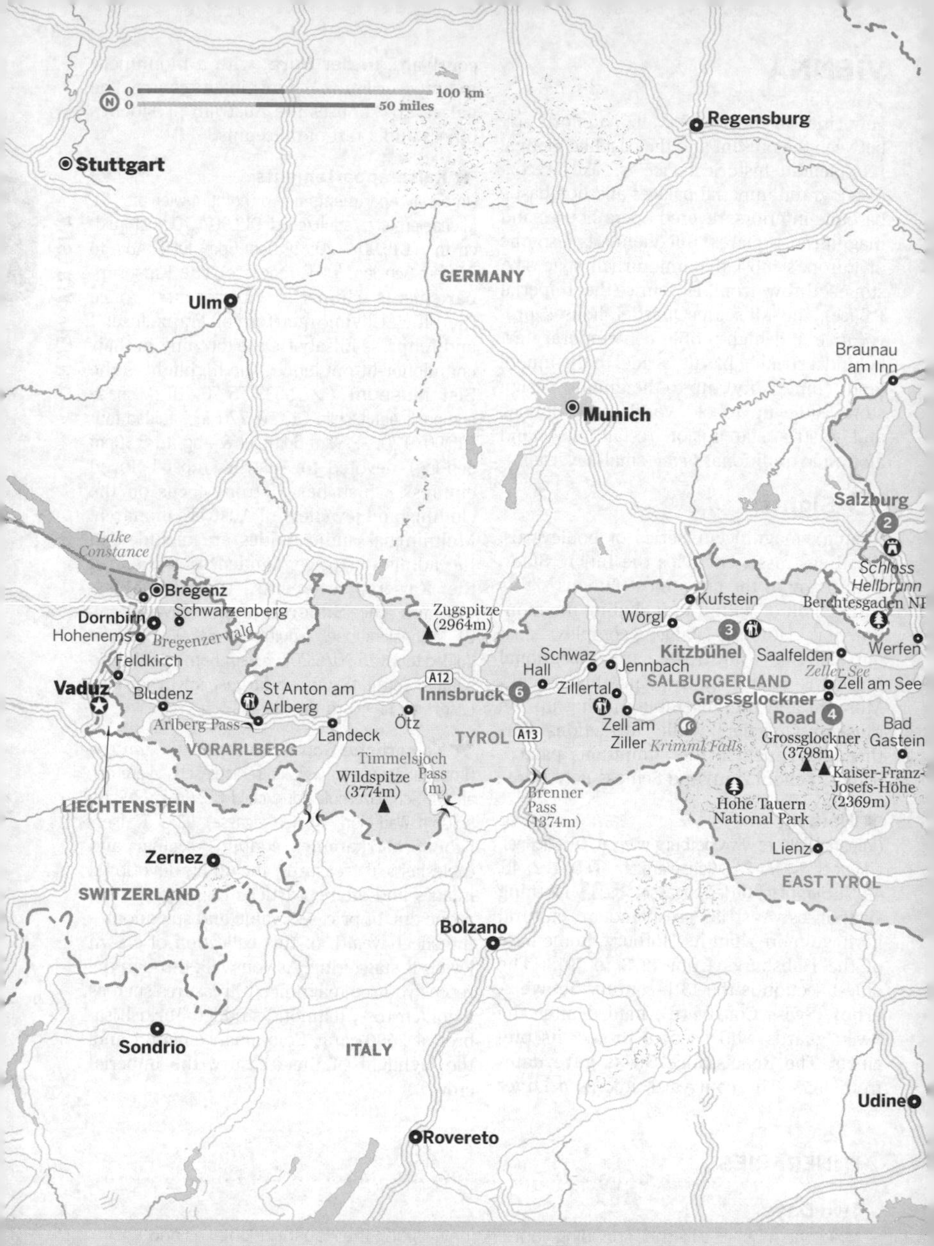

0 100 km
0 50 miles
Stuttgart
Regensburg
GERMANY
Ulm
Braunau am Inn
Munich
Salzburg
Lake Constance
Schloss Hellbrunn
Bregenz
Kufstein
Berchtesgaden NP
Dornbirn
Schwarzenberg
Zugspitze (2964m)
Wörgl
Werfen
Hohenems
Bregenzerwald
Kitzbühel
Saalfelden
Feldkirch
Schwaz
Jennbach
Zeller See
Hall
SALBURGERLAND
Zell am See
Vaduz
St Anton am Arlberg
A12
Zillertal
Bluden
Innsbruck
Grossglockner Road
Bad Gastein
Arlberg Pass
Ötz
Zell am Ziller
Landeck
TYROL
A13
Krimml Falls
Grossglockner (3798m)
VORARLBERG
Timmelsjoch Pass (m)
Kaiser-Franz-Josefs-Höhe (2369m)
Wildspitze (3774m)
Brenner Pass (1374m)
Hohe Tauern National Park
LIECHTENSTEIN
Lienz
Zernez
EAST TYROL
SWITZERLAND
Bolzano
Sondrio
ITALY
Udine
Rovereto

Austria Highlights

1 **Vienna** (p59) Discover opulent Habsburg palaces, coffee houses and cutting-edge galleries.

2 **Salzburg** (p56) Survey the baroque cityscape from the giddy height of 900-year-old Festung Hohensalzburg.

3 **Kitzbühel** (p66) Send your spirits soaring from peak to peak hiking and skiing.

4 **Grossglockner Road** (p67) Buckle up for a rollercoaster ride of Alps and glaciers on one of Austria's greatest drives.

5 Salzkammergut (p61) Dive into the crystal-clear lakes of Austria's summer playground.

6 Innsbruck (p62) Whiz up to the Tyrolean Alps in Zaha Hadid's space-age funicular.

7 Danube Valley (p51) Explore the romantic Wachau and technology trailblazer Linz.

★ **Stephansdom** CATHEDRAL

(St Stephen's Cathedral; ☎tours 01-515 323 054; www.stephanskirche.at; 01, Stephansplatz; main nave adult & one child €6, additional child €1.50; ⊙public visits 9-11.30am & 1-4.30pm Mon-Sat, 1-4.30pm Sun; Ⓤ Stephansplatz) Vienna's Gothic masterpiece Stephansdom – or Steffl (Little Stephan), as it's ironically nicknamed – is Vienna's pride and joy. A church has stood here since the 12th century, and reminders of this are the Romanesque **Riesentor** (Giant Gate) and **Heidentürme**. From the exterior, the first thing that will strike you is the glorious tiled **roof**, with its dazzling row of chevrons and Austrian eagle. Inside, the magnificent Gothic stone **pulpit** presides over the main nave, fashioned in 1515 by Anton Pilgrim.

★ **Kunsthistorisches Museum** MUSEUM

(KHM, Museum of Art History; www.khm.at; 01, Maria-Theresien-Platz; adult/child incl Neue Burg museums €15/free; ⊙10am-6pm Fri-Wed, to 9pm Thu Jun-Aug, closed Mon Sep-May; Ⓤ Museumsquartier, Volkstheater) One of the unforgettable experiences of any trip to Vienna is a visit to the Kunsthistorisches Museum, brimming with works by Europe's finest painters, sculptors and artisans. Occupying a neoclassical building as sumptuous as the art it contains, the museum takes you on a time-travel treasure hunt from Classical Rome to Egypt and the Renaissance. If your time's limited, skip straight to the **Picture Gallery**, where you'll want to dedicate at least an hour or two to Old Masters.

SPIN OF THE RING

One of the best deals in Vienna is a self-guided tour on tram 1 or 2 of the monumental **Ringstrasse** boulevard encircling much of the Innere Stadt, which turned 150 in 2015. For the price of a single ticket you'll take in the neo-Gothic **Rathaus** (City Hall; www.wien.gv.at; 01, Rathausplatz 1; ⊙tours 1pm Mon, Wed & Fri Sep-Jun, 1pm Mon-Fri Jul & Aug; 🚋D, 1, 2 Rathaus, Ⓤ Rathaus) FREE, the Greek Revival–style parliament, the 19th-century **Burgtheater** (National Theatre; ☎01-514 44 4440; www.burgtheater.at; 01, Universitätsring 2; seats €7.50-61, standing room €3.50, students €9; ⊙box office 9am-5pm Mon-Fri; 🚋D, 1, 2 Rathaus, Ⓤ Rathaus) and the baroque **Karlskirche** (St Charles Church; www.karlskirche.at; 04, Karlsplatz; adult/child €8/free; ⊙9am-6pm Mon-Sat, noon-7pm Sun; Ⓤ Karlsplatz), among other sights.

★ **MuseumsQuartier** MUSEUM

(Museum Quarter; MQ; www.mqw.at; 07, Museumsplatz; ⊙information & ticket centre 10am-7pm; Ⓤ Museumsquartier, Volkstheater) The MuseumsQuartier is a remarkable ensemble of museums, cafes, restaurants and bars inside former imperial stables designed by Fischer von Erlach. This breeding ground of Viennese cultural life is the perfect place to hang out and watch or meet people on warm evenings. With over 60,000 sq metres of exhibition space – including the Leopold Museum, MUMOK, Kunsthalle (p51), **Architekturzentrum** (Vienna Architecture Centre; ☎01-522 31 15; www.azw.at; exhibition prices vary, library admission free; ⊙architecture centre 10am-7pm, library 10am-5.30pm Mon, Wed & Fri, to 7pm Sat & Sun, closed Thu) and **Zoom** (☎01-524 79 08; www.kindermuseum.at; exhibition adult/child €4/free, activities child €4-6, accompanying adult free; ⊙12.45-5pm Tue-Sun Jul & Aug, 8.30am-4pm Tue-Fri, 9.45am-4pm Sat & Sun Sep-Jun, activity times vary) – the complex is one of the world's most ambitious cultural hubs.

★ **MUMOK** GALLERY

(Museum Moderner Kunst; Museum of Modern Art; www.mumok.at; 07, Museumsplatz 1; adult/child €11/free; ⊙2-7pm Mon, 10am-7pm Tue, Wed & Fri-Sun, 10am-9pm Thu; 🚋49 Volkstheater, Ⓤ Volkstheater, Museumsquartier) The dark basalt edifice and sharp corners of the Museum Moderner Kunst are a complete contrast to the MuseumsQuartier's historical sleeve. Inside, MUMOK contains Vienna's finest collection of 20th-century art, centred on fluxus, nouveau realism, pop art and photo-realism. The best of expressionism, cubism, minimal art and Viennese Actionism is represented in a collection of 9000 works that are rotated and exhibited by theme – but note that sometimes all this Actionism is packed away to make room for temporary exhibitions.

Leopold Museum MUSEUM

(www.leopoldmuseum.org; 07, Museumsplatz 1; adult/child €13/8; ⊙10am-6pm Fri-Wed, to 9pm Thu Jun-Aug, 10am-6pm Wed & Fri-Mon, to 9pm Thu Sep-May; Ⓤ Volkstheater, Museumsquartier) Part of the MuseumsQuartier (p42), the Leopold Museum is named after ophthalmologist Rudolf Leopold, who, after buying his first Egon Schiele for a song as a young student in 1950, amassed a huge private collection of mainly 19th-century and modernist Austrian artworks. In 1994 he sold the lot – 5266 paintings – to the Austrian government for €160 million (individually, the paintings would have made him €574 million), and the Leopold Museum was born. **Café Leopold** (www.cafe-leopold.at; ⏲10am-midnight Sun-Wed, to 4am Thu, to 6am Fri & Sat; 📶) is located on the top floor.

Haus der Musik MUSEUM
(www.hausdermusik.com; 01, Seilerstätte 30; adult/child €13/6, with Mozarthaus Vienna €18/8; ⏲10am-10pm; 🚋D, 1, 2, 71, Ⓤ Karlsplatz) The Haus der Musik explains the world of sound and music to adults and children alike in an amusing and interactive way (in English and German). Exhibits are spread over four floors and cover everything from how sound is created, from Vienna's Philharmonic Orchestra to street noises. The staircase between floors acts as a piano; its glassed-in ground-floor courtyard hosts musical events. Admission is discounted after 8pm. The nearest tram stop is Kärntner Ring/Oper.

Secession MUSEUM
(www.secession.at; 01, Friedrichstrasse 12; adult/child €9/5.50; ⏲10am-6pm Tue-Sun; Ⓤ Karlsplatz) In 1897, 19 progressive artists swam away from the mainstream Künstlerhaus artistic establishment to form the *Wiener Secession* (Vienna Secession). Among their number were Klimt, Josef Hoffman, Kolo Moser and Joseph M Olbrich. Olbrich designed the new exhibition centre of the Secessionists, which combined sparse functionality with stylistic motifs. Its biggest draw is Klimt's exquisitely gilded *Beethoven Frieze*. Guided tours in English (€3) lasting one hour take place at 11am Saturday. An audio guide costs €3.

★ Schloss Belvedere PALACE
(www.belvedere.at; adult/child Oberes Belvedere €14/free, Unteres Belvedere €12/free, combined ticket €20/free; ⏲10am-6pm; 🚋D, 71 Schwarzenbergplatz, Ⓤ Taubstummengasse, Südtiroler Platz) A masterpiece of total art, Schloss Belvedere is one of the world's finest baroque palaces. Designed by Johann Lukas von Hildebrandt (1668–1745), it was built for the brilliant military strategist Prince Eugene of Savoy, conqueror of the Turks in 1718. What giddy romance is evoked in its sumptuously frescoed halls, replete with artworks by Klimt, Schiele and Kokoschka; what stories are conjured in its landscaped gardens, which drop like the fall of a theatre curtain to reveal Vienna's skyline.

ℹ MORE FOR YOUR MONEY

The **Vienna Card** (Die Wien-Karte; 48/72 hours €21.90/24.90) gives you unlimited travel plus discounts at selected museums, cafes and shops as well as the City Airport Train (CAT). It's available from hotels and the tourist office.

★ Sigmund Freud Museum MUSEUM, HOUSE
(www.freud-museum.at; 09, Berggasse 19; adult/child €10/4; ⏲10am-6pm; 🚋D, Ⓤ Schottentor, Schottenring) Sigmund Freud is a bit like the telephone – once he happened, there was no going back. This is where Freud spent his most prolific years and developed the most significant of his groundbreaking theories; he moved here with his family in 1891 and stayed until forced into exile by the Nazis in 1938.

★ Schloss Schönbrunn PALACE
(www.schoenbrunn.at; 13, Schönbrunner Schlossstrasse 47; adult/child Imperial Tour €13.30/9.80, Grand Tour €16.40/10.80, Grand Tour with guide €19.40/12.30; ⏲8.30am-6.30pm Jul & Aug, to 5.30pm Sep, Oct & Apr-Jun, to 5pm Nov-Mar; Ⓤ Hietzing) The Habsburgs' overwhelmingly opulent summer palace is now a Unesco World Heritage site. Of the palace's 1441 rooms, 40 are open to the public; the Imperial Tour takes you into 26 of these, including the private apartments of Franz Josef and Sisi, while the Grand Tour covers all 40 and includes the precious 18th-century interiors from the time of Maria-Theresia. These mandatory tours are done with an audio guide or, for an additional charge, a tour guide.

Activities

The **Donauinsel** (Danube Island) features swimming areas and paths for walking and cycling. The **Alte Donau** is a landlocked arm of the Danube, a favourite of sailing and boating enthusiasts, swimmers, walkers, fisherfolk and, in winter (when it's cold enough), ice skaters.

Central Vienna

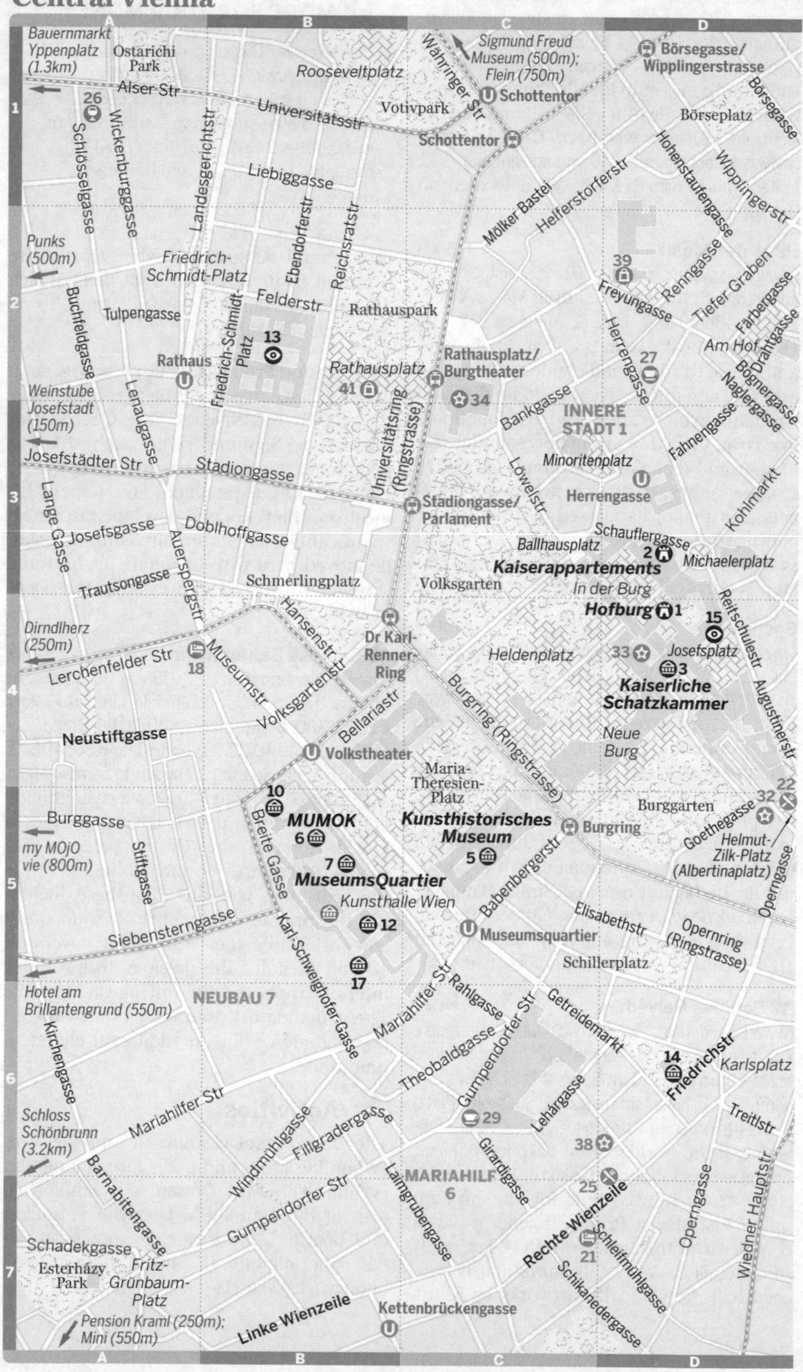

500 m
0.25 miles
Karmelitermarkt (300m)
MuTh (500m); Sperlhof (600m)
Nestroyplatz
Supersense (300m); Fluc (750m); Prater (1km)
LEOPOLDSTADT 2
INNERE STADT 1
Salztorbrücke
Rudolfsplatz
Morzinplatz
Holocaust-Denkmal
Judenplatz
Danube Canal
Obere Donaustr
Franz-Josefs-Kai (Ringstrasse)
Schwedenplatz
Untere Donaustr
Julius-Raab-Platz
Magdas (850m)
Stephansdom
Stock-im-Eisen-Platz
Stephansplatz
Dr-Ignaz-Seipel-Platz
Domgasse
Franziskanerplatz
Stubentor
Wien Mitte
Landstrasse
Lingenhel (700m)
Weihburggasse
Stadtpark
Beethovenplatz
Schwartzenbergstrasse
Kärntner Ring/Oper
Kärntner Ring (Ringstrasse)
Karlsplatz
Resselpark
Schwarzenbergplatz
Karlskirche
Oberes Belvedere (650m)
Schloss Belvedere
Wien
Rennweg

Central Vienna

Top Sights

1 Hofburg ... D4
2 Kaiserappartements ... D3
3 Kaiserliche Schatzkammer ... D4
4 Karlskirche ... E7
5 Kunsthistorisches Museum ... C5
6 MUMOK ... B5
7 MuseumsQuartier ... B5
8 Schloss Belvedere ... G7
9 Stephansdom ... E3

Sights

10 Architekturzentrum Wien ... B5
11 Haus der Musik ... F5
12 Leopold Museum ... B5
13 Rathaus ... B2
14 Secession ... D6
Silberkammer ... (see 2)
Sisi Museum ... (see 2)
15 Spanish Riding School ... D4
16 Unteres Belvedere ... G7
17 Zoom ... B5

Sleeping

18 25hours Hotel ... A4
19 Grand Ferdinand Hotel ... F5
20 Hotel Capricorno ... G2
21 Hotel Drei Kronen ... C7

Eating

22 Bitzinger Würstelstand am Albertinaplatz ... D5
23 Griechenbeisl ... G2
24 Meierei im Stadtpark ... H4
25 Naschmarkt ... D6

Drinking & Nightlife

26 Achtundzwanzig ... A1
27 Café Central ... D2
Café Leopold ... (see 12)
28 Café Leopold Hawelka ... E3
29 Café Sperl ... C6
Dachboden ... (see 18)
30 Loos American Bar ... E4
31 Strandbar Herrmann ... H2

Entertainment

32 Bundestheaterkassen ... D5
33 Burgkapelle Vienna Boys' Choir Tickets ... D4
34 Burgtheater ... C2
35 Jazzland ... F2
36 Musikverein ... E6
37 Staatsoper ... E5
38 Theater an der Wien ... D6

Shopping

39 Bio-Markt Freyung ... D2
40 Dorotheum ... E4
41 Rathausplatz Christkindlmarkt ... B2

Festivals & Events

Pick up a copy of the monthly booklet of events from the tourist office.

★Christkindlmärkte CHRISTMAS MARKET

(www.wien.info/en/shopping-wining-dining/markets/christmas-markets; mid-Nov–25 Dec) Vienna's much-loved Christmas market season runs from around mid-November to Christmas Eve. Magical *Christkindlmärkte* set up in streets and squares, with stalls selling wooden toys, holiday decorations and traditional food such as *Wurst* (sausages) and *Glühwein* (mulled wine). The centrepiece is the **Rathausplatz Christkindlmarkt** (www.christkindlmarkt.at; 10am-10pm 13 Nov–26 Dec; D, 1, 2 Rathaus, U Rathaus).

Wiener Festwochen ART

(Vienna Festival; www.festwochen.at; mid-May–mid-Jun) A wide-ranging program of theatrical productions, concerts, dance performances and visual arts from around the world, the month-long Wiener Festwochen takes place from mid-May to mid-June at various venues city-wide.

Donauinselfest MUSIC

(https://donauinselfest.at; late Jun) FREE Held over three days on a weekend in late June, the Donauinselfest features a feast of rock, pop, folk and country performers, and attracts almost three million onlookers. Best of all, it's free!

Musikfilm Festival FILM

(http://filmfestival-rathausplatz.at; 01, Rathausplatz; mid-Jul–early Sep; D, 1, 2 Rathaus, U Rathaus) Once the sun sets, the Rathausplatz is home to free screenings of operas, operettas and concerts. Turn up early for a good seat. Food stands and bars create a carnival-like atmosphere.

Sleeping

★my MOjO vie HOSTEL €

(0676-551 11 55; www.mymojovie.at; 07, Kaiserstrasse 77; dm €24-28, d/tr/q with private bathroom €80/120/160, s/d/tr/q with shared bathroom €40/60/90/116; @; U Burggasse-Stadthalle) An old-fashioned cage lift rattles up to these design-focused backpacker digs.

Everything you could wish for is here – well-equipped dorms with two power points per bed, a self-catering kitchen, netbooks for surfing, guidebooks for browsing and musical instruments for your own jam session. There's no air-con but fans are available in summer.

Hotel am Brillantengrund HOTEL €
(☎01-523 36 62; www.brillantengrund.com; 07, Bandgasse 4; s/d/tr/q from €69/79/99/119; @ 📶; 🚌49 Westbahnstrasse/Zieglergasse, U Zieglergasse) In a lemon-yellow building set around a sociable courtyard strewn with potted palms, this community linchpin works with local artists and hosts regular exhibitions, along with DJs, live music and other events such as pop-up markets and shops. Parquet-floored rooms are simple but decorated with vintage furniture, which variously incorporate local artworks, funky wallpapers and retro light fittings. Breakfast included.

Hotel Drei Kronen PENSION €
(☎01-587 32 89; www.hotel3kronen.at; 04, Schleifmühlegasse 25; s/d from €69/92; @ 📶; U Kettenbrückengasse) Within stumbling distance of the Naschmarkt (some rooms overlook it), this family-owned abode is one of Vienna's best-kept secrets. Palatial touches (shiny marble, polished brass, white-and-gold wallpaper) are distinctly Viennese, but nonetheless a casual feel prevails. Rooms are fitted with *Jugendstil* (Art Nouveau) furniture and art (including many prints by Gustav Klimt).

★**Grand Ferdinand Hotel** DESIGN HOTEL €€€
(☎01-918 804 00; www.grandferdinand.com; 01, Schubertring 10-12; dm/d/ste from €30/180/500; ❄ 📶 🏊; 🚌2, 71) An enormous taxidermied horse stands in the reception area of this ultrahip newcomer, which is shaking up Vienna's accommodation scene by offering parquet-floored dorms with mahogany bunks alongside richly coloured designer rooms with chaises longues and chandeliered suites with private champagne bars. Breakfast (€29) is served on the panoramic rooftop terrace, adjacent to the heated, open-air infinity pool.

★**Hotel Capricorno** HOTEL €€
(☎01-533 31 04-0; www.schick-hotels.com/hotel-capricorno; 01, Schwedenplatz 3-4; s/d incl breakfast from €118/146; P 📶; 🚌1, 2, U Schwedenplatz) Set behind an unpromising mid-20th-century facade, Hotel Capricorno was stunningly made over in 2015 in lustrous velveteens in zesty lime, orange, lemon and aubergine shades. Most of its 42 rooms have balconies (front rooms overlook the Danube Canal; rear rooms are quieter). On-site parking – rare for Vienna – is available for just €24 per day. It's a 10-minute walk from Stephansdom.

★**Magdas** BOUTIQUE HOTEL €€
(☎01-720 02 88; www.magdas-hotel.at; 02, Laufbergergasse 2; d €70-150) How clever: the Magdas is a hotel making a social difference as here the staff who welcome guests are refugees. The former retirement home turned boutique hotel opened its doors in 2016 and hit the ground running. The rooms are retro cool, with one-of-a-kind murals, knitted cushions and upcycling. The pick of them have balconies overlooking the Prater, just around the corner.

Eating

Würstelstande (sausage stands) are great for a cheap bite on the run, and the city has a booming international restaurant scene and many multiethnic markets. Self-caterers can also stock up at central Hofer, Billa and Spar supermarkets. Some have delis that make sandwiches to order.

DON'T MISS

FOOD MARKET FINDS

The sprawling **Naschmarkt** (06, Linke & Rechte Wienzeile; ⏲6am-7.30pm Mon-Fri, to 6pm Sat; U Karlsplatz, Kettenbrückengasse) is the place to *nasch* (snack) in Vienna. Stalls are piled high with meats, fruits, vegetables, cheeses, olives, spices and wine. There are also plenty of cafes dishing up good-value lunches, along with delis and takeaway stands.

Bio-Markt Freyung (01, Freyungasse; ⏲9am-6pm Fri & Sat; U Herrengasse, Schottentor) 🍃 sells farm-fresh produce, as does the bustling **Karmelitermarkt** (02, Karmelitermarkt; ⏲6am-7.30pm Mon-Fri, to 5pm Sat; 🚌2 Karmeliterplatz, U Taborstrasse). Head to the Saturday farmers market at the latter for brunch at one of the excellent deli-cafes or, if you like you're markets with a little more edge, head to **Bauernmarkt Yppenplatz.** (16, Yppenplatz; ⏲9am-1pm Sat; 🚌2, U Josefstädter Strasse).

★Bitzinger Würstelstand am Albertinaplatz STREET FOOD €

(www.bitzinger-wien.at; 01, Albertinaplatz; sausages €3.40-4.40; ⌚8am-4am; 🚋Kärntner Ring/Oper, Ⓤ Karlsplatz, Stephansplatz) Behind the Staatsoper, Vienna's best sausage stand has cult status. Bitzinger offers the contrasting spectacle of ladies and gents dressed to the nines, sipping beer, wine (from €2.30) or Joseph Perrier Champagne (€19.90 for 0.2L) while tucking into sausages at outdoor tables or the heated counter after performances. Mustard (€0.40) comes in *süss* (sweet, ie mild) or *scharf* (fiercely hot).

★Griechenbeisl BISTRO €€

(☎01-533 19 77; www.griechenbeisl.at; 01, Fleischmarkt 11; mains €15-28; ⌚11.30am-11.30pm; ✎; 🚋1, 2, Ⓤ Schwedenplatz) Dating from 1447 and frequented by Beethoven, Brahms, Schubert and Strauss among other luminaries, Vienna's oldest restaurant has vaulted rooms, wood panelling and a figure of Augustin trapped at the bottom of a well inside the front door. Every classic Viennese dish is on the menu, along with three daily vegetarian options. In summer, head to the plant-fringed front garden.

★Lingenhel MODERN EUROPEAN €€

(☎01-710 15 66; www.lingenhel.com; 03, Landstrasser Hauptstrasse 74; mains €19-24; ⌚shop 8am-8pm, restaurant 8am-10pm Mon-Sat; Ⓤ Rochusgasse) One of Vienna's most exciting gastro newcomers, Lingenhel is an ultra-slick deli-shop-bar-restaurant, lodged in a 200-year-old house. Salamis, wines and own-dairy cheeses tempt in the shop, while much-lauded chef Daniel Hoffmeister helms the kitchen in the pared-back, whitewashed restaurant. The season-inflected food – simple as char with kohlrabi and pork belly with aubergines – tastes profoundly of what it ought to.

★Punks MODERN EUROPEAN €€

(☎0664 275 70 72; www.punks.wien; 08, Florianigasse 50; small plates €4.50) The name might be a giveaway, but this guerilla-style restaurant *is* indeed shaking up an otherwise genteel neighbourhood. Patrick Müller, Anna Schwab and René Steindachner have 'occupied' a former wine bar and eschewed the usual refit or any form of interior decoration; the focus is, quite literally, on the kitchen, with a menu of inventive small dishes prepared behind the bar.

Meierei im Stadtpark AUSTRIAN €€

(☎01-713 31 68; http://steirereck.at; 03, Am Heumarkt 2a; set breakfasts €20-24, mains €11.50-22; ⌚8am-11pm Mon-Fri, 9am-7pm Sat & Sun; ✎; Ⓤ Stadtpark) In the green surrounds of Stadtpark, the Meierei is most famous for its goulash served with lemon, capers and creamy dumplings (€18) and its selection of 120 types of cheese. Served until noon, the bountiful breakfast features gastronomic show-stoppers such as poached duck egg with sweet potato, cress and wild mushrooms, and warm curd-cheese strudel with elderberry compote.

DON'T MISS

COFFEE HOUSE CULTURE

Vienna's legendary *Kaffeehäuser* (coffee houses) rank on the Unesco list of Intangible Cultural Heritage, which defines them as 'places where time and space are consumed, but only the coffee is found on the bill'. Grand or humble, poster-plastered or chandelier-lit, this is where you can join the locals for coffee, cake and a slice of living history.

Café Sperl (www.cafesperl.at; 06, Gumpendorfer Strasse 11; ⌚7am-11pm Mon-Sat, 11am-8pm Sun; 📶; Ⓤ Museumsquartier, Kettenbrückengasse)

Café Central (www.palaisevents.at; 01, Herrengasse 14; ⌚7.30am-10pm Mon-Sat, 10am-10pm Sun; 📶; Ⓤ Herrengasse)

Café Leopold Hawelka (www.hawelka.at; 01, Dorotheergasse 6; ⌚8am-midnight Mon-Wed, to 1am Thu-Sat, 10am-midnight Sun; Ⓤ Stephansplatz)

Sperlhof (02, Grosse Sperlgasse 41; ⌚4pm-1.30am; Ⓤ Taborstrasse)

Supersense (02, Praterstrasse 70; lunch special €5.50-6.50, breakfast €3.80-8; ⌚9am-7pm Mon-Fri, 10am-5pm Sat)

Drinking & Nightlife

Bars pump north and south of the Naschmarkt, around Spittelberg and along the Gürtel (mainly around the U6 stops of Josefstädter Strasse and Nussdorfer Strasse). Vienna's great-value *Heurigen*, or wine taverns, cluster in the wine-growing suburbs to the north, southwest, west and northwest of the city.

★Loos American Bar COCKTAIL BAR
(www.loosbar.at; 01, Kärntner Durchgang 10; ⏲noon-5am Thu-Sat, to 4am Sun-Wed; U Stephansplatz) Loos is *the* spot in the Innere Stadt for a classic cocktail such as its signature dry martini, expertly whipped up by talented mixologists. Designed by Adolf Loos in 1908, this tiny 27-sq-metre box (seating just 20-or-so patrons) is bedecked from head to toe in onyx and polished brass, with mirrored walls that make it appear far larger.

Dachboden BAR
(www.25hours-hotels.com; 07, Lerchenfelder Strasse 1-3; ⏲3pm-1am; 📶; U Volkstheater) Housed in the **25hours Hotel** (☎01-521 51; www.25hours-hotels.com; 07, Lerchenfelder Strasse 1-3; d €160-190, ste €195-330; P📶; U Volkstheater), Dachboden has stunning views of Vienna's skyline from its beach bar–style decked terrace. DJs spins jazz, soul and funk on Wednesday and Friday nights. Inside, wooden crates and mismatched vintage furniture are scattered across the raw-concrete floor beneath chandeliers. Besides Fritz cola and an array of wines, beers and speciality teas, there are tapas-style snacks.

★Achtundzwanzig WINE BAR
(www.achtundzwanzig.at; 08, Schlösslegasse 28; ⏲4pm-1am Mon-Thu, to 2am Fri, 7pm-2am Sat; 🚋5, 43, 44, U Schottentor) Austrian wine fans with a rock-and-roll sensibility will feel like they've found heaven at this black-daubed *vinothek* (wine bar) that vibes casual but takes its wines super seriously. Wines by the glass are all sourced from small producers – many of them are organic or minimal-intervention and friends of the owners – and are well priced at under €4 a glass.

★Strandbar Herrmann BAR
(www.strandbarherrmann.at; 03, Herrmannpark; ⏲10am-2am Apr-early Oct; 📶; 🚋O Hintere Zollamstrasse, U Schwedenplatz) You'd swear you're by the sea at this hopping canalside beach bar, with beach chairs, sand, DJ beats and hordes of Viennese livin' it up on summer evenings. Cool trivia: it's located on Herrmannpark, named after picture-postcard inventor Emanuel Herrmann (1839–1902).

Weinstube Josefstadt WINE BAR
(08, Piaristengasse 27; ⏲4pm-midnight Apr-Dec, closed Jan-Mar; U Rathaus) Weinstube Josefstadt is one of the loveliest *Stadtheurigen* (city wine taverns) in Vienna. A leafy green oasis spliced between towering residential blocks, its tables of friendly, well-liquored locals are squeezed in between the trees and shrubs looking onto a pretty, painted *Salettl*, or wooden summerhouse. Wine is local and cheap, food is typical, with a buffet-style meat and fritter selection.

Fluc CLUB
(www.fluc.at; 02, Praterstern 5; ⏲6pm-4am; U Praterstern) Located on the wrong side of the tracks (Praterstern can be rough around the edges at times) and housed in a converted pedestrian passage, Fluc is the closest that Vienna's nightlife scene comes to anarchy – without the fear of physical violence.

☆ Entertainment

Vienna is, was and will always be the European capital of opera and classical music. The line-up of music events is never-ending and even the city's buskers are often classically trained musicians.

Box offices generally open from Monday to Saturday and sell cheap (€3 to €6) standing-room tickets around an hour before performances.

For weekly listings, visit Flater (www.falter.at), while Tourist Info Wien (http://events.wien.info/en) lists concerts up to 18 months in advance.

★Staatsoper OPERA
(☎01-514 44 7880; www.wiener-staatsoper.at; 01, Opernring 2; tickets €10-208, standing room €3-4; 🚋D 1, 2, 71 Kärntner Ring/Oper, U Karlsplatz) The glorious Staatsoper is Vienna's premiere opera and classical-music venue. Productions are lavish, formal affairs, where people dress up accordingly. In the interval, wander the foyer and refreshment rooms to fully appreciate the gold-and-crystal interior. Opera is not performed here in July and August (tours still take place). Tickets can be purchased (☎01-514 44 7810; www.bundestheater.at; 01, Operngasse 2; ⏲8am-6pm Mon-Fri, 9am-noon Sat & Sun; U Stephansplatz) up to two months in advance.

IMPERIAL ENTERTAINMENT

The world-famous Vienna Boys' Choir performs on Sunday at 9.15am (late September to June) in the **Burgkapelle** (Royal Chapel) in the Hofburg. **Tickets** (01-533 99 27; www.hofmusikkapelle.gv.at; 01, Schweizerhof; tickets €10-36; U Herrengasse) should be booked around six weeks in advance. The group also performs on Friday afternoons at the **MuTh** (01-347 80 80; www.muth.at; 02, Obere Augartenstrasse 1e; Vienna Boys' Choir Fri performance €39-89; 4-6pm Mon-Fri & 1 hour before performances; U Taborstrasse).

Another Habsburg legacy is the **Spanish Riding School** (Spanische Hofreitschule; 01-533 90 31-0; www.srs.at; 01, Michaelerplatz 1; performances €25-217; hours vary; 1A, 2A Michaelerplatz, U Herrengasse), where Lipizzaner stallions gracefully perform equine ballet to classical music. For morning training sessions, same-day tickets are available at the nearby visitor centre.

★Musikverein — CONCERT VENUE

(01-505 81 90; www.musikverein.at; 01, Musikvereinsplatz 1; tickets €24-95, standing room €4-6; box office 9am-8pm Mon-Fri, to 1pm Sat Sep-Jun, 9am-noon Mon-Fri Jul & Aug; U Karlsplatz) The opulent Musikverein holds the proud title of the best acoustics of any concert hall in Austria, which the Vienna Philharmonic Orchestra embraces. The lavish interior can be visited by 45-minute guided tour (in English and German; adult/child €6.50/4) at 10am, 11am and noon Monday to Saturday. Smaller-scale performances are held in the Brahms Saal. There are no student tickets.

Theater an der Wien — THEATRE

(01-588 85; www.theater-wien.at; 06, Linke Wienzeile 6; tickets €10-160, standing room €7, student tickets €10-15; box office 10am-6pm Mon-Sat, 2-6pm Sun; U Karlsplatz) The Theater an der Wien has hosted some monumental premiere performances, including Beethoven's *Fidelio,* Mozart's *Die Zauberflöte* and Strauss Jnr's *Die Fledermaus*. These days, besides staging musicals, dance and concerts, it's re-established its reputation for high-quality opera, with one premiere each month.

Student tickets go on sale 30 minutes before shows; standing-room tickets are available one hour prior to performances.

Jazzland — LIVE MUSIC

(01-533 25 75; www.jazzland.at; 01, Franz-Josefs-Kai 29; cover €11-20; 7pm-2am Mon-Sat mid-Aug–mid-Jul, live music from 9pm; 1, 2, U Schwedenplatz) Buried in a former wine cellar beneath Ruprechtskirche, Jazzland is Vienna's oldest jazz club, dating back nearly 50 years. The music covers the whole jazz spectrum, and features both local and international acts. Past performers have included Ray Brown, Teddy Wilson, Big Joe Williams and Max Kaminsky.

Shopping

In the alley-woven Innere Stadt, go to Kohlmarkt for designer chic, Herrengasse for antiques and Kärntnerstrasse for high-street brands. Tune into Vienna's creative pulse in the idiosyncratic boutiques and concept stores in Neubau, especially along Kirchengasse and Lindengasse along with the edgier still around Yppenplatz.

Dorotheum — ANTIQUES

(www.dorotheum.com; 01, Dorotheergasse 17; 10am-6pm Mon-Fri, 9am-5pm Sat; U Stephansplatz) The Dorotheum is among the largest auction houses in Europe and for the casual visitor it's more like a museum, housing everything from antique toys and tableware to autographs, antique guns and, above all, lots of quality paintings. You can bid at the regular auctions held here, otherwise just drop by (it's free) and enjoy browsing.

★Dirndlherz — CLOTHING

(http://dirndlherz.at; 07, Lerchenfelder Strasse 50; 11am-6pm Thu & Fri, to 4pm Sat; U Volkstheater) Putting her own spin on Alpine fashion, Austrian designer Gabriela Urabl creates one-of-a-kind, high-fashion *Dirndls* (women's traditional dress), from sassy purple-velvet bosom-lifters to 1950s-style gingham numbers and *Dirndls* emblazoned with quirky motifs like pop-art and punk-like conical metal studs. T-shirts with tag-lines like *'Mei Dirndl is in da Wäsch'* ('My *Dirndl* is in the wash') are also available.

Information

Most hostels and hotels in Vienna offer free wi-fi, called WLAN (pronounced vee-lan) in German. As well as 400 city hotspots which can be found at www.wien.gv.at/stadtplan, cafes, coffee houses and bars also offer free wi-fi; check locations at www.freewave.at/en/hotspots.

Tourist Info Wien (☎01-245 55; www.wien.info; 01, Albertinaplatz; ⏰9am-7pm; 📶; 🚊D, 1, 2, 71 Kärntner Ring/Oper, Ⓤ Stephansplatz) Vienna's main tourist office has free maps and racks of brochures.

ℹ Getting There & Away

AIR

Located 19km southwest of the city centre, **Vienna International Airport** (VIE; ☎01-700 722 233; www.viennaairport.com; 📶) is a well-serviced international hub. The fastest transport into the centre is **City Airport Train** (CAT; www.cityairporttrain.com; single/return €11/19), which runs every 30 minutes and takes 16 minutes between the airport and Wien Mitte; book online for a discount. The S-Bahn (S7) does the same journey (single €4.40) but in 25 minutes.

BOAT

Fast hydrofoils travel eastwards to Bratislava (one way €20 to €35, 1¼ hours) daily from April to October. From May to September, they also travel twice weekly to Budapest (one way/return €109/125, 5½ hours). Bookings can be made through **DDSG Blue Danube** (☎01-58 880; www.ddsg-blue-danube.at; Handelskai 265, Vienna; Ⓜ Vorgartenstrasse).

BUS

National Bundesbuses arrive and depart from several different locations, depending on the destination. Bus lines serving Vienna include **Eurolines** (☎0900 128 712; www.eurolines.at; 03, Erdbergstrasse 200; ⏰office 8am-6pm; Ⓤ Erdberg).

CAR & MOTORCYCLE

The Gürtel is an outer ring road that joins up with the A22 on the north bank of the Danube and the A23 southeast of town. All the main road routes intersect with this system, including the A1 from Linz and Salzburg, and the A2 from Graz.

TRAIN

Vienna is one of central Europe's main rail hubs. Österreichische Bundesbahn has connections to many European cities, including Budapest (€29 to €37, 2½ to 3¼ hours), Munich (€93, 4½ to five hours), Paris (€51 to €142, 11½ to 13 hours), Prague (€49, 4¼ hours) and Venice (€49 to €108, seven to 11 hours).

Vienna's main train station, the Wien Hauptbahnhof, 3km south of Stephansdom, handles all international trains as well as trains Austria's provincial capitals, apart from Salzburg.

ℹ Getting Around

BICYCLE

Citybike Wien (Vienna City Bike; www.citybikewien.at; 1st/2nd/3rd hr free/€1/2, per hr thereafter €4) has more than 120 bicycle stands across the city. A credit card is required and after a €1 registration fee bikes are free for the first hour.

PUBLIC TRANSPORT

Vienna's unified public transport network encompasses trains, trams, buses, and underground (U-Bahn) and suburban (S-Bahn) trains. Free maps and information pamphlets are available from **Wiener Linien** (☎01-7909-100; www.wienerlinien.at).

All tickets must be validated at the entrance to U-Bahn stations and on buses and trams (except for weekly and monthly tickets).

Singles cost €2.20. A 24-hour ticket costs €7.60, a 48-hour ticket €13.30 and a 72-hour ticket €16.50. Weekly tickets (valid Monday to Sunday) cost €16.20.

THE DANUBE VALLEY

The stretch of Danube between Krems and Melk, known locally as the Wachau, is arguably the loveliest along the entire length of the long, long river. Both banks are dotted with ruined castles and medieval towns, and lined with terraced vineyards. Further upstream is the industrial city of Linz, Austria's avant-garde art and new technology trailblazer.

Krems an der Donau

☎02732 / POP 23,900

Sitting on the northern bank of the Danube against a backdrop of terraced vineyards, Krems marks the beginning of the Wachau. It has an attractive cobbled centre, some good restaurants and the gallery-dotted Kunstmeile.

👁 Sights & Activities

Kunsthalle Krems GALLERY

(www.kunsthalle.at; Franz-Zeller-Platz 3; €10; ⏰10am-5pm Tue-Sun) The flagship of Krems' Kunstmeile, an eclectic collection of galleries and museums, the Kunsthalle has a program of changing exhibitions. These might be mid-19th-century landscapes or hardcore conceptual works, but are always well curated. Guided tours (€3) run on Sundays at 2pm.

ON YOUR BIKE

Register online for Danube Valley's bike-hire network **Nextbike** (02742-229 901; www.nextbike.at; per hr €1, 24hr €8).

Domäne Wachau WINE
(02711-371 15; www.domaene-wachau.at; 10am-5pm Mon-Sat Apr-Oct, closed Sat Nov-Mar) If you're intent on tasting the best of what the Wachau has to offer, it's a good idea to do a broad range of vineyards, from the innovative family-run operations to the big boys like Domäne Wachau, one of the region's most well known producers internationally. A large modern tasting room is set back just from the river and staffed by an army of keen young assistants. It also stocks some nice local food products if wine's not your thing.

Sleeping

Hotel-Garni Schauhuber HOTEL €
(0660 4003 412; Steiner Landstrasse 16; s/d €40/72;) The Schauhuber is charmingly old-fashioned, with sparkling tiled surfaces, whitewashed walls and large rooms. Breakfast is hearty.

Kolpinghaus ACCOMMODATION SERVICES €
(02732-835 41; www.kolpingkrems.at; Alauntalstrasse 95 & 97; s/d €40/75; reception 8am-5pm Mon-Fri, to noon Sat & Sun; P) These super student quarters are available to travellers any time of year: a great deal if you don't mind the trek up to the university. Some of the basic but comfortable rooms are huge, with bathrooms the size of some hotel singles, as well as their own kitchens. Only con is the institutional checkout time of 10am.

Information

Krems Tourismus (02732-82 676; www.krems.info; Utzstrasse 1; 9am-6pm Mon-Fri, 11am-6pm Sat, 11am-4pm Sun, shorter hours in winter) Helpful office well stocked with info and maps.

Getting There & Away

Frequent daily trains connect Krems with Vienna (€17.60, one hour). **Wachau Linien** (0810 222 324; www.vor.at) runs buses along the Danube Valley and the Wachau Ticket (€10, purchase from the driver) gives you a day's unlimited travel on all buses and the Danube ferries.

Melk

02752 / POP 5260

With its blockbuster abbey-fortress set high above the valley, Melk is a high point of any visit to the Danube Valley. Separated from the river by a stretch of woodland, this pretty town makes for an easy and rewarding day trip from Krems or even Vienna. Post abbey visit, you'll find plenty of restaurants and cafes with alfresco seating line the Rathausplatz.

Sights

Stift Melk ABBEY
(Benedictine Abbey of Melk; www.stiftmelk.at; Abt Berthold Dietmayr Strasse 1; adult/child €11/6, with guided tour €13/8; 9am-5.30pm, tours 10.55am & 2.55pm May-Sep, tours only 11am & 2pm Nov-Mar) Of the many abbeys in Austria, Stift Melk is the most famous. Possibly Lower Austria's finest, the monastery church dominates the complex with its twin spires and high octagonal dome. The interior is baroque gone barmy, with regiments of smirking cherubs, gilt twirls and polished faux marble. The theatrical high-altar scene, depicting St Peter and St Paul (the church's two patron saints), is by Peter Widerin. Johann Michael Rottmayr created most of the ceiling paintings, including those in the dome.

Information

Melk Tourist Office (02752-511 60; www.stadt-melk.at; Kremser Strasse 5; 9.30am-6pm Mon-Sat, to 4pm Sun Apr-Oct, 9am-5pm Mon-Thu, to 2.30pm Fri Nov-Mar)

Getting There & Away

Boats leave from the canal by Pionierstrasse, 400m north of the abbey. There are hourly trains to Vienna (€16.50, 1¼ hours).

Linz

0732 / POP 197,500

'It begins in Linz' goes the Austrian saying, and it's true. The technology trailblazer and European Capital of Culture 2009 is blessed with a leading-edge cyber centre and world-class contemporary-art gallery.

Sights & Activities

★ Ars Electronica Center MUSEUM
(www.aec.at; Ars-Electronica-Strasse 1; adult/child €9.50/7.50; 9am-5pm Tue, Wed & Fri, 9am-9pm Thu, 10am-6pm Sat & Sun) The technology, science and digital media of the future are in the spotlight at Linz' biggest crowd-puller. In the labs you can interact with robots, animate digital objects, print 3D structures, turn your body into musical instruments, and (virtually) travel to outer space. Kids love it. Designed by Vienna-based architectural firm Treusch, the centre resembles a futuristic ship by the Danube after dark, when its LED glass skin kaleidoscopically changes colour.

★ Lentos GALLERY
(www.lentos.at; Ernst-Koref-Promenade 1; adult/child €8/4.50, guided tours €3; 10am-6pm Tue, Wed & Fri-Sun, 10am-9pm Thu) Overlooking the Danube, the rectangular glass-and-steel Lentos is strikingly illuminated by night. The gallery guards one of Austria's finest modern-art collections, including works by Warhol, Schiele, Klimt, Kokoschka and Lovis Corinth, which sometimes feature in the large-scale exhibitions. There are regular guided tours in German and 30-minute tours in English at 4pm on the first Saturday of the month. Alternatively, download Lentos' app from the website.

Sleeping & Eating

★ Hotel am Domplatz DESIGN HOTEL €€
(0732-77 30 00; www.hotelamdomplatz.at; Stifterstrasse 4; d €111-175, ste €280-340;) Adjacent to the neo-Gothic Mariendom (ask for a room overlooking the cathedral), this glass-and-concrete cube filled with striking metal sculptures has streamlined, Nordic-style pristine-white and blonde-wood rooms with semi-open bathrooms. Wind down with a view at the rooftop spa. In fine weather, the cathedral-facing terrace is a prime spot for breakfast (€18), which includes a glass of bubbly.

★ Cafe Jindrak CAFE €
(www.jindrak.at; Herrenstrasse 22; dishes €3-8.80; 8am-6pm Mon-Sat, 8.30am-6pm Sun;) Join the cake-loving locals at this celebrated cafe – the original shop (1929) of a now nine-strong chain that produces over 100,000 of its famous *Linzer Torte* each year made to its family recipe. You'd need a huge fork (and appetite) to tackle the torte that set a Guinness World Record in 1999, measuring 4m high and weighing 650kg.

LINZ CARD

The Linz Card, giving entry to major sights and unlimited use of public transport, costs €18/15 for one/three days.

Information

Tourist Information Linz (0732-7070 2009; www.linztourismus.at; Hauptplatz 1; 9am-7pm Mon-Sat, 10am-7pm Sun May-Sep, 9am-5pm Mon-Sat, 10am-5pm Sun Oct-Apr) Upper Austria information as well as brochures and accommodation listings.

Getting There & Around

AIR

Ryanair flies to the **Blue Danube Airport** (LNZ; 07221-60 00; www.linz-airport.at; Flughafenstrasse 1, Hörsching), 13km southwest of Linz. An hourly shuttle bus (€3.10, 20 minutes) links the airport to the main train station.

PUBLIC TRANSPORT

Single bus and tram tickets cost €1.10, and day passes €4.40 and must be pre-purchased.

TRAIN

Linz is halfway between Salzburg and Vienna on the main road and rail routes. Trains to Salzburg (€12.80, 1¼ hours) and Vienna (€18.90, 1½ hours) leave at least twice hourly.

THE SOUTH

Austria's southern states often feel worlds apart from the rest of the country, both in climate and attitude. Styria (Steiermark) is a blissful amalgamation of genteel architecture, rolling green hills, vine-covered slopes and soaring mountains. Its capital, Graz, is one of Austria's most attractive cities. A glamorous crowd heads to sun-drenched Carinthia (Kärnten) in summer. Sidling up to Italy, its sparkling lakes and pretty lidos are as close to Mediterranean as this landlocked country gets.

Graz

0316 / POP 265,780

Austria's second-largest city is relaxed and good-looking, with ample green spaces, red rooftops and a narrow, fast-flowing river gushing through its centre. Architecturally, Graz hints at nearby Italy with its Renaissance courtyards and baroque palaces. But there's a youthful, almost Eastern European energy too, with a handful of edgily modern buildings, a vibrant arts scene and great nightlife (thanks in part to its large student population).

Sights

Graz is a city easily enjoyed by simply wandering aimlessly. Admission to all of the Joanneum museums with a 24-hour ticket costs €11/4 for adults/children.

★Kunsthaus Graz GALLERY
(www.kunsthausgraz.at; Lendkai 1; adult/child €9/3; 10am-5pm Tue-Sun; 1, 3, 6, 7 Südtiroler Platz) Designed by British architects Peter Cook and Colin Fournier, this world-class contemporary-art space is known as the 'friendly alien' by locals. The building is signature Cook, a photovoltaic-skinned sexy biomorphic blob that is at once completely at odds with its pristine historic surroundings but sits rather lyrically within in it as well. Exhibitions change every three to four months.

Neue Galerie Graz GALLERY
(www.museum-joanneum.at; Joanneumsviertel; adult/child €9/3; 10am-5pm Tue-Sun; ; 1, 3, 4, 5, 6, 7 Hauptplatz) The Neue Galerie is the crowning glory of the three museums inside the Joanneumsviertel complex. The stunning collection on level 0 is the highlight. Though not enormous, it showcases vibrant works by painters such as Ernst Christian Moser, Ferdinand Georg Waldmüller and Johann Nepomuk Passini. Egon Schiele is also represented here.

★Schlossberg VIEWPOINT
(1hr ticket for lift or funicular €2.10, lift adult/child €1.40/0.90; 4, 5 Schlossbergplatz) FREE Rising to 473m, Schlossberg is the site of the original fortress where Graz was founded and is marked by the city's most visible icon – the **Uhrturm** (Clock Tower; 4, 5 Schlossplatz/Murinse, for lift) FREE. Its wooded slopes can be reached by a number of bucolic and strenuous paths, but also by lift or Schlossbergbahn funicular. It's a brief walk or take tram 4 or 5 to Schlossplatz/Murinsel for the lift.

Schloss Eggenberg PALACE
(www.museum-joanneum.at; Eggenberger Allee 90; adult/child €11.50/5.50; tours hourly 10am-4pm, apart from 1pm Tue-Sun late Mar-Oct, exhibitions 10am-5pm Wed-Sun; 1 Schloss Eggenberg) Graz' elegant palace was created for the Eggenberg dynasty in 1625 by Giovanni Pietro de Pomis (1565–1633) at the request of Johann Ulrich (1568–1634). Admission is on a highly worthwhile guided tour during which you learn about the idiosyncrasies of each room, the stories told by the frescoes and about the Eggenberg family itself.

Sleeping

★Hotel Wiesler HOTEL €€
(0316-70 66-0; www.hotelwiesler.com; Grieskai 4; d €155-210; P @; 1, 3, 6, 7 Südtiroler Platz) The riverside Wiesler, a *Jugenstil* (art nouveau) gem from 1901, has been recently transformed into Graz' most glamorous hotel. Hotelier Florian Weltzer has shaken up everything, including the notion of room categories, and ensured that this is a luxury experience that is far from stuffy.

Hotel Daniel HOTEL €
(0316-71 10 80; www.hoteldaniel.com; Europaplatz 1; d €65-350; P @; 1, 3, 6, 7 Hauptbahnhof) The Daniel's rooms are well designed and super simple, and while its small 'smart' rooms scrape into budget territory, it also now offers the super exclusive loft cube on the roof if you're looking for something out of the ordinary. The lobby area is a lot of fun, a great space to work or just hang out.

Eating

Graz does fine dining with aplomb, but you'll also find plenty of cheap eats near Universität Graz, particularly on Halbärthgasse, Zinzendorfgasse and Harrachgasse.

Stock up for a picnic at the farmers markets on Kaiser-Josef-Platz and Lendplatz. For fast-food stands, head for Hauptplatz and Jakominiplatz.

★Aiola Upstairs INTERNATIONAL €€
(www.aiola.at; Schlossberg 2; pasta €14.50-16.50, mains €19.50-27.50; 9am-midnight Mon-Sat; ; 4, 5 Schlossbergplatz/Murinsel (for lift)) Ask locals for the best outdoor dining experience in Graz, and they'll direct you to Aiola. This wonderful restaurant on Schlossberg has great views from both its glass box interior and its beautiful summer terrace. Even better, the cooking up here is some of the city's best, with interesting international flavours and seasonal ingredients.

★Der Steirer AUSTRIAN, TAPAS €€

(☎0316-70 36 54; www.dersteirer.at; Belgiergasse 1; weekday lunch menu €8.90, mains €10.90-22; ⌚11am-midnight; ✎; 🚊1, 3, 6, 7 Südtiroler Platz) This neo-*Beisl* (bistro pub) and wine bar has a beautiful selection of Styrian dishes, including a great goulash, lamb cutlets and stuffed peppers, all done in a simple, contemporary style. Its Styrian tapas concept works, and is a nice way to sample local flavours if you just feel like nibbling.

Kunsthauscafé INTERNATIONAL €

(☎0316-71 49 57; www.kunsthauscafe.co.at; Südtirolerplatz 2; mains €6-16.50; ⌚9am-11pm Sun-Thu, to 1am Fri & Sat) A happy, young crowd fills the long tables here for a menu that incorporates burgers (from big beef to goat cheese), vaguely Mexican dishes, main-sized salads and the house special 'Styrian Sandwich', a combination of crispy pork belly, creamy sauerkraut and horseradish. It's very, very loud, but fun if you're in the mood.

Drinking & Nightlife

The bar scene in Graz is split between three main areas: around the university; east of the Kunsthaus in hipster Lend; and on Mehlplatz and Prokopigasse (dubbed the 'Bermuda Triangle').

Blendend COFFEE

(www.blendend.at; Mariahilferstrasse 24; ⌚4pm-2am Mon-Fri, from 9am Sat & Sun) A rambling, warm and endearingly boho addition to Lend's usual lineup of grungy bars, Blendend is a great drinking and snacking spot during the week and then turns all day cafe on weekends with beautiful homemade cakes and desserts competing with the spritzs and excellent local beers. In warmer weather all the action happens at the courtyard tables.

Freiblick Tagescafe ROOFTOP BAR

(☎0316-83 53 02; freiblick.co.at; Sackstrasse 7-11, Kastner & Öhler; ⌚9.30am-7pm Mon-Fri, to 6pm Sat) This huge terrace cafe-bar tops the Kastner & Öhler department store and has the best view in the city. Enjoy the clouds and rooftops over breakfast platter and coffee or a lunchtime soup or salad. Or stop by in the afternoon for something from the Prosecco spritz menu or a Hugo Royal – Moët Chandon splashed with elderflower (€15).

OFF THE BEATEN TRACK

STYRIAN TUSCANY

Head south of Graz to what's known as *Steirische Toskana* (Styrian Tuscany), for lush wine country that's reminiscent of Chianti: gentle rolling hills cultivated with vineyards or patchwork farmland, dotted with small forests where deer roam. Apart from its stellar whites, it's also famous for Kürbiskernöl, the rich pumpkin-seed oil generously used in Styrian cooking. The picturesque 'capital' of **Ehrenhausen**, on the road to the Slovenian border, makes a fine base for wine tasting and exploring.

Information

Graz Tourismus (☎0316-807 50; www.graztourismus.at; Herrengasse 16; ⌚10am-7pm Apr-Oct & Dec, to 6pm Nov & Jan-Mar; phone line 10am-5pm; 📶; 🚊1, 3, 4, 5, 6, 7 Hauptplatz) Graz' main tourist office, with loads of free information on the city and helpful and knowledgeable staff.

Getting There & Away

AIR

Graz airport (GRZ; ☎0316-290 20; www.flughafen-graz.at) is located 10km south of the centre and is served by European carriers including Air Berlin, which connects the city with Berlin.

TRAIN

Trains to Vienna depart hourly (€37.30, 2½ hours), and six daily go to Salzburg (€48, four hours). International train connections from Graz include Ljubljana (€41, 3½ hours) and Budapest (€70, 5½ hours).

Getting Around

BICYCLE

Bicycle rental is available from **Bicycle** (☎0316-82 13 57; www.bicycle.at; Körösistrasse 5; per 24hr €10, Fri-Mon €16, per week €49; ⌚7am-1pm & 2-6pm Mon-Fri).

PUBLIC TRANSPORT

Single tickets (€2.10) for buses, trams and the Schlossbergbahn are valid for one hour, but you're usually better off buying a 24-hour pass (€4.70).

Klagenfurt

0463 / POP 95,450

With its captivating location on Wörthersee and more Renaissance than baroque beauty, Klagenfurt has a distinct Mediterranean feel and is suprisingly lively. Carinthia's capital makes a handy base for exploring Wörthersee's lakeside villages and elegant medieval towns to the north.

Sights & Activities

Boating and swimming are usually possible from May to September.

Europapark PARK

The green expanse and its *Strandbad* (beach) on the shores of the Wörthersee are centres for aquatic fun and especially great for kids. The park's biggest draw is **Minimundus** (www.minimundus.at; Villacher Strasse 241; adult/child €18/10; 9am-7pm Mar & Apr, to 8pm May-Sep;), a 'miniature world' with 140 replicas of the world's architectural icons, downsized to a scale of 1:25. To get here, take bus 10, 11, 12 or 22 from Heiligengeistplatz.

Sleeping & Eating

When you check into accommodation in Klagenfurt, ask for a *Gästekarte* (guest card), entitling you to discounts.

★Stand No. 17 ITALIAN, AUSTRIAN €

(0677 617 129 65; Benediktiner Platz; €8-14; 8am-4pm Tue-Sat) Nini Loudon's kitchen springs in to service from 11.30am to 2pm. Her small, market-fresh menu has beloved regional specialities but more often crosses the border to include seasonal Italian classics (white truffle risotto if you're lucky) as well as occasionally ranging further to include couscous and tagines.

REACHING EUROPAPARK

Take bus 10 from Heiligengeistplatz via Minimundus to Strandbad. To get to Wörthersee by bicycle, avoid Villacher Strasse and take the bicycle path running along the northern side of Lendl Canal. Access from the small streets running west from Villacher Ring and Villacher Strasse.

★Das Domizil APARTMENT €€

(0664 843 30 50; www.das-domizil.at; Bahnhofstrasse 51; apt €98; P) This large, light and sweetly decorated apartment is in a grand 19th-century building just beyond the ring of the historic centre. It's extremely well equipped with a full kitchen, laundry facilities and lots of space. Owner Ingo Dietrich is a friendly and fashionable young local who is generous with his insider tips and time. Courtyard parking is €12 per day extra.

Information

Tourist Office (0463-537 22 23; www.visitklagenfurt.at; Neuer Platz 1, Rathaus; 8am-6pm Mon-Fri, 10am-5pm Sat, to 3pm Sun) Sells Kärnten Cards and books accommodation.

Getting There & Around

AIR

Klagenfurt's **airport** (www.klagenfurt-airport.com; Flughafenstrasse 60-66) is 3km north of town. Germanwings flies to Vienna and Berlin, Hamburg and Cologne in Germany.

BUS

Bus drivers sell single, hourly or 24-hour tickets (€1.40/2.10/4.80).

TRAIN

Two hourly direct trains run from Klagenfurt to Vienna (€52.60, four hours) and Salzburg (€41.25, 3¼ hours). Trains to Graz depart every two to three hours (€41.25, 2¾ hours). Trains to western Austria, Italy, Slovenia and Germany go via Villach (€7.10, 24 to 37 minutes, two to four per hour).

SALZBURG

0662 / POP

The joke 'If it's baroque, don't fix it' is a perfect maxim for Salzburg; the tranquil Old Town burrowed below steep hills looks much as it did when Mozart lived here 250 years ago.

A Unesco World Heritage site, Salzburg's overwhelmingly 17th-century Altstadt – old town – is entrancing both at ground level and from Hohensalzburg fortress high above. Across the fast-flowing Salzach River rests Schloss Mirabell, surrounded by gorgeous manicured gardens.

You can of course, bypass the baroque grandeur and head straight for kitsch-country via a tour of *The Sound of Music* film locations.

Sights

Dom CATHEDRAL
(Cathedral; www.salzburger-dom.at; Domplatz; 8am-7pm Mon-Sat, 1-7pm Sun May-Sep, shorter hours rest of year) FREE Gracefully crowned by a bulbous copper dome and twin spires, the Dom stands out as a masterpiece of baroque art. Bronze portals symbolising faith, hope and charity lead into the cathedral. In the nave, both the intricate stucco and Arsenio Mascagni's ceiling frescoes recounting the Passion of Christ guide the eye to the polychrome dome.

★ **Residenz** PALACE
(www.domquartier.at; Residenzplatz 1; DomQuartier ticket adult/child €12/5; 10am-5pm Wed-Mon) The crowning glory of Salzburg's new DomQuartier, the Residenz is where the prince-archbishops held court until Salzburg became part of the Habsburg Empire in the 19th century. An audio-guide tour takes in the exuberant **state rooms**, lavishly adorned with tapestries, stucco and frescoes by Johann Michael Rottmayr. The 3rd floor is given over to the **Residenzgalerie**, where the focus is on Flemish and Dutch masters. Must-sees include Rubens' *Allegory on Emperor Charles V* and Rembrandt's chiaroscuro *Old Woman Praying*.

★ **Salzburg Museum** MUSEUM
(www.salzburgmuseum.at; Mozartplatz 1; adult/child €8.50/3; 9am-5pm Tue-Sun, to 8pm Thu;) Housed in the baroque Neue Residenz palace, this flagship museum takes you on a fascinating romp through Salzburg past and present. Ornate rooms showcase everything from Roman excavations to royal portraits. There are free **guided tours** at 6pm every Thursday.

★ **Festung Hohensalzburg** FORT
(www.salzburg-burgen.at; Mönchsberg 34; adult/child/family €12/6.80/26.20, incl funicular €15.20/8.70/33.70; 9am-7pm) Salzburg's most visible icon is this mighty, 900-year-old cliff-top fortress, one of the biggest and best preserved in Europe. It's easy to spend half a day up here, roaming the ramparts for far-reaching views over the city's spires, the Salzach River and the mountains. The fortress is a steep 15-minute jaunt from the centre or a speedy ride up in the glass Festungsbahn funicular.

Stift Nonnberg CONVENT
(Nonnberg Convent; Nonnberggasse 2; 7am-dusk) FREE A short climb up the Nonnbergstiege staircase from Kaigasse or along Festungsgasse brings you to this Benedictine convent, founded 1300 years ago and made famous as the nunnery in *The Sound of Music*. You can visit the beautiful rib-vaulted **church**, but the rest of the convent is off-limits. Take €0.50 to switch on the light that illuminates the beautiful **Romanesque frescoes**.

Mozarts Geburtshaus MUSEUM
(Mozart's Birthplace; www.mozarteum.at; Getreidegasse 9; adult/child €10/3.50; 8.30am-7pm Jul & Aug, 9am-5.30pm Sep-Jun) Wolfgang Amadeus Mozart, Salzburg's most famous son, was born in this bright yellow townhouse in 1756 and spent the first 17 years of his life here. Today's museum harbours a collection of instruments, documents and portraits. Highlights include the mini-violin he played as a toddler, plus a lock of his hair and buttons from his jacket. In one room, Mozart is shown as a holy babe beneath a neon-blue halo – we'll leave you to draw your own analogies.

Mozart-Wohnhaus MUSEUM
(Mozart's Residence; www.mozarteum.at; Makartplatz 8; adult/child €10/3.50; 8.30am-7pm Jul & Aug, 9am-5.30pm Sep-Jun) Tired of the cramped living conditions on Getreidegasse, the Mozart family moved to this more spacious abode in 1773, where a prolific Wolfgang composed works such as the *Shepherd King* (K208) and *Idomeneo* (K366). Emanuel Schikaneder, a close friend of Mozart and the librettist of *The Magic Flute*, was

DOMQUARTIER

Salzburg shines more brightly than ever since the opening of the DomQuartier (www.domquartier.at) in 2014, showcasing the most fabulous baroque monuments and museums in the historic centre. A single ticket (adult/child €12/5) gives you access to the **Residenz** state rooms and gallery, the upper galleries of the **Dom**, the **Dommuseum** and **Erzabtei St Peter**. The multilingual audio guide whisks you through the quarter in 90 minutes, though you could easily spend half a day absorbing all of its sights.

Salzburg

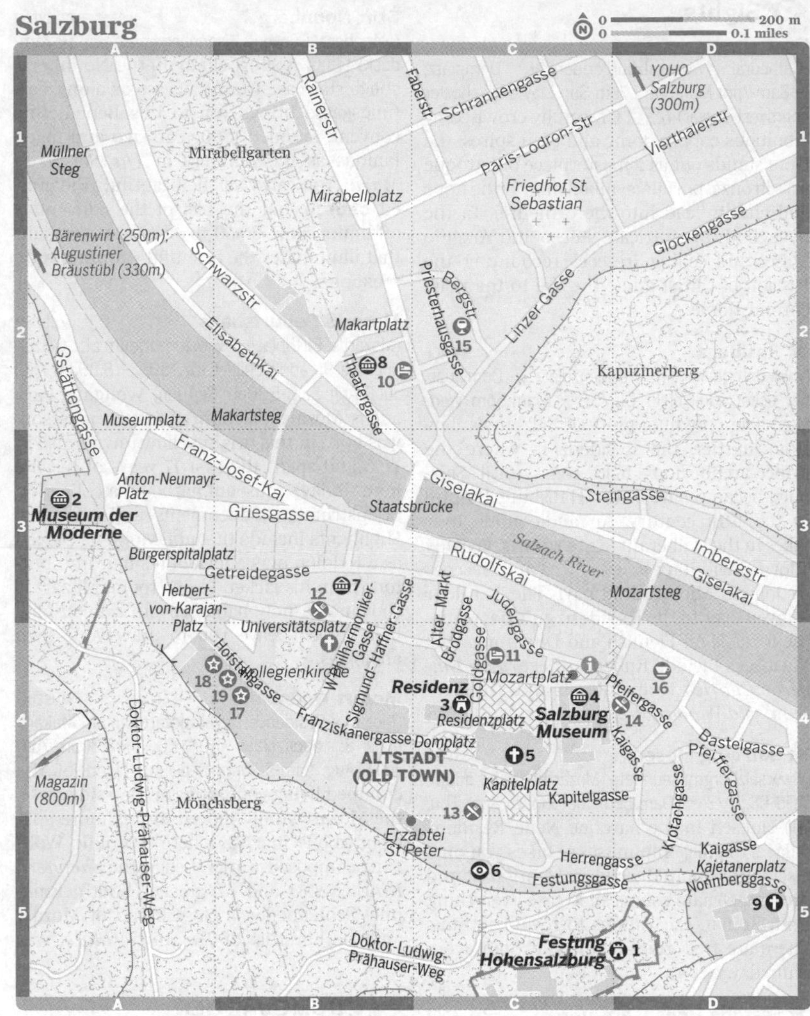

a regular guest here. An audio guide accompanies your visit, serenading you with opera excerpts. Alongside family portraits and documents, you'll find Mozart's original fortepiano.

★Museum der Moderne GALLERY
(www.museumdermoderne.at; Mönchsberg 32; adult/child €8/6; ⏲10am-6pm Tue-Sun, to 8pm Wed) Straddling Mönchsberg's cliffs, this contemporary glass-and-marble oblong of a gallery stands in stark contrast to the fortress, and shows first-rate temporary exhibitions of 20th- and 21st-century art. The works of Alberto Giacometti, Dieter Roth, Emil Nolde and John Cage have previously been featured. There's a free **guided tour** of the gallery at 6.30pm every Wednesday. The **Mönchsberg Lift** (Gstättengasse 13; one-way/return €2.30/3.60, incl gallery entry €9.10/6.50; ⏲8am-7pm Mon, to 9pm Tue-Sun) whizzes up to the gallery year-round.

Tours

One-hour guided tours (in German and English; €10) of the historic centre depart daily at 12.15pm and 2pm from Mozartplatz.

Salzburg

Top Sights
1 Festung Hohensalzburg D5
2 Museum der Moderne A3
3 Residenz C4
4 Salzburg Museum C4

Sights
5 Dom C4
6 Festungsbahn Funicular C5
7 Mozarts Geburtshaus B3
8 Mozart-Wohnhaus B2
9 Stift Nonnberg D5

Sleeping
10 Arte Vida B2
11 Hotel Am Dom C4

Eating
12 Grünmarkt B3
M32 .... (see 2)
13 Stiftsbäckerei St Peter C4
14 Zwettler's D4

Drinking & Nightlife
15 Enoteca Settemila C2
16 Kaffee Alchemie D4

Entertainment
17 Felsenreitschule B4
18 Grosses Festpielhaus A4
19 Haus für Mozart B4

Festivals & Events

Salzburg Festival ART
(Salzburger Festspiele; www.salzburgerfestspiele.at; Jul & Aug) The absolute highlight of the city's events calendar is the Salzburg Festival. It's a grand affair, with some 200 productions – including theatre, classical music and opera – staged in the impressive surrounds of the **Grosses Festpielhaus** (0662-804 50; Hofstallgasse 1), **Haus für Mozart** (House for Mozart; 0662-804 55 00; www.salzburgerfestspiele.at; Hofstallgasse 1) and the baroque **Felsenreitschule** (Summer Riding School; Hofstallgasse 1). Tickets vary in price between €11 and €430; book well ahead.

Sleeping

★ **Haus Ballwein** GUESTHOUSE €
(0662-82 40 29; www.haus-ballwein.at; Moosstrasse 69a; s €55-59, d €69-83, tr €85-90, q €90-98; P wi-fi) With its bright, pine-filled rooms, mountain views, free bike hire and garden, this place is big on charm. The largest, quietest rooms face the back and have balconies and kitchenettes. It's a 10-minute trundle from the *Altstadt;* take bus 21 to Gsengerweg. Breakfast is a wholesome spread of fresh rolls, eggs, fruit, muesli and cold cuts.

YOHO Salzburg HOSTEL €
(0662-87 96 49; www.yoho.at; Paracelsusstrasse 9; dm €19-23, d €72-93; @ wi-fi) Free wi-fi, secure lockers, comfy bunks, plenty of cheap beer and good-value schnitzels – what more could a backpacker ask for? Except, perhaps, a merry sing-along with *The Sound of Music* screened daily (yes, *every* day) at 7pm. The friendly crew can arrange tours, adventure sports such as rafting and canyoning, and bike hire.

Hotel Am Dom BOUTIQUE HOTEL €€
(0662-84 27 65; www.hotelamdom.at; Goldgasse 17; s €109-219, d €119-349; air-con wi-fi) Antique meets boutique at this *Altstadt* hotel, where the original vaults and beams of the 800-year-old building contrast with razor-sharp design features. Artworks inspired by the musical legends of the Salzburg Festival grace the rooms, which sport caramel-champagne colour schemes, funky lighting, velvet throws and ultra-glam bathrooms.

Arte Vida GUESTHOUSE €€
(0662-87 31 85; www.artevida.at; Dreifaltigkeitsgasse 9; s €69-129, d €89-145, apt €160-220; wi-fi) Arte Vida has the boho-chic feel of a Marrakech *riad*, with its lantern-lit salon, communal kitchen and serene garden. Asia and Africa have provided the inspiration for the rich colours and fabrics that dress the individually designed rooms. Your affable hosts Herbert and Karoline happily give tips on Salzburg and its surrounds, and can arrange massages and private yoga sessions.

★ **Villa Trapp** HOTEL €€€
(0662-63 08 60; www.villa-trapp.com; Traunstrasse 34; s €65-130, d €114-280, ste €290-580; P wi-fi) Marianne and Christopher have transformed the original von Trapp family home into a beautiful guesthouse (for guests only, we might add). The 19th-century villa is elegant, if not *quite* as palatial as in the movie, with tasteful wood-floored rooms and a balustrade for sweeping down à la Baroness Schräder.

Eating

Self-caterers can find picnic fixings at the **Grünmarkt** (Green Market; Universitätsplatz; ⏲7am-7pm Mon-Fri, to 3pm Sat).

★Magazin MODERN EUROPEAN €€€
(☎0662-841 584 20; www.magazin.co.at; Augustinergasse 13a; 2-course lunch €16, mains €27-41, tasting menus €71-85; ⏲11.30am-2pm & 6-10pm Tue-Sat) In a courtyard below Mönchsberg's sheer rock wall, Magazin shelters a deli, wine store, cookery school and restaurant. Chef Richard Brunnauer's menus fizz with seasonal flavours: dishes like marinated alpine char with avocado and herb salad and saddle of venison with boletus mushrooms are matched with wines from the 850-bottle cellar, and served alfresco or in the industrial-chic, cave-like interior.

Bärenwirt AUSTRIAN €€
(☎0662-42 24 04; www.baerenwirt-salzburg.at; Müllner Hauptstrasse 8; mains €9-19; ⏲11am-11pm) Sizzling and stirring since 1663, Bärenwirt is Austrian through and through. Go for hearty *Bierbraten* (beer roast) with dumplings, locally caught trout or organic wild-boar *Bratwurst*. A tiled oven warms the woody, hunting-lodge-style interior in winter, while the river-facing terrace is a summer crowd-puller. The restaurant is 500m north of Museumplatz.

Zwettler's AUSTRIAN €€
(☎0662-84 41 99; www.zwettlers.com; Kaigasse 3; mains €9.50-21; ⏲11.30am-1am Tue-Sat, to midnight Sun) This gastro-pub has a lively buzz on its pavement terrace. Local grub such as schnitzel with parsley potatoes and venison ragout goes well with a cold, foamy Kaiser Karl wheat beer. The two-course lunch is a snip at €7.90.

M32 FUSION €€
(☎0662-84 10 00; www.m32.at; Mönchsberg 32; 2-course lunch €16, mains €23-40; ⏲9am-1am Tue-Sun; 🛜👪) Bold colours and a veritable forest of stag antlers reveal architect Matteo Thun's imprint at the Museum der Moderne's ultra-sleek restaurant. The food goes with the seasons with specialities like organic local beef with sautéed porcini and lime-chilli risotto with roasted octopus. The glass-walled restaurant and terrace take in the full sweep of Salzburg's mountain-backed skyline.

Stiftsbäckerei St Peter BAKERY €
(Kapitelplatz 8; ⏲7am-5pm Mon-Tue & Thu-Fri, to 1pm Sat) Next to the monastery, where the watermill turns, this 700-year-old bakery turns out Salzburg's best sourdough loaves from a wood-fired oven.

SALZBURG CARD

If you're planning on doing lots of sightseeing, grab a Salzburg Card (1-/2-/3-day card €27/36/42) and get free entry to all of the major sights and attractions, unlimited use of public transport (including cable cars) and numerous discounts on tours and events. The card is half-price for children and €3 cheaper in the low season.

Drinking & Nightlife

You'll find the biggest concentration of bars along both banks of the Salzach, the most lively are around Gstättengasse.

★Augustiner Bräustübl BREWERY
(www.augustinerbier.at; Augustinergasse 4-6; ⏲3-11pm Mon-Fri, from 2.30pm Sat & Sun) Who says monks can't enjoy themselves? Since 1621, this cheery, monastery-run brewery has been serving potent homebrews in beer steins in the vaulted hall and beneath the chestnut trees in the 1000-seat beer garden. Get your tankard filled at the foyer pump and visit the snack stands for hearty, beer-swigging grub like *Stelzen* (ham hock), pork belly and giant pretzels.

★Enoteca Settemila WINE BAR
(Bergstrasse 9; ⏲5-11pm Tue-Sat) This bijou wine shop and bar brims with the enthusiasm and passion of Rafael Peil and Nina Corti. Go to sample their well-curated selection of wines, including Austrian, organic and biodynamic ones, with *taglieri* – sharing plates of cheese and *salumi* – salami, ham, prosciutto and the like – from small Italian producers.

★Kaffee Alchemie CAFE
(www.kaffee-alchemie.at; Rudolfskai 38; ⏲7.30am-6pm Mon-Fri, 10am-6pm Sat & Sun) Making coffee really is rocket science at this vintage-cool cafe by the river, which plays up high-quality, fair-trade, single-origin beans. Talented baristas knock up spot-on espressos (on a Marzocco GB5, in case you wondered), cappuccinos and speciality coffees, which go nicely with the selection of cakes and brownies. Not a coffee fan? Try the super-smooth coffee-leaf tea.

Information

Most hotels and bars offer free wi-fi, and there are several cheap internet cafes near the train station. *Bankomaten* (ATMs) are all over the place.

Tourist Office (☎0662-88 98 70; www.salzburg.info; Mozartplatz 5; ⏰9am-7pm Mon-Sat, 10am-6pm Sun) Helpful tourist office with a ticket-booking service (www.salzburgticket.com) in the same building.

Getting There & Away

AIR

Flights from the UK and the rest of Europe, including low-cost airlines **Ryanair** (www.ryanair.com) and **easyJet** (www.easyjet.com) service **Salzburg airport** (☎0662-858 00; www.salzburg-airport.com; Innsbrucker Bundesstrasse 95; 📶), 5.5km west of the city centre.

BUS

Salzburger Verkehrsverbund (☎24hr hotline 0662-63 29 00; www.svv-info.at) Coaches depart from just outside the Hauptbahnhof on Südtiroler Platz.

TRAIN

Fast trains leave frequently for Vienna (€51, 2½ hours) via Linz (€25, 1¼ hours). There is a two-hourly express service to Klagenfurt (€39, three hours). There are hourly trains to Innsbruck (€45, two hours).

Getting Around

BICYCLE

A Velo (Mozartplatz; bicycle rental half-day/full day/week €12/18/55, e-bike €18/25/120; ⏰9am-6pm mid-Apr–Oct) Just across the way from the tourist office.

BUS

Buses 1 and 4 start from the Hauptbahnhof and skirt the pedestrian-only Altstadt, Bus 2 runs to the airport. Bus drivers sell single (€2.40) and 24-hour (€5.30) tickets; these are cheaper when purchased in advance from machines and cheaper still in packs of five from *Tabak* (€1.60 each).

SALZKAMMERGUT

A wonderland of deep blue lakes and tall craggy peaks, the Lake District has long been a favourite holiday destination for Austrians, luring a throng of summertime visitors to boat, fish, swim, hike or just laze on the shore.

WORTH A TRIP

SCHLOSS HELLBRUNN

A prince-archbishop with a wicked sense of humour, Markus Sittikus built Italianate **Schloss Hellbrunn** (www.hellbrunn.at; Fürstenweg 37; adult/child/family €12.50/5.50/26.50, gardens free; ⏰9am-5.30pm Apr-Oct, to 9pm Jul & Aug; 👪) as a 17th-century summer palace and an escape from his Residenz functions.

While the whimsical palace interior is worth a peek, the eccentric Wasserspiele (trick fountains) are the big draw in summer. Be prepared to get soaked with no statue quite as it seems, including the emblematic tongue-poking-out Germaul mask.

Look out for *The Sound of Music* pavilion of 'Sixteen Going on Seventeen' fame.

Bus 25 ((€2, every 20 minutes) runs to Hellbrunn, 4.5km south of Salzburg, from Mozartsteg/Rudolfskai in the Altstadt.

Bad Ischl is the region's hub, but Hallstatt is its true jewel. For info visit **Salzkammergut Touristik** (☎06132-24 00 00; www.salzkammergut.co.at; Götzstrasse 12; ⏰9am-7pm summer, 9am-6pm Mon-Fri, to 5am Sat rest of year). The Salzkammergut Card (€4.90, available May to October) provides up to 30% discounts on sights, ferries, cable cars and some buses.

Hallstatt

☎06134 / POP 790

With pastel-coloured houses that cast shimmering reflections onto the glassy waters of the lake and with towering mountains on all sides, Hallstatt is a beauty with a great back story. Now a Unesco World Heritage site, Hallstatt was settled 4500 years ago and over 2000 Iron Age graves have been discovered in the area, most of them dating from 1000 to 500 BC.

Sights & Activities

Salzwelten MINE

(☎06134-200 24 00; www.salzwelten.at; Salzbergstrasse 21; return funicular plus tour adult/child/family €30/10/75; ⏰9.30am-4.30pm Apr-Sep, to 3pm Oct, to 2.30pm Nov) The fascinating *Salzbergwerk* (salt mine) is situated high above

WORTH A TRIP

OBERTRAUN

Across the lake from the Hallstatt throngs, down-to-earth Obertraun is the gateway for some geological fun. The many 1000 year old caves of the **Dachstein Rieseneishöhle** (www.dachstein-salzkammergut.com; tour packages adult €12.30-37.40, child €10.80-20.60; ⌚9am-4pm May-Sep) extend into the mountain for almost 80km in places.

From Obertraun it's also possible to catch a cable car to **Krippenstein** (www.dachstein-salzkammergut.com; cable car return adult/child €29.30/16.10; ⌚mid-Jun–Oct), where you'll find the freaky but fabulous **5 Fingers viewing platform**, which protrudes over a sheer cliff face – not for sufferers of vertigo.

Hallstatt on **Salzberg** (Salt Mountain) and is the lake's major cultural attraction. The bilingual German-English tour details how salt is formed and the history of mining, and takes visitors down into the depths on miners' slides – the largest is 60m (on which you can get your photo taken).

Beinhaus CHURCH
(Bone House; Kirchenweg 40; €1.50; ⌚10am-6pm May-Oct) This small ossuary contains rows of neatly stacked skulls, painted with decorative designs and the names of their former owners. Bones have been exhumed from the overcrowded graveyard since 1600, and although the practice waned in the 20th century, the last joined the collection in 1995. It stands in the grounds of the 15th-century Catholic **Pfarrkirche** (parish church), which has some attractive Gothic frescoes and three winged altars inside.

Sleeping & Eating

Pension Sarstein GUESTHOUSE €€
(☎06134-82 17; Gosaumühlstrasse 83; d €81-101, apt for 2/3/4 people excl breakfast €100/130/150; ⓦ) The affable Fischer family take pride in their little guesthouse, a few minutes' walk along the lakefront from central Hallstatt. The old-fashioned rooms are not flash, but they are neat, cosy and have balconies with dreamy lake and mountain views. Family-sized apartments come with kitchenettes.

Balthazar im Rudolfsturm AUSTRIAN €€
(Rudolfsturm; mains €10.50-20; ⌚9am-5pm May-Oct) Balthazar is situated 855m above Hallstatt and has the most spectacular terrace in the region. The menu is Austrian comfort food and the service is charming, but you're here for the gobsmacking views. It's best accessed by the funicular.

Heritage Hotel Hallstatt HOTEL €€€
(☎06134-20 03 60; www.heritagehotel.at; Landungsplatz 102; s €145, d €200-335; ⓦ) Rooms in this luxury hotel are spread across three buildings. The main building may claim the town's prime position at the landing stage on the lake, but 500-year-old Stocker House, a greystone beauty up the hill, is by far the most atmospheric. Rooms across all three buildings offer stunning views and have modern, rather reserved, decor.

Getting There & Away

BOAT

Ferry excursions do the circuit of Hallstatt Lahn via Hallstatt Markt, Obersee, Untersee and Steeg return (€10, 90 minutes) three times daily from July to early September.

TRAIN

About a dozen trains daily connect Hallstatt and Bad Ischl (€4.30, 27 minutes). Hallstatt Bahnhof (train station) is across the lake from the village, and boat services coincide with train arrivals (€2.40, 10 minutes, last ferry to Hallstatt Markt 6.50pm).

TYROL

Tyrol (or *Tirol*) is as pure Alpine as Austria gets, with mountains that make you want to yodel out loud and patchwork pastures chiming with cowbells. Nowhere else in the country is the downhill skiing as exhilarating, the après-ski as pumping, the wooden chalets as chocolate box, the food as hearty.

Innsbruck

☎0512 / POP 124,580

Tyrol's capital is a sight to behold. Jagged rock spires are so close that within 25 minutes it's possible to travel from the heart of the city to over 2000m above sea level. Summer and winter outdoor activities abound, and it's understandable why some visitors only take a peek at Innsbruck proper before heading for the hills. But to do so is a shame, for Innsbruck is in many ways Austria in microcosm, with an authentic late-medieval Altstadt (Old Town), inventive architecture and vibrant student driven nightlife.

Sights

★Hofkirche CHURCH
(www.tiroler-landesmuseum.at; Universitätstrasse 2; adult/child €7/free; 9am-5pm Mon-Sat, 12.30-5pm Sun) Innsbruck's pride and joy is the Gothic Hofkirche, one of Europe's finest royal court churches. It was commissioned in 1553 by Ferdinand I, who enlisted top artists of the age such as Albrecht Dürer, Alexander Colin and Peter Vischer the Elder. Top billing goes to the empty **sarcophagus of Emperor Maximilian I** (1459–1519), a masterpiece of German Renaissance sculpture, elaborately carved from black marble.

★Goldenes Dachl Museum MUSEUM
(Golden Roof Museum; Herzog-Friedrich-Strasse 15; adult/child €4.80/2.40; 10am-5pm May-Sep, closed Mon Oct-Apr) Innsbruck's golden wonder and most distinctive landmark is this Gothic oriel, built for Holy Roman Emperor Maximilian I (1459–1519), lavishly festooned with murals and glittering with 2657 fire-gilt copper tiles. It is most impressive from the exterior, but the museum is worth a look – especially if you have the Innsbruck Card – with an audio guide whisking you through the history. Keep an eye out for the grotesque tournament helmets designed to resemble the Turks of the rival Ottoman Empire.

★Hofburg PALACE
(Imperial Palace; www.hofburg-innsbruck.at; Rennweg 1; adult/child €9/free; 9am-5pm) Grabbing attention with its pearly white facade and cupolas, the Hofburg was built as a castle for Archduke Sigmund the Rich in the 15th century, expanded by Emperor Maximilian I in the 16th century and given a baroque makeover by Empress Maria Theresia in the 18th century. The centrepiece of the lavish rococo state apartments is the 31m-long **Riesensaal** (Giant's Hall).

Bergisel VIEWPOINT
(www.bergisel.info; adult/child €9.50/4.50; 9am-6pm Jun-Oct, 10am-5pm Nov-May) Rising above Innsbruck like a celestial staircase, this glass-and-steel ski jump was designed by much-lauded Iraqi architect Zaha Hadid. It's 455 steps or a two-minute funicular ride to the 50m-high **viewing platform**, with a breathtaking panorama of the Nordkette range, Inntal and Innsbruck. Tram 1 trundles here from central Innsbruck.

DON'T MISS

FREE GUIDED HIKES

From late May to October, Innsbruck Information (p65) arranges daily guided hikes, from sunrise walks to half-day mountain jaunts. The hikes are free with a Club Innsbruck Card, which you receive automatically when you stay overnight in Innsbruck. Pop into the tourist office to register and browse the program.

★Schloss Ambras PALACE
(www.schlossambras-innsbruck.at; Schlosstrasse 20; palace adult/child €10/free, gardens free; palace 10am-5pm, gardens 6am-8pm;) Picturesquely perched on a hill and set among beautiful gardens, this Renaissance pile was acquired in 1564 by Archduke Ferdinand II, then ruler of Tyrol, who transformed it from a fortress into a palace. Don't miss the centrepiece **Spanische Saal** (Spanish Hall), the dazzling **Armour Collection** and the gallery's Velázquez and Van Dyck originals.

Activities

Anyone who loves playing in the great outdoors will be itching to head up into the Alps in Innsbruck.

Nordkettenbahnen FUNICULAR
(www.nordkette.com; 1 way/return to Hungerburg €4.80/8, to Seegrube €17.30/28.80, to Hafelekar €19.20/32; Hungerburg 7am-7.15pm Mon-Fri, 8am-7.15pm Sat & Sun, Seegrube 8.30am-5.30pm daily, Hafelekar 9am-5pm daily) Zaha Hadid's space-age funicular runs every 15 minutes, whizzing you from the Congress Centre to the slopes in no time. Walking trails head off in all directions from **Hungerburg** and **Seegrube**. For more of a challenge, there is a downhill track for mountain bikers and two fixed-rope routes *(Klettersteige)* for climbers.

Inntour ADVENTURE SPORTS
(www.inntour.com; Leopoldstrasse 4; 9am-6pm Mon-Sat) Based at Die Börse, Inntour arranges all manner of thrillseeking pursuits, including canyoning (€80), tandem paragliding (€105), whitewater rafting (€45) and bungee jumping from the 192m Europabrücke (€140).

CITY SAVERS

The **Innsbruck Card** allows single entrance to Innsbruck's main sights and attractions, a return journey on lifts and cable cars, unlimited use of public transport including the Sightseer bus, five-hour bike rental and numerous discounts. It's available at the tourist office and costs €38/48/55 for 24/48/72 hours.

Sleeping

The tourist office has lists of private rooms costing between €20 and €40 per person.

Nepomuk's HOSTEL €
(0512-584 118; www.nepomuks.at; Kiebachgasse 16; dm/d from €24/58;) Could this be backpacker heaven? Nepomuk's sure comes close, with its Altstadt location, well-stocked kitchen and high-ceilinged dorms with homely touches like CD players. The delicious breakfast in attached Cafe Munding, with homemade pastries, jam and fresh-roasted coffee, gets your day off to a grand start.

Pension Paula GUESTHOUSE €
(0512-292 262; www.pensionpaula.at; Weiherburggasse 15; s €36-48, d €62-72; P) This pension occupies an alpine chalet and has super-clean, homely rooms (most with balcony). It's up the hill towards the zoo and has great vistas across the city.

★**Hotel Weisses Kreuz** HISTORIC HOTEL €€
(0512-594 79; www.weisseskreuz.at; Herzog-Friedrich-Strasse 31; s/d from €77/119, with shared bathroom from €41/75; P@) Beneath the arcades, this atmospheric Altstadt hotel has played host to guests for 500 years, including a 13-year-old Mozart. With its wood-panelled parlours, antiques and twisting staircase, the hotel oozes history with every creaking beam. Rooms are supremely comfortable, staff charming and breakfast is a lavish spread.

Eating

★**Breakfast Club** BREAKFAST €
(www.breakfast-club.at; Maria-Theresien-Strasse 49; breakfast €5-13; 7.30am-4pm;) Hip, wholesome and nicely chilled, the Breakfast Club does what it says on the tin: all-day breakfast and brunch. And boy are you in for a treat: free-range eggs, Tyrolean mountain cheese, organic breads, homemade spreads, cinnamon-dusted waffles with cranberries and cream, French toast, Greek omelette – take your pick. It also does fresh-pressed juices and proper Italian coffee.

★**Die Wilderin** AUSTRIAN €€
(0512-562 728; www.diewilderin.at; Seilergasse 5; mains €9.50-20; 5pm-2am Tue-Sat, to midnight Sun) Take a gastronomic walk on the wild side at this modern-day hunter-gatherer of a restaurant, where chefs take pride in local sourcing and using top-notch farm-fresh and foraged ingredients. The menu sings of the seasons, be it asparagus, game, strawberries or winter veg. The vibe is urbane and relaxed.

Chez Nico VEGETARIAN €€
(0650 4510624; www.chez-nico.at; Maria-Theresien-Strasse 49; 2-course lunch €14.50, 7-course menu €60; 6.30-10pm Mon & Sat, noon-2pm & 6.30-10pm Tue-Fri;) Take a petit bistro and a Parisian chef with a passion for herbs, *et voilà*, you get Chez Nico. Nicolas Curtil (Nico) cooks seasonal, all-vegetarian

OTHER TOWNS WORTH A VISIT

Fancy exploring further? Here are some towns, resorts and valleys in Austria that you may want to consider for day trips or longer visits.

Zillertal Storybook Tyrol, with a steam train, snow-capped Alps and outdoor activities aplenty.

Zell am See An alpine beauty on the shores of its namesake lake. Gateway to the epic Grossglockner Road.

Eisenstadt The petite capital of Burgenland is known for its wonderful palace and famous former resident, composer Haydn.

Schladming Laid-back Styrian gem in the glacial Dachstein mountains. Great for skiing, hiking, biking and white-water rafting on the Enns River.

WORTH A TRIP

KRIMML FALLS

The thunderous, three-tier **Krimmler Wasserfälle** (Krimml Falls; ☎06564-72 12; www.wasserfaelle-krimml.at; adult/child €9.20/4.60 incl WasserWelten Krimml; ⊙9am-5pm May-Oct) is Europe's highest waterfall at 380m, and one of Austria's most unforgettable sights. The **Wasserfallweg** (Waterfall Trail), which starts at the ticket office and weaves gently uphill through mixed forest, has numerous viewpoints with photogenic close-ups of the falls. It's about a two-hour round-trip walk.

The pretty Alpine village of Krimml has a handful of places to sleep and eat – contact the **tourist office** (☎06564-72 39; www.krimml.at; Oberkrimml 37; ⊙8am-6pm Mon-Fri, 8.30-11.30am Sat) for more information.

Buses run year-round from Krimml to Zell am See (€10.20, 1¼ hours, every two hours), with frequent onward train connections to Salzburg (€19.60, 1½ hours). The village is about 500m north of the waterfall, on a side turning from the B165. There are parking spaces near the falls.

delights along the lines of tomato and argan oil consommé and watermelon and chanterelle carpaccio with pine nuts and parmesan. You won't miss the meat, we swear.

Il Convento ITALIAN €€
(☎0512-581 354; www.ilconvento.at; Burggraben 29; mains €13.50-25, 2-course lunch €17.50-18.50; ⊙11am-3pm & 5pm-midnight Mon-Sat) Neatly tucked into the old city walls, this Italian newcomer is run with passion by Peppino and Angelika. It's a winner, with its refined look (white tablecloths, wood beams, Franciscan monastery views from the terrace) and menu. Dishes such as clam linguine, braised veal and salt-crusted cod are cooked to a T and served with wines drawn from the well-stocked cellar.

Drinking & Nightlife

Tribaun CRAFT BEER
(www.tribaun.com; Museumstrasse 5; ⊙6pm-2am Mon-Sat) This cracking new bar taps into craft-beer culture, with a wide variety of brews – from stouts and porters to IPA, sour, amber, honey and red ales. The easygoing vibe and fun-loving crew add to its appeal. For more insight, hook onto a 90-minute, seven-beer tasting (€19).

Moustache BAR
(www.cafe-moustache.at; Herzog-Otto-Strasse 8; ⊙11am-2am Tue-Sun; 📶) Playing Spot-the-Moustache (Einstein, Charlie Chaplin and co) is the preferred pastime at this retro bolthole, with table football and a terrace overlooking pretty Domplatz. They knock up a mean pisco sour.

360° BAR
(Rathaus Galerien; ⊙10am-1am Mon-Sat) Grab a cushion and drink in 360-degree views of the city and Alps from the balcony that skirts this spherical, glass-walled bar. It's a nicely chilled spot for a coffee or sundowner.

Information

Innsbruck Information (☎0512-53 56-0, 0512-59 850; www.innsbruck.info; Burggraben 3; ⊙9am-6pm) Main tourist office with truckloads of info on the city and surrounds, including skiing and walking.

Getting There & Away

AIR

EasyJet flies to **Innsbruck Airport** (INN; ☎22 52 50; www.innsbruck-airport.com; Fürstenweg 180), 4km west of the city centre.

CAR & MOTORCYCLE

The A12 and the parallel Hwy 171 are the main roads heading west and east. The B177, to the west of Innsbruck, continues north to Germany and Munich whilte the A13 toll road (€8.50) runs south through the Brenner Pass to Italy.

TRAIN

Fast trains depart daily every two hours for Bregenz (€37.50, 2¾ hours) and Salzburg (€45.50, two hours); from Innsbruck to the Arlberg, the best views are on the right-hand side of the train. Express trains serve Munich (€41.20, 1¾ hours) and Verona (€40.20, 3½ hours). Direct services to Kitzbühel also run every two hours (€15.80, 1¼ hours) and hourly to Lienz (€23.50, three to five hours).

WORTH A TRIP

BREGENZERWALD

Only a few kilometres southeast of Bregenz, the forest-cloaked slopes, velvet-green pastures and limestone peaks of the Bregenzerwald unfold. In summer it's a glorious place to spend a few days hiking the hills and filling up on homemade cheeses in alpine dairies. Winter brings plenty of snow, and the area is noted for its downhill and cross-country skiing. The **Bregenzerwald tourist office** (05512-23 65; www.bregenzerwald.at; Impulszentrum 1135, Egg; 9am-5pm Mon-Fri, 8am-1pm Sat) has information on the region.

Getting Around

Single tickets on buses and trams cost €2, day passes are €4.

Kitzbühel

05356 / POP 8135

Ever since Franz Reisch slipped on skis and whizzed down the slopes of Kitzbüheler Horn way back in 1893, so christening the first alpine ski run in Austria, Kitzbühel has carved out its reputation as one of Europe's foremost ski resorts. It's renowned for the white-knuckled Hahnenkamm downhill ski race in January and the reliable excellence of its slopes.

Activities

In winter there's first-rate intermediate skiing and freeriding on **Kitzbüheler Horn** to the north and **Hahnenkamm** to the south of town. One-/three-/six-day passes cost €53/147/256 in the high winter season and €47.50/132.50/230.50 at all other times.

Dozens of summer **hiking trails** thread through the Kitzbühel Alps; the tourist office gives walking maps and runs free guided hikes for guests staying in town. Cable cars cost €18.80/23.50 one way/return in summer.

Sleeping & Eating

Rates leap by up to 50% in the winter season.

Snowbunny's Hostel HOSTEL €
(067 67940233; www.snowbunnys.co.uk; Bichlstrasse 30; dm €22-25, d €66;) This friendly, laid-back hostel is a bunny-hop from the slopes. Dorms are fine, if a tad dark; breakfast is DIY-style in the kitchen. There's a TV lounge, a ski storage room and cats to stroke.

★**Villa Licht** HOTEL €€
(05356-622 93; www.villa-licht.at; Franz-Reisch-Strasse 8; apt €120-210;) Pretty gardens, spruce modern apartments with pine trappings, living rooms with kitchenettes, balconies with mountain views, peace – this charming Tyrolean chalet has the lot, and owner Renate goes out of her way to please. Kids love the outdoor pool in summer.

★**Restaurant Zur Tenne** AUSTRIAN €€
(05356-644 44-0; www.hotelzurtenne.com; Vorderstadt 8-10; mains €18-43; 11.30am-1.30pm & 6.30-9.30pm) Choose between the rustic, beamed interior where an open fire crackles and the more summery conservatory at Hotel Tenne's highly regarded restaurant. Service is polished and the menu puts a sophisticated twist on seasonal Tyrolean dishes such as catfish with wild garlic pasta and artichokes.

Getting There & Away

Trains run frequently from Kitzbühel to Innsbruck (€15.80, 1¼ hours) and Salzburg (€30.30, 2½ hours). For Kufstein (€10.20, one hour), change at Wörgl.

Lienz

04852 / POP 11,900

The Dolomites rise like an amphitheatre around Lienz, which straddles the Isel and Drau Rivers just 40km north of Italy. The capital of East Tyrol is a scenic staging point for travels through the Hohe Tauern National Park.

Sights & Activities

A €45 day pass covers skiing on the nearby **Zettersfeld** and **Hochstein** peaks. However, the area is more renowned for its many kilometres of cross-country trails; the town fills up for the annual Dolomitenlauf cross-country skiing race in mid-January.

Sleeping & Eating

The tourist office can point you in the direction of good-value guesthouses and camping grounds.

Gasthof Schlossberghof HOTEL €€

(☎04852-632 33; schlossberghof.at; Iseltalerstrasse 21; s/d €65/100) The location of this simple, freshly renovated hotel might seem unprepossessing at first, but it's great if you're in a car (free parking and undercover parks for bikes), plus the ten-minute stroll into the centre takes you past Tyrolean 19th-century villas watched over by the Dolomites.

Weinphilo WINE BAR

(☎04852-612 53; www.weinphilo.com; Messinggasse 11; ⏲10am-10pm Mon-Fri, to 3pm Sat) A proper Italian wine shop and bar, where you can join locals for a glass of a beautiful small-producer wine from the Veneto, Friuli, Südtirol or even further south. There are meat and cheese platters and you can also pop in here in the morning for an expertly made coffee from Tuscany's Cafe Baratto beans.

ℹ Information

Tourist Office (Lienzer Dolomiten; ☎050 212 400; www.osttirol.com; Europaplatz 1; ⏲8am-6pm Mon-Fri, 9am-noon & 4-6pm Sat, 9.30-midnight Sun mid-June–end Sep, closed Sat afternoon & Sun Oct-May) Staff will help you find accommodation (even private rooms) free of charge. They also have hiking maps and brochures on all the adventure sports operators.

ℹ Getting There & Away

There are several daily services to Innsbruck (€15.40 to €20.40, 3¼ to 4½ hours). Trains run every two hours to Salzburg (€38.90, 3½ hours). To head south by car, you must first divert west or east along Hwy 100.

Hohe Tauern National Park

Straddling Tyrol, Salzburg and Carinthia, this national park is the largest in the Alps; a 1786-sq-km wilderness of 3000m peaks, alpine meadows and waterfalls. At its heart lies **Grossglockner** (3798m), Austria's highest mountain, which towers over the 8km-long Pasterze Glacier, best seen from the outlook at **Kaiser-Franz-Josefs-Höhe** (2369m).

The 48km **Grossglockner Road** (www.grossglockner.at; day ticket car/motorbike €35/25; ⏲5am-9.30pm) from Bruck in Salzburgerland to Heiligenblut in Carinthia is one of Europe's greatest Alpine drives. A feat of 1930s engineering, the road swings giddily around 36 switchbacks, passing jewel-coloured lakes, forested slopes and wondrous glaciers.

The major village on the Grossglockner Road is **Heiligenblut**, famous for its 15th-century pilgrimage church. Here the **tourist office** (☎04824-27 00; www.heiligenblut.at; Hof 4; ⏲9am-6pm Mon-Fri, 2-6pm Sat & Sun) can advise on guided ranger hikes, mountain hiking and skiing. The village also has a spick-and-span **Jugendherberge** (☎04824-22 59; www.oejhv.or.at; Hof 36; dm/s/d €22.50/30.50/52; P ᯤ).

Bus 5002 runs frequently between Lienz and Heiligenblut on weekdays (€16.40, one hour), less frequently at weekends.

NATIONAL PARKS IN THE AUSTRIAN ALPS

For an area of such mind-blowing natural beauty, it may come as a surprise to learn that there are just three national parks (Hohe Tauern, Kalkalpen and Gesäuse) as well as one major nature reserve (Nockberge) in the Austrian Alps. But statistics aren't everything, particularly when one of these national parks is the magnificent Hohe Tauern, the Alps' largest and Europe's second-largest national park, which is a tour de force of 3000m peaks, immense glaciers and waterfalls.

The national-park authorities have managed to strike a good balance between preserving the wildlife and keeping local economic endeavours such as farming, hunting and tourism alive. The website www.nationalparksaustria.at has links to all national parks and a brochure in English to download.

Aside from national parks, protected areas and nature reserves are dotted all over the Austrian Alps, from the mesmerising mountainscapes of Naturpark Zillertaler Alpen in Tyrol to the lakes of the Salzkammergut. See www.naturparke.at for the lowdown on Austria's nature parks.

VORARLBERG

Cut off from the rest of Austria by the snow-capped Arlberg massif, the westerly region of Vorarlberg has more than the touch of nearby Switzerland about it.

The capital, **Bregenz**, sits prettily on the shores of Lake Constance and holds the **Bregenzer Festspiele** (Bregenz Festival; ☎05574-40 76; www.bregenzerfestspiele.com; ⊙mid-Jul-late Aug) in July/August, when opera is performed on a floating stage on the lake.

The real action here, though, is in the Arlberg region, shared by Vorarlberg and neighbouring Tyrol. Some of the country's best downhill and off-piste skiing – not to mention après-ski partying – is in **St Anton am Arlberg**, where the first ski club in the Alps was founded in 1901. The centrally located **tourist office** (☎05446-226 90; www.stantonamarlberg.com; Dorfstrasse 8; ⊙8am-6pm Mon-Fri, 9am-6pm Sat, 9am-noon & 2-5pm Sun) has maps, and information on accommodation and activities.

A single ski pass (one-/three-/six-day pass €52/148/262) covers the whole Arlberg region and is valid for all 87 ski lifts.

Accommodation is mainly in small B&Bs. Most budget places book out months in advance.

St Anton is on the main railway route between Bregenz (€12.80, 1¼ hours) and Innsbruck (€16.80, 1¼ hours). It's close to the eastern entrance of the Arlberg Tunnel, the toll road connecting Vorarlberg and Tyrol (€8.50). This region is also a convenient gateway to Germany and Liechtenstein.

SURVIVAL GUIDE

Directory A–Z

ACCOMMODATION

From simple mountain huts to five-star hotels fit for kings – you'll find the lot in Austria. Tourist offices invariably keep lists and details, as do the sites listed here.

> **SLEEPING PRICE RANGES**
>
> The following price ranges refer to a double room with a bathroom for two people, including breakfast.
>
> **€** less than €80
>
> **€€** €80–€200
>
> **€€€** more than €200

Austrian Hotelreservation (www.austrian-hotelreservation.at)

Austrian National Tourist Office (www.austria.info)

Bergfex (www.bergfex.com)

Camping in Österreich (https://www.camping.info/österreich)

Accommodation Types

Hostels In Austria around 100 hostels (*Jugendherberge*) are affiliated with Hostelling International (HI). Facilities are often excellent. Four- to six-bed dorms with shower/toilet are the norm, though some places also have doubles and family rooms. See www.oejhv.or.at or www.oejhw.at for details.

Private rooms *Privatzimmer* (private rooms) are cheap (often about €50 per double). On top of this, you will find *Bauernhof* (farmhouses) in rural areas, and some *Öko-Bauernhöfe* (organic farms).

Alpine huts There are over 400 huts maintained by the Österreichischer Alpenverein. Bed prices for nonmembers are from €20. Open roughly late June to mid-September with advance bookings essential; meals or cooking facilities are often available.

Rental accommodation *Ferienwohnungen* (self-catering apartments) are ubiquitous in Austrian mountain resorts. Contact a local tourist office for lists and prices.

Camping Austria has some 500 camping grounds, many well equipped and scenically located. Prices can be as low as €5 per person or small tent and as high as €20. Many close in winter, so phone ahead to check.

DISCOUNT CARDS

Student & Youth Cards International Student Identity Cards (ISIC) and European Youth Card (formerly Euro<26; check www.euro26.org for discounts) will get you discounts at most museums, galleries and theatres. Admission is generally a little higher than the price for children.

Discount Rail Cards See the Getting Around section.

MONEY

Austria's currency is the euro. An approximate 10% tip is expected in restaurants. Pay it directly to the server; don't leave it on the table.

OPENING HOURS

Banks 8am or 9am to 3pm Monday to Friday, to 5.30pm Thursday

Cafes 7am to 8pm; hours vary widely

Clubs 10pm to late

Post offices 8am to noon and 2pm to 6pm Monday to Friday, 8am to noon Saturday

Pubs 6pm to 1am or later

Restaurants 11am to 2.30pm and 6pm to 11pm
Shops 9am to 6.30pm Monday to Friday, 9am to 5pm Saturday
Supermarkets 9am to 8pm Monday to Saturday

PUBLIC HOLIDAYS

New Year's Day (Neujahr) 1 January
Epiphany (Heilige Drei Könige) 6 January
Easter Monday (Ostermontag) March/April
Labour Day (Tag der Arbeit) 1 May
Whit Monday (Pfingstmontag) Sixth Monday after Easter
Ascension Day (Christi Himmelfahrt) Sixth Thursday after Easter
Corpus Christi (Fronleichnam) Second Thursday after Whitsunday
Assumption (Maria Himmelfahrt) 15 August
National Day (Nationalfeiertag) 26 October
All Saints' Day (Allerheiligen) 1 November
Immaculate Conception (Mariä Empfängnis) 8 December
Christmas Day (Christfest) 25 December
St Stephen's Day (Stephanitag) 26 December

TELEPHONE

- Austrian telephone numbers consist of an area code followed by the local number.
- The country code is ☎43 and the international access code is ☎00.
- Phone shops sell prepaid SIM cards from around €15.
- Phone cards in different denominations are sold at post offices and *Tabak* (tobacconist) shops. Call centres are widespread in cities, and many internet cafes are geared for Skype calls.

TOURIST INFORMATION

Tourist offices, which are dispersed far and wide in Austria, tend to adjust their hours from one year to the next, so business hours may have changed slightly by the time you arrive. Most offices have at least one English speaker on staff.

VISAS

Schengen visa rules apply. The Austrian Foreign Ministry website www.bmeia.gv.at lists embassies.

Getting There & Away

AIR

Among the low-cost airlines, Air Berlin and Nikki flys to Graz, Innsbruck, Linz, Salzburg and Vienna, easyJet to Innsbruck, Salzburg and Vienna, and Ryanair to Linz, Salzburg and Bratislava (for Vienna).

COUNTRY FACTS

Area 83,879 sq km
Population 8.5 million
Capital Vienna
Country Code ☎43
Currency Euro (€)
Emergencies ☎112
Language German
Money ATMs widely available; banks open Monday to Friday.
Visas Schengen rules apply

LAND

Bus

Buses depart from Austria for as far afield as England, the Baltic countries, the Netherlands, Germany and Switzerland. Most significantly, they provide access to Eastern European cities small and large – from the likes of Sofia and Warsaw, to Banja Luka, Mostar and Sarajevo.

Services operated by **Eurolines** (www.eurolines.at) leave from Vienna and from several regional cities.

Car & Motorcycle

There are numerous entry points into Austria by road from Germany, the Czech Republic, Slovakia, Hungary, Slovenia, Italy and Switzerland. All border-crossing points are open 24 hours.

Standard European insurance and paperwork rules apply.

CONNECTIONS

Bang in the heart of Europe, Austria has speedy connections to its eight neighbouring countries. Trains from Vienna run to many Eastern European destinations, including Bratislava, Budapest, Prague and Warsaw; there are also connections south to Italy via Klagenfurt and north to Berlin. Salzburg is within sight of the Bavarian border, with many Munich-bound trains. Innsbruck is on the main rail line from Vienna to Switzerland, and two routes also lead to Munich. Look out for the fast, comfortable RailJet services to Germany and Switzerland.

EATING PRICE RANGES

The following price ranges refer to the cost of a two-course meal, excluding drinks.

€ less than €15

€€ €15–€30

€€€ more than €30

Train

Austria has excellent rail connections. The main services in and out of the country from the west normally pass through Bregenz, Innsbruck or Salzburg en route to Vienna. Trains to Eastern Europe leave from Vienna. Express services to Italy go via Innsbruck or Villach; trains to Slovenia are routed through Graz.

For online timetables and tickets, visit the **ÖBB** (Österreichische Bundesbahnen; Austrian Federal Railways; ☎24hr hotline 05 1717; www.oebb.at) website. SparSchiene (discounted tickets) are often available when you book online in advance. Deutsche Bahn (www.bahn.com) is also useful.

RIVER & LAKE

Hydrofoils run to Bratislava and Budapest from Vienna; slower boats cruise the Danube between the capital and Passau. The **Danube Tourist Commission** (www.danube-river.org) has a country-by-country list of operators and agents who can book tours.

Getting Around

AIR

Austrian Airlines (www.austrian.com) offers several flights daily between Vienna and Innsbruck, Graz, Klagenfurt, Linz and Salzburg.

BICYCLE

- All cities have at least one bike shop that doubles as a rental centre; expect to pay around €15 to €25 per day.
- You can take bicycles on any train with a bicycle symbol at the top of its timetable. Bikes cost an extra 10% on your ticket price on regional and S-Bahn trains, or reserve ahead (€3.50) for a space on long-distance trains.

BOAT

Services along the Danube are generally slow, scenic excursions rather than functional means of transport.

BUS

Rail routes are often complemented by **Postbus** (☎24hr hotline 0810 222 333; www.postbus.at) services, which really come into their own in the more inaccessible mountainous regions.

CAR & MOTORCYCLE

A *Vignette* (toll sticker) is imposed on all motorways; charges for cars/motorbikes are €8.80/5.10 for 10 days and €25.70/12.90 for two months. *Vignette* can be purchased at border crossings, petrol stations and *Tabak* shops. There are additional tolls (usually €2.50 to €10) for some mountain tunnels.

Speed limits are 50km/h in built-up areas, 130km/h on autobahn and 100km/h on other roads.

ESSENTIAL FOOD & DRINK

Make it meaty Go for a classic Wiener schnitzel, *Tafelspitz* (boiled beef with horseradish sauce) or *Schweinebraten* (pork roast). The humble *Wurst* (sausage) comes in various guises.

On the side Lashings of potatoes, either fried *(Pommes)*, roasted *(Bratkartoffeln)*, in a salad *(Erdapfelsalat)* or boiled in their skins *(Quellmänner)*; or try *Knödel* (dumplings) and *Nudeln* (flat egg noodles).

Kaffee und Kuchen Coffee and cake is Austria's sweetest tradition. Must-tries: flaky apple strudel, rich, chocolatey *Sacher Torte* and *Kaiserschmarrn* (sweet 'scrambled' pancakes with raisins).

Wine at the source Jovial locals gather in rustic *Heurigen* (wine taverns) in the wine-producing east, identified by an evergreen branch above the door. Sip crisp Grüner Veltliner whites and spicy Blaufränkisch wines.

Cheese fest Dig into gooey *Käsnudeln* (cheese noodles) in Carinthia, *Kaspressknodel* (fried cheese dumplings) in Tyrol and *Käsekrainer* (cheesy sausages) in Vienna. The hilly Bregenzerwald is studded with dairies.

The minimum age for hiring small cars is 19 years, or 25 years for larger, 'prestige' cars. Customers must have held a driving licence for at least a year. Many contracts forbid customers to take cars outside Austria, particularly into Eastern Europe.

Crash helmets are compulsory for motorcyclists.

TRAIN

Austria has a clean, efficient rail system, and if you use a discount card it's very inexpensive.

- **ÖBB** (p70) is the main operator, supplemented with a handful of private lines. Tickets and timetables are available online.
- Disabled passengers can use the 24-hour 05-17 17 customer number for special travel assistance; do this at least 24 hours ahead of travel (48 hours ahead for international services). Staff at stations will help with boarding and alighting.

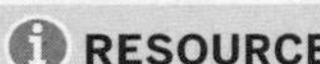

RESOURCES

ÖAV (www.alpenverein.at) Austrian Alpine Club

ÖBB (www.oebb.at) Austrian Federal Railways

Österreich Werbung (www.austria.info) National tourism authority

- It's worth seeking out RailJet train services connecting Vienna, Graz, Villach, Salzburg, Innsbruck, Linz and Klagenfurt, as they travel up to 200km/h.
- Reservations in 2nd class within Austria cost €3.50 for most express services; recommended for travel on weekends.
- Fares quoted are for 2nd-class tickets.

Belgium & Luxembourg

Includes ➡

Best Places to Eat

- ➡ L'Ogenblik (p81)
- ➡ La Cristallerie (p102)
- ➡ Den Gouden Harynck (p95)
- ➡ De Stove (p95)
- ➡ De Ruyffelaer (p98)

Best Places to Stay

- ➡ Chambres d'Hôtes du Vaudeville (p77)
- ➡ Main Street Hotel (p97)
- ➡ Guesthouse Nuit Blanche (p93)
- ➡ Auberge Aal Veinen (p103)
- ➡ Bed, Bad & Brood (p87)

Why Go?

Stereotypes of comic books, chips and sublime chocolates are just the start in eccentric little Belgium, its self-deprecating people have quietly spent centuries producing some of Europe's finest art and architecture. Bilingual Brussels is the dynamic yet personable EU capital, but also sports what's arguably the world's most beautiful city square. Flat, Flemish Flanders has many other alluring medieval cities, all easily linked by regular train hops. In hilly, French-speaking Wallonia, the attractions are contrastingly rural – castle villages, outdoor activities and extensive cave systems. Independent Luxembourg, the EU's richest country, is compact and hilly with its own wealth of castle villages. The grand duchy's capital city is famed for banking but also sports a fairy-tale Unesco-listed historic Old Town. And from the brilliant beers of Belgium to the sparkling wines of Luxembourg's Moselle Valley, there's plenty to lubricate some of Europe's best dining.

When to Go

Brussels

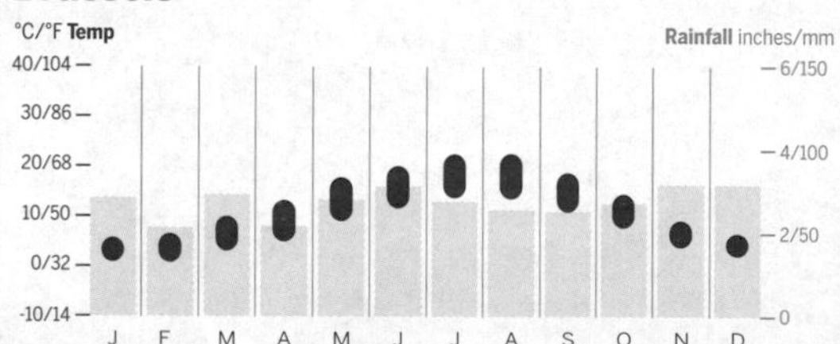

Pre-Easter weekends Belgium hosts many of Europe's weirdest carnivals, not just at Mardi Gras.

Feb–Mar Both countries symbolically burn the spirit of winter on the first weekend after Carnival.

Jul–Aug Countless festivals, hotels packed at the coast but cheaper in Brussels and Luxembourg City.

BRUSSELS

POP 1.2 MILLION

Belgium's fascinating capital, and the administrative capital of the EU, Brussels is historic yet hip, bureaucratic yet bizarre, self-confident yet unshowy, and multicultural to its roots. All this plays out in a cityscape that swings from majestic to quirky to rundown and back again. Organic art nouveau facades face off against 1960s concrete developments, and regal 19th-century mansions contrast with the brutal glass of the EU's Gotham City. This whole maelstrom swirls out from Brussels' medieval core, where the Grand Place is surely one of the world's most beautiful squares.

One constant is the enviable quality of everyday life, with a *café*–bar scene that never gets old.

Sights

Central Brussels

Grand Place SQUARE

(Ⓜ Gare Centrale) Brussels' magnificent Grand Place is one of the world's most unforgettable urban ensembles. Oddly hidden, the enclosed cobblestone square is only revealed as you enter on foot from one of six narrow side alleys: Rue des Harengs is the best first approach. The focal point is the spired 15th-century city hall, but each of the antique guildhalls (mostly 1697–1705) has a charm of its own. Most are unashamed exhibitionists, with fine baroque gables, gilded statues and elaborate guild symbols.

Manneken Pis MONUMENT

(cnr Rue de l'Étuve & Rue du Chêne; Ⓜ Gare Centrale) Rue Charles Buls – Brussels' most unashamedly touristy shopping street, lined with chocolate and trinket shops – leads the hordes three blocks from the Grand Place to the Manneken Pis. This fountain-statue of a little boy taking a leak is comically tiny and a perversely perfect national symbol for surreal Belgium. Most of the time the statue's nakedness is hidden beneath a costume relevant to an anniversary, national day or local event: his ever-growing wardrobe is partly displayed at the **Maison du Roi** (Musée de la Ville de Bruxelles; Grand Place; Ⓜ Gare Centrale).

Musées Royaux des Beaux-Arts GALLERY

(Royal Museums of Fine Arts; ☎ 02-508 32 11; www.fine-arts-museum.be; Rue de la Régence 3; adult/6-25yr/BrusselsCard €8/2/free, with Magritte Museum €13; ⏰ 10am-5pm Tue-Fri, 11am-6pm Sat & Sun; Ⓜ Gare Centrale, Parc) This prestigious museum incorporates the Musée d'Art Ancien (ancient art); the Musée d'Art Moderne (modern art), with works by surrealist Paul Delvaux and Fauvist Rik Wouters; and the purpose-built Musée Magritte (p73). The 15th-century Flemish Primitives are wonderfully represented in the Musée d'Art Ancien: there's Rogier Van der Weyden's *Pietà* with its hallucinatory sky, Hans Memling's refined portraits, and the richly textured *Madonna With Saints* by the Master of the Legend of St Lucy.

Musée Magritte MUSEUM

(☎ 02-508 32 11; www.musee-magritte-museum.be; Rue de la Régence 3; adult/under 26yr/BrusselsCard €8/2/free; ⏰ 10am-5pm Tue-Fri, 11am-6pm Sat & Sun; Ⓜ Gare Centrale, Parc) The beautifully presented Magritte Museum holds the world's largest collection of the surrealist pioneer's paintings and drawings. Watch his style develop from colourful Braque-style cubism in 1920 through a Dali-esque phase and a late-1940s period of Kandinsky-like brushwork to his trademark bowler hats of the 1960s. Regular screenings of a 50-minute documentary provide insights into the artist's unconventionally conventional life.

MIM MUSEUM

(Musée des Instruments de Musique; ☎ 02-545 01 30; www.mim.be; Rue Montagne de la Cour 2; adult/concession €8/6; ⏰ 9.30am-5pm Tue-Fri, 10am-5pm Sat & Sun; Ⓜ Gare Centrale, Parc) Strap on a pair of headphones, then step on the automated floor panels in front of the precious instruments (including world instruments and Adolphe Sax's inventions) to hear them being played. As much of a highlight as the museum itself are the premises – the art-nouveau Old England Building. This former department store was built in 1899 by Paul Saintenoy and has a panoramic rooftop *café* and outdoor terrace.

★ **Musée du Costume et de la Dentelle** MUSEUM

(Costume & Lace Museum; ☎ 02-213 44 50; www.costumeandlacemuseum.brussels; Rue de la Violette 12; adult/child/BrusselsCard €8/free/free; ⏰ 10am-5pm Tue-Sun; Ⓜ Gare Centrale) Lace making has been one of Flanders' finest crafts since the 16th century. While *kloskant* (bobbin lace) originated in Bruges, *naaldkant* (needlepoint lace) was developed in Italy but was predominantly made in Brussels. This

Belgium & Luxembourg Highlights

1 Bruges (p92) Coming on weekdays off-season to appreciate the picture-perfect canal scenes of this medieval city, without the tourist overload.

2 Ghent (p89) Being wooed by one of Europe's greatest underappreciated all-round discoveries.

3 Brussels (p73) Savouring the 'world's most beautiful square', then seeking out remarkable *cafés*, chocolate shops and art nouveau survivors.

4 Antwerp (p85) Following fashion to this hip yet historic city.

5 Luxembourg City (p99) Spending the weekend in the UNESCO-listed Old Town then heading out to the grand duchy's evocative castle villages.

6 Ypres (p96) Pondering the heartbreaking futility of WWI in Flanders' fields around its meticulously rebuilt medieval core.

7 Wallonia (p98) Exploring the caves and castles of Belgium's rural southern half.

0 30 km
0 20 miles
NETHERLANDS
Tilburg
Roosendaal
Eindhoven
Venlo
A1
N1
A12
Turnhout
A21
Antwerp
4
Antwerp Airport
Herentals
Mol
Neerpelt
Roermond
Lier
Fort van Breendonk
E313
GERMANY
National Park Hoge Kempen
Mechelen
Diest
A2
Genk
Hasselt
Bokrijk Openluchtmuseum
E19
Brussels Airport
Leuven
Maastricht
3
Brussels
E313
A2
Aachen
Waterloo
Louvain- la-Neuve
A3
Braine l'Alleud
Ottignies
Liège Airport
Liège
Verviers
Hautes Fagnes-Eifel Nature Park
Nivelles
E411
Jehay
Huy
Hautes Fagnes
Charleroi Airport
E42
Remouchamps
BELGIUM
Herzogenhugel
Hautes Fagnes Nature Reserve
Namur
Modave
Coo
Stavelot
Charleroi
Durbuy
Barvaux
Wallonia
7
Godinne
E25
Hotton
N5
E421
Dinant
Marloie
Houyet
Rochefort
La Roche-en-Ardenne
Jemelle
Lavaux-Ste-Anne
Han-sur-Lesse
Champlon
Clervaux
GERMANY
Chimay
Couvin
E46
Bastogne
Wiltz
E411
ARDENNES
Parc Naturel de la Haute Sûre
Vianden
Libramont
Diekirch
Rochehaut
E46
Ettelbrück
LUXEMBOURG
Echternach
Gutland
Bouillon
Mersch
Bourglinster
Charleville-Mezières
Arlon
Grevenmacher
Findel Airport
Orval
5
Luxembourg City
Virton
Rodange
Dudelange

excellent museum reveals lace's applications for under- and outerwear over the centuries, as well as displaying other luxury textiles in beautifully presented changing exhibitions. Ask for an English-language booklet.

Beyond the Centre

Musée Horta MUSEUM
(☎02-543 04 90; www.hortamuseum.be; Rue Américaine 25; adult/child €10/3; ⊙2-5.30pm Tue-Sun; Ⓜ Horta, 🚊91, 92) The typically austere exterior doesn't give much away, but Victor Horta's former home (designed and built 1898–1901) is an art nouveau jewel. The stairwell is the structural triumph of the house: follow the playful knots and curlicues of the banister, which become more exuberant as you ascend, ending at a tangle of swirls and glass lamps at the skylight, glazed with citrus-coloured and plain glass.

Cantillon Brewery BREWERY
(Musée Bruxellois de la Gueuze; ☎02-520 28 91; www.cantillon.be; Rue Gheude 56; admission €7; ⊙10am-5pm Mon, Tue & Thu-Sat; Ⓜ Clemenceau) Beer lovers shouldn't miss this unique living brewery-museum. Atmospheric and family run, it's Brussels' last operating lambic brewery and still uses much of the original 19th-century equipment. After hearing a brief explanation, visitors take a self-guided tour, including the barrel rooms where the beers mature for up to three years in chestnut wine casks. The entry fee includes two taster glasses of Cantillon's startlingly acidic brews.

★**Musée du Cinquantenaire** MUSEUM
(☎02-741 73 01; www.kmkg-mrah.be; Parc du Cinquantenaire 10; adult/child/BrusselsCard €8/2/free; ⊙9.30am-5pm Tue-Fri, from 10am Sat & Sun; Ⓜ Mérode) This astonishingly rich collection ranges from ancient Egyptian sarcophagi to Meso-American masks to icons to wooden bicycles. Decide what you want to see before coming or the sheer scope can prove overwhelming. Visually attractive spaces include the medieval stone carvings set around a neo-Gothic cloister and the soaring Corinthian columns (convincing fibreglass props) that bring atmosphere to an original AD 420 mosaic from Roman Syria. Labelling is in French and Dutch, so the English-language audio guide (€3) is worth considering.

★**Musée des Sciences Naturelles** MUSEUM
(☎02-627 42 11; www.naturalsciences.be; Rue Vautier 29; adult/concession/child/BrusselsCard €7/6/4.50/free; ⊙9.30am-5pm Tue-Fri, 10am-6pm Sat & Sun; 🚌38 (direction Homborch, departs from next to Gare Centrale) to De Meeus on Rue du Luxembourg) Thought-provoking and highly interactive, this museum has far more than the usual selection of stuffed animals. But the undoubted highlight is a unique 'family' of iguanodons – 10m-high dinosaurs found in a Hainaut coal mine in 1878. A computer simulation shows the mudslide that might have covered them, sand boxes allow you to play dino hunter and multilingual videos give a wonderfully nuanced debate on recent palaeontology.

ITINERARIES

Four Days

Just long enough to get a first taste of Belgium's four finest 'art cities': Bruges, Ghent, Brussels and Antwerp, all easy jump-offs or short excursions while you're train-hopping between Paris and Amsterdam. **Bruges** is the fairy-tale 'Venice of the north', **Ghent** has similar canalside charms without the tourist hordes, and **Brussels**' incomparable Grand Place is worth jumping off any train for, even if you have only a few hours to spare. Cosmopolitan **Antwerp** goes one further, adding in fashion and diamonds. If you're overnighting make sure to hit Brussels on a weekend and Bruges on a weekday to get the best deals on accommodation.

Ten Days

Add in a side trip to **Leuven**, then swing into Wallonia, visiting **Waterloo**, the excellent museums of **Mons**, the picturesque castles and views of the Ardennes, especially **Bouillon**, then pretty **Luxembourg**. All while trying the excellent local beers along the way, of course.

Atomium MONUMENT
(☎02-475 47 75; www.atomium.be; Av de l'Atomium; adult/teen/child €12/8/6; ⏰10am-6pm; Ⓜ Heysel, 🚊51) The space-age Atomium looms 102m over north Brussels' suburbia, resembling a steel alien from a '60s Hollywood movie. It consists of nine house-sized metallic balls linked by steel tube-columns containing escalators and lifts. The balls are arranged like a school chemistry set to represent iron atoms in their crystal lattice… except these are 165 billion times bigger. It was built as a symbol of postwar progress for the 1958 World's Fair and became an architectural icon, receiving a makeover in 2006.

Tours

Groovy Brussels Bike Tours CYCLING
(☎0484 89 89 36; www.groovybrussels.com/bike; tour incl bicycle rental €25; ⏰10am daily Apr-Oct, plus 2pm weekends) Many first-time visitors love this tour for the ride and for the beer and *frites* stops along the way (food and drink cost extra). Tours start from the Grand Place and take 3½ hours; the maximum group size is 12. The outfit also offers chocolate and beer walking tours.

Sleeping

Many business hotels drop their rates dramatically at weekends and in summer. Double rooms with September midweek rates of €240 might cost as little as €69 in August. Brussels has a reasonable network of B&Bs, many listed and bookable through Bed & Brussels (www.bnb-brussels.be), or try sites like Airbnb (www.airbnb.com) and Wimdu (www.wimdu.co.uk).

★**Captaincy Guesthouse** HOSTEL €
(☎0496 59 93 79; www.thecaptaincybrussels.be; Quai à la Chaux 8; dm €31-37, d €90; Ⓜ Ste-Catherine) An idiosyncratic, warm and friendly venture, housed in a 17th-century mansion with a hip Ste-Catherine location and a mix of dorms (some mixed sex) and rooms. A generous €7.50 breakfast is served in the spacious living area. The wooden attic housing an en-suite four-bed female dorm has a fabulous boutique-hotel feel, and the attic double is a winner too.

Centre Vincent van Gogh HOSTEL €
(☎02-217 01 58; www.chab.be; Rue Traversière 8; dm €22-26, s/tw/tr €35/60/90; @📶; Ⓜ Botanique) The lobby bar and pool-table veranda are unusually hip for a hostel, but rooms are less glamorous and, from some, reaching the toilets means crossing the garden courtyard. No membership is required, but you have to be under 35 years unless in a group.

★**Chambres d'Hôtes du Vaudeville** B&B €€
(☎0484 59 46 69; www.theatreduvaudeville.be; Galerie de la Reine 11; d from €120; 📶; 🚊Bruxelles Central) This classy B&B has an incredible location right within the gorgeous (if reverberant) Galeries St-Hubert. Delectable decor styles include African, modernist and 'Madame Loulou' (with 1920s nude sketches). Larger front rooms have claw-foot bathtubs and *galerie* views but can be noisy, with clatter that continues all night. Get keys via the art deco–influenced Café du Vaudeville, where breakfast is included.

Vaudeville's unique house beer is provided free in the minibar.

La Vieille Lanterne B&B €€
(☎02-512 74 94; www.lavieillelanterne.be; Rue des Grands Carmes 29; s €118-168, d €130-180; 📶; 🚊Anneessens) Look out at the Manneken Pis from the window of room 5 in this neat, unsophisticated six-room B&B-style 'hotel', accessed by steep spiral stairs from an archetypal gift shop. Check in before 10pm.

Downtown-BXL B&B €€
(☎0475 29 07 21; www.downtownbxl.com; Rue du Marché au Charbon 118-120; r €109-119; 📶; 🚊Anneessens) Near the capital's gay district, this B&B is superbly located if you're dancing the night away. From the communal breakfast table and help-yourself coffee bar, a classic staircase winds up to good-value rooms featuring zebra-striped cushions and Warhol Marilyn prints. One room features a round bed. Adjacent **Casa-BXL** (r €109-119) offers three rooms in a more Moroccan-Asian style.

★**Hôtel Métropole** HOTEL €€€
(☎02-217 23 00, reservations 02-214 2424; www.metropolehotel.com; Place de Brouckère 31; r €170-350, weekend rates from €130; 🚭❄📶; Ⓜ De Brouckère) This 1895 showpiece has a jaw-droppingly sumptuous French Renaissance-style foyer with marble walls, coffered ceiling and beautifully etched stained-glass back windows. The *café* is indulgent and the bar (with frequent live music) features recently 'rediscovered' murals by a student of Horta. One of the lifts is an 1895 original.

Central Brussels

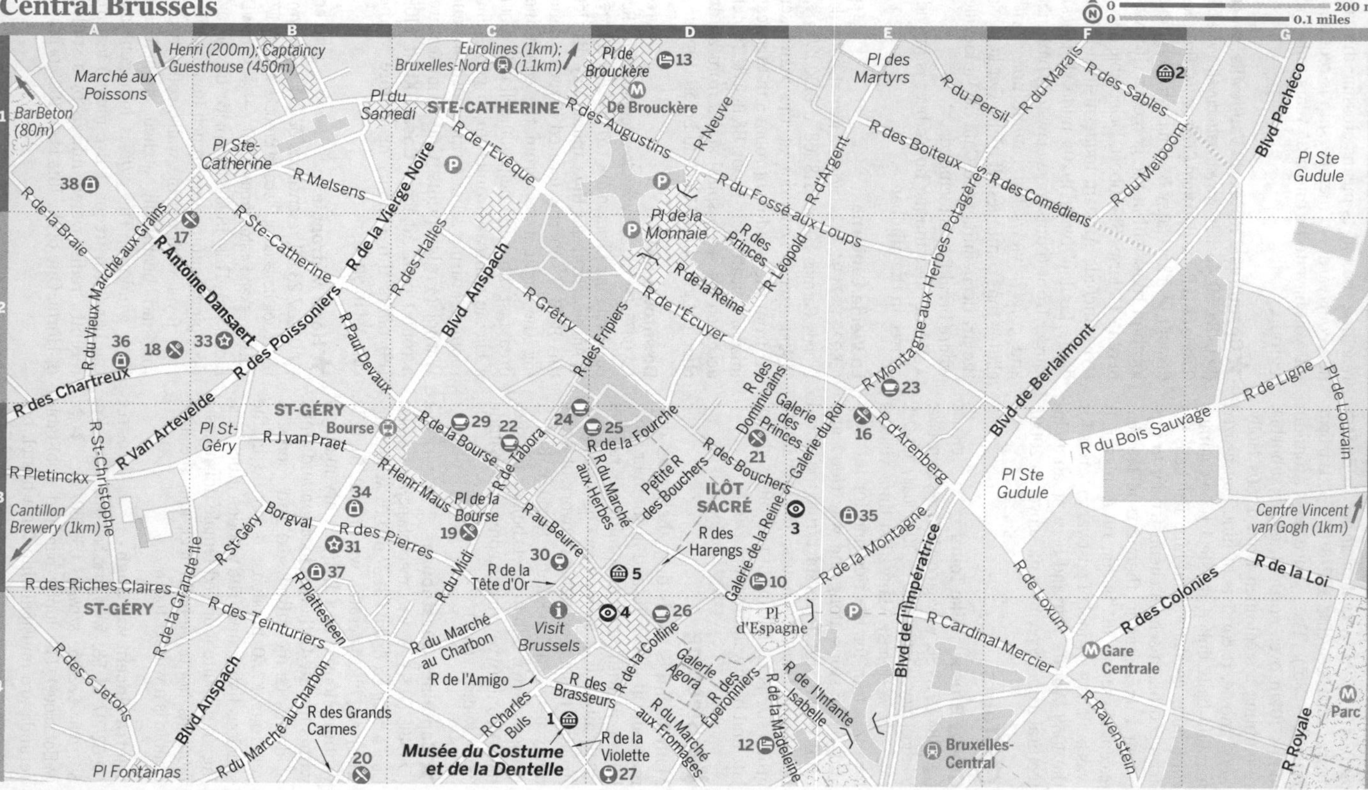

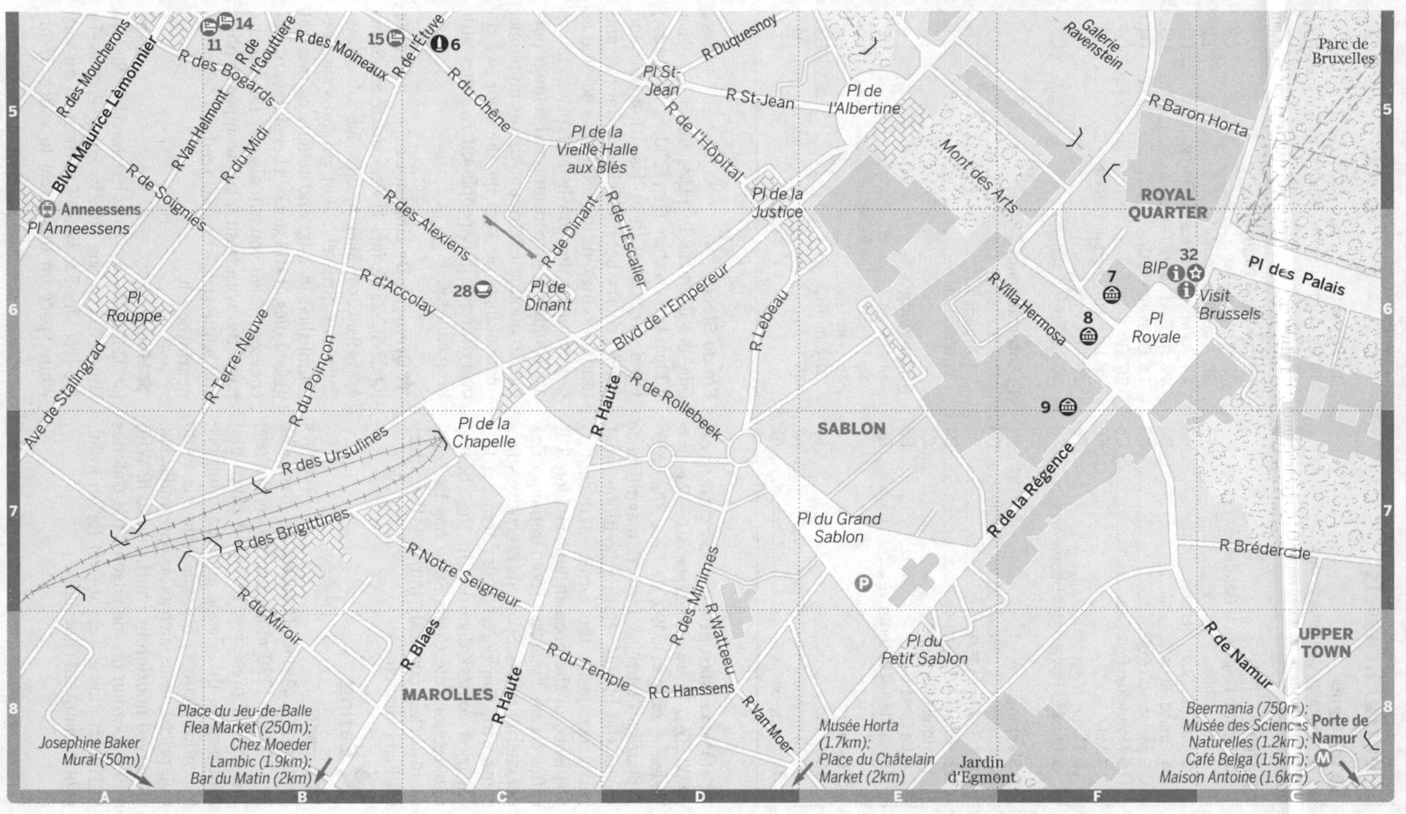
R des Moucherons
Blvd Maurice Lemonnier
14
11
R de l'Gouttière
R des Bogards
R Van Helmont
R du Midi
R de Soignies
Anneessens
Pl Anneessens
Pl Rouppe
Ave de Stalingrad
R Terre-Neuve
R du Poinçon
R des Moineaux
15
R de l'Etuve
6
R du Chêne
R des Alexiens
R d'Accolay
28
Pl de Dinant
R de Dinant
R de l'Escalier
Pl de la Vieille Halle aux Blés
R Duquesnoy
Pl St-Jean
R St-Jean
R de l'Hôpital
Pl de l'Albertine
Pl de la Justice
Galerie Ravenstein
Parc de Bruxelles
R Baron Horta
Mont des Arts
ROYAL QUARTER
32
BIP
Visit Brussels
Pl des Palais
7
8
Pl Royale
R Villa Hermosa
9
Blvd de l'Empereur
R Lebeau
R Haute
R de Rollebeek
SABLON
Pl de la Chapelle
R des Ursulines
R des Brigittines
R du Miroir
R Notre Seigneur
R Blaes
MAROLLES
R du Temple
R des Minimes
R Watteeu
R C Hanssens
R Van Moer
Pl du Grand Sablon
Pl du Petit Sablon
R de la Régence
R Brederode
R de Namur
UPPER TOWN
Jardin d'Egmont
Josephine Baker Mural (50m)
Place du Jeu-de-Balle Flea Market (250m); Chez Moeder Lambic (1.9km); Bar du Matin (2km)
Musée Horta (1.7km); Place du Châtelain Market (2km)
Beermania (750m); Musée des Sciences Naturelles (1.2km); Café Belga (1.5km); Maison Antoine (1.6km)
Porte de Namur

Central Brussels

Top Sights
1 Musée du Costume et de la Dentelle ... C4

Sights
2 Centre Belge de la Bande Dessinée ... F1
3 Galeries St-Hubert ... E3
4 Grand Place ... D4
5 Maison du Roi ... D3
6 Manneken Pis ... C5
7 MIM ... F6
8 Musée Magritte ... F6
9 Musées Royaux des Beaux-Arts ... F6

Sleeping
10 Chambres d'Hôtes du Vaudeville ... D3
11 Downtown-BXL ... B5
12 Hôtel Le Dixseptième ... D4
13 Hôtel Métropole ... D1
14 La Casa-BXL ... B5
15 La Vieille Lanterne ... B5

Eating
16 Arcadi ... E3
17 Cremerie De Linkebeek ... A2
18 Fin de Siècle ... A2
19 Fritland ... C3
20 Le Cercle des Voyageurs ... B4
21 L'Ogenblik ... D3

Drinking & Nightlife
22 À la Bécasse ... C3
23 À la Mort Subite ... E2
24 A l'Image de Nostre-Dame ... C3
25 Au Bon Vieux Temps ... D3
26 Chaloupe d'Or ... D4
27 Goupil le Fol ... D4
28 La Fleur en Papier Doré ... C6
29 Le Cirio ... C3
30 Le Roy d'Espagne ... C3

Entertainment
31 AB ... B3
32 Arsène50 ... F6
33 L'Archiduc ... B2

Shopping
34 Brüsel ... B3
35 Délices et Caprices ... E3
36 Gabriele ... A2
37 Multi-BD ... B3
38 Stijl ... A1

★ **Hôtel Le Dixseptième** BOUTIQUE HOTEL €€€

(☎02-517 17 17; www.ledixseptieme.be; Rue de la Madeleine 25; r €130-190, ste €200-370; ❄📶; 🚉Bruxelles Central) A hushed magnificence greets you in this alluring boutique hotel, partly occupying the former 17th-century residence of the Spanish ambassador. The coffee-cream breakfast room retains original cherub reliefs. Spacious executive suites come with four-poster beds. Across a tiny enclosed courtyard-garden in the cheaper rear section, the Creuz Suite has its bathroom tucked curiously into a 14th-century vaulted basement.

Eating

★ **Arcadi** BRASSERIE €

(☎02-511 33 43; Rue d'Arenberg 1b; mains €10-15; ⏲9.30am-10.30pm Tue-Sun; Ⓜ Gare Centrale) The jars of preserves, beautiful cakes and fruit tarts of this classic and charming bistro entice plenty of Brussels residents, as do well-priced meals such as lasagne and steak, all served nonstop by courteous staff. With a nice location on the edge of the Galeries St-Hubert, this is a great spot for an indulgent, creamy hot chocolate.

Fin de Siècle BELGIAN €

(Rue des Chartreux 9; mains €11.25-20; ⏲bar 4.30pm-1am, kitchen 6pm-12.30am; 🚉Bourse) From *carbonade* (beer-based hot pot) and *kriek* (cherry beer) chicken to mezzes and tandoori chicken, the food is as eclectic as the decor in this low-lit cult place. Tables are rough, music constant and ceilings purple. To quote the barman, 'there's no phone, no bookings, no sign on the door...we do everything to put people off but they still keep coming'.

★ **Cremerie De Linkebeek** DELI €

(☎02-512 35 10; Rue du Vieux Marché aux Grains 4; ⏲9am-3pm Mon, to 6pm Tue-Sat; Ⓜ Ste-Catherine) Brussels' best *fromagerie* was established in 1902 and retains its original glazed tiles. It still stocks a beguiling array of cheeses, which you can also try on crunchy baguettes with fresh salad, wrapped in blue-and-white-striped paper ready to take to a nearby bench.

★ **Henri** FUSION €€

(☎02-218 00 08; www.restohenri.be; Rue de Flandre 113; mains €16-23; ⏲noon-2pm Tue-Fri & 6-10pm Tue-Sat; Ⓜ Ste-Catherine) In an airy white space on this street to watch, Henri

DON'T MISS

BOURSE CAFES

Many of Brussels' most iconic *cafés* are within stumbling distance of the Bourse. Don't miss **Le Cirio** (02-512 13 05; Rue de la Bourse 18; 10am-midnight; Bourse), a sumptuous yet affordable 1866 marvel full of polished brasswork serving great-value pub meals. Three more classics are hidden up shoulder-wide alleys: the medieval yet unpretentious **A l'Image de Nostre-Dame** (Rue du Marais 3; noon-midnight Mon-Fri, 3pm-1am Sat, 4-10.30pm Sun; Bourse); the 1695 Rubenseque **Au Bon Vieux Temps** (02-217 26 26; Impasse St-Nicolas; 11am-midnight; Bourse), which sometimes stocks ultra-rare Westvleteren beers (€10!); and lambic specialist **À la Bécasse** (02-511 00 06; www.alabecasse.com; Rue de Tabora 11; 11am-midnight, to 1am Fri & Sat; M Gare Centrale), with its vaguely Puritanical rows of wooden tables.

concocts tangy fusion dishes such as tuna with ginger, soy and lime, artichokes with scampi, lime and olive tapenade, or Argentine fillet steak. There's an astute wine list, and staff who know their stuff.

Le Cercle des Voyageurs BRASSERIE €€
(02-514 39 49; www.lecercledesvoyageurs.com; Rue des Grands Carmes 18; mains €15-21; 11am-midnight; ; Bourse, Anneessens) Delightful bistro featuring globes, an antique-map ceiling and a travel library. If your date's late, flick through an old *National Geographic* in your colonial leather chair. The global brasserie food is pretty good, and there are documentary screenings and free live music: piano jazz on Tuesday and experimental on Thursday. Other gigs in the cave have a small entrance fee.

★ **L'Ogenblik** FRENCH €€€
(02-511 61 51; www.ogenblik.be; Galerie des Princes 1; mains €25-33; noon-2.30pm & 6.30pm-midnight Mon-Sat; Bourse) It may be only a stone's throw from Rue des Bouchers, but this timeless bistro with its lace curtains, resident cat, marble-topped tables and magnificent wrought-iron lamp feels a world away. They've been producing French classics here for more than 30 years, and the expertise shows. Worth the price for a special meal in the heart of town.

Drinking & Nightlife

Café culture is one of Brussels' greatest attractions. On the Grand Place itself, 300-year-old gems, like **Le Roy d'Espagne** (02-513 08 07; www.roydespagne.be; Grand Place 1; 9.30am-1am; M Gare Centrale) and **Chaloupe d'Or** (02-511 41 61; Grand Place 24; 11am-1am; M Gare Centrale) are magnificent but predictably pricey. Go out of the centre a little to explore the city's new brand of laid-back hipster bars, most decorated in minimal upcycled style, and hosting DJ nights and live music events: try **Café Belga** (02-640 35 08; Place Eugène Flagey 18; 8am-2am Sun-Thu, to 3am Fri & Sat; 81, 82), **BarBeton** (02-513 83 63; www.barbeton.be; Rue Antoine Dansaert 114; 10am-midnight; ; M Ste-Catherine) or **Bar du Matin** (02-537 71 59; bardumatin.blogspot.com; Chaussée d'Alsemberg 172; 8am-1am Sun-Thu, 8am-2am Fri & Sat; M Albert).

★ **Chez Moeder Lambic** PUB
(02-544 16 99; www.moederlambic.com; Rue de Savoie 68; 4pm-3am; M Horta) An institution. Behind windows plastered with beer stickers, this tattered, quirky old brown *café* is the ultimate beer spot in Brussels. Sample some of its hundreds of brews while flipping through its collection of dog-eared comics.

DON'T MISS

CHIP CHAMPS

Frying since 1948, **Maison Antoine** (02-230 54 56; www.maisonantoine.be; Place Jourdan; chips €2.60-3; 11.30am-1am Sun-Thu, to 2am Fri & Sat; M Schuman) is a classic little *fritkot* (take-away chip kiosk) whose reputation as 'Brussels' best' is self-perpetuating. 'Best' or not, its chips are certainly top notch and such is their popularity that *cafés* on the surrounding square (including beautifully wrought-iron-fronted L'Autobus) allow *frites* eaters to sit and snack so long as they buy a drink. Handily central **Fritland** (02-514 06 27; www.fritlandbrussels.be; Rue Henri Maus 49; 11am-1am Sun-Thu, 10am-dawn Fri & Sat; Bourse) keeps frying till the wee hours.

★ **Goupil le Fol** BAR
(☎02-511 13 96; www.goupillefol.com; Rue de la Violette 22; ⌚4pm-2am Sun & Mon, 4pm-3am Tue-Sat; Ⓜ Gare Centrale) Overwhelming weirdness hits you as you acid-trip your way through this sensory overload of rambling passageways, ragged old sofas and inexplicable beverages mostly based on madly fruit-flavoured wines (no beer is served). Unmissable.

La Fleur en Papier Doré CAFE
(☎02-511 16 59; www.goudblommekeinpapier.be; Rue des Alexiens 53; ⌚11am-midnight Tue-Sat, to 7pm Sun; 🚊 Bruxelles Central) The nicotine-stained walls of this tiny *café*, adored by artists and locals, are covered with writings, art and scribbles by Magritte and his surrealist pals, some of which were reputedly traded for free drinks. *'Ceci n'est pas un musée'*, quips a sign on the door reminding visitors to buy a drink and not just look around.

À la Mort Subite CAFE
(☎02-513 13 18; www.alamortsubite.com; Rue Montagne aux Herbes Potagères 7; ⌚11am-1am Mon-Sat, noon-midnight Sun; Ⓜ Gare Centrale) An absolute classic unchanged since 1928, with lined-up wooden tables, arched mirror panels and entertainingly brusque service.

☆ Entertainment

L'Archiduc JAZZ
(☎02-512 06 52; www.archiduc.net; Rue Antoine Dansaert 6; ⌚4pm-5am; 🚊 Bourse) This intimate, split-level art deco bar has been playing jazz since 1937. It's an unusual two-tiered circular space that can get incredibly packed but remains convivial. You might need to ring the doorbell. Saturday concerts (5pm) are free; Sunday brings in international talent and admission charges vary.

AB LIVE MUSIC
(Ancienne Belgique; ☎02-548 24 84; www.abconcerts.be; Blvd Anspach 110; 🚊 Bourse) The AB's two auditoriums are favourite venues for mid-level international rock bands and acts such as Jools Holland and Madeleine Peyroux, plus plenty of home-grown talent. The ticket office is located on Rue des Pierres. There's a good on-site bar-restaurant that opens at 6pm (bookings essential).

Shopping

Tourist-oriented shops selling chocolate, beer, lace and Atomium baubles stretch between the Grand Place and Manneken Pis. For better chocolate shops in calmer, grander settings, peruse the resplendent **Galeries St-Hubert** (☎02-545 09 90; www.grsh.be; Rue du Marché aux Herbes; Ⓜ Gare Centrale) or the upmarket Sablon area, or visit the daily flea market (p83). Antwerp more than Brussels is Belgium's fashion capital, but Rue Antoine Dansaert has several cutting-edge boutiques including **Stijl** (☎02-512 03 13; www.stijl.be; Rue Antoine Dansaert 74; ⌚10.30am-6.30pm Mon-Sat; Ⓜ Ste-Catherine).

Supermarkets sell a range of Belgian beers relatively cheaply but for wider selections and the relevant glasses, try **Beermania** (☎02-512 17 88; www.beermania.be; Chaussée de Wavre 174; ⌚11am-9pm Mon-Sat; Ⓜ Porte de Namur) or the very personal little **Délices et Caprices** (☎02-512 14 51; www.the-belgian-beer-tasting-shop.be; Rue des Bouchers 68; ⌚2-8pm Thu-Sat & Mon; Ⓜ Gare Centrale).

COMIC-STRIP CULTURE

In Belgium, comic strips *(bandes dessinées)* are revered as the 'ninth art'. Serious comic fans might enjoy Brussels' comprehensive **Centre Belge de la Bande Dessinée** (Belgian Comic Strip Centre; ☎02-219 19 80; www.comicscenter.net; Rue des Sables 20; adult/concession €10/7; ⌚10am-6pm Tue-Sun; Ⓜ Rogier) in a distinctive Horta-designed art-nouveau building.

Dozens of cartoon murals enliven Brussels buildings. Comic shops include **Brüsel** (www.brusel.com; Blvd Anspach 100; ⌚10.30am-6.30pm Mon-Sat, from noon Sun; 🚊 Bourse) and **Multi-BD** (☎02-513 72 35; www.multibd.com; Blvd Anspach 122-124; ⌚10.30am-7pm Mon-Sat, 12.30-6.30pm Sun; 🚊 Bourse).

For an immersive Tintin experience, a trip to Louvain-la-Neuve's **Musée Hergé** (☎010-48 84 21; www.museeherge.com; Rue du Labrador 26; adult/child €9.50/5; ⌚10.30am-5.30pm Tue-Fri, 10am-6pm Sat & Sun) is highly recommended. Trains from Brussels (€5.30, 50 minutes) generally require a change at Ottignies.

★ Place du Jeu-de-Balle Flea Market MARKET
(www.marcheauxpuces.be; Place du Jeu-de-Balle; ⏲6am-2pm Mon-Fri, 6am-3pm Sat & Sun; Ⓜ Porte de Hal, 🚋 Lemonnier) The quintessential Marolles experience is haggling at this chaotic flea market, established in 1919. Weekends see it at its liveliest, but for the best bargains, head here early morning midweek.

★ Place du Châtelain Market MARKET
(Place du Châtelain; ⏲afternoon Wed; Ⓜ Louise) Fabulous food stalls cluster around an elongated, leafy square at this market. Cheese, charcuterie, fresh fruit and veg, seasonal fodder – truffles, mushrooms, berries and so on – a Middle Eastern food van, Turkish bread, vats of Congolese stew, a wine bar and cake stalls: it's a true foodie heaven, well worth a special trip.

★ Gabriele VINTAGE
(☎02-512 67 43; www.gabrielevintage.com; Rue des Chartreux 27; ⏲1-7pm Mon & Tue, 11am-7pm Wed-Sat; 🚋 Bourse) For amazing vintage finds, try eccentric, elegant Gabriele. There's a gorgeous jumble of cocktail dresses, hats, Chinese shawls and accessories; only original clothes from the '20s to the '80s are stocked.

ℹ Information

Exchange agency rates are usually best around the Bourse. As well as the following there are info counters at Brussels Airport and Bruxelles-Midi station.

BIP (☎02-563 63 99; bip.brussels; Rue Royale 2-4; ⏲9.30am-5.30pm Mon-Fri, 10am-6pm Sat & Sun; Ⓜ Parc) Official Brussels-region tourist office. Hotel bookings and lots of information.

Visit Brussels (☎02-513 89 40; www.visit.brussels; Hôtel de Ville, Grand Place; ⏲9am-6pm; 🚋 Bourse) Visit Brussels has stacks of city-specific information as well as handy fold-out guides (independently researched) to the best shops, restaurants and pubs in town. The Rue Royale (☎02-513 89 40; www.visit.brussels; Rue Royale 2; ⏲9am-6pm; Ⓜ Parc) office is much less crowded than the Grand Place one. Here you'll also find the Arsène50 (www.arsene50.be; Rue Royale 2; ⏲12.30-5pm Tue-Sat; Ⓜ Parc) desk, which provides great discounts for cultural events.

ℹ Getting There & Away

BUS

Eurolines (☎02-274 13 50; www.eurolines.be; Rue du Progrès 80; 🚋 Gare du Nord) International bus service Eurolines has buses departing from Bruxelles-Nord train station.

WORTH A TRIP

BRUSSELS TO ANTWERP

Direct Brussels–Antwerp trains take just over half an hour. But if you're not in a hurry consider stopping en route at a couple of other historic cities, not more than a minor diversion by train: Leuven (30 minutes) then Mechelen (22 minutes). In both towns the station is around 15 minutes' walk from the centre. And both have imaginative accommodation, including hostels, if you're too charmed to move on.

TRAIN

Bruxelles-Midi (Gare du Midi; luggage office per article per day €2.50, luggage lockers per 24hr small/large €3/4; ⏲luggage office 6am-9pm; Ⓜ Gare du Midi, 🚆 Bruxelles-Midi) is the main station for international connections; high-speed trains only stop here. Most other mainline trains stop in quick succession at Bruxelles-Midi, **Bruxelles-Central** (Gare Centrale) and, except for Amsterdam trains, also at **Bruxelles-Nord** (Gare du Nord). For all enquiries, consult www.b-rail.be.

The following fares (one way, 2nd class) are for standard trains from Bruxelles-Central:

DESTINATION	FARE (€)	DURATION (MIN)	FREQUENCY (HR)
Antwerp	7.30	35-49	5
Bruges	14.10	62	2
Ghent	8.90	36	2
Leuven	5.30	24-36	4
Luxembourg City	37.80	180	1
Mechelen	4.50	15-28	2
Mons	9.40	55	2
Ypres	17.50	105	1

ℹ Getting Around

TO/FROM BRUSSELS AIRPORT

Taxi

Fares start around €40. Very bad idea in rush-hour traffic.

Train

Airport City Express (tickets €8.70; ⏲5.30am-12.20am) trains run four times hourly to the city's three main stations, Bruxelles-Nord (15 minutes), Bruxelles-Central (€8.50, 20 minutes) and Bruxelles-Midi (25 minutes).

TO/FROM CHARLEROI AIRPORT

Around 6km north of Charleroi, **Charleroi Airport** (www.charleroi-airport.com;), also known as Brussels-South, is Belgium's main hub for budget airlines, notably Ryanair. Two or three **coaches** (www.brussels-city-shuttle.com; around €14; 7.50am-midnight) per hour take 55 minutes to Brussels.

BICYCLE

FietsPunt/PointVelo (02-513 04 09; www.recyclo.org; Carrefour de l'Europe 2; per 1/3 days €7.50/15; 7am-7pm Mon-Fri; Bruxelles-Central) Rents long term: it's on the left as you leave Bruxelles-Central station by the (daytime-only) Madeleine exit.

Villo! (078-05 11 10; en.villo.be; subscription day/week €1.60/7.90) Has 180 automated pickup/drop-off short-term-rental stands. Credit card required; read the online instructions carefully.

PUBLIC TRANSPORT

STIB/MIVB (www.stib-mivb.be) tickets are sold at metro stations, newsagents and on buses and trams. Single-/five-/10-journey tickets valid for one hour from validation cost €2.10/8/14 including transfers. Unlimited one-/two-/three-day passes cost €7.50/14/18. Airport buses are excluded.

FLANDERS

Leuven

POP 97,600

Lively, self-confident Leuven (Louvain in French; www.leuven.be) is Flanders' oldest university town and home to the vast **Stella Artois brewery** (www.breweryvisits.com; Vuurkruisenlaan; adult/concession €8.50/7.50; 9am-7.30pm Tue-Sat). Its greatest attraction is a flamboyant 15th-century **Stadhuis** (Grote Markt 9; tours €4; tours 3pm) lavished with exterior statuary. Other architectural attractions are patchy due to heavy damage sustained in 20th-century wars, but the iconic **university library** (University Library; http://bib.kuleuven.be; Monseigneur Ladeuzeplein 21; tower entrance €7; tower 10am-5pm) FREE has been rebuilt. Twice. **Muntstraat** is a loveable medieval alley popular with locals and visitors alike and **Oude Markt** is a very lively square of wall-to-wall bars that hum till the wee hours.

The most interesting option for accommodation is the grand mansion housing **Oude Brouwerei Keyser Carel** (016-22 14 81; www.keysercarel.be; Lei 15; s/d €115/130), while homely **Leuven City Hostel** (016-84 30 33; www.leuvencityhostel.com; Ravenstraat 37; dm/d from €25/55; reception 4-8pm;) and peaceful **Martin's Klooster Hotel** (016-21 31 41; www.martins-hotels.com; Onze-Lieve-Vrouwstraat 18; d €169-209;) are good, relatively central accommodation choices.

Terrace cafes surround the stadhuis, and perpetually packed, casually stylish restaurants and bars spill tables onto cosy flag-decked Munstraat.

Mechelen

POP 82,300

Belgium's religious capital, Mechelen (Malines in French) has the **St-Romboutskathedraal cathedral** (http://sintromboutstoren.mechelen.be; Grote Markt; tower adult/youth €8/3; 1-6pm Mon-Fri, 10am-6pm Sat) FREE featuring a 97m, 15th-century tower that soars above a particularly memorable central market square. There are other splendid churches on Keizerstraat where the courthouse and theatre were both once royal palaces in the days when the Low Countries were effectively run from Mechelen. Other top sights include the brilliant **Speelgoedmuseum Toy Museum** (015-55 70 75; www.speelgoedmuseum.be; Nekkerstraat 21; adult/child €9.80/7.30; 10am-5pm Tue-Sun) and the **Schepenhuis gallery tower** (015-29 40 30; Steenweg 1) on IJzerenleen, a street of fine baroque facades leading towards the main station passing close to **Vismarkt**, the compact bar-cafe zone. There's a modern HI Hostel, the **Hostel De Zandpoort** (015-27 85 39; www.mechelen-hostel.com; Zandpoortvest 70; dm €23-26, tw €55-58; check-in 5-10pm;), or try stylish **Martins Patershof** (015-46 46 46; www.martinshotels.com; Karmelietenstraat 4; d €149-249;), set in a 1867 Franciscan monastery.

Mechelen's agricultural specialities include *witloof* (endives) and especially *asperges* (asparagus), prominent on restaurant menus mid-April to late June.

WORTH A TRIP

WATERLOO

Tourists have been swarming to Waterloo ever since Napoleon's 1815 defeat, a seminal event in European history. Inaugurated for the 2015 bicentenary, **Memorial 1815** (☎02-385 19 12; www.waterloo1815.be; Rte du Lion, Hameau du Lion; adult/child €16/13, with Wellington & Napoleon headquarters museums €19/15; ⏲9.30am-6.30pm Apr-Sep, 9.30am-5.30pm Oct-Mar) is a showpiece underground museum and visitor centre at the main battlefield area (known as Hameau du Lion). There's a detailed audio guide and some enjoyable technological effects. The climax is an impressive 3D film that sticks you right into the middle of the cavalry charges. It includes admission to various other battlefield attractions, including the Butte du Lion, a memorial hill from which you can survey the terrain, and the recently restored Hougoumont farmhouse that played a key part in the battle.

TEC bus W runs every 30 minutes from Ave Fonsny at Bruxelles-Midi to Braine-l'Alleud train station, passing through Waterloo town and stopping near Hameau du Lion (€3.20, one hour). If coming by train, get off at Braine-l'Alleud rather than awkwardly located Waterloo station, then switch to bus W to reach the battlefield.

Antwerp

POP 503,200

Belgium's second city and biggest port is Antwerp (Antwerpen/Anvers in Dutch/French) and without a doubt, this charming city is the country's capital of cool. It's long been a powerful magnet for everyone from fashion moguls and club queens to art lovers and diamond dealers. In the mid-16th century it was one of Europe's most important cities and home to baroque superstar painter Pieter Paul Rubens – there are numerous places to admire his works across the city.

Sights

City Centre

★Grote Markt SQUARE

As with every great Flemish city, Antwerp's medieval heart is a classic Grote Markt (Market Sq). Here the triangular, pedestrianised space features the voluptuous, baroque **Brabo Fountain** depicting Antwerp's giant-killing, hand-throwing legend. Flanked on two sides by very photogenic guildhalls, the square is dominated by an impressive Italo-Flemish Renaissance-style **stadhuis** (Town Hall; Grote Markt), completed in 1565.

Het Steen CASTLE

(Steenplein) On a riverside knoll, Het Steen is a dinky but photogenic castle dating from 1200 and occupying the site of Antwerp's original Gallo-Roman settlement. Outside is a humorous **statue of Lange Wapper**, a tall folkloric 'peeping Tom' figure showing off his codpiece to two diminutive onlookers. Directly north, the misnamed **Maritime Park** is a long, open-sided wrought-iron shed displaying a historic barge collection. There is nothing to see inside the castle.

★Onze-Lieve-Vrouwekathedraal CATHEDRAL

(☎03-213 99 51; www.dekathedraal.be; Handschoenmarkt; adult/reduced €6/4; ⏲10am-5pm Mon-Fri, to 3pm Sat, 1-4pm Sun) Belgium's finest Gothic cathedral was 169 years in the making (1352–1521). Wherever you wander in Antwerp, its gracious, 123m-high spire has a habit of popping unexpectedly into view and it rarely fails to prompt a gasp of awe. The sight is particularly well framed when looking up Pelgrimstraat in the afternoon light.

★Museum Plantin-Moretus HISTORIC BUILDING

(☎03-221 14 50; www.museumplantinmoretus.be; Vrijdag Markt 22; adult/reduced/child €8/6/free; ⏲10am-5pm Tue-Sun) Giving a museum Unesco World Heritage status might seem odd – until you've seen this astonishing, recently renovated place. Once home to the world's first industrial printing works, it's been a museum since 1876. The medieval building and 1622 courtyard garden alone would be worth a visit, but the world's oldest printing press, priceless manuscripts and original type sets make for a giddy experience indeed. Other highlights include the 1640 library, a bookshop dating to 1700 and rooms lined with gilt leather.

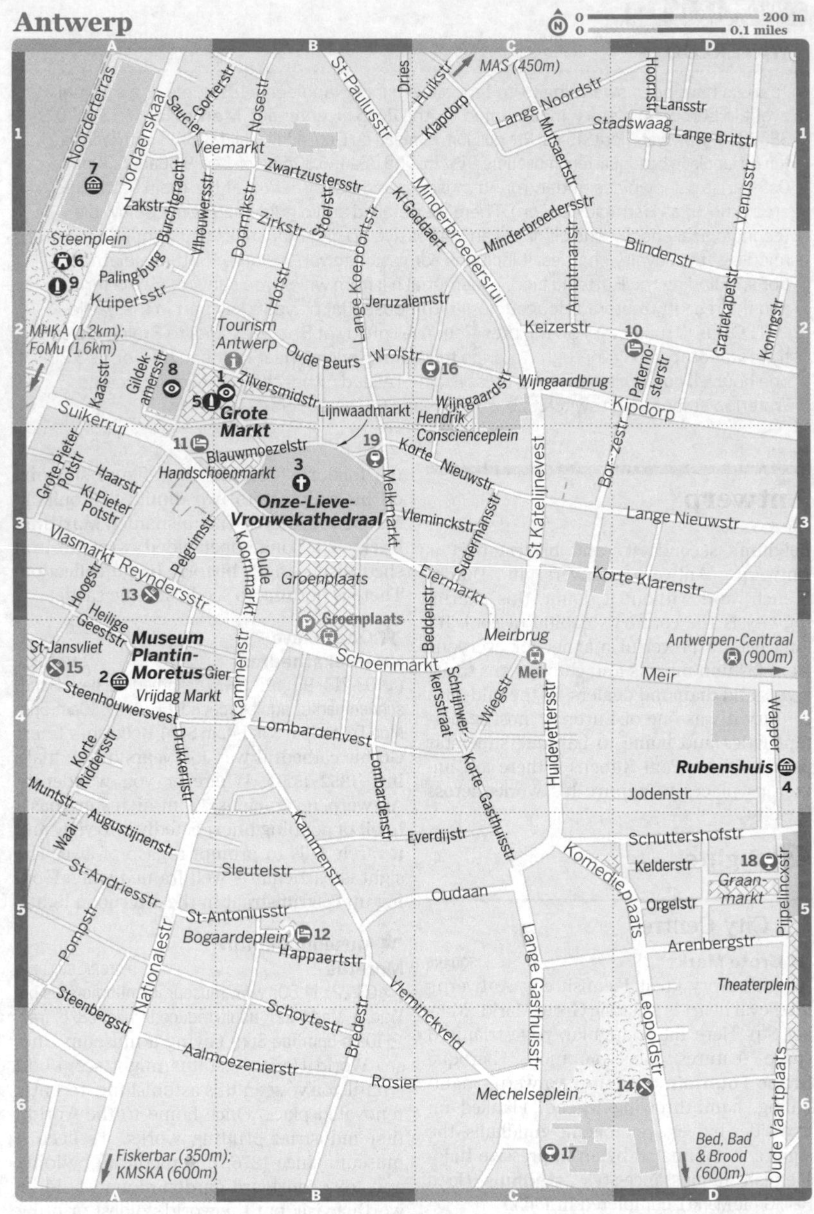

★**Rubenshuis** MUSEUM

(☎03-201 15 55; www.rubenshuis.be; Wapper 9-11; adult/concession €8/6, audioguide €2; ⊙10am-5pm Tue-Sun) The 1611 building was built as home and studio by celebrated painter Pieter Paul Rubens. Rescued from ruins in 1937, and extensively and sensitively restored, the building is a delightfully indulgent one, with baroque portico, rear facade and exquisite formal garden. The furniture all dates from Rubens' era, although it's not part of the original decor. Fourteen Rubens canvases

Antwerp

Top Sights

Sights

Sleeping

Eating

Drinking & Nightlife

are displayed, along with some wonderful period ephemera, such as the metal frame of a ruff collar and a linen press.

★Antwerpen-Centraal LANDMARK
(Koningin Astridplein 27) With its neo-Gothic facade, vast main hall and splendidly proportioned dome, the 1905 Antwerpen-Centraal train station is one of the city's premier landmarks. It was rated by *Newsweek* as one of the world's five most beautiful stations. It's also very practical, the multilevel platforms having had a full 21st-century makeover.

't Zuid

South of the centre, this is a conspicuously prosperous area dotted with century-old architecture, hip bars, fine restaurants and museums. The classic centrepiece art gallery, **KMSKA** (www.kmska.be; Leopold de Waelplaats), is closed for renovation until late 2017, but meanwhile there's still **MHKA** (☎03-238 59 60; www.muhka.be; Leuvenstraat 32; adult/child €10/1; ⊙11am-6pm Tue-Sun, to 9pm Thu) for contemporary conceptual art and outstanding **FoMu** (FotoMuseum; ☎03-242 93 00; www.fotomuseum.be; Waalsekaai 47; adult/child €8/3; ⊙10am-6pm Tue-Sun) for photography.

't Eilandje

★MAS MUSEUM
(Museum aan de Stroom; ☎03-338 44 00; www.mas.be; Hanzestedenplaats; adult/reduced €10/8; ⊙10am-5pm Tue-Sun, to 6pm Sat & Sun Apr-Oct) Opened in 2011, MAS is a 10-storey complex that redefines the idea of a museum-gallery. Floors are designed around big-idea themes using a barrage of media, from old master paintings through to tribal artefacts to video installations.

Sleeping

Antwerp offers a staggering range of stylish, well-priced B&Bs. Many are listed on www.bedandbreakfast.eu.

Pulcinella HOSTEL €
(☎03-234 03 14; www.jeugdherbergen.be; Bogaardeplein 1; dm €25-28, tw €60-63; @) This giant, tailor-made HI hostel is hard to beat for its Fashion District location and cool modernist decor. It's a little cheaper for HI members and under-30s; breakfast is included.

★Bed, Bad & Brood B&B €€
(☎03-248 15 39; www.bbantwerp.com; Justitiestraat 43; s/d/q €70/80/120, budget s/d €57/68; @) In a 1910, belle époque–era townhouse near the vast Gerechtshof (former courthouse), this B&B impresses with authentic wooden floors, high ceilings and beautifully eclectic furniture. Rooms are remarkably spacious and comfortable for the price – all but the budget rooms have a bath, and the family room is a separate two-bedder tucked away up a mysterious little staircase.

Hotel O HOTEL €€
(☎03-500 89 50; www.hotelokathedral.com; Handschoenmarkt 3; s €99, d €119-159) The immediate selling point here is an unbeatable location, staring across a square at the cathedral frontage. A little foyer bar lined with 1950s radios and audio equipment leads to midsize rooms with black and moody decor, giant Rubens reproductions spilling onto the ceilings, and baths in black-framed glass boxes.

★De Witte Lelie DESIGN HOTEL €€€
(☎03-226 19 66; www.dewittelelie.be; Keizerstraat 16-18; d €245-525;) A trio of renovated 16th-century mansions houses 10 luxurious rooms at this elegant family-run hotel. Design choices are bold, mixing 20th-century

DON'T MISS

THE FASHION DISTRICT

Antwerp may seem far more sartorially laid-back than fashion heavyweights Paris or Milan, but it punches above its weight. In the space of just a few streets you'll find dozens of designer boutiques, along with a variety of streetwear, end-of-line discounters, upmarket vintage and designer consignment shops and more mainstream labels. Few places in the world have such a convenient and covetable concentration.

The tourist office has a fashion-walk directory pamphlet. Or simply stroll Nationalestraat, Lombardenvest, Huidevettersstraat and Schuttershofstraat, not missing Kammenstraat for streetwear and up-and-coming designers.

pieces with grand original features and each of the rooms has a distinct look and layout. The public areas – two salons, a reading room, a pretty courtyard and a super-sexy private bar – are incredibly lavish considering the hotel's handful of guests.

Eating

Locals head to 't Zuid to dine, with restaurants lining Leopold de Waelplaats, Vlaamsekaai and Marnixplaats and fanning out through surrounding streets.

LOA INTERNATIONAL, FAST FOOD €

(☎03-291 64 85; www.loa.be; Hoogstraat 77; dishes €5-10; ⏰noon-10pm Mon & Wed-Thu, to 11pm Fri & Sat, to 8pm Sun) International 'street food' – pad thai, Moroccan pancakes, tortillas, croquettes – are made with love and care in this bright cafe. There's complimentary mint tea to sip with your meal and front-row seats onto the square.

De Groote Witte Arend BELGIAN €€

(☎03-233 50 33; www.degrootewittearend.be; Reyndersstraat 18; mains €15-24; ⏰11.30am-midnight, kitchen 11.30am-3pm & 5-10pm; 📶) Retaining the Tuscan stone arcade of a 15th- and 17th-century convent building, as well as a little family chapel, this place combines the joys of a good beer bar with the satisfaction of well-cooked, sensibly priced Flemish home cuisine, notably *stoemp* (potato hash), *stoofvlees/carbonade* (beef, beer and onion stew) and huge portions of rabbit in rich Westmalle sauce.

Fiskebar SEAFOOD €€

(☎03-257 13 57; http://fiskebar.be; Marnixplaats 12; mains €24-36; ⏰restaurant 6-8.30pm Mon-Thu, 6-9.30pm Fri, noon-3pm & 6-9.30pm Sat, noon-3pm & 6-8pm Sun) Locals swear that Fiskebar serves Antwerp's best seafood, meaning there's always an almighty crush for tables in this bustling, fashionably dishevelled former fishmongers' shop. If you can't get a booking, try its oyster bar next door, which serves a more limited selection and works without reservations.

★ **Het Gebaar** BELGIAN €€€

(☎03-232 37 10; www.hetgebaar.be; Leopoldstraat 24; mains €34-48; ⏰noon-5.30pm) Chef Roger van Damme only does fancy and only does lunch. At the entrance to Antwerp's petite botanical gardens, the former gardener's house is a deeply romantic setting to write off an afternoon. The Flemish stew and tartars retain the essence of the original but use the best produce and are prettily presented. Highly theatrical desserts are a house speciality.

Drinking & Nightlife

To sound like a local, stride into a pub and ask for a *bolleke*. Don't worry, that means a 'little bowl' (ie glass) of De Koninck, the city's favourite ale. Cheap places to try it include classic *cafés* **Oud Arsenaal** (Pijpelincxstraat 4; ⏰10am-10pm Wed-Fri, 7.30am-7.30pm Sat & Sun), **De Kat** (☎03-233 08 92; www.facebook.com/cafeDeKat; Wolstraat 22; ⏰noon-2am Mon-Sat, 5pm-2am Sun) and the livelier **Pelikaan** (Melkmarkt 14; ⏰8.30am-3am). Mechelseplein bars including **Korsåkov** (☎0485 46 45 06; facebook.com/vokasrov; Mechelseplein 21; ⏰11am-3am Mon-Wed, to 4am Thu, to 5am Fri & Sat, noon-midnight Sun) open till very late as do countless other great options around KMSKA in the 't Zuid area.

Information

Tourism Antwerp (☎03-232 01 03; www.visitantwerpen.be; Grote Markt 13; ⏰9am-5.45pm Mon-Sat, to 4.45pm Sun) Tourism Antwerp has a large, central office with helpful staff – pick up maps, buy tram/bus passes and book tickets here. There is also a booth on the ground floor of Antwerpen-Centraal station.

Getting There & Away

BUS

Buses for Lier and many other destinations start from Antwerpen-Berchem bus station, although trains are generally much faster.

TRAIN

Regular services to Bruges (€14.80, 75 minutes), Brussels (€7.30, 35 to 49 minutes) and Ghent (€9.40, 46 minutes). High speed service to Amsterdam.

Getting Around

Franklin Rooseveltplaats and Koningin Astridplein are hubs for the integrated network of De Lijn (www.delijn.be) buses and trams (some running underground metro-style).

Ghent

POP 247,500

Ghent (www.visitgent.be) is one of Europe's greatest discoveries – small enough to feel cosy but big enough to stay vibrant. It has enough medieval frivolity to create a spectacle but retains a gritty industrial edge that keeps things 'real'. Tourists remain surprisingly thin on the ground, yet with its fabulous canalside architecture, wealth of quirky bars and some of Belgium's most fascinating museums, this is a city you really won't want to miss.

Sights

Most major sights are strolling distance from Korenmarkt, the westernmost of three interlinked squares that form the heart of Ghent's historic core.

St-Baafskathedraal CATHEDRAL

(www.sintbaafskathedraal.be; St-Baafsplein; ⌚8.30am-6pm Mon-Sat, 10am-6pm Sun Apr-Oct, to 5pm Nov-Mar) St-Baafs cathedral's towering interior has some fine stained glass and an unusual combination of brick vaulting with stone tracery. A €0.20 leaflet guides you round the cathedral's numerous art treasures, including a big original Rubens opposite the stairway that leads down into the partly muralled crypts. However, most visitors come to see just one magnificent work – the Van Eycks' 1432 'Flemish Primitive' masterpiece, *The Adoration of the Mystic Lamb* (adult/child/audio guide €4/1.50/1).

Belfort HISTORIC BUILDING

(☎09-375 31 61; www.belfortgent.be; Botermarkt; adult/concession/child €8/2.70/free; ⌚10am-6pm) Ghent's soaring, Unesco-listed, 14th-century belfry is topped by a large dragon. That's a weathervane not a fire breather and it's become something of a city mascot. You'll meet two previous dragon incarnations on the climb to the top (mostly by lift) but other than some bell-making exhibits, the real attraction is the view. Enter through the **Lakenhalle**, Ghent's cloth hall that was left half-built in 1445 and only completed in 1903.

Gravensteen CASTLE

(http://gravensteen.stad.gent; St-Veerleplein; adult/concession/child €10/6/free; ⌚10am-6pm Apr-Oct, 9am-5pm Nov-Mar) The counts of Flanders' quintessential 12th-century stone castle comes complete with moat, turrets and arrow slits. It's all the more remarkable considering that during the 19th century the site was converted into a cotton mill. Meticulously restored since, the interior sports the odd suit of armour, a guillotine and torture devices. The relative lack of furnishings is compensated with a hand-held 45-minute movie guide, which sets a tongue-in-cheek historical costumed drama in the rooms, prison pit and battlements.

★**MSK** GALLERY

(Museum voor Schone Kunsten; ☎09-323 67 00; www.mskgent.be; Citadelpark; adult/youth/child €8/2/free; ⌚9.30am-5.30pm Tue-Fri, 10am-6pm Sat & Sun) Styled like a Greek temple, this superb 1903 fine-art gallery introduces a veritable A-Z of great Belgian and Low Countries' painters from the 14th to mid-20th centuries. Highlights include a happy family of coffins by Magritte, Luminist canvases by Emile Claus, and Pieter Breughel the Younger's 1621 *Dorpsadvocaat* – a brilliant portrait of a village lawyer oozing with arrogance. English-language explanation cards are available in each room.

PARTY TIME IN GHENT

During mid-July's raucous **Gentse Feesten** (http://gentsefeesten.stad.gent; ⌚Jul) festival, the city's many squares become venues for a variety of street-theatre performances and there are big associated techno and jazz festivals. Those wanting a merrily boozy party atmosphere will love it. But consider avoiding Ghent at this time if you don't.

Ghent Centre

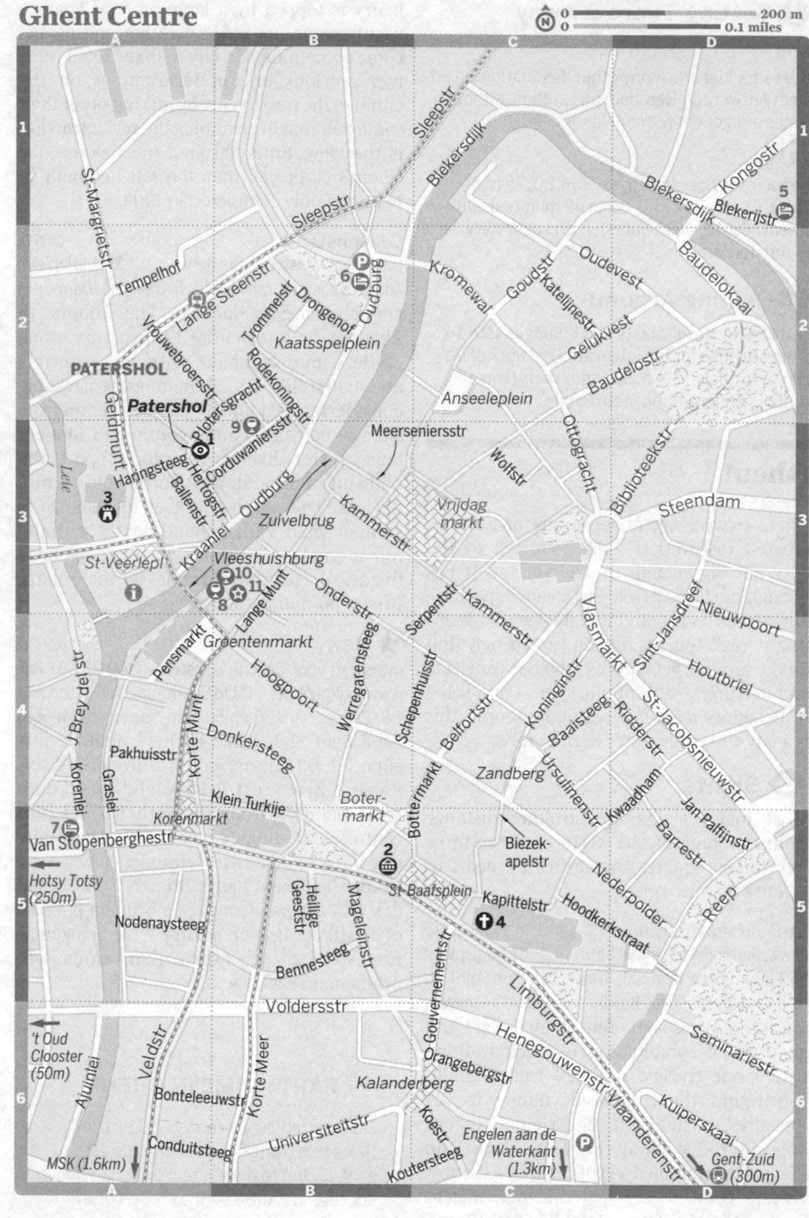

★The Adoration of the Mystic Lamb ARTWORK

(Het Lam Gods; www.sintbaafskathedraal.be; St- Baafskathedraal; adult/child/audio guide €4/1.50/1; ⏰9.30am-5pm Mon-Sat, 1-5pm Sun Apr-Oct, 10.30am-4pm Mon-Sat, 1-4pm Sun Nov-Mar) Formidable queues form to see *The Adoration of the Mystic Lamb (De Aanbidding van het Lams God)*, a lavish representation of medieval religious thinking that is one of

Ghent Centre

Top Sights

Sights

Sleeping

Drinking & Nightlife

Entertainment

the earliest-known oil paintings. Completed in 1432, it was painted as an altarpiece by the Flemish Primitive artists, the Van Eyck brothers, and has 20 panels (originally the interior panels were displayed only on important religious occasions, but these days they're always open to view).

Sleeping

Ghent offers innovative accommodation in all budget ranges. Websites www.gent-accommodations.be and www.bedandbreakfast-gent.be help you gauge availability in the city's numerous appealing B&Bs.

★ **Uppelink** HOSTEL €
(09-279 44 77; www.hosteluppelink.com; Sint-Michielsplein 21; dm €21-37) Within a classic step-gabled canalside house, the showstopping attraction at this super-central new hostel is the unbeatable view of Ghent's main towers as seen from the breakfast room and from the biggest, cheapest dorms. Smaller rooms have little view, if any.

Hostel 47 HOSTEL €
(0478 71 28 27; www.hostel47.com; Blekerijstraat 47-51; dm €26.50-29.50, d/tr €66/€90;) Unusually calm yet pretty central, this inviting hostel has revamped a high-ceilinged historic house with virginal white walls, spacious bunk rooms and designer fittings. Free lockers and cursory breakfast with Nespresso coffee; no bar.

★ **Engelen aan de Waterkant** B&B €€
(0476 40 25 23; www.engelenaandewaterkant.be; Ter Platen 30; r €110) Two 'angel' rooms are an opportunity for the interior-designer owner to experiment and for guests to soak up the special atmosphere in a 1900 townhouse overlooking the tree-lined canal.

★ **Simon Says** GUESTHOUSE €€
(09-233 03 43; www.simon-says.be; Sluizeken 8; d from €130;) Two fashionably styled guest rooms above an excellent coffee shop in a brightly coloured corner house with art nouveau facade.

Eating

Enchanting **Patershol** is a web of twisting cobbled lanes with old-world houses that are now interspersed with small restaurants. Others jostle for summer terrace space on Graslei's gorgeous canalside terrace. There's fast food around Korenmarkt and great-value Turkish options along Sleepstraat. Numerous vegetarian and organic choices feature on the tourist office's free *Veggieplan Gent* guide map.

't Oud Clooster CAFE €
(09-233 78 02; www.toudclooster.be; Zwartezusterstraat 5; mains €12-21; 11.45am-2.30pm & 6-10.30pm Mon-Fri, 11.45am-2.30pm & 5.30-10.30pm Sat, 5.30-9.30pm Sun) Mostly candlelit at night, this atmospheric double-level 'pratcafe' is built into sections of what was long ago a nunnery, hence the sprinkling of religious statues and cherub lampholders. Well-priced *café* food is presented with unexpected style.

Drinking & Entertainment

Try the snug **Hot Club de Gand** (09-256 71 99; www.hotclub.gent; Schuddevisstraatje - Groentenmarkt 15b; 3pm-late) for live jazz, gyspy or blues music; **Hotsy Totsy** (09-224 20 12; www.facebook.com/Hotsy.Totsy.Gent; Hoogstraat 1; 6pm-1am Mon-Fri, 8pm-2am Sat & Sun, opens 8pm Jul & Aug) for free Thursday jazz; and beautifully panelled **Rococo** (09-224 30 35; Corduwaniersstraat 5; 9pm-late Tue-Sun) for candle-lit conversation. **Het Waterhuis aan de Bierkant** (09-225 06 80; www.waterhuisaandebierkant.be; Groentenmarkt 12; 11am-1am) has the best beer choice including their own brews, while **'t Dreupelkot** (09-224 21 20; www.dreupelkot.be; Groentenmarkt 12; 4pm-late Mon-Sat) is a traditional *jenever* bar with a hundred concoctions.

Information

Ghent Tourist Office (☎09-266 56 60; www.visit.gent.be; Oude Vismijn, St-Veerleplein 5; ⊙9.30am-6.30pm mid-Mar–mid-Oct, to 4.30pm mid-Oct–mid-Mar) Very helpful for free maps and accommodation bookings.

Getting There & Away

BUS

Some longer distance buses depart from **Gent-Zuid bus station** (Woodrow Wilsonplein), others from various points around Gent-St-Pieters train station.

TRAIN

Gent-Dampoort, 1km west of the old city, is the handiest station with useful trains to the following destinations:

Antwerp (€9.40, fast/slow 42/64 minutes, three per hour)

Bruges (€6.50, 36 minutes, hourly)

Gent-St-Pieters, 2.5km south of the centre and Ghent's main station, has more choices:

Bruges (€6.50, fast/slow 24/42 minutes, five per hour)

Brussels (€8.90, 36 minutes, twice hourly)

Getting Around

BICYCLE

Biker (☎09-224 29 03; www.bikerfietsen.be; Steendam 16; per day €9; ⊙9am-12.30pm & 1.30-6pm Tue-Sat)

Max Mobiel (☎09-242 80 40; www.max-mobiel.be; Vokselslaan 27; per half-day/day/week €7/10/30) Two minutes' walk south of Gent-St-Pieters station. Branch kiosk at Gent-Dampoort station.

BUS & TRAM

Tickets are cheaper bought from machines, De Lijn (www.delijn.be) or the **ticket kiosk** (www.delijn.be; ⊙7am-1.30pm & 2-7pm Mon-Fri) outside Gent-St-Pieters. **Tram 1** runs from Gent-St-Pieters to and through the centre, passing walkably close to most major sites.

Bruges

POP 117,000

Cobblestone lanes, dreamy canals, soaring spires and whitewashed almshouses combine to make central Bruges (Brugge in Dutch) one of Europe's most picture-perfect historic cities. The only problem is that everyone knows of these charms, and the place gets mobbed.

Sights

The real joy of Bruges is simply wandering alongside the canals, soaking up the atmosphere. To avoid the worst crowds, explore east of pretty Jan van Eyckplein.

Markt SQUARE

The heart of ancient Bruges, the old market square is lined with pavement cafes beneath step-gabled facades. The buildings aren't always quite as medieval as they look, but together they create a fabulous scene and even the neo-Gothic **post office** is architecturally magnificent. The scene is dominated by the **Belfort**, Belgium's most famous belfry, whose iconic octagonal tower is arguably better appreciated from afar than by climbing 366 claustrophobic steps to the top.

Historium MUSEUM

(☎050-27 03 11; www.historium.be; Markt; adult/child €13/7.50; ⊙10am-6pm) The Historium occupies a neo-Gothic building on the northern side of the Markt. Taking visitors back to 1435, it is a multimedia experience, claiming to be more medieval movie than museum. The 'immersive' one-hour audio and video tour aims to take you back to medieval Bruges: a fictional love story gives narrative structure, and you can nose around Van Eyck's studio, among other pseudo historic experiences.

Brugse Vrije HISTORIC BUILDING

(Burg 11a; included in Stadhuis entry; ⊙9.30am-noon & 1.30-5pm) Most eye-catching with its early baroque gabling, gilt highlights and golden statuettes, this was once the palace of the 'Liberty of Bruges', the large autonomous territory and administrative body that ruled from Bruges (1121–1794). Much of the building is still used for city offices, but you can visit the former aldermen's room, the **Renaissancezaal**, to admire its remarkable 1531 carved chimney piece.

Stadhuis HISTORIC BUILDING

(City Hall; Burg 12; adult/child €4/3; ⊙9.30am-5pm) The beautiful 1420 stadhuis features a fanciful facade that's second only to Leuven's for exquisitely turreted Gothic excess. Inside, an audio guide explains numerous portraits in somewhat excessive detail before leading you upstairs to the astonishing **Gotische Zaal** (Gothic Hall). Few rooms anywhere achieve such a jaw-dropping first impression as this dazzling hall with its polychrome ceiling, hanging vaults, romantically historic murals and upper frieze of gilt figures.

★Groeningemuseum GALLERY

(☎050-44 87 43; www.museabrugge.be; Dijver 12; adult/concession €8/6; ⏲9.30am-5pm Tue-Sun) Bruges' most celebrated art gallery boasts an astonishingly rich collection whose strengths are in superb Flemish Primitive and Renaissance works, depicting the conspicuous wealth of the city with glitteringly realistic artistry. In room 2 are meditative works including Jan Van Eyck's 1436 radiant masterpiece *Madonna with Canon George Van der Paele* (1436) and the *Madonna* by the Master of the Embroidered Foliage, where the rich fabric of the Madonna's robe meets the 'real' foliage at her feet with exquisite detail.

Begijnhof HISTORIC BUILDING

(Wijngaardstraat; ⏲6.30am-6.30pm) FREE Bruges' delightful *begijnhof* originally dates from the 13th century. Although the last *begijn* has long since passed away, today residents of the pretty, whitewashed garden complex include a convent of Benedictine nuns. Despite the hordes of summer tourists, the *begijnhof* remains a remarkably tranquil haven. In spring, a carpet of daffodils adds to the quaintness of the scene. Outside the 1776 gateway bridge lies a tempting, if predictably tourist-priced, array of terraced restaurants, lace shops and waffle peddlers.

Tours

Canal Tour BOATING

(☎050-33 32 93; www.boottochten-brugge.be; adult/child €8/4; ⏲10am-6pm Mar–mid-Nov) Taking a Canal Tour is a must. Yep, it's touristy, but what isn't in Bruges? Viewing the city from the water gives it a totally different feel than by foot. Cruise down Spiegelrei towards Jan Van Eyckplein and it's possible to imagine Venetian merchants entering the city centuries ago and meeting under the slender turret of the Poortersloge building up ahead.

Sleeping

Almost all options can get seriously overbooked from Easter to October and over Christmas. Things get especially tough at weekends when two-night minimum stays are often required. Many cheaper B&Bs charge around €10 per room less if you stay more than one night.

't Keizershof HOTEL €

(☎050-33 87 28; www.hotelkeizershof.be; Oostermeers 126; s €40-50, d €54-65; P 📶) Remarkably tasteful and well kept for this price, the seven simple rooms with shared bathrooms are above a former brasserie-cafe decorated with old radios (now used as the breakfast room). Free parking.

Bauhaus HOSTEL €

(St Christopher's Hostel; ☎050-34 10 93; www.bauhaus.be; Langestraat 145; dm €21-31, d €87-97; @📶) One of Belgium's most popular hangouts for young travellers, this backpacker 'village' incorporates a hostel, apartments, a nightclub, internet cafe and a little chill-out room that's well hidden behind the reception and laundrette section at Langestraat 145. Simple and slightly cramped dorms are operated with key cards; hotel-section double rooms have private shower cubicles; bike hire is also available.

★B&B SintNik B&B €€

(☎050-61 03 08; www.sintnik.be; St-Niklaasstraat 18; s €125-155, d €135-165; 📶) Room 1 has a claw-foot bath and antique glass panel, but it's the other two rooms' remarkable Pisa-like belfry views that make this welcoming B&B so special and popular.

★B&B Dieltiens B&B €€

(☎050-33 42 94; www.bedandbreakfastbruges.be; Waalsestraat 40; s €60-80, d €70-90, tr €90-115) Old and new art fills this lovingly restored classical mansion, which remains an appealingly real home run by charming musician hosts. Superbly central yet quiet. It also operates a holiday flat (from €75 per night) nearby in a 17th-century house.

★Guesthouse Nuit Blanche B&B €€€

(☎0494 40 04 47; www.bb-nuitblanche.com; Groeninge 2; d €175-195) Pay what you like, nowhere else in Bruges can get you a more romantic location than this fabulous B&B, which started life as a 15th-century tannery. It oozes history, retaining original Gothic fireplaces, stained-glass roundels and some historic furniture, while bathrooms and beds are luxury-hotel standard.

★B&B Huyze Hertsberge B&B €€€

(☎050-33 35 42; www.bruges-bedandbreakfast.be; Hertsbergestraat 8; d €165-175) Very spacious and oozing good taste, this late-17th-century house has a gorgeous period salon decked with antiques and sepia photos of the charming owner's great-great-grandparents (who first moved in here in 1901). The four guest rooms are comfortably grand, each with at least partial views of the tranquil little canalside garden.

Bruges

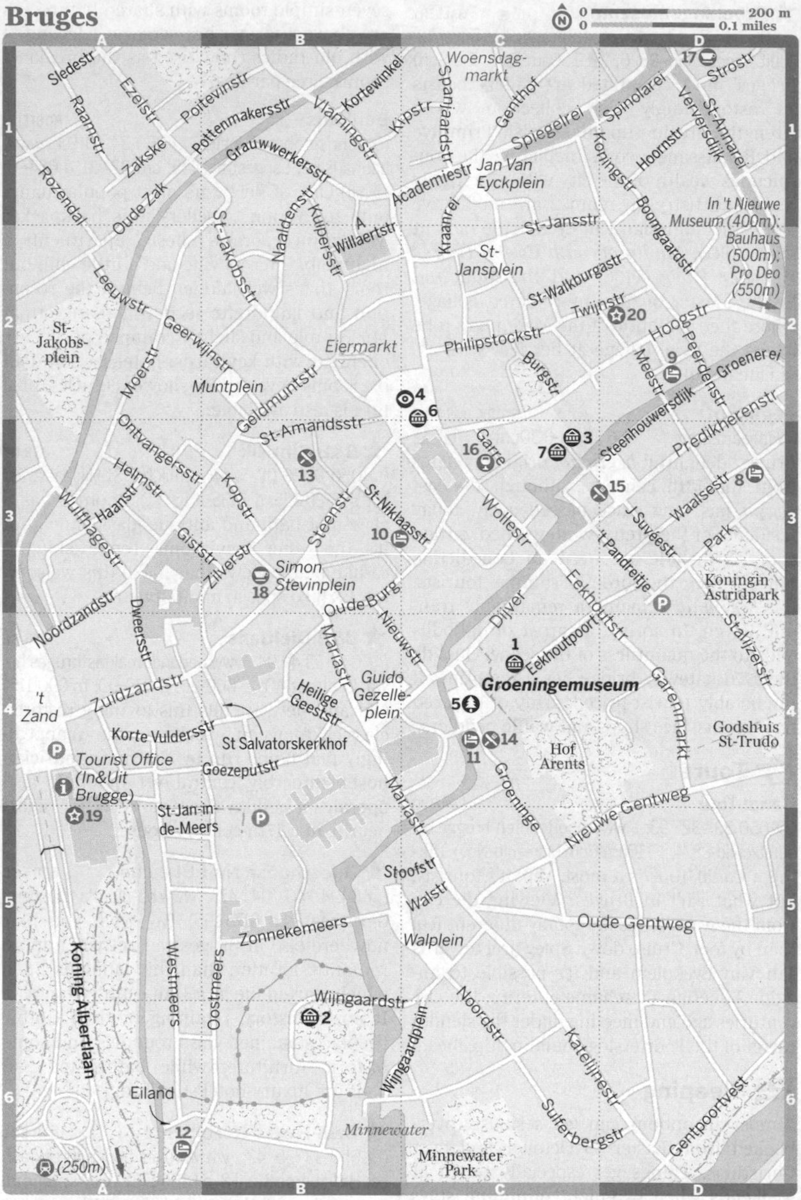

Eating

Den Gouden Karpel SEAFOOD €

(050-33 33 89; www.dengoudenkarpel.be; Vismarkt 9-11; dishes from €4; 11am-6pm Tue-Sat) Takeaway or eat in, this sleek little *café*-bar is a great location for a jumpingly fresh seafood lunch, right by the fish market. Crab sandwiches, smoked salmon salads, shrimp croquettes and oysters are on the menu.

Bruges

Top Sights

1 Groeningemuseum C4

Sights

2 Begijnhof B6
3 Brugse Vrije C3
4 Historium C2
5 Hof Arents C4
6 Markt C2
7 Stadhuis C3

Sleeping

8 B&B Dieltiens D3
9 B&B Huyze Hertsberge D2
10 B&B SintNik B3
11 Guesthouse Nuit Blanche C4
12 't Keizershof A6

Eating

13 De Stove B3
14 Den Gouden Harynck C4
15 Den Gouden Karpel D3

Drinking & Nightlife

16 De Garre C3
17 Herberg Vlissinghe D1
18 't Brugs Beertje B3

Entertainment

19 Concertgebouw A5
20 Retsin's Lucifernum D2

★ **De Stove** INTERNATIONAL €€

(☎050-33 78 35; www.restaurantdestove.be; Kleine St-Amandsstraat 4; mains €19-36, menu without/with wine €51/69; ⏰7-9pm Fri-Tue, plus noon-1.30pm Sun) Just 20 seats keep this gem intimate. Fish caught daily is the house speciality, but the monthly changing menu also includes the likes of wild boar fillet on oyster mushrooms. Everything, from the bread to the ice cream, is homemade. Despite perennially rave reviews, this calm, one-room, family restaurant remains friendly, reliable and inventive, without a hint of tourist-tweeness.

★ **In 't Nieuwe Museum** CAFE €€

(☎050-33 12 80; www.nieuw-museum.com; Hooistraat 42; mains €17-25; ⏰6-11pm Fri-Tue, plus 12.30-2.30pm Sun) So called because of the museum-like collection of brewery plaques, money boxes and other mementos of *café* life adorning the walls, this family-owned local favourite serves succulent meat cooked on a 17th-century open fire. Specials include veggie burgers, eel dishes, ribs, steaks and creamy *vispannetje* (fish casserole).

★ **Pro Deo** BELGIAN €€

(☎050-33 73 55; www.bistroprodeo.be; Langestraat 161; mains €17-27; ⏰11.45am-1.45pm & 6-9.30pm Tue-Fri, 6-10pm Sat) A snug and romantic restaurant in a 16th-century whitewashed gabled building. The owner couple brings a personal touch, and serve up superb Belgian dishes such as *stoofvlees* (traditional stew).

★ **Den Gouden Harynck** INTERNATIONAL €€€

(☎050-33 76 37; www.goudenharynck.be; Groeninge 25; set lunch menu €45, midweek dinner €65, surprise menu €95; ⏰noon-1.30pm & 7-8.30pm Tue-Fri, 7-8.30pm Sat) Behind an ivy-clad facade, this uncluttered Michelin-starred restaurant garners consistent praise and won't hurt the purse quite as severely as certain better-known competitors. A lovely location: both central and secluded; exquisite dishes might include noisettes of venison topped with lardo and quince purée or seed-crusted fillet of bream.

Drinking & Nightlife

Beer-specialist *cafés* include **'t Brugs Beertje** (☎050-33 96 16; www.brugsbeertje.be; Kemelstraat 5; ⏰4pm-midnight Mon, Thu & Sun, to 1am Fri & Sat) and alley-hidden **De Garre** (☎050-34 10 29; www.degarre.be; Garre 1; ⏰noon-midnight Sun-Thu, noon-12.30am Fri, 11am-12.30am Sat) serving its own fabulous 11% Garre house brew. Old-world classic **Herberg Vlissinghe** (☎050-34 37 37; www.cafevlissinghe.be; Blekerstraat 2; ⏰11am-10pm Wed-Sat, to 7pm Sun) dates from 1515. Eiermarkt, just north of Markt, has many plain but lively bars, with DJs and seemingly endless happy hours.

Entertainment

★ **Retsin's Lucifernum** LIVE MUSIC

(☎0476 35 06 51; www.lucifernum.be; Twijnstraat 6-8; admission incl drink €10; ⏰8-11pm Sun) A former Masonic lodge owned by a self-proclaimed vampire: ring the bell on a Sunday night, pass the voodoo temple and hope you're invited inside where an otherworldly candle-lit bar may be serving potent rum cocktails and serenading you with live Latin music. Or maybe not. It's always a surprise. Don't miss the graves in the tropical garden.

Concertgebouw CONCERT VENUE

(☎070-22 33 02; www.concertgebouw.be; 't Zand 34; tickets from €10) Bruges' stunning 21st-century concert hall is the work of architects Paul Robbrecht and Hilde Daem and takes its design cues from the city's three famous towers and red bricks. Theatre, classical music and dance are regularly staged. The tourist office is situated at street level.

Information

There are two offices; both sell extensive €2 guide booklets and €0.50 city maps.

Tourist Information Counter (050-44 46 46; www.visitbruges.be; Train Station; 10am-5pm)

Tourist Office (In&Uit Brugge) (050-44 46 46; www.visitbruges.be; 't Zand 34; 10am-5pm Mon-Sat, 10am-2pm Sun)

Getting There & Away

Bruges' train station is about 1.5km south of the Markt, a lovely walk via the Begijnhof.

Antwerp (€14.80, 75 minutes) Twice hourly.

Brussels (€14.10, one hour) Twice hourly.

Ghent (€6.50, fast/slow 24/42 minutes) Five hourly, two continue to more central Gent-Dampoort.

Ypres (Ieper in Dutch) Take a train to Roeselare (€5, fast/slow 22/33 minutes), then bus 94 or 95: both buses pass key WWI sites en route.

Getting Around

BICYCLE

B-Bike (0479 971 28; www.b-bike.be; Zand Parking 26; per hr/day €5/15; 10am-7pm Apr-Oct)

Rijwielhandel Erik Popelier (050-34 32 62; www.fietsenpopelier.be; Mariastraat 26; per hr/half-/full day €5/10/15, tandem €10/20/30; 10am-6pm) Good bicycles for adults and kids; helmets for hire, free map, no deposit.

WHAT'S A BEGIJNHOF?

Usually enclosed around a central garden, a *begijnhof* (*béguinage* in French) is a pretty cluster of historic houses originally built to house lay sisters. The idea originated in the 12th century when many such women were left widowed by their crusader-knight husbands. Today 14 of Flanders' historic *begijnhoven* have been declared Unesco World Heritage Sites with great examples at Diest, Lier, Turnhout, Kortrijk and Bruges, which also has dozens of smaller *godshuizen* (almshouses).

BUS

To get from the train station to Markt, take any bus marked 'Centrum'. For the way back, buses stop at Biekorf, just northwest of Markt on Kuiperstraat.

Ypres

POP 35,100

Only the hardest of hearts are unmoved by historic Ypres (Ieper in Dutch). In the Middle Ages it was an important cloth town ranking alongside Bruges and Ghent. In WWI some 300,000 Allied soldiers died in the 'Salient', a bow-shaped bulge that formed the front line around town. Ypres remained unoccupied by German forces, but was utterly flattened by bombardment. After the war, the beautiful medieval core was convincingly rebuilt and the restored Ypres Lakenhalle is today one of the most spectacular buildings in Belgium. Most tourism still revolves around WWI; the Salient is dotted with cemeteries, memorials, bunkers and war museums.

Sights

Central Ypres

★In Flanders Fields MUSEUM

(057-23 92 20; www.inflandersfields.be; Lakenhalle, Grote Markt 34; adult/under 26yr/child €9/5/4; 10am-6pm Apr–mid-Nov, to 5pm Tue-Sun mid-Nov–Mar) No museum gives a more balanced yet moving and user-friendly introduction to WWI history. It's a multi-sensory experience combining soundscapes, videos, well-chosen exhibits and interactive learning stations at which you 'become' a character and follow his/her progress through the wartime period. An electronic 'identity' bracelet activates certain displays.

Lakenhalle HISTORIC BUILDING

(Cloth Hall; Grote Markt 34) Dominating the Grote Markt, the enormous reconstructed Lakenhalle is one of Belgium's most impressive buildings. Its 70m-high belfry has the vague appearance of a medieval Big Ben. The original version was completed in 1304 beside the Ieperslee, a river that, now covered over, once allowed ships to sail right up to the Lakenhalle to unload their cargoes of wool. These were stored beneath the high gables of the 1st floor, where you'll find the unmissable In Flanders Fields museum.

Menin Gate MEMORIAL

(Menenpoort) A block east of Grote Markt, the famous Menin Gate is a huge stone gateway straddling the main road at the city moat. It's inscribed with the names of 54,896 'lost' British and Commonwealth WWI troops whose bodies were never found.

Ypres Salient

Many WWI sites are in rural locations that are awkward to reach without a car or tour bus. But the following are all within 600m of Ypres–Roeselare bus routes 94 and 95 (once or twice hourly weekdays, five daily weekends), so could be visited en route between Ypres and Bruges.

Memorial Museum Passchendaele 1917 MUSEUM

(www.passchendaele.be; Ieperstraat 5; admission €8.50; 9am-6pm Feb–mid-Dec; 94) In central Zonnebeke village, **Kasteel Zonnebeke** (www.zonnebeke.be) is a lake-fronted Normandy chalet-style mansion built in 1922 to replace a castle bombarded into rubble during WWI. It hosts a tourist office, cafe and particularly polished WWI museum charting local battle progressions with plenty of multilingual commentaries. The big attraction here is descending into its multiroom 'trench experience' with low-lit, wooden-clad subterranean bunk rooms and a soundtrack. Explanations are much more helpful here than in 'real' trenches elsewhere.

Tyne Cot CEMETERY

(24hr, visitor centre 9am-6pm Feb-Nov; 94) FREE Probably the most visited Salient site, this is the world's biggest British Commonwealth war cemetery, with 11,956 graves. A huge semicircular wall commemorates another 34,857 lost-in-action soldiers whose names wouldn't fit on Ypres' Menin Gate. The name Tyne Cot was coined by Northumberland Fusiliers who fancied that German bunkers on the hillside here looked like Tyneside cottages. Two such dumpy concrete bunkers sit amid the graves, with a third visible through the metal wreath beneath the white Cross of Sacrifice.

Deutscher Soldatenfriedhof CEMETERY

FREE The area's main German WWI cemetery is smaller than Tyne Cot but arguably more memorable, amid oak trees and trios of squat, mossy crosses. Some 44,000 corpses were grouped together here, up to 10 per granite grave slab, and four eerie silhouette statues survey the site. Entering takes you through a black concrete 'tunnel' that clanks and hisses with distant war sounds, while four short video montages commemorate the tragedy of war.

DON'T MISS

LAST POST

At 8pm daily, traffic through the Menin Gate is halted while buglers sound the **Last Post** (www.lastpost.be) in remembrance of the WWI dead, a moving tradition started in 1928. Every evening the scene is different, possibly accompanied by pipers, troops of cadets or maybe a military band.

Tours

Over the Top BUS

(057-42 43 20; www.overthetoptours.be; Meensestraat 41; tours €40; tours 9am-1.30pm & 2.30-5.30pm) A WWI specialist bookshop towards the Menin Gate, offering twice-daily, half-day guided minibus tours of the Ypres Salient, the north salient tour is in the morning, the south in the afternoon.

British Grenadier BUS

(057 21 46 57; www.salienttours.be; Meensestraat 5; standard tour €38; 10am-1.30pm & 2.15-5.45pm) Offers three different Ypres tours, with morning and afternoon departures for various sites on the Salient. It also offers full-day tours (€110) around the Somme region and/or Vimy Ridge.

Sleeping & Eating

Ariane Hotel HOTEL €€

(057-21 82 18; www.ariane.be; Slachthuisstraat 58; r €125-167; P) This peaceful, professionally managed, large hotel has a designer feel to the rooms and popular restaurant, while wartime memorabilia dots the spacious common areas.

B&B Ter Thuyne B&B €€

(057-36 00 42; www.terthuyne.be; Gustave de Stuersstraat 19; s/d from €80/95; @) Three comfortable rooms that are luminously bright and scrupulously clean, but not overly fashion-conscious.

★**Main Street Hotel** GUESTHOUSE €€€

(057-46 96 33; www.mainstreet-hotel.be; Rijselstraat 136; d €180-260;) Jumbling funky eccentricity with historical twists and luxurious comfort, this is a one-off that simply oozes character. The smallest room is designed like a mad professor's experiment, the breakfast room has a Tiffany glass ceiling…and so it goes on!

★ **De Ruyffelaer** FLEMISH €€
(057-36 60 06; www.deruyffelaer.be; Gustave de Stuersstraat 9; mains €15-21; 11.30am-3.30pm Sun, 5.30-9.30pm Fri-Sun) Traditional local dishes served in an adorable, wood-panelled interior with old chequerboard floors and a brocante decor, including dried flowers, old radios and antique biscuit tins.

Information

Tourist Office (057-23 92 20; www.toerismeieper.be; Lakenhalle; 9am-6pm Mon-Fri, 10am-6pm Sat & Sun Apr–mid-Nov, to 5pm mid-Nov–Mar) Tourist office for Ypres and surrounds with an extensive bookshop.

Getting There & Around

BICYCLE

Hire bikes from **Hotel Ambrosia** (057-36 63 66; www.ambrosiahotel.be; D'Hondtstraat 54; bike per day €15; 7.30am-7.30pm).

BUS

Services pick up passengers in Grote Markt's northeast corner (check the direction carefully!). For Bruges take Roeselare-bound routes 94 or 95 then change to train.

TRAIN

Services run hourly to Ghent (€11.50, one hour) and Brussels (€17.50, 1¾ hours) via Kortrijk (€5.30, 30 minutes), where you could change for Bruges or Antwerp.

WALLONIA

Make some time for hilly Wallonia, Belgium's French-speaking southern half. Wallonia's cities have plenty of charm, but the region's standout attractions are mostly rural – outdoor activities, fabulous caves and venerable castles.

Mons

POP 93,400

With a characterful medieval centre climbing up a hill and a fine Grand Place, Mons (Bergen in Dutch) had a substantial facelift in 2015, when it was a European Capital of Culture. The legacy is a handful of entertaining modern museums that make Mons an excellent visit, with plenty to keep you busy for two or three days. One museum covers war in excellent fashion, while another celebrates the riotous Doudou festival, which stars St George, a dragon, St Waudru, devils and thousands of beery revellers.

Sights

★ **Mons Memorial Museum** MUSEUM
(065-40 53 20; www.monsmemorialmuseum.mons.be; Blvd Dolez 51; adult/child €9/2; 10am-6pm Tue-Sun;) A superb new museum, this extensive display mostly covers Mons' experience of the two world wars, though the constant sieges of this town's turbulent history are also mentioned. It gets the balance just right between military history, personal testimony of civilians and soldiers, and thought-provoking items on display. Some seriously good visuals make the to-and-fro (and stuck for years in the mud) of WWI instantly comprehensible, and there's an animated 3D film on the legend of the Angels of Mons.

Musée du Doudou MUSEUM
(065-40 53 18; www.museedudoudou.mons.be; Jardin du Mayeur; adult/child €9/2; 10am-6pm Tue-Sun) Head through the Hôtel de Ville on the Grand Place to reach this museum, dedicated to Mons' riotous **Ducasse festival** (www.doudou.mons.be). All aspects of this curious event, as well as background on St George, St Waudru and dragons, are covered in entertaining interactive fashion, and there are interesting cultural musings on the festival's changing nature over time. During the audiovisual, showing the climactic Lumeçon battle, you can almost smell the beer and sweat. There's audio content in French, Dutch and English.

Sleeping & Eating

Auberge de Jeunesse HOSTEL €
(065-87 55 70; www.lesaubergesdejeunesse.be; Rampe du Château 2; dm/s/d €28/46/68; P@) Just before the base of the belfry, this modern, well-equipped HI hostel has an attractive tiered design making good use of the sloping terrain. Worth booking ahead. Prices drop significantly in quieter months. Rates are €2 less per person for those aged 26 and under; 10% HI discount.

WORTH A TRIP

BOUILLON

Wallonia has some magnificent castles dotted right across it. If you're only going to visit one, though, make it this. Dreamily arrayed around a tight loop of the Semois River, Bouillon is protected by its gloriously medieval stronghold, gnarled and grim up on the hill. On a summer evening, limpid light and reflections in the water can make this one of Belgium's prettiest towns. The **Château de Bouillon** (☎061 46 62 57; www.bouillon-initiative.be; Rue du Château; adult/child €7/5; ⏰10am-6.30pm Jul & Aug, 10am-5pm or 6pm Mar-Jun & Sep-Nov, see website for winter opening; P 👪), Belgium's finest feudal castle, accessed by two stone bridges between crags, harks back to 988, but is especially associated with Crusader knight Godefroid (Godefroy) de Bouillon. The super-atmospheric castle still has everything you might wish for – dank dripping passageways tunnelling into the hillside, musty half-lit cell rooms, rough-hewn stairwells and many an eerie nook and cranny to discover. To reach Bouillon, train to Libramont, then take bus 8 (€3.20, 45 minutes, roughly hourly weekdays, two-hourly weekends).

★**Dream Hôtel** HOTEL **€€**
(☎065-32 97 20; www.dream-mons.be; Rue de la Grand Triperie 17; s/d €94/113; P ❄ @ 📶) Centrally located in a revamped 19th-century chapel, Dream Hôtel combines a good level of comfort with more than a dash of Belgian eccentricity, including multilingual murals, bowler-hat lamps and side tables made from drums. Bathrooms, with separate toilet, are excellent, and noise insulation is relatively good. There's a lovely little spa to wallow in, and free (valet) parking.

★**Vilaine Fille, Mauvais Garçon** MODERN FRENCH **€€€**
(Naughty Girl, Bad Boy; ☎065-66 67 62; www.vilainefillemauvaisgarcon.be; Rue de Nimy 55; mains €25-28, set meals €27-55; ⏰noon-3pm & 7-10.30pm Tue-Fri, 7-10.30pm Sat, noon-3pm Sun) Artful gastronomic takes on traditional plates, with familiar ingredients appearing in surprising ways, are the hallmarks of this enjoyable restaurant. The smart contemporary interior in a historic building makes for relaxed, quality dining. The menu is short, and there are various set meals depending on which day it is.

ℹ Information

Maison du Tourisme (☎065-33 55 80; www.visitmons.be; Grand Place 27; ⏰9am-5.30pm daily; 📶) On the main square, with lots of booklets and information, and bike rental.

ℹ Getting There & Away

Mons' **train station** (Place Léopold; provisional until the new Calatrava design is finally finished) and neighbouring **TEC bus station** (☎065-38 88 15) are 700m west of the Grand Place. There are very regular services to Brussels (€9.40, 50 minutes), among other destinations.

LUXEMBOURG

Ruled by its own monarchy, the Grand Duchy of Luxembourg is famed for its banks but visually it's mostly an undulating series of pretty wooded hills dotted with castle villages. These are made accessible from the attractive capital city by excellent roads and a very well-organised single-price public transport system. Luxembourg has its own language, Lëtzebuergesch, but most Luxembourgers also speak French and German.

Luxembourg City

POP 111,300

If you thought that the Grand Duchy's capital was nothing more than banks and EU offices, you'll be delighted at discovering the attractive reality. The Unesco-listed Old Town is one of Europe's most scenic capitals, thanks largely to its unusual setting, draped across the deep gorges of the Alzette and Pétrusse rivers. It's full of weird spaces, tunnels and surprising nooks to explore. Good museums and a great dining scene makes this a top city to visit. It's worth visiting on a weekend, when hotel prices drop and on-street parking is free.

👁 Sights

The Old Town counterpoints some fine old buildings with modern museums and an offering of high-end restaurants. The picturesque

Luxembourg City

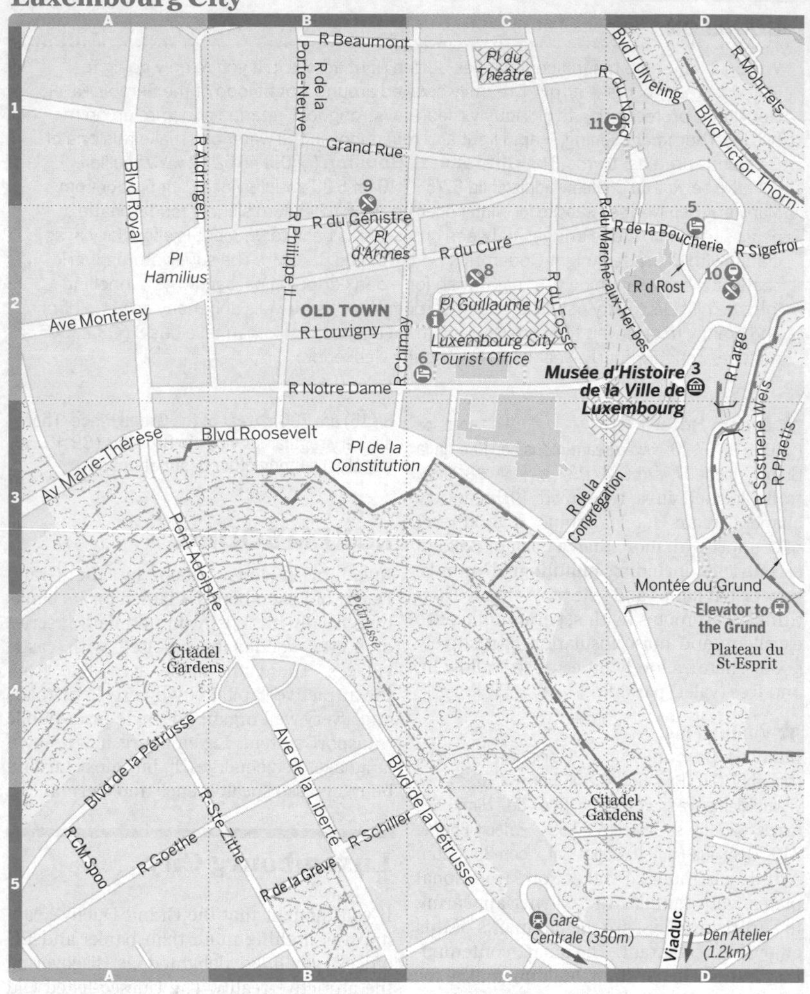

Grund area lies riverside, way below at the base of a dramatic fortified escarpment.

★Chemin de la Corniche AREA

This pedestrian promenade has been hailed as 'Europe's most beautiful balcony'. It winds along the course of the 17th-century city ramparts with views across the river canyon towards the hefty fortifications of the Wenzelsmauer (Wenceslas Wall). The rampart-top walk continues along Blvd Victor Thorn to the Dräi Tier (Triple Gate) tower.

★Bock Casemates FORTRESS

(www.lcto.lu; Montée de Clausen; adult/child €6/3; ⏲10am-5.30pm mid-Feb–Mar & Oct-early Nov, 10am-8.30pm Apr-Sep) Beneath the Montée de Clausen, the cliff-top site of Count Sigefroi's once-mighty fort, the Bock Casemates are a picturesque, atmospheric honeycomb of rock galleries and passages – yes, kids will love it – initially carved by the Spaniards between 1737 and 1746. Over the years the casemates have housed everything from garrisons to bakeries to slaughterhouses; during WWI and WWII they sheltered 35,000 locals.

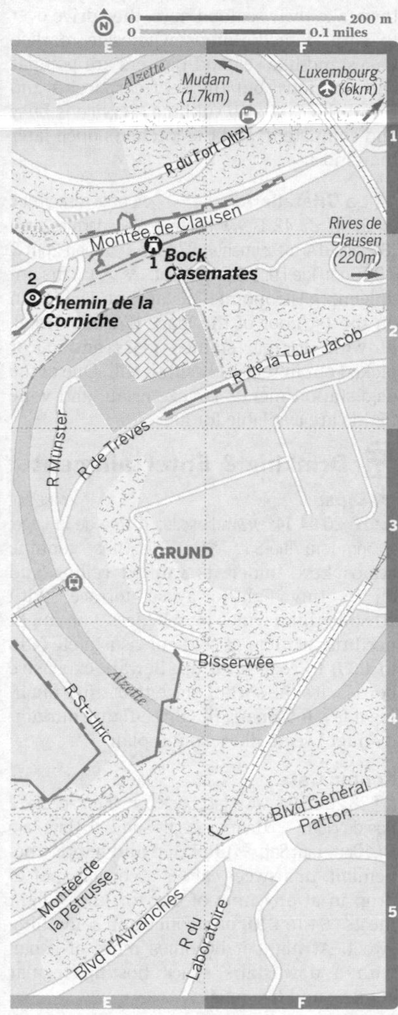

Luxembourg City

Top Sights
1 Bock Casemates E2
2 Chemin de la Corniche E2
3 Musée d'Histoire de la Ville de Luxembourg D2

Sleeping
4 Auberge de Jeunesse F1
5 Hôtel Parc Beaux-Arts D2
6 Hôtel Simoncini C2

Eating
7 Am Tiirmschen D2
8 Brasserie Guillaume C2
9 La Cristallerie B1

Drinking & Nightlife
10 Dipso D2
11 Konrad Cafe D1

★Musée d'Histoire de la Ville de Luxembourg MUSEUM
(Luxembourg City History Museum; ☎47 96 45 00; www.mhvl.lu; 14 Rue du St-Esprit; adult/under 21 yr €5/free; ⊙10am-6pm Tue-Sun, to 8pm Thu) This remarkably engrossing and interactive museum hides within a series of 17th-century houses, including a former 'holiday home' of the Bishop of Orval. A lovely garden and open terrace offers great views.

★Mudam GALLERY
(Musée d'Art Moderne; ☎45 37 85 1; www.mudam.lu; 3 Parc Dräi Eechelen; adult/under-21 €7/free; ⊙10am-8pm Wed, 10am-6pm Thu-Mon; 📶) Groundbreaking exhibitions of modern, installation and experiential art are hosted in this airy architectural icon designed by IM Pei. The collection includes everything from photography to fashion, design and multimedia. The glass-roofed cafe makes a decent lunch/snack spot. To reach Mudam, take bus 1, 8 or 16.

★US Military Cemetery CEMETERY
(www.abmc.gov; 50 Val du Scheid; ⊙9am-5pm) In a beautifully maintained graveyard near Hamm lie over 5000 US WWII war dead, including George Patton, the audacious general of the US Third Army who played a large part in Luxembourg's 1944 liberation. It's a humbling sight, with its long rows of white crosses (and the odd Star of David). It's just near the airport off the N2; bus 15 gets you close. Take it to the second-last stop, Käschtewee.

Sleeping

Luxembourg City's accommodation scene is heavy with business options but online rates are slashed at weekends and in summer.

Auberge de Jeunesse HOSTEL €
(☎26 27 66 650; www.youthhostels.lu; 5 Rue du Fort Olisy; dm/s/d €25/40/60, €3 per person off for HI members; P❄@📶) This state-of-the-art hostel has very comfortable, sex-segregated dorms with electronic entry. There are good-sized lockers (bring padlock), laundry facilities and masses of space including a great terrace from which

to admire views to the Old Town. En-suite dorms cost €1 more.

★Hôtel Simoncini HOTEL €€€
(☎22 28 44; www.hotelsimoncini.lu; 6 Rue Notre-Dame; s/d incl breakfast Mon-Thu from €160/180, Fri-Sun €130/150; @ 📶) A delightful contemporary option in the city centre, the Simoncini's foyer is a modern art gallery and the smart, bright rooms have slight touches of retro-cool. As it's not very big, and prices are pretty low for central Luxembourg, it gets booked up midweek well ahead.

★Hôtel Parc Beaux-Arts BOUTIQUE HOTEL €€€
(☎44 23 23 23 23; www.parcbeauxarts.lu; 1 Rue Sigefroi; ste Mon-Thu advance/rack rates €229/430, Fri-Sun from €159; @ 📶) Exuding understated luxury, this charming little hotel comprises a trio of 18th-century houses containing 10 gorgeous suites. Each features original artworks by contemporary artists, oak floors, Murano crystal lamps and a fresh rose daily. Seek out the 'secret' lounge hidden away in the original timber eaves. In the heart of the bar and restaurant zone, so expect some street noise at weekends.

Eating

Eating is expensive in Luxembourg, but there's a lively dining scene. For characterful options, hunt around in the alleys and passages collectively nicknamed 'Ilôt Gourmand' directly behind the Royal Palace. There are interesting alternatives in Grund and the Clausen area. Daily in summer, tables spill merrily onto leafy Place d'Armes, with everything from burger chains to classy seafood on offer. Inexpensive but mostly characterless places for Asian food are in the train station area.

Am Tiirmschen FRENCH €€
(☎26 27 07 33; www.amtiirmschen.lu; 32 Rue de l'Eau, Ilôt Gourmand; mains €18-25; ⊙noon-2pm Tue-Fri, 7-10.30pm Mon-Sat) This is a great place to sample typical Luxembourg dishes, but it also serves good fish and French options in case your companions don't fancy *kniddelen* (dumplings) or smoked pork. It has a semi-successful mix of old and pseudo-old decor, with heavy, bowed beams.

Brasserie Guillaume SEAFOOD €€€
(☎26 20 20 20; www.brasserieguillaume.lu; 12 Place Guillaume II; mains €18-40; ⊙11.30am-midnight; 📶 👪) With tables on this emblematic square, this could be another tourist trap eatery. But far from it: so seriously do they take their seafood here, they drive over to Paris' famed Rungis wholesale market. Cakestand-like seafood platters are popular and delicious, but the beef carpaccios and fish dishes are also sublime. Service is busy and competent, and the kitchen's open later than most.

★La Cristallerie MODERN FRENCH €€€
(☎27 47 37 42 1; www.hotel-leplacedarmes.com; 18 Place d'Armes; menus €78-178; ⊙noon-2pm & 7-9.30pm Tue-Fri, 7-9.30pm Sat; 📶 🖉) This indulgent gastronomic restaurant is hidden on the 1st floor of the Place d'Armes Hotel, lit with original stained glass and decor picked out in relatively subtle gilt. One of the degustation menus is vegetarian, and wine flights are available for all.

Drinking & Entertainment

★Dipso WINE BAR
(☎26 20 14 14; www.dipso.lu; 4 Rue de la Loge; ⊙5pm-1am Tue-Sat; 📶) This has genuine atmosphere under its vaulted ceiling and on its tiny, fight-for-a-seat terrace. With 20-something wines by the glass, you might need the platters of cold cuts, sushi etc (€18 to €25) to soak it all up. Beware expensive bottles: it's the sort of place that, after quaffing a few looseners, the three-figure burgundy might seem like a sound plan.

Konrad Cafe BAR
(☎26 20 18 94; www.facebook.com/Konradcafe; 7 Rue du Nord; ⊙11am-midnight Sun-Thu, 11am-1am Fri, 10am-1am Sat; 📶) Relaxed and happily bohemian, this sweet cafe is a cordial spot to drop in at any time of day for juices, light meals (€4 to €10) or a coffee and something sweet. At night it becomes more of a bar, with a downstairs space hosting regular comedy and live music.

Information

Luxembourg City Tourist Office (LCTO; ☎22 28 09; www.lcto.lu; Place Guillaume II; ⊙9am-6pm Mon-Sat, 10am-6pm Sun Oct-Mar, 9am-7pm Mon-Sat, 10am-6pm Sun Apr-Nov) Sells city guides (€2), and has maps, walking-tour pamphlets and event guides.

Getting There & Away

BUS

Useful international connections from beside the train station include Bitburg (bus 401, 1¼ hours) and Trier (bus 118, one hour).

TRAIN

Trains are run by CFL (www.cfl.lu), with good connections all through northern Europe. Sample fares from Gare Centrale, 1km south of the Old Town:

Brussels (€39, three hours, hourly) Via Arlon and Namur.

Paris (2¼ hours, €82-€104) Direct five to six times daily via Metz.

Trier (€18, one hour, hourly) Continuing to Koblenz (€46.20, 2½ hours).

Getting Around

TO/FROM LUXEMBOURG AIRPORT

Luxembourg Airport (www.lux-airport.lu) is 6km east of Place d'Armes, 20 minutes by bus 16.

BICYCLE

Velóh (800 611 00; www.en.veloh.lu; subscription per week/year €1/15, plus €1 per hour.; 24hr) Short-hop bike-rental scheme.

Vélo en Ville (47 96 23 83; 8 Bisserwée; per half-/full day/weekend/week €12.50/20/37.50/100; 8am-noon & 1-8pm Mon-Fri, 10am-noon & 1-8pm Sat & Sun Apr-Sep, 7am-3pm Mon-Fri Oct-Mar) Hires mountain bikes and city bikes.

BUS

Frequent buses shuttle to Gare Centrale (the train station) and Kirchberg (for Mudam) from Place Hamilius, the main bus stand for the Old Town. Fewer on Sundays.

Northern Luxembourg

Understandably popular as a weekend getaway, magical little **Vianden** (www.vianden-info.lu) is dominated by a vast slate-roofed **castle** (83 41 08; www.castle-vianden.lu; adult/child €7/2; 10am-4pm Nov-Feb, to 5pm Mar & Oct, to 6pm Apr-Sep) and its impregnable stone walls glow golden in the evening's floodlights. Cobbled Grand Rue descends 700m from there to the riverside tourist office passing the HI Hostel, **Auberge de Jeunesse** (26 27 66 80 0; www.youthhostels.lu; 3 Montée du Château; HI members dm/s/d €19.20/34.20/49.40, nonmembers €22.20/37.20/55.40;), and several appealing family hotels, notably unique **Auberge Aal Veinen** (83 43 68; http://vianden.beimhunn.lu; 114 Grand Rue; s/d €60/80; closed mid-Dec–mid-Jan;) and **Hôtel Heintz** (83 41 55; www.hotel-heintz.lu; 55 Grand Rue; s €65-95, d €75-105; Easter-Sep; P).

Bus 570 (18 minutes) connects at least hourly to **Diekirch,** which is home to **Musée National d'Histoire Militaire** (80 89 08; www.mnhm.net; 10 Rue Bamertal; adult/child €5/3; 10am-6pm Tue-Sun), the most comprehensive and visual of many museums commemorating 1944's devastating midwinter Battle of the Ardennes. Diekirch has twice-hourly trains to Luxembourg City (40 minutes) via **Ettelbrück** (10 minutes). From there you can catch buses to **Bastogne** (Belgium) for other major WWII sites and the excellent new **Bastogne War Museum** (061 21 02 20; www.bastognewarmuseum.be; Colline du Mardasson, 5; adult/child €14/8; 9.30am-6pm, to 7pm Jul & Aug, closed Jan & Mon mid-Nov–mid-Mar).

Bus 545 from Ettelbrück gets you within 2km of isolated **Château de Bourscheid** (www.chateau.bourscheid.lu; adult/youth/child €5/4/3; 9.30am-5.30pm Apr–mid-Oct, 11am-3.30pm mid-Oct–Mar), Luxembourg's most evocative medieval ruined castle, and trains run north towards Liège via pretty **Clervaux**, home to a convincingly rebuilt castle that hosts the world-famous **Family of Man photography exhibition** (92 96 57; www.steichencollections.lu; Château de Clervaux; over /under 21 €6/free; noon-6pm Wed-Sun Mar-Dec), established in 1955 and intended as a manifesto for peace. Bus 663 (32 minutes) departs for Vianden at 8.30am, 10am, 2pm and 5pm.

Moselle Valley

Smothering the Moselle River's steeply rising banks are the neatly clipped vineyards that produce Luxembourg's balanced Rieslings, fruity rivaners and excellent *crémants* (sparkling *méthode traditionelle* wines). Taste a selection at the grand **Caves Bernard-Massard** (75 05 45 1; www.bernard-massard.lu; 8 Rue du Pont; tours €6-9; tours 9.30am-6pm Tue-Sun Apr-Oct) in central **Grevenmacher** where frequent 20-minute winery tours are multilingual and spiced with humour. The Enner der Bréck bus stop outside is on bus routes 130 from Rue Heine in Luxembourg City (55 minutes, once or twice hourly).

A good way of visiting the wine route is renting a bicycle with **Rentabike Miselerland** (www.entente-moselle.lu/rentabike-miselerland; per day €10), free if you have a Luxembourg Card. Pick-up at one of numerous points and drop off at another: just make sure that you check closing times and take ID.

SURVIVAL GUIDE

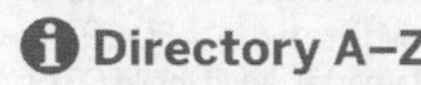

Directory A–Z

ACCOMMODATION

Tourist offices often provide free accommodation-booking assistance.

Hotels Availability and prices vary markedly by area. Bruges, for example, is terribly busy in summer and weekends, while Brussels and Luxembourg City are quieter at those times.

B&Bs Rooms rented in local homes *(gastenkamers/chambres d'hôtes)* can be cheap and cheerful but some offer standards and prices equivalent to a boutique hotel.

Holiday houses *(gîtes)* Are easily rented in **Wallonia** (www.gitesdewallonie.be) and **Luxembourg** (www.gites.lu), but minimum stays apply and there's a hefty 'cleaning fee' on top of quoted rates.

Hostels Typically charge around €18 to €28 for dormitory beds. Luxembourg has an excellent network of HI hostels (http://youthhostels.lu).

Camping Opportunities are plentiful, especially in the Ardennes. For extensive listings see www.campingbelgique.be (Wallonia), www.camping.be (Flanders) and www.camping.lu (Luxembourg).

ACTIVITIES

In mostly-flat **Flanders** (www.fietsroute.org), bicycles are a popular means of everyday travel and many roads have dedicated cycle lanes. In **Wallonia** (www.wallonie.be), the hilly terrain favours mountain bikes (VTT).

Canoeing and kayaking are best in the Ardennes, but don't expect rapids of any magnitude.

Local tourist offices have copious information about footpaths and sell regional hiking maps.

MONEY

- Credit cards are widely accepted. ATMs are plentiful, and are the best way of accessing cash.
- Tipping is not expected in restaurants or cabs: service and VAT are always included.

SLEEPING PRICE RANGES

Ranges are based on the cost of a double room in high season.

€ less than €60

€€ €60–€140

€€€ more than €140

EATING PRICE RANGES

The following price ranges are based on the cost of a typical main course.

€ less than €15

€€ €15 to €25

€€€ more than €25

OPENING HOURS

Many sights close on Monday. Restaurants normally close one full day per week. Opening hours for shops, bars and cafes vary widely.

Banks 8.30am–3.30pm or later Monday to Friday, some also Saturday morning

Bars 10am–1am, but hours very flexible

Restaurants noon–2.30pm and 7pm–9.30pm

Shops 10am–6.30pm Monday to Saturday, sometimes closed for an hour at lunchtime

PUBLIC HOLIDAYS

New Year's Day 1 January

Easter Monday March/April

Labour Day 1 May

Iris Day 8 May (Brussels region only)

Ascension Day 39 days after Easter Sunday (always a Thursday)

Pentecost Monday 50 days after Easter Sunday

Luxembourg National Day 23 June (Luxembourg only)

Flemish Community Day 11 July (Flanders only)

Belgium National Day 21 July (Belgium only)

Assumption Day 15 August

Francophone Community Day 27 September (Wallonia only)

All Saints' Day 1 November

Armistice Day 11 November (Belgium only)

Christmas Day 25 December

TELEPHONE

- Country code 32 (Belgium), 352 (Luxembourg). International access code 00.
- If you've got an unlocked smartphone, you can pick up a local SIM card for a few euros and charge it with a month's worth of data at a decent speed for under €20.

TOURIST INFORMATION

Almost every town and village has its own tourist office – *dienst voor toerisme, toeristische dienst* or simply *toerisme* (in Flanders), *maison du tourisme, office du tourisme* or *syndicat d'initiative* (in Wallonia and Luxembourg).

Useful contacts:

Visit Wallonia (www.belgiumtheplaceto.be) Wallonia and Brussels

Visit Flanders (www.visitflanders.com) Flanders

Visit Luxembourg (www.visitluxembourg.com) Luxembourg

VISAS

Schengen visa rules apply. Embassies are listed at www.diplomatie.belgium.be/en and www.mae.lu.

> **COUNTRY FACTS**
>
> **Area** 30,278 sq km (Belgium), 2586 sq km (Luxembourg)
>
> **Capitals** Brussels (Belgium), Luxembourg City (Luxembourg)
>
> **Country Codes** 32 (Belgium); 352 (Luxembourg)
>
> **Currency** Euro (€)
>
> **Emergency** 112
>
> **Languages** Dutch, French, German, Lëtzebuergesch
>
> **Money** ATMs widely available; banks open Monday to Friday
>
> **Visas** Schengen rules apply

Getting There & Away

AIR

Brussels airport (BRU; www.brusselsairport.be) is Belgium's main long-haul gateway.

Budget airlines use Charleroi Airport (p84), 55km south of Brussels.

Luxembourg airport (www.lux-airport.lu) has various European connections.

You may sometimes find it cheaper or more convenient to fly into one of the major airports in neighbouring countries – in Frankfurt, Amsterdam or Paris, for example – and continue into Belgium/Luxembourg by train.

LAND

Bus

Eurolines (www.eurolines.eu) Large international bus network; usually cheaper than equivalent train tickets. Useful routes served at least daily include London–Brussels (seven to eight hours), London--Bruges/Ghent (six to seven hours), Brussels–Paris (four hours), Brussels–Amsterdam (three to four hours) and Brussels–Berlin (10 hours). Liège and Antwerp also served.

Ecolines (www.ecolines.net) Consortium of mostly Baltic or Eastern European coach lines.

Car & Motorcycle

- Northern Europe is one vast web of motorways, so Belgium and Luxembourg are easily accessed from anywhere.
- There's no problem bringing foreign vehicles into Belgium or Luxembourg, provided you have registration papers and valid insurance ('Green Card').
- Most car-hire companies in the Netherlands, France, Germany or other EU nations won't have a problem with your taking their car into Belgium or Luxembourg, but check rental conditions before you do so.

Train

There are excellent train links with neighbouring countries.

- Internet bookings save you a few euros over Belgian pay-and-go tickets for most international tickets. Check out www.b-europe.com and www.cfl.lu or operator websites of the country of origin.
- Railcards are valid on standard services but there are surcharges for high-speed lines including **Eurostar** (www.eurostar.com) to London (two hours) and Lille, **Thalys** (www.thalys.com) to Cologne, Amsterdam and Paris.
- **Deutsche Bahn** (www.bahn.com) runs high-speed ICE trains Brussels Midi–Liège–Aachen–Cologne–Frankfurt (3 hours) while **SNCF** (www.sncf.com) has TGV links to numerous French destinations, albeit bypassing central Paris.
- To avoid high-speed surcharges, useful 'ordinary' cross-border services include Liège–Aachen, Liège–Maastricht, Tournai–Lille, Brussels Central–Amsterdam and Luxembourg–Trier.

SEA

P&O (www.poferries.com) operates a Zeebrugge–Hull route. Fourteen hours overnight. The quickest way across the Channel is to travel via the French port of Calais, around an hour's drive west of Ostend.

> **LUXEMBOURG'S SIMPLIFIED TRANSPORT SYSTEM**
>
> Luxembourg has a one-price domestic ticket system. Wherever you go by public transport within Luxembourg the price is the same, €2 for up to two hours, €4 for the day. See www.cfl.lu for timetables.

ESSENTIAL FOOD & DRINK

Belgium's famous lagers (eg Stella Artois) and white beers (Hoegaarden) are now global brands. But what has connoisseurs really drooling are the robust, rich 'abbey' beers (originally brewed in monasteries), and the 'Trappist beers' (that still are). Chimay, Rochefort, Westmalle and Orval are the best known. But for beer maniacs the one that really counts is ultra-rare Westvleteren XII.

Dining is a treat in Belgium and Luxembourg, where meals are often described as being French in quality, German in quantity. Classic, home-style dishes include the following:

Chicons au gratin Endive rolled in ham and cooked in cheese/béchamel sauce.

Filet Américain A blob of raw minced beef, typically topped with equally raw egg yolk.

Judd mat gaardebounen Luxembourg's national dish; smoked pork neck in a cream-based sauce with chunks of potato and broad beans.

Kniddelen Dumplings.

Mosselen/moules Steaming cauldrons of in-the-shell mussels, typically cooked in white wine and served with a mountain of *frites* (chips).

Paling in 't groen Eel in a sorrel or spinach sauce.

Stoemp Mashed veg-and-potato dish.

Vlaamse stoverij/carbonade flamande Semi-sweet beer-based meat casserole.

Waterzooi A cream-based chicken or fish stew.

Getting Around

BICYCLE

Cycling is a great way to get around in flat Flanders, less so in chaotic Brussels or undulating Wallonia. The Belgian countryside is riddled with cycling routes and most tourist offices sell helpful regional cycling maps.

- Bike hire is available in or near most major train stations. Short-hop hire schemes are available in cities.
- Bikes on the train are free in Luxembourg. In Belgium it costs €5 one-way (or €8 all day) on top of the rail fare. A few busy city-centre train stations don't allow bicycle transportation.

BUS & TRAM

Regional buses are well coordinated with Belgium's rail network, but in rural regions you can still find that relatively short distances can involve long waits. In Brussels and Antwerp, trams that run underground are called *premetro*.

The route planner at www.belgianrail.be gives useful bus suggestions where that's the logical choice for your route. In Luxembourg, use www.mobiliteit.lu.

CAR & MOTORCYCLE

- Motorways are toll free.
- Speed limits are 50km/h in most towns (30km/h near schools), 70km/h to 90km/h on inter-town roads, and 120km/h on motorways in Belgium (130km/h in Luxembourg).
- The maximum legal blood alcohol limit is 0.05%.
- Car hire is available at airports and major train stations, but is usually cheaper from city-centre offices.
- Fill up in Luxembourg for big savings.

CONNECTIONS

Amsterdam, Paris, Cologne and London are all under 2½ hours from Brussels by high-speed train. Liège, Luxembourg City and Antwerp are also on high-speed international routes. Go via Tournai to reach France, or via Luxembourg City to reach Germany by train if you want to avoid such lines and their compulsory reservations. Budget airlines offer cheap deals to numerous European destinations, particularly from Charleroi.

TAXI

Taxis must usually be pre-booked but there are ranks near main stations. Tips and taxes are always included in metered fares.

TRAIN

Belgium's trains are run by **SNCB** (Belgian Railways; ☎02-528 28 28; www.belgianrail.be; domestic trains). Luxembourg's joint railway-bus network is coordinated by **CFL** (☎24 89 24 89; www.cfl.lu).

Return tickets are normally twice the price of singles except on weekends from 7pm Friday, when a return ticket getting back by Sunday night costs little more than a single.

Under-26s can buy a Go-Pass 1, which costs €6 and is valid for any one-way trip within Belgium.

LUXEMBOURG CARD

The worthwhile **Luxembourg Card** (www.visitluxembourg.com; 1-/2-/3-day adult €13/20/28, family €28/48/68) gives free admission to over 50 of the country's top attractions, discounts on some others, plus unlimited use of public transport. You'll save money if visiting more than two museums or castles a day. Purchase online, from tourist offices, train stations or major hotels. The website details what's included.

Britain

Includes ➡

Best Traditional British Pubs

- ➡ Star Inn (p145)
- ➡ Bear Inn (p148)
- ➡ Old Thatch Tavern (p150)
- ➡ Blue Bell (p155)
- ➡ Café Royal Circle Bar (p165)

Best Museums

- ➡ Victoria & Albert Museum (p117)
- ➡ Ashmolean Museum (p146)
- ➡ National Railway Museum (p154)
- ➡ Kelvingrove Art Gallery & Museum (p167)
- ➡ Science Museum (p117)

Why Go?

Few places cram so much history, heritage and scenery into such a compact space as Britain. Twelve hours is all you'll need to travel from one end to the other, but you could spend a lifetime exploring – from the ancient relics of Stonehenge and Avebury, to the great medieval cathedrals of Westminster and Canterbury, and the magnificent mountain landscapes of Snowdonia and Skye.

In fact, Britain isn't really one country at all, but three. While they haven't always been easy bedfellows, the contrasts between England, Wales and Scotland make this a rewarding place to visit. With a wealth of rolling countryside, stately cities, world-class museums and national parks to explore, Britain really is one of Europe's most unmissable destinations. And despite what you may have heard, it doesn't rain *all* the time – but even so, a brolly and a raincoat will certainly come in handy.

When to Go

London

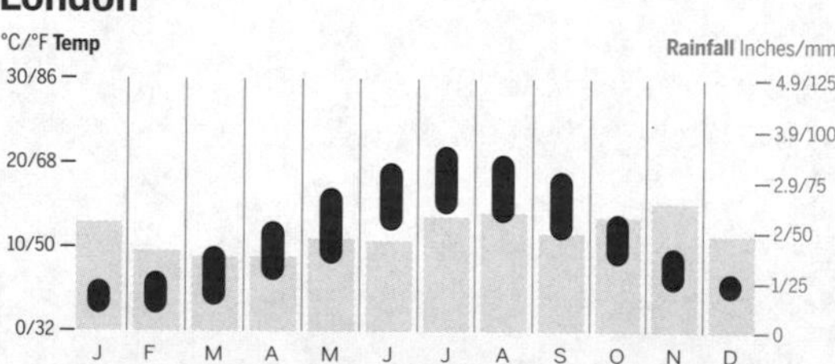

Easter–May Fewer crowds, especially in popular spots like Bath, York and Edinburgh.

Jun–Aug The weather is at its best but the coast and national parks are busy.

Mid-Sep–Oct Prices drop and the weather is often surprisingly good.

ENGLAND

By far the biggest of the three nations that comprise Great Britain, England offers a tempting spread of classic travel experiences, from London's vibrant theatre scene and the historic colleges of Oxford, to the grand cathedrals of Canterbury and York and the mountain landscapes of the Lake District.

London

POP 8.7 MILLION

Everyone comes to London with preconceptions shaped by a multitude of books, movies, TV shows and pop songs. Whatever yours are, prepare to have them exploded by this endlessly intriguing city. Its streets are steeped in fascinating history, magnificent art, imposing architecture and popular culture. When you add a bottomless reserve of cool to this mix, it's hard not to conclude that London is one of the world's great cities, if not the greatest.

The only downside is increasing cost: London is now Europe's most expensive city for visitors, whatever their budget. But with some careful planning and a bit of common sense, you can find excellent bargains and freebies among the popular attractions. And many of London's finest assets – its wonderful parks, bridges, squares and boulevards, not to mention many of its landmark museums – come completely free.

History

London first came into being as a Celtic village near a ford across the River Thames, but the city really only took off after the Roman invasion in AD 43. The Romans enclosed Londinium in walls that still find an echo in the shape of the City of London (the city's central financial district) today. Next came the Saxons, and the town they called Lundenwic prospered.

London grew in global importance throughout the medieval period, surviving devastating challenges such as the 1665 plague and the 1666 Great Fire. Many of its important landmarks such as St Paul's Cathedral were built at this time by visionary architect Christopher Wren.

By the early 1700s, Georgian London had become one of Europe's largest and richest cities. It was during the Victorian era that London really hit its stride, fuelled by vast mercantile wealth and a huge global empire.

The ravages of WWI were followed by the economic troubles of the 1920s and 1930s, but it was WWII that wrought the greatest damage: huge swathes of the city were reduced to rubble during a series of devastating bombings known as the Blitz.

During the 1960s, Swinging London became the world's undisputed cultural capital, with an explosion of provocative art, music, writing, theatre and fashion. The 1970s proved more turbulent than innovative, with widespread unrest and economic discontent, while the 1980s were marked by an economic boom in London's financial district (known as the City), which brought a forest of skyscrapers to the city's skyline.

In 2000 London got its first elected Mayor, left-wing Ken Livingstone, who served for two terms before being ousted in 2008 by his Eton-educated Conservative rival, Boris Johnson, who oversaw the city's hugely successful stint as Olympics host. The pendulum swung back leftwards in 2016 when former Labour MP Sadiq Khan took office, the first Muslim to be mayor of a major Western capital city.

ITINERARIES

One Week

With just seven days, you're pretty much limited to sights in England. Spend three days seeing the sights in **London**, then head to **Oxford** for a day, followed by a day each at **Stonehenge** and historic **Bath**, before returning for a final day in London.

Two Weeks

Follow the one-week itinerary, but instead of returning to London on day seven, head north to **Stratford-upon-Avon** for everything Shakespeare. Continue north with a day in the **Lake District**, followed by two days in Scotland's capital, **Edinburgh**. After a day trip to **Loch Ness**, recross the border for two days to see **York** and **Castle Howard**. Next, stop off in **Cambridge** on the way back to London.

Britain Highlights

1 **London** (p109) Exploring the streets of one of the world's greatest capital cities.

2 **Bath** (p143) Visiting Roman baths and admiring grand Georgian architecture.

3 **Stratford-upon-Avon** (p149) Enjoying a Shakepeare play in the town of his birth.

4 **Snowdonia National Park** (p161) Marvelling at the mountainous landscape of Wales' first national park.

5 **York** (p153) Delving into the city's history – Roman, Viking and medieval .

6 **Oxford** (p145) Getting lost among the city's dreaming spires.

7 Stonehenge (p142) Stepping back in time wandering around the great trilithons of this ancient site.

8 Edinburgh (p161) Joining the party in Scotland's festival city.

9 Isle of Skye (p173) Heading north through the Scottish Highlands to experience the epic scenery of this rugged island.

10 Lake District National Park (p157) Following in the footsteps of Romantic poet William Wordsworth.

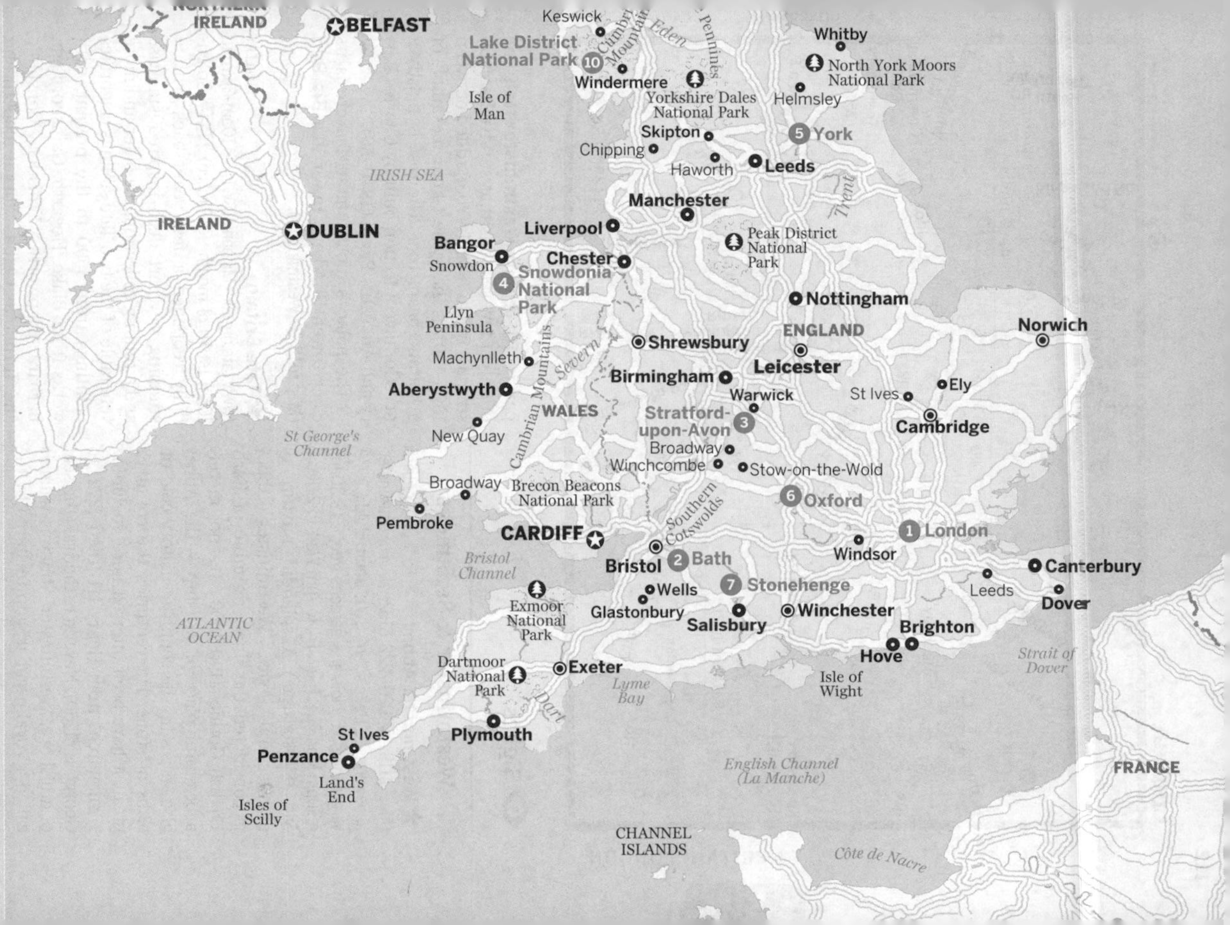

NORTHERN IRELAND
BELFAST
Keswick
Lake District National Park 10
Cumbrian Mountains
Eden
Pennines
Whitby
North York Moors National Park
Windermere
Yorkshire Dales National Park
Helmsley
Isle of Man
Skipton
5 York
Chipping
Haworth
Leeds
IRISH SEA
Trent
Manchester
IRELAND
DUBLIN
Liverpool
Peak District National Park
Bangor
Chester
Snowdon
4 Snowdonia National Park
Nottingham
Llyn Peninsula
Shrewsbury
ENGLAND
Norwich
Machynlleth
Severn
Leicester
Birmingham
Aberystwyth
Warwick
St Ives
Ely
WALES
Stratford-upon-Avon 3
Cambridge
Cambrian Mountains
New Quay
St George's Channel
Broadway
Winchcombe
Stow-on-the-Wold
Broadway
Brecon Beacons National Park
6 Oxford
Southern Cotswolds
Pembroke
1 London
CARDIFF
Windsor
Bristol
2 Bath
Canterbury
Bristol Channel
Wells
7 Stonehenge
Leeds
Dover
ATLANTIC OCEAN
Exmoor National Park
Glastonbury
Salisbury
Winchester
Brighton
Hove
Strait of Dover
Dartmoor National Park
Exeter
Lyme Bay
Isle of Wight
Dart
St Ives
Plymouth
Penzance
Land's End
English Channel (La Manche)
FRANCE
Isles of Scilly
CHANNEL ISLANDS
Côte de Nacre

London

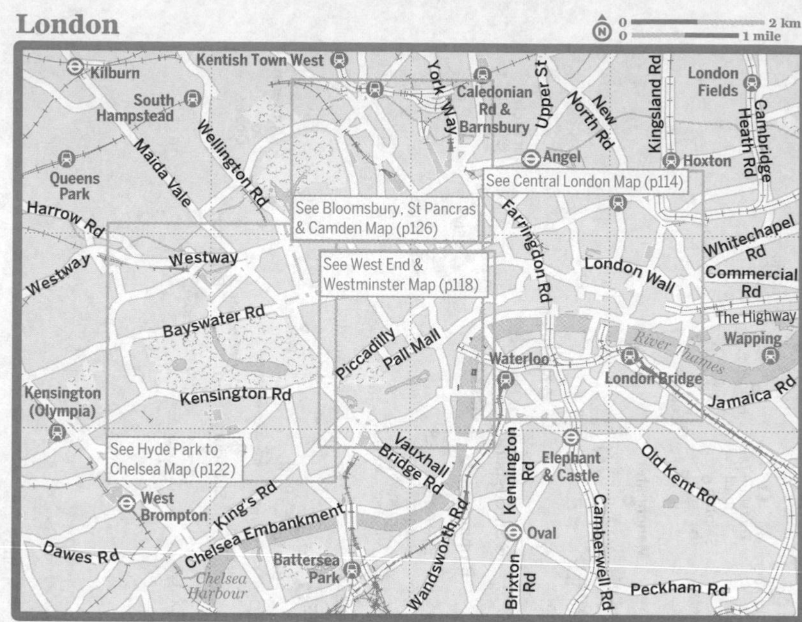

Sights

Westminster & St James's

★Westminster Abbey CHURCH

(Map p118; ☎020-7222 5152; www.westminster-abbey.org; 20 Dean's Yard, SW1; adult/child £20/9, verger tours £5, cloister & gardens free; ⊙9.30am-4.30pm Mon, Tue, Thu & Fri, to 7pm Wed, to 2.30pm Sat; ⊖Westminster) A splendid mixture of architectural styles, Westminster Abbey is considered the finest example of Early English Gothic (1190–1300). It's not merely a beautiful place of worship – the Abbey also serves up the country's history cold on slabs of stone. For centuries the country's greatest have been interred here, including 17 monarchs from Henry III (died 1272) to George II (1760). Never a cathedral (the seat of a bishop), Westminster Abbey is what is called a 'royal peculiar', administered by the Crown.

★Houses of Parliament HISTORIC BUILDING

(Palace of Westminster; Map p118; www.parliament.uk; Parliament Sq, SW1; ⊖Westminster) FREE A visit here is a journey to the heart of UK democracy. Officially called the Palace of Westminster, the Houses of Parliament's oldest part is 11th-century **Westminster Hall**, one of only a few sections that survived a catastrophic fire in 1834. Its roof, added between 1394–1401, is the earliest-known example of a hammerbeam roof. The rest is mostly a neo-Gothic confection built by Charles Barry and Augustus Pugin (1840–58).

The palace's most famous feature is its clock tower, Elizabeth Tower, aka **Big Ben** (Map p118; ⊖Westminster).

★Tate Britain GALLERY

(www.tate.org.uk; Millbank, SW1; ⊙10am-6pm, to 10pm 1st Fri of month; ⊖Pimlico) FREE Splendidly reopened a few years back with a stunning new art deco–inspired staircase and a rehung collection, the older and more venerable of the two Tate siblings celebrates paintings from 1500 to the present, with works from Blake, Hogarth, Gainsborough, Barbara Hepworth, Whistler, Constable and Turner, as well as vibrant modern and contemporary pieces from Lucian Freud, Francis Bacon and Henry Moore. Join a free 45-minute **thematic tour** (11am daily) and 15-minute **Art in Focus talks** (1.15pm Tuesday, Thursday and Saturday).

West End

★Trafalgar Square SQUARE
(Map p118; ⊖Charing Cross) In many ways Trafalgar Sq is is the centre of London, where rallies and marches take place, tens of thousands of revellers usher in the New Year and locals congregate for anything from communal open-air cinema and Christmas celebrations to various political protests. It is dominated by the 52m-high **Nelson's Column** and ringed by many splendid buildings, including the National Gallery and St Martin-in-the-Fields. The Nazis once planned to shift Nelson's Column to Berlin in the wake of a successful invasion.

★National Gallery GALLERY
(Map p118; www.nationalgallery.org.uk; Trafalgar Sq, WC2; 10am-6pm Sat-Thu, to 9pm Fri; ⊖Charing Cross) FREE With some 2300 European paintings on display, this is one of the world's great art collections, with seminal works from every important epoch in the history of art – from the mid-13th to the early 20th century, including masterpieces by Leonardo da Vinci, Michelangelo, Titian, Van Gogh and Renoir.

Many visitors flock to the East Wing (1700–1900), where works by 18th-century British artists such as Gainsborough, Constable and Turner, and seminal Impressionist and post-Impressionist masterpieces by Van Gogh, Renoir and Monet await.

★National Portrait Gallery GALLERY
(Map p118; 020-7321 0055; www.npg.org.uk; St Martin's Pl, WC2; 10am-6pm Sat-Wed, to 9pm Thu & Fri; ⊖Charing Cross, Leicester Sq) FREE What makes the National Portrait Gallery so compelling is its familiarity; in many cases you'll have heard of the subject (royals, scientists, politicians, celebrities) or the artist (Andy Warhol, Annie Leibovitz, Lucian Freud). Highlights include the famous 'Chandos portrait' of William Shakespeare, the first artwork the gallery acquired (in 1856) and believed to be the only likeness made during the playwright's lifetime, and a touching sketch of novelist Jane Austen by her sister.

★Madame Tussauds MUSEUM
(0870 400 3000; www.madame-tussauds.com/london; Marylebone Rd, NW1; adult/child 4-15yr £35/30; 8.30/10am-4/6pm (seasonal); ⊖Baker St) It may be kitschy and pricey (book online for much cheaper rates), but Madame Tussauds makes for a fun-filled day. There are photo ops with your dream celebrity (Daniel Craig, Miley Cyrus, Audrey Hepburn, the Beckhams), the Bollywood gathering (studs Hrithik Roshan and Salman Khan) and the Royal Appointment (the Queen, Harry, William and Kate).

BIG BEN

The Houses of Parliament's most famous feature is the clock tower known as Big Ben. Strictly speaking, however, Big Ben is the tower's 13-ton bell, named after Benjamin Hall, commissioner of works when the tower was completed in 1858.

Piccadilly Circus SQUARE
(Map p118; ⊖Piccadilly Circus) John Nash had originally designed Regent St and Piccadilly in the 1820s to be the two most elegant streets in town but, curbed by city planners, couldn't realise his dream to the full. He may be disappointed, but suitably astonished, with Piccadilly Circus today: a traffic maelstrom, deluged with visitors and flanked by flashing advertisements. 'It's like Piccadilly Circus', as the expression goes, but it's certainly fun.

The City

★Tower of London CASTLE
(Map p114; 0844 482 7777; www.hrp.org.uk/toweroflondon; Petty Wales, EC3; adult/child £25/12, audio guide £4/3; 9.30am-5pm; ⊖Tower Hill) The unmissable Tower of London (actually a castle of 22 towers) offers a window into a gruesome and compelling history. This was where two kings and three queens met their death and countless others were imprisoned. Come here to see the colourful Yeoman Warders (or Beefeaters), the spectacular Crown Jewels, the soothsaying ravens and armour fit for a *very* large king.

★Tower Bridge BRIDGE
(Map p114; ⊖Tower Hill) London was a thriving port in 1894 when elegant Tower Bridge was built. Designed to be raised to allow ships to pass, electricity has now taken over from the original steam and hydraulic engines. A lift leads up from the northern tower to the **Tower Bridge Exhibition**, where the story of its building is recounted within the upper walkway. You then walk down to the fascinating Victorian Engine Rooms, which powered the bridge lifts.

Central London

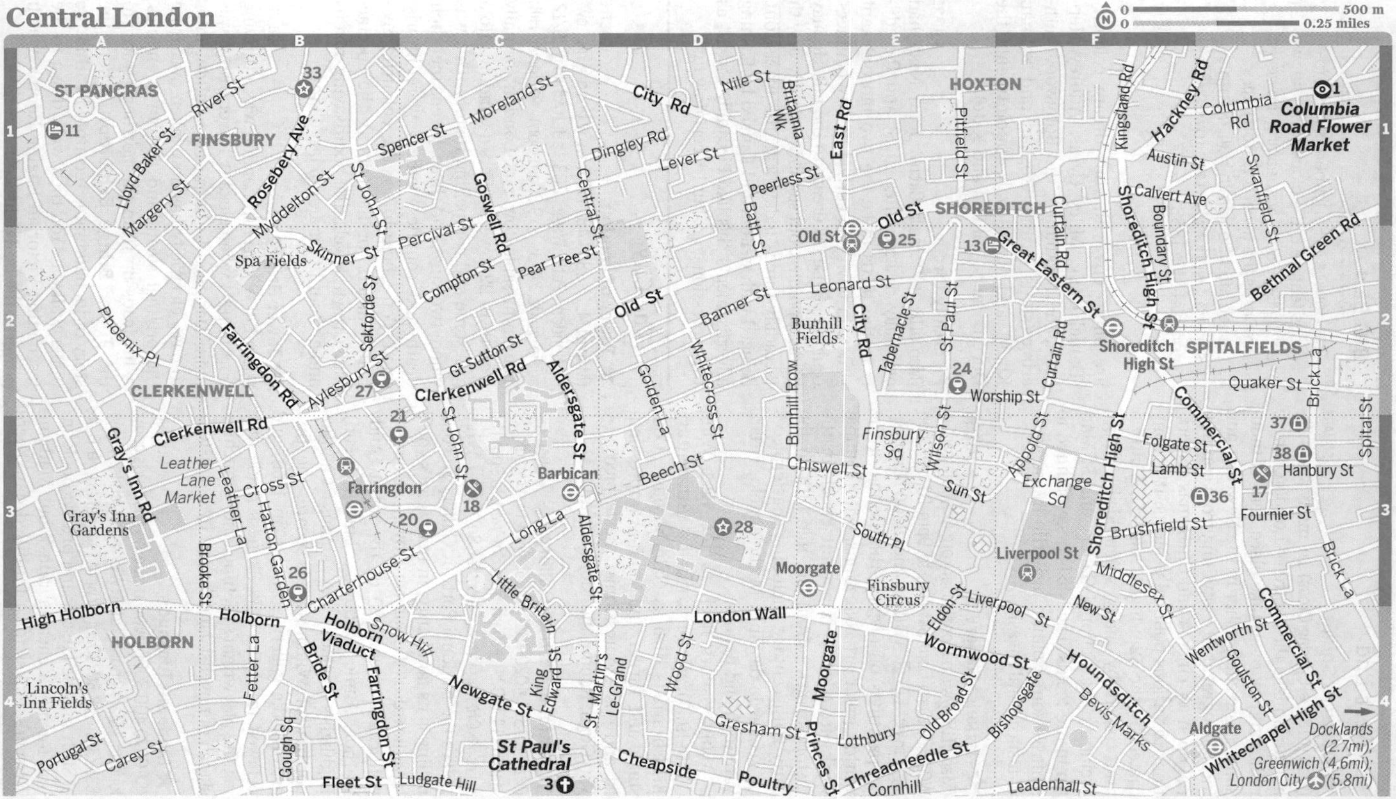

0 — 500 m
0 — 0.25 miles

ST PANCRAS
FINSBURY
CLERKENWELL
HOLBORN
HOXTON
SHOREDITCH
SPITALFIELDS

1 Columbia Road Flower Market
3 St Paul's Cathedral
11
13
17
18
20
21
24
25
26
27
28
33
36
37
38

River St
Lloyd Baker St
Margery St
Rosebery Ave
Myddelton St
Spa Fields
Skinner St
St John St
Spencer St
Moreland St
Percival St
Goswell Rd
Compton St
Pear Tree St
Central St
Dingley Rd
Lever St
City Rd
Nile St
Britannia Wk
East Rd
Peerless St
Bath St
Old St
Pitfield St
Curtain Rd
Kingsland Rd
Hackney Rd
Columbia Rd
Austin St
Calvert Ave
Boundary St
Swanfield St
Shoreditch High St
Bethnal Green Rd
Great Eastern St
Leonard St
Banner St
Phoenix Pl
Farringdon Rd
Sekforde St
Aylesbury St
Gt Sutton St
Clerkenwell Rd
Aldersgate St
Golden La
Whitecross St
Bunhill Row
Bunhill Fields
City Rd
Tabernacle St
St Paul St
Worship St
Quaker St
Brick La
Spital St
Commercial St
Folgate St
Lamb St
Hanbury St
Fournier St
Brushfield St
Gray's Inn Rd
Leather Lane Market
Leather La
Cross St
Hatton Garden
Farringdon
Barbican
Beech St
Chiswell St
Finsbury Sq
Wilson St
Sun St
Appold St
Exchange Sq
Gray's Inn Gardens
Brooke St
Long La
South Pl
Liverpool St
Moorgate
Finsbury Circus
Middlesex St
Charterhouse St
Little Britain
High Holborn
Holborn
Holborn Viaduct
Snow Hill
London Wall
Eldon St
New St
Wentworth St
Goulston St
Fetter La
Bride St
Farringdon St
Newgate St
King Edward St
St Martin's Le-Grand
Wood St
Wormwood St
Houndsditch
Bevis Marks
Aldgate
Whitechapel High St
Lincoln's Inn Fields
Portugal St
Carey St
Gough Sq
Fleet St
Ludgate Hill
Cheapside
Poultry
Gresham St
Princes St
Lothbury
Old Broad St
Bishopsgate
Threadneedle St
Cornhill
Leadenhall St

Docklands (2.7mi); Greenwich (4.6mi); London City (5.8mi)

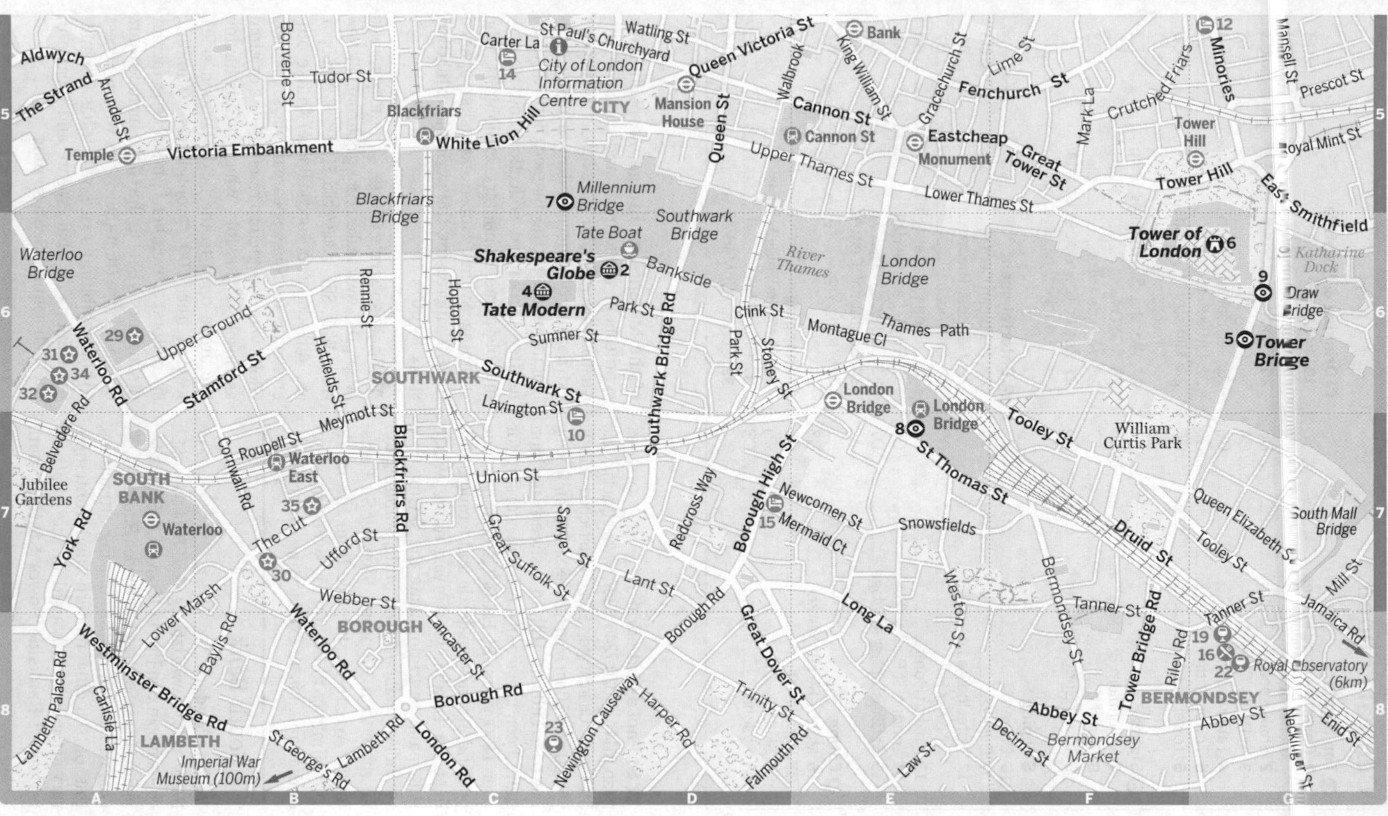
Aldwych
The Strand
Arundel St
Temple
Victoria Embankment
Bouverie St
Tudor St
Blackfriars
White Lion Hill
Carter La
14
St Paul's Churchyard
City of London Information Centre
CITY
Watling St
Mansion House
Queen Victoria St
Queen St
Walbrook
Cannon St
Cannon St
King William St
Bank
Gracechurch St
Eastcheap
Monument
Fenchurch St
Lime St
Great Tower St
Mark La
Crutched Friars
Tower Hill
Tower Hill
Minories
12
East Smithfield
Mansell St
Prescot St
Royal Mint St
Upper Thames St
Lower Thames St
Waterloo Bridge
Blackfriars Bridge
Millennium Bridge
7
Southwark Bridge
London Bridge
River Thames
Tower of London
6
Tower Bridge
5
9
Draw Bridge
Katharine Dock
Tate Boat
Shakespeare's Globe
2
Tate Modern
4
Bankside
Southwark Bridge Rd
Park St
Clink St
Stoney St
Montague Cl
Thames Path
London Bridge
London Bridge
8
St Thomas St
Tooley St
William Curtis Park
Druid St
Queen Elizabeth St
Tooley St
South Mall Bridge
Mill St
Jamaica Rd
Royal Observatory (6km)
Enid St
Neckinger St
Tanner St
19
16
22
Riley Rd
BERMONDSEY
Abbey St
Tower Bridge Rd
Tanner St
Bermondsey St
Bermondsey Market
Abbey St
Decima St
Weston St
Snowsfields
Law St
Long La
Newcomen St
Mermaid Ct
15
Borough High St
Great Dover St
Trinity St
Falmouth Rd
Redcross Way
Borough Rd
Lant St
Harper Rd
Newington Causeway
23
Sawyer St
Great Suffolk St
Union St
Southwark St
Lavington St
10
Sumner St
Hopton St
SOUTHWARK
Blackfriars Rd
Rennie St
Hatfields St
Meymott St
Roupell St
Waterloo East
35
Ufford St
The Cut
30
Webber St
BOROUGH
Lancaster St
Borough Rd
London Rd
Waterloo Rd
Lambeth Rd
St George's Rd
Imperial War Museum (100m)
Baylis Rd
Lower Marsh
Cornwall Rd
Stamford St
Upper Ground
29
Waterloo Rd
31
34
32
Belvedere Rd
Jubilee Gardens
SOUTH BANK
Waterloo
York Rd
Westminster Bridge Rd
LAMBETH
Carlisle La
Lambeth Palace Rd
A
B
C
D
E
F
G
5
6
7
8

Central London

Top Sights
1 Columbia Road Flower Market ... G1
2 Shakespeare's Globe ... D6
3 St Paul's Cathedral ... C4
4 Tate Modern ... C6
5 Tower Bridge ... G6
6 Tower of London ... G6

Sights
7 Millennium Bridge ... C5
8 Shard ... E7
9 Tower Bridge Exhibition ... G6

Sleeping
10 Citizen M ... C7
11 Clink78 ... A1
12 Hotel Indigo London – Tower Hill ... G5
13 Hoxton Hotel ... E2
14 London St Paul's YHA ... C5
15 St Christopher's Village ... D7

Eating
16 Maltby Street Market ... G8
17 Poppies ... G3
Skylon ... (see 32)
18 St John ... C3

Drinking & Nightlife
19 40 Maltby Street ... G8
Aqua Shard ... (see 8)
20 Fabric ... C3
Gŏng ... (see 8)
21 Jerusalem Tavern ... B3
22 Little Bird Gin ... G8
23 Ministry of Sound ... C8
Oblix ... (see 8)
24 Worship St Whistling Shop ... E2
25 XOYO ... E2
26 Ye Olde Mitre ... B3
27 Zetter Townhouse Cocktail Lounge ... B2

Entertainment
28 Barbican Centre ... D3
29 National Theatre ... A6
30 Old Vic ... B7
31 Queen Elizabeth Hall ... A6
32 Royal Festival Hall ... A6
33 Sadler's Wells ... B1
34 Southbank Centre ... A6
35 Young Vic ... B7

Shopping
36 Old Spitalfields Market ... G3
37 Rough Trade East ... G3
38 Sunday UpMarket ... G3

★ **St Paul's Cathedral** CATHEDRAL
(Map p114; 020-7246 8357; www.stpauls.co.uk; St Paul's Churchyard, EC4; adult/child £18/8; 8.30am-4.30pm Mon-Sat; St Paul's) Towering over Ludgate Hill, in a superb position that's been a place of Christian worship for over 1400 years, St Paul's Cathedral is one of London's most majestic and iconic buildings. For Londoners, the vast dome, which still manages to dominate the skyline, is a symbol of resilience and pride, standing tall for more than 300 years. Viewing Sir Christopher Wren's masterpiece from the inside and climbing to the top for sweeping views of the capital is an exhilarating experience.

South Bank

★ **Tate Modern** MUSEUM
(Map p114; www.tate.org.uk; Bankside, SE1; 10am-6pm Sun-Thu, to 10pm Fri & Sat; ; Blackfriars, Southwark or London Bridge) FREE One of London's most amazing attractions, this outstanding modern- and contemporary-art gallery is housed in the creatively revamped **Bankside Power Station** south of the **Millennium Bridge**. A spellbinding synthesis of modern art and capacious industrial brick design, Tate Modern has been extraordinarily successful in bringing challenging work to the masses, both through its free permanent collection and fee-paying big-name temporary exhibitions. The stunning Switch House extension opened in 2016, increasing the available exhibition space by 60%.

★ **Shakespeare's Globe** HISTORIC BUILDING
(Map p114; www.shakespearesglobe.com; 21 New Globe Walk, SE1; adult/child £16/9; 9am-5pm; ; Blackfriars or London Bridge) Unlike other venues for Shakespearean plays, the new Globe was designed to resemble the original as closely as possible, which means having the arena open to the fickle London skies, leaving the 700 'groundlings' (standing spectators) to weather London's spectacular downpours. Visits to the Globe include tours of the theatre (half-hourly) as well as access to the exhibition space, which has fascinating exhibits on Shakespeare and theatre in the 17th century. See also p134.

★London Eye VIEWPOINT
(Map p118; ☎0871-222 4002; www.londoneye.com; adult/child £23.45/18.95; ⊙11am-6pm Sep-May, 10am-8.30pm Jun-Aug; ⊖Waterloo or Westminster) Standing 135m high in a fairly flat city, the London Eye affords views 25 miles in every direction, weather permitting. Interactive tablets provide great information (in six languages) about landmarks as they appear in the skyline. Each rotation – or 'flight' – takes a gracefully slow 30 minutes. At peak times (July, August and school holidays) it can feel like you'll spend more time in the queue than in the capsule; book premium fast-track tickets to jump the queue.

★Imperial War Museum MUSEUM
(www.iwm.org.uk; Lambeth Rd, SE1; ⊙10am-6pm; ⊖Lambeth North) FREE Fronted by a pair of intimidating 15in naval guns, this riveting museum is housed in what was the Bethlehem Royal Hospital, a psychiatric hospital also known as Bedlam. Although the museum's focus is on military action involving British or Commonwealth troops largely during the 20th century, it rolls out the carpet to war in the wider sense. Highlights include the state-of-the-art **First World War Galleries** and **Witnesses to War** in the forecourt and atrium above.

Shard NOTABLE BUILDING
(Map p114; www.theviewfromtheshard.com; 32 London Bridge St, SE1; adult/child £30.95/24.95; ⊙10am-10pm; ⊖London Bridge) Puncturing the skies above London, the dramatic splinter-like form of the Shard has rapidly become an icon of London. The viewing platforms on floors 69 and 72 are open to the public and the views are, as you'd expect from a 244m vantage point, sweeping, but they come at a hefty price – book online at least a day in advance to save £5.

Kensington & Hyde Park

This area is called the Royal Borough of Kensington and Chelsea, and residents are certainly paid royally, earning the highest incomes in the UK (shops and restaurants will presume you do too).

★Natural History Museum MUSEUM
(Map p122; www.nhm.ac.uk; Cromwell Rd, SW7; ⊙10am-5.50pm; 📶; ⊖South Kensington) FREE This colossal and magnificent-looking building is infused with the irrepressible Victorian spirit of collecting, cataloguing and interpreting the natural world. The **Dinosaurs Gallery** (Blue Zone) is a must for children, who gawp at the animatronic T-Rex, fossils and excellent displays. Adults for their part will love the intriguing Treasures exhibition in the **Cadogan Gallery** (Green Zone), which houses a host of unrelated objects each telling its own unique story, from a chunk of moon rock to a dodo skeleton.

★Science Museum MUSEUM
(Map p122; www.sciencemuseum.org.uk; Exhibition Rd, SW7; ⊙10am-6pm; 📶; ⊖South Kensington) FREE With seven floors of interactive and educational exhibits, this scientifically spellbinding museum will mesmerise adults and children alike, covering everything from early technology to space travel. A perennial favourite is **Exploring Space**, a gallery featuring genuine rockets and satellites and a full-size replica of 'Eagle', the lander that took Neil Armstrong and Buzz Aldrin to the Moon in 1969. The **Making the Modern World Gallery** next door is a visual feast of locomotives, planes, cars and other revolutionary inventions.

★Victoria & Albert Museum MUSEUM
(V&A; Map p122; ☎020-7942 2000; www.vam.ac.uk; Cromwell Rd, SW7; ⊙10am-5.40pm Sat-Thu, to 10pm Fri; ⊖South Kensington) FREE The Museum of Manufactures, as the V&A was known when it opened in 1852, was part of Prince Albert's legacy to the nation in the aftermath of the successful Great Exhibition of 1851. It houses the world's largest collection of decorative arts, from Asian ceramics to Middle Eastern rugs, Chinese paintings, Western furniture, fashion from all ages and modern-day domestic appliances. The temporary exhibitions are another highlight, covering anything from David Bowie retrospectives to designer Alexander McQueen, special materials and trends.

★Hyde Park PARK
(Map p122; www.royalparks.org.uk/parks/hyde-park; ⊙5am-midnight; ⊖Marble Arch, Hyde Park Corner or Queensway) At 145 hectares, Hyde Park is central London's largest open space, expropriated from the Church in 1536 by Henry VIII and turned into a hunting ground and later a venue for duels, executions and horse racing. The 1851 Great Exhibition was held here, and during WWII the park became an enormous potato field. These days, there's boating on the **Serpentine**, summer concerts (Bruce Springsteen, Florence + The Machine, Patti Smith), film nights and other warm-weather events.

West End & Westminster

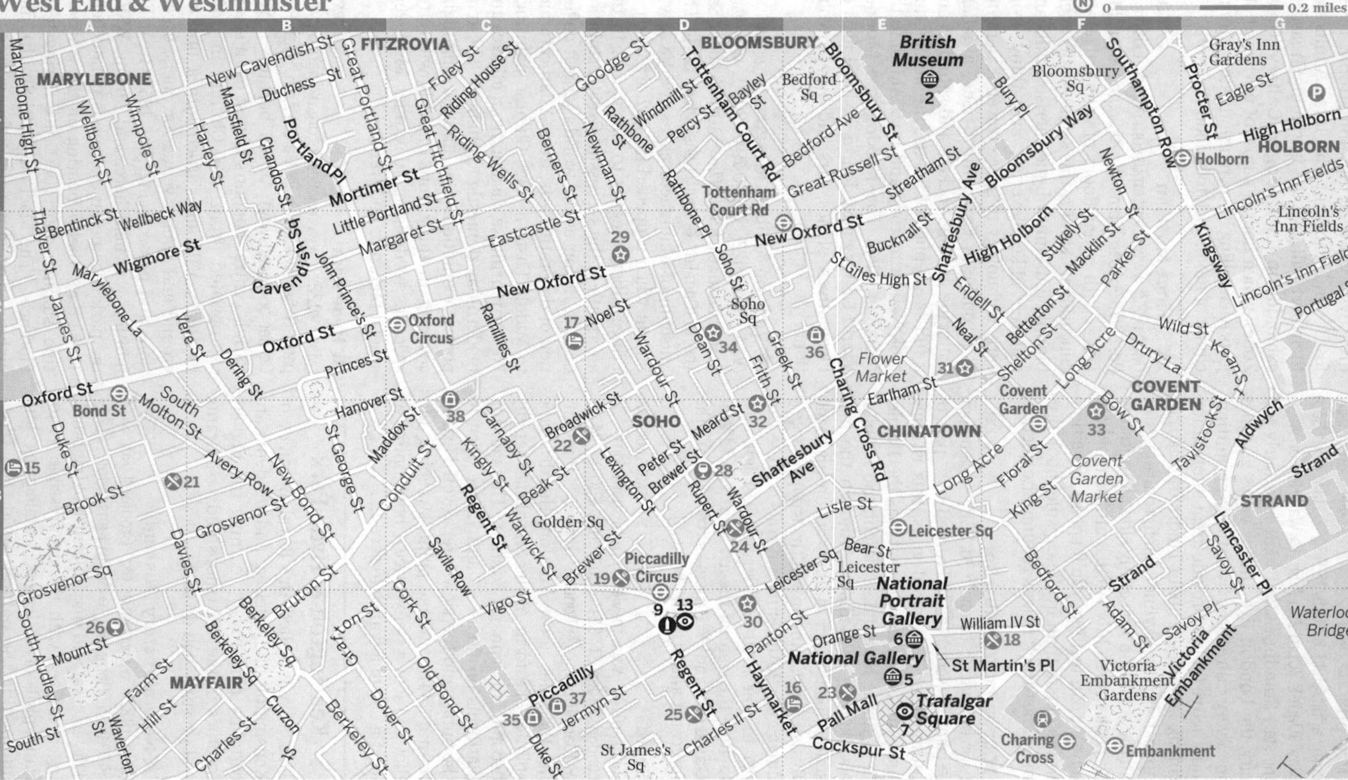

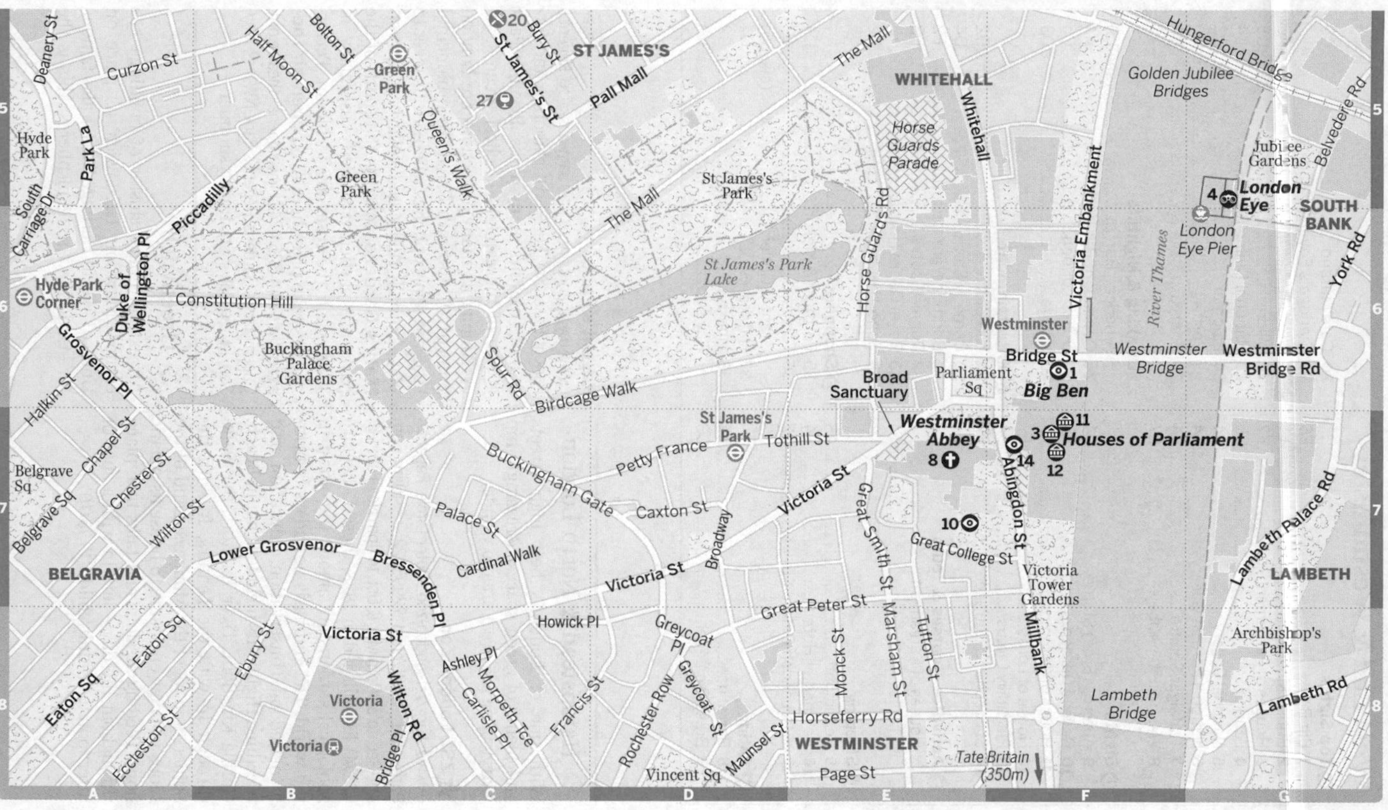
Deanery St
Curzon St
Half Moon St
Bolton St
Green Park
Queen's Walk
20
Bury St
St James's St
27
ST JAMES'S
Pall Mall
The Mall
WHITEHALL
Whitehall
Horse Guards Parade
Hungerford Bridge
Golden Jubilee Bridges
Belvedere Rd
Jubilee Gardens
4 London Eye
SOUTH BANK
London Eye Pier
River Thames
York Rd
Hyde Park
Park La
South Carriage Dr
Piccadilly
Green Park
The Mall
St James's Park
St James's Park Lake
Horse Guards Rd
Victoria Embankment
Hyde Park Corner
Duke of Wellington Pl
Constitution Hill
Westminster
Bridge St
1 Big Ben
Westminster Bridge
Westminster Bridge Rd
Grosvenor Pl
Buckingham Palace Gardens
Spur Rd
Birdcage Walk
Broad Sanctuary
Parliament Sq
Westminster Abbey
8
3
11
Houses of Parliament
14
12
Halkin St
Chapel St
Belgrave Sq
Chester St
Belgrave Sq
St James's Park
Tothill St
Petty France
Buckingham Gate
Caxton St
Victoria St
Abingdon St
Great Smith St
10
Great College St
Lambeth Palace Rd
Wilton St
Palace St
Cardinal Walk
Broadway
Victoria Tower Gardens
LAMBETH
BELGRAVIA
Lower Grosvenor
Bressenden Pl
Victoria St
Great Peter St
Howick Pl
Greycoat Pl
Monck St
Marsham St
Tufton St
Millbank
Archbishop's Park
Eaton Sq
Ebury St
Victoria St
Ashley Pl
Morpeth Tce
Carlisle Pl
Francis St
Rochester Row
Greycoat St
Lambeth Bridge
Lambeth Rd
Eaton Sq
Victoria
Victoria
Wilton Rd
Bridge Pl
Eccleston St
Horseferry Rd
Maunsel St
WESTMINSTER
Vincent Sq
Page St
Tate Britain (350m)

West End & Westminster

Top Sights
1 Big Ben ... F6
2 British Museum ... E1
3 Houses of Parliament ... F7
4 London Eye ... G5
5 National Gallery ... E4
6 National Portrait Gallery ... E4
7 Trafalgar Square ... E4
8 Westminster Abbey ... E7

Sights
9 Anteros (Eros) Statue ... D4
10 College Garden ... E7
11 House of Commons ... F7
12 House of Lords ... F7
13 Piccadilly Circus ... D4
14 St Stephen's Entrance ... F7

Activities, Courses & Tours
Houses of Parliament Tours ... (see 3)

Sleeping
15 Beaumont ... A3
16 Haymarket Hotel ... E4
17 YHA London Oxford Street ... C2

Eating
18 Barrafina ... F4
19 Brasserie Zédel ... D3
20 Cafe Murano ... C5
21 Claridge's Foyer & Reading Room ... A3
22 Mildreds ... C3
23 National Dining Rooms ... E4
24 Palomar ... D3
Portrait ... (see 6)
25 Shoryu ... D4

Drinking & Nightlife
American Bar ... (see 15)
26 Connaught Bar ... A4
27 Dukes London ... C5
28 Village ... D3

Entertainment
29 100 Club ... D2
30 Comedy Store ... D4
31 Donmar Warehouse ... E2
32 Ronnie Scott's ... D3
33 Royal Opera House ... F3
34 Soho Theatre ... D2

Shopping
35 Fortnum & Mason ... C4
36 Foyles ... E2
Grant & Cutler ... (see 36)
37 Hatchards ... C4
38 Liberty ... C2
Ray's Jazz ... (see 36)

Hampstead & North London

With one of London's best high streets and plenty of green space, increasingly hip Marylebone is a great area to wander.

★ZSL London Zoo ZOO
(www.zsl.org/zsl-london-zoo; Outer Circle, Regent's Park, NW1; adult/child £29.75/22; 10am-6pm Apr-Sep, to 5.30pm Mar & Oct, to 4pm Nov-Feb; ; 274) Established in 1828, these 15-hectare zoological gardens are among the oldest in the world. The emphasis nowadays is firmly placed on conservation, education and breeding. Highlights include Penguin Beach, Gorilla Kingdom, Tiger Territory, the walk-through In with the Lemurs, In with the Spiders and Meet the Monkeys. Land of the Lions is a new enclosure to house its Asiatic lions. Feeding sessions and talks take place throughout the day – join in with a spot of afternoon tea (adult/child £19.75/10).

Regent's Park PARK
(www.royalparks.org.uk; 5am-dusk; Regent's Park or Baker St) The most elaborate and formal of London's many parks, Regent's Park is one of the capital's loveliest green spaces. Among its many attractions are London Zoo (p120), Regent's Canal, an ornamental lake and sports pitches where locals meet to play football, rugby and volleyball. **Queen Mary's Gardens**, towards the south of the park, are particularly pretty, especially in June when the roses are in bloom. Performances take place here in an **open-air theatre** (0844 826 4242; www.openairtheatre.org; Queen Mary's Gardens, Regent's Park, NW1; May-Sep; ; Baker St) during summer.

Greenwich

An extraordinary cluster of buildings has earned 'Maritime Greenwich' its place on Unesco's World Heritage list. It's also famous for straddling the hemispheres; this is the degree zero of longitude, home of the Greenwich Meridian and Greenwich Mean Time.

Greenwich is easily reached on the DLR train (to Cutty Sark station), or by boat – **Thames Clippers** (www.thamesclippers.com; all zones adult/child £9/4.50) depart from the London Eye every 20 minutes.

★**Royal Observatory** HISTORIC BUILDING
(www.rmg.co.uk; Greenwich Park, Blackheath Ave, SE10; adult/child £9.50/5, with Cutty Sark £18.50/8.50; ⏰10am-5pm Sep-Jun, to 6pm Jul & Aug; 🚆DLR Cutty Sark, DLR Greenwich or Greenwich) Rising south of Queen's House, idyllic **Greenwich Park** (www.royalparks.org.uk; King George St, SE10; ⏰6am-6pm winter, to 8pm spring & autumn, to 9pm summer; 🚆DLR Cutty Sark, 🚆Greenwich or Maze Hill) climbs up the hill, affording stunning views of London from the Royal Observatory, which Charles II had built in 1675 to help solve the riddle of longitude. To the north is lovely **Flamsteed House** and the **Meridian Courtyard**, where you can stand with your feet straddling the western and eastern hemispheres; admission is by ticket. The southern half contains the highly informative and free **Weller Astronomy Galleries** and the **Peter Harrison Planetarium** (☎020-8312 6608; www.rmg.co.uk/whats-on/planetarium-shows; Greenwich Park, SE10; adult/child £7.50/5.50; 🚆Greenwich or DLR Cutty Sark).

★**Old Royal Naval College** HISTORIC BUILDING
(www.ornc.org; 2 Cutty Sark Gardens, SE10; ⏰grounds 8am-6pm, to 11pm in summer; 🚆DLR Cutty Sark) FREE Designed by Christopher Wren, the Old Royal Naval College is a magnificent example of monumental classical architecture. Parts are now used by the University of Greenwich and Trinity College of Music, but you can still visit the **chapel** and the extraordinary **Painted Hall**, which took artist Sir James Thornhill 19 years to complete. Hour-long, yeomen-led tours (£6) leave at noon daily, taking in areas not otherwise open to the public. Free 45-minute tours take place at least four times daily.

★**National Maritime Museum** MUSEUM
(www.rmg.co.uk/national-maritime-museum; Romney Rd, SE10; ⏰10am-5pm; 🚆DLR Cutty Sark) FREE Narrating the long, briny and eventful history of seafaring Britain, this excellent museum's exhibits are arranged thematically, with highlights including *Miss Britain III* (the first boat to top 100mph on open water) from 1933, the 19m-long golden state barge built in 1732 for Frederick, Prince of Wales, the huge ship's propeller and the colourful figureheads installed on the ground floor. Families will love these, as well as the ship simulator and the 'All Hands' children's gallery on the 2nd floor.

DON'T MISS

BRITISH MUSEUM

The vast **British Museum** (Map p118; ☎020-7323 8299; www.britishmuseum.org; Great Russell St, WC1; ⏰10am-5.30pm Sat-Thu, to 8.30pm Fri; ⊖Russell Sq or Tottenham Court Rd) FREE isn't just the nation's largest museum, it's one of the oldest and finest anywhere in the world. Among the must-see antiquities are the **Rosetta Stone**, the key to deciphering Egyptian hieroglyphics, discovered in 1799; the controversial **Parthenon Sculptures**, stripped from the walls of the Parthenon in Athens by Lord Elgin (the British ambassador to the Ottoman Empire); and the Anglo-Saxon **Sutton Hoo relics**. The **Great Court** was restored and augmented by Norman Foster in 2000 and now has a spectacular glass-and-steel roof.

You'll need multiple visits to savour even the highlights here; take advantage of the 15 free 30- to 40-minute **eye-opener tours** of individual galleries per day. Audio guides (£5) can be found at the audio-guide desk in the Great Court.

★**Cutty Sark** MUSEUM
(☎020-8312 6608; www.rmg.co.uk/cuttysark; King William Walk, SE10; adult/child £13.50/7; ⏰10am-5pm Sep-Jun, to 6pm Jul & Aug; 🚆DLR Cutty Sark) This Greenwich landmark, the last of the great clipper ships to sail between China and England in the 19th century, saw £25 million of extensive renovations largely precipitated by a disastrous fire in 2007. The exhibition in the ship's hold tells her story as a tea clipper at the end of the 19th century (and then wool and mixed cargo).

Outside Central London

★**Kew Gardens** GARDENS
(www.kew.org; Kew Rd; adult/child £15/3.50; ⏰10am-6.30pm Apr-Aug, closes earlier Sep-Mar; ⛴Kew Pier, 🚆Kew Bridge, ⊖Kew Gardens) In 1759 botanists began rummaging around the

Hyde Park to Chelsea

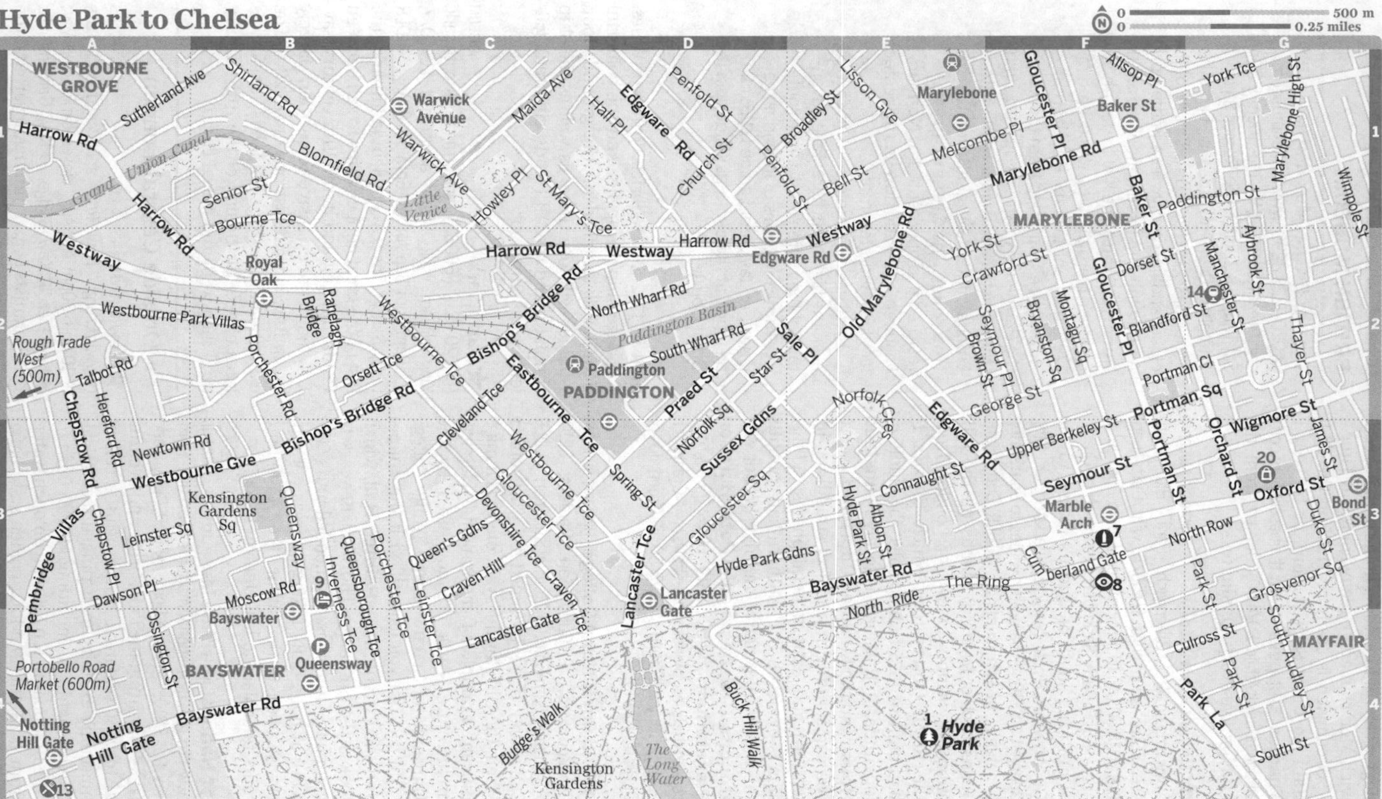

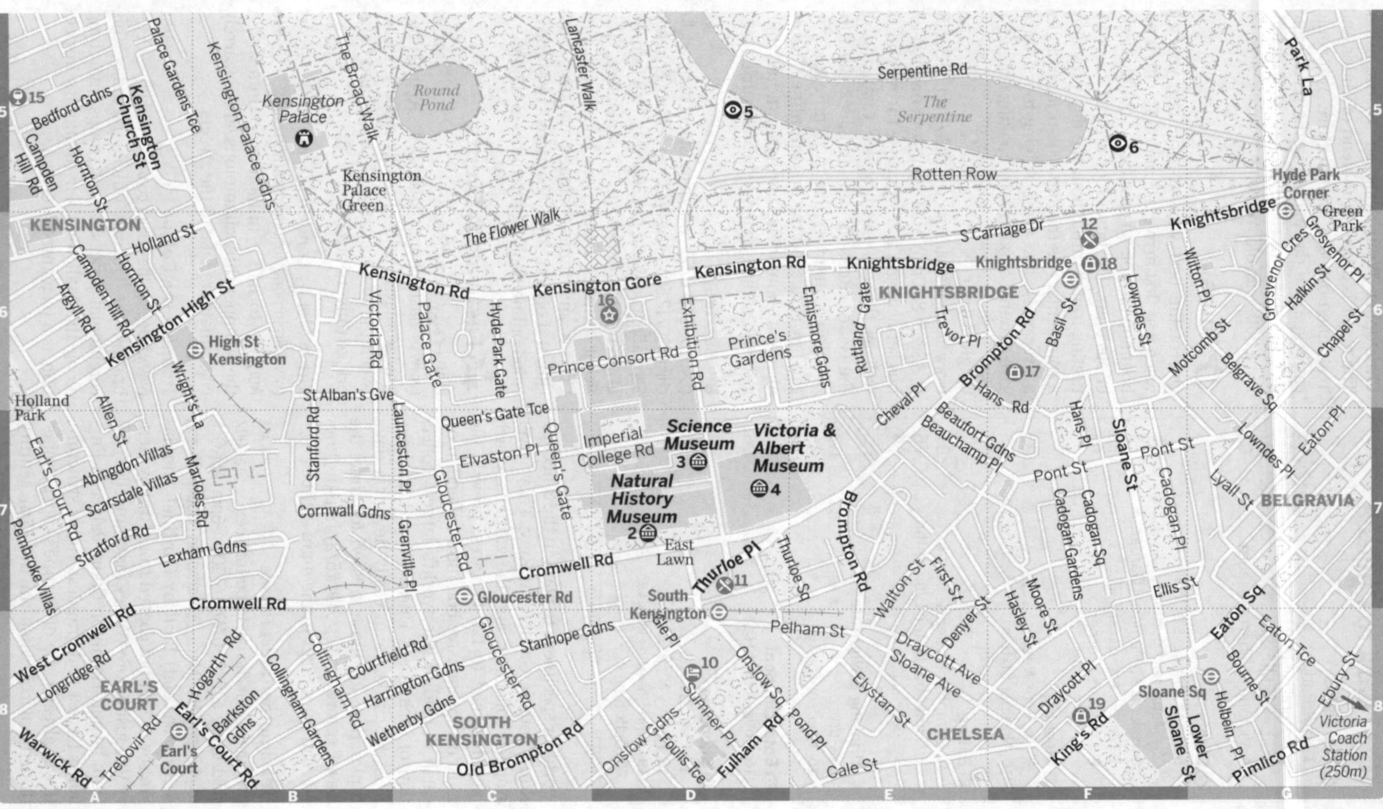
Palace Gardens Tce
Kensington Palace Gdns
The Broad Walk
Round Pond
Lancaster Walk
Serpentine Rd
The Serpentine
Park La
Bedford Gdns
Kensington Church St
Kensington Palace
Campden Hill Rd
Hornton St
Kensington Palace Green
Rotten Row
Hyde Park Corner
Green Park
KENSINGTON
Holland St
The Flower Walk
S Carriage Dr
Knightsbridge
Grosvenor Cres
Grosvenor Pl
Halkin St
Chapel St
Wilton Pl
Kensington Rd
Kensington Gore
Knightsbridge
KNIGHTSBRIDGE
Lowndes St
Argyll Rd
Kensington High St
Victoria Rd
Palace Gate
Hyde Park Gate
Exhibition Rd
Ennismore Gdns
Rutland Gate
Trevor Pl
Brompton Rd
Basil St
Motcomb St
Belgrave Sq
High St Kensington
Prince Consort Rd
Prince's Gardens
Hans Rd
Holland Park
Allen St
Wright's La
St Alban's Gve
Launceston Pl
Queen's Gate Tce
Imperial College Rd
Science Museum
Victoria & Albert Museum
Cheval Pl
Beaufort Gdns
Beauchamp Pl
Hans Pl
Sloane St
Pont St
Lowndes Pl
Eaton Pl
Earl's Court Rd
Abingdon Villas
Scarsdale Villas
Marloes Rd
Stanford Rd
Elvaston Pl
Gloucester Rd
Queen's Gate
Natural History Museum
Cadogan Gardens
Cadogan Sq
Cadogan Pl
Lyall St
BELGRAVIA
Pembroke Villas
Stratford Rd
Cornwall Gdns
Grenville Pl
East Lawn
Lexham Gdns
Cromwell Rd
Thurloe Pl
Thurloe Sq
Walton St
First St
Ellis St
Gloucester Rd
South Kensington
Denyer St
Hasley St
Moore St
Eaton Sq
West Cromwell Rd
Hogarth Rd
Stanhope Gdns
Gle Pl
Pelham St
Eaton Tce
Longridge Rd
EARL'S COURT
Collingham Gardens
Collingham Rd
Courtfield Rd
Harrington Gdns
Onslow Sq
Draycott Ave
Sloane Ave
Bourne St
Draycott Pl
Sloane Sq
Holbein Pl
Ebury St
Barkston Gdns
Earl's Court Rd
Wetherby Gdns
Sumner Pl
Elystan St
Earl's Court
Warwick Rd
Trebovir Rd
SOUTH KENSINGTON
Onslow Gdns
Foulis Tce
Pond Pl
CHELSEA
King's Rd
Lower Sloane St
Old Brompton Rd
Fulham Rd
Cale St
Pimlico Rd
Victoria Coach Station (250m)

Hyde Park to Chelsea

Top Sights
1 Hyde Park E4
2 Natural History Museum D7
3 Science Museum D7
4 Victoria & Albert Museum D7

Sights
5 Diana, Princess of Wales Memorial Fountain D5
6 Holocaust Memorial Garden F5
7 Marble Arch F3
8 Speakers' Corner F3

Sleeping
9 La Suite West B3
10 Number Sixteen D8

Eating
11 Comptoir Libanais D7
12 Dinner by Heston Blumenthal F6
13 Geales A4

Drinking & Nightlife
14 Purl G2
15 Windsor Castle A5

Entertainment
16 Royal Albert Hall D6

Shopping
17 Harrods F6
18 Harvey Nichols F6
19 John Sandoe Books F8
20 Selfridges G3

world for specimens to plant in the 3-hectare Royal Botanic Gardens at Kew. They never stopped collecting, and the gardens, which have bloomed to 120 hectares, provide the most comprehensive botanical collection on earth (including the world's largest collection of orchids). A Unesco World Heritage Site, the gardens can easily devour a day's exploration; for those pressed for time, the **Kew Explorer** (adult/child £5/2) hop-on/hop-off road train takes in the main sights.

★Hampton Court Palace PALACE
(www.hrp.org.uk/hamptoncourtpalace; adult/child/family £19/9.50/47; 10am-6pm Apr-Oct, to 4.30pm Nov-Mar; Hampton Court Palace, Hampton Court) Built by Cardinal Thomas Wolsey in 1514 but coaxed from him by Henry VIII just before Wolsey (as chancellor) fell from favour, Hampton Court Palace is England's largest and grandest Tudor structure. It was already one of Europe's most sophisticated palaces when, in the 17th century, Christopher Wren designed an extension. The result is a beautiful blend of Tudor and 'restrained baroque' architecture. You could easily spend a day exploring the palace and its 24 hectares of riverside gardens, including a 300-year-old **maze**.

Tours

One of the best ways to orientate yourself when you first arrive in London is with a 24-hour hop-on/hop-off pass for the double-decker bus tours. The buses loop around interconnecting routes throughout the day, providing a commentary as they go. The price includes a river cruise and three walking tours. You'll save a couple of pounds by booking online.

Original Tour BUS
(www.theoriginaltour.com; adult/child £30/15; 8.30am-8.30pm) A 24-hour hop-on, hop-off bus service with a river cruise thrown in, as well as three themed walks: Changing of the Guard, Rock 'n' Roll and Jack the Ripper. Buses run every five to 20 minutes; you can buy tickets on the bus or online. There's also a 48-hour ticket available (adult/child £40/19), with an extended river cruise.

Big Bus Tours BUS
(020-7808 6753; www.bigbustours.com; adult/child £30/12.50; every 20min 8.30am-6pm Apr-Sep, to 5pm Oct & Mar, to 4.30pm Nov-Feb) Informative commentaries in 12 languages. The ticket includes a free river cruise with City Cruises and three thematic walking tours (Royal London, film locations, mysteries). Good online booking discounts available.

Festivals & Events

University Boat Race ROWING
(www.theboatrace.org; late Mar) A posh-boy grudge match held annually since 1829 between the rowing crews of Oxford and Cambridge universities.

Virgin Money London Marathon SPORTS
(www.virginmoneylondonmarathon.com; late Apr) Up to half a million spectators watch the whippet-thin champions and bizarrely clad amateurs take to the streets.

Trooping the Colour PARADE
(www.trooping-the-colour.co.uk; Jun) Celebrating the Queen's official birthday, this ceremonial procession of troops, marching along the Mall for their monarch's inspection, is a pageantry overload.

Meltdown Festival MUSIC
(www.southbankcentre.co.uk; ⏲late Jun) The Southbank Centre hands over the curatorial reigns to a legend of contemporary music (such as Morrissey, Patti Smith or David Byrne) to pull together a full program of concerts, talks and films.

Wimbledon Championships SPECTATOR SPORT
(☎020-8944 1066; www.wimbledon.com; Church Rd, SW19; grounds admission £8-25, tickets £41-190) The world's most splendid tennis event.

Pride GAY & LESBIAN
(www.prideinlondon.org; ⏲late Jun or early Jul) The big event on the gay and lesbian calendar, a technicolour street parade heads through the West End, culminating in a concert in Trafalgar Sq.

Notting Hill Carnival CARNIVAL
(www.thelondonnottinghillcarnival.com; ⏲Aug) Every year, for three days during the last weekend of August, Notting Hill echoes to the calypso, ska, reggae and soca sounds of the Notting Hill Carnival. Launched in 1964 by the local Afro-Caribbean community, keen to celebrate its culture and traditions, it has grown to become Europe's largest street festival (up to one million people) and a highlight of London's calendar.

Sleeping

When it comes to accommodation, London is one of the most expensive places in the world. Budget is pretty much anything below £100 per night for a double; double rooms ranging between £100 and £200 per night are considered midrange; more expensive options fall into the top-end category. Public transport is good, so you don't need to sleep at Buckingham Palace to be at the heart of things.

West End

★**Clink78** HOSTEL £
(Map p114; ☎020-7183 9400; www.clinkhostels.com/london/clink78; 78 King's Cross Rd, WC1; dm/r incl breakfast from £16/65; @📶; ⊖King's Cross St Pancras) This fantastic 630-bed hostel is housed in a 19th-century magistrates courthouse where Dickens once worked as a scribe and members of the Clash stood trial in 1978. Rooms feature pod beds (including overhead storage space) in four- to 16-bed dormitories. There's a top kitchen with a huge dining area and the busy Clash bar in the basement.

YHA London Oxford Street HOSTEL £
(Map p118; ☎020-7734 1618; www.yha.org.uk/hostel/london-oxford-street; 14 Noel St, W1; dm/tw from £18-36, tw £50-85; @📶; ⊖Oxford Circus) The most central of London's eight YHA hostels is also one of the most intimate with just 104 beds, and excellent shared facilities, including the fuchsia kitchen and the bright, funky lounge. Dormitories have three and four beds and there are doubles and twins. The in-house shop sells coffee and beer. Wi-fi (common areas) is free. Free daily walking tours too.

London St Pancras YHA HOSTEL £
(☎0345 371 9344; www.yha.org.uk; 79-81 Euston Rd, NW1; dm/r from £16/60; 📶; ⊖King's Cross St Pancras) This hostel with 186 beds spread over eight floors has modern, clean dorms sleeping four to six (nearly all with private facilities) and some private rooms. There's a good bar and cafe, although there are no self-catering facilities. Check out time is 10am.

Arosfa Hotel B&B ££
(☎020-7636 2115; www.arosfalondon.com; 83 Gower St, WC1; s/tw/tr/f from £90/135/155/210, d £140-175, incl breakfast; @📶; ⊖Goodge St) The Philippe Starck furniture and modern look in the lounge is more lavish than the decor in the hotel's 16 rooms, with cabin-like bathrooms in many of them. About half have been refurbished; they are small but remain good value. There are a couple of family rooms; room 4 looks on to a small but charming garden. Prices rise on Saturdays.

Jesmond Hotel B&B ££
(☎020-7636 3199; www.jesmondhotel.org.uk; 63 Gower St, WC1; s £75-95, d £95-125, tr £140-165, q £150-185, all incl breakfast; @📶; ⊖Goodge St) The rooms – cheapest with shared bathroom – at this popular, 15-room family-run Georgian hotel in Bloomsbury are basic but clean and cheerful, there's a small, pretty garden and the price tag is very attractive indeed. There's also laundry service, free wi-fi and good breakfasts for kicking off your London day. Location is highly central.

★**Haymarket Hotel** HOTEL £££
(Map p118; ☎020-7470 4000; www.firmdalehotels.com/hotels/london/haymarket-hotel; 1 Suffolk Pl, off Haymarket, SW1; r/ste from £335/505; ❄📶🏊; ⊖Piccadilly Circus) With the trademark colours and lines of hoteliers and designers Tim and Kit Kemp, the Haymarket is beautiful, with hand-painted Gournay wallpaper, signature fuchsia and green designs

Bloomsbury, St Pancras & Camden

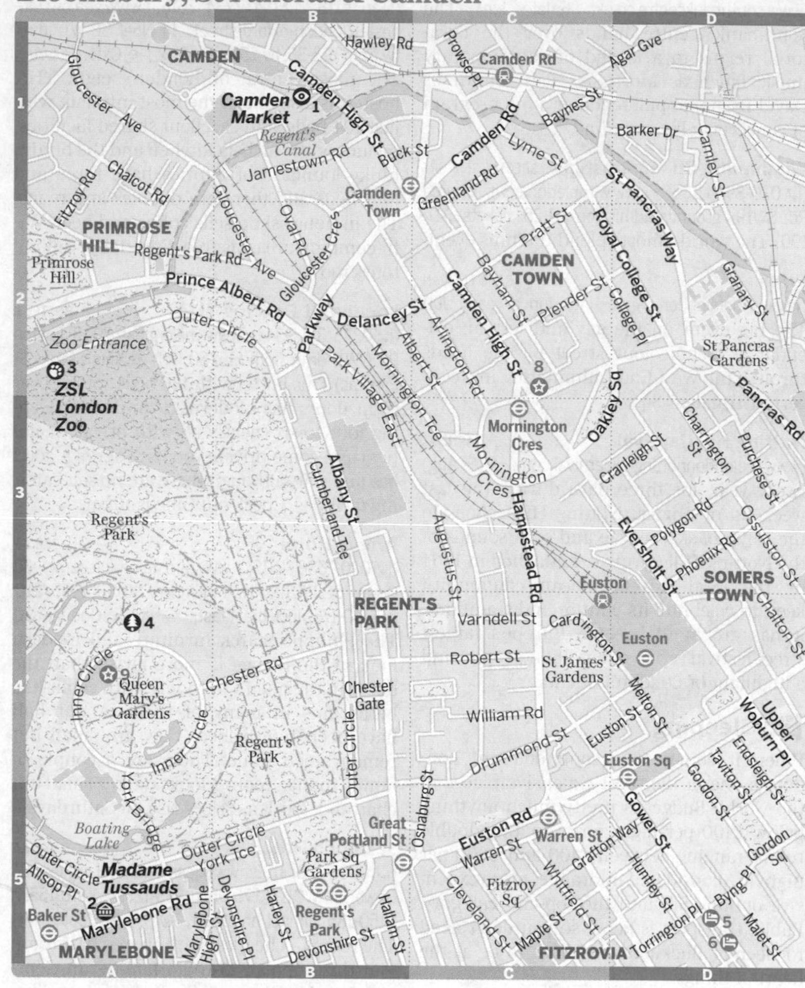

Bloomsbury, St Pancras & Camden

Top Sights

1 Camden Market B1
2 Madame Tussauds A5
3 ZSL London Zoo A2

Sights

4 Regent's Park A4

Sleeping

5 Arosfa Hotel D5
6 Jesmond Hotel D5
7 London St Pancras YHA E4

Entertainment

8 KOKO C2
9 Regent's Park Open Air Theatre A4

in the 50 guest rooms, a sensational 18m pool with mood lighting, an exquisite library lounge with honesty bar, and original artwork throughout. Just love the dog silhouettes on the chairs and bar stools.

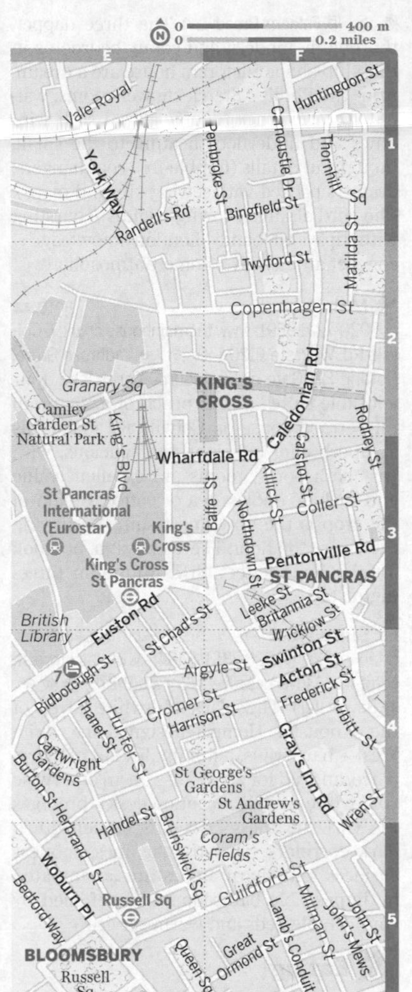

The City

London St Paul's YHA HOSTEL £

(Map p114; ☎020-7236 4965; www.yha.org.uk/hostel/london-st-pauls; 36 Carter Lane, EC4; dm/tw/d from £18/65/89; @ 📶; ⊖St Paul's) This 213-bed hostel is housed in the former boarding school for choirboys from St Paul's Cathedral, almost next door. Dorms have between three and 11 beds, and twins and doubles are available. There's a great lounge, licensed cafeteria (breakfast £5.25, dinner from £7 to £10) but no kitchen – and lots and lots of stairs (and no lift). Seven-night maximum stay.

Hotel Indigo London – Tower Hill HOTEL ££

(Map p114; ☎020-7265 1014; www.hotelindigo.com; 142 Minories, EC3; r from £166; ❄ 📶; ⊖Aldgate) This branch of the US InterContinental group's boutique-hotel chain offers 46 differently styled rooms, all with four-poster beds and iPod docking stations. Larger-than-life drawings and photos of the neighbourhood won't let you forget where you are.

South Bank

Immediately south of the river is good if you want to immerse yourself in workaday London and still be central.

St Christopher's Village HOSTEL £

(Map p114; ☎020-7939 9710; www.st-christophers.co.uk; 163 Borough High St, SE1; dm/r incl breakfast from £11.40/50; 📶; ⊖London Bridge) This 230-bed party-zone hostel has new bathrooms, fresh paint, pod beds with privacy curtains, reading lights, power sockets (British and European) and USB ports, and refurbished common areas. Its two bars, Belushi's and Dugout, are perennially popular. Dorms have four to 33 beds (following the introduction of triple bunks); breakfast and linen are included.

★**Citizen M** BOUTIQUE HOTEL ££

(Map p114; ☎020-3519 1680; www.citizenm.com/london-bankside; 20 Lavington St, SE1; r £109-249; ❄ @ 📶; ⊖Southwark) If Citizen M had a motto, it would be 'Less fuss, more comfort'. The hotel has done away with things it considers superfluous (room service, reception, heaps of space) and instead has gone all out on mattresses and bedding (heavenly super-king-sized beds), state-of-the-art technology (everything from mood lighting to TV is controlled through a tablet computer) and superb decor.

Kensington & Hyde Park

This classy area offers easy access to the museums and big-name fashion stores, but at a price that reflects the upmarket surroundings.

Lime Tree Hotel BOUTIQUE HOTEL ££

(☎020-7730 8191; www.limetreehotel.co.uk; 135-137 Ebury St, SW1; s incl breakfast £120-160, d & tw £180-210, tr £230; @ 📶; ⊖Victoria) Family run for 30 years, this beautiful 25-bedroom Georgian town-house hotel is all comfort, British designs and understated elegance. Rooms are individually decorated, many with open fireplaces and sash windows, but some are smaller than others, so enquire. There is a lovely back garden for late-afternoon rays (picnics encouraged on summer evenings). Rates include a hearty full-English breakfast. No lift.

★**Number Sixteen** HOTEL £££
(Map p122; ☎020-7589 5232; www.firmdalehotels.com/hotels/london/number-sixteen; 16 Sumner Pl, SW7; s from £192, d £240-396; ❄@📶; ⊖South Kensington) With uplifting splashes of colour, choice art and a sophisticated-but-fun design ethos, Number Sixteen is simply ravishing. There are 41 individually designed rooms, a cosy drawing room and a fully stocked library. And wait till you see the idyllic, long back garden set around a fountain, or sit down for breakfast in the light-filled conservatory. Great amenities for families.

Clerkenwell, Shoreditch & Spitalfields

★**Hoxton Hotel** HOTEL ££
(Map p114; ☎020-7550 1000; www.hoxtonhotels.com; 81 Great Eastern St, EC2; r £69-259; ❄📶; ⊖Old St) In the heart of hip Shoreditch, this sleek hotel takes the easyJet approach to selling its rooms – book long enough ahead and you might pay just £49. The 210 renovated rooms are small but stylish, with flatscreen TVs, a desk, fridge with complimentary bottled water and milk, and breakfast (orange juice, granola, yoghurt, banana) in a bag delivered to your door.

Notting Hill & West London

West London's Earl's Court district is lively, cosmopolitan and so popular with travelling Antipodeans that it's been nicknamed Kangaroo Valley.

Safestay Holland Park HOSTEL £
(☎020-3326 8471; www.safestay.co.uk; Holland Walk, W8; dm £20, r from £60; 📶; ⊖High St Kensington or Holland Park) This new place replaced the long-serving YHA hostel running here since 1958. With a bright and bold colour design, the hostel has four- to eight-bunk dorm rooms, twin-bunk and single-bunk rooms, free wi-fi in the lobby and a fabulous location in the Jacobean east wing of Holland House in **Holland Park** (Ilchester Pl).

★**Barclay House** B&B ££
(☎077 6742 0943; www.barclayhouselondon.com; 21 Barclay Rd, SW6; s from £110, d £135-168; @📶; ⊖Fulham Broadway) The three dapper, thoroughly modern and comfy bedrooms in this ship-shape Victorian house are a dream, from the Phillipe Starck shower rooms, walnut furniture, new double-glazed sash windows and underfloor heating to the small, thoughtful details (fumble-free coat hangers, drawers packed with sewing kits and maps). The cordial, music-loving owners – bursting with tips and handy London knowledge – concoct an inclusive, homely atmosphere.

★**Main House** HOTEL ££
(☎020-7221 9691; www.themainhouse.co.uk; 6 Colville Rd, W11; ste £120-150; 📶; ⊖Ladbroke Grove, Notting Hill Gate or Westbourne Park) The four adorable suites at this peach of a Victorian midterrace house on Colville Rd make this a superb choice. Bright and spacious, with vast bathrooms, rooms are excellent value and include endless tea or coffee. Cream of the crop is the uppermost suite, occupying the entire top floor. There's no sign, but look for the huge letters 'SIX'. Minimum three-night stay.

La Suite West BOUTIQUE HOTEL £££
(Map p122; ☎020-7313 8484; www.lasuitewest.com; 41-51 Inverness Tce, W2; r £129-279; ❄@📶; ⊖Bayswater) The black-and-white foyer of the Anouska Hempel–designed La Suite West – bare walls, a minimalist slit of a fireplace, an iPad for guests' use on an otherwise void white-marble reception desk – presages the OCD neatness of rooms hidden down dark corridors. The straight lines, spotless surfaces and sharp angles are accentuated by impeccable bathrooms and softened by comfortable beds and warm service.

Eating

Dining out in London has become so fashionable that you can hardly open a menu without banging into a celebrity chef. The range and quality of eating options has increased enormously over the last few decades.

West End

★**Shoryu** NOODLES £
(Map p118; ☎none; www.shoryuramen.com; 9 Regent St, SW1; mains £9.50-14.90; ⏲11.15am-midnight Mon-Sat, to 10.30pm Sun; ⊖Piccadilly Circus) Compact, well-mannered noodle-parlour Shoryu draws in reams of noodle diners to feast at its wooden counters and small tables. It's busy, friendly and efficient, with helpful

and informative staff. Fantastic *tonkotsu* pork-broth ramen is the name of the game here, sprinkled with *nori* (dried, pressed seaweed), spring onion, *nitamago* (soft-boiled eggs) and sesame seeds. No bookings.

Mildreds VEGETARIAN £

(Map p118; 020-7484 1634; www.mildreds.co.uk; 45 Lexington St, W1; mains £7-12; noon-11pm Mon-Sat; ; Oxford Circus, Piccadilly Circus) Central London's most inventive vegetarian restaurant, Mildred's heaves at lunchtime so don't be shy about sharing a table in the skylit dining room. Expect the likes of Sri Lankan sweet-potato and cashew-nut curry, pumpkin and ricotta ravioli, Middle Eastern meze, wonderfully exotic (and filling) salads and delicious stir-fries. There are also vegan and gluten-free options.

★Brasserie Zédel FRENCH ££

(Map p118; 020-7734 4888; www.brasseriezedel.com; 20 Sherwood St, W1; mains £13.50-25.75; 11.30am-midnight Mon-Sat, to 11pm Sun; ; Piccadilly Circus) This brasserie in the renovated art deco ballroom of a former hotel is the Frenchest eatery west of Calais. Favourites include *choucroute Alsacienne* (sauerkraut with sausages and charcuterie £14) or a straight-up *steak haché, sauce au poivre et frites* (chopped steak with pepper sauce; £9.75). Set menus (£9.75/12.75 for two/three courses) and *plats du jour* (£14.25) offer excellent value, in a terrific setting.

★Palomar ISRAELI ££

(Map p118; 020-7439 8777; http://thepalomar.co.uk; 34 Rupert St, W1; mains £7-16.50; noon-2.30pm & 5.30-11pm Mon-Sat, 12.30-3.30pm & 6-9pm Sun; ; Piccadilly Circus) The buzzing vibe at this good-looking celebration of modern-day Jerusalem cuisine (in all its inflections) is infectious, but we could enjoy the dishes cooked up here in a deserted warehouse and still come back for more. The Jerusalem-style polenta and Josperised aubergine are fantastic, but portions are smallish, so sharing is the way to go. Reservations essential.

★Cafe Murano ITALIAN ££

(Map p118; 020-3371 5559; www.cafemurano.co.uk; 33 St James's St, SW1; mains £18-25, 2/3-course set meal £19/23; noon-3pm & 5.30-11pm Mon-Sat, 11.30am-4pm Sun; Green Park) The setting may seem somewhat demure at this superb and busy restaurant, but with such a sublime North Italian menu on offer, it sees no need to be flash and of-the-moment. You get what you come for, and the beef carpaccio, crab linguine and lamb ragu are as close to culinary perfection as you can get. Reserve.

★Barrafina SPANISH ££

(Map p118; 020-7440 1456; www.barrafina.co.uk; 10 Adelaide St, WC2; tapas £6.50-15.80; noon-3pm & 5-11pm Mon-Sat, 1-3.30pm & 5.30-10pm Sun; Embankment or Leicester Sq) With no reservations, you may need to get in line for an hour or so at this restaurant that does a brisk service in some of the best tapas in town. Divine mouthfuls are served on each plate, from the stuffed courgette flower to the suckling pig and crab on toast, so diners dig their heels in, prepared to wait.

★Claridge's Foyer & Reading Room BRITISH £££

(Map p118; 020-7107 8886; www.claridges.co.uk; 49-53 Brook St, W1; afternoon tea £68, with champagne £79; afternoon tea 2.45-5.30pm; ; Bond St) Extend that pinkie finger to partake in afternoon tea within the classic art deco–style foyer of this landmark hotel where the gentle clink of fine porcelain and champagne glasses could be a defining memory of your trip to London. The setting is gorgeous and dress is elegant, smart casual (ripped jeans and baseball caps won't get served).

South Bank

For a feed with a local feel, head to Borough Market or Bermondsey St.

M Manze BRITISH £

(www.manze.co.uk; 87 Tower Bridge Rd, SE1; mains from £2.95; 11am-2pm Mon, 10.30am-2pm Tue-Thu, 10am-2.30pm Fri & Sat; Borough) Dating to 1902, M Manze started off as an ice-cream seller before moving on to selling its legendary staples: minced-beef pies. It's a classic operation, from the ageing tilework to the traditional workers' menu: pie and mash, pie and liquor (a parsley-based sauce), and you can take your eels jellied or stewed. Vegetarian pies available. Eat in or take away.

★Skylon MODERN EUROPEAN ££

(Map p114; 020-7654 7800; www.skylon-restaurant.co.uk; 3rd fl, Royal Festival Hall, Southbank Centre, Belvedere Rd, SE1; 3-course menu grill/restaurant £25/30; grill noon-11pm Mon-Sat, to 10.30pm Sun, restaurant noon-2.30pm & 5.30-10.30pm Mon-Sat & noon-4pm Sun; ; Waterloo) This excellent restaurant inside the Royal Festival Hall is divided into grill and fine-dining sections by a large **bar** (noon-1am Mon-Sat, to 10.30pm Sun). The decor is cutting-edge 1950s: muted colours and period chairs (trendy then, trendier now) while floor-to-ceiling windows bathe you in magnificent views of the Thames and the city. The six-course restaurant tasting menu costs £59. Booking is advised.

Kensington & Hyde Park

★Pimlico Fresh CAFE £
(020-7932 0030; 86 Wilton Rd, SW1; mains from £4.50; 7.30am-7.30pm Mon-Fri, 9am-6pm Sat & Sun; Victoria) This friendly two-room cafe will see you right whether you need breakfast (French toast, bowls of porridge laced with honey or maple syrup), lunch (homemade quiches and soups, 'things' on toast) or just a good old latte and cake.

Comptoir Libanais LEBANESE £
(Map p122; 020-7225 5006; www.comptoirlibanais.com; 1-5 Exhibition Rd, SW7; mains from £8.50; 8.30am-midnight Mon-Sat, to 10.30pm Sun; ; South Kensington) If your battery's flat hoovering up South Kensington's museums, this colourful, good-looking and brisk restaurant just round the corner from the tube station is excellent for Lebanese meze, wraps, tagine (slow-cooked casseroles), *mana'esh* (flatbreads), salads and fine breakfasts. When the sun's shining, the outside tables quickly fill with munchers and people-watchers. There are no reservations, so just pitch up (elbows sharpened).

★Rabbit MODERN BRITISH ££
(020-3750 0172; www.rabbit-restaurant.com; 172 King's Rd, SW3; mains £6-24, set lunch £13.50; noon-midnight Tue-Sat, 6-11pm Mon, noon-6pm Sun; ; Sloane Sq) Three brothers grew up on a farm. One became a farmer, another a butcher, while the third worked in hospitality. So they pooled their skills and came up with Rabbit, a breath of fresh air in upmarket Chelsea. The restaurant rocks the agri-chic (yes) look and the creative, seasonal modern British cuisine is fabulous.

★Dinner by Heston Blumenthal MODERN BRITISH £££
(Map p122; 020-7201 3833; www.dinnerbyheston.com; Mandarin Oriental Hyde Park, 66 Knightsbridge, SW1; 3-course set lunch £45, mains £28-44; noon-2pm & 6-10.15pm Mon-Fri, noon-2.30pm & 6-10.30pm Sat & Sun; ; Knightsbridge) Sumptuously presented Dinner is a gastronomic tour de force, taking diners on a journey through British culinary history (with inventive modern inflections). Dishes carry historical dates to convey context, while the restaurant interior is a design triumph, from the glass-walled kitchen and its overhead clock mechanism to the large windows looking onto the park. Book ahead.

Clerkenwell, Shoreditch & Spitalfields

From the hit-and-miss Bangladeshi restaurants of Brick Lane to the Vietnamese strip on Kingsland Rd, the East End's cuisine is as multicultural as its residents. Clerkenwell's hidden gems are well worth digging for; Exmouth Market is a good place to start.

★St John BRITISH ££
(Map p114; 020-7251 0848; www.stjohngroup.uk.com/spitalfields; 26 St John St, EC1M; mains £14.80-24.90; noon-3pm & 6-11pm Mon-Fri, 6-11pm Sat, 12.30-4pm Sun; Farringdon) Whitewashed brick walls, high ceilings and simple wooden furniture keep diners free to concentrate on St John's famous nose-to-tail dishes. Serves are big, hearty and a celebration of England's culinary past. Don't miss the signature roast bone marrow and parsley salad (£8.90).

Poppie's FISH & CHIPS ££
(Map p114; www.poppiesfishandchips.co.uk; 6-8 Hanbury St, E1; mains £12.20-15.90; 11am-11pm; Liverpool St) This glorious re-creation of a 1950s East End chippy comes complete with waitresses in pinnies and hairnets, and Blitz memorabilia. As well as the usual fishy suspects, it does those old-time London staples – jellied eels and mushy peas – plus kid-pleasing, sweet-tooth desserts (sticky toffee pudding or apple pie with ice cream) and a wine list.

Notting Hill & West London

★Potli INDIAN £
(020-8741 4328; www.potli.co.uk; 319-321 King St, W6; weekday 1-/2-course set lunch £7.95/10.95, mains £7.50-15; noon-2.30pm Mon-Sat, 6-10.15pm Mon-Thu, 5.30-10.30pm Fri & Sat, noon-10pm Sun; ; Stamford Brook or Ravenscourt Park) With its scattered pieces from Mumbai's Thieves Market, Indian-market-kitchen/bazaar cuisine, home-made pickles and spice mixes, plus an accent on genuine flavour, tantalising

ROLL OUT THE BARROW

London has more than 350 markets selling everything from antiques and curios to flowers and fish. Some, such as Camden and Portobello Road, are full of tourists, while others exist just for the locals.

Portobello Road Market (www.portobellomarket.org; Portobello Rd, W10; ⏲8am-6.30pm Mon-Wed, Fri & Sat, to 1pm Thu; ⊖Notting Hill Gate or Ladbroke Grove) Lovely on a warm summer's day, Portobello Road Market is an iconic London attraction with an eclectic mix of street food, fruit and veg, antiques, curios, collectables, vibrant fashion and trinkets. Although the shops along Portobello Rd open daily and the fruit and veg stalls (from Elgin Cres to Talbot Rd) only close on Sunday, the busiest day by far is Saturday, when antique dealers set up shop (from Chepstow Villas to Elgin Cres).

Columbia Road Flower Market (Map p114; www.columbiaroad.info; Columbia Rd, E2; ⏲8am-3pm Sun; ⊖Hoxton) A wonderful explosion of colour and life, this weekly market sells a beautiful array of flowers, pot plants, bulbs, seeds and everything you might need for the garden. It's a lot of fun and the best place to hear proper Cockney barrow-boy banter ('We got flowers cheap enough for ya muvver-in-law's grave' etc). It gets really packed, so go as early as you can, or later on, when the vendors sell off the cut flowers cheaply.

Camden Market (www.camdenmarket.com; Camden High St, NW1; ⏲10am-6pm; ⊖Camden Town or Chalk Farm) Although – or perhaps because – it stopped being cutting-edge several thousand cheap leather jackets ago, Camden Market attracts millions of visitors each year and is one of London's most popular attractions. What started out as a collection of attractive craft stalls by Camden Lock on the Regent's Canal now extends most of the way from Camden Town tube station to Chalk Farm tube station.

Old Spitalfields Market (Map p114; www.oldspitalfieldsmarket.com; Commercial St, E1; ⏲10am-5pm Mon-Fri & Sun, 11am-5pm Sat; ⊖Liverpool St) Traders have been hawking their wares here since 1638 and it's still one of London's best markets. Today's covered market was built in the late 19th century, with the more modern development added in 2006. Sundays are the biggest and best days, but Thursdays are good for antiques and Fridays for independent fashion. There are plenty of food stalls, too.

Sunday UpMarket (Map p114; www.sundayupmarket.co.uk; Old Truman Brewery, 91 Brick Lane, E1; ⏲11am-6pm Sat, 10am-5pm Sun; ⊖Shoreditch High St) The best of all the Sunday markets, this workaday covered car park fills up with young designers selling their wares, quirky crafts and a drool-inducing array of food stalls.

Broadway Market (www.broadwaymarket.co.uk; Broadway Market, E8; ⏲9am-5pm Sat; 🚌394) There's been a market down this pretty street since the late 19th century. The focus these days is artisan food, arty knick-knacks, books, records and vintage clothing. Stock up on edible treats then head to **London Fields** (Richmond Rd, E8; ⊖Hackney Central) for a picnic.

Potli deftly captures the aromas of its culinary home. Downstairs there's an open kitchen and service is friendly, but it's the alluring menu – where flavours are teased into a rich and authentic India culinary experience – that's the real crowd-pleaser.

★**Geales** SEAFOOD ££
(Map p122; ☎020-7727 7528; www.geales.com; 2 Farmer St, W8; 2-course express lunch £9.95, mains £9-37.50; ⏲noon-3pm & 6-10.30pm Tue-Fri, noon-10.30pm Sat, noon-4pm Sun; 📶; ⊖Notting Hill Gate) Frying since 1939 – a bad year for the restaurant trade – Geales has endured with its quiet location on the corner of Farmer St in Hillgate Village. The succulent fish in crispy batter is a fine catch from a menu which also runs to other British faves such as pork belly with apple sauce and crackling, and beef and bacon pie.

Drinking & Nightlife

As long as there's been a city, Londoners have loved to drink, and – as history shows – often immoderately. Clubland is no longer confined to the West End, with megaclubs scattered throughout the city wherever there's a venue big enough, cheap enough or quirky enough to hold them. The big nights are Friday and Saturday. Admission prices vary widely; it's often cheaper to arrive early or pre-book tickets.

West End

★Dukes London COCKTAIL BAR

(Map p118; 020-7491 4840; www.dukeshotel.com/dukes-bar; Dukes Hotel, 35 St James's Pl, SW1; 2-11pm Mon-Sat, 4-10.30pm Sun; ; Green Park) Sip to-die-for martinis like royalty in a gentleman's-club-like ambience at this tidily tucked-away classic bar where white-jacketed masters mix up some awesomely good preparations. Ian Fleming used to drink here, perhaps perfecting his 'shaken, not stirred' Bond maxim. Smokers can ease into the secluded Cognac and Cigar Garden to light up (but cigars must be purchased here).

★American Bar BAR

(Map p118; www.thebeaumont.com/dining/american-bar; The Beaumont, Brown Hart Gardens, W1; 11.30am-midnight Mon-Sat, to 11pm Sun; ; Bond St) Sip a bourbon or a classic cocktail in the classic 1930s art-deco striped-walnut ambience of this stylish bar at the hallmark **Beaumont hotel** (020-7499 1001; d/studio/ste incl breakfast from £395/625/900;). It's central, period and like a gentleman's club, but far from stuffy. Only a few years old, the American Bar feels like its been pouring drinks since the days of the Eton Crop and the Jazz Age.

Purl COCKTAIL BAR

(Map p122; 020-7935 0835; www.purl-london.com; 50-54 Blandford St, W1; 5-11.30pm Mon-Thu, to midnight Fri & Sat; Baker St, Bond St) Purl is a fabulous underground drinking den. Decked out in vintage furniture, it serves original and intriguingly named cocktails (What's Your Poison? or Mr Hyde's No 2) and a punch of the day. It's all subdued lighting and hushed-tone conversations, which only adds to the mysterious air. Booking recommended.

Connaught Bar COCKTAIL BAR

(Map p118; 020-7314 3419; www.the-connaught.co.uk/mayfair-bars/connaught-bar; Connaught Hotel, Carlos Pl, W1; 11am-1am Mon-Sat, to midnight Sun; Bond St) Drinkers who know their stuff single out the Martini trolley for particular praise, but almost everything at this sumptuous bar at the exclusive and very British Connaught Hotel gets the nod: lavish deco-inspired lines, excruciating attention to detail, faultless service, and some of the best drinks in town. Cocktails, classic and those given a thoroughly contemporary twist, start at £17.

Village GAY

(Map p118; 020-7478 0530; www.village-soho.co.uk; 81 Wardour St, W1; 5pm-1am Mon & Tue, to 2am Wed-Sat, to 11.30pm Sun; Piccadilly Circus) The Village is always up for a party, whatever the night of the week. There are karaoke nights, 'discolicious' nights, go-go-dancer nights – take your pick. And if you can't wait to strut your stuff until the clubs open, there is a dance floor downstairs, complete with pole, of course. Open till 3am on the last weekend of the month.

South Bank

★Little Bird Gin COCKTAIL BAR

(Map p114; www.littlebirdgin.com; Maltby St, SE1; 10am-4pm Sat, from 11am Sun; London Bridge) This South London–based distillery opens a pop-up bar in a workshop at **Maltby Street Market** (www.maltby.st; dishes £5-10; 9am-4pm Sat, 11am-4pm Sun) to ply merry punters with devilishly good cocktails (£5 to £7), served in jam jars or apothecary's glass bottles.

★Oblix BAR

(Map p114; www.oblixrestaurant.com; 32nd fl, Shard, 31 St Thomas St, SE1; noon-11pm; London Bridge) On the 32nd floor of the Shard (p117), Oblix offers mesmerising vistas of London. You can come for anything from a coffee (£3.50) to a cocktail (from £10) and enjoy virtually the same views as the official viewing galleries of the Shard (but at a reduced cost and with the added bonus of a drink). Live music every night from 7pm.

★40 Maltby Street WINE BAR

(Map p114; www.40maltbystreet.com; 40 Maltby St, SE1; 5.30-10pm Wed & Thu, 12.30-2.30pm & 5.30-10pm Fri, 11am-10pm Sat; London Bridge) This tunnel-like wine-bar-cum-kitchen sits under the railway arches that take trains in and out of London Bridge. It is first and foremost a wine importer focusing on organic vintages but its hospitality venture has become incredibly popular. The wine recommendations are obviously top-notch (most of them by the glass) and the food – simple, gourmet bistro fare – is spot on.

GAY & LESBIAN LONDON

Generally, London's a safe place for lesbians and gays. It's rare to encounter any problem with sharing rooms or holding hands in the inner city, although it would pay to keep your wits about you at night and be conscious of your surroundings.

The West End, particularly Soho, is the visible centre of gay and lesbian London, with numerous venues clustered around Old Compton St – but many other areas have their own miniscenes.

The easiest way to find out what's going on is to pick up the free press from a venue *(Boyz, QX)*; the gay section of *Time Out* (www.timeout.com/london/lgbt) is also useful.

Clerkenwell, Shoreditch & Spitalfields

★XOYO CLUB

(Map p114; www.xoyo.co.uk; 32-37 Cowper St, EC2A; 9pm-4am Fri & Sat, hours vary Sun-Thu; Old St) This fantastic Shoreditch warehouse club throws together a pulsingly popular mix of gigs, club nights and art events. Always buzzing, the varied line-up – expect indie bands, hip-hop, electro, dubstep and much in between – attracts a mix of clubbers, from skinny-jeaned hipsters to more mature hedonists (but no suits).

★Zetter Townhouse Cocktail Lounge COCKTAIL BAR

(Map p114; 020-7324 4545; www.thezettertownhouse.com; 49-50 St John's Sq, EC1V; 7.30am-12.45am; ; Farringdon) Tucked away behind an unassuming door on St John's Sq, this ground-floor bar is quirkily decorated with plush armchairs, stuffed animal heads and a legion of lamps. The cocktail list takes its theme from the area's distilling history – recipes of yesteryear and homemade tinctures and cordials are used to create interesting and unusual tipples. House cocktails are all £10.50.

Fabric CLUB

(www.fabriclondon.com; 77a Charterhouse Street, EC1M; £5-25; 11pm-7am Fri-Sun; Farringdon or Barbican) London's leading club, Fabric's three separate dance floors in a huge converted cold store opposite Smithfield meat market draws impressive queues (buy tickets online). FabricLive (on selected Fridays) rumbles with drum and bass and dubstep, while Fabric (usually on Saturdays but also on selected Fridays) is the club's signature live DJ night. Sunday's WetYourSelf! delivers house, techno and electronica.

★Jerusalem Tavern PUB

(Map p114; www.stpetersbrewery.co.uk; 55 Britton St, EC1M; 11am-11pm Mon-Fri; ; Farringdon) Pick a wood-panelled cubicle to park yourself in at this tiny and highly atmospheric pub housed in a building dating to 1720, and select from the fantastic beverages brewed by St Peter's Brewery in North Suffolk. Be warned, it's hugely popular and often very crowded.

★Ye Olde Mitre PUB

(Map p114; www.yeoldemitreholborn.co.uk; 1 Ely Ct, EC1N; 11am-11pm Mon-Fri; ; Farringdon) A delightfully cosy historic pub with an extensive beer selection, tucked away in a backstreet off Hatton Garden, Ye Olde Mitre was built in 1546 for the servants of Ely Palace. There's no music, so the rooms only echo with amiable chit-chat. Queen Elizabeth I danced around the cherry tree by the bar, they say. Closed Saturday and Sunday.

★Worship St Whistling Shop COCKTAIL BAR

(Map p114; 020-7247 0015; www.whistlingshop.com; 63 Worship St, EC2A; 5pm-midnight Mon & Tue, to 1am Wed & Thu, to 2am Fri & Sat; Old St) While the name is Victorian slang for a place selling illicit booze, this subterranean drinking den's master mixologists explore the experimental outer limits of cocktail chemistry and aromatic science, as well as concocting the classics. Many ingredients are made with the rotary evaporators in the on-site lab. Cocktail masterclasses also run.

Notting Hill, Bayswater & Paddington

★Troubadour BAR

(020-7341 6333; www.troubadour.co.uk; 263-267 Old Brompton Rd, SW5; cafe 8.30am-12.30am, club 8pm-12.30am or 2am; ; Earl's Court) On a compatible spiritual plane to Paris' Shakespeare and Company Bookshop, this eccentric, time-warped and convivial boho bar-cafe has been serenading drinkers since the 1950s. (Deep breath) Adele, Paolo Nutini, Joni Mitchell and (deeper breath) Jimi Hendrix and Bob Dylan have performed here, and there's still live music (folk, blues) and a large, pleasant garden open in summer.

Windsor Castle PUB

(Map p122; www.thewindsorcastlekensington.co.uk; 114 Campden Hill Rd, W11; ⏲noon-11pm Mon-Sat, to 10.30pm Sun; ; Notting Hill Gate) A classic tavern on the brow of Campden Hill Rd, this place has history, nooks and charm on tap. It's worth the search for its historic compartmentalised interior, roaring fire (in winter), delightful beer garden (in summer) and affable regulars (most always). According to legend, the bones of Thomas Paine (author of *Rights of Man*) are in the cellar.

Earl of Lonsdale PUB

(277-281 Portobello Rd, W11; ⏲noon-11pm Mon-Fri, 10am-11pm Sat, noon-10.30pm Sun; Notting Hill Gate or Ladbroke Grove) Named after the *bon vivant* founder of the AA (Automobile Association, *not* Alcoholics Anonymous), the Earl is peaceful during the day, with both old biddies and young hipsters inhabiting the reintroduced snugs. There are Samuel Smith's ales, a fantastic backroom with sofas, banquettes, open fires and a magnificent beer garden: all in all, a perfect bolthole for those traipsing Portobello Rd.

Greenwich & South London

★Cutty Sark Tavern PUB

(020-8858 3146; www.cuttysarkse10.co.uk; 4-6 Ballast Quay, SE10; ⏲11.30am-11pm Mon-Sat, noon-10.30pm Sun; ; DLR Cutty Sark) Housed in a delightful bow-windowed, wood-beamed Georgian building directly on the Thames, the Cutty Sark is one of the few independent pubs left in Greenwich. Half a dozen cask-conditioned ales on tap line the bar, there's an inviting riverside seating area opposite and an upstairs dining room looking out on to glorious views. It's a 10-minute walk from the DLR station.

Ministry of Sound CLUB

(Map p114; 020-7740 8600; www.ministryofsound.com; 103 Gaunt St, SE1; £10-22; ⏲10pm-6.30am Fri, 11am-7am Sat; ; Elephant & Castle) This legendary club-cum-enormous-global-brand (four bars, three dance floors) lost some 'edge' in the early noughties but, after pumping in top DJs, firmly rejoined the top club ranks. Fridays is the Gallery trance night, while Saturday sessions offer the crème de la crème of house, electro and techno DJs.

☆ Entertainment

Theatre

London is a world capital for theatre and there's a lot more than mammoth musicals to tempt you into the West End. On performance days, you can buy half-price tickets for West End productions (cash only) from the official agency **Tkts Leicester Sq** (www.tkts.co.uk/leicester-square; The Lodge, Leicester Square, WC2; ⏲10am-7pm Mon-Sat, 11am-4.30pm Sun; Leicester Sq). The booth is the one with the clock tower; beware of touts selling dodgy tickets. For more, see www.officiallondontheatre.co.uk or www.theatremonkey.com.

★Shakespeare's Globe THEATRE

(Map p114; 020-7401 9919; www.shakespearesglobe.com; 21 New Globe Walk, SE1; seats £20-45, standing £5; Blackfriars or London Bridge) If you love Shakespeare and the theatre, the Globe (p116) will knock your theatrical socks off. This authentic Shakespearean theatre is a wooden 'O' without a roof over the central stage area, and although there are covered wooden bench seats in tiers around the stage, many people (there's room for 700) do as 17th-century 'groundlings' did, and stand in front of the stage.

National Theatre THEATRE

(Royal National Theatre; Map p114; 020-7452 3000; www.nationaltheatre.org.uk; South Bank, SE1; Waterloo) England's flagship theatre showcases a mix of classic and contemporary plays performed by excellent casts in three theatres (Olivier, Lyttelton and Dorfman). Artistic director Rufus Norris, who started in April 2015, made headlines in 2016 for announcing plans to stage a Brexit-based drama.

Old Vic THEATRE

(Map p114; 0844 871 7628; www.oldvictheatre.com; The Cut, SE1; Waterloo) American actor Kevin Spacey took the theatrical helm of this London theatre in 2003, giving it a new lease of life. He was succeeded in April 2015 by Matthew Warchus (who directed *Matilda the Musical* and the film *Pride*), whose aim is to bring an eclectic program to the theatre: expect new writing, as well as dynamic revivals of old works and musicals.

Young Vic THEATRE

(Map p114; ☎020-7922 2922; www.youngvic.org; 66 The Cut, SE1; ⊖Southwark or Waterloo) This ground breaking theatre is as much about showcasing and discovering new talent as it is about people discovering theatre. The Young Vic features actors, directors and plays from across the world, many tackling contemporary political and cultural issues, such as the death penalty, racism or corruption, and often blending dance and music with acting.

Donmar Warehouse THEATRE

(Map p118; ☎0844 871 7624; www.donmarwarehouse.com; 41 Earlham St, WC2; ⊖Covent Garden) The cosy Donmar Warehouse is London's 'thinking person's theatre'. Current artistic director Josie Rourke has staged some intriguing and successful productions, including the well-received comedy *My Night with Reg*.

Live Music

★606 Club BLUES, JAZZ

(☎020-7352 5953; www.606club.co.uk; 90 Lots Rd, SW10; ⏲7-11.15pm Sun-Thu, 8pm-12.30am Fri & Sat; 🚆Imperial Wharf) Named after its old address on King's Rd, which cast a spell over jazz lovers London-wide back in the '80s, this fantastic, tucked-away basement jazz club and restaurant gives centre stage to contemporary British-based jazz musicians nightly. The club can only serve alcohol to people who are dining and it is highly advisable to book to get a table.

★KOKO LIVE MUSIC

(www.koko.uk.com; 1a Camden High St, NW1; ⊖Mornington Cres) Once the legendary Camden Palace, where Charlie Chaplin, the Goons and the Sex Pistols performed, KOKO is maintaining its reputation as one of London's better gig venues. The theatre has a dance floor and decadent balconies and attracts an indie crowd with Club NME on Friday. There are live bands most nights and it has a great roof terrace.

Ronnie Scott's JAZZ

(Map p118; ☎020-7439 0747; www.ronniescotts.co.uk; 47 Frith St, W1; ⏲7pm-3am Mon-Sat, 1-4pm & 8pm-midnight Sun; ⊖Leicester Sq or Tottenham Court Rd) Ronnie Scott originally opened his jazz club on Gerrard St in 1959 under a Chinese gambling den. It moved here six years later and became widely known as Britain's best jazz club. Gigs are at 8.15pm (8pm Sunday) with a second sitting at 11.15pm Friday and Saturday (check though), followed by the more informal Late, Late Show until 3am.

100 Club LIVE MUSIC

(Map p118; ☎020 7636 0933; www.the100club.co.uk; 100 Oxford St, W1; admission £8-20; ⏲check website for gig times; ⊖Oxford Circus or Tottenham Court Rd) This legendary London venue has always concentrated on jazz, but also features swing and rock. It's showcased Chris Barber, BB King and the Stones, and was at the centre of the punk revolution and the '90s indie scene. It hosts dancing swing gigs and local jazz musicians, the occasional big-name, where-are-they-now bands and top-league tributes.

Comedy

Comedy Store COMEDY

(Map p118; ☎0844 871 7699; www.thecomedystore.co.uk; 1a Oxendon St, SW1; admission £8-22.50; ⊖Piccadilly Circus) One of the first (and still one of the best) comedy clubs in London. Wednesday and Sunday night's Comedy Store Players is the most famous improvisation outfit in town, with the wonderful Josie Lawrence; on Thursdays, Fridays and Saturdays Best in Stand Up features the best on London's comedy circuit.

Soho Theatre COMEDY

(Map p118; ☎020-7478 0100; www.sohotheatre.com; 21 Dean St, W1; admission £8-25; ⊖Tottenham Court Rd) The Soho Theatre has developed a superb reputation for showcasing new comedy-writing talent and comedians. It's also hosted some top-notch stand-up or sketch-based comedians including Alexei Sayle and Doctor Brown, plus cabaret.

Classical Music, Opera & Dance

Royal Albert Hall CONCERT VENUE

(Map p122; ☎0845 401 5034; www.royalalberthall.com; Kensington Gore, SW7; ⊖South Kensington) This splendid Victorian concert hall hosts classical-music, rock and other performances, but is famously the venue for the BBC-sponsored Proms. Booking is possible, but from mid-July to mid-September Proms punters queue for £5 standing (or 'promenading') tickets that go on sale one hour before curtain-up. Otherwise, the box office and prepaid-ticket collection counter are through door 12 (south side of the hall).

Royal Festival Hall CONCERT VENUE

(Map p114; ☎020-7960 4200; www.southbankcentre.co.uk; Southbank Centre, Belvedere Rd, SE1; 📶; ⊖Waterloo) Royal Festival Hall's amphitheatre seats 2500 and is one of the best places for catching world- and classical-music artists. The sound is fantastic, the programming impeccable and there are frequent free gigs in the wonderfully expansive foyer.

Barbican Centre PERFORMING ARTS
(Map p114; 020-7638 8891; www.barbican.org.uk; Silk St, EC2; box office 10am-8pm; Barbican) Home to the wonderful London Symphony Orchestra and its associate orchestra, the lesser-known BBC Symphony Orchestra, the arts centre also hosts scores of other leading musicians, focusing in particular on jazz, folk, world and soul artists. Dance is another strong point here, while film covers recent releases as well as film festivals and seasons.

Royal Opera House OPERA
(Map p118; 020-7304 4000; www.roh.org.uk; Bow St, WC2; tickets £4-270; Covent Garden) The £210 million redevelopment for the millennium gave classic opera a fantastic setting in London, and coming here for a night is a sumptuous – if pricey – affair. Although the program has been fluffed up by modern influences, the main attractions are still the opera and classical ballet – all are wonderful productions and feature world-class performers.

Sadler's Wells DANCE
(Map p114; 020-7863 8000; www.sadlerswells.com; Rosebery Ave, EC1R; Angel) A glittering modern venue that was, in fact, first established in 1683, Sadler's Wells is the most eclectic modern-dance and ballet venue in town, with experimental dance shows of all genres and from all corners of the globe. The Lilian Baylis Studio stages smaller productions.

Southbank Centre CONCERT VENUE
(Map p114; 0844 875 0073; www.southbankcentre.co.uk; Belvedere Rd, SE1; Waterloo) The Southbank Centre comprises several venues – Royal Festival Hall (p136), **Queen Elizabeth Hall** (QEH) and Purcell Room – hosting a wide range of performing arts. As well as regular programming, it organises fantastic festivals, including **London Wonderground** (circus and cabaret), **Udderbelly** (a festival of comedy in all its guises) and **Meltdown** (a music event curated by the best and most eclectic names in music).

Shopping

Department Stores

London's famous department stores are an attraction in themselves, even if you're not interested in buying.

★ **Fortnum & Mason** DEPARTMENT STORE
(Map p118; 020-7734 8040; www.fortnumandmason.com; 181 Piccadilly, W1; 10am-8pm Mon-Sat, 11.30am-6pm Sun; Piccadilly Circus) With its classic eau de nil colour scheme, London's oldest grocery store (established 1707), refuses to yield to modern times. Its staff still clad in old-fashioned tailcoats, its glamorous food hall supplied with hampers, cut marmalade, speciality teas and so forth, Fortnum and Mason is *the* quintessential London shopping experience.

Harrods DEPARTMENT STORE
(Map p122; 020-7730 1234; www.harrods.com; 87-135 Brompton Rd, SW1; 10am-9pm Mon-Sat, 11.30am-6pm Sun; Knightsbridge) Garish and stylish in equal measures, perennially crowded Harrods is an obligatory stop for visitors, from the cash-strapped to the big spenders. The stock is astonishing, as are many of the price tags. High on kitsch, the 'Egyptian Elevator' resembles something out of an *Indiana Jones* epic, while the memorial fountain to Dodi and Di (lower ground floor) merely adds surrealism.

Selfridges DEPARTMENT STORE
(Map p122; www.selfridges.com; 400 Oxford St, W1; 9.30am-10pm Mon-Sat, 11.30am-6pm Sun; Bond St) Selfridges loves innovation – it's famed for its inventive window displays by international artists, gala shows and, above all, its amazing range of products. It's the trendiest of London's one-stop shops, with labels such as Boudicca, Luella Bartley, Emma Cook, Chloé and Missoni; an unparalleled food hall; and Europe's largest cosmetics department.

Liberty DEPARTMENT STORE
(Map p118; www.liberty.co.uk; Great Marlborough St, W1; 10am-8pm Mon-Sat, noon-6pm Sun; Oxford Circus) An irresistible blend of contemporary styles in an old-fashioned mock-Tudor atmosphere, Liberty has a huge cosmetics department and an accessories floor, along with a breathtaking lingerie section, all at very inflated prices. A classic London souvenir is a Liberty fabric print, especially in the form of a scarf.

Harvey Nichols DEPARTMENT STORE

(Map p122; www.harveynichols.com; 109-125 Knightsbridge, SW1; ⏲10am-8pm Mon-Sat, 11.30am-6pm Sun; ⊖Knightsbridge) At London's temple of high fashion, you'll find Chloe and Balenciaga bags, the city's best denim range, a massive make-up hall with exclusive lines and great jewellery. The food hall and in-house restaurant, **Fifth Floor**, are, you guessed it, on the 5th floor. From 11.30am to midday, it's browsing time only.

Music

As befitting a global music capital, London has a wide range of music stores.

★Rough Trade East MUSIC

(Map p114; www.roughtrade.com; Old Truman Brewery, 91 Brick Lane, E1; ⏲9am-9pm Mon-Thu, to 8pm Fri, 10am-8pm Sat, 11am-7pm Sun; ⊖Shoreditch High St) No longer directly associated with the legendary record label (home to The Smiths, The Libertines and The Strokes, among many others), but this huge record store is still the best place to come for music of an indie, soul, electronica and alternative bent. Apart from the impressive selection of CDs and vinyl, it also dispenses coffee and stages promotional gigs.

Ray's Jazz MUSIC

(Map p118; www.foyles.co.uk; 2nd fl, 107 Charing Cross Rd, WC2; ⏲9.30am-9pm Mon-Sat, 11.30am-6pm Sun; ⊖Tottenham Court Rd) Quiet and serene with friendly and helpful staff, this shop on the 2nd floor of Foyles (p137) bookshop has one of the best jazz selections in London.

Bookshops

★John Sandoe Books BOOKS

(Map p122; ☎020-7589 9473; www.johnsandoe.com; 10 Blacklands Tce, SW3; ⏲9.30am-6.30pm Mon-Sat, 11am-5pm Sun; ⊖Sloane Sq) The perfect antidote to impersonal book superstores, this atmospheric three-storey bookshop in 18th-century premises is a treasure trove of literary gems and hidden surprises. It's been in business for almost 60 years and loyal customers swear by it, while knowledgeable booksellers spill forth with well-read pointers and helpful advice.

Hatchards BOOKS

(Map p118; ☎020-7439 9921; www.hatchards.co.uk; 187 Piccadilly, W1; ⏲9.30am-8pm Mon-Sat, noon-6.30pm Sun; ⊖Green Park or Piccadilly Circus) London's oldest bookshop dates to 1797. Holding three royal warrants (hence the portrait of the Queen), it's a stupendous independent bookstore, with a solid supply of signed editions and bursting at its smart seams with very browsable stock. There's a strong selection of first editions on the ground floor as well as regular literary events.

Foyles BOOKS

(Map p118; ☎020-7434 1574; www.foyles.co.uk; 107 Charing Cross Rd, WC2; ⏲9.30am-9pm Mon-Sat, 11.30am-6pm Sun; ⊖Tottenham Court Rd) With four miles of shelving, you can bet on finding even the most obscure of titles in London's most legendary bookshop. Once synonymous with chaos, Foyles long ago got its act together and in 2014 moved just down the road into the spacious former home of Central St Martins. Thoroughly redesigned, its stunning new home is a joy to explore.

ℹ Information

City of London Information Centre (Map p114; www.visitthecity.co.uk; St Paul's Churchyard, EC4; ⏲9.30am-5.30pm Mon-Sat, 10am-4pm Sun; 📶; ⊖St Paul's) Multilingual tourist information, fast-track tickets to City attractions and guided walks (adult/child £7/6).

ℹ Getting There & Away

BUS & COACH

The London terminus for long-distance buses (called 'coaches' in Britain) is **Victoria Coach Station** (164 Buckingham Palace Rd, SW1; ⊖Victoria).

TRAIN

Most of London's main-line rail terminals are linked by the Circle line on the tube. The terminals listed here serve the following destinations:

Charing Cross Canterbury

Euston Manchester, Liverpool, Carlisle, Glasgow

King's Cross Cambridge, Hull, York, Newcastle, Edinburgh, Aberdeen

Liverpool Street Stansted airport (Express), Cambridge

London Bridge Gatwick airport, Brighton

Marylebone Birmingham

Paddington Heathrow airport (Express), Oxford, Bath, Bristol, Exeter, Plymouth, Cardiff

St Pancras Gatwick and Luton airports, Brighton, Nottingham, Sheffield, Leicester, Leeds, Paris Eurostar

Victoria Gatwick airport (Express), Brighton, Canterbury

Waterloo Windsor, Winchester, Exeter, Plymouth

Getting Around

TO/FROM THE AIRPORTS

Gatwick

National Rail (www.nationalrail.co.uk) has regular train services to/from London Bridge (30 minutes, every 15 to 30 minutes), London King's Cross (55 minutes, every 15 to 30 minutes) and London Victoria (30 minutes, every 10 to 15 minutes). Fares vary depending on the time of travel and the train company, but allow £10 to £20 for a single.

EasyBus (www.easybus.co.uk) runs 19-seater minibuses to Gatwick every 15 to 20 minutes on two routes: one from Earl's Court/West Brompton and from Waterloo (one-way from £5.95). The service runs round the clock. Journey time averages 75 minutes.

Heathrow

The cheapest option from Heathrow is the Underground (tube). The Piccadilly line is accessible from every terminal (£6, one hour to central London, departing from Heathrow every five minutes from around 5am to 11.30pm).

Faster, and much more expensive, is the **Heathrow Express** (www.heathrowexpress.com; 1-way/return £22/36) train to Paddington station (15 minutes, every 15 minutes, 5.12am to 11.48pm). You can purchase tickets on board (£5 extra), from self-service machines (cash and credit cards accepted) at both stations, or online.

London City

The Docklands Light Railway (DLR) connects London City Airport to the tube network, taking 22 minutes to reach Bank station (£4 to £5). A black taxi costs around £35 to/from central London.

Luton

National Rail (www.nationalrail.co.uk) services (one-way from £10, 35 to 50 minutes, every six to 30 minutes, from 7am to 10pm) run from London Bridge and London King's Cross to Luton Airport Parkway station, where an airport shuttle bus (one-way £1.60) will take you to the airport in 10 minutes.

MAPS

There was a time when no Londoner would be without a pocket-sized *London A–Z* map-book. It's a great resource if you don't have a smartphone. You can buy them at newsstands and shops everywhere. For getting around the London Underground system (the tube), maps are free at underground stations.

EasyBus (www.easybus.co.uk) minibuses head from Victoria, Earl's Court and Baker St to Luton (from £4.95); allow 1½ hours, every 30 minutes. A taxi costs around £110 to £110.

Stansted

The **Stansted Express** (☎0845 8500150; www.stanstedexpress.com; one-way/return £19/32) train connects with Liverpool Street station (one way/return £19.10/31, 45 minutes, every 15 to 30 minutes, 5.30am to 12.30am).

EasyBus (www.easybus.co.uk) has services between Stansted and Baker St (from £4.95, 1¼ hours, every 15 minutes).

National Express (www.nationalexpress.com) runs buses to Stansted – the A9 goes to Liverpool Street station (from £10, 80 minutes, every 30 minutes). The A6 links with Victoria Coach Station (from £12, allow 1¾ hours, every 20 minutes).

BICYCLE

Central London is mostly flat, relatively compact and the traffic moves slowly – all of which makes it surprisingly good for cyclists. It can get terribly congested though, so you'll need to keep your wits about you – and lock your bike (including both wheels) securely.

Bikes can be hired from numerous self-service docking stations through **Santander Cycles** (☎0343 222 6666; www.tfl.gov.uk/modes/cycling/santander-cycles). The access fee is £2 for 24 hours. All you need is a credit or debit card. The first 30 minutes are free. It's then £2 for any additional period of 30 minutes.

CAR

Don't. As a visitor, it's very unlikely you'll need to drive in London. If you do, you'll incur an £11.50 per day congestion charge (7am to 6pm weekdays) simply to take a car into central London. If you're hiring a car to continue your trip around Britain, take the tube or train to a major airport and pick it up from there.

PUBLIC TRANSPORT

London's public transport is excellent, with tubes, trains, buses and boats getting you wherever you need to go. **TFL** (www.tfl.gov.uk), the city's public transport provider, is the glue that binds the network together. Its website has a handy journey planner and information on all services, including taxis.

Boat

Thames Clippers (www.thamesclippers.com) run regular services between Embankment, Waterloo, Blackfriars, Bankside, London Bridge, Tower Bridge, Canary Wharf, Greenwich, North Greenwich and Woolwich piers (adult/child £7.50/3.75), from 6.55am to around midnight (from 9.29am weekends).

OYSTER CARD

The Oyster Card is a smart card on which you can store credit towards 'prepay' fares, as well as Travelcards valid for periods from a day to a year. Oyster Cards are valid across the entire public transport network in London. When entering a station, simply touch your card on a reader (they have a yellow circle with the image of an Oyster Card on them) and then touch again on your way out. The system will deduct the appropriate amount of credit from your card. For bus journeys, you only need to touch once upon boarding.

The benefit is that fares for Oyster Card users are lower than standard ones. If you make many journeys during the day, you will never pay more than the appropriate Travelcard (peak or off peak) once the daily 'price cap' has been reached.

Oyster Cards can be bought (£5 refundable deposit required) and topped up at any Underground station, travel information centre or shop displaying the Oyster logo.

To get your deposit back along with any remaining credit, simply return your Oyster Card at a ticket booth.

Bus

Buses run regularly during the day, while less-frequent night buses (prefixed with the letter 'N') wheel into action when the tube stops. Cash is not accepted; instead you must pay with an Oyster Card, Travelcard or a contactless payment card. Fares are a flat £1.50, no matter the distance travelled. Buses stop on request, so clearly signal the driver with an outstretched arm.

Underground & Docklands Light Railway

The tube extends its subterranean tentacles throughout London and into the surrounding counties, with services running every few minutes from roughly 5.30am to 12.30am (7am to 11.30pm Sunday). Selected lines (the Victoria and Jubilee lines, plus most of the Piccadilly, Central and Northern lines) run all night on Fridays and Saturdays, with trains every 10 minutes or so.

The Docklands Light Railway (DLR) links the City to Docklands, Greenwich and London City Airport.

Lines are colour-coded (red for the Central Line, yellow for the Circle Line, black for the Northern Line and so on). It helps to know the direction you're travelling in (ie northbound or southbound, eastbound or westbound) as well as the terminus of the line you're travelling on. If you get confused, don't worry, as copies of the tube's famous map are posted everywhere, showing how the 14 different routes intersect. Be warned, however – the distances between stations on the tube map aren't remotely to scale.

Single fares cost from £2.40/4.90 with/without an Oyster Card.

TAXI

London's famous black cabs are available for hire when the yellow light above the windscreen is lit. Fares are metered, with flag fall of £2.60 and the additional rate dependent on time of day, distance travelled and taxi speed. A 1-mile trip will cost between £6 and £9.

Minicabs are a cheaper alternative to black cabs and will quote trip fares in advance. Only use drivers from proper agencies; licensed minicabs aren't allowed to tout for business or pick you up off the street without a booking. Apps such as **Uber** (www.uber.com) or **Kabbee** (www.kabbee.com) allow you to book a minicab in double-quick time.

Around London

'When you're tired of London, you're tired of life' said 18th-century Londoner Samuel Johnson. But he wasn't living in an age when too many days on the tube can leave you exhausted and grouchy. Luckily, the capital is surprisingly close to some excellent day trips; Windsor and Eton are two gems that are an easy train ride from the capital.

Windsor & Eton

POP 31,225

Dominated by the massive bulk of Windsor Castle, these twin towns have a rather surreal atmosphere, with the morning pomp and ceremony of the changing of the guards in Windsor and the sight of school boys dressed in formal tailcoats wandering the streets of Eton.

Sights

★Windsor Castle CASTLE

(☎0303 123 7304; www.royalcollection.org.uk; Castle Hill; adult/child £20.50/12; ⏱9.30am-5.30pm Mar-Oct, 9.45am-4.15pm Nov-Feb; ♿; 🚌702 from London Victoria, 🚆London Waterloo to Windsor & Eton Riverside, 🚆London Paddington to Windsor & Eton Central via Slough) The world's largest and oldest continuously occupied fortress, Windsor Castle is a majestic vision of battlements and towers. It's used for state occasions and

WORTH A TRIP

THE MAKING OF HARRY POTTER

Whether you're a fairweather fan or a full-on Pothead, this studio **tour** (☎0345 084 0900; www.wbstudiotour.co.uk; Studio Tour Dr, Leavesden, WD25; adult/child £39/31; ⏲9am-8pm, hours vary; Ⓟ) is well worth the admittedly hefty admission price. You'll need to pre-book your visit for an allocated timeslot and then allow two- to three hours to do the complex justice. It starts with a short film before you're ushered through giant doors into the actual set of Hogwarts' Great Hall – the first of many 'wow' moments. It's near Watford, northwest of London.

is one of the Queen's principal residences; if she's at home, the Royal Standard flies from the Round Tower. Join a free guided tour (every half-hour) of the wards or take a handheld multimedia tour of the lavish State Apartments and beautiful chapels. Some sections may be off-limits if in use. Book tickets online to avoid queues.

Eton College NOTABLE BUILDING
(☎01753-370100; www.etoncollege.com; High St, Eton; adult/child £10/free; ⏲tours Fri 2pm & 4pm May-Aug) Eton College is the largest and most famous public (meaning private and fee-paying) boys' school in England, and arguably the most enduring symbol of England's class system. High-profile alumni include 19 British prime ministers, countless princes, kings and maharajas, famous explorers, authors, actors and economists – among them Princes William and Harry, George Orwell, Ian Fleming, John Maynard Keynes, Bear Grylls and Eddie Redmayne.

Information

Tourist Office (☎01753-743900; www.windsor.gov.uk; Old Booking Hall, Windsor Royal Shopping Arcade, Thames St; ⏲10am-5pm Apr-Sep, to 4pm Oct-Mar) Pick up a heritage walk map (£2.20).

Getting There & Away

Trains from Windsor & Eton Riverside (Dachet Rd) go directly to London Waterloo (£10, one hour). Trains from Windsor & Eton Central (Thames St), changing at Slough for London Paddington (£10, 28 to 46 minutes), are quicker.

Canterbury

POP 55,240

Canterbury tops the charts for English cathedral cities. Many consider the World Heritage–listed cathedral that dominates its centre to be one of Europe's finest, and the town's narrow medieval alleyways, riverside gardens and ancient city walls are a joy to explore.

Sights

★Canterbury Cathedral CATHEDRAL
(www.canterbury-cathedral.org; adult/concession £12/10.50, tours £5/4, audio guide £4/3; ⏲9am-5.30pm Mon-Sat, 12.30-2.30pm Sun) A rich repository of more than 1400 years of Christian history, the Church of England's mother ship is a truly extraordinary place with an absorbing history. This Gothic cathedral, the highlight of the city's World Heritage Sites, is southeast England's top tourist attraction as well as a place of worship. It's also the site of English history's most famous murder: Archbishop Thomas Becket was done in here in 1170. Allow at least two hours to do the cathedral justice.

Sleeping

Kipp's Independent Hostel HOSTEL £
(☎01227-786121; www.kipps-hostel.com; 40 Nunnery Fields; dm £16.50-24.50, s £25-35, d £50-70; @📶) Occupying a red-brick town house in a quietish residential area less than a mile from the city centre, these superb backpacker digs enjoy a homely atmosphere, clean (though cramped) dorms and rave reviews.

Arthouse B&B B&B ££
(☎07976-725457; www.arthousebandb.com; 24 London Rd; r from £65; Ⓟ📶) A night at Canterbury's most laid-back digs, housed in a 19th-century fire station, is a bit like sleeping over at a really cool art student's pad. The theme is funky and eclectic, with furniture by local designers and artwork by the instantly likeable artist owners, who have a house-studio out the back.

Eating & Drinking

★Tiny Tim's Tearoom CAFE £
(www.tinytimstearoom.com; 34 St Margaret's St; mains £6-10.50; ⏲9.30am-5pm Tue-Sat, 10.30am-4pm Sun) It's no mean feat to be declared 'Kent Tearoom of the Year', but this swish 1930s cafe was awarded the accolade in 2015. It offers hungry shoppers big breakfasts

bursting with Kentish ingredients, and tiers of cakes, crumpets, cucumber sandwiches and scones plastered in clotted cream. On busy shopping days you are guaranteed to queue for a table.

★ **Deeson's** BRITISH ££

(☎ 01227-767854; www.deesonsrestaurant.co.uk; 25-26 Sun St; mains £15-24; ⌚ noon-3pm & 5-10pm) Put the words 'local', 'seasonal' and 'tasty' together and you have this superb British eatery. Local fruit and veg; award-winning wines, beers and ciders; fish from Kent's coastal waters; and the odd ingredient from the proprietor's own allotment are all served in a straightforward, contemporary setting just a Kentish apple's throw from the Canterbury Cathedral gates.

Information

Tourist Office (☎ 01227-862162; www.canterbury.co.uk; 18 High St; ⌚ 9am-5pm Mon-Wed, Fri & Sat, to 7pm Thu, 10am-5pm Sun) Located in the Beaney House of Art & Knowledge. Staff can help book accommodation, excursions and theatre tickets.

Getting There & Away

There are two train stations: Canterbury East for London Victoria and Dover; and Canterbury West for London's Charing Cross and St Pancras stations. Connections include Dover Priory (£8, 25 minutes, half-hourly), London St Pancras (£34.80, one hour, hourly) and London Victoria/Charing Cross (£29.30, 1¾ hours, two hourly).

Salisbury

POP 40,300

Centred on a majestic cathedral topped by the tallest spire in England, the gracious city of Salisbury has been an important provincial city for more than 1000 years.

Sights

★ **Salisbury Cathedral** CATHEDRAL

(☎ 01722-555120; www.salisburycathedral.org.uk; Cathedral Close; requested donation adult/child £7.50/free; ⌚ 9am-5pm Mon-Sat, noon-4pm Sun) England is endowed with countless stunning churches, but few can hold a candle to the grandeur and sheer spectacle of 13th-century Salisbury Cathedral. This early English Gothic-style structure has an elaborate exterior decorated with pointed arches and flying buttresses, and a sombre, austere interior designed to keep its congregation suitably pious. Its statuary and tombs are outstanding; don't miss the daily tower tours (p141) and the cathedral's original, 13th-century copy of the **Magna Carta** (⌚ 9.30am-4.30pm Mon-Sat, noon-3.45pm Sun).

DON'T MISS

AVEBURY

While the tour buses usually head straight to Stonehenge, prehistoric purists make for **Avebury Stone Circle**. Though it lacks the dramatic trilithons ('gateways') of its sister site across the plain, Avebury is the largest stone circle in the world and a more rewarding place to visit simply because you can get closer to the giant boulders.

A large section of Avebury village is actually inside the circle, meaning you can sleep, or at least have lunch and a pint, inside the mystic ring.

Buses run from Salisbury via Devizes (£7.50, 1¾ hours, hourly Monday to Saturday, five on Sunday).

★ **Salisbury Museum** MUSEUM

(☎ 01722-332151; www.salisburymuseum.org.uk; 65 Cathedral Close; adult/child £8/4; ⌚ 10am-5pm Mon-Sat year-round, plus noon-5pm Sun Jun-Sep) The hugely important archaeological finds here include the Stonehenge Archer, the bones of a man found in the ditch surrounding the stone circle – one of the arrows found alongside probably killed him. With gold coins dating from 100 BC and a Bronze Age gold necklace, it's a powerful introduction to Wiltshire's prehistory.

Sleeping & Eating

★ **Chapter House** INN ££

(☎ 01722-412028; www.thechapterhouseuk.com; 9 St Johns St; r £100-140) In this 800-year-old boutique beauty, wood panels and wildly wonky stairs sit beside duck-your-head beams. The cheaper bedrooms are swish but the posher ones are stunning, starring slipper baths and the odd heraldic crest. The pick is room 6, where King Charles is reputed to have stayed. Lucky him.

Cathedral View B&B ££

(☎ 01722-502254; www.cathedral-viewbandb.co.uk; 83 Exeter St; s £75-85, d £80-100; P 🛜) Admirable attention to detail defines this Georgian town house, where miniature flower displays and home-baked biscuits sit in quietly elegant rooms. Breakfasts include prime Wiltshire sausages and the B&B's own bread and jam, while homemade lemon drizzle cake will be waiting for your afternoon tea.

Cloisters PUB FOOD ££
(www.cloisterspubsalisbury.co.uk; 83 Catherine St; mains £9-19; ⏲noon-9pm) The building dates from 1350, it's been a pub since the 1600s and, today, improbably warped beams reinforce an age-old vibe. It's a convivial spot for beefy burgers and homemade pies, or classier evening fare such as pesto-dusted salmon fillet, and lamb steaks with redcurrant sauce.

Information

Tourist Office (☎01722-342860; www.visitsalisbury.co.uk; Fish Row; ⏲9am-5pm Mon-Fri, 10am-4pm Sat, 10am-2pm Sun)

Getting There & Away

BUS

National Express services include Bath (£11, 1¼ hours, one daily), Bristol (£11, 2¼ hours, one daily) and London (£17, three hours, three daily) via Heathrow. Tour buses leave Salisbury for Stonehenge regularly.

TRAIN

Trains run half-hourly from London Waterloo (£25, 1½ hours), Bath (£10, one hour), Bristol (£15, 1¼ hours) and Exeter (£20, two hours).

Stonehenge

This compelling ring of monolithic stones has been attracting a steady stream of pilgrims, poets and philosophers for the last 5000 years and is easily Britain's most iconic archaeological site.

An ultramodern makeover at ancient **Stonehenge** (EH; ☎0370 333 1181; www.english-heritage.org.uk; adult/child same-day tickets £18/11, advance booking £15.50/9.30; ⏲9am-8pm Jun-Aug, 9.30am-7pm Apr, May & Sep, 9.30am-5pm Oct-Mar; Ⓟ) has brought an impressive visitor centre and the closure of an intrusive road (now restored to grassland). The result is a far stronger sense of historical context; dignity and mystery returned to an archaeological gem.

Stonehenge is one of Britain's great archaeological mysteries: despite countless theories about the site's purpose, ranging from a sacrificial centre to a celestial timepiece, in truth, no one knows for sure what drove prehistoric Britons to expend so much time and effort on its construction.

Stonehenge now operates by timed tickets, meaning if you want guaranteed entry you have to book in advance. If you're planning a high-season visit, it's best to secure your ticket well in advance.

STONE CIRCLE ACCESS VISITS

Visitors to Stonehenge normally have to stay outside the stone circle. But on **Stone Circle Access Visits** (☎0370 333 0605; www.english-heritage.org.uk; adult/child £32/19) you get to wander round the core of the site, getting up-close views of the bluestones and trilithons. The walks take place in the evening or early morning, so the quieter atmosphere and the slanting sunlight add to the effect. Each visit only takes 26 people; to secure a place book at least two months in advance.

Getting There & Around

BUS

There is no public transport to the site. The **Stonehenge Tour** (☎01202-338420; www.thestonehengetour.info; adult/child £27/17) leaves Salisbury's train station half-hourly from June to August, and hourly from September to May.

Bath

POP 88,900

Britain is littered with beautiful cities, but precious few compare to Bath, founded on top of natural hot springs that led the Romans to build a magnificent bathhouse here. Bath's heyday was during the 18th century, when local entrepreneur Ralph Allen and the father-and-son architects John Wood the Elder and Younger turned this sleepy backwater into the toast of Georgian society, and constructed fabulous landmarks such as the Circus and Royal Crescent.

Sights

★**Roman Baths** HISTORIC BUILDING
(☎01225-477785; www.romanbaths.co.uk; Abbey Churchyard; adult/child £15.50/9.80; ⏲9.30am-6pm Sep-Jun, 9am-10pm Jul & Aug) In typically ostentatious style, the Romans constructed a complex of bathhouses above Bath's three natural hot springs, which emerge at a steady

46°C (115°F). Situated alongside a temple dedicated to the healing goddess Sulis-Minerva, the baths now form one of the best-preserved ancient Roman spas in the world, and are encircled by 18th- and 19th-century buildings. Bath's premier attraction can get very busy. To dodge the worst crowds, avoid weekends, July and August.

★Royal Crescent ARCHITECTURE
(Royal Cres) Bath is famous for its glorious Georgian architecture, and it doesn't get any grander than this semicircular terrace of majestic town houses overlooking the green sweep of Royal Victoria Park. Designed by John Wood the Younger (1728–82) and built between 1767 and 1775, the houses appear perfectly symmetrical from the outside, but the owners were allowed to tweak the interiors, so no two houses are quite the same. **No 1 Royal Crescent** (☎01225-428126; www.no1royalcrescent.org.uk; 1 Royal Cres; adult/child/family £10/4/22; ⏲noon-5.30pm Mon & 10.30am-5.30pm Tue-Sun Feb–early Dec) offers you an intriguing insight into life inside.

Jane Austen Centre MUSEUM
(☎01225-443000; www.janeausten.co.uk; 40 Gay St; adult/child £11/5.50; ⏲9.45am-5.30pm Apr-Oct, 10am-4pm Nov-Mar) Bath is known to many as a location in Jane Austen's novels, including *Persuasion* and *Northanger Abbey*. Although Austen lived in Bath for only five years, from 1801 to 1806, she remained a regular visitor and a keen student of the city's social scene. Here, guides in Regency costumes regale you with Austen-esque tales as you tour memorabilia relating to the writer's life in Bath.

Sleeping

Bath YHA HOSTEL £
(☎0845 371 9303; www.yha.org.uk; Bathwick Hill; dm £13-22, d from £39; ⏲reception 7am-11pm; P@) Split across an Italianate mansion and a modern annex, this impressive hostel is a steep climb (or a short hop on bus U1 or U18) from the city. The listed building means the rooms are huge, and some have period features such as cornicing and bay windows.

★Three Abbey Green B&B ££
(☎01225-428558; www.threeabbeygreen.com; 3 Abbey Green; d £90-200, apt £160;) Rarely in Bath do you get somewhere as central as this Georgian town house with such spacious rooms. Elegant, 18th-century-style furnishings are teamed with swish wet-room bathrooms, and the opulent Lord Nelson suite features a vast four-poster bed. There's also a two-person, self-catering apartment nearby (two-night minimum stay).

★Queensberry Hotel HOTEL £££
(☎01225-447928; www.thequeensberry.co.uk; 4 Russell St; r £125-185, ste £225-275;) Award-winning, quirky Queensberry is Bath's best boutique spoil. Four Georgian town houses have been combined into one seamlessly stylish whole, where heritage roots meet snazzy designs; expect everything from gingham checks and country creams to bright upholstery, original fireplaces and free-standing tubs. Rates exclude breakfast; parking is £7.

DON'T MISS

THE THERMAE BATH SPA

Taking a dip in the Roman Baths might be off-limits, but you can still sample the city's curative waters at this fantastic modern **spa complex** (☎01225-331234; www.thermaebathspa.com; Hot Bath St; Mon-Fri £35, Sat & Sun £38; ⏲9am-9.30pm, last entry 7pm), housed in a shell of local stone and plate glass. Ticket includes steam rooms, waterfall showers and a choice of two swimming pools. The showpiece attraction is the open-air rooftop pool, where you can bathe with a backdrop of Bath's cityscape – a don't-miss experience, best enjoyed at dusk.

Eating & Drinking

Adventure Cafe Bar CAFE £
(www.adventurecafebar.co.uk; 5 Princes Bldgs, George St; mains £5-10; ⏲8am-3am Mon-Fri, 9am-3am Sat & Sun;) This cool cafe-bar, just a slipper's throw from the Assembly Rooms, offers something to everyone at most times of the day: morning cappuccino, lunchtime ciabatta and late-night beer and cocktails. There's great outdoor seating in the back.

Café Retro CAFE £
(☎01225-339347; www.caferetro.co.uk; 18 York St; mains £5-11; ⏲9am-5pm Mon-Sun) A poke in the eye for the corporate coffee chains. The paint job's scruffy, the crockery's ancient and none of the furniture matches, but that's all part of the charm: this is a cafe from the old school, and there are few places better for burgers, butties or cake. Takeaways (in biodegradable containers) are available from Retro-to-Go next door.

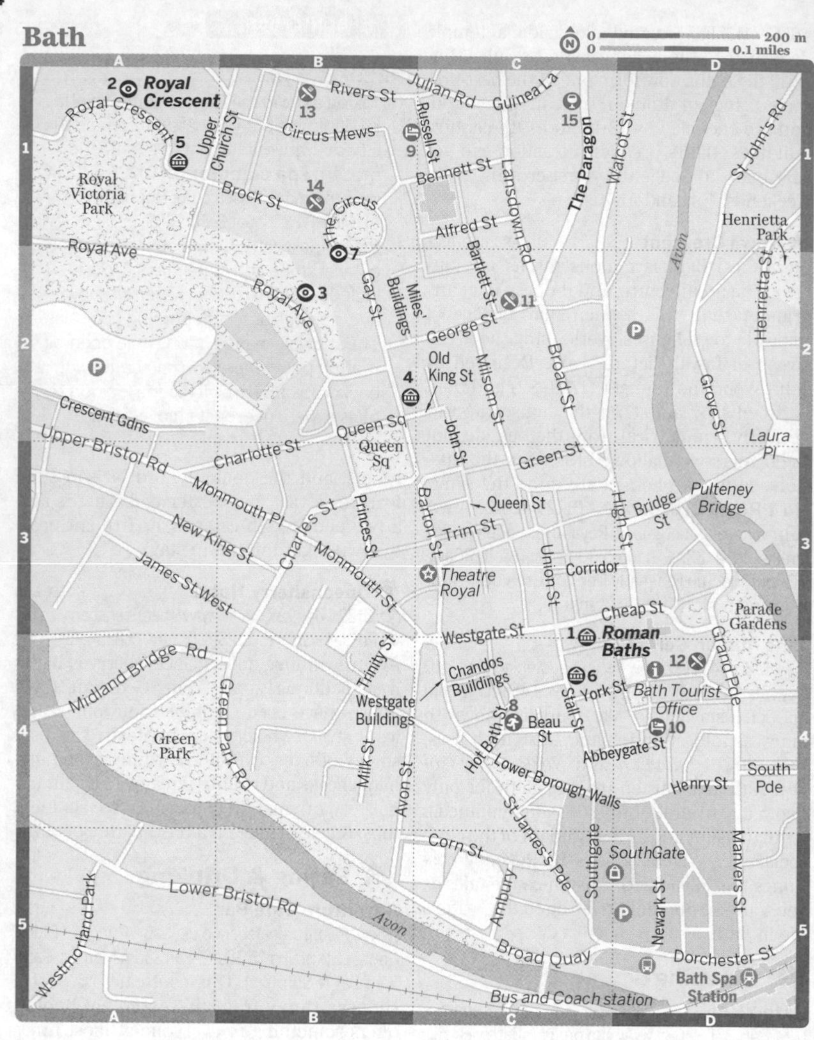

★Circus MODERN BRITISH ££

(☎01225-466020; www.thecircusrestaurant.co.uk; 34 Brock St; mains lunch £10-15, dinner £17-21; ⏲10am-midnight Mon-Sat) Chef Ali Golden has turned this bistro into one of Bath's destination addresses. Her taste is for British dishes with a continental twist, à la Elizabeth David: rabbit, Wiltshire lamb and West Country fish are all infused with herby flavours and rich sauces. It occupies an elegant town house near the Circus. Reservations recommended.

Chequers GASTROPUB ££

(☎01225-360017; www.thechequersbar.com; 50 Rivers St; mains £10-25; ⏲bar noon-11pm daily, food 6-9pm daily, noon-2.30pm Sat & Sun) A discerning crowd inhabits Chequers, a pub that's been in business since 1776, but which has a menu that's bang up to date thanks to head chef Tony Casey. Forget bar-food staples, here it's hake with octopus and wild rice.

★Menu Gordon Jones MODERN BRITISH £££

(☎01225-480871; www.menugordonjones.co.uk; 2 Wellsway; 5-course lunch £40, 6-course dinner

Bath

Top Sights

1	Roman Baths	C3
2	Royal Crescent	A1

Sights

3	Georgian Garden	B2
4	Jane Austen Centre	B2
5	No 1 Royal Crescent	A1
6	Pump Room	C4
7	The Circus	B2

Activities, Courses & Tours

8	Thermae Bath Spa	C4

Sleeping

9	Queensberry Hotel	B1
10	Three Abbey Green	D4

Eating

11	Adventure Cafe Bar	C2
12	Café Retro	D4
13	Chequers	B1
14	Circus	B1
	Pump Room Restaurant	(see 6)

Drinking & Nightlife

15	Star Inn	C1

£55; 12.30-2pm & 7-9pm Tue-Sat) If you enjoy dining with an element of surprise, then Gordon Jones' restaurant will be right up your culinary boulevard. Menus are dreamt up daily and showcase the chef's taste for experimental ingredients (eel, haggis and smoked milk foam) and madcap presentation (test tubes, edible cups, slate plates). It's superb value given the skill on show. Reservations essential.

★Star Inn PUB

(www.abbeyales.co.uk; 23 The Vineyards, off the Paragon; noon-2.30pm & 5.30-11pm Mon-Fri, noon-midnight Sat, to 10.30pm Sun) Not many pubs are registered relics, but the Star is – it still has many of its 19th-century bar fittings. It's the brewery tap for Bath-based Abbey Ales; some ales are served in traditional jugs, and you can even ask for a pinch of snuff in the 'smaller bar'.

Information

Bath Tourist Office (0844 847 5256; www.visitbath.co.uk; Abbey Chambers, Abbey Churchyard; 9.30am-5.30pm Mon-Sat, 10am-4pm Sun) Calls are charged at the premium rate of 50p per minute.

Getting There & Away

BUS

Bath's **bus and coach station** (Dorchester St) is near the train station. National Express coaches run directly to London (£33, 3½ hours, eight to 10 daily) via Heathrow.

TRAIN

Bath Spa station is at the end of Manvers St. Many services connect through Bristol (£7.30, 15 minutes, three per hour), especially to the north of England. Direct services include London Paddington/London Waterloo (£38, 1½ hours, half-hourly) and Salisbury (£18, one hour, hourly).

Oxford

POP 159,994

One of the world's most famous university cities, Oxford is both beautiful and privileged. It's a wonderful place to wander: the elegant honey-toned buildings of the university's 38 colleges wrap around tranquil courtyards and narrow cobbled lanes where a studious calm reigns. But along with the rich history, tradition and energetic academic life, there is a busy, lively town beyond the college walls.

Sights

Not all of Oxford's colleges are open to the public. Check www.ox.ac.uk/colleges for full details.

★Bodleian Library LIBRARY

(01865-277162; www.bodleian.ox.ac.uk/bodley; Catte St; tours £6-14; 9am-5pm Mon-Sat, 11am-5pm Sun) Oxford's Bodleian Library is one of the oldest public libraries in the world and quite possibly the most impressive one you'll ever see. Visitors are welcome to wander around the central quad and the foyer exhibition space. For £1 you can visit the Divinity School, but the rest of the complex is only accessible on guided tours. Check timings online or at the information desk. Advance tickets are only available for extended tours; others must be purchased on the day.

★Christ Church COLLEGE

(01865-276492; www.chch.ox.ac.uk; St Aldate's; adult/child £9/8; 10am-5pm Mon-Sat, 2-5pm Sun) The largest of all of Oxford's colleges, with 650 students, and the one with the grandest quad, Christ Church is also its most popular. Its magnificent buildings, illustrious history and latter-day fame as a location for the *Harry Potter* films have tourists visiting in droves. The college was founded in 1524 by Cardinal Thomas Wolsey, who suppressed the 9th-century monastery existing on the site to acquire the funds for his lavish building project.

★**Pitt Rivers Museum** MUSEUM
(01865-270927; www.prm.ox.ac.uk; South Parks Rd; noon-4.30pm Mon, 10am-4.30pm Tue-Sun) FREE Hidden away through a door at the back of the **Oxford University Museum of Natural History** (01865-272950; www.oum.ox.ac.uk; Parks Rd; 10am-5pm;) FREE, this wonderfully creepy anthropological museum houses a treasure trove of half a million objects from around the world – more than enough to satisfy any armchair adventurer. One of the reasons it's so brilliant is the fact there are no computers, interactive displays or shiny modern gimmicks. Dim lighting lends an air of mystery to glass cases stuffed with the prized booty of Victorian explorers.

★**Ashmolean Museum** MUSEUM
(01865-278000; www.ashmolean.org; Beaumont St; 10am-5pm Tue-Sun) FREE Britain's oldest public museum, second in repute only to London's British Museum, was established in 1683 when Elias Ashmole presented the university with the collection of curiosities amassed by the well-travelled John Tradescant, gardener to Charles I. Today its four floors feature interactive displays, a giant atrium, glass walls revealing galleries on different levels and a beautifully sited rooftop restaurant. Collections, displayed in bright, spacious, attractive galleries within one of Britain's best examples of neoclassical architecture, span the world.

MESSING ABOUT ON THE RIVER

An unmissable Oxford experience, punting is all about sitting back and quaffing Pimms (the quintessential English summer drink) as you watch the city's glorious architecture float by. Which, of course, requires someone else to do the hard work – punting is far more difficult than it appears. If you decide to go it alone, a deposit is usually charged. Most punts hold five people including the punter. Hire them from **Magdalen Bridge Boathouse** (01865-202643; www.oxfordpunting.co.uk; High St; chauffeured 4-person punts per 30min £32, punt rental per hr £22; 9.30am-dusk Feb-Nov) or **Cherwell Boat House** (01865-515978; www.cherwellboathouse.co.uk; 50 Bardwell Rd; punt rental per hour £16-18; 10am-dusk mid-Mar–mid-Oct).

Magdalen College COLLEGE
(01865-276000; www.magd.ox.ac.uk; High St; adult/child £6/5; 1pm-dusk Oct-Jun, 10am-7pm Jul & Aug, noon-7pm Sep) Set amid 40 hectares of private lawns, woodlands, river walks and deer park, Magdalen (*mawd*-lin), founded in 1458, is one of the wealthiest and most beautiful of Oxford's colleges. It has a reputation as an artistic college. Some of its notable students have included writers Julian Barnes, Alan Hollinghurst, CS Lewis, John Betjeman, Seamus Heaney and Oscar Wilde, not to mention Edward VIII, TE Lawrence 'of Arabia', Dudley Moore and Cardinal Thomas Wolsey.

Sleeping

Central Backpackers HOSTEL £
(01865-242288; www.centralbackpackers.co.uk; 13 Park End St; dm £20-25;) A welcoming budget option between the train station and town centre, above a bar. This small hostel has basic, bright and cheerful dorms, with lockers, for four to 12 people, a rooftop terrace and a small TV lounge. There's a six-bed girls-only dorm.

★**Oxford Coach & Horses** B&B ££
(01865-200017; www.oxfordcoachandhorses.co.uk; 62 St Clement's St; s/d/tr £125/135/165; P) Once an 18th-century coaching inn, this fabulous English-Mexican-owned boutique B&B hides behind a fresh powder-blue exterior, just a few metres from the Cowley Rd action. The eight light-filled rooms are cosy, spacious and individually styled in soothing pastels with the odd splash of purple, turquoise or exposed wood. The converted ground floor houses an airy, attractive breakfast room.

Galaxie Hotel B&B ££
(01865-515688; www.galaxie.co.uk; 180 Banbury Rd, Summertown; s/d from £82/88;) A breezy reception hall leads past black-and-white photos to homey, boutique-y rooms at this smartly updated B&B, spread across two interconnecting Victorian town houses. Rooms, in various sizes, are styled in creams and greys offset by lime-green cushions; some come equipped with desks, fridges and

WORTH A TRIP

GLASTONBURY

To many people, Glastonbury is synonymous with the **Glastonbury Festival of Contemporary Performing Arts** (www.glastonburyfestivals.co.uk; tickets from £228; ⊙ Jun or Jul), a majestic (and frequently mud-soaked) extravaganza of music, theatre, dance, cabaret, carnival, spirituality and general all-round weirdness that's been held on and off farmland in Pilton, just outside Glastonbury, for the last 40-something years (bar the occasional off year to let the farm recover).

The town owes much of its spiritual fame to nearby **Glastonbury Tor** (NT; www.nationaltrust.org.uk) FREE, a grassy hump about a mile from town, topped by the ruins of St Michael's Church. According to local legend, the tor is said to be the mythical Isle of Avalon, King Arthur's last resting place. It's also allegedly one of the world's great spiritual nodes, marking the meeting point of many mystical lines of power known as ley lines.

There is no train station in Glastonbury, but bus 37/375/376 runs to Wells (£3.50, 15 minutes, several times per hour) and Bristol (£5.50, 1½ hours, every half hour).

kitchenettes. Sculptures, fire burners and tiki-bar-style benches dot the garden. It's 1.5 miles north of the centre.

Burlington House B&B ££
(☎01865-513513; www.burlington-hotel-oxford.co.uk; 374 Banbury Rd, Summertown; s/d from £70/96; P 📶) Twelve elegantly contemporary rooms with patterned wallpaper, immaculate bathrooms, dashes of colour and luxury touches are available at this beautifully refreshed Victorian merchant's house. Personal service is as sensational as the delicious breakfast, complete with organic eggs, fresh orange juice and homemade bread, yoghurt and granola. It's 2 miles north of central Oxford, with good public transport links.

Eating

★**Edamamé** JAPANESE £
(☎01865-246916; www.edamame.co.uk; 15 Holywell St; mains £6-9.50; ⊙11.30am-2.30pm Wed, 11.30am-2.30pm & 5-8.30pm Thu-Sat, noon-3.30pm Sun; 🌿) The queue out the door speaks volumes about the food quality at this tiny, deliciously authentic place. All light wood, dainty trays and friendly bustle, this is Oxford's top spot for gracefully simple, flavour-packed Japanese cuisine. Dishes include fragrant chicken-miso ramen, tofu stir-fry and, on Thursday night, sushi. No bookings; arrive early and be prepared to wait. Cash only at lunch.

★**Vaults & Garden** CAFE £
(☎01865-279112; www.thevaultsandgarden.com; University Church of St Mary the Virgin, Radcliffe Sq; mains £7-10; ⊙8.30am-6pm; 📶🌿) Hidden away in the vaulted 14th-century Old Congregation House of the University Church, this buzzy local favourite serves a wholesome seasonal selection of soups, salads, pastas, curries, sandwiches and cakes, including plenty of vegetarian and gluten-free options. It's one of Oxford's most beautiful lunch venues, with additional tables in a pretty garden overlooking Radcliffe Sq. Arrive early to grab a seat.

Turl St Kitchen MODERN BRITISH ££
(☎01865-264171; www.turlstreetkitchen.co.uk; 16-17 Turl St; mains £11-19; ⊙8-10am, noon-2.30pm & 6.30-10pm; 🌿) 🍃 A twice-daily-changing menu transforms meals into exquisite surprises at this lively, super-central multilevel cafe-restaurant. Fresh, organic, sustainable and locally sourced produce is thrown into creative contemporary combinations, perhaps starring veggie tajines, roast beef, hake-and-chorizo skewers or fennel-infused salads. Proceeds support a local charity. The interior is a rustic-chic mix of blue-tiled floors, faded-wood tables and fairy lights. Good cakes and coffee.

Café Coco MEDITERRANEAN ££
(☎01865-200232; www.cafecoco.co.uk; 23 Cowley Rd; breakfast £4.50-9, mains £7-12; ⊙10am-10pm Mon-Thu, to midnight Fri, 9am-midnight Sat, 9am-10pm Sun; 🌿) This Cowley Rd institution is a hugely popular brunching destination, decorated with classic posters, warm yellow walls, chunky mirrors and a plaster-cast clown in an ice bath. The globetrotting menu ranges from cooked and 'healthy' breakfasts to pizzas, salads, burgers, pastas, meze platters, Mediterranean mains and zingy fresh juices. Or just swing by for cocktails (happy hour 5pm to 7.30pm).

DON'T MISS

BLENHEIM PALACE

One of the country's greatest stately homes, **Blenheim Palace** (☎01993-810530; www.blenheimpalace.com; Woodstock; adult/child £24.90/13.90, park & gardens only £14.90/6.90; ⏰palace 10.30am-5.30pm, park & gardens 9am-6pm; P) is a monumental baroque fantasy designed by Sir John Vanbrugh and Nicholas Hawksmoor between 1705 and 1722. Now a Unesco World Heritage Site, it's home to the 12th Duke of Marlborough. Highlights include the **Great Hall**, a vast space topped by 20m-high ceilings adorned with images of the first duke in battle; the most important public room, the various grand **state rooms** with their plush decor and priceless china cabinets; and the magnificent 55m **Long Library**. You can also visit the **Churchill Exhibition**, dedicated to the life, work and writings of Sir Winston, who was born at Blenheim in 1874.

Blenheim Palace is near the town of Woodstock, a few miles northwest of Oxford. To get there, Stagecoach bus S3 (£3.70, 30 minutes, every half hour, hourly on Sunday) runs from George St in Oxford.

Drinking & Nightlife

Eagle & Child PUB

(☎01865-302925; www.nicholsonspubs.co.uk/theeagleandchildoxford; 49 St Giles; ⏰noon-11pm) Affectionately known as the 'Bird & Baby', this quirky pub dates from 1650 and was once a favourite haunt of authors JRR Tolkien and CS Lewis and a few other Inklings. Its narrow wood-panelled rooms and selection of real ales, craft beers and gins still attracts a mellow crowd.

Bear Inn PUB

(☎01865-728164; www.bearoxford.co.uk; 6 Alfred St; ⏰11am-11pm Sun-Thu, to midnight Fri & Sat) Arguably Oxford's oldest pub (there's been a pub on this site since 1242), the atmospherically creaky Bear requires all but the most vertically challenged to duck their heads when passing through doorways. A curious tie collection covers the walls and ceilings, and there are usually a couple of worthy guest ales and artisan beers.

Turf Tavern PUB

(☎01865-243235; www.turftavern-oxford.co.uk; 4-5 Bath Pl; ⏰11am-11pm; 📶) Squeezed down a narrow alleyway, this tiny medieval pub (from at least 1381) is one of Oxford's best loved. It's where US president Bill Clinton famously 'did not inhale'; other patrons have included Oscar Wilde, Stephen Hawking and Margaret Thatcher. Home to 11 real ales, it's always crammed with students, professionals and the odd tourist. Plenty of outdoor seating.

Information

Tourist Office (☎01865-686430; www.experienceoxfordshire.com; 15-16 Broad St; ⏰9.30am-5pm Mon-Sat, 10am-4pm Sun) Covers the whole of Oxfordshire, stocks printed Oxford walking guides and books official walking tours.

Getting There & Away

BUS

Oxford's main bus/coach station is at Gloucester Green, with frequent services to London (£15, 1¾ hours, every 15 minutes). There are also regular buses to/from Heathrow and Gatwick airports.

TRAIN

Oxford's train station has half-hourly services to London Paddington (£25, 1¼ hours) and roughly hourly trains to Birmingham (£18, 1¼ hours). Hourly services also run to Bath (£28, 1½ hours) and Bristol (£30, one to two hours), but require a change at Didcot Parkway.

Stratford-upon-Avon

POP 27,455

The author of some of the most quoted lines ever written in the English language, William Shakespeare was born in Stratford in 1564 and died here in 1616. Experiences linked to his life in this unmistakably Tudor town range from the touristy (medieval re-creations and Bard-themed tearooms) to the humbling (Shakespeare's modest grave in Holy Trinity Church) and the sublime (taking in a play by the world-famous Royal Shakespeare Company).

Sights

★Shakespeare's Birthplace
HISTORIC BUILDING

(☎01789 204016; www.shakespeare.org.uk; Henley St; incl Shakespeare's New Place & Halls Croft adult/child £17.50/11.50; ⏲9am-5.30pm Jul & Aug, to 5pm Sep-Jun) Start your Shakespeare quest at the house where the world's most popular playwright supposedly spent his childhood days. In fact, the jury is still out on whether this really was Shakespeare's birthplace, but devotees of the Bard have been dropping in since at least the 19th century, leaving their signatures scratched on to the windows. Set behind a modern facade, the house has restored Tudor rooms, live presentations from famous Shakespearean characters and an engaging exhibition on Stratford's favourite son.

★Shakespeare's New Place
HISTORIC SITE

(☎01789-204016; www.shakespeare.org.uk; cnr Chapel St & Chapel Lane; incl Shakespeare's Birthplace & Hall's Croft adult/child £17.50/11.50; ⏲9am-5.30pm Jul & Aug, 9am-5pm mid-Mar–Jun, Sep & Oct, 10am-4pm Nov–mid-Mar) When Shakespeare retired, he swapped the bright lights of London for a comfortable town house at New Place, where he died of unknown causes in April 1616. The house was demolished in 1759, but an attractive Elizabethan knot garden occupies part of the grounds. A major restoration project has uncovered Shakespeare's kitchen and incorporated new exhibits in a reimagining of the house as it would have been. You can also explore the adjacent Nash's House, where Shakespeare's granddaughter Elizabeth lived.

Shakespeare's School Room
HISTORIC SITE

(www.shakespearesschoolroom.org; King Edward VI School, Church St; adult/child £8.90/5.50; ⏲11am-5pm Mon-Fri during school term, 10am-5pm Sat, Sun & school holidays) Shakespeare's alma mater, King Edward VI School (still a prestigious grammar school today), incorporates a vast black-and-white timbered building, dating from 1420, that was once the town's guildhall. Upstairs, in the Bard's former classroom, you can sit in on mock-Tudor lessons, watch a short film and test yourself on Tudor-style homework.

It's adjacent to the 1269-built **Guild Chapel** (cnr Chapel Lane & Church St; ⏲services 10am Wed, noon 1st Sat of month Apr-Sep).

WORTH A TRIP

THE COTSWOLDS

Rolling gracefully across six counties, the Cotswolds are a delightful tangle of gloriously golden villages, thatch-roofed cottages, evocative churches, rickety almshouses and ancient mansions of honey-coloured stone. If you've ever lusted after exposed beams, cream teas or cuisine crammed full of local produce, look no further.

Travel by public transport requires careful planning and patience; for the most flexibility and the option of getting off the beaten track, your own car is unbeatable. Alternatively, the **Cotswolds Discoverer card** (www.escapetothecotswolds.org.uk/discoverer; one-/three-day pass £10/25) gives you unlimited travel on participating bus or train routes.

Anne Hathaway's Cottage
HISTORIC BUILDING

(☎01789-204016; www.shakespeare.org.uk; Cottage Lane, Shottery; adult/child £10.25/6.50; ⏲9am-5pm mid-Mar–Oct, closed Nov–mid Mar) Before tying the knot with Shakespeare, Anne Hathaway lived in Shottery, 1 mile west of the centre of Stratford, in this delightful thatched farmhouse. As well as period furniture, it has gorgeous gardens and an orchard and arboretum, with examples of all the trees mentioned in Shakespeare's plays. A footpath (no bikes allowed) leads to Shottery from Evesham Pl. The **City Sightseeing** (☎01789-299123; www.city-sightseeing.com; adult/child £13.90/6.95; ⏲every 30min Apr-Sep, less frequently Oct-Mar) bus stops here.

Holy Trinity Church
CHURCH

(☎01789-266316; www.stratford-upon-avon.org; Old Town; Shakespeare's grave adult/child £2/1; ⏲8.30am-6pm Mon-Sat, 12.30-5pm Sun Apr-Sep, shorter hours Oct-Mar) The final resting place of the Bard is said to be the most visited parish church in all of England. Inside are handsome 16th- and 17th-century tombs (particularly in the Clopton Chapel), some fabulous carvings on the choir stalls and, of course, the grave of William Shakespeare, with its ominous epitaph: 'cvrst be he yt moves my bones'.

Sleeping

Stratford-upon-Avon YHA HOSTEL £
(☎0845 371 9661; www.yha.org.uk; Hemmingford House, Wellesbourne, Alveston; dm/d/camping pod from £19/90/89; P@) Set in a large 200-year-old mansion 1.5 miles east of the town centre, this superior hostel attracts travellers of all ages. Of its 32 rooms and dorms, 16 are en suite, as are four-person camping pods with kitchenettes. There's a canteen, bar and kitchen. Buses X15, X18 and 18A run here from Bridge St. Wi-fi is available in common areas.

Falcon Hotel HOTEL ££
(☎01789-279953; www.sjhotels.co.uk; Chapel St; d/f from £85/145; P) Definitely request a room in the original 15th-century building, not the soulless modern annex or dingy 17th-century garden house of this epicentral hotel. This way you'll get the full Tudor experience – creaky floorboards, wonky timbered walls and all. Open fires blaze in the public areas but the best asset is the bargain-priced-for-Stratford car park (£5). Family rooms sleep three people.

Church Street Townhouse BOUTIQUE HOTEL £££
(☎01789-262222; www.churchstreet-th.co.uk; 16 Church St; d from £110;) Some of the dozen rooms at this exquisite hotel have free-standing claw-foot bathtubs, and all have iPod docks, flatscreen TVs and luxurious furnishings. Light sleepers should avoid room 1, nearest the bar. The building itself is a centrally located 400-year-old gem with a first-rate restaurant and bar. There's a minimum two-night stay on weekends.

SHAKESPEARE HISTORIC HOMES

Five of the most important buildings associated with Shakespeare contain museums that form the core of the visitor experience at Stratford. All are run by the **Shakespeare Birthplace Trust** (www.shakespeare.org.uk).

Tickets for the three houses in town – **Shakespeare's Birthplace**, **Shakespeare's New Place** and **Halls Croft** – cost adult/child £17.50/11.50. If you also visit **Anne Hathaway's Cottage** and **Mary Arden's Farm**, buy a combination ticket covering all five properties (adult/child £26.25/17).

Eating & Drinking

Sheep St is clustered with eating options, mostly aimed at theatregoers (look out for good-value pretheatre menus).

Fourteas CAFE £
(☎01789-293908; www.thefourteas.co.uk; 24 Sheep St; dishes £4-7, afternoon tea with/without Prosecco £18.50/14; ⌚9.30am-5pm Mon-Sat, 11am-4pm Sun) Breaking with Stratford's Shakespearean theme, this tearoom takes the 1940s as its inspiration with beautiful old teapots, framed posters and staff in period costume. As well as premium loose-leaf teas and homemade cakes, there are hearty breakfasts, delicious sandwiches (fresh poached salmon, brie and grape), a hot dish of the day and indulgent afternoon teas (gluten-free options available).

Church Street Townhouse BISTRO ££
(☎01789-262222; www.churchstreettownhouse.com; 16 Church St; mains £11-24; ⌚kitchen noon-3pm & 5-9.45pm, bar 8am-midnight Mon-Sat, to 10.30pm Sun;) This lovely restaurant is a fantastic place for immersing yourself in Stratford's historic charms. The food is delightful and the ambience impeccably congenial and well presented. Music students from Shakespeare's old grammar school across the way tinkle the piano ivories daily at 5.30pm, though it can be hard to hear over the bar noise.

★**Old Thatch Tavern** PUB
(www.oldthatchtavernstratford.co.uk; Greenhill St; ⌚11.30am-11pm Mon-Sat, noon-6pm Sun;) To truly appreciate Stratford's olde-worlde atmosphere, join the locals for a pint at the town's oldest pub. Built in 1470, this thatched-roofed, low-ceilinged treasure has great real ales and a gorgeous summertime courtyard.

Dirty Duck PUB
(Black Swan; Waterside; ⌚11am-11pm Mon-Sat, to 10.30pm Sun) Also called the 'Black Swan', this enchanting riverside alehouse is the only pub in England to be licensed under two names. It's a favourite thespian watering hole, with a roll-call of former regulars (Olivier, Attenborough et al) that reads like a who's who of actors.

Entertainment

★**Royal Shakespeare Company** THEATRE
(RSC; ☎box office 01789-403493; www.rsc.org.uk; Waterside; tours adult £6.50-8.50, child £3-4.50, tower adult/child £2.50/1.25; ⌚tour times

vary, tower 10am-6.15pm Sun-Fri, 10am-12.15pm & 2-6.15pm Sat Apr-Sep, 10am-4.30pm Sun-Fri, 10am-12.15pm & 2-4.30pm Sat Oct-Mar) Stratford has two grand stages run by the world-renowned Royal Shakespeare Company – the **Royal Shakespeare Theatre** and the **Swan Theatre** (☎01789-403493) on Waterside – as well as the smaller **Other Place** (☎box office 01789-403493; www.rsc.org.uk; 22 Southern Lane). The theatres have witnessed performances by such legends as Lawrence Olivier, Richard Burton, Judi Dench, Helen Mirren, Ian McKellan and Patrick Stewart. Various one-hour **guided tours** take you behind the scenes.

Information

Tourist Office (☎01789-264293; www.discover-stratford.com; Bridge Foot; ⏲9am-5.30pm Mon-Sat, 10am-4pm Sun) Just west of Clopton Bridge.

Getting There & Away

BUS

National Express coaches and other bus companies run from Stratford's Riverside bus station (behind the Stratford Leisure Centre on Bridgeway). Destinations include Birmingham (£8.50, one hour, twice daily), London Victoria (£7, three hours, three daily) and Oxford (£10.80, one hour, twice daily).

TRAIN

From Stratford train station, trains run to Birmingham (£7.70, 50 minutes, half-hourly), and London Marylebone (£28.90, two hours, up to two per hour) and Warwick (£6.60, 30 minutes, hourly).

WORTH A TRIP

WARWICK

Regularly namechecked by Shakespeare, the town of Warwick is a treasure-house of medieval architecture. It is dominated by the soaring turrets of **Warwick Castle** (☎0871 265 2000; www.warwick-castle.com; Castle Lane; castle adult/child £25.20/22.20, castle & dungeon £30.20/27.20; ⏲10am-6pm Apr-Sep, to 5pm Oct-Mar; P ᯤ), founded in 1068 by William the Conqueror, and later the ancestral home of the Earls of Warwick. It's now been transformed into a major tourist attraction by the owners of Madame Tussauds, with family-friendly activities and waxworks populating the private apartments.

Stagecoach bus 18A goes to Stratford-upon-Avon (£4.30, 45 minutes, half-hourly). Trains run to Birmingham (£6.80, 40 minutes, half-hourly), Stratford-upon-Avon (£6.60, 30 minutes, hourly) and London Marylebone (£31.80, 1½ hours, every 20 minutes).

Cambridge

POP 123,900

Abounding with exquisite architecture, oozing history and tradition, and renowned for its quirky rituals, Cambridge is a university town extraordinaire. The tightly packed core of ancient colleges, the picturesque 'Backs' (college gardens) leading on to the river and the leafy green meadows that surround the city give it a far more tranquil appeal than its historic rival Oxford.

Sights

Cambridge University comprises 31 colleges, though not all are open to the public. Opening hours are only a rough guide, so contact the colleges or the tourist office for more information.

★King's College Chapel CHURCH

(☎01223-331212; www.kings.cam.ac.uk; King's Pde; adult/child £9/free; ⏲9.30am-3.30pm Mon-Sat & 1.15-2.30pm Sun term time, 9.30am-4.30pm daily university holidays) In a city crammed with showstopping buildings, this is the scene-stealer. Grandiose, 16th-century King's College Chapel is one of England's most extraordinary examples of Gothic architecture. Its inspirational, intricate 80m-long, fan-vaulted ceiling is the world's largest and soars upwards before exploding into a series of stone fireworks. This hugely atmospheric space is a fitting stage for the chapel's world-famous choir; hear it during the magnificent, free, **evensong** (term time only; 5.30pm Monday to Saturday, 10.30am and 3.30pm Sunday).

★Trinity College COLLEGE

(www.trin.cam.ac.uk; Trinity St; adult/child £3/1; ⏲10am-3.30pm Nov-Mar, to 5pm Jul-Oct) The largest of Cambridge's colleges, Trinity offers an extraordinary Tudor gateway, an air of supreme elegance and a sweeping Great Court – the largest of its kind in the world. It also boasts the renowned and suitably musty **Wren Library** (⏲noon-2pm Mon-Fri year-round, plus 10.30am-12.30pm Sat term time) FREE, containing 55,000 books dated before 1820 and

DON'T MISS

PUNTING ON THE BACKS

Gliding a self-propelled punt along the Backs is a blissful experience – once you've got the hang of it. It can also be a manic challenge to begin. If you wimp out you can always opt for a relaxing chauffeured punt.

Punt hire costs around £20 to £28 per hour; 45-minute chauffeured trips of the Backs cost about £15 to £19 per person. One-way trips to Grantchester (1½ hours) start at around £18 per person.

more than 2500 manuscripts. Works include those by Shakespeare, St Jerome, Newton and Swift – and AA Milne's original *Winnie the Pooh;* both Milne and his son, Christopher Robin, were graduates.

★The Backs PARK

Behind the Cambridge colleges' grandiose facades and stately courts, a series of gardens and parks line up beside the river. Collectively known as the Backs, the tranquil green spaces and shimmering waters offer unparalleled views of the colleges and are often the most enduring image of Cambridge for visitors. The picture-postcard snapshots of student life and graceful bridges can be seen from the riverside pathways and pedestrian bridges – or the comfort of a chauffeur-driven punt.

★Fitzwilliam Museum MUSEUM

(www.fitzmuseum.cam.ac.uk; Trumpington St; by donation; ⏲10am-5pm Tue-Sat, noon-5pm Sun) FREE Fondly dubbed 'the Fitz' by locals, this colossal neoclassical pile was one of the first public art museums in Britain, built to house the fabulous treasures that the seventh Viscount Fitzwilliam bequeathed to his old university. Expect Roman and Egyptian grave goods, artworks by many of the great masters and some more-quirky collections: banknotes, literary autographs, watches and armour.

Sleeping

Cambridge YHA HOSTEL £

(☎0845-371 9728; www.yha.org.uk; 97 Tenison Rd; dm £18-26, d £39-59; @☎) Smart, friendly, recently renovated, deservedly popular hostel with compact dorms and good facilities. Handily, it's near the train station.

Benson House B&B ££

(☎01223-311594; www.bensonhouse.co.uk; 24 Huntingdon Rd; s £75-115, d £110-115; P☎) Lots of little things lift Benson a cut above – sleep among feather pillows and Egyptian cotton linen, sip tea from Royal Doulton bone china, then tuck into award-winning breakfasts featuring kippers, croissants and fresh fruit.

★Varsity BOUTIQUE HOTEL £££

(☎01223-306030; www.thevarsityhotel.co.uk; Thompson's Lane; d £190-350; @☎) In the 44 individually styled rooms of riverside Varsity, wondrous furnishings and witty features (Union Jack footstools, mock-flock wallpaper) sit beside floor-to-ceiling glass windows, espresso machines and smartphone docks. The views out over the colleges from the roof terrace are frankly gorgeous.

Eating & Drinking

★Urban Shed SANDWICHES £

(www.theurbanshed.com; 62 King St; sandwiches from £4.25; ⏲8.30am-5pm Mon-Thu, 8.30am-4.30pm Fri, 9am-6pm Sat, 10am-4pm Sun) Somewhere between a retro goods shop and a sandwich bar, at unorthodox Urban Shed the personal service ethos is so strong regular customers have a locker for their own mug. Decor teams old aeroplane seats with cable-drum tables, their own-blend coffee is mellow and the sandwiches range is superb.

Chop House BRITISH ££

(www.cambscuisine.com/cambridge-chop-house; 1 King's Pde; mains £15-22; ⏲noon-10.30pm Mon-Sat, to 9.30pm Sun) The window seats here deliver some of the best views in town – on to King's College's hallowed walls. The food is pure English establishment too: hearty steaks and chops and chips, plus a scattering of fish dishes and suet puddings. It's also open from 10am to noon for coffee and cakes.

Pint Shop MODERN BRITISH ££

(☎01223-352293; www.pintshop.co.uk; 10 Peas Hill; mains £12.50-25.50; ⏲noon-10pm Mon-Fri, 11am-10.30pm Sat, 11am-10pm Sun) Popular Pint Shop's vision is to embrace eating and drinking equally. So it's created both a busy bar specialising in craft beer (10 on keg and six on draft) and a stylish dining room serving classy versions of traditional grub (dry aged steaks, gin-cured sea trout, charcoal-grilled plaice). All in all, hard to resist.

★**Midsummer House** MODERN BRITISH £££
(☎01223-369299; www.midsummerhouse.co.uk; Midsummer Common; 5/8 courses £56.50/120; ⊙noon-1.30pm Wed-Sat, 7-8.30pm Tue-Thu, 6.30-9.30pm Fri & Sat;) At the region's top table Chef Daniel Clifford's double Michelin-starred creations are distinguished by depth of flavour and immense technical skill. Sample transformations of coal-baked celeriac, Cornish crab, and roast pigeon with wild garlic before a pear, blueberry and white chocolate delight.

★**Eagle** PUB
(www.eagle-cambridge.co.uk; Benet St; ⊙8am-11pm Mon-Sat, to 10.30pm Sun;) Cambridge's most famous pub has loosened the tongues and pickled the grey cells of many an illustrious academic; among them Nobel Prize–winning scientists Crick and Watson, who discussed their research into DNA here (note the blue plaque by the door). Fifteenth-century, wood-panelled and rambling, its cosy rooms include one with WWII airmen's signatures on the ceiling.

Information

Tourist Office (☎01223-791500; www.visitcambridge.org; The Guildhall, Peas Hill; ⊙10am-5pm Mon-Sat Nov-Mar, 10am-5pm Mon-Sat, 11am-3pm Sun Apr-Oct)

Getting There & Away

BUS

From Parkside there are regular National Express buses to London Gatwick airport (£37, 3¾ hours, nine daily), Heathrow airport (£25, 2¾ hours, hourly) and Oxford (£12, 3½ hours, every 30 minutes).

TRAIN

The train station is off Station Rd, which is off Hills Rd. Destinations include London Kings Cross (£23, one hour, two to four per hour) and Stansted airport (£10, 35 minutes/hourly).

York

POP 198,000

Nowhere in northern England says 'medieval' quite like York, a city of extraordinary historical wealth that has lost little of its preindustrial lustre. Its spider's web of narrow streets is enclosed by a magnificent circuit of 13th-century walls and the city's rich heritage is woven into virtually every brick and beam.

Sights

If the weather's good, don't miss the chance to walk York's **City Walls** (www.yorkwalls.org.uk), which follow the line of the original Roman walls and give a whole new perspective on the city. Allow 1½ to two hours for the full circuit of 4.5 miles or, if you're pushed for time, the short stretch from Bootham Bar to Monk Bar is worth doing for the views of the minster.

★**York Minster** CATHEDRAL
(www.yorkminster.org; Deangate; adult/child £10/free, incl tower £15/5; ⊙9am-5.30pm Mon-Sat, 12.45-5pm Sun, last admission 30min before closing) The remarkable York Minster is the largest medieval cathedral in all of Northern Europe, and one of the world's most beautiful Gothic buildings. Seat of the archbishop of York, primate of England, it is second in importance only to Canterbury, seat of the primate of *all* England – the separate titles were created to settle a debate over the true centre of the English church. If this is the only cathedral you visit in England, you'll still walk away satisfied.

★**Jorvik Viking Centre** MUSEUM
(www.jorvik-viking-centre.co.uk; Coppergate; adult/child £10.25/7.25; ⊙10am-5pm Apr-Oct, to 4pm Nov-Mar) Interactive multimedia exhibits aimed at bringing history to life often achieve exactly the opposite, but the much-hyped Jorvik manages to pull it off with aplomb. Thoroughly restored and reimagined following flood damage in 2015, it's a smells-and-all reconstruction of the Viking settlement unearthed here during excavations in the late 1970s, experienced via a 'time-car' monorail that transports you through 9th-century Jorvik (the Viking name for York). You can reduce time waiting in the queue by booking your tickets online.

★**National Railway Museum** MUSEUM
(www.nrm.org.uk; Leeman Rd; ⊙10am-6pm;) FREE While many railway museums are the sole preserve of lone men in anoraks comparing dog-eared notebooks and getting high on the smell of machine oil, coal smoke and nostalgia, this place is different. York's National Railway Museum – the biggest in the world, with more than 100 locomotives – is so well presented and crammed with fascinating stuff that it's interesting even to folk whose eyes don't mist over at the thought of a 4-6-2 A1 Pacific class thundering into a tunnel.

YORK PASS

If you plan on visiting a number of sights, you can save yourself some money by using a YorkPass (www.yorkpass.com). It gives you free access to more than 30 pay-to-visit sights in and around York, including York Minster, Jorvik and Castle Howard. You can buy it at York tourist office or online; prices for one/two/three days are adult £38/50/60, child £20/26/30.

Yorkshire Museum MUSEUM
(www.yorkshiremuseum.org.uk; Museum St; adult/child £7.50/free; 10am-5pm) Most of York's Roman archaeology is hidden beneath the medieval city, so the superb displays in the Yorkshire Museum are invaluable if you want to get an idea of what Eboracum was like. There are maps and models of Roman York, funerary monuments, mosaic floors and wall paintings, and a 4th-century bust of Emperor Constantine. Kids will enjoy the dinosaur exhibit, centred around giant ichthyosaur fossils from Yorkshire's Jurassic coast.

The Shambles STREET
The Shambles takes its name from the Saxon word *shamel,* meaning 'slaughterhouse' – in 1862 there were 26 butcher shops on this street. Today the butchers are long gone, but this narrow cobbled lane, lined with 15th-century Tudor buildings that overhang so much they seem to meet above your head, is the most picturesque in Britain, and one of the most visited in Europe, often crammed with visitors intent on buying a tacky souvenir before rushing back to the tour bus.

Tours

Ghost Hunt of York WALKING
(www.ghosthunt.co.uk; adult/child £6/4; tours 7.30pm) The kids will just love this award-winning and highly entertaining 75-minute tour laced with authentic ghost stories. It begins at the top end of The Shambles, whatever the weather (it's never cancelled) and there's no need to book, just turn up and wait till you hear the handbell ringing…

Yorkwalk WALKING
(www.yorkwalk.co.uk; adult/child £6/5; tours 10.30am & 2.15pm Feb-Nov) Offers a series of two-hour walks on a range of themes, from the classics – Roman York, the snickelways (narrow alleys) and City Walls – to walks focused on chocolates and sweets, women in York, and the inevitable graveyard, coffin and plague tour. Walks depart from Museum Gardens Gate on Museum St; there's no need to book.

Sleeping

Despite the inflated prices of the high season, it is still tough to find a bed during midsummer.

★**Fort** HOSTEL £
(01904-620222; www.thefortyork.co.uk; 1 Little Stonegate; dm/d from £18/74;) This boutique hostel showcases the work of young British designers, creating affordable accommodation with a dash of character and flair. There are six- and eight-bed dorms, along with half a dozen doubles, but don't expect a peaceful retreat – the central location is in the middle of York's nightlife, and there's a lively club downstairs (earplugs are provided!).

Safestay York HOSTEL £
(01904-627720; www.safestayyork.co.uk; 88-90 Micklegate; dm/tw from £18/75; @) Housed in a Grade I Georgian building that was once home to the High Sheriff of Yorkshire, this is a large and well-equipped boutique hostel with cool decor and good facilities. It's popular with school groups and stag and hen parties – don't come here looking for peace and quiet!

★**Hedley House Hotel** HOTEL ££
(01904-637404; www.hedleyhouse.com; 3 Bootham Tce; d/f from £105/115; P) This red-brick terrace-house hotel sports a variety of smartly refurbished, family-friendly accommodation, including rooms that sleep up to five, and some self-catering apartments – plus it has a sauna and spa bath on the outdoor terrace at the back, and is barely five minutes' walk from the city centre through the Museum Gardens.

Bar Convent B&B ££
(01904-643238; www.bar-convent.org.uk; 17 Blossom St; s/d £67/96;) This elegant Georgian mansion just outside Micklegate Bar, less than 10 minutes' walk from the train station, houses a working convent, a cafe, a conference centre and exhibition, and also offers excellent B&B accommodation. Open to visitors of all faiths and none. Charming bedrooms are modern and well equipped, breakfasts are superb, and there's a garden and hidden chapel to enjoy.

★ Middlethorpe Hall HOTEL £££

(☎01904-641241; www.middlethorpe.com; Bishopthorpe Rd; s/d from £118/126; P ☜ ≋) This breathtaking 17th-century country house is set in 8 hectares of parkland, once the home of diarist Lady Mary Wortley Montagu. The rooms are divided between the main house, restored courtyard buildings and three cottage suites. All are beautifully decorated with original antiques and oil paintings that have been carefully selected to reflect the period.

Eating & Drinking

★ Mannion's CAFE, BISTRO £

(☎01904-631030; www.mannionandco.co.uk; 1 Blake St; mains £6-11; ⊙9am-5.30pm Mon-Fri, to 6pm Sat, 10am-5pm Sun) Expect to queue for a table at this busy bistro (no reservations), with its maze of rustic, wood-panelled rooms and selection of daily specials. Regulars on the menu include eggs Benedict for breakfast, a chunky Yorkshire rarebit made with home-baked bread, and lunch platters of cheese and charcuterie from the attached deli. Oh, and pavlova for pudding.

★ No 8 Bistro BISTRO ££

(☎01904-653074; www.no8york.co.uk/bistro; 8 Gillygate; 3-course lunch/dinner £16/25; ⊙noon-10pm Mon-Thu, 9am-10pm Fri-Sun; ☜ ☺) A cool little place with modern artwork mimicking the Edwardian stained glass at the front, No 8 offers a day-long menu of classic bistro dishes using fresh local produce, including Jerusalem artichoke risotto with fresh herbs, and Yorkshire lamb slow-cooked in hay and lavender. It also does breakfast daily (mains £6 to £9) and Sunday lunch (two courses £18). Booking recommended.

★ Parlour at Grays Court CAFE, BRITISH ££

(www.grayscourtyork.com; Chapter House St; mains £9-20; ⊙10am-5pm & 6-9pm; ☜) An unexpected pleasure in the heart of York, this 16th-century mansion (now a hotel) has more of a country house atmosphere. Relax with coffee and cake in the sunny garden, enjoy a light lunch of Yorkshire rarebit, or indulge in a dinner of scallops and sea bass in the oak-panelled Jacobean gallery. The daytime menu includes traditional afternoon tea (£18.50).

★ Cochon Aveugle FRENCH £££

(☎01904-640222; www.lecochonaveugle.uk; 37 Walmgate; 6-/9-course tasting menu £40/60; ⊙6-9pm Tue-Sat) Black pudding macaroon? Strawberry and elderflower sandwich? Blowtorched mackerel with melon gazpacho? Fussy eaters beware – this small restaurant with huge ambition serves an ever-changing tasting menu (no á la carte) of infinite imagination and invention. You never know what will come next, except that it will be delicious. Bookings essential.

★ Blue Bell PUB

(☎01904-654904; bluebellyork@gmail.com; 53 Fossgate; ⊙11am-11pm Mon-Thu, to midnight Fri-Sat, noon-10.30pm Sun) This is what a proper English pub looks like – a tiny, 200-year-old wood-panelled room with a smouldering fireplace, decor untouched since 1903, a pile of ancient board games in the corner, friendly and efficient bar staff, and Timothy Taylor and Black Sheep ales on tap. Bliss, with froth on top – if you can get in (it's often full).

Information

York Tourist Office (☎01904-550099; www.visityork.org; 1 Museum St; ⊙9am-5pm Mon-Sat, 10am-4pm Sun) Visitor and transport info for all of Yorkshire, plus accommodation bookings, ticket sales and internet access.

Getting There & Away

BUS

York does not have a bus station; intercity buses stop outside the train station, while local and regional buses stop here and also on Rougier St, about 200m northeast of the train station.

There are **National Express** (☎08717 818181; www.nationalexpress.com) coaches to London (from £25, 5½ hours, three daily), Birmingham (£29, 3½ hours, one daily) and Newcastle (£15.40, 2¼ hours, two daily).

TRAIN

York is a major railway hub with frequent direct services to Birmingham (£45, 2¼ hours, half-hourly), Newcastle (£25, one hour, half-hourly), Leeds (£13.90, 25 minutes, four per hour), London's King's Cross (£80, two hours, half-hourly), Manchester (£25, 1½ hours, four per hour) and Scarborough (£14, 50 minutes, hourly). There are also trains to Cambridge (£71, three hours, hourly), changing at Peterborough.

Castle Howard

Stately homes may be two a penny in England, but you'll have to try hard to find one as breathtakingly stately as **Castle Howard** (www.castlehoward.co.uk; adult/child house & grounds £17.50/9, grounds only £9.95/7; ⊙house

10.30am-4pm (last admission), grounds 10am-5pm; P), a work of theatrical grandeur and audacity, and one of the world's most beautiful buildings. It's instantly recognisable from its starring role in the 1980s TV series *Brideshead Revisited* and in the 2008 film of the same name. It's 15 miles northeast of York; **Stephenson's of Easingwold** (www.stephensonsofeasingwold.co.uk) bus 181 links York with Castle Howard (£10 return, 40 minutes, four times daily Monday to Saturday year-round, three on Sunday May to September).

Chester

POP 79,645

With a red-sandstone, Roman wall wrapped around a tidy collection of Tudor and Victorian buildings, Chester is one of English history's greatest gifts to the contemporary visitor. The walls were built when this was Castra Devana, the largest Roman fortress in Britain.

Sights

★City Walls LANDMARK

A good way to get a sense of Chester's unique character is to walk the 2-mile circuit along the walls that surround the historic centre. Originally built by the Romans around AD 70, the walls were altered substantially over the following centuries but have retained their current position since around 1200. The tourist office's *Walk Around Chester Walls* leaflet is an excellent guide and you can also take a 90-minute guided walk.

★Rows ARCHITECTURE

Besides the City Walls, Chester's other great draw is the Rows, a series of two-level galleried arcades along the four streets that fan out in each direction from the **Central Cross**. The architecture is a handsome mix of Victorian and Tudor (original and mock) buildings that house a fantastic collection of individually owned shops.

Chester Cathedral CATHEDRAL

(01244-324756; www.chestercathedral.com; 12 Abbey Sq; 9am-6pm Mon-Sat, 11am-4pm Sun) FREE Originally a Benedictine abbey built on the remains of an earlier Saxon church dedicated to St Werburgh (the city's patron saint), it was shut down in 1540 as part of Henry VIII's dissolution frenzy, but reconsecrated as a cathedral the following year. Despite a substantial Victorian facelift, the cathedral retains much of its original 12th-century structure. You can amble about freely, but the **tours** (adult/child full tour £8/6, short tour £6; full tour 11am & 3pm daily, half tour 12.30pm & 1.15pm Mon-Tue, also 2pm & 4pm Wed-Sat) are excellent, as they bring you to to the top of the panoramic bell tower.

Sleeping

Chester Backpackers HOSTEL £

(01244-400185; www.chesterbackpackers.co.uk; 67 Boughton; dm/s/d from £16/22/34;) Comfortable dorm rooms with nice pine beds in a typically Tudor white-and-black building. It's just a short walk from the city walls and there's also a pleasant garden.

★Stone Villa B&B ££

(01244-345014; www.stonevillachester.co.uk; 3 Stone Pl, Hoole Rd; s/d from £60/85; P; 9) This award-winning, beautiful 1850 villa has everything you need for a memorable stay. Elegant bedrooms, a fabulous breakfast and welcoming, friendly owners all add up to one of the best lodgings in town. The property is about a mile from the city centre.

Eating

Joseph Benjamin MODERN BRITISH ££

(01244-344295; www.josephbenjamin.co.uk; 140 Northgate St; mains £13-17; noon-3pm Tue-Sat, also 6-9.30pm Thu-Sat & noon-4pm Sun) A bright star in Chester's culinary firmament is this combo restaurant, bar and deli that delivers carefully prepared local produce to take out or eat in. Excellent sandwiches and gorgeous salads are the mainstay of the takeaway menu, while the more formal dinner menu features fine examples of modern British cuisine.

★Simon Radley at the Grosvenor MODERN BRITISH £££

(01244-324024; www.chestergrosvenor.com; 58 Eastgate St, Chester Grosvenor Hotel; tasting menu £99, à la carte menu £75; 6.30-9pm Tue-Sat) Simon Radley's formal restaurant (you're instructed to arrive 30 minutes early for drinks and canapés) has served near-perfect Modern British cuisine since 1990, when it was first awarded the Michelin star that it has kept ever since. The food is divine and the wine list extensive. One of Britain's best, but why no second star? Smart attire, no children under 12.

Information

Tourist Office (01244-402111; www.visitchester.com; Town Hall, Northgate St; 9am-5.30pm Mon-Sat, 10am-5pm Sun Mar-Oct, 9.30am-4.30pm Mon-Fri, 9am-4pm Sat, 10am-4pm Sun Nov-Feb)

Getting There & Away

BUS

National Express (08717 81 81 81; www.nationalexpress.com) coaches stop on Vicar's Lane, opposite the tourist office. Destinations include Liverpool (£8, one hour, four daily), London (£27.60, 5½ hours, three daily) and Manchester (£7.60, 1¼ hours, three daily).

TRAIN

The train station is about a mile from the city centre. City Rail Link buses are free for people with rail tickets. Destinations include Liverpool (£6.90, 45 minutes, hourly), London Euston (£69, 2½ hours, hourly) and Manchester (£12.60, one hour, hourly).

Lake District National Park

A dramatic landscape of ridges, lakes and peaks, including England's highest mountain, Scafell Pike (978m), the Lake District is one of Britain's most scenic corners. The awe-inspiring geography here shaped the literary personae of some of Britain's best-known poets, including William Wordsworth.

Often called simply the Lakes, the national park and surrounding area attract around 15 million visitors annually. But if you avoid summer weekends it's easy enough to miss the crush, especially if you do a bit of hiking.

There's a host of B&Bs and country-house hotels in the Lakes, plus more than 20 YHA hostels, many of which can be linked by foot if you wish to hike.

Information

Brockhole National Park Visitor Centre (015394-46601; www.lake-district.gov.uk; 10am-5pm Easter-Oct, to 4pm Nov-Easter) In a 19th-century mansion 3 miles north of Windermere on the A591, this is the Lake District's flagship visitor centre. It also has a teashop, an adventure playground and gardens.

Getting There & Around

BUS

There's one daily National Express coach from London Victoria to Windermere (£31.50, eight hours) via Lancaster and Kendal. Local bus services include the following:

Bus 555/556 Lakeslink Runs hourly between Kendal and Windermere, stopping at all the main towns including Keswick, Grasmere and Ambleside.

Bus 505 Coniston Rambler Runs hourly between Kendal, Windermere, Ambleside and Coniston.

TRAIN

To get to the Lake District by train, you need to change at Oxenholme (on the London Euston to Glasgow line) for Kendal and Windermere, which has connections from London Euston (£103, 3½ hours), Manchester Piccadilly (£36.20, 1½ hours) and Glasgow (£54, 2¾ hours).

Windermere

POP 5423

Stretching for 10.5 miles between Ambleside and Newby Bridge, Windermere isn't just the queen of Lake District lakes – it's also the largest body of water anywhere in England. It's been a centre for tourism since the first trains chugged into town in 1847 and it's still one of the national park's busiest spots.

Windermere Lake Cruises (015394-43360; www.windermere-lakecruises.co.uk; tickets from £2.70) offers scheduled boat trips across the lake from the lakeside settlement of Bowness-on-Windermere.

Sleeping

Lake District Backpackers Lodge HOSTEL £
(015394-46374; www.lakedistrictbackpackers.co.uk; High St, Windermere Town; dm/r £16.50/39; @) In a small, old-style house down a little lane near the train station, this basic hostel lacks pizazz, but it's pretty much the only option in town for budgeteers. There are two small four-bed dorms, plus two private rooms with a double bed and a single bed above. The kitchen is tiny but the lounge is cosy.

★**Boundary** B&B ££
(015394-48978; www.boundaryonline.com; Lake Rd, Windermere Town; d £99-210; P) A refined choice, sleek and chic, with neutral-toned rooms all named after great English cricketers: top picks are Hobbs, with bay window and vast bathroom, and Ranji, with cute flamingo wallpaper and a free-standing in-room bathtub. The downstairs lounge has a trendy wood burner and copies of *Wisden's Almanac* to browse.

★Rum Doodle B&B ££

(☎015394-45967; www.rumdoodlewindermere.com; Sunny Bank Rd, Windermere Town; d £85-119; P 📶) Named after a classic travel novel about a fictional mountain in the Himalayas, this B&B zings with imagination. Its rooms are themed after places and characters in the book, with details like book-effect wallpaper, vintage maps and old suitcases. Top of the heap is The Summit, snug under the eaves with a separate sitting room. Two-night minimum in summer.

Grasmere

POP 1458

Grasmere is a gorgeous little Lakeland village, all the more famous because of its links with Britain's leading Romantic poet, William Wordsworth.

Literary pilgrims come to **Dove Cottage** (☎015394-35544; www.wordsworth.org.uk; adult/child £7.50/4.50; ⏲9.30am-5.30pm), his former home, where highlights include some fine portraits of the man himself, a cabinet containing his spectacles, and a set of scales used by his pal de Quincey to weigh out opium. At **St Oswald's Church** (Church Stile) you'll see a memorial to the poet, and in the churchyard you'll find his grave.

To cure any sombre thoughts, head for **Sarah Nelson's Gingerbread Shop** (☎015394-35428; www.grasmeregingerbread.co.uk; Church Cottage; ⏲9.15am-5.30pm Mon-Sat, 12.30-5pm Sun) and stock up on Grasmere's famous confectionery.

DON'T MISS

HILL TOP

The cute-as-a-button farmhouse of **Hill Top** (NT; ☎015394-36269; www.nationaltrust.org.uk/hill-top; adult/child £10/5, admission to garden & shop free; ⏲house 10am-5.30pm Mon-Thu, 10am-4.30pm Fri-Sun, garden to 5.45pm Mon-Thu, to 5pm Fri-Sun) is a must for Beatrix Potter fans: it was her first house in the Lake District, and is also where she wrote and illustrated several of her famous tales.

The cottage is in Near Sawrey, 2 miles from Hawkshead and Ferry House. The **Cross Lakes Experience** (www.mountain-goat.co.uk/Cross-Lakes-Experience; adult/child return £12.45/7.15; ⏲Apr-Nov) stops en route from Ferry House to Hawkshead.

Keswick

POP 4821

The main town of the north Lakes, Keswick sits beside lovely Derwent Water, a silvery curve studded by wooded islands and criss-crossed by puttering cruise boats, operated by the **Keswick Launch** (☎017687-72263; www.keswick-launch.co.uk; round-the-lake adult/child/family £10.25/5.15/24).

Sleeping

Keswick YHA HOSTEL £

(☎0845-371 9746; www.yha.org.uk; Station Rd; dm £18-30; ⏲reception 7am-11pm; 📶) Right along the River Greta, the town's YHA took a battering during the 2015 storms; much of the ground floor, including the cafe, was swamped and is yet to reopen (although the self-catering kitchen remains). The upper levels of the hostel largely escaped damage: choose from two- to six-bed dorms and relax in the lounge overlooking Fitz Park.

★Howe Keld B&B ££

(☎017687-72417; www.howekeld.co.uk; 5-7 The Heads; s £60-85, d £112-130; P 📶) This gold-standard B&B pulls out all the stops: goose-down duvets, slate-floored bathrooms, chic colours and locally made furniture. The best rooms have views across Crow Park and the golf course, and the breakfast is a pick-and-mix delight. Free parking is available on The Heads if there's space.

★Lookout B&B ££

(☎017687-80407; www.thelookoutkeswick.co.uk; Chestnut Hill; d £95-120; P 📶) The clue's in the name: this fine B&B is all about the views – there's a stunning panorama of fells filling every window. It's in a gabled 1920s house but feels modern with cappuccino-and-cream colour schemes, wooden beds and minimalist glass showers. Take Penrith Rd west and turn right onto Chestnut Hill; the B&B is on the left.

WALES

Lying to the west of England, Wales is a nation with Celtic roots, its own language and a rich historic legacy. While some areas in the south are undeniably scarred by coal mining and heavy industry, Wales boasts a scenic landscape of wild mountains, rolling hills and rich farmland, and the bustling capital city of Cardiff.

OTHER BRITISH PLACES WORTH A VISIT

Some places in Britain we recommend for day trips or longer visits:

Cornwall The southwestern tip of Britain is ringed with rugged granite seacliffs, sparkling bays, picturesque fishing villages and white sandy beaches.

Liverpool The city's waterfront is a World Heritage Site crammed with top museums, including the International Slavery Museum and the Beatles Story.

Hadrian's Wall One of the country's most dramatic Roman ruins, a 2000-year-old procession of abandoned forts and towers marching across the lonely landscape of northern England.

Glen Coe Scotland's most famous glen combines those two essential qualities of Highlands landscape: dramatic scenery and deep history.

Pembrokeshire Wales' western extremity is famous for its beaches and coastal walks, as well as being home to one of Britain's finest Norman castles.

Cardiff

POP 346,000

The capital of Wales since only 1955, Cardiff has embraced its new role with vigour, emerging as one of Britain's leading urban centres in the 21st century.

Sights

★Cardiff Castle CASTLE

(029-2087 8100; www.cardiffcastle.com; Castle St; adult/child £12/9, incl guided tour £15/11; 9am-5pm) There's a medieval keep at its heart, but it's the later additions to Cardiff Castle that really capture the imagination. During the Victorian era, extravagant mock-Gothic features were grafted onto this relic, including a clock tower and a lavish banqueting hall. Some but not all of this flamboyant fantasy world can be accessed with a regular castle entry; the rest can be visited as part of a guided tour.

★National Museum Cardiff MUSEUM

(0300 111 2 333; www.museumwales.ac.uk; Gorsedd Gardens Rd; 10am-4pm Tue-Sun) FREE Devoted mainly to natural history and art, this grand neoclassical building is the centrepiece of the seven institutions dotted around the country that together form the Welsh National Museum. It's one of Britain's best museums; you'll need at least three hours to do it justice, but it could easily consume the best part of a rainy day.

★Wales Millennium Centre ARTS CENTRE

(029-2063 6464; www.wmc.org.uk; Bute Pl, Cardiff Bay; tours adult/child £6/free; 9am-7pm) The centrepiece and symbol of Cardiff Bay's regeneration is the superb Wales Millennium Centre, an architectural masterpiece of stacked Welsh slate in shades of purple, green and grey topped with an overarching bronzed steel shell. Designed by Welsh architect Jonathan Adams, it opened in 2004 as Wales' premier arts complex, housing major cultural organisations such as the Welsh National Opera, National Dance Company, BBC National Orchestra of Wales, Literature Wales, HiJinx Theatre and Tŷ Cerdd (Music Centre Wales).

Doctor Who Experience GALLERY

(0844 801 2279; www.doctorwhoexperience.com; Porth Teigr; adult/child £15/11; 10am-5pm (last admission 3.30pm) daily Jul & Aug, Tue-Sun Mar-Jun, Sep & Oct, Wed-Sun Nov-Feb) The huge success of the reinvented classic TV series *Doctor Who*, produced by BBC Wales, has brought Cardiff to the attention of sci-fi fans worldwide. City locations have featured in many episodes; and the first two series of the spin-off *Torchwood* were also set in Cardiff Bay. Capitalising on Timelord tourism, this interactive exhibition is located right next to the BBC studios where the series is filmed – look out for the Tardis hovering outside.

Sleeping

★Safehouse HOSTEL £

(029-2037 2833; www.safehousehostel.com; 3 Westgate St; dm/s/d without bathroom from £14/35/37;) There aren't too many hostels with a grand Victorian sitting room to rival Safehouse's. Built in 1889, this lovely red-brick office building has been thoughtfully converted into a boutique hostel with private rooms and four- to 12-bed dorms.

WORTH A TRIP

CONWY CASTLE

On the north coast of Wales, the historic town of Conwy is utterly dominated by the Unesco-designated cultural treasure of **Conwy Castle** (Cadw; 01492-592358; www.cadw.wales.gov.uk; Castle Sq; adult/child £7.95/5.60; 9.30am-5pm Mar-Jun, Sep & Oct, to 6pm Jul & Aug, to 4pm Nov-Feb; P), the most stunning of all Edward I's Welsh fortresses. Built between 1277 and 1307 on a rocky outcrop, it has commanding views across the estuary and Snowdonia National Park.

Each bunk bed has its own built-in locker and electrical socket. It's on a busy road, so earplugs are a sensible precaution.

★Lincoln House HOTEL ££
(029-2039 5558; www.lincolnhotel.co.uk; 118 Cathedral Rd, Pontcanna; r £90-150; P) Walking a middle line between a large B&B and a small hotel, Lincoln House is a generously proportioned Victorian property with heraldic emblems in the stained-glass windows of its sitting room, and a separate bar. For added romance, book a four-poster room.

★Number 62 GUESTHOUSE ££
(07974 571348; www.number62.com; 62 Cathedral Rd, Pontcanna; s/d from £68/77;) The only thing stopping us calling Number 62 a B&B is that breakfast is only offered as an add-on. The cosy, comfortable rooms come with thoughtful extras such as body lotion, make-up wipes and cotton buds. It also has one of the most lovingly tended front gardens of all of the converted town houses on this strip.

Eating

★Riverside Market MARKET £
(www.riversidemarket.org.uk; Fitzhamon Embankment, Riverside; 10am-2pm Sun;) What it lacks in size, Riverside Market makes up for in sheer yumminess, its stalls heaving with cooked meals, cakes, cheese, organic meat, charcuterie and bread. There are lots of options for vegetarians and an excellent coffee stall.

★Mint & Mustard INDIAN ££
(029-2062 0333; www.mintandmustard.com; 134 Whitchurch Rd, Cathays; mains £8.25-15; noon-2pm & 5-11pm;) Specialising in seafood dishes from India's southern state of Kerala, this excellent restaurant combines an upmarket ambience with attentive service and delicious, beautifully presented food. If you're not enticed by the lobster, prawn and fish dishes, there are plenty of vegetarian options and an excellent crusted lamb biryani.

★Fish at 85 SEAFOOD £££
(029-2023 5666; www.fishat85.co.uk; 85 Pontcanna Rd, Pontcanna; mains £19-24; noon-2.30pm & 6-9pm Tue-Sat) By day a fishmongers (hence the lingering smell), by night an elegant restaurant with Cape Cod-ish decor and candles floating in water-filled jars, Fish at 85 is Cardiff's premier spot for a seafood dinner. The menu cherry-picks the best of the day's catch, offering half-a-dozen varieties, exquisitely cooked and in huge portions.

Information

Tourist Office (029-2087 3573; www.visitcardiff.com; Wales Millennium Centre, Bute Pl, Cardiff Bay; 10am-6pm Mon-Sat, to 4pm Sun) Information, advice and souvenirs.

Getting There & Away

BUS

Cardiff's central bus station has closed for a major redevelopment and is due to reopen near the train station in a revitalised Central Sq in 2018.

National Express coaches travel to London (from £5, 3½ hours, four daily) and Bristol (£6.10, one hour, four daily).

TRAIN

Direct services from Cardiff include London Paddington (from £40, two hours, two per hour) and Bristol (£12.50, 50 minutes, half-hourly).

Snowdonia National Park

Snowdonia National Park (Parc Cenedlaethol Eryri; www.eryri-npa.gov.uk) was founded in 1951 (making it Wales' first national park). Around 350,000 people travel to the national park to climb, walk or take the train to the summit of Mt Snowdon, Wales' highest mountain.

Snowdon (Yr Wyddfa)

No Snowdonia experience is complete without coming face-to-face with Snowdon (1085m) – 'Yr Wyddfa' in Welsh (pronounced uhr-*with*-vuh, meaning 'the Tomb'). On a clear day the views stretch to Ireland and the Isle of Man. Even on a gloomy day you could find yourself above the clouds. At the top is the striking **Hafod Eryri** (⏲10am–20min before last train departure; 📶) visitor centre, opened in 2009 by Prince Charles.

Six paths of varying length and difficulty lead to the summit, all taking around six hours return, or you can cheat and catch the **Snowdon Mountain Railway** (☎01286-870223; www.snowdonrailway.co.uk; Llanberis; adult/child return diesel £29/20, steam £37/27; ⏲9am-5pm mid-Mar–Nov), opened in 1896 and still the UK's only public rack-and-pinion railway.

However you get to the summit, take warm, waterproof clothing, wear sturdy footwear and check the weather forecast before setting out.

Sleeping

YHA Snowdon Ranger HOSTEL £

(☎08453-719659; www.yha.org.uk; Rhyd Ddu; d/tw £29/55; P 📶) On the A4085, 5 miles north of Beddgelert at the trailhead for the Snowdon Ranger Path, this former inn has its own adjoining lakeside beach, and is close to Llanberis too. Accommodation is basic but dependable.

Pen-y-Gwryd HOTEL ££

(☎01286-870211; www.pyg.co.uk; Nant Gwynant; s/d from £45/90; P 📶) Eccentric but full of atmosphere, this Georgian coaching inn was used as a training base by the 1953 Everest team, and memorabilia from their stay includes signatures on the restaurant ceiling. TV, wi-fi and mobile-phone signals don't penetrate here; instead, there's a comfy games room, sauna and a lake for those hardy enough to swim.

Getting There & Away

The **Welsh Highland Railway** (☎01766-516000; www.festrail.co.uk; adult/child return £38/34.20; ⏲Easter-Oct, limited winter service) and Snowdon Sherpa buses link various places in Snowdonia with the town of Caernarfon, which can be reached by train from London Euston (£86, 3¼ hours, hourly).

SCOTLAND

Despite its small size, Scotland has many treasures crammed into its compact territory – big skies, lonely landscapes, spectacular wildlife, superb seafood and hospitable, down-to-earth people. From the cultural attractions of Edinburgh to the heather-clad hills of the Highlands, there's something for everyone.

Edinburgh

POP 498,810

Edinburgh is a city that just begs to be explored. From the imposing castle to the Palace of Holyroodhouse to the Royal Yacht Britannia, every corner turned reveals sudden views and unexpected vistas – green sunlit hills, a glimpse of rust-red crags, a blue flash of distant sea. But there's more to Edinburgh than sightseeing – there are top shops, world-class restaurants and a bacchanalia of bars to enjoy.

Sights

★**Edinburgh Castle** CASTLE

(www.edinburghcastle.gov.uk; Castle Esplanade; adult/child £16.50/9.90, audioguide additional £3.50; ⏲9.30am-6pm Apr-Sep, to 5pm Oct-Mar, last admission 1hr before closing; 🚌23, 27, 41, 42) Edinburgh Castle has played a pivotal role in Scottish history, both as a royal residence – King Malcolm Canmore (r 1058–93) and Queen Margaret first made their home here in the 11th century – and as a military stronghold. The castle last saw military action in 1745; from then until the 1920s it served as the British army's main base in Scotland. Today it is one of Scotland's most atmospheric and popular tourist attractions.

★**Real Mary King's Close** HISTORIC BUILDING

(☎0845 070 6244; www.realmarykingsclose.com; 2 Warriston's Close, High St; adult/child £14.50/8.75; ⏲10am-9pm daily Apr-Oct, 10am-5pm Sun-Thu, 10am-9pm Fri & Sat Nov-Mar; 🚌23, 27, 41, 42) Edinburgh's 18th-century City Chambers were built over the sealed-off remains of Mary King's Close, and the lower levels of this medieval Old Town alley have survived almost unchanged amid the foundations for 250 years. Now open to the public, this spooky, subterranean labyrinth gives a fascinating insight into the everyday life of 17th-century Edinburgh. Costumed characters lead tours through a 16th-century town house and the plague-stricken home of a 17th-century gravedigger. Advance booking recommended.

★**National Museum of Scotland** MUSEUM

(www.nms.ac.uk; Chambers St; fee for special exhibitions varies; ⏲10am-5pm; 👪; 🚌2, 23, 27, 35, 41, 42, 45) FREE Broad, elegant Chambers St is dominated by the long facade of the National

Museum of Scotland. Its extensive collections are spread between two buildings, one modern, one Victorian – the golden stone and striking modern architecture of the new building, opened in 1998, is one of the city's most distinctive landmarks. The five floors of the museum trace the history of Scotland from its geological beginnings to the 1990s, with many imaginative and stimulating exhibits. Audio-guides are available in several languages.

★Scottish Parliament Building NOTABLE BUILDING
(☎0131-348 5200; www.scottish.parliament.uk; Horse Wynd; ⏲9am-6.30pm Tue-Thu & 10am-5pm Mon, Fri & Sat in session, 10am-5pm Mon-Sat in recess; 📶; 🚌6, 35) FREE The Scottish parliament building, on the site of a former brewery, was officially opened by HM the Queen in October 2005. Designed by Catalan architect Enric Miralles (1955–2000), the ground plan of the parliament complex is said to represent a 'flower of democracy rooted in Scottish soil' (best seen looking down from Salisbury Crags). Free, one-hour guided tours (advance booking recommended) include a visit to the Debating Chamber, a committee room, the Garden Lobby and an MSP's (Member of the Scottish Parliament) office.

★Royal Yacht Britannia SHIP
(www.royalyachtbritannia.co.uk; Ocean Terminal; adult/child £15/8.50; ⏲9.30am-6pm Jul-Sep, to 5.30pm Apr-Jun & Oct, 10am-5pm Nov-Mar, last admission 90min before closing; 📶; 🚌11, 22, 34, 35, 36) Built on Clydeside, the former Royal Yacht *Britannia* was the British royal family's floating holiday home during their foreign travels from the time of her launch in 1953 until her decommissioning in 1997, and is now moored permanently in front of **Ocean Terminal** (☎0131-555 8888; www.oceanterminal.com; Ocean Dr; ⏲10am-8pm Mon-Fri, to 7pm Sat, 11am-6pm Sun; 📶). The tour, which you take at your own pace with an audioguide (included in the admission fee and available in 20 languages), lifts the curtain on the everyday lives of the royals, and gives an intriguing insight into the Queen's private tastes.

★Palace of Holyroodhouse PALACE
(www.royalcollection.org.uk; Horse Wynd; adult/child incl audioguide £12/7.20; ⏲9.30am-6pm Apr-Oct, to 4.30pm Nov-Mar; 📶; 🚌6, 35) This palace is the royal family's official residence in Scotland, but is more famous as the 16th-century home of the ill-fated Mary, Queen of Scots. The highlight of the tour is **Mary's Bed Chamber**, home to the unfortunate queen from 1561 to 1567. It was here that her jealous second husband, Lord Darnley, restrained the pregnant queen while his henchmen murdered her secretary – and favourite – Rizzio. A plaque in the neighbouring room marks the spot where he bled to death.

THE QUEENSFERRY CROSSING

The famous Forth Bridge (1890) and Forth Road Bridge (1964), which soar across the Firth of Forth to the west of Edinburgh have been joined by the impressive Queensferry Crossing (a new bridge opening May 2017).

Sleeping

★Malone's Old Town Hostel HOSTEL £
(☎0131-226 7648; www.maloneshostel.com; 14 Forrest Rd; dm £12-20; @📶; 🚌2, 23, 27, 41, 42, 45) No fancy decor or style credentials here, but they've got the basics right: it's clean, comfortable and friendly, and set upstairs from an Irish pub where guests get discounts on food and drink. The cherry on the cake is its superbly central location, an easy walk from the Royal Mile, the castle, the Grassmarket and Princes St.

Code Hostel HOSTEL £
(☎0131-659 9883; www.codehostel.com; 50 Rose St N Lane; dm from £25, d £99; 📶; 🚋Princes St) This upmarket hostel, bang in the middle of the New Town, combines cute designer decor with innovative sleeping cubicles that offer more privacy than bunks (four to six people per dorm, each with en suite shower room). There's also a luxurious double apartment called the Penthouse, complete with kitchenette and roof terrace.

★Southside Guest House B&B ££
(☎0131-668 4422; www.southsideguesthouse.co.uk; 8 Newington Rd; s/d from £80/105; 📶; 🚌all Newington buses) Though set in a typical Victorian terrace, the Southside transcends the traditional guesthouse category and feels more like a modern boutique hotel. Its eight stylish rooms ooze interior design, standing out from other Newington B&Bs through the clever use of bold colours and modern

furniture. Breakfast is an event, with Bucks Fizz (cava mixed with orange juice) on offer to ease the hangover!

★ Wallace's Arthouse B&B ££
(☎ 07941 343714; www.wallacesarthousescotland.com; 41/4 Constitution St; s/d £99/120; ; 12, 16) This Georgian apartment, housed in the neoclassical Leith Assembly Rooms (a Grade A listed building), offers two beautifully nostalgic bedrooms styled by former fashion designer Wallace, who comes as part of the package – your charming host and breakfast chef is an unfailing source of colourful anecdotes and local knowledge.

★ Sheridan Guest House B&B ££
(☎ 0131-554 4107; www.sheridanedinburgh.com; 1 Bonnington Tce, Newhaven Rd; r from £95; P ; 7, 11, 14) Flowerpots filled with colourful blooms line the steps of this little haven hidden away to the north of the New Town. The eight bedrooms (all en suite) blend crisp colours with contemporary furniture, stylish lighting and colourful paintings, which complement the house's clean-cut Georgian lines, while the breakfast menu adds omelettes, pancakes with maple syrup, and scrambled eggs with smoked salmon to the usual offerings.

Eating

★ Mums CAFE £
(☎ 0131-260 9806; www.monstermashcafe.co.uk; 4a Forrest Rd; mains £8-11; 9am-10pm Mon-Sat, 10am-10pm Sun; ; 23, 27, 41, 42) This nostalgia-fuelled cafe serves up classic British comfort food that wouldn't look out of place on a 1950s menu – bacon and eggs, bangers and mash, shepherd's pie, fish and chips. But there's a twist – the food is all top-quality nosh freshly prepared from local produce. There's also a good selection of bottled craft beers and Scottish-brewed cider.

★ Aizle SCOTTISH ££
(☎ 0131-662 9349; http://aizle.co.uk; 107-109 St Leonard's St; 5-course dinner £45; 6-9.30pm Wed, Thu & Sun, 5-9.30pm Fri & Sat; ; 14) If you're the sort who has trouble deciding what to eat, Aizle will do it for you (the name is an old Scots word for 'spark' or 'ember'). There's no menu, just a five-course dinner conjured from a monthly 'harvest' of the finest and freshest of local produce (listed on a blackboard), and presented beautifully – art on a plate.

FESTIVAL CITY

Edinburgh boasts a frenzy of festivals throughout the year, including the world-famous **Edinburgh Festival Fringe** (☎ 0131-226 0026; www.edfringe.com), held over 3½ weeks in August. The last two weeks overlap with the first two weeks of the **Edinburgh International Festival** (☎ 0131-473 2000; www.eif.co.uk). See www.edinburghfestivals.co.uk for more.

★ Cannonball Restaurant SCOTTISH ££
(☎ 0131-225 1550; www.contini.com/contini-cannonball; 356 Castlehill, Royal Mile; mains £15-25; noon-5pm & 5.30-10pm Tue-Sat; ; 23, 27, 41, 42) The historic Cannonball House next to Edinburgh Castle's esplanade has been transformed into a sophisticated restaurant (and whisky bar) where the Contini family work their Italian magic on Scottish classics to produce dishes such as haggis balls with spiced pickled turnip and whisky marmalade, and lobster with wild garlic and lemon butter.

★ Gardener's Cottage SCOTTISH ££
(☎ 0131-558 1221; www.thegardenerscottage.co; 1 Royal Terrace Gardens, London Rd; lunch mains £16-17, dinner set menu £40; noon-2pm & 5-10pm Mon & Wed-Fri, 10am-2pm & 5-10pm Sat & Sun; all London Rd buses) This country cottage in the heart of the city, bedecked with flowers and fairy lights, offers one of Edinburgh's most interesting dining experiences – two tiny rooms with communal tables made of salvaged timber, and a menu based on fresh local produce (most of the vegetables and fruit are grown in a local organic garden). Bookings essential; brunch served at weekends.

★ Ondine SEAFOOD £££
(☎ 0131-226 1888; www.ondinerestaurant.co.uk; 2 George IV Bridge; mains £17-40, 2-/3-course lunch £25/30; noon-3pm & 5.30-10pm Mon-Sat; ; 23, 27, 41, 42) Ondine is one of Edinburgh's finest seafood restaurants, with a menu based on sustainably sourced fish. Take a seat at the curved Oyster Bar and tuck into oysters Kilpatrick, smoked haddock chowder, lobster thermidor, a roast shellfish platter or just good old haddock and chips (with minted pea purée, just to keep things posh).

Central Edinburgh

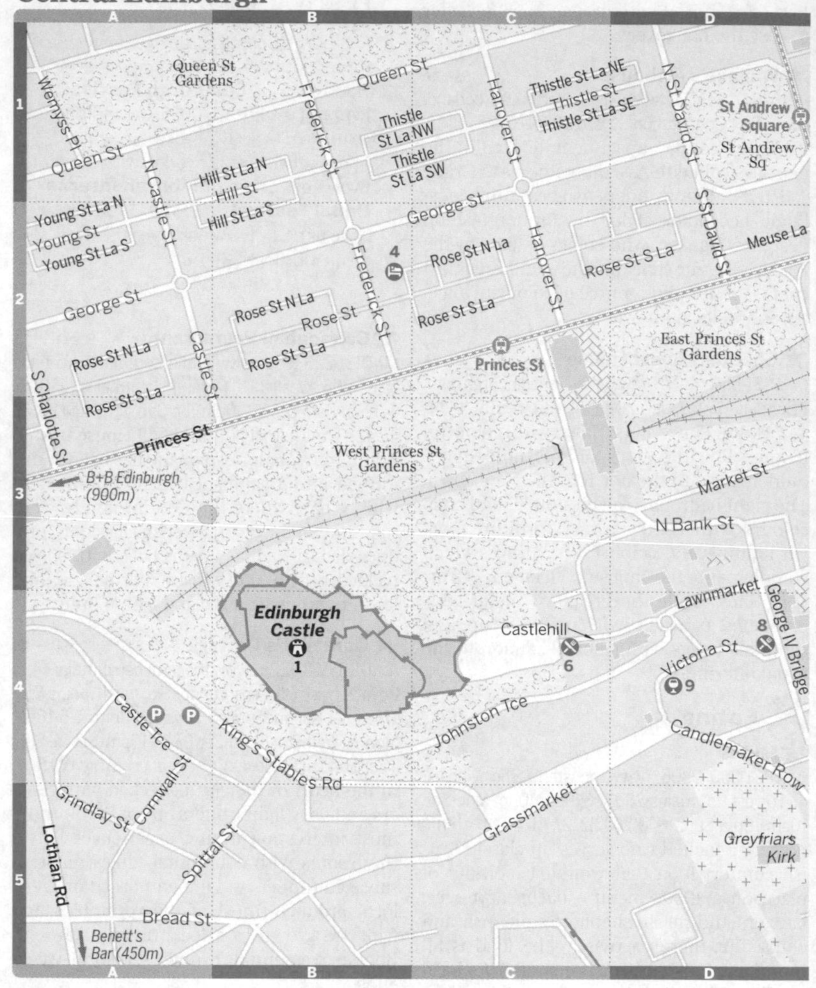

Drinking & Nightlife

Café Royal Circle Bar PUB

(www.caferoyaledinburgh.co.uk; 17 West Register St; 11am-11pm Mon-Wed, to midnight Thu, to 1am Fri & Sat, 12.30-11pm Sun; ; Princes St) Perhaps *the* classic Edinburgh pub, the Café Royal's main claims to fame are its magnificent oval bar and its Doulton tile portraits of famous Victorian inventors. Sit at the bar or claim one of the cosy leather booths beneath the stained-glass windows, and choose from the seven real ales on tap.

★Bow Bar PUB

(www.thebowbar.co.uk; 80 West Bow; noon-midnight Mon-Sat, to 11.30pm Sun; 2, 23, 27, 41, 42) One of the city's best traditional-style pubs (it's not as old as it looks), serving a range of excellent real ales, Scottish craft gins and a vast selection of malt whiskies, the Bow Bar often has standing-room only on Friday and Saturday evenings.

★Bennet's Bar PUB

(0131-229 5143; www.bennetsbaredinburgh.co.uk; 8 Leven St; 11am-1am; all Tollcross buses) Situated beside the King's Theatre, Ben-

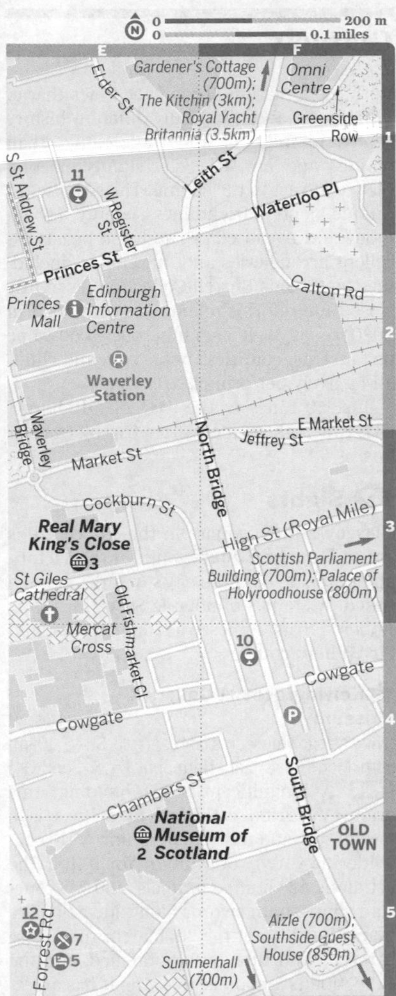

net's has managed to hang on to almost all of its beautiful Victorian fittings, from the leaded stained-glass windows and ornate mirrors to the wooden gantry and the brass water taps on the bar (for your whisky – there are over 100 malts from which to choose).

★ **Roseleaf** BAR

(0131-476 5268; www.roseleaf.co.uk; 23-24 Sandport Pl; 10am-1am; ; 16, 22, 35, 36) Cute, quaint and verging on chintzy, the Roseleaf could hardly be further from the average Leith bar. Decked out in flowered wallpaper, old furniture and rose-patterned

Central Edinburgh

china (cocktails are served in teapots), the real ales and bottled beers are complemented by a range of speciality teas, coffees and fruit drinks (including rose lemonade), and well-above-average pub grub (served from 10am to 10pm).

★ **Cabaret Voltaire** CLUB

(www.thecabaretvoltaire.com; 36-38 Blair St; 5pm-3am Mon-Thu, noon-3am Fri-Sun; ; all South Bridge buses) An atmospheric warren of stone-lined vaults houses this self-consciously 'alternative' club, which eschews huge dance floors and egotistical DJ worship in favour of a 'creative crucible' hosting an eclectic mix of DJs, live acts, comedy, theatre, visual arts and the spoken word. Well worth a look.

☆ Entertainment

The comprehensive source for what's on is *The List* (www.list.co.uk).

★ **Sandy Bell's** TRADITIONAL MUSIC

(www.sandybellsedinburgh.co.uk; 25 Forrest Rd; noon-1am Mon-Sat, 12.30pm-midnight Sun; 2, 23, 27, 41, 42, 45) This unassuming pub is a stalwart of the traditional music scene (the founder's wife sang with the Corries). There's music almost every evening at 9pm, and from 3pm Saturday and Sunday, plus lots of impromptu sessions.

★ **Summerhall** THEATRE

(0131-560 1580; www.summerhall.co.uk; 1 Summerhall; 41, 42, 67) Formerly Edinburgh

University's veterinary school, the Summerhall complex is a major cultural centre and entertainment venue, with old halls and lecture theatres (including an original anatomy lecture theatre) now serving as venues for drama, dance, cinema and comedy performances. It's also one of the main venues for Edinburgh Festival events.

Information

Edinburgh Information Centre (0131-473 3868; www.edinburgh.org; Waverley Mall, 3 Princes St; 9am-7pm Mon-Sat, 10am-7pm Sun Jul & Aug, to 6pm Jun, to 5pm Sep-May; ; St Andrew Sq) Includes an accommodation booking service, currency exchange, gift and bookshop, internet access and counters selling tickets for Edinburgh city tours and Scottish Citylink bus services.

Getting There & Away

AIR

Edinburgh Airport (EDI; 0844 448 8833; www.edinburghairport.com), 8 miles west of the city, has numerous flights to other parts of Scotland and the UK, Ireland and mainland Europe.

BUS

Scottish Citylink (0871 266 3333; www.citylink.co.uk) buses connect Edinburgh with all of Scotland's cities and major towns, including Glasgow (£7.50, 1¼ hours, every 15 minutes), Stirling (£8.20, one hour, hourly) and Inverness (£31, 3½ to 4½ hours, hourly). National Express operates a direct coach service from London (from £28, 10 hours, two daily).

It's also worth checking with **Megabus** (0141-352 4444; www.megabus.com) for cheap intercity bus fares from Edinburgh to London, Glasgow and Inverness.

TRAIN

The main terminus in Edinburgh is Waverley train station, in the heart of the city. Trains arriving from, and departing for, the west also stop at Haymarket station, which is more convenient for the West End.

ScotRail (0344-811 0141; www.scotrail.co.uk) operates a regular shuttle service between Edinburgh and Glasgow (£12.50, 50 minutes, every 15 minutes), and frequent daily services to all Scottish cities, including Stirling (£8.60, one hour, twice hourly Monday to Saturday, hourly Sunday) and Inverness (£38, 3½ hours, eight daily). There are also regular trains to London Kings Cross (from £82, 4½ hours, at least hourly) via York.

Glasgow

POP 596,500

With a population around 1½ times that of Edinburgh, and a radically different history rooted in industry and trade rather than politics and law, Glasgow stands in complete contrast to the capital. The city offers a unique blend of friendliness, energy, dry humour and urban chaos, and also boasts excellent art galleries and museums – including the famous Burrell Collection (currently closed for refurbishment, due to reopen in 2020) – as well as numerous good-value restaurants, countless pubs, bars and clubs, and a lively performing-arts scene.

Just 50 miles to the west of Edinburgh, Glasgow makes an easy day trip by train or bus.

Sights

Glasgow's main square in the city centre is grand **George Square**, built in the Victorian era to show off the city's wealth, and dignified by statues of notable Scots, including Robert Burns, James Watt, John Moore and Sir Walter Scott.

★Kelvingrove Art Gallery & Museum — GALLERY, MUSEUM

(www.glasgowmuseums.com; Argyle St; 10am-5pm Mon-Thu & Sat, 11am-5pm Fri & Sun;) FREE A magnificent stone building, this grand Victorian cathedral of culture is a fascinating and unusual museum, with a bewildering variety of exhibits. You'll find fine art alongside stuffed animals, and Micronesian shark-tooth swords alongside a Spitfire plane, but it's not mix 'n' match: rooms are carefully and thoughtfully themed, and the collection is a manageable size. It has an excellent room of Scottish art, a room of fine French Impressionist works, and quality Renaissance paintings from Italy and Flanders.

★Riverside Museum — MUSEUM

(0141-287 2720; www.glasgowmuseums.com; 100 Pointhouse Pl; 10am-5pm Mon-Thu & Sat, 11am-5pm Fri & Sun;) FREE This visually impressive modern museum at Glasgow Harbour owes its striking curved forms to late British-Iraqi architect Zaha Hadid. A transport museum forms the main part of the collection, featuring a fascinating series of cars made in Scotland, plus assorted railway locos, trams, bikes (including the world's first pedal-powered bicycle from

DON'T MISS

STIRLING CASTLE

Hold Stirling and you control Scotland. This maxim has ensured that a fortress of some kind has existed here since prehistoric times. You cannot help drawing parallels with Edinburgh Castle, but many find **Stirling Castle** (HS; www.stirlingcastle.gov.uk; Castle Wynd; adult/child £14.50/8.70; 9.30am-6pm Apr-Sep, to 5pm Oct-Mar; P) more atmospheric – the location, architecture, historical significance and commanding views combine to make it a grand and memorable sight.

The current castle dates from the late 14th to the 16th century, when it was a residence of the Stuart monarchs. The undisputed highlight of a visit is the fabulous, recently restored **Royal Palace**. The idea was that it should look brand new, just as when it was constructed by French masons under the orders of James V in the mid-16th century with the aim of impressing his new (also French) bride and other crowned heads of Europe.

The suite of six rooms – three for the king, three for the queen – is a sumptuous riot of colour. Particularly notable are the fine fireplaces, the **Stirling Heads** – modern reproductions of painted oak discs in the ceiling of the king's audience chamber – and the fabulous series of **tapestries** that have been painstakingly woven over many years.

Stirling is 35 miles northwest of Edinburgh, and easily reached by train (£8.60, one hour, half-hourly Monday to Saturday, hourly Sunday).

1847) and model Clyde-built ships. An atmospheric recreation of a Glasgow shopping street from the early 20th century puts the vintage vehicles into a social context. There's also a cafe.

★Glasgow Cathedral CATHEDRAL
(HES; 0141-552 8198; www.historicenvironment.scot; Cathedral Sq; 9.30am-5.30pm Mon-Sat & 1-5pm Sun Apr-Sep, 10am-4pm Mon-Sat & 1-4pm Sun Oct-Mar) FREE Glasgow Cathedral has a rare timelessness. The dark, imposing interior conjures up medieval might and can send a shiver down the spine. It's a shining example of Gothic architecture, and unlike nearly all of Scotland's cathedrals, survived the turmoil of the Reformation mobs almost intact. Most of the current building dates from the 15th century.

★Glasgow Science Centre MUSEUM
(0141-420 5000; www.glasgowsciencecentre.org; 50 Pacific Quay; adult/child £11/9, IMAX, tower or planetarium extra £2.50-3.50; 10am-5pm Wed-Sun Nov-Mar, 10am-5pm daily Apr-Oct;) This ultramodern science museum will keep the kids entertained for hours (that's middle-aged kids, too!). It brings science and technology alive through hundreds of interactive exhibits on four floors: a bounty of discovery for inquisitive minds. There's also an **IMAX theatre** (see www.cineworld.com for current screenings), a rotating 127m-high **observation tower**; a **planetarium**, and a **Science Theatre**, with live science demonstrations. To get here, take bus 89 or 90 from Union St.

Eating & Drinking

★Ox & Finch FUSION £
(0141-339 8627; www.oxandfinch.com; 920 Sauchiehall St; portions £4-8; noon-10pm;) This fashionable place could almost sum up the thriving modern Glasgow eating scene, with a faux-pub name, sleek but comfortable contemporary decor, tapas-sized dishes and an open kitchen. Grab a cosy booth and be prepared to have your tastebuds wowed with innovative, delicious creations aimed at sharing, drawing on French and Mediterreanean influences but focusing on quality Scottish produce.

★Saramago Café Bar CAFE £
(0141-352 4920; www.facebook.com/saramagocafebar; 350 Sauchiehall St; light meals £3-9; food noon-10pm Sun-Wed, noon-11.30pm Thu-Sat;) In the airy atrium of the Centre for Contemporary Arts, this place does a great line in eclectic vegan fusion food, with a range of top flavour combinations from around the globe. The upstairs bar has a great deck on steep Scott St and packs out inside with a friendly hipstery crowd enjoying the DJ sets and quality tap beers.

★Mother India INDIAN ££
(0141-221 1663; www.motherindia.co.uk; 28 Westminster Tce, Sauchiehall St; mains £8-16; 5.30-10.30pm Mon-Thu, noon-11pm Fri, 1-11pm Sat, 1-10pm Sun;) Glasgow curry buffs forever debate the merits of the city's numerous excellent South Asian restaurants, and this features in every discussion. It may lack the

Glasgow

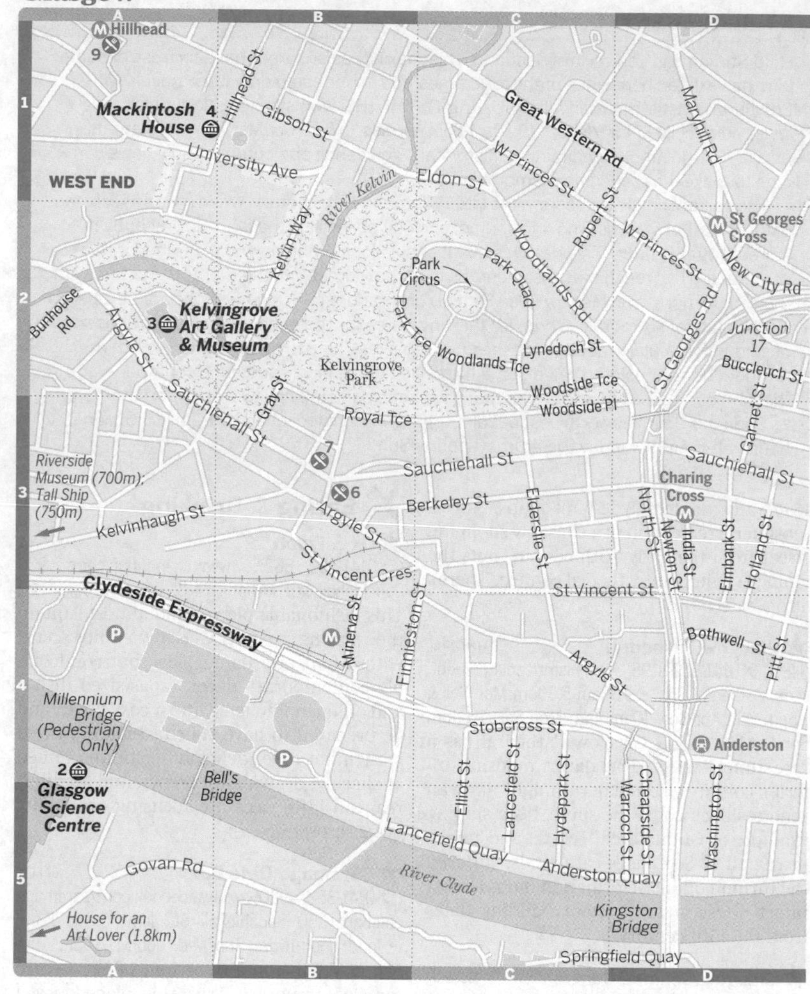

trendiness of some of the up-and-comers, but it's been a stalwart for years, and the quality and innovation on show are superb. The three dining areas are all attractive and it makes an effort for kids, with a separate menu.

★Ubiquitous Chip SCOTTISH £££
(0141-334 5007; www.ubiquitouschip.co.uk; 12 Ashton Lane; 2-/3-course lunch £17/21, mains £22-35, brasserie mains £10-15; noon-2.30pm & 5-11pm Mon-Sat, 12.30-3pm & 5-11pm Sun;) The original champion of Scottish produce, this is legendary for its unparalleled Scottish cuisine and lengthy wine list. Named to poke fun at Scotland's culinary reputation, it offers a French touch but resolutely Scottish ingredients, carefully selected and following sustainable principles. The elegant courtyard space offers some of Glasgow's best dining, while, above, the cheaper brasserie offers exceptional value for money.

Horse Shoe PUB
(www.horseshoebar.co.uk; 17 Drury St; 10am-midnight Sun-Fri, 9am-midnight Sat) This legendary city pub and popular meeting

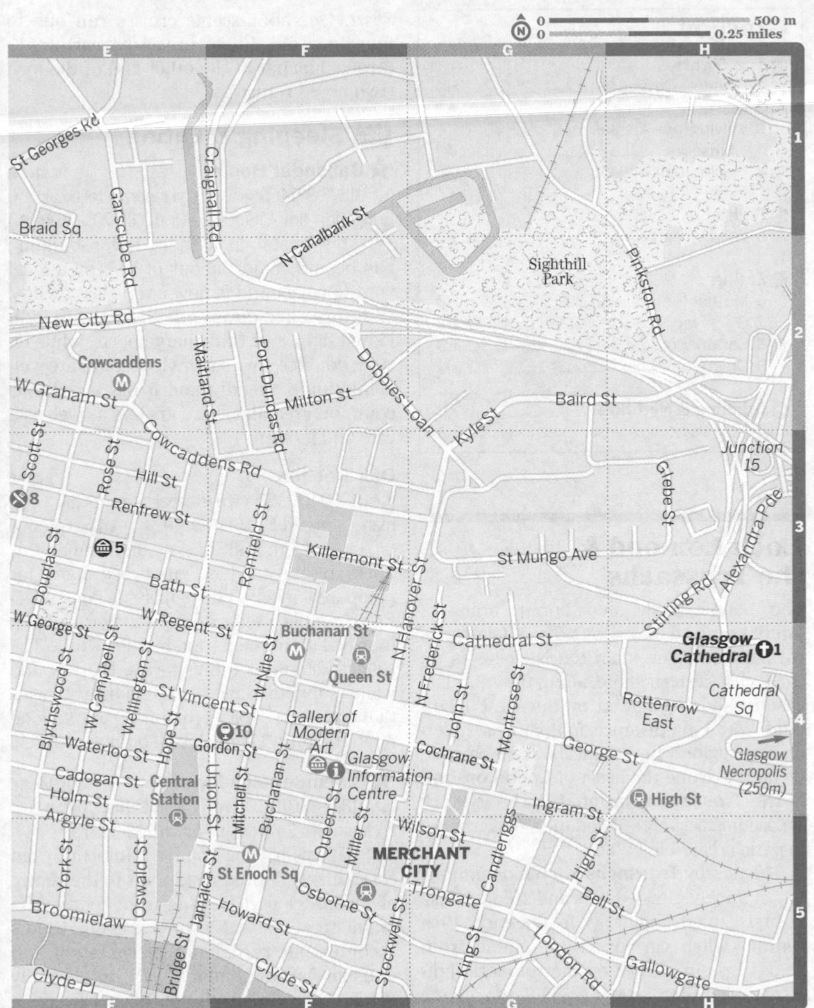

place dates from the late 19th century and is largely unchanged. It's a picturesque spot, with the longest continuous bar in the UK, but its main attraction is what's served over it – real ale and good cheer. Upstairs in the lounge is some of the best-value pub food (three-course lunch £4.50) in town.

Information

Glasgow Information Centre (www.visitscotland.com; Gallery of Modern Art, Royal Exchange Sq; ⏲10am-4.45pm, till 7.45pm Thu, from 11am Fri & Sun; 📶) In the **Gallery of Modern Art** (GoMA; ☎0141-287 3050; www.glasgowmuseums.com; Royal Exchange Sq; ⏲10am-5pm Mon-Thu & Sat, until 8pm Thu, 11am-5pm Fri & Sun; 📶).

Getting There & Away

Glasgow is easily reached from Edinburgh by bus (£7.50, 1¼ hours, every 15 minutes) or train (£13.60, 50 minutes, every 15 minutes).

Glasgow

Top Sights

1 Glasgow Cathedral H4
2 Glasgow Science Centre A4
3 Kelvingrove Art Gallery & Museum A2
4 Mackintosh House A1

Sights

5 Willow Tearooms E3

Eating

6 Mother India B3
7 Ox & Finch B3
8 Saramago Café Bar E3
9 Ubiquitous Chip A1

Drinking & Nightlife

10 Horse Shoe F4

Loch Lomond & the Trossachs

The 'bonnie banks' and 'bonnie braes' of **Loch Lomond** have long been Glasgow's rural retreat. The main tourist focus is on the loch's western shore, along the A82. The eastern shore, followed by the West Highland Way long-distance footpath, is quieter. The region's importance was recognised when it became the heart of **Loch Lomond & the Trossachs National Park** (www.lochlomond-trossachs.org) – Scotland's first national park, created in 2002.

The nearby **Trossachs** is a region famous for its thickly forested hills and scenic lochs. It first gained popularity in the early 19th century when curious visitors came from across Britain, drawn by the romantic language of Walter Scott's poem *Lady of the Lake,* inspired by Loch Katrine, and his novel *Rob Roy,* about the derring-do of the region's most famous son.

The main centre for Loch Lomond boat trips is Balloch, where **Sweeney's Cruises** (☎01389-752376; www.sweeneyscruiseco.com; Balloch Rd) offers a range of outings, including a one-hour cruise to Inchmurrin and back (adult/child £10.20/7, five times daily April to October, twice daily November to March).

Loch Katrine Cruises (☎01877-376315; www.lochkatrine.com; Trossachs Pier; 1hr cruise adult £11-13, child £5.50-6.50; ⏰Easter-Oct) runs boat trips from Trossachs Pier at the eastern end of Loch Katrine, some aboard the fabulous centenarian steamship *Sir Walter Scott*. One-hour scenic cruises run one to four times daily; there are also departures to Stronachlachar at the other end of the loch (two hours return).

Sleeping & Eating

★Callander Hostel HOSTEL £

(☎01877-331465; www.callanderhostel.co.uk; 6 Bridgend; dm £18.50-23.50, d £60-70; P @ 📶) This hostel in a mock-Tudor building has been a major labour of love by a local youth project and is now a top-class facility. Well-furnished dorms offer bunks with individual light and USB charge ports, while en suite doubles have super views. Staff are welcoming and friendly, and it has a spacious common area and share kitchen as well as a cafe and garden.

Oak Tree Inn INN ££

(☎01360-870357; www.theoaktreeinn.co.uk; Balmaha; dm/s/d £30/70/90; P 📶) An attractive traditional inn built in slate and timber, this offers bright modern guest bedrooms for pampered hikers, plus super-spacious superior chambers, self-catering cottages and two four-bed bunkrooms for hardier souls. The rustic restaurant brings locals, tourists and walkers together and dishes up hearty meals that cover lots of bases (mains £9 to £12; food noon to 9pm). There's lots of outdoor seating.

★Callander Meadows SCOTTISH ££

(☎01877-330181; www.callandermeadows.co.uk; 24 Main St; 2-/3-course lunch £12/17, mains £13-17; ⏰10am-9pm Thu-Mon; 📶) Informal and cosy, this well-loved restaurant in the centre of Callander occupies the front rooms of a main-street house. It's truly excellent; there's a contemporary flair for presentation and unusual flavour combinations, but a solidly British base underpins the cuisine. There's a great beer/coffee garden out the back, where you can also eat. Opens daily from June to September.

Drover's Inn PUB FOOD ££

(☎01301-704234; www.thedroversinn.co.uk; Ardlui; bar meals £9-14; ⏰11.30am-10pm Mon-Sat, 11.30am-9.30pm or 10pm Sun; 📶) Don't miss this low-ceilinged howff (drinking den) just north of Ardlui with its smoke-blackened stone, kilted bartenders, and walls festooned with moth-eaten stags' heads and stuffed birds. The bar, where Rob Roy allegedly dropped by for pints, serves hearty hill-walking fuel and hosts live folk music at weekends. Recommended more as an atmospheric place to eat and drink than somewhere to stay.

Getting There & Away

Balloch, at the southern end of Loch Lomond, can be easily reached from Glasgow by bus (£5, 1½ hours, at least two per hour) or train (£5.30, 45 minutes, every 30 minutes).

For exploring the Trossachs, your own transport is recommended.

Inverness

Inverness, the primary city and shopping centre of the Highlands, has a great location astride the River Ness at the northern end of the Great Glen. It's a jumping-off point for exploring Loch Ness and northern Scotland, with the railway line from Edinburgh branching east to Elgin and Aberdeen, north to Thurso and Wick, and west to Kyle of Lochalsh (the nearest train station to the Isle of Skye). The latter route is one of Britain's great scenic rail journeys.

Sleeping

Bazpackers Backpackers Hotel HOSTEL £
(☎01463-717663; www.bazpackershostel.co.uk; 4 Culduthel Rd; dm/tw £18/50; @ wi-fi) This may be Inverness' smallest hostel (34 beds), but it's hugely popular. It's a friendly, quiet place – the main building has a convivial lounge centred on a wood-burning stove, and a small garden and great views (some rooms are in a separate building with no garden). The dorms and kitchen can be a bit cramped, but the showers are great.

★ **Trafford Bank** B&B ££
(☎01463-241414; www.traffordbankguesthouse.co.uk; 96 Fairfield Rd; d £120-140; P wi-fi) Lots of word-of-mouth rave reviews for this elegant Victorian villa, which was once home to a bishop, just a mitre-toss from the Caledonian Canal and 10 minutes' walk west from the city centre. The luxurious rooms include fresh flowers and fruit, bathrobes and fluffy towels – ask for the Tartan Room, which has a wrought-iron king-size bed and Victorian roll-top bath.

★ **Rocpool Reserve** BOUTIQUE HOTEL £££
(☎01463-240089; www.rocpool.com; Culduthel Rd; s/d from £195/230; P wi-fi) Boutique chic meets the Highlands in this slick and sophisticated little hotel, where an elegant Georgian exterior conceals an oasis of contemporary cool. A gleaming white entrance hall lined with red carpet and contemporary art leads to designer rooms in shades of chocolate, cream and gold; a restaurant by Albert Roux completes the luxury package.

Eating

★ **Café 1** BISTRO ££
(☎01463-226200; www.cafe1.net; 75 Castle St; mains £13-25; ⊙noon-2.30pm & 5-9.30pm Mon-Fri, noon-2.30pm & 6-9.30pm Sat;) Café 1 is a friendly, appealing bistro with candlelit tables amid elegant blonde-wood and wrought-iron decor. There is an international menu based on quality Scottish produce, from Aberdeen Angus steaks to crisp pan-fried sea bass and meltingly tender pork belly. The set lunch menu (two courses for £12) is served noon to 2.30pm Monday to Saturday.

THE GENIUS OF CHARLES RENNIE MACKINTOSH

Charles Rennie Mackintosh (1868–1928) is to Glasgow what Gaudí is to Barcelona. A designer, architect and master of the art nouveau style, his quirky, linear and geometric designs are seen all over Glasgow.

Many of his buildings are open to the public, though his masterpiece, the **Glasgow School of Art**, was extensively damaged by fire in 2014 and is due to reopen in 2018. If you're a fan, the **Mackintosh Trail ticket** (£10), available at the tourist office or any Mackintosh building, gives you a day's free admission to all his creations, plus unlimited bus and subway travel. Highlights include the following:

Willow Tearooms (217 Sauchiehall St; wi-fi) FREE

Mackintosh House (www.hunterian.gla.ac.uk; 82 Hillhead St; adult/child £5/3; ⊙10am-5pm Tue-Sat, 11am-4pm Sun)

House for an Art Lover (☎0141-353 4770; www.houseforanartlover.co.uk; Bellahouston Park, Dumbreck Rd; adult/child £4.50/3; ⊙10am-4pm Mon-Wed, to 12.30pm Thu-Sun)

THE NORTH COAST 500

This 500-mile circuit of northern Scotland's stunning coastline (www.northcoast500.com) has become hugely popular, with thousands of people completing the route by car, campervan, motorbike or bicycle.

Kitchen Brasserie MODERN SCOTTISH ££
(☎01463-259119; www.kitchenrestaurant.co.uk; 15 Huntly St; mains £9-20; ⏰noon-3pm & 5-10pm; 📶 👪) This spectacular glass-fronted restaurant offers a great menu of top Scottish produce with a Mediterranean or Asian touch, and a view over the River Ness – try to get a table upstairs. Great value two-course lunch (£9, noon to 3pm) and early-bird menu (£13, 5pm to 7pm).

ℹ Information

Inverness Tourist Office (☎01463-252401; www.visithighlands.com; Castle Wynd; internet access per 20min £1; ⏰9am-5pm Mon-Sat, 10am-3pm Sun, longer hours Mar-Oct) Bureau de change and accommodation booking service; also sells tickets for tours and cruises.

ℹ Getting There & Away

BUS

Buses depart from **Inverness bus station** (Margaret St). Coaches from London (£45, 13 hours, one daily direct) are operated by **National Express** (☎08717-818181; www.nationalexpress.com); more frequent services require a change at Glasgow. Other routes include Edinburgh (£31, 3½ to 4½ hours, hourly) and Portree on the Isle of Skye (£25, 3¼ hours, three daily).

TRAIN

Trains depart from Inverness for Kyle of Lochalsh (£18, 2½ hours, four daily Monday to Saturday, two Sunday), one of Britain's most scenic railway lines.

There's one direct train from London each day (£120, eight to nine hours); others require a change at Edinburgh.

Loch Ness

Deep, dark and narrow, Loch Ness stretches for 23 miles between Inverness and Fort Augustus. Its bitterly cold waters have been extensively explored in search of the elusive Loch Ness monster, but most visitors see her only in cardboard cut-out form at the monster exhibitions. The village of **Drumnadrochit** is a hotbed of beastie fever, with two monster exhibitions battling it out for the tourist dollar.

👁 Sights & Activities

Loch Ness Centre & Exhibition MUSEUM
(☎01456-450573; www.lochness.com; adult/child £7.95/4.95; ⏰9.30am-6pm Jul & Aug, to 5pm Easter-Jun, Sep & Oct, 10am-3.30pm Nov-Easter; P 👪) This Nessie-themed attraction adopts a scientific approach that allows you to weigh the evidence for yourself. Exhibits include the original equipment – sonar survey vessels, miniature submarines, cameras and sediment coring tools – used in various monster hunts, as well as original photographs and film footage of sightings. You'll find out about hoaxes and optical illusions, as well as learning a lot about the ecology of Loch Ness – is there enough food in the loch to support even one 'monster', let alone a breeding population?

Urquhart Castle CASTLE
(HS; ☎01456-450551; adult/child £8.50/5.10; ⏰9.30am-6pm Apr-Sep, to 5pm Oct, to 4.30pm Nov-Mar; P) Commanding a superb location 1.5 miles east of Drumnadrochit, with outstanding views (on a clear day), Urquhart Castle is a popular Nessie-hunting hot spot. A huge visitor centre (most of which is beneath ground level) includes a video theatre (with a dramatic 'reveal' of the castle at the end of the film) and displays of medieval items discovered in the castle. The site includes a huge gift shop and a restaurant, and is often very crowded in summer.

Nessie Hunter BOATING
(☎01456-450395; www.lochness-cruises.com; adult/child £15/10; ⏰Easter-Oct) One-hour monster-hunting cruises, complete with sonar and underwater cameras. Cruises depart from Drumnadrochit hourly (except 1pm) from 9am to 6pm daily.

ℹ Getting There & Away

Scottish Citylink (☎0871-266 3333; www.citylink.co.uk) and Stagecoach buses from Inverness to Fort William run along the shores of Loch Ness (six to eight daily, five on Sunday); those headed for Skye turn off at Invermoriston. There are bus stops at Drumnadrochit (£3.30, 30 minutes) and Urquhart Castle car park (£3.60, 35 minutes).

Isle of Skye

POP 10,000

The Isle of Skye is the biggest of Scotland's islands (now linked to the mainland by a bridge at Kyle of Lochalsh), a 50-mile-long smorgasbord of velvet moors, jagged mountains, sparkling lochs and towering sea cliffs. It takes its name from the old Norse *sky-a*, meaning 'cloud island', a Viking reference to the often mist-enshrouded **Cuillin Hills**, Britain's most spectacular mountain range. The stunning scenery is the main attraction, including the cliffs and pinnacles of the **Old Man of Storr**, **Kilt Rock** and the **Quiraing**, but there are plenty of cosy pubs to retire to when the rainclouds close in.

Portree is the main town, with Broadford a close second; both have banks, ATMs, supermarkets and petrol stations.

Sights & Activities

Dunvegan Castle CASTLE

(01470-521206; www.dunvegancastle.com; adult/child £12/9; 10am-5.30pm Apr–mid-Oct; P) Skye's most famous historic building, and one of its most popular tourist attractions, Dunvegan Castle is the seat of the chief of Clan MacLeod. In addition to the usual castle stuff – swords, silver and family portraits – there are some interesting artefacts, including the Fairy Flag, a diaphanous silk banner that dates from some time between the 4th and 7th centuries, and Bonnie Prince Charlie's waistcoat and a lock of his hair, donated by Flora MacDonald's granddaughter.

Skye Tours BUS

(01471-822716; www.skye-tours.co.uk; adult/child £35/30; Mon-Sat) Five-hour sightseeing tours of Skye in a minibus, taking in the Old Man of Storr, Kilt Rock and Dunvegan Castle. Depart from Kyle of Lochalsh train station at 11.30am (connects with 8.55am train from Inverness, returns to Kyle by 4.45pm in time to catch the return train at 5.13pm).

Sleeping

Portree, the island's capital, has the largest selection of accommodation, eating places and other services.

★ **Cowshed Boutique Bunkhouse** HOSTEL £

(07917 536820; www.skyecowshed.co.uk; Uig; dm/tw £20/80, pod £70; P) This new hostel enjoys a glorious setting overlooking Uig Bay, with superb views from its ultra-stylish lounge. The dorms have custom-built wooden bunks that offer comfort and privacy, while the camping pods (sleeping up to four, but more comfortable with two) have heating and en suite shower rooms; there are even mini 'dog pods' for your canine companions.

Portree Youth Hostel HOSTEL £

(SYHA; 01478-612231; www.syha.org.uk; Bayfield Rd; dm/tw £24/66; P) This brand-new SYHA hostel (formerly Bayfield Backpackers) has been completely renovated and offers brightly decorated dorms and private rooms, a stylish lounge with views over the bay, and outdoor seating areas, with an ideal location in the town centre just 100m from the bus stop.

★ **Tigh an Dochais** B&B ££

(01471-820022; www.skyebedbreakfast.co.uk; 13 Harrapool; d £105; P) A cleverly designed modern building, Tigh an Dochais is one of Skye's best B&Bs – a little footbridge leads to the front door, which is on the 1st floor. Here you'll find the dining room (gorgeous breakfasts) and lounge offering a stunning view of sea and hills; the bedrooms (downstairs) open onto an outdoor deck with that same wonderful view.

★ **Toravaig House Hotel** HOTEL ££

(01471-820200; www.toravaig.com; Toravaig; d £110-149; P) This hotel, 3 miles south of Isleornsay, is one of those places where the owners know a thing or two about hospitality – as soon as you arrive you'll feel right at home, whether relaxing on the sofas by the log fire in the lounge or admiring the view across the Sound of Sleat from the lawn chairs in the garden.

Eating

★ **Scorrybreac** MODERN SCOTTISH ££

(01478-612069; www.scorrybreac.com; 7 Bosville Tce; 2-/3-course dinner £27.50/32.50; 5-9.30pm Tue-Sat) Set in the front rooms of what was once a private house, and with just eight tables, Scorrybreac is snug and intimate, offering fine dining without the faff. Chef Calum Munro (son of Donnie Munro, of Gaelic rock band Runrig fame) sources as much produce as possible from Skye, including foraged herbs and mushrooms, and creates the most exquisite concoctions.

★ **Creelers** SEAFOOD ££

(01471-822281; www.skye-seafood-restaurant.co.uk; Lower Harrapool; mains £14-19; noon-8.30pm Tue-Sat Mar-Oct;) Broadford has several places to eat but one really stands out: Creelers is a small, bustling, no-frills restaurant that serves some of the best seafood on Skye. The house speciality is traditional Marseille *bouillabaisse* (a rich, spicy seafood stew). Best to book ahead.

Getting There & Away

BOAT

Despite the bridge, there are still a couple of ferry links between Skye and the mainland. Ferries also operate from Uig on Skye to the Outer Hebrides.

The **CalMac** (☎ 0800 066 5000; www.calmac.co.uk; per person/car £2.80/9.40) ferry between Mallaig and Armadale (30 minutes, eight daily Monday to Saturday, five to seven on Sunday) is very popular on weekends and in July and August. Book ahead if you're travelling by car.

Skye Ferry (www.skyeferry.co.uk; car with up to 4 passengers £15; ⏲ Easter–mid Oct) runs a tiny vessel (six cars only) on the short Kylerhea to Glenelg crossing (five minutes, every 20 minutes). The ferry operates from 10am to 6pm daily (till 7pm June to August).

BUS

There are buses from Glasgow to Portree (£42, seven hours, three daily), plus a service from Inverness to Portree (£25, 3¼ hours, three daily).

SURVIVAL GUIDE

Directory A–Z

ACCOMMODATION

Accommodation can be difficult to find during holidays (especially around Easter and New Year) and major events (such as the Edinburgh Festival). In summer, popular spots (York, Canterbury, Bath etc) get very crowded, so booking ahead is essential. Local TICs often provide an accommodation booking service for a small fee.

> **SLEEPING PRICE RANGES**
>
> Reviews of places to stay use the following price ranges, all based on double room with private bathroom in high season. Hotels in London are more expensive than the rest of the country, so have different price ranges.
>
> **£** less than £65 (London less than £100)
>
> **££** £65–£130 (London £100–£200)
>
> **£££** more than £130 (London more than £200)

Hostels There are two types of hostels in Britain: those run by the **Youth Hostels Association** (www.yha.org.uk) and **Scottish Youth Hostels Association** (www.syha.org.uk), and independent hostels, most of which are listed in the **Independent Hostels Guide** (www.independenthostelguide.co.uk). The simplest hostels cost around £15 per person per night. Larger hostels with more facilities are £18 to £30. London's YHA hostels cost from £32.

B&Bs The B&B (bed and breakfast) is a great British institution. At smaller places it's pretty much a room in somebody's house; larger places may be called a 'guesthouse' (halfway between a B&B and a full hotel). Prices start from around £30 per person for a simple bedroom and shared bathroom; for around £35 to £45 per person you get a private bathroom – either down the hall or an en suite.

Hotels There's a massive choice of hotels in Britain, from small town houses to grand country mansions, from no-frills locations to boutique hideaways. At the bargain end, single/double rooms cost from £45/60. Move up the scale and you'll pay £100/150 or beyond.

Camping Campsites range from farmers' fields with a tap and basic toilet, costing from £5 per person per night, to smarter affairs with hot showers and many other facilities, charging up to £15. You usually need all your own equipment.

ACTIVITIES

Britain is a great destination for outdoor enthusiasts. Walking and cycling are the most popular activities – you can do them on a whim, and they're the perfect way to open up some beautiful corners of the country.

Cycling

Compact Britain is an excellent destination to explore by bike. Popular regions to tour include southwest England, the Yorkshire Dales, Derbyshire's Peak District, Mid-Wales and the Scottish Borders. Bike-hire outlets are widespread; rates are typically around £15 per day or £80 per week.

The 10,000-mile **National Cycle Network** (www.nationalcyclenetwork.org.uk) is a web of quiet roads and traffic-free tracks that pass through busy cities and remote rural areas.

Sustrans (www.sustrans.org.uk) is another useful organisation, and publishes a wide range of maps, guides and planning tools.

Walking & Hiking

Hiking is a hugely popular pastime in Britain, especially in scenic areas such as Snowdonia, the Lake District, the Yorkshire Dales and the Scottish Highlands. Various long-distance routes cross the countryside, including the **Coast to Coast** (www.wainwright.org.uk/coasttocoast.html), the **Cotswold Way** (www.nationaltrail.co.uk/cotswold), the **West Highland Way** (www.

west-highland-way.co.uk) and the **South West Coast Path** (www.southwestcoastpath.com).

The **Ramblers Association** (www.ramblers.org.uk) is the country's leading walkers' organisation.

GAY & LESBIAN TRAVELLERS

Britain is a generally tolerant place for gays and lesbians. London, Manchester and Brighton have flourishing gay scenes, and in other sizeable cities (even some small towns), you'll find communities not entirely in the closet. That said, you'll still find pockets of homophobic hostility in some areas. Resources include the following:

Diva (www.divamag.co.uk)

Gay Times (www.gaytimes.co.uk)

Switchboard LGBT+ Helpline (www.switchboard.lgbt; ☎ 0300 330 0630)

INTERNET RESOURCES

Visit Britain (www.visitbritain.com) Comprehensive national tourism website.

Traveline (www.traveline.org.uk) Timetables and travel advice for public transport across Britain.

Lonely Planet (www.lonelyplanet.com/great-britain) Destination info, hotel bookings, traveller forum and more.

MONEY

- The currency of Britain is the pound sterling (£). Paper money (notes) comes in £5, £10, £20 and £50 denominations, although some shops don't accept £50 notes.
- ATMs, often called cash machines, are easy to find in towns and cities.
- Most banks and some post offices offer currency exchange.
- Visa and MasterCard credit and debit cards are widely accepted in Britain. Nearly everywhere uses a 'Chip and PIN' system (instead of signing).
- Smaller businesses may charge a fee for credit-card use, and some take cash or cheque only.
- Tipping is not obligatory. A 10% to 15% tip is fine for restaurants, cafes, taxi drivers and pub meals; if you order drinks and food at the bar, there's no need to tip.
- Travellers cheques are rarely used.

OPENING HOURS

Standard opening hours:

Banks 9.30am–4pm or 5pm Monday to Friday; main branches 9.30am–1pm Saturday

Post offices 9am–5pm (5.30pm or 6pm in cities) Monday to Friday, 9am–12.30pm Saturday (main branches to 5pm)

Pubs Noon–11pm Monday to Saturday (many till midnight or 1am Friday and Saturday, especially in Scotland), 12.30pm–11pm Sunday

Restaurants Lunch is noon–3pm, dinner 6pm–9pm or 10pm (or later in cities)

Shops 9am–5.30pm (or 6pm in cities) Monday to Saturday, and often 11am–5pm Sunday. Big city convenience stores open 24/7

PUBLIC HOLIDAYS

In many areas of Britain, bank holidays are just for the banks – many businesses and visitor attractions stay open.

New Year's Day 1 January (plus 2 January in Scotland)

Easter March/April (Good Friday to Easter Monday inclusive)

May Day First Monday in May

Spring Bank Holiday Last Monday in May

Summer Bank Holiday Last Monday in August

Christmas Day 25 December

Boxing Day 26 December

COUNTRY FACTS

Area 88,500 sq miles

Capitals London (England and the United Kingdom), Cardiff (Wales), Edinburgh (Scotland)

Country Code ☎ 44

Currency Pound sterling (£)

Emergency ☎ 999 or ☎ 112

Languages English, Welsh, Scottish Gaelic

Money ATMs widespread; credit cards widely accepted

Population 61.4 million

Visas Schengen rules do not apply

SCHOOL HOLIDAYS

Roads get busy and hotel prices go up during school holidays.

Easter Holiday Week before and week after Easter.

Summer Holiday Third week of July to first week of September.

Christmas Holiday Mid-December to first week of January.

There are also three week-long 'half-term' school holidays – usually late February (or early March), late May and late October. These vary between Scotland, England and Wales.

SCOTTISH POUNDS

Scottish banks issue their own sterling banknotes. They are interchangeable with Bank of England notes, but you'll sometimes run into problems outside Scotland – shops in the south of England may refuse to accept them. They are also harder to exchange once you get outside the UK, though British banks will always exchange them.

SAFE TRAVEL

Britain is a remarkably safe country, but crime is not unknown in London and other cities.

- Watch out for pickpockets and hustlers in crowded areas popular with tourists, such as around Westminster Bridge in London.
- When travelling by tube, tram or urban train services at night, choose a carriage containing other people.
- Many town centres can be rowdy on Friday and Saturday nights when the pubs and clubs are emptying.
- Unlicensed minicabs – a bloke with a car earning money on the side – operate in large cities, and are worth avoiding unless you know what you're doing.

TELEPHONE

The UK uses the GSM 900/1800 network, which covers the rest of Europe, Australia and New Zealand, but isn't compatible with the North American GSM 1900. Most modern mobiles can function on both networks – but check before you leave home just in case.

Though roaming charges within Britain and the EU were entirely eliminated in June 2017, other international roaming charges can be prohibitively high.

Area codes in the UK do not have a standard format or length (eg Edinburgh 0131, London 020, Ambleside 015394). In our reviews, area codes and phone numbers have been listed together, separated by a hyphen.

EATING PRICE RANGES

In reviews, the following price ranges refer to a main dish.

£ less than £10 (London less than £12)

££ £10–£20 (London £12–£25)

£££ more than £20 (London more than £25)

- Dial ☎100 for an operator and ☎155 for an international operator as well as reverse-charge (collect) calls.
- To call outside the UK, dial ☎00, then the country code (1 for USA, 61 for Australia etc), the area code (you usually drop the initial zero) and the number.
- For directory enquiries, a host of agencies offer this service – numbers include ☎118 118, ☎118 500 and ☎118 811 – but fees are extortionate (around £6 for a 45-second call); search online for free at www.thephonebook.bt.com.

TIME

Britain is on GMT/UTC. The clocks go forward for 'summer time' one hour at the end of March and go back at the end of October. The 24-hour clock is used for transport timetables.

VISAS

- Generally not needed for stays of up to six months. Not a member of the Schengen Zone.
- If you're a citizen of the EEA (European Economic Area) nations or Switzerland, you don't need a visa to enter or work in Britain – you can enter using your national identity card.
- Currently, if you're a citizen of Australia, Canada, New Zealand, Japan, Israel, the USA and several other countries, you can stay for up to six months (no visa required), but are not allowed to work.
- For more info see www.gov.uk/check-uk-visa.

Getting There & Away

AIR

London Airports

London is served by five airports; Heathrow and Gatwick are the busiest.

Gatwick (LGW; www.gatwickairport.com) Britain's number-two airport, mainly for international flights, 30 miles south of central London.

London City (LCY; www.londoncityairport.com)

London Heathrow Airport (LHR; www.heathrow airport.com) The UK's major hub welcoming flights from all over the world.

Luton (LTN; www.london-luton.co.uk) Some 35 miles north of central London, well known as a holiday-flight airport.

Stansted (STN; www.stanstedairport.com) About 35 miles northeast of central London, mainly handling charter and budget European flights.

Regional Airports

Bristol Airport (BRS; www.bristolairport.co.uk) Flights from all over Europe.

Cardiff Airport (CWL; www.cardiff-airport.com) 12 miles southwest of Cardiff, past Barry.

Edinburgh Airport (EDI; www. edinburghairport.com) Numerous flights to other parts of the UK, Ireland and mainland Europe. Daily flights to Inverness, Wick, Orkney, Shetland and Stornoway.

Glasgow International Airport (GLA; www.glasgowairport.com) Handles domestic traffic and international flights.

Liverpool John Lennon Airport (LPL; www.liverpoolairport.com) Serves a variety of UK and international destinations.

Manchester Airport (MHT; www.manchesterairport.co.uk) The largest airport outside London with flights to the US and Canada.

Newcastle International Airport (NCL; www.newcastleairport.com) Direct services to many UK and European cities.

LAND

Bus & Coach

The international network **Eurolines** (www.eurolines.com) connects a huge number of European destinations via the Channel Tunnel or ferry crossings.

Services to and from Britain are operated by **National Express** (www.nationalexpress.com).

Train

High-speed **Eurostar** (www.eurostar.com) passenger services shuttle at least 10 times daily between London and Paris (2½ hours) or Brussels (two hours) via the Channel Tunnel. The normal one-way fare between London and Paris/Brussels costs around £145; advance booking and off-peak travel gets cheaper fares as low as £29 one-way.

Vehicles use the **Eurotunnel** (www.eurotunnel.com) at Folkestone in England or Calais in France. The trains run four times an hour from 6am to 10pm, then hourly. The journey takes 35 minutes. The one-way cost for a car and passengers is between £75 and £100 depending on time of day; promotional fares often bring it down to £50 or less.

Travelling between Ireland and Britain, the main train–ferry–train route is Dublin to London, via Dun Laoghaire and Holyhead. Ferries also run between Rosslare and Fishguard or Pembroke (Wales), with train connections on either side.

SEA

The main ferry routes between Britain and mainland Europe include Dover to Calais or Boulogne (France), Harwich to Hook of Holland (Netherlands), Hull to Zeebrugge (Belgium) or Rotterdam (Netherlands), and Portsmouth to Santander or Bilbao (Spain). Routes to and from Ireland include Holyhead to Dun Laoghaire.

Competition from the Eurotunnel and budget airlines means ferry operators discount heavily at certain times of year. The short cross-channel routes such as Dover to Calais or Boulogne can be as low as £45 for a car plus two passengers, although around £75 to £105 is more likely. If you're a foot passenger, or cycling, fares cost about £30 to £50 each way.

Broker sites covering all routes and options include www.ferrybooker.com and www.directferries.co.uk. Ferry companies include the following:

Brittany Ferries (www.brittany-ferries.com)

DFDS Seaways (www.dfds.co.uk)

Irish Ferries (www.irishferries.com)

P&O Ferries (www.poferries.com)

Stena Line (www.stenaline.com)

ESSENTIAL FOOD & DRINK

Britain once had a reputation for bad food, but the nation has enjoyed something of a culinary revolution in the last decade or so, and you can often find fine dining based on fresh local produce.

Fish and chips Long-standing favourite, best sampled in coastal towns.

Haggis Scottish icon, mainly offal and oatmeal, traditionally served with 'tatties and neeps' (potatoes and turnips).

Sandwich Global snack today, but an English invention from the 18th century.

Laverbread Laver is a type of seaweed, mixed with oatmeal and fried to create this traditional Welsh speciality.

Ploughman's lunch Bread and cheese – pub menu regular, perfect with a pint.

Roast beef & Yorkshire pudding Traditional lunch on Sunday for the English.

Cornish pasty Savoury pastry, southwest speciality, now available countrywide.

Real ale Traditionally brewed beer, flavoured with malt and hops and served at room temperature.

Scotch whisky Spirit distilled from malted and fermented barley, then aged in oak barrels for at least three years.

CONNECTIONS

The quickest way to Europe from Britain is via the Channel Tunnel, which has direct Eurostar rail services from London to Paris and Brussels. Ferries sail from southern England to French ports in a couple of hours; other routes connect eastern England to the Netherlands, Germany and northern Spain, and Ireland from southwest Scotland and Wales.

Getting Around

For getting around Britain, your first choice is car or public transport. Having your own car makes the best use of time and helps reach remote places, but rental, fuel costs and parking can be expensive – so public transport is often the better way to go.

Cheapest but slowest are long-distance buses (called coaches in Britain). Trains are faster but much more expensive.

AIR

Britain's domestic air companies include the following:

British Airways (www.britishairways.com)

EasyJet (www.easyjet.com)

FlyBe (www.flybe.com)

Loganair (www.loganair.co.uk)

Ryanair (www.ryanair.com)

On most shorter routes (eg London to Newcastle, or Manchester to Bristol), it's often faster to take the train once airport downtime is factored in.

BUS

Long-distance buses (coaches) nearly always offer the cheapest way to get around. Many towns have separate stations for local buses and intercity coaches; make sure you're in the right one.

National Express (www.nationalexpress.com) is England's main coach operator. North of the border, **Scottish Citylink** (www.citylink.co.uk) is the leading coach company. Tickets are cheaper if you book in advance and travel at quieter times. As a rough guide, a 200-mile trip (eg London to York) will cost around £15 to £25 if booked a few days in advance.

Also offering cheap fares is **Megabus** (www.megabus.com), which serves about 30 destinations around Britain.

Bus Passes

National Express offers discount passes to full-time students and under-26s, called **Young Persons Coachcards**. They cost £10 and give 30% off standard adult fares. Also available are coachcards for people over 60 years, families and travellers with a disability.

For touring the country, National Express offers **Brit Xplorer** passes, allowing unlimited travel for seven days (£79), 14 days (£139) and 28 days (£219).

CAR & MOTORCYCLE

Most overseas driving licences are valid in Britain for up to 12 months from the date of entry.

Rental

Car rental is expensive in Britain; you'll pay from around £130 per week for the smallest model, or £190 per week and upward for a medium-sized car (including insurance and unlimited mileage). All the major players including Avis, Hertz and Budget operate here.

Using a rental-broker site such as **UK Car Hire** (www.ukcarhire.net) or **Kayak** (www.kayak.com) can help find bargains.

It's illegal to drive a car or motorbike in Britain without (at least) third-party insurance. This is included with all rental cars.

Road Rules

The *Highway Code*, available in bookshops (or at www.gov.uk/highway-code), contains everything you need to know about Britain's road rules. The main ones to remember:

- Always drive on the left.
- Give way to your right at junctions and roundabouts.
- Always use the left-hand lane on motorways and dual carriageways, unless overtaking (passing).
- Wear seat belts in cars and crash helmets on motorcycles.
- Don't use a mobile phone while driving.
- Don't drink and drive; the maximum blood-alcohol level allowed is 80mg/100mL (0.08%) in England and Wales, 50mg/100mL (0.05%) in Scotland.
- Yellow lines (single or double) along the edge of the road indicate parking restrictions, red lines mean no stopping whatsoever.
- Speed limits are 30mph in built-up areas, 60mph on main roads, and 70mph on motorways and dual carriageways.

TRAIN

About 20 different companies operate train services in Britain, while Network Rail operates track and stations. For some passengers this system can be confusing at first, but information and ticket-buying services are mostly centralised. If you have to change trains, or use two or more train operators, you still buy one ticket – valid for the whole journey. The main railcards and passes are also accepted by all train operators.

National Rail Enquiries (www.nationalrail.co.uk) provides booking and timetable information for Britain's entire rail network.

Classes

Rail travel has two classes: 1st and standard. Travelling 1st class costs around 50% more than standard. At weekends some train operators offer 'upgrades' to 1st class for an extra £5 to £25 on top of your standard class fare, payable on the spot.

Costs & Reservations

The earlier you book, the cheaper it gets. You can also save if you travel 'off-peak' (ie the days and times that aren't busy). If you buy online, you can have the ticket posted (UK addresses only), or collect it from station machines on the day of travel.

There are three main fare types:

Anytime Buy anytime, travel anytime – usually the most expensive option.

Off-peak Buy anytime, travel off-peak (what is off-peak depends on the journey).

Advance Buy in advance, travel only on specific trains (usually the cheapest option).

Train Passes

If you're staying in Britain for a while, passes known as railcards (www.railcard.co.uk) are available:

16–25 Railcard For those aged 16 to 25, or a full-time UK student.

Senior Railcard For anyone aged over 60.

Family & Friends Railcard Covers up to four adults and four children travelling together.

Railcards cost £30 (valid for one year, available from major stations or online) and get 33% discount on most train fares, except those already heavily discounted. With the Family card, adults get 33% and children get 60% discounts, so the fee is easily repaid in a couple of journeys.

The following train passes are available:

Regional Passes Various local train passes are available covering specific areas and lines – ask at a local train station to get an idea of what's available.

National Passes For country-wide travel, **BritRail** (www.britrail.net) passes are available for visitors from overseas. They must be bought in your country of origin (not in Britain) from a specialist travel agency. Available in seven different versions (eg England only; Scotland only; all Britain; UK and Ireland) for periods from four to 30 days.

TRAVELINE

Traveline (www.traveline.info) is a very useful information service covering bus, coach, taxi and train services nationwide.

France

Includes ➡

Best Places to Stay

➡ Joke Hôtel (p194)

➡ L'Hôtel Particulier (p231)

➡ Villa des Consuls (p229)

➡ Cour des Loges (p224)

➡ Nice Garden Hôtel (p246)

Best Places for History

➡ Musée du Louvre (p185)

➡ Château de Versailles (p204)

➡ D-Day Beaches (p209)

➡ Château de Chambord (p217)

➡ Pont du Gard (p237)

Why Go?

France has so much to entice travellers – renowned gastronomy, iconic sights, splendid art heritage, a fabulous outdoors: you could sample it all in a week, but you'll invariably feel as though you've only scratched the surface of this big country.

Visiting France is certainly about seeing the big sights, but it's just as much about savouring life's little pleasures: a stroll through an elegant city square, a coffee on a sunny pavement terrace, a meal that lasts well into the afternoon or night, a scenic drive punctuated with photo stops and impromptu farm or vineyard visits. The French are big on their *art de vivre* (art of living) and you should embrace it too – whether you're wandering the boulevards of Paris, exploring the vineyards of Bordeaux and Burgundy or cruising the cliffs of the Côte d'Azur.

On y va, as they say in France!

When to Go

Paris

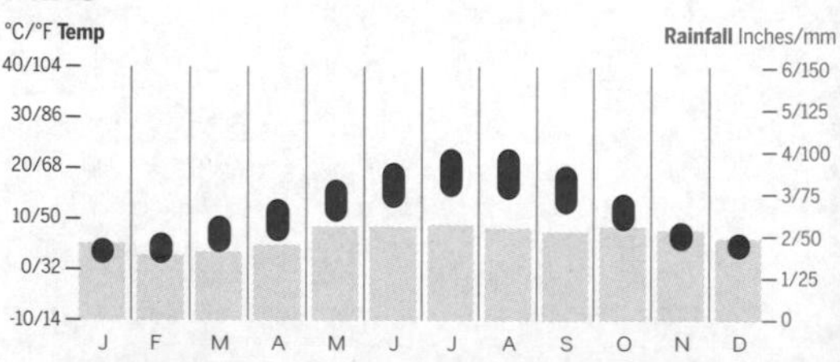

Dec–Mar Christmas markets in Alsace, snow in the Alps and truffles in the south.

Apr–Jun France is at its springtime best, with good weather and far fewer crowds.

Sep Cooling temperatures, abundant local produce and the *vendange* (grape harvest).

PARIS

POP 2.2 MILLION

What can be said about the sexy, sophisticated City of Lights that hasn't already been said myriad times before? Quite simply, this is one of the world's great metropolises – a trendsetter, market leader and cultural capital for over a thousand years and still going strong.

As you might expect, Paris is strewn with historic architecture, glorious galleries and cultural treasures galore. But the modern-day city is much more than just a museum piece: it's a heady hodgepodge of cultures and ideas – a place to stroll the boulevards, shop till you drop, flop riverside or simply do as the Parisians do and watch the world buzz by from a streetside cafe. Savour every moment.

Sights

Left Bank

★Eiffel Tower LANDMARK

(Map p186; ☎08 92 70 12 39; www.toureiffel.paris; Champ de Mars, 5 av Anatole France, 7e; adult/child lift to top €17/8, lift to 2nd fl €11/4, stairs to 2nd fl €7/3; ⏰lifts & stairs 9am-12.45am mid-Jun–Aug, lifts 9.30am-11pm, stairs 9.30am-6.30pm Sep–mid-Jun; Ⓜ Bir Hakeim or RER Champ de Mars–Tour Eiffel) No one could imagine Paris today without it. But Gustave Eiffel only constructed this elegant, 320m-tall signature spire as a temporary exhibit for the 1889 World's Fair. Luckily, the art-nouveau tower's popularity assured its survival. Prebook tickets online to avoid long queues.

Lifts ascend to the tower's three floors; change lifts on the 2nd floor for the final ascent to the top. Energetic visitors can climb as far as the 2nd floor via the south pillar's 704 stairs.

★Musée d'Orsay MUSEUM

(Map p186; www.musee-orsay.fr; 1 rue de la Légion d'Honneur, 7e; adult/child €12/free; ⏰9.30am-6pm Tue, Wed & Fri-Sun, to 9.45pm Thu; Ⓜ Assemblée Nationale, RER Musée d'Orsay) The home of France's national collection from the impressionist, postimpressionist and art-nouveau movements spanning from 1848 to 1914 is the glorious former Gare d'Orsay railway station – itself an art-nouveau showpiece – where a roll-call of masters and their world-famous works are on display.

Top of every visitor's must-see list is the museum's painting collections, centred on the world's largest collection of impressionist and postimpressionist art.

Musée du Quai Branly MUSEUM

(Map p186; ☎01 56 61 70 00; www.quaibranly.fr; 37 quai Branly, 7e; adult/child €10/free; ⏰11am-7pm Tue, Wed & Sun, 11am-9pm Thu-Sat; Ⓜ Alma Marceau or RER Pont de l'Alma) A tribute to the diversity of human culture, Musée du Quai Branly inspires travellers, armchair anthropologists, and anyone who appreciates the beauty of traditional craftsmanship, through an overview of indigenous and folk art. Spanning four main sections – Oceania, Asia, Africa and the Americas – an impressive array of masks, carvings, weapons, jewellery and more make up the body of the rich collection, displayed in a refreshingly unique interior without rooms or high walls.

ITINERARIES

One Week

Start with a couple of days exploring **Paris**, taking in the Louvre, the Eiffel Tower, Notre Dame, Montmartre and a boat trip along the Seine. Day trip to magnificent **Versailles** and then spend the rest of the week in **Normandy** to visit WWII's D-Day beaches and glorious Mont St-Michel. Or head east to **Champagne** to sample the famous bubbly and visit Reims' magnificent cathedral.

Two Weeks

With Paris and surrounds having taken up much of the first week, hop on a high-speed TGV to **Avignon** or **Marseille** and take in the delights of Provence's Roman heritage, its beautiful hilltop villages and its famous artistic legacy. Finish your stay with a few days in **Nice**, enjoying its glittering Mediterranean landscapes and sunny cuisine. Alternatively, head southwest to elegant **Bordeaux** and its world-famous vineyards before pushing inland to the **Dordogne** with its hearty gastronomy and unique prehistoric-art heritage.

France Highlights

❶ **Paris** (p181) Gorging on the iconic sights and sophistication of Europe's most hopelessly romantic city.

❷ **Loire Valley** (p215) Reliving the French Renaissance with extraordinary châteaux built by kings and queens.

❸ **Chamonix** (p226) Doing a Bond and swooshing down slopes in the shadow of Mont Blanc.

❹ **Mont St-Michel** (p209) Dodging tides, strolling moonlit sand and immersing yourself in legend at this island abbey.

❺ **Provence** (p237) Savouring ancient ruins, modern art, markets, lavender and hilltop villages.

❻ **Épernay** (p213) Tasting bubbly in ancient *caves* (cellars) in the heart of Champagne.

❼ **Lyon** (p221) Tucking into France's piggy-driven cuisine in a traditional *bouchon*.

❽ **Casino de Monte Carlo** (p250) Hitting the big time in Monaco's sumptuous gaming house.

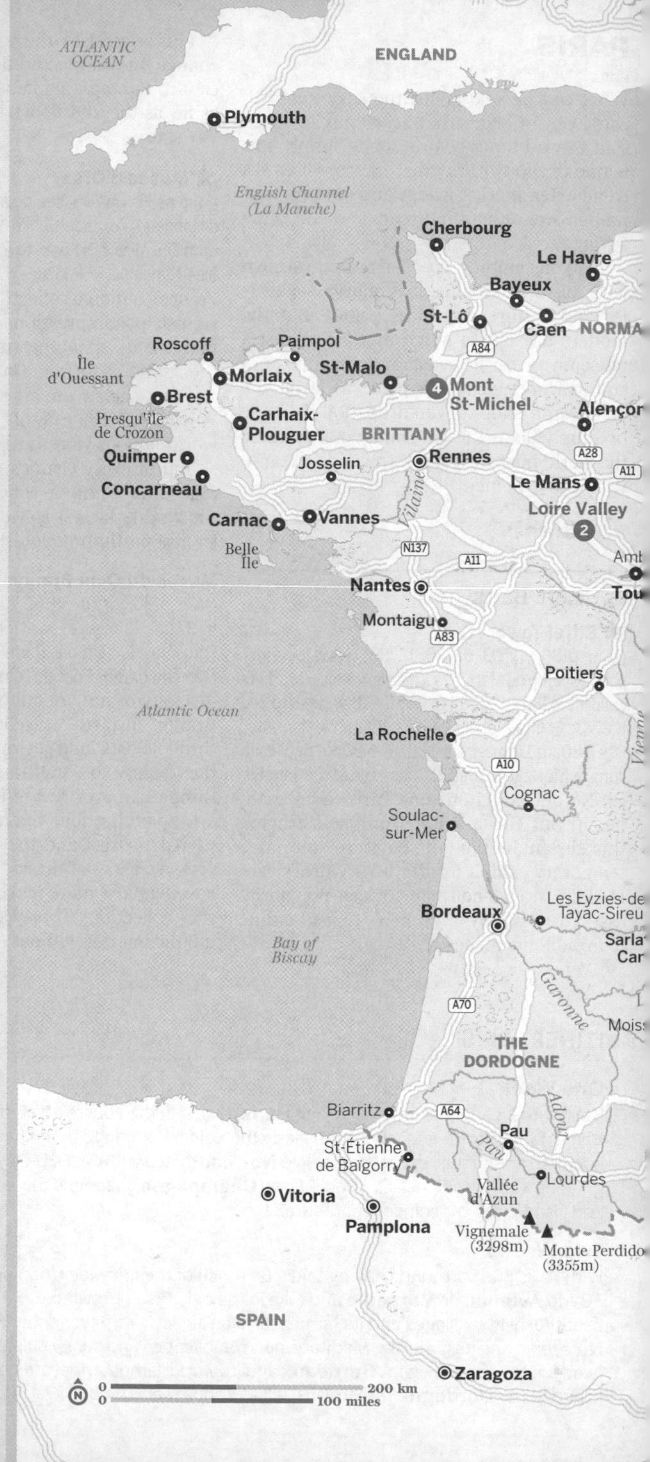

BRUSSELS
NETHERLANDS
BELGIUM
GERMANY
Dunkirk
Calais
Lille
Meuse
Mainz
LUXEMBOURG
LUXEMBOURG CITY
SOMME
Somme
Authie
A28
A1
Oise
Aisne
Reims
A4
Marne
Épernay
Vernon
Paris
Metz
ALSACE
Stuttgart
Strasbourg
Nancy
Seine
Marne
Moselle
Dreux
A5
Sélestat
Schnellenbuhl
Katzenthal
Troyes
LORRAINE
A31
A10
A6
BURGUNDY
Orléans
Beaugency
Chambord
Auxerre
Saône
Basel
LIECHTENSTEIN
AUSTRIA
VADUZ
Dijon
Besançon
Doubs
LA SOLOGNE
CÔTE D'OR
A86
Beaune
Arc-et-Senans
BERN
SWITZERLAND
Cher
Loire
Arbois
Métabief Mont d'Or
Le Creusot
JURA
Les Rousses
Lausanne
Lake Geneva
A6
A71
Les Portes du Soleil
Chamonix
Gueret
Annecy
Mont Blanc (4810m)
Lyon
Clermont-Ferrand
A72
Rhône
Chambéry
Milan
Dordogne
St-Étienne
A48
FRENCH ALPS
ITALY
Moissac
Turenne
Puy Mary (1787m)
Allier
Rhône
A49
Drac
Grenoble
Turin
Valence
Sestriere
D921
A7
Genoa
Vaison la Romaine
Durance
Mt Lozère (1699m)
Mt Ventoux (1912m)
THE LOT
Pont du Gard
Avignon
Nîmes
Tarn
A75
Les Baux de Provence
Nice
Monaco
Ligurian Sea
Provence
Montpellier
Arles
Cannes
LANGUEDOC
Aix-en-Provence
A61
Marseille
St-Tropez
ROUSILLON
A9
Golfe de Beauduc
Île Rousse
Bastia
Perpignan
Calvi
Monte Cinto (2706m)
ANDORRA
Puig Neulós
Mediterranean Sea
CORSICA
SPAIN
Ajaccio
Bonifacio
Barcelona
ITALY
1
3
5
6
7
8

MUSEUM DISCOUNTS & FREEBIES

Almost all museums and monuments in Paris have discounted tickets *(tarif réduit)* for students and seniors with valid ID; children and students who are EU citizens under 26 usually qualify for free admission. National museums are also free on the first Sunday of each month, except the Arc de Triomphe, Conciergerie, Musée du Louvre, Panthéon and Tours de Notre Dame, which are only free on the first Sunday of the month November to March.

Paris Museum Pass (www.parismuseumpass.com; 2/4/6 days €48/62/74) Gets you into 50-odd venues in and around Paris, and often enables you to bypass (or substantially reduce) long ticket queues.

Paris Passlib' (www.parisinfo.com; 2/3/5 days €109/129/155) Sold at the **Paris Convention & Visitors Bureau** (p202) and on its website, this handy city pass includes unlimited public transport in zones 1 to 3, a Paris Museum Pass, a one-hour boat cruise, and a one-day bus tour with **L'Open Tour** (☎01 42 66 56 56; www.paris.opentour.com; 1-day pass adult/child €33/17). There's an optional €15 supplement for a skip-the-line ticket to levels one and two of the Eiffel Tower, or €21.50 for all three Eiffel Tower platforms.

Look out for excellent temporary exhibitions and performances.

Musée Rodin MUSEUM, GARDEN

(Map p186; www.musee-rodin.fr; 79 rue de Varenne, 7e; adult/child museum incl garden €10/free, garden only €4/free; ⏲10am-5.45pm Tue-Sun; Ⓜ Varenne) Sculptor, painter, sketcher, engraver and collector Auguste Rodin donated his entire collection to the French state in 1908 on the proviso that they dedicate his former workshop and showroom, the beautiful 1730 Hôtel Biron, to displaying his works. They're now installed not only in the magnificently restored mansion itself, but in its rose-filled garden – one of the most peaceful places in central Paris and a wonderful spot to contemplate his famous work *The Thinker*. Prepurchase tickets online to avoid queuing.

Panthéon MAUSOLEUM

(Map p190; www.paris-pantheon.fr; place du Panthéon, 5e; adult/child €9/free; ⏲10am-6.30pm Apr-Sep, to 6pm Oct-Mar; Ⓜ Maubert-Mutualité or RER Luxembourg) Overlooking the city from its Left Bank perch, the Panthéon's stately neoclassical dome is an icon of the Parisian skyline. The vast interior is an architectural masterpiece: originally a church and now a mausoleum, it has served since 1791 as the resting place of some of France's greatest thinkers, including Voltaire, Rousseau, Braille and Hugo. A copy of Foucault's pendulum, first hung from the dome in 1851 to demonstrate the rotation of the earth, takes pride of place.

Jardin du Luxembourg PARK

(Map p190; www.senat.fr/visite/jardin; numerous entrances; ⏲hours vary; Ⓜ Mabillon, St-Sulpice, Rennes, Notre Dame des Champs, RER Luxembourg) This inner-city oasis of formal terraces, chestnut groves and lush lawns has a special place in Parisians' hearts. Napoléon dedicated the 23 gracefully laid-out hectares of the Luxembourg Gardens to the children of Paris, and many residents spent their childhood prodding 1920s wooden **sailboats** (sailboat rental per 30min €3.50; ⏲Apr-Oct) with long sticks on the octagonal **Grand Bassin** pond, watching puppets perform *Punch & Judy*-type shows at the **Théâtre du Luxembourg** (www.marionnettesduluxembourg.fr; tickets €6; ⏲usually 11am & 3.30pm Wed, Sat & Sun, 11am, 3pm & 4.15pm daily during school holidays), and riding the *carrousel* (merry-go-round) or **ponies** (pony rides €3.50; ⏲3-6pm Wed, Sat, Sun & school holidays).

Église St-Germain des Prés CHURCH

(Map p190; www.eglise-stgermaindespres.fr; 3 place St-Germain des Prés, 6e; ⏲8am-7.45pm; Ⓜ St-Germain des Prés) Paris' oldest standing church, the Romanesque St Germanus of the Fields, was built in the 11th century on the site of a 6th-century abbey and was the main place of worship in Paris until the arrival of Notre Dame. It's since been altered many times, but the **Chapelle de St-Symphorien** (to the right as you enter) was part of the original abbey and is believed to be the resting place of St Germanus (496–576), the first bishop of Paris.

★**Les Catacombes** CEMETERY

(Map p186; www.catacombes.paris.fr; 1 av Colonel Henri Roi-Tanguy, 14e; adult/child €12/free, online booking incl audioguide €27/5; ⌚10am-8pm Tue-Sun; Ⓜ Denfert Rochereau) Paris' most macabre sight is its underground tunnels lined with skulls and bones. In 1785 it was decided to rectify the hygiene problems of Paris' overflowing cemeteries by exhuming the bones and storing them in disused quarry tunnels and the Catacombes were created in 1810.

After descending 20m (via 130 narrow, dizzying spiral steps) below street level, you follow the dark, subterranean passages to reach the ossuary (2km in all). Exit back up 83 steps onto rue Remy Dumoncel, 14e.

The Islands

Paris' twin set of islands could not be more different. **Île de la Cité** is bigger, full of sights and very touristy (few people live here).

Smaller **Île St-Louis** is residential and quieter, with just enough boutiques and restaurants – and legendary ice-cream maker Berthillon – to attract visitors. The area around **Pont St-Louis**, the bridge across to the Île de la Cité, and **Pont Louis-Philippe**, the bridge to Le Marais, is one of the most romantic spots in Paris.

★**Cathédrale Notre Dame de Paris** CATHEDRAL

(Map p190; ☎01 42 34 56 10; www.notredamedeparis.fr; 6 place du Parvis Notre Dame, 4e; cathedral free, adult/child towers €10/free, treasury €4/2; ⌚cathedral 7.45am-6.45pm Mon-Fri, to 7.15pm Sat & Sun, towers 10am-6.30pm Sun-Thu, to 11pm Fri & Sat Jul & Aug, 10am-6.30pm Apr-Jun & Sep, 10am-5.30pm Oct-Mar, treasury 9.30am-6pm Apr-Sep, 10am-5.30pm Oct-Mar; Ⓜ Cité) Paris' most visited unticketed site, with upwards of 14 million visitors per year, is a masterpiece of French Gothic architecture. The focus of Catholic Paris for seven centuries, its vast interior accommodates 6000 worshippers.

Highlights include its three spectacular **rose windows**, **treasury**, and **bell towers**, which can be climbed. From the North Tower, 400-odd steps spiral to the top of the western façade, where you'll find yourself face-to-face with frightening gargoyles and a spectacular view of Paris.

Sainte-Chapelle CHAPEL

(Map p190; ☎01 53 40 60 80, concerts 01 42 77 65 65; www.sainte-chapelle.fr; 8 bd du Palais, 1er; adult/child €10/free, joint ticket with Conciergerie €15; ⌚9am-7pm Apr-Sep, to 5pm Oct-Mar; Ⓜ Cité) Try to save Sainte-Chapelle for a sunny day, when Paris' oldest, finest stained glass is at its dazzling best. Enshrined within the Palais de Justice (Law Courts), this gemlike Holy Chapel is Paris' most exquisite Gothic monument. Sainte-Chapelle was built in just six years (compared with nearly 200 years for Notre Dame) and consecrated in 1248.

The chapel was conceived by Louis IX to house his personal collection of holy relics, including the famous Holy Crown (now in Notre Dame).

Right Bank

★**Musée du Louvre** MUSEUM

(Map p190; ☎01 40 20 53 17; www.louvre.fr; rue de Rivoli & quai des Tuileries, 1er; adult/child €15/free; ⌚9am-6pm Mon, Thu, Sat & Sun, to 9.45pm Wed & Fri; Ⓜ Palais Royal–Musée du Louvre) Few art galleries are as prized as the Musée du Louvre, Paris' pièce de résistance and the world's most visited museum. The palace rambles over four floors, up and down innumerable staircases, and through three wings. Showcasing 35,000 works of art – from Mesopotamian, Egyptian and Greek antiquities to masterpieces by artists such as Leonardo

THE LOUVRE: TICKETS & TOURS

To best navigate the collection, opt for a self-guided **thematic trail** (1½ to three hours; download trail brochures in advance from the website) or a self-paced **multimedia guide** (€5). More formal, English-language **guided tours** depart from the Hall Napoléon, which also has free English-language maps.

The main entrance and ticket windows are covered by the 21m-high **Grande Pyramide**, a glass pyramid designed by the Chinese-born American architect IM Pei. If you don't have the Museum Pass (which gives you priority), you can avoid the longest queues (for security) outside the pyramid by entering the Louvre complex via the underground shopping centre **Carrousel du Louvre** (Map p190; http://carrouseldulouvre.com; 99 rue de Rivoli, 1er; ⌚8.30am-11pm, shops 10am-8pm; 📶; Ⓜ Palais Royal–Musée du Louvre). You'll need to queue up again to buy your ticket once inside.

Greater Paris

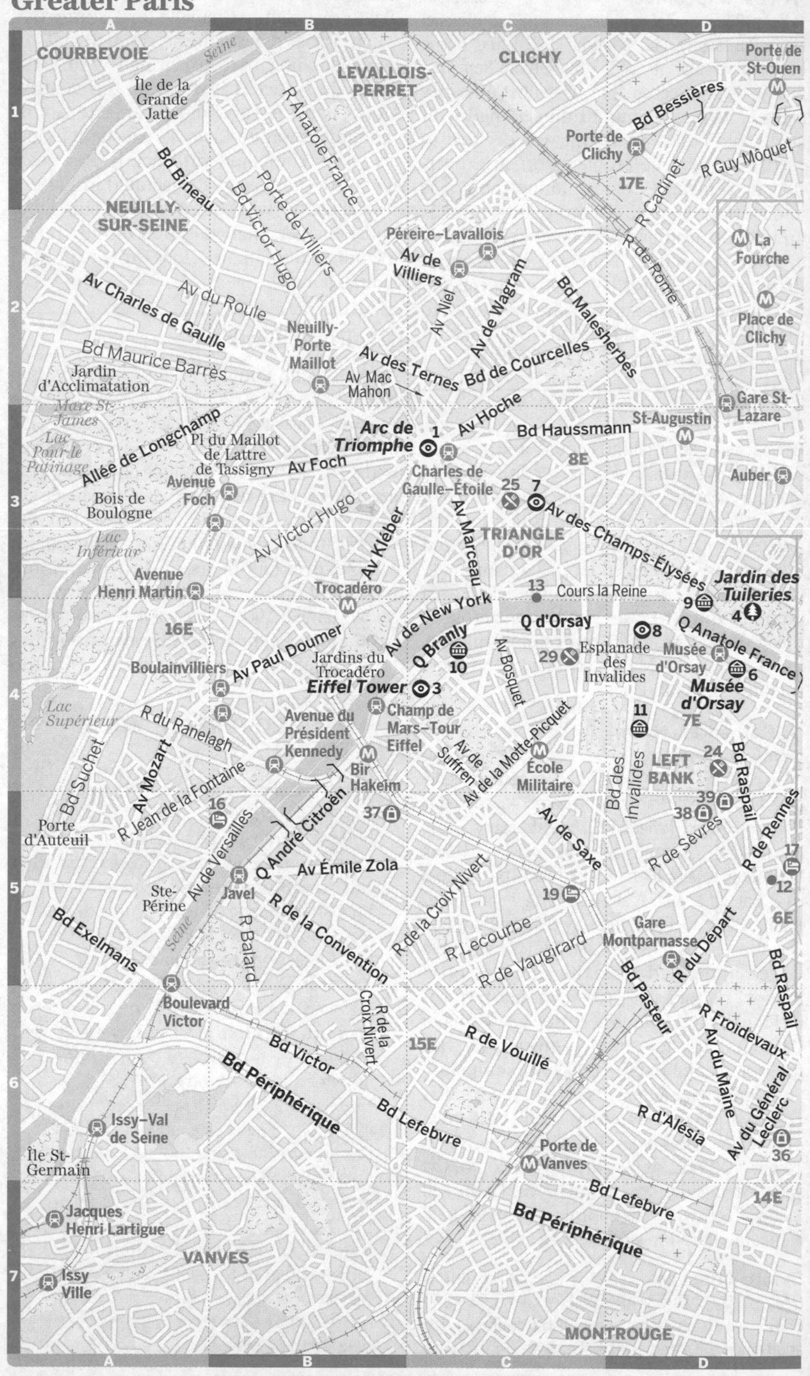

FRANCE PARIS

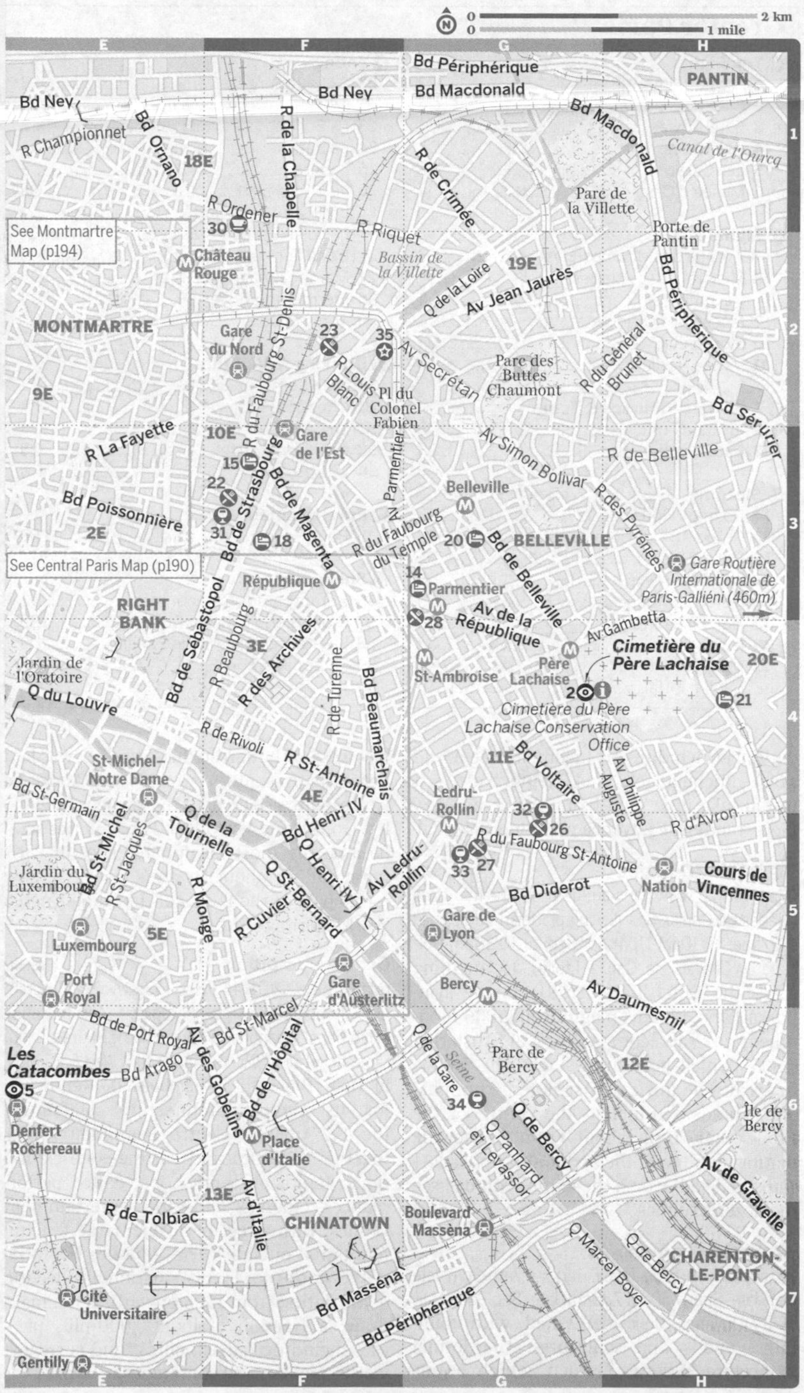
Bd Périphérique
Bd Ney
Bd Macdonald
PANTIN
R Championnet
Bd Ornano
18E
R de la Chapelle
R de Crimée
Canal de l'Ourcq
Parc de la Villette
R Ordener
30
See Montmartre Map (p194)
Château Rouge
R Riquet
Bassin de la Villette
Porte de Pantin
19E
Q de la Loire
Av Jean Jaurès
MONTMARTRE
Gare du Nord
R du Faubourg St-Denis
23
35
Av Secrétan
Parc des Buttes Chaumont
R du Général Brunet
R Louis Blanc
Pl du Colonel Fabien
9E
Bd Sérurier
10E
Gare de l'Est
R La Fayette
Av Parmentier
Av Simon Bolivar
R de Belleville
15
Bd de Strasbourg
22
Bd de Magenta
Belleville
R des Pyrénées
Bd Poissonnière
31
2E
18
R du Faubourg du Temple
20
BELLEVILLE
Bd de Belleville
Gare Routière Internationale de Paris-Galliéni (460m)
See Central Paris Map (p190)
République
14
Parmentier
Bd de Sébastopol
RIGHT BANK
R Beaubourg
28
Av de la République
Av Gambetta
3E
R des Archives
Cimetière du Père Lachaise
Jardin de l'Oratoire
Père Lachaise
20E
St-Ambroise
2
21
Q du Louvre
R de Turenne
Bd Beaumarchais
Cimetière du Père Lachaise Conservation Office
R de Rivoli
11E
R St-Antoine
Bd Voltaire
St-Michel–Notre Dame
Av Philippe Auguste
4E
Ledru-Rollin
32
Bd St-Germain
Bd Henri IV
26
R d'Avron
Q de la Tournelle
Bd St-Michel
R St-Jacques
Q Henri IV
R du Faubourg St-Antoine
33
27
Jardin du Luxembourg
Q St-Bernard
Av Ledru-Rollin
Nation
Cours de Vincennes
R Monge
Bd Diderot
R Cuvier
Gare de Lyon
Luxembourg
5E
Gare d'Austerlitz
Bercy
Port Royal
Av Daumesnil
Bd de Port Royal
Bd St-Marcel
Av des Gobelins
Les Catacombes
5
Bd Arago
Bd de l'Hôpital
Q de la Gare
Seine
Parc de Bercy
12E
34
Denfert Rochereau
Q de Bercy
Île de Bercy
Place d'Italie
Q Panhard et Levassor
13E
Av d'Italie
Av de Gravelle
R de Tolbiac
CHINATOWN
Boulevard Masséna
Q Marcel Boyer
Q de Bercy
CHARENTON-LE-PONT
Bd Masséna
Bd Périphérique
Cité Universitaire
Gentilly
FRANCE PARIS

Greater Paris

Top Sights
1 Arc de Triomphe C3
2 Cimetière du Père Lachaise G4
3 Eiffel Tower C4
4 Jardin des Tuileries D4
5 Les Catacombes E6
6 Musée d'Orsay D4

Sights
7 Avenue des Champs-Élysées C3
8 Ministère des Affaires Étrangères D4
9 Musée de l'Orangerie D4
10 Musée du Quai Branly C4
11 Musée Rodin D4

Activities, Courses & Tours
12 Alliance Française D5
13 Bateaux-Mouches C3

Sleeping
14 Cosmos Hôtel G3
15 Grand Amour Hôtel F3
16 Hôtel Félicien B5
17 Hôtel Perreyve D5
18 Hôtel Providence F3
19 Hôtel Vic Eiffel C5
20 Les Piaules G3
21 Mama Shelter H4
Sublim Eiffel ..... (see 19)

Eating
22 52 Faubourg St-Denis F3
58 Tour Eiffel ..... (see 3)
23 La Bulle F2
24 La Pâtisserie des Rêves D4
25 Ladurée C3
26 Le 6 Paul Bert G5
Le Bistrot Paul Bert ..... (see 32)
Le Jules Verne ..... (see 3)
L'Écailler du Bistrot ..... (see 32)
27 Marché d'Aligre G5
28 Pierre Sang Boyer G3
29 Tomy & Co C4

Drinking & Nightlife
30 Café Lomi F1
31 Chez Jeannette F3
32 La Cave Paul Bert G4
33 Le Baron Rouge G5
34 Le Batofar G6

Entertainment
35 Point Éphémère F2

Shopping
36 Comptoir des Catacombes D6
37 Fromagerie Laurent Dubois B5
38 La Grande Épicerie de Paris D5
39 Le Bon Marché D5

da Vinci (including his incomparable *Mona Lisa*), Michelangelo and Rembrandt – it would take nine months to glance at every piece, rendering advance planning essential.

★Arc de Triomphe LANDMARK

(Map p186; www.paris-arc-de-triomphe.fr; place Charles de Gaulle, 8e; viewing platform adult/child €12/free; 10am-11pm Apr-Sep, to 10.30pm Oct-Mar; M Charles de Gaulle–Étoile) If anything rivals the Eiffel Tower (p181) as the symbol of Paris, it's this magnificent 1836 monument to Napoléon's victory at Austerlitz (1805), which he commissioned the following year. The intricately sculpted triumphal arch stands sentinel in the centre of the Étoile ('Star') roundabout. From the viewing platform on top of the arch (50m up via 284 steps and well worth the climb) you can see the dozen avenues.

★Jardin des Tuileries PARK

(Map p186; rue de Rivoli, 1er; 7am-9pm late Mar–late Sep, 7.30am-7.30pm late Sep–late Mar; ; M Tuileries, Concorde) Filled with fountains, ponds and sculptures, the formal 28-hectare Tuileries Garden, which begins just west of the Jardin du Carrousel, was laid out in its present form in 1664 by André Le Nôtre, who also created the gardens at Vaux-le-Vicomte and Versailles. The Tuileries soon became the most fashionable spot in Paris for parading about in one's finery. It now forms part of the Banks of the Seine Unesco World Heritage Site.

Centre Pompidou MUSEUM

(Map p190; 01 44 78 12 33; www.centrepompidou.fr; place Georges Pompidou, 4e; museum, exhibitions & panorama adult/child €14/free, panorama ticket only €5; 11am-10pm Wed & Fri-Mon, to 11pm Thu; ; M Rambuteau) Renowned for its radical architectural statement, the 1977-opened Centre Pompidou brings together galleries and cutting-edge exhibitions, hands-on workshops, dance performances, cinemas and other entertainment venues, with street performers and fanciful fountains outside. The **Musée National d'Art Moderne**, France's national collection of art dating from 1905 onward, is the main draw; a fraction of its 100,000-plus pieces – including fauvist, cubist and surrealist works, pop art and contemporary works – is on display. Don't miss the spectacular Parisian panorama from the rooftop.

Basilique du Sacré-Cœur BASILICA
(Map p194; ☎01 53 41 89 00; www.sacre-cocurmontmartre.com; Parvis du Sacré-Cœur; basilica free, dome adult/child €6/4, cash only; ⊙basilica 6am-10.30pm, dome 8.30am-8pm May-Sep, to 5pm Oct-Apr; Ⓜ Anvers, Abbesses) Begun in 1875 in the wake of the Franco-Prussian War and the chaos of the Paris Commune, Sacré-Cœur is a symbol of the former struggle between the conservative Catholic old guard and the secular, republican radicals. It was finally consecrated in 1919, standing in utter contrast to the bohemian lifestyle that surrounded it. The view over Paris from its parvis is breathtaking. If you don't want to walk the hill, you can use a regular metro ticket aboard the **funicular** (place St-Pierre, 18e; ⊙6am-12.45am; Ⓜ Anvers, Abbesses).

★**Place des Vosges** SQUARE
(Map p190; 4e; Ⓜ St-Paul, Bastille) Inaugurated in 1612 as place Royale and thus Paris' oldest square, place des Vosges is a strikingly elegant ensemble of 36 symmetrical houses with ground-floor arcades, steep slate roofs and large dormer windows arranged around a leafy square with four symmetrical fountains and an 1829 copy of a mounted statue of Louis XIII. The square received its present name in 1800 to honour the Vosges *département* (administrative division) for being the first in France to pay its taxes.

★**Musée National Picasso** GALLERY
(Map p190; ☎01 85 56 00 36; www.museepicassoparis.fr; 5 rue de Thorigny, 3e; adult/child €12.50/free; ⊙10.30am-6pm Tue-Fri, 9.30am-6pm Sat & Sun; Ⓜ St-Paul, Chemin Vert) One of Paris' most beloved art collections is showcased inside the mid-17th-century Hôtel Salé, an exquisite private mansion owned by the city since 1964. The Musée National Picasso is a staggering art museum devoted to Spanish artist Pablo Picasso (1881–1973), who spent much of his life living and working in Paris. The collection includes more than 5000 drawings, engravings, paintings, ceramic works and sculptures by the *grand maître* (great master), although they're not all displayed at the same time.

★**Cimetière du Père Lachaise** CEMETERY
(Map p186; ☎01 55 25 82 10; www.pere-lachaise.com; 16 rue du Repos & 8 bd de Ménilmontant, 20e; ⊙8am-6pm Mon-Fri, 8.30am-6pm Sat, 9am-6pm Sun mid-Mar–Oct, shorter hours Nov–mid-Mar; Ⓜ Père Lachaise, Gambetta) The world's most visited cemetery, Père Lachaise opened in 1804. Its 70,000 ornate and ostentatious tombs of the rich and famous form a verdant, 44-hectare sculpture garden. The most visited are those of 1960s rock star Jim Morrison (division 6) and Oscar Wilde (division 89). Pick up cemetery maps at the **conservation office** (Bureaux de la Conservation; Map p186; ☎01 55 25 82 10; 16 rue du Repos, 20e; ⊙8.30am-12.30pm & 2-5pm Mon-Fri; Ⓜ Philippe Auguste, Père Lachaise) near the main bd de Ménilmontant entrance. Other notables buried here include composer Chopin; playwright Molière; poet Apollinaire; and writers Balzac, Proust, Gertrude Stein and Colette.

☞ Tours

★**Parisien d'un Jour – Paris Greeters** WALKING
(www.greeters.paris; by donation) See Paris through local eyes with these two- to three-hour city tours. Volunteers – mainly knowledgable Parisians passionate about their city – lead groups (maximum six people) to their favourite spots. Minimum two weeks' notice is needed.

Meeting the French CULTURAL, TOURS
(☎01 42 51 19 80; www.meetingthefrench.com; tours & courses from €25) Cosmetics workshops, backstage cabaret tours, fashion designer showroom visits, French table decoration, art embroidery classes, market tours, baking with a Parisian baker – the repertoire of cultural and gourmet tours and behind-the-scenes experiences offered by Meeting the French is truly outstanding. All courses and tours are in English.

Fat Tire Bike Tours CYCLING
(☎01 82 88 80 96; www.fattiretours.com; tours from €29) Offers day and night bicycle tours of the city, both in central Paris and further afield to Versailles and Monet's Garden (p205) in Giverny.

It also runs a host of other tours and activities, from cookery lessons to flea and food market tours, walking tours, and tours of the Louvre and Château de Versailles.

Bateaux-Mouches BOATING
(Map p186; ☎01 42 25 96 10; www.bateaux-mouches.fr; Port de la Conférence, 8e; adult/child €13.50/6; Ⓜ Alma Marceau) Bateaux-Mouches, the largest river cruise company in Paris, is a favourite with tour groups. Departing just

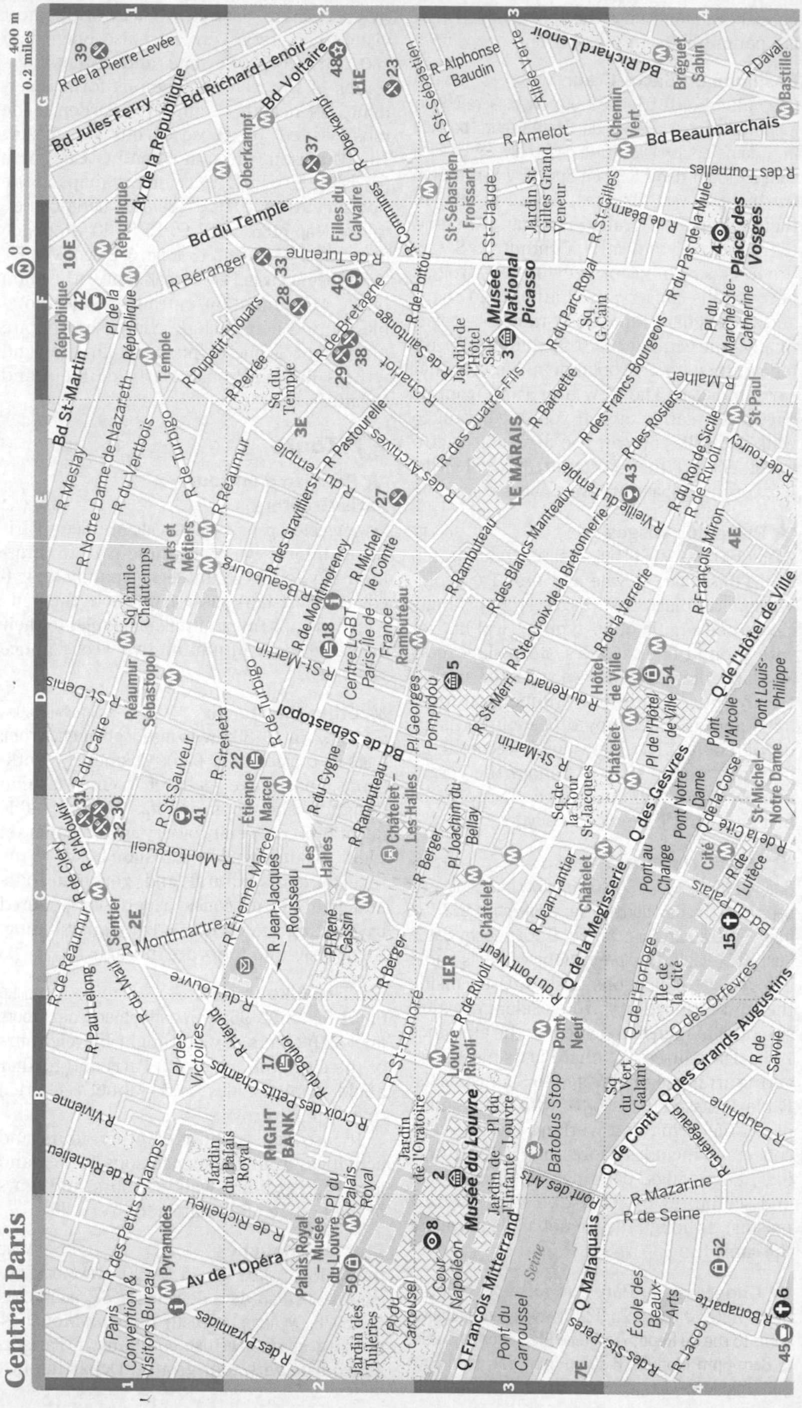

Central Paris

0 400 m
0 0.2 miles

A B C D E F G
1 2 3 4

R de Réaumur
R de Cléry
R d'Aboukir
31
R du Caire
R St-Denis
R Meslay
Bd St-Martin
République
42
10E
Bd Jules Ferry
R de la Pierre Levée
39
R de Richelieu
R Vivienne
R Paul Lelong
Sentier
2E
32 30
Réaumur Sébastopol
Sq Emile Chautemps
R Notre Dame de Nazareth
Pl de la République
République
Paris Convention & Visitors Bureau
R des Petits Champs
R du Mail
R Montmartre
R Montorgueil
R St-Sauveur
41
R du Vertbois
Temple
Av de la République
Pyramides
Pl des Victoires
Arts et Métiers
R de Turbigo
R Dupetit Thouars
R Béranger
Bd du Temple
Bd Richard Lenoir
R des Pyramides
Av de l'Opéra
R de Richelieu
Jardin du Palais Royal
R Hérold
R du Louvre
R Étienne Marcel
R Greneta
22
Étienne Marcel
R Réaumur
R Perrée
Oberkampf
RIGHT BANK
R Croix des Petits Champs
17
R du Bouloi
R Jean-Jacques Rousseau
R de Turbigo
R St-Martin
R Beaubourg
R des Gravilliers
Sq du Temple
28
33
Bd Voltaire
Palais Royal – Musée du Louvre
Les Halles
R du Cygne
Bd de Sébastopol
18
R de Montmorency
R du Temple
3E
37
Pl du Palais Royal
Pl René Cassin
Centre LGBT Paris-Île de France
R Michel le Comte
R Pastourelle
29
R de Bretagne
40
Filles du Calvaire
R Oberkampf
48
Jardin des Tuileries
50
R Rambuteau
38
R de Turenne
11E
Pl du Carrousel
R Berger
Châtelet – Les Halles
Rambuteau
27
R des Archives
R Charlot
R de Saintonge
R Commines
23
R St-Honoré
Jardin de l'Oratoire
Pl Georges Pompidou
R de Poitou
R St-Sébastien
Cour Napoléon
8
2
R Berger
Louvre Rivoli
1ER
Pl Joachim du Bellay
5
R Rambuteau
R des Quatre-Fils
Jardin de l'Hôtel Salé
St-Sébastien Froissart
R Alphonse Baudin
Musée du Louvre
R de Rivoli
Châtelet
R St-Merri
R Ste-Croix de la Bretonnerie
LE MARAIS
3
Musée National Picasso
R St-Claude
Q Francois Mitterrand
Jardin de l'Infante
Pl du Louvre
R du Pont Neuf
R St-Martin
R des Blancs Manteaux
R Barbette
Jardin St-Gilles Grand Veneur
R Amelot
Allée Verte
Pont du Carroussel
Seine
Pont des Arts
Batobus Stop
Pont Neuf
R Jean Lantier
Sq de la Tour St-Jacques
R du Renard
R du Parc Royal
Sq G Cain
Bd Richard Lenoir
7E
Q Malaquais
R des Sts-Pères
Q de la Megisserie
Châtelet
Hôtel de Ville
R de la Verrerie
R Vieille du Temple
R des Francs Bourgeois
R St-Gilles
Chemin Vert
École des Beaux-Arts
R de Seine
R Mazarine
Q de Conti
Sq du Vert Galant
Q de l'Horloge
Pont au Change
Q des Gesvres
Pl de l'Hôtel de Ville
54
43
R des Rosiers
R du Pas de la Mule
R de Béarn
Bd Beaumarchais
Bréguet Sabin
R Jacob
R Guénégaud
Q des Grands Augustins
Île de la Cité
Pont Notre Dame
R François Miron
R du Roi de Sicile
R de Rivoli
R Malher
Pl du Marché Ste-Catherine
4
Place des Vosges
R Bonaparte
52
Q des Orfèvres
15
Bd du Palais
R de Lutèce
Cité
Q de la Corse
R de la Cité
Pont d'Arcole
Q de l'Hôtel de Ville
4E
St-Paul
R de Fourcy
R des Tournelles
R Daval
Bastille
45
6
R Dauphine
R de Savoie
St-Michel–Notre Dame
Pont Louis-Philippe

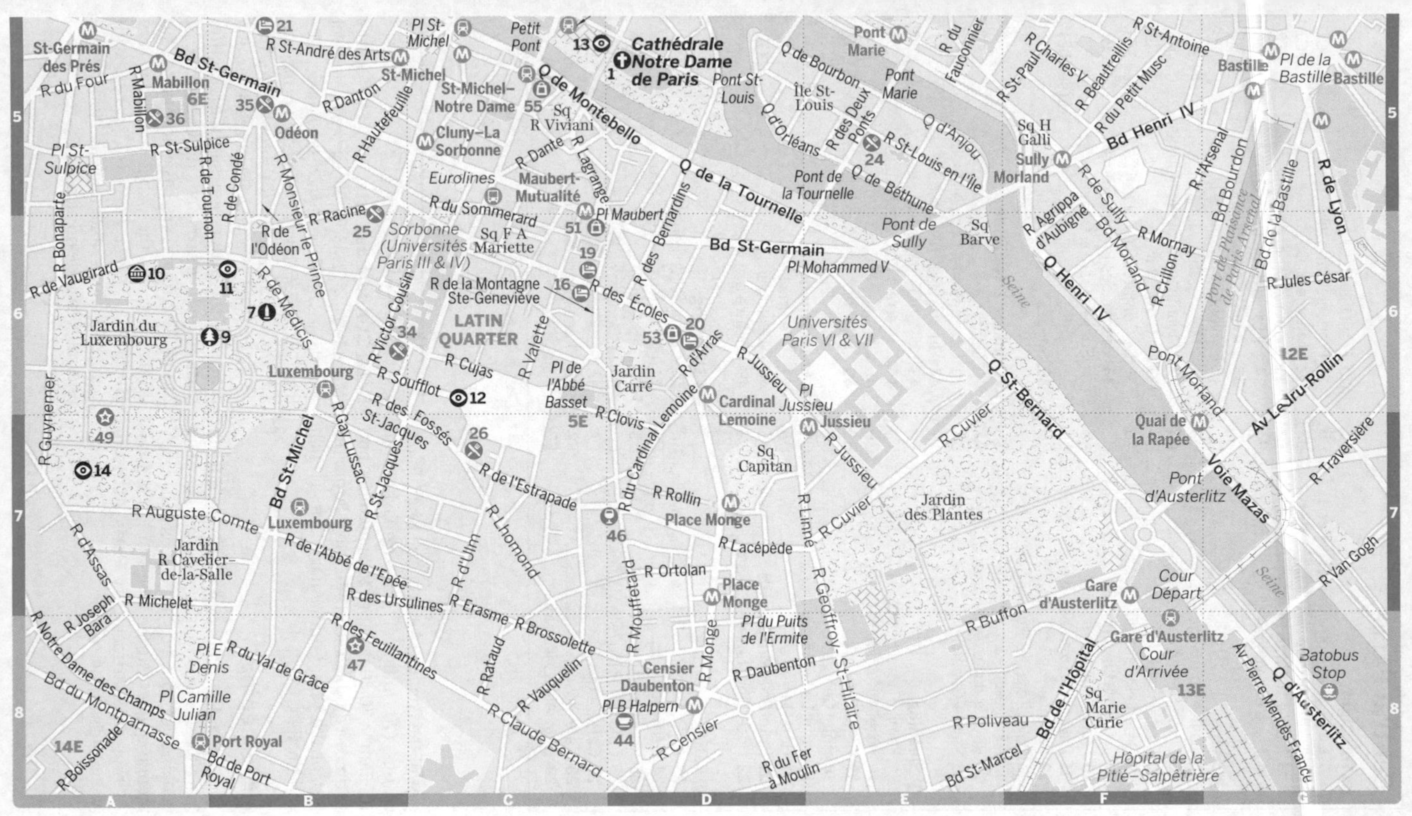
St-Germain des Prés
R du Four
R Mabillon
Mabillon
6E
36
Bd St-Germain
35
Odéon
21
R St-André des Arts
Pl St-Michel
St-Michel
R Danton
R Hautefeuille
St-Michel–Notre Dame
55
Petit Pont
13
Cathédrale Notre Dame de Paris
1
Q de Montebello
Sq R Viviani
Cluny–La Sorbonne
R Dante
R Lagrange
Eurolines
Maubert-Mutualité
Pl Maubert
51
R du Sommerard
Sorbonne (Universités Paris III & IV)
Sq F A Mariette
R Racine
25
Pl St-Sulpice
R St-Sulpice
R de Tournon
R de Condé
R de l'Odéon
R Monsieur le Prince
R Bonaparte
R de Vaugirard
10
11
R de Médicis
7
9
Jardin du Luxembourg
R Victor Cousin
34
R de la Montagne Ste-Geneviève
16
19
R des Écoles
LATIN QUARTER
R Cujas
R Valette
Luxembourg
R Soufflot
12
R des Fossés St-Jacques
26
R Gay Lussac
R St-Jacques
Bd St-Michel
R Guynemer
49
14
Pl de l'Abbé Basset
5E
Jardin Carré
R Clovis
R d'Arras
53
20
R des Bernardins
Q de la Tournelle
Bd St-Germain
Pl Mohammed V
Pont de la Tournelle
Q de Béthune
Pont de Sully
Sq Barye
Pont St-Louis
Île St-Louis
Q d'Orléans
Q de Bourbon
R des Deux Ponts
24
R St-Louis en l'Île
Q d'Anjou
Pont Marie
R du Fauconnier
R St-Paul
R Charles V
R Beautreillis
R du Petit Musc
R St-Antoine
Bastille
Pl de la Bastille
Sq H Galli
Sully Morland
Bd Henri IV
R de Sully
R Agrippa d'Aubigné
Bd Morland
R Mornay
R Crillon
R de l'Arsenal
Bd Bourdon
Port de Plaisance de Paris Arsenal
Bd de la Bastille
R de Lyon
R Jules César
Seine
Q Henri IV
Universités Paris VI & VII
R Jussieu
Pl Jussieu
Cardinal Lemoine
Jussieu
R du Cardinal Lemoine
Sq Capitan
R Rollin
Place Monge
R de l'Estrapade
R Lhomond
R Auguste Comte
Luxembourg
Jardin R Cavelier-de-la-Salle
R de l'Abbé de l'Epée
R d'Ulm
46
R Mouffetard
R Ortolan
R Lacépède
R Linné
R Cuvier
Q St-Bernard
Jardin des Plantes
Pont Morland
Quai de la Rapée
Av Ledru-Rollin
12E
R Traversière
Voie Mazas
Pont d'Austerlitz
R Van Gogh
Cour Départ
Gare d'Austerlitz
R Buffon
R Geoffroy-St-Hilaire
Pl du Puits de l'Ermite
R Monge
R Daubenton
Censier Daubenton
Pl B Halpern
44
R Censier
R du Fer à Moulin
R d'Assas
R Joseph Bara
R Michelet
R des Ursulines
R Erasme
R Brossolette
R des Feuillantines
47
R Rataud
R Vauquelin
R Claude Bernard
Pl E Denis
R du Val de Grâce
Pl Camille Julian
Port Royal
Bd de Port Royal
R Notre Dame des Champs
Bd du Montparnasse
14E
R Boissonade
Bd St-Marcel
R Poliveau
Bd de l'Hôpital
Sq Marie Curie
Hôpital de la Pitié–Salpêtrière
Gare d'Austerlitz
Cour d'Arrivée
13E
Av Pierre Mendès France
Q d'Austerlitz
Batobus Stop

Central Paris

Top Sights

1 Cathédrale Notre Dame de Paris.......... D5
2 Musée du Louvre B3
3 Musée National Picasso.................. F3
4 Place des Vosges.................... F4

Sights

5 Centre Pompidou.................... D3
6 Église St-Germain des Prés.............. A4
7 Fontaine des Médici B6
8 Grande Pyramide.................... A3
9 Jardin du Luxembourg.................. B6
10 Musée du Luxembourg.................. A6
11 Palais du Luxembourg B6
12 Panthéon.................... C6
13 Point Zéro des Routes de France.................... C5
14 Rucher du Luxembourg.................. A7
15 Sainte-Chapelle.................... C4

Sleeping

Familia Hôtel.................. (see 20)
16 Hôtel Atmosphères C6
17 Hôtel Crayon B2
18 Hôtel Georgette D2
19 Hôtel La Lanterne C6
20 Hôtel Minerve.................... D6
21 Hôtel St-André des Arts.................. B5
22 Hôtel Tiquetonne.................... D2

Eating

23 Au Passage.................... G2
24 Berthillon.................... E5
25 Bouillon Racine B5
26 Café de la Nouvelle Mairie.................. C7
27 Café Marais.................... E2
28 Café Pinson.................... F2
29 Chez Alain Miam Miam F2
30 Frenchie.................... C1
31 Frenchie Bar à Vins C1
32 Frenchie to Go C1
33 Jacques Genin F2
34 La Table de Marie-Jeanne.................. B6
35 L'Avant Comptoir.................... B5
L'Avant Comptoir de la Mer .... (see 35)
36 L'Avant Comptoir du Marché A5
37 Le Clown Bar.................... G2
Le Comptoir du Relais .... (see 35)
38 Marché des Enfants Rouges.................. F2
Shakespeare & Company Café.................. (see 55)
39 Soya G1

Drinking & Nightlife

40 Candelaria.................... F2
41 Experimental Cocktail Club C1
42 Fluctuat Nec Mergitur.................. F1
43 Le Petit Fer à Cheval E4
44 Le Verre à Pied.................... D8
45 Les Deux Magots.................... A4
46 Little Bastards D7

Entertainment

47 Café Universel.................... B8
48 Le Bataclan.................... G2
49 Théâtre du Luxembourg.................. A7

Shopping

50 Carrousel du Louvre A2
51 Fromagerie Laurent Dubois.................. C6
52 Gab & Jo A4
53 Le Bonbon au Palais.................. D6
54 Paris Rendez-Vous.................. D4
55 Shakespeare & Company C5

east of the Pont de l'Alma on the Right Bank, cruises (70 minutes) run regularly from 10.15am to 10.30pm April to September and 13 times a day between 11am and 9.20pm the rest of the year. Commentary is in French and English.

Sleeping

The Paris Convention & Visitors Bureau (p202) can find you a place to stay (no booking fee, but you need a credit card), though queues can be long in high season. To rent an apartment, try **Paris Attitude** (www.parisattitude.com).

Left Bank

Hôtel St-André des Arts HOTEL **€**

(Map p190; 01 43 26 96 16; www.hotel-saintandredesarts.fr; 66 rue St-André des Arts, 6e; s/d/tr/q €95/115/156/181; ; M Odéon) Located on a lively, restaurant-lined thoroughfare, this 31-room hotel is a veritable bargain in the centre of the action opposite the beautiful glass-roofed passage Cour du Commerce St André. The rooms are basic and there's no lift/elevator, but the public areas are very evocative of *vieux Paris* (old Paris), with beamed ceilings and ancient stone walls, and rates include breakfast.

★Familia Hôtel HOTEL €€
(Map p190; ☎01 43 54 55 27; www.familiahotel.com; 11 rue des Écoles, 5e; s €110, d €134-152, tr €191, f €214; ❄📶; Ⓜ Cardinal Lemoine) Sepia murals of Parisian landmarks, flower-bedecked windows and exposed rafters and stone walls make this friendly third-generation family-run hotel one of the most attractive 'almost budget' options on this side of the Seine. Eight rooms (on the 2nd, 5th and 6th floors; there's a lift) have little balconies offering glimpses of Notre Dame. Breakfast costs €7.

Hôtel La Lanterne BOUTIQUE HOTEL €€
(Map p190; ☎01 53 19 88 39; www.hotel-la-lanterne.com; 12 rue de la Montagne Ste-Geneviève, 5e; d/ste from €170/390; ❄@📶; Ⓜ Maubert-Mutualité) A stunning swimming pool and *hammam* (Turkish steambath) in a vaulted stone cellar, a topiary-filled courtyard garden, contemporary guest rooms (some with small balconies) with B&W photos of Parisian architecture, and amenities, including Nespresso machines, and an honesty bar make this a jewel of a boutique hotel. Breakfast (€19) lets you choose from hot and cold buffets and includes Mariage Frères teas.

Hôtel Atmosphères DESIGN HOTEL €€
(Map p190; ☎01 43 26 56 02; www.hotelatmospheres.com; 31 rue des Écoles, 5e; s/d/tr/ste from €126/144/174/229; ❄@📶; Ⓜ Maubert-Mutualité) Striking images by award-winning French photographer Thierry des Ouches are permanently exhibited at this haven, where cocooning rooms evoke different Parisian 'atmospheres', such as 'nature', 'monuments', the metro-inspired 'urban' and colourful *salon de thé* (tearoom)-style 'macaron'. There's a small gym and a sauna as well as an honesty bar. Breakfast costs €16.

Hôtel Minerve HOTEL €€
(Map p190; ☎01 43 26 26 04; www.parishotelminerve.com; 13 rue des Écoles, 5e; s/d/f from €161/197/394; ❄@📶; Ⓜ Cardinal Lemoine) Oriental carpets, antique books, frescoes of French monuments and wall tapestries make this family-run hotel a lovely place to stay. Room styles are a mix of traditional and modern (renovated earlier this decade); some have small balconies with views of Notre Dame, while the 1st-floor rooms all have parquet floors.

Hôtel Perreyve HOTEL €€
(Map p186; ☎01 45 48 35 01; www.perreyve-hotel-paris-luxembourg.com; 63 rue Madame, 6e; s/d €152/197; ❄📶; Ⓜ Rennes) A hop, skip and a jump from the Jardin du Luxembourg, this welcoming 1920s hotel is superb value given its coveted location. Cosy, carpeted rooms have enormous frescoes; on the ground floor, start the day in the pretty breakfast room with herringbone floors and fire-engine-red tables and chairs.

★Sublim Eiffel DESIGN HOTEL €€
(Map p186; ☎01 40 65 95 95; www.sublimeiffel.com; 94 bd Garibaldi, 15e; d from €146; ❄📶; Ⓜ Sèvres-Lecourbe) There's no forgetting what city you're in with the Eiffel Tower motifs in reception and rooms (along with Parisian street-map carpets and metro-tunnel-shaped bedheads) plus glittering tower views from upper-floor windows. Edgy design elements also include cobblestone staircase carpeting (there's also a lift) and, fittingly in *la ville lumière* (the City of Lights), technicoloured in-room fibre-optic lighting. The small wellness centre/*hammam* offers massages.

Right Bank

★Les Piaules HOSTEL €
(Map p186; ☎01 43 55 09 97; www.lespiaules.com; 59 bd de Belleville, 11e; dm €23-58, d €130-200; @📶; Ⓜ Couronnes) This thoroughly contemporary hostel is the Belleville hot spot to mingle with locals over Parisian craft beer, cosy up in front of the wood-burner with a good book, or lap up sun and stunning views from the 5th-floor rooftop terrace. Dorms are bright and cheery, with custom bunks and ample bedside plugs, but it's the sleek all-white rooftop doubles everyone really gushes over.

Cosmos Hôtel HOTEL €
(Map p186; ☎01 43 57 25 88; www.cosmos-hotel-paris.com; 35 rue Jean-Pierre Timbaud, 11e; s €66, d €72-82, tr €93; 📶; Ⓜ République) Cheap, brilliant value and just footsteps from the nightlife of rue JPT, Cosmos is a shiny star with retro style on the budget-hotel scene. It has been around for 30-odd years but, unlike most other hotels in the same price bracket, Cosmos has been treated to a thoroughly modern makeover this century. Breakfast costs €8.

Hôtel Tiquetonne HOTEL €
(Map p190; ☎01 42 36 94 58; www.hoteltiquetonne.fr; 6 rue Tiquetonne, 2e; d €80, without shower €65; 📶; Ⓜ Étienne Marcel) What heart-warmingly good value this 45-room cheapie is. This serious, well-tended address has been

in the hotel biz since the 1900s and is much loved by a loyal clientele of all ages. Rooms range across seven floors, are spick and span, and sport an inoffensive mix of vintage decor – roughly 1930s to 1980s, with brand-new bathrooms and parquet flooring in recently renovated rooms.

Mama Shelter DESIGN HOTEL **€**
(Map p186; ☎01 43 48 48 48; www.mamashelter.com; 109 rue de Bagnolet, 20e; s/d/tr from €89/99/139; ❄@📶; 🚌76, Ⓜ Alexandre Dumas, Gambetta) This former car park was coaxed into its current zany incarnation by uber-designer Philippe Starck. Its 170 cutting-edge rooms feature iMacs, catchy colour schemes, polished-concrete walls and free movies on demand. A rooftop terrace, pizzeria, and huge restaurant with live music and Sunday brunch only add to its street cred. Book as early as possible to get the best deal. Breakfast is €16.

★ **Joke Hôtel** DESIGN HOTEL **€€**
(Map p194; ☎01 40 40 71 71; www.astotel.com/hotel; rue Blanche, 9e; s/d €129/150; ❄@📶; Ⓜ Place de Clichy, Pigalle) No joke. This hotel is a serious contender for Paris' best-value, most fun address. Play 'scrabble' or spin the wheel of fortune above your bed each night, hunt

Montmartre

for coins stuck in the floor, and generally frolic in the youthful ambience and striking design of this fabulous, childhood-themed hotel. Rates include breakfast and all-day complimentary drinks, cakes and fruit

★**Hôtel Crayon** BOUTIQUE HOTEL €€
(Map p190; ☎01 42 36 54 19; www.hotelcrayon.com; 25 rue du Bouloi, 1er; s/d €203/229; ❄📶; Ⓜ Les Halles, Sentier) Line drawings by French artist Julie Gauthron bedeck walls and doors at this creative boutique hotel. *Le crayon* (the pencil) is the theme, with 26 rooms sporting a different shade of each floor's chosen colour – we love the coloured-glass shower doors, and the books on the bedside table guests can swap and take home. Online deals often slash rates by up to 50%.

★**Hôtel Providence** BOUTIQUE HOTEL €€
(Map p186; ☎01 46 34 34 04; www.hotelprovidenceparis.com; 90 rue René Boulanger, 10e; d from €170; ❄📶; Ⓜ Strasbourg-St-Denis, République) This luxurious hideaway, in a 19th-century townhouse in the increasingly trendy 10e, is exquisite. Its 18 individually decorated rooms come with rich House of Hackney velvet wallpaper and vintage flea-market finds; the smallest rooms are not nearly as 'Mini' (by Paris standards) as the name suggests. Utterly glorious is the bespoke cocktail bar gracing each room, complete with suggested recipes and ingredients.

★**Hôtel Georgette** DESIGN HOTEL €€
(Map p190; ☎01 44 61 10 10; www.hotelgeorgette.com; 36 rue du Grenier St-Lazare, 3e; d from €190; ❄📶; Ⓜ Rambuteau) Clearly seeking inspiration from the Centre Pompidou around the corner, this sweet little neighbourhood hotel is a steal. The lobby is bright and appealing, and rooms are a decorative ode to either Pop Art, Op Art, Dada or New Realism with lots of bold colours and funky touches like Andy Warhol–inspired Campbell's-soup-can lampshades.

Grand Amour Hôtel DESIGN HOTEL €€
(Map p186; ☎01 44 16 03 10; www.hotelamourparis.fr; 18 rue de la Fidelité, 10e; s/d from €145/230; 📶; Ⓜ Château d'Eau) Younger sister to Pigalle's **Hôtel Amour** (Map p194; ☎01 48 78 31 80; 8 rue Navarin, 9e; d €170-230; 📶; Ⓜ St-Georges, Pigalle), this hipster lifestyle hotel mixes vintage furniture from the flea market with phallic-symbol carpets and the striking B&W nude photography of graffiti artist André Saraiva. The result is an edgy hideaway for lovers in one of the city's most up-and-coming neighbourhoods. Breakfast is served in the hotel bistro, a trendy drinking and dining address in itself.

Hôtel Vic Eiffel BOUTIQUE HOTEL €€
(Map p186; ☎01 53 86 83 83; www.hotelviceiffel.com; 92 bd Garibaldi, 15e; s/d €190/220; 📶; Ⓜ Sèvres-Lecourbe) A short walk from the Eiffel Tower, with the metro on the doorstep, this pristine hotel has chic orange and oyster-grey rooms (two of which are wheelchair accessible). Classic rooms are small but perfectly functional; Superior and Privilege rooms offer increased space. All have Nespresso coffee-making machines. Rates plummet outside high season. Breakfast, served in an atrium-style courtyard, costs €14.

★**Hôtel Félicien** BOUTIQUE HOTEL €€€
(Map p186; ☎01 55 74 00 00; www.hotelfelicienparis.com; 21 rue Félicien David, 16e; d €280-330, ste from €470; ❄@📶; Ⓜ Mirabeau) The price-quality ratio at this chic boutique hotel, squirrelled away in a 1930s building, is outstanding. Exquisitely designed rooms feel more five-star than four, with 'White' and 'Silver' suites on the hotel's top 'Sky floor' more than satisfying their promise of indulgent cocooning. Romantics, eat your heart out.

Montmartre

Sights
1 Basilique du Sacré-Cœur C1

Sleeping
2 Hôtel Amour C3
3 Joke Hôtel B2

Eating
4 Bambou D5
5 L'Office D4
6 Richer D4
7 Soul Kitchen C1

Drinking & Nightlife
La Fourmi .... (see 10)
8 Le Très Particulier B1

Entertainment
9 Kiosque Théâtre Madeleine A5
10 La Cigale C2
11 Moulin Rouge B2

Left Bank

★Shakespeare & Company Café CAFE €

(Map p190; www.shakespeareandcompany.com; 2 rue St-Julien le Pauvre, 5e; dishes €3.50-10.50; 9.30am-7pm Mon-Fri, to 8pm Sat & Sun; ; St-Michel) Instant history was made when this light-filled, literary-inspired cafe opened in 2015 adjacent to magical bookshop Shakespeare & Company (p201), designed from long-lost sketches to fulfil a dream of late bookshop founder George Whitman from the 1960s. Its primarily vegetarian menu (with vegan and gluten-free dishes available) includes homemade bagels, rye bread, soups, salads and pastries, plus Parisian-roasted **Café Lomi** (Map p186; 09 80 39 56 24; www.lomi.paris; 3ter rue Marcadet, 18e; 10am-7pm; Marcadet–Poissonniers) coffee.

★L'Avant Comptoir du Marché TAPAS €

(Map p190; 15 rue Lobineau, 6e; tapas €3.50-19; noon-11pm; Mabillon) The latest of Yves Camdeborde's casual 'small plates' eateries is this porcine-specialist tapas bar wedged in one corner of the Marché St-Germain covered market–shopping complex. A flying, fire-engine-red pig is the ceiling's centrepiece, surrounded by suspended menus listing dishes such as Bayonne ham croquettes, Bigorre pâté, and shots of Béarnaise pig's blood; wines are chalked on the blackboard. No reservations.

Camdeborde's neighbouring addresses include bistro **Le Comptoir du Relais** (Map p190; 01 44 27 07 97; www.hotel-paris-relais-saint-germain.com; 9 Carrefour de l'Odéon, 6e; lunch mains €14-28, dinner menu €60; noon-6pm & 8.30-11.30pm Mon-Fri, noon-11pm Sat & Sun; Odéon), tapas bar **L'Avant Comptoir** (Map p190; www.hotel-paris-relais-saint-germain.com; 3 Carrefour de l'Odéon, 6e; tapas €4-10; noon-midnight; Odéon) and seafood tapas bar **L'Avant Comptoir de la Mer** (Map p190; www.hotel-paris-relais-saint-germain.com; 3 Carrefour de l'Odéon, 6e; tapas €5-25; 11am-11pm; Odéon).

★Café de la Nouvelle Mairie CAFE €

(Map p190; 01 44 07 04 41; 19 rue des Fossés St-Jacques, 5e; mains €9-19; kitchen noon-2.30pm & 8-10.30pm Mon-Thu, 8-10pm Fri; Cardinal Lemoine) Shhhh…just around the corner from the Panthéon (p184) but hidden away on a small, fountained square, this narrow wine bar is a neighbourhood secret, serving blackboard-chalked natural wines by the glass and delicious seasonal bistro fare from oysters and ribs *(à la française)* to grilled lamb sausage over lentils. It takes reservations for dinner but not lunch – arrive early.

★Bouillon Racine BRASSERIE €€

(Map p190; 01 44 32 15 60; www.bouillon-racine.com; 3 rue Racine, 6e; weekday 2-course lunch menu €17, menus €33-46, mains €18.50-29; noon-11pm; ; Cluny-La Sorbonne) Inconspicuously situated in a quiet street, this heritage-listed 1906 art-nouveau 'soup kitchen', with mirrored walls, floral motifs and ceramic tiling, was built in 1906 to feed market workers. Despite the magnificent interior, the food – inspired by age-old recipes – is no afterthought but superbly executed (stuffed, spit-roasted suckling pig, pork shank in Rodenbach red beer, scallops and shrimps with lobster coulis).

★Tomy & Co GASTRONOMY €€

(Map p186; 01 45 51 46 93; 22 rue Surcouf, 7e; 2-course lunch menu €25, 3-course dinner menu €45, tasting menu €65, with paired wines €100; noon-2pm & 7.30-9.30pm Mon-Fri; Invalides) The talk-of-the-town address of the moment is Tomy Gousset's inaugural restaurant (book ahead). Gousset previously cooked in some of Paris' top kitchens and now works his magic here on inspired seasonal dishes like roast duck with candied yellow beets and pickled grapes, and pork neck with spinach, black olives, micro herbs and raw mushrooms, using produce from his organic garden.

La Table de Marie-Jeanne ROTISSERIE €€

(Map p190; 01 42 49 87 31; www.latabledemariejeanne.fr; 4 rue Toullier, 5e; 2-/3-course menus lunch €17/21, dinner €26/31; noon-2.15pm & 7-10.30pm Tue-Sat; Cluny–La Sorbonne or RER Luxembourg) Free-range chickens and prime cuts of lamb, beef, pork, duck and veal (plus venison in season) are spit-roasted on these chic Left Bank premises. Adorned with stencilled animals on blond wood-panelled walls, exposed stone and suspended topaz and jade-green glass lights, accompanying sides here include roasted potatoes, salads and fragrant sauces such as rosemary and pepper.

LOCAL KNOWLEDGE

TOP FIVE SWEET TREATS

You couldn't come to Paris and not indulge in something sweet, sticky and delicious. From light-as-air macarons to creamy éclairs, fruity tarts and sinful chocolate confections, the Parisians really know how to indulge a sweet tooth.

Ladurée (Map p186; www.laduree.com; 75 av des Champs-Élysées, 8e; pastries from €1.90,; ⊙7.30am-11.30pm Mon-Thu, 7.30am-12.30am Fri, 8.30am-12.30am Sat, 8.30am-11.30pm Sun; Ⓜ George V) Famous across Paris for its multi-flavoured macarons.

Berthillon (Map p190; www.berthillon.fr; 31 rue St-Louis en l'Île, 4e; 1/2/3 scoops take away €3/4/6.50, eat-in €4.50/7.50/10.50; ⊙10am-8pm Wed-Sun, closed Aug; Ⓜ Pont Marie) Seventy-odd flavours of ice-cream, including seasonal ones.

Jacques Genin (Map p190; ☎01 45 77 29 01; www.jacquesgenin.fr; 133 rue de Turenne, 3e; pastries €9; ⊙11am-7pm Tue-Sun; Ⓜ Oberkampf, Filles du Calvaire) A wildly creative chocolatier with a delightful tea-room.

La Patisserie des Rêves (Map p186; www.lapatisseriedesreves.com; 93 rue du Bac, 7e; ⊙9am-7pm Tue-Thu, to 8pm Fri & Sat, to 2pm Sun; Ⓜ Rue du Bac) The cakes on show here are almost too dreamy to eat.

Le Bonbon au Palais (Map p190; www.bonbonsaupalais.fr; 19 rue Monge, 5e; ⊙10.30am-7.30pm Tue-Sat; Ⓜ Cardinal Lemoine) From stripey *berlingots* to almondy *calissons*, this is Paris' favourite sweet-shop.

Right Bank

★Chez Alain Miam Miam SANDWICHES, CRÊPERIE €
(Map p190; www.facebook.com/ChezAlainMiamMiam; Marché des Enfants Rouges, 39 rue de Bretagne & 33bis rue Charlot, 3e; dishes €3-9.50; ⊙9am-3.30pm Wed-Fri, to 5.30pm Sat, to 3pm Sun; ; Ⓜ Filles du Calvaire) Weave your way through the makeshift kitchens inside Marché des Enfants Rouges to find Alain, a retired baker sporting T-shirts with attitude, whose passion, humour and food are legendary. Watch him prepare you a monster sandwich or *galette* (savoury pancake) on a sizzling griddle a fresh, organic ingredients – grated fennel, smoked air-dried beef, avocado, sesame salt and prized honeys.

★Café Pinson CAFE, VEGETARIAN €
(Map p190; ☎09 83 82 53 53; www.cafepinson.fr; 6 rue du Forez, 3e; 2-course lunch menu €17.50, mains €14; ⊙9am-10pm Mon-Fri, 10am-10pm Sat, noon-6pm Sun; ; Ⓜ Filles du Calvaire) Tucked down a narrow side street in the fashionable Haut Marais, with an interior by celebrity designer Dorothée Meilichzon, this spacious cafe sees a stylish lunchtime crowd flock for its organic vegetarian and vegan dishes such as almond, carrot and ginger soup and dark-chocolate pear crumble. Freshly squeezed juices are excellent, as is Sunday brunch (€27; 12.15pm and 2pm).

★52 Faubourg St-Denis MODERN FRENCH €
(Map p186; www.faubourgstdenis.com; 52 rue du Faubourg St-Denis, 10e; mains €16-20; ⊙8am-midnight, kitchen noon-2.30pm & 7-11pm; ; Ⓜ Château d'Eau) This thoroughly contemporary, neighbourhood cafe-restaurant is simply a brilliant space to hang out in at any time of day. Be it for breakfast, coffee, a zingy fresh-sage infusion, dinner or drinks, 52 Faubourg, as locals call it, gets it just right. Cuisine is modern and creative, and the chef is not shy in mixing veg with fruit in every course – including dessert. No reservations.

★Richer BISTRO €
(Map p194; www.lericher.com; 2 rue Richer, 9e; mains €18-20; ⊙noon-2.30pm and 7.30-10.30pm; Ⓜ Poissonière, Bonne Nouvelle) Richer's pared-back, exposed-brick decor is a smart setting for genius creations like smoked duck breast ravioli in miso broth, and quince and lime cheesecake for dessert. It doesn't take reservations, but it serves up snacks and Chinese tea, and has a full bar (open until midnight). Fantastic value. Run by the same team as across-the-street neighbour **L'Office** (☎01 47 70 67 31; www.office-resto.com; 2-/3-course lunch menus €22/27, mains €19-32; ⊙noon-2pm & 7.30-10.30pm Mon-Fri).

Café Marais MODERN FRENCH €
(Map p190; ☎01 42 71 61 46; www.cafemarais.fr; 10 rue des Haudriettes, 3e; 2-course lunch/

dinner menu €17.50/19.50; ⏲noon-3pm Mon-Thu, noon-3pm & 7-11.30pm Fri & Sat; Ⓜ Rambuteau) Exposed stone, a beamed ceiling and silent B&W movies (Charlie Chaplin et al) screened on one wall create an appealing vintage feel in this small and excellent bistro – one of the best-value spots for dining in Le Marais. The round of Camembert roasted with honey, homemade courgette gratin and parmesan crème brûlée are all excellent.

Soul Kitchen VEGETARIAN €

(Map p194; www.soulkitchenparis.fr; 33 rue Lamarck, 18e; lunch menu €13.90; ⏲8.45am-6pm Mon-Fri; ; Ⓜ Lamarck–Caulaincourt) This vegetarian eatery with shabby-chic vintage interior and tiny open kitchen serves market-driven dishes including feisty bowls of creative salads, homemade soups, savoury tarts, burritos and wraps – all gargantuan in size and packed with seasonal veggies. Round off lunch or snack between meals on muffins, cakes and mint-laced *citronnade maison* (homemade lemonade). Families should check out the sage-green 'games' cupboard.

★Au Passage BISTRO €€

(Map p190; ☎01 73 20 23 23; www.restaurant-aupassage.fr; 1bis passage St-Sébastien, 11e; small plates €7-14, meats to share €18-70; ⏲7-11.30pm Mon-Sat; Ⓜ St-Sébastien-Froissart) Spawned by talented Australian chef James Henry, who went on to open Bones then Parisian bistro Belon in Hong Kong, this *petit bar de quartier* (neighbourhood bar) is still raved about. Pick from a good-value, uncomplicated choice selection *of petites assiettes* (small plates designed to be shared) featuring various market produce – cold meats, raw or cooked fish, vegetables and so on. Advance reservations essential.

★Bambou SOUTHEAST ASIAN €€

(Map p194; ☎01 40 28 98 30; www.bambou-paris.com; 23 rue des Jeûneurs, 2e; mains €19-28; ⏲noon-2.30pm & 7-11pm, bar to midnight; ; Ⓜ Sentier) One of Paris' most sizzling recent openings, this spectacular Southeast Asian restaurant occupies a 500-sq-metre former fabric warehouse, with vintage birdcages and a giant metal dragon adorning the main dining room, a downstairs billiards room and bar, vast terrace and Zen-like garden. Chef Antonin Bonnet's specialities include squid with black pepper and basil, and aromatic shrimp pad thai.

★La Bulle MODERN FRENCH €€

(Map p186; ☎01 85 15 21 58; www.restolabulle.fr; 48 rue Louis Blanc, 10e; 2-/3-course lunch menus €18.50/24, 3-/6-course dinner menus €36/55, mains €19-28; ⏲noon-2.30pm & 7.30-10.30pm Mon-Sat; Ⓜ Louis Blanc) It's worth the short detour to this contemporary corner bistro with lime-green seating on a sunny pavement terrace, and talented young chef Romain Perrollaz in the kitchen. His cuisine is creative and strictly *fait maison* (homemade), with lots of tempting combos like poached salmon and artichoke mousse, squid stuffed with konbu (Japanese seaweed), or pork, pistachio and cuttlefish ink terrine.

★Le Clown Bar MODERN FRENCH €€

(Map p190; ☎01 43 55 87 35; www.clown-bar-paris.com; 114 rue Amelot, 11e; mains €28-36; ⏲kitchen noon-2.30pm & 7-10.30pm Wed-Sun, bar 7.30am-1.30am; Ⓜ Filles du Calvaire) The former staff dining room of the city's winter circus, the 1852-built Cirque d'Hiver, is a historic monument with colourful clown-themed ceramics and mosaics, painted glass ceilings and its original zinc bar. Fabulous modern French cuisine spans scallops with smoked rosemary ricotta to Mesquer pigeon, smoked eel with pear and mushrooms and sautéed veal's brains, accompanied by excellent natural wines.

★Pierre Sang Boyer MODERN FRENCH €€

(Map p186; ☎09 67 31 96 80; www.pierresang-boyer.com; 55 rue Oberkampf, 11e; 2-/3-/5-course lunch €20/25/35, 4-/6-course dinner €35/50; ⏲noon-3pm & 7-11pm Tue-Sat; Ⓜ Oberkampf) *Top Chef* finalist Pierre Sang Boyer stars at his kitchen restaurant where foodies sit on bar stools and watch the French–South Korean chef perform. Cuisine is modern French with a strong fusion lilt, and the vibe is fun and casual. If the place is full, nip around the corner to Sang's 'atelier' annexe on rue Gambey.

Le Bistrot Paul Bert BISTRO €€

(Map p186; ☎01 43 72 24 01; 18 rue Paul Bert, 11e; 2-/3-course lunch/dinner menu €19/41; ⏲noon-2pm & 7.30-11pm Tue-Sat; Ⓜ Faidherbe-Chaligny) When food writers list Paris' best bistros, Paul Bert's name consistently pops up. The timeless vintage decor and classic dishes like *steak-frites* and hazelnut-cream Paris-Brest pastry merit booking ahead. Look for its siblings in the same street: **L'Écailler du Bistrot** (☎01 43 72 76 77; 22 rue Paul Bert, 11e; weekday lunch menu €19, mains €17-38; ⏲noon-

2.30pm & 7.30-11pm Tue-Sat) for seafood; **La Cave Paul Bert** (01 58 53 30 92; 16 rue Paul Bert, 11e; noon-midnight, kitchen noon-2pm & 7.30-11.30pm), a wine bar with small plates; and **Le 6 Paul Bert** (01 43 79 14 32; 6 rue Paul Bert, 12e; 6-course menu €60; 7-11pm Tue-Sat) for modern cuisine.

Soya VEGETARIAN, VEGAN €€
(Map p190; 01 48 06 33 02; www.facebook.com/soyacantinebio; 20 rue de la Pierre Levée, 11e; weekday lunch menu €15-22, brunch €27; 7-11pm Tue, noon-3.30pm & 7-11pm Wed-Fri, 11.30am-11pm Sat, 11.30am-4pm Sun; ; Goncourt, République) A favourite for its ubercool location in an industrial atelier (with bare cement, metal columns and big windows), Soya is a full-on *cantine bio* (organic eatery) in what was once a staunchly working-class district. Dishes, many tofu-based, are vegetarian and the weekend brunch buffet is deliciously lazy and languid. A glass floor floods the basement area with light.

★**Frenchie** BISTRO €€€
(Map p190; 01 40 39 96 19; www.frenchie-restaurant.com; 5 rue du Nil, 2e; 4-course lunch menu €45, 5-course dinner menu €74, with wine €175; 6.30-11pm Mon-Wed, noon-2.30pm & 6.30-11pm Fri; Sentier) Tucked down an inconspicuous alley, this tiny bistro with wooden tables and old stone walls is always packed and for good reason: excellent-value dishes are modern, market-driven and prepared with unpretentious flair by French chef Gregory Marchand. Reserve well in advance; arrive at 6.30pm and pray for a cancellation (it does happen); or head to neighbouring **Frenchie Bar à Vins** (6 rue du Nil, 2e; dishes €9-23; 6.30-11pm Mon-Fri).

Drinking & Nightlife

The line between bars, cafes and bistros is blurred at best. It costs more to sit at a table than to stand at the counter, more on a fancy square than a backstreet, more in the 8e than in the 18e. After 10pm many cafes charge a pricier *tarif de nuit* (night rate).

Left Bank

★**Little Bastards** COCKTAIL BAR
(Map p190; 5 rue Blainville, 5e; 7pm-2am Mon, 6pm-2am Tue-Thu, 6pm-4am Fri & Sat; Place Monge) Only house-creation cocktails are listed on the menu at uberhip Little Bastards – among them Fal' in Love (Beefeater gin, cranberry juice, lime, mint, guava purée and Falernum clove-, ginger- and almond-syrup), Be a Beet Smooth (Jameson whisky, coriander, sherry, egg white and pepper) and Deep Throat (Absolut vodka, watermelon syrup and Pernod) – but they'll also mix up classics if you ask.

★**Les Deux Magots** CAFE
(Map p190; www.lesdeuxmagots.fr; 170 bd St-Germain, 6e; 7.30am-1am; St-Germain des Prés) If ever there was a cafe that summed up St-Germain des Prés' early 20th-century literary scene, it's this former hang-out of anyone who was anyone. You will spend *beaucoup* to sip a coffee in a wicker chair on the terrace shaded by dark-green awnings and geraniums spilling from window boxes, but it's an undeniable piece of Parisian history.

Le Verre à Pied CAFE
(Map p190; 118bis rue Mouffetard, 5e; 9am-9pm Tue-Sat, 9.30am-4pm Sun; Censier Daubenton) This *café-tabac* is a pearl of a place where little has changed since 1870. Its nicotine-hued mirrored wall, moulded cornices and original bar make it part of a dying breed, but it epitomises the charm, glamour and romance of an old Paris everyone loves, including stallholders from the rue Mouffetard market who yo-yo in and out.

Right Bank

★**Le Baron Rouge** WINE BAR
(Map p186; 01 43 43 14 32; www.lebaronrouge.net; 1 rue Théophile Roussel, 12e; 5-10pm Mon, 10am-2pm & 5-10pm Tue-Fri, 10am-10pm Sat, 10am-4pm Sun; Ledru-Rollin) Just about the ultimate Parisian wine-bar experience, this wonderfully unpretentious local meeting place where everyone is welcome has barrels

BAR-HOPPING STREETS

Prime Parisian streets for a soirée:

Rue Vieille du Temple, 4e Marais cocktail of gay bars and chic cafes.

Rue Oberkampf, 11e Edgy urban hangouts.

Rue de Lappe, 11e Boisterous Bastille bars and clubs.

Rue de la Butte aux Cailles, 13e Village atmosphere and fun local haunts.

Rue Princesse, 6e Student and sports bars.

stacked against the bottle-lined walls and serves cheese, charcuterie and oysters. It's especially busy on Sunday after the **Marché d'Aligre** (Map p186; rue d'Aligre, 12e; ⌚8am-1pm Tue-Sun) wraps up. For a small deposit, you can fill up 1L bottles straight from the barrel for under €5.

★**Experimental Cocktail Club** COCKTAIL BAR
(ECC; Map p190; www.experimentalevents.com; 37 rue St-Sauveur, 2e; ⌚7pm-2am; Ⓜ Réaumur–Sébastopol) With a black-curtain façade, this retro-chic speakeasy – with sister bars in London, Ibiza and New York – is a sophisticated flashback to those *années folles* (crazy years) of Prohibition New York. Cocktails (€13 to €15) are individual and fabulous, and DJs keep the party going until dawn at weekends. It's not a large space, however, and fills to capacity quickly.

★**Candelaria** COCKTAIL BAR
(Map p190; www.quixotic-projects.com; 52 rue de Saintonge, 3e; ⌚bar 6pm-2am Mon-Fri, noon-4pm & 6pm-2am Sat & Sun, taqueria noon-10.30pm Sun-Wed, noon-11.30pm Thu-Sat; Ⓜ Filles du Calvaire) A lime-green *taqueria* serving homemade tacos, quesadillas and tostadas (dishes €3.50 to €9) conceals one of Paris' coolest cocktail bars through an unmarked internal door. Evenings kick off with occasional DJ sets, tastings, post-gallery drinks and phenomenal cocktails made from agave spirits including mezcal. Reserve online for cocktail-fuelled weekend brunch (€20; noon to 4pm), featuring a feisty tequila-laced Bloody Maria.

★**Le Très Particulier** COCKTAIL BAR
(Map p194; ☎01 53 41 81 40; www.hotel-particulier-montmartre.com; Pavillon D, 23 av Junot, 18e; ⌚6pm-2am; Ⓜ Lamarck-Caulaincourt) The clandestine cocktail bar of boutique Hôtel Particulier Montmartre is an enchanting spot for a summertime alfresco cocktail. Ring the buzzer at the unmarked black gated entrance and make a beeline for the 1871 mansion's flowery walled garden (or, if it's raining, the adjacent conservatory-style interior). DJs spin tunes from 9.30pm Wednesday to Saturday and from 7pm on Sunday.

★**Le Petit Fer à Cheval** BAR
(Map p190; www.cafeine.com/petit-fer-a-cheval; 30 rue Vieille du Temple, 4e; ⌚9am-2am; Ⓜ Hôtel de Ville, St-Paul) A Marais institution, the Little Horseshoe is a minute cafe-bar with an original horseshoe-shaped zinc bar from 1903. The place overflows with regulars from dawn to dark. Great *apéro* (predinner drink) spot and great WC – stainless-steel toilet stalls straight out of a Flash Gordon film (actually inspired by the interior of the *Nautilus* submarine in Jules Verne's *20,000 Leagues under the Sea*).

★**Fluctuat Nec Mergitur** CAFE
(Map p190; ☎01 42 06 44 07; www.fluctuat-cafe.paris; place de la République, 10e; ⌚7.30am-2am; 📶; Ⓜ République) No address guarantees a fuller immersion into local life than Fluctuat (formerly Café Monde et Média), all shiny, new and rebranded with an edgy name after a kitchen fire in February 2015 wrecked the popular cafe and after-work hot spot. Its enviable location on pedestrian esplanade place de la République means it's always buzzing with Parisians chatting over drinks.

Chez Jeannette BAR
(Map p186; 47 rue du Faubourg St-Denis, 10e; ⌚8am-2am; Ⓜ Château d'Eau) For vintage vibe you don't get better than Jeannette's. Cracked tile floors and original 1950s decor have turned this local neighbourhood cafe-bar into one of the 10e's most popular hot spots. Local hang-out by day, pints by night and reasonably priced meals around the clock.

La Fourmi BAR
(Map p194; 74 rue des Martyrs, 18e; ⌚8.30am-2am Sun-Thu, to 4am Fri & Sat; Ⓜ Pigalle) A Pigalle institution, sociable La Fourmi hits the mark with its high ceilings, long zinc bar, timber-panelled walls and unpretentious vibe. It's a great place to find out about live music and club nights or grab a drink before heading out to a show. Bonus: table football.

☆ Entertainment

To find out what's on, buy *Pariscope* (€0.50) or *L'Officiel des Spectacles* (€0.50; www.offi.fr) at Parisian news kiosks. Both are published on Wednesday. The most convenient place to buy concert, performance or event tickets is megastore **Fnac** (☎08 92 68 36 22; www.fnactickets.com), which has numerous branches in town.

If you go on the day of a performance, you can snag a half-price ticket (plus €3 commission) for ballet, theatre, opera and other performances at the discount-ticket outlet **Kiosque Théâtre Madeleine** (Map p194; www.kiosqueculture.com; opposite 15 place de la

Madeleine, 8e; 12.30-7.30pm Tue-Sat, to 3.45pm Sun; M Madeleine).

★Café Universel JAZZ, BLUES

(Map p190; 01 43 25 74 20; www.cafeuniversel.com; 267 rue St Jacques, 5e; 9pm-2am Tue-Sat; ; M Censier Daubenton or RER Port Royal) Café Universel hosts a brilliant array of live concerts with everything from bebop and Latin sounds to vocal jazz sessions. Plenty of freedom is given to young producers and artists, and its convivial relaxed atmosphere attracts a mix of students and jazz lovers. Concerts are free, but tip the artists when they pass the hat around.

★Le Batofar CLUB

(Map p186; www.batofar.fr; opposite 11 quai François Mauriac, 13e; club 11.30pm-6am Tue-Sat, bar 6-11pm Tue-Sat May-Sep, 7pm-midnight Tue-Sat Oct-Apr; M Quai de la Gare, Bibliothèque) This much-loved, red-metal tugboat has a rooftop bar that's terrific in summer, and a respected restaurant, while the club underneath provides memorable underwater acoustics between its metal walls and portholes. Le Batofar is known for its edgy, experimental music policy and live performances from 7pm, mostly electro-oriented but also incorporating hip hop, new wave, rock, punk and jazz.

Le Bataclan LIVE MUSIC

(Map p190; www.bataclan.fr; 50 bd Voltaire, 11e; M Oberkampf, St-Ambroise) Built in 1864, intimate concert, theatre and dance hall Le Bataclan was Maurice Chevalier's debut venue in 1910. The 1497-capacity venue reopened with a concert by Sting on 12 November 2016, almost a year to the day following the tragic 13 November 2015 terrorist attacks that took place here, and once again hosts French and international rock and pop legends.

La Cigale LIVE MUSIC

(Map p194; 01 49 25 89 99; www.lacigale.fr; 120 bd de Rochechouart, 18e; M Pigalle) Now classed as a historical monument, this music hall dates from 1887 but was redecorated 100 years later by Philippe Starck. Artists who have performed here include Ryan Adams, Ibrahim Maalouf and the Dandy Warhols.

Moulin Rouge CABARET

(Map p194; 01 53 09 82 82; www.moulinrouge.fr; 82 bd de Clichy, 18e; show/dinner show from €87/165; shows 7pm, 9pm & 11pm; M Blanche) Immortalised in Toulouse-Lautrec's posters and later in Baz Luhrmann's film, Paris' legendary cabaret twinkles beneath a 1925 replica of its original red windmill. Yes, it's packed with bus-tour crowds. But from the opening bars of music to the last high cancan-girl kick, it's a whirl of fantastical costumes, sets, choreography and Champagne. Book in advance online and dress smartly (no sneakers). No entry for children under six.

Point Éphémère LIVE MUSIC

(Map p186; 01 40 34 02 48; www.pointephemere.org; 200 quai de Valmy, 10e; 12.30pm-2am Mon-Sat, to 10pm Sun; ; M Louis Blanc) On the banks of Canal St-Martin in a former fire station and later squat, this arts and music venue attracts an underground crowd for concerts, dance nights and art exhibitions. Its rockin' restaurant, Animal Kitchen, fuses gourmet cuisine with music from Animal Records (Sunday brunch from 1pm is a highlight); the rooftop bar, Le Top, opens in fine weather.

GAY & LESBIAN PARIS

Le Marais (4e), especially the areas around the intersection of rue Ste Croix de la Bretonnerie and rue des Archives, and eastwards to rue Vieille du Temple, has been Paris' main centre of gay nightlife for some three decades.

The single best source of info on gay and lesbian Paris is the **Centre Gai et Lesbien de Paris** (Map p190; 01 43 57 21 47; www.centrelgbtparis.org; 63 rue Beaubourg, 3e; centre & bar 3.30-8pm Mon-Fri, 1-7pm Sat, library 2-8pm Mon, Tue & Wed, 5-7pm Fri & Sat; M Rambuteau), with a large library and happening bar.

Shopping

★Shakespeare & Company BOOKS

(Map p190; 01 43 25 40 93; www.shakespeareandcompany.com; 37 rue de la Bûcherie, 5e; 10am-11pm; M St-Michel) Shakespeare's enchanting nooks and crannies overflow with new and secondhand English-language books. The original shop (12 rue l'Odéon, 6e; closed by the Nazis in 1941) was run by Sylvia Beach and became the meeting point for Hemingway's 'Lost Generation'. Readings by emerging and illustrious authors take place at 7pm most Mondays. There's a wonderful cafe (p196) and various workshops and festivals.

★ **Marché aux Puces de St-Ouen** MARKET
(www.marcheauxpuces-saintouen.com; rue des Rosiers, St-Ouen; ⏲ Sat-Mon; Ⓜ Porte de Clignancourt) This vast flea market, founded in the late 19th century and said to be Europe's largest, has more than 2500 stalls grouped into 15 *marchés* (markets), each with its own speciality (eg Marché Paul Bert Serpette for 17th-century furniture, Marché Malik for casual clothing, Marché Biron for Asian art). Each market has different opening hours – check the website for details.

★ **Paris Rendez-Vous** GIFTS & SOUVENIRS
(Map p190; www.rendezvous.paris.fr; 29 rue de Rivoli, 4e; ⏲ 10am-7pm Mon-Sat; Ⓜ Hôtel de Ville) This chic city has its own designer line of souvenirs, sold in its own ubercool concept store inside Hôtel de Ville (city hall). Shop here for everything from clothing and homewares to Paris-themed books, wooden toy sailing boats and signature Jardin du Luxembourg Fermob chairs. *Quel style!*

★ **Gab & Jo** FASHION & ACCESSORIES
(Map p190; www.gabjo.fr; 28 rue Jacob, 6e; ⏲ 11am-7pm Mon-Sat; Ⓜ St-Germain des Prés) Forget mass-produced, imported souvenirs: for quality local gifts, browse the shelves of the country's first-ever concept store stocking only made-in-France items. Designers include La Note Parisienne (scented candles for each Parisian *arrondissement*, such as the 6e, with notes of lipstick, cognac, orange blossom, tuberose, jasmine, rose and fig), Marius Fabre (Marseille soaps), Germaine-des-Prés (lingerie), MILF (sunglasses) and Monsieur Marcel (T-shirts).

★ **La Grande Épicerie de Paris** FOOD & DRINKS
(Map p186; www.lagrandeepicerie.com; 36 rue de Sèvres, 7e; ⏲ 8.30am-9pm Mon-Sat, 10am-8pm Sun; Ⓜ Sèvres-Babylone) The magnificent food hall of department store **Le Bon Marché** (Map p186; www.bonmarche.com; 24 rue de Sèvres, 7e; ⏲ 10am-8pm Mon-Wed & Sat, to 8.45pm Thu & Fri, 11am-8pm Sun; Ⓜ Sèvres-Babylone) sells 30,000 rare and/or luxury gourmet products, including 60 different types of bread baked on site and delicacies such as caviar ravioli. Its fantastical displays of chocolates, pastries, biscuits, cheeses, fresh fruit and vegetables and deli goods are a Parisian sight in themselves. Wine tastings regularly take place in the basement.

Fromagerie Laurent Dubois CHEESE
(Map p190; www.fromageslaurentdubois.fr; 47ter bd St-Germain, 5e; ⏲ 8am-7.45pm Tue-Sat, 8.30am-1pm Sun; Ⓜ Maubert-Mutualité) One of the best *fromageries* in Paris, this cheese-lover's nirvana is filled with to-die-for delicacies, such as St-Félicien with Périgord truffles. Rare, limited-production cheeses include blue Termignon and Tarentaise goat's cheese. All are appropriately cellared in warm, humid or cold environments. There's also a 15e **branch** (Map p186; 2 rue de Lourmel, 15e; ⏲ 9am-1pm & 4-7.45pm Tue-Fri, 8.30am-7.45pm Sat, 9am-1pm Sun; Ⓜ Dupleix).

ℹ Information

DANGERS & ANNOYANCES

Metro stations best avoided late at night include Châtelet–Les Halles and its corridors; Château Rouge in Montmartre; Gare du Nord; Strasbourg St-Denis; Réaumur Sébastopol; and Montparnasse Bienvenüe.

Pickpocketing and thefts from handbags and packs is a problem wherever there are crowds (especially of tourists).

MEDICAL SERVICES

Paris has some 50 hospitals including the following:

American Hospital of Paris (☎ 01 46 41 25 25; www.american-hospital.org; 63 bd Victor Hugo, Neuilly-sur-Seine; Ⓜ Pont de Levallois) Private hospital; emergency 24-hour medical and dental care.

Hertford British Hospital (IHFB; ☎ 01 46 39 22 00; www.ihfb.org; 4 rue Kléber, Levallois-Perret; Ⓜ Anatole France) Less expensive, private, English-speaking option.

Hôpital Hôtel Dieu (☎ 01 42 34 88 19; www.aphp.fr; 1 place du Parvis Notre Dame, 4e; Ⓜ Cité) One of the city's main government-run public hospitals; after 8pm use the emergency entrance on rue de la Cité.

TOURIST INFORMATION

Paris Convention & Visitors Bureau (Office du Tourisme et des Congrès de Paris; Map p190; www.parisinfo.com; 25 rue des Pyramides, 1er; ⏲ 9am-7pm May-Oct, 10am-7pm Nov-Apr; Ⓜ Pyramides) The main branch is 500m northwest of the Louvre. It sells tickets for tours and several attractions, plus museum and transport passes. Also books accommodation.

ℹ Getting There & Away

AIR

There are three main airports in Paris:

Aéroport de Charles de Gaulle (CDG; ☎ 01 70 36 39 50; www.parisaeroport.fr) Most international airlines fly to CDG, 28km northeast of the centre of Paris. In French, the airport is commonly called 'Roissy'.

Aéroport d'Orly (ORY; ☎01 70 36 39 50; www.parisaeroport.fr) Located 19km south of Paris but not as frequently used by international airlines.

Aéroport de Beauvais (BVA; ☎08 92 68 20 66; www.aeroportbeauvais.com) Not really in Paris at all (it's 75km north of Paris) but used by some low-cost carriers.

BUS

Eurolines (Map p190; www.eurolines.fr; 55 rue St-Jacques, 5e; ⊙ticket office 9.30am-6.30pm Mon-Fri, 10am-1pm & 2-5pm Sat; Ⓜ Cluny-La Sorbonne) connects all major European capitals to Paris' international bus terminal, **Gare Routiére Internationale de Paris-Galliéni** (☎08 92 89 90 91; 28 av du Général de Gaulle, Bagnolet; Ⓜ Galliéni). The terminal is in the eastern suburb of Bagnolet; it's about a 15-minute metro ride to the more central République station.

TRAIN

Paris has six major train stations serving both national and international destinations. For mainline train information, check **SNCF** (www.sncf-voyages.com).

Gare du Nord (rue de Dunkerque, 10e; Ⓜ Gare du Nord) Trains to/from the UK, Belgium, Germany and northern France.

Gare de l'Est (bd de Strasbourg, 10e; Ⓜ Gare de l'Est) Trains to/from Germany, Switzerland and eastern areas of France.

Gare de Lyon (bd Diderot, 12e; Ⓜ Gare de Lyon) Trains to/from Provence, the Riviera, the Alps and Italy. Also serves Geneva.

Gare d'Austerlitz (bd de l'Hôpital, 13e; Ⓜ Gare d'Austerlitz) Trains to/from Spain and Portugal, and non-TGV trains to southwestern France.

Gare Montparnasse (av du Maine & bd de Vaugirard, 15e; Ⓜ Montparnasse Bienvenüe) Trains to/from western France (Brittany, Atlantic coast) and southwestern France.

Gare St-Lazare Trains to Normandy.

ℹ Getting Around

TO/FROM THE AIRPORTS

Getting into town is straightforward and inexpensive thanks to a fleet of public-transport options. Bus drivers sell tickets. Children aged four to 11 years pay half-price on most services.

Aéroport de Charles de Gaulle

RER B line (€10, 50 minutes, every 10 to 20 minutes) Stops at Gare du Nord, Châtelet–Les Halles and St-Michel–Notre Dame stations. Trains run from 5am to 11pm; there are fewer trains on weekends.

Le Bus Direct line 2 (€17; one hour; every 30 minutes, 5.45am to 11pm) Links the airport with the Arc de Triomphe via the Eiffel Tower and Trocadéro.

Le Bus Direct line 4 (€17; 50 to 80 minutes, every 30 minutes, 6am to 10.30pm from the airport, 5.30am to 10.30pm from Montparnasse) Links the airport with Gare Montparnasse (80 minutes) in southern Paris via Gare de Lyon (50 minutes) in eastern Paris.

RATP bus 350 (€6; 70 minutes; every 30 minutes, 5.30am to 11pm) Links the airport with Gare de l'Est in northern Paris.

Taxi (40 minutes to city centre) €50 to Right Bank and €55 to Left Bank, plus 15% surcharge between 5pm and 10am and on Sundays.

Aéroport d'Orly

RER B and Orlyval (€12.05, 35 minutes, every four to 12 minutes, 6am to 11pm) The nearest RER station to the airport is Antony, where you connect on the dedicated Orlyval.

Le Bus Direct line 1 (€12; one hour, every 20 minutes 5.50am to 11.30pm from Orly, 4.50am to 10.30pm from the Arc de Triomphe) Runs to/from the Arc de Triomphe (one hour) via Gare Montparnasse (40 minutes), La Motte-Picquet and Trocadéro.

Taxi (30 minutes to city centre) €30 to the Left Bank and €35 to the Right Bank, plus 15% between 5pm and 10am and on Sundays.

Aéroport de Beauvais

Beauvais shuttle (€17, 1¼ hours) links the airport with metro station Porte Maillot.

BICYCLE

The **Vélib'** (☎01 30 79 79 30; www.velib.paris.fr; day/week subscription €1.70/8, bike hire up to 30/60/90/120min free/€1/2/4) bike-share scheme puts 20,000-odd bikes at the disposal of Parisians and visitors to get around the city. There are about 1800 docking stations; bikes are available around the clock.

BOAT

Batobus (www.batobus.com; adult/child 1-day pass €17/8, 2-day pass €19/10; ⊙10am-9.30pm Apr-Aug, to 7pm Sep-Mar) runs glassed-in trimarans that dock every 20 to 25 minutes at nine small piers along the Seine: Beaugrenelle, Eiffel Tower, Musée d'Orsay, St-Germain des Prés, Notre Dame, Jardin des Plantes/Cité de la Mode et du Design, Hôtel de Ville, Musée du Louvre and Champs-Élysées.

Buy tickets online, at ferry stops or at tourist offices. You can also buy a two- or three-day Paris À La Carte Pass that includes L'Open Tour buses for €45 or €49.

PUBLIC TRANSPORT

➡ Paris' public transit system is operated by the **RATP** (www.ratp.fr).

➡ The same RATP tickets are valid on the metro, RER, buses, trams and Montmartre funicular. A ticket – white in colour and called Le Ticket t+ – costs €1.90 (half price for children aged four to nine years) if bought individually and €14.50 for adults for a carnet (book) of 10.

➡ One ticket covers travel between any two metro stations (no return journeys) for 1½ hours; you can transfer between buses and between buses and trams, but not from metro to bus or vice versa.

➡ Keep your ticket until you exit the station or risk a fine.

Bus

➡ Buses run from 5.30am to 8.30pm Monday to Saturday, with certain evening lines continuing until midnight or 12.30am, when the hourly Noctilien (www.noctilien.fr) night buses kick in.

➡ Short bus rides (ie rides in one or two bus zones) cost one ticket; longer rides require two.

➡ Remember to punch single-journey tickets in the *composteur* (ticket machine) next to the driver.

Metro & RER

Paris' underground network consists of 14 numbered metro lines and the five suburban RER lines (designated by the letters A to E).

Trains usually start around 5.30am and finish sometime between 12.35am and 1.15am (2.15am Friday and Saturday).

Tourist Passes

Mobilis Allows unlimited travel for one day and costs €7.30 (two zones) to €17.30 (five zones). Buy it at any metro, RER or SNCF station in the Paris region.

Paris Visite Allows unlimited travel as well as discounted entry to certain museums and other discounts and bonuses. The 'Paris+Suburbs+Airports' pass includes transport to/from the airports and costs €24.50/37.25/52.20/63.90 for one/two/three/five days. The cheaper 'Paris Centre' pass, valid for zones 1 to 3, costs €11.65/18.95/25.85/37.25 for one/two/three/five days.

Travel Passes

If you're staying in Paris more than three or four days, the cheapest and easiest way to use public transport is to get a rechargeable **Navigo** (www.navigo.fr) pass.

A weekly pass costs €22.15 and is valid Monday to Sunday. You'll also need to pay €5 for the Navigo card and provide a passport photo.

TAXI

➡ The *prise en charge* (flagfall) is €2.60. Within the city limits, it costs €1.04 per kilometre for travel between 10am and 5pm Monday to Saturday (*Tarif A;* white light on taxi roof and meter).

➡ At night (5pm to 10am), on Sunday from 7am to midnight, and in the inner suburbs the rate is €1.27 per kilometre (*Tarif B;* orange light).

➡ The minimum taxi fare for a short trip is €6.86.

➡ There's a €3 surcharge for taking a fourth passenger. The first piece of baggage is free; additional pieces over 5kg cost €1 extra.

➡ To order a taxi, call or reserve online with **Taxis G7** (☎3607, 01 41 27 66 99; www.taxisg7.fr), **Taxis Bleus** (☎08 91 70 10 10, 3609; www.taxis-bleus.com) or **Alpha Taxis** (☎01 45 85 85 85; www.alpha-taxis-paris.fr).

➡ An alternative is the private driver system, Uber taxi (www.uber.com/cities/paris), whereby you order and pay via your smartphone.

AROUND PARIS

Versailles

POP 87,400

Louis XIV – the Roi Soleil (Sun King) – transformed his father's hunting lodge into the monumental Château de Versailles in the mid-17th century, and it remains France's most famous, grandest palace. Situated in the prosperous, leafy and bourgeois suburb of Versailles, 28km southwest of Paris, the baroque château was the kingdom's political capital and the seat of the royal court from 1682 up until the fateful events of 1789, when revolutionaries massacred the palace guard and dragged Louis XVI and Marie Antoinette back to Paris, where they were ingloriously guillotined.

The current €400 million restoration program is the most ambitious yet, and until it's completed in 2020, at least a part of the palace is likely to be clad in scaffolding when you visit.

Sights

★**Château de Versailles** PALACE

(☎01 30 83 78 00; www.chateauversailles.fr; place d'Armes; adult/child passport ticket incl estate-wide access €20/free, with musical events €27/free, palace €15/free; ⏲9am-6.30pm Tue-Sun Apr-Oct, to 5.30pm Tue-Sun Nov-Mar; Ⓜ RER Versailles-Château–Rive Gauche) Amid magnificently landscaped formal gardens, this splendid and enormous palace was built in the mid-17th century during the reign of Louis XIV – the Roi Soleil (Sun King) – to project the absolute power of the French monarchy, which was then at the height of its glory. The château has undergone relatively few alterations since its construction, though almost all the interior furnishings disappeared during the Revolution and many of the rooms were rebuilt by Louis-Philippe (r 1830–48).

Getting There & Away

RER C5 (€4.20, 40 minutes, frequent) goes from Paris' Left Bank RER stations to Versailles-Château–Rive Gauche station. The less convenient RER C8 links Paris with Versailles-Chantiers station, a 1.3km walk from the château.

Chartres

POP 40,216

The magnificent 13th-century **Cathédrale Notre Dame** (www.cathedrale-chartres.org; place de la Cathédrale; 8.30am-7.30pm daily year-round, also to 10pm Tue, Fri & Sun Jun-Aug) of Chartres, crowned by two very different spires – one Gothic, the other Romanesque – rises from rich farmland 88km southwest of Paris and dominates the medieval town.

The cathedral's west, north and south entrances have superbly ornamented triple portals and its 105m-high **Clocher Vieux** (Old Bell Tower), also called the Tour Sud (South Tower), is the tallest Romanesque steeple still standing. Superb views of three-tiered flying buttresses and the 19th-century copper roof, turned green by verdigris, reward the 350-step hike up the 112m-high **Clocher Neuf** (New Bell Tower, also known as North Tower).

Inside, 172 extraordinary stained-glass windows, mainly from the 13th century, form one of the most important ensembles of medieval stained glass in the world. The three most exquisite – renowned for the depth and intensity of their tones, famously known as 'Chartres blue' – are above the west entrance and below the rose window.

Getting There & Away

Frequent SNCF trains link Paris' Gare Montparnasse (€16, 55 to 70 minutes) with Chartres, some of which stop at Versailles-Chantiers (€13.50, 45 to 60 minutes).

VERSAILLES TIPS

Versailles is one of the country's most popular destinations, with over five million visitors annually; advance planning will make visiting more enjoyable.

- Monday is out for obvious reasons (it's closed).
- Arrive early morning and avoid Tuesday, Saturday and Sunday, its busiest days.
- Prepurchase tickets on the château's website or at **Fnac** (p200) branches and head straight to **Entrance A** (Château de Versailles).
- Versailles is free on the first Sunday of every month from November to March.
- Pre-book a **guided tour** (01 30 83 77 88; www.chateauversailles.fr; Château de Versailles; tours €7, plus palace entry; English-language tours 9.30am Tue-Sun) to access areas that are otherwise off limits as well as the most famous parts of the palace.
- Free apps can be downloaded from the website.

Giverny

518

The tiny village of Giverny, 74km northwest of Paris, was the **home of impressionist Claude Monet** (02 32 51 28 21; http://fondation-monet.com; 84 rue Claude Monet; adult/child €9.50/5.50, incl Musée des Impressionnismes Giverny €16.50/8.50; 9.30am-6pm Easter-Oct) for the last 43 years of his life. You can visit the artist's pastel-pink house and famous gardens with lily pond, Japanese bridge draped in purple wisteria, and so on. Early to late spring, daffodils, tulips, rhododendrons, wisteria and irises bloom in the flowery gardens, followed by poppies and lilies. By June, nasturtiums, roses and sweet peas are in flower, while September is the month to see dahlias, sunflowers and hollyhocks.

The closest train station is at Vernon, from where buses, taxis and cycle/walking tracks run to Giverny. Shuttle buses (€8 return, 20 minutes, four daily Easter to October) meet most trains from Paris at Vernon. From Paris' Gare St-Lazare there are up to 15 daily trains to Vernon (€14.70, 45 minutes to one hour).

WORTH A TRIP

MODERN ART MUSEUMS

Two of Paris' foremost art institutions, the Louvre and the Centre Pompidou, have satellite outposts in northern France that art lovers definitely won't want to miss.

Louvre-Lens (☎ 03 21 18 62 62; www.louvrelens.fr; 99 rue Paul Bert; multimedia guide €3; ⏲10am-6pm Wed-Mon) FREE Showcases hundreds of the Louvre's treasures in a purpose-built, state-of-the-art exhibition space in Lens, 35km southwest of Lille. A second building, the glass-walled **Pavillon de Verre**, displays temporary themed exhibits. Lens is easily reached by train from Paris' Gare du Nord (€40, 1¼ hours) and Lille-Flandres (from €8.30, 45 minutes)

Centre Pompidou-Metz (www.centrepompidou-metz.fr; 1 parvis des Droits de l'Homme; adult/child €7/free; ⏲10am-6pm Mon & Wed-Thu, to 7pm Fri-Sun) Concentrates mainly on abstract and experimental art. The building itself is worth the trip, designed by Japanese architect Shigeru Ban, with a curved roof resembling a space-age Chinese hat. Trains run direct from from Paris (€33 to €81, 1½ hours) and Strasbourg (€27.10, 1½ hours).

LILLE & THE SOMME

When it comes to culture, cuisine, beer, shopping and dramatic views of land and sea, the friendly Ch'tis (residents of France's northern tip) and their region compete with the best France has to offer. Highlights include Flemish-style Lille, the cross-Channel shopping centre of Calais, and the moving battlefields and cemeteries of WWI.

Lille

POP 231,500

Lille may be the country's most underrated major city. In recent decades, this once-grimy industrial metropolis has transformed itself – with generous government help – into a glittering and self-confident cultural and commercial hub. Highlights of the city include an attractive old town with a strong Flemish accent, renowned art museums, stylish shopping and a cutting-edge, student-driven nightlife.

Sights

Palais des Beaux Arts GALLERY
(Fine Arts Museum; ☎ 03 20 06 78 00; www.pba-lille.fr; place de la République; adult/child €7/4; ⏲2-5.50pm Mon, 10am-5.50pm Wed-Sun; 📶 👪; Ⓜ République Beaux-Arts) Lille's illustrious Fine Arts Museum displays a truly first-rate collection of 15th- to 20th-century paintings, including works by Rubens, Van Dyck and Manet. Exquisite porcelain and faience (pottery), much of it of local provenance, is on the ground floor, while in the basement you'll find classical archaeology, medieval statuary and 18th-century scale models of the fortified cities of northern France and Belgium.

Vieille Bourse HISTORIC BUILDING
Ornamented with caryatids and cornucopia, this Flemish Renaissance extravaganza was built in 1653. It consists of 24 separate houses set around a richly ornamented interior courtyard that hosts a used-book market and chess games.

Musée d'Art Moderne, d'Art Contemporain et d'Art Brut – LaM GALLERY
(☎ 03 20 19 68 88; www.musee-lam.fr; 1 allée du Musée, Villeneuve-d'Ascq; adult/child €7/5; ⏲10am-6pm Tue-Sun) Colourful, playful and just plain weird works of modern and contemporary art by masters such as Braque, Calder, Léger, Miró, Modigliani and Picasso are the big draw at this renowned museum and sculpture park in the Lille suburb of Villeneuve-d'Ascq, 9km east of Gare Lille-Europe. Take metro line 1 to Pont de Bois, then bus L4 six stops to 'LAM'.

Sleeping

Auberge de Jeunesse HOSTEL €
(☎ 03 20 57 08 94; www.hifrance.org; 235 bd Paul Painlevé; dm incl breakfast & sheets €25; @📶; Ⓜ Porte de Valenciennes) The good news is that Lille has a youth hostel, opened in 2015, with a façade sporting the colours of Europe. The bad news is that while all 55 rooms have showers, only 12 have attached toilets, and instead of faucets the showers have annoying timer-buttons. Wi-fi is available only in the lobby.

Hôtel de la Treille HOTEL €€

(☎03 20 55 45 46; www.hoteldelatreille.com; 7-9 place Louise de Bettignies; d €90-140; 📶) In a superb spot smack in the middle of Vieux Lille, a few steps from dining and shopping options galore. The 42 stylish rooms, totally redecorated in 2014, offer views of the lively square out front, the cathedral or a quiet interior courtyard.

Eating

★Meert PASTRIES €

(☎03 20 57 93 93; www.meert.fr; 27 rue Esquermoise; waffles from €3; ⊙shop 9.30am-7.30pm Tue-Sat, 9am-1pm & 3-7pm Sun, tearoom 9.30am-10pm Tue-Sat, 9am-6pm Sun; 📶; Ⓜ Rihour) Famed for its *gaufres* (waffles) made with Madagascar vanilla, Meert has served kings, viceroys and generals since 1761. The sumptuous chocolate shop's coffered ceiling, painted wooden panels, wrought-iron balcony and mosaic floor date from 1839. Inside, the historic *salon de thé* is a delightful spot for a morning Arabica or a mid-afternoon tea. Also has a French gourmet restaurant.

La Petite Table MODERN FRENCH €

(☎03 20 55 60 47; www.lapetitetable-vieuxlille.com; 59 rue de la Monnaie; mains €1-16; ⊙noon-2.30pm Tue-Sun, 7.30-10pm or 10.30pm Tue-Sat; 📶) Inspired by the 34 countries he visited during nine years in the French navy, chef Arnaud Duhamel – a Lonely Planet fan – prepares both local (Flemish) favourites and dishes inspired by the tastes he encountered in the Americas, Africa and around the Indian Ocean. A favourite of locals in search of good value.

ℹ Information

Tourist Office (☎03 59 57 94 00; www.lilletourism.com; place Rihour; ⊙9am-6pm Mon-Sat, 10am-4.30pm Sun & holidays; Ⓜ Rihour) Has walking itineraries of the city (€3).

ℹ Getting There & Away

AIR

Aéroport de Lille (www.lille.aeroport.fr) is connected to all major French cities and a number of European destinations too.

TRAIN

Lille's two main train stations, Gare Lille-Flandres and newer Gare Lille-Europe, are 400m apart on the eastern edge of the city centre.

Gare Lille-Europe (📶; Ⓜ Gare Lille-Europe) Topped by what looks like a 20-storey ski boot, this ultramodern station handles Eurostar trains to London, TGV/Thalys/Eurostar trains to Brussels-Midi, half of the TGVs to Paris Gare du Nord and most province-to-province TGVs.

Gare Lille-Flandres (📶; Ⓜ Gare Lille-Flandres) This old-fashioned station, recently spruced up, is used by half of the TGVs to Paris Gare du Nord and all intra-regional TER services.

WORTH A TRIP

THE SOMME BATTLEFIELDS

The First Battle of the Somme, a WWI Allied offensive waged in the villages and woodlands northeast of Amiens, was designed to relieve pressure on the beleaguered French troops at Verdun. On 1 July 1916, British, Commonwealth and French troops 'went over the top' in a massive assault along a 34km front. But German positions proved virtually unbreachable, and on the first day of the battle an astounding 21,392 British troops were killed and another 35,492 were wounded. By the time the offensive was called off in mid-November, a total of 1.2 million lives had been lost on both sides. The British had advanced 12km, the French 8km.

The battlefields and memorials are numerous and scattered – joining a tour can therefore be a good option, especially if you don't have your own transport. Respected operators include the **Battlefields Experience** (☎03 22 76 29 60; www.thebattleofthesomme.co.uk), **Chemins d'Histoire** (☎06 31 31 85 02; www.cheminsdhistoire.com) and **Terres de Mémoire** (☎03 22 84 23 05; www.terresdememoire.com).

Between 2014 and 2018, a number of events will commemorate the Centenary of WWI throughout the region.

The tourist offices in **Péronne** (☎03 22 84 42 38; www.hautesomme-tourisme.com; 16 place André Audinot; ⊙10am-noon & 2-5pm or 6pm Mon-Sat Sep-Jun, plus 9am-12.30pm & 1.30-6.30pm Sun Jul & Aug) and **Albert** (☎03 22 75 16 42; www.tourisme-paysducoquelicot.com; 9 rue Gambetta; ⊙9am-12.30pm & 1.30-5pm or 6.30pm Mon-Fri, 9am-noon & 2-5pm or 6.30pm Sat Sep-Apr, plus 9am-1pm Sun May-Aug) can help with booking tours and accommodation.

Services include the following:

Brussels-Midi TGV €30, 35 minutes, at least a dozen daily; regular train €22.50, two hours

London (St Pancras International) Eurostar €110 to €180, 90 minutes, 10 daily

Paris Gare du Nord €50 to €67, one hour, 16 to 24 daily

NORMANDY

Famous for cows, cider and Camembert, this largely rural region (www.normandie-tourisme.fr) is one of France's most traditional, and most visited, thanks to world-renowned sights such as the Bayeux Tapestry, the historic D-Day beaches and spectacular Mont St-Michel.

Bayeux

POP 13,900

Bayeux has become famous throughout the English-speaking world thanks to a 68.3m-long piece of painstakingly embroidered cloth: the 11th-century Bayeux Tapestry, with its 58 scenes that vividly tell the story of the Norman invasion of England in 1066.

The town is also one of the few in Normandy to have survived WWII practically unscathed, with a centre crammed with 13th- to 18th-century buildings, wooden-framed Norman-style houses, and a spectacular Norman Gothic cathedral. It makes a great base for exploring D-Day beaches.

Sights

★Bayeux Tapestry TAPESTRY

(☎02 31 51 25 50; www.bayeuxmuseum.com; rue de Nesmond; adult/child incl audioguide €9/4; ⏲9am-6.30pm Mar-Oct, to 7pm May-Aug, 9.30am-12.30pm & 2-6pm Nov-Feb) The world's most celebrated work of embroidery depicts the conquest of England by William the Conqueror in 1066 from an unashamedly Norman perspective. Commissioned by Bishop Odo of Bayeux, William's half-brother, for the opening of Bayeux' cathedral in 1077, the 68.3m-long cartoon strip tells the dramatic, bloody tale with verve and vividness.

Sleeping

Hôtel d'Argouges HOTEL €€

(☎02 31 92 88 86; www.hotel-dargouges.com; 21 rue St-Patrice; s/d/tr/f €115/132/175/205; ⏲closed Dec & Jan; P 📶) Occupying a stately 18th-century residence with a lush little garden, this graceful hotel has 28 comfortable rooms with exposed beams, thick walls and Louis XVI–style furniture. The breakfast room, hardly changed since 1734, still has its original wood panels and parquet floors.

Villa Lara BOUTIQUE HOTEL €€€

(☎02 31 92 00 55; www.hotel-villalara.com; 6 place de Québec; d €190-360, ste €390-520; P ❄ 📶) Newly constructed in the past decade, this 28-room hotel, Bayeux' most luxurious, sports minimalist colour schemes, top-quality fabrics and decor that juxtaposes 18th- and 21st-century tastes. Amenities include a bar and a gym. Most rooms have cathedral views.

Eating

★La Reine Mathilde PASTRIES €

(47 rue St-Martin; cakes from €2.50; ⏲9am-7.30pm Tue-Sun) This sumptuously decorated patisserie and *salon de thé*, ideal for a sweet breakfast or a relaxing cup of afternoon tea, hasn't changed much since it was built in 1898.

Au Ptit Bistrot MODERN FRENCH €€

(☎02 31 92 30 08; 31 rue Larcher; lunch menu €17-20, dinner menu €27-33, mains €16-19; ⏲noon-2pm & 7-9pm Tue-Sat) Near the cathedral, this friendly, welcoming eatery whips up creative, beautifully prepared dishes that highlight the Norman bounty without a lick of pretension. Recent hits include chestnut soup, duck breast and bulgur with seasonal fruits and roasted pineapple, and black cod with spinach and spicy guacamole. Reservations essential.

Alchimie MODERN FRENCH €€

(lunch menu €12) On a street lined with restaurants, Alchimie has a simple but elegant design that takes nothing from the beautifully presented dishes. Choose from the day's specials listed on a chalkboard menu, which might include hits like *brandade de morue* (baked codfish pie). It's a local favourite, so call ahead.

Information

Tourist Office (☎02 31 51 28 28; www.bayeux-bessin-tourisme.com; pont St-Jean; ⏲9.30am-12.30pm & 2-6pm) Covers both Bayeux and the surrounding region, including D-Day beaches.

Getting There & Away

Trains link Bayeux with Caen (€7, 20 minutes, hourly), from where there are connections to Paris' Gare St-Lazare and Rouen.

D-Day Beaches

Early on 6 June 1944, Allied troops stormed 80km of beaches north of Bayeux, code-named (from west to east) Utah, Omaha, Gold, Juno and Sword. The landings on D-Day – called *Jour J* in French – ultimately led to the liberation of Europe from Nazi occupation. For context, see www.normandiememoire.com and www.6juin1944.com.

The most brutal fighting on D-Day took place 15km northwest of Bayeux along the stretch of coastline now known as **Omaha Beach**, today a glorious stretch of fine golden sand partly lined with sand dunes and summer homes. **Circuit de la Plage d'Omaha**, a trail marked with a yellow stripe, is a self-guided tour along the beach, surveyed from a bluff above by the huge **Normandy American Cemetery & Memorial** (☎02 31 51 62 00; www.abmc.gov; Colleville-sur-Mer; ⏲9am-6pm mid-Apr–mid-Sep, to 5pm mid-Sep–mid-Apr). Featured in the opening scenes of Steven Spielberg's *Saving Private Ryan*, this is the largest American cemetery in Europe.

Caen's high-tech, hugely impressive **Mémorial – Un Musée pour la Paix** (Memorial – A Museum for Peace; ☎02 31 06 06 44; www.memorial-caen.fr; esplanade Général Eisenhower; adult/child €20/17; ⏲9am-7pm early Feb-early Nov, 9.30am-6.30pm Tue-Sun early Nov-early Feb, closed 3 weeks in Jan) uses sound, lighting, film, animation and lots of exhibits to graphically explore and evoke the events of WWII, the D-Day landings and the ensuing Cold War.

Tours

Tours by Le Mémorial – Un Musée pour la Paix BUS

(☎02 31 06 06 45; www.memorial-caen.fr; tour morning/afternoon €65/85; ⏲9am & 2pm Apr-Sep, 1pm Oct-Mar, closed 3 weeks in Jan) Excellent year-round minibus tours (four to five hours), take in Pointe du Hoc, Omaha Beach, the American cemetery and the artificial port at Arromanches. There are cheaper tours in full-size buses (€45) from June to August. Rates include entry to Le Mémorial – Un Musée pour la Paix. Book online.

Normandy Tours TOURS

(☎02 31 92 10 70; www.normandy-landing-tours.com; 26 place de la Gare, Bayeux; adult/student €62/55) Offers well-regarded four- to five-hour tours of the main sites starting at 8.15am and 1.15pm on most days, as well as personally tailored trips. Based at Bayeux' Hôtel de la Gare, facing the train station.

Mont St-Michel

It's one of France's most iconic images: the slender spires, stout ramparts and rocky slopes of Mont St-Michel rising dramatically from the sea – or towering over sands laid bare by the receding tide. Despite huge numbers of tourists, both the abbey and the narrow alleys below still manage to transport visitors back to the Middle Ages.

The bay around Mont St-Michel is famed for having Europe's highest tidal variations; the difference between low and high tides – only about six hours apart – can reach an astonishing 15m.

Sights

Abbaye du Mont St-Michel ABBEY

(☎02 33 89 80 00; www.monuments-nationaux.fr; adult/child incl guided tour €9/free; ⏲9am-7pm, last entry 1hr before closing) The Mont's star attraction is the stunning architectural ensemble high up on top: the abbey. Most areas can be visited without a guide, but it's well worth taking the one-hour tour included in the ticket price; English tours (usually) begin at 11am and 3pm from October to March, with three or four daily tours in spring and summer. You can also take a 1½-hour audioguide tour (one/two people €4.50/6), available in six languages.

Sleeping

La Jacotière B&B €€

(☎02 33 60 22 94; www.lajacotiere.fr; 46 rue de la Côte, Ardevon; d incl breakfast €75-90, studio €80-95; P 📶) Built as a farmhouse in 1906, this superbly situated, family-run B&B has five comfortable rooms and one studio apartment. Situated just 300m east of the shuttle stop in La Caserne.

Hôtel Du Guesclin HOTEL €€

(☎02 33 60 14 10; www.hoteldguesclin.com; Grande Rue, Mont St-Michel; d €95-125; ⏲closed Wed night & Thu Apr-Jun & Oct–mid-Nov, hotel closed mid-Nov–Mar) One of the most affordable hotels on the Mont itself, the Hôtel Du

Guesclin (geck-*la*) has 10 charming rooms, five with priceless views of the bay.

Getting There & Away

Transdev bus 1 links the Mont St-Michel La Caserne parking lot (2.5km from the Mont itself, which you access by free shuttle) with **Pontorson** (€3.20, 18 minutes), the nearest train station. From Pontorson, there are two to three daily trains to/from Bayeux (€25, 1¾ hours) and Caen (€26.10, 1¾ hours).

BRITTANY

Brittany is for explorers. Its wild, dramatic coastline, medieval towns, thick forests and the eeriest stone circles this side of Stonehenge make a trip here well worth the detour from the beaten track. This is a land of prehistoric mysticism, proud tradition and culinary wealth, where locals remain fiercely independent, where Breton culture (and cider) is celebrated and where Paris feels a very long way away indeed.

Quimper

POP 66,926

Small enough to feel like a village – with its slanted half-timbered houses and narrow cobbled streets – and large enough to buzz as the troubadour of Breton culture, Quimper (pronounced *kam-pair*) is the thriving capital of Finistère (meaning 'land's end').

Sights

★Cathédrale St-Corentin CHURCH
(place St-Corentin; 8.30am-noon & 1.30-6.30pm Mon-Sat, 8.30am-noon & 2-6.30pm Sun) At the centre of the city is Quimper's Gothic cathedral with its distinctive dip in the middle where it was built to conform to the land, said to symbolise Christ's inclined head as he was dying on the cross. Construction began in 1239, but the cathedral's dramatic twin spires weren't added until the 19th century. High on the west façade, look out for an equestrian statue of King Gradlon, the city's mythical 5th-century founder.

★Musée Départemental Breton MUSEUM
(02 98 95 21 60; www.museedepartementalbreton.fr; 1 rue du Roi Gradlon; adult/child €5/free; 9am-12.30pm & 1.30-5pm Tue-Sat, 2-5pm Sun Sep-Jun, 9am-6pm daily Jul & Aug) Beside the Cathédrale St-Corentin, recessed behind a magnificent stone courtyard, this superb museum showcases Breton history, furniture, costumes, crafts and archaeology, in a former bishop's palace.

Sleeping & Eating

Hôtel Gradlon HOTEL €€
(02 98 95 04 39; www.hotel-gradlon.com; 30 rue de Brest; d €130-150; mid-Jan–mid-Dec; P) The rather bland, modern façade belies a charming country manor interior, with excellent service. The smallish but well-furnished rooms differ, but all have plenty of character and individual touches, and bathrooms tend towards the large and modern. Costs drop dramatically in winter; breakfast costs €12. No lift.

★L'Épée CAFE €€
(02 98 95 28 97; www.quimper-lepee.com; 14 rue du Parc; mains €12-24, lunch menus €24, other menus €29-46; brasserie noon-2.30pm & 7-10.30pm, cafe 10.30am-midnight) A Quimper institution – it's one of Brittany's oldest brasseries – L'Épée hits the mark with its buzzy, contemporary dining areas, efficient service and good vibe. Despite the hip interior, the food is by no means an afterthought. Superbly executed dishes include duck breast, lamb shank, shellfish and salads. You can also just stop in for a drink.

Information

Tourist office (02 98 53 04 05; www.quimper-tourisme.com; place de la Résistance; 9am-7pm Mon-Sat, 10am-12.45pm & 3-5.45pm Sun Jul & Aug, 9.30am-12.30pm & 1.30-6.30pm Mon-Sat Sep-Jun, plus 10am-12.45pm Sun Apr-Jun & Sep;) Has information about the wider area.

Getting There & Away

Frequent trains serve Paris' Gare Montparnasse (€30 to €96, 4¾ hours).

St-Malo

POP 46,589

The mast-filled port of fortified St-Malo is inextricably tied up with the deep briny blue: the town became a key harbour during the 17th and 18th centuries, functioning as a base for merchant ships and government-sanctioned privateers, and these days it's a busy cross-Channel ferry port and summertime getaway.

Sights

Walking on top of the sturdy 17th-century ramparts (1.8km) affords fine views of the old walled city known as **Intra-Muros** (Within the Walls), or Ville Close; access the ramparts from any of the city gates.

★Château de St-Malo CASTLE
Château de St-Malo was built by the dukes of Brittany in the 15th and 16th centuries, and now holds **Musée d'Histoire de St-Malo** (☎02 99 40 71 57; www.ville-saint-malo.fr/culture/les-musees; Château; adult/child €6/3; ⊙10am-12.30pm & 2-6pm daily Apr-Sep, Tue-Sun Oct-Mar), which looks at the life and history of the city. The castle's lookout tower offers eye-popping views of the old city.

Île du Grand Bé & Fort du Petit Bé ISLAND, CASTLE
(☎06 08 27 51 20; www.petit-be.com; fort guided tours adult/child €5/3; ⊙fort by reservation, depending on tides) At low tide, cross the beach to walk out via Porte des Bés to Île du Grand Bé, the rocky islet where the great St-Malo-born, 18th-century writer Chateaubriand is buried. About 100m beyond the Île du Grand Bé is the privately owned, Vauban-built, 17th-century Fort du Petit Bé. The owner runs 30-minute guided tours in French; leaflets are available in English. Once the tide rushes in, the causeway remains impassable for about six hours; check tide times with the tourist office.

Sleeping & Eating

★La Maison des Armateurs HOTEL €€
(☎02 99 40 87 70; www.maisondesarmateurs.com; 6 Grand Rue; d €110-210, f/ste from €190/230; ⊙closed Dec; ❄📶) No language barrier here – La Maison des Armateurs is run by a helpful French-American couple. Despite the austere granite-fronted setting, the inside of this sassy four-star hotel is all sexy, modern minimalism: modern furniture throughout, gleaming bathrooms with power showers and cool chocolate, pale orange and neutral grey tones. Families can plump for the super-sized suites. Check the website for deals.

★Bistro Autour du Beurre BISTRO €€
(☎02 23 18 25 81; www.lebeurrebordier.com; 7 rue de l'Orme; lunch menu €19, mains €18-24; ⊙noon-2pm Tue-Sat, 7-10pm Thu-Sat) This casual bistro showcases the cheeses and butters handmade by the world-famous Jean-Yves Bordier; you'll find his **shop** (www.lebeurrebordier.com; 7 rue de l'Orme; ⊙9am-1pm & 3.30-7.30pm Tue-Sat, 9am-1pm Mon & Sun) next door. His products are shipped to renowned restaurants around the globe. At the bistro, the butter sampler (€15 in the shop, but included in meals) and bottomless bread basket are just the start to creative, local meals that change with the seasons.

Information

Tourist Office (☎08 25 13 52 00; www.saint-malo-tourisme.com; esplanade St-Vincent; ⊙9am-7.30pm Mon-Sat, 10am-6pm Sun Jul & Aug, shorter hours Sep-Jun; 📶) Just outside the walls, near Porte St-Vincent. Has smartphone app, transport info and loads of local advice.

Getting There & Away

Brittany Ferries (www.brittany-ferries.com) sails between St-Malo and Portsmouth; Condor Ferries (www.condorferries.co.uk) runs to/from Poole via Jersey or Guernsey.

TGV train services go to Paris' Gare Montparnasse (€45 to €79, 3½ hours, three direct TGVs daily).

CHAMPAGNE

Known in Roman times as Campania, meaning 'plain', the agricultural region of Champagne is synonymous these days with its world-famous bubbly. This multimillion-dollar industry is strictly protected under French law, ensuring that only grapes grown in designated Champagne vineyards can truly lay claim to the hallowed title. The town of Épernay, 30km south of the regional capital of Reims, is the best place to head for *dégustation* (tasting); a self-drive **Champagne Routes** (www.tourisme-en-champagne.com) wends its way through the region's most celebrated vineyards.

Reims

POP 186,505

Over the course of a millennium (816 to 1825), some 34 sovereigns – among them two dozen kings – began their reigns in Reims' famed cathedral. Meticulously reconstructed after WWI and again following WWII, the city – whose name is pronounced something like 'rance' and is often anglicised as Rheims – is endowed with handsome pedestrian zones, well-tended parks, lively nightlife and a state-of-the-art tramway.

Sights

★Cathédrale Notre Dame CATHEDRAL

(www.cathedrale-reims.culture.fr; place du Cardinal Luçon; tower adult/child €7.50/free, incl Palais du Tau €11/free; ⌚7.30am-7.15pm, tower tours hourly 10am-4pm Tue-Sat, 2-4pm Sun May-Sep, 10am-4pm Sat, 2-4pm Sun mid-Mar–Apr) Imagine the egos and extravagance of a French royal coronation. The focal point of such bejewelled pomposity was Reims' resplendent Gothic cathedral, begun in 1211 on a site occupied by churches since the 5th century. The interior is a rainbow of stained-glass windows; the finest are the western façade's 12-petalled **great rose window** – under restoration at the time of research – the north transept's **rose window** and the vivid **Chagall** creations (1974) in the central axial chapel. The tourist office rents audioguides (€6) for self-paced cathedral tours.

★Basilique St-Rémi BASILICA

(place du Chanoine Ladame; ⌚8am-7pm) FREE This 121m-long former Benedictine abbey church, a Unesco World Heritage Site, mixes Romanesque elements from the mid-11th century (the worn but stunning nave and transept) with early Gothic features from the latter half of the 12th century (the choir, with a large triforium gallery and, way up top, tiny clerestory windows).

Next door, **Musée St-Rémi** (53 rue Simon; adult/child €4/free; ⌚2-6.30pm Mon-Fri, to 7pm Sat & Sun), in a 17th- and 18th-century abbey, features local Gallo-Roman archaeology, tapestries and 16th- to 19th-century military history.

★Palais du Tau MUSEUM

(www.palais-du-tau.fr; 2 place du Cardinal Luçon; adult/child €7.50/free, incl cathedral tower €11/free; ⌚9.30am-12.30pm & 2-5.30pm Tue-Sun) A Unesco World Heritage Site, this lavish former archbishop's residence, redesigned in neoclassical style between 1671 and 1710, was where French princes stayed before their coronations – and where they threw sumptuous banquets afterwards. Now a museum, it displays truly exceptional statuary, liturgical objects and tapestries from the cathedral, some in the impressive, Gothic-style Salle de Tau (Great Hall). Treasures worth seeking out include the 9th-century talisman of Charlemagne and Saint Remi's golden, gem-encrusted chalice, which dates to the 12th century.

★Taittinger WINERY

(☎03 26 85 45 35; www.taittinger.com; 9 place St-Niçaise; tours €17-45; ⌚9.30am-5.30pm, shorter hours & closed weekends Oct-Mar) The headquarters of Taittinger are an excellent place to come for a clear, straightforward presentation on how Champagne is actually made – there's no claptrap about 'the Champagne mystique' here. Parts of the cellars occupy 4th-century Roman stone quarries; other bits were excavated by 13th-century Benedictine monks. No need to reserve. Situated 1.5km southeast of Reims centre; take the Citadine 1 or 2 bus to the St-Niçaise or Salines stops.

Sleeping

★Les Telliers B&B €€

(☎09 53 79 80 74; www.telliers.fr; 18 rue des Telliers; s €67-84, d €79-120, tr €116-141, q €132-162; P 📶) Enticingly positioned down a quiet alley near the cathedral, this bijou B&B extends one of Reims' warmest *bienvenues*. The high-ceilinged rooms are big on art deco character, and handsomely decorated with ornamental fireplaces, polished oak floors and the odd antique. Breakfast costs an extra €9 and is a generous spread of pastries, fruit, fresh-pressed juice and coffee.

La Demeure des Sacres B&B €€

(☎06 79 06 80 68; www.la-demeure-des-sacres.com; 29 rue Libergier; d €145, ste €220-245; 📶) Nuzzled in an art deco townhouse close to the cathedral, this B&B harbours four wood-floored rooms and suites, with pleasing original features like marble fireplaces and free-standing bath-tubs. The Royal Suite has cracking cathedral views. Homemade treats (preserves, crêpes and the like) appear at breakfast, which is included in the room rate. There is a secluded garden for post-sightseeing moments.

Eating

Anna-S – La Table Amoureuse FRENCH €€

(☎03 26 89 12 12; www.annas-latableamoureuse.com; 6 rue Gambetta; 3-course lunch €17.50, dinner menus €29-47; ⌚noon-1.30pm & 7-9pm Tue & Thu-Sat, noon-1.30pm Wed & Sun) So what if the decor is chintzy – there is a reason why this bistro is as busy as a beehive. Friendly service and a menu packed with well-done classics – Arctic char with Champagne jus, fillet of veal in rich, earthy morel sauce – hit the mark every time. The three-course lunch is a steal at €17.50.

Brasserie Le Boulingrin BRASSERIE €€
(☎03 26 40 96 22; www.boulingrin.fr; 29-31 rue de Mars; menus €20-29; ⊙noon-2.30pm & 7-10.30pm Mon-Sat) A genuine, old-time brasserie – the decor and zinc bar date back to 1925 – whose ambience and cuisine make it an enduring favourite. From September to June, the culinary focus is on *fruits de mer* (seafood) such as Breton oysters. There's always a €9.50 lunch special.

Information

Tourist Office (☎03 26 77 45 00; www.reims-tourisme.com; 6 rue Rockefeller; ⊙10am-6pm Mon-Sat, 10am-12.30pm & 1.30-5pm Sun) Find stacks of information on Reims (plus free city maps) and the Champagne region here.

Getting There & Away

From Reims' train station, 1km northwest of the cathedral, there are services to Paris' Gare de l'Est (€19 to €63, 46 minutes to one hour, 12 to 17 daily) and Épernay (€7, 20 to 42 minutes, 16 daily).

Épernay

POP 23,529

Prosperous Épernay, 25km south of Reims, is the self-proclaimed *capitale du champagne* and home to many of the world's most celebrated Champagne houses. Beneath the town's streets, some 200 million bottles of Champagne are slowly being aged, just waiting to be popped open for some fizz-fuelled celebration.

Sights & Activities

★Avenue de Champagne STREET
Épernay's handsome av de Champagne fizzes with *maisons de champagne* (Champagne houses). The boulevard is lined with mansions and neoclassical villas, rebuilt after WWI. Peek through wrought-iron gates at Moët's private **Hôtel Chandon**, an early 19th-century pavilion-style residence set in landscaped gardens, which counts Wagner among its famous past guests. The haunted-looking **Château Perrier**, a red-brick mansion built in 1854 in neo–Louis XIII style, is aptly placed at No13! The roundabout presents photo ops with its giant cork and bottle-top.

★Moët & Chandon WINERY
(☎03 26 51 20 20; www.moet.com; 20 av de Champagne; adult incl 1/2 glasses €23/28, 10-18yr €10; ⊙tours 9.30-11.30am & 2-4.30pm Apr–mid-Nov, 9.30-11.30am & 2-4.30pm Mon-Fri mid-Nov–Mar) Flying the Moët, French, European and Russian flags, this prestigious *maison* offers frequent one-hour tours that are among the region's most impressive, offering a peek at part of its 28km labyrinth of *caves* (cellars). At the shop, you can pick up a 15L bottle of Brut Impérial for just €1500; a standard bottle will set you back €31.

Mercier WINERY
(☎03 26 51 22 22; www.champagnemercier.fr; 68-70 av de Champagne; adult incl 1/2/3 glasses €14/19/22 Mon-Fri, €16/21/25 Sat & Sun, 12-17yr €8; ⊙tours 9.30-11.30am & 2-4.30pm, closed mid-Dec–mid-Feb) France's most popular brand was founded in 1847 by Eugène Mercier, a trailblazer in the field of eye-catching publicity stunts and the virtual creator of the cellar tour. Everything here is flashy, including the 160,000L barrel that took two decades to build (for the Universal Exposition of 1889), the lift that transports you 30m underground and the laser-guided touring train.

Sleeping

Magna Quies B&B €€
(☎06 73 25 66 60; www.magnaquies-epernay.jimdo.com; 49 av de Champagne; d/tr/q €140/180/200; P) Nestled in a shuttered manor house on the av de Champagne, this family-run B&B extends the warmest of welcomes. The trio of sunny, wood-floored rooms command fine views of the vineyards. Rates include a generous breakfast spread of pastries, fresh fruit and cold cuts.

Hôtel Jean Moët HISTORIC HOTEL €€
(☎03 26 32 19 22; www.hoteljeanmoet.com; 7 rue Jean Moët; d €140-205, ste €230-260; ❄📶🏊) Housed in a beautifully converted 18th-century mansion, this old-town hotel is big on atmosphere, with its skylit tearoom, antique-meets-boutique-chic rooms and cellar, C. Comme (p214). Spa treatments and a swimming pool await after a hard day's Champagne-tasting.

Eating & Drinking

★La Grillade Gourmande FRENCH €€
(☎03 26 55 44 22; www.lagrilladegourmande.com; 16 rue de Reims; menus €19-59; ⊙noon-2pm & 7.30-10pm Tue-Sat) This chic, red-walled bistro

is an inviting spot to try chargrilled meats and dishes rich in texture and flavour, such as crayfish pan-fried in Champagne and lamb cooked in rosemary and honey until meltingly tender. Diners spill out onto the covered terrace in the warm months.

★C. Comme WINE BAR
(www.c-comme.fr; 8 rue Gambetta; light meals €7.50-14.50, 6-glass Champagne tasting €33-39; ⏲10am-8.30pm Sun-Wed, to 11pm Thu, to midnight Fri & Sat) The downstairs cellar has a stash of 300 different varieties of Champagne; sample them (from €6 a glass) in the softly lit bar-bistro upstairs. Accompany with a tasting plate of regional cheese, charcuterie and *rillettes* (pork pâté). We love the funky bottle-top tables and relaxed ambience.

Information

Tourist office (☎03 26 53 33 00; www.ot-epernay.fr; 7 av de Champagne; ⏲9am-12.30pm & 1.30-7pm Mon-Sat, 10.30am-1pm & 2-4.30pm Sun, closed Sun mid-Oct–mid-Apr; 📶) Has English brochures and maps.

Getting There & Away

The **train station** (place Mendès-France) has direct services to Reims (€7, 24 to 37 minutes, 14 daily) and Paris Gare de l'Est (€24 to €65, 1¼ hours to 2¾ hours, eight daily).

ALSACE & LORRAINE

Teetering on the tempestuous frontier between France and Germany, the neighbouring regions of Alsace and Lorraine are where the worlds of Gallic and Germanic culture collide. Half-timbered houses, lush vineyards and forest-clad mountains hint at Alsace's Teutonic leanings, while Lorraine is indisputably Francophile.

Strasbourg

POP 280,114

Strasbourg is the perfect overture to all that is idiosyncratic about Alsace – walking a fine tightrope between France and Germany and between a medieval past and a progressive future, it pulls off its act in inimitable Alsatian style. Roam the old town's twisting alleys lined with crooked half-timbered houses à la Grimm, feast in cosy *winstubs* (Alsatian taverns), and marvel at how a city that does Christmas markets and gingerbread so well can also be home to the glittering EU Quarter and France's second-largest student population.

Sights

★Cathédrale Notre-Dame CATHEDRAL
(www.cathedrale-strasbourg.fr; place de la Cathédrale; adult/child astronomical clock €2/1.50, platform €5/2.50; ⏲7-11.15am & 12.45-7pm, astronomical clock tickets sold 11.30am-12.25pm Mon-Sat, platform 9am-7.15pm; 🚊Grand'Rue) Nothing prepares you for your first glimpse of Strasbourg's Cathédrale Notre-Dame, completed in all its Gothic grandeur in 1439. The lace-fine façade lifts the gaze little by little to flying buttresses, leering gargoyles and a 142m spire. The interior is exquisitely lit by 12th- to 14th-century **stained-glass windows**, including the western portal's jewel-like rose window. The Gothic-meets-Renaissance **astronomical clock** strikes solar noon at 12.30pm with a parade of figures portraying the different stages of life and Jesus with his Apostles.

★Grande Île HISTORIC SITE
(🚊Grand'Rue) History seeps through the twisting lanes and cafe-rimmed plazas of Grande Île, Strasbourg's Unesco World Heritage–listed island bordered by the River Ill. These streets – with their photogenic line-up of wonky, timber-framed houses in sherbet colours – are made for aimless ambling. They cower beneath the soaring magnificence of the cathedral (p214) and its sidekick, the gingerbready 15th-century **Maison Kammerzell** (rue des Hallebardes; 🚊Grand'Rue), with its ornate carvings and leaded windows. The alleys are at their most atmospheric when lantern lit at night.

Petite France AREA
(🚊Grand'Rue) Criss-crossed by narrow lanes, canals and locks, Petite France is where artisans plied their trades in the Middle Ages. The half-timbered houses, sprouting veritable thickets of scarlet geraniums in summer, and the riverside parks attract the masses, but the area still manages to retain its Alsatian charm, especially in the early morning and late evening. Drink in views of the River Ill and the **Barrage Vauban** (Vauban Dam; ⏲viewing terrace 7.15am-9pm, shorter hours winter; 🚊Faubourg National) FREE from the much-photographed **Ponts Couverts** (Covered Bridges; 🚊Musée d'Art Moderne) and their trio of 13th-century towers.

★Palais Rohan HISTORIC BUILDING
(2 place du Château; adult/child per museum €6.50/free, all 3 museums €12/free; ⊙10am-6pm Wed-Mon; Grand'Rue) Hailed a 'Versailles in miniature', this opulent 18th-century residence is replete with treasures. The basement **Musée Archéologique** takes you from the Palaeolithic period to AD 800. On the ground floor is the **Musée des Arts Décoratifs**, where rooms adorned with Hannong ceramics and gleaming silverware evoke the lavish lifestyle of the nobility in the 18th century. On the 1st floor, the **Musée des Beaux-Arts** collection of 14th- to 19th-century art includes El Greco, Botticelli and Flemish Primitive works.

Sleeping

Les Artistes GUESTHOUSE €
(03 88 77 15 53; www.chambre-hotes-les-artistes.fr; 22 rue Vermeer; d €60-80, tr €80-100; ; Elsau) Les Artistes offers clean, simple quarters and a good old-fashioned *bienvenue*. Rates include a fab breakfast, with fresh pastries and homemade jam. It's a homely pick, with a garden and barbecue area. Central Strasbourg, 3km away, can be reached on a cycle path or by tram (take B or C from rue du Faubourg National to the Elsau stop).

Hotel D BOUTIQUE HOTEL €€
(03 88 15 13 67; www.hoteld.fr; 15 rue du Fossé des Treize; d €129-189, ste €219-309; P; République) Splashes of bold colour and daring design have transformed this townhouse into a nouveau-chic boutique hotel. The slick, spacious rooms are dressed in soothing tones and no comfort stone has been left unturned – you'll find robes, Nespresso machines and iPod docks even in the standard ones. A fitness room and sauna invite relaxation.

Eating

★Vince'Stub FRENCH €€
(03 88 52 02 91; www.vincestub.com; 10 Petite rue des Dentelles; mains €14-17; ⊙11.30am-2pm & 7-10.30pm Tue-Sat; Grand'Rue) This sweet, petite bistro has a cosy beamed interior, a nicely down-to-earth vibe and a menu packed with Alsatian classics – see the blackboard for daily specials. It does a roaring trade in comfort food, from spot-on *steak-frites* to pork knuckles with Munster cheese.

La Cuiller à Pot FRENCH €€
(03 88 35 56 30; www.lacuillerapot.com; 18b rue Finkwiller; mains €19.50-26.50; ⊙noon-2.30pm & 7-10.30pm Tue-Fri, 7-10.30pm Sat; Musée d'Art Moderne) Run by a talented husband-and-wife team, this little Alsatian dream of a restaurant rustles up fresh regional cuisine. Its well-edited menu goes with the seasons but might include such dishes as fillet of beef with wild mushrooms, and homemade gnocchi and escargots in parsley jus. Quality is second to none.

Information

Tourist office (03 88 52 28 28; www.otstrasbourg.fr; 17 place de la Cathédrale; ⊙9am-7pm daily; Grand'Rue) Has maps in English (€1).

Getting There & Away

AIR

Strasbourg's international **airport** (www.strasbourg.aeroport.fr) is 17km southwest of the city centre (towards Molsheim).

TRAIN

Destinations within France:

Lille €98 to €151, four hours, 17 daily
Lyon €38 to €182, 4½ hours, 14 daily
Metz €27.10, 1½ hours, 16 daily
Nancy €26 to €31, 1½ hours, 12 daily
Paris €77 to €144, 2¼ hours, 19 daily

THE LOIRE VALLEY

One step removed from the French capital, the Loire was historically the place where princes, dukes and notable nobles established their country getaways, and the countryside is littered with some of the most extravagant architecture outside Versailles.

Blois

POP 47,500

Blois' historic château was the feudal seat of the powerful counts of Blois, and its grand halls, spiral staircases and sweeping courtyards provide a whistle-stop tour through the key periods of French architecture.

Sights

★Château Royal de Blois CHATEAU
(02 54 90 33 33; www.chateaudeblois.fr; place du Château; adult/child €10/5, audioguide €4/3; ⊙9am-6pm or 7pm Apr-Oct, 9am-noon & 1.30-5.30pm Nov-Mar) Seven French kings lived in Blois' royal château, whose four grand

wings were built during four distinct periods in French architecture: Gothic (13th century), Flamboyant Gothic (1498–1501), early Renaissance (1515–20) and classical (1630s). You can easily spend a half-day immersing yourself in the château's dramatic and bloody history and its extraordinary architecture. In July and August there are free tours in English.

★Maison de la Magie MUSEUM
(☎02 54 90 33 33; www.maisondelamagie.fr; 1 place du Château; adult/child €9/5; ⏲10am-12.30pm & 2-6.30pm Apr-Aug & mid-Oct–2 Nov, 2-6.30pm 1st half Sep; 👪) Across the square from the château, this museum of magic occupies the one-time home of watchmaker, inventor and conjurer Jean Eugène Robert-Houdin (1805–71), after whom the American magician Harry Houdini named himself. Dragons emerge roaring from the windows every half-hour, while inside the museum has exhibits on Houdin and the history of magic, displays of optical trickery, and several daily magic shows.

Sleeping

Hôtel Anne de Bretagne HOTEL €
(☎02 54 78 05 38; www.hotelannedebretagne.com; 31 av du Dr Jean Laigret; s/d/q €60/69/95; P📶) This ivy-covered hotel, in a great location midway between the train station and the château, has friendly staff, a cosy piano-equipped salon and 29 brightly coloured rooms with bold bedspreads. A packed three-course picnic lunch costs €11.50. It also rents out bicycles.

★La Maison de Thomas B&B €€
(☎09 81 84 44 59; www.lamaisondethomas.fr; 12 rue Beauvoir; s/d/tr incl breakfast €90/100/140; 📶) A friendly welcome and five spacious rooms with large windows, high ceilings and exposed beams await you at this beautiful B&B, on a pedestrianised street midway between the château and the cathedral. There's bike storage in the interior courtyard and a wine cellar where you can sample local vintages.

Eating

Les Banquettes Rouges MODERN FRENCH €€
(☎02 54 78 74 92; www.lesbanquettesrouges.com; 16 rue des Trois Marchands; lunch/dinner menus from €17.50/27.50; ⏲noon-1.30pm & 7-9.30pm Tue-Sat) In the St-Nicolas quarter below the château, this restaurant – easy to spot thanks to its bright-red façade – serves French *semi-gastronomique* cuisine. Favourites often available here include pan-fried veal liver with morello cherry and bitter-orange gravy, and *fondant au chocolat*.

L'Orangerie du Château GASTRONOMY €€€
(☎02 54 78 05 36; www.orangerie-du-chateau.fr; 1 av Dr Jean Laigret; menus €38-84; ⏲noon-1.45pm & 7-9.15pm Tue-Sat) This Michelin-starred restaurant serves *cuisine gastronomique inventive* inspired by both French tradition and culinary ideas from faraway lands. The wine list comes on a tablet computer. For dessert try the speciality, soufflé.

Information

Tourist Office (☎02 54 90 41 41; www.bloischambord.co.uk; 23 place du Château; ⏲9am-7pm Easter-Sep, 10am-5pm Oct-Easter) Has maps of town and sells châteaux combo and concert tickets. Download its smartphone app via the website. Situated across the square from the château.

CHÂTEAUX TOURS

If you don't have your own car, minibus tours are a good way to see the châteaux without being dependent on sometimes infrequent public transport. A variety of private companies offer well-organised itineraries, taking in various combinations of Azay-le-Rideau, Villandry, Cheverny, Chambord, Chenonceau and vineyards offering wine tasting. Many are also happy to create custom-designed tours. Half-day trips cost between €23 and €36 per person; full-day trips range from €50 to €54. These prices don't include admission to the châteaux, though you often get slightly discounted tickets. Reserve online or via the **Tours** (☎02 47 70 37 37; www.tours-tourisme.fr; 78-82 rue Bernard Palissy; ⏲8.30am-7pm Mon-Sat, 10am-12.30pm & 2.30-5pm Sun Apr-Sep, 9am-12.30pm & 1.30-6pm Mon-Sat, 10am-1pm Sun Oct-Mar) or **Amboise** (p218) tourist offices, from where most tours depart.

Getting There & Away

BUS

The tourist office has a brochure detailing public-transport options to nearby châteaux.

A *navette* (shuttle bus; €6) run by **Route 41** (TLC; ☎02 54 58 55 44; www.route41.fr) makes it possible to do a Blois-Chambord-Cheverny-Beauregard-Blois circuit on Wednesday, Saturday and Sunday from early April to 1 November; it also runs daily during school vacation periods and on holidays from early April to August.

TRAIN

The **Blois-Chambord train station** (av Dr Jean Laigret) is 600m west (up the hill) from Blois' château. Destinations include the following:

Amboise €7.20, 15 minutes, 16 to 25 daily

Paris Gare d'Austerlitz €29.40, 1½ hours, five direct daily

Tours €11.20, 40 minutes, 14 to 22 daily

Around Blois

Château de Chambord

For full-blown château splendour, you can't top **Chambord** (☎info 02 54 50 40 00, tour & show reservations 02 54 50 50 40; www.chambord.org; adult/child €11/9, parking near/distant €6/4; ⏲9am-5pm or 6pm; 👪), constructed from 1519 by François I as a lavish base for hunting game in the Sologne forests but eventually used for just 42 days during the king's 32-year reign (1515–47).

The château's most famous feature is its **double-helix staircase**, attributed by some to Leonardo da Vinci, who lived in Amboise (34km southwest) from 1516 until his death three years later. The most interesting rooms are on the 1st floor, including the **king's and queen's chambers** (complete with interconnecting passages to enable late-night hijinks) and a wing devoted to the thwarted attempts of the Comte de Chambord to be crowned Henri V after the fall of the Second Empire.

In summer there may be hour-long guided tours (€5/3 per adult/child) in English – ask at the new Halle d'Acceuil (entrance pavilion).

Chambord is 16km east of Blois.

Château de Cheverny

Thought by many to be the most perfectly proportioned château of all, **Cheverny** (☎02 54 79 96 29; www.chateau-cheverny.fr; av du Château; château & gardens adult/child €10.50/7.50; ⏲9.15am-7pm Apr-Sep, 10am-5.30pm Oct-Mar) has hardly been altered since its construction between 1625 and 1634. Inside is a formal dining room, bridal chamber and children's playroom (complete with Napoléon III–era toys), as well as a guards' room full of pikestaffs, claymores and suits of armour.

Many priceless art works (including the *Mona Lisa*) were stashed in the château's 18th-century **Orangerie** during WWII.

Near the château's gateway, the **kennels** house pedigreed French pointer/English foxhound hunting dogs still used by the owners of Cheverny; feeding time, the **Soupe des Chiens**, takes place daily at 5pm April to September.

Cheverny is 14km southeast of Blois and 18km southwest of Chambord.

Amboise

POP 13,200

The childhood home of Charles VIII and the final resting place of Leonardo da Vinci, elegant Amboise, 23km northeast of Tours, is pleasantly perched along the southern bank of the Loire and overlooked by its fortified château.

Sights

★ Château Royal d'Amboise CHATEAU

(☎02 47 57 00 98; www.chateau-amboise.com; place Michel Debré; adult/child €11.20/7.50, incl audioguide €15.20/10.50; ⏲9am-6pm or 7.30pm Mar–mid-Nov, 9am-12.30pm & 2-5.15pm mid-Nov–Feb) Perched on a rocky escarpment above town, Amboise's castle was a favoured retreat for all of France's Valois and Bourbon kings. Only a few of the château's original structures survive, but you can still visit the furnished Logis (Lodge) – Gothic except for the top half of one wing, which is Renaissance – and the Flamboyant Gothic Chapelle St-Hubert (1493), where Leonardo da Vinci's presumed remains have been buried since 1863. The ramparts afford thrilling views of the town and river.

★ Le Clos Lucé HISTORIC BUILDING

(☎02 47 57 00 73; www.vinci-closluce.com; 2 rue du Clos Lucé; adult/child €15/10.50; ⏲9am-7pm or 8pm Feb-Oct, 9am or 10am-5pm or 6pm Nov-Jan; 👪) It was on the invitation of François I that Leonardo da Vinci (1452–1519), aged 64, took up residence at this grand manor house (built 1471). An admirer of the Italian Renaissance, the French monarch named Da Vinci 'first painter, engineer and king's architect', and the Italian spent his time here sketching, tinkering and dreaming up ingenious contraptions. Fascinating models of his many inventions are on display inside the home and around its lovely 7-hectare gardens.

Sleeping

★Le Vieux Manoir B&B €€

(02 47 30 41 27; www.le-vieux-manoir.com; 13 rue Rabelais; d incl breakfast €150-220, f €330, cottages €260-310; late Mar-Oct; P) Set in a lovely walled garden, this restored mansion has oodles of old-time charm. The six rooms and two cottages, decorated with antiques, get lots of natural light, and owners Gloria and Bob (expat Americans who once ran an award-winning Boston B&B) are generous with their knowledge of the area.

Le Clos d'Amboise HISTORIC HOTEL €€€

(02 47 30 10 20; www.leclosamboise.com; 27 rue Rabelais; r €189-239, 6-person ste €239-289; P@) Overlooking a lovely garden with 200-year-old fir trees and a heated pool, this posh pad – most of it built in the 17th century – offers country living in the heart of town. Stylish features abound, from luxurious fabrics to antique furnishings. Half of the 20 rooms still have their original, now non-functioning, fireplaces.

Eating

★Food Market MARKET €

(quai du Général de Gaulle; 8am-1pm Sun) Voted France's *marché préféré* (favourite market) in 2015, this riverfront extravaganza, 400m southwest of the château, draws 200 to 300 stalls selling both edibles and durables. Worth timing your visit around.

La Fourchette FRENCH €€

(06 11 78 16 98; 9 rue Malebranche; lunch/dinner menus €17/30; noon-1.30pm Tue-Sat, 7-8.30pm Fri & Sat, plus Tue & Wed evenings summer) Hidden away in a back alley off rue Nationale, this is Amboise's favourite address for family-style French cooking – chef Christine will make you feel as though you've been invited to her house for lunch. The *menu* has just two entrées, two mains and two desserts. The restaurant is small, so reserve ahead.

Information

Tourist office (02 47 57 09 28; www.amboise-valdeloire.co.uk; cnr quai du Général de Gaulle & allée du Sergent Turpin; internet access per 30min €4; 9am or 10am-6pm or 7pm Mon-Sat, 10am-12.30pm Sun Apr-Oct, 10am-12.30pm & 2-5pm Mon-Sat Nov-Mar;) Offers walking tours.

Getting There & Around

Amboise's **train station** (bd Gambetta) is 1.5km north of the château, on the opposite side of the Loire.

Destinations include the following:

Blois €7.20, 15 minutes, 16 to 25 daily

Paris Gare d'Austerlitz €33.20, 1¾ hours, four direct daily

Tours €5.70, 17 minutes, 13 to 23 daily

Around Amboise

Château de Chenonceau

Spanning the languid Cher River via a series of supremely graceful arches, the castle of **Chenonceau** (02 47 23 90 07; www.chenonceau.com; adult/child €13/10, with audioguide €17.50/14; 9am-7pm or later Apr-Sep, to 5pm or 6pm Oct-Mar;) is one of the most elegant and unusual in the Loire Valley.

The château's interior is crammed with wonderful furniture and tapestries, stunning original tiled floors and a fabulous art collection including works by Tintoretto, Correggio, Rubens, Murillo, Van Dyck and Ribera. The pièce de résistance is the 60m-long window-lined **Grande Gallerie** spanning the Cher.

Make time to visit the **gardens** too: it seems as if there's one of every kind imaginable (maze, English, vegetable, playground, flower...).

The château is 33km east of Tours, 13km southeast of Amboise and 40km southwest of Blois. From the town of Chenonceaux (spelt with an x), just outside the château grounds, trains go to Tours (€7, 25 minutes, nine to 12 daily).

Château d'Azay-le-Rideau

Romantic, moat-ringed **Azay-le-Rideau** (02 47 45 42 04; www.azay-le-rideau.fr; adult/child €8.50/free, audioguide €4.50; 9.30am-6pm Apr-Sep, to 7pm Jul & Aug, 10am-5.15pm Oct-Mar) is wonderfully adorned with slender turrets, geometric windows and decorative stonework, wrapped up within a shady landscaped park. Built in the 1500s on a natural island in the middle of a river, the château is one of the Loire's loveliest: Honoré de Balzac called it a 'multifaceted diamond set in the River Indre'.

Its most famous feature is its open **loggia staircase**, in the Italian style, overlooking the central courtyard and decorated with the salamanders and ermines of François I and Queen Claude.

Azay-le-Rideau is 26km southwest of Tours. The château is 2.5km from the train station, where there are eight daily services to Tours (€5.90, 30 minutes).

BURGUNDY & THE RHÔNE VALLEY

If there's one place in France where you're really going to find out what makes the nation tick, it's Burgundy. Two of the country's enduring passions – food and wine – come together in this gorgeously rural region; if you're a sucker for hearty food and the fruits of the vine, you'll be in seventh heaven.

Dijon

POP 157,200

Filled with elegant medieval and Renaissance buildings, dashing Dijon is Burgundy's capital, and the spiritual home of French mustard. Its lively old town is wonderful for strolling and shopping, interspersed with some snappy drinking and dining.

Sights

Palais des Ducs et des États de Bourgogne PALACE

(Palace of the Dukes & States of Burgundy; place de la Libération) Once home to Burgundy's powerful dukes, this monumental palace with a neoclassical façade overlooks place de la Libération, Old Dijon's magnificent central square dating from 1686. The palace's eastern wing houses the outstanding Musée des Beaux-Arts, whose entrance is next to the **Tour de Bar**, a squat 14th-century tower that once served as a prison. The remainder of the palace houses municipal offices that are off-limits to the public.

★Musée des Beaux-Arts MUSEUM

(☎03 80 74 52 09; http://mba.dijon.fr; 1 rue Rameau; audioguide €4, guided tour €6; ⏲9.30am-6pm May-Oct, 10am-5pm Nov-Apr, closed Tue year-round) FREE Housed in the monumental Palais des Ducs, these sprawling galleries (works of art in themselves) constitute one of France's most outstanding museums. The star attraction, reopened in September 2013 after extensive renovations, is the wood-panelled **Salle des Gardes**, which houses the ornate, carved late-medieval sepulchres of dukes John the Fearless and Philip the Bold. Other sections focus on Egyptian art, the Middle Ages in Burgundy and Europe, and six centuries of European painting, from the Renaissance to modern times.

Sleeping

Hôtel du Palais HOTEL €

(☎03 80 65 51 43; www.hoteldupalais-dijon.fr; 23 rue du Palais; s €59-79, d €65-95, q €109, breakfast €9.90; ❄📶) Newly remodelled and upgraded to three-star status, this inviting hotel in a 17th-century *hôtel particulier* (private mansion) offers excellent value. The 13 rooms range from cosy, inexpensive 3rd-floor doubles tucked under the eaves to spacious, high-ceilinged family suites with abundant natural light. The location is unbeatable, on a quiet side street five minutes' walk from central place de la Libération.

★La Cour Berbisey B&B €€€

(☎03 45 83 12 38; www.lacourberbisey.fr; 31 rue Berbisey; r €129-159, junior ste €189-219, ste €249-279; 📶🏊) An arched red doorway in an ivy-draped wall leads to this luxurious B&B, easily Dijon's classiest midcity accommodation. Three enormous suites with parquet floors, beamed ceilings and tall French-shuttered windows are complemented by a lone junior suite and one smaller but equally comfortable double. Other upscale touches include an indoor swimming pool, sauna and an antique-filled salon. Breakfast is included.

Eating

Chez le Bougnat BURGUNDIAN €

(☎03 80 43 31 17; www.facebook.com/chezlebougnat; 53 rue Berbisey; menus €10.50-18; ⏲noon-2.30pm & 7pm-1am) Chef-owner (and former TV scriptwriter) Cyrille Doudies serves up copious plates of authentic Burgundian food at insanely low prices in this one-room eatery decorated with concert posters and old 45rpm records. It's one of the few eateries in Dijon that opens dependably on Sundays.

DZ'Envies BURGUNDIAN €€

(☎03 80 50 09 26; www.dzenvies.com; 12 rue Odebert; mains €16-22, lunch menus €13-20, dinner menus €29-36; ⏲noon-2pm & 7-10pm Mon-Sat) This zinging restaurant with cheery decorative touches is a good choice if you're tired of heavy Burgundian classics. The menu always involves seasonal, fresh ingredients, and dishes are imaginatively prepared and beautifully presented. At €18, the lunchtime 'I love Dijon' *menu* is a steal.

Shopping

Moutarde Maille FOOD

(☎03 80 30 41 02; www.maille.com; 32 rue de la Liberté; ⏲10am-7pm Mon-Sat) When you enter the factory boutique of this mustard company, tangy odours assault your nostrils. Three-dozen varieties of mustard fill the shelves (cassis, truffle, celery etc), along with three rotating flavours on tap for you to sample.

Information

Tourist office (☎08 92 70 05 58; www.visitdijon.com; 11 rue des Forges; ⏲9.30am-6.30pm Mon-Sat, 10am-6pm Sun Apr-Sep, 9.30am-1pm & 2-6pm Mon-Sat, 10am-4pm Sun Oct-Mar; 📶) Offers tours and maps.

Getting There & Away

BUS

Transco (☎03 80 11 29 29; www.cotedor.fr/cms/transco-horaires) Buses stop in front of the train station. Tickets are sold on board (€1.50). Bus 44 goes to Nuits-St-Georges (45 minutes) and Beaune (1¼ hours).

TRAIN

Connections from Dijon's train station include the following:

Lyon-Part Dieu Regional train/TGV from €32/39, two/1½ hours, 25 daily

Marseille TGV from €82, 3½ hours, six direct daily

Paris Gare de Lyon Regional train/TGV from €46/59, three/1½ hours, 25 daily

Beaune

POP 22,540

Beaune (pronounced 'bone'), 44km south of Dijon, is the unofficial capital of the Côte d'Or. This thriving town's *raison d'être* and the source of its *joie de vivre* is wine.

Sights & Activities

Beaune's amoeba-shaped old city is enclosed by **stone ramparts** sheltering wine cellars.

Hôtel-Dieu des Hospices de Beaune HISTORIC BUILDING

(☎03 80 24 45 00; www.hospices-de-beaune.com; rue de l'Hôtel-Dieu; adult/child €7.50/3; ⏲9am-6.30pm mid-Mar–mid-Nov, 9-11.30am & 2-5.30pm mid-Nov–mid-Mar) Built in 1443, this magnificent Gothic hospital (until 1971) is famously topped by stunning turrets and pitched rooftops covered in multicoloured tiles. Interior highlights include the barrel-vaulted **Grande Salle** (look for the dragons and peasant heads up on the roof beams); the mural-covered **St-Hughes Room**; an 18th-century **pharmacy** lined with flasks once filled with elixirs and powders; and the multipanelled masterpiece **Polyptych of the Last Judgement** by 15th-century Flemish painter Rogier van der Weyden, depicting Judgment Day in glorious technicolour.

Sleeping

★**Les Jardins de Loïs** B&B €€

(☎03 80 22 41 97; www.jardinsdelois.com; 8 bd Bretonnière; r €160, ste €185-195, 2-/4-person apt €280/350; 📶) An unexpected oasis in the middle of the city, this luxurious B&B encompasses several ample rooms, including two suites and a 135-sq-metre top-floor apartment with drop-dead gorgeous views of Beaune's rooftops. The vast garden, complete with rose bushes and fruit trees, makes a dreamy place to sit and enjoy wine grown on the hotel's private domaine. Free parking.

Hôtel des Remparts HISTORIC HOTEL €€

(☎03 80 24 94 94; www.hotel-remparts-beaune.com; 48 rue Thiers; d €97-129, ste €134-179; P❄📶) Set around two delightful courtyards, rooms in this 17th-century townhouse have red-tiled or parquet floors and simple antique furniture. Some rooms come with exposed beams and a fireplace while others have air-con. Most bathrooms have been renovated. Friendly staff can also hire out bikes. Parking costs €10.

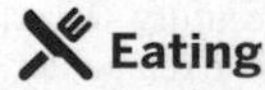

Eating

Food Market MARKET €

(place de la Halle; ⏲7am-1pm Wed & Sat) Beaune's Saturday food market is an elaborate affair, with vendors displaying their wares both indoors and on the cobblestones of place de la Halle. There's a much smaller *marché*

WORTH A TRIP

A TRIP BETWEEN VINES

Burgundy's most renowned vintages come from the **Côte d'Or** (Golden Hillside), a range of hills made of limestone, flint and clay that runs south from Dijon for about 60km. The northern section, the **Côte de Nuits**, stretches from Marsannay-la-Côte south to Corgoloin and produces reds known for their robust, full-bodied character. The southern section, the **Côte de Beaune**, lies between Ladoix-Serrigny and Santenay and produces great reds and whites.

Tourist offices provide brochures. The signposted **Route des Grands Crus** (www.road-of-the-fine-burgundy-wines.com) visits some of the most celebrated Côte de Nuits vineyards; mandatory tasting stops for oenophiles seeking nirvana include 16th-century **Château du Clos de Vougeot** (☎03 80 62 86 09; www.closdevougeot.fr; Vougeot; adult/child €7.50/2.50; ⏲9am-6.30pm Sun-Fri & to 5pm Sat Apr-Oct, 10am-5pm Nov-Mar), which offers excellent guided tours, and **L'Imaginarium** (☎03 80 62 61 40; www.imaginarium-bourgogne.com; av du Jura, Nuits-St-Georges; adult incl basic/grand cru tasting €9/17, child €6; ⏲2-7pm Mon, 10am-7pm Tue-Sun), an entertaining wine museum in **Nuits-St-Georges**.

Wine & Voyages (☎03 80 61 15 15; www.wineandvoyages.com; tours €58-114) and **Authentica Tours** (☎06 87 01 43 78; www.authentica-tours.com; tours €65-130) run minibus tours in English; reserve online or at the Dijon tourist office.

gourmand (gourmet market) on Wednesday morning.

Le Bacchus BURGUNDIAN **€€**
(☎03 80 24 07 78; 6 rue du Faubourg Madeleine; menus lunch €14-16.50, dinner €29-31; ⏲noon-2pm & 7-10pm Tue-Sat) The welcome is warm and the food exceptional at this small restaurant just outside Beaune's centre. Multilingual co-owner Anna works the tables while her partner Olivier whips up market-fresh *menus* that blend classic flavours (steak with Fallot mustard) with tasty surprises (gazpacho with tomato-basil ice cream). Save room for desserts such as Bourbon vanilla crème brûlée, flambéed at your table.

Information

Tourist office (☎03 80 26 21 30; www.beaune-tourisme.fr; 6 bd Perpreuil; ⏲9am-6.30pm Mon-Sat, to 6pm Sun Apr-Oct, shorter hours Nov-Mar) Has lots of info about nearby vineyards.

Getting There & Away

BUS

Bus 44, operated by Transco (www.cotedor.fr), links Beaune with Dijon (€1.50, 1¼ hours, two to seven daily), stopping at Côte d'Or villages such as Gevrey-Chambertin, Vougeot, Nuits-St-Georges and Aloxe-Corton.

TRAIN

Trains connect the following places:

Dijon €8, 20 to 30 minutes, 40 daily

Nuits-St-Georges €3.70, 10 minutes, eight daily

Paris €50, 3½ hours, seven direct daily

Lyon

POP 509,000

Gourmets, eat your heart out: Lyon is *the* gastronomic capital of France, with a lavish table of piggy-driven dishes and delicacies to savour. The city has been a commercial, industrial and banking powerhouse for the past 500 years, and is France's third-largest city, with outstanding art museums, a dynamic nightlife, green parks and a Unesco-listed old town.

Sights

Vieux Lyon

Old Lyon, with its cobblestone streets and medieval and Renaissance houses below Fourvière hill, is divided into three quarters: St-Paul (north), St-Jean (middle) and St-Georges (south). Lovely old buildings languish on **rue du Bœuf**, **rue St-Jean** and **rue des Trois Maries**.

Deep within Vieux Lyon and Croix Rousse, dark, dingy *traboules* (secret passages) wind their way through apartment blocks, under streets and into courtyards. In all, 315 passages link 230 streets, with a combined length of 50km. The tourist office includes *traboules* on many of its guided walking **tours** (☎ 04 72 77 69 69; www.lyon-france.com; tours adult/child €12/7; ⏱ by reservation).

Cathédrale St-Jean CATHEDRAL
(place St-Jean, 5e; ⏱ 8.15am-7.45pm Mon-Fri, to 7pm Sat & Sun; Ⓜ Vieux Lyon) Lyon's partly Romanesque cathedral was built between the late 11th and early 16th centuries. The portals of its Flamboyant Gothic façade, completed in 1480 (and recently renovated), are decorated with 280 square stone medallions. Inside, the highlight is the **astronomical clock** in the north transept.

Fourvière

Over two millennia ago, the Romans built the city of Lugdunum on the slopes of Fourvière. Footpaths wind uphill, but the funicular is less taxing.

Basilique Notre Dame de Fourvière CHURCH
(www.fourviere.org; place de Fourvière, 5e; rooftop tour adult/child €7/4; ⏱ 8am-6.45pm, guided tours Apr-Nov; 🚊 Fourvière) Crowning the hill, with stunning city panoramas from its terrace, this superb example of late 19th-century French ecclesiastical architecture is lined

Lyon

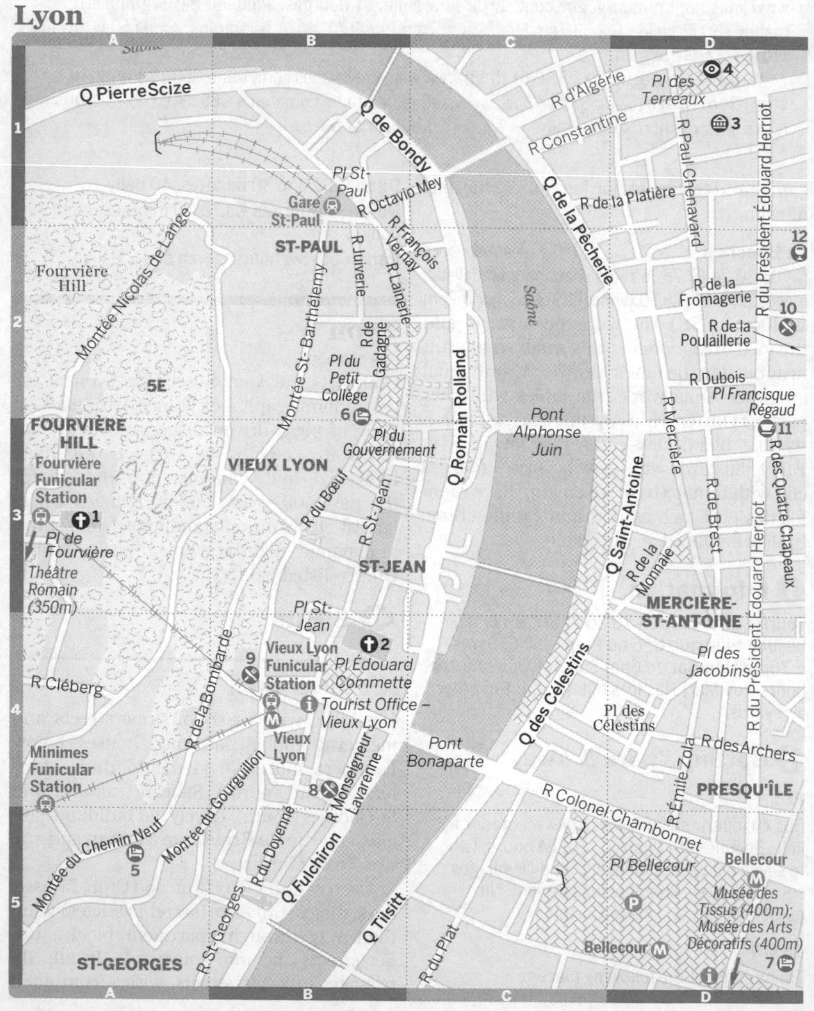

with intricate mosaics. One-hour discovery visits take in the main features of the basilica and crypt; 75-minute rooftop tours ('Visite Insolite') climax on the stone-sculpted roof.

Théâtre Romain ARCHAEOLOGICAL SITE
(rue Cléberg, 5e; Fourvière, Minimes) Lyon's Roman theatre, built around 15 BC and enlarged in AD 120, sat an audience of 10,000. Romans held poetry readings and musical recitals in the smaller, adjacent *odéon*.

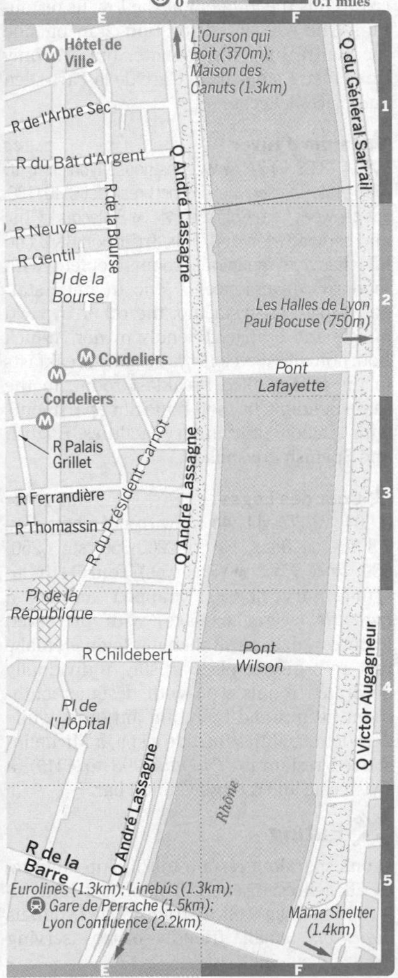

Presqu'île, Confluence & Croix-Rousse

Lyon's city centre lies on this 500m- to 800m-wide peninsula bounded by the rivers Rhône and Saône. Past **Gare de Perrache** lies **Lyon Confluence** (www.lyon-confluence.fr) the city's newest neighbourhood. The hilltop quarter of Croix Rousse slinks north up the steep *pentes* (slopes) from place des Terreaux.

Musée des Beaux-Arts MUSEUM
(04 72 10 17 40; www.mba-lyon.fr; 20 place des Terreaux, 1er; adult/child €8/free; 10am-6pm Wed, Thu & Sat-Mon, 10.30am-6pm Fri; M Hôtel de Ville) This stunning and eminently manageable museum showcases France's finest collection of sculptures and paintings outside of Paris from antiquity onwards. Highlights include works by Monet, Matisse and Picasso. Pick up a free audioguide and be sure to stop for a drink or meal on the delightful stone terrace off its cafe-restaurant or take time out in its tranquil **cloister garden**.

Place des Terreaux SQUARE
(M Hôtel de Ville) The centrepiece of the Presqu'île's beautiful central square is a 19th-century **fountain** made of 21 tonnes of lead and sculpted by Frédéric-Auguste Bartholdi (of Statue of Liberty fame). The four horses pulling the chariot symbolise rivers galloping seawards. The **Hôtel de Ville** fronting the square was built in 1655 but was given its present ornate façade in 1702.

Lyon

Sights
1 Basilique Notre Dame de Fourvière A3
2 Cathédrale St-Jean B4
3 Musée des Beaux-Arts D1
4 Place des Terreaux D1

Sleeping
5 Auberge de Jeunesse du Vieux Lyon A5
6 Cour des Loges B2
7 Jardin d'Hiver D5

Eating
8 Cinq Mains B4
9 Daniel et Denise B4
10 Le Musée D2

Drinking & Nightlife
11 Grand Café des Négociants D3
12 Harmonie des Vins D2

Daniel Buren's polka-dot 'forest' of 69 **granite fountains** are embedded in the ground across much of the square.

Musée des Tissus MUSEUM
(☎04 78 38 42 00; www.mtmad.fr; 34 rue de la Charité, 2e; adult/child €10/7.50; ⏲10am-5.30pm Tue-Sun; Ⓜ Ampère) Extraordinary Lyonnais and international silks are showcased here. Ticket includes admission to the adjoining Musée des Arts Décoratifs (p224), which displays 18th-century furniture, tapestries, wallpaper, ceramics and silver.

Musée des Arts Décoratifs MUSEUM
(☎04 78 38 42 00; www.mtmad.fr; 34 rue de la Charité, 2e; adult/child €10/7.50; ⏲10am-5.30pm Tue-Sun; Ⓜ Ampère) This well-organised museum displays 18th-century furniture, tapestries, wallpaper, ceramics and silver. Ticket includes admission to the adjoining Musée des Tissus (p224), which showcases extraordinary Lyonnais and international silks.

Musée des Confluences MUSEUM
(☎04 28 38 11 90; www.museedesconfluences.fr; 86 quai Perrache, 6e; adult/child €9/free; ⏲11am-6.15pm Tue, Wed & Fri, 11am-9.15pm Thu, 10am-6.15pm Sat & Sun; 🚊T1) Opened in late 2014, this recent building, designed by the Viennese firm Coop Himmelb(l)au, is the crowning glory of Lyon's newest neighbourhood, the Confluence, at Presqu'île's southern tip. Lying at the confluence of the Rhône and Saône rivers, this ambitious science-and-humanities museum is housed in a futuristic steel-and-glass transparent crystal. Its distorted structure is one of the city's iconic landmarks.

Tours

★Walking Tours WALKING
(☎04 72 77 69 69; www.en.lyon-france.com/Guided-Tours-Excursions; adult/child €12/7; ⏲by reservation) The tourist office organises a variety of excellent tours through Vieux Lyon and Croix Rousse with local English-speaking guides. Book in advance (online, by phone or in person at the tourist office).

Sleeping

Auberge de Jeunesse du Vieux Lyon HOSTEL €
(☎04 78 15 05 50; www.hifrance.org; 41-45 montée du Chemin Neuf, 5e; dm incl breakfast €19.50-25.60; ⏲reception 7am-1pm, 2-8pm & 9pm-1am; @📶; Ⓜ Vieux Lyon, 🚊Minimes) Stunning city views unfold from the terrace of Lyon's HI-affiliated hostel, and from many of the (mostly four- and six-bed) dorms. Bike parking and kitchen facilities are available, and there's an on-site bar. Try for a dorm with city views. To avoid the tiring 10-minute climb from Vieux Lyon metro station, take the funicular to Minimes station and walk downhill.

★Mama Shelter HOTEL €€
(☎04 78 02 58 00; www.mamashelter.com/en/lyon; 13 rue Domer, 7e; r €69-299; P❄@📶; Ⓜ Jean Macé) Lyon's branch of this trendy hotel chain has sleek decor, carpets splashed with calli-graffiti, firm beds, plush pillows, modernist lighting and big-screen Macs offering free in-room movies. A youthful crowd fills the long bar at the low-lit restaurant. The residential location 2km outside the centre may feel remote, but it's only three metro stops from Gare de la Part-Dieu and place Bellecour.

★Jardin d'Hiver B&B €€
(☎04 78 28 69 34; www.guesthouse-lyon.com; 10 rue des Marronniers, 2e; s/d incl breakfast €110/130, apt per week from €520; ❄📶; Ⓜ Bellecour) Chic and centrally located, this 3rd-floor B&B (no lift) has two spacious rooms replete with modern conveniences – one in understated purple and pistachio, the other in vivid purple and orange. Friendly owner Annick Bournonville serves 100% organic breakfasts in the foliage-filled breakfast room. In the same building, her son rents out apartments with kitchen and laundry facilities. English and Spanish are spoken.

★Cour des Loges HOTEL €€€
(☎04 72 77 44 44; www.courdesloges.com; 2-8 rue du Bœuf, 5e; d €200-350, ste €250-600; ❄@📶🏊; Ⓜ Vieux Lyon) Four 14th- to 17th-century houses wrapped around a *traboule* (secret passage) with preserved features such as Italianate loggias make this an exquisite place to stay. Individually decorated rooms woo with designer bathroom fittings and bountiful antiques, while decadent facilities include a spa, a Michelin-starred restaurant (*menus* €95 to €115), a swish cafe and a cross-vaulted bar.

Eating

Lyon's sparkling restaurant line-up embraces all genres: French, fusion, fast and international, as well as traditional Lyonnais *bouchons* (small, friendly bistros serving local city cuisine).

★Les Halles de Lyon Paul Bocuse MARKET €
(☎04 78 62 39 33; www.hallespaulbocuse.lyon.fr; 102 cours Lafayette, 3e; ⊙7am-10.30pm Tue-Sat, to 4.30pm Sun; Ⓜ Part-Dieu) Lyon's famed indoor food market has nearly five-dozen stalls selling countless gourmet delights. Pick up a round of runny St Marcellin from legendary cheesemonger Mère Richard, and a knobbly Jésus de Lyon from Charcuterie Sibilia. Or enjoy a sit-down lunch of local produce, especially enjoyable on Sundays when local families congregate for shellfish and white-wine brunches.

★L'Instant CAFE €
(☎04 78 29 85 08; www.linstant-patisserie.fr; 3 place Marcel Bertone, 4e; breakfast €6.50, lunch mains €6.50-13, weekend brunch €20; ⊙8am-7pm Mon-Sat, to 1pm Sun; ; Ⓜ Croix Rousse) The best spot in Croix Rousse to start the day, this hybrid cafe–pastry shop overlooking lovely place Marcel Bertone packs a punch. The continental breakfast (and brunch on weekends) is the highlight, while the pastries and pies will leave your taste buds reeling. The wonderfully mellow setting and relaxed urban vibe add to the appeal. Ample outdoor seating on warm days.

★Le Musée BOUCHON €€
(☎04 78 37 71 54; 2 rue des Forces, 2e; lunch mains €14, lunch menus €19-26, dinner menus €23-32; ⊙noon-1.30pm & 7.30-9.30pm Tue-Sat; Ⓜ Cordeliers) Housed in the stables of Lyon's former Hôtel de Ville, this delightful *bouchon* serves a splendid array of meat-heavy Lyonnais classics, including a divine *poulet au vinaigre* (chicken cooked in vinegar). The daily changing *menu* features 10 appetisers and 10 main dishes, plus five scrumptious desserts, all served on cute china plates at long family-style tables.

★Daniel et Denise BOUCHON €€
(☎04 78 42 24 62; www.danieletdenise-stjean.fr; 36 rue Tramassac, 5e; mains €15-25, lunch menu €21, dinner menus €30-40; ⊙noon-2pm & 7.30-9.30pm Tue-Sat) One of Vieux Lyon's most dependable and traditional eateries, this classic spot is run by award-winning chef Joseph Viola, who was elected president of Lyon's *bouchon* association in 2014. Come here for elaborate variations on traditional Lyonnais themes.

★Cinq Mains NEOBISTRO €€
(☎04 37 57 30 52; www.facebook.com/cinqmains; 12 rue Monseigneur Lavarenne, 5e; lunch menus €12-19, dinner menus €28-35; ⊙noon-2pm & 8-10pm daily) When young Lyonnais Grégory Cuilleron and his two friends opened this neobistro in early 2016, it was an instant hit. They're working wonders at this cool loft-like space with a mezzanine, serving up tantalising creations based on what they find at the market. A new generation of chefs and a new spin for Lyonnais cuisine.

Drinking & Entertainment

Grand Café des Négociants CAFE
(www.lesnegociants.com; 1 place Francisque Régaud, 2e; ⊙7am-4am; Ⓜ Cordeliers) The tree-shaded terrace and Second Empire decor of chandeliers and mirror-lined walls are the big draws at this centrally located cafe-brasserie, a Lyonnais institution since 1864. Food is served from noon to midnight.

Harmonie des Vins WINE BAR
(www.harmoniedesvins.fr; 9 rue Neuve, 1er; ⊙10am-2.30pm & 6.30pm-1am Tue-Fri, 6.30pm-1am Sat; ; Ⓜ Hôtel de Ville, Cordeliers) Find out all about French wine at this charm-laden wine bar replete with old stone walls, contemporary furnishings and tasty food. A cheese or charcuterie platter will set you back €14.

Information

Tourist Office (☎04 72 77 69 69; www.lyon-france.com; place Bellecour, 2e; ⊙9am-6pm; Ⓜ Bellecour) In the centre of Presqu'île, Lyon's exceptionally helpful, multilingual and well-staffed main tourist office offers a variety of city walking tours and sells the Lyon City Card. It can also book accommodation.

LYON CITY CARD

The excellent-value Lyon City Card (www.lyon-france.com; 1/2/3 days adult €22/32/42, child €13.50/18.50/23.50) offers free admission to every Lyon museum and a number of attractions. The card also includes unlimited city-wide transport on buses, trams, the funicular and the metro. Full-price cards are available at the tourist office, or save 10% by booking online.

Tourist Office – Vieux Lyon (☎04 72 77 69 69; www.lyon-france.com; 4 av du Doyenné, 5e; ⌚10am-5.30pm; Ⓜ Vieux Lyon) A smaller branch of the main tourist office, just outside the Vieux Lyon metro station.

ℹ Getting There & Away

AIR

Lyon-St-Exupéry Airport (www.lyonaeroports.com), 25km east of the city, serves 120 direct destinations across Europe and beyond, including many budget carriers.

BUS

In the Perrache complex, **Eurolines** (☎08 92 89 90 91, 04 72 56 95 30; www.eurolines.fr; Gare de Perrache, 2e; Ⓜ Perrache) and Spain-oriented **Linebús** (☎04 72 41 72 27; www.linebus.com; Gare de Perrache) have offices on the bus-station level of the Centre d'Échange (follow the 'Lignes Internationales' signs).

TRAIN

Lyon has two main-line train stations: **Gare de la Part-Dieu** (place Charles Béraudier, 3e; Ⓜ Part-Dieu), 1.5km east of the Rhône, and **Gare de Perrache** (cours de Verdun Rambaud, 2e; Ⓜ Perrache).

Destinations by direct TGV include the following:

Dijon €37, 1½ hours, at least six daily

Marseille €53, 1¾ hours, every 30 to 60 minutes

Paris Charles de Gaulle Airport €97, two hours, at least 11 daily

Paris Gare de Lyon €75, two hours, every 30 to 60 minutes

ℹ Getting Around

Buses, trams, a four-line metro and two funiculars linking Vieux Lyon to Fourvière and St-Just are operated by TCL (www.tcl.fr). Public transport runs from around 5am to midnight.

Tickets cost €1.80 (€16.20 for a *carnet* of 10) and are available from bus and tram drivers as well as machines at metro entrances. An all-day ticket costs €5.50. Bring coins, as machines don't accept notes (or some international credit cards). Time-stamp tickets on all forms of public transport or risk a fine.

Pick up a red-and-silver bike at one of 200-odd bike stations throughout the city and drop it off at another with Lyon's **Vélo'v** (www.velov.grandlyon.com; 1st 30min free, next 30min €1, each subsequent 30min period €2) bike rental scheme.

THE FRENCH ALPS

Hiking, skiing, majestic panoramas – the French Alps have it all when it comes to the great outdoors. But you'll also find excellent gastronomy, good nightlife and plenty of history.

Chamonix

POP 9050 / ELEV 1037M

With the pearly white peaks of the Mont Blanc massif as a sensational backdrop, being an icon comes naturally to Chamonix. First 'discovered' by Brits William Windham and Richard Pococke in 1741, this is the mecca of mountaineering. Its knife-edge peaks, plunging slopes and massive glaciers have enthralled generations of adventurers and thrill-seekers ever since. Its après-ski scene is equally pumping.

👁 Sights

★Aiguille du Midi VIEWPOINT

A great broken tooth of rock rearing among the Alpine fastness of the Mont Blanc massif, the Aiguille du Midi (3842m) is one of Chamonix' most distinctive geographical features. If you can handle the altitude, the 360-degree views of the French, Swiss and Italian Alps from the summit are (quite literally) breathtaking. Year-round, you can float in a cable car from Chamonix to the Aiguille du Midi on the vertiginous **Téléphérique de l'Aiguille du Midi** (www.compagniedumontblanc.co.uk; place de l'Aiguille du Midi; adult/child return to Aiguille du Midi €58.50/49.70, to Plan de l'Aiguille summer €31/26.40, winter €17/14.50; ⌚1st ascent btwn 7.10am & 8.30am, last btwn 3.30pm & 5pm).

Le Brévent VIEWPOINT

The highest peak on the western side of the Chamonix Valley, Le Brévent (2525m) has tremendous views of the Mont Blanc massif, myriad hiking trails through a nature reserve, ledges to paraglide from and some vertiginous black runs. Reach it by linking the **Télécabine de Planpraz** (☎04 50 53 22 75; www.compagniedumontblanc.co.uk; 29 rue Henriette d'Angeville; adult/child return €30.50/25.90; ⌚from 8.50am Dec-Apr, Jun-Sep & late Oct-Nov), 400m west of the tourist office, with the **Téléphérique du Brévent** (www.compagniedumontblanc.co.uk; 29 rue Henriette d'Angeville; adult/child one way €23/19.60, return €31/26.40; ⌚mid-Dec–mid-Apr & mid-Jun–mid-Sep). Plenty of family-friendly trails begin at **Planpraz** (2000m), and the Liaison cable car connects to the adjacent ski fields of La Flégère.

Mer de Glace VIEWPOINT

France's largest glacier, the 200m-deep 'Sea of Ice', flows 7km down the northern side of Mont Blanc, moving up to 1cm an hour (about 90m a year). The **Train du Montenvers** (☎04 50 53 22 75; www.compagniedumont-blanc.fr; 35 place de la Mer de Glace; adult/child return €31/26.40; ⏰10am-4.30pm), a picturesque, 5km-long cog railway opened in 1909, links Gare du Montenvers with Montenvers (1913m), from where a cable car takes you down to the glacier and the **Grotte de Glace** (⏰closed last half of May & late Sep–mid-Oct). Your ticket also gets you into the Glaciorium, which looks at the birth, life and future of glaciers.

Activities

The ski season runs from mid-December to mid-April. Summer activities – hiking, canyoning, mountaineering etc – generally start in June and end in September. The **Compagnie des Guides de Chamonix** (☎04 50 53 00 88; www.chamonix-guides.com; 190 place de l'Église, Maison de la Montagne; ⏰8.30am-noon & 2.30-7.30pm, closed Sun & Mon late Apr–mid-Jun & mid-Sep–mid-Dec) is the most famous of all the guide companies and has guides for virtually every activity, whatever the season.

Sleeping

★**Hôtel Richemond** HOTEL €€

(☎04 50 53 08 85; www.richemond.fr; 228 rue du Docteur Paccard; s/d/tr €66/103/136; ⏰mid-Dec–mid-Apr & mid-Jun–mid-Sep; 📶) In a grand old building constructed in 1914 (and run by the same family ever since), this hotel – as friendly as it is central – has 52 spacious rooms with views of either Mont Blanc or Le Brévent; some are pleasantly old-fashioned (retaining original furniture and cast-iron bath-tubs), others are recently renovated in white, black and beige. Outstanding value.

★**Hôtel Aiguille du Midi** HOTEL €€

(☎04 50 53 00 65; www.hotel-aiguilledumidi.com; 479 chemin Napoléon, Les Bossons; d €77-158, q €198; ⏰mid-Dec–early Apr & mid-May–Sep; 📶🏊) Run by the same family since 1908, this welcoming hotel has stunning views of the Aiguille du Midi and Mont Blanc. There are 39 cosy, pine-panelled rooms, an outdoor heated pool and a clay tennis court for summer fun, and a very good restaurant, accessible on half-board packages. Bus and train stops to Chamonix are right around the corner.

Eating

Hibou Deli DELI €

(☎04 50 96 65 13; www.hibou-chamonix.com; 416 rue Joseph Vallot; mains €8-10; ⏰11am-9pm mid-Dec–early May & mid-Jun–early Oct; 🖉) This tiny shopfront kitchen, owned by a British chef, pumps out fantastic Asian and North African–inflected dishes to takeaway. The lamb *mechoui* is rubbed with spices and cooked over 24 hours to an almost buttery consistency, the Bangkok chicken is fragrant with limes leaves and coconut, and there's always plenty of veggie options and an interesting *plat de jour*.

★**Le Cap Horn** MODERN FRENCH €€

(☎04 50 21 80 80; www.caphorn-chamonix.com; 78 rue des Moulins; menus lunch €20, dinner €32-39; ⏰noon-3pm & 7-10.30pm) Housed in a gorgeous, two-storey chalet decorated with model sailing boats – joint homage to the Alps and Cape Horn – this highly praised restaurant, opened in 2012, serves French and Asian-inflected dishes such as pan-seared duck breast with honey and soy sauce, fisherman's stew and, for dessert, *soufflé au Grand Marnier*. Reserve for dinner Friday and Saturday in winter and summer.

Munchie FUSION €€

(☎04 50 53 45 41; www.munchie.eu; 87 rue des Moulins; mains €22-24; ⏰7pm-2am winter & summer) Franco-Asian-Scandinavian fusion may not be a tried-and-true recipe for success, but this casual, Swedish-skippered restaurant has been making diners happy since 1997. Dishes such as Sichuan-spiced lamb tataki, Japanese coconut rice with egg-yolk confit and Thai 'pesto', and cod with ash and leek are so popular that reservations are recommended during the ski season.

Drinking & Nightlife

★**MBC** MICROBREWERY

(Micro Brasserie de Chamonix; ☎04 50 53 61 59; www.mbchx.com; 350 rte du Bouchet; ⏰4pm-2am winter & summer, to 1am spring & autumn) Run by the last man standing of four Canadian founders, this buzzing microbrewery is one of Chamonix' most unpretentious and gregarious watering holes. Be it with their phenomenal burgers (€10 to €15), chilli-licked wings (12 for €5.25 – half-price – on Monday), live music (from 9pm) or great craft beer, MBC delivers. It's busiest from 5pm to 11pm.

Chambre Neuf BAR

(☎04 50 53 00 31; www.hotelgustavia.eu; 272 av Michel Croz; ⏲7am-1am; 📶) Chamonix' most spirited après-ski party (4pm to 8pm), fuelled by a Swedish band and dancing on the tables, spills out the front door of Chambre Neuf. Wildly popular with seasonal workers, it opens its terrace in spring.

Jekyll & Hyde PUB

(☎04 50 55 99 70; www.thejekyll.com; 71 rte des Pélerins, Chamonix Sud; ⏲4pm-2am Mon-Fri, opens earlier Sat & Sun; 📶) This British-owned après-ski mainstay has a split personality: upstairs the 'Jekyll' has really good pub food (try the steak-and-Guinness pie), live music (Wednesday, Thursday and Sunday from 9.30pm) and DJs; downstairs, the 'Hyde' is cosier and more relaxed. Both have good Irish beer and a friendly vibe, and can be found 350m southwest of the Téléphérique de l'Aiguille du Midi.

ℹ Information

Tourist Office (☎04 50 53 00 24; www.chamonix.com; 85 place du Triangle de l'Amitié; ⏲8.30am-7pm winter & summer, 9am-12.30pm & 2-6pm in low season; 📶) The tourist office has information on accommodation (including various types of B&Bs and *gîtes* in the valley), activities, weather and cultural events.

ℹ Getting There & Away

BUS

Chamonix' **bus station** (☎04 50 53 01 15; 234 av Courmayeur, Chamonix Sud; ⏲8am-noon & 1.15-6.30pm in winter, shorter hours rest of year) has moved to av Courmayeur, Chamonix Sud.

Geneva, Switzerland (airport and bus station) One way/return €25/50, 1½ to two hours, eight daily in winter, six at other times. Operated by **Starshipper** (☎04 56 12 40 59; www.starshipper.com).

Courmayeur, Italy One way/return €15/21, 45 minutes, four daily. Run by **Savda** (☎+39 01 65 36 70 11; www.savda.it), with onward connections to Aosta and Milan.

TRAIN

The scenic, narrow-gauge **Mont Blanc Express** glides from St-Gervais-Le-Fayet to the Swiss town of Martigny, taking in Les Houches, Chamonix, Argentière and Vallorcine en route.

From St-Gervais-Le-Fayet, there are somewhat infrequent trains to cities around France, often with a change in Bellegarde or Annecy.

Annecy €15.70, 1½ hours, 12 daily

Lyon €36.60, 3½ to five hours, 10 daily

Paris €98.50 to €128, 4¾ to seven hours, 11 daily

THE DORDOGNE

Tucked in the country's southwestern corner, the Dordogne fuses history, culture and culinary sophistication in one unforgettably scenic package. The region is best known for its sturdy *bastides* (fortified towns), clifftop châteaux and spectacular prehistoric cave paintings.

Sarlat-La-Canéda

POP 9414

A picturesque tangle of honey-coloured buildings and medieval architecture, Sarlat-La-Canéda is incredibly scenic and perennially popular with visitors.

Sights

Part of the fun of Sarlat is getting lost in its twisting alleyways and backstreets. **Rue Jean-Jacques Rousseau** and **rue Landry** are good starting points, but for the grandest buildings and *hôtels particuliers* explore **rue des Consuls**.

★**Weekly Markets** MARKET

(place de la Liberté & rue de la République; ⏲8.30am-1pm Wed, 8.30am-6pm Sat) For an introductory French market experience, visit Sarlat's heavily touristed Saturday market, which takes over the streets around Cathédrale St-Sacerdos. Depending on the season, delicacies include local mushrooms and duck- and goose-based products such as foie gras. The Wednesday version is a smaller affair. An atmospheric largely organic **night market** (⏲6-10pm) operates on Thursdays.

★**Église Ste-Marie** CHURCH, MARKET

(place de la Liberté) Église Ste-Marie was ingeniously converted by acclaimed architect Jean Nouvel, whose parents still live in Sarlat, into the town's touristy **Marché Couvert** (Covered Market; ⏲8.30am-2pm daily mid-Apr–mid-Nov, closed Mon, Thu & Sun rest of year).

DON'T MISS

PREHISTORIC CAVE ART

The Vézère Valley is littered with some of the most spectacular prehistoric cave art anywhere in Europe, spread over some 175 known sites. The most famous of all is **Grotte de Lascaux**, 2km from Montignac, which features the largest collection of paintings ever discovered. The original cave was closed in 1963 to prevent damage, but in December 2016, an amazing, millimetre-perfect facsimile was opened just a few steps from the site of the original cave. Known as **Lascaux IV** (05 53 50 15 63, reservations 05 53 05 65 60; Montignac; www.lascaux.fr; adult/child €16/10.40; 9am-10pm Jul & Aug, 9.30am-8pm Apr-Jun & Sep,10am-5pm rest of the year), it uses the latest laser technology to re-create the rock paintings in what feels like a real cave – complete with muffled sounds, semi-darkness, damp smells, prehistoric fauna and all.

Several other caves around the valley remain open to the public. Visitor numbers are limited, so you'll need to reserve well ahead.

Grotte de Font de Gaume (05 53 06 86 00; www.eyzies.monuments-nationaux.fr; 4 av des Grottes; adult/child €7.50/free; guided tours 9.30am-5.30pm Sun-Fri mid-May–mid-Sep, 9.30am-12.30pm & 2-5.30pm Sun-Fri mid-Sep–mid-May) About 14,000 years ago, prehistoric artists created the gallery of over 230 figures, including bison, reindeer, horses, mammoths, bears and wolves, of which 25 are on permanent display. Located about 1km northeast of LEs Eyzies.

Abri du Cap Blanc (05 53 06 86 00; www.eyzies.monuments-nationaux.fr; adult/child €7.50/free; guided tours 10am-6pm Sun-Fri mid-May–mid-Sep, 10am-12.30pm & 2-5.30pm Sun-Fri mid-Sep–mid-May) Showcases an unusual sculpture gallery of horses, bison and deer. It's 7km east of Les Eyzies.

Grotte de Rouffignac (05 53 05 41 71; www.grottederouffignac.fr; Rouffignac-St-Cernin-de-Reilhac; adult/child €7.50/4.80; 9-11.30am & 2-6pm Jul & Aug, 10-11.30am & 2-5pm Apr-Jun, Sep & Oct, closed Nov-Mar) Sometimes known as the 'Cave of 100 Mammoths' because of its painted mammoths. Access to the caves, hidden in woodland 15km north of Les Eyzies, is aboard a trundling electric train.

Its panoramic lift offers 360-degree views across Sarlat's countryside.

Sleeping

★La Maison des Peyrat HOTEL €€
(05 53 59 00 32; www.maisondespeyrat.com; Le Lac de la Plane; r €70-112) This beautifully renovated 17th-century house, formerly a nuns' hospital and later an aristocratic hunting lodge, is set on a hill about 1.5km from Sarlat centre. Eleven generously sized rooms are decorated in modern farmhouse style; the best have views over gardens and the countryside beyond. Good restaurant, too.

★Villa des Consuls B&B €€
(05 53 31 90 05; www.villaconsuls.fr; 3 rue Jean-Jacques Rousseau; d €95-110, apt €150-190;) Despite its Renaissance exterior, the enormous rooms here are modern through and through, with shiny wood floors and sleek furnishings. Several delightful self-contained apartments dot the town, all offering the same mix of period plushness – some also have terraces overlooking the town's rooftops.

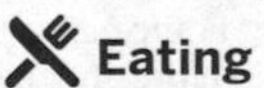

Eating

Le Petit Manoir FRENCH €€
(05 53 29 82 14; 13 rue de la République; mains €20; 12.40-2pm & 7-9pm Tue-Sun;) Book ahead for a seat in the ornate 15th-century mansion where the cuisine combines creative Dordogne specialities with a touch of Asian fusion. The Vietnamese chef creates a *menu* that changes with the seasons, and there are always vegetarian options (*menu* €27).

Le Bistrot FRENCH €€
(05 53 28 28 40; www.le-bistrot-sarlat.com; 14 place du Peyrou; menus €18-30; noon-2pm & 6.30-10pm mid-Mar–Sep) This touristy little bistro is the best of the bunch on cafe-clad place du Peyrou. The menu's heavy on Sarlat classics, especially walnuts, duck breast and finger-lickin' *pommes sarlardaises* (potatoes cooked in duck fat).

Information

Tourist Office (☎05 53 31 45 45; www.sarlat-tourisme.com; 3 rue Tourny; ⏲9am-7pm Mon-Sat, 10am-1pm & 2-6pm Sun May-Sep, shorter hours Oct-Apr; 📶) Sarlat's tourist office is packed with info, but often gets overwhelmed by visitors; the website has it all.

Getting There & Away

The **train station** (av de la Gare) is 1.3km south of the old city. Many destinations require a change at Le Buisson or Libourne.

Destinations include the following:

Bordeaux €27.70, 2¾ hours, six daily

Les Eyzies €10.10, 1½ to two hours depending on connections, four daily

Périgueux €16.30, 1½ to 2½ hours depending on connections, five daily

THE ATLANTIC COAST

With quiet country roads winding through vine-striped hills and wild stretches of coastal sands interspersed with misty islands, the Atlantic coast is where France gets back to nature. If you're a surf nut or beach bum, the sandy bays around Biarritz will be right up your alley, while oenophiles can sample the fruits of the vine in the high temple of French winemaking, Bordeaux.

Bordeaux

POP 242,945

The city of Bordeaux is among France's most exciting, vibrant and dynamic cities. In the last decade and a half, it's shed its languid, *Belle au Bois Dormant* (Sleeping Beauty) image thanks to the vision of city mayor Alain Juppé who has pedestrianised boulevards, restored neoclassical architecture, created a high-tech public transport system and reclaimed Bordeaux' former industrial wet docks at Bassin à Flots. Half the city (18 sq km) is Unesco-listed, making it the largest urban World Heritage Site; while world-class architects have designed a bevy of striking new buildings – the Herzog & de Meuron stadium (2015), decanter-shaped La Cité du Vin (2016) and Jean-Jacques Bosc bridge (2018) across the Garonne River included.

Sights

Thirsty? The 1000-sq-km wine-growing area around the city of Bordeaux is, along with Burgundy, France's most important producer of top-quality wines. Whet your palate with one of the tourist office's two-hour introductory courses (€14), or head for the nearby wine villages like St-Émilion and Pauillac, where many châteaux accept visitors.

★La Cité du Vin MUSEUM

(☎05 56 81 38 47; www.laciteduvin.com; 1 Esplanade de Pontac; adult/child €20/free; ⏲9.30am-7.30pm Apr-Oct, Tue-Sun Nov-Mar) The complex world of wine is explored in depth at ground-breaking La Cité du Vin, a stunning piece of contemporary architecture resembling a wine decanter on the banks of the River Garonne. The curvaceous gold building glitters in the sun and its 3000 sq metres of exhibits are equally sensory and sensational. Digital guides lead visitors around 20 different themed sections covering everything from vine cultivation, grape varieties and wine production to ancient wine trade, 21st-century wine trends and celebrated personalities.

Cathédrale St-André CATHEDRAL

(www.cathedrale-bordeaux.fr; place Jean Moulin; ⏲2-6pm Mon, 10am-noon & 2-6pm Tue-Sun) Lording over the city, and a Unesco World Heritage Site prior to the city's classification, the cathedral's oldest section dates from 1096; most of what you see today was built in the 13th and 14th centuries. Enjoy exceptional masonry carvings in the north portal.

Musée des Beaux-Arts GALLERY

(☎05 56 96 51 60; www.musba-bordeaux.fr; 20 cours d'Albret; adult/child €4/2; ⏲11am-6pm mid-Jul–mid-Aug, closed Tue rest of year) The evolution of Occidental art from the Renaissance to the mid-20th century is on view at Bordeaux' Museum of Fine Arts, which occupies two wings of the 1770s-built Hôtel de Ville, either side of elegant city park Jardin de la Mairie. The museum was established in 1801; highlights include 17th-century Flemish, Dutch and Italian paintings. Temporary exhibitions are regularly hosted at its nearby annexe, **Galerie des Beaux-Arts** (place du Colonel Raynal; adult/child €6.50/3.50; ⏲11am-6pm mid-Jul–mid-Aug, closed Tue rest of year).

Sleeping

Chez Dupont B&B €€

(☎05 56 81 49 59; www.chez-dupont.com; 45 rue Notre Dame; s/d from €85/100) Five impeccably decorated rooms, peppered with a wonderful collection of vintage curiosities, inspires love at first sight at this thoroughly contemporary, design-driven B&B in the trendy former wine-merchant quarter of Chartrons. Across the road from, and run by, the bistro of the same name, Chez Dupont is one of the best deals in town.

La Maison du Lierre BOUTIQUE HOTEL €€
(☎05 56 51 92 71; www.hotel-maisondulierre-bordeaux.com; 57 rue Huguerie; d €95-149; 📶) The delightfully restored 'House of Ivy' has a welcoming *chambre d'hôte* feel. A beautiful Bordelaise stone staircase (no lift) leads to small, sunlit rooms with polished floorboards, rose-printed fabrics and sparkling bathrooms. The vine-draped garden is a perfect spot to sip fresh orange juice at breakfast (€10).

★**L'Hôtel Particulier** BOUTIQUE HOTEL €€€
(☎05 57 88 28 80; www.lhotel-particulier.com; 44 rue Vital-Carles; d €189-299; 📶) Step into this fabulous boutique hotel and be wowed by period furnishings mixed with contemporary design, extravagant decorative touches and an atmospheric courtyard garden. Its five individually designed hotel rooms (breakfast €12) match up to expectations with vintage fireplaces, carved ceilings and bath-tubs with legs. Exceptional value are the suite of equally well-furnished self-catering apartments, sleeping one (€89), two (€109) or four people (€179).

Eating

Place du Parlement, rue du Pas St-Georges, rue des Faussets and place de la Victoire are loaded with dining addresses, as is the old waterfront warehouse district around quai des Marques – great for a sunset meal or drink.

★**Magasin Général** INTERNATIONAL €
(☎05 56 77 88 35; www.magasingeneral.camp; 87 quai des Queyries; 2-/3-course menu €14/18, mains €9-19; ⏲8.30am-6pm Wed-Fri, 8.30am-midnight Sat, 10am-midnight Sun, kitchen noon-2.15pm & 7-10pm; 📶) Follow the hip crowd across the river to this huge industrial hangar on the right bank, France's biggest and best organic restaurant with gargantuan terrace complete with vintage sofa seating, ping-pong table and table football. Everything here, from the vegan burgers and super-food salads to smoothies, pizzas, wine and French bistro fare, is *bio* (organic) and sourced locally. Sunday brunch (€24) is a bottomless feast.

★**Le Petit Commerce** SEAFOOD €€
(05 56 79 76 58; 22 rue Parlement St-Pierre; 2-course lunch menu €14, mains €15-25; ⏲noon-midnight) This iconic bistro, with dining rooms both sides of a narrow pedestrian street and former Michelin-starred chef Stéphane Carrade in the kitchen, is the star turn of the trendy St-Pierre quarter. It's best known for its excellent seafood *menu* that embraces everything from Arcachon sole and oysters to eels, lobsters and *chipirons* (baby squid) fresh from St-Jean de Luz.

★**Potato Head** MODERN FRENCH €€
(www.potatoheadbordeaux.com; 27 rue Buhan; mains lunch €13, dinner €18-25, 5-course tasting menu €41; ⏲11am-3pm Sun) With its eclectic mix of seating (bar stool, bistro and armchair), moss-clad vegetal wall and industrial-style lighting, this trendy bistro is a fabulous space to dine in. Throw in a creative kitchen known for surprise combos (foie gras, beetroot, ginger and chocolate, anyone?) and the finest summer garden in the city and, well, you need to reserve well in advance.

DON'T MISS

DUNE DU PILAT

This colossal sand dune (sometimes referred to as the Dune de Pyla because of its location in the resort town of Pyla-sur-Mer), 65km west of Bordeaux, stretches from the mouth of the Bassin d'Arcachon southwards for almost 3km. Already the largest in Europe, it's spreading eastwards at 4.5m a year – it has swallowed trees, a road junction and even a hotel. Take care swimming in this area: powerful currents swirl out to sea from the deceptively tranquil *baïnes* (little bays).

Although an easy day trip from Bordeaux, the area around the dune is an enjoyable place to kick back for a while. Most people camp in one of the swag of seasonal campgrounds; see www.bassin-arcachon.com.

Information

Tourist Office (05 56 00 66 00; www.bordeaux-tourisme.com; 12 cours du 30 Juillet; 9am-7.30pm Mon-Sat, 9.30am-6.30pm Sun Jul & Aug, shorter hours Sep-Jun) Runs an excellent range of city and regional tours; reserve online or in situ. It also rents pocket modems to hook you up with wi-fi. There's a small but helpful branch (05 56 91 64 70; rue Charles Domercq, Parvis Louis Armand; 9am-noon & 1-6pm Mon-Sat, 10am-noon & 1-3pm Sun Jul & Aug, shorter hours rest of year) at the train station.

Getting There & Away

AIR

Bordeaux airport (www.bordeaux.aeroport.fr) is in Mérignac, 10km west of the city centre, with domestic and international services.

TRAIN

Bordeaux is one of France's major rail-transit points. The station, **Gare St-Jean** (cours de la Marne), is about 3km from the city centre at the southern terminus of cours de la Marne.

Destinations include the following:

Nantes €52.40, five hours, three daily
Paris Gare Montparnasse €79, 3¼ hours, at least 16 daily
Poitiers €42, 1¾ hours, at least hourly
Toulouse €40 to €50, 2¼ hours, hourly

Biarritz

POP 26,000

Edge your way south along the coast towards Spain and you arrive in stylish Biarritz, just as ritzy as its name suggests. The resort took off in the mid-19th century (Napoléon III had a rather soft spot for the place) and it still shimmers with architectural treasures from the belle époque and art deco eras. Big waves – some of Europe's best – and a beachy lifestyle are a magnet for Europe's hip surfing set.

Sights & Activities

Biarritz' raison d'être is its fashionable beaches, particularly central **Grande Plage** and **Plage Miramar**, lined end to end with sunbathing bodies on hot summer days. North of Pointe St-Martin, the adrenaline-pumping surfing beaches of **Anglet** (the final 't' is pronounced) continue northwards for more than 4km. Take bus 10 or 13 from the bottom of av Verdun (just near av Édouard VII).

Chapelle Impériale CHURCH
(05 59 22 37 10; 15 rue des 100 Gardes; €3; 2.30-6pm) Built in 1864 on the instructions of Empress Eugénie, this glitzy church mixes Byzantine and Moorish styles, and the plaza in front has a great view of the Grande Plage. You can buy tickets online at the tourist office to avoid queues.

Cité de l'Océan MUSEUM
(05 59 22 75 40; www.citedelocean.com; 1 av de la Plage; adult/child/family €11.50/7.50/39, joint ticket with Musée de la Mer €18.50/13/63; 10am-10pm Jul & Aug, 10am-7pm Easter, Apr-Jun, Sep & Oct, shorter hours rest of year) Biarritz' newest sea-themed attraction is part museum, part theme park, part educational centre. It takes a fun approach to learning about the sea in all its forms – attractions range from a chance to explore a marine lab to a simulated dive into the depths in an underwater bathysphere. It's good fun, but probably more of interest to older kids.

Sleeping

Maison du Lierre HERITAGE HOTEL €€
(05 59 24 06 00; www.hotel-maisondulierre-biarritz.com; 3 av du Jardin Public; d €129-169;) What a beauty this mansion is, impressively detached, with a balcony and park view from nearly every room (apart from the very cheapest, which overlook a neighbouring building). It's elegantly simple – wooden floors, cool furnishings, rooms named after flowers – and the central staircase is a listed monument. It's not even expensive for Biarritz. Recommended.

Hôtel St-James HOTEL €€
(05 59 24 06 36; www.hotel-saintjames.com; 1 rue des Halles; s €55-105, d €65-120, tr €75-140;) This one won't suit all, but it offers some of the best value in town. It's directly above the Café du Commerce, so inevitably it's got a buzzier (read: noisier) vibe than some of the pricier places – but the simple, smart rooms and central location make it well worthy of consideration.

Eating

Bar Jean TAPAS €
(05 59 24 80 38; www.barjean-biarritz.fr; 5 rue des Halles; tapas €2-6; noon-3.30pm & 6.30pm-midnight) One of the oldest tapas venues in town (in business since the '30s), traditional and full of atmosphere – from the flamenco soundtrack to the Andalucian murals. Try

the calamari rings wrapped around a stack of lardons and drizzled in olive oil.

★ **Restaurant Le Pim'pi** FRENCH €€
(05 59 24 12 62; 14 av Verdun; menus €14-28, mains €15-18; noon-2pm Tue, noon-2pm & 7-9.30pm Wed-Sat) A small and resolutely old-fashioned place unfazed by all the razzmatazz around it. The daily specials are chalked up on a blackboard – most are of the classic French bistro style but are produced with such unusual skill and passion that many consider this one of the town's better places to eat.

Information

Tourist Office (05 59 22 37 10; www.tourisme.biarritz.fr; square d'Ixelles; 9am-7pm Jul & Aug, shorter hours rest of year) In July and August there are tourist-office annexes at the airport, train station and at the roundabout just off the Biarritz *sortie* (exit) 4 from the A63.

Getting There & Away

AIR

Biarritz-Anglet-Bayonne Airport (05 59 43 83 83; www.biarritz.aeroport.fr), 3km southeast of Biarritz, is served by several low-cost carriers.

BUS

ATCRB (09 70 80 90 74; www.transports-atcrb.com) line 816 buses travel down the coast to St-Jean de Luz, Urrugne and Hendaye. The fare is a flat-rate €2, and buses leave from the **stop** just near the tourist office beside square d'Ixelles.

Buses to Spain, including San Sebastián and Bilbao, also depart from the same stop.

TRAIN

Biarritz-La Négresse train station, 3km south of town, is linked to the centre by bus A1.

TGVs run direct to Paris Gare Montparnasse (€69 to €109, five to six hours, eight daily). Other destinations include Bordeaux and Toulouse. For destinations further south, trains run at least hourly including services to St-Jean de Luz (€4.50, 20 minutes) and Hendaye (€6, 28 minutes), and twice daily to Irún (€6.50, 43 minutes).

LANGUEDOC-ROUSSILLON

Languedoc-Roussillon comes in three distinct flavours: Bas-Languedoc (Lower Languedoc), land of bullfighting, rugby and robust red wines; Haut Languedoc (Upper Languedoc), a mountainous, sparsely populated terrain made for lovers of the great outdoors; and Roussillon, to the south, snug against the rugged Pyrenees and frontier to Spanish Catalonia.

Languedoc's traditional centre, Toulouse, was shaved off when regional boundaries were redrawn almost half a century ago, but we've chosen to include it in this section.

Toulouse

POP 458,298

Elegantly set at the confluence of the Canal du Midi and the Garonne River , this vibrant southern city – nicknamed *la ville rose* (the pink city) after the distinctive hot-pink stone used in many buildings – is one of France's liveliest metropolises. Busy, buzzy and bustling with students, this riverside dame has a history stretching back over 2000 years and has been a hub for the aerospace industry since the 1930s. With a thriving cafe and cultural scene, a wealth of impressive *hôtels particuliers* and an enormously atmospheric old quarter, France's fourth-largest city is one place where you'll love to linger.

Sights & Activities

Place du Capitole SQUARE
Toulouse's magnificent main square is the city's literal and metaphorical heart, where Toulousiens turn out en masse on sunny evenings to sip a coffee or an early aperitif at a pavement cafe. On the eastern side is the 128m-long façade of the **Capitole** (place du Capitole; 8.30am-7pm Mon-Sat, 10am-7pm Sun) FREE, the city hall, built in the 1750s. Inside is the **Théâtre du Capitole**, one of France's most prestigious opera venues, and the over-the-top, late 19th-century **Salle des Illustres** (Hall of the Illustrious).

To the south of the square is the city's **Vieux Quartier** (Old Quarter), a tangle of lanes and leafy squares brimming with cafes, shops and eateries.

Musée des Augustins GALLERY
(www.augustins.org; 21 rue de Metz; adult/child €5/free; 10am-6pm Thu-Mon, to 9pm Wed) Located within a former Augustinian monastery, this fine-arts museum spans the Roman era through to the early 20th century. Echoing stairwells and high-vaulted chambers are part of the fun, but artistic highlights include the French rooms – with works by Delacroix, Ingres and Courbet – and works

by Toulouse-Lautrec and Monet, among the standouts from the 20th-century collection. Don't skip the 14th-century **cloister gardens**, with gurning gargoyle statues that seem to pose around the courtyard. Temporary exhibitions are €4 extra.

Basilique St-Sernin CHURCH
(place St-Sernin; ambulatory €2.50; ⌚8.30am-6pm Mon-Sat, to 7.30pm Sun) This well-preserved Romanesque edifice is built from golden and rose-hued stonework up to the tip of the octogonal bell tower. Entry is free, but it's worth the additional charge to explore the **ambulatory**, where marble statues stare out from alcoves in the pink brick walls. The tomb of the basilica's namesake St Sernin (also known as St Saturnin) has pride of place: he was Toulouse's first bishop and met a gruesome end when pagan priests tied him to a bull.

★Couvent des Jacobins CHURCH, MONASTERY
(www.jacobins.mairie-toulouse.fr; rue Lakanal; cloister adult/child €4/2; ⌚9am-6pm Tue-Sun) Fresh from celebrating its eighth centenary, this elegant ecclesiastical structure is the mother church of the Dominican order, founded in 1215. First admire the **Église des Jacobins**' ornate stained-glass windows before wandering through the **Cloitre des Jacobins**, in which graceful russet-brick columns surround a green courtyard. Pause in chapels and side rooms along the way, like the echoing **Salle Capitulaire**, a 14th-century hall ornamented with a haloed lamb. Don't miss **Chapelle St-Antonin**, with its 14th-century ceiling frescoes showing apocalyptic scenes.

★Cité de l'Espace MUSEUM
(www.cite-espace.com; av Jean Gonord; adult €21-25.50, child €15.50-19; ⌚10am-7pm daily Jul & Aug, to 5pm or 6pm Sep-Dec & Feb-Jun, closed Mon in Feb, Mar & Sep-Dec, closed Jan; 👪) The fantastic space museum on the city's eastern outskirts brings Toulouse's illustrious aeronautical history to life through hands-on exhibits, including a moon-running simulator, a rotating pod to test your tolerance for space travel, a planetarium and an observatory, plus a vast cinema to immerse you in a space mission. The showpieces are the full-scale replicas of iconic spacecraft, including the Mars Rover and a 52m-high Ariane 5 space rocket.

Sleeping

La Petite Auberge de St-Sernin HOSTEL €
(☎09 81 26 63 00; www.lapetiteaubergedesaint-sernin.com; 17 rue d'Embarthe; dm €22, r €45-55; ❄📶) No-frills but friendly, this backpacker-filled hostel offers boxy dorm rooms of four, six and eight beds, plus a few doubles (winter only). The decor's very plain – tiled floors, bare walls – but there's a garden for barbecues, and you're only a minute's walk from the Basilique St-Sernin. Some rooms have air-conditioning; ask when you book.

★Hôtel Albert 1er HOTEL €€
(☎05 61 21 47 49; www.hotel-albert1.com; 8 rue Rivals; d €65-145; ❄📶) 🍃 The Albert's central location and eager-to-please staff are a winning combination. A palette of maroon and cream, with marble flourishes here and there, bestows a regal feel on comfortable rooms. Bathrooms are lavished with ecofriendly products. The breakfast buffet is largely organic. Some recently upgraded rooms have mod cons such as USB ports and coffee makers.

Hôtel St-Sernin BOUTIQUE HOTEL €€
(☎05 61 21 73 08; www.hotelstsernin.com; 2 rue St-Bernard; d €79-119; P📶) Red-velvet furnishings and white walls give a classic feel to this hotel's small but sleek rooms. The best rooms have floor-to-ceiling windows overlooking the Basilique St-Sernin. Ask in advance about parking; there's a limited number of on-site spaces.

Eating

Bd de Strasbourg, place St-Georges and place du Capitole are perfect spots for summer dining alfresco. Rue Pargaminières is the street for kebabs, burgers and other late-night student grub.

Faim des Haricots VEGETARIAN €
(☎05 61 22 49 25; www.lafaimdesharicots.fr; 3 rue du Puits Vert; menus €12-14; ⌚noon-3pm & 6-10pm; 🖉) With confit duck and pâté featuring prominently on restaurant menus across Toulouse, this budget vegetarian canteen provides a much-needed palate cleanser. Faim des Haricots serves everything *à volonté* (all you can eat); simply choose whether you'd prefer to tuck into salads, quiches or the dish of the day.

Les Halles Victor Hugo MARKET
(☎05 61 22 76 92; www.marchevictorhugo.fr; place Victor Hugo; ⌚7am-1.30pm Tue-Sun) The beating

heart of Toulouse's food scene is this covered market, packed with local producers busily selling cheeses, fresh pasta, meats and take-away nibbles from sushi to spicy curries. For a great-value local dining experience, join streams of hungry market-goers at one of the tiny restaurants on the 1st floor (arrive just before noon or prepare to fight for a table).

La Braisière BISTRO **€€**
(☎05 61 52 37 13; www.labraisiere.fr; 42 rue Pharaon; mains €14-22; ⊙noon-2.30pm & 6.30-10pm Mon-Sat, 6.30-11pm Sun) This carnivorous bistro flame-grills beef to perfection, lavishing fine cuts of meat with sauces from green pepper to pungent Roquefort. Right in the middle of one of Toulouse's most historic streets, its interior decorated with watercolours of the city's past, La Braisière exudes comfort and nostalgia. Come hungry.

If you can't muster the appetite for hulking steaks, adjoining **L'Annexe** serves tapas.

★**Le Genty Magre** FRENCH **€€€**
(☎05 61 21 38 60; www.legentymagre.com; 3 rue Genty Magre; mains €18-30, menu €38; ⊙12.30-2.30pm & 8-10pm Tue-Sat) Classic French cuisine is the order of the day here, but lauded chef Romain Brard has plenty of modern tricks up his sleeve, too. The dining room feels inviting, with brick walls, burnished wood and sultry lighting. It's arguably the best place in the city to try rich, traditional dishes such as *confit de canard* (duck confit) or *cassoulet* (stew).

Solides FRENCH **€€€**
(☎05 61 53 34 88; www.solides.fr; 38 rue des Polinaires; lunch menu €18, dinner menus €31-60; ⊙noon-2pm & 8-10pm Mon-Fri) Ex-contestant on French *MasterChef* Simon Carlier has two excellent restaurants in Toulouse. **Solides Comme Cochons** (☎09 67 36 58 16; 49 rue Pargaminières; mains €15-20; ⊙noon-2pm & 8-10pm Tue-Sat), a diner with a piggy focus, and his flagship, this newly renovated bistro inside the old Rotisserie des Carmes restaurant. Both showcase his imaginative, playful style. Tables here are red-hot, so book ahead.

ℹ Information

Tourist Office (☎€0.45 per min 08 92 18 01 80; www.toulouse-tourisme.com; square Charles de Gaulle; ⊙9am-7pm Mon-Sat, 10.30am-5.15pm Sun Jun-Sep, 9am-6pm Mon-Fri, 9am-12.30pm & 2-6pm Sat, 10am-12.30pm & 2-5pm Sun Oct-Mar) The modern, multilingual tourist office is housed within a spiky, 16th-century belfry on square Charles de Gaulle.

ℹ Getting There & Away

AIR

Toulouse-Blagnac Airport (TLS; www.toulouse.aeroport.fr/en), 8km northwest of the centre, has frequent domestic and European flights. A **Navette Aéroport Flybus** (Airport Shuttle; www.tisseo.fr; single/return €8/15) links it with town.

TRAIN

Gare Matabiau (bd Pierre Sémard), 1km northeast of the centre, is served by frequent TGVs to Bordeaux (€26 to €44 via TGV, two hours, 15 daily) and east to Carcassonne (€16.50 to €22, 45 minutes to 1 hour, 12 to 20 daily).

DON'T MISS

CARCASSONNE

Perched on a rocky hilltop and bristling with zigzag battlements, stout walls and spiky turrets, the fortified city of Carcassonne looks like something out of a children's storybook from afar. It's most people's perfect idea of a medieval castle, and it's undoubtedly an impressive spectacle – not to mention one of the Languedoc's biggest tourist draws.

The town's main attraction is its rampart-ringed fortress, known as La Cité. Encircled by two sets of battlements and 52 stone towers, it's topped by distinctive 'witch's hat' roofs (added by architect Viollet-le-Duc during 19th-century restorations). Inside the gates, there's a maze of cobbled lanes and courtyards to explore, now mostly lined by shops and restaurants.

Carcassonne also has one of France's oldest bridges: the Pont-Vieux, built during the 14th century.

Carcassonne is on the main train line from Toulouse (€16, 50 minutes, up to three hourly).

Nîmes

POP 154,000

This lively city boasts some of France's best-preserved classical buildings, including a famous Roman amphitheatre, although the city is most famous for its sartorial export, *serge de Nîmes* – better known to cowboys, clubbers and couturiers as denim.

Sights

A **Pass Nîmes Romaine** (adult/child €11.50/9), valid for three days, covers all three sights; buy one at the first place you visit.

★ **Les Arènes** ROMAN SITE

(www.arenes-nimes.com; place des Arènes; adult/child incl audioguide €10/8; 9am-8pm Jul & Aug, shorter hours Sep-Jun) Nîmes' twin-tiered amphitheatre is the best preserved in France. Built around 100 BC, the arena once seated 24,000 spectators and staged gladiatorial contests and public executions, and it's still an impressive venue for gigs, events and summer bullfights (during which it's closed for visits). An audioguide provides context as you explore the arena, seating areas, stairwells and corridors (known to Romans as *vomitories*), and afterwards you can view replicas of gladiatorial armour and original bullfighters' costumes in the museum.

Sleeping

Hôtel des Tuileries HOTEL €

(04 66 21 31 15; www.hoteldestuileries.com; 22 rue Roussy; d/tr/f from €72/90/115; P ❄) Nîmes' best deal is this delightful, bargain-priced 11-room hotel strolling distance from Les Arènes. Individually decorated rooms are spacious and spotless, and some have covered balconies. Breakfast costs €8. Its private parking garage (€10) is located just down the street, but there are only five car spaces, so reserve ahead.

Hôtel de l'Amphithéâtre HOTEL €€

(04 66 67 28 51; www.hoteldelamphitheatre.com; 4 rue des Arènes; s/d €70/90) Down a narrow backstreet leading away from Les Arènes, this tall town house has rooms in greys, whites and taupes, some with balconies overlooking place du Marché (light sleepers, beware: it can be noisy at night), and great buffet breakfasts (€10) including organic honey and homemade jam. It's run by an ex-pat Cornishman and his French wife.

Eating

La Petite Fadette CAFE €

(04 66 67 53 05; 34 rue du Grand Couvent; menus €10-14.50, tapas €3.30-7.50; 11am-2.30pm Mon-Wed, 11am-2.30pm & 6-10.30pm Thu-Sat) *Tartines* (open-face toasted sandwiches) such as smoked salmon or cured ham and goat's cheese, as well as huge salads, are specialities of this cosy cafe, which has a cute rococo interior lined with vintage photos, and outside tables on a small courtyard. Contemporary tapas takes over the menu of an evening: crispy duck hearts, mini burgers, courgette *frites* (fries)...

★ **Le Cerf à Moustache** BISTRO €€

(09 81 83 44 33; www.lecerfamoustache.com; 38 bd Victor Hugo; 2-/3-course menus lunch €15.80/19.90, dinner €25.90/30.90; 11.45am-2pm & 7.45-10pm Mon-Sat) The Deer with the Moustache has established itself as one of Nîmes' best bistros, with quirky decor (including reclaimed furniture and a wall of sketch-covered old books), matched by chef Julien Salem's creative take on the classics (Aveyronnais steak with St-Marcellin cream, rabbit ballotine with crushed potatoes and garlic, white-chocolate mousse with mandarin meringue) and 60 wines by the glass.

Information

Tourist Office (04 66 58 38 00; www.ot-nimes.fr; 6 rue Auguste; 9am-7.30pm Mon-Fri, 9am-7pm Sat, 10am-6pm Sun Jul & Aug, shorter hours rest of year;) There's also a seasonal annexe (04 66 58 38 00; www.ot-nimes.fr; esplanade Charles de Gaulle; 10am-5pm Jul & Aug) on esplanade Charles de Gaulle.

Getting There & Away

AIR

Aéroport de Nîmes Alès Camargue Cévennes (FNI; 04 66 70 49 49; www.aeroport-nimes.fr) 10km southeast of the city on the A54, is served only by Ryanair, which flies to/from London Luton, Liverpool, Brussels and Fez.

An airport bus (€6.50, 30 minutes) to/from the train station connects with all flights.

BUS

Edgard runs services to Pont du Gard (Line B21, €1.50, 40 minutes, hourly Monday to Saturday, two on Sunday) from the **bus station** (next to the train station).

TRAIN

TGVs run hourly to/from Paris' Gare de Lyon (€77, three hours) from the **train station** (bd Sergent Triaire).

Local destinations, with at least hourly departures, include the following:

Arles €8.80, 35 minutes

Avignon €10.60, one hour

Montpellier €9.90, 30 minutes

Pont du Gard

Southern France has some fine Roman sites, but for audacious engineering, nothing can top Unesco World Heritage Site **Pont du Gard** (☎04 66 37 50 99; www.pontdugard.fr; car & up to 5 passengers €18, after 8pm €10, by bicycle or on foot €7, after 8pm €3.50; ⏰site 24hr year-round, visitor centre & museum 9am-8pm Jul & Aug, shorter hours Sep–mid-Jan & mid-Feb–Jun), 21km northeast of Nîmes. This three-tiered aqueduct was once part of a 50km-long system of water channels, built around 19 BC to transport water from Uzès to Nîmes. The scale is huge: 48.8m high, 275m long and graced with 35 precision-built arches, the bridge was sturdy enough to carry up to 20,000 cu metres of water per day. Each block was carved by hand and transported here from nearby quarries – no mean feat, considering the largest blocks weigh over 5 tonnes.

The **Musée de la Romanité** provides background on the bridge's construction, while kids can try out educational activities in the **Ludo** play area. Nearby, the 1.4km **Mémoires de Garrigue** walking trail winds upstream through typically Mediterranean scrubland, and offers some of the best bridge views.

There are large car parks on both banks of the river, about a 400m walk from the bridge.

PROVENCE

Provence conjures up images of rolling lavender fields, blue skies, gorgeous villages, wonderful food and superb wine. It certainly delivers on all those fronts, but it's not just worth visiting for its good looks – dig a little deeper and you'll also discover the multicultural metropolis of Marseille, the artistic haven of Aix-en-Provence and the old Roman city of Arles.

Marseille

POP 858,902

Marseille grows on you with its fusion of cultures, souk-like markets, millennia-old port and *corniches* (coastal roads) along rocky inlets and sun-baked beaches. Once the butt of French jokes, the *cité phocéenne* (in reference to Phocaea, the ancient Greek city located in modern-day Turkey, from where Marseille's settlers, the Massiliots, came) is looking fabulous after its facelift as the European Capital of Culture in 2013.

Sights

★Vieux Port HISTORIC SITE

(Ⓜ Vieux Port) Ships have docked for more than 26 centuries at the city's birthplace, the colourful old port. The main commercial docks were transferred to the Joliette area north of here in the 1840s, but the old port remains a thriving harbour for fishing boats, pleasure yachts and tourists. Guarding either side of the harbour are **Fort St-Nicolas** (⏰8am-7.45pm May-Aug, shorter hours rest of year; Ⓜ Vieux Port) and **Fort St-Jean** (Ⓜ Vieux Port), founded in the 13th century by the Knights Hospitaller of St John of Jerusalem (and now home to the city's flagship MuCEM museum).

★Musée des Civilisations de l'Europe et de la Méditerranée MUSEUM

(MuCEM, Museum of European & Mediterranean Civilisations; ☎04 84 35 13 13; www.mucem.org; 7 Promenade Robert Laffont; adult/family/child incl exhibitions €9.50/14/free, 1st Sun of month free; ⏰10am-8pm Wed-Mon Jul & Aug, 11am-7pm Wed-Mon May, Jun, Sep & Oct, 11am-6pm Wed-Mon Nov-Apr; 👪; Ⓜ Vieux Port, Joliette) The icon of modern Marseille, this stunning museum explores the history, culture and civilisation of the Mediterranean region through anthropological exhibits, rotating art exhibitions and film. The collection sits in a bold, contemporary building, J4, designed by Algerian-born, Marseille-educated architect Rudi Ricciotti. It is linked by a vertigo-inducing footbridge to the 13th-century Fort St-Jean, from which there are stupendous views of the Vieux Port and the Mediterranean. The fort grounds and their gardens are free to explore.

★Villa Méditerranée MUSEUM

(www.villa-mediterranee.org; bd du Littoral, esplanade du J4; ⏰noon-6pm Tue-Fri, 10am-6pm Sat & Sun; 👪; Ⓜ Vieux Port, Joliette) FREE This eye-catching white structure next to MuCEM is no ordinary 'villa'. Designed by architect Stefano Boeri in 2013, the sleek white edifice sports a spectacular cantilever overhanging an ornamental pool. Inside, a viewing gallery with glass-panelled floor (look down if you dare!), and two or three temporary multimedia exhibitions evoke aspects of the Mediterranean, be they sea life, history or environmental. But it's the building itself that's the undisputed highlight here.

★Le Panier HISTORIC SITE

(M Vieux Port) From the Vieux Port, hike north up to this fantastic history-woven quarter, which is fabulous for a wander with its artsy ambience, cool hidden squares and sun-baked cafes. In Greek Massilia it was the site of the agora (marketplace), hence its name, which means 'the basket'. During WWII the quarter was dynamited and afterwards rebuilt. Today it's a mishmash of lanes hiding artisan shops, ateliers (workshops) and terraced houses strung with drying washing.

★Basilique Notre Dame de la Garde CHURCH

(Montée de la Bonne Mère; www.notredamedelagarde.com; rue Fort du Sanctuaire; 7am-8pm Apr-Sep, to 7pm Oct-Mar; 60) This opulent 19th-century Romano-Byzantine basilica occupies Marseille's highest point, La Garde (162m). Built between 1853 and 1864, it is ornamented with coloured marble, murals depicting the safe passage of sailing vessels and superb mosaics. The hilltop gives 360-degree panoramas of the city. The church's bell tower is crowned by a 9.7m-tall gilded statue of the Virgin Mary on a 12m-high pedestal. It's a 1km walk from the Vieux Port, or take bus 60 or the tourist train.

Château d'If ISLAND, CASTLE

(www.if.monuments-nationaux.fr; adult/child €5.50/free; 10am-6pm Apr-Oct, to 5pm rest of year) Located 3.5km west of the Vieux Port, this island fortress-prison was immortalised in Alexandre Dumas' classic 1844 novel *The Count of Monte Cristo*. Many political prisoners were incarcerated here including the Revolutionary hero Mirabeau and the Communards of 1871. Other than the island itself there's not a great deal to see, but it's worth the trip just for the views of the Vieux Port. **Frioul If Express** (www.frioul-if-express.com; 1 quai des Belges) runs boats (€10.50 return, 20 minutes, around nine daily) from the quay.

MARSEILLE CITY PASS

The **Marseille City Pass** (www.resamarseille.com; 24/48/72hr €24/31/39) covers admission to city museums, public transport, a guided city tour, a Château d'If boat trip and more, plus other discounts. It's not necessary for children under 12, as many attractions are greatly reduced or free. Buy it online or at the tourist office.

Sleeping

★Mama Shelter DESIGN HOTEL €€

(01 43 48 48 48; www.mamashelter.com; 64 rue de la Loubière; d €79-129; ; M Notre Dame du Mont-Cours Julien) This funky mini-chain of design-forward hotels recently opened its outpost in Marseille, and if you're a cool kid in search of sexy sleeps, this is the address for you. It's all about the details here – Philippe Starck furniture, sleek white-and-chrome colour schemes, in-room iMacs. Smaller rooms are oddly shaped, though, and it's a walk from the old port.

★Hôtel St-Louis HOTEL €€

(04 91 54 02 74; www.hotel-st-louis.com; 2 rue des Récollettes; r €89-140; ; M Noailles, Canebière Garibaldi) With its balconies and curlicues, the handsome 19th-century façade of this old-style hotel sets the vintage tone for the whole place. It's full of imagination: each of the rooms has its own individual style, from flea-market chic to English cottage-cosy, and a few have little balconies.

Hotel Carré Vieux Port HOTEL €€

(04 91 33 02 33; www.hotel-carre-vieux-port.com; 6 rue Beauvau; s €99-112, d €106-119, tr €137-150;) Fresh from a comprehensive refurb, this ultra-central hotel now rates as one of the old port's top choices. It's a block from the buzzy quayside of the Vieux Port, and its rooms are bright, spacious and comfortable, with nice touches like frying-pan-sized shower heads, cube-shaped bath goodies, kettles in every room, and – er – a fibreglass bull in reception.

Eating

The Vieux Port overflows with restaurants, but choose carefully. Head to cours Julien and its surrounding streets for world cuisine.

★ Les Buffets du Vieux Port FRENCH €
(☎04 13 20 11 32; www.clubhousevieuxport.com; 158 quai du Port; adult/child menu €23/13; ⏲noon-2.30pm & 7.30-10.30pm; 👪; Ⓜ Vieux Port) What a great idea – a high-class, on trend self-service canteen, with a vast array of starters, mains, salads and desserts laid out like a banquet for diners to help themselves to. Premium cold cuts, fresh seafood, bouillabaisse, mussels, fish soup – it's all here and more. Portside tables go fast, but there's plenty of room inside.

★ Café Populaire BISTRO €€
(☎04 91 02 53 96; www.cafepopulaire.com; 110 rue Paradis; tapas €6-16, mains €17-22; ⏲noon-2.30pm & 8-11pm Tue-Sat; Ⓜ Estrangin-Préfecture) Vintage furniture, old books on the shelves and a fine collection of glass soda bottles lend a retro air to this trendy, 1950s-styled *jazz comptoir* (counter) – a restaurant despite its name. The crowd is chic and smiling chefs in the open kitchen mesmerise with daily specials like king prawns *à la plancha* (grilled) or beetroot and coriander salad.

★ L'Arome MODERN FRENCH €€
(☎04 91 42 88 80; rue de Trois Rois; mains €16-25; ⏲7.30-10pm; Ⓜ Notre Dame du Mont) The current hot tip in the trendy area around cours Julien is this tiny bistro, on a graffiti-clad street flanked by ethnic restaurants. The no-frills decor, relaxed service and focused menu of French market classics have made this diner deservedly popular. Chef-owner Romain has worked in plenty of fancy restaurants, but aims for sophisticated simplicity here. Reservations essential.

★ Le Café des Épices MODERN FRENCH €€
(☎04 91 91 22 69; www.cafedesepices.com; 4 rue du Lacydon; lunch/dinner menus from €25/45; ⏲noon-3pm & 6-11pm Tue-Fri, noon-3pm Sat; 👪; Ⓜ Vieux Port) One of Marseille's best chefs, Arnaud de Grammont infuses his cooking with a panoply of flavours: squid-ink spaghetti with sesame and perfectly cooked scallops, or coriander- and citrus-spiced potatoes topped with the catch of the day. Presentation is impeccable, the decor playful, and the colourful outdoor terrace between giant potted olive trees nothing short of superb.

Drinking & Entertainment

Options for a coffee or something stronger abound on both quays at the Vieux Port. Cafes crowd cours Honoré d'Estienne d'Orves, 1er, a large open square two blocks south of quai de Rive Neuve.

Au Petit Nice BAR
(☎04 91 48 43 04; 28 place Jean Jaurès; ⏲6.30pm-2am Tue-Sat; Ⓜ Notre Dame du Mont-Cours Julien) This popular pub has loads of beers on tap and a pleasant courtyard to chill in (note that this is *not* the hotel of the same name).

Le Montmartre CAFE
(☎04 91 56 03 24; 4 place de Lenche; mains from €6; ⏲9am-11pm; Ⓜ Vieux Port, Joliette) Place de Lenche is a lovely, small square in Le Panier with glimpses of the Vieux Port. Among several cafes here, this one captures the neighbourhood vibe and is a fine place to hang out with a drink on a lazy afternoon.

Dock des Suds LIVE MUSIC
(☎04 91 99 00 00; www.dock-des-suds.org; 12 rue Urbain V; ⏲closed Aug; Ⓜ National, 🚊 Arenc

WORTH A TRIP

LES CALANQUES

Marseille abuts the wild and spectacular **Parc National des Calanques** (www.calanques-parcnational.fr), a 20km stretch of high, rocky promontories, rising from brilliant-turquoise Mediterranean waters.

The sheer cliffs are occasionally interrupted by small idyllic beaches, some impossible to reach without a kayak. Amongst the most famous are the calanques of Sormiou, Port-Miou, Port-Pin and En-Vau.

October to June, the best way to see the Calanques is to hike and the best access is from the small town of Cassis. The **tourist office** (☎08 92 39 01 03; www.ot-cassis.com; quai des Moulins; ⏲9am-7pm Mon-Sat, 9.30am-12.30pm & 3-6pm Sun Jul & Aug, shorter hours rest of year; 📶) has maps. In July and August, trails close because of fire danger: take a boat tour from Marseille or Cassis; sea kayak with **Raskas Kayak** (☎04 91 73 27 16; www.raskas-kayak.com; Marseille; half-/full day €35/65); drive; or take a bus.

le Silo) Eclectic live music in a large venue in the Joliette neighbourhood north of the Vieux Port.

Tourist Information

Tourist Office (04 91 13 89 00; www.marseille-tourisme.com; 11 La Canebière; 9am-7pm Mon-Sat, 10am-5pm Sun; M Vieux Port) Has plenty of information about the city and the Calanques.

Getting There & Away

AIR

Aéroport Marseille-Provence (Aéroport Marseille-Marignane; MRS; 04 42 14 14 14; www.marseille.aeroport.fr) is located 25km northwest of Marseille in Marignane. There are regular year-round flights to nearly all major French cities, plus major conurbations in the UK, Germany, Belgium, Italy and Spain.

Navette Marseille (www.navettemarseille-aeroport.com; 4.30am-11.30pm) buses link the airport and Gare St-Charles (adult/child €8.20/4.10) every 15 to 20 minutes.

The airport's train station has direct services to several cities including Arles and Avignon; a free shuttle bus runs to/from the airport terminal.

BOAT

The **passenger ferry terminal** (www.marseille-port.fr; M Joliette) is 250m south of place de la Joliette, 1er. **SNCM** (08 91 70 18 01; www.sncm.fr; 61 bd des Dames; M Joliette) boats sail to Corsica, Sardinia and North Africa.

TRAIN

Eurostar (www.eurostar.com) has services one to five times weekly between Marseille and London (from €99, 6½ hours) via Avignon and Lyon. As always, the earlier you book, the cheaper the potential fare.

Regular and TGV trains serve **Gare St-Charles** (ticket office 5.15am-10pm; M Gare St-Charles SNCF), which is a junction for both metro lines. The **left-luggage office** (8.15am-9pm) is next to platform A. Sample fares:

Avignon €17 to €20.50, 35 minutes

Nice €28, 2½ hours

Paris Gare de Lyon from €75, three hours on TGV

Getting Around

Marseille has two metro lines, two tram lines and an extensive bus network, all run by **RTM** (04 91 91 92 10; www.rtm.fr; 6 rue des Fabres; 8.30am-6pm Mon-Fri, 8.30am-noon & 1-4.30pm Sat; M Vieux Port), where you can obtain information and transport tickets (€1.60).

Pick up a bike from 100-plus stations across the city with **Le Vélo** (www.levelo-mpm.fr).

Aix-en-Provence

POP 145,300

Aix-en-Provence is to Provence what the Left Bank is to Paris: a pocket of bohemian chic crawling with students. It's hard to believe that 'Aix' (pronounced ex) is just 25km from chaotic, exotic Marseille. The city has been a cultural centre since the Middle Ages (two of the town's most famous sons are painter Paul Cézanne and novelist Émile Zola), but for all its polish, it's still a laid-back Provençal town at heart.

Sights

A stroller's paradise, Aix highlight is the mostly pedestrian old city, **Vieil Aix**. South of cours Mirabeau, the **Quartier Mazarin** was laid out in the 17th century, and is home to some of Aix finest buildings.

★Musée Granet MUSEUM
(04 42 52 88 32; www.museegranet-aixenprovence.fr; place St-Jean de Malte; adult/child €5/free; 11am-7pm Tue-Sun) This fabulous art museum sits right near the top of France's artistic must-sees, housing works by some of the most iconic artists associated with Provence, including Picasso, Léger, Matisse, Monet, Klee, Van Gogh and, perhaps most importantly of all in Aix, nine works by local boy Cézanne. The collection is named after the Provençal painter François Marius Granet (1775–1849), who donated a large number of works, and housed inside a dramatic 17th-century priory.

★Caumont Centre d'Art HISTORIC BUILDING
(04 42 20 70 01; www.caumont-centredart.com; 3 rue Joseph Cabassol; temporary exhibitions €8.50-11; 10am-7pm May-Sep, to 6pm Oct-Apr) Aix' newest pride and joy is also one of its oldest: a stellar art space housed inside the Mazarin Quarter's grandest 17th-century *hôtel particulier*. There are three exhibitions every year exploring the region's rich artistic and cultural heritage, but it's the building itself that's the star of the show. Built from honey-coloured stone, its palatial rooms are stuffed with antiques and objets d'art that illustrate the aristocratic lifestyle of the house's most celebrated owner, the Marquise de Caumont.

Atelier Cézanne MUSEUM
(☎04 42 21 06 53; www.atelier-cezanne.com; 9 av Paul Cézanne; adult/child €6/free; ⊙10am-6pm Jul & Aug, shorter hours Sep-Jun) Cézanne's last studio, 1.5km north of the tourist office on a hilltop, was painstakingly preserved (and re-created: not all the tools and still-life models strewn around the room were his) as it was at the time of this death. Though the studio is inspiring, none of his works hang there. Take bus 1 or 20 to the Atelier Cézanne stop or walk from town.

Sleeping

Hôtel Cardinal HOTEL €
(☎04 42 38 32 30; www.hotel-cardinal-aix.com; 24 rue Cardinale; s €69, d €79-119;) Pleasantly removed from the hustle and bustle of central Aix, this quaint Mazarin Quarter hotel is surprisingly elegant considering the price, with heritage rooms featuring original fireplaces, antiques and a surfeit of swag curtains. There are also six large suites in the annexe up the street, each with a kitchenette and dining room – ideal for longer stays.

★**L'Épicerie** B&B €€
(☎06 08 85 38 68; www.unechambreenville.eu; 12 rue du Cancel; d €100-140;) This intimate B&B on a backstreet in Vieil Aix is the creation of born-and-bred Aixois lad Luc. His breakfast room re-creates a 1950s grocery store, and the flowery garden out the back is perfect for excellent evening dining and weekend brunch (book ahead for both). Breakfast is a veritable feast. Two rooms accommodate families of four.

Eating

★**Farinoman Fou** BAKERY €
(www.farinomanfou.fr; 3 rue Mignet; breads €1-3; ⊙7am-7pm Tue-Sat) Tucked just off place des Prêcheurs is this truly phenomenal bakery, with a constant queue outside its door. The different crunchy breads baked by artisanal *boulanger* Benoît Fradette are reason enough to sell up and move to Aix. The bakery has no shop as such; customers jostle for space with bread ovens and dough-mixing tubs.

★**Le Petit Verdot** FRENCH €€
(☎04 42 27 30 12; www.lepetitverdot.fr; 7 rue d'Entrecasteaux; mains €19-25; ⊙7pm-midnight Mon-Sat) Great Provençal food and great Provençal wines – really, what more do you want from a meal in this part of France? It's all about hearty, honest dining here, with table tops made out of old wine crates, and a lively chef-patron who runs the place with huge enthusiasm. Expect slow-braised meats, seasonal veg, sinful desserts and some super wines to go with.

Information

Tourist Office (☎04 42 16 11 61; www.aixenprovencetourism.com; 300 av Giuseppe Verdi; ⊙8.30am-7pm Mon-Sat, 10am-1pm & 2-6pm Sun, to 8pm Mon-Sat Jun-Sep;) Sells tickets for guided tours and events.

Getting There & Away

BUS

Aix' **bus station** (☎08 91 02 40 25, 04 42 91 26 80; place Marius Bastard) is a 10-minute walk southwest from La Rotonde. Sunday service is limited.

Avignon Line 23, €17.40, 1¼ hours, six daily

Marseille Line 20, €5.60, 25 minutes, every 10 minutes, five daily, three on Sunday

Nice Line 20, €29.40, 3¼ hours, five daily, three on Sunday

TRAIN

The **city centre train station**, at the southern end of av Victor Hugo, serves Marseille (€6.50, 45 minutes).

Aix' **TGV station**, 15km from the centre, is a stop on the high-speed Paris–Marseille line. Bus 40 runs from the TGV station to Aix' bus station (€4.10, 15 minutes, every 15 minutes).

Avignon

POP 91,250

Hooped by 4.3km of superbly preserved stone ramparts, this graceful city is the belle of Provence's ball. Its turn as the papal seat of power has bestowed Avignon with a treasury of magnificent art and architecture, none grander than the massive medieval fortress and papal palace, the Palais des Papes. Famed for its annual performing arts festival, these days Avignon is a lively student city and an ideal spot from which to step out into the surrounding region.

Sights

★**Palais des Papes** PALACE
(Papal Palace; www.palais-des-papes.com; place du Palais; adult/child €11/9, with Pont St-Bénezet €13.50/10.50; ⊙9am-8pm Jul, to 8.30pm Aug, shorter hours Sep-Jun) The largest Gothic palace ever built, the Palais des Papes was

WORTH A TRIP

VAN GOGH'S ARLES

If the winding streets and colourful houses of Arles seem familiar, it's hardly surprising – Vincent van Gogh lived here for much of his life in a yellow house on place Lamartine, and the town regularly featured in his canvases. His original house was destroyed during WWII, but you can still follow in Vincent's footsteps on the evocative **Van Gogh walking circuit** – the **tourist office** (☎04 90 18 41 20; www.arlestourisme.com; esplanade Charles de Gaulle, Blvd des Lices; ⏲9am-6.45pm Apr-Sep, 9am-4.45pm or 5.45pm Mon-Fri, 10am-1pm Sun Oct-Mar; 📶) sells maps (€1). You won't see many of the artist's masterpieces in Arles, however, although the modern art gallery **Fondation Vincent Van Gogh** (☎04 90 49 94 04; www.fondation-vincentvangogh-arles.org; 35ter rue du Docteur Fanton; adult/child €9/4; ⏲11am-7pm Tue-Sun Apr–mid-Sep, to 6pm mid-Sep–Mar) always has one on show, as well as contemporary exhibitions inspired by the Impressionist.

Two millennia ago, Arles was a major Roman settlement. The town's 20,000-seat amphitheatre, known as the **Arènes** (Amphithéâtre; ☎08 91 70 03 70; www.arenes-arles.com; Rond-Point des Arènes; adult/child €6/free, incl Théâtre Antique €9/free; ⏲9am-8pm Jul & Aug, to 7pm May, Jun & Sep, shorter hours Oct-Apr), is nowadays used for bullfights.

There are buses to/from Aix-en-Provence (€11, 1½ hours) and regular trains to/from Nîmes (€7.50, 30 minutes), Marseille (€13, 55 minutes) and Avignon (€6, 20 minutes).

erected by Pope Clement V, who abandoned Rome in 1309 as a result of violent disorder following his election. It served as the seat of papal power for seven decades, and its immense scale provides ample testament to the medieval might of the Roman Catholic church. Ringed by 3m-thick walls, its cavernous halls, chapels and antechambers are largely bare today, but an audioguide (€2) provides a useful backstory.

★Pont St-Bénezet BRIDGE
(bd du Rhône; adult/child 24hr ticket €5/4, with Palais des Papes €13.50/10.50; ⏲9am-8pm Jul, to 8.30pm Aug, shorter hours Sep-Jun) Legend says Pastor Bénezet had three saintly visions urging him to build a bridge across the Rhône. Completed in 1185, the 900m-long bridge with 20 arches linked Avignon with Villeneuve-lès-Avignon. It was rebuilt several times before all but four of its spans were washed away in the 1600s.

If you don't want to pay to visit the bridge, admire it for free from Rocher des Doms park or Pont Édouard Daladier or on Île de la Barthelasse's chemin des Berges.

Festivals & Events

Hundreds of artists take to the stage and streets during the world-famous **Festival d'Avignon** (www.festival-avignon.com; ⏲Jul) and the fringe **Festival Off** (www.avignonleoff.com; ⏲Jul), held early July to early August.

Sleeping

Les Jardins de Baracane B&B €€
(☎06 11 14 88 54; www.lesjardinsdebaracane.fr; 12 rue Baracane; r €125-205; P❄📶🏊) This 18th-century house near place des Corps-Saints is owned by an architect, so it's been sensitively and tastefully renovated. Wood beams, stone walls and period detailing feature in all rooms, but the best are the two suites, which are posh enough for a pope. There's a great pool, and breakfast is served in the garden under a huge wisteria tree.

Hotel Central HOTEL €€
(☎04 90 86 07 81; www.hotel-central-avignon.com; 31 rue de la République; d €89-119) As its name suggests, this efficient hotel is right in the heart of things, smack bang beside the main thoroughfare of rue de la Republique. It's modern throughout, with smallish but smart rooms, minimal clutter, and tasteful tones of cream and slate predominating, although a few rooms are more floral in style. The interior breakfast courtyard is a boon.

Hôtel de l'Horloge HOTEL €€
(☎04 90 16 42 00; www.hotels-ocre-azur.com; place de l'Horloge; d €130-220; ❄📶) A refined choice: a spacious and well-run hotel in a lovely building near the town hall just off Avignon's main thoroughfare. The decor is fairly standard – beige walls, tasteful prints – but the terrace rooms are worth the extra for their knockout views (room 505 overlooks the Palais des Papes).

Eating

Maison Violette BAKERY €
(☎ 06 59 44 62 94; place des Corps Saints; ⊙ 7am-7.30pm Mon-Sat) We simply defy you to walk into this bakery and not instantly be tempted by the stacks of baguettes, *ficelles* and *pains de campagnes* loaded up on the counter, not to mention the orderly ranks of éclairs, *millefeuilles,* fruit tarts and cookies lined up irresistibly behind the glass. Go on, a little bit of what you fancy does you good, *non*?

★ **Restaurant L'Essentiel** FRENCH €€
(☎ 04 90 85 87 12; www.restaurantlessentiel.com; 2 rue Petite Fusterie; menus €32-46; ⊙ noon-2pm & 7-9.45pm Tue-Sat) Snug in an elegant, caramel-stone *hôtel particulier,* the Essential is one of the finest places to eat in town – inside or in the wonderful courtyard garden. Begin with courgette flowers poached in a crayfish and truffle sauce, then continue with rabbit stuffed with candied aubergine, perhaps.

L'Épicerie BISTRO €€
(☎ 04 90 82 74 22; www.restaurantlepicerie.fr; 10 place St-Pierre; lunch/dinner menus from €16/23; ⊙ noon-2.30pm & 8-10pm) Traditional and unashamedly so, this cosy bistro is a fine spot for hearty French dishes, from homemade foie gras to a mixed platter of Provençal produce (€19). All the bistro boxes receive a big tick: checked tablecloths, vintage signs, friendly waiters, great local wines by the glass.

Information

Tourist Office (☎ 04 32 74 32 74; www.avignon-tourisme.com; 41 cours Jean Jaurès; ⊙ 9am-6pm Mon-Sat, 10am-5pm Sun Apr-Oct, shorter hours Nov-Mar) Offers a range of excellent guided walking tours covering the town's history, architecture and papal buildings. It can also book tickets for boat trips on the Rhône and wine-tasting trips to nearby vineyards.

Getting There & Away

BUS

The **bus station** (bd St-Roch; ⊙ information window 8am-7pm Mon-Fri, to 1pm Sat) is next to the central train station.

Destinations include the following:

Aix-en-Provence €17.40, LER Line 23, 1¼ hours, six daily Monday to Saturday, two on Sunday

Arles €7.10, LER Line 18, 50 minutes, at least seven daily

TRAIN

Avignon has two train stations: **Gare Avignon Centre** (42 bd St-Roch), on the southern edge of the walled town, and **Gare Avignon TGV** (Courtine), 4km southwest in Courtine. Local shuttle trains link the two every 20 minutes (€1.60, five minutes, 6am to 11pm). Note that there is no luggage storage at the train station.

Destinations served by TGV include Paris Gare du Lyon (€35 to €80, 3½ hours), Marseille (€17.50, 35 minutes) and Nice (€31 to €40, 3¼ hours).

THE FRENCH RIVIERA & MONACO

With its glistening seas, idyllic beaches and fabulous weather, the French Riviera (Côte d'Azur in French) screams exclusivity, extravagance and excess. It has been a favourite getaway for the European jet set since Victorian times and there is nowhere more chichi or glam in France than St-Tropez, Cannes and super-rich, sovereign Monaco.

Nice

POP 343,000

Riviera queen Nice is what good living is all about – shimmering shores, the very best of Mediterranean food, a unique historical heritage, free museums, a charming old town, exceptional art and alpine wilderness within an hour's drive.

Sights & Activities

★ **Promenade des Anglais** ARCHITECTURE
The most famous stretch of seafront in Nice – if not France – is this vast paved promenade, which gets its name from the English expat patrons who paid for it in 1822. It runs for the whole 4km sweep of the Baie des Anges with a dedicated lane for cyclists and skaters; if you fancy joining them, you can rent skates, scooters and bikes from **Roller Station** (☎ 04 93 62 99 05; www.roller-station.fr; 49 quai des États-Unis; skates, boards & scooters per hr/day €5/10, bicycles €5/15; ⊙ 9am-8pm Jul & Aug, 10am-7pm Sep-Jun).

★ **Vieux Nice** HISTORIC SITE
Getting lost among the dark, narrow, winding alleyways of Nice's old town is a highlight. The layout has barely changed since

the 1700s, and it's now packed with delis, restaurants, boutiques and bars, but the centrepiece remains **cours Saleya**: a massive market square that's permanently thronging in summer. The **food market** (cours Saleya; ⏲6am-1.30pm Tue-Sun) is perfect for fresh produce and foodie souvenirs, while the **flower market** is worth visiting just for the colours and fragrances. A **flea market** (cours Saleya; ⏲8am-5pm Mon) is held on Monday.

★Musée d'Art Moderne et d'Art Contemporain GALLERY
(MAMAC; ☎04 97 13 42 01; www.mamac-nice.org; place Yves Klein; ⏲10am-6pm Tue-Sun) FREE European and American avant-garde works from the 1950s to the present are the focus of this museum. Highlights include many works by Christo and Nice's New Realists: Niki de Saint Phalle, César, Arman and Yves Klein. The building's rooftop also works as an exhibition space (with knockout panoramas of Nice to boot).

Musée Matisse GALLERY
(☎04 93 81 08 08; www.musee-matisse-nice.org; 164 av des Arènes de Cimiez; ⏲10am-6pm Wed-Mon) FREE This museum, 2km north in the leafy Cimiez quarter, houses a fascinating assortment of works by Matisse, including

Nice

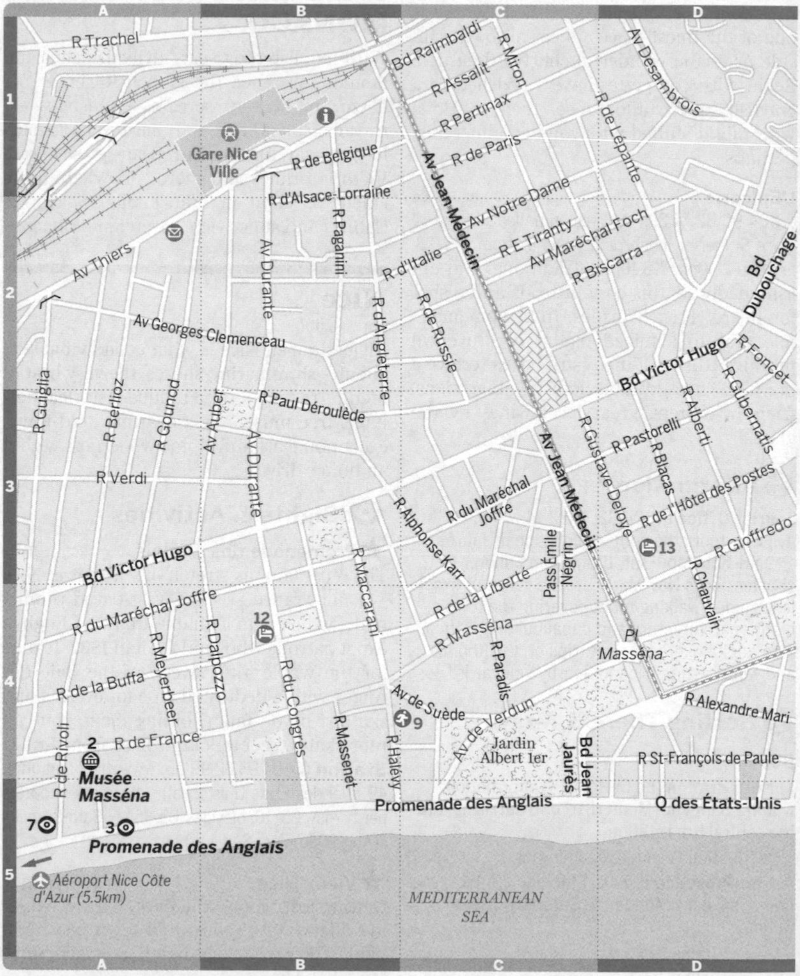

A B C D
1 2 3 4 5
R Trachel
Bd Raimbaldi
R Assalit
R Miron
Av Desambrois
R Pertinax
R de Lépante
Gare Nice Ville
R de Belgique
R de Paris
Av Jean Médecin
R d'Alsace-Lorraine
Av Notre Dame
R Paganini
R E Tiranty
Av Maréchal Foch
Av Thiers
Av Durante
R d'Italie
R Biscarra
Bd Dubouchage
R d'Angleterre
R de Russie
Av Georges Clemenceau
Bd Victor Hugo
R Foncet
R Guiglia
R Berlioz
R Gounod
Av Auber
R Paul Déroulède
R Alberti
R Gubernatis
R Gustave Deloye
R Pastorelli
R Blacas
R Verdi
R Alphonse Karr
R du Maréchal Joffre
R de l'Hôtel des Postes
13
R Gioffredo
Pass Émile Négrin
R Maccarani
R de la Liberté
R Chauvain
R du Maréchal Joffre
R Dalpozzo
12
R Masséna
Pl Masséna
R Meyerbeer
R du Congrès
R Paradis
R de la Buffa
Av de Suède
R Alexandre Mari
9
Av de Verdun
R de Rivoli
2
R de France
R Massenet
R Halévy
Jardin Albert 1er
Bd Jean Jaurès
R St-François de Paule
Musée Masséna
Promenade des Anglais
Q des États-Unis
7
3
Promenade des Anglais
Aéroport Nice Côte d'Azur (5.5km)
MEDITERRANEAN SEA

oil paintings, drawings, sculptures, tapestries and Matisse's famous paper cut-outs. The permanent collection is displayed in a red-ochre 17th-century Genoese villa in an olive grove. Temporary exhibitions are in the futuristic basement building. Matisse is buried in the **Monastère Notre Dame de Cimiez** (place du Monastère; ⌚8.30am-12.30pm & 2.30-6.30pm) cemetery, across the park from the museum.

★ **Musée Masséna** MUSEUM
(☎04 93 91 19 10; 65 rue de France; adult/child €6/free; ⌚10am-6pm Wed-Mon) Originally built as a holiday home for Prince Victor d'Essling (the grandson of one of Napoléon's favourite generals, Maréchal Massena), this lavish belle époque building is another of the city's iconic architectural landmarks. Built between 1898 and 1901 in grand neoclassical style with an Italianate twist, it's now a fascinating museum dedicated to the history of the Riviera – taking in everything from holidaying monarchs to expat Americans, the boom of tourism and the enduring importance of Carnival.

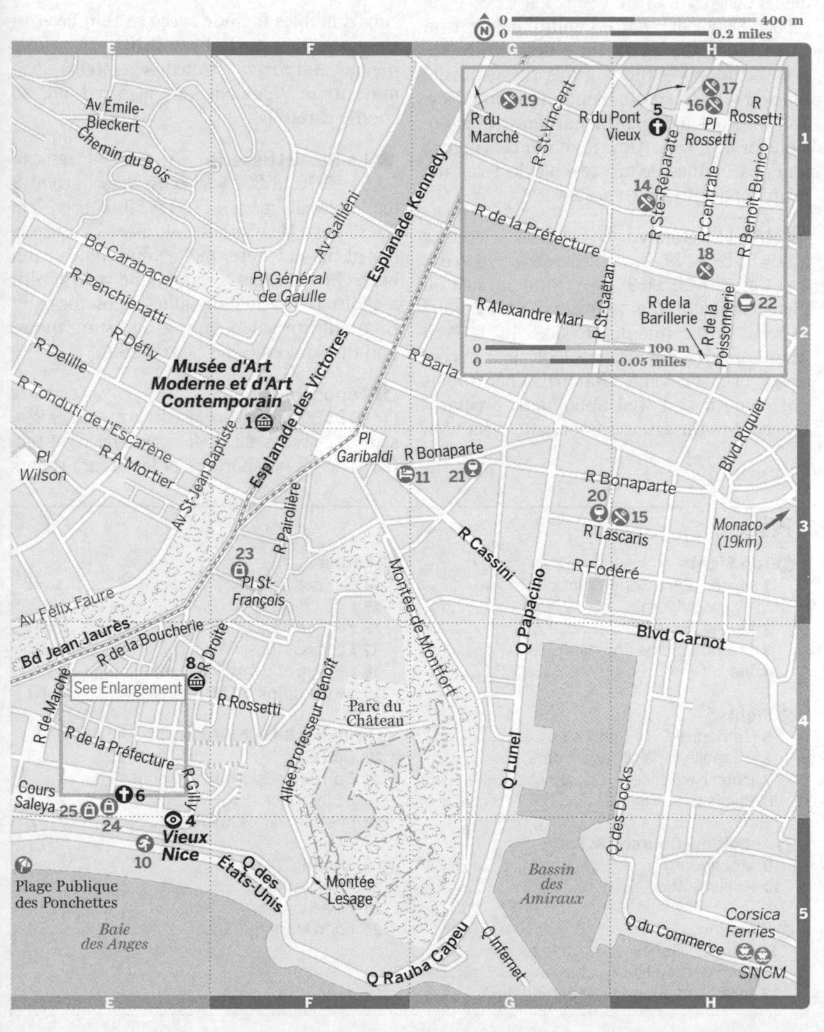

Sleeping

Villa Saint-Exupéry Beach Hostel HOSTEL €
(04 93 16 13 45; www.villahostels.com; 6 rue Sacha Guitry; dm €40-50, d/tr €120/150;) It's actually a few blocks from the beach, but this longstanding city hostel has plenty of other pluses: bar, kitchen, free wi-fi, gym, games room etc, plus friendly multilingual staff and a great location. The downside? High prices (at least for a hostel) and occasionally drab decor. All dorms have a private ensuite bathroom, and sleep from three to 14.

★**Nice Garden Hôtel** BOUTIQUE HOTEL €€
(04 93 87 35 62; www.nicegardenhotel.com; 11 rue du Congrès; s €75, d €90-123, tr €138; reception 8am-9pm;) Behind heavy iron gates hides this gem: nine beautifully appointed rooms – the work of the exquisite Marion – are a subtle blend of old and new and overlook a delightful garden with a glorious orange tree. Amazingly, all this charm and peacefulness is just two blocks from the promenade. Breakfast costs €9.

★**Hôtel Le Genève** HOTEL €€
(04 93 56 84 79; www.hotel-le-geneve-nice.com; 1 rue Cassini; r €135-169;) Situated just off place Garibaldi, this renovated corner hotel is bang in the middle of Nice's lively Petit Marais *quartier*. Bedrooms look sleek in cool greys, crimsons and charcoals; bathrooms are modern and well appointed. Breakfast is served in the ground-floor cafe, brimful of vintage bric-a-brac and mismatched furniture. Bars and cafes abound here.

★**Nice Pebbles** APARTMENT €€
(04 97 20 27 30; www.nicepebbles.com; 1-/2-/3-bedroom apt from €110/130/200;) Nice Pebbles offers nearly a hundred apartments and villas to choose from, from one to five bedrooms: all chosen for quirkiness and design, though sizes and location vary. Wi-fi, DVD players and proper kitchens are standard, and some also have luxuries such as a swimming pool, patio or garden. Rates vary widely; low-season deals can be very good.

Eating

Niçois nibbles include *socca* (a thin layer of chickpea flour and olive oil batter), *salade niçoise* and *farcis* (stuffed vegetables). Restaurants in Vieux Nice are a mixed bag, so choose carefully.

★**La Rossettisserie** FRENCH €
(04 93 76 18 80; www.larossettisserie.com; 8 rue Mascoïnat; mains €13.50-14.50; noon-2pm & 7.30-10pm Mon-Sat) Roast meat is the order of the day here: make your choice from beef, chicken, veal or lamb, and pair it with a choice of mashed or sautéed potatoes and ratatouille or salad. Simple and sumptuous, and the vaulted cellar is a delight.

★**Fenocchio** ICE CREAM €
(04 93 80 72 52; www.fenocchio.fr; 2 place Rossetti; 1/2 scoops €2.50/4; 9am-midnight Feb-Oct) There's no shortage of ice-cream sellers

Nice

Top Sights
1 Musée d'Art Moderne et d'Art Contemporain ... F2
2 Musée Masséna ... A4
3 Promenade des Anglais ... A5
4 Vieux Nice ... E5

Sights
5 Cathédrale Ste-Réparate ... H1
6 Chapelle de la Miséricorde ... E4
7 Hôtel Negresco ... A5
8 Palais Lascaris ... E4

Activities, Courses & Tours
9 Mobilboard Nice ... C4
10 Roller Station ... E5

Sleeping
11 Hôtel Le Genève ... F3
12 Nice Garden Hôtel ... B4
13 Villa Saint-Exupéry Beach Hostel ... D3

Eating
14 Bar des Oiseaux ... H1
15 Chez Pipo ... H3
16 Fenocchio ... H1
17 La Rossettisserie ... H1
18 Le Bistrot d'Antoine ... H2
19 Le Comptoir du Marché ... G1

Drinking & Nightlife
20 BaR'Oc ... G3
21 Comptoir Central Électrique ... G3
22 Les Distilleries Idéales ... H2

Shopping
23 Fish Market ... F3
24 Flea Market ... E4
25 Food Market ... E4

DON'T MISS

THE CORNICHES

Some of the Riviera's most spectacular scenery stretches east between Nice and Monaco. A trio of *corniches* (coastal roads) hugs the cliffs between the two seaside cities, each higher up the hill than the last. The middle *corniche* ends in Monaco; the upper and lower continue to Menton near the France/Italy border.

Corniche Inférieure (lower) Skimming the glittering, villa-studded shoreline, this road is all about belle époque glamour, the height of which can be seen at the extravagant **Villa Ephrussi de Rothschild** (☎04 93 01 33 09; www.villa-ephrussi.com/en; St-Jean-Cap Ferrat; adult/child €13/10; ⏱10am-7pm Jul & Aug, 10am-6pm Feb-Jun Sep & Oct, 2-6pm Mon-Fri, 10am-6pm Sat & Sun Nov-Jan) in St-Jean-Cap Ferrat.

Moyenne (middle) Corniche The jewel in the Riviera crown undoubtedly goes to **Èze**, a medieval village spectacularly located on a rocky outcrop with dazzling views of the Med.

Grande (upper) Corniche The epitomy of 'scenic drive', with sublime panoramas unfolding at every bend. Stop in **La Turbie** for dramatic views of Monaco.

in the old town, but this *maître glacier* (master ice-cream maker) has been king of the scoops since 1966. The array of flavours is mind-boggling – olive, tomato, fig, beer, lavender and violet are just a few to try. Dither too long over the 70-plus flavours and you'll never make it to the front of the queue. For a Niçois twist, ask for *tourte de blette* (a sweet chard tart with raisins, pine kernels and parmesan).

Chez Pipo FRENCH €

(☎04 93 55 88 82; 13 rue Bavastro; socca €2.70; ⏱11.30am-2.30pm & 5.30-11pm Tue-Sun) Everyone says the best *socca* (chickpea-flour pancakes) can be found in the old town, but don't believe them – this place near Port Lympia has been in the biz since 1923 and, for our money, knocks *socca*-shaped spots off anywhere else in Nice.

★Le Bistrot d'Antoine MODERN FRENCH €€

(☎04 93 85 29 57; 27 rue de la Préfecture; menus €25-43, mains €15-25; ⏱noon-2pm & 7-10pm Tue-Sat) A quintessential French bistro, right down to the checked tablecloths, streetside tables and impeccable service – not to mention the handwritten blackboard, loaded with classic dishes such as rabbit pâté, pot-cooked pork, blood sausage and duck breast. If you've never eaten classic French food, this is definitely the place to start; and if you have, you're in for a treat.

Bar des Oiseaux FRENCH €€

(☎04 93 80 27 33; 5 rue Saint-Vincent; mains €16-25; ⏱noon-1.45pm & 7.15-9.45pm Tue-Sat) An old town classic, in business since 1961 on a corner of a shady backstreet (expect to get lost en route). It's been various things down the years, including a bar and nightclub, and still has a few of its original saucy murals left in situ. But today it's a lively bistro serving trad French cuisine spiced up with a modern twist or two. Bookings recommended.

Drinking & Nightlife

Les Distilleries Idéales CAFE

(☎04 93 62 10 66; www.lesdistilleriesideales.fr; 24 rue de la Préfecture; ⏱9am-12.30am) The most atmospheric spot for a tipple in the old town, whether you're after one of the many beers on tap or a local wine by the glass. Brick-lined and set out over two floors (with a little balcony that's great for people-watching), it's packed until late. Happy hour is from 6pm to 8pm.

Comptoir Central Électrique BAR

(☎04 93 14 09 62; www.comptoircentralelectrique.fr; 10 rue Bonaparte; ⏱8.30am-12.30am Mon-Sat) Once a lighting factory (check out the lighbulb collection inside), now a hip-and-happening Port Lympia bar with slouchy sofas, industrial-chic decor and loads of beers and wines by the glass. There's a blackboard menu of snacks to share too.

BaR'Oc WINE BAR

(☎06 43 64 68 05; 10 rue Bavastro; ⏱7pm-12.30am) Fine wine and even finer tapas – from parma ham to oven-baked *figatelli* (a type of salami from Corsica) – plus tasting platters of cheese and cold cuts.

Information

Tourist Office (Gare de Nice; ☎08 92 70 74 07; av Thiers; ⏲9am-7pm daily Jun-Sep, 9am-6pm Mon-Sat & 10-5pm Sun Oct-May) In a booth right beside the train station.

Getting There & Away

AIR

Nice-Côte d'Azur Airport (☎08 20 42 33 33; www.nice.aeroport.fr; 📶) is France's second-largest airport and has international flights to Europe, North Africa and the US, with regular and low-cost airlines. The airport has two terminals, linked by a free shuttle bus.

Buses 98 and 99 link the airport's terminal with Promenade des Anglais and Nice train station respectively (€6, 35 minutes, every 20 minutes).

BOAT

Nice is the main port for ferries to Corsica. **SNCM** (www.sncm.fr; quai du Commerce) and **Corsica Ferries** (www.corsicaferries.com; quai du Commerce) are the two main companies.

TRAIN

From Nice's train station, 1.2km north of the beach, there are frequent services to Cannes (€5.90, 40 minutes), Marseille (€35 to €38, 2½ hours), Monaco (€3.30, 25 minutes) and other Riviera destinations.

Cannes

POP 74,626

Most have heard of Cannes and its celebrity film festival. The latter only lasts for two weeks in May, but the buzz and glitz linger all year thanks to regular visits from celebrities who come here to indulge in designer shopping, beaches and the palace hotels of the Riviera's glammest seafront, bd de la Croisette.

Sights & Activities

★La Croisette — ARCHITECTURE

The multi-starred hotels and couture shops lining the iconic bd de la Croisette (aka La Croisette) may be the preserve of the rich and famous, but anyone can enjoy strolling the palm-shaded promenade – a favourite pastime among Cannois at night, when it twinkles with bright lights. Views of the Baie de Cannes and nearby Estérel mountains are beautiful, and seafront hotel palaces dazzle in all their stunning art deco glory.

Le Suquet — HISTORIC SITE

Follow rue St-Antoine and snake your way up Le Suquet, Cannes' oldest district, for great views of the bay.

Îles de Lérins — ISLAND

Although just 20 minutes away by boat, these tranquil islands feel far from the madding crowd. **Île Ste-Marguerite**, where the mysterious Man in the Iron Mask was incarcerated during the late 17th century, is known for its bone-white beaches, eucalyptus groves and small marine museum. Tiny **Île St-Honorat** has been a monastery since the 5th century: you can visit the church and small chapels and stroll through the monks' vineyards.

Boats leave Cannes from quai des Îles on the western side of the harbour. **Riviera Lines** (☎04 92 98 71 31; www.riviera-lines.com; quai Max Laubeuf) runs ferries to Île Ste-Marguerite and **Compagnie Planaria** (www.cannes-ilesdelerins.com; quai Max Laubeuf) covers Île St-Honorat.

Sleeping

Hôtel Le Mistral — BOUTIQUE HOTEL €€

(☎04 93 39 91 46; www.mistral-hotel.com; 13 rue des Belges; s €89-109, d €99-129; ❄📶) For super-pricey Cannes, this little 10-roomer is quite amazing value. Rooms are small but decked out in flattering red and plum tones – Privilege rooms have quite a bit more space, plus a fold-out sofa bed. There are sea views from the top floor, and the hotel is just 50m from La Croisette. There's no lift, though.

Hôtel 7e Art — BOUTIQUE HOTEL €€

(☎04 93 68 66 66; www.7arthotel.com; 23 rue du Maréchal Joffre; r €82-115; ❄📶) Cinema-themed in name and nature: the hotel's styled after the '7th Art' (as French people call film), and the rooms are divided into three filmic categories (Short Film, Long Film and Palme d'Or). Space is tight, but additions like iPod docks and vintage film posters add character. The very noisy road is a major drawback.

Eating

★La Boulangerie par Jean-Luc Pelé — BAKERY €

(☎04 93 38 06 10; www.jeanlucpele.com; 3 rue du 24 août; lunch menus €6-9.50; ⏲7.30am-7.30pm Mon-Sat) This swanky bakery by Cannois *chocolatier* and *pâtissier* Jean-Luc Pelé casts a whole new spin on eating cheap in Cannes. Creative salads, sandwiches, wraps and bagels – to eat in or out – burst with local flavours and provide the perfect prelude to the utterly sensational cakes and desserts Pelé is best known for.

★ Bobo Bistro MEDITERRANEAN €
(☎ 04 93 99 97 33; 21 rue du Commandant André; pizza €12-16, mains €15-20; ⏱ noon-3pm & 7-11pm Mon-Sat, 7-11pm Sun) Predictably, it's a 'bobo' (bourgeois bohemian) crowd that gathers at this achingly cool bistro in Cannes' fashionable Carré d'Or (Golden Sq). Decor is stylishly retro, with attention-grabbing objets d'art including a tableau of dozens of spindles of coloured yarn. Cuisine is local, seasonal and invariably organic: artichoke salad, tuna carpaccio with passion fruit, roasted cod with mash *fait masion* (homemade).

Aux Bons Enfants FRENCH €€
(☎ 06 18 81 37 47; www.aux-bons-enfants.com; 80 rue Meynadier; menus €29, mains €16; ⏱ noon-2pm & 7-10pm Tue-Sat) A people's-choice place since 1935, this informal restaurant cooks up regional dishes, such as *aïoli garni* (garlic and saffron mayonnaise served with fish and vegetables), *daube* (a Provençal beef stew) and *rascasse meunière* (pan-fried rockfish), all in a convivial atmosphere. No credit cards or reservations.

Information

Tourist Office (☎ 04 92 99 84 22; www.cannes-destination.fr; 1 bd de la Croisette; ⏱ 9am-8pm Jun-Aug, 9am or 10am-7pm Sep-May; 📶) Runs an informative guided walking tour (€6) of the city at 2.30pm every Monday, and at 9.15am in July and August; there are simultaneous tours in English and French. It also runs a guided tour of the Palais des Festivals, but at the moment it's only run in French.

Getting There & Away

Cannes' gleaming white train station is well connected with other towns along the coast:

Marseille €25, two hours, half-hourly
Monaco €8, one hour, at least twice hourly
Nice €6, 40 minutes, every 15 minutes

St-Tropez

POP 4903

In the soft autumn or winter light, it's hard to believe the pretty terracotta fishing village of St-Tropez is a stop on the Riviera celebrity circuit. It seems far removed from its glitzy siblings further up the coast, but come spring or summer, it's a different world: the population increases tenfold, prices triple and fun-seekers pile in to party till dawn, strut around the luxury-yacht-packed Vieux Port and enjoy the creature comforts of exclusive A-listers' beaches in the Baie de Pampelonne.

Sights & Activities

About 4km southeast of town is the start of **Plage de Tahiti** and its continuation, the famous **Plage de Pampelonne**, studded with St-Tropez' most legendary drinking and dining haunts.

★ Citadelle de St-Tropez MUSEUM
(☎ 04 94 54 84 14; admission €3; ⏱ 10am-6.30pm Apr-Sep, to 5.30pm Oct-Mar) Built in 1602 to defend the coast against Spain, the citadel dominates the hillside overlooking St-Tropez to the east. The views are fantastic. Its dungeons are home to the excellent **Musée de l'Histoire Maritime**, an all-interactive museum inaugurated in July 2013 retracing the history of humans at sea, from fishing, trading, exploration, travel and the navy.

★ La Ponche HISTORIC SITE
Shrug off the hustle of the port in St-Tropez' historic fishing quarter, La Ponche, northeast of the Vieux Port. From the southern end of quai Frédéric Mistral, place Garrezio sprawls east from 10th-century **Tour Suffren** to place de l'Hôtel de Ville. From here, rue Guichard leads southeast to sweet-chiming **Église de St-Tropez** (place de l'Ormeau), a St-Trop landmark built in 1785 in Italian baroque style. Inside is a bust of St Torpes, honoured during Les Bravades in May.

Sleeping

Hôtel Lou Cagnard HOTEL €€
(☎ 04 94 97 04 24; www.hotel-lou-cagnard.com; 18 av Paul Roussel; d €83-176; ⏱ Mar-Oct; ❄📶) This old-school hotel stands out in stark contrast against most of the swanky hotels around St-Tropez. Located in an old house shaded by lemon and fig trees, its rooms are unashamedly frilly and floral, but some have garden patios, and the lovely jasmine-scented garden and welcoming family feel make it a home away from home. The cheapest rooms share toilets.

Hôtel Le Colombier HOTEL €€
(☎ 04 94 97 05 31; http://lecolombierhotel.free.fr; impasse des Conquettes; d €105-185, tr €235-285;

⏲mid-Apr–mid-Nov; ❄📶) An immaculately clean converted house, a five-minute walk from place des Lices, the Colombier's fresh, summery decor is feminine and uncluttered. Rooms are in shades of white and furnished with vintage furniture.

Eating

★La Tarte Tropézienne CAFE €
(☎04 94 97 04 69; www.latartetropezienne.fr; place des Lices; mains €13-15, cakes €3-5; ⏲6.30am-7.30pm & noon-3pm) This newly renovated cafe-bakery is the creator of the eponymous sugar-crusted, orange-perfumed cake. There are smaller branches on **rue Clémenceau** (☎04 94 97 71 42; www.latartetropezienne.fr; 36 rue Clémenceau; mains €13-15, cakes €3-5; ⏲7am-7pm) and near the **new port** (☎04 94 97 19 77; www.latartetropezienne.fr; 9 bd Louis Blanc; mains €13-15, cakes €3-5; ⏲6.30am-7.30pm), plus various other towns around the Côte d'Azur.

La Pesquière SEAFOOD €
(☎04 94 97 05 92; 1 rue des Remparts; menu €29, mains €14-20; ⏲9am-midnight mid-Mar–Nov) This is the kind of place you wouldn't think could still exist in swanky St-Tropez – a down-to-earth, honest-as-they-come seafood restaurant, which has been been serving up bowls of mussels, stuffed sardines and Provençal vegetables for going on five decades. It's near the old fishing quays of La Ponche, so the fish is guaranteed fresh – but don't expect any frills.

Le Café CAFE €€
(☎04 94 97 44 69; www.lecafe.fr; place des Lices; lunch/dinner menus €18/32; ⏲8am-11pm) Whetting whistles since 1789, this historic cafe is where artists and painters preferred to hang out back in the days when St-Trop was still a sleepy port. Happily, it's clung on to its no-nonsense roots – you'll find solid dishes such as pot-roasted chicken, mussels and grilled fish on the menu, as well as a lovely interior bar with globe lights and wooden fixtures that still give it a cosy fin-de-siècle vibe. They'll lend you a set of boules if you want to take on some *pétanque* players on the square.

Information

Tourist Office (☎08 92 68 48 28; www.sainttropeztourisme.com; quai Jean Jaurès; ⏲9.30am-1.30pm & 3-7.30pm Jul & Aug, 9.30am-12.30pm & 2-7pm Apr-Jun, Sep & Oct, to 6pm Mon-Sat Nov-Mar) Runs occasional walking tours April to October, and also has a kiosk in Parking du Port in July and August. Rather stingily, you have to pay for a town map (€2).

Getting There & Away

VarLib (☎04 94 24 60 00; www.varlib.fr) tickets cost €3 from the **bus station** (☎04 94 56 25 74; av du Général de Gaulle) for anywhere within the Var département (except Toulon-Hyères airport), including Ramatuelle (35 minutes), St-Raphaël (1¼ hours to three hours, depending on traffic) via Grimaud and Port Grimaud, and Fréjus.

Buses serve Toulon-Hyères airport (€15, 1½ hours), but some require a transfer.

Monaco

POP 37,800

Squeezed into just 200 hectares, this confetti principality might be the world's second-smallest country (the Vatican is smaller), but what it lacks in size it makes up for in attitude. Glitzy, glam and screaming hedonism, Monaco is truly beguiling.

It is a sovereign state but has no border control. It has its own flag (red and white) and national holiday (19 November), and it uses the euro even though it's not part of the EU.

You can easily visit Monaco as a day trip from Nice, a short train ride away.

Sights

★Casino de Monte Carlo CASINO
(☎98 06 21 21; www.montecarlocasinos.com; place du Casino; 9am-noon €10, from 2pm Salons Ordinaires/Salons Privées €10/20; ⏲visits 9am-noon, gaming 2pm-2am or 4am or when last game ends) Peeping inside Monte Carlo's legendary marble-and-gold casino is a Monaco essential. The building, open to visitors every morning, is Europe's most lavish example of belle époque architecture. Prince Charles III came up with the idea of the casino and in 1866, three years after its inauguration, the name 'Monte Carlo' – Ligurian for 'Mount Charles' in honour of the prince – was coined. To gamble or watch the poker-faced play, visit after 2pm (when a strict over-18s-only admission rule kicks in).

★Le Rocher HISTORIC SITE
Monaco Ville, also called Le Rocher, is the only part of Monaco to have retained its original old town, complete with small,

winding medieval lanes. The old town thrusts skywards on a pistol-shaped rock, its strategic location overlooking the sea that became the stronghold of the Grimaldi dynasty. There are various staircases up to Le Rocher; the best route up is via Rampe Major, which starts from place aux Armes near the port.

★Musée Océanographique de Monaco AQUARIUM
(☎93 15 36 00; www.oceano.mc; av St-Martin; adult €11-16, child €7-12; ⊙9.30am-8pm Jul & Aug, 10am-7pm Apr-Jun & Sep, to 6pm Oct-Mar) Stuck dramatically to the edge of a cliff since 1910, the world-renowned Musée Océanographique de Monaco, founded by Prince Albert I (1848–1922), is a stunner. Its centrepiece is its **aquarium** with a 6m-deep lagoon where sharks and marine predators are separated from colourful tropical fishes by a coral reef. Upstairs, two huge colonnaded rooms retrace the history of oceanography and marine biology (and Prince Albert's contribution to the field) through photographs, old equipment, numerous specimens and interactive displays.

Sleeping

Monaco is no budget destination when it comes to accommodation. Budget-conscious travellers should stay in nearby Nice and visit it as a day trip.

Relais International de la Jeunesse Thalassa HOSTEL €
(☎04 93 78 18 58; www.clajsud.fr; 2 av Gramaglia, Cap d'Ail; dm €20; ⊙Apr-Oct) This hostel isn't actually in Monaco, it's 2km along the coast at Cap d'Ail, but it's only a quick bus or train ride into the principality. It's got a lot going for it: a fab beachside location, clean four- to 10-bed dorms, home-cooked meals (€12) and takeaway picnics (€9), and a handy location 300m from the station.

Novotel Monte Carlo HOTEL €€€
(☎99 99 83 00; www.novotel.com/5275; 16 bd Princesse Charlotte; d from €175; ❄@🛜🏊) Put all your chain-hotel preconceptions aside, for the Novotel Monte Carlo is no ordinary chain hotel. Rooms are bright, spacious and colourful, with bath and shower in every bathroom. Even better, up to two children under 16 can stay for free with their parents (and they throw the breakfast in too). The pool is open June to September.

Eating

★Marché de la Condamine MARKET €
(www.facebook.com/marche.condamine; 15 place d'Armes; ⊙7am-3pm Mon-Sat, to 2pm Sun) For tasty, excellent-value fare around shared tables, hit Monaco's fabulous market food court, tucked beneath the arches behind the open-air market stalls on place d'Armes. Fresh pasta (€5.50 to €9) from Maison des Pâtes, truffle cuisine from Truffle Gourmet and traditional Niçois *socca* (€2.80 per slice) from Chez Roger steal the show. Check its Facebook page for what's cooking.

★La Montgolfière FUSION €€€
(☎97 98 61 59; www.lamontgolfiere.mc; 16 rue Basse; 3-/4-course menu €47/54; ⊙noon-2pm & 7.30-9.30pm Mon, Tue & Thu-Sat) Monegasque chef Henri Geraci has worked in some of the Riviera's top restaurants, but he's now happily settled at his own establishment down a shady alleyway near the palace. Escoffier-trained, he's faithful to the French classics, but his travels have given him a taste for Asian flavours too, so expect some exotic twists. The restaurant's small and sought after, so reserve ahead.

Information

TELEPHONE

Calls between Monaco and France are international calls. Dial 00 followed by Monaco's country code (☎377) when calling Monaco from France or elsewhere abroad. To phone France from Monaco, dial ☎00 and France's country code (☎33).

TOURIST INFORMATION

Tourist Office (www.visitmonaco.com; 2a bd des Moulins; ⊙9am-7pm Mon-Sat, 11am-1pm Sun) For tourist information by the port, head to the seasonal kiosk run by the tourist office near the cruise-ship terminal on Esplanade des Pêcheurs.

Getting There & Away

Services run about every 20 minutes east to Menton (€2, 15 minutes) and west to Nice (€3, 25 minutes). Bus 100 (€1.50, every 15 minutes from 6am to 9pm) goes to Nice (45 minutes) and Menton (40 minutes) along the Corniche Inférieure.

CORSICA

The rugged island of Corsica (Corse in French) is officially a part of France but remains fiercely proud of its own culture, history and language. It's one of the Mediterranean's most dramatic islands, with a bevy of beautiful beaches, glitzy ports and a mountainous, maquis-covered interior to explore, as well as a wild, independent spirit all of its own.

Ajaccio

POP 68,265

Ajaccio, Corsica's main metropolis, is all class and seduction. Looming over this elegant port city is the spectre of Corsica's great general: Napoléon Bonaparte was born here in 1769 and the city is dotted with statues and museums relating to him (starting with the main street in Ajaccio, cours Napoléon).

Sights & Activities

Kiosks on the quayside opposite place du Maréchal Foch sell tickets for seasonal **boat trips** around the Golfe d'Ajaccio and Îles Sanguinaires (adult/child €25/15), and excursions to the Réserve Naturelle de Scandola (adult/child €55/35).

Maison Bonaparte MUSEUM

(☎04 95 21 43 89; www.musees-nationaux-napoleoniens.org; rue St-Charles; adult/child €7/free; ⏲10.30am-12.30pm & 1.15-6pm Tue-Sun Apr-Sep, to 4.30pm Oct-Mar) Napoléon spent his first nine years in this house. Ransacked by Corsican nationalists in 1793, requisitioned by English troops from 1794 to 1796, and eventually rebuilt by Napoléon's mother, the house became a place of pilgrimage for French revolutionaries. It hosts memorabilia of the emperor and his siblings, including a glass medallion containing a lock of his hair. A comprehensive audioguide (included in admission price for adults, €2 for children) is available in several languages.

Palais Fesch – Musée des Beaux-Arts GALLERY

(☎04 95 26 26 26; www.musee-fesch.com; 50-52 rue du Cardinal Fesch; adult/child €8/5; ⏲10.30am-6pm Mon, Wed & Sat, noon-6pm Thu, Fri & Sun May-Sep, to 5pm Oct-Apr) One of the island's must-sees, this superb museum established by Napoléon's uncle has France's largest collection of Italian paintings outside the Louvre. Mostly the works of minor or anonymous 14th- to 19th-century artists, there are also canvases by Titian, Fra Bartolomeo, Veronese, Botticelli and Bellini. Look out for *La Vierge à l'Enfant Soutenu par un Ange* (Mother and Child Supported by an Angel), one of Botticelli's masterpieces. The museum also houses temporary exhibitions.

Sleeping & Eating

Hôtel Marengo HOTEL €

(☎04 95 21 43 66; www.hotel-marengo.com; 2 rue Marengo; d €78-98; ⏲Apr-Oct; ❄📶) For something near to the sand, try this charmingly eccentric small hotel. Rooms have a balcony, there's a quiet flower-filled courtyard and reception is an agreeable clutter of tasteful prints and personal objects. Find it down a cul-de-sac off bd Madame Mère.

Hôtel Kallisté HOTEL €

(☎04 95 51 34 45; www.hotel-kalliste-ajaccio.com; 51 cours Napoléon; s/d €68/88; ❄📶) Low prices and a central location on Ajaccio's main street, midway between the train station and the port, are the twin draws at this 19th-century Ajaccio town house. The front desk closes after 8pm, but there's an automated reception system for late arrivals.

★**L'Altru Versu** BISTRO €€

(☎04 95 50 05 22; rte des Sanguinaires; mains €20-29; ⏲12.30-2pm Thu-Mon, 7.30-10.30pm daily mid-Jun–mid-Oct, 12.30-2pm Thu-Tue, 7.30-10.30pm Mon, Tue & Thu-Sat rest of year) A phoenix rising from the ashes, this perennial favourite reopened in 2015 on Ajaccio's western waterfront after suffering two devastating winter storms and a fire. Magnificent sea views complement the exquisite gastronomic creations of the Mezzacqui brothers (Jean-Pierre front of house, David powering the kitchen), from crispy minted prawns with pistachio cream to pork with honey and clementine zest.

Information

Tourist Office (☎04 95 51 53 03; www.ajaccio-tourisme.com; 3 bd du Roi Jérôme; ⏲8am-7pm Mon-Sat, 9am-1pm Sun Apr-Oct, shorter hours Nov-Mar; 📶)

Getting There & Away

AIR

Aéroport d'Ajaccio Napoléon Bonaparte (☎04 95 23 56 56; www.2a.cci.fr/Aeroport-Napoleon-Bonaparte-Ajaccio.html), 7km east of town, is linked by bus 8 (€4.50, 15 minutes) with Ajaccio's train station (bus stop marked Marconajo). Count on around €25 for a taxi into town.

BOAT

Boats to/from Toulon, Nice and Marseille depart from Ajaccio's **Terminal Maritime et Routier** (☎04 95 51 55 45; quai L'Herminier).

BUS

Local bus companies have ticket kiosks inside the ferry terminal building, the arrival/departure point for buses.

Bonifacio €20, 3hr, two daily Mon-Sat

Porto €12, 2hr, two daily Mon-Sat

Porto-Vecchio €20, 3¼hr, two daily Mon-Sat

Zonza €12, 2hr, two daily Mon-Sat

TRAIN

From the **train station** (place de la Gare), 500m north of town, services include the following:

Bastia €21.60, 3¾ hours, five daily

Calvi €25.10, 4¾ hours, two daily (change at Ponte Leccia)

Bastia

POP 42,948

The bustling old port of Bastia has an irresistible magnetism. Allow yourself at least a day to drink in the narrow old-town alleyways of Terra Vecchia, the seething Vieux Port, the dramatic 16th-century citadel perched up high, and the compelling history museum.

Sights & Activities

★Terra Vecchia — HISTORIC SITE

A spiderweb of narrow lanes, Terra Vecchia is Bastia's heart and soul. Shady **place de l'Hôtel de Ville** hosts a lively morning market on Saturday and Sunday. One block west, baroque **Chapelle de l'Immaculée Conception** (rue des Terrasses), with its elaborately painted barrel-vaulted ceiling, briefly served as the seat of the short-lived Anglo-Corsican parliament in 1795. Further north is **Chapelle St-Roch** (rue Napoléon), with an 18th-century organ and *trompe l'œil* roof.

★Terra Nova — HISTORIC SITE

Above Jardin Romieu looms Bastia's amber-hued citadel, built from the 15th to 17th centuries as a stronghold for the city's Genoese masters. Inside, the Palais des Gouverneurs houses the **Musée de Bastia** (☎04 95 31 09 12; www.musee-bastia.com; place du Donjon; adult/child €5/2.50, Oct-Apr free; ⏲10am-6.30pm Tue-Sun May-Sep, daily Jul & Aug, shorter hours rest of year), which retraces the city's history. A few streets south, don't miss the majestic **Cathédrale Ste-Marie** (rue de l'Évêché) and nearby **Église Ste-Croix** (rue de l'Évêché), featuring gilded ceilings and a mysterious black-oak crucifix found in the sea in 1428.

Sleeping & Eating

★Hôtel-Restaurant La Corniche — HOTEL €€

(☎04 95 31 40 98; www.hotel-lacorniche.com; San Martino di Lota; d €78-106; ⏲mid-Feb–Dec; ❄📶🏊) Perched high in the hilltop village of San Martino di Lota, Hôtel-Restaurant La Corniche is a brilliant halfway house between city convenience (it's just 8km from Bastia) and Cap Corse wilderness: the sea views will leave you smitten. A family-run hotel since 1934, it woos travellers with its fabulous location and gourmet food (mains €18 to €29, *menus* €24.50 to €31.50).

Hôtel Central — HOTEL €€

(☎04 95 31 71 12; www.centralhotel.fr; 3 rue Miot; s €80-90, d €90-110, apt €130; ❄📶) From the vintage, black-and-white tiled floor in the entrance to the sweeping staircase and eclectic jumble of plant pots in the minuscule interior courtyard, this family-run address oozes 1940s grace. The hotel's pedigree dates to 1941 and the vintage furnishings inside the 19th-century building don't disappoint. The three apartments, with fully equipped kitchen, are great for longer stays.

A Scudella — CORSICAN €€

(☎04 95 46 25 31, 09 51 70 79 46; 10 rue Pino; menu €25; ⏲7pm-2am Tue-Sat) Tucked down a back alley between place de l'Hôtel de Ville and the Vieux Port, this is a superb spot to sample traditional mountain fare, from appetisers of fine Corsican charcuterie and *beignets de brocciu* (fritters filled with *fromage frais)* to *veau aux olives* (stewed veal with olives) to *flan à la châtaigne* (chestnut flan).

Information

Tourist Office (☎04 95 54 20 40; www.bastia-tourisme.com; place St-Nicolas; ⏲8am-6pm Mon-Sat, to noon Sun; 📶) Organises guided tours of the city and has plenty of information about Cap Corse.

Getting There & Away

AIR

Aéroport Bastia-Poretta (www.bastia.aeroport.fr) is 24km south of the city. **Société des Autobus Bastiais** (☎04 95 31 06 65;

bastiabus.com) operates shuttles (€9, 35 minutes) every hour or two between the airport and Bastia's downtown Préfecture building. **Taxi Aéroport Poretta** (☎04 95 36 04 65; www.corsica-taxis.com) charges €48/66 by day/night.

BOAT

Ferry companies have information offices at **Bastia Port** (www.bastia.port.fr); they are usually open for same-day ticket sales a couple of hours before sailings. Ferries sail to/from Marseille, Toulon and Nice (mainland France), and Livorno, Savona, Piombino and Genoa (Italy).

BUS & TRAIN

From the **train station** (av Maréchal Sébastiani), there are daily services to Ajaccio (€21.60, 3¾ hours, four daily) via Corte (€10.10, 1¾ hours), and Calvi (€16.40, 3¼ hours, two daily) via Île Rousse (€13.50, 2¾ hours).

Bonifacio

POP 3016

With its glittering harbour, dramatic perch atop creamy white cliffs, and a stout citadel teetering above the cornflower-blue waters of the Bouches de Bonifacio, this dazzling port is an essential stop. Just a short hop from Sardinia, Bonifacio has a distinctly Italianate feel: sun-bleached townhouses, dangling washing lines and murky chapels cram the web of alleyways of the old citadel, while, down below on the harbourside, brasseries and boat kiosks tout their wares to the droves of day trippers.

Sights

★Citadel HISTORIC SITE

(Haute Ville) Much of Bonifacio's charm comes from strolling the citadel's shady streets, several spanned by arched aqueducts designed to collect rainwater to fill the communal cistern opposite **Église Ste-Marie Majeure**. From the marina, the paved steps of **montée du Rastello** and **montée St-Roch** bring you up to the citadel's old gateway, **Porte de Gênes**, complete with an original 16th-century drawbridge.

Îles Lavezzi ISLAND

Paradise! This protected clutch of uninhabited islets were made for those who love nothing better than splashing in tranquil lapis-lazuli waters. The 65-hectare Île Lavezzi, which gives its name to the whole archipelago, is the most accessible of the islands.

In summer, various companies organise **boat trips** here; buy tickets at the booths located on Bonifacio's marina and bring your own picnic lunch. Boats also sail to the island from Porto-Vecchio.

Sleeping & Eating

Hôtel Le Colomba HOTEL €€

(☎04 95 73 73 44; www.hotel-bonifacio-corse.fr; 4-6 rue Simon Varsi; d €112-167; ❄📶) Occupying a tastefully renovated 14th-century building, this hotel enjoys a prime location on a picturesque (steep) street, bang in the heart of the old town. Rooms are simple and smallish, but fresh and individually decorated with amenities including wrought-iron bedsteads, country fabrics, carved bedheads and/or checkerboard tiles. Other pluses include friendly staff and breakfast served in a medieval vaulted cellar.

★Kissing Pigs CORSICAN €

(☎04 95 73 56 09; 15 quai Banda del Ferro; mains €11-23, menus €20-22; ⏲noon-2.30pm & 7-10.30pm Tue-Sun) Soothingly positioned by the harbour, this widely acclaimed restaurant and wine bar serves savoury fare in a seductively cosy interior, complete with wooden fixtures and swinging sausages. It's famed for its cheese and charcuterie platters; for the indecisive, the combination *moitié-moitié* (half-half) is perfect. The Corsican wine list is another hit.

Information

Tourist Office (☎04 95 73 11 88; www.bonifacio.fr; 2 rue Fred Scamaroni; ⏲9am-8pm Jul & Aug, shorter hours rest of year; 📶)

Getting There & Away

AIR

A taxi into town from **Aéroport de Figari-Sud-Corse** (☎04 95 71 10 10; www.2a.cci.fr/Aeroport-Figari-Sud-Corse.html), 20km north, costs about €45.

BOAT

Sardinia's main ferry operator, **Moby** (☎04 95 73 00 29; www.mobycorse.com) runs seasonal boats between Bonifacio and Santa Teresa Gallura (Sardinia); sailing time is 50 minutes.

SURVIVAL GUIDE

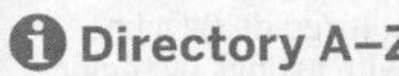

Directory A–Z

ACCOMMODATION

Many tourist offices make room reservations, often for a fee of €5; many only do so if you stop by in person. In the French Alps, ski-resort tourist offices operate a central reservation service.

B&Bs

For charm, a heartfelt *bienvenue* (welcome) and home cooking, it's hard to beat a *chambre d'hôte* (B&B). Pick up lists at local tourist offices or online.

Fleurs de Soleil (www.fleursdesoleil.fr) Selective collection of 550 stylish *maisons d'hôte*, mainly in rural France.

Gîtes de France (www.gites-de-france.com) France's primary umbrella organisation for B&Bs and self-catering properties (*gîtes*). Search by region, theme (charm, with kids, by the sea, gourmet, great garden etc), activity (fishing, wine tasting etc) or facilities (pool, dishwasher, fireplace, baby equipment etc).

Samedi Midi Éditions (www.samedimidi.com) Country, mountain, seaside... Choose your *chambre d'hôte* by location or theme (romance, golf, design, cooking courses).

Camping

- Most campgrounds open March or April to October.
- Euro-economisers should look for good-value but no-frills *campings municipaux* (municipal camping grounds).
- Accessing campgrounds without your own transport can be difficult in many areas.
- Camping in nondesignated spots (*camping sauvage*) is illegal in France.

> **SLEEPING PRICE RANGES**
>
> The following price ranges refer to a double room in high season, with private bathroom (any combination of toilet, bath-tub, shower and washbasin), excluding breakfast unless otherwise noted.
>
> **€** less than €90 (less than €130 in Paris)
>
> **€€** €90–190 (€130–250 in Paris)
>
> **€€€** more than €190 (more than €250 in Paris)

Hostels

Hostels range from funky to threadbare.

- A dorm bed in an *auberge de jeunesse* (youth hostel) costs €20 to €50 in Paris, and anything from €15 to €40 in the provinces, depending on location, amenities and facilities; sheets are always included, breakfast more often than not.
- To prevent outbreaks of bed bugs, sleeping bags are no longer permitted.
- All hostels are nonsmoking.

Hotels

- French hotels almost never include breakfast in their advertised nightly rates.
- Hotels in France are rated with one to five stars; ratings are based on objective criteria (eg size of entry hall), not service, decor or cleanliness.
- A double room has one double bed (or two singles pushed together); a room with twin beds is more expensive, as is a room with bath-tub instead of shower.

> **ESSENTIAL FOOD & DRINK**
>
> **Bordeaux & Burgundy wines** You'll find France's signature reds in every restaurant; now find out more by touring the vineyards.
>
> **Bouillabaisse** Marseille's signature hearty fish stew, eaten with croutons and rouille (garlic-and-chilli mayonnaise).
>
> **Champagne Tasting** in century-old cellars is an essential part of Champagne's bubbly experience.
>
> **Foie gras & truffles** The Dordogne features goose and 'black diamonds' from December to March. Provence is also good for indulging in the aphrodisiacal fungi.
>
> **Fondue & raclette** Warming cheese dishes in the French Alps.
>
> **Oysters & white wine** Everywhere on the Atlantic coast, but especially in Cancale and Bordeaux.
>
> **Piggy-part cuisine** Lyon is famous for its juicy *andouillette* (pig-intestine sausage), a perfect marriage with a local Côtes du Rhône red.

COUNTRY FACTS

Area 551,000 sq km

Capital Paris

Country Code ☎33

Currency Euro (€)

Emergency ☎112

Language French

Money ATMs everywhere.

Visas Schengen rules apply.

ACTIVITIES

From glaciers, rivers and canyons in the Alps to porcelain-smooth cycling trails in the Dordogne and Loire Valley – not to mention 3200km of coastline stretching from Italy to Spain and from the Basque country to the Straits of Dover – France's landscapes are ripe for exhilarating outdoor escapes.

- The French countryside is crisscrossed by a staggering 120,000km of *sentiers balisés* (marked walking paths), which pass through every imaginable terrain in every region of the country. No permit is needed to hike.
- The best-known trails are the *sentiers de grande randonnée* (GR), long-distance paths marked by red-and-white-striped track indicators.
- For complete details on regional activities, courses, equipment rental, clubs, companies and organisations, contact local tourist offices.

FOOD

Price indicators refer to the average cost of a two-course meal.

€ less than €20

€€ €20–40

€€€ more than €40

GAY & LESBIAN TRAVELLERS

The rainbow flag flies high in France, one of Europe's most liberal countries when it comes to homosexuality.

- Paris has been a thriving gay and lesbian centre since the late 1970s.
- Bordeaux, Lille, Lyon, Toulouse and many other towns have active communities.
- Attitudes towards homosexuality tend to be more conservative in the countryside and villages.
- Same-sex marriage has been legal in France since May 2013.
- Gay Pride marches are held in major French cities from mid-May to early July.

Online, try the following websites:

France Queer Resources Directory (www.france.qrd.org) Gay and lesbian directory.

Gaipied (www.gayvox.com/guide3) Online travel guide to France, with listings by region, by Gayvox.

LANGUAGE COURSES

- All manner of French-language courses are available in Paris and provincial towns and cities; most also arrange accommodation.
- Prices and courses vary greatly; the content can often be tailored to your specific needs (for a fee).
- The website www.europa-pages.com/france lists language schools in France.

Alliance Française (Map p186; ☎01 42 84 90 00; www.alliancefr.org; 101 bd Raspail, 6e; intensif/extensif courses per week from €202/91; Ⓜ St-Placide) French courses (minimum one week) for all levels. *Intensif* courses meet for four hours a day five days a week; *extensif* courses involve nine hours' tuition a week.

Eurocentres (www.eurocentres.com) This affiliation of small, well-organised schools has three addresses in France: in Amboise in the charming Loire Valley, in La Rochelle and Paris.

LEGAL MATTERS

- French police have wide powers of stop-and-search and can demand proof of identity at any time.
- Foreigners must be able to prove their legal status in France (eg passport, visa, residency permit).
- French law doesn't distinguish between hard and soft drugs; penalties can be severe (including fines and jail sentences).

MONEY

- Credit and debit cards are accepted almost everywhere in France.
- Some places (eg 24-hour petrol stations and some *autoroute* toll machines) only take credit cards with chips and PINs.
- In Paris and major cities, *bureaux de change* (exchange bureaux) are fast and easy, are open longer hours and offer competitive exchange rates.

OPENING HOURS

- French business hours are regulated by a maze of government regulations, including the 35-hour working week.
- The midday break is uncommon in Paris but, in general, gets longer the further south you go.
- French law requires most businesses to close Sunday; exceptions include grocery stores, *boulangeries*, florists and businesses catering to the tourist trade.
- In many places shops close on Monday.

- Many service stations open 24 hours a day and stock basic groceries.
- Restaurants generally close one or two days of the week.
- Museums tend to close on Monday or Tuesday.

PUBLIC HOLIDAYS

The following *jours fériés* (public holidays) are observed in France:

New Year's Day (Jour de l'An) 1 January

Easter Sunday & Monday (Pâques & Lundi de Pâques) Late March/April

May Day (Fête du Travail) 1 May

Victoire 1945 8 May – WWII armistice

Ascension Thursday (Ascension) May – celebrated on the 40th day after Easter

Pentecost/Whit Sunday & Whit Monday (Pentecôte & Lundi de Pentecôte) Mid-May to mid-June – celebrated on the seventh Sunday after Easter

Bastille Day/National Day (Fête Nationale) 14 July – *the* national holiday

Assumption Day (Assomption) 15 August

All Saints' Day (Toussaint) 1 November

Remembrance Day (L'onze Novembre) 11 November – WWI armistice

Christmas (Noël) 25 December

TELEPHONE

- French mobile phone numbers begin with ☎06 or 07.
- France uses GSM 900/1800, which is compatible with the rest of Europe and Australia but not with the North American GSM 1900 or the totally different system in Japan (though some North Americans have tri-band phones that work here).
- It is usually cheaper to buy a local SIM card from a French provider such as Orange, SFR, Bouygues and Free Mobile than to use international roaming. To do this, ensure your phone is 'unlocked'.
- Recharge cards are sold at most *tabacs* (tobacconist-newsagents) and supermarkets.
- To call France from abroad dial your country's international access code, then ☎33 (France's country code), then the 10-digit local number without the initial zero.
- To call internationally from France dial ☎00, the *indicatif* (country code), the area code (without the initial zero if there is one) and the local number.

VISAS

For up-to-date details on visa requirements, check the **Ministère des Affaires Étrangères** (Ministry of Foreign Affairs; Map p186; www.diplomatie.gouv.fr; 37 quai d'Orsay, 7e; Ⓜ Assemblée Nationale).

- EU nationals and citizens of Iceland, Norway and Switzerland need only a passport or national identity card to enter France and stay in the country, even for stays of over 90 days. Citizens of new EU member states may be subject to various limitations on living and working in France.
- Citizens of Australia, the USA, Canada, Israel, Hong Kong, Japan, Malaysia, New Zealand, Singapore, South Korea and many Latin American countries do not need visas to visit France as tourists for up to 90 days. For longer stays of over 90 days, contact your nearest French embassy or consulate.
- Other people wishing to come to France as tourists have to apply for a **Schengen Visa**.
- Citizens of Australia, Canada, Japan and New Zealand aged between 18 and 30 are eligible for a 12-month, multiple-entry **Working Holiday Visa** (Permis Vacances Travail).

ℹ Getting There & Away

AIR

International airports include the following; there are many smaller ones serving European destinations only.

Aéroport de Charles de Gaulle, Paris (p202)

Aéroport d'Orly, Paris (p203)

Aéroport Lyon-St-Exupéry (p226)

Aéroport Marseille-Provence (p240)

Aéroport Nice Côte d'Azur (p248)

LAND

Bus

Eurolines (☎08 92 89 90 91; www.eurolines.eu), a grouping of 32 long-haul coach operators, links France with cities all across Europe and in Morocco and Russia. Discounts are available to people under 26 and over 60. Make advance reservations, especially in July and August.

Car & Motorcycle

A right-hand-drive vehicle brought to France from the UK or Ireland must have deflectors affixed to the headlights to avoid dazzling oncoming traffic.

> **CONNECTIONS**
>
> - High-speed trains link Paris' Gare du Nord with London's St Pancras (via the Channel Tunnel/Eurostar rail service) in just over two hours; Gare du Nord is also the point of departure for speedy trains to Brussels, Amsterdam and Cologne.
> - Rail services link France with virtually every country in Europe.

SNCF TRAIN FARES & DISCOUNTS

The Basics

- 1st-class travel, where available, costs 20% to 30% extra.
- Ticket prices for some trains, including most TGVs, are pricier during peak periods.
- The further in advance you reserve, the lower the fares.
- Children under four travel for free, or €9 with a *forfait bambin* to any destination if they need a seat.
- Children aged four to 11 travel for half-price.

Discount Tickets

Prem's The SNCF's most heavily discounted, use-or-lose tickets are sold online, by phone and at ticket windows/machines a maximum of 90 days and a minimum of 14 days before you travel.

Bons Plans A grab-bag of cheap options for different routes/dates, advertised online under the tab 'Dernière Minute' (Last Minute).

iDTGV Cheap tickets on advance-purchase TGV travel between about 30 cities; only sold at www.idtgv.com.

Ouigo (www.ouigo.com) is a low-cost TGV service whereby you can travel on high-speed TGVs for a snip of the usual price.

Discount Cards

Reductions of 25% to 60% are available with several discount cards (valid for one year):

Carte Jeune (€50) Available to travellers aged 12 to 27.

Carte Enfant+ (€75) For one to four adults travelling with a child aged four to 11.

Carte Weekend (€75) For people aged 26 to 59. Discounts on return journeys of at least 200km that either include a Saturday night away or only involve travel on a Saturday or Sunday.

Carte Sénior+ (€60) For travellers over 60.

Departing from the UK, **Eurotunnel Le Shuttle** (☎ in France 08 10 63 03 04, in UK 08443 35 35 35; www.eurotunnel.com) trains whisk bicycles, motorcycles, cars and coaches in 35 minutes from Folkestone through the Channel Tunnel to Coquelles, 5km southwest of Calais. Shuttles run 24 hours a day, with up to three departures an hour during peak periods. The earlier you book, the less you pay. Fares for a car, including up to nine passengers, start at €30.

Train

- Rail services – including a dwindling number of overnight services to/from Spain, Italy and Germany, and Eurostar services to/from the UK – link France with virtually every country in Europe.
- Book tickets and get train information from Rail Europe (www.raileurope.com). In France, ticketing is handled by SNCF (www.voyages-sncf.com); internet bookings are possible, but it won't post tickets outside France.

SEA

Regular ferries travel to France from the UK, Ireland and Italy.

Brittany Ferries (www.brittany-ferries.co.uk) Links between England/Ireland and Brittany and Normandy.

P&O Ferries (www.poferries.com) Ferries between England and northern France.

SNCM (www.sncm.fr) Ferries between France and Sardinia.

Getting Around

AIR

Air France (www.airfrance.com) and its subsidiaries Hop! (www.hop.com) and Transavia (www.transavia.com) control the lion's share of France's domestic airline industry.

Budget carriers offering flights within France include EasyJet (www.easyjet.com), Twin Jet (www.twinjet.net) and Air Corsica (www.aircorsica.com).

BUS

Buses are widely used for short-distance travel within *départements*, especially in rural areas with relatively few train lines (eg Brittany and Normandy). Unfortunately, services in some regions are infrequent and slow, in part because they were designed to get children to school rather than transport visitors around the countryside.

BICYCLE

France is a great place to cycle, and French train company SNCF does its best to make travelling with a bicycle easy; see **www.velo.sncf.com** for full details.

Most French cities and towns have at least one bike shop that rents out mountain bikes (VTT; around €15 a day), road bikes (VTCs) and cheaper city bikes. You have to leave ID and/or a deposit (often a credit-card slip) that you forfeit if the bike is damaged or stolen. A growing number of cities have automatic bike-rental systems.

CAR & MOTORCYCLE

A car gives you exceptional freedom and allows you to visit more remote parts of France.

- All drivers must carry a national ID card or passport; a valid driving licence (*permis de conduire*; most foreign licences can be used in France for up to a year); car-ownership papers, known as a *carte grise* (grey card); and proof of third-party (liability) insurance.
- Many French motorways (*autoroutes*) are fitted with toll (*péage*) stations that charge a fee based on the distance you've travelled; factor in these costs when driving.
- To hire a car you'll usually need to be over 21 and in possession of a valid driving licence and a credit card. Automatic transmissions are very rare in France; you'll need to order one well in advance.

TRAIN

- France's superb rail network is operated by the state-owned SNCF (www.sncf.com); many rural towns not on the SNCF train network are served by SNCF buses.
- The flagship trains on French railways are the superfast TGVs, which reach speeds in excess of 200mph and can whisk you from Paris to the Côte d'Azur in as little as three hours.
- Before boarding any train, you must validate (*composter*) your ticket by time-stamping it in a *composteur*, one of those yellow posts located on the way to the platform.

Rail Passes

Residents of Europe (who do not live in France) can purchase an InterRail One Country Pass (www.interrailnet.com; three/four/six/eight days €203/223/283/313, 12–25 years €154/164/208/232), which entitles its bearer to unlimited travel on SNCF trains for three to eight days over the course of a month.

For non-European residents, Rail Europe (www.raileurope-world.com) offers the France Rail Pass (www.francerailpass.com; two/four/five days over one month €102/153/172, 12–25 years €81/123/138).

You need to really rack up the kilometres to make these passes worthwhile.

Germany

Best Castles & Palaces

- ➡ Schloss Neuschwanstein (p295)
- ➡ Wartburg (p283)
- ➡ Burg Eltz (p314)
- ➡ Schloss Sanssouci (p274)

Best Iconic Sights

- ➡ Brandenburger Tor (p261)
- ➡ Kölner Dom (p314)
- ➡ Holstentor (p328)
- ➡ Hofbräuhaus (p291)

Why Go?

Few countries have had as much impact on the world as Germany. It has given us the printing press, the automobile, aspirin and historic heavyweights from Luther to Bach to Hitler. You'll encounter history in towns where streets were laid out long before Columbus set sail, and in castles that loom above prim, half-timbered villages.

The great cities – Berlin, Munich and Hamburg among them – come in more flavours than a jar of jelly beans but will all wow you with a cultural kaleidoscope that spans the arc from art museums and high-brow opera to naughty cabaret and underground clubs.

Germany's storybook landscapes will also likely leave an even bigger imprint on your memories. There's something undeniably artistic in the way Germany's scenery unfolds from the dune-fringed northern coasts via romantic river valleys to the off-the-charts Alpine splendour. As much fun as it may be to rev up the engines on the autobahn, do slow down to better appreciate this complex and fascinating country.

When to Go

Berlin

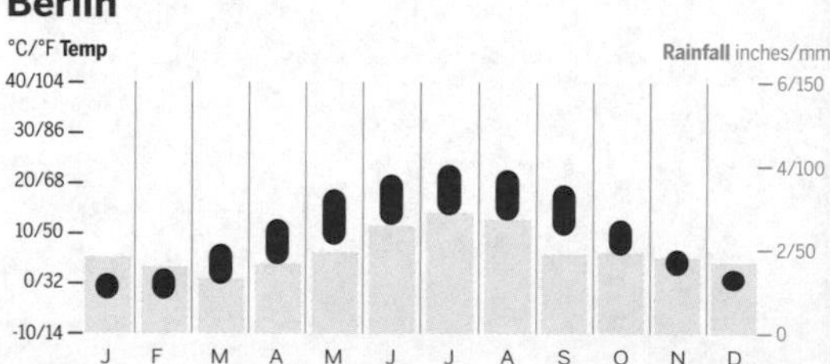

Jun–Aug Warm summers cause Germans to shed their clothes; night never seems to come.

Sep Radiant foliage and often-sunny skies invite outdoor pursuits; festivals galore.

Dec It's icy, it's cold but lines are short and Alpine slopes and twinkly Christmas markets beckon.

BERLIN

030 / POP 3.61 MILLION

Berlin is a bon vivant, passionately feasting on the smorgasbord of life, never taking things – or itself – too seriously. Its unique blend of glamour and grit is bound to mesmerise anyone keen to connect with its vibrant culture, superb museums, fabulous food, intense nightlife and tangible history.

When it comes to creativity, the sky's the limit in Berlin, Europe's newest start-up capital. In the last 20 years, the city has become a giant lab of cultural experimentation thanks to an abundance of space, cheap rent and a free-wheeling spirit that nurtures and encourages new ideas.

All this trendiness is a triumph for a city that staged a revolution, was headquartered by Nazis, bombed to bits, divided in two and finally reunited – and that was just in the 20th century! Must-sees and aimless explorations – Berlin delivers it all in one exciting and memorable package.

Sights

Key sights such as the Reichstag, Brandenburger Tor and Museumsinsel cluster in the walkable historic city centre – **Mitte** – which also cradles the **Scheunenviertel**, a maze-like hipster quarter around Hackescher Markt. Further north, residential **Prenzlauer Berg** has a lively cafe and restaurant scene, while to the south loom the contemporary high-rises of **Potsdamer Platz**. Further south, gritty but cool **Kreuzberg** and **Neukölln** are party central, as is student-flavoured **Friedrichshain** east across the Spree River. Western Berlin's hub is **Charlottenburg**, with great shopping and a swish royal palace.

Historic Mitte

★Reichstag HISTORIC BUILDING
(www.bundestag.de; Platz der Republik 1, Visitors' Service, Scheidemannstrasse; lift ride 8am-midnight, last entry 10pm, Visitors' Service 8am-8pm Apr-Oct, to 6pm Nov-Mar; 100, S Brandenburger Tor, Hauptbahnhof, U Brandenburger Tor, Bundestag) FREE It's been burned, bombed, rebuilt, buttressed by the Wall, wrapped in fabric and finally turned into the modern home of the German parliament by Norman Foster: the 1894 Reichstag is indeed one of Berlin's most iconic buildings. Its most distinctive feature, the glittering glass dome, is serviced by a lift and affords fabulous 360-degree city views. For guaranteed access, make free reservations online, otherwise try scoring tickets at the Reichstag Service Centre for the same or next day. Bring ID.

★Brandenburger Tor LANDMARK
(Brandenburger Gate; Pariser Platz; S Brandenburger Tor, U Brandenburger Tor) A symbol of division during the Cold War, the landmark Brandenburg Gate now epitomises German reunification. Carl Gotthard Langhans found inspiration in Athens' Acropolis for the elegant triumphal arch, completed in 1791 as the royal city gate. It stands sentinel over Pariser Platz, a harmoniously proportioned square once again framed by banks, a hotel and the US, British and French embassies, just as it was during its 19th-century heyday.

★Holocaust Memorial MEMORIAL
(Memorial to the Murdered Jews of Europe; Map p270; 030-2639 4336; www.stiftung-denkmal.de; Cora-Berliner-Strasse 1; audioguide adult/

ITINERARIES

Three Days

Come on, is that all you got? If the answer is really yes, drive down the **Romantic Road**, stopping in Rothenburg ob der Tauber and Füssen, then spend the rest of your time in **Munich**.

Five Days

Spend a couple of days in **Berlin**, head south to **Dresden** and **Nuremberg** or **Bamberg** for half a day each and wrap up your trip in **Munich** and surrounds.

One Week

This gives you a little bit of time to tailor a tour beyond the highlights mentioned above. Art fans might want to build **Cologne** or **Düsseldorf** into their itinerary; romantics could consider **Heidelberg**, a Rhine cruise or a trip down the **Romantic Road**; while outdoorsy types are likely to be lured by **Garmisch-Partenkirchen**, **Berchtesgaden** or the **Black Forest**.

Germany Highlights

1 Berlin (261) Discovering your inner party animal in the capital; save sleep for somewhere else as there's no time here with the clubs, museums and bars.

2 Munich (p285) Experiencing Oktoberfest,a bacchanale of suds, or just soaking up the vibe in a beer garden.

3 Bamberg (p300) Going slow in Germany's alluring small towns like this gem, with winding lanes, smoked beer (!) and a lack of cliché.

4 Cologne (p314) Comparing the soaring peaks of the Dom with the slinky glasses of this city's famous beer.

5 Black Forest (p304) Going cuckoo in the Black Forest, discovering its chilly

crags, misty peaks and endless trails.

6 Dresden (p277) Getting into the swing of this city, with a creative culture beyond the restorations.

7 Hamburg (p321) Cruising around one of the world's great harbours, then following the trail of the Beatles.

8 Trier (p313) Discovering the best-preserved Roman ruins north of the Alps in this delightful wine town on the Moselle.

9 Schloss Neuschwanstein (p295) Diving into the mind of a loopy Bavarian monarch at this dreamy palace cradled by the Alps.

10 Nuremberg (p298) Tapping into this city's medieval roots, enjoying the famous local sausages, and pondering its haunting Nazi past.

Berlin

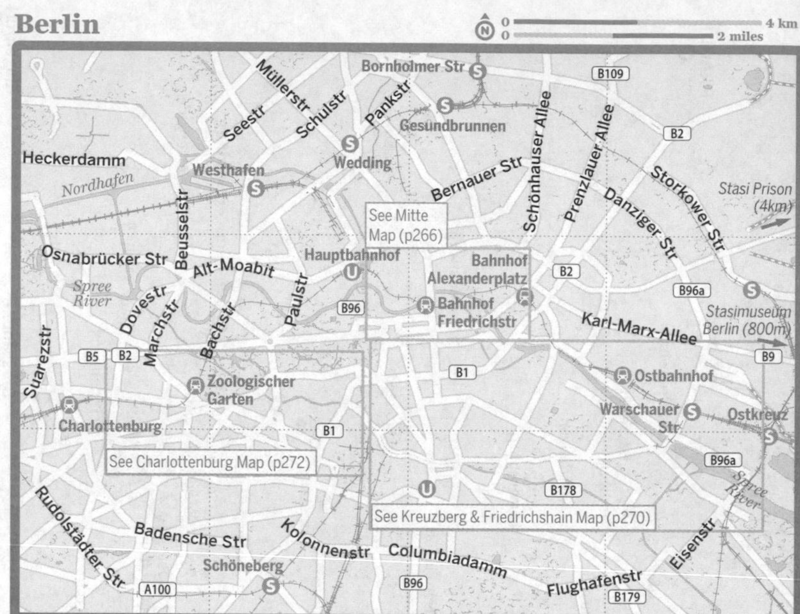

concession €4/2; field 24hr, information centre 10am-8pm Tue-Sun Apr-Sep, to 7pm Oct-Mar, last entry 45min before closing; S Brandenburger Tor, U Brandenburger Tor) FREE Inaugurated in 2005, this football-field-sized memorial by American architect Peter Eisenman consists of 2711 sarcophagi-like concrete columns rising in sombre silence from undulating ground. You're free to access this maze at any point and make your individual journey through it. For context visit the subterranean **Ort der Information** (Information Centre; Map p270; 030-7407 2929; www.holocaust-mahnmal.de; Cora-Berliner-Strasse 1) FREE whose exhibits will leave no one untouched. Audioguides and audio translations of exhibit panels are available.

Hitler's Bunker HISTORIC SITE

(Map p270; cnr In den Ministergärten & Gertrud-Kolmar-Strasse; 24hr; S Brandenburger Tor, U Brandenburger Tor) Berlin was burning and Soviet tanks advancing relentlessly when Adolf Hitler killed himself on 30 April 1945, alongside Eva Braun, his long-time female companion, hours after their marriage. Today, a parking lot covers the site, revealing its dark history only via an information panel with a diagram of the vast bunker network, construction data and the site's post-WWII history.

Checkpoint Charlie HISTORIC SITE

(Map p270; cnr Zimmerstrasse & Friedrichstrasse; 24hr; U Kochstrasse) FREE Checkpoint Charlie was the principal gateway for foreigners and diplomats between the two Berlins from 1961 to 1990. Unfortunately, this potent symbol of the Cold War has degenerated into a tacky tourist trap, though a free open-air exhibit that illustrates milestones in Cold War history is one redeeming aspect.

Museumsinsel & Scheunenviertel

Museumsinsel (Museum Island) is Berlin's most important treasure trove with five museums showcasing 6000 years worth of art, artefacts, sculpture and architecture from Europe and beyond.

★ **Pergamonmuseum** MUSEUM

(030-266 424 242; www.smb.museum; Bodestrasse 1-3; adult/concession €12/6; 10am-6pm Fri-Wed, to 8pm Thu; 100, 200, TXL, S Hackescher Markt, Friedrichstrasse) Opening a fascinating window on to the ancient world, this palatial three-wing complex unites a rich feast of classical sculpture and monumental architecture from Greece, Rome, Babylon and the Middle East, including the radiant-blue **Ishtar Gate** from Babylon, the **Roman Market**

Gate of Miletus and the **Caliph's Palace** of Mshatta. Renovations put the namesake Pergamon Altar off limits until 2019. Budget at least two hours for this amazing place and be sure to pick up the free and excellent audioguide.

★Neues Museum MUSEUM

(New Museum; ☎030-266 424 242; www.smb.museum; Bodestrasse 1-3; adult/concession €12/6; ⊙10am-6pm, to 8pm Thu; 🚌100, 200, TXL, S Hackescher Markt) David Chipperfield's reconstruction of the bombed-out Neues Museum is now the residence of Queen Nefertiti, the showstopper of the **Egyptian Museum**, which also features mummies, sculptures and sarcophagi. Pride of place at the **Museum of Pre- and Early History** (in the same building) goes to Trojan antiquities, a Neanderthal skull and the 3000-year-old 'Berliner Goldhut', a golden conical hat. Skip the queue by buying your timed ticket online. Entry must be made during the designated 30-minute time slot.

Berliner Dom CHURCH

(Berlin Cathedral; ☎030-2026 9136; www.berlinerdom.de; Am Lustgarten; adult/concession/under 18 €7/5/free; ⊙9am-8pm Apr-Oct, to 7pm Nov-Mar; 🚌100, 200, TXL, S Hackescher Markt) Pompous yet majestic, the Italian Renaissance–style former royal court church (1905) does triple duty as house of worship, museum and concert hall. Inside it's gilt to the hilt and outfitted with a lavish marble-and-onyx altar, a 7269-pipe Sauer organ and elaborate royal sarcophagi. Climb up the 267 steps to the gallery for glorious city views.

★DDR Museum MUSEUM

(GDR Museum; ☎030-847 123 731; www.ddr-museum.de; Karl-Liebknecht-Strasse 1; adult/concession €9.50/6; ⊙10am-8pm Sun-Fri, to 10pm Sat; 🚌100, 200, TXL, S Hackescher Markt) This interactive museum does an entertaining job of pulling back the iron curtain on an extinct society. You'll learn how, under communism, kids were put through collective potty training, engineers earned little more than farmers, and everyone, it seems, went on nudist holidays. A highlight is a simulated ride in a Trabi (an East German car).

★Fernsehturm LANDMARK

(TV Tower; ☎030-247 575 875; www.tv-turm.de; Panoramastrasse 1a; adult/child €13/8.50, premium ticket €19.50/12; ⊙9am-midnight Mar-Oct, 10am-midnight Nov-Feb, last ascent 11.30pm; 📶; 🚌100, 200, TXL, U Alexanderplatz, S Alexanderplatz) Germany's tallest structure, the TV Tower has been soaring 368m high since 1969 and is as iconic to Berlin as the Eiffel Tower is to Paris. On clear days, views are stunning from the panorama level at 203m or from the upstairs **restaurant** (☎030-247 5750; www.tv-turm.de/en/bar-restaurant; mains lunch €9.50-18.50, dinner €14.50-28.50; ⊙10am-midnight), which makes one revolution per hour. To shorten the wait, buy a timed ticket online.

★Hackesche Höfe HISTORIC SITE

(☎030-2809 8010; www.hackesche-hoefe.com; enter from Rosenthaler Strasse 40/41 or Sophienstrasse 6; 🚋M1, S Hackescher Markt, U Weinmeisterstrasse) FREE The Hackesche Höfe is the largest and most famous of the courtyard ensembles peppered throughout the Scheunenviertel. Built in 1907, the eight

BERLIN IN...

One Day

Book ahead for an early lift ride to the **Reichstag** dome, then snap a picture of the **Brandenburger Tor (Gate)** before stumbling around the **Holocaust Memorial** and admiring the contemporary architecture of **Potsdamer Platz**. Ponder Cold War madness at **Checkpoint Charlie**, then head to **Museumsinsel** for an audience with Queen Nefertiti and the Ishtar Gate. Finish up with a night of mirth and gaiety around **Hackescher Markt**.

Two Days

Kick off day two coming to grips with what life was like in divided Berlin at the **Gedenkstätte Berliner Mauer**. Intensify the experience at the **DDR Museum** or on a walk along the **East Side Gallery**. Spend the afternoon soaking up the urban spirit of **Kreuzberg** with its sassy shops and street art, grab dinner along the canal, drinks around Kottbusser Tor and finish up with a night of clubbing.

Mitte

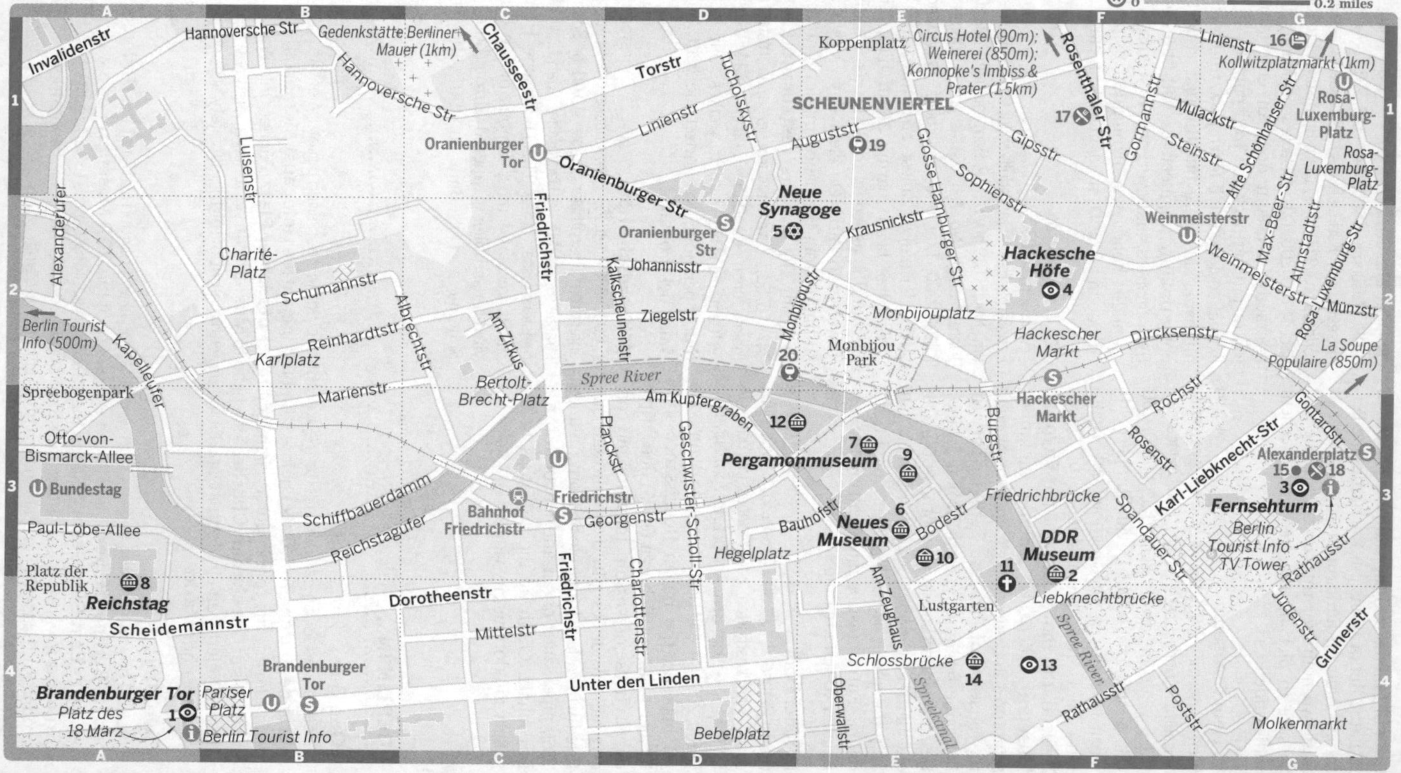

400 m
0.2 miles
Rosa-Luxemburg-Platz
Rosa-Luxemburg-Platz
Kollwitzplatzmarkt (1km)
16
Linienstr
Rosa-Luxemburg-Str
Almstadtstr
Münzstr
La Soupe Populaire (850m)
Max-Beer-Str
Alte Schönhauser Str
Mulackstr
Steinstr
Weinmeisterstr
Weinmeisterstr
Gormannstr
Rosenthaler Str
17
Circus Hotel (90m); Weinerei (850m); Konnopke's Imbiss & Prater (1.5km)
Gipsstr
Sophienstr
Hackesche Höfe
4
Dircksenstr
Hackescher Markt
Hackescher Markt
Gontardstr
Alexanderplatz
15
18
3
Fernsehturm
Berlin Tourist Info
TV Tower
Rathausstr
Jüdenstr
Grunerstr
Molkenmarkt
Rochstr
Rosenstr
Karl-Liebknecht-Str
Spandauer Str
Poststr
Friedrichbrücke
DDR Museum
2
Liebknechtbrücke
Spree River
Rathausstr
13
Burgstr
11
Lustgarten
14
Schlossbrücke
Spreekanal
Koppenplatz
SCHEUNENVIERTEL
Grosse Hamburger Str
Krausnickstr
Monbijouplatz
Bodestr
10
9
7
Pergamonmuseum
6
Neues Museum
Am Zeughaus
Oberwallstr
19
Auguststr
Neue Synagoge
5
Monbijoustr
Monbijou Park
20
12
Am Kupfergraben
Bauhofstr
Hegelplatz
Tucholskystr
Oranienburger Str
Oranienburger Str
Johannisstr
Ziegelstr
Geschwister-Scholl-Str
Bebelplatz
Torstr
Linienstr
Kalkscheunenstr
Spree River
Planckstr
Friedrichstr
Georgenstr
Charlottenstr
Unter den Linden
Chausseestr
Oranienburger Tor
Friedrichstr
Friedrichstr
Am Zirkus
Bertolt-Brecht-Platz
Bahnhof Friedrichstr
Dorotheenstr
Mittelstr
Gedenkstätte Berliner Mauer (1km)
Hannoversche Str
Albrechtstr
Reinhardtstr
Marienstr
Schiffbauerdamm
Reichstagufer
Hannoversche Str
Schumannstr
Karlplatz
Brandenburger Tor
Luisenstr
Charité-Platz
Scheidemannstr
Pariser Platz
Berlin Tourist Info
Invalidenstr
Kapelleufer
Berlin Tourist Info (500m)
Alexanderufer
Spreebogenpark
Otto-von-Bismarck-Allee
Bundestag
Paul-Löbe-Allee
8
Reichstag
Platz der Republik
Brandenburger Tor
1
Platz des 18 März

Mitte

Top Sights

1 Brandenburger Tor....A4
2 DDR Museum....F3
3 Fernsehturm....G3
4 Hackesche Höfe....F2
5 Neue Synagoge....D2
6 Neues Museum....E3
7 Pergamonmuseum....E3
8 Reichstag....A4

Sights

9 Alte Nationalgalerie....E3
10 Altes Museum....E3
11 Berliner Dom....F3
12 Bode-Museum....D3
13 Humboldt Forum....F4
14 Humboldt-Box....E4

Activities, Courses & Tours

15 Fat Tire Tours Berlin....G3

Sleeping

16 Wombat's Berlin....G1

Eating

17 Chèn Chè....F1
18 Sphere....G3

Drinking & Nightlife

19 Clärchens Ballhaus....E1
20 Strandbar Mitte....D2

interlinked *Höfe* reopened in 1996 with a congenial mix of cafes, galleries, boutiques and entertainment venues. The main entrance on Rosenthaler Strasse leads to **Court I**, prettily festooned with art nouveau tiles, while Court VII segues to the romantic **Rosenhöfe** with a sunken rose garden and tendril-like balustrades.

★ **Neue Synagoge** SYNAGOGUE

(030-8802 8300; www.centrumjudaicum.de; Oranienburger Strasse 28-30; adult/concession €5/4; 10am-6pm Mon-Fri, to 7pm Sun, closes 3pm Fri & 6pm Sun Oct-Mar; M1, U Oranienburger Tor, S Oranienburger Strasse) The gleaming gold dome of the Neue Synagoge is the most visible symbol of Berlin's revitalised Jewish community. The 1866 original was Germany's largest synagogue but its modern incarnation is not so much a house of worship (although prayer services do take place), as a museum and place of remembrance called **Centrum Judaicum**. The dome can be climbed from April to September (adult/concession €3/2.50). An audioguide costs €3.

★ **Gedenkstätte Berliner Mauer** MEMORIAL

(Berlin Wall Memorial; 030-467 986 666; www.berliner-mauer-gedenkstaette.de; Bernauer Strasse btwn Schwedter Strasse & Gartenstrasse; visitor & documentation centre 10am-6pm Tue-Sun, open-air exhibit 8am-10pm daily; S Nordbahnhof, Bernauer Strasse, Eberswalder Strasse) FREE For an insightful primer on the Berlin Wall, visit this outdoor memorial, which extends for 1.4km along Bernauer Strasse and integrates an original section of Wall, vestiges of the border installations and escape tunnels, a chapel and a monument. Multimedia stations, panels, excavations and a **Documentation Centre** provide context and explain what the border fortifications looked like and how they shaped the everyday lives of people on both sides of them. There's a great view from the centre's viewing platform.

Potsdamer Platz & Tiergarten

Potsdamer Platz, built from scratch in the 1990s from terrain once bisected by the Berlin Wall, is a showcase of contemporary architecture, with Helmut Jahn's **Sony Center** being the most eye-catching complex. A visit here is easily combined with the **Kulturforum**, a cluster of art museums and the world-famous Berliner Philharmonie. With its rambling paths and hidden beer gardens, the Tiergarten, one of Europe's largest city parks, makes for a perfect sightseeing break.

★ **Gemäldegalerie** GALLERY

(Gallery of Old Masters; Map p272; 030-266 424 242; www.smb.museum/gg; Matthäikirchplatz; adult/concession €10/5; 10am-6pm Tue, Wed & Fri, 10am-8pm Thu, 11am-6pm Sat & Sun; M29, M48, M85, 200, S Potsdamer Platz, U Potsdamer Platz) This museum ranks among the world's finest and most comprehensive collections of European art with about 1500 paintings spanning the arc of artistic vision from the 13th to the 18th century. Wear comfy shoes when exploring the 72 galleries: a walk past masterpieces by Titian, Dürer, Hals, Vermeer, Gainsborough and many more Old Masters covers almost 2km. Don't miss the Rembrandt Room (Room X).

★ **Topographie des Terrors** MUSEUM

(Topography of Terror; Map p270; 030-2548 0950; www.topographie.de; Niederkirchner Strasse 8; 10am-8pm, grounds close at dusk or 8pm at the latest; S Potsdamer Platz, U Potsdamer Platz) FREE In the same spot where the most feared institutions of Nazi Germany (including the

Gestapo headquarters and the SS central command) once stood, this compelling exhibit chronicles the stages of terror and persecution, puts a face on the perpetrators and details the impact these brutal institutions had on all of Europe. A second exhibit outside zeroes in on how life changed for Berlin and its people after the Nazis made it their capital.

Kreuzberg & Friedrichshain

Kreuzberg has a split personality: while its western section (around Bergmannstrasse) has a genteel air, eastern Kreuzberg (around Kottbusser Tor) – as well as northern Neukölln across the canal – is a multicultural mosaic and raucous nightlife hub. You'll find more after-dark action along with some Cold War relics in Friedrichshain across the Spree.

★East Side Gallery LANDMARK

(Map p270; www.eastsidegallery-berlin.de; Mühlenstrasse btwn Oberbaumbrücke & Ostbahnhof; 24hr; U Warschauer Strasse, S Ostbahnhof, Warschauer Strasse) FREE The year was 1989. After 28 years, the Berlin Wall, that grim and grey divider of humanity, finally met its maker. Most of it was quickly dismantled, but along Mühlenstrasse, paralleling the Spree, a 1.3km stretch became the East Side Gallery, the world's largest open-air mural collection. In more than 100 paintings, dozens of international artists translated the era's global euphoria and optimism into a mix of political statements, drug-induced musings and truly artistic visions.

★Jüdisches Museum MUSEUM

(Jewish Museum; Map p270; 030-2599 3300; www.jmberlin.de; Lindenstrasse 9-14; adult/concession €8/3, audioguide €3; 10am-8pm Tue-Sun, to 10pm Mon, last entry 1hr before closing; U Hallesches Tor, Kochstrasse) In a landmark building by American-Polish architect Daniel Libeskind, Berlin's Jewish Museum offers a chronicle of the trials and triumphs in 2000 years of Jewish life in Germany. The exhibit smoothly navigates all major periods, from the Middle Ages via the Enlightenment to the community's post-1990 renaissance. Find out about Jewish cultural contributions, holiday traditions, the difficult road to emancipation and outstanding individuals (eg Moses Mendelssohn, Levi Strauss) and the fates of ordinary people.

Stasimuseum MUSEUM

(030-553 6854; www.stasimuseum.de; Haus 1, Ruschestrasse 103; adult/concession €6/4.50; 10am-6pm Mon-Fri, 11am-6pm Sat & Sun; U Magdalenenstrasse) This exhibit provides an overview of the structure, methods and impact of the Ministry of State Security (Stasi), former East Germany's secret police, inside the feared institution's fortress-like headquarters. Marvel at cunningly low-tech surveillance devices (hidden in watering cans, rocks, even neckties), a prisoner transport van with tiny, lightless cells, and the stuffy offices of Stasi chief Erich Mielke. Panelling is partly in English. Free English tours at 3pm Saturday and Sunday. The museum is in the eastern district of Lichtenberg, just north of U-Bahn station Magdalenenstrasse.

MORE MUSEUM ISLAND TREASURES

While the Pergamonmuseum and the Neues Museum are the highlights of Museum Island, the other three museums are no slouches in the treasure department either. Fronting the Lustgarten park the **Altes Museum** (Old Museum; 030-266 424 242; www.smb.museum; Am Lustgarten; adult/concession €10/5; 10am-6pm Tue, Wed & Fri-Sun, to 8pm Thu; 100, 200, TXL, S Friedrichstrasse, Hackescher Markt) presents Greek, Etruscan and Roman antiquities. At the northern tip of the island, the **Bodemuseum** (030-266 424 242; www.smb.museum; cnr Am Kupfergraben & Monbijoubrücke; adult/concession €12/6; 10am-6pm Tue, Wed & Fri-Sun, to 8pm Thu; S Hackescher Markt, Friedrichstrasse) has a prized collection of European sculpture from the Middle Ages to the 18th century. Finally, there's the **Alte Nationalgalerie** (Old National Gallery; 030-266 424 242; www.smb.museum; Bodestrasse 1-3; adult/concession €12/6; 10am-6pm Tue, Wed & Fri-Sun, to 8pm Thu; 100, 200, TXL, S Hackescher Markt), whose thematic focus is on 19th-century European painting.

A combined day pass for all five museums costs €18 (concession €9).

BERLIN CITY PALACE: BACK TO THE FUTURE PALACE

Across from Museum Island looms Berlin's biggest construction site: the **Humboldt Forum** (Berlin City Palace; Schlossplatz; 100, 200, TXL, U Klosterstrasse), an art and cultural centre built to look like an exact replica of the baroque Berliner Stadtschloss (Berlin City Palace), but with a modern interior. The new space will be a centre of global culture and also harbour famous collections of ethnology and Asian art. If all goes to plan, the entire project should open in 2019.

Although barely damaged in WWII, the palace where Prussian rulers had made their home since 1443 was blown up by East Germany's government in 1950 to drop the final curtain on Prussian and Nazi rule.

Meanwhile, an adjacent information centre called **Humboldt-Box** (0180 503 0707; www.humboldt-box.com; Schlossplatz 5; 10am-7pm Apr-Nov, to 6pm Dec-Mar; 100, 200, TXL, U Hausvogteiplatz) FREE has changing exhibits on the project and panoramic views from its top-level cafe. An exhibition highlight is a fantastically detailed model that shows how the historic palace fit into the old city centre around 1900.

Stasi Prison MEMORIAL

(Gedenkstätte Berlin-Hohenschönhausen; 030-9860 8230; www.stiftung-hsh.de; Genslerstrasse 66; tours adult/concession €6/3, exhibit free; tours in English 10.30am, 12.30pm & 2.30pm Mar-Oct, 2.30pm daily & 11.30am Sat & Sun Nov-Feb, exhibit 9am-6pm, German tours more frequent; P; M5) Victims of Stasi persecution often ended up in this grim remand prison, now a memorial site officially called Gedenkstätte Berlin-Hohenschönhausen. Tours – often conducted by former inmates – reveal the full extent of the terror and cruelty perpetrated upon thousands of suspected regime opponents, many utterly innocent. A permanent exhibit uses photographs, objects and a free audioguide to document daily life behind bars and also opens up the offices of the prison administration.

City West & Charlottenburg

★Schloss Charlottenburg PALACE

(030-320 910; www.spsg.de; Spandauer Damm 10-22; day passes to all 4 buildings adult/concession €12/9; hours vary by building; P; M45, 109, 309, U Richard-Wagner-Platz, Sophie-Charlotte-Platz) Charlottenburg Palace is one of the few sites in Berlin that still reflects the one-time grandeur of the Hohenzollern clan that ruled the region from 1415 to 1918. Originally a petite summer retreat, it grew into an exquisite baroque pile with opulent private apartments, richly festooned festival halls, collections of precious porcelain and paintings by French 18th-century masters. It's lovely in fine weather when you can fold a stroll in the palace park into a day of peeking at royal treasures.

★Kaiser-Wilhelm-Gedächtniskirche CHURCH

(Kaiser Wilhelm Memorial Church; Map p272; 030-218 5023; www.gedaechtniskirche.com; Breitscheidplatz; church 9am-7pm, memorial hall 10am-6pm Mon-Fri, 10am-5.30pm Sat, noon-5.30pm Sun; 100, 200, U Zoologischer Garten, Kurfürstendamm, S Zoologischer Garten) FREE Allied bombing in 1943 left only the husk of the west tower of this once magnificent neo-Romanesque church standing. Now an antiwar memorial, it stands quiet and dignified amid the roaring traffic. Historic photographs displayed in the **Gedenkhalle** (Hall of Remembrance), at the bottom of the tower, help you visualise the former grandeur of this 1895 church. The adjacent octagonal hall of worship, added in 1961, has glowing midnight-blue glass walls and a giant 'floating' Jesus.

Tours

Alternative Berlin Tours WALKING

(0162 819 8264; www.alternativeberlin.com; tours €10-20) Not your run-of-the-mill tour company, this outfit runs tip-based subculture tours that get beneath the skin of the city, plus an excellent street-art tour and workshop, an alternative pub crawl, a craft beer tour, the surreal 'Twilight Tour', an eco-tour, and a food and drink tour.

Fat Tire Tours Berlin CYCLING

(030-2404 7991; www.fattiretours.com/berlin; Panoramastrasse 1a; adult/concession/under 12 incl bicycle from €28/26/14; S Alexanderplatz, U Alexanderplatz) This top-rated outfit runs English-language tours by bike, e-bike and Segway. Options include a classic city spin;

Kreuzberg & Friedrichshain

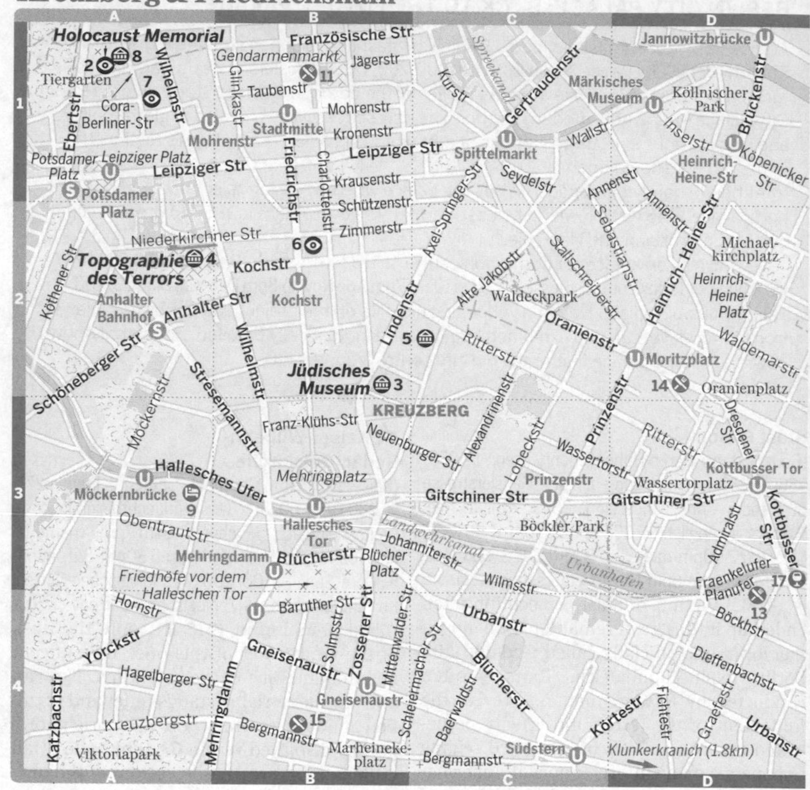

tours with a focus on Nazi Germany, the Cold War or 'Modern Berlin'; a trip to Potsdam; and an evening food tour. Tours leave from the TV Tower main entrance. Reservations advised.

Sleeping

While hotels in Charlottenburg often have special deals, remember that staying here puts you an U-Bahn ride away from most major sights (which are in Mitte) and happening nightlife in Friedrichshain or Kreuzberg.

Historic Mitte & Scheunenviertel

Wombat's Berlin HOSTEL €

(☎030-8471 0820; www.wombats-hostels.com/berlin; Alte Schönhauser Strasse 2; dm €20-26, d €68-78; ; URosa-Luxemburg-Platz) Sociable and central, Wombat's gets hostelling right. From backpack-sized in-room lockers to individual reading lamps and a guest kitchen with dishwasher, the attention to detail here is impressive. Spacious and clean en-suite dorms are as much part of the deal as free linen and a welcome drink, best enjoyed with fellow party pilgrims at sunset on the rooftop.

★Circus Hotel HOTEL €€

(☎030-2000 3939; www.circus-berlin.de; Rosenthaler Strasse 1; d €85-120, apt €120-190; ; URosenthaler Platz) At this super-central budget boutique hotel, none of the compact, mod rooms are alike, but all feature upbeat colours, thoughtful design touches, a small desk, a tea and coffee station and organic bath products. Unexpected perks include a roof terrace, bike rentals and a fabulous breakfast buffet (€9) served until 1pm. Need more space? Go for an apartment.

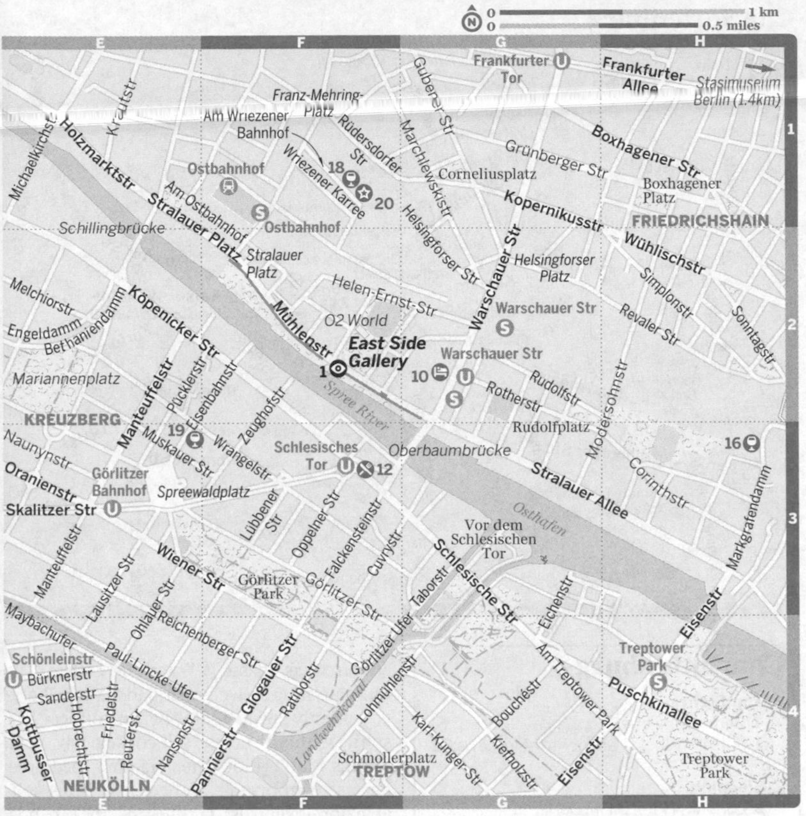

Kreuzberg & Friedrichshain

Top Sights

1 East Side Gallery F2
2 Holocaust Memorial A1
3 Jüdisches Museum B2
4 Topographie des Terrors A2

Sights

5 Berlinische Galerie C2
6 Checkpoint Charlie B2
7 Hitler's Bunker A1
8 Ort der Information A1

Sleeping

9 Grand Hostel Berlin A3
10 Michelberger Hotel G2

Eating

11 Augustiner am Gendarmenmarkt B1
12 Burgermeister F3
13 Defne D4
14 Max und Moritz D2
Michelberger (see 10)
15 Umami B4

Drinking & Nightlife

16 ://about blank H3
17 Ankerklause D3
18 Berghain/Panorama Bar F1
19 Schwarze Traube E3

Entertainment

20 Kantine am Berghain F1

Kreuzberg & Friedrichshain

★ **Grand Hostel Berlin** HOSTEL €

(Map p270; ☎030-2009 5450; www.grandhostel-berlin.de; Tempelhofer Ufer 14; dm €10-32, tw with/without bathroom from €49/38; ; Möckernbrücke) Cocktails in the library bar? Check. Rooms with stucco-ornamented ceilings? Got 'em. Canal views? Yep. Ensconced in a fully renovated 1870s building, the

Charlottenburg

Charlottenburg

Top Sights

1 Gemäldegalerie F1
2 Kaiser-Wilhelm-Gedächtniskirche C2

Sleeping

3 25hours Hotel Bikini Berlin.................C2
4 Sir Savigny A2

Eating

Butcher ....(see 4)
5 Dicke Wirtin B2
Neni...(see 3)

Drinking & Nightlife

Monkey Bar...............................(see 3)

Entertainment

6 Berliner Philharmonie F1

'five-star' Grand Hostel is one of Berlin's most supremely comfortable, convivial and atmospheric hostels. Private rooms are spacious and nicely furnished and dorms come with freestanding quality beds and large lockers. Breakfast is €6.50.

★Michelberger Hotel HOTEL €€
(Map p270; ☎030-2977 8590; www.michelberger hotel.com; Warschauer Strasse 39; d €90-160; 📶; Ⓤ Warschauer Strasse, Ⓢ Warschauer Strasse) The ultimate in creative crash pads, Michelberger perfectly encapsulates Berlin's offbeat DIY spirit without being self-consciously cool. Rooms don't hide their factory pedigree, but are comfortable and come in sizes suitable for lovebirds, families or rock bands. Staff are friendly and clued-up, and the **restaurant** (Map p270; ☎030-2977 8590; www.michelbergerhotel.com; Warschauer Strasse 39-40; mains lunch €8-10, dinner €12-23; ⏲7-11am, noon-3pm & 7-11pm; 🚭📶🍷; Ⓢ Warschauer Strasse, Ⓤ Warschauer Strasse) 🌿 is popular with both guests and locals. Breakfast is €16.

City West & Charlottenburg

Sir Savigny BOUTIQUE HOTEL €€
(Map p272; ☎030-323 015 600; www.hotel-sirsavigny.de; Kantstrasse 144; r €90-160; 🚭❄📶; Ⓢ Savignyplatz) Not only pictures but also hotels tell a story, and this is the story of Sir FK Savigny, a fictional character who welcomes savvy travellers to his cosmopolitan crash pad with a hip bar and burger joint on the ground floor. Smartly dressed rooms are equipped with such lifestyle essentials as smartphone docks, espresso-pod machines and complimentary minibar. Breakfast is €18.

★25hours Hotel Bikini Berlin DESIGN HOTEL €€
(Map p272; 030-120 2210; www.25hours-hotels.com; Budapester Strasse 40; r €130-330; P ; 100, 200, S Zoologischer Garten, U Zoologischer Garten) The 'urban jungle' theme of this lifestyle outpost in the iconic 1950s Bikini Haus plays on its location between the zoo and main shopping district. Rooms are stylish, if a tad compact, with the nicer ones facing the animal park. Quirk factors include an on-site bakery, hammocks in the public areas and a sauna with zoo view.

Eating

Historic Mitte & Scheunenviertel

★Chèn Chè VIETNAMESE €€
(030-2888 4282; www.chenche-berlin.de; Rosenthaler Strasse 13; dishes €6.50-11; noon-midnight; ; M1, U Rosenthaler Platz) In this exotic Vietnamese tearoom you can settle down in the charming Zen garden or beneath the hexagonal chandelier made from the torn pages of a herbal medicine book. The compact menu features healthy and meticulously presented *pho* (soups), curries and noodle dishes served in traditional clay pots. Exquisite tea selection and small shop.

★Augustiner am Gendarmenmarkt GERMAN €€
(Map p270; 030-2045 4020; www.augustiner-braeu-berlin.de; Charlottenstrasse 55; mains €6.50-26.50; 10am-2am; U Französische Strasse) Tourists, concert-goers and hearty-food lovers rub shoulders at rustic tables in this authentic Bavarian beer hall. Soak up the down-to-earth vibe right along with a mug of full-bodied Augustiner brew. Sausages, roast pork and pretzels provide rib-sticking sustenance, but there's also plenty of lighter (even meat-free) fare as well as good-value lunch specials.

★Katz Orange INTERNATIONAL €€€
(030-983 208 430; www.katzorange.com; Bergstrasse 22; mains €18-29; 6-11pm; ; M8, U Rosenthaler Platz) With its gourmet, organic farm-to-table menu, stylish country flair and top-notch cocktails, the 'Orange Cat' hits a gastro grand slam. It will have you purring for such perennial faves as Duroc pork that's been slow-roasted for 12 hours (nicknamed 'candy on bone'). The setting in a castle-like former brewery is stunning, especially in summer when the patio opens.

Prenzlauer Berg

Konnopke's Imbiss GERMAN €
(030-442 7765; www.konnopke-imbiss.de; Schönhauser Allee 44a; sausages €1.30-2; 9am-8pm Mon-Fri, 11.30am-8pm Sat; M1, M10, U Eberswalder Strasse) Brave the inevitable queue at this famous sausage kitchen, ensconced in the same spot below the elevated U-Bahn tracks since 1930, but now equipped with a heated pavilion and an English menu. The 'secret' sauce topping its classic *Currywurst* comes in a four-tier heat scale from mild to wild.

Umami VIETNAMESE €€
(030-2886 0626; www.umami-restaurant.de; Knaackstrasse 16-18; mains €7.50-15; noon-11.30pm; ; M2, U Senefelderplatz) A mellow 1950s lounge-vibe and an inspired menu of Indochine home cooking divided into 'regular' and 'vegetarian' choices are the main draws of this restaurant with large pavement terrace. Leave room for the green-tea apple pie or a Vietnamese cupcake called 'popcake'. The six-course family meal is a steal at €20.

WORTH A TRIP

SCHLOSS & PARK SANSSOUCI

Easily reached in half an hour from central Berlin, the former royal Prussian seat of Potsdam lures visitors to its splendid Unesco-recognised palaces and parks dreamed up by 18th-century King Friedrich II (Frederick the Great).

Headlining the roll call of royal pads is **Schloss Sanssouci** (☎0331-969 4200; www.spsg.de; Maulbeerallee; adult/concession incl tour or audioguide €12/8; ⊙10am-6pm Tue-Sun Apr-Oct, to 5pm Nov-Mar; 🚌614, 650, 695), a celebrated rococo palace and the king's favourite summer retreat. Standouts on the audio-guided tour include the whimsically decorated concert hall, the intimate library and the domed Marble Hall. Admission is limited and by timed ticket only; book online (tickets.spsg.de) to avoid wait times and/or disappointment. Tickets must be printed out. Tours run by the Potsdam **tourist office** (☎0331-2755 8899; www.potsdam-tourism.com; Potsdam Hauptbahnhof; ⊙9.30am-6pm Mon-Sat; S Potsdam Hauptbahnhof) guarantee entry.

Schloss Sanssouci is surrounded by a sprawling park dotted with numerous other palaces, buildings, fountains, statues and romantic corners. The one building not to be missed is the **Chinesisches Haus** (Chinese House; ☎0331-969 4200; www.spsg.de; Am Grünen Gitter; adult/concession €3/2; ⊙10am-6pm Tue-Sun May-Oct; 🚌605, 606, 🚊91), an adorable clover-leaf-shaped pavilion whose exterior is decorated with exotically dressed gilded figures shown sipping tea, dancing and playing musical instruments.

Another park highlight is the **Neues Palais** (New Palace; ☎0331-969 4200; www.spsg.de; Am Neuen Palais; adult/concession incl tour or audioguide €8/6; ⊙10am-6pm Wed-Mon Apr-Oct, to 5pm Nov-Mar; 🚌605, 606, 695, S Potsdam Charlottenhof) at the far western end. It has built-to-impress dimensions and is filled with opulent private and representative rooms.

Each building charges separate admission; a day pass to all costs €19 (concession €14).

On a nice day, it's worth exploring Potsdam's watery landscape and numerous other palaces on a **boat cruise** (☎0331-275 9210; www.schiffahrt-in-potsdam.de; Lange Brücke 6; ⊙Apr-Oct; 🚌605, 610, 631, 694, 🚊91, 92, 93, 98). The most popular one is the 90-minute *Schlösserundfahrt* (palace cruise; €14). Boats leave from docks near the Hauptbahnhof.

Regional trains leaving from Berlin-Hauptbahnhof and Zoologischer Garten need only 25 minutes to reach Potsdam Hauptbahnhof. The S-Bahn S7 from central Berlin makes the trip in about 40 minutes. You need an ABC ticket (€3.30) for either service.

Kreuzberg

★Burgermeister — BURGERS €

(Map p270; ☎030-2388 3840; www.burgermeister.de; Oberbaumstrasse 8; burgers €3.50-4.80; ⊙11am-3am Sun-Thu, to 4am Fri & Sat; U Schlesisches Tor) It's green, ornate, a century old and…it used to be a toilet. Now it's a burger joint beneath the elevated U-Bahn tracks. Get in line for the plump all-beef patties (try the Meisterburger with fried onions, bacon and barbecue sauce) paired with cheese fries and such homemade dips as peanut or mango curry.

Max und Moritz — GERMAN €€

(Map p270; ☎030-6951 5911; www.maxundmoritzberlin.de; Oranienstrasse 162; mains €9.50-17; ⊙5pm-midnight; ⊜📶; U Moritzplatz) The patina of yesteryear hangs over this ode to old-school brewpub named for the cheeky Wilhelm Busch cartoon characters. Since 1902 it has packed hungry diners and drinkers into its rustic tile-and-stucco ornamented rooms for sudsy home brews and granny-style Berlin fare. A menu favourite is the *Königsberger Klopse* (veal meatballs in caper sauce).

Defne — TURKISH €€

(Map p270; ☎030-8179 7111; www.defne-restaurant.de; Planufer 92c; mains €8.50-20; ⊙4pm-1am Apr-Sep, 5pm-1am Oct-Mar; ⊜🌶; U Kottbusser Tor, Schönleinstrasse) If you thought Turkish cuisine stopped at the doner kebab, canal-side Defne will teach you otherwise. The appetiser platter alone elicits intense cravings (fabulous walnut-chilli paste!), but inventive mains such as *ali nacik* (sliced lamb with puréed eggplant and yoghurt) also warrant repeat visits. Good vegetarian choices too. Lovely summer terrace.

City West & Charlottenburg

Butcher BURGERS €€

(Map p272; 030-323 015 600; www.the-butcher.com; Kantstrasse 144; burgers €9-11.50; 7am-late; ; S Savignyplatz) No matter if you fancy the Daddy, the Cow Boy or the Ugly – this place knows how to build one hell of a burger. Prime ingredients like Aberdeen Angus beef, house-baked buns and a secret (what else?) sauce make these patty-and-bun combos shine. With its bar and DJ line-up, the Butcher also injects a dose of hip into the 'hood.

Dicke Wirtin GERMAN €€

(Map p272; 030-312 4952; www.dicke-wirtin.de; Carmerstrasse 9; mains €6-16.50; 11am-late; ; S Savignyplatz) Old Berlin charm oozes from every nook and cranny of this been-here-forever pub, which pours nine draught beers (including the superb Kloster Andechs) and nearly three dozen homemade schnapps varieties. Hearty local and German fare like smoked veal dumplings, boiled eel, beef liver and pork roast keeps brains balanced. Bargain lunches, too.

Drinking & Nightlife

★**Prater Biergarten** BEER GARDEN

(030-448 5688; www.pratergarten.de; Kastanienallee 7-9; snacks €2.50-6; noon-late Apr-Sep, weather permitting; U Eberswalder Strasse) Berlin's oldest beer garden has seen beer-soaked nights since 1837 and is still a charismatic spot for guzzling a custom-brewed Prater Pilsner beneath the ancient chestnut trees (self-service). Kids can romp around the small play area.

★**Schwarze Traube** COCKTAIL BAR

(Map p270; 030-2313 5569; www.schwarzetraube.de; Wrangelstrasse 24; 7pm-2am Sun-Thu, to 5am Fri & Sat; U Görlitzer Bahnhof) Mixologist Atalay Aktas was Germany's Best Bartender of 2013 and this pint-sized drinking parlour is where he and his staff create their magic potions. Since there's no menu, each drink is calibrated to the taste and mood of each patron using premium spirits, expertise and a dash of psychology.

★**Strandbar Mitte** BAR

(030-2838 5588; www.strandbar-mitte.de; Monbijoustrasse 3; dancing €4; 10am-late May-Sep; M1, S Oranienburger Strasse) With a full-on view of the Bodemuseum, palm trees and a relaxed ambience, Germany's first beach bar (since 2002) is great for balancing a surfeit of sightseeing stimulus with a reviving drink and thin-crust pizza. At night, there's dancing under the stars with tango, cha-cha, swing and salsa, often preceded by dance lessons.

★**Clärchens Ballhaus** CLUB

(030-282 9295; www.ballhaus.de; Auguststrasse 24; 11am-late; ; M1, S Oranienburger Strasse) Yesteryear is right now at this late, great 19th-century dance hall where groovers and grannies hoof it across the parquet without even a touch of irony. There are different sounds nightly – salsa to swing, tango to disco – and a live band on Saturday. Dancing kicks off from 9pm or 9.30pm. Easy door but often packed, so book a table.

Ankerklause PUB

(Map p270; 030-693 5649; www.ankerklause.de; Kottbusser Damm 104; from 4pm Mon, from 10am Tue-Sun; U Schönleinstrasse) Ahoy there! Drop anchor at this nautical kitsch tavern in an old harbour master's shack and enjoy the arse-kicking jukebox, cold beers and surprisingly good German pub fare. The best seats are on the geranium-festooned terrace where you can wave to the boats puttering along the canal. A cult pit stop until the wee hours.

Klunkerkranich BAR

(www.klunkerkranich.de; Karl-Marx-Strasse 66; 10am-1.30am Mon-Sat, noon-1.30am Sun, weather permitting; ; U Rathaus Neukölln) During the warmer months, this club-garden-bar combo is mostly a fab place for day-drinking

GAY & LESBIAN BERLIN

Berlin's legendary liberalism has spawned one of the world's biggest and most diverse GLBT playgrounds. The historic 'gay village' is near Nollendorfplatz in Schöneberg (Motzstrasse and Fuggerstrasse especially; get off at U-Bahn station Nollendorfplatz), where the rainbow flag has proudly flown since the 1920s. The crowd skews older and leather. Current hipster central is Kreuzberg, where freewheeling party pens cluster along Oranienstrasse. Check *Siegessäule* (www.siegessaeule.de), the weekly freebie 'bible' to all things gay and lesbian in town, for the latest happenings.

and chilling to local DJs or bands up on the rooftop parking deck of the Neukölln Arcaden shopping mall. It also does breakfast, light lunches and tapas. Check the website – these folks come up with new ideas all the time (gardening workshops anyone?).

To get up here, take the lifts just inside the 'Bibliothek/Post' entrance on Karl-Marx-Strasse to the 5th floor.

★://about blank CLUB
(Map p270; www.aboutparty.net; Markgrafendamm 24c; ⏲hours vary, always Fri & Sat; S Ostkreuz) At this gritty multifloor party pen with lots of nooks and crannies, a steady line-up of top DJs feeds a diverse bunch of revellers dance-worthy electronic gruel. Intense club nights usually segue into the morning and beyond. Run by a collective, the venue also hosts cultural, political and gender events.

★Berghain/Panorama Bar CLUB
(Map p270; www.berghain.de; Am Wriezener Bahnhof; ⏲midnight Fri-Mon morning; S Ostbahnhof) Only world-class spinmasters heat up this hedonistic bass-junkie hellhole inside a labyrinthine ex-power plant. Hard-edged minimal techno dominates the ex-turbine hall (Berghain) while house dominates at Panorama Bar, one floor up. Strict door, no cameras. Check the website for midweek concerts and record-release parties at the main venue and the adjacent **Kantine am Berghain** (☎030-2936 0210; admission varies; ⏲hours vary).

☆ Entertainment

Berliner Philharmonie CLASSICAL MUSIC
(Map p272; ☎tickets 030-254 888 999; www.berliner-philharmoniker.de; Herbert-von-Karajan-Strasse 1; tickets €30-100; 🚌M29, M48, M85, 200, S Potsdamer Platz, U Potsdamer Platz) This world-famous concert hall has supreme acoustics and, thanks to Hans Scharoun's terraced vineyard configuration, not a bad seat in the house. It's the home turf of the Berliner Philharmoniker, which will be led by Sir Simon Rattle until 2018. One year later, Russia-born Kirill Petrenko will pick up the baton as music director.

ℹ Information

Brandenburger Tor (☎030-250 025; www.visitberlin.de; Brandenburger Tor, south wing, Pariser Platz; ⏲9.30am-7pm Apr-Oct, to 6pm Nov-Mar; S Brandenburger Tor, U Brandenburger Tor)

DISCOUNT CARDS

Berlin Welcome Card (www.berlin-welcomecard.de; travel in AB zones 48/72 hours €19.50/27.50, AB zones 72 hours plus admission to Museumsinsel €42) Valid for unlimited public transport for one adult and up to three children under 14 plus up to 50% discount to 200 sights, attractions and tours. Sold online, at the tourist offices, from U-Bahn and S-Bahn station ticket vending machines and on buses.

Museumspass Berlin (adult/concession €24/12) Buys admission to the permanent exhibits of about 50 museums for three consecutive days, including big draws like the Pergamonmuseum. Sold at tourist offices and participating museums.

Europa-Center (Map p272; ☎030-250 025; Tauentzienstrasse 9, Europa-Center, ground fl; ⏲10am-8pm Mon-Sat; 🚌100, 200, U Kurfürstendamm)

Hauptbahnhof (☎030-250 025; www.visitberlin.de; Hauptbahnhof, Europaplatz entrance, ground fl; ⏲8am-10pm; S Hauptbahnhof, 🚆Hauptbahnhof)

TV Tower (☎030-250 025; www.visitberlin.de; Panoramastrasse 1a, TV Tower, ground fl; ⏲10am-6pm Apr-Oct, to 4pm Nov-Mar; 🚌100, 200, TXL, U Alexanderplatz, S Alexanderplatz)

ℹ Getting There & Away

AIR

Since the opening of the new Berlin Brandenburg Airport has been delayed indefinitely, flights continue to land at the city's **Tegel** (TXL; ☎030-6091 1150; www.berlin-airport.de; 🚌Tegel Flughafen) and **Schönefeld** (SXF; ☎030-6091 1150; www.berlin-airport.de; 🚆Airport-Express, RE7 & RB14) airports.

BUS

Most long-haul buses arrive at the **Zentraler Omnibusbahnhof** (ZOB; ☎030-3010 0175; www.iob-berlin.de; Masurenallee 4-6; S Messe/ICC Nord, U Kaiserdamm) near the trade fair grounds in far western Berlin. The U2 U-Bahn line links to the city centre. Some bus operators also stop at Alexanderplatz and other points around town.

TRAIN

Berlin has several train stations but most trains converge at the Hauptbahnhof (main train station) in the heart of the city.

Getting Around

TO/FROM THE AIRPORT

Tegel

Bus TXL bus to Alexanderplatz (Tariff AB, 40 minutes) via Hauptbahnhof (central train station) every 10 minutes. Bus X9 for Charlottenburg (eg Zoo station; Tariff AB, 20 minutes).

U-Bahn Closest U-station is Jakob-Kaiser-Platz, served by bus 109 and X9. From here, the U7 goes straight to Schöneberg and Kreuzberg (Tariff AB).

Schönefeld

The airport train station is about 400m from the terminals. Free shuttle buses run every 10 minutes; walking takes five to 10 minutes.

Airport-Express Regular Deutsche Bahn regional trains, identified as RE7 and RB14 in timetables, go to central Berlin twice hourly (Tariff ABC, 30 minutes).

S-Bahn S9 runs every 20 minutes and is handy for Friedrichshain or Prenzlauer Berg. For the Messe (trade-fair grounds), take the S45 to Südkreuz and change to the S41.Tariff ABC.

PUBLIC TRANSPORT

➡ One ticket is valid on all forms of public transport, including the U-Bahn, buses, trams and ferries. Most rides require a Tariff AB ticket, which is valid for two hours (interruptions and transfers allowed, but not round trips).

➡ Tickets are available from bus drivers, vending machines at U- and S-Bahn stations and on trams and at station offices. Expect to pay cash (change given) and be sure to validate (stamp) your ticket or risk a €60 fine during spot-checks.

➡ Services operate from 4am until just after midnight on weekdays, with half-hourly *Nachtbuses* (night buses) in between. At weekends the U-Bahn and S-Bahn run all night long (except the U4 and U55).

➡ For trip planning, check the website (www.bvg.de) or call the 24-hour hotline.

BUS TOUR ON THE CHEAP

Get a crash course in 'Berlinology' by hopping on bus 100 or 200 at Zoologischer Garten or Alexanderplatz and letting the landmarks whoosh by for the price of a standard bus ticket (€2.70, day pass €7). Bus 100 goes via the Tiergarten, 200 via Potsdamer Platz. Without traffic and getting off, trips take about 30 minutes.

CENTRAL GERMANY

Central Germany straddles the states of Thuringia and Saxony, both in the former eastern Germany. It takes in towns like Weimar, Eisenach and Erfurt that have been shaped by some of the biggest names in German history and culture, including Goethe and Martin Luther. Further east, Dresden is a town that defines survival while Leipzig can be justifiably proud of doing its part in bringing about the downfall of East Germany. Expect this region to enlighten, inspire and, above all, surprise you.

Dresden

☎0351 / POP 512,000

Proof that there is life after death, Dresden has become one of Germany's most visited cities, and for good reason. Restorations have returned its historic core to its 18th-century heyday when it was famous throughout Europe as 'Florence on the Elbe'. Scores of Italian artists, musicians, actors and master craftsmen flocked to the court of Augustus the Strong, bestowing countless masterpieces upon the city.

The devastating bombing raids in 1945 levelled most of these treasures. But Dresden is a survivor and many of the most important landmarks have since been rebuilt, including the elegant Frauenkirche. Today, there's a constantly evolving arts and cultural scene and zinging pub and nightlife quarters, especially in the Outer Neustadt.

Sights

Dresden straddles the Elbe River, with the attraction-studded Altstadt (old town) in the south and the Neustadt (new town) pub and student quarter to the north.

★Zwinger PALACE
(☎0351-4914 2000; www.der-dresdner-zwinger.de; Theaterplatz 1; adult/concession €10/7.50; ⏲10am-6pm Tue-Sun) FREE A collaboration between the architect Matthäus Pöppelmann and the sculptor Balthasar Permoser, the Zwinger was built between 1710 and 1728 on the orders of Augustus the Strong, who, having returned from seeing Louis XIV's palace at Versailles, wanted something similar for himself. Primarily a party palace for royals, the Zwinger has ornate portals that lead into the vast fountain-studded courtyard, which is framed by buildings

WORTH A TRIP

SACHSENHAUSEN CONCENTRATION CAMP

A mere 35km north of Berlin, Sachsenhausen was built by prisoners and opened in 1936 as a prototype for other concentration camps. By 1945 some 200,000 people had passed through its sinister gates, most of them political opponents, Jews, Roma people and, after 1939, POWs. Tens of thousands died from hunger, exhaustion, illness, exposure, medical experiments and executions. The camp became a **memorial site** (Memorial & Museum Sachsenhausen; ☎03301-200 200; www.stiftung-bg.de; Strasse der Nationen 22, Oranienburg; ⊙8.30am-6pm mid-Mar–mid-Oct, to 4.30pm mid-Oct–mid-Mar, museums closed Mon mid-Oct–mid-Mar; P; S Oranienburg) FREE in 1961. A tour of the grounds, remaining buildings and exhibits will leave no one untouched.

Unless you're on a guided tour, pick up a leaflet (€0.50) or, better yet, an audioguide (€3, including leaflet) at the visitor centre to get a better grasp of this huge site. Between mid-October and mid-March avoid visiting on a Monday when all indoor exhibits are closed.

The S-Bahn S1 makes the trip to Oranienburg train station thrice hourly (ABC ticket €3.30, 45 minutes), from where it's a 2km signposted walk or a ride on hourly bus 804 to the site.

lavishly festooned with evocative sculpture. Today, it houses three superb museums within its baroque walls.

★Historisches Grünes Gewölbe MUSEUM
(Historic Green Vault; ☎0351-4914 2000; www.skd.museum; Residenzschloss; admission incl audioguide €15; ⊙10am-6pm Wed-Mon) The Historic Green Vault displays some 3000 precious items in the same fashion as during the time of August der Starke, namely on shelves and tables without glass protection in a series of increasingly lavish rooms. Admission is by timed ticket only, and only a limited number of visitors per hour may pass through the 'dust lock'. Get advance tickets online or by phone since only 40% are sold at the palace box office for same-day admission.

Neues Grünes Gewölbe MUSEUM
(New Green Vault; ☎0351-4914 2000; www.skd.museum; Residenzschloss; adult/under 17yr incl audioguide €15/free; ⊙10am-6pm Wed-Mon) The New Green Vault presents some 1000 objects in 10 modern rooms. Key sights include a frigate fashioned from ivory with wafer-thin sails, a cherry pit with 185 faces carved into it and an exotic ensemble of 132 gem-studded figurines representing a royal court in India. The artistry of each item is dazzling. To avoid the worst crush of people, visit during lunchtime.

Frauenkirche CHURCH
(☎0351-6560 6100; www.frauenkirche-dresden.de; Neumarkt; audioguide €2.50, cupola adult/student €8/5; ⊙10am-noon & 1-6pm) FREE The domed Frauenkirche – Dresden's most beloved symbol – has literally risen from the city's ashes. The original graced its skyline for two centuries before collapsing after the February 1945 bombing, and was rebuilt from a pile of rubble between 1994 and 2005. A spitting image of the original, it may not bear the gravitas of age but that only slightly detracts from its festive beauty inside and out. The altar, reassembled from nearly 2000 fragments, is especially striking.

★Albertinum MUSEUM
(☎0351-4914 2000; www.skd.museum; enter from Brühlsche Terrasse or Georg-Treu-Platz 2; adult/concession/under 17yr €10/7.50/free; ⊙10am-6pm Tue-Sun) After massive renovations following severe 2002 flood damage, the Renaissance-era former arsenal became the stunning home of the **Galerie Neue Meister** (New Masters Gallery), which displays an arc of paintings by some of the great names in art from the 18th century onwards. Caspar David Friedrich and Claude Monet's landscapes compete with the abstract visions of Marc Chagall and Gerhard Richter, all in gorgeous rooms orbiting a light-filled courtyard. There's also a superb sculpture collection spread over the lower floors.

Semperoper HISTORIC BUILDING
(☎0351-320 7360; www.semperoper-erleben.de; Theaterplatz 2; tour adult/concession €11/7; ⊙hours vary) One of Germany's most famous opera houses, the Semperoper opened in 1841 and has hosted premieres of famous

works by Richard Strauss, Carl Maria von Weber and Richard Wagner. Guided 45-minute tours operate almost daily (the 3pm tour is in English); exact times depend on the rehearsal and performance schedule. Buy advance tickets online to skip the queue.

Sleeping

Hostel Mondpalast HOSTEL €
(☎0351-563 4050; www.mondpalast.de; Louisenstrasse 77; dm/d from €14/37, linen €2; @ 📶) A funky location in the thick of the Äussere Neustadt is the main draw of this out-of-this-world hostel-bar-cafe (with cheap drinks). Each funky and playful room is designed to reflect a sign of the zodiac. Bonus points for the bike rentals and the well-equipped kitchen. Breakfast is €7.

Aparthotel am Zwinger APARTMENT €
(☎0351-8990 0100; www.aparthotel-zwinger.de; Maxstrasse 3; apt from €60; ⏲reception 7am-10pm Mon-Fri, 9.30am-6pm Sat & Sun, or by arrangement; P 📶) This excellent option has bright, functional and spacious apartments with kitchens that even come equipped with Nespresso machines. Units are spread over several buildings, but all are super-central and quiet. Access to the buffet breakfast costs €12.90, and it's a good option unless you're self-catering, as the neighbourhood is pretty low on breakfast options.

★**Gewandhaus Hotel** BOUTIQUE HOTEL €€
(☎0351-494 90; www.gewandhaus-hotel.de; Ringstrasse 1; d from €137; P ❄ @ 📶 ≋) Revamped as a boutique hotel a few years ago, the stunning Gewandhaus, an 18th-century trading house of tailors and fabric merchants that burned down in 1945, boasts sleek public areas, beautiful and bright rooms, and a breakfast that sets a high bar for anything else offered in the city. Part of the Marriott group.

Eating & Drinking

The Neustadt has oodles of cafes and restaurants, especially along Königstrasse and the streets north of Albertplatz. The latter is also the centre of Dresden's nightlife. Altstadt restaurants are more tourist-geared and pricier.

★**Raskolnikoff** INTERNATIONAL €€
(☎0351-804 5706; www.raskolnikoff.de; Böhmische Strasse 34; mains €10-15; ⏲11am-2am Mon-Fri, 9am-2am Sat & Sun) An artist squat before the Wall came down, Raskolnikoff now brims with grown-up artsy-bohemian flair, especially in the sweet little garden at the back, complete with bizarre water feature. The seasonally calibrated menu showcases the fruits of the surrounding land in globally inspired dishes, and the beer is brewed locally. Breakfast is served until 2pm, with an excellent brunch (€14.90) on Sundays.

Lila Sosse GERMAN €€
(☎0351-803 6723; www.lilasosse.de; Alaunstrasse 70, Kunsthofpassage; appetisers €3.50-9.50, mains €13-15; ⏲4pm-late Mon-Fri, from noon Sat & Sun) This jumping joint puts a new spin on modern German cooking by serving intriguing appetisers in glass preserve jars. You're free to order just a couple (the fennel-orange salad and carp with capers are recommended) or, if your tummy needs silencing, pair them with a meaty main and dessert. Reservations essential. It's part of the charming **Kunsthofpassage courtyard complex** (enter from Alaunstrasse 70 or Görlitzer Strasse 23; ⏲24hr) FREE.

brennNessel VEGETARIAN €€
(☎0351-494 3319; www.brennnessel-dresden.de; Schützengasse 18; mains €9-15; ⏲11am-midnight) This popular, largely vegetarian gastropub in a miraculously surviving 350-year-old building is an oasis in the otherwise empty and anodyne streets of the Altstadt. Indeed, reserve for lunch if you'd like to eat outside in the charming, sun-dappled courtyard as it's something of a favourite hang-out for off-duty Semperoper musicians and nearby office workers.

★**Restaurant Genuss-Atelier** GERMAN €€€
(☎0351-2502 8337; www.genuss-atelier.net; Bautzner Strasse 149; mains €15-27; ⏲noon-11pm Wed-Fri, from noon Sat & Sun; 🚊11 to Waldschlösschen) Lighting up Dresden's culinary scene of late is this fantastic place that's well worth the trip on the 11 tram. The creative menu is streets ahead of most offerings elsewhere, although the best way to experience the 'Pleasure-Atelier' is to book a surprise menu (three/four/five courses €38/48/58) and let the chefs show off their craft. Reservations essential.

Information

There are tourist office branches inside the **Hauptbahnhof** (☎0351-501 501; www.dresden.de; main train station, Wiener Platz; ⏲8am-8pm) and near the **Frauenkirche** (☎0351-501

WORTH A TRIP

MEISSEN

Straddling the Elbe around 25km upstream from Dresden, Meissen is the cradle of European porcelain, which was first cooked up in 1710 in its imposing castle, the **Albrechtsburg** (☎03521-470 70; www.albrechtsburg-meissen.de; Domplatz 1; adult/concession incl audioguide €8/4, with Dom €10.50/5.50; ⊙10am-6pm Mar-Oct, 10am-5pm Nov-Feb). An exhibit on the 2nd floor chronicles how it all began. Highlights of the adjacent **cathedral** (☎03521-452 490; www.dom-zu-meissen.de; Domplatz 7; adult/concession €4/2.50, with Albrechtsburg €10.50/5.50; ⊙9am-6pm Apr-Oct, 10am-4pm Nov-Mar) include medieval stained-glass windows and an altarpiece by Lucas Cranach the Elder. Both squat atop a ridge overlooking Meissen's handsome Altstadt (old town).

Since 1863, porcelain production has taken place in a custom-built factory, about 1km south of the Altstadt. Next to it is the **Erlebniswelt Haus Meissen** (☎03521-468 208; www.meissen.com; Talstrasse 9; adult/concession €9/5; ⊙9am-6pm May-Oct, 9am-5pm Nov-Apr), a vastly popular porcelain museum where you can witness the astonishing artistry and craftsmanship that makes Meissen porcelain unique. Note that entry is timed and only in groups, so you may have to wait a while during high season.

For details and further information about the town, stop by the **tourist office** (☎03521-419 40; www.touristinfo-meissen.de; Markt 3; ⊙10am-6pm Mon-Fri, 10am-4pm Sat & Sun Apr-Oct, 10am-5pm Mon-Fri, 10am-3pm Sat Nov, Dec, Feb & Mar).

Half-hourly S1 trains run to Meissen from Dresden's Hauptbahnhof and Neustadt train stations (€6, 40 minutes). For the Erlebniswelt, get off at Meissen-Triebischtal. Boats operated by **Sächsische Dampfschiffahrt** (☎03521-866 090; www.saechsische-dampfschiffahrt.de; one way/return €16/21.50; ⊙May-Sep) make the trip to Meissen from the Terrassenufer in Dresden in two hours. Consider going one way by boat and the other by train.

501; www.dresden.de; QF Passage, Neumarkt 2; ⊙10am-7pm Mon-Fri, to 6pm Sat, to 3pm Sun). Both book rooms and tours and rent out audioguides.

Getting There & Away

Dresden Airport (DRS; ☎0351-881 3360; www.dresden-airport.de) is about 9km north of the city centre and linked by the S2 train several times hourly (€2.20, 20 minutes).

Fast trains make the trip to Dresden from Berlin-Hauptbahnhof in two hours (€40) and Leipzig in 1¼ hours (€24.50). The S1 local train runs half-hourly to Meissen (€6.40, 40 minutes) and Bad Schandau in Saxon Switzerland (€6.40, 45 minutes).

Leipzig

☎0341 / POP 532,000

Hypezig! cry the papers. The New Berlin, says just about everybody. Yes, Leipzig is Saxony's coolest city, a playground for nomadic young creatives who have been displaced even by the fast-gentrifying German capital. But Leipzig is also a city of enormous history known as the Stadt der Helden (City of Heroes) for its leading role in the 1989 'Peaceful Revolution' that helped bring the Cold War to an end. A trade-fair mecca since medieval times, the city is solidly in the sights of music lovers due to its intrinsic connection to the lives and work of Bach, Mendelssohn and Wagner.

Sights

Don't rush from sight to sight – wandering around Leipzig is a pleasure in itself, with many of the blocks around the central Markt criss-crossed by historic shopping arcades, including the classic **Mädlerpassage**.

★Nikolaikirche CHURCH

(Church of St Nicholas; www.nikolaikirche-leipzig.de; Nikolaikirchhof 3; ⊙10am-6pm Mon-Sat, to 4pm Sun) This church has Romanesque and Gothic roots but since 1797 has sported a striking neoclassical interior with palm-like pillars and cream-coloured pews. The design is certainly gorgeous but the church is most famous for playing a key role in the nonviolent movement that led to the downfall of the East German government. As early as 1982 it hosted 'peace prayers' every Monday at 5pm (still held today), which over time inspired and empowered local citizens to confront the injustices plaguing their country.

★ Museum der Bildenden Künste MUSEUM
(☎0341-216 990; www.mdbk.de; Katharinenstrasse 10; adult/concession €5/4; ⏲10am-6pm Tue & Thu-Sun, noon-8pm Wed) This imposing modernist glass cube is the home of Leipzig's fine arts museum and its world-class collection of paintings from the 15th century to today, including works by Caspar David Friedrich, Cranach, Munch and Monet. Highlights include rooms dedicated to native sons Max Beckmann, Max Klinger and Neo Rauch. Exhibits are playfully juxtaposed and range from sculpture and installation to religious art. The collection is enormous, so set aside at least two hours to do it justice.

Zeitgeschichtliches Forum MUSEUM
(Forum of Contemporary History; ☎0341-222 0400; www.hdg.de/leipzig; Grimmaische Strasse 6; ⏲9am-6pm Tue-Fri, 10am-6pm Sat & Sun) FREE This fascinating, enormous and very well curated exhibit tells the political history of the GDR, from division and dictatorship to fall-of-the-Wall ecstasy and post-*Wende* blues. It's essential viewing for anyone seeking to understand the late country's political power apparatus, the systematic oppression of regime critics, milestones in inter-German and international relations, and the opposition movement that led to its downfall.

Stasi Museum MUSEUM
(☎0341-961 2443; www.runde-ecke-leipzig.de; Dittrichring 24; ⏲10am-6pm) FREE In the GDR the walls had ears, as is chillingly documented in this exhibit in the former Leipzig headquarters of the East German secret police (the Stasi), a building known as the Runde Ecke (Round Corner). English-language audioguides (€4) aid in understanding the all-German displays on propaganda, preposterous disguises, cunning surveillance devices, recruitment (even among children), scent storage and other chilling machinations that reveal the GDR's all-out zeal when it came to controlling, manipulating and repressing its own people.

Thomaskirche CHURCH
(☎0341-222 240; www.thomaskirche.org; Thomaskirchhof 18; tower €2; ⏲church 9am-6pm, tower 1pm, 2pm & 4.30pm Sat, 2pm & 3pm Sun Apr-Nov) Johann Sebastian Bach worked as a cantor in the Thomaskirche from 1723 until his death in 1750, and his remains lie buried beneath a bronze plate in front of the altar. The Thomanerchor, once led by Bach, has been going strong since 1212 and now includes 100 boys aged eight to 18. The church tower can be climbed, though the real reason to come here is to absorb the great man's legacy, often played on the church's giant organ.

Bach-Museum Leipzig MUSEUM
(☎0341-913 70; www.bachmuseumleipzig.de; Thomaskirchhof 16; adult/concession/under 16yr €8/6/free; ⏲10am-6pm Tue-Sun) This interactive museum does more than tell you about the life and accomplishments of Johann Sebastian Bach. Learn how to date a Bach manuscript, listen to baroque instruments or treat your ears to any composition he ever wrote. The 'treasure room' downstairs displays rare original manuscripts.

Sleeping

Hostel Blauer Stern HOSTEL €
(☎0341-4927 6166; www.hostelblauerstern.de; Lindenauer Markt 20; dm/s/d/ €18/25/35; 📶) If you're interested in exploring Leipzig's alternative scene, then this is a great option, in the western district of Plagwitz, a fast up-and-coming, young and arty slice of town. The thoughtfully decorated rooms all have an East German retro style, and big weekly discounts can make them a steal. Take tram 7 or 15 from Hauptbahnhof.

arcona Living Bach14 HOTEL €€
(☎0341-496 140; http://bach14.arcona.de; Thomaskirchhof 13/14; d from €105; 📶) In this musically themed marvel, you'll sleep sweetly in sleek rooms decorated with sound-sculpture lamps, Bach manuscript wallpaper and colours ranging from subdued olive to perky raspberry. The quietest rooms are in the garden wing, while those in the historic front section have views of the famous Thomaskirche.

Eating

Pilot INTERNATIONAL €€
(☎0341-9628 9550; Bosestrasse 1; mains €7-20; ⏲9am-late; 📶) This retro-styled and quite charming establishment draws a bohemian crowd with its rustic menu, back-to-basic Saxon dishes and a splash of more contemporary specials and fresh salads. Its extensive drinks selection, including rich espresso from Trieste and a long tea list, is a further draw.

Cafe Puschkin CAFE €€
(☎0341-392 0105; www.cafepuschkin.de; Karl-Liebknecht-Strasse 74; mains €5-12; ⏲9am-2am) This charming old pub on the Südvorstadt's

super cool Karl-Liebknecht-Strasse (aka 'Karli') is a bit of a local institution. The selection of burgers, nachos and sausages won't blow you away, but it's good comfort food in a friendly and somewhat eccentric atmosphere. It's also a great breakfast spot following a night out here.

★ **Auerbachs Keller** GERMAN €€€
(☎0341-216 100; www.auerbachs-keller-leipzig.de; Mädlerpassage, Grimmaische Strasse 2-4; mains Keller €10-26, Weinstuben €33-35; ⏲Keller noon-11pm daily, Weinstuben 6-11pm Mon-Sat) Founded in 1525, Auerbachs Keller is one of Germany's best-known restaurants. It's cosy and touristy but the food's actually quite good and the setting memorable. There are two sections: the vaulted Grosser Keller for hearty Saxonian dishes and the four historic rooms of the Historische Weinstuben for upscale German fare. Reservations highly advised.

Drinking & Nightlife

Leipzig is Saxony's liveliest city, with several areas noted for their going out options: in the city centre there's the boisterous Barfussgässchen and the more upmarket theatre district around Gottschedstrasse. Younger crowds gravitate towards Karl-Liebknecht-Strasse (aka 'Karli') south of the centre and Karl-Heine-Strasse in the up-and-coming southwestern suburb of Plagwitz.

Moritzbastei BAR
(☎0341-702 590; www.moritzbastei.de; Universitätsstrasse 9; ⏲10am-late Mon-Fri, noon-late Sat; 📶) This legendary (sub)cultural centre in a warren of cellars of the old city fortifications keeps an all-ages crowd happy with parties (almost nightly), concerts, art and readings. It harbours stylish cocktail and wine bars as well as a daytime cafe (dishes €2 to €5) that serves delicious coffee, along with healthy and wallet-friendly fare. Summer terrace, too.

★ **Distillery** CLUB
(☎0341-3559 7400; www.distillery.de; Kurt-Eisner-Strasse 91; ⏲from 11.30pm Fri & Sat; 🚋9 to Kurt-Eisner/A-Hoffmann-Strasse) One of the oldest techno clubs in eastern Germany, Distillery has been going for over 20 years and remains among the best. With an unpretentious crowd, cool location, decent drinks prices and occasional star DJs (Ellen Allien, Carl Craig, Richie Hawtin), its popularity is easy to understand. As well as techno, there's house, drum'n'bass and hip hop to be had here.

Noch Besser Leben PUB
(www.nochbesserleben.com; Merseburger Strasse 25; ⏲4.30pm-late) Despite the address, this locally beloved bar can be found on Plagwitz' main drag, Karl-Heine-Strasse, and is a great, if smokey, spot to join a cool local crowd drinking an impressive selection of beer. It has a communal, friendly atmosphere, for which only the German word *gemütlich* (approximately translated as cosy) will do.

Information

Tourist Office (☎0341-710 4260; www.leipzig.travel; Katharinenstrasse 8; ⏲9.30am-6pm Mon-Fri, to 4pm Sat, to 3pm Sun) Room referral, ticket sales, maps and general information. Also sells the **Leipzig Card** (one/three days €11.90/23.50); good for free or discounted admission to attractions, plus free travel on public transport.

Getting There & Away

Leipzig-Halle Airport (LEJ; ☎0341-2240; www.leipzig-halle-airport.de) is about 21km west of Leipzig and linked to town by half-hourly S-Bahn trains (€4.30, 35 minutes).

High-speed trains frequently serve Frankfurt (€76, 3½ hours), Dresden (€24.50, 1¼ hours) and Berlin (€47, 1¼ hours), among other cities.

Weimar

☎03643 / POP 63,320

Historical epicentre of the German Enlightenment, Weimar is an essential stop for anyone with a passion for German history and culture. A pantheon of intellectual and creative giants lived and worked here: Goethe, Schiller, Bach, Cranach, Liszt, Nietzsche, Gropius, Herder, Feininger, Kandinsky…the list goes on. In summer, Weimar's many parks and gardens lend themselves to quiet contemplation of the town's intellectual and cultural onslaught, or to taking a break from it.

Sights

★ **Goethe-Nationalmuseum** MUSEUM
(☎03643-545 400; www.klassik-stiftung.de; Frauenplan 1; adult/concession €12/8.50; ⏲9.30am-6pm Tue-Sun Apr-Oct, to 4pm Nov-Mar) This museum has the most comprehensive and insightful exhibit about Johann Wolfgang von Goethe, Germany's literary icon. It incorporates his home of 50 years, left pretty much as it was upon his death in 1832. This is where Goethe worked, studied, researched

WORTH A TRIP

EISENACH

On the edge of the Thuringian forest, Eisenach is the birthplace of Johann Sebastian Bach, but even the town's **museum** (03691-793 40; www.bachhaus.de; Frauenplan 21; adult/concession €9/5; 10am-6pm) dedicated to the great composer plays second fiddle to its main attraction: the awe-inspiring 11th-century **Wartburg** (03691-2500; www.wartburg-eisenach.de; Auf der Wartburg 1; tour adult/concession €9/5, museum & Luther study only €5/3; tours 8.30am-5pm Apr-Oct, 9am-3.30pm Nov-Mar, English tour 1.30pm) castle.

Perched high above the town (views!), the humungous pile hosted medieval minstrel song contests and was the home of Elisabeth, a Hungarian princess later canonised for her charitable deeds. Its most famous resident, however, was **Martin Luther**, who went into hiding here in 1521 after being excommunicated and placed under papal ban. During this 10-month stay, he translated the New Testament from Greek into German, contributing enormously to the development of the written German language. His modest study is part of the guided tour. Back in town, there's an exhibit about the man and his historical impact in the **Lutherhaus** (03691-298 30; www.lutherhaus-eisenach.com; Lutherplatz 8; adult/concession €6/4; 10am-5pm, closed Mon Nov-Mar), where he lived as a school boy.

In summer, arrive before 11am to avoid the worst of the crowds. From April to October, bus 10 runs hourly from 9am to 5pm from the Hauptbahnhof to the Eselstation stop, from where it's a steep 10-minute walk up to the castle.

Regional trains run frequently to Erfurt (€12.10, 45 minutes) and Weimar (€15, one hour). The **tourist office** (03691-792 30; www.eisenach.info; Markt 24; 10am-6pm Mon-Fri, to 5pm Sat & Sun) can help with finding accommodation.

and penned *Faust* and other immortal works. In a modern annexe, documents and objects shed light on the man and his achievements, not only in literature, but also in art, science and politics.

★Herzogin Anna Amalia Bibliothek LIBRARY

(03643-545 400; www.anna-amalia-bibliothek.de; Platz der Demokratie 1; adult/concession incl audioguide €7.50/6; 9.30am-2.30pm Tue-Sun) Assembled by literature-loving local duchess Anna Amalia (1739–1807), this Unesco World Heritage library has been beautifully reconstructed after a monumental fire in 2004 destroyed much of the building and its priceless contents. Some of the most precious tomes are housed in the magnificent **Rokokosaal** (Rococo Hall), and were once used by Goethe, Schiller and other Weimar hot shots, who are depicted in busts and paintings.

Bauhaus Museum MUSEUM

(03643-545 400; www.klassik-stiftung.de; Theaterplatz 1; adult/concession €4/3; 10am-6pm Apr-Oct, to 4pm Nov-Mar) Considering that Weimar is the 1919 birthplace of the influential Bauhaus school of art, design and architecture, this museum is a rather modest affair. A new, representative museum is expected to open in 2018.

Sleeping & Eating

★Design Apartments Weimar APARTMENT €€

(03643-251 8426; www.hier-war-goethe-nie.de; Fuldaer Strasse 85; apt per person from €61;) Get in quick to snap up one of these enormous, self-contained, fully renovated heritage apartments that could have been plucked from the pages of a Taschen design book. Even better is that you'd be hard-pressed to find friendlier, kinder hosts anywhere. This is surely the perfect home base from which to explore the delights of Weimar and Thuringia. Exceptional value.

Residenz-Café INTERNATIONAL €€

(03643-594 08; www.residenz-cafe.de; Grüner Markt 4; breakfast €3.90-8.60, mains €5-18; 8am-1am;) Locally adored 'Resi' is a Viennese-style coffeehouse and a jack of all trades – everyone should find something to their taste here, no matter where the hand's on the clock. The 'Lovers' Breakfast' comes with sparkling wine, the cakes are delicious and the salads crisp, but perhaps the most creativity goes into the weekly specials.

Hans und Franz GERMAN €€

(03643-457 3987; www.hanzundfranz.com; Erfurter Strasse 23; mains €8-14; 6-11pm Mon-Sat, to 9pm Sun;) There's something of a mid-century vibe at this happy haunt serving up local specialities such as *Thuringian Klösse* (dumplings) with red cabbage, and meaty German favourites, intelligently balanced with a few nice options for vegetarians and vegans. And, yes, the schnitzel here is good.

Zum Weissen Schwan GERMAN €€
(03643-908 751; Frauentorstrasse 23; mains €9-24; noon-10pm Tue-Sat) At this venerable inn, you can fill your tummy with Goethe's favourite dish, which actually hails from his home town of Frankfurt (boiled beef with herb sauce, red beet salad and potatoes). The rest of the menu, though, is midrange Thuringian.

Information

Tourist Office (03643-7450; www.weimar.de; Markt 10; 9.30am-7pm Mon-Sat, to 3pm Sun Apr-Oct, 9.30am-6pm Mon-Fri, to 2pm Sat & Sun Nov-Mar) Pick up a great-value WeimarCard (€27.50 for two days) for free admission to most museums, free iGuides, free travel on city buses and discounted tours.

Getting There & Away

Frequent regional trains go to Erfurt (€5, 15 minutes), Eisenach (€15, one hour), Gotha (€13, 35 minutes) and Jena (€5, 15 minutes). The town centre is a 20-minute walk or ride on bus 1 away.

Erfurt

0361 / POP 204,880

A little river courses through this Instagram-pretty medieval pastiche of sweeping squares, time-worn alleyways, a house-lined bridge and lofty church spires. Erfurt also boasts one of Germany's oldest universities, founded by rich merchants in 1392, where Martin Luther studied philosophy before becoming a monk at the local monastery. It's a refreshingly untouristed spot and well worth exploring.

Sights

Erfurt's main sights cluster in the old town, about a 10-minute walk from the train station (or quick ride on tram 3, 4 or 6).

Erfurter Dom CATHEDRAL
(Mariendom; 0361-646 1265; www.dom-erfurt.de; Domplatz; 9.30am-6pm Mon-Sat, 1-6pm Sun May-Oct, to 5pm Nov-Apr) Erfurt's cathedral, where Martin Luther was ordained a priest, has origins as a simple 8th-century chapel that grew into the stately Gothic pile you see today. Standouts in its treasure-filled interior include the stained-glass windows; the Wolfram, an 850-year-old bronze candelabrum in the shape of a man; the Gloriosa bell (1497); a Romanesque stucco Madonna; and the intricately carved choir stalls.

★Zitadelle Petersberg FORTRESS
(0361-664 00; tour adult/concession €8/4; 7pm Fri & Sat May-Oct) Situated on the Petersberg hill northwest of Domplatz, this citadel ranks among Europe's largest and best-preserved baroque fortresses. It sits above a honeycomb of tunnels, which can be explored on two-hour guided tours run by the tourist office. Otherwise, it's free to roam the external grounds and to enjoy fabulous views over Erfurt.

Krämerbrücke BRIDGE
(Merchants' Bridge) Flanked by cute half-timbered houses on both sides, this charming 1325 stone bridge is the only one north of the Alps that's still inhabited. To this day people live above little shops with attractive displays of chocolate and pottery, jewellery and basic souvenirs. See the bridge from above by climbing the tower of the **Ägidienkirche** (usually open 11am to 5pm) punctuating its eastern end.

Sleeping

Opera Hostel HOSTEL €
(0361-6013 1360; www.opera-hostel.de; Walkmühlstrasse 13; dm €15-22, s/d/tr €49/60/81, linen €2.50; @) This upmarket hostel in a historic building scores big with wallet-watching global nomads. Rooms are bright and spacious, many with an extra sofa for chilling. Make friends in the communal kitchen and on-site lounge-bar.

★Hotel Brühlerhöhe BOUTIQUE HOTEL €€
(0361-241 4990; www.hotel-bruehlerhoehe-erfurt.de; Rudolfstrasse 48; s/d from €80/95; P) This Prussian officers' casino turned chic city hotel gets high marks for its opulent breakfast spread (€12.50) and smiling, quick-on-their-feet staff. Rooms are cosy and modern with chocolate-brown furniture, thick carpets and sparkling baths. It's a short tram ride into the town centre.

Eating & Drinking

Faustfood BARBECUE €
(0361-6443 6300; www.faustfood.de; Waagegasse 1; items from €3.50; 11am-11pm Tue-Sat, to 7pm Sun) It's a clever name and a clever con-

cept: traditional Thuringian grills (*Rostbrätel* and bratwurst) alongside more international meaty treats such as spare ribs, steak and cheeseburgers. Dine in or take away, but you might want to head elsewhere if you're vegetarian.

★ Zum Wenigemarkt 13 GERMAN **€€**
(☎0361-642 2379; www.wenigemarkt-13.de; Wenigemarkt 13; mains €10-18; ⏲11.30am-11pm) This upbeat restaurant in a delightful spot serves traditional and updated takes on Thuringian cuisine, starring regionally hunted and gathered ingredients where possible. Tender salt-encrusted pork roast and trout drizzled with tangy caper-and-white-wine sauce are both menu stars.

Modern Masters COCKTAIL BAR
(☎0361-550 7255; www.modern-masters.de; Michaelisstrasse 48; ⏲6pm-2am Tue-Sat) Urbane and sophisticated, this cocktail bar has been shaking up Erfurt with flights of fancy in libation, offering an impressive range of more than 220 concoctions.

Information

Tourist Office Erfurt (☎0361-664 00; www.erfurt-tourismus.de; Benediktsplatz 1; ⏲10am-6pm Mon-Sat, to 3pm Sun) Sells the ErfurtCard (€14.90 per 48 hours), which includes a city tour, public transport, and free or discounted admissions.

Getting There & Away

Direct IC/ICE trains connect Erfurt with Berlin (€61, 2½ hours), Dresden (€53, 2½ hours) and Frankfurt am Main (€55, 2¼ hours). Regional trains to Weimar (€5, 15 minutes) and Eisenach (€12.10, 45 minutes) run at least hourly.

BAVARIA

From the cloud-shredding Alps to the fertile Danube plain, Bavaria (Bayern) is a place that keeps its clichéd promises. Storybook castles bequeathed by an oddball king poke through dark forest, cowbells tinkle in flower-filled meadows, the thwack of palm on Lederhosen accompanies the clump of frothy stein on timber, and medieval walled towns go about their time-warped business.

But there's so much more than the chocolate-box idyll. Learn about Bavaria's state-of-the-art motor industry in Munich, discover its Nazi past in Nuremberg and Berchtesgaden, sip world-class wines in Würzburg or take a mindboggling train ride up Germany's highest mountains. Destinations are often described as possessing 'something for everyone'. In Bavaria, this is no exaggeration.

Munich

☎089 / POP 1.38 MILLION

If you're looking for Alpine clichés, they're all here, but Munich also has plenty of unexpected cards down its Dirndl. Munich's walkable centre retains a small-town air but holds some world-class sights, especially art galleries and museums. Throw in royal Bavarian heritage, an entire suburb of Olympic legacy and a kitbag of dark tourism, and it's clear why southern Germany's metropolis is such a favourite among those who seek out the past but like to hit the town once they're done.

Sights

Munich's major sights cluster around the Altstadt, with the main museum district just north of the Residenz. However, it will take another day or two to explore bohemian Schwabing, the sprawling Englischer Garten and trendy Haidhausen to the east. Northwest of the Altstadt you'll find cosmopolitan Neuhausen, the Olympiapark and Schloss Nymphenburg.

Altstadt

★ Munich Residenz PALACE
(☎089-290 671; www.residenz-muenchen.de; Max-Joseph-Platz 3; Museum & Schatzkammer each adult/concession/under 18 €7/6/free, combination ticket €11/9/free; ⏲9am-6pm Apr–mid-Oct, 10am-5pm mid-Oct–Mar, last entry 1hr before closing) Generations of Bavarian rulers expanded a medieval fortress into this vast and palatial compound that served as their primary residence and seat of government from 1508 to 1918. Today it's an Aladdin's cave of fanciful rooms and collections through the ages that can be seen on an audio-guided tour of what is called the **Residenzmuseum**. Allow at least two hours to see everything at a gallop.

Highlights include the fresco-smothered **Antiquarium** banqueting hall and the exuberantly rococo **Reiche Zimmer** (Ornate Rooms). **The Schatzkammer** (Treasure Chamber) displays a veritable banker's

Central Munich

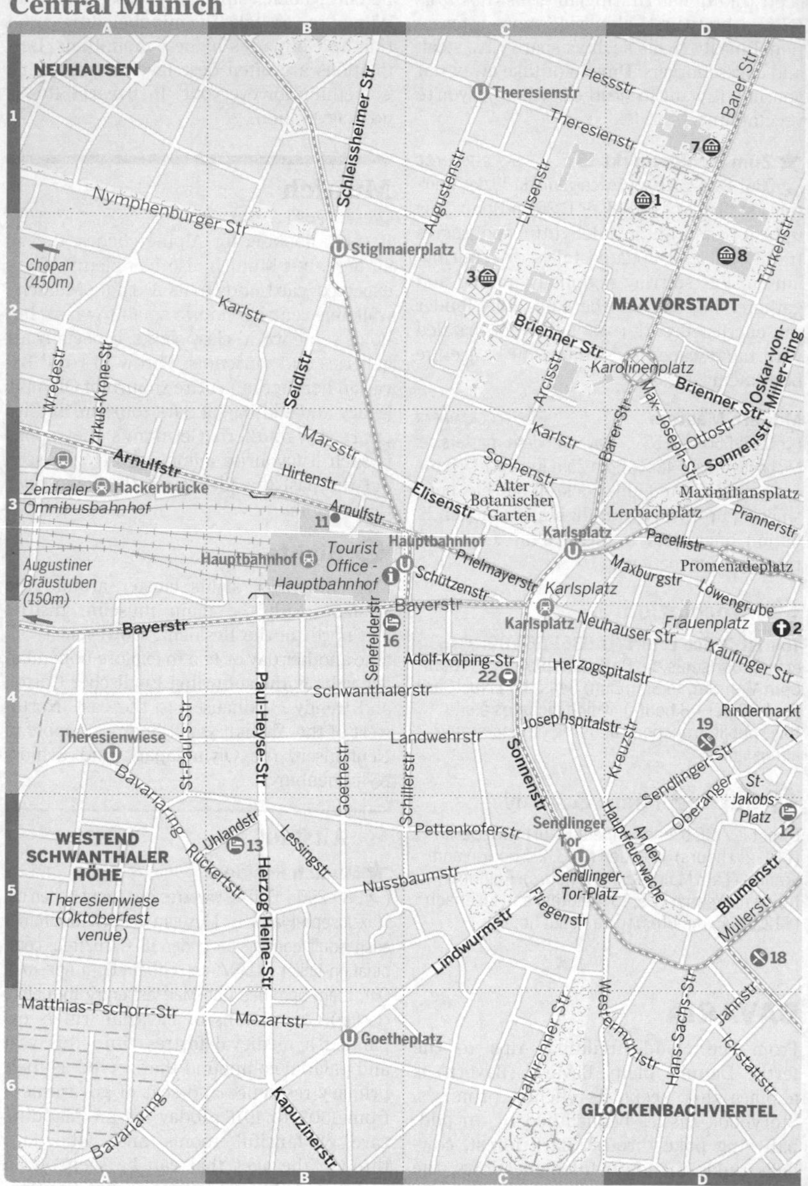

bonus worth of jewel-encrusted bling of yesteryear, from golden toothpicks to finely crafted swords, miniatures in ivory to gold entombed cosmetics trunks.

Marienplatz SQUARE

(S Marienplatz, U Marienplatz) The epicentral heart and soul of the Altstadt, Marienplatz is a popular gathering spot and packs a lot of personality into a compact frame. It's

anchored by the **Mariensäule** (Mary's Column), built in 1638 to celebrate victory over Swedish forces during the Thirty Years' War. This is the busiest spot in all Munich, with throngs of tourists swarming across its expanse from early morning till late at night.

Central Munich

Sights

1 Alte Pinakothek D1
2 Frauenkirche D4
3 Lenbachhaus C2
4 Marienplatz E4
5 Mariensäule E4
6 Munich Residenz E3
7 Neue Pinakothek D1
8 Pinakothek der Moderne D2
9 St Peterskirche E4
10 Viktualienmarkt E4

Activities, Courses & Tours

11 Radius Tours & Bike Rental B3

Sleeping

12 Hotel Blauer Bock D5
13 Hotel Uhland B5
14 Louis Hotel E4
15 The Flushing Meadows E6
16 Wombats City Hostel Munich B4

Eating

17 Alois Dallmayr E4
18 Fraunhofer D5
19 Prinz Myshkin D4
20 Schmalznudel E4
21 Tegernseer Tal E4

Drinking & Nightlife

22 Harry Klein C4
23 Hofbräuhaus E4
24 Niederlassung E5
25 Zephyr Bar E6

St Peterskirche CHURCH

(Church of St Peter; Rindermarkt 1; church free, tower adult/concession €3/1; tower 9am-6.30pm Mon-Fri, from 10am Sat & Sun; U Marienplatz, S Marienplatz) Some 306 steps divide you from the best view of central Munich from the 92m tower of St Peterskirche, Munich's oldest church (1150). Inside awaits a virtual textbook of art through the centuries. Worth a closer peek are the Gothic St-Martin-Altar, the baroque ceiling fresco by Johann Baptist Zimmermann and rococo sculptures by Ignaz Günther.

Viktualienmarkt MARKET

(Mon-Fri & morning Sat; U Marienplatz, S Marienplatz) Fresh fruit and vegetables, piles of artisan cheeses, tubs of exotic olives, hams and jams, chanterelles and truffles – Viktualienmarkt is a feast of flavours and one of central Europe's finest gourmet markets.

Frauenkirche CHURCH

(Church of Our Lady; www.muenchner-dom.de; Frauenplatz 1; ⌚7am-7pm Sat-Wed, to 8.30pm Thu, to 6pm Fri; S Marienplatz) The landmark Frauenkirche, built between 1468 and 1488, is Munich's spiritual heart and the Mt Everest among its churches. No other building in the central city may stand taller than its onion-domed twin towers, which reach a skyscraping 99m. The south tower can be climbed but was under urgent renovation at the time of writing.

Maxvorstadt, Schwabing & Englischer Garten

North of the Altstadt, Maxvorstadt is home to Munich's main university and top-drawer art museums. It segues into equally cafe-filled Schwabing, which rubs up against the vast Englischer Garten, one of Europe's biggest city parks and a favourite playground for locals and visitors alike.

Note that many major museums, including all the Pinakothek galleries, charge just €1 admission on Sundays.

Alte Pinakothek MUSEUM

(☎089-238 0526; www.pinakothek.de; Barer Strasse 27; adult/child €4/2, Sun €1, audio-guide €4.50; ⌚10am-8pm Tue, to 6pm Wed-Sun; 🚌 Pinakotheken, 🚋 Pinakotheken) Munich's main repository of Old European Masters is crammed with all the major players that decorated canvases between the 14th and 18th centuries. This neoclassical temple was masterminded by Leo von Klenze and is a delicacy even if you can't tell your Rembrandt from your Rubens. The collection is world famous for its exceptional quality and depth, especially when it comes to German masters.

Neue Pinakothek MUSEUM

(☎089-2380 5195; www.pinakothek.de; Barer Strasse 29; adult/child €7/5, Sun €1; ⌚10am-6pm Thu-Mon, to 8pm Wed; 🚌 Pinakotheken, 🚋 Pinakotheken) The Neue Pinakothek harbours a well-respected collection of 19th- and early-20th-century paintings and sculpture, from rococo to *Jugendstil* (art nouveau). All the world-famous household names get wall space here, including crowd-pleasing French impressionists such as Monet, Cézanne and Degas as well as Van Gogh, whose boldly pigmented *Sunflowers* (1888) radiates cheer.

Pinakothek der Moderne MUSEUM

(☎089-2380 5360; www.pinakothek.de; Barer Strasse 40; adult/child €10/7, Sun €1; ⌚10am-6pm Tue, Wed & Fri-Sun, to 8pm Thu; 🚌 Pinakotheken, 🚋 Pinakotheken) Germany's largest modern-art museum unites four significant collections under a single roof: 20th-century art, applied design from the 19th century to today, a graphics collection and an architecture museum. It's housed in a spectacular building by Stephan Braunfels, whose four-storey interior centres on a vast eye-like dome through which soft natural light filters throughout the blanched white galleries.

Lenbachhaus MUSEUM

(Municipal Gallery; ☎089-2333 2000; www.lenbachhaus.de; Luisenstrasse 33; adult/concession incl audioguide €10/5; ⌚10am-9pm Tue, to 6pm Wed-Sun; 🚌 Königsplatz, U Königsplatz) Reopened in 2013 to rave reviews after a four-year renovation that saw the addition of a new wing by noted architect Norman Foster, this glorious gallery is once again the go-to place to admire the vibrant canvases of Kandinsky, Franz Marc, Paul Klee and other members of ground-breaking modernist group Der Blaue Reiter (The Blue Rider), founded in Munich in 1911.

Further Afield

Schloss Nymphenburg PALACE

(www.schloss-nymphenburg.de; castle adult/concession €6/5, all sites €11.50/9; ⌚9am-6pm Apr–mid-Oct, 10am-4pm mid-Oct–Mar; 🚋 Schloss Nymphenburg) This commanding palace and its lavish gardens sprawl around 5km northwest of the Altstadt. Begun in 1664 as a villa for Electress Adelaide of Savoy, the stately pile was extended over the next century to create the royal family's summer residence. Franz Duke of Bavaria, head of the once royal Wittelsbach family, still occupies an apartment here.

BMW Museum MUSEUM

(www.bmw-welt.de; Am Olympiapark 2; adult/concession €10/7; ⌚10am-6pm Tue-Sun; U Olympiazentrum) This silver, bowl-shaped museum comprises seven themed 'houses' that examine the development of BMW's product line and include sections on motorcycles and motor racing. Even if you can't tell a head gasket from a crankshaft, the interior design – with its curvy retro feel, futuristic bridges, squares

OKTOBERFEST

Hordes come to Munich for **Oktoberfest** (www.oktoberfest.de), running the 15 days before the first Sunday in October. Reserve accommodation well ahead and go early in the day so you can grab a seat in one of the hangar-sized beer tents spread across the Theresienwiese grounds, about 1km southwest of the Hauptbahnhof. While there is no entrance fee, those €11 1L steins of beer (called *Mass*) add up fast. Although its origins are in the marriage celebrations of Crown Prince Ludwig in 1810, there's nothing regal about this beery bacchanalia now: expect mobs, expect to meet new and drunken friends, expect decorum to vanish as night sets in and you'll have a blast.

and huge backlit wall screens – is reason enough to visit.

Tours

★Radius Tours & Bike Rental TOURS
(☎089-543 487 7740; www.radiustours.com; Arnulfstrasse 3; S Hauptbahnhof, Ⓣ Hauptbahnhof, U Hauptbahnhof) Entertaining and informative English-language tours include the two-hour Discover Munich walk (€14), the fascinating 2½-hour Third Reich tour (€16), and the three-hour Bavarian Beer tour (€33). The company also runs popular excursions to Neuschwanstein, Salzburg and Dachau and has hundreds of bikes for hire (€14.50 per day).

City Bus 100 BUS
(www.mvv-muenchen.de) Ordinary city bus that runs from the Hauptbahnhof to the Ostbahnhof via 21 sights, including the Residenz and the Pinakothek museums.

Sleeping

Room rates in Munich tend to be high, and they skyrocket during the Oktoberfest. Book well ahead.

Wombats City Hostel Munich HOSTEL €
(☎089-5998 9180; www.wombats-hostels.com; Senefelderstrasse 1; dm/d from €19/74; P @ Wi-Fi; Ⓣ Hauptbahnhof, U Hauptbahnhof) Munich's top hostel is a professionally run affair with a whopping 300 dorm beds plus private rooms. Dorms are painted in cheerful pastels and outfitted with wooden floors, en-suite facilities, sturdy lockers and comfy pine bunks, all in a central location near the train station. A free welcome drink awaits in the bar. Buffet breakfast costs €4.50.

Hotel Uhland HOTEL €€
(☎089-543 350; www.hotel-uhland.de; Uhlandstrasse 1; s/d incl breakfast from €75/95; P Wi-Fi; U Theresienwiese) The Uhland is an enduring favourite with regulars who like their hotel to feel like a home away from home. Free parking, a breakfast buffet with organic products, and minibar drinks that won't dent your budget are just some of the thoughtful features.

Hotel Blauer Bock HOTEL €€
(☎089-231 780; www.hotelblauerbock.de; Sebastiansplatz 9; s/d from €47/79; Wi-Fi; U Marienplatz, S Marienplatz) A pretzel's throw from the Viktualienmarkt, this simple hotel has cunningly slipped through the net of Altstadt gentrification to become one of the city centre's best deals. The cheapest, unmodernised rooms have shared facilities, the updated en-suite chambers are of a 21st-century vintage, and all are quiet, despite the location. Superb restaurant.

Flushing Meadows DESIGN HOTEL €€
(☎089-5527 9170; www.flushingmeadowshotel.com; Fraunhoferstrasse 32; studios €115-165; ⏲reception 6am-11pm; P ❄ Wi-Fi; S Fraunhoferstrasse) Urban explorers keen on up-to-the-minute design cherish this new contender on the top two floors of a former postal office in the hip Glockenbachviertel. Each of the 11 concrete-ceilinged lofts reflects the vision of a locally known creative type, while three of the five penthouse studios have a private terrace. Breakfast costs €10.50.

NO WAVE GOODBYE

Possibly the last sport you might expect to see being practised in Munich is surfing, but go to the southern tip of the English Garden at Prinzregentenstrasse and you'll see scores of people leaning over a bridge to cheer on wetsuit-clad daredevils as they hang on an artificially created wave in the Eisbach. It's only a single wave, but it's a damn fine one!

Louis Hotel HOTEL €€€

(089-411 9080; www.louis-hotel.com; Viktualienmarkt 6/Rindermarkt 2; r €159-289; S Marienplatz) An air of relaxed sophistication pervades the scene-savvy Louis, where good-sized rooms are furnished in nut and oak, natural stone and elegant tiles and equipped with the gamut of 'electronica', including iPod docks and flat screens with Sky TV. All have small balconies facing either the courtyard or the Viktualienmarkt. Views are also terrific from the rooftop bar and restaurant.

Eating

Schmalznudel CAFE €

(Cafe Frischhut; Prälat-Zistl-Strasse 8; pastries €2; 8am-6pm; U Marienplatz, S Marienplatz) This incredibly popular institution serves just four traditional pastries, one of which, the *Schmalznudel* (an oily type of doughnut), gives the place its local nickname. Every baked goodie you munch here is crisp and fragrant, as they're always fresh off the hotplate. They're best eaten with a steaming pot of coffee on a winter's day.

Tegernseer Tal BAVARIAN €€

(089-222 626; www.tegernseer-tal8.com; Tal 8; mains €7-20.50; 9.30am-1am Sun-Wed, to 3am Thu-Sat; ; U Marienplatz, S Marienplatz) A blond-wood interior illuminated by a huge skylight makes this a bright alternative to Munich's dark-panelled taverns. And with Alpine Tegernseer beer on tap and an imaginative menu of regional food, this is generally a lighter, calmer beer-hall experience with a less raucous ambience.

★ **Fraunhofer** BAVARIAN €€

(089-266 460; www.fraunhofertheater.de; Fraunhoferstrasse 9; mains €7-25; 4.30pm-1am Mon-Fri, 10am-1am Sat; ; Müllerstrasse) With its screechy parquet floors, stuccoed ceilings, wood panelling and virtually no trace that the last century even happened, this wonderfully characterful inn is perfect for exploring the region with a fork. The menu is a seasonally adapted checklist of southern German favourites but also features at least a dozen vegetarian dishes and the odd exotic ingredient.

Prinz Myshkin VEGETARIAN €€

(089-265 596; www.prinzmyshkin.com; Hackenstrasse 2; mains €10-20; 11am-12.30am; ; U Marienplatz, S Marienplatz) This place is proof, if any were needed, that the vegetarian experience has well and truly left the sandals, beards and lentils era. Ensconced in a former brewery, Munich's premier meat-free dining spot occupies a gleamingly whitewashed, vaulted space where health-conscious eaters come to savour imaginative dishes such as curry-orange-carrot soup, unexpectedly good curries and 'wellness desserts'.

Chopan AFGHANI €€

(089-1895 6459; www.chopan.de; Elvirasstrasse 18a; mains €7-19.50; 6pm-midnight; U Maillingerstrasse) Munich has a huge Afghan community, whose most respected eatery is this much-lauded restaurant done out Central Asian caravanserai style with rich fabrics, multihued glass lanterns and geometric patterns. In this culinary Aladdin's cave you'll discover an exotic menu of lamb, lentils, rice, spinach and flatbread in various combinations, but there are no alcoholic beverages to see things on their way.

Alois Dallmayr FOOD HALL €€

(089-213 5104; www.dallmayr.de; Dienerstrasse 14; 9.30am-7pm Mon-Sat) A pricey gourmet delicatessen right in the thick of the Altstadt action, best known for its coffee but has so much more, including cheeses, ham, truffles, wine, caviar and exotic foods from every corner of the globe.

Drinking & Nightlife

Generally speaking, student-flavoured places abound in Maxvorstadt and Schwabing, while traditional beer halls and taverns cluster in the Altstadt. Haidhausen attracts trendy types, and the Gärtnerplatzviertel and Glockenbachviertel are alive with gay bars and hipster haunts.

Niederlassung BAR

(089-3260 0307; www.niederlassung.org; Buttermelcherstrasse 6; 7pm-1am Tue-Thu, to 3am Fri & Sat, to midnight Sun; S Fraunhoferstrasse,

GAY & LESBIAN MUNICH

In Munich, the rainbow flag flies especially proudly along Müllerstrasse and the adjoining Glockenbachviertel. Keep an eye out for the freebie mags *Our Munich* and *Sergej*, which contain up-to-date listings and news about the community and gay-friendly establishments around town. Another source of info is www.gaytouristoffice.com.

LOCAL KNOWLEDGE

BEER HALLS & BEER GARDENS

Beer drinking is not just an integral part of Munich's entertainment scene, it's a reason to visit. A few enduring faves:

Augustiner Bräustuben (089-507 047; www.braeustuben.de; Landsberger Strasse 19; 10am-midnight; Holzapfelstrasse) Depending on the wind, an aroma of hops envelops you as you approach this traditional beer hall inside the Augustiner brewery. The Bavarian fare is superb, especially the *Schweinshaxe* (pork knuckle). Due to the location the atmosphere in the evenings is slightly more authentic than that of its city-centre cousins, with fewer tourists at the long tables.

Chinesischer Turm (089-383 8730; www.chinaturm.de; Englischer Garten 3; 10am-11pm; Chinesischer Turm, Tivolistrasse) This one's hard to ignore because of its English Garden location and pedigree as Munich's oldest beer garden (open since 1791). Camera-toting tourists and laid-back locals, picnicking families and businessmen sneaking a sly brew clomp around the wooden pagoda, showered by the strained sounds of possibly the world's drunkest oompah band.

Hofbräuhaus (089-2901 3610; www.hofbraeuhaus.de; Am Platzl 9; 1L beer €8.40, mains €9-19; 9am-11.30pm; Kammerspiele, S Marienplatz, U Marienplatz) Every visitor to Munich should make a pilgrimage to this mothership of all beer halls, if only once. Within this major tourist attraction you'll discover a range of spaces in which to do your mass lifting: the horse chestnut–shaded garden, the main hall next to the oompah band, tables opposite the industrial-scale kitchen and quieter corners.

Isartor) From Adler Dry to Zephyr, this gin joint stocks an impressive 80 varieties of juniper juice in an unpretentious setting filled with books and sofas and humming with indie sounds. There's even a selection of different tonic waters to choose from. Happy hour from 7pm to 9pm and after midnight.

Zephyr Bar COCKTAIL BAR
(www.zephyr-bar.de; Baaderstrasse 68; 8pm-1am Mon-Thu, to 3am Fri & Sat; S Fraunhoferstrasse) At one of Munich's best bars, Alex Schmaltz whips up courageous potions with unusual ingredients such as homemade cucumber-dill juice, sesame oil or banana-parsley purée. Cocktail alchemy at its finest, and a top gin selection to boot. No reservations.

Harry Klein CLUB
(089-4028 7400; www.harrykleinclub.de; Sonnenstrasse 8; from 11pm; Karlsplatz, S Karlsplatz, U Karlsplatz) Follow the gold-lined passageway off Sonnenstrasse to what some regard as one of the best *Elektro-clubs* in the world. Nights here are an alchemy of electro sound and visuals, with live video art projected onto the walls Kraftwerk style blending to awe-inspiring effect with the music.

Entertainment

FC Bayern München FOOTBALL
(089-6993 1333; www.fcbayern.de; Allianz Arena, Werner-Heisenberg-Allee 25, Fröttmaning; U Fröttmaning) Germany's most successful team both domestically and on a European level plays home games at the impressive Allianz Arena, built for the 2006 World Cup. Tickets can be ordered online.

Information

Tourist office branches include **Hauptbahnhof** (089-2339 6500; www.muenchen.de; Bahnhofplatz 2; 9am-8pm Mon-Sat, 10am-6pm Sun; Hauptbahnhof, U Hauptbahnhof, S Hauptbahnhof) and **Marienplatz** (089-2339 6500; www.muenchen.de; Marienplatz 2; 9am-7.30pm Mon-Fri, 9am-4pm Sat, 10am-2pm Sun; U Marienplatz, S Marienplatz).

Getting There & Away

AIR

Munich Airport (MUC; 089-975 00; www.munich-airport.de) is about 30km northeast of town and linked to the Hauptbahnhof every 10 minutes by S-Bahn (S1 and S8; €10.40, 40 minutes) and every 20 minutes by the Lufthansa Airport Bus (€10.50, 45 minutes, between 5am and 8pm).

WORTH A TRIP

DACHAU CONCENTRATION CAMP

Officially called the **KZ-Gedenkstätte Dachau** (Dachau Concentration Camp Memorial Site; ☎08131-669 970; www.kz-gedenkstaette-dachau.de; Peter-Roth-Strasse 2a, Dachau; museum admission free; ⏱9am-5pm), the first Nazi concentration camp opened in 1933 in a bucolic village about 16km northwest of central Munich. All in all, it 'processed' more than 200,000 inmates, killing at least 43,000, and is now a haunting memorial. Expect to spend two to three hours exploring the grounds and exhibits. For deeper understanding, pick up an audioguide (€3), join a 2½-hour tour (€3) or watch the 22-minute English-language documentary at the main museum.

From the Hauptbahnhof take the S2 to Dachau station (two-zone ticket; €5.20, 21 minutes), then catch frequent bus 726 (direction: Saubachsiedlung) to the camp.

Ryanair flies into Memmingen's **Allgäu Airport** (FMM; ☎08331-984 2000; www.allgaeu-airport.de; Am Flughafen 35, Memmingen), 125km to the west. The Allgäu-Airport-Express bus travels up to seven times daily between here and Munich Hauptbahnhof (€13.50, 1¾ hours).

BUS

Buses, including the Romantic Road Coach, depart from **Zentraler Omnibusbahnhof** (Central Bus Station, ZOB; www.muenchen-zob.de; Arnulfstrasse 21; Ⓢ Hackerbrücke) at S-Bahn station Hackerbrücke near the main train station.

TRAIN

All services leave from the Hauptbahnhof, where **Euraide** (www.euraide.de; Desk 1, Reisezentrum, Hauptbahnhof; ⏱10am-7pm Mon-Fri Mar-Apr & Aug-Dec, to 8pm May-Jul; 🚊Hauptbahnhof, Ⓤ Hauptbahnhof, Ⓢ Hauptbahnhof) is a friendly English-speaking travel agency. Frequent fast and direct services include trains to Nuremberg (€55, 1¼ hours), Frankfurt (€101, 3¼ hours), Berlin (€130, 6½ hours) and Vienna (€93, 4½ hours), as well as thrice-daily trains to Prague (€74, 6¼ hours).

Getting Around

For public transport information, consult www.mvv-muenchen.de.

Garmisch-Partenkirchen

☎08821 / POP 26,000

A paradise for skiers and hikers, Garmisch-Partenkirchen is blessed with a fabled setting a snowball's throw from Germany's highest peak, the 2962m-high Zugspitze. Garmisch has a more cosmopolitan feel, while Partenkirchen retains an old-world Alpine village vibe. The towns were merged for the 1936 Winter Olympics.

Sights

Zugspitze MOUNTAIN

(www.zugspitze.de; return adult/child €53/31; ⏱train 8.15am-3.15pm) On good days, views from Germany's rooftop extend into four countries. The round trip starts in Garmisch aboard a cogwheel train (Zahnradbahn) that chugs along the mountain base to the Eibsee, an idyllic forest lake. From here, the Eibsee-Seilbahn, a super-steep cable car, swings to the top at 2962m. When you're done admiring the views, the Gletscherbahn cable car takes you to the Zugspitze glacier at 2600m, from where the cogwheel train heads back to Garmisch.

Partnachklamm CANYON

(www.partnachklamm.eu; adult/concession €4/2.50; ⏱8am-6pm May, Jun & Oct, to 7pm Jul-Sep, 9am-6pm Nov-Apr) A top attraction around Garmisch is this narrow and dramatically beautiful 700m-long gorge with walls rising up to 80m. The trail hewn into the rock is especially spectacular in winter when you can walk beneath curtains of icicles and frozen waterfalls.

Sleeping & Eating

Hotel Garmischer Hof HOTEL €€

(☎08821-9110; www.garmischer-hof.de; Chamonixstrasse 10; s €65-80, d €98-138; 📶🏊) In the ownership of the Seiwald family since 1928, many a climber, skier and Alpine adventurer has creased the sheets at this welcoming inn. Rooms are elegant and cosy with some traditional Alpine touches, the buffet breakfast is served in the vaulted cafe-restaurant and there's a spa and sauna providing après-ski relief.

★ Gasthof Fraundorfer BAVARIAN €€
(www.gasthof-fraundorfer.de; Ludwigstrasse 24; mains €8-19; ⏲7am-midnight Thu-Mon, from 5pm Wed) If you came to the Alps to experience yodelling, knee slapping and red-faced locals in lederhosen, you just arrived at the right address. Steins of frothing ale fuel the increasingly raucous atmosphere as the evening progresses and monster portions of plattered pig meat push belt buckles to the limit. Decor ranges from baroque cherubs to hunting trophies and the 'Sports Corner'. Unmissable.

ℹ Information

Tourist Office (☎08821-180 700; www.gapa.de; Richard-Strauss-Platz 2; ⏲9am-6pm Mon-Sat, 10am-noon Sun, closed Sun Nov-Mar) Friendly staff hands out map, brochures and advice.

ℹ Getting There & Away

Numerous tour operators run day trips to Garmisch-Partenkirchen from Munich but there's also at least hourly direct train service (€20.70, 1¼ hours).

Berchtesgaden

☎08652 / POP 7800

Steeped in myth and legend, Berchtesgaden's and the surrounding countryside (the Berchtesgadener Land) is almost preternaturally beautiful. Framed by six formidable mountain ranges and home to Germany's second-highest mountain, the Watzmann (2713m), its dreamy, fir-lined valleys are filled with gurgling streams and peaceful Alpine villages. Alas, Berchtesgaden's history is also indelibly tainted by the Nazi period. The area is easily visited on a day trip from Salzburg.

Sights

Berchtesgaden main sights are all a car or bus ride away from town. Seeing everything in a day without your own transport is virtually impossible.

Eagle's Nest HISTORIC SITE
(Kehlsteinhaus; ☎08652-2969; www.kehlsteinhaus.de; Obersalzberg; adult/child €16.10/9.30; ⏲buses 8.30am-4.50pm mid-May–Oct) The Eagle's Nest was built as a mountaintop retreat for Hitler, and gifted to him on his 50th birthday. It took some 3000 workers only two years to carve the precipitous 6km-long mountain road, cut a 124m-long tunnel and a brass-panelled lift through the rock, and build the lodge itself (now a restaurant). It can only be reached by special shuttle bus from the Kehlsteinhaus bus station.

Dokumentation Obersalzberg MUSEUM
(☎08652-947 960; www.obersalzberg.de; Salzbergstrasse 41, Obersalzberg; adult/concession €3/free, audioguide €2; ⏲9am-5pm daily Apr-Oct, 10am-3pm Tue-Sun Nov-Mar, last entry 1hr before closing) In 1933 the quiet mountain village of Obersalzberg (3km from Berchtesgaden) became the second seat of Nazi power after Berlin, a dark period that's given the full historical treatment at this excellent exhibit. It documents the forced takeover of the area, the construction of the compound and the daily life of the Nazi elite. All facets of Nazi terror are dealt with, including Hitler's near-mythical appeal, his racial politics, the resistance movement, foreign policy and the death camps.

Königssee LAKE
Crossing the serenely picturesque, emerald-green Königssee makes for some unforgettable memories and once-in-a-lifetime photo opportunities. Cradled by steep mountain walls some 5km south of Berchtesgaden, the emerald-green Königssee is Germany's highest lake (603m), with drinkably pure waters shimmering into fjordlike depths. Bus 841/842 makes the trip out here from the Berchtesgaden train station roughly every hour.

Tours

Eagle's Nest Tours TOURS
(☎08652-649 71; www.eagles-nest-tours.com; adult/child €53/35; ⏲1.15pm mid-May–Oct) This highly reputable outfit offers a fascinating overview of Berchtesgaden's Nazi legacy. Guests are taken not only to the Eagle's Nest but around the Obersalzberg area and into the underground bunker system. The four-hour English-language tour departs from the tourist office, across the roundabout opposite the train station. Booking ahead is advisable in July and August.

Sleeping & Eating

Hotel Vier Jahreszeiten HOTEL €€
(☎08652-9520; www.hotel-vierjahreszeiten-berchtesgaden.de; Maximilianstrasse 20; s €59-89, d €89-119; ⏲reception 7am-11pm; P 📶 🏊) For a

HITLER'S MOUNTAIN RETREAT

Of all the German towns tainted by the Third Reich, the Berchtesgaden area carries a burden heavier than most. Hitler fell in love with the secluded alpine village of Obersalzberg while vacationing here in the 1920s and later bought a small country home that was enlarged into an imposing residence – the Berghof.

After seizing power in 1933, the 'Führer' established a second seat of power here and brought much of the party brass with him. They drove out the local villagers and turned the compound into a *Führersperrgebiet* (an off-limits area). Many important decisions, about war and peace and the Holocaust, were made here.

In the final days of WWII, British and American bombers levelled much of Obersalzberg, although the Eagle's Nest, Hitler's mountaintop eyrie, was left strangely unscathed.

taste of Berchtesgaden's storied past, stay at this traditional lodge where Bavarian royalty once crumpled the sheets. Rooms have been updated in the last decade and the south-facing (more-expensive) rooms offer dramatic mountain views. After a day's sightseeing, dinner in the hunting lodge-style Hubertusstube restaurant is a real treat.

Bräustübl BAVARIAN **€€**
(☎08652-976 724; www.braeustueberl-berchtesgaden.de; Bräuhausstrasse 13; mains €7-17; ⌚10am-midnight) Past the vaulted entrance painted in Bavaria's white and blue diamonds, this cosy beer hall-beer garden is run by the local brewery. Expect a carnivorous feast with such favourite rib-stickers as pork roast and the house speciality: breaded calf's head (tastes better than it sounds). On Friday and Saturday, an oompah band launches into knee-slapping action.

ℹ Information

Tourist Office (☎08652-896 70; www.berchtesgaden.com; Königsseer Strasse; ⌚8.30am-6pm Mon-Fri, 9am-5pm Sat, 9am-3pm Sun, reduced hours mid-Oct–Mar) Near the train station, this very helpful office has detailed information on the entire Berchtesgaden region.

ℹ Getting There & Away

Travelling from Munich by train involves a change from Meridian to BLB (Berchtesgadener Land Bahn) trains at Freilassing (€33.80, 2½ hours, at least hourly connections). The best option between Berchtesgaden and Salzburg is hourly RVO bus 840 (45 minutes).

Romantic Road

Stretching 400km from the vineyards of Würzburg to the foot of the Alps, the Romantic Road (Romantische Strasse) is by far the most popular of Germany's themed holiday routes. It passes through more than two dozen cities and towns, including Rothenburg ob der Tauber and also takes in Schloss Neuschwanstein, the country's most famous palace.

ℹ Getting There & Around

Frankfurt and Munich are the most popular gateways for exploring the Romantic Road. The ideal way to travel is by car, though many foreign travellers prefer to take Deutsche Touring's **Romantic Road Coach** (☎09851-551 387; www.romanticroadcoach.de), which can get incredibly crowded in summer. From April to October this special coach runs daily in each direction between Frankfurt and Füssen (for Neuschwanstein); the entire journey takes around 12 hours. There's no charge for breaking the journey and continuing the next day.

Tickets are available for the entire route or for short segments, and reservations are only necessary during peak-season weekends. Buy tickets online or from travel agents, **EurAide** (p292) in Munich or Reisezentrum offices in larger train stations.

Füssen

☎08362 / POP 14,600

In the foothills of the Alps, Füssen itself is a charming town, although most visitors skip it and head straight to Schloss Neuschwanstein and Hohenschwangau, the two most famous castles associated with King Ludwig II. You can see both on a long day trip from Munich, although only when spending the night, after all the day-trippers have gone, will you sense a certain Alpine serenity.

Sights

The castles are served by buses 78 and 73 from Füssen Bahnhof (€4.40 return, eight minutes, at least hourly).

CASTLE TICKETS & TOURS

Both Hohenschwangau and Neuschwanstein must be seen on guided 35-minute tours (in German or English). Timed tickets are only available from the **Ticket-Center** (☎08362-930 830; www.hohenschwangau.de; Alpenseestrasse 12; ⏰8am-5pm Apr–mid-Oct, 9am-3.30pm mid-Oct–Mar) at the foot of the castles and may be reserved online until two days prior to your visit (recommended).

If visiting both castles on the same day, the Hohenschwangau tour is scheduled first with enough time for the steep 30- to 40-minute walk between the castles. The footsore can travel by bus or by horsedrawn carriage.

★Schloss Neuschwanstein CASTLE
(☎tickets 08362-930 830; www.neuschwanstein.de; Neuschwansteinstrasse 20; adult/concession €12/11, incl Hohenschwangau €23/21; ⏰9am-6pm Apr–mid-Oct, 10am-4pm mid-Oct–Mar) Appearing through the mountaintops like a mirage, Schloss Neuschwanstein was the model for Disney's *Sleeping Beauty* castle. King Ludwig II planned this fairy-tale pile himself, with the help of a stage designer rather than an architect. He envisioned it as a giant stage on which to recreate the world of Germanic mythology, inspired by the operatic works of his friend Richard Wagner. The most impressive room is the **Sängersaal** (Minstrels' Hall), whose frescos depict scenes from the opera *Tannhäuser*.

Built as a romantic medieval castle, work started in 1869 and, like so many of Ludwig's grand schemes, was never finished. For all the coffer-depleting sums spent on it, the king spent just over 170 days in residence.

Completed sections include Ludwig's Tristan and Isolde–themed bedroom, dominated by a huge Gothic-style bed crowned with intricately carved cathedral-like spires; a gaudy artificial grotto (another allusion to *Tannhäuser*); and the Byzantine-style **Thronsaal** (Throne Room) with an incredible mosaic floor containing over two million stones. The painting opposite the (throneless) throne platform depicts another castle dreamed up by Ludwig that was never built. Almost every window provides tour-halting views across the plain below.

The tour ends with a 20-minute film on the castle and its creator, and there's a reasonably priced cafe and the inevitable gift shops.

For the postcard view of Neuschwanstein and the plains beyond, walk 10 minutes up to **Marienbrücke** (Mary's Bridge), which spans the spectacular Pöllat Gorge over a waterfall just above the castle. It's said Ludwig enjoyed coming up here after dark to watch the candlelight radiating from the Sängersaal.

Schloss Hohenschwangau CASTLE
(☎08362-930 830; www.hohenschwangau.de; Alpseestrasse 30; adult/concession €12/11, incl Neuschwanstein €23/21; ⏰8am-5pm Apr–mid-Oct, 9am-3.30pm mid-Oct–Mar) King Ludwig II grew up at the sun-yellow Schloss Hohenschwangau and later enjoyed summers here until his death in 1886. His father, Maximilian II, built this palace in a neo-Gothic style atop 12th-century ruins left by Schwangau knights. Far less showy than Neuschwanstein, Hohenschwangau has a distinctly lived-in feel where every piece of furniture is a used original. After his father died, Ludwig's main alteration was having stars, illuminated with hidden oil lamps, painted on the ceiling of his bedroom.

Sleeping & Eating

★Hotel Sonne DESIGN HOTEL €€
(☎08362-9080; www.hotel-fuessen.de; Prinzregentenplatz 1; s/d from €89/109; P 📶) Although traditional looking from outside, this Altstadt favourite offers an unexpected design-hotel experience within. Themed rooms feature everything from swooping bed canopies to big-print wallpaper, huge pieces of wall art to sumptious fabrics. The public spaces are littered with pieces of art, period costumes and design features – the overall effect is impressive and unusual for this part of Germany.

Restaurant Ritterstub'n GERMAN €€
(☎08362-7759; www.restaurant-ritterstuben.de; Ritterstrasse 4; mains €6.80-18.50; ⏰11.30am-10pm Tue-Sun) This convivial pit stop has value-priced salads, snacks, lunch specials, fish, schnitzel and gluten-free dishes, and even a cute kids' menu. The medieval knight

theme can be a bit grating but kids often love eating their fishsticks with their fingers or seeing mum and dad draped in a big bib.

Information

Tourist Office (☎08362-938 50; www.fuessen.de; Kaiser-Maximilian-Platz; ⊙9am-5pm Mon-Fri, 9.30am-3.30pm Sat) Can help find rooms.

Getting There & Away

Füssen is the southern terminus of the Romantic Road Coach.

If you want to do the castles in a single day from Munich, you'll need to start early. The first train leaves Munich at 5.53am (€26.20, change in Buchloe), reaching Füssen at 7.52am. Otherwise, direct trains leave Munich once every two hours throughout the day.

Rothenburg ob der Tauber

☎09861 / POP 10,900

With its jumble of half-timbered houses enclosed by Germany's best-preserved ramparts, Rothenburg ob der Tauber lays on the medieval cuteness with a trowel. It's an essential stop on the Romantic Road but, alas, overcrowding can detract from its charm. Visit early or late in the day (or, ideally, stay overnight) to experience this historic wonderland sans crowds.

Sights

Jakobskirche CHURCH

(Church of St Jacob; Klingengasse 1; adult/concession €2.50/1.50; ⊙9am-5.15pm Mon-Sat, 10.45am-5.15pm Sun Apr-Oct, shorter hours Nov-Mar) One of the few places of worship in Bavaria to charge admission, Rothenburg's Lutheran parish church was begun in the 14th century and finished in the 15th. The building sports some wonderfully aged stained-glass windows but the top attraction is Tilman Riemenschneider's **Heilig Blut Altar** (Altar of the Holy Blood). The gilded cross above the main scene depicting the Last Supper incorporates Rothenburg's most treasured reliquary – a rock crystal capsule said to contain three drops of Christ's blood.

Rathausturm HISTORIC BUILDING

(Town Hall Tower; Marktplatz; adult/concession €2/0.50; ⊙9.30am-12.30pm & 1-5pm daily Apr-Oct, 10.30am-2pm & 2.30-6pm daily Dec, noon-3pm Sat & Sun rest of year) The Rathaus on Marktplatz was begun in Gothic style in the 14th century and was completed during the Renaissance. Climb the 220 steps of the medieval town hall to the viewing platform of the Rathausturm to be rewarded with widescreen views of the Tauber.

Stadtmauer HISTORIC SITE

(Town Wall) With time and fresh legs, a 2.5km circular walk around the unbroken ring of town walls gives a sense of the importance medieval people placed on defending their settlement. A great lookout point is the eastern tower, the **Röderturm** (Rödergasse; adult/child €1.50/1; ⊙9am-5pm Mar-Nov), but for the most impressive views head to the west side of town, where a sweeping view of the Tauber Valley includes the Doppelbrücke, a double-decker bridge.

Mittelalterliches Kriminalmuseum MUSEUM

(Medieval Crime & Punishment Museum; www.kriminalmuseum.eu; Burggasse 3; adult/concession €7/4; ⊙10am-6pm May-Oct, 1-4pm Nov-Apr) Medieval implements of torture and punishment are on show at this gruesomely fascinating museum. Exhibits include chastity belts, masks of disgrace for gossips, a cage for cheating bakers, a neck brace for quarrelsome women and a beer-barrel pen for drunks. You can even snap a selfie in the stocks!

Sleeping & Eating

★**Burg-Hotel** HOTEL €€

(☎09861-948 90; www.burghotel.eu; Klostergasse 1-3; s €100-135, d €125-195; P ⊖ ❄ ☎) Each of the 17 elegantly furnished guest rooms at this boutique hotel built into the town walls has its own private sitting area. The lower floors shelter a decadent spa with tanning beds, saunas and rainforest showers, and a cellar with a Steinway piano, while phenomenal valley views unfurl from the breakfast room and stone terrace.

Gasthof Butz GERMAN €

(☎09861-2201; Kapellenplatz 4; mains €7-15; ⊙noon-11pm Fri-Wed; ☎) For a quick, no-nonsense goulash, schnitzel or roast pork, lug your weary legs to this locally adored, family-run inn in a former brewery. In summer two flowery beer gardens beckon. It also rents a dozen simply furnished rooms (doubles €36 to €75).

Zur Höll FRANCONIAN €€
(☎09861-4229; www.hoell.rothenburg.de; Burggasse 8; mains €7-20; ⏰5-11pm Mon-Sat) This medieval wine tavern is in the town's oldest original building, with sections dating back to the year 900. The menu of regional specialities is limited but refined, though it's the superb selection of Franconian wines that people really come for.

Information

Tourist Office (☎09861-404 800; www.tourismus.rothenburg.de; Marktplatz 2; ⏰9am-6pm Mon-Fri, 10am-5pm Sat & Sun May-Oct, 9am-5pm Mon-Fri, 10am-1pm Sat Nov-Apr) Helpful office offering free internet access.

Getting There & Away

The Romantic Road Coach pauses in town for 45 minutes.

You can go anywhere by train from Rothenburg, as long as it's Steinach. Change there for services to Würzburg (€13.30, one hour and 10 minutes). Travel to and from Munich (from €31, three hours) can involve up to three different trains.

Würzburg

☎0931 / POP 133,800

Tucked in among river valleys lined with vineyards, Würzburg beguiles long before you reach the city centre and is renowned for its art, architecture and delicate wines. Its crowning architectural glory is the Residenz, one of the finest baroque structures in Germany and a Unesco World Heritage site.

Sights

★**Würzburg Residenz** PALACE
(www.residenz-wuerzburg.de; Balthasar-Neumann-Promenade; adult/concession/under 18yr €7.50/6.50/free; ⏰9am-6pm Apr-Oct, 10am-4.30pm Nov-Mar, 45min English tours 11am & 3pm, also 4.30pm Apr-Oct) The vast Unesco-listed Residenz, built by 18th-century architect Balthasar Neumann as the home of the local prince-bishops, is one of Germany's most important and beautiful baroque palaces. Top billing goes to the brilliant zigzagging **Treppenhaus** (Staircase) lidded by what still is the world's largest fresco, a masterpiece by Giovanni Battista Tiepolo depicting allegories of the four then-known continents (Europe, Africa, America and Asia).

The structure was commissioned in 1720 by prince-bishop Johann Philipp Franz von Schönborn, who was unhappy with his old-fashioned digs up in Marienberg Fortress, and took almost 60 years to complete. Today, the 360 rooms are home to government institutions, university faculties and a museum, but the grandest 40 have been restored for visitors to admire.

Besides the Grand Staircase, feast your eyes on the ice-white stucco-adorned **Weisser Saal** (White Hall) before entering the **Kaisersaal** (Imperial Hall), canopied by yet another impressive Tiepolo fresco. Other stunners include the gilded stucco **Spiegelkabinett** (Mirror Hall), covered with a unique mirror-like glass painted with figural, floral and animal motifs (accessible by tour only).

In the residence's south wing, the **Hofkirche** (Court Church) is another Neumann and Tiepolo co-production. Its marble columns, gold leaf and profusion of angels match the Residenz in splendour and proportions.

Entered via frilly wrought-iron gates, the **Hofgarten** (Court Garden; open until dusk, free) is a smooth blend of French- and English-style landscaping teeming with whimsical sculptures of children, mostly by court sculptor Peter Wagner. Concerts, festivals and special events take place here during the warmer months.

The complex also houses collections of antiques, paintings and drawings in the **Martin-von-Wagner Museum** (no relation to Peter) and, handily, a winery in the atmospheric cellar, the **Staatlicher Hofkeller Würzburg**, that is open for tours with tasting.

Dom St Kilian CHURCH
(www.dom-wuerzburg.de; Domstrasse 40; ⏰8am-7pm Mon-Sat, 8am-8pm Sun) FREE Würzburg's highly unusual cathedral has a Romanesque core that has been altered many times over the centuries. Recently renovated, the elaborate stucco work of the chancel contrasts starkly with the bare whitewash of the austere Romanesque nave, which is capped with a ceiling that wouldn't look out of place in a 1960s bus station.

The whole mishmash creates quite an impression and is possibly Germany's oddest cathedral interior. The **Schönbornkapelle** by Balthasar Neumann returns a little baroque order to things.

Festung Marienberg FORTRESS
(tour adult/concession €3.50/2.50; ⊙tours 11am, 2pm, 3pm & 4pm Tue-Sun, also 10am & 1pm Sat & Sun mid-Mar–Oct, 11am, 2pm & 3pm Sat & Sun Nov–mid-Mar) Enjoy panoramic city and vineyard views from this hulking fortress whose construction was initiated around 1200 by the local prince-bishops who governed here until 1719. Dramatically illuminated at night, the structure was only penetrated once, by Swedish troops during the Thirty Years' War, in 1631. Inside, the **Fürstenbaumuseum** (closed November to mid-March) sheds light on its former residents' pompous lifestyle, while the **Mainfränkisches Museum** presents city history and works by local late-Gothic master carver Tilmann Riemenschneider and other famous artists.

Sleeping & Eating

Hotel Rebstock HOTEL €€€
(☎0931-309 30; www.rebstock.com; Neubaustrasse 7; s/d from €131/241; ❄@📶) Würzburg's top digs, in a squarely renovated rococo townhouse, has 70 unique, stylishly finished rooms with the gamut of amenities, impeccable service and an Altstadt location. A pillow selection and supercomfy 'gel' beds should ease you into slumberland, perhaps after a fine meal in the dramatic bistro or the slick Michelin-star Kuno 1408 restaurant.

Backöfele FRANCONIAN €€
(☎0931-590 59; www.backoefele.de; Ursulinergasse 2; mains €8-20; ⊙noon-midnight Mon-Thu, to 1am Fri & Sat, to 11pm Sun) This old-timey warren has been serving hearty Franconian food for nearly 50 years. Find a table in the cobbled courtyard or one of four historic rooms, each candlelit and uniquely furnished with local flair. Featuring schnitzel, snails, bratwurst in wine, wine soup with cinnamon croutons, grilled meat and other local faves, the menu makes for mouth-watering reading. Bookings recommended.

Alte Mainmühle FRANCONIAN €€
(☎0931-167 77; www.alte-mainmuehle.de; Mainkai 1; mains €8-25; ⊙10am-midnight) Accessed straight from the old bridge, tourists and locals alike cram into this old mill to savour modern twists on Franconian classics (including popular river fish). In summer the double terrace beckons – the upper one delivers pretty views of the bridge and Marienberg Fortress; in winter retreat to the snug timber dining room. Year round, guests spill out onto the bridge itself, Aperol Sprizz in hand.

Information

Tourist Office (☎0931-372 398; www.wuerzburg.de; Marktplatz 9; ⊙10am-5pm Mon-Fri, 10am-3pm Sat & Sun May-Oct, closed Sun and slightly shorter hours Nov-Apr) Within the attractive Falkenhaus, this efficient office can help you with room reservations and tour booking.

Getting There & Away

Frequent trains run to Bamberg (€20.70, one hour), Frankfurt (€35, one hour), Nuremberg (from €20.90, one hour) and Rothenburg ob der Tauber (via Steinach; €13.30, one hour).

Nuremberg

☎0911 / POP 510,600

Nuremberg (Nürnberg) woos visitors with its wonderfully restored medieval Altstadt, its grand castle and, in December, its magical *Christkindlmarkt* (Christmas market).

The town played a key role during the Nazi years. It was here that the fanatical party rallies were held, the boycott of Jewish businesses began and the anti-Semitic Nuremberg Laws were enacted. After WWII the city was chosen as the site of the Nuremberg Trials of Nazi war criminals.

Sights

Nuremberg's city centre is best explored on foot but the Nazi-related sights are a tram ride away.

Hauptmarkt SQUARE
This bustling square in the heart of the Altstadt is the site of daily markets as well as the famous *Christkindlmarkt* (Christmas market). At the eastern end is the ornate Gothic **Frauenkirche** (church). Daily at noon crowds crane their necks to witness the clock's figures enact a spectacle called the *Männleinlaufen* (Little Men Dancing). Rising from the square like a Gothic spire is the sculpture-festooned **Schöner Brunnen** (Beautiful Fountain). Touch the golden ring in the ornate wrought-iron gate for good luck.

★**Kaiserburg** CASTLE
(Imperial Castle; ☎0911-244 6590; www.kaiserburg-nuernberg.de; Auf der Burg; adult/concession incl Sinwell Tower €7/6, Palas & Museum €5.50/4.50; ⊙9am-6pm Apr-Sep, 10am-4pm Oct-Mar) This enormous castle complex above the

CHRISTMAS MARKETS

Beginning in late November every year, central squares across Germany are transformed into Christmas markets or *Christkindlmarkt* (also known as *Weihnachtsmärkte*). Folks stamp about between the wooden stalls, perusing seasonal trinkets (from hand-carved ornaments to plastic angels) while warming themselves with *Glühwein* (mulled, spiced red wine) and grilled sausages. Locals love 'em and, not surprisingly, the markets are popular with tourists, so bundle up and carouse for hours. Markets in Nuremberg, Dresden, Cologne and Munich are especially famous.

Altstadt poignantly reflects Nuremberg's medieval might. The main attraction is a tour of the newly renovated residential wing (**Palas**) to see the lavish Knights' and Imperial Hall, a Romanesque double chapel and an exhibit on the inner workings of the Holy Roman Empire. This segues to the **Kaiserburg Museum**, which focuses on the castle's military and building history. Elsewhere, enjoy panoramic views from the **Sinwell Tower** or peer 48m down into the **Deep Well**.

Memorium Nuremberg Trials MEMORIAL
(☎0911-3217 9372; www.memorium-nuremberg.de; Bärenschanzstrasse 72; adult/concession incl audioguide €5/3; ⏲9am-6pm Mon & Wed-Fri, 10am-6pm Sat & Sun Apr-Oct, slightly shorter hours Nov-Mar) Göring, Hess, Speer and 21 other Nazi leaders were tried for crimes against peace and humanity by the Allies in **Schwurgerichtssaal 600** (Court Room 600) of this still-working courthouse. Today the room forms part of an engaging exhibit detailing the background, progression and impact of the trials using film, photographs, audiotape and even the original defendants' dock. To get here, take the U1 towards Bärenschanze and get off at Sielstrasse.

Reichsparteitagsgelände HISTORIC SITE
(Luitpoldhain; ☎0911-231 7538; www.museen.nuernberg.de/dokuzentrum/; Bayernstrasse 110; grounds free, Documentation Centre adult/concession incl audioguide €5/3; ⏲grounds 24hr, Documentation Centre 9am-6pm Mon-Fri, 10am-6pm Sat & Sun) If you've ever wondered where the infamous black-and-white images of ecstatic Nazi supporters hailing their Führer were taken, it was here in Nuremberg. Much of the grounds were destroyed during Allied bombing raids, but enough remains to get a sense of the megalomania behind the regime. The excellent **Dokumentationszentrum** (Documentation Centre) is especially enlightening; it's served by tram 9 from the Hauptbahnhof.

Sleeping

Hotel Victoria HOTEL €€
(☎0911-240 50; www.hotelvictoria.de; Königstrasse 80; s/d from €82/98; P @) A hotel since 1896, the Victoria is a solid option with a central location. With its early-21st-century bathrooms and now ever-so-slightly-dated decor, the price is about right. Popular with business travellers. Parking costs €12.

Hotel Drei Raben BOUTIQUE HOTEL €€€
(☎0911-274 380; www.hoteldreiraben.de; Königstrasse 63; d incl breakfast from €175; P) The design of this classy charmer builds upon the legend of the three ravens perched on the building's chimney stack, who tell stories from Nuremberg lore. Art and decor in the 'mythical theme' rooms reflect a particular tale, from the life of Albrecht Dürer to the first railway.

Eating & Drinking

Don't leave Nuremberg without trying its famous finger-sized *Nürnberger Bratwürste*. You'll find them everywhere around town.

★**Albrecht Dürer Stube** FRANCONIAN €€
(☎0911-227 209; www.albrecht-duerer-stube.de; cnr Albrecht-Dürer-Strasse & Agnesgasse; mains €6-15; ⏲6pm-midnight Mon-Sat, 11.30am-2.30pm Fri & Sun) This unpretentious and intimate restaurant has a Dürer-inspired dining room, prettily laid tables, a ceramic stove keeping things toasty when they're not outside and a menu of Nuremberg sausages, steaks, sea fish, seasonal specials, Franconian wine and *Landbier* (regional beer). There aren't many tables so booking ahead at weekends is recommended.

Heilig-Geist-Spital BAVARIAN €€
(☎0911-221 761; www.heilig-geist-spital.de; Spitalgasse 16; mains €7-18; ⏲11.30am-11pm) Lots of dark carved wood, a herd of hunting trophies and a romantic candlelit half-light make this former hospital, suspended over the Pegnitz, one of the most atmospheric dining rooms in town. Sample the delicious, seasonally changing menu inside or out in

the pretty courtyard, a real treat if you are looking for somewhere traditional to dine.

Kloster PUB
(Obere Wörthstrasse 19; 5pm-1am) One of Nuremberg's best drinking dens is all dressed up as a monastery replete with ecclesiastic knick-knacks including coffins emerging from the walls. The monks here pray to the god of *Landbier* (regional beer) and won't be up at 5am for matins, that's for sure.

Information

Tourist Office – Hauptmarkt (0911-233 60; www.tourismus.nuernberg.de; Hauptmarkt 18; 9am-6pm Mon-Sat year-round, also 10am-4pm Sun Apr-Oct)

Tourist Office – Künstlerhaus (0911-233 60; www.tourismus.nuernberg.de; Königstrasse 93; 9am-7pm Mon-Sat, 10am-4pm Sun) Publishes the excellent *See & Enjoy* booklet, a comprehensive guide to the city.

Getting There & Away

Rail connections from Nuremberg include Frankfurt (€55, 2½ hours) and Munich (from €36, one hour).

Bamberg

0951 / POP 71,200

Off the major tourist routes, Bamberg is one of Germany's most delightful and authentic towns. It has a bevy of beautifully preserved historic buildings, palaces and churches in its Unesco-recognised Altstadt, a lively student population and its own style of beer.

Sights

Bamberger Dom CATHEDRAL
(www.erzbistum-bamberg.de; Domplatz; 8am-6pm Apr-Oct, to 5pm Nov-Mar) FREE Beneath the quartet of spires, Bamberg's cathedral is packed with artistic treasures, most famously the life-size equestrian statue of the **Bamberger Reiter** (Bamberg Horseman), whose true identity remains a mystery. It overlooks the **tomb of cathedral founders**, Emperor Heinrich II and his wife Kunigunde, splendidly carved by Tilmann Riemenschneider. The **marble tomb of Clemens II** in the west choir is the only papal buried site north of the Alps. Nearby, the **Virgin Mary altar** by Veit Stoss also warrants closer inspection.

Altes Rathaus HISTORIC BUILDING
(Old Town Hall; Obere Brücke; adult/concession €4.50/4; 9.30am-4.30pm Tue-Sun) Like a ship in dry dock, Bamberg's 1462 Old Town Hall was built on an artificial island in the Regnitz River, allegedly because the local bishop had refused to give the town's citizens any land for its construction. Inside is a collection of precious porcelain but even more enchanting are the richly detailed frescos adorning its facades – note the cherub's leg cheekily sticking out from its east facade.

Neue Residenz PALACE
(New Residence; 0951-519 390; Domplatz 8; adult/concession €4/3; 9am-6pm Apr-Sep, 10am-4pm Oct-Mar) This splendid episcopal palace gives you an eyeful of the lavish lifestyle of Bamberg's prince-bishops who, between 1703 and 1802, occupied its 40-odd rooms that can only be seen on guided 45-minute tours (in German). Tickets are also good for the **Bavarian State Gallery**, with works by Lucas Cranach the Elder and other old masters. The baroque **Rose Garden** delivers fabulous views over the town.

Sleeping

Hotel Wohnbar BOUTIQUE HOTEL €
(0951-5099 8844; www.wohnbar-bamberg.de; Stangsstrasse 3; s/d from €59/79; P) 'Carpe Noctem' (Seize the Night) is the motto of this charming 10-room retreat with boldly coloured, contemporary rooms near the university quarter. Those in the 'economy' category are a very tight squeeze. Parking costs €10 per day.

Barockhotel am Dom HOTEL €€
(0951-540 31; www.barockhotel.de; Vorderer Bach 4; s/d from €84/99; P) The sugary facade, a sceptre's swipe from the Dom, gives a hint of the baroque heritage and original details within. The 19 rooms have sweeping views of the Dom or the roofs of the Altstadt, and breakfast is served in a 14th-century vault.

Eating & Drinking

Obere Sandstrasse near the cathedral and Austrasse near the university are both good eat and drink streets. Try Bamberg's unique style of beer called *Rauchbier* (smoked beer).

Zum Sternla FRANCONIAN €
(0951-287 50; www.sternla.de; Lange Strasse 46; mains €5-12; 4-11pm Tue, 11am-11pm Wed-Sun) Bamberg's oldest *Wirtshaus* (inn; es-

tablished 1380) bangs down bargain-priced staples including pork dishes, steaks, dumplings and sauerkraut, as well as specials, but it's a great, non-touristy place for a traditional *Brotzeit* (snack), or just a pretzel and a beer. The menu is helpfully translated from Franconian into German.

Schlenkerla GERMAN €€
(☎0951-560 60; www.schlenkerla.de; Dominikanerstrasse 6; mains €6.50-13; ⏰9.30am-11.30pm) Beneath wooden beams as dark as the superb *Rauchbier* poured straight from oak barrels, locals and visitors dig into scrumptious Franconian fare at this legendary flower-festooned tavern near the cathedral.

Information

Tourist Office (☎0951-297 6200; www.bamberg.info; Geyerswörthstrasse 5; ⏰9.30am-6pm Mon-Fri, to 4pm Sat, to 2.30pm Sun) Staff sell the Bambergcard (€14.90), valid for three days of free bus rides and free museum entry.

Getting There & Away

Getting to and from Bamberg by train usually involves a change in Würzburg.

Regensburg

☎0941 / POP 140,300

In a scene-stealing locale on the wide Danube River, Regensburg has relics of historic periods reaching back to the Romans, yet doesn't get the tourist mobs you'll find in other equally attractive German cities. Though big on the historical wow factor, today's Regensburg is a laid-back and unpretentious student town with a distinct Italianate flair.

Sights

Altes Rathaus HISTORIC BUILDING
(Old Town Hall; Rathausplatz; adult/concession €7.50/4; ⏰tours in English 3pm Easter-Oct, 2pm Nov & Dec, in German every 30min) From 1663 to 1806, the Reichstag (imperial assembly) held its gatherings at Regensburg's old town hall, an important role commemorated by an exhibit in today's **Reichstagsmuseum**. Tours take in the lavish assembly hall and the original **torture chambers** in the cellar.

Buy tickets at the tourist office in the same building. Note that access is by tour only. Audioguides are available for English speakers in January and February.

Dom St Peter CHURCH
(www.bistum-regensburg.de; Domplatz; ⏰6.30am-7pm Jun-Sep, to 6pm Apr, May & Oct, to 5pm Nov-Mar) It takes a few seconds for your eyes to adjust to the dim interior of Regensburg's soaring landmark, the Dom St Peter, one of Bavaria's grandest Gothic cathedrals with stunning kaleidoscopic stained-glass windows and an opulent, silver-sheathed main altar.

The cathedral is home of the **Domspatzen**, a 1000-year-old boys' choir that accompanies the 10am Sunday service (only during the school year). The **Domschatzmuseum** (Cathedral Treasury) brims with monstrances, tapestries and other church treasures.

Steinerne Brücke BRIDGE
(Stone Bridge) An incredible feat of engineering for its day, Regensburg's 900-year-old Stone Bridge was at one time the only fortified crossing of the Danube. Damaged and neglected for centuries, the entire expanse has undergone renovation in recent years.

Sleeping

Brook Lane Hostel HOSTEL €
(☎0941-696 5521; www.hostel-regensburg.de; Obere Bachgasse 21; dm/s/d from €16/40/50, apt per person €55; 📶) Regensburg's only backpacker hostel has its very own convenience store, which doubles up as reception, but isn't open 24 hours, so late landers should let staff know in advance. Dorms do the minimum required, but the apartments and doubles here are applaudable deals, especially if you're travelling in a two- or moresome. Access to kitchens and washing machines throughout.

★**Elements Hotel** HOTEL €€
(☎941-2007 2275; www.hotel-elements.de; Alter Kornmarkt 3; d from €105; 📶) Four elements, four rooms, and what rooms they are! 'Fire' blazes in plush crimson, while 'Water' is a wellness suite with a Jacuzzi; 'Air' is playful and light and natural wood; and stone and leather reign in colonial-inspired 'Earth'. Breakfast costs an extra €15.

Eating & Drinking

Historische Wurstkuchl GERMAN €
(☎0941-466 210; www.wurstkuchl.de; Thundorferstrasse 3; 6 sausages €9; ⏰9am-7pm) Completely submerged several times by the Danube's fickle floods, this titchy eatery has been serving the city's traditional finger-size sausages, grilled over beech wood and dished up with the restaurant's own sauerkraut and sweet

grainy mustard, since 1135 and lays claim to being the world's oldest sausage kitchen.

Weltenburger am Dom BAVARIAN €€
(☎0941-586 1460; www.weltenburger-am-dom.de; Domplatz 3; dishes €6.40-20.80; ⏲11am-11pm) Tightly packed gastropub with a mouth-watering menu card of huge gourmet burgers, sausage dishes, beer hall and garden favourites such as *Obazda* (cream cheese on pretzels) and *Sauerbraten* (marinated roast meat), dark beer goulash and a few token desserts. Make sure you are hungry before you come as portions are big.

Information

Tourist Office (☎0941-507 4410; www.regensburg.de; Rathausplatz 4; ⏲9am-6pm Mon-Fri, 9am-4pm Sat, 9.30am-4pm Sun Apr-Oct, closes 2.30pm Sun Nov-Mar; 📶) In the historic Altes Rathaus. Sells tickets, tours, rooms and an audioguide for self-guided tours.

Getting There & Away

Frequent trains leave for Munich (€27.50, 1½ hours) and Nuremberg (€20.70, one to two hours), among other cities.

STUTTGART & THE BLACK FOREST

The high-tech urbanite pleasures of Stuttgart, one of the engines of the German economy, form an appealing contrast to the historic charms of Heidelberg, home to the country's oldest university and a romantic ruined castle. Beyond lies the myth-shrouded Black Forest (Schwarzwald in German), a pretty land of misty hills, thick forest and cute villages with youthful and vibrant Freiburg as its only major town.

Stuttgart

☎0711 / POP 600,000

Stuttgart residents enjoy an enviable quality of life that's to no small degree rooted in its fabled car companies – Porsche and Mercedes – which show off their pedigree in two excellent museums. Hemmed in by vine-covered hills the city also has plenty in store for fans of European art.

Sights

Königsstrasse, a long, pedestrianised shopping strip, links the Hauptbahnhof to the city centre with the Schloss and the art museums. The Mercedes-Benz Museum is about 5km northeast and the Porsche Museum 7km north of here.

Kunstmuseum Stuttgart GALLERY
(☎0711-2161 9600; www.kunstmuseum-stuttgart.de; Kleiner Schlossplatz 1; adult/concession €6/4; ⏲10am-6pm Tue-Thu, Sat & Sun, to 9pm Fri) Occupying a shimmering glass cube, this gallery presents high-calibre special exhibits alongside a permanent gallery filled with a prized collection of works by Otto Dix, Willi Baumeister and Alfred Höltzel. For a great view, head up to the Cube cafe.

Mercedes-Benz Museum MUSEUM
(☎0711-173 0000; www.mercedes-benz-classic.com; Mercedesstrasse 100; adult/concession/under 15yr €10/5/free; ⏲9am-6pm Tue-Sun, last admission 5pm; 🚇S1 to Neckarpark) A futuristic swirl on the cityscape, the Mercedes-Benz Museum takes a chronological spin through the Mercedes empire. Look out for legends like the 1885 Daimler Riding Car, the world's first gasoline-powered vehicle, and the record-breaking Lightning Benz that hit 228km/h at Daytona Beach in 1909.

Porsche Museum MUSEUM
(☎0711-9112 0911; www.porsche.com/museum; Porscheplatz 1; adult/concession €8/4; ⏲9am-6pm Tue-Sun; 🚇Neuwirtshaus) Like a pearly white spaceship preparing for lift-off, the barrier-free Porsche Museum is every little boy's dream. Groovy audioguides race you through the history of Porsche from its 1948 beginnings. Stop to glimpse the 911 GT1 that won Le Mans in 1998.

Sleeping

Hostel Alex 30 HOSTEL €
(☎0711-838 8950; www.alex30-hostel.de; Alexanderstrasse 30; dm €25-29, s/d €43/64; P📶) Fun-seekers on a budget should thrive at this popular hostel within walking distance of the city centre. Rooms are kept spick and span, and the bar, sun deck and communal kitchen are ideal for swapping stories with fellow travellers. Light sleepers might want to pack earplugs for thin walls and street noise. Breakfast costs €8.

Kronen Hotel HOTEL €€€
(☎0711-225 10; www.kronenhotel-stuttgart.de; Kronenstrasse 48; s €115-125, d €160-190; P❄@📶) Right on the lap of Königstrasse, this hotel outclasses most in Stuttgart with its terrific location, good-natured staff, well-appointed rooms and funkily lit sauna. Breakfast is

above par, with fresh fruit, eggs and bacon, smoked fish and pastries.

Eating & Drinking

Hans-im-Glück Platz is a hub of bars, while clubs line Theodor-Heuss-Strasse and wine taverns abound in the Bohnenviertel.

Stuttgarter Markthalle MARKET €
(Market Hall; 0711-480 410; www.markthalle-stuttgart.de; Dorotheenstrasse 4; 7am-6.30pm Mon-Fri, 7am-5pm Sat) Olives, regional cheeses, spices, patisserie, fruit and veg, wine and tapas – you'll find it all under one roof at Stuttgart's large art-nouveau market hall, which also has snack stands.

Ochs'n'Willi GERMAN €€
(0711-226 5191; www.ochsn-willi.de; Kleiner Schlossplatz 4; mains €11.50-30; 11am-11.30pm) A warm, woody hunter's cottage restaurant just this side of twee, Ochs'n'Willi delivers gutsy portions of Swabian and Bavarian fare. Dig into pork knuckles with lashings of dumplings and kraut, spot-on *Maultaschen* (pasta pockets) or rich, brothy *Gaisburger Marsch* (beef stew). There's a terrace for warm-weather dining.

Weinhaus Stetter GERMAN €€
(0711-240 163; www.weinhaus-stetter.de; Rosenstrasse 32; snacks & mains €4-14; 3-11pm Mon-Fri, noon-3pm & 5.30-11pm Sat) This traditional wine tavern in the Bohnenviertel quarter serves up no-nonsense Swabian cooking, including flavoursome *Linsen und Saiten* (lentils with sausage) and beef roast with onion, in a convivial ambience. The attached wine shop sells around 500 different vintages.

Cube INTERNATIONAL €€€
(0711-280 4441; www.cube-restaurant.de; Kleiner Schlossplatz 1; mains €29-37; 10am-midnight Sun-Thu, 10am-2am Fri & Sat) The food is stellar but it actually plays second fiddle to the dazzling decor, refined ambience and stunning views at this glass-fronted cube atop the Kunstmuseum. Lunches are perky, fresh and international, while dinners feature more complex Pacific Rim–inspired cuisine. The lunch special is a steal at around €10.

Information

Tourist Office (0711-22 280; www.stuttgart-tourist.de; Königstrasse 1a; 9am-8pm Mon-Fri, to 6pm Sat, 11am-6pm Sun)

LOCAL KNOWLEDGE

BOHEMIAN BEANS

To really slip under Stuttgart's skin, mosey through the **Bohnenviertel** (Bean District), one of the city's lesser-known neighbourhoods. Walk south to Hans-im-Glück Platz, centred on a fountain depicting the caged Grimm's fairytale character Lucky Hans, and you'll soon reach the boho-flavoured Bohnenviertel, named after beans introduced in the 16th century. Back then they were grown everywhere as the staple food of the poor tanners, dyers and craftsmen who lived here.

Getting There & Away

Stuttgart Airport (SGT; 0711-9480; www.stuttgart-airport.com), a major hub for Germanwings, is 13km south of the city and linked to the Hauptbahnhof by S2 and S3 trains (€3.90, 30 minutes).

There are train services to all major German cities, including Frankfurt (€63, 1¼ hours) and Munich (€57, 2¼ hours).

Heidelberg

06221 / POP 152,435

Germany's oldest and most famous university town is renowned for its lovely Altstadt, its plethora of pubs and its evocative half-ruined castle. Millions of visitors are drawn each year to this photogenic assemblage, thereby following in the footsteps of Mark Twain who kicked off his European travels in 1878 in Heidelberg, later recounting his bemused observations in *A Tramp Abroad*.

Sights

Heidelberg's sites cluster in the Altstadt, which starts to reveal itself only after a charm-free 15-minute walk east from the main train station or a short ride on bus 32 or 38.

★**Schloss Heidelberg** CASTLE
(072 5174 2770; www.schloss-heidelberg.de; adult/child incl Bergbahn €7/4, tours €4/2, audioguide €4; grounds 24hr, castle 8am-6pm, English tours hourly 11.15am-4.15pm Mon-Fri, 10.15am-4.15pm Sat & Sun Apr-Oct, reduced tours Nov-Mar) Towering over the Altstadt, Heidelberg's ruined Renaissance castle cuts a romantic figure, especially across the Neckar River when illuminated at night. Attractions

include the world's largest wine cask and fabulous views. It's reached either via a steep, cobbled trail in about 10 minutes or by taking the **Bergbahn** (cogwheel train) from Kornmarkt station. The only way to see the less-than-scintillating interior is by tour, which can be safely skipped. After 6pm you can stroll the grounds for free.

Alte Brücke BRIDGE
(Karl-Theodor-Brücke) Heidelberg's 200m-long 'old bridge', built in 1786, connects the Altstadt with the river's right bank and the **Schlangenweg** (Snake Path), whose switchbacks lead to the **Philosophenweg** (Philosophers' Walk; south bank of the Neckar River).

Next to the tower gate on the Altstadt side of the bridge, look for the brass sculpture of a monkey holding a mirror. It's the 1979 replacement of the 17th-century original sculpture.

Studentenkarzer HISTORIC SITE
(Student Jail; 06221-543 593; www.uni-heidelberg.de; Augustinergasse 2; adult/child incl Universitätsmuseum €3/2.50; 10am-6pm Tue-Sun Apr-Sep, 10am-4pm Tue-Sat Oct-Mar) From 1823 to 1914, students convicted of misdeeds such as public inebriation, loud nocturnal singing, freeing the local pigs or duelling were sent to this student jail for at least 24 hours. Judging by the inventive wall graffiti, some found their stay highly amusing. Delinquents were let out to attend lectures or take exams. In certain circles, a stint in the Karzer was considered a rite of passage.

Sleeping

Steffis Hostel HOSTEL €
(06221-778 2772; www.hostelheidelberg.de; Alte Eppelheimer Strasse 50; dm from €18, s/d/f without bathroom from €45/56/100; reception 8am-10pm; P @) In a 19th-century tobacco factory a block north of the Hauptbahnhof, accessed via an industrial-size lift/elevator, Steffis offers bright, well-lit dorms and rooms (all with shared bathrooms), a colourful lounge that's great for meeting fellow travellers, a spacious kitchen and an old-school hostel vibe. Breakfast costs €3. Perks include tea, coffee and free bike rental.

★**Hotel Villa Marstall** HISTORIC HOTEL €€
(06221-655 570; www.villamarstall.de; Lauerstrasse 1; s €95-165, d €115-185; reception 7am-10pm Mon-Sat, 8am-6pm Sun;) A 19th-century neoclassical mansion directly overlooking the Neckar River, Villa Marstall is a jewel with cherrywood floors, solid-timber furniture and amenities including a lift/elevator. Exquisite rooms are decorated in whites, creams and bronzes, and come with in-room fridges (perfect for chilling a bottle of regional wine). A sumptuous breakfast buffet (€12) is served in the red-sandstone vaulted cellar.

Eating & Drinking

★**'S' Kastanie** GERMAN €€
(06221-728 0343; www.restaurant-s-kastanie.de; Elisabethenweg 1; 2-course lunch menu €10, mains €12-30; 11.30am-2.30pm & 6-10pm Wed-Fri, 5-10pm Sat, 11.30am-8pm Sun) A panoramic terrace provides sweeping views of the river at this gorgeous 1904-built former hunting lodge, with stained glass and timber panelling, set in the forest near the castle. Chef Sven Schönig's stunning creations include a sweet potato and goat's cheese tower with papaya, and goose-stuffed ravioli.

Schnitzelbank GERMAN €€
(06221-211 89; www.schnitzelbank-heidelberg.de; Baumamtsgasse 7; mains €15-22; 5pm-1am Mon-Fri, from 11.30am Sat & Sun) Small and often jam-packed, this cosy wine tavern has you sampling the local tipples (all wines are regional) and cuisine while crouched on wooden workbenches from the time when this was still a cooperage. It's these benches that give the place its name, incidentally, not the veal and pork schnitzel on the menu. Other specialities include *Saumagen* (stuffed pig's stomach).

Information

Tourist Office – Hauptbahnhof (06221-584 4444; www.heidelberg-marketing.de; Willy-Brandt-Platz 1; 9am-7pm Mon-Sat, 10am-6pm Sun Apr-Oct, 9am-6pm Mon-Sat Nov-Mar) Right outside the main train station.

Tourist Office – Marktplatz (www.heidelberg-marketing.de; Marktplatz 10; 8am-5pm Mon-Fri year-round, 10am-5pm Sat Apr-Oct) In the old town.

Getting There & Away

There are at least hourly IC trains to/from Frankfurt (€18 to €29, one hour) and Stuttgart (€19 to €39, 40 minutes).

Black Forest

The Black Forest (Schwarzwald) gets its name from its dark canopy of evergreens. Let winding backroads take you through misty vales, fairy-tale woodlands and villages that radiate earthy authenticity. It's not nature wild and remote, but bucolic and picturesque.

Many of the Black Forest's most impressive sights are in the triangle delimited by the lively university city of Freiburg, 15km east of the Rhine in the southwest; Triberg, cuckoo-clock capital in the north; and the charming river-valley city of St Blasien in the southeast.

Baden-Baden

07221 / POP 54,500

The northern gateway to the Black Forest, Baden-Baden is one of Europe's most famous spa towns whose mineral-rich waters have cured the ills of celebs from Queen Victoria to Victoria Beckham. An air of old-world luxury hangs over this beautiful town that's also home to a palatial casino.

Activities

★Friedrichsbad SPA

(07221-275 920; www.carasana.de; Römerplatz 1; 3hr ticket €25, incl soap-&-brush massage €37; 9am-10pm, last admission 7pm) If it's the body of Venus and the complexion of Cleopatra you desire, abandon modesty (and clothing) to wallow in thermal waters at this palatial 19th-century marble-and-mosaic-festooned spa. As Mark Twain put it, 'after 10 minutes you forget time; after 20 minutes, the world', as you slip into the regime of steaming, scrubbing, hot-cold bathing and dunking in the Roman-Irish bath.

Caracalla Spa SPA

(07221-275 940; www.carasana.de; Römerplatz 11; 2/3hr €16/19, day ticket €23; 8am-10pm, last admission 8pm) This modern, glass-fronted spa has a cluster of indoor and outdoor pools, grottos and surge channels, making the most of the mineral-rich spring water. For those who dare to bare, saunas range from the rustic 'forest' to the roasting 95°C 'fire' variety.

Sleeping & Eating

Schweizer Hof HOTEL €€

(07221-304 60; www.schweizerhof.de; Lange Strasse 73; s €69-89, d €99-135) Sitting on one of Baden-Baden's smartest streets, this above-par hotel is a real find, with 34 dapper en-suite rooms, chandelier-lit spaces, and a garden with sun lounges for chilling. The buffet breakfast is a rich affair.

★Weinstube im Baldreit GERMAN €€

(07221-231 36; Küferstrasse 3; mains €12.50-19; 5-10pm Tue-Sat) Well hidden down cobbled lanes, this wine-cellar restaurant is tricky to find, but worth looking for. Baden-Alsatian fare such as *Flammkuchen* (Alsatian pizza) topped with Black Forest ham, Roquefort and pears is expertly matched with local wines. Eat in the ivy-swathed courtyard in summer, and the vaulted interior in winter.

Information

Main Tourist Office (07221-275 200; www.baden-baden.com; Schwarzwaldstrasse 52; 9am-6pm Mon-Sat, 9am-1pm Sun) Situated 2km northwest of the centre. If you're driving from the northwest (from the A5), this place is on the way into town. Sells event tickets.

Triberg

07722 / POP 5000

Cuckoo-clock capital, Black Forest–cake pilgrimage site and Germany's highest waterfall – Triberg is a torrent of Schwarzwald superlatives and attracts gushes of guests.

Sights

★Triberger Wasserfälle WATERFALL

(adult/concession/family €4/3.50/9.50; 9am-7pm Mar-early Nov & 25-30 Dec) Niagara they ain't but Germany's highest waterfalls do exude their own wild romanticism. The Gutach River feeds the seven-tiered falls, which drop a total of 163m and are illuminated until 10pm.

Sleeping & Eating

★Parkhotel Wehrle HISTORIC HOTEL €€€

(07722-860 20; www.parkhotel-wehrle.de; Gartenstrasse 24; s €95-105, d €155-179; P) This 400-year-old hotel has a recommended integrated day spa. Often with a baroque or Biedermeier touch, quarters are roomy and beautifully furnished with antiques; the best have Duravit whirlpool tubs. Hemingway once waxed lyrical about the trout he ordered at the hotel's venerable **restaurant** (mains €15-24; 6-9pm daily, noon-2pm Sun).

★Café Schäfer CAFE €

(07722-4465; www.cafe-schaefer-triberg.de; Hauptstrasse 33; cakes €3-4; 9am-6pm Mon, Tue, Thu & Fri, 8am-6pm Sat, 11am-6pm Sun) Confectioner Claus Schäfer uses the original 1915 recipe for Black Forest gateau to prepare this sinful treat that layers chocolate cake perfumed with cherry brandy, whipped cream and sour cherries and wraps it all in more cream and shaved chocolate. Trust us, it's worth the calories.

Information

Tourist Office (07722-866 490; www.triberg.de; Wallfahrtstrasse 4; 9am-5pm Mon-Fri, 10am-5pm Sat & Sun) Inside the Schwarzwald-Museum. Stocks walking, cross-country skiing and mountain-biking maps.

Freiburg im Breisgau

0761 / POP 224,190

Sitting plump at the foot of the Black Forest's wooded slopes and vineyards, Freiburg is a sunny, cheerful university town whose Altstadt is a storybook tableau of gabled townhouses, cobblestone lanes and cafe-rimmed plazas. Party-loving students spice up the local nightlife and give Freiburg its relaxed air.

Sights

★**Freiburger Münster** CATHEDRAL

(Freiburg Minster; 0761-202 790; www.freiburgermuenster.info; Münsterplatz; tower adult/concession €2/1.50; 10am-5pm Mon-Sat, 1-7.30pm Sun, tower 9.30am-4.45pm Mon-Sat, 1-5pm Sun) With its lacy spires, cheeky gargoyles and intricate entrance portal, Freiburg's 11th-century minster cuts an impressive figure above the central market square. It has dazzling kaleidoscopic stained-glass windows that were mostly financed by medieval guilds and a high altar with a masterful triptych by Dürer protégé Hans Baldung Grien. Square at the base, the tower becomes an octagon higher up and is crowned by a filigreed 116m-high spire. On clear days you can spy the Vosges Mountains in France.

Rathausplatz SQUARE

(Town Hall Square) Join locals relaxing in a cafe by the fountain in chestnut-shaded Rathausplatz, Freiburg's prettiest square. Pull out your camera to snap pictures of the ox-blood-red 16th-century **Altes Rathaus** (Old Town Hall) with the tourist office, the step-gabled 19th-century **Neues Rathaus** (New Town Hall) and the medieval **Martinskirche** with its modern interior.

Augustinermuseum MUSEUM

(0761-201 2531; Auginerplatz 1; adult/concession/under 18yr €7/5/free; 10am-5pm Tue-Sun) Dip into the past as represented by artists working from the Middle Ages to the 19th century at this superb museum in a sensitively modernised monastery. The **Sculpture Hall** on the ground floor is especially impressive for its fine medieval sculpture and masterpieces by Renaissance artists Hans Baldung Grien and Lucas Cranach the Elder. Head upstairs for eye-level views of mounted gargoyles.

Sleeping

Black Forest Hostel HOSTEL €

(0761-881 7870; www.blackforest-hostel.de; Kartäuserstrasse 33; dm €17-28, s/d €36/60, linen €4; reception 7am-1am; @) Boho budget digs with chilled common areas, a shared kitchen, bike rental and spacey stainless-steel showers. It's a five-minute walk from the town centre.

Hotel Schwarzwälder Hof HOTEL €€

(0761-380 30; www.schwarzwaelder-hof.com; Herrenstrasse 43; s €68-80, d €99-125;) This bijou hotel has an unrivalled style-for-euro ratio. A wrought-iron staircase sweeps up to snazzy rooms furnished in classic, modern or traditional style. Some have postcard

THE BATTLE OF THE BIRDS

Triberg being Germany's undisputed cuckoo-clock capital, it's not surprising that two giant timepieces battle for title of world's largest cuckoo clock.

The older and more charming contender calls itself the **1. Weltgrösste Kuckucksuhr** (First World's Largest Cuckoo Clock; www.1weltgroesstekuckucksuhr.de; Untertalstrasse 28, Schonach; adult/concession €1.20/0.60; 10am-noon & 1-5pm) and can be found in Schonach. It kicked into gear in 1980 and took a local clockmaker three years to build by hand. A Dold family member is usually around to the explain the mechanism.

It has since been eclipsed in size by its cousin at the **Eble Uhren-Park** (07722-962 20; www.uhren-park.de; Schonachbach 27; €2; 9am-6pm Mon-Sat, 10am-6pm Sun), which occupies an entire house on the B33 between Triberg and Hornberg. Although undeniably bigger (and listed in the *Guinness Book of World Records*), it's more of a gimmick to lure shoppers inside a large clock shop.

views of the Altstadt. There's also an on-site restaurant.

Eating & Drinking

Markthalle MARKET €
(www.markthalle-freiburg.de; Martinsgasse 235; light meals €4-8; ⌚8am-8pm Mon-Thu, to midnight Fri & Sat) Eat your way around the world – from curry to sushi, oysters to antipasti – at the food counters in this historic market hall, nicknamed 'Fressgässle'.

Gasthaus zum Kranz GERMAN €€
(☎0761-217 1967; www.gasthauszumkranz.de; Herrenstrasse 40; mains €13-25; ⌚11.30am-3pm & 5.30pm-midnight Mon-Sat, noon-3pm & 5.30pm-midnight Sun) There's always a good buzz at this quintessentially rustic Badisch tavern. Pull up a hefty chair at one of the even heftier timber tables for well-prepared regional faves such as roast suckling pig, *Maultaschen* and *Sauerbraten* (beef pot roast with vinegar, onions and peppercorns).

Hausbrauerei Feierling PUB FOOD €€
(☎0761-243 480; www.feierling.de; Gerberau 46; mains €5-15; ⌚11am-midnight Mon-Thu, to 1am Fri & Sun; 🌶) Thumbs up for the Feierling house brew, which has kept beer lovers lubricated for over a quarter century. In summer grab a table in the lovely beer garden and stave off a hangover with honest-to-goodness German classics or try one of the flavour-packed vegetarian alternatives.

Schlappen PUB
(☎0761-334 94▯; www.schlappen.com; Löwenstrasse 2; ⌚11am-1am Mon-Wed, to 2am Thu, to 3am Fri & Sat, 3pm-1am Sun) In historic digs and crammed with antiques and vintage theatre posters, this rocking, evergreen pub has made the magic happen for generations of students. Check out the skeleton in the men's toilet. Summer terrace.

Information

Tourist Office (☎0761-388 1880; www.freiburg.de; Rathausplatz 2-4; ⌚8am-8pm Mon-Fri, 9.30am-5pm Sat, 10.30am-3.30pm Sun) Pick up the three-day WelcomeKarte (€25), covering all public transport and the Schauinslandbahn, at Freiburg's central tourist office.

Getting There & Away

Connections include ICE trains to Basel (from €19, 45 minutes) and Baden-Baden (from €18.10, 45 minutes).

LOCAL KNOWLEDGE

SOARING ABOVE THE FOREST

Freiburg seems tiny as you drift up above the city and a tapestry of meadows and forest on the **Schauinslandbahn** (☎451 1777; www.schauinslandbahn.de; return adult/child €12.50/8, one way €9/6; ⌚9am-5pm Oct-Jun, to 6pm Jul-Sep) to the 1284m Schauinsland peak. The lift provides a speedy link between Freiburg and the Black Forest highlands.

FRANKFURT & THE RHINELAND

Defined by the mighty Rhine, fine wines, medieval castles and romantic villages, Germany's heartland speaks to the imagination. Even Frankfurt, which may seem all buttoned-up business, reveals itself as a laidback metropolis with fabulous museums and pulsating nightlife.

Frankfurt-am-Main

☎069 / POP 709,395

Unashamedly high-rise, Frankfurt-on-the-Main (pronounced 'mine') is a true capital of finance and business and hosts some of Europe's key trade fairs. But despite its business demeanour, Frankfurt consistently ranks high among Germany's most liveable cities thanks to its rich collection of museums, expansive parks and greenery, a lively student scene and excellent public transport.

Sights

★**Kaiserdom** CATHEDRAL
(Imperial/Frankfurt Cathedral; www.dom-frankfurt.de; Domplatz 1; tower adult/concession €3.50/1.50; ⌚church 8am-8pm Mon-Thu, noon-8pm Fri, 9am-8pm Sat & Sun, tower 9am-6pm Apr-Oct, 11am-5pm Thu-Mon Nov-Mar; Ⓢ Dom/Römer) Frankfurt's red-sandstone cathedral is dominated by a 95m-high Gothic **tower**, which can be climbed via 324 steps. Construction began in the 13th century; from 1356 to 1792, the Holy Roman Emperors were elected (and, after 1562, consecrated and crowned) in the **Wahlkapelle** at the end of the right aisle (look for the 'skull' altar). The cathedral was rebuilt both after an 1867 fire and after the bombings of 1944, which left it a burnt-out shell.

Frankfurt-am-Main

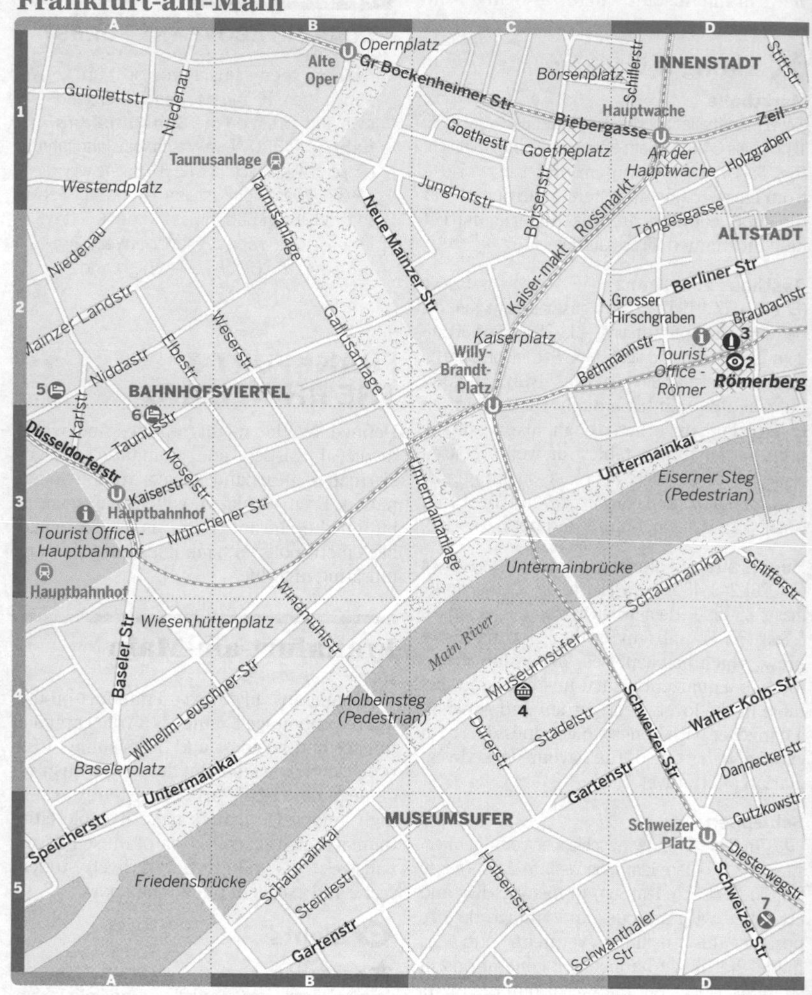

★Römerberg SQUARE

(S Dom/Römer) The Römerberg is Frankfurt's old central square. Ornately gabled half-timbered buildings, reconstructed after WWII, give an idea of how beautiful the city's medieval core once was.

In the square's centre is the **Gerechtigkeitsbrunnen** (Fountain of Justice; Römerberg); in 1612, at the coronation of Matthias, the fountain ran with wine. The Römerberg is especially lovely as a backdrop for the **Christmas market** (Weihnachtsmarkt; ⏲10am-9pm Mon-Sat, 11am-9pm Sun late Nov-23 Dec).

Museumsufer Frankfurt MUSEUM

(www.museumsufer-frankfurt.de; south bank of the Main River, btwn Eiserner Steg & Friedensbrücke; S Schweizer Platz) More than a dozen museums line up along the south bank of the Main River, collectively known as the Museumsufer. The most famous is the **Städel Museum** (☎069-605 098; www.staedelmuseum.de; Schaumainkai 63; adult/child €14/12; ⏲10am-7pm Tue, Wed, Sat & Sun, to 9pm Thu & Fri May-Jun & Sep, 10am-9pm daily Jul & Aug, 10am-6pm Tue, Wed, Sat & Sun, to 9pm Thu & Fri Oct-Apr; 📶; 🚊16 Otto-Hahn-Platz), a renowned art gallery, but fans of architecture, archaeology, applied arts,

Frankfurt-am-Main

Top Sights
1 Kaiserdom E2
2 Römerberg D2

Sights
Dommuseum .... (see 1)
3 Gerechtigkeitsbrunnen D2
4 Museumsufer Frankfurt C4

Sleeping
5 25hours Hotel by Levi's A2
6 Five Elements A3

Eating
7 Adolf Wagner D5
8 Bitter & Zart E2
9 Dauth-Schneider F4
10 Kleinmarkthalle E1

Drinking & Nightlife
11 Fichtekränzi F4

film and ethnology will also get their fill. Bus 46, which leaves from the Hauptbahnhof several times hourly, links most museums.

Sleeping

If a big trade show is in town (and it often is) prices can triple. In general, rates drop on weekends.

Five Elements HOSTEL €
(069-2400 5885; www.5elementshostel.de; Moselstrasse 40; dm/s/d from €18/45/56; ; Hauptbahnhof) The location mightn't be Frankfurt's most salubrious, but once you're inside the turn-of-the-20th-century gabled building it's a sanctuary of parquet floors, boldly coloured walls and designer furniture. Facilities include a laundry and 24-hour bar with a billiard table; breakfast costs €4.50. A private apartment sleeping up to four people with a private bathroom and kitchen costs €426 per week.

25hours Hotel by Levi's DESIGN HOTEL €€
(069-256 6770; www.25hours-hotels.com; Niddastrasse 58; d weekday/weekend from €149/89; P; Hauptbahnhof) Inspired by Levi's (yes, the jeans brand), this hipster haven has a rooftop terrace, free bike hire, and a Gibson Music Room for jamming on drums and guitars. Rooms are themed by decade, from the 1930s (calm colours) to the 1980s (tiger-print walls, optical-illusion carpets). Breakfast costs a whopping €18.

★ **Villa Orange** BOUTIQUE HOTEL €€
(069-405 840; www.villa-orange.de; Hebelstrasse 1; s/d weekday from €130/160, weekend from €105/129; P; 12/18 Friedberger Platz) Offering a winning combination of tranquillity, modern German design and small-hotel comforts (such as a quiet corner library), this century-old, tangerine-coloured villa has 38 spacious rooms, some with free-standing baths and four-poster beds. Everything is organic – the sheets, the soap and the bountiful buffet breakfast.

LOCAL KNOWLEDGE

APPLE-WINE TAVERNS

Apple-wine taverns are Frankfurt's great local tradition. They serve *Ebbelwei* (Frankfurt dialect for *Apfelwein*), an alcoholic apple cider, along with local specialities like *Handkäse mit Musik* (literally, 'hand-cheese with music'). This is a round cheese soaked in oil and vinegar and topped with onions; your bowel supplies the music. Anything with *Grüne Sosse*, a herb sauce, is also a winner. **Fichtekränzi** (☎069-612 778; www.fichtekraenzi.de; Wallstrasse 5; ⏰5pm-1am Mon-Sat, 4pm-1am Sun; 🚋14/18 Frankensteiner Platz) and **Adolf Wagner** (☎069-612 565; www.apfelwein-wagner.com; Schweizer Strasse 71; mains €8-18; ⏰11am-midnight; S Schweizer Platz) in Alt-Sachsenhausen are recommended traditional taverns.

Eating & Drinking

The pedestrian strip west of Hauptwache square is nicknamed Fressgass (literally 'Grazing Street') thanks to its many (average) eateries. Cosy apple-wine taverns cluster in Alt-Sachsenhausen south of the Main.

★**Kleinmarkthalle** MARKET €
(www.kleinmarkthalle.de; Hasengasse 5-7; ⏰8am-6pm Mon-Fri, to 4pm Sat; S Dom/Römer) Aromatic stalls inside this bustling traditional market hall sell artisan smoked sausages, cheeses, roasted nuts, breads, pretzels, loose-leaf teas, and pastries, cakes and chocolates, as well as fruit, vegetables, spices, fresh Italian pastas, Greek olives, meat, poultry and, downstairs, fish. It's unmissable for picnickers or self-caterers, or anyone wanting to experience Frankfurt life. The upper-level wine bar opens to a terrace.

Bitter & Zart CAFE €
(☎069-9494 2846; www.bitterundzart.de; Braubachstrasse 14; dishes €4-8; ⏰10am-7pm Mon-Sat, 11am-6pm Sun; S Dom/Römer) Walk past the shelves piled high with chocolate pralines to order espresso, hot chocolate and luscious cakes such as lemon cake, carrot cake and *Frankfurt Kränze* (butter-cream cake), with gluten-free options.

★**Dauth-Schneider** GERMAN €€
(☎069-613 533; www.dauth-schneider.de; Neuer Wall 5; mains €4-14.50; ⏰kitchen 11.30am-midnight; 🚆Lokalbahnhof) With a history stretching back to 1849 (the basement housed an apple winery), this convivial tavern is not only a wonderful place to sample the local drop but also classic regional specialities such as *Sulz Fleisch* (cold meat and jelly terrine), pork knuckle with sauerkraut, Frankfurter schnitzel, sausages and various tasting platters. Tables fill the tree-shaded terrace in summer.

Information

Tourist Office – Hauptbahnhof (☎069-2123 8800; www.frankfurt-tourismus.de; Main Hall, Hauptbahnhof; ⏰8am-9pm Mon-Fri, 9am-6pm Sat & Sun; 🚆Hauptbahnhof) At the main train station.

Tourist Office – Römer (☎069-2123 8800; www.frankfurt-tourismus.de; Römerberg 27; ⏰9.30am-5.30pm Mon-Fri, to 4pm Sat & Sun; S Dom/Römer) Smallish office in the central square.

Getting There & Away

AIR

Frankfurt Airport (FRA; www.frankfurt-airport.com; 📶; 🚆Flughafen Regionalbahnhof), 12km southwest of the city centre, is Germany's busiest. S-Bahn lines S8 and S9 shuttle between the airport's regional train station (Regionalbahnhof) and the city centre (€4.55, 15 minutes) several times hourly.

Note that **Frankfurt-Hahn Airport** (HHN; www.hahn-airport.de), served by Ryanair, is actually 125km west of Frankfurt, near the Mosel Valley. Buses to Frankfurt's Hauptbahnhof take 1¾ hours and should be booked ahead.

BUS

The Romantic Road Coach and long-distance buses leave from the south side of the Hauptbahnhof.

TRAIN

There are direct trains to pretty much everywhere, including Berlin (€123, 4¼ hours) and Munich (from €82, 3½ hours).

The Romantic Rhine Valley

Between Bingen and Koblenz, the Rhine cuts deeply through the Rhenish slate mountains. Forested hillsides cradle craggy cliffs and nearly vertical terraced vineyards. Idyllic villages appear around each bend, their neat half-timbered houses and church steeples seemingly plucked from the world of fairy tales. High above the river, busy with barge traffic, are the famous medieval castles, some ruined, some restored, all vestiges from a mysterious past.

Although Koblenz and Mainz are logical starting points, the area can also be explored on a long day trip from Frankfurt.

Bacharach

One of the prettiest of the Rhine villages, Bacharach conceals its considerable charms behind a 14th-century town wall. Beyond the thick arched gateways awaits a beautiful medieval old town graced with half-timbered townhouses lining Oberstrasse, the main thoroughfare. There's no shortage of atmospheric places to eat and sample the local vintages.

For gorgeous views of village, vineyards and river, take a stroll atop the **medieval ramparts**, which are punctuated by guard towers. An especially scenic panorama unfolds from the **Postenturm** at the north end of town, from where you can also espy the filigreed ruins of the **Wernerkapelle**, a medieval chapel, and the turrets of the 12th-century hilltop **Burg Stahleck**, a castle turned **youth hostel** (06743-1266; www.jugendherberge.de; dm/s/d €22/27/54; P @).

Another good place to stay is the **Rhein Hotel** (06743-1243; www.rhein-hotel-bacharach.de; Langstrasse 50; s €39-68, d €78-136; P ❄ ᯤ), which has 14 well-lit rooms with original artwork and a respected restaurant.

St Goar & St Goarshausen

These twin towns face each other across the Rhine. On the left bank, St Goar is lorded over by **Burg Rheinfels** (06741-7753; www.st-goar.de; adult/child €5/2.50; 9am-6pm mid-Mar–late Oct, 11am-5pm late Oct–mid-Nov). Once the mightiest fortress on the Rhine, Burg Rheinfels was built in 1245 by Count Dieter V of Katzenelnbogen as a base for his toll-collecting operations. Its size and labyrinthine layout are astonishing.

A ferry links St Goar with St Goarshausen and the most fabled spot along the Romantic Rhine, the **Loreley Rock**. This vertical slab of slate owes its fame to a mythical maiden whose siren songs are said to have lured sailors to their death in the river's treacherous currents. A **Besucherzentrum** (06771-599 093; www.loreley-besucherzentrum.de; Loreleyring 7; adult/child €2.50/1.50, parking €2; 10am-6pm Apr-Oct, 10am-5pm Mar, 11am-4pm Sat & Sun Nov-Feb) at the top of the rock reveals more.

A classy spot to spend the night is **Romantik Hotel Schloss Rheinfels** (06741-8020; www.schloss-rheinfels.de; Schlossberg 47; s/d weekday from €95/130, weekend €110/140; P @ ᯤ), right by the castle. Its three restaurants enjoy a fine reputation but there are plenty more down in the village.

Braubach

Framed by forested hillsides, vineyards and rose gardens, the 1300-year-old town of Braubach, 8km south of Koblenz, centres on a small, half-timbered market square. High above are the dramatic towers, turrets and crenellations of the 700-year-old **Marksburg** (02627-206; www.marksburg.de; adult/child €7/5; 10am-5pm mid-Mar–Oct, 11am-4pm Nov–mid-Mar), which – unique among the Rhine fortresses – was never destroyed. Tours (in English at 1pm and 4pm from late March to October) take in the citadel, the Gothic hall, the kitchen and the torture chamber.

Koblenz

Founded by the Romans, Koblenz sits at the confluence of the Rhine and Moselle Rivers, a point known as **Deutsches Eck** (German Corner) and dominated by a bombastic 19th-century statue of Kaiser Wilhelm I on horseback. On the right Rhine bank high above the Deutsches Eck – and reached by an 850m-long **Seilbahn** (cable car; www.seilbahn-koblenz.de; return adult/child

ROMANCING THE RHINE

The Romantic Rhine Valley villages have plenty more charmers that deserve at least a quick spin. Just pick one at random and make your own discoveries. Here are some teasers:

Boppard Roman ruins and a cable car to the stunning Vierseenblick viewpoint (left bank).

Oberwesel Famous for its 3km-long medieval town wall punctuated by 16 guard towers (left bank).

Assmannhausen Relatively untouristed village known for its red wines, sweeping views and good hikes (right bank).

Rüdesheim Day-tripper-deluged but handy launchpad for the mighty Niederwalddenkmal monument and Eberbach Monastery (right bank).

EXPLORING THE ROMANTIC RHINE

Each mode of transport on the Rhine has its own advantages and all are equally enjoyable. Try combining several.

Boat From about Easter to October (winter services are very limited), passenger ships run by **Köln-Düsseldorfer** (☎0221-208 8318; www.k-d.com) link villages on a set timetable. You're free to get on and off as you like.

Car No bridges span the Rhine between Koblenz and Bingen but you can easily change banks by using a car ferry *(Autofähre)*. There are five routes: Bingen–Rüdesheim, Niederheimbach–Lorch, Boppard–Filsen, Oberwesel–Kaub and St Goar–Goarshausen.

Train Villages on the Rhine's left bank (eg Bacharach and Boppard) are served regularly by local trains on the Koblenz–Mainz run. Right-bank villages such as Rüdesheim, St Goarshausen and Braubach are linked hourly to Koblenz' Hauptbahnhof and Frankfurt by the RheingauLinie train.

€9/4, incl fortress €11.80/5.60; ⏲10am-6pm or 7pm Apr-Oct, to 5pm Nov-Mar) – is the **Festung Ehrenbreitstein** (☎0261-6675 4000; www.diefestungehrenbreitstein.de; adult/child €6/3, incl cable car €11.80/5.60; ⏲10am-6pm Apr-Oct, to 5pm Nov-Mar), one of Europe's mightiest citadels. Views are great and there's a restaurant and a regional museum inside.

Moselle Valley

Like a vine right before harvest, the Moselle hangs heavy with visitor fruit. Castles and towns with half-timbered buildings are built along the sinuous river below steep, rocky cliffs planted with vineyards. It's one of Germany's most evocative regions, with stunning views revealed at every river bend. Unlike the Romantic Rhine, it's spanned by plenty of bridges. The most scenic section unravels between Bernkastel-Kues and Cochem, 50km apart and linked by the B421.

Cochem

Easily reached by train or boat from Koblenz, Cochem is one of the most popular destinations on the Moselle thanks to its fairy-tale-like **Reichsburg** (☎02671-255; www.burg-cochem.de; Schlossstrasse 36; tours adult/child €6/3; ⏲tours 9am-5pm mid-Mar–Oct, 10am-3pm Nov & Dec, 11am, noon & 1pm Wed, Sat & Sun Jan–mid-Mar). Like many others, the 11th-century original fell victim to frenzied Frenchmen in 1689, then stood ruined for centuries until a wealthy Berliner snapped it up for a pittance in 1868 and had it restored to its current – if not always architecturally faithful – glory. The 40-minute tours (in German but English leaflet available) take in decorative rooms reflecting 1000 years' worth of tastes and styles.

The **tourist office** (☎02671-600 40; www.cochem.de; Endertplatz 1; ⏲9am-5pm Mon-Sat, 10am-3pm Sun May-Oct, 9am-5pm Mon-Fri Apr, 9am-1pm & 2-5pm Mon-Fri Nov-Mar) has information about the entire region.

Cochem is 55km from Koblenz via the scenic B327 and B49. Regional trains shuttling between Trier (€15.90, 45 minutes) and Koblenz (€11.90, 50 minutes) stop here as well.

Beilstein

Picture-perfect Beilstein is little more than a cluster of higgledy-piggledy houses surrounded by steep vineyards. Its historic highlights include the **Marktplatz** and the ruined hilltop castle **Burg Metternich** (☎02673-936 39; admission €2.50; ⏲9am-6pm Apr-Nov) – oh the views! The **Zehnthauskeller** (☎02673-900 907; www.zehnthauskeller.de; Marktplatz; ⏲11am-10pm Tue-Sat, noon-10pm Sun) houses a romantically dark, vaulted wine tavern owned by the same family that also runs two local hotels. There is no tourist office nor an ATM.

Bus 716 goes from Cochem to Beilstein (€3.65, 20 minutes) almost hourly in season, although the approach by boat is more scenic (€12, one hour).

Bernkastel-Kues

This charming twin town straddles the Moselle about 50km downriver from Trier and is close to some of the river's most famous vineyards. The prettier of the two – Bernkastel on the right bank – is a symphony in half-timber, stone and slate and teems with wine taverns.

Get your heart pumping by hoofing it up to **Burg Landshut**, a ruined 13th-century castle on a bluff above town. Allow 30 minutes to be rewarded with glorious valley views and a cold drink at the beer garden. Alternatively, shuttle buses leave from the riverfront.

The **tourist office** (☎06531-500 190; www.bernkastel.de; Gestade 6; ⏰9am-5pm Mon-Fri, 10am-5pm Sat, 10am-1pm Sun May-Oct, 9.30am-4pm Mon-Fri Nov-Apr) is in Bernkastel.

Coming from Trier, drivers should follow the B53. Using public transport involves catching the regional train to Wittlich and switching to bus 300.

Trier

☎0651 / POP 106,544

A Unesco World Heritage site since 1986, Germany's oldest city is home to its finest ensemble of ancient Roman monuments, among them a mighty gate, amphitheater and thermal baths. Architectural treasures from later ages include Germany's oldest Gothic church and Karl Marx' birthplace.

Sights

★Porta Nigra GATE

(adult/child €4/3; ⏰9am-6pm Apr-Sep, to 5pm Mar & Oct, to 4pm Nov-Feb) This brooding 2nd-century Roman city gate – blackened by time (hence the name, Latin for 'black gate') – is a marvel of engineering since it's held together by nothing but gravity and iron clamps.

In the 11th century, the structure was turned into a church to honour Simeon, a Greek hermit who spent six years walled up in its east tower. After his death in 1134, he was buried inside the gate and later became a saint.

★Konstantin Basilika CHURCH

(☎0651-9949 1200; www.ekkt.ekir.de; Konstantinplatz 10; ⏰10am-6pm Mon-Sat, 1-6pm Sun Apr-Oct, 10am-noon & 2-4pm Mon-Sat, 1-4pm Sun Nov-Mar) Constructed around AD 310 as Constantine's throne room, the brick-built basilica is now an austere Protestant church. With built-to-impress dimensions (some 67m long, 27m wide and 33m high), it's the largest single-room Roman structure still in existence. A new organ, with 87 registers and 6500 pipes, generates a seven-fold echo.

★Amphitheatre ROMAN SITE

(Olewiger Strasse; adult/child €4/3; ⏰9am-6pm Apr-Sep, to 5pm Mar & Oct, to 4pm Nov-Feb) Trier's Roman amphitheatre could accommodate 20,000 spectators for gladiator tournaments and animal fights. Beneath the arena are dungeons where prisoners sentenced to death waited next to starving beasts for the final showdown.

★Kaiserthermen ROMAN SITE

(Imperial Baths; Weberbachstrasse 41; adult/child €4/3; ⏰9am-6pm Apr-Sep, to 5pm Mar & Oct, to 4pm Nov-Feb) Get a sense of the layout of this vast Roman thermal bathing complex with its striped brick-and-stone arches from the corner lookout tower, then descend into an underground labyrinth consisting of cavernous hot and cold water baths, boiler rooms and heating channels.

★Trierer Dom CATHEDRAL

(☎0651-979 0790; www.dominformation.de; Liebfrauenstrasse 12, cnr of Domfreihof; ⏰6.30am-6pm Apr-Oct, to 5.30pm Nov-Mar) FREE Looming above the Roman palace of Helena (Emperor Constantine's mother), this cathedral is Germany's oldest bishop's church and still retains Roman sections. Today's edifice is a study in nearly 1700 years of church architecture with Romanesque, Gothic and baroque elements. Intriguingly, its floor plan is of a 12-petalled flower, symbolising the Virgin Mary.

To see some dazzling ecclesiastical equipment and peer into early Christian history, head upstairs to the **Domschatz** (Cathedral Treasury; ☎0651-710 5378; adult/child €1.50/0.50; ⏰10am-5pm Mon-Sat, 12.30-5pm Sun Mar-Oct & Dec, 11am-4pm Tue-Sat, 12.30-4pm Sun & Mon Nov, Jan & Feb) or around the corner to the **Museum am Dom Trier** (☎0651-710 5255; www.bistum-trier.de/museum; Bischof-Stein-Platz 1; adult/child €3.50/2; ⏰9am-5pm Tue-Sat, 1-5pm Sun).

Sleeping

Evergreen Hostel HOSTEL €

(☎0651-6998 7026, outside office hours 0157 8856 9594; www.evergreen-hostel.de; Gartenfeldstrasse 7; dm from €17, s/d from €42/52, without bathroom from €38/50; ⏰reception 8-11am & 2-7pm May-Oct, 9-11am & 3-6pm Nov-Apr; @ 📶) This laid-back indie hostel has a piano in the common kitchen and 12 attractive, spacious rooms, most with private bathrooms. Breakfast costs €6. Outside office hours, call ahead to arrange your arrival.

WORTH A TRIP

BURG ELTZ

At the head of the beautiful Eltz Valley, **Burg Eltz** (☎02672-950 500; www.burg-eltz.de; Burg-Eltz-Strasse 1, Wierschem; tour adult/child €9/6.50; ⏰9.30am-5.30pm Apr-Oct) is one of Germany's most romantic medieval castles. Never destroyed, this vision of turrets, towers, oriels, gables and half-timber has squatted atop a rock framed by thick forest for nearly 900 years and is still owned by the original family. The decorations, furnishings, tapestries, fireplaces, paintings and armour you see during the 45-minute tour are also centuries old.

By car, you can reach Burg Eltz via Munstermaifeld. From the car park it's a shuttle bus ride (€2) or 1.3km walk to the castle. Alternatively, take a boat or train to Moselkern village and approach the castle via a lovely 5km walk (or €24 taxi ride).

Hotel Villa Hügel BOUTIQUE HOTEL €€
(☎0651-937 100; www.hotel-villa-huegel.de; Bernhardstrasse 14; s/d from €108/148; P@🛜≋) Begin the day with sparkling wine at a lavish breakfast buffet at this stylish hillside villa, and end it luxuriating in the 12m indoor pool and Finnish sauna. The 36 rooms are decorated with honey-toned woods.

Eating & Drinking

de Winkel PUB FOOD €
(☎0651-436 1878; www.de-winkel.de; Johannisstrasse 25; mains €6-9.50; ⏰6pm-1am Tue-Thu, to 2am Fri & Sat) Winny and Morris have presided over this locally adored watering hole for years. Join the locals for Pils and a bite, for instance the crispy chicken wings called 'Flieten' in Trier dialect.

★**Weinwirtschaft Friedrich-Wilhelm** GERMAN €€
(☎0651-9947 4800; www.weinwirtschaft-fw.de; Weberbach 75; mains €11-26; ⏰kitchen noon-2pm & 6-10pm Mon-Sat, wine shop 11.30am-3pm & 5.30-8pm Tue-Sat) A historic former wine warehouse with exposed brick and hoists now houses this superb restaurant. Creative dishes incorporate local wines, such as trout poached in sparkling white wine with mustard sauce and white asparagus; and local sausage with Riesling sauerkraut and fried potatoes. Vines trail over the trellis-covered garden; the attached wine shop is a great place to stock up.

Information

Tourist Office (☎0651-978 080; www.trier-info.de; An der Porta Nigra; ⏰9am-6pm Mon-Sat, 10am-5pm Sun May-Oct, shorter hours Nov-Apr)

Getting There & Away

Frequent direct train connections include Koblenz (€12 to €24, 1½ to two hours), Cologne (€19 to €45, three hours) and Luxembourg (€14 to €30, 50 minutes).

Cologne

☎0221 / POP 1 MILLION

Cologne (Köln) offers lots of attractions, led by its famous cathedral whose filigree twin spires dominate the skyline. The city's museum landscape is especially strong when it comes to art but also has something in store for fans of chocolate, sports and Roman history. Its people are well known for their joie de vivre and it's easy to have a good time right along with them year-round in the beer halls of the Altstadt.

Sights

★**Kölner Dom** CATHEDRAL
(Cologne Cathedral; ☎0221-9258 4720; www.koelner-dom.de; tower adult/concession €4/2; ⏰6am-9pm May-Oct, to 7.30pm Nov-Apr, tower 9am-6pm May-Sep, to 5pm Mar, Apr & Oct, to 4pm Nov-Feb) Cologne's geographical and spiritual heart – and its single-biggest tourist draw – is the magnificent Kölner Dom. With its soaring twin spires, this is the Mt Everest of cathedrals, jam-packed with art and treasures. For an exercise fix, climb the 533 steps up the Dom's south tower to the base of the steeple that dwarfed all buildings in Europe until Gustave Eiffel built a certain tower in Paris. The underground Domforum visitor centre is a good source of info and tickets.

The Dom is Germany's largest cathedral and must be circled to truly appreciate its dimensions. Note how its lacy spires and flying buttresses create a sensation of lightness and fragility despite its mass and height.

This sensation continues inside, where a phalanx of pillars and arches supports the lofty nave. Soft light filters through the medieval stained-glass windows, as well as a much-lauded recent window by contemporary artist Gerhard Richter in the transept. A kaleidoscope of 11,500 squares in 72 colours, Richter's abstract design has been called a 'symphony of light'. In the afternoon especially, when the sun hits it just so, it's easy to understand why.

The pièce de résistance among the cathedral's bevy of treasures is the **Shrine of the Three Kings** behind the main altar, a richly bejewelled and gilded sarcophagus said to hold the remains of the kings who followed the star to the stable in Bethlehem where Jesus was born. The bones were spirited out of Milan in 1164 as spoils of war by Emperor Barbarossa's chancellor and instantly turned Cologne into a major pilgrimage site.

Other highlights include the **Gero Crucifix** (970), notable for its monumental size and an emotional intensity rarely achieved in those early medieval days; the choir stalls from 1310, richly carved from oak; and the altar painting (c 1450) by Cologne artist Stephan Lochner.

During your climb up to the 95m-high viewing platform, take a breather and admire the 24-tonne **Peter Bell** (1923), the largest free-swinging working bell in the world.

★Römisch-Germanisches Museum MUSEUM

(Roman Germanic Museum; ☎0221-2212 4438; www.museenkoeln.de; Roncalliplatz 4; adult/concession €9/5; ⏰10am-5pm Tue-Sun) Sculptures and ruins displayed outside the entrance are merely the overture to a full symphony of Roman artefacts found along the Rhine. Highlights include the giant **Poblicius tomb** (AD 30–40), the magnificent 3rd-century **Dionysus mosaic**, and astonishingly well-preserved glass items. Insight into daily Roman life is gained from toys, tweezers, lamps and jewellery, the designs of which have changed surprisingly little since Roman times.

Museum Ludwig MUSEUM

(☎0221-2212 6165; www.museum-ludwig.de; Heinrich-Böll-Platz; adult/concession €11/7.50, more during special exhibits; ⏰10am-6pm Tue-Sun) A mecca of contemporary art, Museum Ludwig presents a tantalising mix of works from all major phases. Fans of German expressionism (Beckmann, Dix, Kirchner) will get their fill here as much as those with a penchant for Picasso, American pop art (Warhol, Lichtenstein) and Russian avant-garde painter Alexander Rodchenko. Rothko and Pollock are highlights of the abstract collection, while Gursky and Tillmanns are among the reasons the photography section is a must stop.

Wallraf-Richartz-Museum & Fondation Corboud MUSEUM

(☎0221-2212 1119; www.wallraf.museum; Obenmarspforten; adult/concession €12/8; ⏰10am-6pm Tue-Sun) A famous collection of European paintings from the 13th to the 19th centuries, the Wallraf-Richartz-Museum occupies a postmodern cube designed by the late OM Ungers. Works are presented chronologically, with the oldest on the 1st floor where standouts include brilliant examples from the Cologne School, known for its distinctive use of colour. The most famous painting is Stefan Lochner's *Madonna of the Rose Bower*.

Schokoladenmuseum MUSEUM

(Chocolate Museum; ☎0221-931 8880; www.schokoladenmuseum.de; Am Schokoladenmuseum 1a; adult/concession €9/6.50; ⏰10am-6pm Tue-Fri, 11am-7pm Sat & Sun, last entry 1hr before closing; 👪) At this high-tech temple to the art of chocolate-making, exhibits on the origin of the 'elixir of the gods', as the Aztecs called it, and the cocoa-growing process are followed by a live-production factory tour and a stop at a chocolate fountain for a sample.

COLOGNE CARNIVAL

Carnival in Cologne is one of the best parties in Europe and a thumb in the eye of the German work ethic. It all starts with *Weiberfastnacht*, the Thursday before Ash Wednesday, when women rule the day (and do things like chop off the ties of their male colleagues/bosses). The party continues through the weekend, with more than 50 parades of ingenious floats and wildly dressed lunatics dancing in the streets. By the time it all comes to a head with the big parade on *Rosenmontag* (Rose Monday), the entire city has come unglued. Those still capable of swaying and singing will live it up one last time on Shrove Tuesday before the curtain comes down on Ash Wednesday.

Cologne

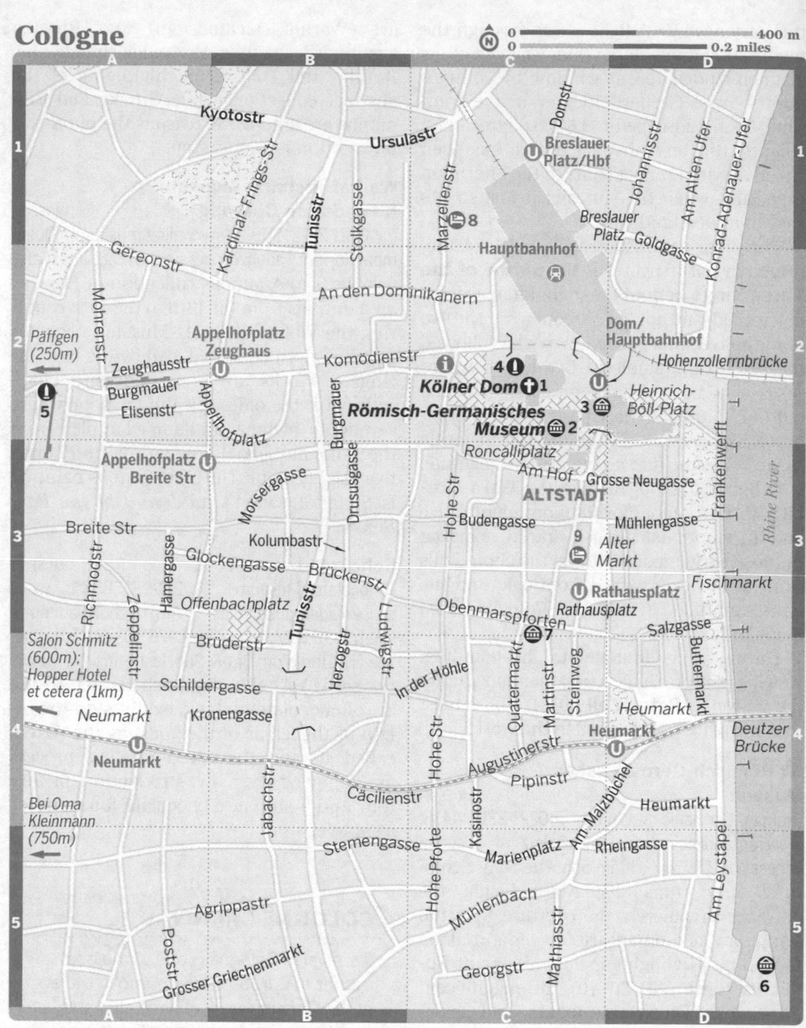

Sleeping

Station Hostel for Backpackers HOSTEL €
(☎0221-912 5301; www.hostel-cologne.de; Marzellenstrasse 44-56; dm €17-24, s/d from €32/48; @) Near the Hauptbahnhof, this is a hostel as hostels should be: central, convivial and economical. A lounge gives way to clean, colourful rooms sleeping one to six people. There's lots of free stuff, including linen, internet access, lockers, city maps and guest kitchen. Some private rooms have their own bathrooms.

★**Hopper Hotel et cetera** HOTEL €€
(☎0221-924 400; www.hopper.de; Brüsseler Strasse 26; s/d from €75/110; P @) A waxen monk welcomes you to this former monastery whose 49 rooms sport eucalyptus floors, cherry furniture and marble baths along with lots of useful features like fridges. The sauna and bar, both in the vaulted cellars, are great places for reliving the day's exploits. The cheapest singles are dubbed 'monastic cells'.

Cologne

Top Sights

1 Kölner Dom C2
2 Römisch Germanisches Museum C2

Sights

3 Museum Ludwig C2
4 Roman Arch C2
5 Römerturm A2
6 Schokoladenmuseum D5
7 Wallraf-Richartz-Museum & Fondation Corboud C3

Sleeping

8 Station Hostel for Backpackers C1
9 Stern am Rathaus C3

Stern am Rathaus HOTEL €€

(☎0221-2225 1750; www.stern-am-rathaus.de; Bürgerstrasse 6; s/d from €75/105; ❄📶) This small, contemporary hotel has eight nicely spruced-up, luxuriously panelled rooms spread over three floors. It's in a quiet side street smack dab in the Altstadt yet close to sights and plenty of restaurants. Kudos for the extra-comfortable beds, the personalised service and the high-quality breakfast buffet.

Eating & Drinking

There are plenty of beer halls and restaurants in the tourist-adored Altstadt, but for a more local vibe head to student-flavoured Zülpicher Viertel or the Belgisches Viertel, both in the city centre. Local breweries turn out a variety called *Kölsch*, which is relatively light and served in skinny 200mL glasses.

★ **Salon Schmitz** MODERN EUROPEAN €€

(☎0221-9229 9594; www.salonschmitz.com; Aachener Strasse 28; mains from €10; ⏲9am-late, hours vary by venue) Spread over three historic row houses, the Schmitz empire is your one-stop for excellent food and drink. From the casual bistro to excellent seasonal meals in the restaurant to the takeaway deli, you'll find something you like at Schmitz almost any time of day. Wash it all down with the house-brand *Kölsch*.

★ **Bei Oma Kleinmann** GERMAN €€

(☎0221-232 346; www.beiomakleinmann.de; Zülpicher Strasse 9; mains €13-22; ⏲5pm-midnight Tue-Thu & Sun, to 1am Fri & Sat) Named for its long-time owner, who was still cooking almost to her last day at age 95 in 2009, this perennially booked, graffiti-covered restaurant serves oodles of schnitzel, made either with pork or veal and paired with homemade sauces and sides. Pull up a seat at the small wooden tables for a classic Cologne night out.

★ **Päffgen** BEER HALL

(☎0221-135 461; www.paeffgen-koelsch.de; Friesenstrasse 64-66; mains €6-20; ⏲10am-midnight Sun-Thu, to 12.30am Fri & Sat) Busy, loud and boisterous, Päffgen has been pouring *Kölsch* since 1883 and hasn't lost a step since. In summer you can enjoy the refreshing brew and local specialities (€1.10 to €10.70) beneath starry skies in the beer garden.

Information

Tourist Office (☎0221-346 430; www.cologne-tourism.com; Kardinal-Höffner-Platz 1; ⏲9am-8pm Mon-Sat, 10am-5pm Sun) Excellent; near the cathedral. The app is well done.

Getting There & Away

AIR

Köln Bonn Airport (CGN; Cologne-Bonn Airport; ☎02203-404 001; www.koeln-bonn-airport.de; Kennedystrasse) is about 18km southeast of the city centre and connected to the Hauptbahnhof by the S-Bahn S13 train every 20 minutes (€2.80, 15 minutes).

TRAIN

Services to and from Cologne are fast and frequent in all directions. A sampling: Berlin (€117, 4¼ hours), Frankfurt (€71, 1¼ hours) and Munich (€142, 4½ hours). In addition there are fast Thalys and ICE trains to Brussels (where you can connect to the Eurostar for London) and Paris.

Düsseldorf

☎0211 / POP 594,000

Düsseldorf dazzles with boundary-pushing architecture, zinging nightlife and an art scene to rival many a metropolis. It's a posh and modern city whose economy is dominated by banking, advertising, fashion and telecommunications. However, a couple of hours of partying in the boisterous pubs of the Altstadt, the historical quarter along the Rhine, is all you need to realise that locals have no problem letting their hair down once they slip out of those Boss jackets.

WORTH A TRIP

BONN

South of Cologne on the Rhine River, Bonn served as West Germany's capital from 1949 until 1990. For visitors, the birthplace of Ludwig van Beethoven has plenty in store, not least the great composer's birth house, a string of top-rated museums and the lovely riverside setting.

The **Beethoven-Haus** (☎0228-981 7525; www.beethoven-haus-bonn.de; Bonngasse 24-26; adult/concession €6/4.50; ⏰10am-6pm Apr-Oct, 10am-5pm Mon-Sat, 11am-5pm Sun Nov-Mar), where the composer was born in 1770, is big on memorabilia concerning his life and music. A highlight is his last piano, which was outfitted with an amplified sounding board to accommodate his deafness. Tickets are also good for an adjacent interactive Beethoven-themed 3D multimedia show.

Bonn's most stellar museums line up neatly on Museumsmeile (Museum Mile) in the heart of the former government quarter along Willy-Brandt-Allee just south of the city centre (take U-Bahn lines 16, 63 and 66). A top contender is the **Kunstmuseum Bonn** (Bonn Art Museum; ☎0228-776 260; www.kunstmuseum-bonn.de; Friedrich-Ebert-Allee 2; adult/concession €7/3.50; ⏰11am-6pm Tue & Thu-Sun, to 9pm Wed), which presents 20th-century art, including a standout collection of works by August Macke and other Rhenish expressionists. History buffs gravitate to the **Haus der Geschichte** (Museum of History; ☎0228-916 50; www.hdg.de; Willy-Brandt-Allee 14; ⏰9am-7pm Tue-Fri, 10am-6pm Sat & Sun) FREE for an engaging romp through Germany's post-WWII history.

The **tourist office** (☎0228-775 000; www.bonn-region.de; Windeckstrasse 1; ⏰10am-6pm Mon-Fri, to 4pm Sat, to 2pm Sun) is just off Münsterplatz and a three-minute walk, along Poststrasse, from the Hauptbahnhof.

The U-Bahn lines 16 and 18 (€7.70, one hour) and regional trains (€7.70, 30 minutes) link Cologne and Bonn several times hourly.

Sights

K20 Grabbeplatz MUSEUM

(☎0211-838 1204; Grabbeplatz 5; adult/child €12/2.50; ⏰10am-6pm Tue-Fri, 11am-6pm Sat & Sun) A collection that spans the arc of 20th-century artistic vision gives the K20 an enviable edge in the art world. It encompasses major works by Picasso, Matisse and Mondrian and more than 100 paintings and drawings by Paul Klee. Americans represented include Jackson Pollock, Andy Warhol and Jasper John. Düsseldorf's own Joseph Beuys has a major presence as well.

K21 Ständehaus MUSEUM

(☎0211-838 1204; Ständehausstrasse 1; adult/child €12/2.50; ⏰10am-6pm Tue-Fri, 11am-6pm Sat & Sun) A stately 19th-century parliament building forms a fabulous dichotomy to the cutting-edge art of the K21 – a collection showcasing only works created after the 1980s. Large-scale film and video installations and groups of works share space with site-specific rooms by an international cast of artists including Andreas Gursky, Candida Höfer, Bill Viola and Nam June Paik.

Medienhafen ARCHITECTURE

(Am Handelshafen) This once-dead old harbour area has been reborn as the Medienhafen, an increasingly hip quarter filled with architecture, restaurants, bars, hotels and clubs. Once-crumbling warehouses have turned into high-tech office buildings and now rub shoulders with bold new structures designed by celebrated international architects, including Frank Gehry.

Sleeping

Max Hotel Garni PENSION €€

(☎0211-386 800; www.max-hotelgarni.de; Adersstrasse 65; s/d €75/90; @☜) Upbeat, contemporary and run with personal flair, this charmer is a favourite Düsseldorf bargain. The 11 rooms are good-sized and decked out in bright hues and warm woods. Rates include coffee, tea, soft drinks and a regional public transport pass; breakfast costs €7.50. The reception isn't always staffed, so call ahead to arrange an arrival time.

★Hotel Windsor HOTEL €€

(☎0211-914 680; www.sir-astor.de; Grafenberger Allee 36; s/d from €89/94; P⊖@☜) With the same owner as the Sir & Lady Astor, the

Windsor commits itself to the British country tradition. Behind the sandstone facade of this 100-year-old mansion await 18 rooms where you can unwind beneath stucco-ornamented ceilings surrounded by antiques and sedate prints.

Eating & Drinking

The local beverage of choice is *Altbier*, a dark and semisweet beer typical of Düsseldorf.

★Brauerei im Füchschen GERMAN €€
(☎0211-137 4716; www.fuechschen.de; Ratinger Strasse 28; mains €6-16; ⏲9am-1am Mon-Thu, to 2am Fri & Sat, to midnight Sun) Boisterous, packed and drenched with local colour, the 'Little Fox' in the Altstadt is all you expect a Rhenish beer hall to be. The kitchen makes a mean *Schweinshaxe* (roast pork leg). The high-ceilinged interior echoes with the mirthful roar of people enjoying their meals. This is one of the best *Altbier* breweries in town.

★Zum Uerige BEER HALL
(☎0211-866 990; www.uerige.de; Berger Strasse 1; ⏲10am-midnight) This cavernous brewpub is the quintessential Düsseldorf haunt to try the city's typical *Altbier*. The suds flow so quickly from giant copper vats that the waiters – called *Köbes* – simply carry huge trays of brew and plonk down a glass whenever they spy an empty. Even on a cold day, the outside tables are alive with merriment.

Information

Tourist Office – Altstadt (☎0211-1720 2840; www.duesseldorf-tourismus.de; cnr Marktstrasse & Rheinstrasse; ⏲10am-6pm) Right in the heart of the old centre.
Tourist Office – Hauptbahnhof (☎0211-1720 2844; www.duesseldorf-tourismus.de; Immermannstrasse 65b; ⏲9.30am-7pm Mon-Fri, to 5pm Sat) The main tourist office, across from the train station; has an exchange window.

Getting There & Away

Düsseldorf International Airport (DUS; ☎0211-4210; www.dus.com) is linked to the city centre by the S-Bahn line 1 (€2.60, 10 minutes).

Regional trains travel to Cologne (€12, 30 minutes), Bonn (€19, one hour) and Aachen (€23, 1½ hours). Fast ICE train links include Berlin (€111, 4¼ hours), Hamburg (€82, 3½ hours) and Frankfurt (€82, 1½ hours).

LOCAL KNOWLEDGE

FLINGERN FLING

Once all working-class, Flingern, a neighbourhood east of the Hauptbahnhof, is now the centre of Düsseldorf's stylish hipness. The main strip is a 1km-stretch of leafy Ackerstrasse, where retail therapy gets a unique twist in indie boutiques stocked with vintage frocks, edgy jewellery, whimsical tees, handmade accessories and gourmet foods.

There are cafes by the dozen; try arty, punky **Café Hüftgold** (www.cafehueftgold.de; Ackerstrasse 113; snacks from €3; ⏲8am-7pm Mon-Wed, to 10pm Thu & Fri, 9am-10pm Sat, 10am-10pm Sun) or join the mixed and merry mobs on the terrace at **Beethoven** (☎0211-2339 8687; Ackerstrasse 106; ⏲10am-midnight).

Aachen

☎0241 / POP 240,100

Aachen makes for an excellent day trip from Cologne or Düsseldorf as well as a worthy overnight stop. The Romans nursed their war wounds and stiff joints in the steaming waters of Aachen's mineral springs, but it was Charlemagne who put the city firmly on the European map. His legacy lives on in the stunning Dom, which in 1978 became Germany's first Unesco World Heritage site, as well as the new Centre Charlemagne.

Sights

★Aachener Dom CATHEDRAL
(☎0241-447 090; www.aachendom.de; Münsterplatz; ⏲7am-7pm Apr-Dec, to 6pm Jan-Mar) It's impossible to overestimate the significance of Aachen's magnificent cathedral. The burial place of Charlemagne, it's where more than 30 German kings were crowned and where pilgrims have flocked since the 12th century. Before entering the church, stop by **Dom Information** (☎0241-4770 9145; www.aachendom.de; Johannes-Paul-II-Strasse; ⏲10am-5pm Jan-Mar, to 6pm Apr-Dec) for info and tickets for tours and the cathedral treasury.

The oldest and most impressive section is Charlemagne's palace chapel, the **Pfalzkapelle**, an outstanding example of Carolingian architecture. Completed in 800, the year of the emperor's coronation, it's an octagonal dome encircled by a 16-sided ambulatory supported by antique Italian pillars. The colossal brass chandelier was a gift from Emperor Friedrich Barbarossa, during whose reign Charlemagne was canonised in 1165.

Pilgrims have poured into town ever since that time, drawn as much by the cult surrounding Charlemagne as by his prized relics: Christ's loincloth from when he was crucified, Mary's cloak, the clothes used for John the Baptist when he was beheaded and swaddling clothes from when Jesus was an infant. These are displayed once every seven years (next in 2021) and draw 100,000 or more of the faithful.

To accommodate these regular floods of visitors, a Gothic choir was docked to the chapel in 1414 and filled with such priceless treasures as the **pala d'oro**, a gold-plated altar-front depicting Christ's Passion, and the jewel-encrusted gilded copper pulpit, both fashioned in the 11th century. At the far end is the gilded **shrine of Charlemagne** that has held the emperor's remains since 1215. In front, the equally fanciful **shrine of St Mary** shelters the cathedral's four prized relics.

Unless you join a **guided tour** (adult/concession €4/3; ⌚tours 11am-5.30pm Mon-Fri, 1-5pm Sat & Sun, 2pm tour in English daily), you'll barely get a glimpse of the white marble of Charlemagne's **imperial throne** in the upstairs gallery. Reached via six steps – just like King Solomon's throne – it served as the coronation throne of those 30 German kings between 936 and 1531.

Rathaus HISTORIC BUILDING

(Town Hall; ☎0241-432 7310; Markt; adult/concession incl audioguide €5/3; ⌚10am-6pm) Fifty life-size statues of German rulers, including 30 kings crowned in town between 936 and 1531 AD, adorn the facade of Aachen's splendid Gothic town hall. It was built in the 14th century atop the foundations of Charlemagne's palace, of which only the eastern tower, the **Granusturm**, survives. Inside, the undisputed highlight is the **Krönungssaal** (Coronation Hall) with its epic 19th-century frescos and replicas of the imperial insignia: a crown, orb and sword (the originals are in Vienna). The Rathaus faces the Markt.

Centre Charlemagne MUSEUM

(☎0241-432 4994; www.route-charlemagne.eu; Katschhof 1; adult/concession €6/3; ⌚10am-5pm Tue-Sat) Overlooking the Katschhof square and right in the midst of where the great man walked, this museum looks at not only the life and times of Charlemagne but also Aachen's dramatic history. Multimedia exhibits bring the Roman era to life, and significant moments ever since. Begin your Route Charlemagne walk here; there is a huge amount of info in English.

Sleeping & Eating

Aachen's students have their own 'Latin Quarter' along Pontstrasse northeast of the Markt.

A&O Aachen HOSTEL, HOTEL €

(☎0241-463 073 300; www.aohostels.com; Hackländerstrasse 5; dm/s/d from €24/60/70; 📶) Vast and utilitarian, you can't beat this flashpacker haven's location next to the train station and close to the centre. All rooms have private bathrooms and there is a lift. At busy times rates can soar past those of plusher digs in town.

★**Hotel Drei Könige** HOTEL €€

(☎0241-483 93; www.h3k-aachen.de; Büchel 5; s €109-139, d €139-169; 📶) The radiant Mediterranean decor is an instant mood-warmer at this family-run favourite with its doesn't-get-more-central location. Some of the nine rooms are a tad twee; the four two-room apartments sleep up to four. Breakfast, on the 4th floor, comes with dreamy views over the rooftops and the cathedral.

Alt-Aachener Café-Stuben CAFE €

(Van den Daele; ☎0241-357 24; Büchel 18; treats from €3; ⌚9am-6.30pm Mon-Fri, 10am-6pm Sat & Sun) Leather-covered walls, tiled stoves and antiques forge the yesteryear flair of this rambling cafe institution that dates from 1890 (the building goes back to 1655). Come for all-day breakfast, a light lunch, divine cakes or just to pick up the house-made *Printen*, Aachen's riff on traditional *Lebkuchen*.

★**Am Knipp** GERMAN €€

(☎0241-331 68; www.amknipp.de; Bergdriesch 3; mains €9-23; ⌚5-11pm Mon & Wed-Fri, from 6pm Sat & Sun) Hungry grazers have stopped by this traditional inn since 1698, and you too will have a fine time enjoying hearty German cuisine served amid a flea market's worth of knick-knacks or, if weather permits, in the big beer garden.

Information

Tourist Office (☎0241-180 2950; www.aachen-tourist.de; Friedrich-Wilhelm-Platz; ⊙9am-6pm Mon-Fri, to 3pm Sat & Sun Apr-Dec, shorter hours Jan-Mar) Local tourist information.

Getting There & Away

Regional trains to Cologne (€17, one hour) run twice hourly, with some proceeding beyond. Aachen is a stop for high-speed trains to/from Brussels and Paris.

HAMBURG & THE NORTH

Germany's windswept and maritime-flavoured north is dominated by Hamburg, a metropolis shaped by water and commerce since the Middle Ages. Bremen is a fabulous stop with fairy-tale character, and not only because of the famous Brothers' Grimm fairy tale starring a certain donkey, dog, cat and rooster. Those with a sweet tooth should not miss a side trip to Lübeck, renowned for its superb marzipan.

Hamburg

☎040 / POP 1.8 MILLION

Hamburg's historic label, 'The gateway to the world', might be a bold claim, but Germany's second-largest city and biggest port has never been shy. Hamburg has engaged in business with the world ever since it joined the Hanseatic League back in the Middle Ages. Its maritime spirit infuses the entire city; from architecture to menus to the cry of gulls, you always know you're near the water. The city has given rise to vibrant neighbourhoods awash with multicultural eateries, as well as the gloriously seedy Reeperbahn red-light district. Hamburg nurtured the early promise of the Beatles, and today its distinctive live- and electronic-music scene thrives in unique harbourside venues.

Sights

★Speicherstadt AREA

(Am Sandtorkai; ⊙24hr; SRödingsmarkt, Messberg) The seven-storey red-brick warehouses lining the Speicherstadt archipelago are a famous Hamburg symbol and the largest continuous warehouse complex in the world, recognised by Unesco as a World Heritage Site. Its distinctive architecture is best appreciated on a leisurely wander or a ride on a flat tour boat (called *Barkasse*). Many buildings contain shops, cafes and small museums.

★Fischmarkt MARKET

(Grosse Elbstrasse 9; ⊙5-9.30am Sun Apr-Oct, 7-9.30am Sun Nov-Mar; 112 to Fischmarkt, Reeperbahn) Here's the perfect excuse to stay up all Saturday night. Every Sunday in the wee hours, some 70,000 locals and visitors descend upon the famous Fischmarkt in St Pauli. The market has been running since 1703, and its undisputed stars are the boisterous *Marktschreier* (market criers) who hawk their wares at full volume. Live bands also entertainingly crank out cover versions of ancient German pop songs in the adjoining **Fischauktionshalle** (Fish Auction Hall).

★Miniatur Wunderland MUSEUM

(☎040-300 6800; www.miniatur-wunderland.de; Kehrwieder 2; adult/child €13/6.50; ⊙9.30am-6pm Mon, Wed & Thu, to 9pm Tue, to 7pm Fri, 8am-9pm Sat, 8.30am-8pm Sun; SMessberg) Even the worst cynics are quickly transformed into fans of this vast miniature world that goes on and on. The model trains wending their way through the Alps are impressive – but slightly predictable. But when you see a model A380 swoop out of the sky and land at the fully functional model of Hamburg's airport, you can't help but gasp and say OMG! On weekends and in summer holidays, prepurchase your ticket online to skip the queues.

★Hamburger Kunsthalle MUSEUM

(☎040-428 131 257; www.hamburger-kunsthalle.de; Glockengiesserwall; adult/child weekdays €12/free, weekends €14/free, Thu 6-9pm €8/free; ⊙10am-6pm Tue, Wed & Fri-Sun, to 9pm Thu; SHauptbahnhof) A treasure trove of art from the Renaissance to the present day, the Kunsthalle spans two buildings linked by an underground passage. The main building houses works ranging from medieval portraiture to 20th-century classics, such as Klee and Kokoschka. There's also a memorable room of 19th-century landscapes by Caspar David Friedrich. Its stark white modern cube, the **Galerie der Gegenwart**, showcases contemporary German artists.

St Michaelis Kirche CHURCH

(Church of St Michael; ☎040-376 780; www.st-michaelis.de; Englische Planke 1; tower adult/child €5/3.50, crypt €4/2.50, combo ticket

Hamburg

A B C D
1
Sternschanzenpark
Schröderstiftstr
Bundesstr
Altonaer Str
12
Sternschanze
Sternschanze
Sternschanze
Max-Brauer-Allee
Bartelsstr
22
16
Lagerstr
Rentzelstr
Planten un Blomen
SCHANZENVIERTEL
Susannenstr
Schulterblatt
Schanzenstr
17
Kampstr
St Petersburger Str
Karolinenstr
Lippmannstr
15
Stresemannstr
Grabenstr
2
Neuer Pferdemarkt
Sternstr
SCHANZENVIERTEL
Holstenglacis
Wohlers Allee
Bernstorffstr
Marktstr
Messehallen
Kleine Wallanlagen
Neuer Kamp
Feldstrasse
23
Feldstr
Thadenstr
Johannes Brahms Platz
3
Otzenstr
HEILIGENGEISTFELD
Kaiser-Wilhelm-Str
Pilatuspool
Gilbertstr
Annenstr
Budapester Str
Paul-Roosen-Str
Holstenwall
Clemens-Schultz-Str
Glacischaussee
Grosse Wallanlagen
Holstenstr
Grosse Freiheit
21
Simon-von-Utrecht-Str
Peterstr
ST PAULI
4
Hein-Hoyer-Str
Talstr
St Pauli
Hütten
Grossneumarkt
Seilerstr
Reeperbahn
Millerntorplatz
Reeperbahn
Hans-Albers-Platz
Reeperbahn
Ludwig-Erhard-Str
Zirkusweg
Kastanienallee
9
Balduinstr
Herbertstr
Davidstr
Hopfenstr
Elbpark
Friedrichstr
Seewartenstr
Böhmkenstr
Venusberg
5
Bernhard-Nocht-Str
Tourist Information am Hafen
Landungsbrücken
Stubbenhuk
Herrengraben
Hafenklang (200m)
St-Pauli-Hafenstr
Ditmar-Koel-Str
St-Pauli-Fischmarkt
18
Fischmarkt
2
Johannisbollwerk
Wolfgangsweg
Baumwall
Vorsetzen
St Pauli Elbtunnel
Elbe River
St Pauli Harbour
6
A B C D

€7/4; ⏲9am-7.30pm May-Oct, 10am-5.30pm Nov-Apr, last admission 30min before closing; 🚌Stadthausbrücke) 'Der Michel', as it is affectionately called, is one of Hamburg's most recognisable landmarks and northern Germany's largest Protestant baroque church. Ascending the tower (by steps or lift) rewards visitors with great panoramas across the city and canals. The crypt has an engaging multimedia exhibit on the city's history.

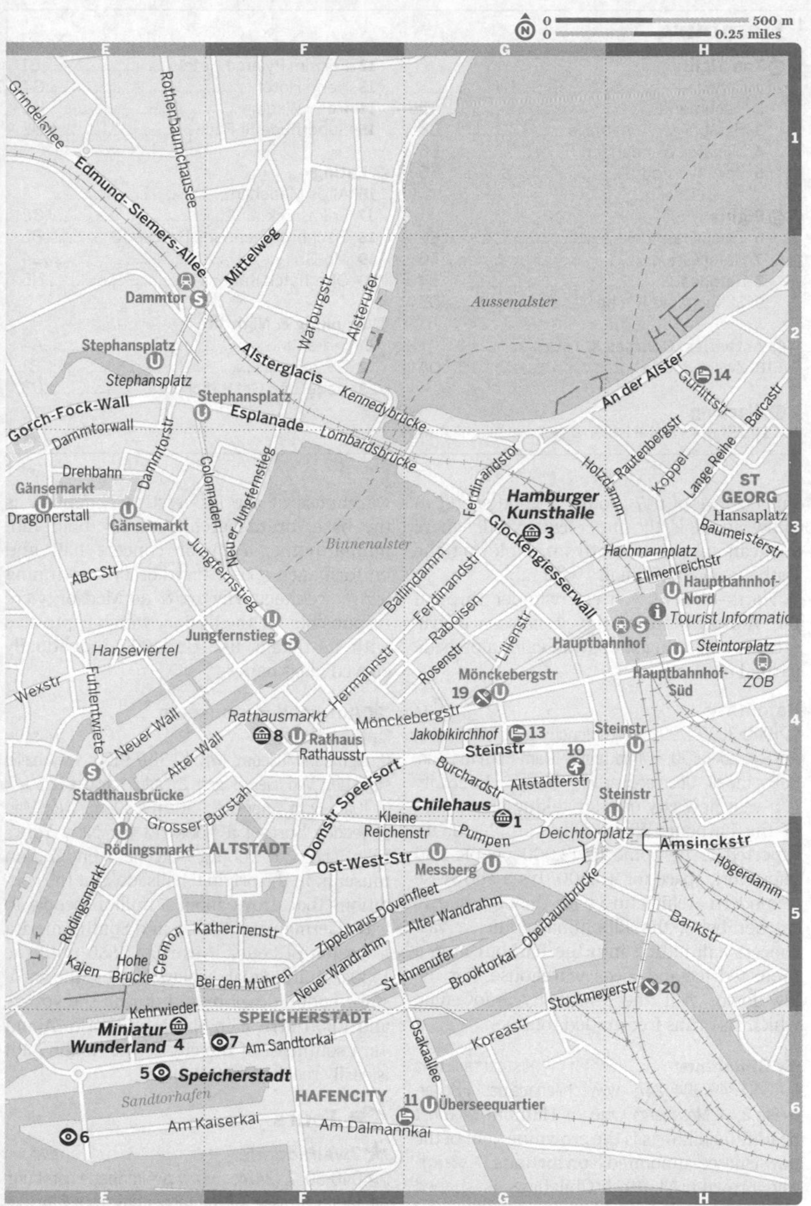

Rathaus HISTORIC BUILDING

(☎040-428 312 064; Rathausmarkt 1; tours adult/under 14yr €4/free; ⏱tours half-hourly 11am-4pm Mon-Fri, 10am-5pm Sat, to 4pm Sun, English tours depend on demand; Ⓢ Rathausmarkt, Jungfernstieg) With its spectacular coffered ceiling, Hamburg's baroque Rathaus is one of Europe's most opulent, and is renowned for its **Emperor's Hall** and **Great Hall**. The 40-minute tours take in only a fraction of

Hamburg

Top Sights
1 Chilehaus ... G5
2 Fischmarkt ... A5
3 Hamburger Kunsthalle ... G3
4 Miniatur Wunderland ... E6
5 Speicherstadt ... E6

Sights
6 Elbphilharmonie ... E6
7 HafenCity ... F6
8 Rathaus ... F4
9 St Michaelis Kirche ... D5

Activities, Courses & Tours
10 Zweiradperle ... G4

Sleeping
11 25hours Hotel HafenCity ... G6
12 Fritz im Pyjama Hotel ... B1
13 Henri Hotel ... G4
14 Hotel Wedina ... H2
15 Superbude St Pauli ... B2

Eating
16 Altes Mädchen ... C1
17 Erikas Eck ... C2
18 Fischbrötchenbude Brücke 10 ... B5
19 Mö-Grill ... G4
20 Oberhafen Kantine ... H5

Drinking & Nightlife
21 Indra Club ... A4
22 Katze ... B1
23 Uebel und Gefährlich ... C3

this beehive of 647 rooms. A good secret to know about is the inner courtyard, where you can take a break from exploring the Rathaus on comfy chairs with tables.

North of here, you can wander through the **Alsterarkaden**, the Renaissance-style arcades sheltering shops and cafes alongside a canal or 'fleet'.

HafenCity AREA

(☎040-3690 1799; www.hafencity.com; InfoCenter, Am Sandtorkai 30; ⊙InfoCenter 10am-6pm Tue-Sun; S Baumwall, Überseequartier) FREE HafenCity is a vast new city quarter taking shape east of the harbour. When fully completed, it's expected to be home to 12,000 people and offer work space for 40,000. It's a showcase of modern architecture with the biggest eye-catcher being the Elbphilharmonie, a vast concert hall jutting into the harbour atop a protected tea-and-cocoa warehouse. For the low-down, visit the HafenCity InfoCenter, which also runs free guided tours.

★**Chilehaus** HISTORIC BUILDING

(☎040-349 194 247; www.chilehaus.de; Fischertwiete 2; S Messberg) One of Hamburg's most beautiful buildings is the crowning gem of the new Unesco-annointed **Kontorhaus District**. The brown-brick 1924 Chilehaus is shaped like an ocean liner, with remarkable curved walls meeting in the shape of a ship's bow and staggered balconies that look like decks.

Elbphilharmonie ARTS CENTRE

(Elbe Philharmonic Hall; ☎040-3576 6666; www.elbphilharmonie.de; Platz der Deutschen Einheit 4; S Baumwall) A squat brown-brick former warehouse at the far west of HafenCity is the base for the architecturally bold Elbphilharmonie, a major concert hall and performance space. Pritzker Prize-winning Swiss architects Herzog & de Meuron were responsible for the design, which captivates with its details like the 1096 individually curved glass panes.

★**Auswanderermuseum BallinStadt** MUSEUM

(Emigration Museum; ☎040-3197 9160; www.ballinstadt.de; Veddeler Bogen 2; adult/child €12.50/7; ⊙10am-6pm Apr-Oct, 10am-4.30pm Nov-Mar; R Veddel) Sort of a bookend for New York's Ellis Island, Hamburg's excellent emigration museum in the original halls looks at the conditions that drove about 5 million people to leave Germany for the US and South America in search of better lives from 1850 until the 1930s. Multilingual displays address the hardships endured before and during the voyage and upon arrival in the New World. About 4km southeast of the city centre, BallinStadt is easily reached by S-Bahn.

Tours

★**Zweiradperle** CYCLING

(☎040-3037 3474; www.zweiradperle.hamburg; Altstädter Strasse 3-7; rental per day from €14, tour incl rental from €25; ⊙10am-6pm daily Apr–mid-Oct, from 11am Tue-Fri, to 3pm Sat mid-Oct–Mar, tour 10.30am daily; U Steinstrasse) Offers a range of rental bikes (including helmets and locks), as well as tours. The three-hour tour is a great introduction to the city. Has a cool cafe and plenty of cycling info.

Sleeping

★Superbude St Pauli HOTEL, HOSTEL €
(☎040-807 915 820; www.superbude.de; Juliusstrasse 1-7; dm/r from €16/60; @ 📶; S Sternschanze, 🚇 Sternschanze, Holstenstrasse) The young and forever-young mix and mingle without a shred of prejudice at this rocking design hotel-hostel combo that's all about living, laughing, partying and, yes, even sleeping well. All rooms have comfy beds and sleek private baths, breakfast is served until noon and there's even a 'rock star suite' with an Astra beer as a pillow treat.

★Henri Hotel HOTEL €€
(☎040-554 357 557; www.henri-hotel.com; Bugenhagenstrasse 21; r €110-180; 📶; S Mönckebergstrasse) Kidney-shaped tables, plush armchairs, vintage typewriters – the Henri channels the 1950s so successfully that you half expect to run into Don Draper. Its 65 rooms and studios are a good fit for urban lifestyle junkies who like the alchemy of modern comforts and retro design. For more elbow room get an L-sized room with a king-size bed.

★Fritz im Pyjama Hotel BOUTIQUE HOTEL €€
(☎040-314 838; www.fritz-im-pyjama.de; Schanzenstrasse 101-103; s/d from €77/120; 📶; S Sternschanze) This stylish townhouse hotel sits smack dab in the heart of the Schanzenviertel party zone. Rooms are smallish, with wooden floors, angular furniture and large windows; seven of the 17 have a balcony. Those without are quieter as they face the courtyard.

25hours Hotel HafenCity HOTEL €€
(☎040-257 7770; www.25hours-hotel.de; Überseeallee 5; r €100-200; P ⊖ 📶; S Überseequartier) Offbeat decor, an infectious irreverence and postmodern vintage flair make this pad a top choice among global nomads. Sporting maritime flourishes, the decor channels an old-timey seaman's club in the lobby. There's an excellent restaurant and 170 cabin-style rooms. Enjoy views of the emerging HafenCity neighbourhood from the rooftop sauna.

★Hotel Wedina HOTEL €€€
(☎040-280 8900; www.hotelwedina.de; Gurlittstrasse 23; r €125-245; P @ 📶; S Hauptbahnhof) Margaret Atwood, Jonathan Franzen and Martin Walser are among the literary greats who've stayed at this lovable lair. Rooms are spread over five brightly pigmented buildings that in different ways express the owners' love for literature, architecture and art. It's close to the train station and the Alster lakes. The breakfasts are especially good.

LOCAL KNOWLEDGE

SIGHTSEEING LIKE A REAL HAMBURGER

This maritime city offers a bewildering array of boat trips, but locals will tell you that you don't have to book a cruise to see the port – the city's **harbour ferries** will take you up the river on a regular public transport ticket, and you can avoid hokey narration!

One oft-recommended route is to catch **ferry 62** from Landungsbrücken to Finkenwerder, then change for the 64 to Teufelsbrücke. From Teufelsbrücke, you can wander along the Elbe eastwards to Neumühlen, from where you can catch bus 112 back to the Altona S-Bahn station or ferry 62 back to Landungsbrücken.

On land, the **U3 U-Bahn line** is particularly scenic, especially the elevated track between the St Pauli and Rathaus U-Bahn stations.

Eating

The **Schanzenviertel** (U-Bahn to Feldstrasse or Schanzenstern) swarms with cheap eateries; try Schulterblatt for Portuguese outlets or Susannenstrasse for Asian and Turkish. St Georg's **Lange Reihe** (U-Bahn to Hauptbahnhof) offers many characterful eating spots to suit every budget. Fish restaurants around the Landungsbrücken tend to be overrated and touristy.

★Fischbrötchenbude Brücke 10 SEAFOOD €
(☎040-3339 9339; www.bruecke-10.de; Landungsbrücken, Pier 10; sandwiches €3-9.50; ⏰10am-10pm Apr-Oct, to 8pm Nov-Mar; S Landungsbrücken, 🚇 Landungsbrücken) There are a gazillion fish sandwich vendors in Hamburg, but we're going to stick our neck out and say that this vibrant, clean and contemporary outpost makes the best. Try a classic *Bismarck* (pickled herring) or *Matjes* (brined), or treat yourself to a bulging shrimp sandwich. Lovely tables outside.

LOCAL KNOWLEDGE

ST PAULI & THE REEPERBAHN

No discussion of Hamburg is complete without mentioning St Pauli, home to one of Europe's most (in)famous red-light districts. Sex shops, table-dance bars and strip clubs still line its main drag, the Reeperbahn, and side streets, but the popularity of prostitution has declined dramatically in the internet age. Today St Pauli is Hamburg's main nightlife district, drawing people of all ages and walks of life to live music and dance clubs, chic bars and theatres.

In fact, street walkers are not even allowed to hit the pavement before 8pm and then are confined to certain areas, the most notorious being the gated Herbertstrasse (no women and men under 18 years allowed). Nearby, the cops of the Davidwache police station keep an eye on the lurid surrounds. A short walk west is the side street called Grosse Freiheit, where the Beatles cut their teeth at the Indra Club (No 64) and the Kaiserkeller (No 36). Both are vastly different venues today, but there's a small monument to the Fab Four in a courtyard behind No 35.

★Mö-Grill GERMAN €

(Mönckebergstrasse 11; mains from €4; ⏲10am-7pm; Ⓢ Mönckebergstrasse) You can smell the curry and see the crowds from two streets away at this very popular venue for that beloved German fast food, the *Currywurst*. Locals agree that the versions here (and at a second stand across the street) are about the best anywhere.

★Altes Mädchen MODERN EUROPEAN €€

(☎040-800 077 750; www.altes-maedchen.com; Lagerstrasse 28b; mains €6-29; ⏲noon-late Mon-Sat, from 10am Sun; Ⓢ Sternschanze) The lofty red-brick halls of a 19th-century animal market have been upcycled into a hip culinary destination that includes a coffee roastery, a celebrity chef restaurant, and this beguiling brewpub with a central bar, in-house bakery and garden.

Oberhafen Kantine GERMAN €€

(☎040-3280 9984; www.oberhafenkantine-hamburg.de; Stockmeyerstrasse 39; mains €8.50-19.50; ⏲noon-10pm Mon-Sat, to 5.30pm Sun; Ⓤ Steinstrasse) Since 1925, this slightly tilted brick restaurant has served up the most traditional Hamburg fare. Here you can order a 'Hamburger' and you get the real thing: a patty made with various seasonings and onions. Roast beef and fish round out a trip back to the days when the surrounding piers echoed to the shouts of seafarers.

Erikas Eck GERMAN €€

(☎040-433 545; www.erikas-eck.de; Sternstrasse 98; mains €6-21; ⏲5pm-2pm Mon-Fri, to 9am Sat & Sun; Ⓤ Sternschanze) This pit-stop institution originally fed hungry workers from the nearby abattoir (today the central meat market) and now serves wallet-friendly but waist-expanding portions of schnitzel and other German fare to a motley crowd of clubbers, cabbies and cops 21 hours a day (weekdays).

Drinking & Entertainment

Partying in Hamburg concentrates on the Schanzenviertel and St Pauli, a few streets further south. Most people start the night in the former, then move on to the clubs and bars of the latter around midnight. Online sources: www.szene-hamburg.de and www.neu.clubkombinat.de.

★Katze BAR

(☎040-5577 5910; Schulterblatt 88; ⏲3pm-midnight Mon-Thu, 6pm-3am Fri, 1pm-3am Sat, 3pm-midnight Sun; Ⓢ Sternschanze) Small and sleek, this 'kitty' (*Katze* = cat) gets the crowd purring for well-priced cocktails (best caipirinhas in town) and great music (there's dancing on weekends). It's one of the most popular among the watering holes on this main Schanzenviertel booze strip.

★Indra Club CLUB

(www.indramusikclub.com; 64 Grosse Freiheit; ⏲9pm-late Wed-Sun; Ⓤ Reeperbahn) The Beatles' small first venue is open again and has live acts many nights. The interior is vastly different from the 1960s and there is a fine beer garden.

★Hafenklang MUSIC BAR

(☎040-388 744; www.hafenklang.org; Grosse Elbstrasse 84; Ⓤ Königstrasse) A collective of Hamburg industry insiders present established and emerging DJs and bands, as well as clubbing events and parties. Look for the spray-painted name on the graffiti-covered dark-brick harbour store above a blank metal door.

★ Strandperle BAR

(☎ 040-8809 9508; www.strandperle-hamburg.de; Oevelgönne 60; ⏲ 10am-11pm Mon-Fri, 9am-11pm Sat & Sun May-Sep, shorter hours & Fri-Sun only Oct-Apr; 🚌 112) Hamburg's original beach bar is a must for primo beer, burgers and people-watching. All ages and classes gather, mingle and wriggle their toes in the sand, especially at sunset, right on the Elbe as huge freighters glide past. Get here by taking ferry 62 from Landungsbrücken or bus 112 from Altona station to Neumühlen/Oevelgönne.

Uebel und Gefährlich CLUB

(☎ 040-3179 3610; www.uebelundgefaehrlich.com; Feldstrasse 66; S Feldstrasse) DJ sets, live music and parties rock this soundproof WWII bunker. Doors open around 7pm weekdays but as late as midnight on Friday and Saturday.

ℹ Information

Tourist Information am Hafen (☎ 040-3005 1701; www.hamburg-travel.com; btwn piers 4 & 5, St Pauli Landungsbrücken; ⏲ 9am-6pm Sun-Wed, to 7pm Thu-Sat; S Landungsbrücken) No hotel bookings.

Tourist Information Hauptbahnhof (☎ 040-3005 1701; www.hamburg-travel.com; Hauptbahnhof, near Kirchenallee exit; ⏲ 9am-7pm Mon-Sat, 10am-6pm Sun; S Hauptbahnhof, R Hauptbahnhof) Busy all the time.

ℹ Getting There & Away

AIR

Hamburg's **airport** (HAM; ☎ 040-507 50; www.hamburg-airport.de; R Hamburg Airport) is linked to the city centre every 10 minutes by the S-Bahn line S1 (€3.10, 25 minutes). A taxi takes about a half hour and cost around €30.

BUS

The **Zentraler Omnibusbahnhof** (Zentraler Omnibusbahnhof, Central Bus Station; ☎ 040-247 576; www.zob-hamburg.de; Adenauerallee 78; R Hauptbahnhof), southeast of the Hauptbahnhof, has many domestic and international departures by Eurolines, Flixbus and many other operators.

TRAIN

Hamburg is a major train hub with four mainline train stations: the Hauptbahnhof, Altona, Dammtor and Harburg. Frequent trains serve Lübeck (€17, 45 minutes), Bremen (from €26, 55 minutes), Berlin-Hauptbahnhof (€78, 1¾ hours), Copenhagen (€110, 4¾ hours) and many other cities.

ℹ Getting Around

For public transport information, go to www.hvv.de. The city is divided into zones. Fare zone A covers the city centre, inner suburbs and airport.

Lübeck

☎ 0451 / POP 211,700

Compact and charming Lübeck makes for a great day trip from Hamburg. Looking like a pair of witches' hats, the pointed towers of its landmark Holstentor (Holsten Gate) form the gateway to its historic centre that sits on an island embraced by the arms of the Trave River. The Unesco-recognised web of cobbled lanes flanked by gabled merchants' homes and spired churches is an enduring reminder of Lübeck's role as the one-time capital of the medieval Hanseatic League trading power. Today, it enjoys fame as Germany's marzipan capital.

OFF THE BEATEN TRACK

ANNE FRANK & BERGEN-BELSEN

Nazi-built **Bergen-Belsen** (Bergen-Belsen Memorial Site; ☎ 05051-475 90; www.bergen-belsen.de; Anne-Frank-Platz, Lohheide; ⏲ Documentation Centre 10am-6pm Apr-Sep, 10am-5pm Oct-Mar, grounds until dusk) began its existence in 1940 as a POW camp, but became a concentration camp after being taken over by the SS in 1943, initially to imprison Jews as hostages in exchange for German POWs held abroad. In all, 70,000 prisoners perished here, most famously Anne Frank. A modern **Documentation Centre** chronicles the fates of the people who passed through here. A small section deals with Anne Frank, and there's also a **memorial grave stone** for her and her sister, Margot, near the cemetery's Jewish Monument.

The memorial site is in the countryside about 60km northeast of Hanover and a bit complicated to reach if you don't have your own wheels. See the website for detailed driving and public transport directions.

Sights

★Holstentor LANDMARK

(Holsten Gate) Built in 1464 and looking so settled-in that it appears to sag, Lübeck's charming red-brick city gate is a national icon. Its twin pointed cylindrical towers, leaning together across the stepped gable that joins them, captivated Andy Warhol (his print is in the St Annen Museum), and have graced postcards, paintings, posters and marzipan souvenirs. Discover this and more inside the **Museum Holstentor** (0451-122 4129; www.museum-holstentor.de; adult/child €7/2.50; 10am-6pm Apr-Dec, 11am-5pm Tue-Sun Jan-Mar), which sheds light on the history of the gate and on Lübeck's medieval mercantile glory days.

★Museumsquartier St Annen MUSEUM

(Museum Quarter St Annen; 0451-122 4137; www.museumsquartier-st-annen.de; St-Annen-Strasse; adult/child €12/6; 10am-5pm Tue-Sun Apr-Dec, 11am-5pm Tue-Sun Jan-Mar) This museum quarter includes an old synagogue, church and medieval buildings along its uneven streets. The namesake **St Annen Museum** details the diverse history of the neighbourhood as it traces 700 years of art and culture. The adjoining **St Annen Kunstalle** has ecclesiastical art (including Hans Memling's 1491 *Passion Altar*) and contemporary art including Andy Warhol's print of Lübeck's Holstentor. There's a chic little cafe in the courtyard.

Marienkirche CHURCH

(St Mary's Church; 0451-397 700; www.st-marien-luebeck.com; Marienkirchhof 1; adult/child €2/1.50; 10am-6pm Apr-Sep, to 5pm Oct, to 4pm Tue-Sun Nov-Mar) This fine Gothic church boasts the world's highest brick-vaulted roof and was the model for dozens of churches in northern Germany. Crane your neck to take in the painted cross-vaulted ceilings supported by slender, ribbed pillars. A WWII bombing raid brought down the church's bells, which have been left where they fell in 1942 and have become a famous symbol of the city.

Sleeping

★Klassik Altstadt Hotel BOUTIQUE HOTEL €€

(0451-702 980; www.klassik-altstadt-hotel.de; Fischergrube 52; s/d from €50/120;) Each of the 29 rooms at this elegantly furnished boutique hotel is dedicated to a different, mostly German, writer or artist, such as Thomas Mann and Johann Sebastian Bach. Single rooms (some share baths and are great value) feature travelogues by famous authors.

DON'T MISS

SWEET TEMPTATIONS

Niederegger (0451-530 1126; www.niederegger.de; Breite Strasse 89; 9am-8pm Mon-Sat, 10am-6pm Sun) is Lübeck's mecca for marzipan, which has been made locally for centuries. The shop's elaborate displays are a feast for the eyes, and there's even a small museum where you'll learn that marzipan was considered medicine in the Middle Ages. The on-site cafe serves sandwiches and salads alongside sweet treats.

★Hotel zur Alten Stadtmauer HOTEL €€

(0451-737 02; www.hotelstadtmauer.de; An der Mauer 57; s/d from €67/98; P) With pine furniture and splashes of red and yellow, this simple 24-room hotel is a great place to wake up. Back rooms overlook the lakes and three are in a historic guesthouse. The real star of your stay, however, is the bounteous breakfast buffet, with many homemade preserves and other touches. Be aware that the hotel parking is 200m away.

Eating & Drinking

★Grenadine BISTRO €€

(0451-307 2950; www.grenadine-hl.de; Wahmstrasse 40; mains €7-15.50; 9am-4pm Mon, to 10pm Tue-Thu, to midnight Fri & Sat, to 3pm Sun;) This narrow, elongated bar leads through to a garden out the back. Enjoy bistro fare amid chic, retro-minimalist style. The long drinks menu goes well with tapas choices. Sandwiches, salads and pasta plus a gorgeous breakfast buffet are served.

Brauberger GERMAN €€

(0451-714 44; www.brauberger.de; Alfstrasse 36; mains €9-20; 5pm-midnight Mon-Thu, 5pm-late Fri & Sat) The air is redolent of hops at this traditional German brewery. Get a stein of the one house brew, the superbly sweet, cloudy *Zwickelbier,* and tuck into a sizeable schnitzel or other traditional fare. There are outside tables out the back and student specials for pitchers.

Information

Tourist Office (0451-889 9700; www.luebeck-tourismus.de; Holstentorplatz 1; 9am-7pm Mon-Fri, 10am-4pm Sat, 10am-3pm Sun May-Aug, reduced hours Sep-Apr) Sells the HappyDay Card (€12/14/17 per

24/48/72 hours) with discounts and free public transport. Also has a cafe and internet terminals.

Getting There & Away

Ryanair and Wizzair serve **Lübeck Airport** (LBC; ☎0451-583 010; www.flughafen-luebeck.de; Blankenseer Strasse 101).

Regional trains connect to Hamburg hourly (€14, 45 minutes).

Bremen

☎0421 / POP 546,450

It's a shame the donkey, dog, cat and rooster in Grimm's *Town Musicians of Bremen* never actually made it here – they would have fallen in love with the place. This little city is big on charm, from the fairy-tale character statue to a jaw-dropping expressionist laneway and impressive town hall. On top of that, the Weser riverside promenade is a relaxing, bistro and beer garden–lined refuge and the lively student district ('Das Viertel') along Ostertorsteinweg is filled with indie boutiques, cafes, art-house cinemas and alt-flavoured cultural venues.

Sights

Bremen's key historic sights cluster around Markt and can easily be explored on foot.

Markt SQUARE

Bremen's Unesco World Heritage–protected Markt is striking, especially for its ornate, gabled and sculpture-festooned **Rathaus** (town hall; 1410). In front stands a 5.5m-high medieval statue of the knight Roland (1404), the symbolic protector of Bremen's civic rights and freedoms.

Dom St Petri CHURCH

(St Petri Cathedral; ☎0421-334 7142; www.stpetridom.de; Sandstrasse 10-12; tower adult/concession €2/1, museum free; ⏰10am-5pm Mon-Fri, to 2pm Sat, 2-5pm Sun) Bremen's Protestant main church has origins in the 8th century and got its ribbed vaulting, chapels and two high towers in the 13th century. Aside from the imposing architecture, the intricately carved pulpit and the baptismal font in the western crypt deserve a closer look. For panoramic views, climb the 265 steps to the top of the south tower (April to October). The Dom-museum displays religious artefacts and treasures found here in a 1970s archaeological dig.

Böttcherstrasse STREET

(www.boettcherstrasse.de) The charming medieval coopers' lane was transformed into a prime example of mostly expressionist architecture in the 1920s at the instigation of coffee merchant Ludwig Roselius. Its red-brick houses sport unique facades, whimsical fountains, statues and a carillon; many house artisanal shops and art museums. Its most striking feature is Bernhard Hoetger's golden **Lichtbringer** (Bringer of Light) relief that keeps an eye on the north entrance.

★**Beck's Brewery** BREWERY

(☎0421-5094 5555; www.becks.de/besucherzentrum; Am Deich 18/19; tours €11.90; ⏰tours 1pm, 3pm & 4.30pm Mon-Wed, 10am, 11.30am, 1pm,

WORTH A TRIP

BACK TO THE ROOTS IN BREMERHAVEN

Standing on the spot where more than 7.2 million emigrants set sail for the US, South America and Australia between 1830 and 1942, the spectacular **Deutsches Auswandererhaus** (German Emigration Centre; ☎0471-902 200; www.dah-bremerhaven.de; Columbusstrasse 65; adult/concession €13.80/11.80; ⏰10am-6pm Mar-Oct, 10am-5pm Nov-Feb) museum does a superb job commemorating some of their stories. The visitor relives stages of their journey, which begins at the wharf where passengers huddle together before boarding 'the ship', clutching the biographical details of one particular traveller and heading toward their new life. A second exhibit, opened in 2012, reverses the theme and tells of immigration to Germany since the 17th century. Everything is available in both German and English.

Bremerhaven is some 70km north of Bremen and is served by regional train (€12.10, 40 minutes). From the station, take bus 502, 505, 506, 508 or 509 to 'Havenwelten' to get to the museum and the harbour with its many old vessels (including a WWII sub) and striking contemporary architecture.

WORTH A TRIP

HANOVER'S HERRENHÄUSER GÄRTEN

Proof that Hanover is not all buttoned-down business are the grandiose baroque **Royal Gardens of Herrenhausen** (☎0511-1683 4000; www.hannover.de/Herrenhausen; Herrenhäuser Strasse 4; general admission free; ⏰9am-6pm Apr-Oct, to 4.30pm Nov-Mar, grotto 9am-5.30pm Apr-Oct, to 4pm Nov-Mar; Ⓤ Hannover Herrenhäuser Gärten), which rank among the most important historic garden landscapes in Europe. Inspired by the park at Versailles, the sprawling grounds are perfect for slowing down and smelling the roses for a couple of hours, especially on a blue-sky day.

With its fountains, neat flowerbeds, trimmed hedges and shaped lawns, the 300-year-old **Grosser Garten** (Great Garden) is the centrepiece of the experience. Don't miss the **Niki de Saint Phalle Grotto** near the northern end, which provides a magical backdrop for the whimsical statues, fountains and coloured tiles by this late French artist (1930–2002). South of here, the **Grosse Fontäne** (Big Fountain; the tallest in Europe) jets water up to 80m high. In summer, fountains are synchronised during the **Wasserspiele** (water games). During the **Illuminations** the gardens and fountains are atmospherically lit at night.

Across Herrenhäuser Strasse, the **Berggarten** is redolent with a mindboggling assortment of global flora, while east of the Grosser Garten, beyond a small canal, the lake-dotted **Georgengarten** counts the **Wilhelm-Busch-Museum** (☎0511-1699 9911; www.karikatur-museum.de; adult/concession €6/4; ⏰11am-6pm Tue-Sun), with its wealth of caricatures by Busch, Honoré Daumier, William Hogarth and many others' among its treasures.

If you're curious about Hanover's other sights, stop by the **tourist office** (☎information 0511-1234 5111, room reservations 12 34 55 55; www.hannover.de; Ernst-Aug-Platz 8; ⏰9am-6pm Mon-Fri, 10am-3pm Sat & Sun).

3pm, 4.30pm & 6pm Thu-Sat) Two-hour tours of one of Germany's most internationally famous breweries must be booked online. The 3pm tour is also in English. Minimum age 16. Meet at the brewery's visitor centre, reached by taking tram 1, 2 or 3 to Am Brill.

Schnoor AREA

This maze of narrow, winding alleys was once the fishermen's quarter and later a red-light district. Now its doll's house–sized cottages contain boutiques, restaurants, cafes and galleries. Though tourist-geared, there are some lovely corners to explore around here on a leisurely amble.

Sleeping

Prizeotel Bremen City HOTEL €

(☎0421-222 2100; www.prizeotel.com/bremen; Theodor-Heuss-Allee 12; s/d from €59/64; P ❄ 📶) This funky, fresh and fluoro design hotel won't be everyone's cup of tea, but if you like it, you'll love it. Ultra-modern, compact rooms are quiet despite their proximity to the rail lines (the hotel is a five-minute walk from the station). All rooms feature 32-inch TVs, 'mega beds' and 'maxi showers'.

★Atlantic Grand HOTEL €€

(☎0421-620 620; www.atlantic-hotels.de; Bredenstrasse 2; r from €114) Pitched around a central courtyard, moments from Bremen's quirky Böttcherstrasse, the simple, effortlessly stylish, dark-wooded rooms with chocolate leather armchairs and top-notch service from attentive staff make this classy hotel an excellent choice.

Eating & Drinking

Tourist-oriented places cluster around Markt, which is pretty dead after dark. Das Viertel has an alternative, student-flavoured feel, while the waterfront promenade, Schlachte, is pricier and more mainstream.

Engel Weincafe CAFE €

(☎0421-6964 2390; www.engelweincafe-bremen.de; Ostertorsteinweg 31; dishes €4.50-12; ⏰9am-1am Mon-Fri, 10am-1am Sat & Sun; 📶 🖉) Exuding the nostalgic vibe of a former pharmacy, this popular hang-out gets a good crowd no matter where the hand's on the clock. Come for breakfast, a hot lunch special, crispy *Flammekuche* (French pizza), carpaccio or pasta, or just some cheese and a glass of wine.

★ Bremer Ratskeller
GERMAN €€

(☎0421-321 676; www.ratskeller-bremen.de; Am Markt 11; mains €9-19; ⊙11am-midnight) Ratskellers were traditionally built underneath the Rathaus in every German town to keep the citizens and civil servants fed. Bremen's is quite the experience, with high vaulted ceilings, an atmosphere that's the real deal on the historical Richter scale (in business since 1405!) and good, heavy, no-fuss German food and beer. What's not to like?

★ Kleiner Olymp
GERMAN €€

(☎0421-326 667; www.kleiner-olymp.de; Hinter der Holzpforte 20; mains €7-19; ⊙11am-11pm) This homely kitchen in Schnoor has a wonderful atmosphere, delicious (and not too heavy) North German cuisine and very reasonable prices. With a selection of mouthwatering soups and starters, seafood (not pork, for a change) features predominantly and appropriately on the menu. Enjoy!

☆ Entertainment

★ Lila Eule
LIVE MUSIC

(www.lilaeule.de; Bernhardstrasse 10; ⊙from 8pm) A decade or more is a long time to be a hot tip, but this gem off Sielwall has pulled it off. A student crowd gathers here for parties and events, but it's also a very alternative place to watch the Werder Bremen football team; most Werder matches are shown here. Thursday night is the legendary student bash.

ℹ Information

Tourist Office (☎0421-308 0010; www.bremen-tourism.de) Branches include **Markt** (Langenstrasse 2-4; ⊙9.30am-6.30pm Mon-Fri, to 5pm Sat, 10am-4pm Sun), a full-service tourist office with friendly staff, near Markt, and **Hauptbahnhof** (⊙9am-6.30pm Mon-Fri, to 5pm Sat & Sun), handily located at the main train station.

ℹ Getting There & Around

Bremen's **airport** (BRE; ☎0421-559 50; www.airport-bremen.de) is about 3.5km south of the city and served by tram 6 (€2.60, 15 minutes).

Frequent IC trains go to Hamburg (€28, one hour), Hanover (€33, one hour) and Cologne (€67, three hours). Less frequent IC trains go to Berlin (€79, four hours).

SURVIVAL GUIDE

Directory A–Z

ACCOMMODATION

Reservations are a good idea between June and September, and around major holidays, festivals, cultural events and trade shows.

DISCOUNT CARDS

Tourist offices in many cities sell Welcome Cards, which entitle visitors to discounts on museums, sights and tours, plus unlimited trips on local public transport. They can be good value if you plan on taking advantage of most of the benefits and don't qualify for any of the standard discounts.

GAY & LESBIAN TRAVELLERS

Germany is a magnet for *schwule* (gay) and *lesbische* (lesbian) travellers, with the rainbow flag flying especially proudly in Berlin and Cologne. There are also sizeable communities in Hamburg, Frankfurt and Munich.

INTERNET RESOURCES

Lonely Planet (www.lonelyplanet.com/germany) Hotel bookings, traveller forum and more.

German National Tourist Office (www.germany.travel)

Facts About Germany (www.tatsachen-ueber-deutschland.de/en) Reference tool on all aspects of German society.

Deutschland Online (www.magazine-deutschland.de) Insightful features on culture, business and politics.

Online German course (www.deutsch-lernen.com)

LEGAL MATTERS

- The permissible blood-alcohol limit is 0.05%.
- Drinking in public is legal, but be discreet.

COUNTRY FACTS

Area 356,866 sq km

Capital Berlin

Country Code 49

Currency euro (€)

Emergency ☎112

Language German

Money ATMs common, cash preferred for most purchases

Population 80.7 million

Visas Schengen rules apply

ESSENTIAL FOOD & DRINK

As in Britain, Germany has redeemed itself gastronomically over the past decade. These days culinary offerings are often slimmed down and healthier as many chefs let the trifecta of seasonal-regional-organic ingredients steer their menus. International flavours and cooking techniques further add pizzazz to tried-and-trusted specialities, while vegan and vegetarian selections are becoming commonplace. Of course, if you crave traditional comfort food, you'll still find plenty of pork, potatoes and cabbage on the menus, especially in the countryside. Here are our top-five classic German culinary treats:

Sausage (wurst) Favourite snack food, links come in 1500 varieties, including finger-sized *Nürnbergers*, crunchy *Thüringers* and tomato-sauce-drowned *Currywurst*.

Schweinshaxe The mother of all pork dishes, this one presents itself as entire knuckle roasted to crispy perfection.

Königsberger Klopse A simple but elegant plate of golf-ball-sized veal meatballs in a caper-laced white sauce and served with a side of boiled potatoes and beetroot.

Bread Get Germans talking about bread and often their eyes will water as they describe their favourite type – usually hearty and wholegrained in infinite variations.

Black forest cake (Schwarzwälder Kirschtorte) Multilayered chocolate sponge cake, whipped cream and kirsch confection, topped with cherries and chocolate shavings.

- Cannabis *consumption* is not illegal, but the possession, acquisition, sale and cultivation of it is considered a criminal offence. There is usually no prosecution for possessing 'small quantities'.

MONEY

- Cash is king in Germany. Always carry some with you and plan to pay cash almost everywhere.
- Credit cards are becoming more widely accepted, but it's best not to assume you'll be able to use one – ask first.
- Most ATMs (*Geldautomat*) are linked to international networks such as Cirrus, Plus, Star and Maestro.

OPENING HOURS

The following are typical opening hours in Germany, although these may vary seasonally and between cities and villages.

Banks 9am–4pm Monday to Friday, extended hours usually on Tuesday and Thursday, some open Saturday

Bars 6pm–1am

Cafes 8am–8pm

Clubs 11pm to early morning hours

Restaurants 11am–11pm (food service often stops at 9pm in rural areas)

Major stores and supermarkets 9.30am–8pm Monday to Saturday (shorter hours outside city centres)

PUBLIC HOLIDAYS

The following are nationwide *gesetzliche Feiertage* (public holidays):

Neujahrstag (New Year's Day) 1 January

Ostern (Easter) March/April; Good Friday, Easter Sunday and Easter Monday

Christi Himmelfahrt (Ascension Day) Forty days after Easter

Maifeiertag/Tag der Arbeit (Labour Day) 1 May

Pfingsten (Whit/Pentecost Sunday & Monday) Fifty days after Easter

Tag der Deutschen Einheit (Day of German Unity) 3 October

Weihnachtstag (Christmas Day) 25 December

Zweiter Weihnachtstag (Boxing Day) 26 December

TELEPHONE

German phone numbers consist of an area code (three to six digits), starting with 0, and the local number (three to nine digits). If dialling from a

SLEEPING PRICE RANGES

The price indicators in this book refer to the cost of a double room with private bathroom, including taxes.

€ less than €80

€€ €80–€160

€€€ more than €160

landline within the same city, you don't need to dial the area code. You must dial it if using a mobile.

Country code ☎ 49

International access code ☎ 00

Getting There & Away

AIR

Huge **Frankfurt Airport** (p310) is Germany's busiest, with **Munich** (p291) a close second and **Düsseldorf** (p319) getting a good share of flights as well. Airports in Berlin, Hamburg and Cologne are comparatively small.

LAND

Bus

Long-distance coach travel to Germany from such cities as Milan, Vienna, Amsterdam and Copenhagen has become a viable option thanks to a new crop of companies offering good-value connections aboard comfortable buses with snack bars and free wi-fi. Major operators include **Flixbus** (☎ 030-300 137 300; www.flixbus.com), **Megabus** (☎ in the UK 0900 1600 900; www.megabus.com) and Eurolines (www.eurolines.com). For routes, times and prices, check www.busradar.com.

Car & Motorcycle

➡ When bringing your own vehicle to Germany, you need a valid driving licence, car registration and proof of third-party insurance. Foreign cars must display a nationality sticker unless they have official European plates. You also need to carry a warning (hazard) triangle and a first-aid kit.

➡ Most German cities now have environmental zones that may only be entered by vehicles (including foreign ones) displaying an *Umweltplakette* (emissions sticker). Check with your motoring association or buy one at www.umwelt-plakette.de.

Train

➡ Germany has an efficient railway network with excellent links to other European destinations. Ticketing is handled by **Deutsche Bahn** (☎ 01806 99 66 33; www.bahn.de).

➡ Seat reservations are a good idea for Friday and Sunday travel on long-distance trains and highly recommended during the peak summer season and around major holidays.

➡ Eurail and Interrail passes are valid on all German national trains.

SEA

➡ Germany's main ferry ports are Kiel, Travemünde (near Lübeck), Rostock and Sassnitz (on Rügen Island). All have services to Scandinavia and the Baltic states. There are no direct ferries between Germany and the UK.

➡ For details and tickets, go to www.ferrysavers.com.

Getting Around

Germans are whizzes at moving people around, and the public transport network is one of the best in Europe. The best ways of getting around the country are by car and by train.

AIR

Unless you're flying from one end of the country to the other, say from Berlin or Hamburg to Munich, planes are only marginally quicker than trains once you factor in the check-in and transit times.

BICYCLE

➡ Cycling is allowed on all roads except autobahns (motorways). Helmets are not compulsory (not even for children).

➡ Bicycles may be taken on most trains but require a separate ticket *(Fahrradkarte)* and a reservation if travelling on an IC/EC train. They are not allowed on ICE trains.

➡ Most towns and cities have a private bicycle-hire station, often at or near the train station. A growing number have automated bike-rental systems.

BOAT

➡ From April to October, boats operate on set timetables along sections of the Rhine, the Elbe and the Danube.

BUS

➡ Domestic buses cover an extensive nationwide network. Fierce competition has kept prices extremely low. Flixbus (www.flixbus.com) is the dominant operator.

➡ In some rural areas buses may be your only option for getting around without your own vehicle. The frequency of services varies from 'rarely' to 'constantly'. Commuter-geared routes offer limited or no service in the evenings and on weekends.

➡ In cities, buses generally converge at the *Busbahnhof* or *Zentraler Omnibus Bahnhof*

EATING PRICE RANGES

The following price ranges refer to a standard main course.

€ less than €8

€€ €8–€18

€€€ more than €18

MILESTONES IN GERMAN HISTORY

800 Charlemagne is crowned emperor by the pope, laying the foundation for the Holy Roman Empire, which will last until 1806.

1241 Hamburg and Lübeck sign a trading agreement, creating the base for the powerful Hanseatic League that dominates politics and trade across much of Europe throughout the Middle Ages.

1455 Johannes Gutenberg invents moveable type, which for the first time allows books to be published in larger quantities.

1517 Martin Luther challenges Catholic church practices by posting his Ninety-Five Theses and ushering in the Reformation.

1618–48 The Thirty Years' War pits Protestants against Catholics in a far-reaching, bloody war that leaves Europe's population depleted and vast regions reduced to wasteland.

1871 A united Germany is created with Prussia at its helm, Berlin as its capital and Wilhelm I as its emperor.

1914–18 WWI: Germany, Austria-Hungary and Turkey go to war against Britain, France, Italy and Russia. Germany is defeated.

1933 Hitler comes to power, ushering in 12 years of Nazi terror that culminates in WWII and the systematic annihiliation of Jews, Roma, Sinti and other people deemed 'undesirable'.

1949 Germany is divided into a democratic West Germany under the western Allies (the US, UK and France) and a socialist East Germany under the Soviet Union.

1961 The East German government erects the Berlin Wall, dividing the country into two for the next 28 years.

1989 The Berlin Wall collapses; Germany is reunited the following year.

(ZOB; central bus station), which is often near the Hauptbahnhof (central train station).

➡ From April to October, the tourist-geared **Romantic Road Coach** (☎09851-551 387; www.romantic-road.com) runs one coach daily in each direction between Frankfurt and Füssen (for Schloss Neuschwanstein) via Munich; the entire trip takes around 12 hours.

CAR & MOTORCYCLE

➡ Driving is on the right side of the road.

➡ With few exceptions, no tolls are charged on public roads.

➡ Unless posted otherwise, speed limits are 50km/h in cities, 100km/h on country roads and no limit on the autobahn.

➡ Cars are impractical in urban areas. Leaving your car in a central *Parkhaus* (car park) can cost €20 per day or more.

➡ Visitors from most countries do not need an International Driving Permit to drive in Germany. Automatic transmissions are rare and must be booked well in advance.

LOCAL TRANSPORT

➡ Public transport is excellent within big cities and small towns and may include buses, trams *(Strassenbahn)*, S-Bahn (light rail), U-Bahn (underground/subway trains) and ferries.

➡ Fares are usually determined by zones or time travelled, sometimes both. Multiticket strips *(Streifenkarte)* and day passes *(Tageskarte)* usually offer better value than single-ride tickets.

➡ Most tickets must be validated (stamped) upon boarding.

TRAIN

➡ Germany's train network is almost entirely run by **Deutsche Bahn** (p333), although there is a growing number of routes operated by private companies but integrated into the DB network.

➡ Of the several train types, ICE trains are the fastest and most comfortable. IC trains (EC if they cross borders) are almost as fast but older and less snazzy. RE and RB trains are regional.

S-Bahn are suburban trains operating in large cities and conurbations.

➡ At larger stations, you can store your luggage in a locker (*Schliessfach*) or a left-luggage office (*Gepäckaufbewahrung*).

➡ Seat reservations for long-distance travel are highly recommended, especially if you're travelling on a Friday or Sunday afternoon, during holiday periods or in summer. Reservations can be made online and at ticket counters as late as 10 minutes before departure.

➡ Buy tickets online (www.bahn.de) or at stations from vending machines or ticket offices (*Reisezentrum*). Only conductors on ICE and IC/EC trains sell tickets on board at a surcharge.

TIPPING

Hotels €1 per bag is standard. It's also nice to leave a little cash for the room cleaners, say €1 or €2 per day.

Restaurants Restaurant bills always include *Bedienung* (service charge), but most people add 5% or 10% unless the service was truly abhorrent.

Bars About 5%, rounded to the nearest euro. For drinks brought to your table, tip as for restaurants.

Taxis Tip about 10%, rounded to the nearest euro.

Toilet attendants Loose change.

Greece Ελλάδα

Includes ➡

Best Places to Eat

- Mani Mani (p344)
- Koukoumavlos (p362)
- Thalassino Ageri (p368)
- Klimataria (p380)
- Il Vesuvio (p379)

Best Places to Sleep

- Nafplion 1841 (p348)
- Mill Houses (p362)
- Marco Polo Mansion (p371)
- Bella Venezia (p379)

Why Go?

It's easy to understand how so many myths of gods and giants originated in this vast and varied landscape, with wide open skies and a sea speckled with islands. Endless kilometres of aquamarine coastline, sun-bleached ancient ruins, strong feta and stronger ouzo – the Greek landscape thrills while the culture captivates with a population passionate about everything from politics to art. Magnificent archaeological sites like the Acropolis, Delphi, Delos and Knossos are easilly reached and hiking trails criss-cross Mt Olympus, the Zagorohoria and islands like Crete and Corfu. Meanwhile, the nightlife thrives in Greece's vibrant modern cities and on islands such as Mykonos and Santorini. Add a flourishing arts scene, world-class cuisine and welcoming locals to the mix and it's easy to see why most visitors head home vowing to come back. Travellers to Greece inevitably end up with a favourite site they long to return to – get out there and find yours.

When to Go

Athens

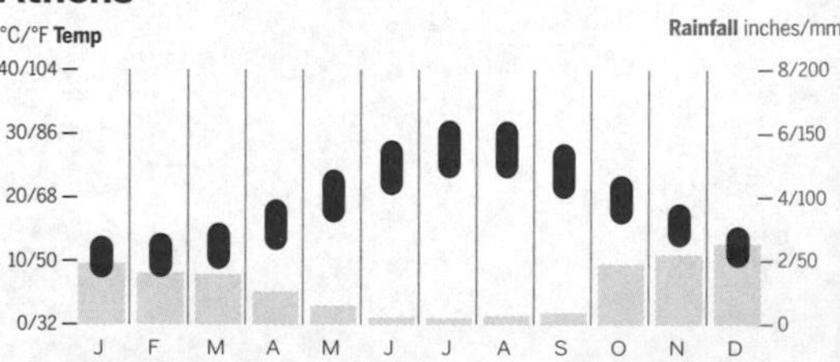

May & Jun Greece opens the shutters in time for Orthodox Easter; the best months to visit.

Jul & Aug Be prepared to battle summer crowds, high prices and soaring temperatures.

Sep & Oct The tourist season winds down; an excellent, relaxing time to head to Greece.

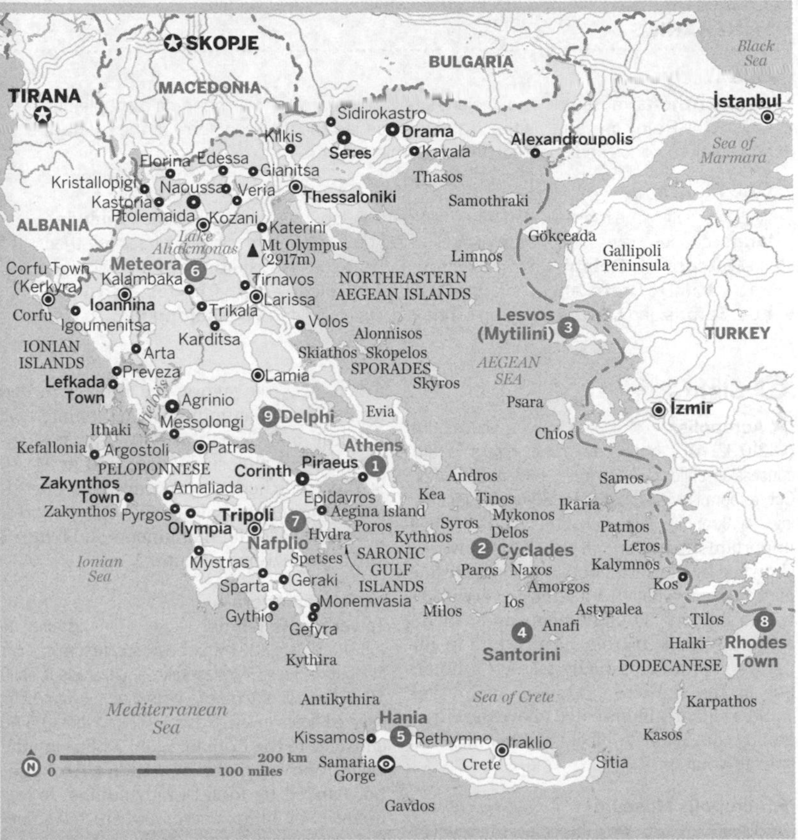

Greece Highlights

1 **Athens** (p337) Tracing the ancient to the modern, from the Acropolis to booming nightclubs.

2 **Cyclades** (p355) Island-hopping under the Aegean sun.

3 **Lesvos (Mytilini)** (p375) Sipping ouzo while munching grilled octopus on this olive-tree-filled island.

4 **Santorini** (p360) Staring dumbfounded at the dramatic volcanic caldera on this incomparable island.

5 **Hania, Crete** (p363) Strolling the lovely Venetian Harbour then supping on some of Greece's best food.

6 **Meteora** (p351)Climbing russet rock pinnacles to exquisite monasteries.

7 **Nafplio** (p348) Basing yourself in this quaint village and exploring the back roads and ruins of the Peloponnese.

8 **Rhodes Town** (p369) Losing yourself within the medieval walls of the Old Town.

9 **Delphi** (p351) Searching for the oracle amid the dazzling ruins.

ATHENS ΑΘΗΝΑ

POP 3.1 MILLION

Ancient and modern, with equal measures of grunge and grace, bustling Athens is a heady mix of history and edginess. Iconic monuments mingle with first-rate museums, bustling shops and stylish, alfresco dining. Even in the face of current financial issues, Athens is more cosmopolitan than ever before with hip hotels, artsy-industrial neighbourhoods and entertainment quarters showing its modern face.

ITINERARIES

One Week

Explore **Athens**' museums and ancient sites on day one before spending a couple of days in the **Peloponnese** visiting Nafplio, Mycenae and Olympia; ferry to the **Cyclades** and enjoy Mykonos and spectacular Santorini.

One Month

Give yourself some more time in Athens and the Peloponnese, then visit the **Ionian Islands** for a few days. Explore the villages of Zagorohoria before travelling back to Athens via **Meteora** and **Delphi**. Take a ferry from Piraeus south to **Mykonos**, then island-hop via Santorini to **Crete**. After exploring Crete, take the ferry east to **Rhodes**, then north to **Kos**, **Samos** and **Lesvos**. Wrap up in relaxed, cosmopolitan **Thessaloniki**.

Sights

★Acropolis HISTORIC SITE

(☎210 321 4172; http://odysseus.culture.gr; adult/concession/child €20/10/free; ⏲8am-8pm Apr-Oct, to 5pm Nov-Mar, last entry 30min before closing; Ⓜ Akropoli) The Acropolis is the most important ancient site in the Western world. Crowned by the Parthenon, it stands sentinel over Athens, visible from almost everywhere within the city. Its monuments and sanctuaries of Pentelic marble gleam white in the midday sun and gradually take on a honey hue as the sun sinks, while at night they stand brilliantly illuminated above the city. A glimpse of this magnificent sight cannot fail to exalt your spirit.

★Acropolis Museum MUSEUM

(☎210 900 0900; www.theacropolismuseum.gr; Dionysiou Areopagitou 15, Makrygianni; adult/child €5/free; ⏲8am-4pm Mon, to 8pm Tue-Sun, to 10pm Fri Apr-Oct, 9am-5pm Mon-Thu, to 10pm Fri, to 8pm Sat & Sun Nov-Mar; Ⓜ Akropoli) This dazzling modernist museum at the foot of the Acropolis' southern slope showcases its surviving treasures still in Greek possession. While the collection covers the Archaic and Roman periods, the emphasis is on the Acropolis of the 5th century BC, considered the apotheosis of Greece's artistic achievement. The museum cleverly reveals layers of history, floating over ruins with the Acropolis visible above, showing the masterpieces in context. The surprisingly good-value restaurant has superb views; there's also a fine museum shop.

★Ancient Agora HISTORIC SITE

(☎210 321 0185; http://odysseus.culture.gr; Adrianou 24; adult/student/child €8/4/free, with Acropolis pass free; ⏲8am-8pm daily May-Oct, 8am-3pm Nov-Apr; Ⓜ Monastiraki) The heart of ancient Athens was the Agora, the lively, crowded focal point of administrative, commercial, political and social activity. Socrates expounded his philosophy here, and in AD 49 St Paul came here to win converts to Christianity. The site today is a lush, refreshing respite, with beautiful monuments and temples and a fascinating museum.

★Roman Agora & Tower of the Winds HISTORIC SITE

(☎210 324 5220; http://odysseus.culture.gr; cnr Pelopida & Eolou, Monastiraki; adult/student/child €6/3/free, with Acropolis pass free; ⏲8am-5pm, reduced hours in low season; Ⓜ Monastiraki) The entrance to the Roman Agora is through the well-preserved **Gate of Athena Archegetis**, flanked by four Doric columns. It was financed by Julius Caesar and erected sometime during the 1st century AD. Restored and reopened in 2016, the extraordinary **Tower of the Winds** was built in the 1st century BC by a Syrian astronomer named Andronicus. The octagonal monument of Pentelic marble is an ingenious construction that functioned as a sundial, weather vane, water clock and compass.

★Temple of Olympian Zeus TEMPLE

(Olympieio; ☎210 922 6330; http://odysseus.culture.gr; Leoforos Vasilissis Olgas, Syntagma; adult/student/child €6/3/free, with Acropolis pass free; ⏲8am-3pm Oct-Apr, 8am-8pm May-Sep, final admission 30min before closing; Ⓜ Akropoli, Syntagma) You can't miss this striking marvel smack in the centre of Athens. It is the largest temple in Greece; begun in the 6th century BC by Peisistratos, it was abandoned for lack of funds. Various other leaders had stabs at completing it, but it was left to Hadrian to complete the work in AD 131 – taking more than 700 years in total to build.

★Panathenaic Stadium HISTORIC SITE

(☎210 752 2984; www.panathenaicstadium.gr; Leoforos Vasileos Konstantinou, Pangrati; adult/student/child €5/2.50/free; ⏲8am-7pm Mar-Oct, to 5pm Nov-Feb; M Akropoli) The grand Panathenaic Stadium lies between two pine-covered hills between the neighbourhoods of Mets and Pangrati. It was originally built in the 4th century BC as a venue for the Panathenaic athletic contests. It's said that at Hadrian's inauguration in AD 120, 1000 wild animals were sacrificed in the arena. Later, the seats were rebuilt in Pentelic marble by Herodes Atticus. There are seats for 70,000 spectators, a running track and a central area for field events.

★Parliament & Changing of the Guard NOTABLE BUILDING

(Plateia Syntagmatos; M Syntagma) FREE In front of the parliament building on Plateia Syntagmatos (Syntagma Sq), the traditionally costumed *evzones* (guards) of the **Tomb of the Unknown Soldier** change every hour on the hour. On Sunday at 11am, a whole platoon marches down Vasilissis Sofias to the tomb, accompanied by a band.

★National Gardens GARDENS

(cnr Leoforos Vasilissis Sofias & Leoforos Vasilissis Amalias, Syntagma; ⏲7am-dusk; M Syntagma) FREE A delightful, shady refuge during summer, the National Gardens were formerly the royal gardens, designed by Queen Amalia. There's a large children's playground, a duck pond and a shady cafe.

★Benaki Museum MUSEUM

(☎210 367 1000; www.benaki.gr; Koumbari 1, cnr Leoforos Vasilissis Sofias, Kolonaki; adult/student/child €9/7/free, Thu free; ⏲9am-5pm Wed & Fri, to midnight Thu & Sat, to 3pm Sun; M Syntagma, Evangelismos) Greece's finest private museum contains the vast collection of Antonis Benakis, accumulated during 35 years of avid collecting in Europe and Asia. The collection includes Bronze Age finds from Mycenae and Thessaly; works by El Greco; ecclesiastical furniture brought from Asia Minor; pottery, copper, silver and woodwork from Egypt, Asia Minor and Mesopotamia; and a stunning collection of Greek regional costumes.

★National Archaeological Museum MUSEUM

(☎213 214 4800; www.namuseum.gr; 28 Oktovriou-Patision 44, Exarhia; adult/child €10/free; ⏲1-8pm Mon, 8am-8pm Tue-Sun Apr-Oct, 1-8pm Mon, 9am-4pm Tue-Sun Nov-Mar; M Viktoria, 🚎2, 4, 5, 9 or 11 to Polytechnio) One of the world's most important museums, the National Archaeological Museum houses the world's finest collection of Greek antiquities. Treasures offering a view of Greek art and history – dating from the Neolithic era to classical periods – include exquisite sculptures, pottery, jewellery, frescoes and artefacts found throughout Greece. The beautifully presented exhibits

CHEAPER BY THE HALF-DOZEN

A €30 unified ticket from the Acropolis (valid for five days) includes entry to the other significant ancient sites: Ancient Agora, Roman Agora, Keramikos, Temple of Olympian Zeus and the Theatre of Dionysos.

Enter the sites free on the first Sunday of the month from November to March, and on certain holidays. Anyone aged under 18 years or with an EU student card gets in free.

CONTEMPORARY ART

Athens is not all about ancient art. For a taste of the contemporary, visit:

Taf (The Art Foundation; ☎210 323 8757; www.theartfoundation.gr; Normanou 5, Monastiraki; ⏲noon-9pm Mon-Sat, to 7pm Sun; M Monastiraki) Eclectic art and music gallery.

Six DOGS (☎210 321 0510; www.sixdogs.gr; Avramiotou 6-8, Monastiraki; ⏲10am-late; M Monastiraki) Theatre meets gallery meets live music venue.

Onassis Cultural Centre (☎info/tickets 210 900 5800; www.sgt.gr; Leoforos Syngrou 107-109, Neos Kosmos; M Syngrou-Fix) Multimillion-euro visual and performing-arts centre.

National Museum of Contemporary Art (☎211 101 9000; www.emst.gr; Kallirrois & Frantzi, Koukaki-Syngrou; adult/student/child €5/3/free, 5-10pm Thu free; ⏲11am-7pm Tue, Wed & Fri-Sun, to 10pm Thu; M Syngrou-Fix) In spectacularly renovated quarters, with top-notch rotating exhibits.

Central Athens

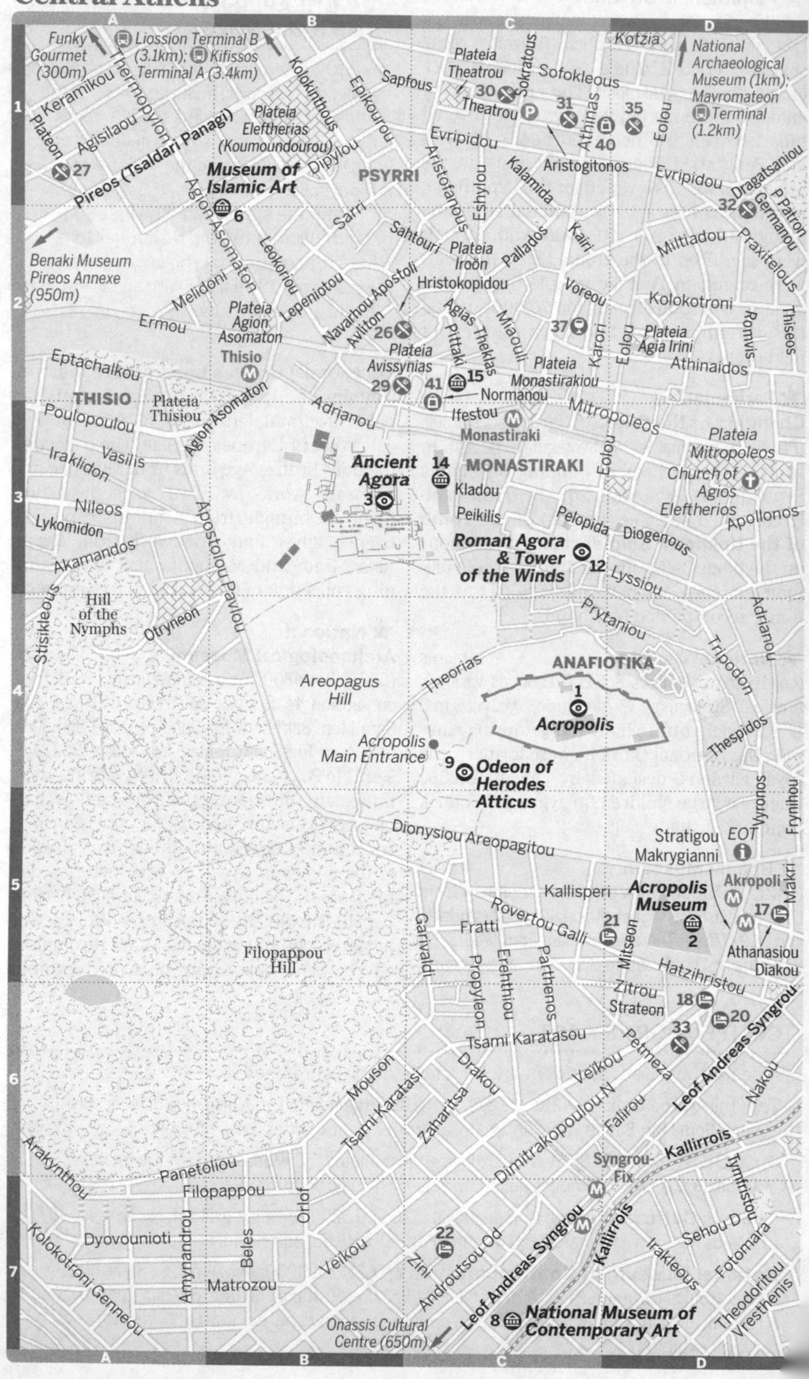

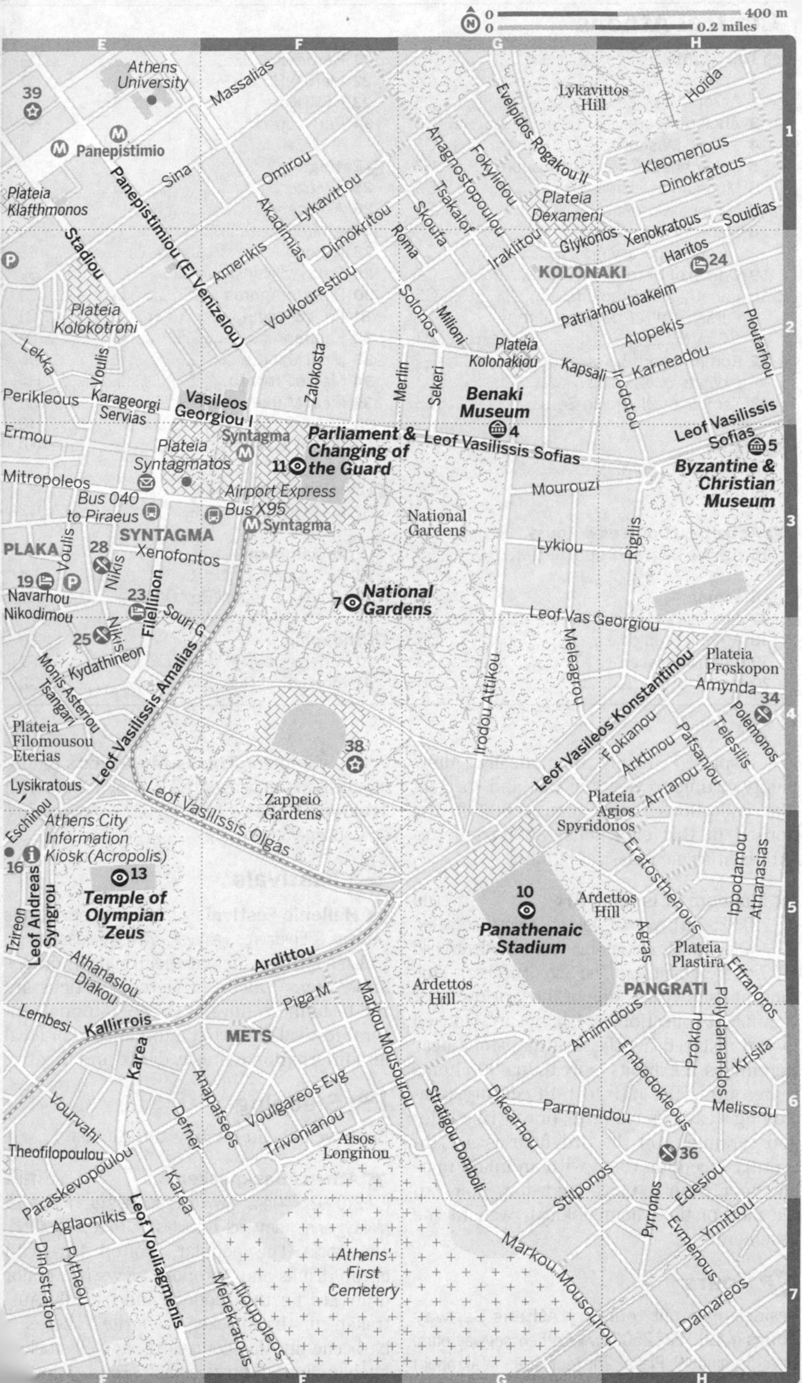

400 m
0.2 miles
Athens University
Massalias
Lykavittos Hill
Hoida
Panepistimio
Sina
Omirou
Evelpidos Rogakou II
Kleomenous
Dinokratous
Plateia Klafthmonos
Panepistimiou (El Venizelou)
Stadiou
Akadimias
Lykavittou
Anagnostopoulou
Fokylidou
Tsakalof
Skoufa
Plateia Dexameni
Xenokratous
Souidias
Amerikis
Dimokritou
Roma
Iraklitou
Glykonos
Haritos
KOLONAKI
Voukourestiou
Solonos
Milioni
Patriarhou Ioakeim
Plateia Kolokotroni
Alopekis
Ploutarhou
Lekka
Voulis
Zalokosta
Merlin
Sekeri
Plateia Kolonakiou
Kapsali
Irodotou
Karneadou
Perikleous
Karageorgi Servias
Vasileos Georgiou I
Benaki Museum
Leof Vasilissis Sofias
Ermou
Syntagma
Parliament & Changing of the Guard
Plateia Syntagmatos
Byzantine & Christian Museum
Mitropoleos
Mourouzi
Bus 040 to Piraeus
Airport Express Bus X95
National Gardens
Rigilis
SYNTAGMA
PLAKA
Xenofontos
Lykiou
Nikis
Navarhou Nikodimou
Filellinon
National Gardens
Souri G
Leof Vas Georgiou
Kydathineon
Meleagrou
Plateia Proskopon
Monis Asteriou
Tsangari
Leof Vasilissis Amalias
Irodou Attikou
Leof Vasileos Konstantinou
Amynda
Polemonos
Telesilis
Plateia Filomousou Eterias
Fokianou
Arktinou
Pafsaniou
Lysikratous
Leof Vasilissis Olgas
Zappeio Gardens
Plateia Agios Spyridonos
Arrianou
Eschinou
Athens City Information Kiosk (Acropolis)
Eratosthenous
Ippodamou
Athanasias
Temple of Olympian Zeus
Panathenaic Stadium
Ardettos Hill
Tzireon
Leof Andreas Syngrou
Agras
Plateia Plastira
Effranoros
Athanasiou Diakou
Arditou
Piga M
Markou Mousourou
Ardettos Hill
PANGRATI
Polydamandos
Lembesi
Kallirrois
METS
Arhimidous
Proklou
Krisila
Karea
Embedokleous
Vourvahi
Anapafseos
Voulgareos Evg
Stratigou Dombol
Dikearhou
Parmenidou
Melissou
Defner
Trivonianou
Alsos Longinou
Theofilopoulou
Paraskevopoulou
Karea
Stilponos
Pyrronos
Edesiou
Aglaonikis
Leof Vouliagmenis
Evmenous
Ymittou
Dinostratou
Pytheou
Athens' First Cemetery
Markou Mousourou
Iliopoleos
Menekratous
Damareos

Central Athens

are displayed mainly thematically. Allow plenty of time to view the vast and spectacular collections (more than 11,000 items) housed in this enormous (8000-sq-metre) 19th-century neoclassical building.

★ **Museum of Islamic Art** MUSEUM
(☎210 325 1311; www.benaki.gr; Agion Asomaton 22 & Dipylou 12, Keramikos; adult/student/child €9/7/free; ⊙8am-6pm Thu-Sun; Ⓜ Thisio) This museum showcases one of the world's most significant collections of Islamic art. Housed in two restored neoclassical mansions near Keramikos, it exhibits more than 8000 items representing the 12th to 19th centuries, including weavings, carvings, prayer rugs, tiles and ceramics. On the 3rd floor is a 17th-century reception room with an inlaid marble floor from a Cairo mansion. You can see part of the Themistoklean wall in the basement.

Tours

Besides open-bus tours try **Athens Segway Tours** (☎210 322 2500; www.athenssegwaytours.com; Eschinou 9, Plaka; 2hr tour €59; Ⓜ Akropoli) or the volunteer **This is My Athens** (http://myathens.thisisathens.org). Hike or kayak with **Trekking Hellas** (☎210 331 0323; www.trekking.gr; Gounari 96, Marousi).

Festivals

★ **Hellenic Festival** PERFORMING ARTS
(Athens & Epidavros Festival; www.greekfestival.gr; ⊙Jun-Aug) The ancient theatre at Epidavros and Athens' Odeon of Herodes Atticus are the headline venues of Greece's annual cultural festival featuring a top line-up of local and international music, dance and theatre.

Sleeping

Book well ahead for July and August.

★ **Athens Backpackers** HOSTEL €
(☎210 922 4044; www.backpackers.gr; Makri 12, Makrygianni; dm incl breakfast €27-30; ❄@📶; Ⓜ Akropoli) The popular rooftop bar with cheap drinks and Acropolis views is a major drawcard for this modern and friendly Australian-run backpacker favourite. There's a barbecue in the courtyard, a well-stocked kitchen and a busy social scene. Spotle

dorms with private bathrooms and lockers have bedding, but towel use costs €2. Management also runs well-priced **Athens Studios** (☎210 923 5811; www.athensstudios.gr; Veïkou 3a, Makrygianni; apt incl breakfast €105; @; M Akropoli), with modern apartments nearby.

Marble House Pension PENSION €
(☎210 923 4058; www.marblehouse.gr; Zini 35a, Koukaki; s/d/tr €35/45/55, d/tr/q with shared bathroom €40/50/65; @; M Syngrou-Fix) Tucked into a quiet cul-de-sac is one of Athens' best-value budget hotels. Rooms have been artfully updated, with wrought-iron beds, and bathrooms are sleek marble. All rooms have a fridge and ceiling fans and some have air-con (€9 extra). It's a fair walk from the tourist drag, but close to the metro. Breakfast available (€5).

★ **Hera Hotel** BOUTIQUE HOTEL €€
(☎210 923 6682; www.herahotel.gr; Falirou 9, Makrygianni; d incl breakfast €160-190, ste €250; @; M Akropoli) This elegant boutique hotel, a short walk from the Acropolis and Plaka, was totally rebuilt – but the formal interior design is in keeping with the lovely neoclassical facade. There's lots of brass and timber, and stylish classic furnishings. The rooftop garden, restaurant and bar have spectacular views.

Periscope BOUTIQUE HOTEL €€
(☎210 729 7200; www.periscope.gr; Haritos 22, Kolonaki; d from €120; M Evangelismos) Right in chic Kolonaki overlooking Lykavittos, Periscope is a design hotel with industrial decor. Clever gadgets are sprinkled throughout, including the lobby slide show and aerial shots of the city on the ceilings. Korres organic toiletries and the trendy **Pbox** restaurant add to the vibe. The penthouse's private rooftop spa has sensational views.

★ **Herodion** HOTEL €€€
(☎210 923 6832; www.herodion.gr; Rovertou Galli 4, Makrygianni; d incl breakfast from €165; @; M Akropoli) This smart four-star hotel is geared towards the well-heeled traveller and business travellers. Rooms are small but decked out with all the trimmings and have super-comfortable beds. The rooftop spa and lounge have unbeatable Acropolis and museum views.

★ **Electra Palace** LUXURY HOTEL €€€
(☎210 337 0000; www.electrahotels.gr; Navarhou Nikodimou 18, Plaka; d/ste incl breakfast from €250/350; P @; M Syntagma) Plaka's smartest hotel is one for the roman[...] have breakfast under the Acropolis on [...] balcony (in higher-end rooms) and din[...] in the chic rooftop restaurant. Complete[...] refurbished with classic elegance, the well-appointed rooms are buffered from the sounds of the city streets. There's a gym and an indoor swimming pool, as well as a rooftop pool with Acropolis views.

★ **NEW Hotel** BOUTIQUE HOTEL €€€
(☎210 327 3000; www.yeshotels.gr; Filellinon 16, Plaka; d from €150; P; M Syntagma) Whether you dig the groovy, top-designer Campana Brothers furniture or the sleeping-pillow menu (tell 'em how you like it!), you'll find some sort of decadent treat here to tickle your fancy. Part of a renowned local design-hotel group, NEW Hotel is the latest entry on the high-end Athens scene.

Eating

Eat streets include Mitropoleos, Adrianou and Navarchou Apostoli in Monastiraki, the area around Plateia Psyrri, and Gazi, near Keramikos metro.

The fruit and vegetable **market** (Varvakios Agora; Athinas, btwn Sofokleous & Evripidou; ⏲7am-3pm Mon-Sat; M Monastiraki, Panepistimio, Omonia) is opposite the meat market.

★ **Akordeon** MEZEDHES €
(☎210 325 3703; Hristokopidou 7, Psyrri; dishes €6-15; ⏲lunch & dinner; M Monastiraki, Thisio) Slide into this charming butter-yellow house across from a church in a quiet Psyrri side street for a warm welcome by musician-chefs Pepi and Achilleas (and their spouses), who run this excellent venue on the local music and mezedhes scene. They'll help you order authentic Greek fare, then (at night and on weekends) surround you with their soulful songs.

★ **Mavro Provato** MEZEDHES €
(☎210 722 3466; www.tomauroprovato.gr; Arrianou 31-33, Pangrati; dishes €5-12; ⏲lunch & dinner; M Evangelismos) Book ahead for this wildly popular modern *mezedhopoleio* (restaurant specialising in mezedhes) in Pangrati, where tables line the footpath and delicious small plates are paired with *raki* (Cretan firewater) or *tsipouro* (distilled spirit similar to ouzo but usually stronger).

★ **Kalnterimi** TAVERNA €
(☎210 331 0049; www.kalnterimi.gr; Plateia Agion Theodoron, cnr Skouleniou, Monastiraki; mains €5-8; ⏲noon-11pm Mon-Sat; M Panepistimio)

RTH A TRIP

LAND IN A DAY: AEGINA & HYDRA

For islands within easy reach of Athens, head to the Saronic Gulf. **Aegina** (eh-yee-nah; www.aeginagreece.com), just a half hour from Piraeus, is home to the impressive **Temple of Aphaia**, said to have served as a model for the construction of the Parthenon. The catwalk queen of the Saronics, **Hydra** (ee-drah; www.hydra.gr, www.hydraislandgreece.com) is a delight, an hour and a half from Piraeus. Its picturesque horseshoe-shaped harbour town with gracious stone mansions stacked up the rocky hillsides is known as a retreat for artists, writers and celebrities. There are no motorised vehicles – apart from sanitation trucks – leading to unspoilt trails along the coast and into the mountains.

From Hydra, you can return to Piraeus, or carry on to Spetses and the Peloponnese (Metohi, Ermione and Porto Heli). Check **Hellenic Seaways** (www.hsw.gr) and **Aegina Flying Dolphins** (www.aegeanflyingdolphins.gr).

Find your way behind the Church of Agii Theodori to this hidden, open-air taverna offering Greek food at its most authentic. Everything is freshly cooked and delicious: you can't go wrong. Hand-painted tables spill onto the footpath along a pedestrian street and give a feeling of peace in one of the busiest parts of the city.

★Diporto Agoras TAVERNA €

(☎210 321 1463; cnr Theatrou & Sokratous; plates €5-7; ⏲7am-7pm Mon-Sat, closed 1-20 Aug; Ⓜ Omonia, Monastiraki) This quirky old taverna is one of the dining gems of Athens. There's no signage, only two doors leading to a rustic cellar where there's no menu, just a few dishes that haven't changed in years. The house speciality is *revythia* (chickpeas), usually followed by grilled fish and washed down with wine from one of the giant barrels lining the wall. The often erratic service is part of the appeal.

★Avocado VEGETARIAN €

(☎210 323 7878; www.avocadoathens.com; Nikis 30, Plaka; mains €8-13; ⏲noon-11pm Mon-Fri, 11am-11pm Sat, noon-7pm Sun; 📶✎; Ⓜ Syntagma) This excellent, popular cafe offers a full array of vegan, gluten-free and organic treats – a rarity in Greece. Next to an organic market, and with a tiny front patio, you can enjoy everything from sandwiches to quinoa with eggplant or mixed-veg coconut curry. Fresh juices and mango lassis are all made on the spot.

★Varvakios Agora MARKET €

(Athens Central Market; Athinas, btwn Sofokleous & Evripidou, Omonia; ⏲7am-6pm Mon-Sat; Ⓜ Monastiraki, Panepistimio, Omonia) The streets around the colourful and bustling Varvakios Agora are a sensory delight. The **meat and fish market** fills the historic building on the eastern side, and the **fruit and vegetable market** is across the road. The meat market might sound like a strange place to go for a meal, but its **tavernas** are an Athenian institution. Clients range from hungry market workers to elegant couples emerging from nightclubs in search of a bowl of hangover-busting *patsas* (tripe soup).

★2 Mazi FUSION €€

(☎210 322 2839; www.2mazi.gr; Nikis 48, Plaka; mains €17-26; ⏲12.30pm-midnight; Ⓜ Syntagma, Akropoli) Inside a neoclassical mansion, this elegant dining room with white linen and proper crystal is the venue for inventive creations by two young chefs. They incorporate fresh local products such as mountain greens, Greek cheeses and freshly caught seafood to make interesting and beautifully presented dishes spanning the cuisines of Asia, France and the Greek islands.

★Athiri GREEK €€

(☎210 346 2983; www.athirirestaurant.gr; Plateon 15, Keramikos; mains €12-19; ⏲8pm-1am Tue-Sat, 1-5pm Sun; Ⓜ Thisio) Athiri's lovely garden courtyard is a verdant surprise in this pocket of Keramikos. The small but innovative menu plays on Greek regional classics. Try Santorini fava and the hearty beef stew with *myzithra* (sheep's-milk cheese) and handmade pasta from Karpathos.

★Mani Mani GREEK €€

(☎210 921 8180; www.manimani.com.gr/english.html; Falirou 10, Makrygianni; mains €15-20; ⏲2-11pm Mon-Sat, 1-6pm Sun; Ⓜ Akropoli) Head upstairs to the relaxing, cheerful dining rooms of this delightful modern restaurant, which specialises in regional cuisine from Mani in the Peloponnese. Standouts include the ravioli with Swiss chard, chervil and cheese, and the tangy Mani sausage with orange. Almost all dishes can be ordered as half portions (at half-price), allowing you to sample widely.

★ Funky Gourmet MEDITERRANEAN €€€
(☎210 524 2727; www.funkygourmet.com; Paramythias 3, cnr Salaminas, Keramikos; set menu from €150; ⏲7.30pm-1am Tue-Sat, last order 10.30pm; Ⓜ Metaxourgio) Nouveau gastronomy meets fresh Mediterranean ingredients at this two-Michelin star restaurant. Elegant lighting, refinement and sheer joy in food make this a worthwhile stop for any foodie. The degustation menus can be paired with wines. Book ahead.

★ Spondi MEDITERRANEAN €€€
(☎210 756 4021; www.spondi.gr; Pyrronos 5, Pangrati; mains €44-52, set menus from €73; ⏲8pm-late) Two Michelin-starred Spondi is frequently voted Athens' best restaurant, and the accolades are deserved. It offers Mediterranean haute cuisine, with heavy French influences, in a relaxed, chic setting in a charming old house. Choose from the menu or a range of set dinner and wine *prix fixes*.

Drinking & Entertainment

One local favoured pastime is going for coffee. Athens' ubiquitous, packed cafes have some of Europe's most expensive coffee (between €3 and €5) – you're essentially hiring the chair and can linger for hours. Many daytime cafes and restaurants turn into bars and clubs at night.

The city's hottest scene masses around Kolokotroni north of Plateia Syntagmatos, and around Plateia Agia Irini in Monastiraki. A cafe-thick area in Monastiraki is Adrianou, along the Ancient Agora, where people fill shady tables. Psyrri has seen a recent resurgence, while Kolonaki steadfastly attracts the trendier set, and Gazi remains tried-and-true. For the best dancing in summer, cab it to beach clubs along the coast near Glyfada – city locations close earlier.

English-language entertainment information appears daily in the 'Kathimerini' supplement in the *International Herald Tribune*; Athens Plus also has listings. For comprehensive events listings, with links to online ticket sales points, try the following: www.breathtakingathens.gr, www.elculture.gr, www.tickethour.com, www.tickethouse.gr, www.ticketservices.gr.

With the current financially strapped climate in Athens, watch your back wherever you go.

DON'T MISS

SUMMER CINEMA

One of the delights of hot summer nights in Athens is the enduring tradition of open-air cinema, where you can watch the latest Hollywood or art-house flick under moonlight. The most historic outdoor cinema is **Aigli** (☎210 336 9369; www.aeglizappiou.gr; Zappeio Gardens, Syntagma; €8.50; ⏲films at 9pm & 11pm; Ⓜ Syntagma), in the verdant Zappeio Gardens, where you can watch a movie in style with a glass of wine.

Shopping

Find boutiques around Syntagma, from the Attica department store past Voukourestiou and on Ermou; designer brands and cool shops in Kolonaki; and souvenirs, folk art and leather in Plaka and Monastiraki with its fun **Monastiraki Flea Market** (btwn Adrianou, Ifestou & Ermou, Monastiraki; ⏲daily May-Oct, closed Thu & Sat Nov-Apr; Ⓜ Monastiraki).

Information

DANGERS & ANNOYANCES

Crime has risen in Athens with the onset of the financial crisis. Though violent crime remains relatively rare, travellers should stay alert on the streets, especially at night.

- Streets surrounding Omonia have become markedly seedier, with an increase in prostitutes and junkies; avoid the area, especially at night.
- Watch for pickpockets on the metro and at the markets.
- When taking taxis, ask the driver to use the meter or negotiate a price in advance. Ignore stories that the hotel you've chosen is closed

REMBETIKA

Athens has some of the best *rembetika* (Greek blues) in intimate, evocative venues. Performances usually include both *rembetika* and *laïka* (urban popular music), start at around 11.30pm and do not have a cover charge, though drinks can be expensive. Most close May to September, so in summer try live-music tavernas around Plaka and Psyrri. There's also live music most weekends at **Café Avyssinia** (☎210 321 7047; Kynetou 7, Monastiraki; mains €10-16; ⏲11am-1am Tue-Sat, to 7pm Sun; Ⓜ Monastiraki) and Akordeon (p343).

UNCERTAIN TIMES

➡ Due to the financial difficulties in Greece, opening hours, prices and even the existence of some establishments have fluctuated much more than usual.

➡ With businesses associated with tourism, opening hours can always be haphazard; if trade is good, they're open, if not, they shut.

➡ 'High season' is usually July and August. If you turn up in 'shoulder seasons' (May and June; September and October) expect to pay significantly less. Things may be dirt cheap or closed in winter.

or full: they're angling for a commission from another hotel.

➡ Bar scams are commonplace, particularly in Plaka and Syntagma. Beware the over-friendly!

➡ With the recent financial reforms in Greece have come strikes in Athens (check http://livingingreece.gr/strikes). Picketers tend to march in Plateia Syntagmatos.

EMERGENCY

Ambulance/First-Aid Advice (☎166)

Pharmacies (☎in Greek 1434) Check pharmacy windows for details of the nearest duty pharmacy. There's a 24-hour pharmacy at the airport.

SOS Doctors (☎1016, 210 821 1888; ⏲24hr) Pay service with English-speaking doctors.

INTERNET RESOURCES

Official visitor site (www.thisisathens.org)

TOURIST INFORMATION

EOT (Greek National Tourist Organisation; ☎210 331 0716, 210 331 0347; www.visitgreece.gr; Dionysiou Areopagitou 18-20, Makrygianni; ⏲8am-8pm Mon-Fri, 10am-4pm Sat & Sun May-Sep, 9am-7pm Mon-Fri Oct-Apr; Ⓜ Akropoli) Free *Athens* map, transport information and *Athens & Attica* booklet. There's also a desk at **Athens Airport** (⏲9am-5pm Mon-Fri & 10am-4pm Sat).

Athens Airport Information Desk (⏲24hr) This 24-hour desk has Athens info, booklets and the Athens Spotlighted discount card for goods and services.

Athens City Information Kiosks (www.breathtakingathens.com) **Airport** (☎210 353 0390; ⏲8am-8pm; Ⓜ Airport); **Acropolis** (☎210 321 7116; Dionysiou Areopagitou & Leoforos Syngrou; ⏲9am-9pm May-Sep; Ⓜ Akropoli) Maps, transport information and all Athens info.

Getting There & Away

AIR

Modern **Eleftherios Venizelos International Airport** (ATH; ☎210 353 0000; www.aia.gr) is 27km east of Athens.

BOAT

Most ferries, hydrofoils and high-speed catamarans leave from the massive port at Piraeus. Some depart from smaller ports at Rafina and Lavrio.

Purchase tickets at booths on the quay next to each ferry, over the phone or online; travel agencies selling tickets also surround each port.

BUS

Athens has two main intercity **KTEL** (☎210 880 8000; www.ktelattikis.gr) bus stations: **Liossion Terminal B** (☎210 831 7153; Liossion 260, Thymarakia; Ⓜ Agios Nikolaos, Attiki), 5km north of Omonia with buses to central and northern Greece (Delphi, Meteora), and **Kifissos Terminal A** (☎210 515 0025; Leoforos Kifisou 100, Peristeri; Ⓜ Agios Antonios), 7km north of Omonia, with buses to Thessaloniki, the Peloponnese, Ionian Islands and western Greece. The KTEL website and tourist offices have timetables.

Buses for southern Attica (Rafina, Lavrio, Sounio) leave from the **Mavromateon Terminal** (☎210 880 8080, 210 822 5148, 210 880 8000; www.ktelattikis.gr; cnr Leoforos Alexandras & 28 Oktovriou-Patision, Pedion Areos; Ⓜ Viktoria), about 250m north of the National Archaeological Museum.

CAR & MOTORCYCLE

The airport has car rental, and Syngrou, just south of the Temple of Olympian Zeus, is dotted with car-hire firms, though driving in Athens is treacherous.

TRAIN

Intercity trains to central and northern Greece depart from the central **Larisis train station** (Stathmos Larisis; ☎14511; www.trainose.gr; Ⓜ Larisis), about 1km northwest of Plateia Omonias, and served by the metro. For the Peloponnese, take the suburban rail to Kiato and change for other OSE services, or check for available lines at the Larisis station.

ℹ Getting Around

TO/FROM THE AIRPORT

Bus

Tickets cost €5. Twenty-four-hour services:

Piraeus Port Bus X96, 1½ hours, every 20 minutes

Plateia Syntagmatos Bus X95, 60 to 90 minutes, every 30 minutes (the Syntagma stop is on Othonos)

Terminal A (Kifissos) Bus Station Bus X93, 60 minutes, every 30 to 60 minutes

Metro

Blue line 3 links the airport to the city centre in around 40 minutes; it operates from Monastiraki from 5.50am to midnight, and from the airport from 5.30am to 11.30pm. Tickets (€8) are valid for all public transport for 70 minutes. Fare for two passengers is €14 total.

Taxi

Fixed fares are posted. Expect day/night €35/50 to the city centre, and €47/72 to Piraeus. Both trips often take at least an hour, longer with heavy traffic. Check www.athensairporttaxi.com for more info.

PUBLIC TRANSPORT

The metro, tram and bus system makes getting around central Athens and to Piraeus easy. Athens' road traffic can be horrendous. Get maps and timetables at the tourist offices or **Athens Urban Transport Organisation** (OASA; ☎11185; www.oasa.gr).

Tickets good for 70 minutes (€1.20), or a 24-hour/five-day travel pass (€4/10) are valid for all forms of public transport except for airport services. The three-day tourist ticket (€20) includes airport transport. Bus/trolleybus-o[nly] tickets cannot be used on the metro.

Children under six travel free; people under 18 or over 65 pay half-fare. Buy tickets in metro stations, transport kiosks or most *periptera* (kiosks). Validate the ticket in the machine as you board.

Bus & Trolleybus

Buses and electric trolleybuses operate every 15 minutes from 5am to midnight.

To get to Piraeus: from Syntagma and Filellinon to Akti Xaveriou catch bus 040; from the Omonia end of Athinas to Plateia Themistokleous, catch bus 049.

Metro

Trains operate from 5am to midnight (Friday and Saturday to around 2am), every four to 10 minutes. Get timetables at www.stasy.gr.

TAXI

Taxis are generally reasonable, with small surcharges for port, train and bus station pickups, baggage over 10kg or radio taxi. Insist on a metered rate (except for posted flat rates at the airport). Taxi services include **Athina 1** (☎210 921 2800, 210 921 0417), **Enotita** (☎210 649 5099, 18388; www.athensradiotaxienotita.gr), **Taxibeat** (www.taxibeat.gr) and **Parthenon** (☎210 532 3300; www.radiotaxi-parthenon.gr).

TRAIN

Suburban Rail (☎14511; www.trainose.gr) A fast suburban rail links Athens with the airport, Piraeus, the outer regions and the northern Peloponnese. It connects to the metro at Larisis, Doukissis Plakentias and Nerantziotissa stations, and goes from the airport to Kiato.

PIRAEUS PORT

Greece's main port and ferry hub fills seemingly endless quays with ships, hydrofoils and catamarans heading all over the country. All ferry companies have online timetables and booths on the quays. EOT (p346) in Athens has a weekly schedule, or check www.openseas.gr. Schedules are reduced in April, May and October, and are radically cut in winter, especially to smaller islands. When buying tickets, confirm the departure point – some Cyclades boats leave from Rafina or Lavrio, and Patras port serves Italy and the Ionian Islands. Igoumenitsa also serves Corfu.

The fastest and most convenient link to Athens is the metro (€1.20, 40 minutes, every 10 minutes, 5am to midnight), near the ferries. Piraeus has a station for Athens' suburban rail.

Left luggage at the metro station costs €3 per 24 hours.

The **X96** (Plateia Karaïskaki; tickets €5) Piraeus–Athens Airport Express (€5) leaves from the southwestern corner of Plateia Karaïskaki. Bus 040 goes to Syntagma in downtown Athens.

The Peloponnese encompasses a breathtaking array of landscapes, villages and ruins, where much of Greek history has played out.

Nafplio Ναύπλιο

POP 14,200

Elegant Venetian houses and neoclassical mansions dripping with crimson bougainvillea cascade down Nafplio's hillside to the azure sea. Vibrant cafes, shops and restaurants fill winding pedestrian streets. Crenulated Palamidi Fortress perches above it all. What's not to love?

Sights

★Palamidi Fortress FORTRESS

(☎27520 28036; adult/concession €4/2; ⊙8am-6.45pm May-Oct, 8am-2.45pm Nov-Apr) This vast, spectacular citadel, reachable either by steep ascent on foot or a short drive, stands on a 216m-high outcrop of rock that gives all-encompassing views of Nafplio and the Argolic Gulf. It was built by the Venetians between 1711 and 1714, and is regarded as a masterpiece of military architecture in spite of being successfully stormed in one night by Greek troops in 1822, causing the Turkish garrison within to surrender without a fight.

★Archaeological Museum MUSEUM

(☎27520 27502; Plateia Syntagmatos; adult/child €6/3; ⊙8am-3pm Tue-Sun) Inside a splendid Venetian building, this museum traces the social development of Argolis, from the hunter-gatherers of the Fragthi cave to the sophisticated Mycenaean-era civilisations, through beautifully presented archaeological finds from the surrounding area. Exhibits range from Paleolithic fire middens, dating from 32,000 BC, to elaborately painted amphorae (circa 520 BC). You may also spot the only existing bronze armour from near Mycenae (3500 years old and complete with boar-tusk helmet), a wealth of funereal offerings and ceremonial clay masks.

Peloponnesian Folklore Foundation Museum MUSEUM

(☎27520 28379; www.pli.gr; Vasileos Alexandrou 1; adult/child €2/free; ⊙9am-2:30pm Mon-Sat, 9:30am-3pm Sun) Established by its philanthropic owner, Nafplio's award-winning museum is a beautifully arranged collection of folk costumes and household items from Nafplio's 19th- and early 20th-century history. Be wowed by the intricate embroidery of traditional costumes and the heavy silver adornments; admire the turn-of-the-century couture and see if you can spot a horse-tricycle. The gift shop sells high-quality local crafts.

Sleeping

The Old Town is *the* place to stay, but it has few budget options. Cheaper spots dot the road to Argos and Tolo.

★Nafplion 1841 PENSION €

(☎27520 24622; www.nafplion1841.gr; Kapodistriou 9; s incl breakfast €50, d incl breakfast €55-85, tr incl breakfast €95; ❄📶) Not only does this delightful pension occupy a 19th-century mansion, but its five bright rooms offer contemporary creature comforts without diminishing the building's character. Expect Cocomat mattresses, superior bed linens, climate control, hydro-massage showers and plasma-screen TVs. The hostess is a delight and so is the breakfast.

Amfitriti Pension PENSION €€

(☎27520 96250; www.amfitriti-pension.gr; Kapodistriou 24; d incl breakfast from €90; ❄📶) Quaint antiques fill these intimate rooms in a house in the Old Town. You can also enjoy stellar views at its nearby sister hotel, **Amfitriti Belvedere**, which is chock-full of brightly coloured tapestries and emits a feeling of cheery serenity.

Eating

Nafplio's Old Town streets are loaded with standard tavernas, with best eats around Vasilissis Olgas.

Ta Fanaria GREEK €

(☎27520 27141; www.fanaria.gr; Staikopoulou 14; mains €7-15; ⊙noon-midnight; 🖉) This intimate taverna wins points not just for the attentive service but also for its superior selection of vegetarian dishes (think spinach and feta pie, okra stew, oven-baked veggies) alongside the dolmadhes (vine leaves stuffed with rice and sometimes meat) and other Greek classics.

Faro Taverna SEAFOOD €€

(☎27520 27704; Mili; mains €8-15; ⊙noon-11pm) Locally famous and well worth the 10-minute drive around the bay from Nafplio, this taverna, run by the grandson of the original owner, sits right on Mili Beach. You can't go wrong with the catch of the day, be it freshly grilled squid, red mullet, fresh sardines or anchovies.

★ **3Sixty°** INTERNATIONAL €€€
(☎27525 00501; www.3sixtycafe.gr; Papanikolaou 26 & Koletti; dinner mains €20-64; ⏰9am-1am;) Nafplio punches above its culinary weight at the most imaginative restaurant in town. Sophisticated fare includes the likes of smoky aubergine *imam* with veal, wild mushroom risotto with truffle oil, and lamb stuffed with goat gruyère. Salads are equally creative. The sultry bar serves potent signature cocktails (we're fans of Legendary Star) and numerous Greek wines.

Information

Staikos Tours (☎27520 27950; www.rentacarnafplio.gr; Bouboulinas 50; ⏰8.30am-2.30pm & 5.30-9pm) A helpful outfit offering Avis rental cars and full travel services.

Getting There & Away

KTEL Argolis Bus Station (☎27520 27323; www.ktelargolida.gr; Syngrou) has the following services:

Argos (for Peloponnese connections) €1.60, 30 minutes, hourly

Athens €13.10, 2½ hours, hourly (via Corinth)

Epidavros €2.90, 45 minutes, four to six Monday to Saturday, one Sunday

Mycenae €2.90, one hour, two to three daily

Epidavros Επίδαυρος

In its day **Epidavros** (☎27530 22009; adult/concession incl museum and Sanctuary of Asclepius €12/6; ⏰8am-8pm, reduced hours Sep-Mar; P) was famed as far away as Rome as a place of miraculous healing. Visitors came great distances to this Sanctuary of Asclepius (god of medicine), set amid pine-clad hills, to seek a cure for their ailments. Don't miss the peaceful Sanctuary of Asclepius, an ancient spa and healing centre.

This World Heritage site's remarkably well-preserved theatre remains a venue during the Hellenic Festival (p342) for Classical Greek theatre, first performed here up to 2000 years ago.

Go as a day trip from Nafplio (€2.90, 45 minutes, four to six buses Monday to Saturday, one Sunday).

Mycenae Μυκήνες

Although settled as early as the 6th millennium BC, **Ancient Mycenae** (☎27510 76585; adult/concession incl Ancient Mycenae museum & Agamemon's Tomb €12/6; ⏰8am-8pm Apr-Oct, to 3pm Nov-Mar), pronounced mih-*kee*-nes, was at its most powerful from 1600 to 1200 BC. Mycenae's grand entrance, the Lion Gate, is Europe's oldest monumental sculpture.

Two daily buses (excluding Sundays) head to Mycenae from Nafplio (€2.60, one hour) and Argos (€1.60, 30 minutes).

Mystras Μυστράς

The captivating ruins of churches, libraries, strongholds and palaces in the fortress town of Mystras (miss-*trahss*), a World Heritage-listed site, spill from a spur of the Taÿgetos Mountains 7km west of Sparta. It's among the most important historical sites in the Peloponnese. This is where the Byzantine Empire's richly artistic and intellectual culture made its last stand before an invading Ottoman army, almost 1000 years after its foundation.

Traveller facilities are found in Mystras village, 1km or so below the main gate of ancient Mystras. Staying in the village allows you to beat the crowds and the heat. The stunning **Traditional Guesthouse Mazaraki** (☎27310 20414; www.xenonasmazaraki.gr; Pikoulianika; d €85, ste €120-150, apt €190; incl breakfast; P) is a destination in itself.

Olympia Ολυμπία

POP 1000

The compact modern village of Olympia (o-lim-bee-ah), lined with souvenir shops and eateries, caters to the coach-loads of tourists who pass through on their way to the most famous sight in the Peloponnese: Ancient Olympia. This is where myth and fact merge – where Zeus allegedly held the first Olympic Games and where the first Olympics were staged in 776 BC, and every four years thereafter until AD 393, when Emperor Theodosius I banned them.

Just 500m south of the village, across the Kladeos River, the remains of **Ancient Olympia** (☎26240 22517; adult/concession site & Olympic museums €12/6; ⏰8am-8pm Apr-Oct, to 3pm Nov-Mar) rest amid luxurious greenery. The Olympic Flame is lit here every four

GREEK HISTORY IN A NUTSHELL

With its strategic position at the crossroads of Europe and Asia, Greece has endured a vibrant and turbulent history. During the Bronze Age (3000–1200 BC in Greece), the advanced Cycladic, Minoan and Mycenaean civilisations flourished. The Mycenaeans were swept aside in the 12th century BC by the warrior-like Dorians, who introduced Greece to the Iron Age.

By 800 BC, when Homer's *Odyssey* and *Iliad* were first written down, Greece was undergoing a cultural and military revival with the evolution of the city states, the most powerful of which were Athens and Sparta, and the development of democracy. The unified Greeks repelled the Persians twice, which was followed by an era of unparalleled growth and prosperity known as the Classical (or Golden) Age.

The Golden Age

During this period, Pericles commissioned the Parthenon, Sophocles wrote *Oedipus the King* and Socrates taught young Athenians to think. The era ended with the Peloponnesian War (431–404 BC), when the militaristic Spartans defeated the Athenians. They failed to notice the expansion of Macedonia under King Philip II, who conquered the war-weary city states.

Philip's son, Alexander the Great, marched triumphantly into Asia Minor, Egypt, Persia and parts of what are now Afghanistan and India. In 323 BC he met an untimely death at the age of 33, and his generals divided his empire between themselves.

Roman Rule & the Byzantine Empire

Roman incursions into Greece began in 205 BC. By 146 BC Greece and Macedonia had become Roman provinces. In the centuries that followed, Venetians, Franks, Normans, Slavs, Persians, Arabs and, finally, Turks, took turns chipping away at the Byzantine Empire.

The Ottoman Empire & Independence

After the end of the Byzantine Empire in 1453, when Constantinople fell to the Turks, most of Greece became part of the Ottoman Empire. The Greeks fought the War of Independence from 1821 to 1832, and in 1827 Ioannis Kapodistrias was elected the first Greek president.

years. Don't miss the statue of Hermes of Praxiteles, a classical-sculpture masterpiece, at the exceptional **Archaeological Museum** (adult/concession site & Olympic museums €12/6; ⌚8am-8pm May-Oct, 8am-3pm Nov-Apr).

Sparkling-clean **Pension Posidon** (☎26240 22567; www.pensionposidon.gr; Stefanopoulou 9; s/d/tr incl breakfast €35/40/45; ❄) and quiet, spacious **Hotel Pelops** (☎26240 22543; www.hotelpelops.gr; Varela 2; s/d/tr incl breakfast €45/60/80; ❄@📶) offer the best value in the centre. Family-run **Best Western Europa** (☎26240 22650; www.hoteleuropa.gr; Drouva 1; s/d/tr incl breakfast €75/94/105; P❄@📶🏊) above town has sweeping vistas from room balconies and the wonderful swimming pool.

Buses depart from in front of the train station. There are services to Pyrgos (€2.30, 30 minutes, eight to 13 daily), with four or five handy Athens connections, and to Tripoli (€14.30, three hours) – reserve your seat with KTEL Pyrgos one day in advance. Train services head to/from Pyrgos only – there are five departures daily (€2, 30 minutes).

CENTRAL GREECE
ΚΕΝΤΡΙΚΗ ΕΛΛΑΔΑ

Central Greece's dramatic landscape of deep gorges, rugged mountains and fertile valleys is home to the magical stone pinnacle-topping monasteries of Meteora and the iconic ruins of ancient Delphi, where Alexander the Great sought advice from the Delphic oracle. Established in 1938, **Parnassos National Park** (☎22340 23529; http://en.parnassosnp.gr), to the north of Delphi, attracts naturalists, hikers (it's part of the E4 European long-distance path) and skiers.

Delphi Δελφοί

POP 854

Modern Delphi and its adjoining ruins hang stunningly on the slopes of Mt Parnassos overlooking the shimmering Gulf of Corinth.

According to mythology, Zeus released two eagles at opposite ends of the world and they met here, thus making Delphi the centre of the world. By the 6th century BC, **Ancient Delphi** (☎22650 82312; site or museum adult/child €6/free, combined €9; ⏲8am-8pm Apr-Oct, 8am-3pm Nov-Mar) had become the Sanctuary of Apollo. Thousands of pilgrims flocked here to consult the female oracle who sat at the mouth of a fume-emitting chasm. After sacrificing a sheep or goat, pilgrims would ask a question, and a priest would translate the oracle's response into verse. Wars, voyages and business transactions were undertaken on the strength of these prophecies.

In the town centre, **Rooms Pitho** (☎22650 82850; www.pithohotel.gr; Vasileon Pavlou & Friderikis 40a; s/d/tr incl breakfast from €45/55/70; ❄📶) is friendly, and cosy **Hotel Sibylla** (☎22650 82335; www.sibylla-hotel.gr; Vasileon Pavlou & Friderikis 9; s/d/tr €30/35/40; ❄📶) has tidy rooms and views across the gulf. Elegant, modern **Hotel Apollonia** (☎22650 82919; www.hotelapollonia.gr; Syngrou 37-39; s/d incl breakfast €75/90; ❄@📶) has balcony views all over Delphi.

Apollon Camping (☎22650 82762; www.apolloncamping.gr; campsites per person/tent €8.50/5; P@📶≋) is just 2km west of town, with a restaurant, pool and minimarket.

At the excellent, family-run **Taverna Vakhos** (☎22650 83186; www.vakhos.com; Apollonos 31; mains €8-15; ⏲noon-late; 📶) they serve traditional dishes while locals pack **Taverna Gargadouas** (Vasileon Pavlou & Friderikis; mains €8-10; ⏲noon-late) for grilled meats and slow-roasted lamb.

Buses depart from the eastern end of Friderikis, opposite the old Hotel Vouza. Tickets must be purchased from The Delphi restaurant between 9am and 8pm. Four to five buses head daily to Athens Liossion Terminal B (€15.10, three hours). For Meteora/Kalambaka, take a bus to Lamia (€9.10, two hours, one daily) to transfer.

Meteora Μετέωρα

Meteora (meh-*teh*-o-rah) should be a certified Wonder of the World with its magnificent late-14th-century monasteries perched dramatically atop enormous rocky pinnacles.

Sights

While there were once monasteries on all 24 pinnacles, only six are still occupied: **Megalou Meteorou** (Grand Meteoron; €3; ⏲9am-1pm & 3.30-6pm Wed-Mon Apr-Oct, to 5pm Thu-Mon Nov-Mar), **Varlaam** (€3; ⏲9am-1pm & 3.30-6pm Sat-Thu Apr-Oct, until 5pm Sat-Wed Nov-Mar), **Agiou Stefanou** (€3; ⏲9am-1.30pm & 3.30-6pm Tue-Sun Apr-Oct, 9.30am-1pm & 3-5pm Tue-Sun Nov-Mar), **Agias Triados** (Holy Trinity; €3; ⏲9am-5.45pm Fri-Wed Apr-Oct, 9am-12.30pm & 3-5pm Sat-Wed Nov-Mar), **Agiou Nikolaou** (Monastery of St Nikolaou Anapafsa; €3; ⏲9am-3.30pm Sat-Thu Nov-Mar, to 2pm Apr-Oct) and **Agias Varvaras Rousanou** (€3; ⏲9am-6pm Thu-Tue Apr-Oct, to 2pm Nov-Mar). Strict dress codes apply (no bare shoulders or knees and women must wear skirts; you can borrow a long skirt at the door). Walk the footpaths between monasteries, drive the back asphalt road, or take the bus (€1.20, 20 minutes) that departs from Kalambaka and Kastraki at 9am, and returns at 1pm (12.40pm on weekends).

Meteora's stunning rocks are also a climbing paradise. **Visit Meteora** (☎24320 23820; www.visitmeteora.travel; Patriarchou Dimitriou 2, Kalambaka; ⏲9am-9pm) offers some excellent opportunities with professional guides Lazaros Botelis and Kostas Liolios.

MT OLYMPUS

Just as it did for the ancients, Greece's highest mountain, **Olympus** (☎23520 83000; www.olympusfd.gr), the cloud-covered lair of the Greek pantheon, fires the visitor's imagination today. The highest of Olympus' eight peaks is **Mytikas** (2917m), popular with trekkers, who use **Litohoro** (305m), 5km inland from the Athens–Thessaloniki highway, as their base. The main route up takes two days, with a stay overnight at one of the **refuges** (⏲May-Oct). Good protective clothing is essential, even in summer. **EOS Litohoro** (Greek Alpine Club; ☎23520 84544, 23520 82444; http://eoslitohorou.blogspot.com; ⏲9.30am-12.30pm & 6-8pm Mon-Sat Jun-Sep) has information.

Sleeping & Eating

The tranquil village of Kastraki, 2km from Kalambaka, is the best base for visiting Meteora.

Pyrgos Adrachti BOUTIQUE HOTEL €€
(☎24320 22275; www.hotel-adrachti.gr; d €55-80, tr €85; P ❄ 📶) Slick and cool sums up this place – think designer-style touches throughout the rooms, bar and common areas, and an up-close-and-personal rock experience. Plus there's a tidy garden to relax in post-activities. It's at the northern end of the village, nestled under the rocks; follow the signs.

Batalogianni TAVERNA €
(☎3202 3253; mains €7-12; ⏰8am-late) You know the type of place you wouldn't look twice at 'cos it's slightly off the road and you don't realise it has an oasis of a garden terrace and serves up delicious 100% homemade *mayirefta* (ready-cooked meals)? This charming little spot is all that. Open all year.

Getting There & Around

Local buses shuttle between Kalambaka and Kastraki (€1.20). Hourly buses go from Kalambaka's **KTEL bus station** (☎24320 22432; www.ktel-trikala.gr; Ikonomou) to the transport hub of Trikala (€2.30, 30 minutes), from where buses go to Ioannina (€12.50, 2½ hours, two daily) and Athens (€29, five hours, seven daily).

From Kalambaka **train station** (☎24320 22451; www.trainose.gr), trains run to Athens (regular/IC €18 to €29, 4½/five hours, both once daily) and Thessaloniki (€15.20, four hours, three daily). You may need to change in Paleofarsalos.

NORTHERN GREECE
ΒΟΡΕΙΑ ΕΛΛΑΔΑ

Northern Greece is graced with magnificent mountains, thick forests, tranquil lakes and archaeological sites. It's easy to get off the beaten track and experience aspects of Greece noticeably different to other mainland areas and the islands.

Thessaloniki Θεσσαλονίκη

POP 325,200

Dodge cherry sellers in the street, smell spices in the air and enjoy waterfront breezes in Thessaloniki (thess-ah-lo-*nee*-kih), also known as Salonica. The second city of Byzantium and of modern Greece boasts countless Byzantine churches, a smattering of Roman ruins, engaging museums, shopping to rival Athens, fine restaurants and a lively cafe scene and nightlife.

Sights

Check out the seafront **White Tower** (Lefkos Pyrgos; ☎2310 267 832; www.lpth.gr; adult/student €3/2; ⏰8.30am-3pm Tue-Sun, to 8pm in summer) with its spine-chillling history, and wander *hammams* (Turkish baths), Ottoman and Roman sites like Galerius' **Rotunda** (☎2310 218 720; Plateia Agiou Georgiou; ⏰9am-5pm Tue-Sun) FREE, and churches such as the enormous, revered 5th-century **Church of Agios Dimitrios** (☎2310 270 008; www.inad.gr; Agiou Dimitriou 97; ⏰8am-10pm) with its crypt containing the relics of the city's patron saint.

The award-winning **Museum of Byzantine Culture** (☎2313 306 400; www.mbp.gr; Leoforos Stratou 2; adult/student €8/4 Apr-Oct, €4 Nov-Mar; ⏰8am-8pm Apr-Oct, 9am-4pm Nov-Mar) beautifully displays splendid sculptures, mosaics, icons and other intriguing artefacts. The outstanding **Archaeological Museum** (☎2310 830 538; www.amth.gr; Manoli Andronikou 6; adult/concession €8/4; ⏰8am-8pm daily) showcases prehistoric, ancient Macedonian and Hellenistic finds.

The compelling **Thessaloniki Centre of Contemporary Art** (☎231 059 3270; www.cact.gr; Warehouse B1; adult/child €3/1.50; ⏰10am-6pm Tue-Sat, hours vary) and hip **Thessaloniki Museum of Photography** (☎2310 566 716; www.thmphoto.gr; Warehouse A, Port; adult/student €2/1; ⏰11am-7pm Tue-Sun, to 10pm Fri), beside the port, are worth a look.

Sleeping

Thess Hostel HOSTEL €
(☎6937320162, 2310 554 120; http://thesshostel.gr; Ag Panton 12; dm/apt €18/49; 📶) This brand-new hostel is a splash of colour tucked into the backstreets behind the train station. The effusive warmth of the staff, the hostel's immaculate cleanliness and its provision of backpacker essentials (good wi-fi, 24-hour reception, a quirkily decorated hang-out area) are all impressive. Thess is well situated if you have an early start at the train or main bus station.

Colors Central Ladadika BOUTIQUE HOTEL €€
(☎2316 007 676; www.colorscentral.gr; Oplopiou 1, cnr Katouni; s/d/ste €70/80/100; ❄ 📶) This stylish boutique hotel, sister to the Colors hotel in Valaoritou, occupies a grand heritage

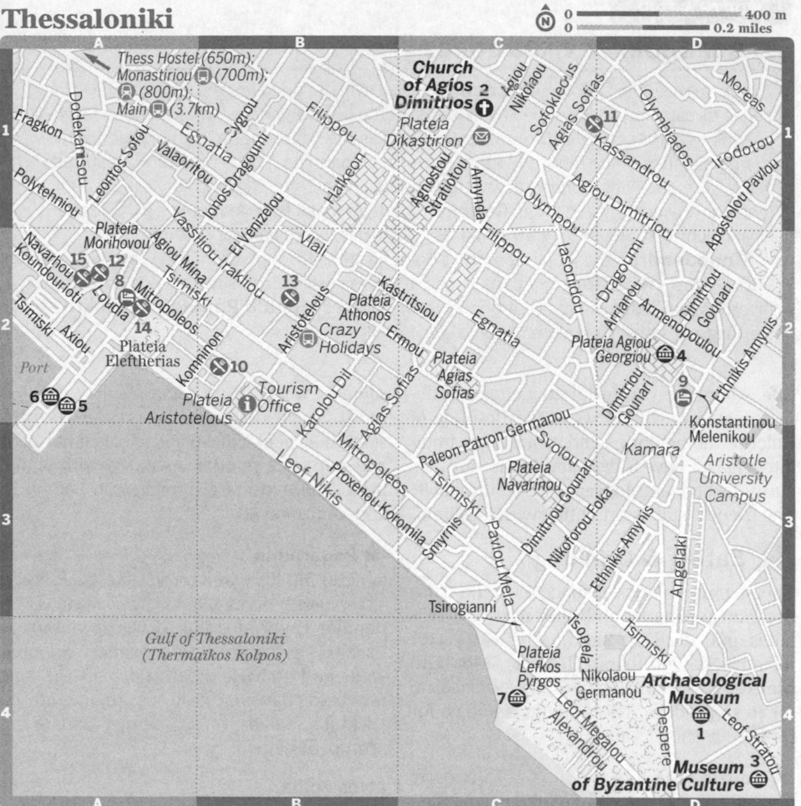

Thessaloniki

Top Sights

1 Archaeological Museum.......D4
2 Church of Agios Dimitrios.......C1
3 Museum of Byzantine Culture.......D4

Sights

4 Rotunda of Galerius.......D2
5 Thessaloniki Centre of Contemporary Art.......A2
6 Thessaloniki Museum of Photography.......A2
7 White Tower.......C4

Sleeping

8 Colors Central Ladadika.......A2
9 Rent Rooms Thessaloniki.......D2

Eating

10 Chatzis.......B2
11 I Nea Follia.......C1
12 Kouzina Kioupia.......A2
13 Modiano Market.......B2
14 Omikron.......A2
15 Paparouna.......A2

house with 12 uniquely decorated rooms. The modern pop-art decor and vibrant tones give it an uplifting, contemporary feel, and its location in the heart of Ladadika's restaurant quarter couldn't be better.

Rent Rooms Thessaloniki HOSTEL €€
(☎2310 204 080; www.rentrooms-thessaloniki.com; Konstantinou Melenikou 9; dm/s/d/tr/q incl breakfast €25/55/70/90/115; ❄📶) This excellent-value hostel and apartment accommodation has a charming back-garden

WORTH A TRIP

ZAGOROHORIA & VIKOS GORGE

Try not to miss the spectacular **Zagori region**, with its deep gorges, abundant wildlife, dense forests and snowcapped mountains. Some 46 charming villages, famous for their grey-slate architecture, and known collectively as the Zagorohoria, are sprinkled across a large expanse of the Pindos Mountains north of Ioannina. These beautifully restored gems were once only connected by stone paths and arching footbridges, but paved roads now wind between them. Get information on walks from Ioannina's **EOS** (Greek Alpine Club; 26510 22138; www.orivatikos.gr; Smyrnis 15; hours vary) office.

Monodendri is a popular departure point for treks through dramatic 12km-long, 900m-deep **Vikos Gorge**, with its sheer limestone walls. Exquisite inns with attached tavernas abound in remote (but popular) twin villages **Megalo Papingo** and **Mikro Papingo**. It's best to explore by rental car from Ioannina.

cafe, where you can tuck into a choice of filling breakfasts with views of the Rotunda of Galerius. Some dorms and rooms have mini-kitchens; all have fridges and bathrooms. Security lockers and luggage storage available. The friendly staff is brimming with local info.

Eating & Drinking

Thessaloniki is a great food town. Tavernas dot Plateia Athonos and cafes pack Leoforos Nikis, and the Ladadika quarter is tops for restaurants and bars. Head to **Modiano Market** (Vassiliou Irakliou or Ermo; 7am-6pm) for fresh produce. Thessaloniki is known for its sweets: shop around!

★Kouzina Kioupia TAVERNA €

(2310 553 239; www.kouzina-kioupia.gr; Plateia Morihovou 3-5; mains €5-10; 1pm-1am Mon-Sat, to 6pm Sun) Bright, friendly and spilling onto the plaza, this welcoming taverna fills with happy local families and tables full of friends. Straightforward taverna dishes are served with flare, and a good time is had by all. Occasional live music.

Omikron GREEK €

(2310 532 774; Oplopiou 3; mains €7-10; 1pm-late) This neat and tidy local favourite does excellent fresh fish and inventive grills, but most mouth-watering are the daily specials on the chalkboard by the door. Expect masterful use of oysters, market fish and herb-strewn salads.

Chatzis SWEETS €

(2310 221 655; http://chatzis.gr; Mitropoleos 24; sweets €1.40-4; 8am-late) Glistening syrup-soaked treats have been luring dessert fans into Chatzis since 1908, back when Thessaloniki was still an Ottoman city. Try the moist, sugar-rush-inducing *revani* (syrupy semolina cake), chickpea and raisin halva, or *rizogalo* (rice pudding) scented with cinnamon. There are also branches on Sofouli 73 and Venizelou 50.

★Paparouna GREEK €€

(2310 510 852; www.paparouna.com; Pangaiou 4, cnr Doxis; mains €9-14; 11am-3am) Ever-popular Paparouna has dishes as vibrant as its interior design. Bright primary-coloured walls and a checkerboard floor set the tone for bold flavours such as thyme-infused cocktails, salads of sea fennel and spice-crumbed seafood.

I Nea Follia GREEK €€

(2310 960 383; cnr Aristomenous & Haritos; mains €9-14; 1-11pm;) This is the kind of place Anthony Bourdain would like to discover. A bare-bones taverna opened in 1966 on a nondescript north-side alley, in recent years it was commandeered by three young chefs who serve classic Greek fare with a contemporary twist. Expertly sautéed shrimp, fig-strewn salads and juicy grills are all beautifully presented.

Information

Check www.enjoythessaloniki.com for current events.

Tourism Office (2310 229 070; www.visitgreece.gr; Plateia Aristotelous; 10am-5pm) The tourism office on Plateia Aristotelous can assist with hotel bookings, local information, and arranging tours and excursions beyond Thessaloniki.

Getting There & Away

AIR

Makedonia International Airport (SKG; ☎2310 985 000; www.thessalonikiairport.com) is 17km southeast of the centre and served by local bus 78 (€2, one hour, half-hourly from 5am to 10pm with a few night buses; www.oasth.gr). Taxis cost €15 to €20 (more from midnight and 5am).

Aegean Airlines and Astra Airlines (p384) fly throughout Greece and many airlines fly internationally.

BOAT

At the time of writing, travellers were being advised to travel to Kavala for ferry connections to the islands. Double-check online through Thesferry (www.thesferry.gr).

BUS

The **main KTEL bus station** (☎2310 595 400; www.ktelmacedonia.gr; Giannitson 244), 3km west of the centre, services Athens (€39, six hours, nine daily), Ioannina (€28, 3½ hours, six daily) and other destinations. For Athens *only* you can also get on buses near the train station at **Monastiriou Bus Station** (☎2310 500 111; http://ktelthes.gr; Monastiriou 67). Buses to the Halkidiki Peninsula leave from the **Halkidiki bus terminal** (☎2310 316 555; www.ktel-chalkidikis.gr; 9km Thessaloniki-Halkidiki road).

KTEL has direct services to Tirana (€30, nine hours, twice weekly) and Sofia (€20 to €23, five hours, four daily). Small bus companies, such as **Simeonidis Tours** (☎2310 540 970; www.simeonidistours.gr; 26 Oktovriou 14; ⌚9am-9pm Mon-Fri, to 2pm Sat), opposite the courthouse, serve international destinations like Turkey, Romania and Hungary. **Crazy Holidays** (☎2310 237 696; www.crazy-holidays.gr; Aristotelous 10, 1st fl) operates daily buses to İstanbul departing at 10am and 10pm.

TRAIN

The **train station** (☎2310 599 421; www.trainose.gr; Monastiriou) serves Athens (€55.40, 5¼ hours, seven daily) and other domestic destinations. International trains go to Skopje and Sofia, and beyond.

CYCLADES ΚΥΚΛΑΔΕΣ

The Cyclades (kih-*klah*-dez) are the Greek islands of postcards. Named after the rough *kyklos* (circle) they form around the island of Delos, they're lapped by the azure Aegean and speckled with white cubist buildings and blue-domed Byzantine churches. Throw in sun-blasted golden beaches, more than a dash of hedonism and history, and it's easy to see why many find the Cyclades irresistible.

Mykonos Μύκονος

POP 10,134

Mykonos is the great glamour island of the Cyclades and happily flaunts its sizzling style and party-hard reputation. The high-season mix of good-time holidaymakers, cruise-ship crowds (which can reach 15,000 a day), and posturing fashionistas throngs through Mykonos Town, a traditional Cycladic maze. While it retains authentic cubist charms, it remains a mecca for gay travellers and the well bankrolled, and can get super-packed in high season.

Sights

The island's most popular beaches, thronged in summer, are on the southern coast. **Platys Gialos** has wall-to-wall sun lounges, while nudity is not uncommon at **Paradise Beach**, **Super Paradise**, **Elia** and more secluded **Agrari**.

Without your own wheels, catch buses from Hora or caïques from Ornos and Platys Gialos to further beaches. Mykonos Cruises (p358) has an online timetable of its sea-taxi services.

Hora TOWN

(Mykonos Town) Hora is a captivating labyrinth that's home to chic boutiques and whiter-than-white houses decked with bougainvillea and geraniums, plus a handful of small museums and photogenic churches. **Little Venice**, where the sea laps up to the edge of the restaurants and bars, and Mykonos' famous hilltop **windmills** should be high on the must-see list.

Sleeping

Book well ahead in high season. Prices plummet outside of July and August, most hotels close in winter.

Mykonos has two **camping** areas, and both on the south coast – Paradise Beach and **Mykonos Camping** (☎22890 25915; www.mycamp.gr; Paraga Beach; campsite per adult/child/tent €10/5/10, dm €25, bungalow per person €35; ⌚May-Sep; @🛜🏊). Minibuses from both meet the ferries and buses go regularly into town.

Mykonos

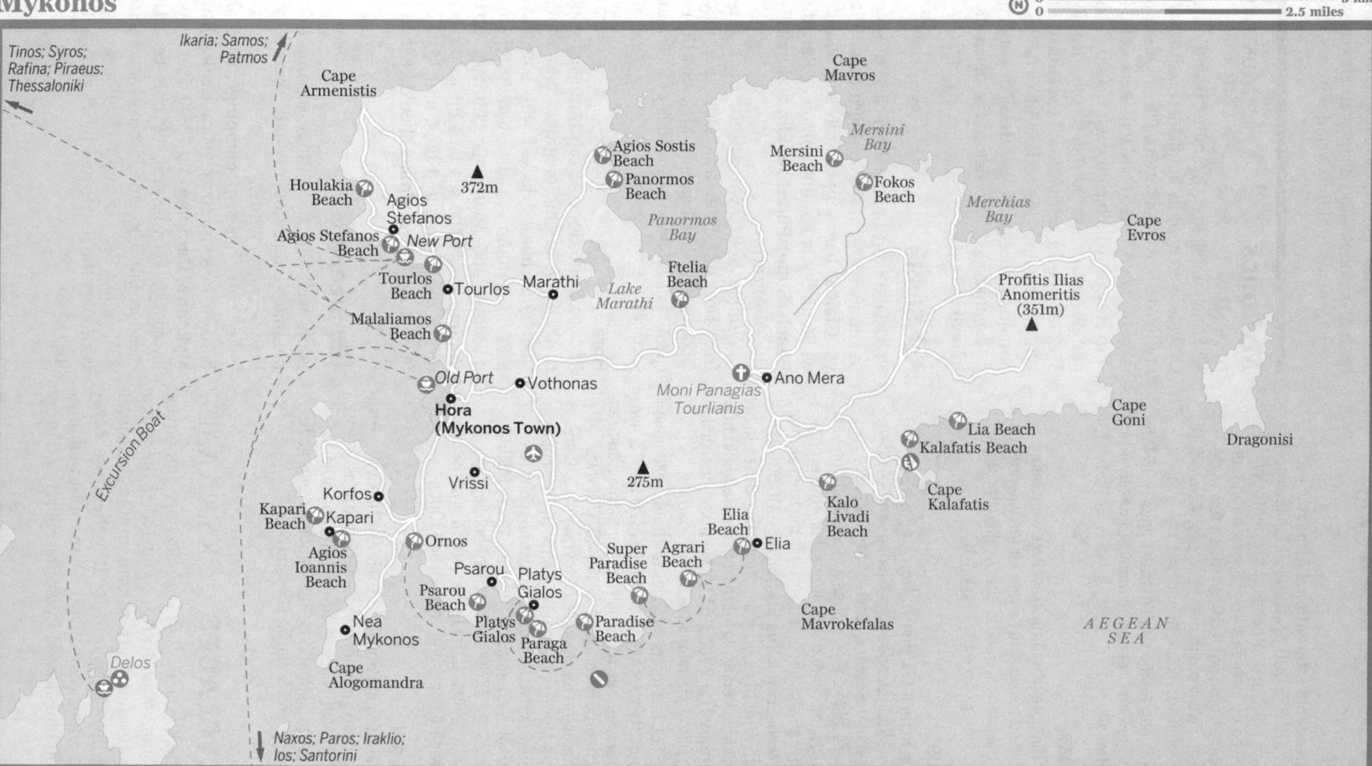
0 5 km
0 2.5 miles
Tinos; Syros; Rafina; Piraeus; Thessaloniki
Ikaria; Samos; Patmos
Cape Armenistis
Houlakia Beach
Agios Stefanos
Agios Stefanos Beach
New Port
Tourlos Beach
Tourlos
372m
Marathi
Lake Marathi
Malaliamos Beach
Old Port
Hora (Mykonos Town)
Vothonas
Agios Sostis Beach
Panormos Beach
Panormos Bay
Ftelia Beach
Mersini Beach
Mersini Bay
Cape Mavros
Fokos Beach
Merchias Bay
Cape Evros
Profitis Ilias Anomeritis (351m)
Ano Mera
Moni Panagias Tourlianis
Cape Goni
Lia Beach
Kalafatis Beach
Cape Kalafatis
Dragonisi
Kalo Livadi Beach
275m
Vrissi
Korfos
Kapari Beach
Kapari
Agios Ioannis Beach
Ornos
Psarou
Psarou Beach
Platys Gialos
Paraga Beach
Paradise Beach
Super Paradise Beach
Agrari Beach
Elia Beach
Elia
Cape Mavrokefalas
AEGEAN SEA
Nea Mykonos
Cape Alogomandra
Delos
Excursion Boat
Naxos; Paros; Iraklio; Ios; Santorini

Hotel Lefteris PENSION €
(☎22890 23128; www.lefterishotel.gr; Apollonas 9; d from €120; ❄📶) Tucked uphill and away from the crowds, a colourful entranceway leads to pristine, compact rooms and a warm welcome. A young family now runs this eight-room guesthouse (established by the owner's grandfather in the 1970s). All rooms have TV and air-con, and there's a roof terrace with views. Winter prices drop to €35.

Fresh Hotel BOUTIQUE HOTEL €€
(☎22890 24670; www.hotelfreshmykonos.com; Kalogera 31; s/d incl breakfast €180/190; ⏱mid-May–Oct; ❄📶) In the heart of town, with a lush and leafy garden and highly regarded on-site restaurant, Fresh is indeed fresh, with compact and stylishly minimalist rooms. Rates fall to €70/80 in the low season.

Carbonaki Hotel BOUTIQUE HOTEL €€
(☎22890 24124; www.carbonaki.gr; 23 Panahrantou; s/d €140/200; ⏱Apr-Oct; ❄📶) This family-run boutique hotel is a delightful oasis with bright, comfortable rooms (of various price categories), relaxing public balconies and sunny central courtyards.

★ **Semeli Hotel** HOTEL €€€
(☎22890 27466; www.semelihotel.gr; off Rohari; d incl breakfast from €355; ❄📶🏊) Expansive grounds, a glamorous restaurant terrace and swimming pool, and stylish, contemporary rooms combine to make this one of Mykonos' loveliest (and more affordable) top-end hotels.

Eating

High prices don't necessarily reflect high quality in Mykonos Town. Cafes line the waterfront; you'll find good food and coffee drinks at **Kadena** (☎22890 29290; Hora; mains €10-20; ⏱8am-late; 📶). Souvlaki shops dot Enoplon Dynameon and Plateia Yialos (Fabrika Sq). Most places stay open late during high season.

To Maereio GREEK €€
(☎22890 28825; Kalogera 16; mains €15-20; ⏱noon-3pm & 7pm-midnight) A busy, cosy and well-priced place favoured by many locals, with a small but selective menu of Mykonian favourites. It's heavy on meat – try the meatballs, local ham and/or spicy sausage.

★ **M-Eating** MEDITERRANEAN €€€
(☎22890 78550; www.m-eating.gr; Kalogera 10; mains €17-35; ⏱7pm-1am daily) Attentive service, soft lighting and relaxed luxury are the hallmarks of this creative restaurant specialising in fresh Greek products prepared with flair. Sample anything from sea bass tartar to rib-eye veal with honey truffle. Don't miss the dessert of Mykonian honey pie.

Drinking & Entertainment

Folks come to Mykonos to party. Each major beach has at least one beach bar which gets going during the day. Night action in town starts around 11pm and warms up by 1am; in the wee hours revellers often relocate from Hora to **Cavo Paradiso** (☎22890 26124; www.cavoparadiso.gr; Paradise Beach; ⏱11.30pm-7am) on Paradise Beach. From cool sunset cocktails to sweaty trance dancing, wherever you go bring a bankroll – the high life doesn't come cheap.

Hora's Little Venice quarter has a swath of colourful bars and some excellent clubs. Another prime spot is the Tria Pigadia (Three Wells) area on Enoplon Dynameon.

Information

Mykonos has no tourist office; visit travel agencies instead. There is information online at www.inmykonos.com and www.mykonos.gr. The **Mykonos Accommodation Centre** (MAC; ☎22890 23408; www.mykonos-accommodation.com; 1st fl, Enoplon Dynameon 10) is helpful for all things Mykonos (accommodation, guided tours, island info). The website is loaded.

Getting There & Around

AIR

Mykonos Airport (☎22890 79000; www.mykonos-airport.com), 3km southeast of the town centre, has flights year-round to Athens and Thessaloniki with Astra Airlines (www.astra-airlines.gr). Summertime connections to European destinations are plentiful.

BOAT

Year-round ferries serve mainland ports Piraeus and Rafina (the latter is usually quicker if you are coming directly from Athens airport), and nearby islands Tinos and Andros. In the high season, Mykonos is well connected with all neighbouring islands, including Paros and Santorini. Hora is loaded with ticket agents.

Mykonos has two ferry quays: the **Old Port**, 400m north of town, where some smaller fast ferries dock, and the **New Port**, 2km north of town, where the bigger fast ferries and all conventional ferries dock. When buying outgoing tickets double-check which quay your ferry leaves from.

WORTH A TRIP

DELOS

Southwest of Mykonos, the island of **Delos** (☎22890 22259; museum & site adult/child €12/ free; ⏰8am-8pm Apr-Oct, to 3pm Nov-Mar), a Unesco World Heritage site, is the Cyclades' archaeological jewel. The mythical birthplace of twins Apollo and Artemis, splendid Ancient Delos was a shrine-turned–sacred treasury and commercial centre. It was inhabited from the 3rd millennium BC and reached its apex of power around the 5th century BC.

Overnight stays are forbidden (as is swimming) and boat schedules allow a maximum of four hours at Delos. A simple cafe is located by the museum, but it pays to bring water and food. Wear a hat, sunscreen and walking shoes.

Boats from Mykonos to Delos (€18 return, 30 minutes) go between 9am and 5pm in summer, and return between noon and 8pm. In Hora (Mykonos Town) buy tickets at the old wharf kiosk or at **Delia Travel** (☎22890 22322; Akti Kambani), **Sea & Sky** (☎22890 22853; www.seasky.gr; Akti Kambani) or **Mykonos Accommodation Centre** (p357). Sometimes in summer boats go from Tinos and Naxos.

Local Boats

Mykonos Cruises (☎22890 23995; www.mykonos-cruises.gr; ⏰8am-7pm Apr-Oct) offers services to the island's best beaches. See the timetables online. The main departure point is Platys Gialos.

Sea Bus (☎6978830355; www.mykonos-seabus.gr; one way €2) connects the New Port with Hora (€2), running hourly from 9am to 10pm.

BUS

Terminal A, the southern bus station (Fabrika Sq), known as Fabrika, serves Ornos and Agios Ioannis Beach, Platys Gialos, Paraga and Super Paradise beaches.

Terminal B, the northern bus station, sometimes called Remezzo, has services to Agios Stefanos via Tourlos, Ano Mera, and Kalo Livadi, Kalafatis, and Elia beaches. Buses for Tourlos and Agios Stefanos stop at the Old and New Ports.

Timetables are on the **KTEL Mykonos** (☎22890 26797, 22890 23360; www.mykonosbus.com) website.

CAR & TAXI

Car hire starts at €45 per day in high season. Scooters/quads are €20/40. Avis and Sixt are among agencies at the airport.

Naxos ΝΑΞΟΣ

POP 12,726

The largest of the Cyclades islands, beautiful, raw Naxos could probably survive without tourism. Green and fertile, with vast central mountains, Naxos produces olives, grapes, figs, citrus, corn and potatoes. Explore its fascinating main town, excellent beaches, remote villages and striking interior.

Naxos Town (Hora), on the west coast, is the island's capital and port.

Sights

★Kastro — AREA

The most alluring part of Hora is the 13th-century residential neighbourhood of Kastro, which Marco Sanudo made the capital of his duchy in 1207. Located behind the waterfront, get lost in its narrow alleyways scrambling up to its spectacular hilltop location.

Several Venetian mansions survive in the centre of Kastro, and you can see the remnants of his castle, the **Tower of Sanoudos**, which was once surrounded by marble balconies.

★Temple of Apollo — ARCHAEOLOGICAL SITE

(The Portara) FREE From Naxos Town harbour, a causeway leads to the Palatia islet and the striking, unfinished Temple of Apollo, Naxos' most famous landmark (also known as the Portara, or 'Doorway'). Simply two marble columns with a crowning lintel, it makes an arresting sight, and people gather at sunset for splendid views.

Panagia Drosiani — CHURCH

(donations appreciated; ⏰10am-7pm May–mid-Oct) Located 2.5km north of Halki, just below Moni, the small, peaceful Panagia Drosiani is among the oldest and most revered churches in Greece. Inside is a series of cavelike chapels. In the darkest chapels, monks and nuns secretly taught Greek language and religion to local children during the Turkish occupation.

Several frescoes still grace the walls and date from the 7th century. Look for the depiction of Mary in the eastern chapter; the clarity and expression is incredible.

Temple of Demeter TEMPLE
(Dimitra's Temple) About 1.5km south of Sangri is the impressive 6th-century BC Temple of Demeter. The ruins and reconstructions are not large, but they are historically fascinating. There's also a good site museum with some fine reconstructions of temple features. Signs point the way from Sangri.

Beaches

The popular beach of **Agios Georgios** is just a 10-minute walk south from the main waterfront. **Agia Anna Beach**, 6km from town, and **Plaka Beach** are lined with accommodation and packed in summer. Beyond, wonderful sandy beaches continue as far south as **Pyrgaki Beach**.

Villages

A hire car or scooter will help reveal Naxos' dramatic and rugged landscape. The **Tragaea** region has tranquil villages, churches atop rocky crags and huge olive groves. Between Melanes and Kinidaros are the island's famous **marble quarries**. You'll find two ancient abandoned **kouros** (youth) statues, signposted a short walk from the road. Little **Apiranthos** settlement perches on the slopes of **Mt Zeus** (1004m), the highest peak in the Cyclades, and has a few intermittently open museums. The historic village of **Halki**, one-time centre of Naxian commerce, is well worth a visit.

Lovely waterside **Apollonas** near Naxos' northern tip has a beach, taverna, and another mysterious 10.5m kouros from the 7th century BC, abandoned and unfinished in an ancient marble quarry.

Sleeping

Nikos Verikokos Studios HOTEL €
(☎22850 22025; www.nikos-verikokos.com; Naxos Town; s/d/tr €90/100/120; ⏰year-round; ❄📶) Friendly Nikos maintains immaculate rooms in the heart of the old town. Some have balconies and sea views, most have little kitchenettes. They offer port pick-up with pre-arrangement.

Hotel Galini HOTEL €€
(☎22850 22114; www.hotelgalini.com; d incl breakfast from €90; ❄📶) A nautical theme lends this super-friendly place loads of character. Updated, spacious rooms have small balconies and wrought-iron beds, plus great decor creatively fashioned from seashells and driftwood. The location is first-rate – close to the old town and the beach – and the breakfast is hearty.

DON'T MISS

KITRON-TASTING IN HALKI

The historic village of **Halki** is a top spot to try *kitron*, a liqueur unique to Naxos. While the exact recipe is top secret, visitors can taste it and stock up on supplies at **Vallindras Distillery** (☎22850 31220; www.facebook.com/media/set/?set=o.140729449272799; ⏰10am-10pm Jul & Aug, to 6pm May-Jun & Sep-Oct) in Halki's main square. There are free tours of the old distillery's atmospheric rooms, which contain ancient jars and copper stills. *Kitron* tastings round off the trip.

Xenia Hotel HOTEL €€
(☎22850 25068; www.hotel-xenia.gr; Plateia Pigadakia; s/d/tr incl breakfast from €85/90/110; ❄📶) Sleek and minimalist, this hotel (built 2012) is right in the old-town scene, close to everything. Balconies overlook the bustle of the streets but thick glass keeps the noise out when you decide to call it a night.

Eating & Drinking

Hora's waterfront is lined with eating and drinking establishments. Head into Market St in the Old Town, just down from the ferry quay, to find quality tavernas. South, only a few minutes' walk away, Main Sq is home to other excellent eateries, some of which stay open year-round.

★**Maro** GREEK €
(☎22850 25113; mains €5-15; ⏰lunch & dinner) There's no sea view here, or old-town romance, but the locals don't care. They're too busy tucking into mammoth portions of delicious, good-value local food (including lots of specialities from the village of Apiranthos). The zucchini balls (fritters, really) are tasty, the *mousakas* (baked layers of eggplant or zucchini, minced meat and potatoes topped with cheese sauce) enormous. It's just south of Plateia Evripeou.

O Apostolis GREEK €€
(☎22850 26777; www.facebook.com/pages/Taverna-O-Apostolis/314061735335882; Old Market St; mains €8-15; ⏰lunch & dinner) Right at the heart of labyrinthine Bourgos, O Apostolis serves up tasty dishes in its pretty flagstone coutyard. The *kleftiko* (lamb wrapped in filo pastry), with sautéed vegetables and feta cheese, is delicious.

L'Osteria ITALIAN €€

(☎22850 24080; www.osterianaxos.com; mains €10-16; ⏰7pm-midnight) This authentic Italian eatery is tucked away in a small alley uphill from the harbour, beneath the Kastro walls. Grab a table in the cute courtyard and prepare to be impressed: the appetising menu changes daily, but there's also an unchanging list of bruschetta, salads and delectable *antipasti*.

Naxos Cafe BAR

(☎22850 26343; www.facebook.com/naxos-cafe-47365083135; Old Market St; ⏰8pm-2am) If you want to drink but don't fancy the club scene, here's your answer. This atmospheric, traditional bar is small and candlelit and spills into the cobbled Bourgos street. Drink Naxian wine with the locals.

Information

There's no official tourist office on Naxos. Travel agencies can deal with most queries. Handy online resources include www.naxos.gr.

Getting There & Around

AIR

Naxos Airport (JNX; www.naxos.net/airport) serves Athens daily. The airport is 3km south of town; there are no buses – a taxi costs €15, or arrange hotel pick-up.

BOAT

There are myriad high-season daily ferry and hydrofoil connections to most Cycladic islands and Crete, plus Piraeus ferries (€34.50, five hours) and catamarans (€57.50, 3¾ hours). Reduced services in winter.

BUS

Buses leave from the end of the ferry quay in Hora; timetables are posted across the road outside the **bus information office** (☎22850 22291; www.naxosdestinations.com; Harbour). You have to buy tickets from the office or from the machine outside (not from the bus driver).

CAR & MOTORCYCLE

Having your own wheels is a good idea for exploring Naxos. Car (€45 to €65) and motorcycle (€25 to €30) rentals line Hora's port and main streets.

Santorini (Thira) ΣΑΝΤΟΡΙΝΗ (ΘΗΡΑ)

POP 15,550

Stunning Santorini may well have conquered a corner of your imagination before you've even set eyes on it. The startling sight of the submerged caldera almost encircled by sheer lava-layered cliffs – topped by clifftop towns that look like a dusting of icing sugar – will grab your attention and not let it go. If you turn up in high season, though, be prepared for relentless crowds and commercialism – Santorini survives on tourism.

Sights & Activities

★**Museum of Prehistoric Thera** MUSEUM

(☎22860 22217; www.santorini.com/museums/prehistoric_museum.htm; Mitropoleos; adult/child €3/free; ⏰8.30am-3pm Wed-Mon) Opposite the bus station, this well-presented museum houses extraordinary finds excavated from Akrotiri and is all the more impressive when you realise just how old they are. Most remarkable is the glowing gold ibex figurine, dating from the 17th century BC and in amazingly mint condition. Also look for fossilised olive tree leaves from within the caldera from 60,000 BC.

★**Ancient Akrotiri** ARCHAEOLOGICAL SITE

(☎22860 81366; http://odysseus.culture.gr/h/3/eh351.jsp?obj_id=2410; adult/child €12/free; ⏰8am-8pm Apr-Oct, 8am-3pm Nov-Mar) In 1967, excavations began at the site of Akrotiri. What they uncovered was phenomenal: an ancient Minoan city buried deep beneath volcanic ash from the catastrophic eruption of 1613 BC. Today, the site retains a strong sense of place. Housed within a cool, protective structure, wooden walkways allow you to pass through various parts of the city.

★**Art Space** GALLERY

(☎22860 32774; www.artspace-santorini.com; Exo Gonia; ⏰11am-sunset) FREE This unmissable, atmospheric gallery is just outside Kamari, in Argyros Canava, one of the oldest wineries on the island. The old wine caverns are hung with superb artworks, while sculptures transform lost corners and niches. The collection features some of Greece's finest modern artists.

Oia VILLAGE

At the north of the island, the postcard-perfect village of Oia (ee-ah), famed for its sunsets, is less hectic than Fira and a must-visit. Its caldera-facing tavernas are superb spots for a meal. A path from Fira to Oia along the top of the caldera takes three to four hours to walk; otherwise take a taxi or bus. Beat the crowds in the early morning or late evening.

Santorini (Thira)

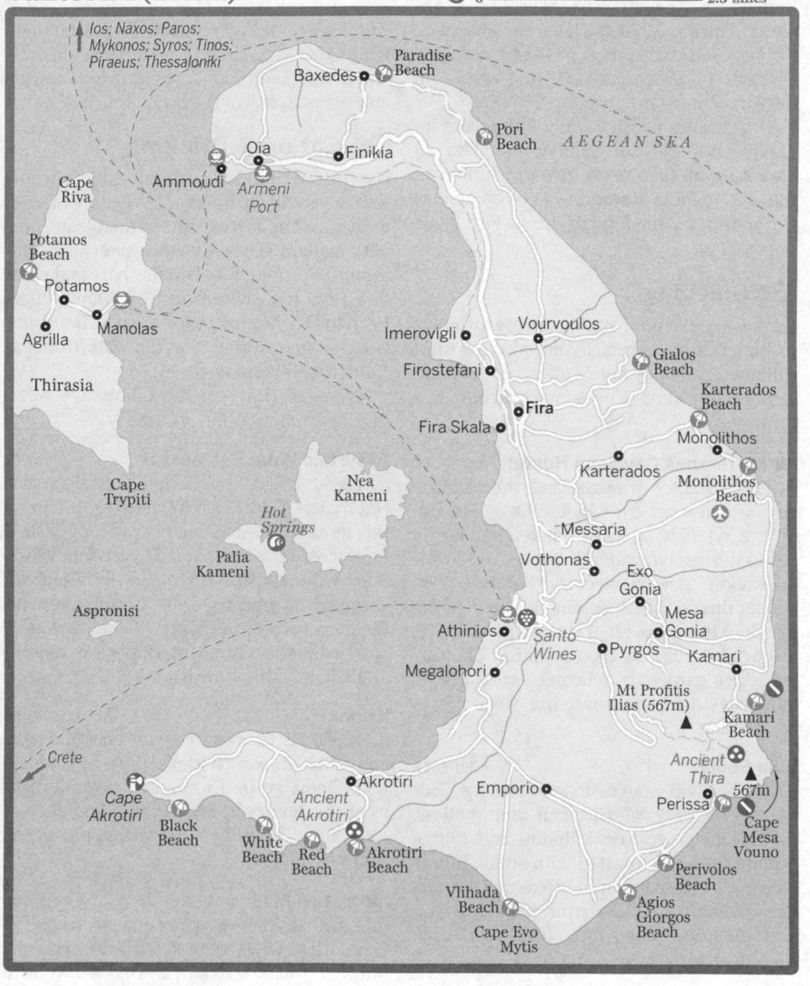

Fira VILLAGE

Santorini's vibrant main town with its snaking narrow streets full of shops and restaurants perches on top of the caldera. The stunning caldera views from Fira and its neighbouring hamlet Firostefani are matched only by tiny Oia.

SantoWines WINERY

(☎22860 22596; www.santowines.gr; tours & tastings from €12.50; ⏲9am-9pm) The best place to start your wine adventure. The island's cooperative of grape-growers, it's a large tourist-focused complex on the caldera edge near the port. It has short tours of the production process and lots of tasting options. There are also superb views, a wine bar with food, and a shop full of choice vintages as well as gourmet local products.

Around the Island

Santorini's known for its multihued beaches. The black-sand beaches of **Perissa**, **Perivolos**, **Agios Giorgos** and **Kamari** sizzle – beach mats are essential. **Red Beach**, near Ancient Akrotiri, has impressive red cliffs and smooth, hand-sized pebbles submerged under clear water.

On a mountain between Perissa and Kamari are the atmospheric ruins of **Ancient Thira** (☎22860 23217; http://odysseus.culture.gr/h/3/eh351.jsp?obj_id=2454; adult/child €4/free; ⊙8am-3pm Tue-Sun), first settled in the 9th century BC.

Of the volcanic islets, only **Thirasia** is inhabited. Visitors can clamber over lava on **Nea Kameni** then swim in warm springs in the sea at **Palia Kameni**. Many excursions get you there; small boats are at Fira Skala port.

Sleeping

Santorini's sleeping options are exorbitant in high season, especially anywhere with a caldera view. Many hotels offer free port and airport transfers. Check www.airbnb.com for deals.

★Karterados Caveland Hostel HOSTEL €€
(☎22860 22122; www.cave-land.com; Karterados; incl breakfast dm €25, d €90; ⊙Mar-Oct; P ❄ 📶 ≋) This fabulous, chilled-out hostel is based in an old winery complex in Karterados about 2km from central Fira (see website for directions). Accommodation is in the big old wine caves, all of them with creative, colourful decor and good facilities. The surrounding garden is relaxing, with weekly barbecues held, and there are yoga classes on offer too.

Villa Soula HOTEL €€
(☎22860 23473; www.santorini-villasoula.gr; Fira; r from €100; ❄ 📶 ≋) Cheerful and spotless, this hotel is a great deal. Rooms aren't large but are freshly renovated with small, breezy balconies. Colourful public areas and a small, well-maintained undercover pool give you room to spread out a little. It's a short walk from the town centre.

★Zorzis Hotel BOUTIQUE HOTEL €€
(☎22860 81104; www.santorinizorzis.com; Perissa; d incl breakfast from €90; ❄ 📶 ≋) Behind a huge bloom of geraniums on Perissa's main street, Hirohiko and Spiros (a Japanese-Greek couple) run an immaculate 10-room hotel. It's a pastel-coloured sea of calm (no kids), with delightful garden, pool and mountain backdrop.

★Mill Houses BOUTIQUE HOTEL €€€
(☎22860 27117; www.millhouses.gr; Firostefani; d incl breakfast from €350; ❄ 📶 ≋) Built right into the side of the caldera at Firostefani, down a long flight of steps, these superb studios and suites are chic and plush. Lots of white linen and whitewashed walls fill them with light. King-sized beds, Bulgari toiletries and private patios looking out over the Aegean are just a few of the lavish touches.

Eating & Drinking

Overpriced, indifferent food geared towards tourists is still an unfortunate feature of summertime Fira. Prices tend to double at spots with caldera views. Cheaper eateries cluster around Fira's square. Popular bars and clubs line Erythrou Stavrou in Fira. Many diners head to Oia, legendary for its superb sunsets. Good-value tavernas line the waterfronts at Kamari and Perissa.

Try Santorini Brewing Company's offerings like Yellow Donkey beer.

Assyrtico Wine Restaurant GREEK €€
(☎22860 22463; www.assyrtico-restaurant.com; Fira; mains €15-30; ⊙lunch & dinner) Settle in on this terrace above the main drag for polished local flavours accompanied by caldera views. Start with, say, the *saganaki* (fried cheese) wrapped in a pastry crust, and follow with the deconstructed gyros or the *mousakas* of Santorini white eggplant. Service is relaxed and friendly; the wine list is big.

Krinaki TAVERNA €€
(☎22860 71993; www.krinaki-santorini.gr; Finikia; mains €12-22; ⊙noon-late) All-fresh, all-local ingredients go into top-notch taverna dishes at this homey taverna in tiny Finikia, just east of Oia. Local beer and wine, plus a sea (but not caldera) view.

★Metaxi Mas TAVERNA €€
(☎22860 31323; www.santorini-metaximas.gr; Exo Gonia; mains €9-19; ⊙lunch & dinner) The *raki* flows at this convivial taverna, a favourite among locals and authenticity-seeking travellers. In the central village of Exo Gonia (between Pyrgos and Kamari), park by the large church and walk down some steps to reach it. Prebooking is a good idea. Enjoy sweeping views and a delicious menu of local and Cretan specialities.

Koukoumavlos GREEK €€€
(☎22860 23807; www.koukoumavlos.com; mains €28-34; ⊙dinner Apr–mid-Oct) This terrace is filled with gleeful diners partaking of fresh, modern, Aegean cuisine (including a worthwhile degustation at €65). Creativity reigns

and the menu is poetic, elevating dishes to new heights: 'slow-cooked shoulder of lamb with potato mousseline flavored with jasmine, fig and Greek coffee sauce'. Look for the pink building and wooden doorway. Book ahead.

Information

Try www.santorini.net for more information.

Dakoutros Travel (22860 22958; www.dakoutrostravel.gr; Fira; 8.30am-10pm) on the main street, just before Plateia Theotokopoulou. Ferry and air tickets sold; assitance with excursions, accommodation and transfers.

Getting There & Around

AIR

Santorini Airport (22860 28400; www.santoriniairport.com) has flights year-round to/from Athens (from €64, 45 minutes). Seasonal European connections are plentiful, including easyJet from London, Rome and Milan.

There are frequent bus connections between Fira's bus station and the airport between 7am and 9pm (€1.60, 20 minutes). Most accommodation providers will arrange (paid) transfers.

BOAT

Thira's main port, Athinios, stands on a cramped shelf of land 10km south of Fira. Buses (and taxis) meet all ferries and then cart passengers up the towering cliffs. Accommodation providers can usually arrange transfers (to Fira per person is around €10).

Multiple boats leave daily for Piraeus (€36 to €59, 5 hours), Naxos (€19.50 to €42, 1½ to two hours) and Mykonos (€60, two to three hours). Less frequent sailing service Rethymno, Rhodes and Kos.

BUS

KTEL Santorini Buses (22860 25404; http://ktel-santorini.gr) has a good website with schedules and prices. Tickets are purchased on the bus.

In summer, buses leave Fira twice-hourly for Oia, with more services pre-sunset (€1.60). There are also numerous daily departures for Akrotiri (€1.80), Kamari (€1.60), Perissa and Perivolos Beach (€2.20), and a few to Monolithos (€1.60).

Buses leave Fira, Perissa and Kamari for the port of Athinios (€2.20, 30 minutes) a half-dozen times per day. Buses for Fira meet all ferries, even late at night.

CAR & MOTORCYCLE

A car (from €50 per day) or scooter is good for getting out of town. Outlets abound.

CRETE ΚΡΗΤΗ

POP 623,000

With its dramatic landscape, myriad mountain villages, unique cultural identity and some of the best food in Greece, Crete is a delight to explore. As Greece's largest, most southerly island, its size, distance and independent history give it the feel of a different country.

The island is split by a spectacular chain of mountains running east to west. Major towns are on the more hospitable northern coast, while most of the southern coast is too precipitous to support large settlements. The rugged mountainous interior, dotted with caves and sliced by dramatic gorges, offers rigorous hiking and climbing. Small villages like Magarites, a potters' village near Mt Idi, offer a glimpse into traditional life.

Iraklio ΗΡΑΚΛΕΙΟ

POP 140,730

Iraklio (ee-*rah*-klee-oh; often spelt Heraklion), Crete's capital and economic hub, is a bustling modern city and the fifth-largest in Greece. It has a lively city centre, an excellent archaeological museum and is close to Knossos, Crete's major visitor attraction. Other towns are more picturesque, but in a pinch, you can stay over in Iraklio.

Iraklio's harbours face north with the landmark **Koules Venetian Fortress**. Plateia Venizelou, known for its **Lion (Morosini) Fountain**, is the heart of the city, 400m south of the old harbour up 25 Avgoustou.

Sights & Activities

★Heraklion Archaeological Museum — MUSEUM

(2810 279000; http://odysseus.culture.gr; Xanthoudidou 2; adult/child €10/free; 8am-8pm Apr-Oct, 11am-5pm Mon, 8am-3pm Tue-Sun Nov-Mar) Reopened in 2014 after a long renovation, the Archaeological Museum of Heraklion is Crete's outstanding jewel. The two floors of the restored 1930s Bauhaus building make a gleaming showcase for the exhibits that span 5500 years, from neolithic to Roman times, and an extensive Minoan collection. The rooms are colour coded and artefacts, displayed both chronologically and thematically, are beautifully presented with descriptions in English. A visit here enhances any understanding of Crete's rich history. Don't skip it.

Crete

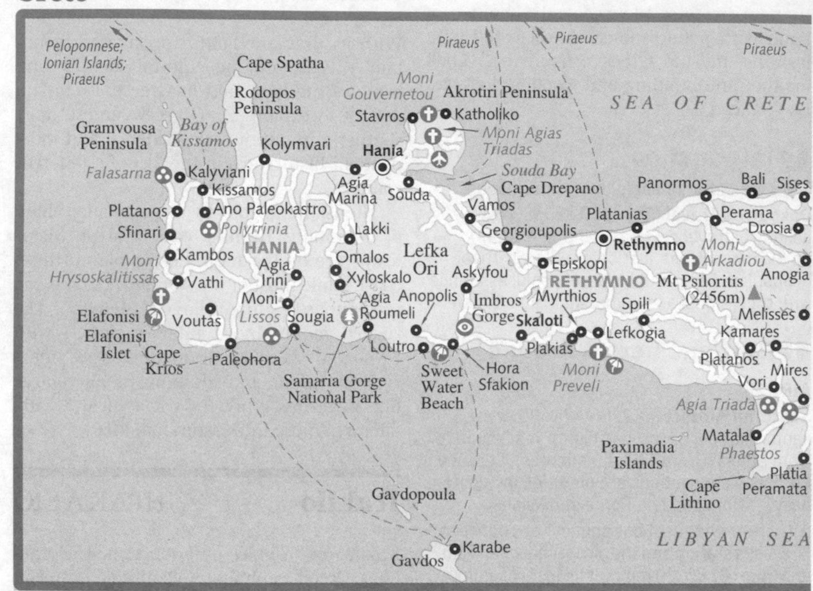

Cretan Adventures OUTDOORS

(☎2810 332772; www.cretanadventures.gr; 3rd fl, Evans 10) This well-regarded local company run by friendly and knowledgeable English-speaking Fondas organises hiking tours, mountain biking and extreme outdoor excursions. It also coordinates fabulous self-guided tours with detailed hiking instructions, plus accommodation with breakfast and luggage transfer (from €740 for one week). Fondas' office is up on the 3rd floor and easy to miss.

Sleeping

Staying in nearby Arhanes offers a chance to see Cretan wine country. Try **Arhontiko** (☎2810 752985; www.arhontikoarhanes.gr; Arhanes; apt €75-95;) with its beautifully kitted-out apartments.

Kronos Hotel HOTEL €

(☎2810 282240; www.kronoshotel.gr; Sofokli Venizelou 2; s €47, d €60-67; @) Good, if noisy, position near the waterfront, the no-frills but pleasant rooms have double-glazed windows to block out noise, as well as a balcony, phone, a tiny TV and a fridge. Some doubles have sea views. An 'only-OK' breakfast costs €7.

Capsis Astoria HOTEL €€

(☎2810 343080; www.capsishotel.gr; Plateia Eleftherias 11; r incl breakfast €100-140; P@) The hulking exterior doesn't impress, but past the front door the Capsis is a class act, all the way to the rooftop pool from where you enjoy a delicious panorama of Iraklio. Rooms sport soothing neutral tones and dashing historic black-and-white photographs. Thirty of the 131 rooms are 'skylight' rooms, meaning windows but no vistas. Fabulous breakfast buffet.

Eating & Drinking

Eateries, bars and cafes surround Plateia Venizelou (Lion Fountain) and the El Greco Park area. The old harbour offers seafood options.

Fyllo...Sofies CAFE €

(☎2810 284774; www.fillosofies.gr; Plateia Venizelou 33; snacks €3-7; 6am-late;) With tables sprawling out towards the Morosini Fountain, this is a great place to sample a breakfast *bougatsa* (creamy semolina pudding wrapped in a pastry envelope and sprinkled with cinnamon and sugar). The less-sweet version is made with *myzithra* (sheep's-milk cheese).

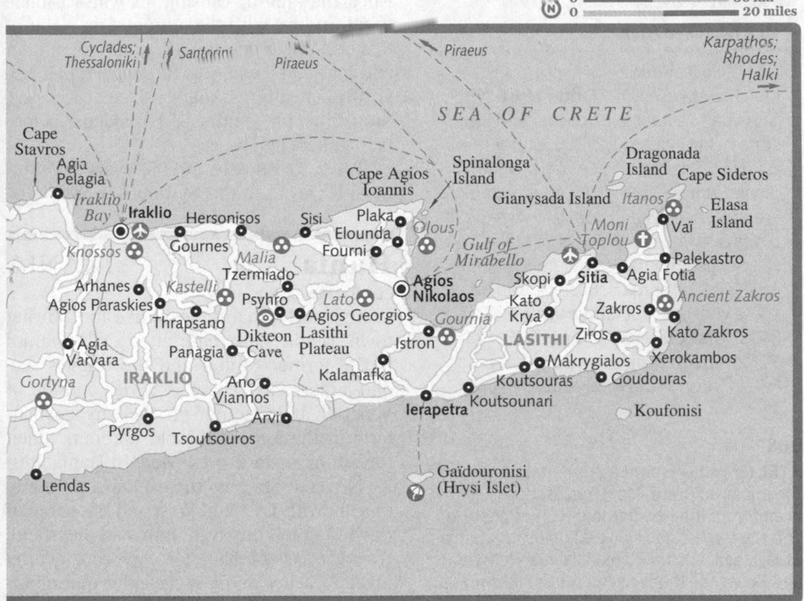

★Peskesi CRETAN €€
(☎2810 288887; www.peskesicrete.gr; mains €8-16; ⊙10am-late) One of Iraklio's recent additions to the city's upmarket dining scene, and housed in a smartly converted cottage, this lovely eatery comes with a large dollop of snob value. It's best described as 'postmodern ancient Greek' (say what? we hear you ask). Think smoked pork (*apaki*) hanging off a butcher's hook with smoking herbs beneath and *kandavlos* (an ancient souvlaki).

Ippokambos SEAFOOD €€
(Sofokli Venizelou 3; mains €6-15; ⊙noon-late Mon-Sat; 📶) Locals give this smart *ouzerie* (place that serves ouzo and light snacks) an enthusiastic thumbs up and we are only too happy to follow suit. Fish is the thing here – it's freshly caught, simply but expertly prepared and sold at fair prices. In summer, park yourself on the covered waterfront terrace. Look for the seahorse *(ippokambos)* sign.

Parasties GREEK €€
(☎2810 225009; www.parasties.gr; Historic Museum Sq, Sofokli Venizelou 19; mains €7-24; ⊙noon-midnight) Parasties' owner Haris is Iraklio's answer to a city's restaurateur who is genuine about serving great-quality local produce and top Cretan wines. And his passion shows in his small but gourmet menu. Beef liver and grilled mushrooms are our top choices, while a great selection of zingy salads and superb meats will keep you munching more than you planned.

ℹ Information

Visit www.heraklion.gr for city information.

ℹ Getting There & Around

AIR

Flights from Iraklio's **Nikos Kazantzakis International Airport** (HER; ☎general 2810 397800, info 2810 397136; www.heraklion-airport.info) serve Athens, Thessaloniki and Rhodes plus destinations all over Europe. The airport is 5km east of town. In summer, bus 1 travels between the airport and city centre (€1.10) every 15 minutes from 6.15am to midnight. A taxi into town costs around €12 to €15.

BOAT

Daily ferries from Iraklio's **ferry port** (☎2810 244956) service Piraeus (€36 to €43, 6½ to 9½ hours), and catamarans head to Santorini and other Cycladic islands. Ferries sail east to Rhodes (€27, 14 hours) via Agios Nikolaos, Sitia, Kasos, Karpathos and Halki. Services are reduced in winter. See www.openseas.gr.

DON'T MISS

IRAKLIO MARKET

An Iraklio institution, just south of the Lion Fountain, narrow **Odos 1866** (1866 St) is part market, part bazaar and, despite being increasingly tourist-oriented, it's a fun place to browse and stock up on picnic supplies from fruit and vegetables, creamy cheeses and honey to succulent olives and fresh breads. Other stalls sell pungent herbs, leather goods, hats, jewellery and some souvenirs. Cap off a spree with lunch at **Giakoumis** (☎28102 84039; Theodosaki 5-8; mains €6-13; ⏲7am-11pm) or another nearby taverna (avoid those in the market itself).

BUS

KTEL (www.bus-service-crete-ktel.com) runs the buses on Crete. Main Bus Station A, just inland from the new harbour, serves eastern and western Crete (Agios Nikolaos, Ierapetra, Sitia, Malia, Lasithi Plateau, Hania, Rethymno and Knossos). It has useful tourist information and a left-luggage service.Bus Station B, 50m beyond the Hania Gate, serves the southern route (Phaestos, Matala and Anogia).

Knossos ΚΝΩΣΣΟΣ

Crete's most famous historical attraction is the **Palace of Knossos** (☎28102 31940; http://odysseus.culture.gr; adult/concession/child €15/8/free, incl Heraklion Archaeological Museum €16; ⏲8am-8pm Apr-Oct, to 5pm Nov-Mar), 5km south of Iraklio, and the grand capital of Minoan Crete. Excavation on Knossos (k-nos-*os*) started in 1878 with Cretan archaeologist Minos Kalokerinos, and continued from 1900 to 1930 with British archaeologist Sir Arthur Evans. Today, it's hard to make sense, in the extensive restorations, of what is Evans' interpretation and what actually existed in Minoan times. But the setting is gorgeous and the ruins and recreations impressive, incorporating an immense palace, courtyards, private apartments, baths, lively frescoes and more. Going to the Heraklion Archaeological Museum (p363) in Iraklio (most treasures are there) and taking a guided tour (€10) add needed context.

Knossos was the setting for the myth of the Minotaur. According to legend, King Minos of Knossos was given a magnificent white bull to sacrifice to the god Poseidon, but decided to keep it. This enraged Poseidon, who punished the king by causing his wife Pasiphae to fall in love with the animal. The result of this odd union was the Minotaur – half-man and half-bull – who was imprisoned in a labyrinth beneath the king's palace at Knossos, munching on youths and maidens, before being killed by Theseus.

Bus 2 to Knossos (€1.50, every 20 minutes) leaves from Bus Station A in Iraklio.

Hania ΧΑΝΙΑ

POP 54,000

Crete's most romantic, evocative and alluring town, Hania (hahn-*yah*; often spelt Chania) is the former capital and the island's second-largest city. There is a rich mosaic of Venetian and Ottoman architecture, particularly in the area of the old harbour, which lures tourists in droves. Modern Hania with its university retains the exoticism of a city playing with East and West and has some of the best hotels and restaurants on the island. It's an excellent base for exploring nearby idyllic beaches and a spectacular mountainous interior.

Sights

★Venetian Harbour HISTORIC SITE

A stroll around the old harbour is a must for any visitor to Hania. Pastel-coloured historic homes and businesses line the harbour, zigzagging back into narrow lanes lined with shops. The entire area is ensconced in impressive **Venetian fortifications**, and it's worth the 1.5km walk around the sea wall to the **Venetian lighthouse**. On the eastern side of the inner harbour the prominent **Mosque of Kioutsouk Hasan** (Mosque of Janissaries) houses regular exhibitions.

★Archaeological Museum MUSEUM

(☎28210 90334; Halidon 30; adult/child €4/free; ⏲8am-8pm Mon-Fri, to 3pm Sat & Sun) The setting alone in the beautifully restored 16th-century Venetian Church of San Francisco is reason to visit this fine collection of artefacts from neolithic to Roman times. The museum's late-Minoan sarcophagi catch the eye as much as a large glass case with an entire herd of clay bulls (used to worship Poseidon). Other standouts include three Roman floor mosaics, Hellenistic gold jewellery, clay tablets with Linear A and Linear B script, and a marble sculpture of Roman emperor Hadrian.

PHAESTOS

Sixty-three kilometres southwest of Iraklio is Crete's second-most important Minoan palatial site, **Phaestos** (☎28920 42315; http://odysseus.culture.gr; adult/concession/child €8/4/free; ⊙8am-8pm Apr-Oct, 8.30am-3pm Nov-Mar). More unreconstructed and moody than Knossos, Phaestos (fes-*tos*) is also worth a visit for its stunning views of the surrounding Mesara plain and Mt Psiloritis (2456m; also known as Mt Ida). The smaller site of **Agia Triada** (☎27230 22448; adult/child €3/free; ⊙9.30am-4.30pm summer, 8.30am-3pm winter) is 3km west.

★Byzantine & Post-Byzantine Collection MUSEUM
(☎28210 96046; Theotokopoulou 82; €2; ⊙8am-3pm Tue-Sun) The Byzantine museum is in the impressively restored Venetian Church of San Salvatore. It has a small but fascinating collection of artefacts, icons, jewellery and coins spanning the period from AD 62 to 1913, including a fine segment of a mosaic floor for an early-Christian basilica and a prized icon of St George slaying the dragon. The building has a mixed bag of interesting architectural features from its various occupiers. A joint ticket with the Archaeological Museum costs adult/child €3/free.

★Maritime Museum of Crete MUSEUM
(☎28210 91875; www.mar-mus-crete.gr; Akti Koundourioti; adult/child €4/free; ⊙9am-5pm Mon-Sat, 10am-6pm Sun) Part of the hulking Venetian-built Firkas Fortress at the western port entrance, this museum celebrates Crete's nautical tradition with model ships, naval instruments, paintings, photographs, maps and memorabilia. One room is dedicated to historical sea battles while upstairs there's thorough documentation on the WWII-era Battle of Crete. The gate to the fortress itself is open from 8am to 2pm.

Sleeping

Hania's Old Harbour is loaded with great hotels which can book up, even on winter weekends; reserve ahead.

Pension Theresa PENSION €
(☎28210 92798; www.pensiontheresa.gr; Angelou 8; r €50-60; ❄📶) Part of the Venetian fortifications, this creaky old house with a steep (and narrow!) spiral staircase and antique furniture delivers snug rooms with character aplenty. The location is excellent and views are stunning from the rooftop terrace with communal kitchen stocked with basic breakfast items. They have another annexe as well.

★Casa Leone BOUTIQUE HOTEL €€€
(☎28210 76762; www.casa-leone.com; Parodos Theotokopoulou 18; d/ste incl breakfast from €135/190; ❄📶) This Venetian residence has been converted into a classy and romantic family-run boutique hotel. The rooms are spacious and well appointed, with balconies overlooking the harbour. There are honeymoon suites, with classic drape-canopy beds and sumptuous curtains. Discounts for prebooking or cash payments.

Eating & Drinking

Look beyond the waterfront tourist-traps for some of the best eats on the island. The Splantzia neighbourhood is popular with discerning locals. Nightclubs dot the port and atmospheric **Fagotto Jazz Bar** (☎28210 71877; Angelou 16; ⊙12-5pm & 9pm-12am) has occasional live music.

★Bougatsa tou Iordanis CRETAN €
(☎28210 88855; Apokoronou 24; bougatsa €3; ⊙6am-2.30pm Mon-Sat, to 1.30pm Sun) You haven't lived until you've eaten the *bougatsa* at this little storefront dedicated to the flaky, sweet-cheesy treat. It's cooked fresh in enormous slabs and carved up in front of your eyes. Pair it with a coffee and you're set for the morning. There's nothing else on the menu!

★Taverna Tamam MEDITERRANEAN €€
(☎28210 96080; Zambeliou 49; mains €7-14; ⊙noon-midnight; 📶🖋) This excellent, convivial taverna in a converted Turkish bathhouse fills with chatting locals at tables spilling out onto the street. Dishes incorporate Middle Eastern spices, and include tasty soups and a superb selection of vegetarian specialities. Cretan delicacies include tender goat with *staka* (a rich goat's milk sauce).

★To Maridaki CRETAN €€
(☎28210 08880; Daskalogianni 33; dishes €7-12; ⊙noon-midnight Mon-Sat) This modern seafood *mezedhopoleio* (restaurant specialising in mezedhes) is not to be missed. In a cheerful, bright dining room, happy visitors and locals alike tuck into impeccable local seafood and Cretan specialities. Ingredients

WORTH A TRIP

RETHYMNO & MONI ARKADIOU

Rethymno (*reth*-im-no), on the coast between Iraklio and Hania, is one of the island's architectural treasures, due to its stunning **fortress** and mix of Venetian and Turkish houses in the **old quarter**. It's worth a stop to explore the area around the old Venetian harbour, and shop in its interesting arts and crafts boutiques.

Moni Arkadiou (Arkadi Monastery; ☎28310 22415, 28310 83136; www.arkadimonastery.gr; €3; ⏰9am-8pm Jun-Aug, shorter hours Sep-May), in the hills some 23km southeast of Rethymno, has deep significance for Cretans. A potent symbol of human resistance, it was the site of a tragic and momentous stand-off between the Turks and the Cretans in 1866, and considered a spark plug in the struggle towards freedom from Turkish occupation. Arkadiou's most impressive structure, its **Venetian church** (1587), has a striking Renaissance facade marked by eight slender Corinthian columns and topped by an ornate triple-belled tower. Its high mountain valley is beautiful, especially around sunset.

are fresh, the fried calamari is to die for, the house white wine is crisp and delicious, and the complimentary panna cotta to finish the meal is sublime. What's not to love?

★**Thalassino Ageri** SEAFOOD **€€€**
(☎28210 51136; www.thalasino-ageri.gr; Vivilaki 35; fish per kg €55; ⏰from 7.30pm Apr–mid-Oct) This solitary fish taverna in a tiny port 2km east of the centre among the ruins of Hania's old tanneries is one of Crete's top eateries. Take in the sunset from the superb setting and peruse the changing menu, dictated by the day's catch. Most dishes, like the fisherman's salad, hum with creativity, or transcendent simplicity like melt-in-your-mouth calamari.

ℹ Information

For information visit www.chania.gr.

ℹ Getting There & Away

AIR

Hania Airport (☎28210 83800; www.chaniaairport.com) serves Athens, Thessaloniki and seasonally cities around Europe. The airport is 14km east of town. KTEL (www.bus-service-crete-ktel.com) buses link the airport with central Hania up to 27 times daily (€2.30, 30 minutes). Taxis cost €20 (plus €2 per bag).

BOAT

The port is at Souda, 7km southeast of Hania. Once-nightly **Anek** (www.anek.gr) ferries serve Piraeus (€35, nine hours). Frequent buses (€1.50) and taxis (€9) connect the town and Souda. Hania buses meet each boat, as do buses to Rethymno.

BUS

Frequent buses from the **main bus station** (☎info 28210 93052, tickets 28210 93306; www.bus-service-crete-ktel.com; Kydonias 73-77; 📶) run along Crete's northern coast to Iraklio (€13.80, 2¾ hours, half-hourly) and Rethymno (€6.20, one hour, half-hourly); buses run less frequently to Paleohora, Omalos and Hora Sfakion. Buses for beaches west of Hania leave from the eastern side of Plateia 1866.

Samaria Gorge
ΦΑΡΑΓΓΙ ΤΗΣ ΣΑΜΑΡΙΑΣ

Samaria Gorge (☎28210 45570, 28210 67179; www.samaria.gr; adult/child €5/free; ⏰7am-sunset May-late Oct) is one of Europe's most spectacular gorges and a superb (very popular) hike. Walkers should take rugged footwear, food, drinks and sun protection for this strenuous five- to six-hour trek. You can do the walk as part of an excursion tour, or independently by taking the Omalos bus from the main bus station in Hania (€6.90, one hour) to the head of the gorge at Xyloskalo (1230m). It's a 16.7km walk (all downhill) to **Agia Roumeli** on the coast, from where you take a boat to Hora Sfakion (€10, 1¼ hours) and then a bus back to Hania (€7.60, 1½ hours). You are not allowed to spend the night in the gorge, so you need to complete the walk in a day, or beat the crowds and stay over in one of the nearby villages. Other gorges, like **Imbros** (€2; ⏰year-round), also make for fine walking, and are less crowded.

DODECANESE
ΔΩΔΕΚΑΝΗΣΑ

Strung out along the coast of western Turkey, the 12 main islands of the Dodecanese (*dodeca* means 12) have suffered a turbulent past of invasions and occupations that have endowed them with a fascinating diversity.

Conquered successively by the Romans, the Arabs, the Knights of St John, the Turks, the Italians, then liberated from the Germans by British and Greek commandos in 1944, the Dodecanese became part of Greece in 1947. These days, tourists rule.

Rhodes ΡΟΔΟΣ

POP 115,000

Rhodes (Rodos in Greek) is the largest island in the Dodecanese. According to mythology, the sun god Helios chose Rhodes as his bride and bestowed light, warmth and vegetation upon her. The blessing seems to have paid off, for Rhodes produces more flowers and sunny days than most Greek islands. Throw in an east coast of virtually uninterrupted sandy beaches and it's easy to understand why sun-starved northern Europeans flock here in droves. The old town is magnificent.

Rhodes Town

POP 86,000

Rhodes' capital is Rhodes Town, on the northern tip of the island. Its magnificent **Old Town**, the largest inhabited medieval town in Europe, is enclosed within massive walls and is a delight to explore. Nowhere else in the Dodecanese can boast so many layers of architectural history, with ruins and relics of the classical, medieval, Ottoman and Italian eras entangled in a mind-boggling maze of twisting alleys.

To the north is **New Town**, the commercial centre. The **town beach**, which looks out at Turkey, runs around the peninsula at the northern end of New Town. The main port, **Commercial Harbour**, is east of the Old Town, and is where the big interisland ferries dock. Northwest of here is **Mandraki Harbour**, lined with excursion boats and smaller ferries, hydrofoils and catamarans. It was the supposed site of the **Colossus of Rhodes**, a 32m-high bronze statue of Apollo built over 12 years (294–282 BC). The statue stood for a mere 65 years before being toppled by an earthquake.

LINDOS

The **Acropolis of Lindos** (☎22413 65200; adult/concession/child €12/6/free; ⏰8am-8pm Tue-Fri, to 3pm Sat-Mon Apr-Oct, 8.30am-3pm Tue-Sun Nov-Mar), 47km south from Rhodes Town, is an ancient city spectacularly perched atop a 116m-high rocky outcrop. Below is the town of Lindos, a tangle of pedestrian streets with elaborately decorated 17th-century captain houses. Nearby is the gorgeous though tiny beach of Agios Pavlos.

Sights

A wander around Rhodes' Unesco World Heritage–listed Old Town is a must. It is reputedly the world's finest surviving example of medieval fortification, with 12m-thick walls. A mesh of Byzantine, Turkish and Latin architecture, the Old Town is divided into the Kollakio (the Knights' Quarter, where the Knights of St John lived during medieval times), the Hora and the Jewish Quarter. The Knights' Quarter contains most of the medieval historical sights while the Hora, often referred to as the Turkish Quarter, is primarily Rhodes Town's commercial sector with shops and restaurants, thronged by tourists.

The Knights of St John lived in the **Knights' Quarter** in the northern end of the Old Town. The cobbled **Avenue of the Knights** (Ippoton) is lined with magnificent medieval buildings, the most imposing of which is the **Palace of the Grand Master**

THE KNIGHTS OF ST JOHN

Island-hopping in the Dodecanese you'll quickly realise that the Knights of St John left behind a passel of castles. Originally formed as the Knights Hospitaller in Jerusalem in 1080 to provide care for poor and sick pilgrims, the knights relocated to Rhodes (via Cyprus) after the loss of Jerusalem in the First Crusade. They ousted the ruling Genoese in 1309, built a stack of castles in the Dodecanese to protect their new home, then set about irking the neighbours by committing acts of piracy against Ottoman shipping. Sultan Süleyman the Magnificent, not a man you'd want to irk, took offence and set about dislodging the knights from their strongholds. Rhodes finally capitulated in 1523 and the remaining knights relocated to Malta. They set up there as the Sovereign Military Hospitaller of Jerusalem, of Rhodes, and of Malta.

WORTH A TRIP

SOUTHWEST COAST VILLAGES

Crete's southern coastline at its western end is dotted with remote, attractive little villages that are brilliant spots to take it easy for a few days.

From Paleohora heading east are Sougia, Agia Roumeli, Loutro and Hora Sfakion. No road links the coastal resorts, but a once-daily boat from Paleohora to Sougia (€9, 50 minutes), Agia Roumeli (€15, 1½ hours), Loutro (€16, 2½ hours) and Hora Sfakion (€17, three hours) connects the villages in summer. See www.sfakia-crete.com/sfakia-crete/ferries.html. In summer three buses daily connect Hania and Hora Sfakion (€7.60, one hour and 40 minutes), two daily to Sougia (€7.10, one hour and 50 minutes). If you're a keen hiker, it's also possible to walk right along this southern coast.

Paleohora This village is isolated on a peninsula with a sandy beach to the west and a pebbly beach to the east. On summer evenings the main street is closed to traffic and the tavernas move onto the road. If you're after a relaxing few days, Paleohora is a great spot to chill out. Stay at **Joanna's** (28230 41801; www.joanna-place.com; studio €50-60; Apr-Nov; P) spacious, spotless studios.

Sougia At the mouth of the **Agia Irini gorge**, Sougia (soo-yah) is a laid-back and refreshingly undeveloped spot with a wide curve of sand-and-pebble beach. The 14.5km (six hours) walk from Paleohora is popular, as is the Agia Irini gorge walk which ends (or starts!) in Sougia. It's possible to get here by ferry, by car or on foot. Stay at **Santa Irene Apartments** (28230 51342; www.santa-irene.gr; apt €60-80; late Mar-early Nov; P), a smart beachside complex with its own cafe.

Agia Roumeli At the mouth of the Samaria Gorge (p368), Agia Roumeli bristles with gorge-walkers from mid-afternoon until the ferry comes to take them away. Once they are gone, this pleasant little town goes into quiet mode until the first walkers turn up in the early afternoon the following day. Right on the waterfront, **Paralia Taverna & Rooms** (28250 91408; www.taverna-paralia.com; d €35-40;) offers excellent views, tasty Cretan cuisine, cold beer and simple, clean rooms.

Loutro This tiny village is a particularly picturesque spot, curled around the only natural harbour on the southern coast of Crete. With no vehicle access, the only way in is by boat or on foot. **Hotel Porto Loutro** (28250 91433, 28250 91001; www.hotelportoloutro.com; s/d/tr incl breakfast €55/65/75; Apr-Oct; @) has tasteful rooms with balconies overlooking the harbour. The village beach, excellent walks, rental kayaks, and boat transfers to excellent Sweetwater Beach fill peaceful days.

Hora Sfakion Renowned in Cretan history for its rebellious streak, Hora Sfakion is an amiable town. WWII history buffs know this as the place where thousands of Allied troops were evacuated by sea after the Battle of Crete. Hora Sfakion's seafront tavernas serve fresh seafood and unique *Sfakianes pites* which look like crêpes filled with sweet or savoury local cheese. **Hotel Stavris** (28250 91220; www.hotel-stavris-sfakia-crete.com; s/d from €28/33;) has simple rooms and breakfast outside in its courtyard.

(22410 23359, 22413 65270; €6; 8am-8pm May-Oct, 8am-4pm Tue-Sun Nov-Apr), which was restored, but never used, as a holiday home for Mussolini. From the palace, explore the **D'Amboise Gate**, the most atmospheric of the fortification gates which takes you across the moat.

The beautiful 15th-century Knights' Hospital, closer to the seafront, now houses the excellent **Archaeological Museum** (22413 65200; Plateia Mousiou; adult/child €8/free; 8am-8pm Tue-Fri, 8am-3pm Sat & Sun, 9am-3pm Mon Apr-Oct, 9am-4pm Tue-Sat Nov-Mar). The splendid building was restored by the Italians and has an impressive collection that includes the ethereal marble statue *Aphrodite of Rhodes*.

The pink-domed **Mosque of Süleyman** (Sokratous), at the top of Sokratous, was built in 1522 to commemorate the Ottoman victory against the knights, then rebuilt in 1808.

Sleeping

★Hotel Anastasia PENSION €€

(22410 28007; www.anastasia-hotel.com; 28 Oktovriou 46; s/d/tr €55/65//85; @) The New Town's friendliest and most peaceful accommodation option, this handsome white-painted villa is set well back from the road and offers charming ochre-coloured ensuite rooms with wooden shutters, tiled floors and traditional furnishings. Some have private balconies and there's an inviting breakfast bar in the lush garden.

★Marco Polo Mansion BOUTIQUE HOTEL €€
(☎22410 25562; www.marcopolomansion.gr; Agiou Fanouriou 40; d incl breakfast €80-260; ⊙Apr-Oct; ❄📶) In the 15th century, this irresistible garden-set mansion, tucked away on an ancient alleyway, was home to a high Ottoman official. Now it's a gloriously romantic B&B hotel, its cool, high-ceilinged rooms decorated with exquisite taste and old-world flair. Amazing buffet breakfasts are spread out in the flower-filled courtyard, which is open to all every evening as a fabulous restaurant.

★Spirit of the Knights BOUTIQUE HOTEL €€€
(☎22410 39765; www.rhodesluxuryhotel.com; Alexandridou 14; s/d incl breakfast €160-200/200-375; 🚭❄📶) Six sumptuous suites in a splendidly transformed old home, nestled close to the Old Town walls. Each has its own historical theme, evoked through lavish linens, hangings and furniture and details such as stained glass, while all share a library inside and a whirlpool spa outside. Linger over breakfast in the tranquil gardens.

Eating & Drinking

Old Rhodes is rife with tourist traps; look in the backstreets. Head further north into New Town for better-value restaurants and bars.

★Koykos GREEK €
(☎22410 73022; http://koukosrodos.com; Mandilana 20-26; mains €3-10; ⊙daily early-late; ❄📶) This inviting complex, off a pedestrian shopping street, consists of several antique-filled rooms – a couple hold vintage jukeboxes – along with two bougainvillea-draped courtyards and a floral roof terrace. Best known for fabulous homemade pies, it also serves all the classic mezedhes, plus meat and fish dishes, or you can drop in for a coffee or sandwich.

★Nireas SEAFOOD €€
(☎22410 21703; Sofokleous 45-47; mains €8-16; ⊙lunch & dinner; ❄) Nireas' status as Rhodes' favourite seafood restaurant owes much to the sheer enthusiasm and verve of genial owner Theo, from Symi – that and the beautifully prepared food, served beneath a vine-shaded canopy outside, or in the candlelit, lemon-walled interior. Be sure to sample the Symi shrimp, salted mackerel and, if you're in the mood, the 'Viagra' salad of small shellfish.

★Marco Polo Cafe MEDITERRANEAN €€
(☎22410 25562; www.marcopolomansion.gr; Agiou Fanouriou 40-42; mains €12-25; ⊙7-11pm) Magical, irresistibly romantic restaurant in a delightful garden courtyard. The passion and flair of the cuisine is astounding, while the service epitomises *filoxenia* (hospitality). Menus change nightly, with specials such as calamari and prawn balls in a couscous crust, tuna in sesame marinated with orange, or lamb souvlaki on a bed of risotto, plus inventive desserts such as semifreddo of tahini.

Petaladika GREEK €€
(☎22410 27319; Menakleous 8; mains €8-15; ⊙noon-late) Petaladika might look like just another tourist trap, tucked into a corner off the main drag, but it has quickly established itself as the finest newcomer on the Old Town dining scene. Locals swoon over highlights such as deep-fried baby squid, zucchini balls and freshly grilled fish.

Information

EOT (Greek Tourist Information Office; ☎22410 44335; www.ando.gr/eot; cnr Makariou & Papagou; ⊙8am-2.45pm Mon-Fri) National tourism information, including brochures, maps and transport details.

Rhodes Tourism Office – New Town (☎22410 35495; www.rhodes.gr; Plateia Rimini; ⊙7.30am-3pm Mon-Fri) Conveniently poised between Mandraki Harbour and the Old Town.

Rhodes Tourism Office – Old Town (☎22410 35945; www.rhodes.gr; cnr Platonos & Ippoton; ⊙7am-3pm Mon-Fri) In an ancient building at the foot of the Street of the Knights, this helpful office supplies excellent street maps, leaflets and brochures.

Getting There & Around

AIR

Many flights daily connect Rhodes' **Diagoras Airport** (RHO; ☎22410 88700; www.rhodes-airport.org) and Athens, plus less-regular flights to Karpathos, Kastellorizo, Thessaloniki, Iraklio, Crete, Santorini and Samos. International flights, budget airlines and charter flights swarm in summer. The airport is on the west coast, 16km southwest of Rhodes Town; 25 minutes and €2.40 by bus, €22 by taxi.

BOATS TO TURKEY

Turkey is so close that it looks like you could swim there from many of the Dodecanese and Northeastern Aegean islands. Here are the boat options:

Bodrum from Kos

Çeşme (near İzmir) from Chios

Dikili (near Ayvalık) from Lesvos

Kuşadasi (near Ephesus) from Samos

Marmaris from Rhodes

BOAT

Rhodes is the main port of the Dodecanese and there is a complex array of departures. Most of the daily boats to Piraeus (€44, 18 hours) sail via the Dodecanese, but some go via Karpathos, Crete and the Cyclades. In summer, catamaran services run up and down the Dodecanese daily from Rhodes to Symi or Halki, Kos, Kalymnos, Nisyros, Tilos, Patmos and Leros. Check www.openseas.gr, **Dodekanisos Seaways** (☎22410 70590; www.12ne.gr; Afstralias 3, Rhodes Town) and **Blue Star Ferries** (☎21089 19800; www.bluestarferries.com). Excursion boats at the harbour also go to Symi.

To Turkey

Catamarans connect Rhodes and Marmaris in Turkey (one-way/return including port taxes €50/75, 50 minutes). Check www.marmarisinfo.com.

BUS

Rhodes Town has two bus stations a block apart next to the New Market. The **Eastern Bus Terminal** (☎22410 27706; www.ktelrodou.gr) has frequent services to the airport (€2.40), Kalithea Thermi (€2.20), Ancient Kamiros (€5) and Monolithos (€6). The **Western Bus Terminal** (☎22410 26300) services Faliraki (€2.20), Tsambika Beach (€3.50), Stegna Beach (€4) and Lindos (€5).

Kos ΚΩΣ

POP 33,300

Bustling Kos, only 5km from the Turkish peninsula of Bodrum, is popular with history buffs as the birthplace of Hippocrates (460–377 BC), the father of medicine. The island also attracts an entirely different crowd – hordes of sun-worshipping beach lovers from northern Europe who pack the long, sandy stretches in summer.

Sights & Activities

Busy Kos Town has lots of **bicycle paths** and renting a bike along the pretty waterfront is great for seeing the sights. Near the Castle of the Knights is **Hippocrates Plane Tree** (Plateia Platanou, Kos Town) FREE, under which the man himself is said to have taught his pupils. The modern town is built on the vast remains of the ancient Greek one – explore the ruins!

★Asklepieion ARCHAEOLOGICAL SITE

(☎22420 28763; adult/child €7/free; ⊗8am-7pm Tue-Sun Apr-Oct, 8am-3pm Tue-Sun Nov-Mar) The island's most important ancient site stands on a pine-covered hill 3km southwest of Kos Town, commanding lovely views across town towards Turkey. A religious sanctuary devoted to Asclepius, the god of healing, it was also a healing centre and a school of medicine. It was founded in the 3rd century BC, according to legend by Hippocrates himself. He was already dead by then, though, and the training here simply followed his teachings.

Castle of the Knights CASTLE

(☎22420 27927; €4; ⊗8am-8pm Apr-Oct, 8am-3pm Tue-Sun Nov-Mar) Kos' magnificent 15th-century castle was constructed not on a hilltop, but right beside the entrance to the harbour. Access it by the bridge from Plateia Platanou, crossing what was once a seawater-filled moat but is now a road. Visitors can stroll atop the intact outer walls, surveying all activity in the port and keeping a watchful eye on Turkey across the strait. The precinct within, however, is now largely overgrown, with cats stalking through a wilderness of wildflowers.

Sleeping

★Hotel Afendoulis HOTEL €

(☎22420 25321; www.afendoulishotel.com; Evripilou 1; s/d €30/50; ⊗Mar-Nov; ❄@📶) Peaceful Afendoulis has unfailingly friendly staff and sparkling rooms with white walls, small balconies and spotless bathrooms. Downstairs, the open breakfast room and flowery terrace have wrought-iron tables and chairs for enjoying the feast of homemade jams and marmalades. There may be more modern, plusher hotels in Kos, but none with the special soul of this fine, family-run establishment.

Hotel Sonia HOTEL €€
(☎22420 28798; www.hotelsonia.gr; Irodotou 9; s/d/tr €45/60/75; ❄📶) A block from the waterfront on a peaceful backstreet, this pension offers a dozen sparkling rooms with parquet floors, fridges, smart bathrooms and an extra bed if required. Room 4 has the best sea view. Breakfast is served on a relaxing communal verandah, there's a decent book exchange and it plans to open up the garden to visitors.

Eating & Drinking

Restaurants line the central waterfront of the old harbour in Kos Town, but backstreets harbour better value. Nightclubs dot Diakon and Nafklirou, just north of the *agora* (market).

★**Pote Tin Kyriaki** TAVERNA €
(☎22420 27872, 6930352099; Pisandrou 9; ⏲7pm-2am) Named for Melina Mercouri's Oscar-winning 1960 song, 'Never on Sunday' is not the sort of place you expect to find in modern Kos – and it takes a lot of finding. This traditional *ouzerie* (place that serves ouzo and light snacks) serves delicious specialities such as stuffed zucchini flowers, dolmadhes (vine leaves stuffed with rice and sometimes meat) with lemongrass, and steamed mussels. It plans to open for breakfast and lunch too – just never on Sunday.

Elia GREEK €€
(☎22420 22133; Appelou Ifestou 27; mains €8-15; ⏲12.30pm-late; ❄📶🍷👪) 🌿 Friendly restaurant with seating in the garden and venerable interior as well as on the lively pedestrian street. The menu draws on traditional dishes from all over Greece, with standouts including the chunky rustic sausage, bream baked with oregano and rosemary, and drunken pork (cooked in wine). Simple starters such as fava and fried onions are equally tasty.

Petrino Meze Restaurant MEZEDHES €€
(☎22420 27251; www.petrino-kos.gr; Plateia Theologou 1; mains €9-28; ⏲lunch & dinner; ❄📶) Peaceful and balmy, this graceful restaurant has a leafy garden shaded by bougainvillea, overlooking Kos Town's western group of archaeological ruins. Highlights on its upscale menu include hearty meat concoctions such as beef stuffed with blue cheese and pork with plums, but it also serves lighter dishes such as steamed swordfish or pasta, as well as mixed mezedhes platters.

Information

Visit www.kos.gr, www.kosinfo.gr or www.travel-to-kos.com for information.

Fanos Travel & Shipping (☎22420 20035; 11 Akti Koundourioti) Tickets for the hydrofoil service to Bodrum and other ferries, plus yachting services.

Kentrikon Travel (☎22420 28914; Akti Kountouriotou 7) The offical agents for Blue Star Ferries also sells all other ferry and air tickets.

Getting There & Around

AIR

From **Ippokratis Airport** (KGS; ☎22420 56000; www.kosairportguide.com), there are up to four daily flights to Athens (from €50, 55 minutes) as well as three weekly to Rhodes (€61, 30 minutes), and once weekly in summer to Heraklion in Crete (€69, 50 minutes). The airport is 24km southwest of Kos Town; buses cost €3.20, taxis €30.

BICYCLE

Hire bikes at the harbour to get around town.

BOAT

Kos has services to Piraeus and all islands in the Dodecanese, the Cyclades, Samos and Thessaloniki. Catamarans are run by Dodekanisos Seaways at the interisland ferry quay. Local passenger and car ferries run to Pothia on Kalymnos from Mastihari. For tickets, visit Fanos Travel & Shipping on the harbour.

To Turkey

Catamarans connect Kos Town with both Bodrum (two daily) and Turgutreis in Turkey (one daily). Both journeys take 20 minutes. Tickets cost €18 each way, with same-day returns €24 and longer-stay returns €32. For schedules and bookings, visit www.rhodes.marmarisinf.

BUS

The main **bus station** (☎22420 22292; Kleopatras 7, Kos Town), well back from the waterfront in Kos Town, is the base for services to all parts of the island, including the airport and south-coast beaches, with **KTEL** (☎22420 22292; www.ktel-kos.gr).

ISLAND SHORTCUTS

If long ferry rides eat into your holiday too much, check Aegean Airlines (p383), Olympic Air (p384), Astra Airlines (p384) and Sky Express (p384) for flights. But beware baggage limits: Sky Express in particular only allows teeny bags.

NORTHEASTERN AEGEAN ISLANDS
ΤΑ ΝΗΣΙΑ ΤΟΥ ΒΟΡΕΙΟ ΑΝΑΤΟΛΙΚΟ ΑΙΓΑΙΟΥ

One of Greece's best-kept secrets, these far-flung islands are strewn across the northeastern corner of the Aegean, closer to Turkey than mainland Greece. They harbour unspoilt scenery, welcoming locals, fascinating independent cultures, and remain relatively calm even when other Greek islands are sagging with tourists at the height of summer.

Samos ΣΑΜΟΣ

POP 32,820

A lush mountainous island only 3km from Turkey, Samos has a glorious history as the legendary birthplace of Hera, wife and sister of god-of-all-gods Zeus. Samos was an important centre of Hellenic culture, and the mathematician Pythagoras and storyteller Aesop are among its sons. The island has beaches that bake in summer, and a hinterland that is superb for hiking. Spring brings with it pink flamingos, wildflowers, and orchids that the island grows for export, while summer brings throngs of package tourists.

Vathy (Samos Town) Βαθύ Σάμος

POP 2025

Busy Vathy is an attractive working port town. Most of the action is along Themistokleous Sofouli, the main street that runs along the waterfront. The main square, Plateia Pythagorou, in the middle of the waterfront, is recognisable by its four palm trees and statue of a lion.

The first-rate **Archaeological Museum** (☎22730 27469; adult/child €4/free, free 1st Sun Nov-Mar; ⌚8am-3pm Tue-Sun) is one of the best in the islands and the **Museum of Samos Wines** (☎22730 87551; www.samoswine.gr; €2; ⌚8am-8pm Mon-Sat) FREE offers tours and taste-testing with one of the island's best vinters. **Cleomenis Hotel** (☎22730 23232; Kallistratous 33; d incl breakfast from €50) offers great, simple rooms close to the beach northeast of town. Elegant **Ino Village Hotel** (☎22730 23241; www.inovillagehotel.com; Kalami; d incl breakfast €67-150; P❄☕≋) in the hills north of the ferry quay has **Elea Restaurant** with views over town and the harbour.

ITSA Travel (☎22730 23605; www.itsatravelsamos.gr; Themistokleous Sofouli 5; ⌚8am-8pm), opposite the quay, is helpful with travel inquiries, excursions, accommodation and luggage storage.

Pythagorio Πυθαγόρειο

POP 1330

Little Pythagorio, 11km south of Vathy, is where you'll disembark if you've come by boat from Patmos. It is a small, enticing town with a yacht-lined harbour and a busy, holiday atmosphere, overwhelming to some.

The 1034m-long **Evpalinos Tunnel** (☎22730 61400; adult/child €4/free; ⌚8am-3pm Tue-Sun), built in the 6th century BC, was dug by political prisoners and used as an aqueduct to bring water from Mt Ampelos (1140m).

Ireon (adult/child €4/free; ⌚8.30am-3pm Tue-Sun), the legendary birthplace of the goddess Hera, is 8km west of Pythagorio. The temple at this World Heritage site was enormous – four times the size of the Parthenon – though only one column remains.

The impeccable **Pension Despina** (☎6938120399, 22730 61677; www.samosrooms.gr/despina/more.html; A Nikolaou; r/studio €35/40; ❄☕) is a relaxing spot with a garden while **Polyxeni Hotel** (☎22730 61590; www.polyxenihotel.com; s/d/tr incl breakfast from €40/55/70; ❄☕) is in the heart of the waterfront action. Tavernas and bars line the waterfront.

The cordial **Tourist Office** (☎22730 61389; Lykourgou Logotheti; ⌚8am-9.30pm, reduced hours in winter) is two blocks from the waterfront on the main street. The bus stop is two blocks further inland on the same street.

Around Samos

Samos is an island of forests, mountains, wildlife and over 30 villages, harbouring excellent, cheap tavernas. The captivating villages of **Vourliotes** and **Manolates**, on the slopes of imposing **Mt Ampelos**, northwest of Vathy, are excellent walking territory and have many marked pathways.

Karlovasi, on the northwest coast, is another ferry port and interesting in its own right. Spend the night at **Studios Angela** (☎22730 62198; www.studiosangela.com; Manolates; d €30-40; ❄), with studios built into a hillside overlooking the sea. The beaches south of Karlovasi, like **Potami Beach**, are tops. Other choice beaches include **Tsamadou** on the north coast, **Votsalakia** in the southwest and **Psili Ammos** to the east of Pythagorio. The latter is sandy and stares straight out at Turkey, barely a couple of kilometres away. Beautiful **Bullos Beach** near Skoureika village is even more off the beaten path.

Hire a car and explore!

Getting There & Around

AIR

Daily flights connect Athens with Samos Airport (SMI), 4km west of Pythagorio. Several weekly flights serve Iraklio, Rhodes, Chios and Thessaloniki. Charters serve Chios from Amsterdam, Oslo and Vienna.

Buses (€2) run three to four times daily and taxis to Vathy/Pythagorio cost €25/6.

BOAT

Samos is home to three ports – Vathy (aka Samos), Pythagorio and Karlovasi. The new ferry terminal in Vathy, for ferries to domestic destinations only, is at the harbour's southeast end, 1.7km from the old ferry terminal, which is only for boats to Turkey. A taxi between the terminals is €5.

A maritime hub, Samos offers daily ferries to Piraeus (€32, 12 hours), plus ferries heading north to Chios and west to the Cyclades. In summer, high-speed services head south to Patmos and Kos.

ITSA Travel (p374), directly opposite Vathy's old ferry terminal, provides detailed information and sells tickets. In Pythagorio, check ferry and hydrofoil schedules with the tourist office (p374), the **port police** (☎22730 61225) or **By Ship Travel** (☎22730 80768; www.byshiptravel.gr).

To Turkey

There are daily ferries to Kuşadasi (for Ephesus) in Turkey (€35/45 one-way/return, plus €10 port taxes). Day excursions are also available from April to October. Check with **ITSA Travel** (p374) for up-to-date details.

BUS

You can get to most of the island's villages and beaches by bus.

CAR & MOTORCYCLE

Opposite the port entrance in Vathy, **Manos Moto-Auto Rental** (☎6974392157, 22730 23309; www.manos-rentals.gr; Grammou & Kounturioti) runs an efficient service. Another good option is **Pegasus Rent-a-Car** (☎22730 24470, 6978536440; www.samos-car-rental.com; Themistoklis Sofouli 5, Vathy), with good rates on car, 4WD and motorcycle hire.

Lesvos (Mytilini) ΛΕΣΒΟΣ (ΜΥΤΙΛΗΝΗ)

POP 95,330

Lesvos, or Mytilini as it is often called, tends to do things in a big way. The third-largest of the Greek islands after Crete and Evia, Lesvos produces half the world's ouzo and is home to over 11 million olive trees. Mountainous yet fertile, the island has world-class local cuisine, and presents excellent hiking and birdwatching opportunities, but remains refreshingly untouched in terms of tourism.

Mytilini Μυτιλήνη

POP 29,650

The capital and main port, Mytilini, is a lively student town with great eating and drinking options, plus eclectic churches and grand 19th-century mansions and museums. It is built between two harbours (north and south) with an imposing fortress on the promontory to the east. All ferries dock at the southern harbour, and most of the town's action is around this waterfront.

Sights

Teriade Museum MUSEUM

(☎22510 23372; http://museumteriade.gr; Varia; adult €2; ⏲9am-2pm & 5-8pm Apr-Oct, 9am-5pm Nov-Mar) Varia, 4km south of Mytilini, is the

SAPPHO, LESBIANS & LESVOS

Sappho, one of Greece's great ancient poets, was born on Lesvos during the 7th century BC. Most of her work was devoted to love and desire, and the objects of her affection were often female. Because of this, Sappho's name and birthplace have come to be associated with female homosexuality.

These days, Lesvos is visited by many lesbians paying homage to Sappho. The whole island is very gay-friendly, in particular the southwestern beach resort of **Skala Eresou**, which is built over ancient Eresos, where Sappho was born. The village is well set up to cater to lesbian needs and has a 'Women Together' festival held annually in September. See www.womensfestival.eu and www.sapphotravel.com for details.

unlikely home of the Teriade Museum with its astonishing collection of paintings by artists such as Picasso, Chagall, Miro, Le Corbusier and Matisse. The museum honours the Lesvos-born artist and critic Stratis Eleftheriadis, who brought the work of primitive painter and Lesvos native Theophilos to international attention.

Archaeological Museum MUSEUM
(☎22510 40223; 8 Noemvriou; adult/child €3/2; ⊙8am-5pm Jun-Oct, 8.30am-5pm Tue-Sun Nov-May) This handsome and refurbished museum, about 500m above the eastern quay (and the now-closed Old Archaeological Museum), portrays island life from the 2nd century BC to the 3rd century AD, including striking floor mosaics with a walking 'trail' across the protective glass surface.

Fortress FORTRESS
(Kastro; adult/child €2/free; ⊙8am-3pm Tue-Sun) Mytilini's imposing early Byzantine fortress was renovated in the 14th century by Genoese overlord Francisco Gatelouzo, and then the Turks enlarged it again. Flanked by pine trees, it's popular for a stroll, with great views included.

Sleeping

★Alkaios Rooms PENSION €
(☎6981314154, 22510 47737; www.alkaiosrooms.gr; Alkaiou 16; s/d/tr incl breakfast €35/45/55; ❄📶) This collection of 30 spotless and well-kept rooms nestled discreetly in two renovated traditional buildings is Mytilini's most attractive budget option. It's a two-minute walk up from the west side of the waterfront (and Kitchen 19 cafe). The reception is in a restored mansion, where breakfast is served in a flowery courtyard.

Theofilos Paradise Boutique Hotel BOUTIQUE HOTEL €€
(☎22510 43300; www.theofilosparadise.gr; Skra 7; d/ste/f incl breakfast from €120/150/170; P❄@📶≋) This smartly restored, 100-year-old mansion is elegant, cheerful and good value, with modern amenities along with a traditional *hammam*. The 22 swanky rooms (plus two luxe suites) are spread among three adjacent buildings surrounding an inviting courtyard.

Hotel Lesvion HOTEL €€
(☎22510 28177; www.lesvion.gr; Kountouriotou 27a, harbour; s/d/tr from €45/60/70; ❄📶) The modern and well-positioned Lesvion, smack on the harbour, has friendly service and attractive and spacious rooms, some with excellent port-view balconies. A breakfast bar overlooks the harbour.

Eating & Drinking

Hit the streets in the bend in the harbour (Plateia Sapphou), around Ladadika, for zippy bars, cafes and creative eats.

★Taverna Efkaliptos SEAFOOD €
(☎22510 32727; old harbour, Panagiouda; mains €6-12; ⊙lunch & dinner) You might be sitting closer to the fishing boats than the kitchen at this first-class fish taverna in Panagiouda, just 4km north of Mytilini but with a distinctly remote feel. Excellent mezedhes and well-priced fresh fish, great service, and white wine from nearby Limnos.

★To Steki tou Yianni TAVERNA €
(☎22510 28244; Agiou Therapodos; mains €5-15; ⊙noon-3pm & 8pm-late) Head up behind the giant Agios Therapon church to this wonderful, welcoming taverna where Yianni dishes out whatever's freshest. All the produce is local, the cheeses delectable, and the fish or meat top quality. Go with the flow...this is a local hang-out, with folks arriving after 9pm. Sip a local ouzo and see what Yianni brings you.

Cafe P CAFE €
(☎22510 55594; Samou 2; mains €2-7; ⊙11am-3am) This hip back-alley bistro draws a mostly university crowd for its unusual and well-priced small plates, small menu, eclectic music mix and all-round chill atmosphere. Oven-cooked pork with leeks or baked feta in a fig balsamic, plus a draught beer is €6. About 50m in from Sappho Sq. Look for the single Greek letter, 'Π'.

Information

See www.lesvos.net and www.greeknet.com for information.

Molyvos (Mithymna) Μόλυβος (Μήθυμνα)

POP 1500

The gracious, historic town of Mithymna (known by locals as Molyvos), 62km north of Mytilini Town, winds beautifully from the picturesque **old harbour**, up through cobbled streets canopied by flowering vines to the impressive **Byzantine-Genoese Castle** (☎22530 71803; €2; ⊙8.30am-3pm) on the hilltop, from which you get tremendous views out to Turkey and around the lush valleys.

Ravishing to the eye, Molyvos is well worth a wander, or is a peaceful place to stay.

Eftalou hot springs (☎22530 71245; old/new bathhouse €4/5; ⊙old bathhouse 6-8am & 6-9pm, new bathhouse 9am-5pm), 4km from town on the beach, is a superb bathhouse complex with steaming, pebbled pools. The scenery on the northern coast is extraordinary, as are its tiny villages.

Airy, friendly **Nassos Guest House** (☎6942046279; www.nassosguesthouse.com; d/tr without bathroom from €25/35; 📶) offers shared facilities and a communal kitchen, in an old Turkish house with rapturous views. **Lela's Studios** (☎22530 71285, 6942928224; www.eftalouolivegrove.com/lelas_studios.htm; studio from €40; ❄📶) is set in a courtyard of roses and geraniums with sunset sea views.

From the bus stop, walk towards town 100m to the helpful **municipal tourist office** (☎22530 71347; ⊙10am-3pm Mon-Sat May-Jun & Sep, 10am-3pm & 4-9pm Mon-Sat, 10am-3pm Sun Jul-Aug).

Buses to Mithymna (€7.50) take 1½ hours from Mytilini; a rental car is a better option with so much to explore.

Around the Island

Hire a car and tour the incredible countryside. Southern Lesvos is dominated by **Mt Olympus** (968m), and grove-covered valleys. Visit wonderful mountain village **Agiasos**, with its artisan workshops making everything from handcrafted furniture to pottery. **Plomari** in the far south is the land of ouzo distilleries; tour fascinating **Varvagianni Ouzo Museum** (☎22520 32741; www.barbayanni-ouzo.com; Plomari; ⊙9am-4pm Mon-Fri Apr-Oct, 10am-2pm Mon-Fri Nov-Mar, by appointment Sat & Sun) FREE.

Western Lesvos is known for its **petrified forest** (☎22510 47033; www.petrifiedforest.gr; €2; ⊙park 8am-4pm Tue-Sun Jul-Sep, museum 9.30am-5.30pm Jul-Sep, 9am-5pm Tue-Sun Oct-Jun), with petrified wood at least 500,000 years old, and for the gay-friendly town of **Skala Eresou**, the birthplace of Sappho. You can stay over in peaceful **Sigri**, with its broad beaches, to the southwest.

ℹ Getting There & Around

AIR

Written up on flight schedules as Mytilene, Lesvos' **Odysseas Airport** (MJT; ☎22510 61212, 22510 38700) has daily connections with Athens and Thessaloniki. **Sky Express** (☎28102 23500; www.skyexpress.gr) flies to Limnos, Chios, Samos and Rhodes (but beware their strict baggage policy). The airport is 8km south of Mytilini town; taxis cost €10, bus €1.60.

BOAT

In summer, daily fast boats leave Mytilini Town for Piraeus (€42, 11 to 13 hours) via Chios. Other ferries serve Chios, Ikaria, Limnos, Thessaloniki and Samos. Check www.openseas.gr.

BUS

The long-distance bus station in Mytilini Town is beside Agia Irinis Park, near the domed church. The local bus station is opposite Plateia Sapphou, the main square.

CAR

It's worth renting a car in Lesvos to explore the vast island. There are several outlets at the airport and many in town.

SPORADES ΣΠΟΡΑΔΕΣ

Scattered to the southeast of the Pelion Peninsula, to which they were joined in prehistoric times, the 11 islands that make up the Sporades group have similarly mountainous terrain and dense vegetation, and are surrounded by scintillatingly clear seas.

The main ports for the Sporades are Volos and Agios Konstantinos on the mainland.

Skiathos ΣΚΙΑΘΟΣ

POP 6110

Lush and green, Skiathos has a beach resort feel about it. Charter flights bring loads of package tourists, but the island still oozes enjoyment and is downright mellow in winter. Skiathos Town, with its quaint **old harbour**, and some excellent beaches are on the hospitable south coast.

👁 Sights & Activities

Moni Evangelistrias (☎24270 22012; museum €2; ⊙10am-dusk), the most famous of the island's monasteries, was a hilltop refuge for freedom fighters during the War of Independence, and the Greek flag was first raised here, in 1807.

Skiathos has superb beaches, particularly on the south coast. **Koukounaries** is popular with families, and has a wonderful protected **marshland** for water fowl. A stroll over the headland, **Big Banana Beach** is stunning, but if you want an all-over tan, head a tad further to **Little Banana Beach**, where bathing suits are a rarity. Beautiful **Lalaria** on the north coast is accessible only by boat.

At the Old Port in Skiathos Town, **boat excursions** go to nearby beaches (€10), around Skiathos Island (€25) and on full-day trips to Skopelos, Alonnisos and the Alonnisos Marine Park (€35).

Sleeping

★Gisela's House-in-Town PENSION €
(☎24270 21370, 6945686542; gisbaunach@hotmail.com; r from €45;) Cosy and quiet on a backstreet off Papadiamanti, this well-managed budget gem has just two rooms, with two twin beds in each, overhead fans, mosquito screens, tables, tea kettles and a flowery verandah.

Hotel Bourtzi BOUTIQUE HOTEL €€
(☎24270 21304; www.hotelbourtzi.gr; Moraitou 8, cnr Papadiamanti; d incl breakfast from €90;) On upper Papadiamanti, the swank Bourtzi features austere-modern rooms, attentive staff, and an inviting garden and pool.

Eating & Drinking

Seafood joints line Skiathos' Old Harbour, cafes and bars wrap around the whole waterfront.

★Taverna-Ouzerie Kabourelia TAVERNA €
(☎24270 21112; Old Harbour; mains €4-12; ⊙noon-midnight;) Poke your nose into the open kitchen to glimpse the day's catch at this popular year-round eatery at the old port. Perfect fish grills and house wine are served at moderate prices. Grilled octopus and *taramasalata* (a thick purée of fish roe, potato, oil and lemon juice) are just two of several standout mezedhes.

★La Cucina di Maria RISTORANTE €€
(☎24270 24168; Plateia Trion Ierarhon; €8-15; ⊙dinner) Excellent thin-crust pizza twirled in the air is just the beginning at this popular spot above the old port. Fresh pasta, fine meat and fish grills in a colourful setting under the mulberry tree.

Information

See skiathosinfo.com for information.

Getting There & Around

AIR

Skiathos Airport (JSI; ☎24270 29100) is 2km northeast of Skiathos Town, and has two summertime daily flights to Athens (€88) and charter flights from northern Europe. Taxis cost €6 to €15 depending on where you're headed.

BOAT

Frequent daily hydrofoils serve mainland ports Volos (€37, 1½ hours) and Agios Konstantinos (€37, 1½ hours), as do cheaper ferries. Hydrofoils/ferries serve Skopelos (€17/10, 20/55 minutes) and Alonnisos (€17/11, 1½/two hours). See **Hellenic Seaways** (☎24270 22209; www.skiathosoe.com; cnr Papadiamantis, waterfront).

Water taxis around Skiathos depart from the Old Harbour.

BUS

Crowded buses ply the south-coast road between Skiathos Town and Koukounaries (€2) every 30 minutes between 7.30am and 11pm year-round, stopping at all the beaches along the way. The bus stop is at the eastern end of the harbour.

IONIAN ISLANDS
ΤΑ ΕΠΤΑΝΗΣΑ

The idyllic cypress- and fir-covered Ionian Islands stretch down the western coast of Greece from Corfu in the north to Kythira, off the southern tip of the Peloponnese. Mountainous, with dramatic cliff-backed beaches, soft light and turquoise water, they're more Italian in feel, offering a contrasting experience to other Greek islands.

Corfu ΚΕΡΚΥΡΑ

POP 102,071

Many consider Corfu, or Kerkyra (*ker*-kih-rah) in Greek, to be Greece's most beautiful island – the unfortunate consequence of which is that it's overbuilt and often overrun with crowds. Look beyond them to find its core splendour.

Corfu Town Κέρκυρα

POP 35,000

Built on a promontory and wedged between two fortresses, Corfu's **Old Town** is a tangle of narrow walking streets through gorgeous Venetian buildings. Explore the winding alleys and surprising plazas in the early morning or late afternoon to avoid the hordes of day trippers seeking souvenirs.

Sights

★Palaio Frourio FORTRESS
(Old Fortress; ☎26610 48310; adult/concession €4/2; ⊙8am-8pm Apr-Oct, 8.30am-3pm Nov-Mar) Constructed by the Venetians in the 15th century on the remains of a Byzantine castle

(and further altered by the British), this spectacular landmark offers respite from the crowds and superb views of the region. Climb to the summit of the inner outcrop, which is crowned by a lighthouse, for a 360-degree panorama. The gatehouse contains a Byzantine **museum**.

★Palace of St Michael & St George PALACE

Originally the residence of a succession of British high commissioners, this palace now houses the world-class **Museum of Asian Art** (☎26610 30443; www.matk.gr; adult/child €6/free, 3-day with Antivouniotissa Museum & Old Fortress €14; ⏰9am-4pm Tue-Sun), founded in 1929. Expertly curated with extensive, informative English-language placards, the collection's approximately 10,000 artefacts, collected from all over Asia, include priceless prehistoric bronzes, ceramics, jade figurines, coins and works of art in onyx, ivory and enamel. Additionally, the palace's **throne room** and **rotunda** are impressively adorned in period furnishings and art.

★Church of Agios Spyridon CHURCH

(Agios Spyridonos; ⏰7am-8pm) FREE The sacred relic of Corfu's beloved patron saint, St Spyridon, lies in an elaborate silver casket in the 16th-century basilica.

Mon Repos Estate PARK

(Kanoni Peninsula; ⏰8am-7pm May-Oct, to 5pm Nov-Apr) FREE On the Kanoni Peninsula on the southern outskirts of town, an extensive, wooded parkland estate surrounds an elegant neoclassical villa. It houses the **Museum of Palaeopolis** (☎26610 41369; adult/concession €4/2; ⏰8am-3pm), with entertaining archaeological displays and exhibits on the history of Corfu Town. Paths lead through lush grounds to the ruins of two Doric temples; the first is truly a ruin, but the southerly **Temple of Artemis** is serenely impressive.

Antivouniotissa Museum MUSEUM

(☎26610 38313; www.antivouniotissamuseum.gr; off Arseniou; adult/child €2/free; ⏰8.30am-3pm Tue-Sun) The exquisite, timber-roofed, 15th-century **Church of Our Lady of Antivouniotissa** holds an outstanding collection of Byzantine and post-Byzantine icons and artefacts dating from the 13th to the 17th centuries.

Sleeping

Accommodation prices fluctuate wildly depending on season; book ahead.

★Bella Venezia BOUTIQUE HOTEL €€

(☎26610 46500; www.bellaveneziahotel.com; N Zambeli 4; s/d incl breakfast from €115/130; ⊖❄📶) From the instant you enter this neoclassical former girls' school – with its elegant lobby decked in candelabras, velvet chairs and grand piano – the place will charm you with its pure old-world charm. The Venezia has plush, high-ceilinged rooms with fine city views (some with balcony). Conscientious staff welcome you, and the gazebo breakfast room in the garden is delightful.

★Siorra Vittoria BOUTIQUE HOTEL €€

(☎26610 36300; www.siorravittoria.com; Stefanou Padova 36; s/d incl breakfast from €118/160; P❄📶) Expect luxury and style at this quiet 19th-century mansion where painstakingly restored traditional architecture meets modern amenities; marble bathrooms, crisp linens and genteel service make for a relaxed stay. Breakfast in the peaceful garden beneath an ancient magnolia tree. The Vittoria suite encompasses the atelier and has views to the sea.

Hermes Hotel HOTEL €€

(☎26610 39268; www.hermes-hotel.gr; Markora 12; s/d/tr from €55/65/75; ❄📶) Peaceful Hermes has cool, lime-hued rooms in a central location (though mercifully the windows are double-glazed), with old-fashioned bathrooms, laminate floors and a classy breakfast area. Rooms have TVs, fridges and CD players. Find it up a stairway, overlooking the market.

Eating & Drinking

Corfu has excellent restaurants. Cafes and bars line the arcaded Liston. Try Corfu Beer.

★Il Vesuvio GREEK €

(☎26610 21284; Guilford; mains from €10; ⏰noon-late) The Neapolitan owner of this classy Italian restaurant, which has premises on both sides of the street, won the 'Best Italian Restaurant in Greece' award for his moreish homemade gnocchi, tortellini and ravioli. Eat on the street or inside but don't neglect a taste of their silky-smooth panna cotta – so fresh it will make your taste buds sing.

WORTH A TRIP

IONIAN PLEASURES

Paxi (Πάξοι) Paxi lives up to its reputation as one of the Ionians' most idyllic and picturesque islands. At only 10km by 4km it's the smallest of the main holiday islands and makes a fine escape from Corfu's quicker-paced pleasures.

Kefallonia (Κεφαλλονιά) Tranquil cypress- and fir-covered Kefallonia, the largest Ionian island, is breathtakingly beautiful with rugged mountain ranges, rich vineyards, soaring coastal cliffs and golden beaches. Not yet overrun with package tourism, it remains low-key outside resort areas and is a perfect spot for kayaking.

Ithaki (Ιθάκη) Odysseus' long-lost home in Homer's *Odyssey*, Ithaki (ancient Ithaca) remains a verdant, pristine island blessed with cypress-covered hills and beautiful turquoise coves. It's a walkers' paradise, best reached from Kefallonia.

Lefkada (Λευκάδα) Lefkada has some of the best beaches in Greece, if not the world, and an easygoing way of life.

★**To Tavernaki tis Marinas** TAVERNA €
(☎69816 56001; 4th Parados, Agias Sofias 1; mains €6-16; ⊙noon-midnight) Restored stone walls, hardwood floors and cheerful staff lift the ambience of this taverna. Check daily specials or choose anything from *mousakas* (baked layers of eggplant or zucchini, minced meat and potatoes topped with cheese sauce) or grilled sardines to steak. Accompany it all with a dram of ouzo or *tsipouro* (a spirit similar to ouzo).

Rouvas TAVERNA €
(☎26610 31182; S Desilla 13; mains €9; ⊙9am-5pm) As authentically Greek as it gets, this earthy gourmand's delight is a Corfiot institution. Look out for dishes like beef stew in tomato sauce and roast salmon with potatoes, as well as plenty of veggie dishes. Even celebrity chef Rick Stein was impressed.

★**La Cucina** ITALIAN €€
(☎26610 45029; Guilford 17; mains €13-25; ⊙7-11pm; ❄📶) A long-established favourite, well-run La Cucina shines for its creative cuisine, with hand-rolled pasta dishes at the fore. The original Guilford location has cosy, warm tones and murals, while the **Moustoxidou** (☎26610 45799; cnr Guilford & Moustoxidou; €10-15; ⊙7-11pm) annexe (with identical menu) is chic in glass and grey.

ℹ Information

Municipal Tourist Kiosk (Palaio Frourio; ⊙9am-4pm Mon-Sat Jun-Sep) Offers helpful information for things to do around Corfu, accommodation and transport timetables.

Pachis Travel (☎26610 28298; www.pachis-travel.com; Guilford 7; ⊙9am-2.30pm & 5.30-9pm, closed Sun) This helpful travel agency can assist with ferry and plane tickets, and hotels. They also organise charter boats and excursions to Paxi.

Around the Island

To explore the island fully your own transport is best. Much of the coast just north of Corfu Town is overwhelmed with beach resorts, the south is quieter, and the west has a beautiful, if popular, coastline. The **Corfu Trail** (www.thecorfutrail.com) traverses the island north to south.

North of Corfu Town, in **Kassiopi**, picturesque **Manessis Apartments** (☎6973918416, 26630 81474; www.manessiskassiopi.com; Kassiopi; 4-person apt €80-110; ❄📶) offers water-view apartments.

South of Corfu Town, **Achillion Palace** (☎26610 56210; www.achillion-corfu.gr; Gastouri; €7, audio guide €3; ⊙8am-8pm Apr-Oct, 8.45am-4pm Nov-Mar) pulls 'em in for over-the-top royal bling. Don't miss a dinner at one of the island's best tavernas, **Klimataria** (☎26610 71201; www.klimataria-restaurant.gr; Benitses; mains €8-15; ⊙7pm-midnight Feb-Nov), in nearby **Benitses**.

To gain an aerial view of the gorgeous cypress-backed bays around **Paleokastritsa**, the west coast's main resort, go to the quiet village of **Lakones**. For beautiful rooms just 20m from the pretty beach, check in to **Hotel Zefiros** (☎26630 41244; www.hotel-zefiros.gr; Paleokastritsa; d/tr/q from €90/130/145; ❄📶). Further south, good beaches surround tiny **Agios Gordios**, which has famous **Pink Palace** (☎26610 53103; www.thepinkpalace.com; Agios Gordios Beach; incl breakfast & dinner dm/d/tr/q from €21/42/63/84, 2-night minimum stay; ❄@) backpackers and party central.

Getting There & Around

AIR

Ioannis Kapodistrias Airport (CFU; ☎26610 89600; www.corfu-airport.com) is 2km southwest of Corfu Town. There are direct flights to Athens daily and regularly to Thessaloniki, throughout the Ionians and (from June to September) to Iraklio, Crete. Charter planes and budget airlines fly internationally in summer. Bus 15 serves the airport (€1.50), taxis cost €10.

BOAT

Neo Limani port lies west of the Neo Frourio (New Fortress). Ferries go to Igoumenitsa (€10, 1¼ hours, hourly). In summer daily ferries and hydrofoils go to Paxi, and ferries to Italy (Bari, Brindisi and Venice) also stop in Patra (€35, six hours); some stop in Kefallonia and Zakynthos. Check www.openseas.gr.

BUS

Blue buses (€1.10 to €1.50) for villages near Corfu Town depart from the **local bus station** (☎26610 31595, 26610 39859; www.astikoktelkerkyras.gr; Plateia San Rocco) in Corfu Old Town. Services to other destinations (around Corfu €1.60 to €4.40) and daily buses to Athens (€45, 8½ hours) and Thessaloniki (€35, eight hours) leave from Corfu's **long-distance bus station** (☎26610 28900; www.greenbuses.gr; Ioannou Theotoki, Corfu Town).

SURVIVAL GUIDE

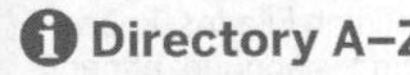

Directory A–Z

ACCOMMODATION

Accommodation Types

Hotels Range from basic business lodging to high-end boutique extravaganzas.

Pensions and guesthouses Often include breakfast and are usually owner-operated.

Domatia Rooms for rent; owners greet ferries and buses shouting 'room!'.

Youth hostels In most major towns and on some islands.

Campgrounds Generally open April to October; standard facilities include hot showers, kitchens, restaurants and minimarkets, often a swimming pool. Check out **Panhellenic Camping Association** (☎21036 21560; www.greececamping.gr). Wild camping is forbidden.

Mountain refuges Listed in *Greece Mountain Refuges & Ski Centres*, available free from EOT and EOS (Ellinikos Orivatikos Syndesmos; Greek Alpine Club) offices.

SLEEPING PRICE RANGES

Based on the rate for a double room in high season (May to August). Unless otherwise stated, all rooms have private bathroom facilities.

€ less than €60 (under €80 in Athens)

€€ €60–€150 (€80–€150 in Athens)

€€€ more than €150

For the Cyclades, budgets are based on the rates in July and August. For Mykonos only, the price ranges are as follows:

€ less than €150

€€ €150–€300

€€€ more than €300

Prices

Accommodation is nearly always negotiable (and deeply reduced) outside peak season, especially for longer stays.

CUSTOMS REGULATIONS

It is strictly forbidden to export antiquities (anything over 100 years old) without an export permit.

INTERNET ACCESS

Wi-fi is common at most sleeping and eating venues, ports, airports and some city squares.

INTERNET RESOURCES

EOT (Greek National Tourist Organisation; www.gnto.gr) Concise tourist information.

Greek Travel Pages (www.gtp.gr) Access to ferry schedules and accommodation.

Lonely Planet (www.lonelyplanet.com/greece) Destination information, hotel bookings and traveller forum.

Ministry of Culture (www.culture.gr) For cultural events and sights.

MONEY

- ATMs are everywhere except small villages.
- Cash is king, especially in the countryside; credit cards are not always accepted in small villages.
- Service charge is included on the bill in restaurants, but it is the custom to 'round up the bill'; same for taxis.

OPENING HOURS

Hours decrease significantly in the shoulder and low seasons, when many places shut completely.

Banks 8.30am–2.30pm Monday to Thursday, 8am–2pm Friday

ESSENTIAL FOOD & DRINK

Nutritious and flavourful, the food is one of the great pleasures of travelling in Greece. The country's rich culinary heritage draws from a fusion of mountain village food, island cuisine, flavours introduced by Greeks from Asia Minor, and influences from various invaders and historical trading partners. The essence of classic Greek cuisine lies in fresh, seasonal home-grown produce and generally simple, unfussy cooking that brings out the rich flavours of the Mediterranean.

Savoury appetisers Known as mezedhes (literally, 'tastes'; meze for short), standards include *tzatziki* (yoghurt, cucumber and garlic), *melitzanosalata* (aubergine dip), *taramasalata* (fish-roe dip), dolmadhes (stuffed vine leaves; dolmas for short), *fasolia* (beans) and *oktapodi* (octopus).

Cheap eats *Gyros* is pork or chicken shaved from a revolving stack of sizzling meat and wrapped in pitta bread with tomato, onion, fried potatoes and lashings of *tzatziki*. Souvlaki is skewered meat, usually pork.

Taverna staples You'll find *mousakas* (layers of aubergine and mince, topped with béchamel sauce and baked) on every menu, alongside *moschari* (oven-baked veal and potatoes), *keftedes* (meatballs), *stifado* (meat stew), *pastitsio* (baked dish of macaroni with minced meat and béchamel sauce) and *yemista* (either tomatoes or green peppers stuffed with minced meat and rice).

Sweets Greeks are serious about their sweets, with *zaharoplasteia* (sweet shops) in even the smallest villages. Try variations on baklava (thin layers of pastry filled with honey and nuts). Or go simple: delicious Greek yoghurt drizzled with honey.

Top Tipples Legendary aniseed-flavoured ouzo, sipped slowly, turns a cloudy white when ice or water is added. *Raki*, the Cretan firewater, is produced from grape skins. Greek coffee, a legacy of Ottoman rule, is a favourite pastime.

Bars 8pm–late
Cafes 10am–midnight
Clubs 10pm–4am
Post Offices 7.30am–2pm Monday to Friday (rural); 7.30am–8pm Monday to Friday, 7.30am–2pm Saturday (urban)
Restaurants 11am–noon and 7pm–1am
Shops 8am–3pm Monday, Wednesday and Saturday; 8am–2.30pm and 5–8pm Tuesday, Thursday and Friday

POST

Tahydromia (post offices; www.elta.gr) are easily identified by their yellow sign.To send post abroad, use the yellow post boxes labelled *exoteriko* (for overseas).

PUBLIC HOLIDAYS

Epiphany 6 January
First Sunday in Lent February
Greek Independence Day 25 March
Good Friday March/April
Orthodox Easter Sunday 8 April 2018, 28 April 2019
May Day (Protomagia) 1 May
Whit Monday (Agiou Pnevmatos) 50 days after Easter Sunday
Feast of the Assumption 15 August
Ohi Day 28 October
Christmas Day 25 December
St Stephen's Day 26 December

TELEPHONE

➡ Organismos Tilepikoinonion Ellados, known as OTE (o-teh), public phones abound; phonecards are sold at OTE shops and newspaper kiosks; pressing the 'i' button brings up instructions in English.

➡ Local SIM cards can be used in European and Australian phones. Most other phones can be set to roaming. US/Canadian phones need to have a dual- or tri-band system.

➡ For directory inquiries within Greece, call ☎131; for international inquiries ☎161. Area codes are part of the 10-digit number within Greece.

TIME

Greece is in the Eastern European time zone: two hours ahead of GMT/UTC and three hours ahead on daylight-saving time (last Sunday in March through to last Sunday in October).

ℹ Getting There & Away

Regular ferry connections shuttle between Greece and the Italian ports of Ancona, Bari, Brindisi and Venice. Similarly, ferries operate between the Greek islands of Rhodes, Kos, Samos, Chios and Lesvos and the Aegean coast of Turkey.

Overland, it's possible to reach Albania, Bulgaria, the Former Yugoslav Republic of Macedonia (FYROM), Romania and Turkey from Greece. If you've got your own wheels, you can drive through border crossings with these four countries. There are train and bus connections with Greece's neighbours, but check ahead, as these have been affected by the financial crisis.

See www.seat61.com for more information on ferry travel.

AIR

Most visitors arrive by air, mostly into Athens. There are 17 international airports in Greece; most handle only summer charter flights to the islands.

There's a growing number of direct scheduled services into Greece by European budget airlines – **Aegean Airlines** (www.aegeanair.com) and its subsidiary, **Olympic Air** (www.olympicair.com), also fly internationally.

LAND

Border Crossings

You can drive or ride through the following border crossings.

Albania Kakavia (60km northwest of Ioannina); Sagiada (28km north of Igoumenitsa); Mertziani (17km west of Konitsa); Krystallopigi (14km west of Kotas)

Bulgaria Promahonas (109km northeast of Thessaloniki); Ormenio (41km from Serres); Exohi (a 448m-tunnel border crossing 50km north of Drama)

Former Yugoslav Republic of Macedonia (FYROM) Evzoni (68km north of Thessaloniki); Niki (16km north of Florina); Doïrani (31km north of Kilkis)

Turkey Kipi (43km east of Alexandroupolis); Kastanies (139km northeast of Alexandroupolis)

Bus

Private companies and KTEL Macedonia run buses from Thessaloniki to İstanbul, Skopje and Sofia.

Albania is served by **Albatrans** (☎ +355 42 259 204; www.albatrans.com.al) and **Euro Interlines** (☎ 21052 34594; www.komatastours.gr).

Bus and tour companies run buses between Greece and Sofia, Bulgaria; Budapest, Hungary; Prague, Czech Republic; and Turkey. See **Simeonidis Tours** (p355), **Dimidis Tours** (☎ 21069 27240; www.dimidistours.gr; 68 Kifissias Av, Athens; ⏲ 9am-8pm Mon-Fri, 9.30am-2.30pm Sat) and **Tourist Service** (www.tourist-service.com).

> **EATING PRICE RANGES**
>
> The following price ranges refer to the average cost of a main course (not including service charges):
>
> **€** less than €10
>
> **€€** €10–€20
>
> **€€€** more than €20

Train

The Greek railways organisation **OSE** (Organismos Sidirodromon Ellados; ☎ 14511; www.trainose.gr) runs daily trains from Thessaloniki to Sofia and to Belgrade (via Skopje), with a weekly onward train to and from Budapest.

SEA

Check ferry routes and schedules at www.greekferries.gr and www.openseas.gr.

If you are travelling on a rail pass, check to see if ferry travel between Italy and Greece is included. Some ferries are free, others give a discount. On some routes you will need to make reservations.

Albania

For Saranda, **Petrakis Lines** (☎ 26610 38690; www.ionian-cruises.com) has daily hydrofoils to Corfu (25 minutes).

Italy

Routes vary, check online.

Ancona Patra (20 hours, three daily, summer)

Bari Patra (15 hours, daily) via Corfu (10 hours) and Keffalonia (14 hours); also to Igoumenitsa (11½ hours, daily)

Brindisi Patra (15 hours, April to early October) via Igoumenitsa (11 hours)

Venice Patra (30 hours, up to 12 weekly, summer) via Corfu (25 hours)

Turkey

Boat services operate between Turkey's Aegean coast and the Greek islands.

ℹ Getting Around

Greece has a comprehensive transport system and is easy to get around.

AIR

It's sometimes cheaper to fly than take the ferry, especially if you book ahead online. Domestic airlines include the following.

Aegean Airlines (A3; ☎ 801 112 0000; www.aegeanair.com)

COUNTRY FACTS

Area 131,944 sq km

Capital Athens

Country Code ☎30

Currency Euro (€)

Emergency ☎112

Language Greek

Money Cash is king. ATMs are common except in small villages, and credit cards only sporadically accepted.

Population 10.9 million

Visas Generally not required for stays up to 90 days. Member of Schengen Convention.

Astra Airlines (A2; ☎2310 489 392, 800 700 7466; www.astra-airlines.gr) Thessaloniki-based airline.

Olympic Air (☎801 801 0101; www.olympicair.com) Partly merged with Aegean.

Sky Express (☎28102 23800; www.skyexpress.gr) Cretan airline with flights around Greece. Beware harsh baggage restrictions.

Hellenic Seaplanes (☎801 505 5050, 210 647 0180; www.hellenic-seaplanes.com) Charters with planned routes to the islands.

BICYCLE

➡ Greece has very hilly terrain and the summer heat can be stifling. In addition, most drivers totally disregard road rules. Bicycles are carried for free on ferries.

➡ See www.cyclegreece.gr for bicycle tour ideas.

➡ Rental bicycles are available at most tourist centres, but are generally for pedalling around town rather than for serious riding. Prices range from €5 to €12 per day.

BOAT

From state-of-the-art 'superferries' that run on the major routes, to ageing open ferries that operate local services to outlying islands, Greece has an extensive network of ferries – the only means of reaching many of the islands. Schedules are often subject to delays due to poor weather and industrial action, and prices fluctuate regularly. In summer, ferries run regular services between all but the most out-of-the-way destinations; however, services seriously slow down in winter (and in some cases stop completely).

Be flexible. Boats seldom arrive early, but often arrive late. And some don't come at all. You may have the option of 'deck class', which is the cheapest ticket, or 'cabin class' with aircon assigned seats. On larger ferries there are lounges and restaurants for everyone serving fast food or snacks.

Tickets can be bought at the dock, but in high season, boats are often full – plan ahead. Check www.openseas.gr or www.gtp.gr for schedules, costs and links to individual boat company websites.

The Greek Ships app for smartphones tracks ferries in real time.

BUS

Long-distance buses are operated by **KTEL** (www.ktel.org). Fares are fixed by the government and service routes can be found on the company's website or regional websites (listed in our coverage). Buses are comfortable, generally run on time, are reasonably priced and offer frequent services on major routes. Buy tickets at least an hour in advance. Buses don't have toilets or refreshments, but stop for a break every couple of hours.

CAR & MOTORCYCLE

➡ A great way to explore areas in Greece that are off the beaten track, but be careful on highways – Greece has the highest road-fatality rate in Europe. The road network is decent, but freeway tolls are fairly hefty.

➡ Almost all islands are served by car ferries, but they are expensive; costs vary by the size of the vehicle.

➡ The Greek automobile club, **ELPA** (www.elpa.gr), generally offers reciprocal services to members of other national motoring associations. If your vehicle breaks down, dial 104.

➡ EU-registered vehicles are allowed free entry into Greece for six months without road taxes being due; a green card (international third-party insurance) is all that's required.

Hire Cars

➡ Available throughout Greece, you'll get better rates with local rental-car companies than with the big multinational outfits. Check insurance waivers closely, and how they assist in a breakdown.

➡ High-season weekly rates start at about €280 for the smallest models, dropping to €200 in winter – add tax and extras. Major companies request a credit-card deposit.

➡ Minimum driving age in Greece is 18, but most firms require a driver of 21 or over.

Hire Mopeds & Motorcycles

➡ Available for hire everywhere. Regulations stipulate that you need a valid motorcycle licence for the size of motorcycle you wish to rent – from 50cc upwards.

➡ Mopeds and 50cc motorcycles start from €15 per day or from €30 per day for a 250cc motorcycle. Outside high season, rates drop considerably.

Main Ferry Routes

Road Rules

- Drive on the right.
- Overtake on the left (not all Greeks do this!).
- Compulsory to wear seatbelts in the front seats, and in the back if they are fitted.
- Drink-driving laws are strict; a blood alcohol content of 0.05% incurs a fine of around €150 and over 0.08% is a criminal offence.

PUBLIC TRANSPORT

All major towns have a local bus system. Athens is the only city with a metro system.

TAXI

- Taxis are widely available and reasonably priced. Yellow city cabs are metered; rates double between midnight and 5am. Grey rural taxis do not have meters; settle on a price before you get in.
- Athens taxi drivers are gifted in their ability to make a little bit extra with every fare. If you have a complaint, note the cab number and contact the Tourist Police. Rural taxi drivers are better.

TRAIN

- Check the **Greek Railways Organisation** (www.trainose.gr) website for the current schedules. Greece has only two main lines: Athens north to Thessaloniki and Alexandroupolis, and Athens to the Peloponnese.
- There are a number of branch lines, eg Pyrgos–Olympia line and the spectacular Diakofto–Kalavryta mountain railway.
- Inter-Rail and Eurail passes are valid; you still need to make a reservation.
- In summer make reservations at least two days in advance.

Ireland

Includes ➡

Best Traditional Pubs

- ➡ Kyteler's Inn (p398)
- ➡ O'Connor's (p403)
- ➡ Crown Liquor Saloon
- ➡ Peadar O'Donnell's (p416)
- ➡ Crane Bar (p407)

Best Places to Eat

- ➡ Fade Street Social (p394)
- ➡ Market Lane (p401)
- ➡ Barking Dog (p411)
- ➡ Oscar's (p407)

Why Go?

Few countries have an image so plagued by cliché. From shamrocks and *shillelaghs* (Irish fighting sticks) to leprechauns and lovable rogues, there's a plethora of platitudes to wade through before you reach the real Ireland. But it's well worth looking beyond the tourist tat, for the Emerald Isle is one of Europe's gems, a scenic extravaganza of lakes, mountains, sea and sky. From picture-postcard County Kerry to the rugged coastline of Northern Ireland (part of the UK, distinct from the Republic of Ireland), there are countless opportunities to get outdoors and explore, whether cycling the Causeway Coast or hiking the hills of Killarney and Connemara.

There are cultural pleasures too in the land of Joyce and Yeats, U2 and the Undertones. Dublin, Cork and Belfast all have world-class art galleries and museums, while you can enjoy foot-stomping traditional music in the bars of Galway and Killarney. So push aside the shamrocks and experience the real Ireland.

When to Go

Dublin

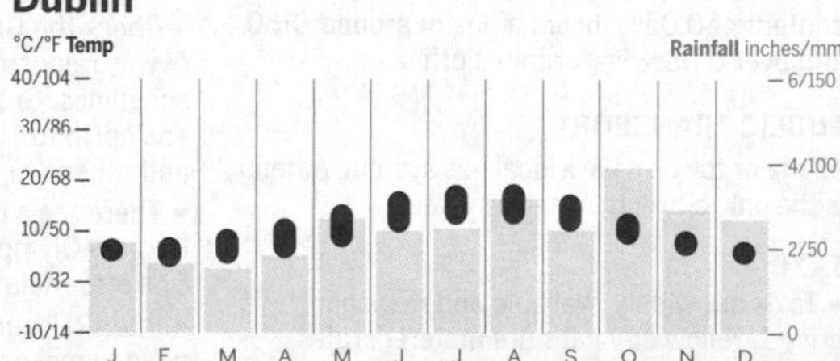

Late Mar Spring flowers everywhere, landscape is greening, St Patrick's Day festivities beckon.

Jun Best chance of dry weather, long summer evenings, Bloomsday in Dublin.

Sep–Oct Summer crowds thin, autumn colours reign, surf's up on the west coast.

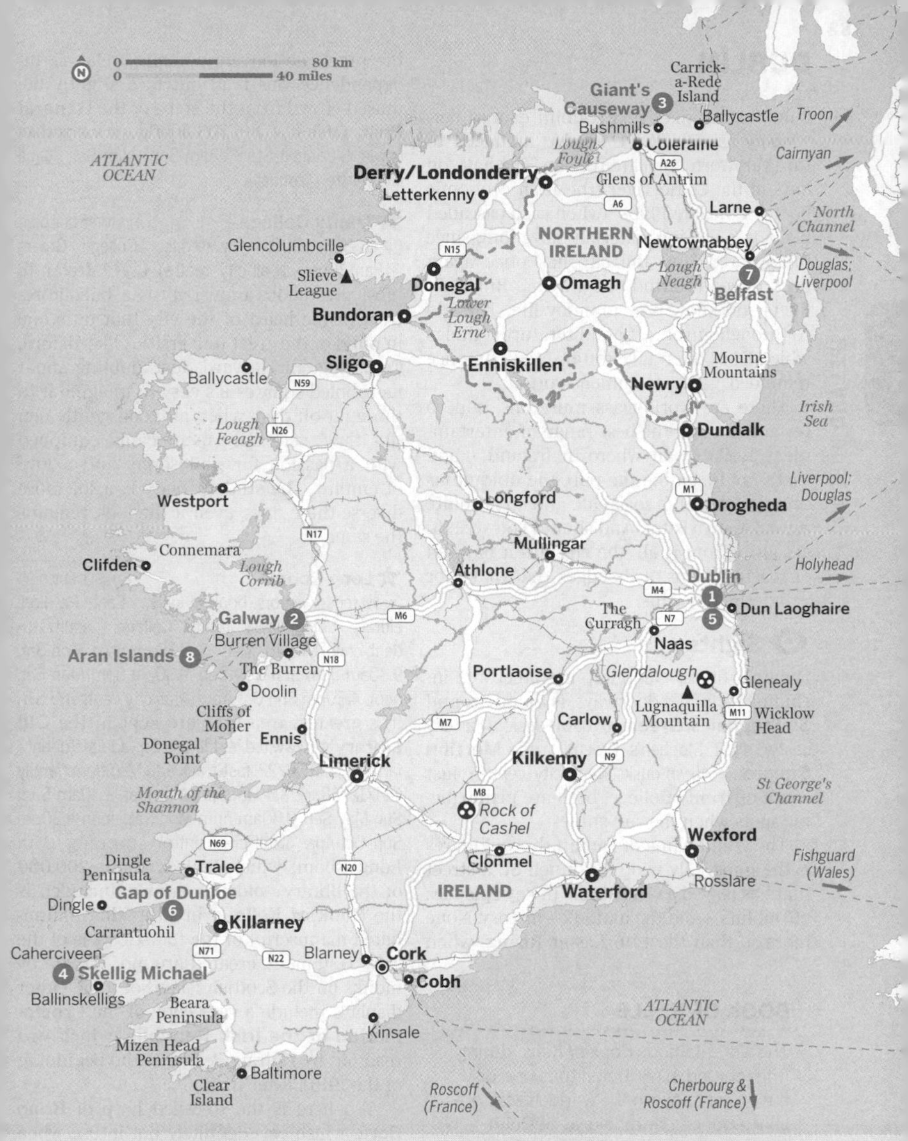

Ireland Highlights

1. **Dublin** (p388) Meandering through the museums, pubs and literary haunts of the Irish capital.
2. **Galway** (p405) Hanging out in bohemian Galway, with its hip cafes and music venues.
3. **Giant's Causeway** (p414) Hiking along the Causeway Coast and clambering across the Giant's Causeway.
4. **Skellig Michael** (p403) Taking a boat trip to the 6th-century monastery perched atop a wild rocky islet.
5. **Irish Pubs** Sipping a pint while tapping your toes to a live music session in one of Dublin's traditional Irish pubs.
6. **Gap of Dunloe** (p402) Cycling through spectacular lake and mountain scenery.
7. **Titanic Belfast** (p410) Discovering the industrial history of the city that built the famous ocean liner.
8. **Aran Islands** (p408) Wandering the wild shores of the remote and craggy islands.

DUBLIN

POP 1,273,069

Sultry rather than sexy, Dublin exudes personality as only those who've managed to turn careworn into carefree can. The halcyon days of the Celtic Tiger (the Irish economic boom of the late 1990s), when cash cascaded like a free-flowing waterfall, have long since disappeared, and the city has once again been forced to grind out a living. But Dubliners still know how to enjoy life. They do so through music, art and literature – things which Dubs often take for granted but, once reminded, generate immense pride.

There are world-class museums, superb restaurants and the best range of entertainment available anywhere in Ireland – and that's not including the pub, the ubiquitous centre of the city's social life and an absolute must for any visitor. And should you wish to get away from it all, the city has a handful of seaside towns at its edges that make for wonderful day trips.

Sights

Dublin's finest Georgian architecture, including its famed doorways, is found around **St Stephen's Green** (dawn-dusk; all city centre, St Stephen's Green) and **Merrion Square** (dawn-dusk; all city centre) just south of Trinity College; both are prime picnic spots when the sun shines.

The grand dame of Dublin thoroughfares is the imperially wide O'Connell St, a street that has played a central role in key episodes of Dublin's – and the nation's – history. None more so than the 1916 Easter Rising, when the proclamation announcing Ireland's independence was read out to a slightly bemused crowd from the steps of the **General Post Office** (01-705 7000; www.anpost.ie; Lower O'Connell St; 8am-8pm Mon-Sat; all city centre, Abbey).

BOOK OF KELLS

The world-famous *Book of Kells*, dating from around AD 800 and thus one of the oldest books in the world, was probably produced by monks at St Colmcille's Monastery on the remote island of Iona, Scotland. It contains the four gospels of the New Testament, written in Latin, as well as prefaces, summaries and other text. If it were merely words, the *Book of Kells* would simply be a very old book – it's the extensive and amazingly complex illustrations (the illuminations) that make it so wonderful. The superbly decorated opening initials are only part of the story, for the book has smaller illustrations between the lines.

★Trinity College — HISTORIC BUILDING

(01-896 1000; www.tcd.ie; College Green; 8am-10pm; all city centre) FREE Ireland's most prestigious university is a bucolic retreat in the heart of the city that puts one in mind of the great universities like Oxford, Cambridge or Harvard. Just ambling about its cobbled squares it's easy to imagine it in those far-off days when all good gentlemen (for they were only men) came equipped with a passion for philosophy and a love of empire. The student body is a lot more diverse these days, even if the look remains the same.

★Long Room — NOTABLE BUILDING

(www.tcd.ie/visitors/book-of-kells; East Pavilion, Library Colonnades, Trinity College; adult/student/child €13/10/free; 8.30am-5pm Mon-Sat, 9.30am-5pm Sun May-Sep, 9.30am-5pm Mon-Sat, noon-4.30pm Sun Oct-Apr; all city centre) Trinity's greatest treasures are kept in the **Old Library's** (www.tcd.ie; Library Sq; adult/student/family €11/9.50/22, fast-track adult/student/family €14/12/28; 8.30am-5pm Mon-Sat, 9.30am-5pm Sun May-Sep, 9.30am-5pm Mon-Sat, noon-4.30pm Sun Oct-Apr; all city centre) stunning 65m Long Room, which houses about 200,000 of the library's oldest volumes. Included is the **Book of Kells**, a breathtaking, illuminated manuscript of the four Gospels of the New Testament, created around AD 800 by monks on the Scottish island of Iona. Other displays include a rare copy of the **Proclamation of the Irish Republic**, which was read out by Pádraig Pearse at the beginning of the 1916 Easter Rising.

Also here is the so-called harp of **Brian Ború**, which was definitely not in use when the army of this early Irish hero defeated the Danes at the Battle of Clontarf in 1014. It does, however, date from around 1400, making it one of the oldest harps in Ireland. Your entry ticket also includes admission to temporary exhibitions on display in the East Pavilion.

The Long Room gets very busy during the summer months, so it's recommended to go online and buy a fast-track ticket (adult/student/family €13/11/26), which gives timed admission to the exhibition and allows visitors to skip the queue. You'll still get only a

ITINERARIES

One Week

Spend a couple of days in **Dublin** ambling through the excellent national museums, and gorging yourself on Guinness and good company in Temple Bar. Get medieval in **Kilkenny** before heading on to **Cork** and discovering why they call it 'The Real Capital'. Head west for a day or two exploring the scenic **Ring of Kerry** and enchanting **Killarney**.

Two Weeks

Follow the one-week itinerary, then make your way north from Killarney to bohemian **Galway**. Using Galway as your base, explore the alluring **Aran Islands** and the hills of **Connemara**. Finally, head north to see the **Giant's Causeway** and experience the optimistic vibe in fast-changing **Belfast**.

fleeting moment with the *Book of Kells*, as the constant flow of viewers is hurried past.

★ **National Museum of Ireland – Archaeology** MUSEUM
(www.museum.ie; Kildare St; ⌚10am-5pm Tue-Sat, 2-5pm Sun; 🚌all city centre) FREE Ireland's most important cultural institution was established in 1877 as the primary repository of the nation's archaeological treasures. These include the most famous of Ireland's crafted artefacts, the **Ardagh Chalice** and the **Tara Brooch**, dating from the 12th and 8th centuries respectively. They are part of the **Treasury**, itself part of Europe's finest collection of Bronze and Iron Age gold artefacts, and the most complete assemblage of medieval Celtic metalwork in the world.

★ **Guinness Storehouse** BREWERY, MUSEUM
(www.guinness-storehouse.com; St James's Gate, South Market St; adult/student/child €18/16/6.50, connoisseur experience €48; ⌚9.30am-5pm Sep-Jun, to 6pm Jul & Aug; 📶; 🚌21A, 51B, 78, 78A, 123 from Fleet St, 🚋James's) The most popular visit in town is this multimedia homage to Guinness, one of Ireland's most enduring symbols. A converted grain storehouse is the only part of the 26-hectare brewery that is open to the public, but it's a suitable cathedral in which to worship the black gold. Across its seven floors you'll discover everything about Guinness before getting to taste it in the top-floor **Gravity Bar**, with its panoramic views. Pre-booking your tickets online will save you money.

★ **Chester Beatty Library** MUSEUM
(☎01-407 0750; www.cbl.ie; Dublin Castle; ⌚10am-5pm Mon-Fri, 11am-5pm Sat, 1-5pm Sun year-round, closed Mon Nov-Feb, free tours 1pm Wed, 2pm Sat & 3pm Sun; 🚌all city centre) FREE This world-famous library, in the grounds of **Dublin Castle** (☎01-677 7129; www.dublincastle.ie; Dame St; guided tours adult/child €10/4; self-guided tour adult/child €7/3; ⌚9.45am-5.45pm, last admission 5.15pm; 🚌all city centre), houses the collection of mining engineer Sir Alfred Chester Beatty (1875–1968), bequeathed to the Irish State on his death. And we're immensely grateful for Chester's patronage: spread over two floors, the breathtaking collection includes more than 20,000 manuscripts, rare books, miniature paintings, clay tablets, costumes and other objects of artistic, historical and aesthetic importance.

★ **Kilmainham Gaol** MUSEUM
(☎01-453 2037; http://kilmainhamgaolmuseum.ie; Inchicore Rd; adult/child €8/4; ⌚9.30am-6.45pm Jul-Aug, to 5.30pm rest of year; 🚌69, 79 from Aston Quay, 13, 40 from O'Connell St) If you have *any* desire to understand Irish history – especially the juicy bits about resistance to British rule – then a visit to this former prison is an absolute must. This threatening grey building, built between 1792 and 1795, played a role in virtually every act of Ireland's painful path to independence, and even today, despite closing in 1924, it still has the power to chill.

★ **National Gallery** MUSEUM
(www.nationalgallery.ie; West Merrion Sq; ⌚9.15am-5.30pm Mon-Wed, Fri & Sat, to 8.30pm Thu, 11am-5.30pm Sun; 🚌4, 7, 8, 46A from city centre) FREE A magnificent Caravaggio and a breathtaking collection of works by Jack B Yeats – William Butler's younger brother – are the main reasons to visit the National Gallery, but not the only ones. Its excellent collection is strong in Irish art, and there are also high-quality collections of every major European school of painting.

★ **St Patrick's Cathedral** CATHEDRAL
(www.stpatrickscathedral.ie; St Patrick's Close; adult/student/child €6.50/5.50/free; ⌚9.30am-5pm Mon-Fri, 9am-6pm Sat, 9-10.30am & 12.30-

Dublin

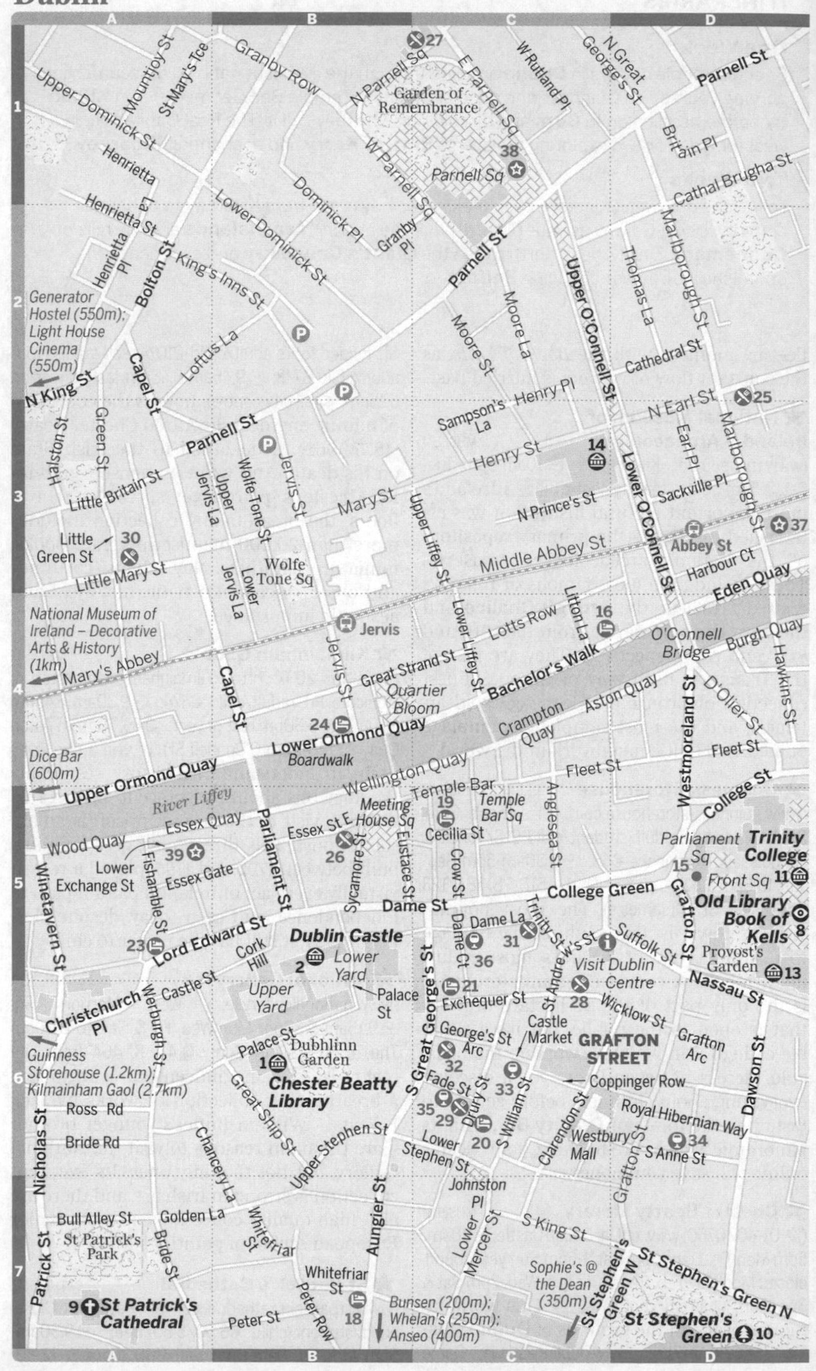

IRELAND DUBLIN

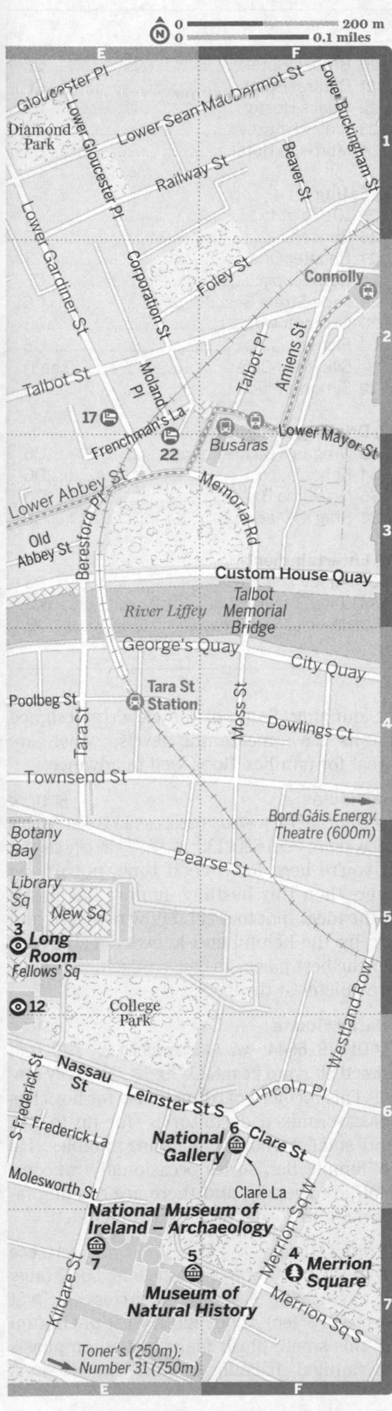

2.30pm Sun; 50, 50A, 56A from Aston Quay, 54, 54A from Burgh Quay) Ireland's largest church is St Patrick's Cathedral, built between 1191 and 1270 on the site of an earlier church that had stood here since the 5th century. It was here that St Patrick himself reputedly baptised the local Celtic chieftains, making this bit of ground some fairly sacred turf: the well in question is in the adjacent **St Patrick's Park**, which was once a slum but is now a lovely spot to sit and take a load off.

Sleeping

Hotel rooms in Dublin aren't as expensive as they were during the Celtic Tiger years, but demand is high and booking is highly recommended, especially if you want to stay in the city centre or within walking distance of it.

North of the Liffey

★ Isaacs Hostel HOSTEL €
(01-855 6215; www.isaacs.ie; 2-5 Frenchman's Lane; dm/tw from €16/70; @ ; all city centre, Connolly) The north side's best hostel – hell, for atmosphere alone it's the best in town – is in a 200-year-old wine vault just around the corner from the main bus station. With summer barbecues, live music in the lounge, internet access and colourful dorms, this terrific place generates consistently good reviews from backpackers and other travellers.

★ Generator Hostel HOSTEL €
(01-901 0222; www.generatorhostels.com; Smithfield Sq; dm/tw from €16/70; @ ; Smithfield) This European chain brings its own brand of funky, fun design to Dublin's hostel scene, with bright colours, comfortable dorms (including women-only) and a lively social scene. It even has a screening room for movies. Good location right on Smithfield Sq, next to the Old Jameson Distillery.

Abbey Court Hostel HOSTEL €
(01-878 0700; www.abbey-court.com; 29 Bachelor's Walk; dm/d from €16/80; ; all city centre) Spread over two buildings, this large, well-run hostel has 33 clean dorm beds with good storage. Its excellent facilities include a dining hall, a conservatory and a barbecue area. Doubles with bathrooms are in the newer building where a light breakfast is provided in the adjacent cafe. Not surprisingly, this is a popular spot; reservations are advised.

Anchor House B&B €€
(01-878 6913; www.anchorhousedublin.com; 49 Lower Gardiner St; r from €125; P ; all city

Dublin

centre, Connolly) While most B&Bs round these parts offer pretty much the same stuff – TV, half-decent shower, tea- and coffee-making facilities and wi-fi – the Anchor does all of that with a certain (frayed) elegance, and also has a friendliness the others can't easily match.

Morrison Hotel HOTEL €€€
(01-887 2400; www.morrisonhotel.ie; Lower Ormond Quay; r from €260; P @ ; all city centre, Jervis) Space-age funky design is the template at this hip hotel, recently taken over by the Hilton Doubletree group. King-size beds (with Serta mattresses), 40in LCD TVs, free wi-fi and Crabtree & Evelyn toiletries are just some of the hotel's offerings. Easily the northside's most luxurious address.

South of the Liffey

Avalon House HOSTEL €
(01-475 0001; www.avalon-house.ie; 55 Aungier St; dm/s/d from €10/34/54; @ ; 15, 16, 16A, 16C, 19, 19A, 19C, 65, 65B, 83 & 122) One of the city's most popular hostels, welcoming Avalon House has pine floors, high ceilings and large, open fireplaces that create the ambience for a good spot of meet-the-backpacker lounging. Some of the cleverly designed rooms have mezzanine levels, which are great for families. Book well in advance.

Barnacles HOSTEL €
(01-671 6277; www.barnacles.ie; 19 Lower Temple Lane; dm/d from €20/130; P ; all city centre) If you're here for a good time, not a long time, then this bustling Temple Bar hostel is the ideal spot to meet fellow revellers, and tap up the helpful and knowledgeable staff for the best places to cause mischief. Rooms are quieter at the back.

Kinlay House HOSTEL €
(01-679 6644; www.kinlaydublin.ie; 2-12 Lord Edward St; dm/d from €20/90; ; all city centre) This former boarding house for boys has massive, mixed dormitories (for up to 24), and smaller rooms, including doubles. It's in Temple Bar, so it's occasionally raucous. Staff are friendly, and there are cooking facilities and a cafe. Breakfast is included.

Brooks Hotel HOTEL €€€
(01-670 4000; www.brookshotel.ie; 59-62 Drury St; r from €200; P @ ; all cross-city, St Stephen's Green) About 120m west of Grafton St, this small, plush place has an emphasis on familial, friendly service. The decor is

nouveau classic with high-veneer-panelled walls, decorative bookcases and old-fashioned sofas, while bedrooms are extremely comfortable and come fitted out in subtly coloured furnishings. The clincher though, is the king- and superking-size beds in all rooms, complete with…a pillow menu.

Central Hotel HOTEL €€
(☎01-679 7302; www.centralhoteldublin.com; 1-5 Exchequer St; r from €110; @📶; 🚌all city centre, 🚋St Stephen's Green) The rooms are a modern – if miniaturised – version of Edwardian luxury. Heavy velvet curtains and custom-made Irish furnishings (including beds with draped backboards) fit a little too snugly into the space afforded them, but they do lend a touch of class. Note that street-facing rooms can get a little noisy. Location-wise, the name says it all.

★**Number 31** GUESTHOUSE €€€
(☎01-676 5011; www.number31.ie; 31 Leeson Close; s/d €220/260; P📶; 🚌all city centre) The city's most distinctive property is the former home of modernist architect Sam Stephenson, who successfully fused '60s style with 18th-century grace. Its 21 bedrooms are split between the retro coach house, with its coolly modern rooms, and the more elegant Georgian house, where rooms are individually furnished with tasteful French antiques and big comfortable beds. Breakfast included. Gourmet breakfasts with kippers, homemade breads and granola are served in the conservatory.

Eating

The most concentrated restaurant area is Temple Bar but, apart from a handful of good places, the bulk of eateries offer bland, unimaginative fodder and cheap set menus for tourists. Better food and service can usually be found on either side of Grafton St, while the top-end restaurants are clustered around Merrion Sq and Fitzwilliam Sq. Fast-food chains dominate the northside, though some fine cafes and eateries are finally appearing there too.

North of the Liffey

★**Oxmantown** CAFE €
(www.oxmantown.com; 16 Mary's Abbey, City Markets; sandwiches €5.50; ⏰7.30am-4pm Mon-Fri; 🚌Four Courts, Jervis) Delicious breakfasts and excellent sandwiches make this relatively new cafe one of the standout places for daytime eating on the north side of the Liffey. Locally baked bread, coffee supplied by Cloud Nine (Dublin's only micro-roastery) and meats sourced from Irish farms are the ingredients, but it's the way it's all put together that makes it so worthwhile.

★**101 Talbot** MODERN IRISH €€
(www.101talbot.ie; 100-102 Talbot St; mains €18-24; ⏰noon-3pm & 5-11pm Tue-Sat; 🚌all city centre) This Dublin classic has expertly resisted every trendy wave and has been a stalwart of good Irish cooking since opening more than two decades ago. Its speciality is traditional meat-and-two-veg dinners, but with vague Mediterranean and even Middle Eastern influences: roast Wicklow venison with sweet potato, lentil and bacon cassoulet and a sensational Morcoccan-style lamb tagine. Superb.

★**Chapter One** MODERN IRISH €€€
(☎01-873 2266; www.chapteronerestaurant.com; 18 N Parnell Sq; 2-course lunch €32.50, 4-course dinner €75; ⏰12.30-2pm Tue-Fri, 7.30-10.30pm Tue-Sat; 🚌3, 10, 11, 13, 16, 19, 22 from city centre) Flawless haute cuisine and a relaxed, welcoming atmosphere make this Michelin-starred restaurant in the basement of the Dublin Writers Museum our choice for best dinner experience in town. The food is French-inspired contemporary Irish, the menus change regularly and the service is top-notch. The three-course pretheatre menu (€37.50) is great if you're going to the **Gate** (www.gatetheatre.ie; 1 Cavendish Row) around the corner.

FREE THRILLS

Dublin is not a cheap city, but there are plenty of attractions that won't bust your budget.

Trinity College (p388) Wander the grounds at Dublin's oldest and most beautiful university.

National Museum of Archaeology (p389) Discover the world's finest collection of prehistoric gold artefacts.

Chester Beatty Library (p389) Explore the library with its collection of oriental and religious art.

National Gallery (p389) Gaze at Irish and European paintings.

St Stephen's Green (p388) Laze at the city's most picturesque public park.

DUBLIN PASS

If you're planning some heavy-duty sightseeing, you'll save a packet by investing in the **Dublin Pass** (www.dublinpass.com; adult/child 1 day €49/29, 3 day €79/49). It provides free entry to more than 30 attractions, including the Guinness Storehouse and Kilmainham Gaol, and you can also skip queues by presenting your card. It also includes free transfer to and from the airport on the Aircoach. Available from any Dublin Tourism office.

South of the Liffey

Cornucopia VEGETARIAN €
(www.cornucopia.ie; 19-20 Wicklow St; salads €5.50-10.95, mains €12.50-€13.95; 8.30am-9pm Mon, 8.30am-10pm Tue-Sat, noon-9pm Sun; ; all city centre) Dublin's best-known vegetarian restaurant is this terrific eatery that serves wholesome salads, sandwiches and a selection of hot main courses from a daily changing menu. It's so popular it's recently expanded onto the 2nd floor.

Bunsen BURGERS €
(www.bunsen.ie; 22 Essex St E; burgers €7-10; noon-9.30pm Mon-Wed, noon-10.30pm Thu-Sat, 1-9.30pm Sun; all city centre) The tagline says Straight Up Burgers, but Bunsen serves only the tastiest, most succulent lumps of prime beef cooked to perfection and served between two halves of a homemade bap. Want fries? You've a choice between skinny, chunky or sweet potato. Order the double at your peril. There are two other branches: on **Wexford Street** (36 Wexford St; noon-9.30pm Mon-Wed, noon-10.30pm Thu-Sat, 1-9.30pm Sun; all city centre) and South Anne St.

Simon's Place CAFE €
(George's St Arcade, S Great George's St; sandwiches €5-6; 8.30am-5pm Mon-Sat; ; all city centre) Simon's soup-and-sandwich joint is a city stalwart, impervious to the fluctuating fortunes of the world mostly because its doorstep sandwiches and wholesome vegetarian soups are delicious and affordable. As trustworthy cafes go, this is the real deal.

★ **Fade Street Social** MODERN IRISH €€
(01-604 0066; www.fadestreetsocial.com; 4-6 Fade St; mains €18-32, tapas €5-12; 12.30-10.30pm Mon-Fri, 5-10.30pm Sat & Sun; ; all city centre) Two eateries in one, courtesy of renowned chef Dylan McGrath: at the front, the buzzy tapas bar, which serves up gourmet bites from a beautiful open kitchen. At the back, the more muted restaurant specialises in Irish cuts of meat – from veal to rabbit – served with home grown, organic vegetables. There's a bar upstairs too. Reservations suggested.

Sophie's @ the Dean ITALIAN €€
(www.sophies.ie; 33 Harcourt St; mains €14-29; 7am-midnight; 10, 11, 13, 14 or 15A, Harcourt) There's perhaps no better setting in all of Dublin – a top-floor glasshouse restaurant with superb views of the city – to enjoy this quirky take on Italian cuisine, where delicious pizzas come with non-traditional toppings (pulled pork with BBQ sauce?) and the 8oz fillet steak is done to perfection. A good spot for breakfast too.

Pichet FRENCH €€
(01-677 1060; www.pichetrestaurant.ie; 15 Trinity St; mains €19-27; noon-3pm & 5-10pm Mon-Sat, 11am-4pm & 5-9pm Sun; all city centre) Head chef Stephen Gibson (formerly of L'Ecrivain) delivers his version of modern French cuisine to this elongated dining room replete with blue leather chairs and lots of windows to stare out of. The result is pretty good indeed, the food excellent – we expected nothing less – and the service impeccable. Sit in the back for atmosphere.

Drinking & Nightlife

Temple Bar, Dublin's 'party district', is almost always packed with raucous stag (bachelor) and hen (bachelorette) parties, scantily clad girls and loud guys from Ohio wearing Guinness T-shirts. If you're looking to get smashed and hook up with someone from another country, there's no better place in Ireland. If that's not your style, there's plenty to enjoy beyond Temple Bar. In fact, most of the best old-fashioned pubs are outside the district.

★ **Toner's** PUB
(01-676 3090; www.tonerspub.ie; 139 Lower Baggot St; 10.30am-11.30pm Mon-Thu, to 12.30am Fri & Sat, 11.30am-11pm Sun; 7, 46 from city centre) Toner's, with its stone floors and antique snugs, has changed little over the years and is the closest thing you'll get to a country pub in the heart of the city. Next door, Toner's Yard is a comfortable outside space. The shelves and drawers are reminders that it once doubled as a grocery shop.

The writer Oliver St John Gogarty once brought WB Yeats here, after the upper-class poet – who lived just around the corner – decided he wanted to visit a pub. After a silent sherry in the noisy bar, Yeats turned to his friend and said, 'I have seen the pub, now please take me home.' We always suspected he was a little too precious for normal people, and he would probably be horrified by the good-natured business crowd making the racket these days too. His loss.

★Grogan's Castle Lounge PUB
(www.groganspub.ie; 15 S William St; ⌚10.30am-11.30pm Mon-Thu, to 12.30am Fri & Sat, 12.30-11pm Sun; 🚌all city centre) This place, known simply as Grogan's (after the original owner), is a city-centre institution. It has long been a favourite haunt of Dublin's writers and painters, as well as others from the alternative bohemian set, who enjoy a fine Guinness while they wait for that inevitable moment when they're discovered.

★No Name Bar BAR
(3 Fade St; ⌚12.30-11.30pm Sun-Wed, to 1am Thu, to 2.30am Fri & Sat; 🚌all city centre) A low-key entrance just next to the trendy French restaurant L'Gueuleton leads upstairs to one of the nicest bar spaces in town, consisting of three huge rooms in a restored Victorian townhouse plus a sizeable heated patio area for smokers. There's no sign or a name – folks just refer to it as the No Name Bar.

★Anseo BAR
(18 Lower Camden St; ⌚10.30am-11.30pm Mon-Thu, to 12.30am Fri & Sat, 11am-11pm Sun; 🚌14, 15, 65 or 83) Unpretentious, unaffected and incredibly popular, this cosy alternative bar – which is pronounced 'an-*shuh*', the Irish for 'here' – is a favourite with those who live by the credo that to try too hard is far worse than not trying at all. The pub's soundtrack is an eclectic mix; you're as likely to hear Peggy Lee as Lee 'Scratch' Perry.

★Kehoe's PUB
(9 S Anne St; ⌚10.30am-11.30pm Mon-Thu, to 12.30am Fri & Sat, noon-11pm Sun; 🚌all city centre) This is one of the most atmospheric pubs in the city centre and a favourite with all kinds of Dubliners. It has a beautiful Victorian bar, a wonderful snug, and plenty of other little nooks and crannies. Upstairs, drinks are served in what was once the publican's living room – and looks it!

Stag's Head PUB
(www.louisfitzgerald.com/stagshead; 1 Dame Ct; ⌚10.30am-1am Mon-Sat, to midnight Sun; 🚌all city centre) The Stag's Head was built in 1770, remodelled in 1895 and thankfully not changed a bit since then. It's a superb pub: so picturesque that it often appears in films, and also featured in a postage-stamp series on Irish bars. A bloody great pub, no doubt.

☆ Entertainment

For events, reviews and club listings, pick up a copy of the fortnightly music review *Hot Press* (www.hotpress.com), or for free cultural events, check out the weekly e-zine *Dublin Event Guide* (www.dublinevent-guide.com). Friday's *Irish Times* has a pull-out section called 'The Ticket' that has reviews and listings of all things arty.

Smock Alley Theatre THEATRE
(☎01-677 0014; www.smockalley.com; 6-7 Exchange St) One of the city's most diverse theatres is hidden in this beautifully restored 17th-century building. It boasts a diverse program events (expect anything from opera to murder mystery nights, puppet shows and Shakespeare) and many events also come with a dinner option. The theatre was built in 1622 and was the only Theatre Royal to ever be built outside London. It's been reinvented as a warehouse and a Catholic church and was lovingly restored in 2012 to become a creative hub once again.

Whelan's LIVE MUSIC
(☎01-478 0766; www.whelanslive.com; 25 Wexford St; 🚌16, 122 from city centre) Perhaps the city's most beloved live-music venue is this midsized room attached to a traditional bar. This is the singer-songwriter's spiritual home: when they're done pouring out the contents of their hearts on stage, you can find them filling up in the bar along with their fans.

Light House Cinema CINEMA
(☎01-872 8006; www.lighthousecinema.ie; Smithfield Plaza; 🚌all city centre, 🚊Smithfield) The most impressive cinema in town is this snazzy four-screener in a stylish building just off Smithfield Plaza. The menu is strictly art house, and the cafe-bar on the ground floor is perfect for discussing the merits of German Expressionism.

Bord Gáis Energy Theatre THEATRE
(☎01-677 7999; www.grandcanaltheatre.ie; Grand Canal Sq; 🚆Grand Canal Dock) Forget the uninviting sponsored name: Daniel Libeskind's masterful design is a three-tiered, 2100-capacity auditorium where you're as likely to be entertained by the Bolshoi or a touring state opera as you are to see *Disney on Ice* or

Barbra Streisand. It's a magnificent venue – designed for classical, paid for by the classics.

Abbey Theatre THEATRE

(☎01-878 7222; www.abbeytheatre.ie; Lower Abbey St; all city centre, Abbey) Ireland's national theatre was founded by WB Yeats in 1904 and was a central player in the development of a consciously native cultural identity. Its relevance has waned dramatically in recent decades but it still provides a mix of Irish classics (Synge, O'Casey etc), established international names (Shepard, Mamet) and contemporary talent (O'Rowe, Carr et al).

Information

All Dublin tourist offices provide walk-in services only – no phone enquiries. For tourist information by phone call ☎1850 230 330 from within the Republic.

Grafton Medical Centre (☎01-671 2122; www.graftonmedical.ie; 34 Grafton St; 8.30am-6pm Mon-Fri, 11am-2pm Sat; all city centre) One-stop shop with male and female doctors and physiotherapists.

Hickey's Pharmacy (☎01-679 0467; 21 Grafton St; 8.30am-8pm Mon-Wed & Fri, to 8.30pm Thu, 9am-7.30pm Sat, 10.30am-6pm Sun)

St James's Hospital (☎01-410 3000; www.stjames.ie; James's St; James's) Dublin's main 24-hour accident and emergency department.

Visit Dublin Centre (www.visitdublin.com; 25 Suffolk St; 9am-5.30pm Mon-Sat, 10.30am-3pm Sun; all city centre) The main tourist information centre, with free maps, guides and itinerary planning, plus booking services for accommodation, attractions and events.

Getting There & Away

AIR

Dublin Airport (p418), about 13km north of the city centre, is Ireland's major international gateway, with direct flights from Europe, North America and Asia. Budget airlines such as Ryanair and Flybe land here.

BOAT

There are direct ferries from Holyhead (Wales) to Dublin Port, 3km northeast of the city centre, and to Dun Laoghaire, 13km southeast. Boats also sail direct to Dublin Port from Liverpool and from Douglas, on the Isle of Man.

BUS

Dublin's main bus station Busáras (☎01-836 6111; www.buseireann.ie; Store St; Connolly) (pronounced buh-*saw*-ras) is just north of the Liffey. **Aircoach** (www.aircoach.ie) operates a service from O'Connell St in the Dublin city centre, via Dublin Airport to Belfast.

Belfast €18.50, 2½ hours, hourly

Cork €16.50, 3¾ hours, six daily

Galway €15.50, 3¾ hours, hourly

Kilkenny €9.50, 1¾ hours, six daily

Rosslare Europort €19, 3½ hours, five daily

The private company Citylink (www.citylink.ie) has nonstop services from Dublin Airport (picking up in the city centre at Bachelor's Walk, near O'Connell Bridge) to Galway (€13, 2½ hours, hourly).

TRAIN

Connolly station is north of the Liffey, with trains to Belfast, Sligo and Rosslare. **Heuston station** is south of the Liffey and west of the city centre, with trains for Cork, Galway, Killarney, Limerick, and most other points to the south and west. Visit www.irishrail.ie for timetables and fares.

Belfast €38, 2¼ hours, eight daily

Cork €66, 2¾ hours, hourly

Galway €37, 2¾ hours, nine daily

Killarney €70, 3¼ hours, seven daily

Getting Around

TO/FROM THE AIRPORT

Aircoach (www.aircoach.ie) Buses every 10 to 15 minutes between 6am and midnight, hourly from midnight until 6am (one way/return €7/12).

Airlink Express (☎01-873 4222; www.dublinbus.ie; one-way/return €10/6) Bus 747 runs every 10 to 20 minutes from 5.45am to 11.30pm between the airport, central bus station (Busáras) and the Dublin Bus office on Upper O'Connell St.

Taxi There is a taxi rank directly outside the arrivals concourse. It should take about 45 minutes to get into the city centre by taxi and cost about €25, including a supplementary charge of €3 (not applied when going to the airport).

BICYCLE

Rental rates begin at around €13/70 per day/week; you'll need a €50 to €200 cash deposit and photo ID.

Neill's Wheels (www.rentabikedublin.com; per day €15) Various outlets, including Avalon House and Isaacs Hostel.

Dublinbikes (www.dublinbikes.ie) A pay-as-you-go service similar to London's: cyclists purchase a Smart Card (€5 for three days, €20 for one year, plus a €150 credit-card deposit) either online or at any of more than 40 stations throughout the city centre, and bike use is then free for the first 30 minutes, increasing gradually thereafter (eg €3.50 for up to three hours).

PUBLIC TRANSPORT

Bus

Dublin Bus (www.dublinbus.ie) Local buses cost from €0.75 to €3.30 for a single journey. You must pay the exact fare when boarding;

drivers don't give change. The Freedom Pass (€33) allows three days' unlimited travel on all Dublin buses including Airlink and Dublin Bus hop-on/hop-off tour buses.

Train

Dublin Area Rapid Transport (DART; ☎01-836 6222; www.irishrail.ie) Provides quick rail access as far north as Howth and south to Bray; Pearse and Tara St stations are handy for central Dublin. Single fares cost €2.20 to €5.95; a one-day pass costs €11.70.

Tram

Luas (www.luas.ie) Runs on two (unconnected) lines; the green line runs from the eastern side of St Stephen's Green southeast to Sandyford, and the red line runs from Tallaght to Connolly station, with stops at Heuston station, the National Museum and Busáras. Single fares range from €2 to €3.30 depending on how many zones you travel through; a one-day pass is €7.

Taxi

Taxis in Dublin are expensive; flag fall costs €4, plus €1.25 per kilometre. For taxi service, call **National Radio Cabs** (☎01-677 2222; www.nrc.ie).

THE SOUTHEAST

Kilkenny

POP 24,400

Kilkenny (Cill Chainnigh) is the Ireland of many visitors' imaginations. Its majestic riverside castle, tangle of 17th-century passageways, rows of colourful, old-fashioned shopfronts and centuries-old pubs with traditional live music all have a timeless appeal, as does its splendid medieval cathedral. But Kilkenny is also famed for its contemporary restaurants and rich cultural life.

Sights

★Kilkenny Castle CASTLE

(☎056-770 4100; www.kilkennycastle.ie; The Parade; adult/child €8/4; ⏰9.30am-5.30pm Apr-Sep, to 5pm Mar, to 4.30pm Oct-Feb) Rising above the River Nore, Kilkenny Castle is one of Ireland's most visited heritage sites. Stronghold of the powerful Butler family, it has a history dating back to the 12th century, though much of its present look dates from Victorian times.

During the winter months (November to January) visits are by 40-minute guided tours only, which shift to self-guided February to October. Highlights include the Long Gallery with its painted roof and carved marble fireplace. There's an excellent tea room in the former castle kitchens, all white marble and gleaming copper.

★St Canice's Cathedral CATHEDRAL

(☎056-776 4971; www.stcanicescathedral.ie; St Canice's Pl; cathedral €4, round tower €3, combined €6; ⏰9am-6pm Mon-Sat, 1-6pm Sun Jun-Aug, shorter hours Sep-May) Ireland's second-largest medieval cathedral (after St Patrick's in Dublin) has a long and fascinating history. The first monastery was built here in the 6th century by St Canice, Kilkenny's patron saint. The present structure dates from the 13th to 16th centuries, with extensive 19th-century reconstruction, its interior housing ancient grave slabs and the tombs of Kilkenny Castle's Butler dynasty. Outside stands a 30m-high round tower, one of only two in Ireland that you can climb.

National Craft Gallery GALLERY

(☎056-779 6147; www.nationalcraftgallery.ie; Castle Yard; ⏰10am-5.30pm Tue-Sun; 👪) FREE Contemporary Irish crafts are showcased at these imaginative galleries, set in former stables across the road from Kilkenny Castle, next to the shops of the **Kilkenny Design Centre** (☎056-772 2118; www.kilkennydesign.com; ⏰10am-7pm). Ceramics dominate, but exhibits often feature furniture, jewellery and weaving from the members of the Crafts Council of Ireland. Family days are held the third Saturday of every month, with a tour of the gallery and free hands-on workshops for children. For additional workshops and events, check the website.

Festivals & Events

Kilkenny is rightly known as the festival capital of Ireland, with several world-class events throughout the year.

Kilkenny Arts Festival ART

(☎056-776 3663; www.kilkennyarts.ie; ⏰Aug; 👪) In August the city comes alive with theatre, cinema, music, literature, visual arts, children's events and street spectacles for 10 action-packed days.

Kilkenny Rhythm & Roots MUSIC

(☎056-776 3669; www.kilkennyroots.com; ⏰Apr/May) More than 30 pubs and other venues participate in hosting this major music festival in late April/early May, with an emphasis on country and 'old-time' American roots music.

Sleeping

Kilkenny Tourist Hostel HOSTEL €

(056-776 3541; www.kilkennyhostel.ie; 35 Parliament St; dm/tw from €17/42; @) Inside an ivy-covered 1770s Georgian town house, this fairly standard, 60-bed IHH hostel has a sitting room warmed by an open fireplace, and a timber- and leadlight-panelled dining room adjoining the self-catering kitchen. Excellent location.

★**Rosquil House** GUESTHOUSE €€

(056-772 1419; www.rosquilhouse.com; Castlecomer Rd; r from €95, 2-person apt from €80; P) Rooms at this immaculately maintained guesthouse are decorated with dark-wood furniture and pretty paisley fabrics, while the guest lounge is similarly tasteful with sink-into sofas, brass-framed mirrors and leafy plants. The breakfast is above average with home-made granola and fluffy omelettes. There's also a well equipped and comfortable self-catering apartment (minimum three-day stay).

Celtic House B&B €€

(056-776 2249; www.celtic-house-bandb.com; 18 Michael St; r €60-80; P @) Artist and author Angela Byrne extends one of Ireland's warmest welcomes at this spick-and-span B&B. Some of the bright rooms have sky-lit bathrooms, others have views of the castle, and Angela's landscapes adorn many of the walls. Book ahead.

Eating

Gourmet Store SANDWICHES €

(056-777 1727; 56 High St; sandwich & coffee €5; 8am-6pm Mon-Sat) In this crowded little deli, takeaway sandwiches are assembled from choice imported meats and cheeses (plus a few top-notch locals).

★**Foodworks** BISTRO, CAFE €€

(056-777 7696; www.foodworks.ie; 7 Parliament St; lunch mains €14, 3-course dinner €30; noon-4.30pm Sun-Wed, noon-9.30pm Thu-Sat;) The owners of this cool and casual bistro keep their own pigs and grow their own salad leaves, so it would be churlish not to try their pork belly stuffed with black pudding, or confit pig's trotter – and you'll be glad you did. Delicious food, excellent coffee and friendly service make this a justifiably popular venue; best to book a table.

Drinking & Nightlife

★**Kyteler's Inn** PUB

(056-772 1064; www.kytelersinn.com; 27 St Kieran's St; 11am-midnight Sun-Thu, to 2am Fri & Sat) Dame Alice Kyteler's old house was built back in 1224 and has seen its share of history: she was charged with witchcraft in 1323. Today the rambling bar includes the original building, complete with vaulted ceiling and arches. There is a beer garden, a courtyard and a large upstairs room for the live bands (nightly March to October), ranging from trad to blues.

Entertainment

Watergate Theatre THEATRE

(box office 056-776 1674; www.watergatetheatre.com; Parliament St) Kilkenny's top theatre venue hosts drama, comedy and musical performances. If you're wondering why intermission lasts 18 minutes, it's so patrons can nip into **John Cleere's pub** (056-776 2573; www.cleeres.com; 22 Parliament St; 11.30am-11.30pm Mon-Thu, to 12.30am Fri & Sat, 1-11pm Sun) for a pint.

Information

Kilkenny Tourist Office (056-775 1500; www.visitkilkenny.ie; Rose Inn St; 9am-6pm Mon-Sat, 10.30am-4pm Sun) Stocks guides and walking maps. Located in Shee Alms House, dating from 1582 and built in local stone by benefactor Sir Richard Shee to help the poor.

Getting There & Away

BUS

Buses depart from the train station. Services include Cork (€19, three hours, two daily) and Dublin (€9.50, 1¾ hours, six daily).

TRAIN

Kilkenny train station (Dublin Rd) is east of the town centre along John St, next to the MacDonagh Junction shopping mall. Services include Dublin Heuston (€26, 1¾ hours, eight daily) and Galway (€63, 3½ hours, two daily, change at Kildare).

THE SOUTHWEST

Cork

POP 119,230

Ireland's second city is first in every important respect, at least according to the locals, who cheerfully refer to it as the 'real capital of Ireland'. The compact city centre is surrounded by interesting waterways and is chock full of great restaurants fed by arguably the best foodie scene in the country.

Sights

★English Market MARKET
(www.englishmarket.ie; main entrance Princes St; 8am-6pm Mon-Sat) It could just as easily be called the Victorian Market for its ornate vaulted ceilings and columns, but the English Market is a true gem, no matter what you name it. Scores of vendors sell some of the region's very best local produce, meats, cheeses and takeaway food. On a sunny day, take your lunch to nearby Bishop Lucey Park, a popular al fresco eating spot.

Cork City Gaol MUSEUM
(021-430 5022; www.corkcitygaol.com; Convent Ave; adult/child €8/5; 9.30am-5pm Apr-Sep, 10am-4pm Oct-Mar) This imposing former prison is well worth a visit, if only to get a sense of how awful life was for prisoners a century ago. An audio tour guides you around the restored cells, which feature models of suffering prisoners and sadistic-looking guards. Take a bus to UCC – from there walk north along Mardyke Walk, cross the river and follow the signs uphill (10 minutes).

Crawford Municipal Art Gallery GALLERY
(021-480 5042; www.crawfordartgallery.ie; Emmet Pl; 10am-5pm Mon-Wed, Fri & Sat, to 8pm Thu) FREE Cork's public gallery houses a small but excellent permanent collection covering the 17th century through to the modern day. Highlights include works by Sir John Lavery, Jack B Yeats and Nathaniel Hone, and a room devoted to Irish women artists from 1886 to 1978 – don't miss the pieces by Mainie Jellet and Evie Hone.

Sleeping

Oscar's Hostel HOSTEL €
(021-241 8380; www.oscarshostel.com; 111 Lower Glanmire Rd; dm €18-22, tw €50-55;) Small (32-bed) but stylish, this relatively new hostel is set on a busy street just 200m east of the train station and 15-minutes' walk from the city centre. Facilities are good, with a well-equipped modern kitchen, comfy common rooms and bike storage, though the bedrooms are basic.

Brú Bar & Hostel HOSTEL €
(021-455 9667; www.bruhostel.com; 57 MacCurtain St; dm/tw incl breakfast from €17/50; @) This buzzing hostel has its own internet cafe, with free access for guests, and a fantastic bar, popular with backpackers and locals alike. The dorms (each with a bathroom) have four to six beds and are both clean and stylish – ask for one on the upper floors to avoid bar noise. Breakfast is free.

★Garnish House B&B €€
(021-427 5111; www.garnish.ie; 18 Western Rd; s/d/tr/f from €92/103/119/134; P) Attention is lavished upon guests at this award-winning B&B where the legendary breakfast menu (30 choices) ranges from fresh fish to French toast. Typical of the touches here is freshly cooked porridge, served with creamed honey and your choice of whiskey or Baileys; enjoy it out on the garden terrace. The 14 rooms are very comfortable; reception is open 24 hours.

★River Lee Hotel HOTEL €€€
(021-425 2700; www.doylecollection.com; Western Rd; r from €195; P) This modern riverside hotel brings a touch of luxury to the city centre. It has gorgeous public areas with huge sofas, a designer fireplace, a stunning five-storey glass-walled atrium, and superb

WORTH A TRIP

ROCK OF CASHEL

The **Rock of Cashel** (www.heritageireland.ie; adult/child €8/4; 9am-7pm early Jun–mid-Sep, to 5.30pm mid-Mar–early Jun & mid-Sep–mid-Oct, to 4.30pm mid-Oct–mid-Mar) is one of Ireland's most spectacular archaeological sites. A prominent green hill, banded with limestone outcrops, it rises from a grassy plain on the outskirts of Cashel town and bristles with ancient fortifications. For more than 1000 years it was a symbol of power, and the seat of kings and churchmen who ruled over the region. Sturdy walls circle an enclosure that contains a complete round tower, a roofless abbey and the finest 12th-century Romanesque chapel in Ireland.

Cashel Lodge & Camping Park (062-61003; www.cashel-lodge.com; Dundrum Rd; campsite per person €10, s/d from €55/85; P) is a good place to stay, with terrific views of the Rock. Bus Éireann services run every two hours between Cashel and Cork (€15.70, 1¾ hours).

Cork

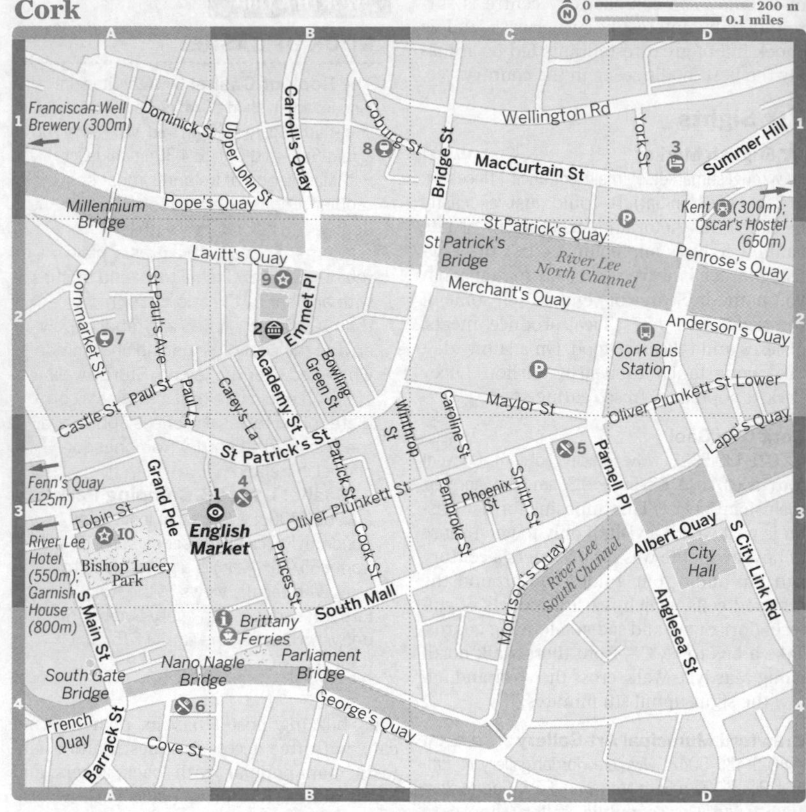

Cork

Top Sights
1 English Market ... B3

Sights
2 Crawford Municipal Art Gallery ... B2

Sleeping
3 Brú Bar & Hostel ... D1

Eating
4 Farmgate Cafe ... B3
5 Market Lane ... C3
6 Quay Co-op ... A4

Drinking & Nightlife
7 Rising Sons ... A2
8 Sin É ... B1

Entertainment
9 Cork Opera House ... B2
10 Triskel Arts Centre ... A3

service. There are well-equipped bedrooms (nice and quiet at the back, but request a corner room for extra space) and possibly the best breakfast buffet in Ireland.

Eating

★ Farmgate Cafe CAFE, BISTRO €

(021-427 8134; www.farmgate.ie; Princes St, English Market; mains €8-14; 8.30am-5pm Mon-Sat) An unmissable experience at the heart of the English Market, the Farmgate is perched on a balcony overlooking the food stalls below, the source of all that fresh local produce on your plate – everything from crab and oysters to the lamb for an Irish stew. Up the stairs and turn left for table service, right for counter service.

Quay Co-op VEGETARIAN €

(021-431 7026; www.quaycoop.com; 24 Sullivan's Quay; mains €5-11; 10am-9pm;) Flying the flag for alternative Cork, this cafeteria offers a range of self-service vegetarian dishes, all organic, including big breakfasts and rib-sticking soups and casseroles. It also caters for gluten-, dairy- and wheat-free needs, and is amazingly child-friendly.

★ Market Lane IRISH, INTERNATIONAL €€
(☎021-427 4710; www.marketlane.ie; 5 Oliver Plunkett St; mains €11-27; ⏰noon-9.30pm Mon-Thu, noon-10.30pm Fri & Sat, 1-9.30pm Sun; 📶👪) It's always hopping at this bright corner bistro. The menu is broad and hearty, changing to reflect what's fresh at the English Market: perhaps gamekeepers pie with celeriac bake, or mushroom and lentil pie with stout gravy? No reservations for fewer than six diners; sip a drink at the bar till a table is free. Lots of wines by the glass.

Fenn's Quay MODERN IRISH €€
(☎021-427 9527; www.fennsquay.net; 5 Fenn's Quay; mains €12-24; ⏰8.15-11.30am & noon-3pm Mon-Fri, 5-8pm Thu, 5-10pm Fri, 8.30am-3pm & 5-10pm Sat; 👪) From breakfast (Rosscarbery black pudding with smoked Gubbeen cheese on home-baked toast) to lunch (spiced beef and pickle sandwiches or fresh fish platters) to dinner (collar of bacon with cabbage and walnuts), this hidden gem of a restaurant serves up the best of local produce, much of it from the English Market – 'Cork on a fork', as their tagline says.

Drinking & Nightlife

In Cork pubs, drink Guinness at your peril, even though Heineken now owns both of the local stout legends, Murphy's and Beamish (and closed down the latter's brewery). Cork's microbrewery, the Franciscan Well Brewery, makes quality beers, including Friar Weisse, popular in summer.

★ Sin É PUB
(www.corkheritagepubs.com; 8 Coburg St; ⏰12.30-11.30pm Mon-Thu, to 12.30am Fri & Sat, to 11pm Sun) You could easily while away an entire day at this great old place, which is everything a craic-filled pub should be – long on atmosphere and short on pretension (Sin É means 'that's it!'). There's music most nights (regular sessions Tuesday at 9.30pm, Friday and Sunday at 6.30pm), much of it traditional, but with the odd surprise.

Franciscan Well Brewery PUB
(www.franciscanwellbrewery.com; 14 North Mall; ⏰1-11.30pm Mon-Thu, to 12.30am Fri & Sat, to 11pm Sun; 📶) The copper vats gleaming behind the bar give the game away: the Franciscan Well brews its own beer. The best place to enjoy it is in the enormous beer garden at the back. The pub holds regular beer festivals together with other small independent Irish breweries.

Rising Sons MICROBREWERY
(☎021-241 1126; www.risingsonsbrewery.com; Cornmarket St; ⏰noon-late) This huge, warehouse-like, red-brick building houses Cork's newest microbrewery. The industrial decor of exposed brick, riveted iron and gleaming copper brewing vessels recalls American West Coast brewpubs. It turns out 50 kegs a week, some of them full of its lip-smacking trademark stout, Mi Daza, and has a food menu that extends as far as pizza, and no further.

☆ Entertainment

Cork's cultural life is generally of a high calibre. To see what's happening grab *WhazOn?* (www.whazon.com), a free monthly booklet available from the tourist office, newsagencies, shops, hostels and B&Bs.

Cork Opera House OPERA
(☎021-427 0022; www.corkoperahouse.ie; Emmet Pl; ⏰box office 10am-5.30pm Mon-Sat, to 7pm preshow, also 6-7pm Sun preshow) Given a modern makeover in the 1990s, this leading venue has been entertaining the city for more than 150 years with everything from opera and ballet to stand-up comedy and puppet shows. Around the back, the **Half Moon Theatre** presents contemporary theatre, dance, art and occasional club nights.

Triskel Arts Centre ARTS CENTRE
(☎021-472 2022; www.triskelart.com; Tobin St; ⏰box office 10am-5pm Mon-Sat; 📶) A fantastic cultural centre housed partly in a renovated church building – expect a varied program of live music, installation art, photography and theatre at this intimate venue. There's also a cinema (from 6.30pm) and a great cafe.

ℹ Information

Cork City Tourist Office (☎021-425 5100; www.discoverireland.ie/corkcity; Grand Pde; ⏰9am-5pm Mon-Sat year-round, plus 10am-5pm Sun Jul & Aug) Souvenir shop and information desk. Sells Ordnance Survey maps.

ℹ Getting There & Around

BIKE

Cycle Scene (☎021-430 1183; www.cyclescene.ie; 396 Blarney St; per day/week from

€15/80) has bikes for hire from €15/80 per day/week.

BOAT

Brittany Ferries (☎021-427 7801; www.brittanyferries.ie; 42 Grand Pde) sails to Roscoff (France) weekly from the end of March to October. The ferry terminal is at Ringaskiddy, about 15 minutes by car southeast of the city centre along the N28.

BUS

Aircoach (☎01-844 7118; www.aircoach.ie) provides a direct service to Dublin city (€16) and Dublin Airport (€20) from St Patrick's Quay (three hours, hourly). **Cork bus station** (cnr Merchant's Quay & Parnell Pl) is east of the city centre. Services include Dublin (€16.50, 3¾ hours, six daily), Kilkenny (€15.70, three hours, five daily) and Killarney (€21, 1½ hours, hourly).

TRAIN

Cork's **Kent train station** (☎021-450 6766) is across the river. Destinations include Dublin (€67, 2¼ hours, eight daily), Galway (€58, four to six hours, seven daily, two or three changes needed) and Killarney (€28, 1½ to two hours, nine daily).

Around Cork

Blarney Castle CASTLE

(☎021-438 5252; www.blarneycastle.ie; adult/child €15/6; ⏲9am-7pm Mon-Sat, to 6pm Sun Jun-Aug, shorter hours Sep-May; Ⓟ) If you need proof of the power of a good yarn, then join the queue to get into this 15th-century castle, one of Ireland's most popular tourist attractions. They're here, of course, to plant their lips on the **Blarney Stone**, which supposedly gives one the gift of the gab – a cliché that has entered every lexicon and tour route. Blarney is 8km northwest of Cork and buses run every half hour from Cork bus station (€7.80 return, 30 minutes).

Killarney

POP 14,220

Killarney is a well-oiled tourism machine set in a sublime landscape of lakes, forests and 1000m peaks. Its manufactured tweeness is renowned, the streets filled with tour-bus visitors shopping for soft-toy shamrocks and countless placards pointing to trad-music sessions. However, it has many charms beyond its proximity to lakes, waterfalls and woodland spreading beneath a skyline of 1000m-plus peaks. In a town that's been practising the tourism game for more than 250 years, competition keeps standards high, and visitors on all budgets can expect to find superb restaurants, great pubs and good accommodation.

Sights & Activities

Most of Killarney's attractions are just outside the town. The mountain backdrop is part of **Killarney National Park** (www.killarneynationalpark.ie) FREE, which takes in beautiful Lough Leane, Muckross Lake and Upper Lake. Besides Ross Castle and Muckross House, the park also has much to explore by foot, bike or boat.

In summer the **Gap of Dunloe**, a gloriously scenic mountain pass squeezed between Purple Mountain and Carrauntouhill (at 1040m, Ireland's highest peak), is a tourist bottleneck. Rather than join the crowds taking pony-and-trap rides, **O'Connors Tours** (☎064-663 0200; www.gapofdunloetours.com; 7 High St; ⏲Mar-Oct) can arrange a bike and boat circuit (€15; highly recommended) or bus and boat tour (€30) taking in the Gap.

Sleeping

Súgán Hostel HOSTEL €

(☎087 718 8237; www.suganhostelkillarney.com; Lewis Rd; dm/tw from €15/40; 📶) Behind its publike front, 250-year-old Súgán is an amiably eccentric hostel with an open fire in the cosy common room, low, crazy-cornered ceilings and hardwood floors. Check in at the next-door pub, a handy spot for a pint of Guinness once you're settled in.

★Fleming's White Bridge Caravan & Camping Park CAMPGROUND €

(☎064-663 1590; http://killarneycamping.com; White Bridge, Ballycasheen Rd; sites per vehicle plus 2 adults €26, hiker €10; ⏲mid-Mar–Oct; 📶) A lovely, sheltered, family-run campsite about 2km southeast of the town centre off the N22, Fleming's has a games room, bike hire, campers' kitchen, laundry and free trout fishing on the river that runs alongside. Your man Hillary at reception can arrange bus, bike and boat tours, if he doesn't talk the legs off you first!

★Crystal Springs B&B €€

(☎064-663 3272; www.crystalspringsbandb.com; Ballycasheen Cross, Woodlawn Rd; s/d €75/115; Ⓟ📶) The timber deck of this wonderfully relaxing B&B overhangs the River Flesk, where trout anglers can fish for free. Rooms are richly furnished with patterned wallpapers and walnut timber; private bathrooms (most with spa baths) are huge. The glass-enclosed breakfast room also overlooks the rushing river. It's about a 15-minute stroll into town.

Eating

Jam CAFE €
(☎064-663 7716; www.jam.ie; Old Market Lane; mains €4-11; ⏱8am-5.30pm Mon-Sat, 9am-5pm Sun; 📶) Duck down the alley to this local hideout for a changing menu of deli sandwiches, coffee and cake, and hot lunch dishes like shepherd's pie. It's all made with locally sourced produce and there are a few tables out front.

Smoke House STEAK, SEAFOOD €€
(☎064-663 9336; https://thesmokehouse.ie; 8 High St; mains €13-31; ⏱5-10pm Mon-Fri, noon-10pm Sat & Sun) One of Killarney's busiest restaurants, this always-crowded bistro was the first establishment in Ireland to cook with a Josper (superhot Spanish charcoal oven). Stylish starters include old-school prawn cocktail, while the Kerry surf'n'turf platter – a half-lobster and fillet steak – is decadence on a plate. Weekend brunch, served from noon till 3pm, includes eggs Florentine and Benedict.

Mareena's Simply Food IRISH €€
(☎066-663 7787; www.mareenassimplyfood.com; East Avenue Rd; mains €19-29; ⏱6-9pm Tue-Sun mid-Feb–Dec) The clue is in the name – Mareena's serves the finest of locally sourced produce, from scallops and sea bass to neck of lamb and pork fillet, cooked plainly and simply to let the quality of the food speak for itself. The decor matches the cuisine – unfussy and understated.

Drinking

★**O'Connor's** PUB
(http://oconnorstraditionalpub.com; 7 High St; ⏱10.30am-11pm Mon-Thu, to 12.30am Fri & Sat, 12.30-11pm Sun) This tiny traditional pub with leaded-glass doors is one of Killarney's most popular haunts. Live music plays every night; good bar food is served daily in summer. In warmer weather, the crowds spill out onto the adjacent lane.

Courtney's PUB
(www.courtneysbar.com; 24 Plunkett St; ⏱2-11.30pm Sun-Thu, to 12.30am Fri & Sat Jun-Sep, from 5pm Oct-May) Inconspicuous on the outside, inside this timeless pub bursts at the seams with Irish music sessions many nights year-round. This is where locals come to see their old mates perform and to kick off a night on the town.

> WORTH A TRIP
>
> ### SKELLIG MICHAEL
>
> Portmagee (an 80km drive west of Killarney) is the jumping-off point for an unforgettable experience: the Skellig Islands, two tiny rocks 12km off the coast. The vertiginous climb up uninhabited **Skellig Michael** inspires an awe that monks could have clung to life in the meagre beehive-shaped stone huts that cluster on the tiny patch of level land on top. From spring to late summer, weather permitting, boat trips run from Portmagee to Skellig Michael; the standard rate is around €60 per person, departing 10am and returning 3pm. Advance booking is essential; there are a dozen boat operators, including **Sea Quest** (☎087 236 2344; www.skelligs-rock.com; Skellig tour €75; ⏱Skellig tour 9am mid-May–Sep).

Information

Tourist Office (☎064-663 1633; http://killarney.ie; Beech Rd; ⏱9am-5pm Mon-Sat; 📶) Can handle most queries, especially good with transport intricacies.

Getting There & Around

BUS

Operating from the bus station on Park Rd, Bus Éireann has regular services to Cork (€21, ½ hours, hourly), Galway via Tralee and Limerick (€28, 3¾ hours, four daily) and Rosslare Harbour (€29, six hours, three daily).

TAXI

Taxis can be found at the taxi rank on College St. A cab from the edge of town (eg Flesk campsite) into the town centre costs around €9 to €10.

TRAIN

Travelling by train to Cork (€28, 1½ to two hours, nine daily) or Dublin (€70, 3¼ hours, seven daily) sometimes involves changing at Mallow.

Ring of Kerry

The Ring of Kerry, a 179km circuit around the dramatic coastal scenery of the Iveragh Peninsula (pronounced eev-raa), is one of Ireland's premier tourist attractions. Most travellers tackle the Ring by bus on guided day trips from Killarney, but you could spend days wandering here.

The Ring is dotted with picturesque villages (**Sneem** and **Portmagee** are worth a stop), **prehistoric sites** (ask for a guide at Killarney tourist office) and spectacular **viewpoints**, notably at Beenarourke just west of Caherdaniel, and Ladies' View (between Kenmare and Killarney). The **Ring of Skellig**, at the end of the peninsula, has fine views of the Skellig Rocks and is not as busy as the main route. You can forgo driving completely by walking part of the 200km **Kerry Way** (www.kerryway.com), which winds through the Macgillycuddy's Reeks mountains past Carrauntuohill (1040m), Ireland's highest mountain.

Sights

Kerry Bog Village Museum MUSEUM
(www.kerrybogvillage.ie; Ballincleave, Glenbeigh; adult/child €6.50/4.50; 9am-6pm) This museum re-creates a 19th-century bog village, typical of the small communities that carved out a precarious living in the harsh environment of Ireland's ubiquitous peat bogs. You'll see the thatched homes of the turf-cutter, blacksmith, thatcher and labourer, as well as a dairy, and meet Kerry bog ponies (a native breed) and Irish wolfhounds. It's on the N70 between Killorglin and Glenbeigh; buy a ticket at the neighbouring Red Fox Inn if no one's at the gate.

Old Barracks Heritage Centre MUSEUM
(066-401 0430; www.oldbarrackscahersiveen.com; Bridge St; adult/child €4/2; 10am-5.30pm Mon-Sat, 11am-5.30pm Sun) Established in response to the Fenian Rising of 1867, the Royal Irish Constabulary barracks at Caherciveen were built in an eccentric Bavarian-schloss style, complete with pointy turret and stepped gables. Burnt down in 1922 by anti-Treaty forces, the imposing building has been restored and now houses fascinating exhibitions on the Fenian Rising and the life and works of local hero Daniel O'Connell.

Derrynane National Historic Park HISTORIC SITE
(066-947 5113; www.heritageireland.ie; Derrynane; adult/child €5/3; 10.30am-5.15pm mid-Mar–Sep, 10am-5pm Wed-Sun Nov–mid-Dec;) Derrynane House was the home of Maurice 'Hunting Cap' O'Connell, a notorious local smuggler who grew rich on trade with France and Spain. He was the uncle of Daniel O'Connell, the 19th-century campaigner for Catholic emancipation, who grew up here in his uncle's care and inherited the property in 1825, when it became his private retreat. The house is furnished with O'Connell memorabilia, including the impressive triumphal chariot in which he lapped Dublin after his release from prison in 1844.

Sleeping & Eating

There are plenty of hostels and B&Bs along the Ring. It's wise to book ahead, though, as some places are closed out of season and others fill up quickly.

★**Mannix Point Camping & Caravan Park** CAMPGROUND €
(066-947 2806; www.campinginkerry.com; Mannix Point, Cahersiveen; hiker €8.50, vehicle plus 2 adults €26; mid-Mar–mid-Oct;) Mortimer Moriarty's award-winning waterfront campsite is one of Ireland's finest, with an inviting kitchen, campers' sitting room with peat fire (no TV but regular music sessions), a barbecue area and even a birdwatching platform. And the sunsets are stunning.

★**Smuggler's Inn** MODERN IRISH €€
(066-947 4330; www.the-smugglers-inn.com; Cliff Rd; d €95-150; Apr-Oct;) The Smuggler's Inn is a diamond find (it's hard to spot if you're coming from the north; head towards the golf course). Rooms are fresh and understated – try for room 15, with a glassed-in balcony overlooking Ballinskelligs Bay. Breakfasts, including a catch of the day, are cooked to order.

The inn also has a gourmet **restaurant** where owner/chef Henry Hunt's creations not only span seafood (including sensational chowder) but locally farmed poultry and meat, and elegant desserts.

Moorings INN €€
(066-947 7108; www.moorings.ie; s/d/tr from €70/110/140;) The Moorings is a friendly local hotel, bar and restaurant, with 16 rooms split between modern sea-view choices and simpler options, most refreshingly white. The nautical-themed **restaurant** (066-947 7108; www.moorings.ie; mains €22-26; 6-10pm Tue-Sun Mar-Oct;) specialises in excellent seafood, while the **Bridge Bar** (066-947 7108; www.moorings.ie; 11am-11.30pm Mon-Sat, noon-11pm Sun) serves superb fish and chips.

QCs Seafood Restaurant & Bar SEAFOOD €€
(☎066-947 2244; http://qcbar.com; 3 Main St; mains €16-26.50, bar food €9-15; ⏲kitchen 12.30-2.30pm & 6-9.30pm Mon-Sat, 5-9pm Sun, bar 12.30pm-midnight Mon-Sat, 5pm-midnight Sun; 📶) QCs is a modern take on a classic pub and as such is open pub hours for pints and craic. But when the kitchen's open, some of the finest food on the Ring pours forth (especially locally sourced seafood). Hours may vary – it's best to call ahead and book a table. Upstairs are six boutique B&B bedrooms (doubles from €109).

Getting Around

Bus Éireann runs a once-daily Ring of Kerry bus service (No 280) from late June to late August. Buses leave Killarney at 11.30am and stop at Killorglin, Glenbeigh, Cahersiveen (€16.60, 1½ hours), Waterville, Caherdaniel and Kenmare (€22, 4½ hours), arriving back at Killarney at 4.45pm.

Travel agencies and hostels in Killarney offer daily coach tours of the Ring for about €25 year-round, lasting from 10.30am to 5pm.

THE WEST COAST

Galway

POP 75,600

Arty and bohemian, Galway (Gaillimh) is legendary around the world for its entertainment scene. Students make up a quarter of the city's population and brightly painted pubs heave with live music on any given night. Here, street life is more important than sightseeing – cafes spill out onto cobblestone streets filled with a frenzy of fiddles, banjos, guitars and *bodhráns* (handheld goatskin drums), while jugglers, painters, puppeteers and magicians in outlandish masks enchant passers-by.

Sights

★Galway City Museum MUSEUM
(www.galwaycitymuseum.ie; Spanish Parade House, Merchant's Rd; ⏲10am-5pm Tue-Sat year-round, noon-5pm Sun Easter-Sep) FREE This modern museum has exhibits on the city's history from 1800 to 1950, including an iconic Galway Hooker fishing boat, a collection of *currachs* (boats made from animal hides) and sections covering Galway and the Great War and the city's cinematic connections.

WORTH A TRIP

CLIFFS OF MOHER

Star of a million tourist brochures, the Cliffs of Moher in County Clare are one of the most popular sights in Ireland. But like many an ageing star, you have to look beyond the famous facade to appreciate its inherent attributes. In summer the site is overrun with day trippers, but there are good rewards if you're willing to walk along the clifftops for 10 minutes to escape the crowds.

The landscaped **Cliffs of Moher Visitor Centre** (☎065-708 6141; www.cliffsofmoher.ie; adult/child including parking €6/free, O'Brien's Tower €2/1; ⏲9am-9pm Jul & Aug, 9am-7.30pm Mon-Fri, to 8pm Sat & Sun June & Sep, shorter hours rest of year; 📶) has exhibitions about the cliffs and their natural history. A number of bus tours leave Galway every morning for the Cliffs of Moher, including Burren Wild Tours.

Also check out rotating displays of works by local artists. The ground floor cafe, with its Spanish Arch views, is a perfect rest stop.

★Spanish Arch HISTORIC SITE
The Spanish Arch is thought to be an extension of Galway's medieval city walls, designed to protect ships moored at the nearby quay while they unloaded goods from Spain, although it was partially destroyed by the tsunami that followed the 1755 Lisbon earthquake. Today it reverberates to the beat of bongo drums, and the lawns and riverside form a gathering place for locals and visitors on sunny days, as kayakers negotiate the tidal rapids of the River Corrib.

Festivals

Galway International Arts Festival ART
(www.giaf.ie; ⏲mid-late Jul) A two-week extravaganza of theatre, music, art and comedy in mid-July.

Galway International Oyster & Seafood Festival FOOD, DRINK
(www.galwayoysterfest.com; ⏲late Sep) Going strong for over 60 years, the world's oldest oyster festival draws thousands of visitors in late September.

Galway City

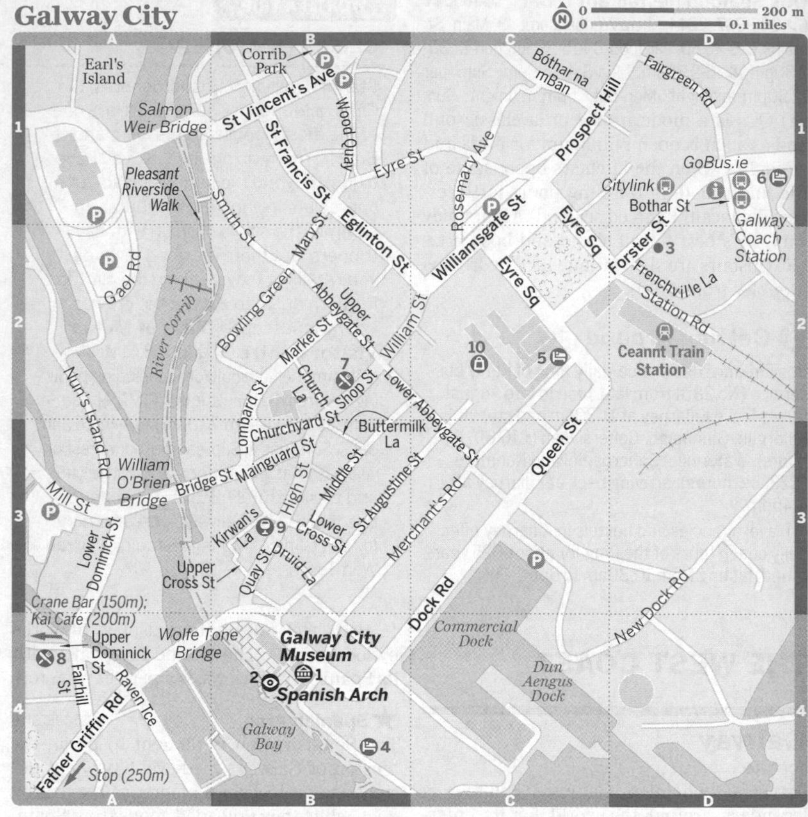

Galway City

Top Sights

1 Galway City Museum B4
2 Spanish Arch B4

Activities, Courses & Tours

3 Lally Tours D2

Sleeping

4 Heron's Rest B4
5 Kinlay House C2
6 Snoozles Tourist Hostel D1

Eating

7 McCambridge's B2
8 Oscar's A4

Drinking & Nightlife

9 Tigh Neachtain B3

Shopping

10 Eyre Square Centre C2

Sleeping

★Kinlay House HOSTEL €
(091-565 244; www.kinlaygalway.ie; Merchant's Rd, Eyre Sq; dm/d €25/70;) Easygoing staff, a full range of facilities and a cream-in-the-doughnut location just off Eyre Sq make this a top choice, with four- to eight-bed dorms and doubles. Spanning two huge, brightly lit floors, amenities include a self-catering kitchen and a cosy TV lounge, with a pool table. Some rooms have bay views and newer beds have electric sockets and USB points.

Snoozles Tourist Hostel HOSTEL €
(091-530 064; http://snoozleshostelgalway.ie; Forster St; dm/d/q from €17.50/90/117;) Dorms and private rooms all have bathrooms at this hostel west of Eyre Sq and not far from the train and bus stations. Continental breakfast is free and facilities include

a barbecue terrace, pool table, lounge with PS2 and kitchen.

★ Stop B&B €€
(☎091-586 736; www.thestopbandb.com; 38 Father Griffin Rd; s/d/tw/tr/f from €70/100/100/140/180; 📶) Done up with funky artwork, fun colours and bare floorboards, this tremendous house pulls out all the stops. The owners keep things fresh as a daisy and neat as a pin with 11 shipshape but never dull rooms. Space – at a premium – is wisely used, so no wardrobes (just hangers), small work desk, no TV, but comfy beds. Brekkie is another forte.

★ Heron's Rest B&B €€
(☎091-539 574; www.theheronsrest.com; 16a Longwalk; d €140-160; 📶) Ideally located in a lovely row of houses on the banks of the Corrib, the thoughtful hosts here give you deck chairs so you can sit outside and enjoy the scene. Other touches include holiday-friendly breakfast times (8am to 11am), decanters of port (enough for a glass or two) and more. Double-glazed rooms, all with water views, are small and cute.

Eating & Drinking

★ McCambridge's CAFE, DELI €
(www.mccambridges.com; 38/39 Shop St; dishes €5-14; ⏲cafe 8.30am-5.30pm Mon-Wed, 8.30am-9pm Thu-Sat, 9.30am-6pm Sun, deli 8am-7pm Mon-Wed, 8am-9pm Thu-Sat, 9.30am-6pm Sun) The long-running food hall here has some superb prepared salads, hot foods and other more exotic treats. Create the perfect picnic or enjoy your pickings at the tables out front. All high ceilings, blond-wood and busy staff, the upstairs cafe is lovely with an ever-changing menu of modern Irish fare plus gourmet sandwiches, salads, silky soups and tip top coffee.

★ Kai Cafe CAFE €€
(☎091-526 003; http://kaicaferestaurant.com; 20 Sea Rd; mains lunch €11-12.50, dinner €18.50-26.50; ⏲cafe 9.30am-3pm Mon-Fri, 10.30am-3pm Sat, restaurant 6.30-10.30pm Tue-Sat; 📶) This fantastic cafe on happening Sea Rd is a delight, whether for a coffee, portions of West Coast Crab or Roscommon hogget and glasses of Galway Hooker Sixty Knots IPA in a relaxed, casual, wholesome and rustic dining environment. Great at any time of the day, but reserve for din-dins.

★ Oscar's SEAFOOD €€
(☎091-582 180; www.oscarsseafoodbistro.com; Upper Dominick St; mains €15.50-25.50; ⏲6-9.30pm Mon-Sat) Galway's best seafood restaurant is just west of the tourist bustle. The long and ever-changing menu has a huge range of local specialities, from shellfish to white fish (which make some superb fish and chips), with some bold flavours. There's a two-course dinner menu from Monday to Thursday (€18.50) before 7pm.

★ Tigh Neachtain PUB
(www.tighneachtain.com; 17 Upper Cross St; ⏲11.30am-midnight Mon-Thu, 11.30am-1am Fri, 10.30am-1am Sat, 12.30-11.30pm Sun) Painted a bright cornflower blue, this 19th-century pub, known simply as Neáchtain's (*nocktans*) or Naughtons, has a wraparound string of tables outside, many shaded by a large tree. It's a place where a polyglot mix of locals plop down and let the world pass them by – or stop and join them for a pint. Good lunches.

★ Crane Bar PUB
(www.thecranebar.com; 2 Sea Rd; ⏲10.30am-11.30pm Mon-Fri, 10.30am-12.30am Sat, 12.30pm-11pm Sun) This atmospheric old pub west of the Corrib is the best spot in Galway to catch an informal *céilidh* (traditional music and dancing) most nights. Talented bands play its rowdy, goodnatured upstairs bar; downstairs at times it seems straight out of *The Far Side.*

Information

Galway Tourist Office (☎091-537 700; www.discoverireland.ie; Forster St; ⏲9am-5pm Mon-Sat) Large, efficient regional information centre that can help arrange local accommodation and tours.

Getting There & Around

BIKE

On Yer Bike (☎091-563 393; http://onyourbikecycles.com; 42 Prospect Hill; bike rental per day from €20; ⏲9am-7pm Mon-Sat, noon-6pm Sun) Bike hire for €15/90 per day/week.

BUS

Bus Éireann Services depart from outside the train station. **Citylink** (www.citylink.ie; ticket office 17 Forster St; ⏲office 9am-6pm; 📶) and **GoBus** (www.gobus.ie; Galway Coach Station; 📶) use the **coach station** (New Coach Station; Fairgreen Rd) a block northeast. Citylink has buses to Clifden (€15, 1½ hours, five daily) and

Dublin (€15, 2½ hours, hourly). Bus Éireann runs buses to Killarney via Limerick (€28, 4½ hours, four daily).

TRAIN

Trains run to and from Dublin (€38, 2¾ hours, nine daily). You can connect with other trains at Athlone.

Aran Islands

The windswept Aran Islands are one of western Ireland's major attractions. As well as their rugged beauty – they are an extension of The Burren's limestone plateau – the Irish-speaking islands have some of the country's oldest Christian and pre-Christian ruins.

There are three main islands in the group, all inhabited year-round. Most visitors head for the long and narrow (14.5km by a maximum 4km) **Inishmór** (or Inishmore). The land slopes up from the relatively sheltered northern shores and plummets on the southern side into the raging Atlantic. **Inishmaan** and **Inisheer** are much smaller and receive far fewer visitors.

The **tourist office** (☎099-61263; www.aranislands.ie; Kilronan; ⊙10am-5pm) operates year-round at Kilronan, the arrival point and major village of Inishmór. You can leave your luggage here and change money. Around the corner is a Spar supermarket with an ATM (many places do not accept credit cards).

Inishmór

Three spectacular forts stand guard over Inishmór, each believed to be around 2000 years old. Chief among them is **Dún Aengus** (Dún Aonghasa; www.heritageireland.ie; site adult/child €5/3, visitor centre €2/1; ⊙9.30am-6pm Apr-Oct, to 4pm Nov-Mar), which has three massive drystone walls that run right up to sheer drops to the ocean below. It is protected by remarkable *chevaux de frise,* fearsome and densely packed defensive stone spikes. A small visitor centre has displays that put everything in context. A slightly strenuous 900m walkway wanders uphill to the fort itself.

Kilronan Hostel (☎099-61255; http://kilronanhostel.com; Kilronan; dm from €30; ⊙late Feb-late Oct; @📶), perched above Tí Joe Mac's pub, is a friendly hostel just a two-minute walk from the ferry. **Kilmurvey House** (☎099-61218; www.aranislands.ie/kilmurvey-house/; Kilmurvey; s/d from €60/95; ⊙Apr–mid-Oct; 📶) offers B&B in a grand 18th-century stone mansion on the path leading to Dún Aengus.

ℹ Getting There & Away

AIR

Aer Arann Islands (☎091-593 034; http://aerarannislands.ie; one-way/return €25/49) Offers return flights to each of the islands three to six times a day for adult/child €49/27; the flights take about 10 minutes, and groups of four or more can get group rates (€44 each adult). A connecting minibus from the Victoria Hotel in Galway costs €3 one-way.

BOAT

Aran Island Ferries (☎091-568 903; www.aranislandferries.com; one-way/return €13/25) Crossings can take up to one hour, subject to cancellation in high seas. Boats leave from Rossaveal, 40km west of Galway City on the

WORTH A TRIP

CONNEMARA

With its shimmering black lakes, pale mountains, lonely valleys and more than the occasional rainbow, Connemara in the northwestern corner of County Galway is one of the most gorgeous corners of Ireland. It's prime hillwalking country with plenty of wild terrain, none more so than the Twelve Bens, a ridge of rugged mountains that form part of **Connemara National Park** (www.connemaranationalpark.ie; off N59; ⊙24hr) FREE.

Connemara's 'capital', **Clifden** (An Clochán), is an appealing Victorian-era country town with an oval of streets offering evocative strolls. Right in the centre of town is cheery **Clifden Town Hostel** (☎087 7769 345; http://clifdenbayhostel; 1 Market St; dm €17-23; ⊙reception 9am-5pm), while the gorgeous **Dolphin Beach B&B** (☎095-21204; www.dolphinbeachhouse.com; Lower Sky Rd; s/d from €90/130, dinner €40; P📶) 🍃 is 5km west of town.

From Galway, **Lally Tours** (☎091-562 905; http://lallytours.com; tours adult/child from €25/15) run day-long coach tours of Connemara.

OTHER IRISH PLACES WORTH A VISIT

Some other places in Ireland you might like to consider for day trips or longer visits:

Dingle (65km west of Killarney) The charms of this special spot have long drawn runaways from across the world, making this port town a surprisingly cosmopolitan and creative place. There are loads of cafes, bookshops and art-and-craft galleries, and a friendly dolphin called Fungie who has lived in the bay for 25 years.

Glendalough (50km south of Dublin) Nestled between two lakes, haunting Glendalough (Gleann dá Loch, meaning 'Valley of the Two Lakes') is one of the most significant monastic sites in Ireland and one of the loveliest spots in the country.

Kinsale (28km south of Cork) This picturesque yachting harbour is one of the many gems that dot the coastline of County Cork, and has been labelled the gourmet capital of Ireland; it certainly contains more than its fair share of international-standard restaurants.

Slieve League (120km southwest of Derry/Londonderry) The awe-inspiring cliffs at Slieve League, rising 300m above the Atlantic Ocean, are one of Ireland's top sights. Experienced hikers can spend a day walking along the top of the cliffs via the slightly terrifying One Man's Path to Malinbeg, near Glencolumbcille.

Sligo (140km north of Galway) William Butler Yeats (1865–1939) was born in Dublin and educated in London, but his poetry is infused with the landscapes, history and folklore of his mother's native Sligo (Sligeach). He returned many times and there are plentiful reminders of his presence in this sweet, sleepy town.

R336. Buses from Queen St in Galway (return adult/child €7/4) connect with most sailings; ask when you book.

Ferries to the Arans (primarily Inisheer) also operate from Doolin.

NORTHERN IRELAND

☎028

Dragged down for decades by the violence and uncertainty of the Troubles, Northern Ireland today is a nation rejuvenated. The 1998 Good Friday Agreement laid the groundwork for peace and raised hopes for the future, and since then this UK province has seen a huge influx of investment and redevelopment. Belfast has become a happening place with a famously wild nightlife, and the stunning Causeway Coast gets more and more visitors each year.

There are plenty of reminders of the Troubles – notably the 'peace lines' that divide Belfast – and the passions that have torn Northern Ireland apart over the decades still run deep. But despite occasional setbacks there is an atmosphere of determined optimism.

When you cross from the Republic into Northern Ireland you notice a couple of changes: the accent is different, the road signs are in miles, and the prices are in pounds sterling. But there's no border checkpoint, no guards, not even a sign to mark the crossing point – the two countries are in a customs union, so there's no passport control and no customs declarations. However, the UK's 2016 decision to leave the EU has introduced a note of uncertainty, and no one is quite sure what its long-term effect on the Ireland/Northern Ireland border will be.

Belfast

POP 280,900

Once lumped with Beirut, Baghdad and Bosnia as one of the four 'B's for travellers to avoid, Belfast has pulled off a remarkable transformation from bombs-and-bullets pariah to hip-hotels-and-hedonism party town. The old shipyards on the Lagan continue to give way to the luxury apartments of the Titanic Quarter, whose centrepiece is the stunning, star-shaped Titanic Belfast centre, the city's number-one tourist draw. New venues keep popping up – historic Crumlin Road Gaol and *SS Nomadic* have opened to the public, and WWI warship HMS *Caroline* is set to become a floating museum. They all add to a list of attractions that includes beautifully restored Victorian architecture, a glittering waterfront lined with modern art, a fantastic foodie scene and music-filled pubs.

The city centre is compact, and the imposing City Hall in Donegall Sq is the central landmark. The principal shopping district is north of the square. North again, around Donegall St and St Anne's Cathedral, is the bohemian Cathedral Quarter.

South of the square, the so-called Golden Mile stretches for 1km along Great Victoria St, Shaftesbury Sq and Botanic Ave to Queen's University and the leafy suburbs of South Belfast; this area has dozens of restaurants and bars, and most of the city's budget and midrange accommodation.

Sights

★Titanic Belfast MUSEUM

(www.titanicbelfast.com; Queen's Rd; adult/child £18/8; 9am-7pm Jun-Aug, to 6pm Apr, May & Sep, 10am-5pm Oct-Mar; Abercorn Basin) The head of the slipway where the *Titanic* was built is now occupied by the gleaming, angular edifice of Titanic Belfast, an unmissable multimedia extravaganza that charts the history of Belfast and the creation of the world's most famous ocean liner. Cleverly designed exhibits enlivened by historic images, animated projections and soundtracks chart Belfast's rise to turn-of-the-20th-century industrial superpower, followed by a high-tech ride through a noisy, smells-and-all re-creation of the city's shipyards.

★SS Nomadic HISTORIC SITE

(www.nomadicbelfast.com; Hamilton Dock, Queen's Rd; adult/child £7/5; 9am-7pm Jun-Aug, to 6pm Apr, May & Sep, 10am-5pm Oct-Mar) Built in Belfast in 1911, the SS *Nomadic* is the last remaining vessel of the White Star Line. The little steamship ferried 1st- and 2nd-class passengers between Cherbourg Harbour and the ocean liners that were too big to dock at the French port. On 10 April 1912 it delivered 172 passengers to the ill-fated *Titanic*. First-come, first-served guided tours run every 30 minutes from 10am until an hour before closing. Alternatively, you're free to roam at will (don't miss the 1st-class toilets!).

> **BELFAST VISITOR PASS**
>
> The Belfast Visitor Pass (one/two/three days £6.50/11/14.50) allows unlimited travel on bus and train services in Belfast and around, and discounts on admission to **Titanic Belfast** and other attractions. You can buy it at airports, main train and bus stations, the Metro kiosk on Donegall Sq and the **Visit Belfast Welcome Centre** (p413).

★Ulster Museum MUSEUM

(www.nmni.com; Botanic Gardens; 10am-5pm Tue-Sun; ; Botanic) FREE You could spend hours browsing this state-of-the-art museum, but if you're pressed for time don't miss the **Armada Room**, with artefacts retrieved from the 1588 wreck of the Spanish galleon *Girona;* the **Egyptian Room**, with Princess Takabuti, a 2500-year-old Egyptian mummy unwrapped in Belfast in 1835; and the **Early Peoples Gallery**, with the bronze Bann Disc, a superb example of Celtic design from the Iron Age.

Free tours (10 people maximum; first-come, first served) run at 2.30pm Tuesday to Friday and 1.30pm Sunday.

★Crown Liquor Saloon HISTORIC BUILDING

(www.nationaltrust.org.uk/the-crown-bar; 46 Great Victoria St; 11.30am-11pm Mon-Sat, 12.30-10pm Sun; Europa Bus Centre) FREE There are not too many historical monuments that you can enjoy while savouring a pint of beer, but the National Trust's Crown Liquor Saloon is one of them. Belfast's most famous bar was refurbished by Patrick Flanagan in the late 19th century and displays Victorian decorative flamboyance at its best (he was looking to pull in a posh clientele from the newfangled train station and Grand Opera House across the street).

West Belfast HISTORIC SITE

(Falls Rd) Though scarred by three decades of civil unrest, the former battleground of West Belfast is one of the most compelling places to visit in Northern Ireland. Falls Rd and Shankill Rd are adorned with famous **murals** expressing local political and religious passions, and divided by the infamous **Peace Line** (Falls Rd) barrier separating Catholic and Protestant districts. Take a taxi tour of the district, or pick up a map from the tourist office and explore on foot.

Festivals & Events

Féile An Phobail CULTURAL

(West Belfast Festival; www.feilebelfast.com; early Aug) Said to be the largest community festival in Ireland, the Féile takes place in West Belfast over 10 days. Events include an opening carnival parade, street parties, theatre performances, concerts and historical tours of the City and Milltown cemeteries.

BELFAST CITY TOURS

Many operators, including **Harpers** (www.harpertaxitours.com; from £30) and **Paddy Campbell's** (07990 955227; www.belfastblackcabtours.co.uk; tour per 1-3 people £30), offer guided taxi tours of West Belfast, with an even-handed account of the Troubles. They run daily for around £10 per person based on a group of three to six, or £30 total for one or two, and pick-up can be arranged.

There are a number of walking tours available, including the three-hour **Belfast Pub Crawl** (07731 977774; www.belfastcrawl.com; per person £10; 8.30pm Fri & Sat; Queen's Sq), taking in four of the city's historic pubs, and the three-hour **Titanic Tour** (028-9065 9971; www.titanictours-belfast.co.uk; ½ day tour £25 per person), visiting various *Titanic* sites.

Belfast International Arts Festival PERFORMING ARTS
(www.belfastinternationalartsfestival.com; mid-late Oct) The UK's second-largest arts festival stretches over two weeks and features theatre, music, dance and talks.

Sleeping

Many B&Bs are concentrated in the pleasant university district of South Belfast, which is well stocked with restaurants and pubs.

★**Vagabonds** HOSTEL €
(028-9023 3017; www.vagabondsbelfast.com; 9 University Rd; dm £15-17, d & tw £50; Shaftesbury Sq) Comfy bunks, lockable luggage baskets, private shower cubicles and a relaxed atmosphere are what you get at one of Belfast's best hostels, run by a couple of experienced travellers. It's conveniently located close to both Queen's and the city centre.

Tara Lodge GUESTHOUSE €€
(028-9059 0900; www.taralodge.com; 36 Cromwell Rd; s/d from £75/85; Upper Crescent Queens University) In a great location on a quiet side street just a few paces from the buzz of Botanic Ave, this B&B feels more like a boutique hotel with its clean-cut, minimalist decor, friendly and efficient staff, and 24 bright and cheerful rooms. Delicious breakfasts include porridge with Bushmills whiskey.

Old Rectory B&B €€
(028-9066 7882; www.anoldrectory.co.uk; 148 Malone Rd; s/d/f from £52/80/132; Myrtlefield Pk) A lovely Victorian villa with lots of original stained glass, this former rectory has five spacious bedrooms, a comfortable drawing room with leather sofa and fancy breakfasts (home-baked bread, home-made Irish-whiskey marmalade, scrambled eggs with smoked salmon, veggie fry-ups, freshly squeezed OJ). A credit card is required to secure your booking but payment is in cash only.

The inconspicuous driveway is on the left, just past Deramore Park S.

Eating

There are lots of inexpensive eating places along Botanic Ave in South Belfast, and many pubs offer good-value meals.

Maggie May's CAFE €
(028-9032 2662; www.maggiemaysbelfastcafe.co.uk; 50 Botanic Ave; mains £4.50-7.50; 8am-11pm Mon-Sat, 9am-11pm Sun; Botanic) This is a classic little cafe with cosy wooden booths, murals of old Belfast and a host of hungover students wolfing down huge Ulster fry-ups. The all-day breakfast menu includes French toast and maple syrup, while lunch can be soup and a sandwich or beef lasagne. BYO.

There's a newer branch in **Stranmillis** (028-9066 8515; www.maggiemaysbelfastcafe.co.uk; 2 Malone Rd; mains £4.50-7.50; 8am-11pm Mon-Sat, 9am-11pm Sun; Methodist College).

★**Barking Dog** BISTRO €€
(028-9066 1885; www.barkingdogbelfast.com; 33-35 Malone Rd; mains £16-30 tapas 5 dishes £15.50; noon-2.30pm & 5-10pm Mon-Thu, to 11pm Fri & Sat, noon-4pm & 5-9pm Sun; Eglantine Ave) Chunky hardwood, bare brick, candlelight and quirky design create the atmosphere of a stylishly restored farmhouse. The menu completes the feeling of cosiness and comfort with simple but sensational dishes such as their signature burger of meltingly tender beef shin with caramelised onion and horseradish cream, and sweet-potato ravioli with carrot and parmesan crisps. It has superb service, too.

Belfast

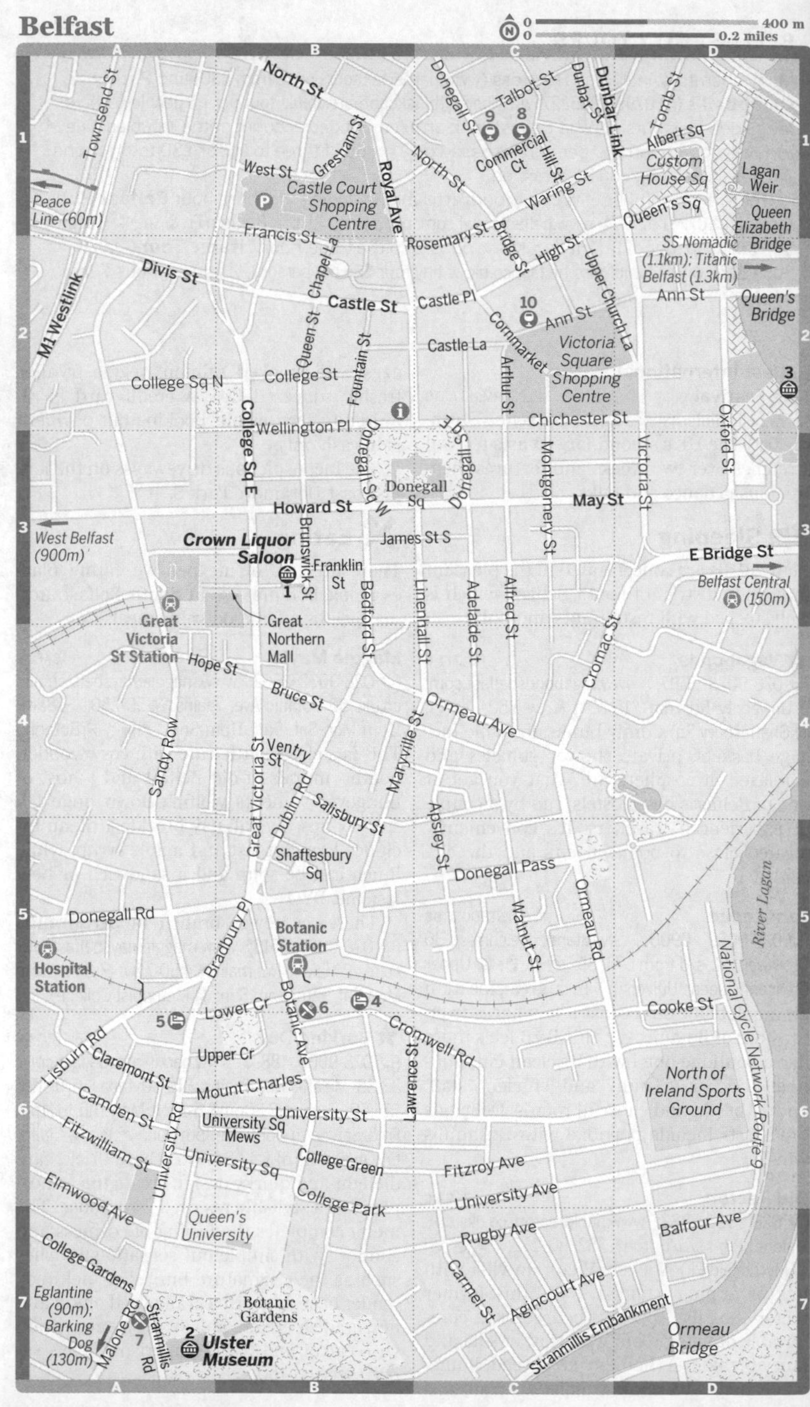
0 400 m
0 0.2 miles
North St
Townsend St
Gresham St
Donegall St
Talbot St
Dunbar St
Dunbar Link
Tomb St
Albert Sq
Custom House Sq
Lagan Weir
West St
Royal Ave
Commercial Ct
Hill St
Castle Court Shopping Centre
Waring St
Queen's Sq
Queen Elizabeth Bridge
Peace Line (60m)
Francis St
Rosemary St
Bridge St
High St
SS Nomadic (1.1km); Titanic Belfast (1.3km)
Divis St
Chapel La
Upper Church La
Ann St
Queen's Bridge
M1 Westlink
Castle St
Castle Pl
Cornmarket
Victoria Square Shopping Centre
Queen St
Fountain St
Castle La
Arthur St
College Sq N
College St
College Sq E
Wellington Pl
Chichester St
Oxford St
Donegall Sq W
Donegall Sq E
Donegall Sq
Montgomery St
Victoria St
Howard St
May St
West Belfast (900m)
Crown Liquor Saloon
Brunswick St
James St S
Franklin St
E Bridge St
Belfast Central (150m)
Bedford St
Linenhall St
Adelaide St
Alfred St
Great Victoria St Station
Great Northern Mall
Cromac St
Hope St
Bruce St
Ormeau Ave
Sandy Row
Maryville St
Ventry St
Great Victoria St
Dublin Rd
Salisbury St
Apsley St
Shaftesbury Sq
Donegall Pass
River Lagan
Donegall Rd
Bradbury Pl
Botanic Station
Walnut St
Ormeau Rd
Hospital Station
National Cycle Network Route 9
Lower Cr
Botanic Ave
Cromwell Rd
Cooke St
Lisburn Rd
Claremont St
Upper Cr
Lawrence St
Mount Charles
North of Ireland Sports Ground
Camden St
University St
University Sq Mews
University Rd
Fitzwilliam St
University Sq
College Green
Fitzroy Ave
Elmwood Ave
College Park
University Ave
Queen's University
Rugby Ave
Balfour Ave
College Gardens
Carmel St
Agincourt Ave
Eglantine (90m); Barking Dog (130m)
Malone Rd
Stranmillis Rd
Botanic Gardens
Ulster Museum
Stranmillis Embankment
Ormeau Bridge

Belfast

Top Sights

Sights

Sleeping

Eating

Drinking & Nightlife

★ **Holohan's at the Barge** MODERN IRISH €€
(☎028-9023 5973; www.holohansatthebarge.co.uk; Belfast Barge, Lanyon Quay; mains lunch £5-9, dinner £15-22; ⏲5-11pm Tue-Sat, 1-7pm Sun; 🚌Oxford St) Aboard the **Belfast Barge** (www.facebook.com/TheBelfastBarge; Lanyon Quay; ⏲10am-4pm Tue-Sat; 🚌Oxford St) FREE, Holohan's is a sensational find for inspired twists on seafood (seared scallops with burnt cauliflower purée; roast hake with crayfish and dulse butter), as well as land-based dishes such as salt-aged beef with heirloom vegetables, desserts such as plum and ginger cake with vanilla ice cream, and by-the-glass wines from around the world.

Drinking & Nightlife

Belfast's pub scene is lively and friendly, with the older traditional pubs complemented by a rising tide of stylish designer bars.

★ **Duke of York** PUB
(☎028-9024 1062; www.dukeofyorkbelfast.com; 11 Commercial Ct; ⏲11.30am-midnight Mon, to 1am Tue-Sat, 1-9pm Sun; 🚌Queen's Sq) Down an inconspicuous alley in the heart of the city's former newspaper district, the snug, traditional Duke was a hang-out for print workers and journalists. Sinn Féin leader Gerry Adams worked behind the bar here during his student days in 1971. The entire alley takes on a street-party atmosphere in warm weather.

★ **Eglantine** PUB
(www.eglantinebar.com; 32 Malone Rd; ⏲11.30am-midnight Sun-Tue, to 1am Wed-Sat; 📶; 🚌Eglantine Ave) The 'Eg' is a local institution, and widely reckoned to be the best of Belfast's many student pubs. It serves good beer and good food, and hosts numerous events: Monday is quiz night, Tuesday is open-mic night; other nights see DJs spin and bands perform. Bonus: Pac-Man machine.

★ **Love & Death Inc** COCKTAIL BAR
(www.loveanddeathinc.com; 10a Ann St; ⏲4pm-1am Mon-Thu, noon-3am Fri-Sat, 2pm-midnight Sun) More like a cool inner-city house party, speakeasy-style Love & Death Inc is secreted up a flight of stairs above a pizza joint. Its living-room-style bar has outrageous decor, feisty Latin American–influenced food, feistier cocktails and a wild nightclub in the attic on weekends.

Information

Visit Belfast Welcome Centre (☎028-9024 6609; http://visit-belfast.com; 9 Donegall Sq N; ⏲9am-7pm Mon-Sat, 11am-4pm Sun Jun-Sep, 9am-5.30pm Mon-Sat, 11am-4pm Sun Oct-May; 📶; 🚌Donegall Sq) Provides information about the whole of Northern Ireland and books accommodation. Services include left luggage (not overnight), currency exchange and free wi-fi.

Getting There & Away

AIR

Belfast International Airport (p418) is 30km northwest of the city, and has flights from the UK, Europe and the USA. George Best Belfast City Airport (p418) is 6km northeast of the city centre, with flights from the UK and Europe.

BOAT

Stena Line ferries to Belfast from Cairnryan and Liverpool dock at Victoria Terminal, 5km north of the city centre; exit the M2 motorway at junction 1. Ferries from the Isle of Man arrive at Albert Quay, 2km north of the centre.

Other car ferries to and from Scotland dock at Larne, 37km north of Belfast.

BUS

Europa Bus Centre, Belfast's main bus station, is behind the Europa Hotel and next door to Great Victoria St train station; it's reached via the Great Northern Mall beside the hotel. It's the main terminus for buses to Derry, Dublin and destinations in the west and south of Northern Ireland.

Ballycastle £12, 2¼ hours, four daily on weekdays, two on Saturday, change at Ballymena

Derry £12, 1¾ hours, half-hourly

Dublin £15, 2½ hours, hourly

Aircoach (www.aircoach.ie) operates a service from Glengall St, near Europa Bus Centre, to Dublin city centre and Dublin Airport.

TRAIN

Belfast has two main train stations: Great Victoria St, next to the Europa Bus Centre, and Belfast Central, east of the city centre. If you arrive by train at Central Station, your rail ticket entitles you to a free bus ride into the city centre. A local train also connects with Great Victoria St.

Derry £12, 2¼ hours, seven or eight daily

Dublin £30, 2¼ hours, eight daily Monday to Saturday, five on Sunday

Larne Harbour £7.20, one hour, hourly

Getting Around

BIKE

Belfast Bike Tours (07812 114235; www.belfastbiketours.com; per person £15; 10.30am & 2pm Mon, Wed, Fri & Sat Apr-Aug, Sat only Sep-Mar; Queen's University) hires out bikes for £15 per day. Credit-card deposit and photo ID are required.

BUS

A short trip on a city bus costs £1.50 to £2.30; a one-day ticket costs £3.90. Most local bus services depart from Donegall Sq, near the City Hall, where there's a ticket kiosk; otherwise, buy a ticket from the driver.

The Causeway Coast

Ireland isn't short of scenic coastlines, but the **Causeway Coast** between Portstewart and Ballycastle – climaxing in the spectacular rock formations of the Giant's Causeway – and the **Antrim Coast** between Ballycastle and Belfast, are as magnificent as they come.

From April to September the **Ulsterbus** (028-9066 6630; www.translink.co.uk) Antrim Coaster (bus 252) links Larne with Coleraine (£12, four hours, two daily) via the Glens of Antrim, Ballycastle, the Giant's Causeway, Bushmills, Portrush and Portstewart.

From Easter to September the Causeway Rambler (bus 402) links Coleraine and Carrick-a-Rede (£6.50, 40 minutes, seven daily) via Bushmills Distillery, the Giant's Causeway, White Park Bay and Ballintoy. The ticket allows unlimited travel in both directions for one day.

There are several hostels along the coast, including **Sheep Island View Hostel** (028-2076 9391; www.sheepislandview.com; 42a Main St; dm/s/tw £18/25/45; P @ wi-fi), **Ballycastle Backpackers** (028-2076 3612; www.ballycastlebackpackers.net; 4 North St; dm/tw from £17.50/35, cottage £80; P @ wi-fi) and **Bushmills Youth Hostel** (028-2073 1222; www.hini.org.uk; 49 Main St; dm £16-20, tr £53; closed 11.30am-2.30pm Jul & Aug, 11.30am-5pm Mar-Jun, Sep & Oct; @ wi-fi).

GAME OF THRONES TOURS

If you're driving around Northern Ireland, there are *Game of Thrones* filming locations aplenty – visit www.discovernorthernireland.com/gameofthrones. Alternatively, day-long bus tours depart from Belfast.

Sights

★Giant's Causeway LANDMARK

(www.nationaltrust.org.uk; dawn-dusk) FREE This spectacular rock formation – Northern Ireland's only Unesco World Heritage site – is one of Ireland's most impressive and atmospheric landscape features, a vast expanse of regular, closely packed, hexagonal stone columns looking for all the world like the handiwork of giants. The phenomenon is explained in the **Giant's Causeway Visitor Experience** (028-2073 1855; www.nationaltrust.org.uk; 60 Causeway Rd; adult/child £10.50/5.25; 9am-7pm Jul-Aug, to 6pm Mar-Jun & Sep-Oct, to 5pm Nov-Feb; wi-fi), a spectacular new ecofriendly building half-hidden in a hillside above the sea.

Visiting the Giant's Causeway itself is free of charge but you pay to use the car park and the visitor centre. (The admission fee is reduced by £2 if you arrive by bus, bike or on foot.)

From the centre it's an easy 10- to 15-minute walk downhill to the Causeway itself, but a more interesting approach is to follow the clifftop path northeast for 2km to the Chimney Tops headland, then descend the Shepherd's Steps to the Causeway. For the less mobile, a minibus shuttles from the visitors centre to the Causeway (£2 return).

★Carrick-a-Rede Rope Bridge BRIDGE

(028-2076 9839; www.nationaltrust.org.uk/carrick-a-rede; 119 Whitepark Rd, Ballintoy; adult/child £7/3.50; 9.30am-6pm Apr-Oct, to 3.30pm Nov-Mar) This 20m-long, 1m-wide bridge of wire rope spans the chasm between the sea cliffs and the little island of Carrick-a-Rede, swaying 30m above the rock-strewn water. Crossing the bridge is perfectly safe, but frightening if you don't have a head for heights, especially if it's breezy (in high winds the bridge is closed). From the island, views take in Rathlin Island and Fair Head to the east.

There's a small National Trust information centre and cafe at the car park.

Derry/Londonderry

POP 84,340

Northern Ireland's second city comes as a pleasant surprise to many visitors. Derry was never the prettiest of places, and it certainly lagged behind Belfast in terms of investment and redevelopment, but in preparation for its year in the limelight as UK City of Culture 2013, the city centre was given a handsome makeover. The new **Peace Bridge**, Ebrington Sq, and the redevelopment of the waterfront and Guildhall area make the most of the city's riverside setting. And Derry's determined air of can-do optimism has made it the powerhouse of the North's cultural revival.

There's a lot of history to absorb here, from the Siege of Derry to the Battle of the Bogside – a stroll around the 17th-century city walls is a must, as is a tour of the Bogside murals. The city's lively pubs are home to a burgeoning live-music scene. But perhaps the biggest attraction is the people themselves: warm, witty and welcoming.

Derry or Londonderry? The name you use for Northern Ireland's second-largest city can be a political statement, but today most people just call it Derry, whatever their politics. The 'London' prefix was added in 1613 in recognition of the Corporation of London's role in the 'plantation' of Ulster with Protestant settlers.

In 1968 resentment at the long-running Protestant domination of the city council boiled over into a series of (Catholic-dominated) civil-rights marches. In August 1969 fighting between police and local youths in the poor Catholic Bogside district prompted the UK government to send British troops into Derry. In January 1972 'Bloody Sunday' resulted in the deaths of 13 unarmed Catholic civil-rights marchers in Derry at the hands of the British army, an event that marked the beginning of the Troubles in earnest.

Sights

★Derry's City Walls WALLS

(dawn-dusk) FREE The best way to get a feel for Derry's layout and history is to walk the 1.5km circumference of the city's walls. Completed in 1619, Derry's city walls are 8m high and 9m thick and are the only city walls in Ireland to survive almost intact. The four original gates (Shipquay, Ferryquay, Bishop's and Butcher's) were rebuilt in the 18th and 19th centuries, when three new gates (New, Magazine and Castle) were added.

★Tower Museum MUSEUM

(www.derrystrabane.com/towermuseum; Union Hall Pl; adult/child £4/2; 10am-5.30pm, last admission 4pm) Head straight to the 5th floor of this award-winning museum inside a replica 16th-century tower house for a view from the top. Then work your way down through the excellent **Armada Shipwreck** exhibition, and the **Story of Derry**, where well-thought-out exhibits and audiovisuals lead you through the city's history from the founding of the monastery of St Colmcille (Columba) in the 6th century to the Battle of the Bogside in the late 1960s. Allow at least two hours.

People's Gallery Murals PUBLIC ART

(Rossville St) The 12 murals that decorate the gable ends of houses along Rossville St, near Free Derry Corner, are popularly referred to as the People's Gallery. They are the work of Tom Kelly, Will Kelly and Kevin Hasson, known as 'the Bogside Artists'. The three men have spent most of their lives in the Bogside, and lived through the worst of the Troubles. The murals can be clearly seen from the northern part of the City Walls.

Sleeping

★Merchant's House B&B €€

(028-7126 9691; www.thesaddlershouse.com; 16 Queen St; s/d/tr/f from £40/65/90/100;) This historic, Georgian-style town house is a gem of a B&B. It has an elegant lounge and dining room with marble fireplaces and antique furniture, TV, coffee-making facilities, homemade marmalade at breakfast and bathrobes in the bedrooms (some rooms have shared bathroom). Call at **Saddler's House** (028-7126 9691; www.thesaddlershouse.com; 36 Great James St; s/d from £55/60;) first to pick up a key.

ESSENTIAL FOOD & DRINK

Ireland's recently acquired reputation as a gourmet destination is thoroughly deserved, with a host of chefs and producers leading a foodie revolution that has made it easy to eat well on all budgets.

Champ Northern Irish dish of mashed potatoes with spring onions (scallions).

Colcannon Potatoes mashed with milk, cabbage and fried onion.

Farl Triangular flatbread in Northern Ireland and Donegal.

Irish stew Lamb stew with potatoes, onions and thyme.

Irish whiskey Around 100 different types are produced by only four distilleries: Jameson, Bushmills, Cooley and recently reopened Kilbeggan.

Soda bread Wonderful bread – white or brown, sweet or savoury – made from very soft Irish flour and buttermilk.

Stout Dark, almost black beer made with roasted barley; famous brands are Guinness in Dublin, and Murphy's and Beamish & Crawford in Cork.

Abbey B&B B&B €€
(☎028-7127 9000; www.abbeyaccommodation.com; 4 Abbey St; s/d/tr from £50/70/90;) There's a warm welcome waiting at this family-run B&B just a short walk from the walled city, on the edge of the Bogside. The six rooms are stylishly decorated.

Eating & Drinking

★**Pyke 'n' Pommes** STREET FOOD €
(www.facebook.com/PykeNPommes; behind Foyle Marina, off Baronet St; mains £4-16; noon-4pm Sun-Thu, to 5pm Fri & Sat;) Derry's single-best eatery is this quayside shipping container. Chef Kevin Pyke's amazing, mostly organic burgers span his signature Notorious Pig (pulled pork, crispy slaw, beetroot and crème fraiche), Cheeky Monkey (monkfish, warm potato and smoked-apple purée) and Veganderry (chickpeas, lemon and coriander) to his Legenderry Burger (wagyu beef, pickled onions and honey-mustard mayo). Seasonal specials might include mackerel or oysters.

★**Peadar O'Donnell's** PUB
(www.peadars.com; 59-63 Waterloo St; 11.30am-1.30am Mon-Sat, 12.30pm-12.30am Sun) Done up as a typical Irish pub/grocery – with shelves of household items, shopkeepers scales on the counter and a museum's-worth of old bric-a-brac – Peadar's has traditional music sessions every night and often on weekend afternoons as well. Its adjacent **Gweedore Bar** (www.peadars.com; 59-61 Waterloo St; 11.30am-1.30am Mon-Sat, noon-12.30am Sun) hosts live rock bands every night, and a Saturday night disco upstairs.

Information

Visit Derry (☎028-7126 7284; www.visitderry.com; 44 Foyle St; 9am-5.30pm Mon-Fri, 10am-5pm Sat & Sun;) Sells books and maps, has a bureau de change and can book accommodation.

Getting There & Away

BUS

The **bus station** (☎028-7126 2261; Foyle St) is just northeast of the walled city.

Belfast £12, 1¾ hours, half-hourly Monday to Friday, hourly Saturday and Sunday

Dublin £20, four hours, every two hours daily

TRAIN

Derry's train station (always referred to as Londonderry in Northern Ireland timetables) is on the eastern side of the River Foyle; a free Rail Link bus connects with the bus station.

Belfast £12, 2½ hours, nine daily Monday to Saturday, six on Sunday

SURVIVAL GUIDE

Directory A–Z

ACCOMMODATION

Hostels in Ireland can be booked solid in the summer.

From June to September a dorm bed at most hostels costs €15 to €25 (£13 to £20), except for the more expensive hostels in Dublin, Belfast and a few other places.

Typical B&Bs cost around €35 to €45 (£25 to £40) per person a night (sharing a double room), though more luxurious B&Bs can cost upwards of €55 (£45) per person. Most B&Bs are small, so in summer they quickly fill up.

Commercial camping grounds typically charge €12 to €25 (£10 to £20) for a tent or campervan and two people. Unless otherwise indicated, prices quoted for 'campsites' are for a tent, car and two people.

The following are useful resources:

An Óige (www.anoige.ie) Hostelling International (HI)–associated national organisation with 26 hostels scattered around the Republic.

Family Homes of Ireland (www.familyhomes.ie) Lists family-run guesthouses and self-catering properties.

HINI (www.hini.org.uk) HI-associated organisation with six hostels in Northern Ireland.

Independent Holiday Hostels of Ireland (IHH; www.hostels-ireland.com) 80 tourist-board approved hostels throughout Ireland.

Independent Hostel Owners of Ireland (IHO; www.independenthostelsireland.com) Independent hostelling association.

ACTIVITIES

Ireland is great for outdoor activities, and tourist offices have a wide selection of information covering birdwatching, surfing (great along the west coast), scuba diving, cycling, fishing, horse riding, sailing, canoeing and many other activities.

Walking is particularly popular, although you must come prepared for wet weather. There are now well over 20 waymarked trails throughout Ireland, one of the more popular being the 214km Kerry Way.

SLEEPING PRICE RANGES

The following price ranges have been used in our reviews of places to stay. Prices are all based on a double room with private bathroom in high season.

Republic

€ less than €80

€€ €80-180

€€€ more than €180

Northern Ireland

€ less than €50

€€ €50-120

€€€ more than €120

COUNTRY FACTS

Area 84,421 sq km

Capitals Dublin (Republic of Ireland), Belfast (Northern Ireland)

Country Code Republic of Ireland ☎353, Northern Ireland ☎44

Currency euro (€) in Republic of Ireland; pound sterling (£) in Northern Ireland

Emergency ☎112

Languages English, Irish Gaelic

Money ATMs widespread; credit cards widely accepted

Population Republic of Ireland 4.76 million; Northern Ireland 1.87 million

Visas Schengen rules do not apply

INTERNET RESOURCES

Entertainment Ireland (www.entertainment.ie) Countrywide listings for every kind of entertainment.

Failte Ireland (www.discoverireland.ie) Official tourist board website – practical info and a huge accommodation database.

Lonely Planet (www.lonelyplanet.com/ireland) Destination information, hotel bookings, traveller forums and more.

Northern Ireland Tourist Board (www.nitb.com) Official tourist site.

MONEY

The Republic of Ireland uses the euro (€), while Northern Ireland uses the British pound sterling (£). Banks offer the best exchange rates; exchange bureaux, open longer, have worse rates and higher commissions. Post offices generally have exchange facilities and are open on Saturday morning.

In Northern Ireland several banks issue their own Northern Irish pound notes, which are equivalent to sterling but not readily accepted in mainland Britain. Many hotels, restaurants and shops in Northern Ireland accept euros.

Tipping

Fancy hotels and restaurants usually add a 10% or 15% service charge onto bills. Simpler places usually don't add a service charge; if you decide to tip, just round up the bill (or add 10% at most). Taxi drivers do not have to be tipped, but if you do, 10% is more than generous.

EATING PRICE RANGES

The following price indicators are used to indicate the cost of a main course at dinner:

Republic

€ less than €12

€€ €12-25

€€€ more than €25

Northern Ireland

€ less than €12

€€ €12-20

€€€ more than €20

OPENING HOURS

Banks 10am–4pm Monday to Friday (to 5pm Thursday)

Pubs 10.30am–11.30pm Monday to Thursday, 10.30am–12.30am Friday and Saturday, noon–11pm Sunday (30 minutes 'drinking up' time allowed); closed Christmas Day and Good Friday

Restaurants noon–10.30pm; many close one day of the week

Shops 9.30am–6pm Monday to Saturday (until 8pm Thursday in cities), noon–6pm Sunday

PUBLIC HOLIDAYS

The main public holidays in the Republic of Ireland and Northern Ireland are:

New Year's Day 1 January

St Patrick's Day 17 March

Easter (Good Friday to Easter Monday inclusive) March/April

May Holiday First Monday in May

Christmas Day 25 December

St Stephen's Day (Boxing Day) 26 December

Northern Ireland

Spring Bank Holiday Last Monday in May

Orangemen's Day 12 July (following Monday if 12th is on the weekend)

August Bank Holiday Last Monday in August

Republic of Ireland

June Holiday First Monday in June

August Holiday First Monday in August

October Holiday Last Monday in October

TELEPHONE

The mobile- (cell-) phone network in Ireland runs on the GSM 900/1800 system compatible with the rest of Europe and Australia, but not the USA. Mobile numbers in the Republic begin with ☎085, ☎086 or ☎087 (07 in Northern Ireland). A local pay-as-you-go SIM for your mobile will cost from around €10, but may work out free after the standard phone-credit refund (make sure your phone is compatible with the local provider).

To call Northern Ireland from the Republic, do not use ☎0044 as for the rest of the UK. Instead, dial ☎048 and then the local number. To dial the Republic from Northern Ireland, however, use the full international code ☎00 353, then the local number.

VISAS

If you're a European Economic Area (EEA) national, you don't need a visa to visit (or work in) either the Republic or Northern Ireland. Citizens of Australia, Canada, New Zealand, South Africa and the US can visit the Republic for up to three months, and Northern Ireland for up to six months.

There are currently no border controls or passport checks bcorketween the Republic of Ireland and Northern Ireland.

Getting There & Away

AIR

There are nonstop flights from Britain, Continental Europe and North America to Dublin, Shannon and Belfast International, and nonstop connections from Britain and Europe to Cork. International departure tax is normally included in the price of your ticket.

International airports in Ireland:

Belfast International Airport (Aldergrove; ☎028-9448 4848; www.belfastairport.com; Airport Rd) Located 30km northwest of the city; flights serve the UK and Europe, and in the USA, Las Vegas, Orlando and New York.

Dublin Airport (☎01-814 1111; www.dublinairport.com) Dublin Airport, 13km north of the centre, is Ireland's major international gateway airport. It has two terminals: most international flights (including most US flights) use the newer Terminal 2; Ryanair and select others use Terminal 1. Both terminals have the usual selection of pubs, restaurants, shops, ATMs and car-hire desks.

There is no train service to/from the airport, but there are bus and taxi options.

George Best Belfast City Airport (BHD; ☎028-9093 9093; www.belfastcityairport.com; Airport Rd) Located 6km northeast of Belfast's city centre; flights serve the UK and Europe.

Shannon Airport (SNN; ☎061-712 000; www.shannonairport.ie; 📶) Has many facilities, including a free observation area for those stuck waiting. Almost everything, including ATMs, currency exchange and car rental, is on one level.

SEA

The main ferry routes between Ireland and the UK and mainland Europe:

- Belfast to Liverpool (England; eight hours)
- Belfast to Cairnryan (Scotland; 1¾ hours)
- Cork to Roscoff (France; 14 hours; April to October only)
- Dublin to Liverpool (England; fast/slow four/8½ hours)
- Dublin & Dun Laoghaire to Holyhead (Wales; fast/slow two hours/3½ hours)
- Larne to Cairnryan (Scotland; two hours)
- Larne to Troon (Scotland; two hours; March to October only)
- Larne to Fleetwood (England; six hours)
- Rosslare to Cherbourg/Roscoff (France; 18/20½ hours)
- Rosslare to Fishguard & Pembroke (Wales; 3½ hours)

Competition from budget airlines has forced ferry operators to discount heavily and offer flexible fares.

A useful website is www.ferrybooker.com, which covers all sea-ferry routes and operators to Ireland.

Main operators include the following:

Brittany Ferries (www.brittanyferries.com) Cork to Roscoff; April to October.

Irish Ferries (www.irishferries.com) It has Dublin to Holyhead ferries (up to four per day year-round); and France to Rosslare (three times per week).

P&O Ferries (www.poferries.com) Daily sailings year-round from Dublin to Liverpool, and Larne to Cairnryan. Larne to Troon runs March to October only.

Stena Line (www.stenaline.com) Daily sailings from Holyhead to Dublin Port, from Belfast to Liverpool and Cairnryan, and from Rosslare to Fishguard.

Discounts & Passes

Eurail Pass Holders get a 50% discount on Irish Ferries crossings to France.

InterRail Pass Holders get a 50% discount on Irish Ferries and Stena Line services.

Britrail Pass Has an option to add on Ireland for an extra fee, including ferry transit.

Getting Around

Travelling around Ireland looks simple, as the distances are short and there's a dense network of roads and railways. But in Ireland, getting from A to B seldom uses a straight line, and public transport can be expensive (particularly trains), infrequent or both. For these reasons having your own transport – either car or bicycle – can be a major advantage.

BICYCLE

Ireland's compact size and scenic landscapes make it a good cycling destination. However, dodgy weather, many very narrow roads and some very fast drivers are major concerns. Special tracks such as the 42km Great Western Greenway in County Mayo are a delight. A good tip for cyclists in the west is that the prevailing winds make it easier to cycle from south to north.

Buses will carry bikes, but only if there's room. For trains, bear in mind:

- Bikes are carried free on Intercity and off-peak commuter trains.
- Book in advance (www.irishrail.ie), as there's only room for two bikes per service.

BUS

The Republic of Ireland's national bus line, **Bus Éireann** (☎1850 836 6111; www.buseireann.ie), operates services all over the Republic and into Northern Ireland. Bus fares are cheaper than train fares. Return trips are usually only slightly more expensive than one-way fares, and special deals (eg same-day returns) are often available. Most intercity buses in Northern Ireland are operated by **Ulsterbus** (☎028-9066 6630; www.translink.co.uk).

CAR & MOTORCYCLE

The majority of hire companies won't rent you a car if you're under 23 years of age and haven't had a valid driving licence for at least a year. Some companies will not hire to those aged 74 or over. Your own local licence is usually sufficient to hire a car for up to three months.

TRAIN

The Republic of Ireland's railway system, **Iarnród Éireann** (Iarnród Éireann; ☎1850 366 222; www.irishrail.ie), has routes radiating out from Dublin, but there is no direct north–south route along the west coast. Tickets can be twice as expensive as the bus, but travel times may be dramatically reduced. Special fares are often available, and a midweek return ticket sometimes costs just a bit more than the single fare; the flip side is that fares may be significantly higher on Friday and Sunday. **Rail Users Ireland** (www.railusers.ie) can be more informative than the official website.

Northern Ireland Railways (NIR; ☎028-9066 6630; www.translink.co.uk/Services/NI-Railways/; Belfast Central Station) has four lines from Belfast, one of which links up with the Republic's rail system.

Italy

Includes ➡

Best Places to Eat

➡ Pizzeria Gino Sorbillo (p482)

➡ All'Osteria Bottega (p463)

➡ Trattoria Mario (p470)

➡ Marina Grande (p489)

➡ Antiche Carampane (p459)

Best Museums & Galleries

➡ Vatican Museums (p428)

➡ Galleria degli Uffizi (p465)

➡ Museo Archeologico Nazionale (p479)

➡ Museo del Novecento (p445)

➡ Museo e Galleria Borghese (p432)

Why Go?

A favourite destination since the days of the 18th-century Grand Tour, Italy may appear to hold few surprises. Its iconic monuments and masterpieces are known the world over, while cities like Rome, Florence and Venice need no introduction.

Yet Italy is far more than the sum of its sights. Its fiercely proud regions maintain customs and culinary traditions dating back centuries, resulting in passionate festivals and delectable food at every turn. And then there are those timeless landscapes, from Tuscany's gentle hillsides to icy Alpine peaks, vertiginous coastlines and spitting southern volcanoes.

Drama is never far away in Italy and its theatrical streets and piazzas provide endless people-watching, ideally over a leisurely lunch or cool evening drink. This is, after all, the land of *dolce far niente* (sweet idleness) where simply hanging out is a pleasure and time seems to matter just that little bit less.

When to Go

Rome

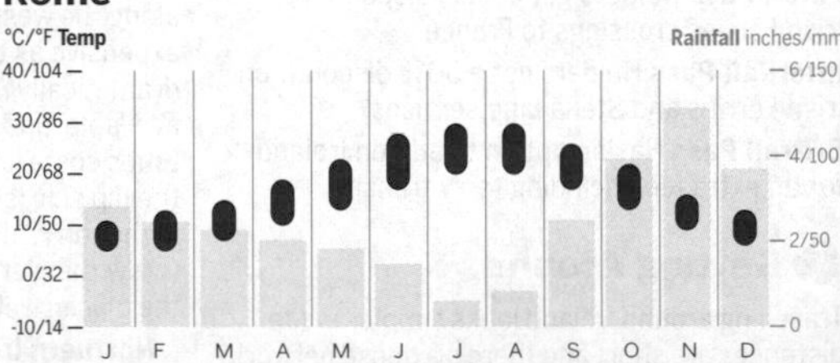

Apr–May Perfect spring weather; ideal for exploring vibrant cities and blooming countryside.

Jun–Jul Summer means beach weather and a packed festival calendar.

Sep–Oct Enjoy mild temperatures, autumn cuisine and the *vendemia* (grape harvest).

Italy Highlights

1. **Rome** (p422) Seeing awe-inspiring art and monuments.
2. **Venice** (p452) Cruising past Gothic palaces, churches and crumbling piazzas.
3. **Florence** (p464) Exploring this exquisite Renaissance time capsule.
4. **Naples** (p479) Working up an appetite for the world's best pizza.
5. **Turin** (p444) Visiting Turin's regal palaces and magnificent museums.
6. **Siena** (p474) Admiring glorious Gothic architecture and Renaissance art.
7. **Amalfi Coast** (p488) Basking in inspiring sea views.
8. **Verona** (p451) Enjoying an open-air opera in one of Italy's most romantic cities.
9. **Bologna** (p462) Feasting on foodie delights and medieval architecture in hedonistic Bologna.
10. **Syracuse** (p493) Revelling in drama at an ancient Greek theatre.

ROME

POP 2.86 MILLION

Ever since its glory days as an ancient superpower, Rome has been astonishing visitors. Its historic cityscape, piled high with haunting ruins and iconic monuments, is achingly beautiful, and its museums and basilicas showcase some of Europe's most celebrated masterpieces. But no list of sights and must-sees can capture the sheer elation of experiencing Rome's operatic streets and baroque piazzas, of turning a corner and stumbling across a world-famous fountain or a colourful neighbourhood market. Its streetside cafes are made for idling and elegant Renaissance *palazzi* (mansions) provide the perfect backdrop for romantic alfresco dining.

Sights

Ancient Rome

★**Colosseum** RUINS

(Colosseo; Map p424; ☎06 3996 7700; www.coopculture.it; Piazza del Colosseo; adult/reduced incl Roman Forum & Palatino €12/7.50; ⏰8.30am-1hr before sunset; Ⓜ Colosseo) Rome's great gladiatorial arena is the most thrilling of the city's ancient sights. Inaugurated in AD 80, the 50,000-seat Colosseum, also known as the Flavian Amphitheatre, was clad in travertine and covered by a huge canvas awning held aloft by 240 masts. Inside, tiered seating encircled the arena, itself built over an underground complex (the hypogeum) where animals were caged and stage sets prepared. Games involved gladiators fighting wild animals or each other.

★**Palatino** ARCHAEOLOGICAL SITE

(Palatine Hill; Map p424; ☎06 3996 7700; www.coopculture.it; Via di San Gregorio 30, Piazza di Santa Maria Nova; adult/reduced incl Colosseum & Roman Forum €12/7.50; ⏰8.30am-1hr before sunset; Ⓜ Colosseo) Sandwiched between the Roman Forum and the Circo Massimo, the Palatino is an atmospheric area of towering pine trees, majestic ruins and memorable views. It was here that Romulus supposedly founded the city in 753 BC and Rome's emperors lived in unabashed luxury. Look out for the **stadio** (stadium), the ruins of the **Domus Flavia** (imperial palace), and grandstand views over the Roman Forum from the **Orti Farnesiani**.

★**Roman Forum** ARCHAEOLOGICAL SITE

(Foro Romano; Map p424; ☎06 3996 7700; www.coopculture.it; Largo della Salara Vecchia, Piazza di Santa Maria Nova; adult/reduced incl Colosseum & Palatino €12/7.50; ⏰8.30am-1hr before sunset; 🚌 Via dei Fori Imperiali) An impressive – if rather confusing – sprawl of ruins, the Roman Forum was ancient Rome's showpiece centre, a grandiose district of temples, basilicas and vibrant public spaces. The site, which was originally an Etruscan burial ground, was first developed in the 7th century BC, growing over time to become the social, political and commercial hub of the Roman Empire. Landmark sights include the **Arco di Settimio Severo** (Arch of Septimius Severus), the **Curia** and the **Casa delle Vestali** (House of the Vestal Virgins).

★**Capitoline Museums** MUSEUM

(Musei Capitolini; Map p424; ☎06 06 08; www.museicapitolini.org; Piazza del Campidoglio 1; adult/reduced €11.50/9.50; ⏰9.30am-7.30pm, last admission 6.30pm; 🚌 Piazza Venezia) Dating to 1471, the Capitoline Museums are the world's oldest public museums. Their collection of classical sculpture is one of Italy's finest, including crowd-pleasers such as the iconic *Lupa capitolina* (Capitoline Wolf), a sculpture of Romulus and Remus under a wolf, and the *Galata morente* (Dying Gaul), a moving depiction of a dying Gaul warrior. There's also a formidable picture gallery with masterpieces by the likes of Titian, Tintoretto, Rubens and Caravaggio.

Ticket prices increase when there's a temporary exhibition on.

ITINERARIES

One Week

A one-week whistle-stop tour of Italy is enough to take in the country's three most famous cities. After a couple of days exploring the unique canalscape of **Venice**, head south to **Florence**, Italy's great Renaissance city. Two days will whet your appetite for the artistic and architectural treasures that await in **Rome**.

Two Weeks

After the first week, continue south for some sea and southern passion. Spend a day admiring art in **Naples**, a day investigating the ruins at **Pompeii**, and a day or two admiring the **Amalfi Coast**. Then backtrack to Naples for a ferry to **Palermo** and the gastronomic delights of Sicily.

> **COLOSSEUM TICKETS**
>
> Long waits are the norm at the Colosseum. You'll have to queue for security checks and then to buy a ticket. To save time, get your ticket at the Palatino entrance (about 250m away at Via di San Gregorio 30) or book online at www.coopculture.it (incurs a €2 booking fee).

Vittoriano MONUMENT
(Victor Emmanuel Monument; Map p424; Piazza Venezia; 9.30am-5.30pm summer, to 4.30pm winter; Piazza Venezia) FREE Love it or loathe it, as many Romans do, you can't ignore the Vittoriano (aka the Altare della Patria; Altar of the Fatherland), the massive mountain of white marble that towers over Piazza Venezia. Begun in 1885 to honour Italy's first king, Victor Emmanuel II – who's immortalised in its vast equestrian statue – it incorporates the **Museo Centrale del Risorgimento** (06 679 35 98; www.risorgimento.it; adult/reduced €5/2.50; 9.30am-6.30pm), a small museum documenting Italian unification, and the **Tomb of the Unknown Soldier**.

For Rome's best 360-degree views, take the **Roma dal Cielo** (adult/reduced €7/3.50; 9.30am-7.30pm, last admission 7pm) lift to the top.

Bocca della Verità MONUMENT
(Mouth of Truth; Map p430; Piazza Bocca della Verità 18; 9.30am-5.50pm; Piazza Bocca della Verità) A bearded face carved into a giant marble disc, the *Bocca della Verità* is one of Rome's most popular curiosities. Legend has it that if you put your hand in the mouth and tell a lie, the Bocca will slam shut and bite your hand off.

The mouth, which was originally part of a fountain, or possibly an ancient manhole cover, now lives in the portico of the **Chiesa di Santa Maria in Cosmedin**, a handsome medieval church.

Centro Storico

★Pantheon CHURCH
(Map p430; www.pantheonroma.com; Piazza della Rotonda; 8.30am-7.15pm Mon-Sat, 9am-5.45pm Sun; Largo di Torre Argentina) FREE A striking 2000-year-old temple, now a church, the Pantheon is the best preserved of Rome's ancient monuments and one of the most influential buildings in the Western world. Built by Hadrian over Marcus Agrippa's earlier 27 BC temple, it has stood since around AD 125, and although its greying, pockmarked exterior looks its age, it's still a unique and exhilarating experience to pass through its vast bronze doors and gaze up at the largest unreinforced concrete dome ever built.

★Piazza Navona PIAZZA
(Map p430; Corso del Rinascimento) With its showy fountains, baroque *palazzi* and colourful cast of street artists, hawkers and tourists, Piazza Navona is central Rome's elegant showcase square. Built over the 1st-century **Stadio di Domiziano** (Domitian's Stadium; 06 4568 6100; www.stadiodomiziano.com; Via di Tor Sanguigna 3; adult/reduced €8/6; 10am-7pm Sun-Fri, to 8pm Sat), it was paved over in the 15th century and for almost 300 years hosted the city's main market. Its grand centrepiece is Bernini's **Fontana del Quattro Fiumi** (Fountain of the Four Rivers), a flamboyant fountain featuring an Egyptian obelisk and muscular personifications of the rivers Nile, Ganges, Danube and Plate.

Campo de' Fiori PIAZZA
(Map p430; Corso Vittorio Emanuele II) Noisy, colourful 'Il Campo' is a major focus of Roman life: by day it hosts one of Rome's best-known markets, while at night it morphs into a raucous open-air pub as drinkers spill out from its many bars and eateries. For centuries the square was the site of public executions, and it was here that philosopher Giordano Bruno was burned for heresy in 1600. The spot is marked by a sinister statue of the hooded monk, which was created by Ettore Ferrari in 1889.

★Galleria Doria Pamphilj GALLERY
(Map p430; 06 679 73 23; www.doriapamphilj.it; Via del Corso 305; adult/reduced €12/8; 9am-7pm, last admission 6pm; Via del Corso) Hidden behind the grimy grey exterior of Palazzo Doria Pamphilj, this wonderful gallery boasts one of Rome's richest private art collections, with works by Raphael, Tintoretto, Titian, Caravaggio, Bernini and Velázquez, as well as several Flemish masters. Masterpieces abound, but the undisputed star is Velázquez' portrait of an implacable Pope Innocent X, who grumbled that the depiction was 'too real'. For a comparison, check out Gian Lorenzo Bernini's sculptural interpretation of the same subject.

Ancient Rome

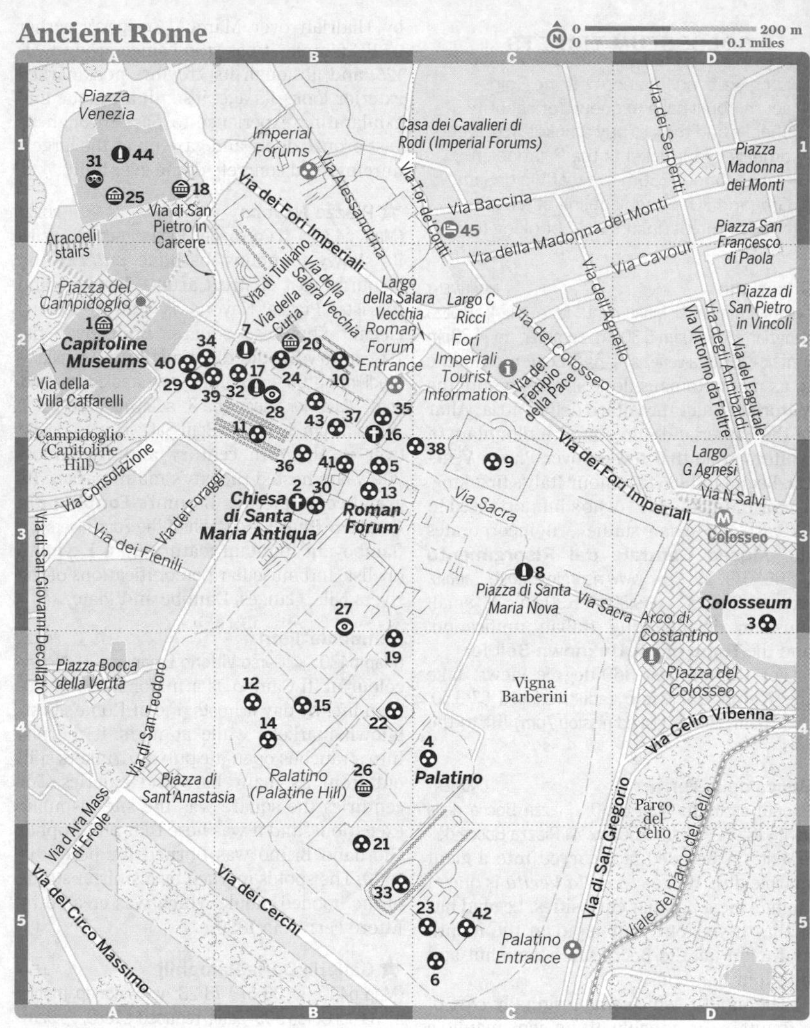

★Trevi Fountain FOUNTAIN

(Fontana di Trevi; Map p434; Piazza di Trevi; M Barberini) The Fontana di Trevi, scene of Anita Ekberg's dip in *La dolce vita*, is a flamboyant baroque ensemble of mythical figures and wild horses taking up the entire side of the 17th-century Palazzo Poli. After a Fendi-sponsored restoration finished in 2015, the fountain gleams brighter than it has for years. The tradition is to toss a coin into the water, thus ensuring that you'll return to Rome – on average about €3000 is thrown in every day.

★Palazzo Barberini GALLERY

(Galleria Nazionale d'Arte Antica; Map p434; 06 481 45 91; www.barberinicorsini.org; Via delle Quattro Fontane 13; adult/reduced €5/2.50, incl Palazzo Corsini €10/5; 8.30am-7pm Tue-Sun; M Barberini) Commissioned to celebrate the Barberini family's rise to papal power, Palazzo Barberini is a sumptuous baroque palace that impresses even before you clap eyes on the breathtaking art. Many high-profile architects worked on it, including rivals Bernini and Borromini; the former contributed a large squared staircase, the latter a helicoidal

Ancient Rome

Top Sights
1 Capitoline Museums........ A2
2 Chiesa di Santa Maria Antiqua........ B3
3 Colosseum........ D3
4 Palatino........ C4
5 Roman Forum........ B3

Sights
6 Arcate Severiane........ C5
7 Arco di Settimio Severo........ B2
8 Arco di Tito........ C3
9 Basilica di Massenzio........ C3
10 Basilica Fulvia Aemilia........ B2
11 Basilica Giulia........ B2
12 Capanne Romulee........ B4
13 Casa delle Vestali........ B3
14 Casa di Augusto........ B4
15 Casa di Livia........ B4
16 Chiesa di San Lorenzo in Miranda........ B2
17 Colonna di Foca........ B2
18 Complesso del Vittoriano........ A1
19 Criptoportico Neroniano........ B4
20 Curia........ B2
21 Domus Augustana........ B5
22 Domus Flavia........ B4
23 Domus Severiana........ C5
24 Lapis Niger........ B2
25 Museo Centrale del Risorgimento........ A1
26 Museo Palatino........ B4
27 Orti Farnesiani........ B3
28 Piazza del Foro........ B2
29 Portico degli Dei Consenti........ A2
30 Rampa imperiale........ B3
31 Roma dal Cielo........ A1
32 Rostri........ B2
33 Stadio........ B5
34 Tempio della Concordia........ A2
35 Tempio di Antonino e Faustina........ B2
36 Tempio di Castore e Polluce........ B3
37 Tempio di Giulio Cesare........ B2
38 Tempio di Romolo........ C3
39 Tempio di Saturno........ A2
40 Tempio di Vespasiano........ A2
41 Tempio di Vesta........ B3
42 Terme di Settimio Severo........ C5
43 Via Sacra........ B2
44 Vittoriano........ A1

Sleeping
45 Residenza Maritti........ C1

one. Amid the masterpieces, don't miss Pietro da Cortona's *Il triChiesa della Trinità dei Montionfo della divina provvidenza* (Triumph of Divine Providence; 1632–39), the most spectacular of the *palazzo*'s ceiling frescoes in the 1st-floor main salon.

★ Piazza di Spagna & the Spanish Steps — PIAZZA

(Map p434; Ⓜ Spagna) A magnet for visitors since the 18th century, the Spanish Steps (Scalinata della Trinità dei Monti) provide a perfect people-watching perch. The 135 steps, gleaming after a recent clean-up, rise from Piazza di Spagna to the landmark Chiesa della Trinità dei Monti.

Piazza di Spagna was named after the Spanish Embassy to the Holy See, although the staircase, designed by the Italian Francesco de Sanctis, was built in 1725 with money bequeathed by a French diplomat.

★ Piazza del Popolo — PIAZZA

(Map p426; Ⓜ Flaminio) This dazzling piazza was laid out in 1538 to provide a grandiose entrance to what was then Rome's main northern gateway. It has since been remodelled several times, most recently by Giuseppe Valadier in 1823. Guarding its southern approach are Carlo Rainaldi's twin 17th-century churches, **Chiesa di Santa Maria dei Miracoli** (Via del Corso 528; ⏰6.45am-12.30pm & 4.30-7.30pm Mon-Sat, 8am-1.15pm & 4.30-7.45 Sun) and **Chiesa di Santa Maria in Montesanto** (Chiesa degli Artisti; www.chiesadegliartisti.it; Via del Babuino 198; ⏰5.30-8pm Mon-Fri, 11am-1.30pm Sun). In the centre, the 36m-high **obelisk** was brought by Augustus from ancient Egypt; it originally stood in Circo Massimo.

Vatican City, Borgo & Prati

★ St Peter's Basilica — BASILICA

(Basilica di San Pietro; Map p426; ☎06 6988 5518; www.vatican.va; St Peter's Square; ⏰7am-7pm summer, to 6.30pm winter; 🚌Piazza del Risorgimento, Ⓜ Ottaviano-San Pietro) FREE In this city of outstanding churches, none can hold a candle to St Peter's (Basilica di San Pietro), Italy's largest, richest and most spectacular basilica. Built atop an earlier 4th-century church, it was consecrated in 1626 after 120 years' construction. Its lavish interior contains many spectacular works of art, including three of Italy's most celebrated masterpieces: Michelangelo's *Pietà*, his soaring dome, and Bernini's 29m-high baldachin over the papal altar.

Expect queues and note that strict dress codes are enforced, so no shorts, miniskirts or bare shoulders.

Greater Rome

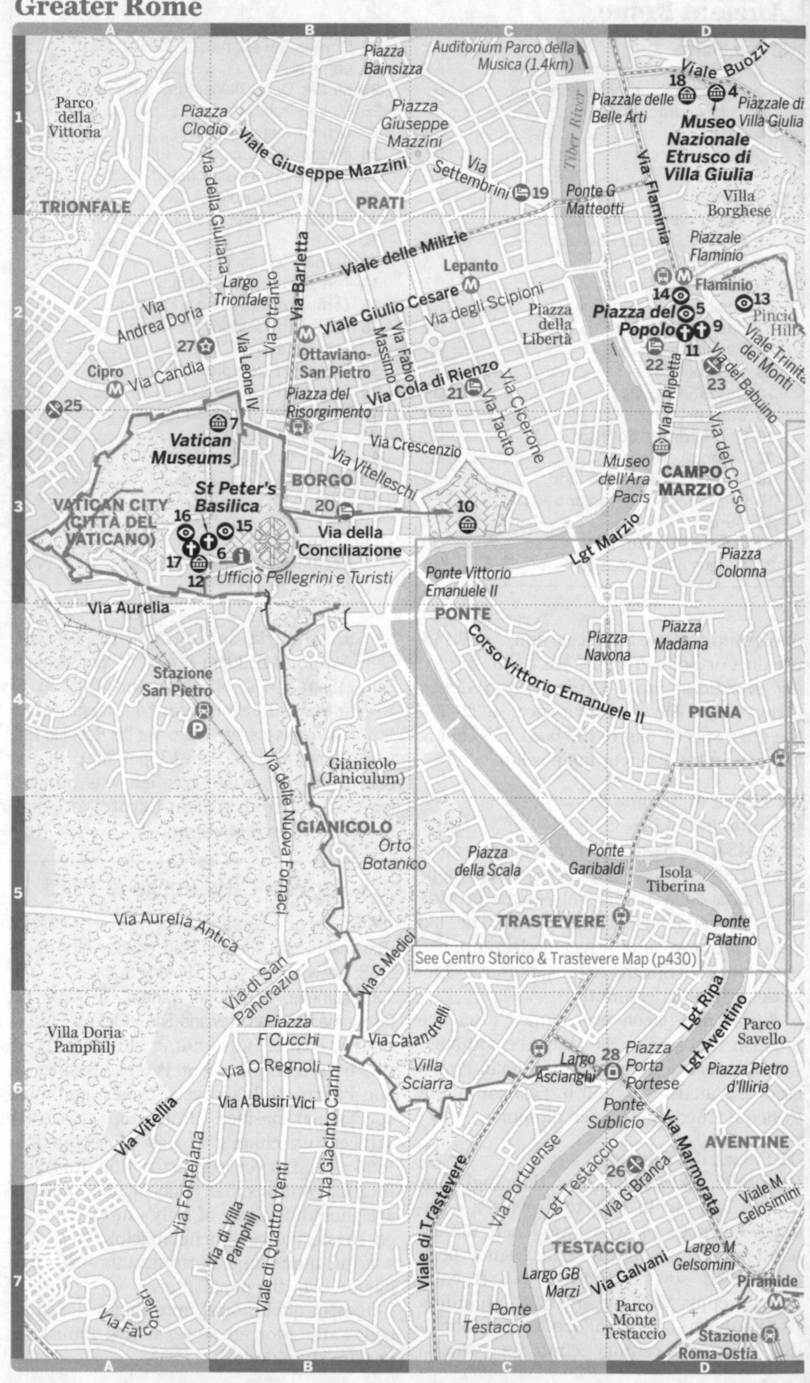

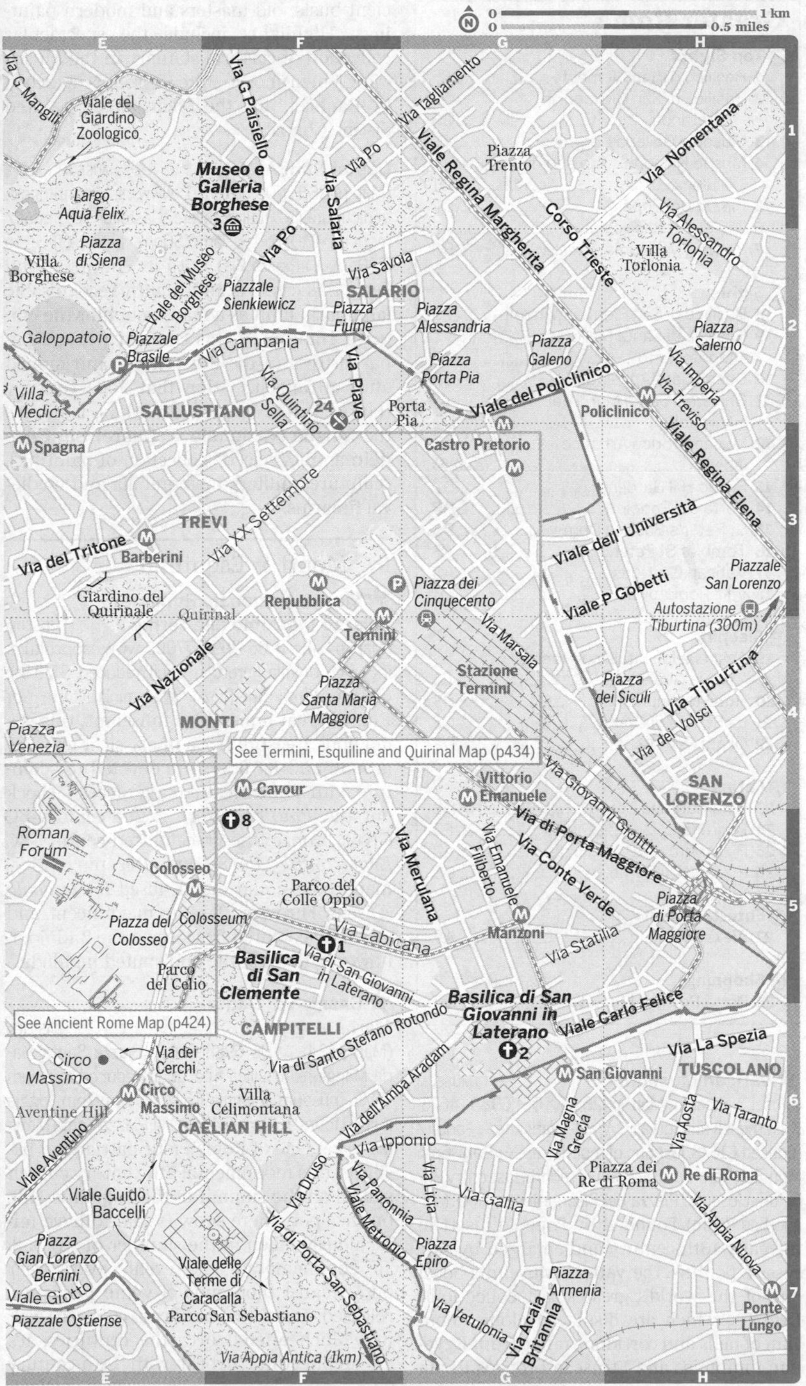

Via G Mangili
Viale del Giardino Zoologico
Via G Paisiello
Museo e Galleria Borghese
Largo Aqua Felix
Piazza di Siena
Villa Borghese
Viale del Museo Borghese
Piazzale Sienkiewicz
Galoppatoio
Piazzale Brasile
Via Campania
Villa Medici
SALLUSTIANO
Via Quintino Sella
Via Po
Via Salaria
Via Savoia
SALARIO
Piazza Fiume
Via Piave
Porta Pia
Via Tagliamento
Viale Regina Margherita
Piazza Trento
Corso Trieste
Via Nomentana
Via Alessandro Torlonia
Villa Torlonia
Piazza Alessandria
Piazza Porta Pia
Piazza Galeno
Viale del Policlinico
Piazza Salerno
Via Imperia
Via Treviso
Policlinico
Viale Regina Elena
Castro Pretorio
Spagna
TREVI
Via XX Settembre
Via del Tritone
Barberini
Giardino del Quirinale
Quirinal
Repubblica
Piazza dei Cinquecento
Termini
Via Marsala
Stazione Termini
Viale dell' Università
Viale P Gobetti
Piazzale San Lorenzo
Autostazione Tiburtina (300m)
Via Tiburtina
Via dei Volsci
Piazza dei Siculi
Via Nazionale
MONTI
Piazza Santa Maria Maggiore
Piazza Venezia
See Termini, Esquiline and Quirinal Map (p434)
Cavour
Vittorio Emanuele
Via Giovanni Giolitti
SAN LORENZO
Roman Forum
Colosseo
Colosseum
Piazza del Colosseo
Parco del Celio
Parco del Colle Oppio
Via Merulana
Via Emanuele Filiberto
Via di Porta Maggiore
Via Conte Verde
Piazza di Porta Maggiore
Manzoni
Via Statilia
Via Labicana
Basilica di San Clemente
Via di San Giovanni in Laterano
Basilica di San Giovanni in Laterano
Viale Carlo Felice
See Ancient Rome Map (p424)
CAMPITELLI
Via di Santo Stefano Rotondo
Via La Spezia
TUSCOLANO
San Giovanni
Circo Massimo
Via dei Cerchi
Aventine Hill
Villa Celimontana
CAELIAN HILL
Via dell'Amba Aradam
Via Taranto
Via Aosta
Via Magna Grecia
Viale Aventino
Via Ipponio
Via Druso
Via Pannonia
Viale Metronio
Via Licia
Via Gallia
Piazza dei Re di Roma
Re di Roma
Via Appia Nuova
Viale Guido Baccelli
Piazza Gian Lorenzo Bernini
Viale Giotto
Piazzale Ostiense
Viale delle Terme di Caracalla
Parco San Sebastiano
Via di Porta San Sebastiano
Piazza Epiro
Via Vetulonia
Via Acaia
Britannia
Piazza Armenia
Ponte Lungo
Via Appia Antica (1km)
0 1 km
0 0.5 miles

Greater Rome

Top Sights
1 Basilica di San Clemente ... F5
2 Basilica di San Giovanni in Laterano ... G6
3 Museo e Galleria Borghese ... F1
4 Museo Nazionale Etrusco di Villa Giulia ... D1
5 Piazza del Popolo ... D2
6 St Peter's Basilica ... A3
7 Vatican Museums ... B3

Sights
8 Basilica di San Pietro in Vincoli ... F5
9 Basilica di Santa Maria in Montesanto ... D2
10 Castel Sant'Angelo ... C3
11 Chiesa di Santa Maria dei Miracoli ... D2
12 Museo Storico Artistico ... A3
Obelisk ... (see 5)
13 Pincio Hill Gardens ... D2
14 Porta del Popolo ... D2
15 St Peter's Basilica Dome ... B3
16 Tomb of St Peter ... A3
17 Vatican Grottoes ... A3
18 Villa Poniatowski ... D1

Sleeping
19 Associazione Italiana Alberghi per la Gioventù ... C1
20 Hotel Bramante ... B3
21 Le Stanze di Orazio ... C2
22 Okapi Rooms ... D2

Eating
23 Fatamorgana Corso ... D2
24 I Caruso ... F2
25 Pizzarium ... A2
26 Pizzeria Da Remo ... D6

Entertainment
27 Alexanderplatz ... A2

Shopping
28 Porta Portese Market ... D6

★**Vatican Museums** MUSEUM
(Musei Vaticani; Map p426; 06 6988 4676; www.museivaticani.va; Viale Vaticano; adult/reduced €16/8, last Sun of month free; 9am-6pm Mon-Sat, 9am-2pm last Sun of month, last entry 2hr before close; Piazza del Risorgimento, M Ottaviano-San Pietro) Founded by Pope Julius II in the early 16th century and enlarged by successive pontiffs, the Vatican Museums boast one of the world's greatest art collections. Exhibits, which are displayed along about 7km of halls and corridors, range from Egyptian mummies and Etruscan bronzes to ancient busts, old masters and modern paintings. Highlights include the spectacular collection of classical statuary in the Museo Pio-Clementino, a suite of rooms frescoed by Raphael, and the Michelangelo-painted Sistine Chapel.

Castel Sant'Angelo MUSEUM, CASTLE
(Map p426; 06 681 91 11; www.castelsantangelo.beniculturali.it; Lungotevere Castello 50; adult/reduced €10/5; 9am-7.30pm, ticket office to 6.30pm; Piazza Pia) With its chunky round keep, this castle is an instantly recognisable landmark. Built as a mausoleum for the emperor Hadrian, it was converted into a papal fortress in the 6th century and named after an angelic vision that Pope Gregory the Great had in 590. Nowadays, it houses the **Museo Nazionale di Castel Sant'Angelo** and its eclectic collection of paintings, sculpture, military memorabilia and medieval firearms.

Monti & Esquilino

★**Museo Nazionale Romano: Palazzo Massimo alle Terme** MUSEUM
(Map p434; 06 3996 7700; www.coopculture.it; Largo di Villa Peretti 1; adult/reduced €7/3.50; 9am-7.45pm Tue-Sun; M Termini) One of Rome's great unheralded museums, this is a fabulous treasure trove of classical art. The ground and 1st floors are devoted to sculpture with some breathtaking pieces – check out the *Pugile* (Boxer), a 2nd-century-BC Greek bronze; the graceful 2nd-century-BC *Ermafrodite dormiente* (Sleeping Hermaphrodite); and the idealised *Il discobolo* (Discus Thrower). It's the magnificent and vibrantly coloured frescoes on the 2nd floor, however, that are the undisputed highlight.

★**Basilica di Santa Maria Maggiore** BASILICA
(Map p434; 06 6988 6800; Piazza Santa Maria Maggiore; basilica free, adult/reduced museum €3/2, museum & loggia €5/4; 7am-7pm, loggia guided tours 9.30am-5.45pm; Piazza Santa Maria Maggiore) One of Rome's four patriarchal basilicas, this monumental 5th-century church stands on the summit of the Esquiline Hill, on the spot where snow is said to have miraculously fallen in the summer of AD 358. To commemorate the event, every year on 5 August thousands of white petals are released from the basilica's coffered ceiling. Much altered over the centuries, it's an architectural hybrid with 14th-century

> **SKIP THE LINE AT THE VATICAN MUSEUMS**
>
> ➡ Book tickets online at http://biglietteriamusei.vatican.va/musei/tickets/do (€4 booking fee).
>
> ➡ Time your visit: Tuesdays and Thursdays are quietest; Wednesday mornings are good as everyone is at the pope's weekly audience; afternoon is better than the morning; avoid Mondays when many other museums are shut.

Romanesque belfry, 18th-century baroque facade, largely baroque interior and a series of glorious 5th-century mosaics.

Basilica di San Pietro in Vincoli BASILICA
(Map p426; Piazza di San Pietro in Vincoli 4a; ⌚8am-12.30pm & 3-7pm summer, to 6pm winter; Ⓜ Cavour) Pilgrims and art lovers flock to this 5th-century basilica for two reasons: to marvel at Michelangelo's colossal *Moses* (1505) sculpture and to see the chains that supposedly bound St Peter when he was imprisoned in the Carcere Mamertino (near the Roman Forum). Access to the church is via a flight of steps through a low arch that leads up from Via Cavour.

Trastevere

Trastevere is one of central Rome's most vivacious neighbourhoods, a tightly packed warren of ochre *palazzi*, ivy-clad facades and photogenic lanes. Originally working class, it's now a trendy hang-out full of bars and restaurants.

★Basilica di Santa Maria in Trastevere BASILICA
(Map p430; ☎06 581 4802; Piazza Santa Maria in Trastevere; ⌚7.30am-9pm Sep-Jul, 8am-noon & 4-9pm Aug; 🚌 Viale di Trastevere, 🚋 Viale di Trastevere) Nestled in a quiet corner of Trastevere's focal square, this is said to be the oldest church dedicated to the Virgin Mary in Rome. In its original form, it dates to the early 3rd century, but a major 12th-century makeover saw the addition of a Romanesque bell tower and glittering facade. The portico came later, added by Carlo Fontana in 1702. Inside, the 12th-century mosaics are the headline feature.

San Giovanni & Testaccio

★Basilica di San Giovanni in Laterano BASILICA
(Map p426; Piazza di San Giovanni in Laterano 4; basilica/cloister free/€5 with audio guide; ⌚7am-6.30pm, cloister 9am-6pm; Ⓜ San Giovanni) For a thousand years this monumental cathedral was the most important church in Christendom. Commissioned by Constantine and consecrated in AD 324, it was the first Christian basilica built in the city and, until the late 14th century, was the pope's main place of worship. It's still Rome's official cathedral and the pope's seat as the bishop of Rome.

The basilica has been revamped several times, most notably by Borromini in the 17th century, and by Alessandro Galilei, who added the immense white facade in 1735.

> **VATICAN MUSEUMS ITINERARY**
>
> Follow this three-hour itinerary for the museums' greatest hits:
>
> At the top of the escalator after the entrance, head out to the **Cortile della Pigna**, a courtyard named after the Augustan-era bronze pine cone in the monumental niche. Cross the courtyard into the long corridor that is the **Museo Chiaramonti** and head left up to the **Museo Pio-Clementino**, home of the Vatican's finest classical statuary. Follow through the **Cortile Ottagono** (Octagonal Courtyard) onto the **Sala Croce Greca** (Greek Cross Room) from where stairs lead up to the 1st floor. Continue through the **Galleria delle Carte Geografiche** (Map Gallery) to the **Sala di Costantino**, the first of the four **Stanze di Raffaello** (Raphael Rooms) – the others are the **Stanza d' Eliodoro**, the **Stanza della Segnatura**, home to Raphael's superlative *La scuola di Atene* (The School of Athens), and the **Stanza dell'Incendio di Borgo**. Anywhere else these frescoed chambers would be the star attraction, but here they're the warm-up act for the museums' grand finale, the **Sistine Chapel**. Originally built in 1484 for Pope Sixtus IV, this towering chapel boasts two of the world's most famous works of art: Michelangelo's ceiling frescoes (1508–12) and his *Giudizio universale* (Last Judgment; 1535–41).

Centro Storico & Trastevere

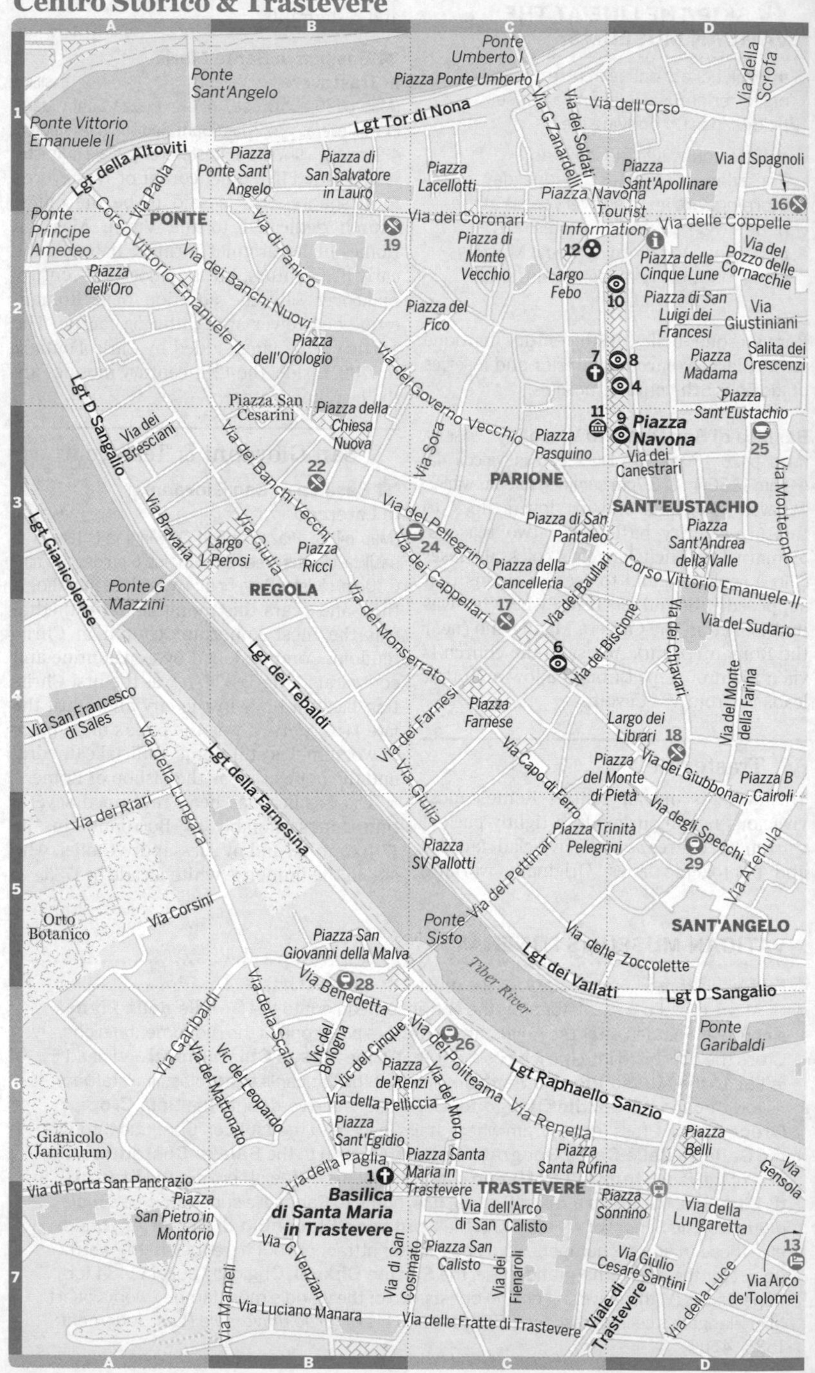

Centro Storico & Trastevere

Top Sights

1 Basilica di Santa Maria in Trastevere B6
2 Galleria Doria Pamphilj F3
3 Pantheon E2
4 Piazza Navona D2

Sights

5 Bocca della Verità F7
6 Campo de' Fiori C4
7 Chiesa di Sant'Agnese in Agone C2
8 Fontana dei Quattro Fiumi D2
9 Fontana del Moro D3
10 Fontana del Nettuno D2
11 Palazzo Pamphilj C3
12 Stadio di Domiziano C2

Sleeping

13 Arco del Lauro D7
14 Hotel Pensione Barrett E4

Eating

15 Armando al Pantheon E2
16 Casa Coppelle D1
17 Forno di Campo de' Fiori C4
18 Forno Roscioli D4
19 Gelateria del Teatro B2
20 La Ciambella E3
21 La Gensola E7
22 Supplizio B3
23 Venchi E2

Drinking & Nightlife

24 Barnum Cafe C3
25 Caffè Sant'Eustachio D3
26 Freni e Frizioni C6
27 La Casa del Caffè Tazza d'Oro E2
28 Ma Che Siete Venuti a Fà B5
29 Open Baladin D5

★ **Basilica di San Clemente** BASILICA

(Map p426; www.basilicasanclemente.com; Piazza San Clemente; excavations adult/reduced €10/5; 9am-12.30pm & 3-6pm Mon-Sat, 12.15-6pm Sun; Via Labicana) Nowhere better illustrates the various stages of Rome's turbulent past than this fascinating multi-layered church. The ground-level 12th-century basilica sits atop a 4th-century church, which, in turn, stands over a 2nd-century pagan temple and a 1st-century Roman house. Beneath everything are foundations dating from the Roman Republic.

Villa Borghese

Accessible from Piazzale Flaminio, Pincio Hill and the top of Via Vittorio Veneto, Villa Borghese is Rome's best-known park.

ROME FOR FREE

Some of Rome's most famous sights are free:

- Trevi Fountain
- Spanish Steps
- Pantheon
- St Peter's Basilica and all of Rome's churches
- Vatican Museums on the last Sunday of the month
- All state museums and monuments on the first Sunday of the month

★Museo e Galleria Borghese MUSEUM
(Map p426; ☎06 3 28 10; www.galleriaborghese.it; Piazzale del Museo Borghese 5; adult/reduced €15/8.50; ⊙9am-7pm Tue-Sun; Via Pinciana) If you only have the time (or inclination) for one art gallery in Rome, make it this one. Housing what's often referred to as the 'queen of all private art collections', it boasts paintings by Caravaggio, Raphael and Titian, as well as some sensational sculptures by Bernini. Highlights abound, but look out for Bernini's *Ratto di Proserpina* (Rape of Proserpina) and Canova's *Venere vincitrice* (Venus Victrix).

To limit numbers, visitors are admitted at two-hourly intervals, so you'll need to prebook your ticket and get an entry time.

★Museo Nazionale Etrusco di Villa Giulia MUSEUM
(Map p426; ☎06 322 65 71; www.villagiulia.beniculturali.it; Piazzale di Villa Giulia; adult/reduced €8/4; ⊙8.30am-7.30pm Tue-Sun; Via delle Belle Arti) Pope Julius III's 16th-century villa provides the charming setting for Italy's finest collection of Etruscan and pre-Roman treasures. Exhibits, many of which came from tombs in the surrounding Lazio region, range from bronze figurines and black *bucchero* tableware to temple decorations, terracotta vases and a dazzling display of sophisticated jewellery.

Must-sees include a polychrome terracotta statue of Apollo from a temple in Veio and the 6th-century-BC *Sarcofago degli sposi* (Sarcophagus of the Betrothed), found in 1881 in Cerveteri.

Sleeping

Ancient Rome

★Residenza Maritti GUESTHOUSE €€
(Map p424; ☎06 678 82 33; www.residenzamaritti.com; Via Tor de' Conti 17; s/d/tr €120/170/190; ; Cavour) Boasting stunning views over the nearby forums and Vittoriano, this hidden gem has rooms spread over several floors. Some are bright and modern, others are more cosy in feel with antiques, original tiled floors and family furniture. There's a fully equipped kitchen and a self-service breakfast is provided.

Centro Storico

Okapi Rooms HOTEL €
(Map p426; ☎06 3260 9815; www.okapirooms.it; Via della Penna 57; s/d/tr/q €80/110/140/170; ; Flaminio) The Okapi is a smart, value-for-money choice near Piazza del Popolo. Rooms, spread over six floors of a narrow townhouse, are simple and airy with cream walls, terracotta floors and the occasional stone frieze. Some are smaller than others and several have little terraces. An optional breakfast (€4.50) is served in a nearby bar; buy a voucher at reception.

Hotel Pensione Barrett PENSION €€
(Map p430; ☎06 686 8481; www.pensionebarrett.com; Largo di Torre Argentina 47; s/d/tr €115/135/165; ; Largo di Torre Argentina) This exuberant *pensione* is quite unique. Boasting a convenient central location, its decor is wonderfully over the top with statues, busts and vibrant stucco set against a forest of leafy potted plants. Rooms are cosy and come with thoughtful extras like foot spas, coffee machines and fully stocked fridges.

Vatican City, Borgo & Prati

Le Stanze di Orazio B&B €€
(Map p426; ☎06 3265 2474; www.lestanzediorazio.com; Via Orazio 3; d €110-135; ; Via Cola di Rienzo, Lepanto) This friendly boutique B&B makes for an attractive home away from home in the heart of the elegant Prati district, a single metro stop from the Vatican. It has five bright, playfully decorated rooms – think shimmering rainbow wallpaper, lilac accents and designer bathrooms – and a small breakfast area.

Hotel Bramante HISTORIC HOTEL €€€
(Map p426; ☎06 6880 6426; www.hotelbramante.com; Vicolo delle Palline 24-25; s €140-180, d €200-240, tr €230-270, q €260-290; ❄📶; 🚌Via Transpontina) Nestled under the Vatican walls, the Bramante exudes country-house charm with its cosy internal courtyard and classically attired rooms complete with wood-beamed ceilings and antique furniture. It's housed in the 16th-century building where architect Domenico Fontana once lived.

Monti & Esquilino

★**Beehive** HOSTEL €
(Map p434; ☎06 4470 4553; www.the-beehive.com; Via Marghera 8; dm €35-40, d with shared €80, s/d/tr €70/100/120; ⏰reception 7am-11pm; ❄📶; Ⓜ Termini) More boutique chic than backpacker dive, the Beehive is a small and stylish hostel with glorious summer garden. Dynamic American owners Linda and Steve exude energy and organise cooking classes, storytelling evenings, weekly hostel dinners around a shared table, pop-up dinners with chefs, and so on. Pick from a spotless eight-bed dorm (mixed), a four-bed female dorm, or private rooms with ceiling fan and honey-based soap.

Blue Hostel GUESTHOUSE €
(Map p434; ☎340 925 85 03; www.bluehostel.it; Via Carlo Alberto 13, 3rd fl; d/tr/q €150/160/190; ❄📶; Ⓜ Vittorio Emanuele) A hostel in name only, this small guesthouse has small, hotel-standard rooms with en suite bathroom and tasteful low-key decor – think beamed ceilings, wooden floors, French windows, framed B&W photos. There's also an apartment with kitchen that sleeps up to four. No lift and no breakfast.

Trastevere

★**Arco del Lauro** GUESTHOUSE €€
(Map p430; ☎06 9784 0350; www.arcodellauro.it; Via Arco de' Tolomei 27; d €95-135, q €135-175; ❄@📶; 🚌Viale di Trastevere, 🚋Viale di Trastevere) Perfectly placed on a peaceful cobbled lane in the 'quiet side' of Trastevere, this ground-floor guesthouse sports six gleaming white rooms with parquet floors, a modern low-key look and well-equipped bathrooms. Guests share a kettle, fridge, complimentary fruit bowl and cakes, and breakfast is served in a nearby cafe. Daniele and Lorenzo who run the place could not be friendlier or more helpful.

Eating

The most atmospheric neighbourhoods to dine in are the *centro storico* (historic centre) and Trastevere. There are also excellent choices in boho Monti and Testaccio. Watch out for overpriced tourist traps around Termini and the Vatican.

Centro Storico

★**Supplizio** FAST FOOD €
(Map p430; ☎06 8987 1920; www.facebook.com/supplizioroma; Via dei Banchi Vecchi 143; supplì €3-7; ⏰noon-8pm Mon-Thu, noon-3.30pm & 6.30-10.30pm Fri & Sat; 🚌Corso Vittorio Emanuele II) Rome's favourite snack, the *supplì* (a fried croquette filled with rice, tomato sauce and mozzarella), gets a gourmet makeover at this elegant street-food joint. Sit back on the vintage leather sofa and dig into a crispy classic or push the boat out and try something different, maybe a little fish number stuffed with fresh anchovies, cheese, bread and raisins.

Forno Roscioli PIZZA, BAKERY €
(Map p430; ☎06 686 4045; www.anticofornoroscioli.it; Via dei Chiavari 34; pizza slices from €2, snacks €2; ⏰6am-8pm Mon-Sat, 9am-7pm Sun; 🚋Via Arenula) This is one of Rome's top bakeries, much loved by lunching locals who crowd here for luscious sliced pizza, prize pastries and hunger-sating *supplì*. The *pizza margherita* is superb, if messy to eat, and there's also a counter serving hot pastas and vegetable side dishes.

Forno di Campo de' Fiori PIZZA, BAKERY €
(Map p430; www.fornocampodefiori.com; Campo de' Fiori 22; pizza slices around €3; ⏰7.30am-2.30pm & 4.45-8pm Mon-Sat, closed Sat dinner Jul

ROMA PASS

A cumulative sightseeing and transport card, available online or from tourist information points and participating museums, the **Roma Pass** (www.romapass.it) comes in two forms:

72 hours (€38.50) Provides free admission to two museums or sites, as well as reduced entry to extra sites, unlimited city transport, and discounted entry to other exhibitions and events.

48 hours (€28) Gives free admission to one museum or site, and then as per the 72-hour pass.

Termini, Esquiline and Quirinal

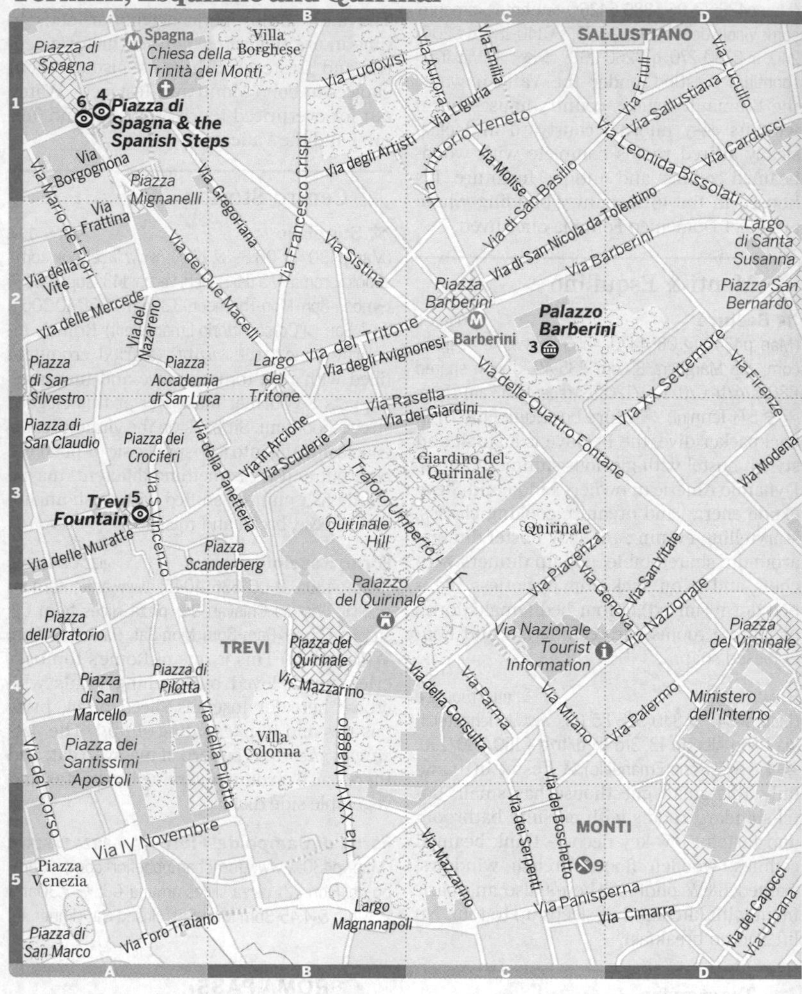

Termini, Esquiline and Quirinal

Top Sights

1 Basilica di Santa Maria Maggiore F5
2 Museo Nazionale Romano: Palazzo Massimo alle Terme F3
3 Palazzo Barberini C2
4 Piazza di Spagna & the Spanish Steps A1
5 Trevi Fountain A3

Sights

6 Fontana della Barcaccia A1

Sleeping

7 Beehive H2
8 Blue Hostel F5

Eating

9 L'Asino d'Oro C5

Entertainment

10 Teatro dell'Opera di Roma E3

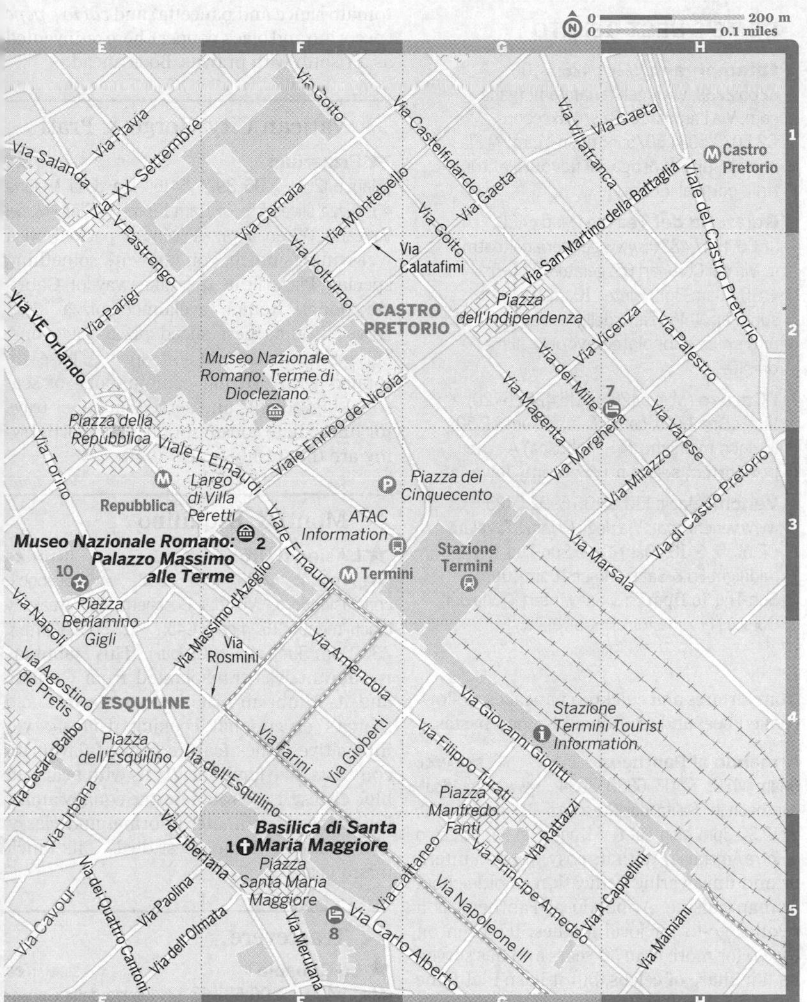

& Aug; Corso Vittorio Emanuele II) This buzzing bakery on Campo de' Fiori, divided into two adjacent shops, does a roaring trade in *panini* and delicious fresh-from-the-oven *pizza al taglio* (pizza by the slice). Aficionados swear by the *pizza bianca* ('white' pizza with olive oil, rosemary and salt), but the *panini* and *pizza rossa* ('red' pizza with olive oil, tomato and oregano) taste plenty good too.

★La Ciambella ITALIAN **€€**

(Map p430; 06 683 2930; www.la-ciambella.it; Via dell'Arco della Ciambella 20; meals €35-45; bar 7.30am-midnight, wine bar & restaurant noon-11pm Tue-Sun; Largo di Torre Argentina) Central but largely undiscovered by the tourist hordes, this friendly wine-bar-cum-restaurant beats much of the neighbourhood competition. Its spacious, light-filled interior is set over the ruins of the Terme di Agrippa, visible through transparent floor panels, and its kitchen sends out some excellent food,

ROME'S BEST GELATO

Fatamorgana (Map p426; ☎06 3265 2238; www.gelateriafatamorgana.com; Via Laurina 10; 2/3/4/5 scoops €2.50/3.50/4.50/5; ⊙noon-11pm; Ⓜ Flaminio) Superb artisanal flavours at multiple central locations.

Gelateria del Teatro (Map p430; ☎06 4547 4880; www.gelateriadelteatro.it; Via dei Coronari 65; gelato €2.50-5; ⊙10.30am-8pm winter, 10am-10.30pm summer; 🚌Via Zanardelli) Seasonal fruit and spicy chocolate flavours, all made on site.

I Caruso (Map p426; ☎06 4201 6420; Via Collina 13-15; cones & tubs from €2.50; ⊙noon-midnight; Ⓜ Repubblica) A small but perfect selection of creamy flavours.

Venchi (Map p430; ☎06 6992 5423; www.venchi.com; Via degli Orfani 87; gelato €2.50-5; ⊙10.30am-11pm Sun-Thu, to midnight Fri & Sat summer, 10am-10pm Sun-Thu, to 11pm Fri & Sat winter; 🚌Via del Corso) Nirvana for chocoholics.

from tartares and chickpea pancakes to slow-cooked beef and traditional Roman pastas.

Armando al Pantheon ROMAN €€
(Map p430; ☎06 6880 3034; www.armandoalpantheon.it; Salita dei Crescenzi 31; meals €40; ⊙12.30-3pm Mon-Sat & 7-11pm Mon-Fri; 🚌Largo di Torre Argentina) With its cosy wooden interior and unwavering dedication to old-school Roman cuisine, Armando al Pantheon is a regular go-to for local foodies. It's been on the go for more than 50 years and has served its fair share of celebs, but it hasn't let fame go to its head and remains as popular as ever. Reservations essential.

★**Casa Coppelle** RISTORANTE €€€
(Map p430; ☎06 6889 1707; www.casacoppelle.it; Piazza delle Coppelle 49; meals €65, tasting menu €85; ⊙noon-3.30pm & 6.30-11.30pm; 🚌Corso del Rinascimento) Boasting an enviable setting near the Pantheon and a plush, theatrical look – think velvet drapes, black lacquer tables and bookshelves – Casa Coppelle sets a romantic stage for high-end Roman-French cuisine. Gallic trademarks like snails and onion soup feature alongside updated Roman favourites such as pasta *amatriciana* (with tomato sauce and pancetta) and *cacio e pepe* (pecorino and black pepper), here re-invented as a risotto with prawns. Book ahead.

Vatican City, Borgo & Prati

★**Pizzarium** PIZZA €
(Map p426; ☎06 3974 5416; Via della Meloria 43; pizza slices €5; ⊙11am-10pm; Ⓜ Cipro-Musei Vaticani) When a pizza joint is packed on a wet winter's lunch, you know it's something special. Pizzarium, the takeaway of Gabriele Bonci, Rome's acclaimed pizza king, serves Rome's best sliced pizza, bar none. Scissor-cut squares of soft, springy base are topped with original combinations of seasonal ingredients and served on paper trays for immediate consumption. Also worth trying are the freshly fried *supplì*.

Monti & Esquilino

★**L'Asino d'Oro** ITALIAN €€
(Map p434; ☎06 4891 3832; www.facebook.com/asinodoro; Via del Boschetto 73; weekday lunch menu €16, meals €45; ⊙12.30-2.30pm & 7.30-11pm Tue-Sat; Ⓜ Cavour) This fabulous restaurant was transplanted from Orvieto, and its Umbrian origins resonate in Lucio Sforza's exceptional cooking. Unfussy yet innovative dishes feature bags of flavourful contrasts, like lamb meatballs with pear and blue cheese. Save room for the equally amazing desserts. Intimate, informal and classy, this is one of Rome's best deals – its lunch menu is a steal.

Trastevere

★**La Gensola** SICILIAN €€
(Map p430; ☎06 581 63 12; Piazza della Gensola 15; meals €45; ⊙12.30-3pm & 7.30-11.30pm, closed Sun summer; 🚌Viale di Trastevere, 🚋Viale di Trastevere) Enjoy delicious traditional cuisine with an emphasis on seafood at this upmarket trattoria, which can feel a tad overpriced. Begin the feast with a half-dozen oysters or wafer-thin slices of raw tuna, amberjack or seabass carpaccio, followed perhaps by a heap of *spaghellini* with fingernail-sized clams or seared anchovies with chicory. Meat lovers, tuck into Roman classics like *coda alla vaccinara* (oxtail stew) or *trippa* (tripe).

San Giovanni & Testaccio

Pizzeria Da Remo PIZZA €
(Map p426; ☎06 574 62 70; Piazza Santa Maria Liberatrice 44; meals €15; ⊙7pm-1am Mon-Sat; 🚌Via Marmorata) For an authentic Roman experience, join the noisy crowds here, one of the city's best-known and most popular pizzerias. It's a spartan-looking place, but the fried starters and thin-crust Roman pizzas are the business, and there's a cheerful, boisterous vibe. Expect to queue after 8.30pm.

Drinking & Nightlife

Much of the drinking action is in the *centro storico*: Campo de' Fiori is popular with students, while the area around Piazza Navona hosts a more upmarket scene. Over the river, Trastevere is another favoured spot with dozens of bars and pubs.

Rome's clubbing scene is centred on Testaccio and the Ostiense area, although you'll also find places in Trastevere and the *centro storico*. Admission to clubs is often free, but drinks are expensive.

★**Il Tiaso** BAR
(☎06 4547 4625; www.iltiaso.com; Via Ascoli Piceno 25; ⊙6pm-2am; 📶; 🚌Circonvallazione Casilina) Think living room with zebra-print chairs, walls of indie art, Lou Reed biographies wedged between wine bottles, and 30-something owner Gabriele playing his latest New York Dolls album to neo-beatnik chicks, corduroy-clad professors and the odd neighbourhood dog. Expect well-priced wine, an intimate chilled vibe, regular live music and lovely pavement terrace.

★**Barnum Cafe** CAFE
(Map p430; ☎06 6476 0483; www.barnumcafe.com; Via del Pellegrino 87; ⊙9am-10pm Mon, to 2am Tue-Sat; 📶; 🚌Corso Vittorio Emanuele II) A laid-back *Friends*-style cafe, evergreen Barnum is the sort of place you could quickly get used to. With its shabby-chic vintage furniture and white bare-brick walls, it's a relaxed spot for a breakfast cappuccino, a light lunch or a late afternoon drink. Come evening, a coolly dressed-down crowd sips seriously good cocktails.

Caffè Sant'Eustachio COFFEE
(Map p430; www.santeustachioilcaffe.it; Piazza Sant'Eustachio 82; ⊙8.30am-1am Sun-Thu, to 1.30am Fri, to 2am Sat; 🚌Corso del Rinascimento) This small, unassuming cafe, generally three deep at the bar, is reckoned by many to serve the best coffee in town. To make it, the bartenders sneakily beat the first drops of an espresso with several teaspoons of sugar to create a frothy paste to which they add the rest of the coffee. It's superbly smooth and guaranteed to put some zing into your sightseeing.

Open Baladin BAR
(Map p430; ☎06 683 8989; www.openbaladinroma.it; Via degli Specchi 6; ⊙noon-2am; 📶; 🚋Via Arenula) For some years, this cool, modern pub near Campo de' Fiori has been a leading light in Rome's craft beer scene, and it's still a top place for a pint with more than 40 beers on tap and up to 100 bottled brews, many from Italian artisanal microbreweries. There's also a decent food menu with *panini*, gourmet burgers and daily specials.

La Casa del Caffè Tazza d'Oro COFFEE
(Map p430; ☎06 678 9792; www.tazzadorocoffeeshop.com; Via degli Orfani 84-86; ⊙7am-8pm Mon-Sat, 10.30am-7.30pm Sun; 🚌Via del Corso) A busy, stand-up affair with burnished 1940s fittings, this is one of Rome's best coffee houses. Its espresso hits the mark nicely and there's a range of delicious coffee concoctions, including a cooling *granita di caffè*, a crushed-ice coffee drink served with whipped cream. There's also a small shop and, outside, a coffee *bancomat* for those out-of-hours caffeine emergencies.

Ma Che Siete Venuti a Fà PUB
(Map p430; ☎06 6456 2046; www.football-pub.com; Via Benedetta 25; ⊙11am-2am; 🚌Piazza Trilussa) Named after a football chant, which translates politely as 'What did you come here for?', this pint-sized Trastevere pub is a beer-buff's paradise, packing in around 15 international craft beers on tap and even more by the bottle. Expect some rowdy drinking.

Freni e Frizioni BAR
(Map p430; ☎06 4549 7499; www.freniefrizioni.com; Via del Politeama 4-6; ⊙7pm-2am; 🚌Piazza Trilussa) This perennially cool Trastevere bar is housed in an old mechanic's workshop – hence its name ('brakes and clutches') and tatty facade. It draws a young *spritz*-loving crowd that swells onto the small piazza outside to sip superbly mixed cocktails (€10) and seasonal punches, and fill up on its lavish early-evening *aperitivo* buffet (7pm to 10pm). Table reservations are essential on Friday and Saturday evenings.

✩ Entertainment

Rome has a thriving cultural scene, with a year-round calendar of concerts, performances and festivals. Upcoming events are also listed on www.turismoroma.it and www.inromenow.com.

Auditorium Parco della Musica CONCERT VENUE
(☎06 8024 1281; www.auditorium.com; Viale Pietro de Coubertin; 🚋Viale Tiziano) The Auditorium is the capital's premier concert venue. Its three concert halls offer superb acoustics, and together with a 3000-seat open-air arena, stage everything from classical music concerts to jazz gigs, public lectures and film screenings. The Auditorium is also home to Rome's world-class **Orchestra dell'Accademia Nazionale di Santa Cecilia** (www.santacecilia.it).

Alexanderplatz JAZZ
(Map p426; ☎06 8377 5604; www.facebook.com/alexander.platz.37; Via Ostia 9; ⏲8.30pm-1.30am; Ⓜ Ottaviano-San Pietro) Intimate, underground, and hard to find – look for the discreet black door – Rome's most celebrated jazz club draws top Italian and international performers and a respectful cosmopolitan crowd. Book a table for the best stage views or to dine here, although note that it's the music that's the star act not the food.

Teatro dell'Opera di Roma OPERA, BALLET
(Map p434; ☎06 48 16 01; www.operaroma.it; Piazza Beniamino Gigli 1; ⏲box office 10am-6pm Mon-Sat, 9am-1.30pm Sun; Ⓜ Repubblica) Rome's premier opera house boasts a plush gilt interior, a Fascist 1920s exterior and an impressive history: it premiered Puccini's *Tosca*, and Maria Callas once sang here. Opera and ballet performances are staged between September and June.

> **WORTH A TRIP**
>
> ### VIA APPIA ANTICA
>
> Completed in 190 BC, the Appian Way connected Rome with Brindisi on Italy's Adriatic coast. It's now a picturesque area of ancient ruins, grassy fields and towering pine trees. But it has a dark history – this is where Spartacus and 6000 of his slave rebels were crucified in 71 BC, and where the ancients buried their dead. Well-to-do Romans built elaborate mausoleums while the early Christians went underground, creating a 300km network of subterranean burial chambers – the catacombs.
>
> Highlights include the **Catacombe di San Sebastiano** (☎06 785 03 50; www.catacombe.org; Via Appia Antica 136; adult/reduced €8/5; ⏲10am-5pm Mon-Sat Jan-Nov; 🚌Via Appia Antica) and the nearby **Catacombe di San Callisto** (☎06 513 01 51; www.catacombe.roma.it; Via Appia Antica 110-126; adult/reduced €8/5; ⏲9am-noon & 2-5pm Thu-Tue Mar-Jan; 🚌Via Appia Antica).
>
> To get to the Via, take bus 660 from Colli Albani metro station (line A) or bus 118 from Circo Massimo (line B).

Shopping

Rome boasts the usual cast of flagship chain stores and glitzy designer outlets, but what makes shopping here fun is its legion of small, independent shops: family-run delis, small-label fashion boutiques, artisans' studios and neighbourhood markets.

Porta Portese Market MARKET
(Map p426; Piazza Porta Portese; ⏲6am-2pm Sun; 🚌Viale di Trastevere, 🚋Viale di Trastevere) To see another side of Rome, head to this mammoth flea market. With thousands of stalls selling everything from rare books and fell-off-a-lorry bikes to Peruvian shawls and MP3 players, it's crazily busy and a lot of fun. Keep your valuables safe and wear your haggling hat.

Information

DANGERS & ANNOYANCES

Rome is not a dangerous city, but petty theft can be a problem. Watch out for pickpockets around the big tourist sites, at Stazione Termini and on crowded public transport – the 64 Vatican bus is notorious.

INTERNET ACCESS

Free wi-fi is widely available in hostels, B&Bs and hotels; some also provide laptops or computers. Many bars and cafes also offer wi-fi .

MEDICAL SERVICES

Farmacrimi Stazione Termini (☎06 474 54 21; Via Marsala 29; ⏲7am-10pm; Ⓜ Termini) Pharmacy located in Stazione Termini, next to Platform 1.

Policlinico Umberto I (☎06 4 99 71; www.policlinicoumberto1.it; Viale del Policlinico 155; Ⓜ Policlinico, Castro Pretorio) Rome's largest hospital is located near Stazione Termini.

WORTH A TRIP

DAY TRIPS FROM ROME

Ostia Antica

An easy train ride from Rome, Ostia Antica is one of Italy's most under-appreciated archaeological sites. The ruins of ancient Rome's main seaport, the **Scavi Archeologici di Ostia Antica** (☎06 5635 0215; www.ostiaantica.beniculturali.it; Viale dei Romagnoli 717; adult/reduced €8/4, exhibitions €3; ⊙8.30am-6.15pm Tue-Sun summer, shorter hours winter), are spread out and you'll need a few hours to do them justice.

To get to Ostia take the Ostia Lido train (25 minutes, half-hourly) from Stazione Porta San Paolo next to Piramide metro station. The journey is covered by standard public-transport tickets.

Tivoli

Tivoli, 30km east of Rome, is home to two Unesco–listed sites. Five kilometres from Tivoli proper, the ruins of the emperor Hadrian's sprawling **Villa Adriana** (☎0774 38 27 33; www.villaadriana.beniculturali.it; adult/reduced €8/4; ⊙9am-1hr before sunset) are quite magnificent. Up in Tivoli's hilltop centre, the Renaissance **Villa d'Este** (☎0774 33 29 20; www.villadestetivoli.info; Piazza Trento; adult/reduced €8/4; ⊙8.30am-1hr before sunset Tue-Sun) is famous for its elaborate gardens and fountains.

Tivoli is accessible by Cotral bus (€1.30, one hour, every 15 to 20 minutes) from Ponte Mammolo metro station. To get to Villa Adriana from Tivoli town centre, take CAT bus 4 or 4X (€1.30, 10 minutes, half-hourly) from Largo Garibaldi.

TOURIST INFORMATION

For phone enquiries, there's a **tourist information line** (☎06 06 08; www.060608.it; ⊙9am-9pm).

For information about the Vatican, contact the **Centro Servizi Pellegrini e Turisti** (Map p426; ☎06 6988 1662; St Peter's Square; ⊙8.30am-6.30pm Mon-Sat; 🚌Piazza del Risorgimento, Ⓜ Ottaviano-San Pietro).

There are **tourist information points** (☎06 06 08; www.turismoroma.it) at **Fiumicino** (International Arrivals, Terminal 3; ⊙8am-8.45pm) and **Ciampino** (Arrivals Hall; ⊙8.30am-6pm) airports, and at locations across town. These include the following:

Stazione Termini Tourist Information (Map p434; Via Giovanni Giolitti 34; ⊙9am-5pm; Ⓜ Termini) Located inside the station next to the Mercato Centrale, not far from the car-rental and left-luggage desk. Pick up city maps and reserve city tours at this efficient tourist office.

Via Nazionale Tourist Information (Map p434; Via Nazionale 184; ⊙9.30am-7pm; 🚌Via Nazionale) Tourist information kiosk in front of Palazzo delle Esposizioni. Handy for city maps and sells the Roma Pass.

Fori Imperiali Tourist Information (Map p424; Via dei Fori Imperiali; ⊙9.30am-7pm; 🚌Via dei Fori Imperiali) Has a panel illustrating the Roman and Imperial Forums – photograph it and you've got a useful guide.

Minghetti Tourist Information (Map p430; Via Marco Minghetti; ⊙9.30am-7pm; 🚌Via del Corso) A tourist information kiosk between Via del Corso and the Trevi Fountain.

Piazza Navona Tourist Information (Map p430; Piazza delle Cinque Lune; ⊙9.30am-7pm; 🚌Corso del Rinascimento) Actually located just off of Piazza Navona, on Piazza delle Cinque Lune.

USEFUL WEBSITES

060608 (www.060608.it) Rome's official tourist website.

Auditorium (www.auditorium.com) Check concert listings.

Coopculture (www.coopculture.it) Information and ticket booking for Rome's monuments.

Lonely Planet (www.lonelyplanet.com/rome) Destination low-down, hotel bookings and traveller forum.

Vatican Museums (www.vatican.va) Book tickets and avoid the queues.

ℹ Getting There & Away

AIR

Rome's main international airport, **Leonardo da Vinci** (☎06 6 59 51; www.adr.it/fiumicino), better known as Fiumicino, is on the coast 30km west of the city.

The much smaller **Ciampino Airport** (☎06 6 59 51; www.adr.it/ciampino), 15km southeast of the city centre, is the hub for European low-cost carrier Ryanair.

BOAT

The nearest port to Rome is Civitavecchia, about 80km north. Ferries sail here from Spain and Tunisia, as well as Sicily and Sardinia. Book tickets at travel agents or online at www.traghettiweb.it. You can also buy directly at the port. Half-hourly trains connect Civitavecchia and Roma Termini (€5 to €15.50, 40 minutes to 1¼ hours).

BUS

Long-distance national and international buses use the **Autostazione Tiburtina** (Tibus; Largo Guido Mazzoni; Ⓜ Tiburtina). Get tickets at the bus station or at travel agencies.

CAR & MOTORCYCLE

Rome is circled by the Grande Raccordo Anulare (GRA), to which all autostrade (motorways) connect, including the main A1 north–south artery, and the A12, which runs to Civitavecchia and Fiumicino airport.

Car hire is available at the airport and Stazione Termini.

TRAIN

Rome's main station is **Stazione Termini** (www.romatermini.com; Piazza dei Cinquecento; Ⓜ Termini). It has regular connections to other European countries, all major Italian cities and many smaller towns. **Left luggage** (Stazione Termini; 1st 5hr €6, 6-12hr per hour €0.90, 13hr & over per hour €0.40; ⏲ 6am-11pm; Ⓜ Termini) is in the wing on the Via Giolitti side of the station, near the tourist office.

Rome's other principal train stations are Stazione Tiburtina and Stazione Roma-Ostiense.

ℹ Getting Around

TO/FROM THE AIRPORTS

Fiumicino

The easiest way to get to/from Fiumicino is by train, but there are also bus services. The set taxi fare to the city centre is €48 (valid for up to four people with luggage).

Leonardo Express Train (one way €14) Runs to/from Stazione Termini. Departures from Fiumicino airport every 30 minutes between 6.23am and 11.23pm; from Termini between 5.35am and 10.35pm. Journey time is 30 minutes.

FL1 Train (one way €8) Connects to Trastevere, Ostiense and Tiburtina stations, but not Termini. Departures from Fiumicino airport every 15 minutes (half-hourly on Sundays and public holidays) between 5.57am and 10.42pm; from Tiburtina every 15 minutes between 5.01am and 7.31pm, then half-hourly to 10.01pm.

Ciampino

The best option from Ciampino is to take one of the regular bus services into the city centre. The set taxi fare to the city centre is €30.

SIT Bus – Ciampino (☎ 06 591 68 26; www.sitbusshuttle.com; from/to airport €5/6, return €9) Regular departures from the airport to Via Marsala outside Stazione Termini between 7.45am and 11.15pm; from Termini between 4.30am and 9.30pm. Get tickets on the bus. Journey time is 45 minutes.

Schiaffini Rome Airport Bus – Ciampino (☎ 06 713 05 31; www.romeairportbus.com; Via Giolitti; one-way/return €4.90/7.90) Regular departures to/from Via Giolitti outside Stazione Termini. From the airport, services are between 4am and 10.50pm; from Via Giolitti, buses run from 4.50am to midnight. Buy tickets onboard, online, at the airport, or at the bus stop. Journey time is approximately 40 minutes.

PUBLIC TRANSPORT

Rome's public transport system includes buses, trams, metro and a suburban train network.

Tickets are valid on all forms of public transport, except for routes to Fiumicino airport. They come in various forms:

BIT (€1.50) Valid for 100 minutes and one metro ride.

Roma 24h (€7) Valid for 24 hours.

Roma 48h (€12.50) Valid for 48 hours.

Roma 72h (€18) Valid for 72 hours.

Buy tickets at *tabacchi* (tobacconist shops), newsstands or from vending machines.

Bus

- Rome's buses and trams are run by **ATAC** (☎ 06 5 70 03; www.atac.roma.it).
- The main bus station is in front of Stazione Termini on Piazza dei Cinquecento, where there's an **information booth** (Map p434; ⏲ 8am-8pm).
- Other important hubs are at Largo di Torre Argentina and Piazza Venezia.
- Buses generally run from about 5.30am until midnight, with limited services throughout the night.

Metro

- Rome has two main metro lines, A (orange) and B (blue), which cross at Termini.
- Trains run between 5.30am and 11.30pm (to 1.30am on Fridays and Saturdays).

TAXI

- Official licensed taxis are white with an ID number and *Roma Capitale* on the sides.
- Always go with the metered fare, never an arranged price (the set fares to and from the airports are exceptions).
- There are taxi ranks at the airports, Stazione Termini, Piazza della Repubblica, Piazza Barberini, Piazza di Spagna, the Pantheon, the Colosseum, Largo di Torre Argentina, Piazza Belli, Piazza Pio XII and Piazza del Risorgimento.

NORTHERN ITALY

Italy's well-heeled north is a fascinating area of historical wealth and natural diversity. Bordered by the northern Alps and boasting some of the country's most spectacular coastline, it also encompasses Italy's largest lowland area, the fertile Po valley plain. Glacial lakes in the far north offer stunning scenery, while cities like Venice, Milan and Turin harbour artistic treasures and lively cultural scenes.

Genoa

POP 586,700

Genoa (Genova) is an absorbing city of aristocratic *palazzi*, dark, malodorous alleyways, Gothic architecture and industrial sprawl. Formerly a powerful maritime republic known as La Superba (Christopher Columbus was born here in 1451), it's still an important transport hub, with ferry links to destinations across the Med and train links to the Cinque Terre.

Sights

★Palazzo Reale PALACE

(☎010 271 02 36; www.palazzorealegenova.beniculturali.it; Via Balbi 10; adult/reduced €4/2; ⏲9am-7pm Tue-Sat, 1.30-7pm Sun) If you only get the chance to visit one of the Palazzi dei Rolli (a group of palaces belonging to the city's most eminent families), make it this one. A former residence of the Savoy dynasty, it has terraced gardens, exquisite furnishings, a fine collection of 17th-century art and a gilded Hall of Mirrors that is worth the entry fee alone.

Musei di Strada Nuova MUSEUM

(☎010 557 21 93; www.museidigenova.it; Via Garibaldi 9; combined ticket adult/reduced €9/7; ⏲9am-7pm Tue-Fri, 10am-7.30pm Sat & Sun summer, to 6.30pm winter) Skirting the northern edge of what was once the city limits, pedestrianised Via Garibaldi (formerly called the Strada Nuova) was planned by Galeazzo Alessi in the 16th century. It quickly became the city's most sought-after quarter, lined with the palaces of Genoa's wealthiest citizens. Three of these *palazzi* – Rosso, Bianco and Doria-Tursi – today comprise the Musei di Strada Nuova. Between them, they hold the city's finest collection of old masters.

Cattedrale di San Lorenzo CATHEDRAL

(Piazza San Lorenzo; ⏲8am-noon & 3-7pm) Genoa's zebra-striped Gothic-Romanesque cathedral owes its continued existence to the poor quality of a British WWII bomb that failed to ignite here in 1941; it still sits on the right side of the nave like an innocuous museum piece.

The cathedral, fronted by three arched portals, twisting columns and crouching lions, was first consecrated in 1118. The two bell towers and cupola were added later in the 16th century.

Sleeping & Eating

★Palazzo Cambiaso APARTMENT €

(☎010 856 61 88; www.palazzocambiaso.it; Via al Ponte Calvi 6; d €80-120, apt €120-240; 📶) A real attention to design is evident in these rooms and apartments, set on the upper floor of a stately *palazzo*. The larger ones (sleeps up to six) come with full marble kitchens, long dining tables and laundries, but even the cheapest double is spacious, soothing and has the signature Frette linen.

★Hotel Cairoli HOTEL €

(☎010 246 14 54; www.hotelcairoligenova.com; Via Cairoli 14/4; d €65-105, tr €85-125, q €90-150; ❄@📶) For five-star service at three-star prices, book at this artful hideaway. Rooms, on the 3rd floor of a towering *palazzo*, are themed on modern artists and feature works inspired by the likes of Mondrian, Dorazio and Alexander Calder. Add in a library, chill-out area, internet point, small gym and terrace, and you have the ideal bolt-hole.

Trattoria Rosmarino TRATTORIA €€

(☎010 251 04 75; www.trattoriarosmarino.it; Salita del Fondaco 30; meals €30-35; ⏲12.30-2.30pm & 7.30-10.30pm Mon-Sat) Rosmarino cooks up the standard local specialities, yes, but the straight-forwardly priced menu has an elegance and vibrancy that sets it apart. With two nightly sittings, there's always a nice buzz (though there's also enough nooks and crannies that a romantic night for two isn't out of the question). Call ahead for an evening table.

Trattoria della Raibetta TRATTORIA €€

(☎010 246 88 77; www.trattoriadellaraibetta.it; Vico Caprettari 10-12; meals €30-35; ⏲noon-2.30pm & 7.30-11pm Tue-Sun) Totally *typica* Genoese food can be found in the family-run joints hidden in the warren of streets near the cathedral. This, a snug trattoria with a low brick-vaulted ceiling, serves regional classics such as *trofiette al pesto* or octopus salad alongside excellent fresh fish.

Information

Tourist Office (☎010 557 29 03; www.visitgenoa.it; Via Garibaldi 12r; ⌚9am-6.20pm) Helpful office in the historic centre.

Getting There & Around

AIR

Genoa's **Cristoforo Colombo Airport** (☎010 6 01 51; www.airport.genova.it) is 6km west of the city.

To get to/from it, the **Volabus** (☎848 000 030; www.amt.genova.it; one-way €6) shuttle connects with Stazione Brignole and Stazione Principe. Buy tickets on board.

BOAT

Ferries sail to Spain, Sicily, Sardinia, Corsica, Morocco and Tunisia from the international passenger terminals, west of the city centre.

Grandi Navi Veloci (GNV; ☎010 209 45 91; www.gnv.it) Ferries to Sardinia (Porto Torres; from €38) and Sicily (Palermo; from €68). Also to Barcelona (Spain) and Tunis (Tunisia).

Moby Lines (☎199 303040; www.mobylines.it) Ferries year-round to the Sardinian ports of Olbia (from €41) and Porto Torres (from €41).

BUS

Buses to international cities depart from Piazza della Vittoria, as does a daily bus to/from Milan's Malpensa airport (€25, three hours) and other interregional services. Tickets are sold at **Geo travels** (☎010 58 71 81; Piazza della Vittoria 57; ⌚9am-12.30pm & 3-7pm Mon-Fri, 9am-noon Sat).

TRAIN

Genoa's Stazione Principe and Stazione Brignole are linked by train to the following destinations:

TO	FARE (€)	DURATION (HR)	FREQUENCY
Milan	13-27	1½	22 daily
Pisa	21-26	2-2½	16 daily
Rome	51-63	4½-5½	9 daily
Turin	12-21	2	19 daily

Cinque Terre

Liguria's eastern Riviera boasts some of Italy's most dramatic coastline, the highlight of which is the Unesco-listed **Parco Nazionale delle Cinque Terre** (Cinque Terre National Park) just west of La Spezia. Running for 18km, this awesome stretch of plunging cliffs and vine-covered hills is named after its five tiny villages: Riomaggiore, Manarola, Corniglia, Vernazza and Monterosso.

In October 2011 flash floods along the Ligurian coast wreaked havoc in Vernazza and Monterosso, burying historic streets under metres of mud and killing half-a-dozen people. The villages recovered swiftly, but some of the walking trails remain closed to visitors.

Activities

The Cinque Terre offers excellent hiking with a 120km network of paths. The best known is the 12km **Sentiero Azzurro** (Blue Trail), a one-time mule trail that links all five villages. To walk it (or any of the national park's trails) you'll need a **Cinque Terre Card** (one/two days €7.50/14.50), or a **Cinque Terre Treno Card** (one/two days €16/29), which also provides unlimited train travel between La Spezia and the five villages. Both cards are available at park offices.

At the time of writing, two legs of the Sentiero Azzurro were closed – Riomaggiore to Manarola (the so-called Via dell'Amore) and Manarola to Corniglia – and will possibly remain so until 2018. Check www.parconazionale5terre.it for the current situation.

If water sports are more your thing, you can hire snorkelling gear and kayaks at the **Diving Center 5 Terre** (☎0187 92 00 11; www.5terrediving.it; Via San Giacomo) in Riomaggiore.

Information

Parco Nazionale (www.parconazionale5terre.it; ⌚8am-8pm summer, 8.30am-12.30pm & 1-5pm winter) Offices in the train stations of all five villages and La Spezia station; has comprehensive information about hiking trail closures.

Getting There & Away

BOAT

Golfo Paradiso SNC (☎0185 77 20 91; www.golfoparadiso.it) In summer, Golfo Paradiso runs boats to the Cinque Terre from Genoa (one way/return €20/35).

Consorzio Marittimo Turistico Cinque Terre Golfo dei Poeti (www.navigazionegolfodeipoeti.it) From late March to October, La Spezia–based Consorzio Marittimo Turistico Cinque Terre Golfo dei Poeti runs daily shuttle boats between all of the Cinque Terre villages (except Corniglia), costing €9 one way, including all stops, or €20 for an all-day ticket.

TRAIN

From Genoa Brignole, direct trains run to Riomaggiore (€6.80, 1½ to two hours, at least 10 daily), stopping at each of the villages.

From La Spezia, one to three trains an hour run up the coast between 4.30am and 11.10pm. If you're using this route and want to stop at all the villages, get the Cinque Terre Treno Card.

Monterosso

The largest and most developed of the villages, Monterosso boasts the coast's only sandy beach, as well as a wealth of eating and accommodation options.

Sleeping & Eating

★ Hotel Pasquale HOTEL €€

(☎0187 81 74 77; www.hotelpasquale.it; Via Fegina 4; s €85-170, d €135-255, tr €170-340; ⏱Mar-Nov; ❄📶) Offering soothing views and 15 unusually stylish, modern guest rooms, this friendly seafront hotel is built into Monterosso's medieval sea walls. To find it, exit the train station and go left through the tunnel towards the *centro storico*.

Trattoria da Oscar TRATTORIA €€

(Via Vittorio Emanuele 67; meals €35; ⏱noon-2pm & 7-10pm) Behind Piazza Matteoti, in the heart of the old town, this vaulted dining room is run by a young, friendly team. The town's famed anchovies dominate the menu; whether you go for the standard fried-with-lemon, with a white wine sauce or deep-fried, they are all good. No credit cards.

Vernazza

Perhaps the most attractive of the five villages, Vernazza overlooks a small, picturesque harbour.

From near the harbour, a steep, narrow staircase leads up to **Castello Doria** (€1.50; ⏱10am-7pm summer, to 6pm winter), the oldest surviving fortification in the Cinque Terre. Dating to around 1000, it's now largely ruined except for the circular tower in the centre of the esplanade, but the castle is well worth a visit for the superb views it commands.

To overnight in Vernazza, try **La Mala** (☎334 287 57 18; www.lamala.it; Via San Giovanni Battista 29; d €140-220; ❄📶), a contemporary boutique hotel in the cliffside heights of the village.

Corniglia

Corniglia, the only village with no direct sea access, sits atop a 100m-high rocky promontory surrounded by vineyards. To reach the village proper from the railway station you must first tackle the **Lardarina**, a 377-step brick stairway, or jump on a shuttle bus (one way €2.50).

Once up in the village, you can enjoy dazzling 180-degree sea views from the **Belvedere di Santa Maria**, a heart-stopping lookout point at the end of Via Fieschi.

Manarola

One of the busiest of the villages, Manarola tumbles down to the sea in a helter-skelter of pastel-coloured buildings, cafes, trattorias and restaurants.

Sleeping & Eating

Hotel Marina Piccola BOUTIQUE HOTEL €€

(☎0187 92 07 70; www.hotelmarinapiccola.com; s/d/tr €125/145/190, ste €160-245; ❄📶) This choice Manarola hotel has 12 big, comfortable, contemporary rooms, with a few looking over the sea. The lovely lobby and lounge area, which sports a surprisingly on-trend interior, is a welcome respite from the busy day-time streets. A real find at this price, although there is a minimum two-day stay in summer.

Da Aristide SEAFOOD €

(☎0187 92 00 00; Via Discovolo 290; meals €25-30; ⏱9am-11pm Fri-Wed) Up the hill, not far from the train station, Aristide has tables in an old village house and in a bright, modern terrace on the square. Order a few of the heaped plates of stuffed anchovies or lemon-doused grilled octopus to share or keep one of the fish ravioli or homemade pappardelle with mussels and eggplant for yourself.

Riomaggiore

The Cinque Terre's largest and easternmost village, Riomaggiore acts as the unofficial HQ.

For a taste of classic seafood and local wine, search out **Dau Cila** (☎0187 76 00 32; www.ristorantedaucila.com; Via San Giacomo 65; meals €40; ⏱noon-midnight, closed Jan & Feb), a smart restaurant-cum-wine bar perched overlooking the twee harbour.

Turin

POP 890,500

With its regal *palazzi*, baroque piazzas, cafes and world-class museums, Turin (Torino) is a dynamic, cultured city. For centuries, it was the seat of the royal Savoy family, and between 1861 and 1864, it was Italy's first post-unification capital. More recently, it hosted the 2006 Winter Olympics and was European Capital of Design in 2008.

Sights

★Museo Egizio MUSEUM

(Egyptian Museum; 011 561 77 76; www.museoegizio.it; Via Accademia delle Scienze 6; adult/reduced €15/11; 9am-6.30pm Tue-Sun, 9am-2pm Mon) Opened in 1824 and housed in the austere Palazzo dell'Accademia delle Scienze, this Turin institution houses the most important collection of Egyptian treasure outside Cairo. Among its many highlights are a statue of Ramses II (one of the world's most important pieces of Egyptian art), the world's largest papyrus collection and over 500 funerary and domestic items found in 1906 in the tomb of royal architect Kha and his wife Merit (from 1400 BC).

Mole Antonelliana LANDMARK

(www.gtt.to.it/cms/turismo/ascensore-mole; Via Montebello 20; lift adult/reduced €7/5, incl Museo €14/11; lift 10am-8pm Sun, Mon & Wed-Fri, to 11pm Sat) The symbol of Turin, this 167m tower with its distinctive aluminium spire appears on the Italian two-cent coin. It was originally intended as a synagogue when construction began in 1862, but was never used as a place of worship, and nowadays houses the **Museo Nazionale del Cinema** (011 813 85 60; www.museocinema.it; adult/reduced €10/8, incl lift €14/11; 9am-8pm Sun, Mon & Wed-Fri, to 11pm Sat). For dazzling 360-degree views, take the **Panoramic Lift** up to the 85m-high outdoor viewing deck.

Cattedrale di San Giovanni Battista CATHEDRAL

(www.duomoditorino.it; Via XX Settembre 87; 9am-12.30pm & 3-7pm) Turin's cathedral was built between 1491 and 1498 on the site of three 14th-century basilicas and, before that, a Roman theatre. Plain interior aside, as home to the famous **Shroud of Turin** (alleged to be the burial cloth in which Jesus' body was wrapped), this is a highly trafficked church. A copy of the cloth is on permanent display to the left of the cathedral altar.

Piazza Castello PIAZZA

Turin's central square is lined with museums, theatres and cafes. The city's Savoy heart, although laid out from the mid-1300s, was mostly constructed from the 16th to 18th centuries. Dominating it is the part-medieval, part-baroque **Palazzo Madama**, the original seat of the Italian parliament. To the north is the exquisite facade of the **Palazzo Reale**, the royal palace built for Carlo Emanuele II in the mid-1600s.

Sleeping & Eating

★Via Stampatori B&B €

(339 258 13 30; www.viastampatori.com; Via Stampatori 4; s/d €90/110;) This utterly lovely B&B occupies the top floor of a frescoed Renaissance building. Six bright, stylish and uniquely furnished rooms overlook either a sunny terrace or a leafy inner courtyard. The owner's personal collection of 20th-century design is used throughout the rooms and several serene common areas. It's central but blissfully quiet.

★DuParc Contemporary Suites DESIGN HOTEL €€

(011 012 00 00; www.duparcsuites.com; Corso Massimo D'Azeglio 21; r/ste from €120/140; P) A business-friendly location doesn't mean this isn't a great choice for all travellers. Staff are young and friendly, and the building's stark modern lines are softened with a fantastic contemporary art collection, bold colour and tactile furnishings. Best of all, even the cheapest rooms here are sumptuously large, with king beds, ample cupboard space, huge bathrooms and floor-to-ceiling windows.

È Cucina MODERN ITALIAN €

(011 562 90 38; www.cesaremarretti.com; Via Bertola 27a; meals €10-30; 12.30-3pm & 8-11pm) Northern Italians are fond of a 'concept' and Bolognese chef Cesare Marretti's concept here is *sorpesa* (surprise). Beyond the choice of meat, fish or vegetables and the number of courses you want, it's up to the kitchen. What *is* certain is the innovative cooking and excellent produce that will arrive. Local's tip: don't be tempted to over order.

★Banco vini e alimenti PIEDMONT €€

(011 764 02 39; www.bancoviniealimenti.it; Via dei Mercanti 13f; meals €25-30; 6.30pm-12.30am Mon, 12.30pm-12.30am Tue-Sat) A hybrid restaurant-bar-deli, this smartly designed but low-key place does clever small-dish dining for

lunch and dinner. While it might vibe casual wine bar, with young staff in T-shirts and boyfriend jeans, don't underestimate the food: this is serious Piedmontese cooking. Open all day, you can grab a single-origin pour-over here in the morning, or a herbal house *spritz* late afternoon.

Drinking & Nightlife

Aperitivi and more substantial *apericenas* are a Turin institution. If you're on a tight budget, you can fill up on a generous buffet of bar snacks for the cost of a drink.

Nightlife concentrates in the riverside area around Piazza Vittoria Veneto, the Quadrilatero Romano district and increasingly the southern neighbourhoods of San Salvarino and Vanchiglia.

Information

Piazza Castello Tourist Office (011 53 51 81; www.turismotorino.org; Piazza Castello; 9am-6pm) Central and multilingual.

Getting There & Around

From **Turin Airport** (011 567 63 61; www.aeroportoditorino.it; Strada Aeroporto 12), 16km northwest of the city centre in Caselle, airlines fly to Italian and European destinations.

Sadem (800 801 600; www.sadem.it) runs an airport shuttle (€6.50 or €7.50 on board, 50 minutes, half-hourly) to/from Porta Nuova train station.

Trains connect with Milan (€12 to €35, one to two hours, 30 daily), Florence (€55 to €116, three hours, 10 daily), Genoa (€12 to €21, two hours, up to 19 daily) and Rome (€60 to €124, 4¼ hours, up to 16 daily).

Milan

POP 1.34 MILLION

Few Italian cities polarise opinion like Milan, Italy's financial and fashion capital. Some people love the cosmopolitan, can-do atmosphere, the vibrant cultural scene and sophisticated shopping; others grumble that it's dirty, ugly and expensive. Certainly, it lacks the picture-postcard beauty of many Italian towns, but in among the urban hustle are some truly great sights – Leonardo da Vinci's *Last Supper*, the immense Duomo and La Scala opera house.

WORTH A TRIP

MUSEO NAZIONALE DELL'AUTOMOBILE

As the historic birthplace of one of the world's leading car manufacturers – the 'T' in Fiat stands for Torino – Turin is the obvious place for a car museum. And the dashing **Museo Nazionale dell'Automobile** (011 67 76 66; www.museoauto.it; Corso Unità d'Italia 40; adult/reduced €12/8; 10am-7pm Wed, Thu & Sun, to 9pm Fri & Sat, to 2pm Mon, 2-7pm Tue; M Lingotto), located roughly 5km south of the city centre, doesn't disappoint with its precious collection of over 200 automobiles – everything from an 1892 Peugeot to a 1980 Ferrari 308 (in red, of course).

Sights

★Duomo CATHEDRAL

(02 7202 3375; www.duomomilano.it; Piazza del Duomo; adult/reduced duomo €2/3, roof terraces via stairs €9/4.50, lift €13/7, archaeological area €7/3; duomo 8am-7pm, roof terraces 9am-7pm; M Duomo) A vision in pink Candoglia marble, Milan's extravagant Gothic cathedral, 600 years in the making, aptly reflects the city's creativity and ambition. Its pearly white facade, adorned with 135 spires and 3400 statues, rises like the filigree of a fairy-tale tiara, wowing the crowds with its extravagant detail. The interior is no less impressive, punctuated by the largest stained-glass windows in Christendom, while in the crypt saintly Carlo Borromeo is interred in a rock-crystal casket.

★Museo del Novecento GALLERY

(02 8844 4061; www.museodelnovecento.org; Via Marconi 1; adult/reduced €10/8; 2.30-7.30pm Mon, 9.30am-7.30pm Tue, Wed, Fri & Sun, to 10.30pm Thu & Sat; ; M Duomo) Overlooking Piazza del Duomo, with fabulous views of the cathedral, is Mussolini's Arengario, from where he would harangue huge crowds in his heyday. Now it houses Milan's museum of 20th-century art. Built around a futuristic spiral ramp (an ode to the Guggenheim), the lower floors are cramped, but the heady collection, which includes the likes of Umberto Boccioni, Campigli, de Chirico and Marinetti, more than distracts.

Central Milan

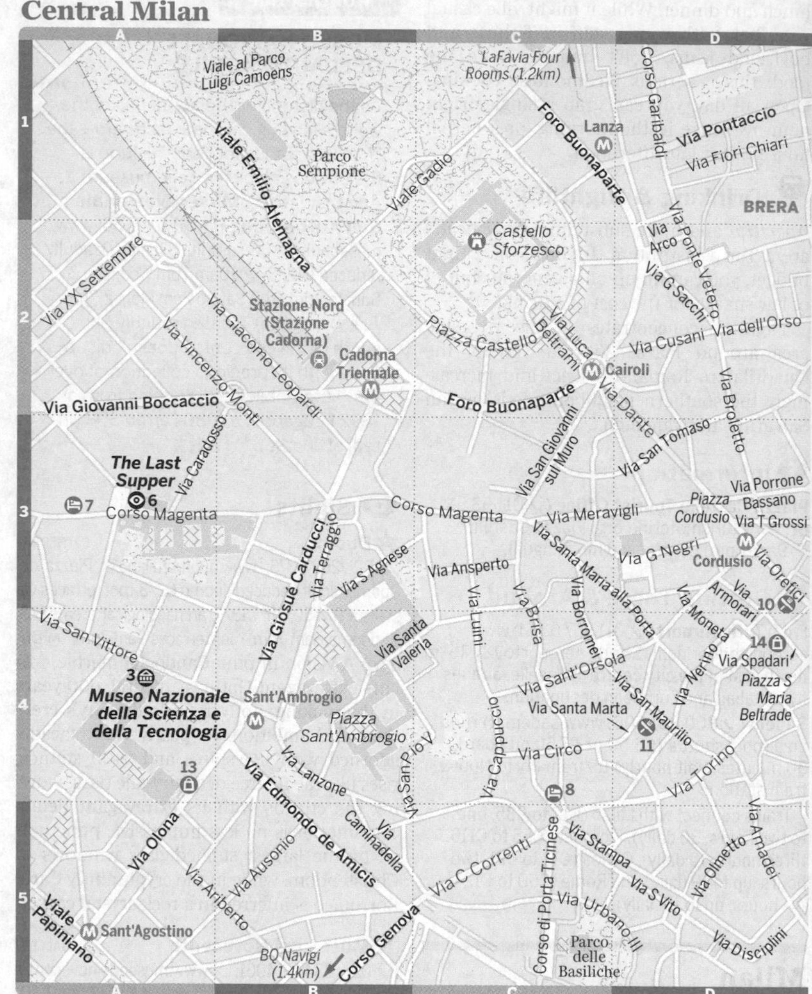

★Pinacoteca di Brera GALLERY

(☎02 722 631; www.pinacotecabrera.org; Via Brera 28; adult/reduced €10/7; ⏱8.30am-7.15pm Tue-Wed & Fri-Sun, to 10.15pm Thu; Ⓜ Lanza, Montenapoleone) Located upstairs from the centuries-old Accademia di Belle Arti (still one of Italy's most prestigious art schools), this gallery houses Milan's impressive collection of Old Masters, much of it 'lifted' from Venice by Napoleon. Rubens, Goya and Van Dyck all have a place in the collection, but you're here for the Italians: Titian, Tintoretto, Veronese, and the Bellini brothers. Much of the work has tremendous emotional clout, most notably Mantegna's brutal *Lamentation over the Dead Christ*.

★The Last Supper ARTWORK

(Il Cenacolo; ☎02 9280 0360; www.cenacolovinciano.net; Piazza Santa Maria delle Grazie 2; adult/reduced €10/5, plus booking fee €2; ⏱8.15am-6.45pm Tue-Sun; Ⓜ Cadorna) Milan's most famous mural, Leonardo da Vinci's *The Last Supper* is hidden away on a wall of the refectory adjoining the **Basilica di Santa Maria delle Grazie** (☎02 467 6111; www.legraziemilano.it; ⏱7am-noon & 3.30-7.30pm Mon-Sat, 7.30am-12.30pm & 4-9pm Sun). Depicting Christ and

Central Milan

Top Sights
1 Duomo ... E3
2 Museo del Novecento ... E4
3 Museo Nazionale della Scienza e della Tecnologia ... A4
4 Pinacoteca di Brera ... E1
5 Quadrilatero d'Oro ... F2
6 The Last Supper ... A3

Sights
Basilica di Santa Maria delle Grazie ... (see 6)

Sleeping
7 Antica Locanda Leonardo ... A3
8 Ostello Bello ... C4

Eating
Giacomo Arengario ... (see 2)
9 Luini ... E3
10 Peck Italian Bar ... D3
11 Trattoria Milanese ... D4

Entertainment
12 Teatro alla Scala ... E2

Shopping
13 MUST Shop ... A4
14 Peck ... D4

his disciples at the dramatic moment when Christ reveals he's aware of his betrayal, it's a masterful psychological study and one of the world's most iconic images. To see it you must book in advance or sign up for a guided city tour.

★ Museo Nazionale della Scienza e della Tecnologia MUSEUM
(☎02 48 55 51; www.museoscienza.org; Via San Vittore 21; adult/child €10/7.50, submarine tours €8, flight simulator €10; ⏲9.30am-5pm Tue-Fri, to 6.30pm Sat & Sun; 📶 👪; Ⓜ Sant'Ambrogio) Kids and would-be inventors will go goggle-eyed at Milan's science museum, the largest of its kind in Italy. It is a fitting tribute in a city where arch-inventor Leonardo da Vinci did much of his finest work. The 16th-century monastery where it is housed features a collection of more than 10,000 items, including models based on da Vinci's sketches, and outdoor hangars housing steam trains, planes and Italy's first submarine, *Enrico Toti*. More recently, the museum added a helicopter flight simulator, in which you can swoop over Milan in a real AW109 cockpit.

Sleeping

★ Ostello Bello HOSTEL €
(☎02 3658 2720; www.ostellobello.com; Via Medici 4; dm/d/tr €45/129/149; ❄📶; 🚊2, 3, 14) A breath of fresh air in Milan's stiffly-suited centre, this is the best hostel in town. Entrance is through its lively bar-cafe, open to nonguests, where you're welcomed with a smile and a complimentary drink. Beds are in mixed dorms or spotless private rooms, and there's a kitchen, a small terrace, and a basement lounge equipped with guitars, board games and table football.

★**LaFavia Four Rooms** B&B €€

(☎347 7842212; www.lafavia4rooms.com; Via Carlo Farini 4; s €90-105, d €100-125; ❄📶; Ⓜ Garibaldi) Marco and Fabio's four-room B&B in the former Rabarbaro Zucca factory is a multicultural treat with rooms inspired by their travels through India, Mexico and Europe. Graphic wallpapers by Manuela Canova in zippy greens and oranges are complemented by lush window views onto plant-filled verandas. Best of all is the rooftop garden, where an organic breakfast is served in summer.

Antica Locanda Leonardo HOTEL €€

(☎02 4801 4197; www.anticalocandaleonardo.com; Corso Magenta 78; s €95-105, d €158; ❄@📶; Ⓜ Conciliazione) An old-school, homely B&B in a 19th-century residence near Leonardo's *The Last Supper*. Rooms are small and decorated in an old-fashioned style with faux period furniture, parquet floors and heavy drapes. Managed by the same family for more than 40 years, it's a convenient, affordable place in a great location, although it's starting to need a little TLC.

Eating & Drinking

Local specialities include *risotto alla milanese* (saffron-infused risotto cooked in bone marrow stock) and *cotoletta alla milanese* (breaded veal cutlet).

Luini FAST FOOD €

(☎02 8646 1917; www.luini.it; Via Santa Radegonda 16; panzerotti €2.70; ⏰10am-3pm Mon, to 8pm Tue-Sat; 👪; Ⓜ Duomo) This historic joint is the go-to place for *panzerotti,* delicious pizza-dough parcels stuffed with a combination of mozzarella, spinach, tomato, ham or spicy salami, and then fried or baked in a wood-fired oven.

★**Un Posto a Milano** MODERN ITALIAN €€

(☎02 545 77 85; www.unpostoamilano.it; Via Cuccagna 2; meals €15-35; ⏰12.30-3pm & 7.30-11pm; 🌿👪; Ⓜ Porta Romana) A few years ago this country *cascina* (farmhouse) was a derelict ruin until a collection of cooperatives and cultural associations returned it to multi-functional use as restaurant, bar, social hub and hostel. Delicious salads, homemade foccacia, soups and snacks are served throughout the day at the bar, while the restaurant serves simple home cooking using locally sourced ingredients.

Trattoria Milanese MILANESE €€

(☎02 8645 1991; Via Santa Marta 11; meals €35-45; ⏰noon-2.45pm & 7-10.45pm Mon-Sat; 🚊2, 14) Like an old friend you haven't seen in years, this trattoria welcomes you with generous goblets of wine, hearty servings of traditional Milanese fare and convivial banter over the vegetable buffet. Regulars slide into their seats, barely needing to order as waiters bring them their usual: meatballs wrapped in cabbage, minestrone or the sinfully good *risotto al salto* (refried risotto).

BQ Navigli BAR

(Birra Artigianale di Qualità; ☎02 8940 3212; www.bqmilano.it; Alzaia Naviglio Grande 44; ⏰6pm-3am Wed-Fri, noon-3am Sat & Sun; Ⓜ Porta Genova) This Navigli canalside bar has a fine selection of craft beers, ranging from light lagers to robust hop-heavy bitters. Soak it all up with *panini* and *piadine* (stuffed pitta breads).

☆ Entertainment

Teatro alla Scala OPERA

(La Scala; ☎02 72 00 3744; www.teatroallascala.org; Piazza della Scala; tickets €30-300; Ⓜ Duomo) The opera season at La Scala, one of the most famous opera stages in the world, runs from early December through July. You can also see theatre, ballet and concerts here year-round (except August). Buy tickets online or by phone up to two months before the performance, or from the central box office. On performance days, tickets for the gallery are available from the box office at Via Filodrammatici 2 (one ticket per customer). Queue early.

San Siro Stadium FOOTBALL

(Stadio Giuseppe Meazza; ☎02 4879 8201; www.sansiro.net; Piazzale Angelo Moratti; tickets from €20; 👪; Ⓜ San Siro Stadio) San Siro Stadium wasn't designed to hold the entire population of Milan, but on a Sunday afternoon amid 80,000 football-mad citizens it can certainly feel like it. The city's two clubs, AC Milan and FC Internazionale Milano (aka Inter), play on alternate weeks from September to May.

Shopping

Beyond the hallowed streets of the Quadrilatero d'Oro, designer outlets and chains can be found along Corso Buenos Aires and Corso Vercelli; younger, hipper labels live along Via Brera and Corso Magenta; while Corso di Porta Ticinese and Navigli are home of the Milan street scene and subculture shops.

Peck FOOD & DRINKS
(02 802 31 61; www.peck.it; Via Spadari 9; 3-8pm Mon, 9am-8pm Tue-Sat, 10am-5pm Sun; ; M Duomo) Milan's historic deli is a bastion of the city's culinary heritage with three floors below ground dedicated to turning out the fabulously colourful display of foods that cram every counter. It showcases a mind-boggling selection of cheeses, chocolates, pralines, pastries, freshly made gelato, seafood, meat, caviar, pâté, fruit and vegetables, olive oils and balsamic vinegars.

Information

Farmacia Essere Benessere (02 669 07 35; 2nd fl, Stazione Centrale; 7am-10pm Mon-Thu, to 10.45pm Fri & Sat, 8am-10.45pm Sun; M Centrale FS) A well-stocked pharmacy with highly qualified staff and long opening hours located in the Central Station shopping arcade.

Milan Tourist Office (02 8845 5555; www.turismo.milano.it; Galleria Vittorio Emanuele II 11-12; 9am-7pm Mon-Fri, to 6pm Sat, 10am-6pm Sun; M Duomo) Centrally located in the Galleria with helpful English-speaking staff and tons of maps and brochures.

Getting There & Away

AIR

Aeroporto Linate (LIN; 02 23 23 23; www.milanolinate-airport.com) Located 7km east of Milan city centre; domestic and European flights only.

Aeroporto Malpensa (MXP; 02 23 23 23; www.milanomalpensa-airport.com; Malpensa Express) About 50km northwest of Milan city; northern Italy's main international airport.

Orio al Serio (035 32 63 23; www.sacbo.it) Low-cost carriers link Bergamo airport with a wide range of European cities. It has direct transport links to Milan.

TRAIN

Fast trains depart Stazione Centrale for Venice (€44, 2½ hours), Bologna (€34 to €84, one to two hours), Florence (€35 to €74, 1¾ hours), Rome (€89, three hours) and other Italian and European cities.

Most regional trains also stop at Stazione Nord in Piazzale Cadorna.

Getting Around

TO/FROM THE AIRPORT

Linate

Airport Bus Express (02 3391 0794; www.airportbusexpress.it; one way/return €5/9; M Centrale) The Autostradale express airport bus departs from Milan's Stazione Centrale for Linate airport every half-hour between 5.30am and 10pm. Buses from the airport to Milan run on the same schedule. Buses from Milan depart from Piazza Luigi di Savoia on the east side of the station. Tickets are sold on board.

Malpensa

Malpensa Shuttle (02 5858 3185; www.malpensashuttle.it; one way/return €10/16; M Centrale) This Malpensa airport shuttle runs at least half-hourly between 5.15am and 10.45pm from Stazione Centrale, and hourly throughout the rest of the night. The journey time is 50 minutes and buses depart from Piazza IV Novembre on the west side of the station. Terminal 2 stops need to be requested.

Malpensa Express (02 7249 4949; www.malpensaexpress.it; one way €13) Half-hourly trains run from Malpensa airport Terminal 1 to Cadorna Stazione Nord (40 minutes) and Stazione Centrale (60 minutes). Services to Cadorna run between 5.26am and 12.26am; to Stazione Centrale from 5.43am to 10.43pm. The train also serves Terminal 2.

Orio al Serio

Orio al Serio Bus Express (02 3008 9300; www.airportbusexpress.it; one way/return €5/9; M Centrale) This Autostradale service departs Piazza Luigi di Savoia at Stazione Centrale approximately every half-hour between 2.45am and 11.15pm, and from Orio al Serio airport between 7.45am and 11.15am. The journey takes one hour.

PUBLIC TRANSPORT

Milan's metro, buses and trams are run by **ATM** (Azienda Trasporti Milano; 02 4860 7607; www.atm.it). Tickets (€1.50) are valid for one underground ride and up to 90 minutes' travel on city buses and trams. A day ticket costs €4.50.

DON'T MISS

QUADRILATERO D'ORO

A stroll around the world's most famous shopping district, **Quadrilatero d'Oro** (Golden Quad; M Monte Napoleone), is a must. This quaintly cobbled quadrangle of streets – bounded by Via Monte Napoleone, Via Sant'Andrea, Via della Spiga and Via Alessandro Manzoni – has always been synonymous with elegance and money (Via Monte Napoleone was where Napoleon's government managed loans). Even if you don't have the slightest urge to buy, the window displays and people-watching are priceless.

The Lakes

Ringed by snowcapped mountains, gracious towns and landscaped gardens, the Italian lake district is an enchanting corner of the country.

Lago Maggiore

Snaking across the Swiss border, Lago Maggiore, the westernmost of the three main lakes, retains the belle époque air of its 19th-century heyday when it was a popular retreat for artists and writers.

Its headline sights are the Borromean islands, accessible from **Stresa** on the lake's western bank. **Isola Bella** is dominated by the 17th-century **Palazzo Borromeo** (☎0323 3 05 56; www.isoleborromee.it; adult/child €16/8.50, incl Palazzo Madre €21/10; ⌚9am-5.30pm mid-Mar–mid-Oct), a grand baroque palace with a wonderful art collection and beautiful tiered gardens. Over the water, **Palazzo Madre** (☎0323 3 05 56; www.isoleborromee.it; adult/child €13/6.50, incl Palazzo Borromeo €21/10; ⌚9am-5.30pm mid-Mar–mid-Oct) lords it over **Isola Madre**.

In Stresa's pedestrianised centre, **Piemontese** (☎0323 3 02 35; www.ristorantepiemontese.com; Via Mazzini 25; meals €40-55; ⌚noon-3pm & 7-11pm Tue-Sun) is a refined restaurant serving excellent regional cooking. Nearby, the **Hotel Saini Meublè** (☎0323 93 45 19; www.hotelsaini.it; Via Garibaldi 10; d €95-125, tr €130-160; 📶) has warm, spacious rooms.

For further information, contact Stresa's **tourist office** (☎0323 3 13 08; www.stresaturismo.it; Piazza Marconi 16; ⌚10am-12.30pm & 3-6.30pm summer, closed Sat pm & Sun winter).

ℹ Getting There & Around

The easiest way to get to Stresa is by train from Milan (€8.60 to €17, one hour, up to 20 daily).

Between April and September, **Saf** (☎0323 55 21 72; www.safduemila.com) operates an Alibus shuttle to/from Malpensa airport (€12, one hour, six daily).

Navigazione Lago Maggiore (☎800 551801; www.navigazionelaghi.it) operates ferries across the lake. From Stresa, a return ticket to Isola Bella costs €6.80, to Isola Madre €10.

Lago di Como

Lago di Como, overshadowed by steep wooded hills and snowcapped peaks, is the most spectacular and least visited of the lakes. At its southwestern tip, **Como** is a prosperous town with an imposing **Duomo** (Cattedrale di Como; ☎031 331 22 75; Piazza del Duomo; ⌚10.30am-5pm Mon-Sat, 1-4.30pm Sun) and a charming medieval core.

For lunch head to the characterful **Osteria del Gallo** (☎031 27 25 91; www.osteriadelgallo-como.it; Via Vitani 16; meals €26-32; ⌚12.30-3pm Mon, to 10pm Tue-Sat).

Also in the medieval centre, the modish **Avenue Hotel** (☎031 27 21 86; www.avenuehotel.it; Piazzolo Terragni 6; d €190-280, ste €280-310; P ❄ 📶) offers slick four-star accommodation.

You can get more information at the **tourist office** (☎342 0076403; www.visitcomo.eu; Como San Giovanni, Piazzale San Gottardo; ⌚9am-5pm summer, 10am-4pm Wed-Mon winter) at San Giovanni train station.

ℹ Getting There & Around

Regional trains run to Como San Giovanni from Milan's Stazione Centrale and Porta Garibaldi (€4.80, one hour, half-hourly).

Navigazione Lago di Como (☎800 551801; www.navigazionelaghi.it) operates year-round ferries from the jetty near Piazza Cavour.

Lago di Garda

The largest and most developed of the lakes, Lago di Garda straddles the border between Lombardy and the Veneto.

A good base is **Sirmione**, a picturesque village on its southern shores. Here you can investigate the **Grotte di Catullo** (☎030 91 61 57; www.grottedicatullo.beniculturali.it; Piazzale Orti Manara 4; adult/reduced €6/3; ⌚8.30am-7.30pm Tue-Sat & 9.30am-6.30pm Sun summer, 8.30am-5pm Tue-Sat & 8.30am-2pm Sun winter), a ruined Roman villa, and enjoy views over the lake's placid blue waters.

There are an inordinate number of eateries crammed into Sirmione's historic centre. One of the best is **La Fiasca** (☎030 990 61 11; www.trattorialafiasca.it; Via Santa Maria Maggiore 11; meals €30-35; ⌚noon-2.30pm & 7-10.30pm Thu-Tue), an authentic trattoria serving flavoursome lake fish.

Sirmione can be visited on a day trip from Verona, but if you want to overnight, **Grifone** (☎030 91 60 14; www.gardalakegrifonehotel.eu; Via Gaetano Bocchio 4; s €50-80, d €70-110) boasts a superb lakeside location and relaxing views.

Get information from the **tourist office** (☎030 91 61 14; iat.sirmione@provincia.brescia.it; Viale Marconi 8; ⌚10am-12.30pm & 3-6.30pm daily summer, 10am-12.30pm & 3-6pm Mon-Fri, 9.30am-12.30pm Sat winter) outside the medieval walls.

Getting There & Around

Regular buses run to Sirmione from Verona (€3.50, one hour, hourly).

Navigazione Lago di Garda (030 914 9511; www.navigazionelaghi.it) operates the lake's ferries.

Verona

POP 258,800

Wander Verona's atmospheric streets and you'll understand why Shakespeare set *Romeo and Juliet* here – this is one of Italy's most beautiful and romantic cities. Known as *piccola Roma* (little Rome) for its importance in ancient times, its heyday came in the 13th and 14th centuries when it was ruled by the Della Scala (aka Scaligeri) family, who built *palazzi* and bridges, sponsored Giotto, Dante and Petrarch, oppressed their subjects, and feuded with everyone else.

Sights

Roman Arena RUINS

(045 800 32 04; Piazza Brà; adult/reduced €10/7.50; 8.30am-7.30pm Tue-Sun, from 1.30pm Mon) Built of pink-tinged marble in the 1st century AD, Verona's Roman amphitheatre survived a 12th-century earthquake to become the city's legendary open-air opera house, with seating for 30,000 people. You can visit the arena year-round, though it's at its best during the summer opera festival. In winter months, concerts are held at the **Teatro Filarmonico** (045 800 28 80; www.arena.it; Via dei Mutilati 4; opera €23-60, concerts €25-50). From January to May and October to December, admission is €1 on the first Sunday of the month.

Casa di Giulietta NOTABLE BUILDING

(Juliet's House; 045 803 43 03; Via Cappello 23; adult/reduced €6/4.50, free with VeronaCard; 1.30-7.30pm Mon, 8.30am-7.30pm Tue-Sun) Never mind that Romeo and Juliet were completely fictional characters, and that there's hardly room for two on the narrow stone balcony: romantics flock to this 14th-century house to add their lovelorn pleas to the sea of sticky notes lining the courtyard gateway. In truth, Juliet's House is altogether underwhelming, so consider a free glance from the courtyard and search for your Romeo elsewhere.

★ **Basilica di Sant'Anastasia** BASILICA

(www.chieseverona.it; Piazza di Sant'Anastasia; €2.50; 9am-6pm Mon-Sat, 1-6pm Sun Mar-Oct, 10am-1pm & 1.30-5pm Mon-Sat, 1-5pm Sun Nov-Feb) Dating from the 13th to 15th centuries and featuring an elegantly decorated vaulted ceiling, the Gothic Sant'Anastasia is Verona's largest church and a showcase for local art. The multitude of frescoes is overwhelming, but don't overlook Pisanello's story-book-quality fresco *St George and the Princess* above the entrance to the **Pellegrini Chapel**, or the 1495 holy water font featuring a hunchback carved by Paolo Veronese's father, Gabriele Caliari.

Sleeping & Eating

★ **Corte delle Pigne** B&B €€

(333 7584141; www.cortedellepigne.it; Via Pigna 6a; s €60-110, d €90-150, tr €110-170, q €130-190; P) In the heart of the historic centre, this three-room B&B is set around a quiet internal courtyard. It offers tasteful rooms and plenty of personal touches: sweet jars, luxury toiletries and even a Jacuzzi for one lucky couple.

Hotel Aurora HOTEL €€

(045 59 47 17; www.hotelaurora.biz; Piazzetta XIV Novembre 2; d €110-280, tr €130-300;) Overlooking Piazza delle Erbe, friendly Aurora offers smart rooms, some with piazza views and all with classic wooden furniture and fresh, modern bathrooms. The open-air terrace makes for a perfect spot to enjoy breakfast or a lazy sundowner.

★ **Locanda 4 Cuochi** MODERN ITALIAN €€

(045 803 03 11; www.locanda4cuochi.it; Via Alberto Mario 12; meals €40, 3-course set menu €25; 12.30-2.30pm & 7.30-10.30pm, closed lunch Mon-Wed;) With its open kitchen, urbane vibe and hotshot chefs, you're right to expect great things from the Locanda. Culinary acrobatics play second fiddle to prime produce cooked with skill and subtle twists. Whether it's perfectly crisp suckling pig lacquered with liquorice, or an epilogue of *gianduia* ganache with sesame crumble and banana, expect to swoon.

La Taverna di Via Stella VENETO €€

(045 800 80 08; www.tavernadiviastella.com; Via Stella 5c; meals €30-35; 12.15-2.30pm & 7.15-11pm, closed Wed & Mon evening) Brush past the haunches of prosciutto dangling over the deli bar and make your way into the dining room, decorated Tiepolo-style with rustic murals of chivalric knights and maidens. This is the place you'll want to sample traditional Veronese dishes such as *pastissada*

(horse stew), *bigoli* with duck *ragù* and DOP Lessinia cheeses from Monte Veronese. Cash only for bills under €30.

☆ Entertainment

Performances during the summer opera festival are held at the **Roman Arena** (☎045 800 51 51; www.arena.it; box office Via Dietro Anfiteatro 6b; opera tickets €22-200; ⊙box office 9am-noon Mon-Sat & 3.15-5.45pm Mon-Fri, longer hours during opera festival).

ℹ Information

Tourist Office (☎045 806 86 80; www.tourism.verona.it; Via degli Alpini 9; ⊙10am-7pm Mon-Sat, to 3pm Sun) Just off Piazza Brà. Knowledgeable and helpful.

ℹ Getting There & Around

Verona-Villafranca airport (☎045 809 56 66; www.aeroportoverona.it) is 12km outside town and accessible by ATV Aerobus to/from the train station (€6, 15 minutes, every 20 minutes 5.35am to 11.10pm).

From the station, buses 11, 12 and 13 (90, 96, 97 and 98 evenings and Sundays) run to Piazza Brà.

Trains connect with Milan (€12 to €64, one hour 20 minutes to two hours, up to three hourly), Venice (€9 to €26, 50 minutes to 2¼ hours, twice hourly) and Bologna (€10 to €24, 50 minutes to 1½ hours, 20 daily).

Venice

POP 263,300

Venice (Venezia) is a hauntingly beautiful city. At every turn you're assailed by unforgettable images – tiny bridges arching over limpid canals; chintzy gondolas sliding past working barges; towers and distant domes silhouetted against the watery horizon. Its celebrated sights are legion, and its labyrinthine alleyways exude a unique, almost eerie atmosphere, redolent of cloaked passions and dark secrets. Many of the city's treasures date to its time as a powerful medieval republic known as La Serenissima.

ℹ NAVIGATING VENICE

Venice is not an easy place to navigate and even with a smartphone and satellite mapping you're bound to get lost. The main area of interest lies between Santa Lucia train station (signposted as the *ferrovia*) and Piazza San Marco (St Mark's Sq). The path between the two – Venice's main drag – is a good 40- to 50-minute walk. It also helps to know that the city is divided into six *sestieri* (districts): Cannaregio, Castello, San Marco, Dorsoduro, San Polo and Santa Croce.

Sights

San Marco

★Basilica di San Marco CATHEDRAL

(St Mark's Basilica; Map p454; ☎041 270 83 11; www.basilicasanmarco.it; Piazza San Marco; ⊙9.45am-5pm Mon-Sat, 2-5pm Sun summer, to 4pm Sun winter; San Marco) FREE With its Byzantine domes and 8500 sq metres of luminous mosaics, Venice's basilica is an unforgettable sight. It dates to the 9th century when, according to legend, two merchants smuggled the corpse of St Mark out of Egypt in a barrel of pork fat. When the original burnt down in 932 Venice rebuilt the basilica in its own cosmopolitan image, with Byzantine domes, a Greek cross layout and walls clad in marbles from Syria, Egypt and Palestine.

Campanile TOWER

(Bell Tower; Map p454; www.basilicasanmarco.it; Piazza San Marco; adult/reduced €8/4; ⊙8.30am-9.30pm summer, 9.30am-5.30pm winter, last entry 45min prior; San Marco) The basilica's 99m-tall bell tower has been rebuilt twice since its initial construction in AD 888. Galileo Galilei tested his telescope here in 1609, but modern-day visitors head to the top for 360-degree lagoon views and close encounters with the Marangona, the booming bronze bell that originally signalled the start and end of the working day for the craftsmen *(marangoni)* at the Arsenale shipyards. Today it rings twice a day, at noon and midnight.

★Palazzo Ducale MUSEUM

(Ducal Palace; Map p454; ☎041 271 59 11; www.palazzoducale.visitmuve.it; Piazzetta San Marco 1; adult/reduced incl Museo Correr €19/12, or with Museum Pass; ⊙8.30am-7pm Apr-Oct, to 5.30pm Nov-Mar; San Zaccaria) This grand Gothic palace was the Doge's official residence from the 9th century, and seat of the Venetian Republic's government (and prisons) for nearly seven centuries. The Doge's Apartments are on the 1st floor, but it's the lavishly decorated 2nd-floor chambers that are the real highlight. These culminate in the echoing **Sala del Maggior Consiglio** (Grand Council Hall), home to the Doge's

Greater Venice

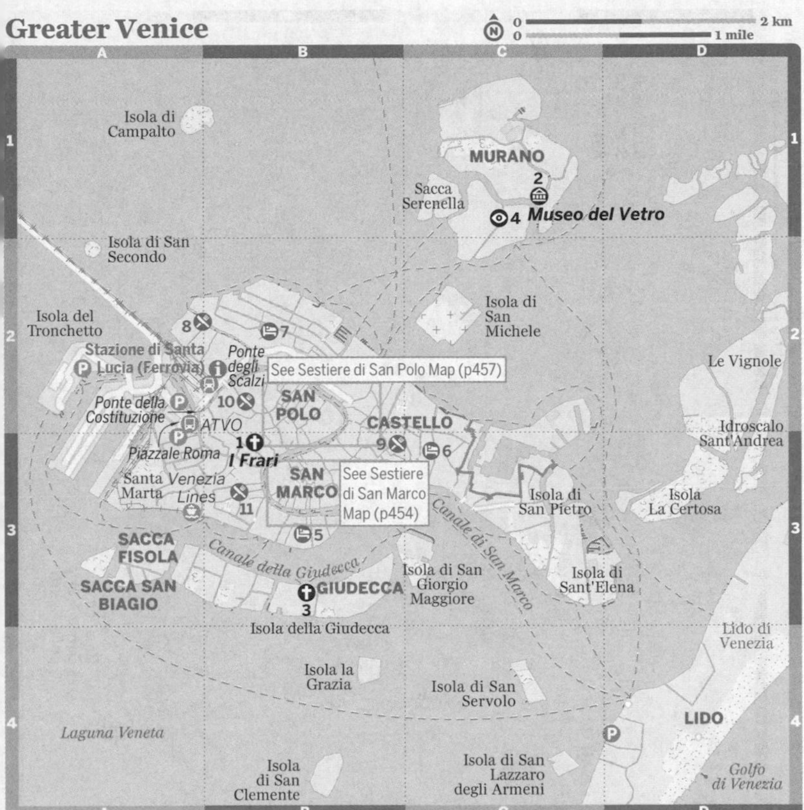

throne and a 22m-by-7m *Paradise* painting by Tintoretto's son Domenico.

Ponte dei Sospiri BRIDGE
(Bridge of Sighs; Map p454; San Zaccaria) One of Venice's most photographed sights, the Bridge of Sighs connects Palazzo Ducale to the 16th-century Priggione Nove (New Prisons). It's named after the sighs that condemned prisoners – including Giacomo Casanova – emitted as they were led down to the cells.

Dorsoduro

★ Gallerie dell'Accademia GALLERY
(Map p454; 041 520 03 45; www.gallerieaccademia.org; Campo della Carità 1050, Dorsoduro; adult/reduced €12/6, 1st Sun of month free; 8.15am-2pm Mon, to 7.15pm Tue-Sun; Accademia) Venice's historic gallery traces the development of Venetian art from the 14th to 18th centuries, with works by Bellini, Titian, Tintoretto, Veronese and Canaletto among others. The former Santa Maria della Carità

Greater Venice

Top Sights
1 I Frari B3
2 Museo del Vetro C1

Sights
3 Chiesa del Santissimo Redentore B3
4 Murano C1

Sleeping
5 B&B Corte Vecchia B3
6 B&B San Marco C3
7 Giardino dei Melograni B2

Eating
8 Dalla Marisa A2
9 Osteria Ruga di Jaffa B3
10 Osteria Trefanti B2
11 Ristorante La Bitta B3

Sestiere di San Marco

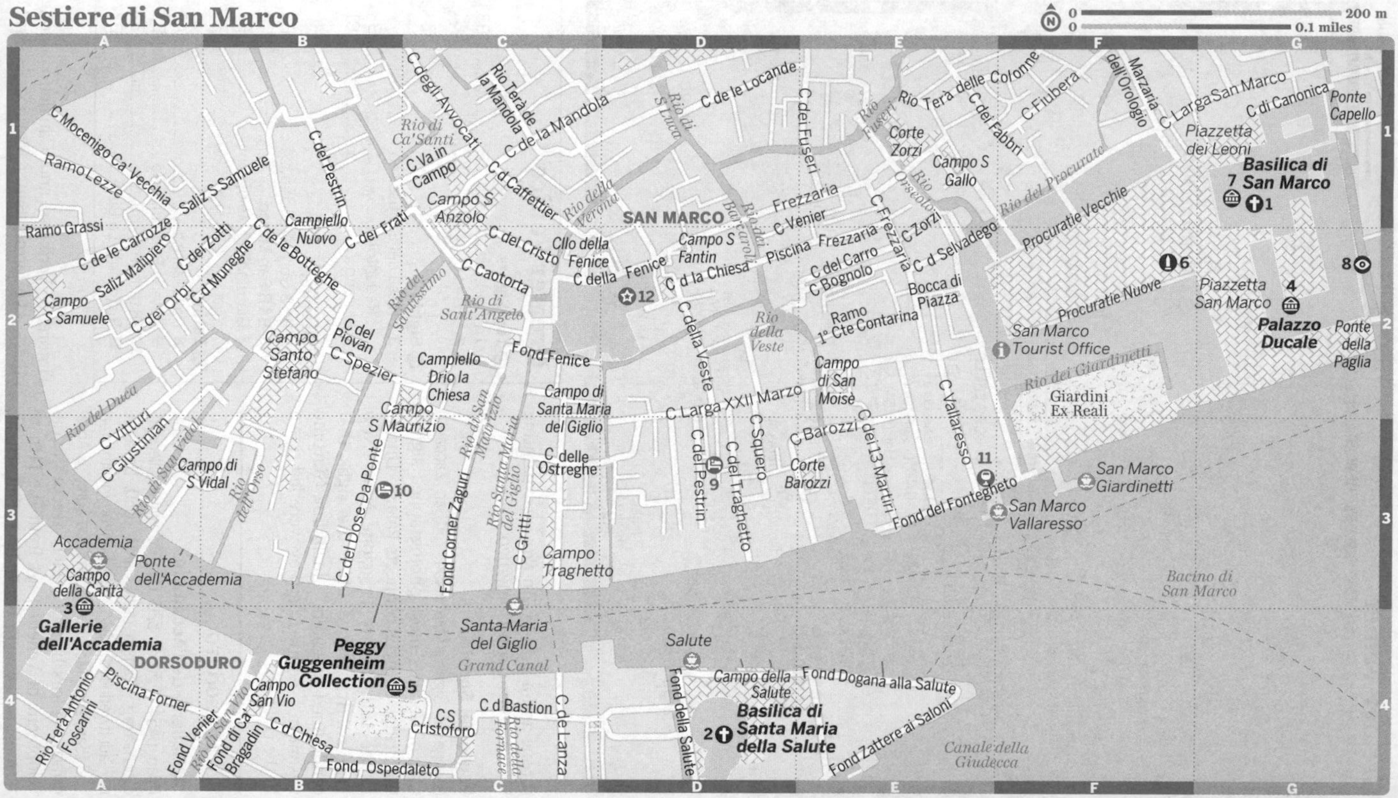

0 200 m
0 0.1 miles

SAN MARCO
DORSODURO
Basilica di San Marco
Palazzo Ducale
Basilica di Santa Maria della Salute
Gallerie dell'Accademia
Peggy Guggenheim Collection
San Marco Tourist Office
Giardini Ex Reali
Grand Canal
Bacino di San Marco
Canale della Giudecca
San Marco Giardinetti
San Marco Vallaresso
Santa Maria del Giglio
Salute
Accademia
Ponte dell'Accademia
Ponte Capello
Ponte della Paglia
Piazzetta dei Leoni
Piazzetta San Marco
Procuratie Vecchie
Procuratie Nuove
Marzaria dell'Orologio
C Larga San Marco
C di Canonica
Rio Terà delle Colonne
C dei Fabbri
C Fiubera
Corte Zorzi
Campo S Gallo
Rio Orseolo
Rio Fuseri
Rio del Procurate
Rio dei Giardinetti
C dei Fuseri
C de le Locande
Rio di S Luca
Rio dei Barcaroli
Frezzaria
C Venier
Campo S Fantin
Piscina Frezzaria
C Frezzaria
C Zorzi
C d Selvadego
C del Carro
C Bognolo
Bocca di Piazza
Ramo 1° Cte Contarina
C della Fenice
C d la Chiesa
Cllo della Fenice
C della Veste
Rio della Veste
Campo di San Moisè
C Vallaresso
C Larga XXII Marzo
C Barozzi
C dei 13 Martiri
Corte Barozzi
C Squero
C del Traghetto
C del Pestrin
Fond del Fontegheto
Rio della Verona
C degli Avvocati
Rio Terà de la Mandola
C de la Mandola
Rio di Ca'Santi
C Va in Campo
C d Caffettier
Campo S Anzolo
C del Cristo
C Caotorta
Rio di Sant'Angelo
Rio del Santissimo
Fond Fenice
Campiello Drio la Chiesa
Campo di Santa Maria del Giglio
C delle Ostreghe
Campo Traghetto
C Gritti
Rio Santa Maria del Giglio
Rio di San Maurizio
Fond Corner Zaguri
Campo S Maurizio
C del Dose Da Ponte
C del Piovan
C Spezier
Campo Santo Stefano
C del Pestrin
Campiello Nuovo
C dei Frati
C de le Botteghe
C d Muneghe
C dei Zotti
C dei Orbi
Saliz Malipiero
C de le Carrozze
Saliz S Samuele
C Mocenigo Ca' Vecchia
Ramo Lezze
Ramo Grassi
Campo S Samuele
Rio del Duca
C Vitturi
C Giustinian
Rio di San Vidal
Campo di S Vidal
Rio dell'Orso
Campo della Carità
Rio Terà Antonio Foscarini
Piscina Forner
Fond Venier
Rio di San Vio
Fond di Ca' Bragadin
Campo San Vio
C d Chiesa
Fond Ospedaleto
CS Cristoforo
C d Bastion
Rio della Fornace
C de Lanza
Fond della Salute
Campo della Salute
Fond Dogana alla Salute
Fond Zattere ai Saloni

1 Basilica di San Marco
2 Basilica di Santa Maria della Salute
3 Gallerie dell'Accademia
4 Palazzo Ducale
5 Peggy Guggenheim Collection
6
7
8
9
10
11
12

Sestiere di San Marco

Top Sights

1 Basilica di San Marco............................G1
2 Basilica di Santa Maria della Salute............................D4
3 Gallerie dell'Accademia............................A4
4 Palazzo Ducale............................G2
5 Peggy Guggenheim Collection............................B4

Sights

6 Campanile............................F2
7 Museo di San Marco............................G1
8 Ponte dei Sospiri............................G2

Sleeping

9 Hotel Flora............................D3
10 Novecento............................B3

Drinking & Nightlife

11 Harry's Bar............................E3

Entertainment

12 La Fenice............................D2

convent complex housing the collection maintained its serene composure for centuries until Napoleon installed his haul of Venetian art trophies here in 1807. Since then there's been nonstop visual drama inside its walls.

★**Peggy Guggenheim Collection** MUSEUM
(Map p454; 041 240 54 11; www.guggenheim-venice.it; Palazzo Venier dei Leoni 704, Dorsoduro; adult/reduced €15/9; 10am-6pm Wed-Mon; Accademia) After losing her father on the *Titanic,* heiress Peggy Guggenheim became one of the great collectors of the 20th century. Her palatial canalside home, Palazzo Venier dei Leoni, showcases her stockpile of surrealist, futurist and abstract expressionist art with works by up to 200 artists, including her ex-husband Max Ernst, Jackson Pollock (among her many rumoured lovers), Picasso and Salvador Dalí.

★**Basilica di Santa Maria della Salute** BASILICA
(La Salute; Map p454; www.basilicasalutevenezia.it; Campo della Salute 1b, Dorsoduro; basilica free, sacristy adult/reduced €4/2; basilica 9.30am-noon & 3-5.30pm, sacristry 10am-noon & 3-5pm Mon-Sat, 3-5pm Sun; Salute) Guarding the entrance to the Grand Canal, this 17th-century domed church was commissioned by Venice's plague survivors as thanks for their salvation. Baldassare Longhena's uplifting design is an engineering feat that defies simple logic; in fact the church is said to have mystical curative properties. Titian eluded the plague until age 94, leaving 12 key paintings in the basilica's art-slung sacristy.

San Polo & Santa Croce

★**I Frari** CHURCH
(Basilica di Santa Maria Gloriosa dei Frari; Map p453; 041 272 86 18; www.basilicadeifrari.it; Campo dei Frari 3072, San Polo; adult/reduced €3/1.50; 9am-6pm Mon-Sat, 1-6pm Sun; San Tomà) A soaring Italian-brick Gothic church, I Frari's assets include marquetry choir stalls, Canova's pyramid mausoleum, Bellini's achingly sweet *Madonna with Child* triptych in the sacristy and Longhena's creepy Doge Pesaro funereal monument. Upstaging them all, however, is the small altarpiece. This is Titian's lauded 1518 *Assunta* (Assumption), in which a radiant red-cloaked Madonna reaches heavenward, steps onto a cloud and escapes this mortal coil. Titian himself – lost to the plague in 1576 at the age 94 – is buried here near his celebrated masterpiece.

Giudecca

Chiesa del Santissimo Redentore CHURCH
(Church of the Most Holy Redeemer; Map p453; www.chorusvenezia.org; Campo del SS Redentore 194, Giudecca; adult/reduced €3/1.50, with Chorus Pass free; 10.30am-4.30pm Mon-Sat; Redentore) Built to celebrate the city's deliverance from the Black Death, Palladio's Il Redentore was completed under Antonio da Ponte (of Rialto bridge fame) in 1592. Inside there are works by Tintoretto, Veronese and Vivarini, but the most striking is Paolo Piazza's 1619 *Gratitude of Venice for Liberation from the Plague.*

The Islands

Murano ISLAND
(Map p453; Faro) Murano has been the home of Venetian glass-making since the 13th century. Today, artisans ply their trade at workshops along **Fondamenta dei Vetrai**.

To learn about local manufacturing traditions and enjoy a collection of historic glassware, visit the **Museo del Vetro** (Glass Museum; Map p453; 041 527 47 18; www.museovetro.visitmuve.it; Fondamenta Giustinian 8, Murano; adult/reduced €10/7.50, free with Museum Pass; 10am-5pm; Museo) near the Museo *vaporetto* stop.

Sestiere di San Polo

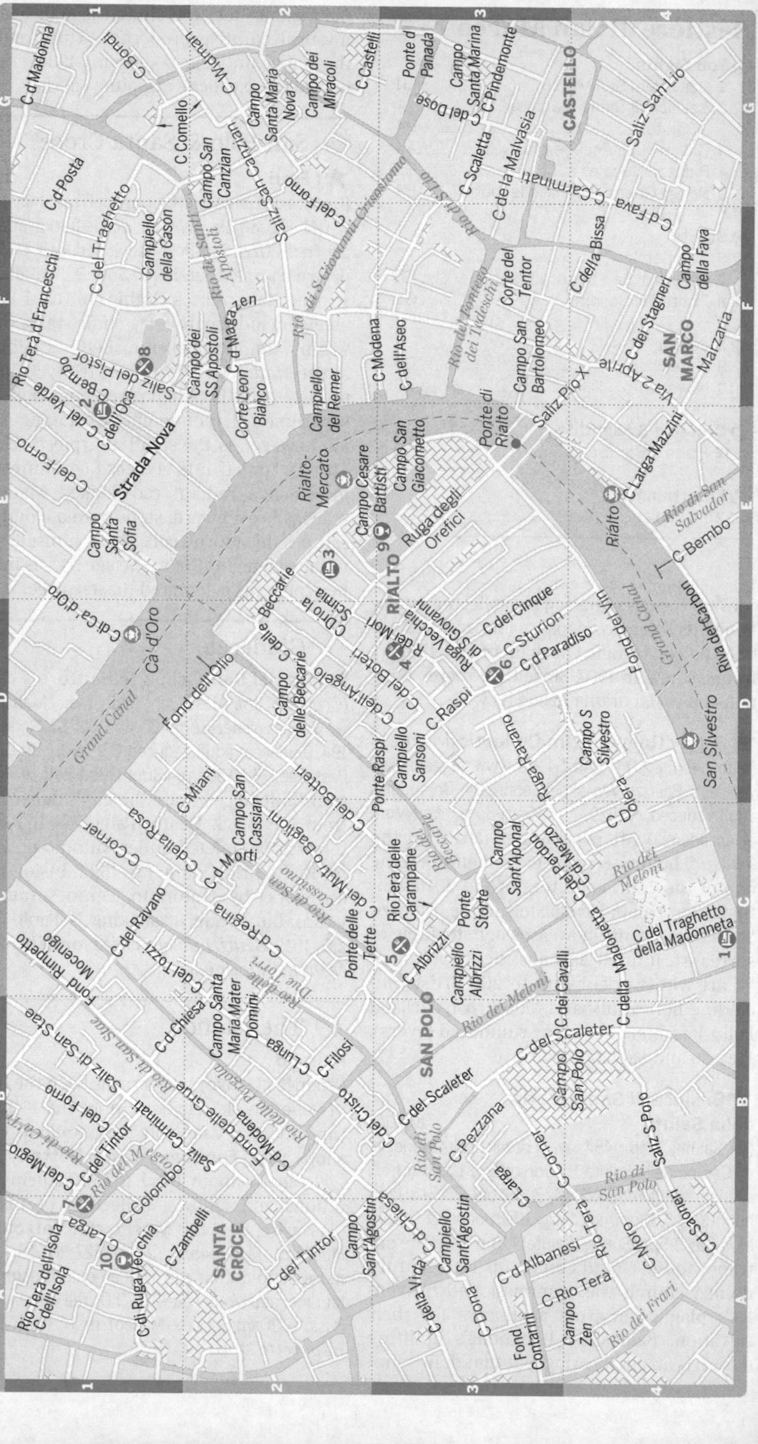

Sestiere di San Polo

Sleeping

1 Ca' Angeli.........C4
2 Hotel Bernardi.........E1
3 Pensione Guerrato.........E2

Eating

4 All'Arco.........D3
5 Antiche Carampane.........C3
6 Dai Zemei.........D3
7 Osteria La Zucca.........A1
8 Trattoria da Bepi Già "54".........F1

Drinking & Nightlife

9 Al Mercà.........E3
10 Al Prosecco.........A1

Burano ISLAND

(Burano) Burano, with its cheery pastel-coloured houses, is renowned for its handmade lace, which once graced the décolletage and ruffs of European aristocracy. These days, however, much of the lace sold in local shops is imported.

Torcello ISLAND

(Torcello) Torcello, the republic's original island settlement, was largely abandoned due to malaria and now counts no more than 10 permanent residents. Its mosaic-clad Byzantine cathedral, the **Basilica di Santa Maria Assunta** (041 73 01 19; Piazza Torcello; adult/reduced €5/4, incl museum €8/6, incl museum, audio guide & campanile €12/10; 10am-5pm), is Venice's oldest.

Activities

Official gondola rates are €80 for 30 minutes (it's €100 for 35 minutes from 7pm to 8am) for up to six people. Additional time is charged in 20-minute increments (day/night €40/50).

Festivals & Events

Carnevale CARNIVAL

(www.carnevale.venezia.it; Feb) Masquerade madness stretches over two weeks in February before Lent. A Grand Canal flotilla marks the outbreak of festivities which feature masked balls, processions, public parties in every *campo* (square), and all manner of dressing up.

Venice Biennale ART

(www.labiennale.org; Giardini della Biennale; mid-May–Nov; Giardini Biennale) Europe's premier arts showcase since 1907 is something of a misnomer: the Venice Biennale is actually held every year, but the spotlight alternates between art (odd-numbered years) and architecture (even-numbered years).

Festa del Redentore RELIGIOUS

(Feast of the Redeemer; http://events.veneziaunica.it; Jul) Walk on water across the Giudecca Canal to Il Redentore via a wobbly pontoon bridge on the third Saturday and Sunday in July, then watch the fireworks from the Zattere.

Venice International Film Festival FILM

(Mostra Internazionale d'Arte Cinematografica; www.labiennale.org/en/cinema; Lido; Aug-Sep) The only thing hotter than a Lido beach in August is the film festival's star-studded red carpet, usually rolled out from the last weekend in August through the first week of September.

Regata Storica CULTURAL

(www.regatastoricavenezia.it; Sep) Sixteenth-century costumes, eight-oared gondolas and ceremonial barques feature in this historical procession (usually held in early September) along the Grand Canal, which re-enacts the arrival of the Queen of Cyprus and precedes gondola races.

Sleeping

San Marco

★Hotel Flora HOTEL €€

(Map p454; 041 520 58 44; www.hotelflora.it; Calle dei Bergamaschi 2283a; s/d from €134/151; ; Giglio) Down a lane from glitzy Calle Larga XXII Marzo, this ivy-covered retreat quietly outclasses brash designer neighbours with its delightful tearoom and breakfasts around the garden fountain. Guest rooms feature antique mirrors, fluffy duvets atop hand-carved beds, and tiled en-suite bathrooms with apothecary-style amenities. Damask-clad superior rooms overlook the garden. Strollers and kids' teatime are complimentary; babysitting available.

★Novecento BOUTIQUE HOTEL €€€

(Map p454; 041 241 37 65; www.novecento.biz; Calle del Dose 2683/84; r from €200; ; Giglio) Sporting a boho-chic look, the Novecento is a real charmer. Its nine individually designed rooms ooze style with Turkish kilim pillows, Fortuny draperies and 19th-century carved bedsteads. You can mingle with creative fellow travellers around the

VENICE DISCOUNT PASSES

Civic Museum Pass (www.visitmuve.it; adult/reduced €24/18) Valid for single entry to 11 civic museums, or just the four museums around Piazza San Marco (€19/12). Buy online or at participating museums.

Chorus Pass (www.chorusvenezia.org; adult/reduced €12/8) Covers admission to 16 churches. Buy at participating sites.

VeneziaUnica (www.veneziaunica.it) A universal pass covering museum admission, transport, wi-fi and more. There's no standard pass; instead you tailor it to your needs and pay according to the services you include on it. See the website for details.

honesty bar, while outside, its garden is a lovely spot to linger over breakfast.

Dorsoduro

★B&B Corte Vecchia B&B €€
(Map p453; ☎335 7449238; www.cortevecchia.net; Rio Terà San Vio 462, Dorsoduro; s €60-80, d €100-130; ❄📶; 🚢Accademia) Corte Vecchia is a stylish steal, run by young architects Antonella and Mauro and a stone's throw from Peggy Guggenheim, Accademia and Punta della Dogana. Choose from a snug single with en suite, or two good-sized doubles: one with en suite, the other with an external private bathroom. All are simple yet understatedly cool, with contemporary and vintage objects, and a tranquil, shared lounge.

San Polo & Santa Croce

Ca' Angeli BOUTIQUE HOTEL €€
(Map p456; ☎041 523 24 80; www.caangeli.it; Calle del Traghetto de la Madoneta 1434, San Polo; d €165-240; ❄📶; 🚢San Silvestro) Murano glass chandeliers, a Louis XIV love-seat and namesake 16th-century angels set a refined tone at this restored, canalside *palazzo*. Guest rooms are a picture with beamed ceilings, antique carpets and big bathrooms, while the dining room looks out onto the Grand Canal. Breakfast includes organic products where possible.

Pensione Guerrato PENSION €€
(Map p456; ☎041 528 59 27; http://hotelguerrato.com; Calle Drio la Scimia 240a, San Polo; d/tr/q €145/165/185, apt €160-280; ❄📶; 🚢Rialto-Mercato) In a 1227 tower that was once a hostel for knights headed to the Third Crusade, the smart guestrooms here haven't lost their sense of history – some have frescoes or glimpses of the Grand Canal. Sparkling modern bathrooms, a prime Rialto Market location and helpful owners add to the package. No lift.

Cannaregio

Hotel Bernardi HOTEL €€
(Map p456; ☎041 522 72 57; www.hotelbernardi.com; SS Apostoli Calle de l'Oca 4366; s/d from €80/110, without bathroom from €32/65; ❄📶; 🚢Ca' d'Oro) Hospitable owners, a convenient location just off the main thoroughfare, and keen prices mean that the Bernardi is always heavily booked. Some of the best rooms – think timber-beamed ceilings, Murano chandeliers and gilt furniture – are in the annexe round the corner.

Giardino dei Melograni HOTEL €€
(Map p453; ☎041 822 61 31; www.pardesrimonim.net; Campo del Ghetto Nuovo 2874; s €80-150, d €100-200; ❄📶; 🚢Guglie) Run by Venice's Jewish community, to which all proceeds go, the 'Garden of Pomegranates' is a sparkling kosher residence. It's located on the charming Campo Ghetto Nuovo just a short walk from the train station, and offers 14 bright modern rooms.

Castello

★B&B San Marco B&B €
(Map p453; ☎041 522 75 89; www.realvenice.it; Fondamente San Giorgio dei Schiavoni 3385l; r with/without bathroom €135/105; ❄; 🚢San Zaccaria) One of the few genuine B&Bs in Venice. Alice and Marco welcome you warmly to their home overlooking Carpaccio's frescoed Scuola di San Giorgio Schiavoni. The 3rd-floor apartment (no lift), with its parquet floors and large windows, is furnished with family antiques and offers photogenic views over the terracotta rooftops and canals. Marco and Alice live upstairs, so they're always on hand with great recommendations.

Eating

Dorsoduro

★Ristorante La Bitta RISTORANTE €€
(Map p453; ☎041 523 05 31; Calle Lunga San Barnaba 2753a, Dorsoduro; meals €35-40; ⌚6.30-11pm

Mon-Sat; Ca' Rezzonico) Recalling a cosy, woody bistro, La Bitta keeps punters purring with hearty rustic fare made using the freshest ingredients – no fish, just meat and seasonal veggies. Scan the daily menu for mouthwatering options like tagliatelle with artichoke thistle and Gorgonzola, or juicy pork *salsiccette* (small sausages) served with *verze* (local cabbage) and warming polenta. Reservations essential. Cash only.

San Polo & Santa Croce

★ Antiche Carampane VENETIAN €€€
(Map p456; 041 524 01 65; www.antiche carampane.com; Rio Terà delle Carampane 1911, San Polo; meals €50; 12.45-2.30pm & 7.30-10.30pm Tue-Sat; San Stae) Hidden in the once-shady lanes behind Ponte delle Tette, this culinary indulgence is a trick to find. Once you do, say goodbye to soggy lasagne and hello to a market-driven menu of silky *crudi* (raw fish/seafood), surprisingly light *fritto misto* (fried seafood) and *caramote* prawn salad with seasonal vegetables. Never short of a smart, convivial crowd; it's a good idea to book ahead.

★ Osteria Trefanti VENETIAN €€
(Map p453; 041 520 17 89; www.osteriatrefanti.it; Fondamenta Garzotti 888, Santa Croce; meals €40; noon-2.30pm & 7-10.30pm Tue-Sun; Riva de Biasio) La Serenissima's spice trade lives on at simple, elegant Trefanti, where a dish of marinated prawns, hazelnuts, berries and caramel might get an intriguing kick from garam masala. Furnished with old pews and recycled copper lamps, it's the domain of the competent Sam Metcalfe and Umberto Slongo, whose passion for quality extends to a small, beautifully curated selection of local and organic wines.

Osteria La Zucca MODERN ITALIAN €€
(Map p456; 041 524 15 70; www.lazucca.it; Calle del Tentor 1762, Santa Croce; meals €35-40; 12.30-2.30pm & 7-10.30pm Mon-Sat; San Stae) With its menu of seasonal vegetarian creations and classic meat dishes, this cosy, woody restaurant consistently hits the mark. Herbs and spices are used to great effect in dishes such as cinnamon-tinged pumpkin flan and chicken curry with yoghurt, lentils and rice. The small interior can get toasty, so reserve canalside seats in summer.

Cannaregio

★ Dalla Marisa VENETIAN €€
(Map p453; 041 72 02 11; Fondamenta di San Giobbe 692b; set menu lunch €15, dinner €35-40; noon-2.15pm daily, 8-11pm Wed-Sat; Crea) At this Cannaregio institution, you'll be seated where there's room and get no menu – you'll have whatever Marisa's cooking. And you'll like it. Lunches are a bargain at €15 for a first, main, side, wine, water and coffee – pace yourself through prawn risotto to finish with steak and grilled zucchini.

Trattoria da Bepi Già "54" VENETIAN €€
(Map p456; 041 528 50 31; www.dabepi.it; Campo SS Apostoli 4550; meals €24-37; noon-3pm & 7-10pm Fri-Wed; Ca' d'Oro) Da Bepi is a traditional trattoria in the very best sense. The interior is a warm, wood-panelled cocoon, and the service is efficient and friendly: host

LOCAL KNOWLEDGE

CICHETI

Venice's answer to tapas, *cicheti* are served at lunch and from around 6pm to 8pm with sensational Veneto wines by the glass. They range from basic bar snacks (spicy meatballs, fresh tomato and basil bruschetta) to highly inventive small plates: think white Bassano asparagus and shrimp wrapped in pancetta at **All'Arco** (Map p456; 041 520 56 66; Calle dell'Ochialer 436, San Polo; cicheti from €2; 8am-2.30pm Mon, Tue & Sat, to 7pm Wed-Fri summer, 8am-2.30pm Mon-Sat winter; Rialto-Mercato); Gorgonzola paired with *peperoncino* (chilli) jam at **Dai Zemei** (Map p456; 041 520 85 96; www.ostariadaizemei.it; Ruga Vecchia San Giovanni 1045, San Polo; cicheti from €1.50; 8.30am-8.30pm Mon-Sat, 9am-7pm Sun; San Silvestro); or bite-sized rolls crammed with tuna, chicory and horseradish at **Al Mercà** (Map p456; 346 8340660; Campo Cesare Battisti 213, San Polo; 10am-2.30pm & 6-8pm Mon-Thu, to 9.30pm Fri & Sat; Rialto-Mercato).

Prices start at €1 for meatballs and range from €3 to €6 for gourmet fantasias, typically devoured standing up or perched atop stools at the bar.

Loris has been welcoming loyal locals and curious culinary travellers for years. Take their advice on the classic Venetian menu and order *spaghetti col nero di seppia* (with cuttlefish ink), grilled turbot and a tiramisu that doesn't disappoint.

Castello

★ Osteria Ruga di Jaffa OSTERIA €€
(Map p453; ☎041 241 10 62; www.osteriaruga-dijaffa.it; Ruga Giuffa 4864; meals €29-41; ⏲7am-11pm; San Zaccaria) Hiding in plain sight on the busy Ruga Giuffa is this excellent *osteria* (casual tavern) with artsy Murano wall lamps. You should be able to spot it by the *gondolieri* packing out the tables at lunchtime; they come to feast on the select menu of housemade pastas and succulent roast pork soaked in its own savoury juices.

Drinking & Nightlife

★ Al Prosecco WINE BAR
(Map p456; ☎041 524 02 22; www.alprosecco.com; Campo San Giacomo dell'Orio 1503, Santa Croce; ⏲10am-8pm Mon-Fri, to 5pm Sat Nov-Mar, to 10.30pm Apr-Oct; San Stae) The urge to toast sunsets in Venice's loveliest *campo* is only natural – and so is the wine at Al Prosecco. This forward-thinking bar specialises in *vini naturi* (natural-process wines) – organic, biodynamic, wild-yeast fermented – from enlightened Italian winemakers like Cinque Campi and Azienda Agricola Barichel. So order a glass of unfiltered 'cloudy' *prosecco* and toast to the good things in life.

★ Timon WINE BAR
(☎041 524 60 66; Fondamenta dei Ormesini 2754; ⏲6pm-1am; San Marcuola) Find a spot on the boat moored out front along the canal and watch the motley parade of drinkers and dreamers arrive for seafood *crostini* (open-face sandwiches) and quality organic and DOC wines by the *ombra* (half-glass of wine) or carafe. Folk singers play sets canalside when the weather obliges; when it's cold, regulars scoot over to make room for newcomers at indoor tables.

Harry's Bar BAR
(Map p454; ☎041 528 57 77; www.harrysbarvenezia.com; Calle Vallaresso 1323; ⏲10.30am-11pm; San Marco) Aspiring auteurs hold court at bistro tables well scuffed by Ernest Hemingway, Charlie Chaplin, Truman Capote and Orson Welles, enjoying the signature bellini (Giuseppe Cipriani's original 1948 recipe: white peach juice and *prosecco*) with a side of reflected glory. Upstairs is one of Italy's most unaccountably expensive restaurants – stick to the bar to save the financing for your breakthrough film.

Entertainment

To find out what's on during your visit, check listings in free mags distributed citywide and online at Venezia da Vivere (www.veneziadavivere.com) and 2Venice (www.2venice.it).

★ La Fenice OPERA
(Map p454; ☎041 78 66 72; www.teatrolafenice.it; Campo San Fantin 1977; restricted view from €30; Giglio) La Fenice, one of Italy's top opera houses, hosts a rich program of opera, ballet and classical music. With advance booking you can tour the theatre, but the best way to see it is with the *loggionisti* – opera buffs in the cheap top-tier seats. Get tickets at the theatre, online or through Vela Venezia Unica ticket offices.

Information

Marco Polo Airport Tourist Office (☎041 24 24; www.veneziaunica.it; Arrivals Hall, Marco Polo Airport; ⏲8.30am-7pm) Tourist information at the airport.

Ospedale SS Giovanni e Paolo (☎041 529 41 11; www.ulss12.ve.it; Campo Zanipolo 6777, Castello; Ospedale) Venice's main hospital; for emergency care and dental treatment.

San Marco Tourist Office (Map p454; ☎041 24 24; www.veneziaunica.it; Piazza San Marco 71f; ⏲9am-7pm; San Marco) Near the entrance to the Museo Correr.

Stazione Santa Lucia Tourist Office (Map p453; ☎041 24 24; www.veneziaunica.it; ⏲7am-9pm; Ferrovia)

Getting There & Away

AIR

Most flights arrive at and depart from **Marco Polo Airport** (☎flight information 041 260 92 60; www.veniceairport.it; Via Galileo Gallilei 30/1, Tessera), 12km outside Venice.

Ryanair flies to/from **Treviso Airport** (☎0422 31 51 11; www.trevisoairport.it; Via Noalese 63), about 30km away.

BOAT

Anek (☎041 528 65 22; www.anekitalia.com; Via Dell 'Elettronica, Fusina) runs regular ferries between Venice and Greece, and **Venezia Lines** (Map p453; ☎041 847 09 03; www.

venezialines.com) runs high-speed boats to/from Croatia in summer.

BUS

ACTV (Azienda del Consorzio Trasporti Veneziano; ☎041 272 21 11; www.actv.it) buses service surrounding areas. Get tickets and information at the **bus station** (Piazzale Roma).

TRAIN

Regular trains serve Venice's Stazione di Santa Lucia from Padua (€4 to €17, 25 minutes) and Verona (€9 to €26, 50 minutes to 2¼ hours) as well as Bologna, Milan, Rome and Florence.

Getting Around

TO/FROM THE AIRPORT

Marco Polo Airport

Alilaguna (☎041 240 17 01; www.alilaguna.it; airport transfer one-way €15) operates three boat lines that link the airport with various parts of Venice at a cost of €8 to Murano and €15 to all other landing stages. It takes approximately 1¼ hours to reach Piazza San Marco. Lines:

Blue Stops at Lido, San Marco, Cruise Terminal and points in-between.

Red Stops include Murano, Lido, San Marco and Giudecca.

Orange To Santa Maria del Giglio via Rialto and the Grand Canal.

An **ATVO** (☎0421 59 46 71; www.atvo.it; Piazzale Roma 497g, Santa Croce; ⊙6.40am-7.45pm) shuttle bus goes to/from Piazzale Roma (one way/return €8/11, 15 minutes, half-hourly), as does ACTV bus 5 (one way/return €8/15, 25 minutes, every 15 minutes).

Treviso Airport

ATVO buses run to/from Piazzale Roma (one way/return €12/22, 70 minutes, 13 daily).

BOAT

The city's main mode of public transport is the *vaporetto* (water bus).

Tickets, available from booths at major landing stations and on Piazzale Roma, cost €7.50 for a single trip. Passes are available for 24/48/72 hours at €20/30/40.

Useful routes:

1 Piazzale Roma to the train station and down the Grand Canal to San Marco and the Lido.

2 San Marco to/from the train station and Piazzale Roma, via the Grand canal and Rialto.

4.1 Joins Murano to Fondamente Nove, then circles the perimeter of Venice in both directions.

Trieste

POP 204,400

Italy's last city before Slovenia, Trieste merits a quick stopover. There are few must-see sights, but its imposing seafront *palazzi* lend it an impressive grandeur and the historic centre buzzes with bars and cafes. Hanging over everything is a palpable Mittel-European air, a hangover of its time as an important Austro-Hungarian port.

Sights & Activities

Piazza dell'Unità d'Italia PIAZZA

This vast public space – Italy's largest sea-facing piazza – is an elegant triumph of Austro-Hungarian town planning and contemporary civil pride. Flanked by the city's grandest *palazzi*, including Palazzo del Municipio, Trieste's 19th-century city hall, it's a good place for a drink or a chat, or simply for a quiet moment staring out at ships on the horizon.

★Castello di Miramare CASTLE

(☎040 22 41 43; www.castello-miramare.it; Viale Miramare; adult/reduced €8/5; ⊙9am-7pm) Sitting on a rocky outcrop 7km from town, Castello di Miramare is Trieste's elegiac bookend, the fanciful neo-Gothic home of the hapless Archduke Maximilian of Austria. Maximilian originally came to Trieste in the 1850s as the commander-in-chief of Austria's imperial navy, an ambitious young aristocrat known for his liberal ideas. But in 1867 he was shot by a republican firing squad in Mexico, after briefly, and rather foolishly, taking up the obsolete crown.

Sleeping & Eating

L'Albero Nascosto BOUTIQUE HOTEL €€

(☎040 30 01 88; www.alberonascosto.it; Via Felice Venezian 18; s €80-95, d €105-170; ❄📶) A delightful little hotel in the middle of the old town, Nascosto is a model of discreet style. Rooms are spacious and tastefully decked out with parquet floors, original artworks, books and a vintage piece or two; most also have a small kitchen corner. Breakfasts are simple but thoughtful, with local cheeses, top-quality preserves and Illy coffee.

Buffet da Siora Rosa BUFFET €

(☎040 30 14 60; Piazza Hortis 3; meals €25; ⊙8am-10pm Tue-Sat) Opened before WWII, the family-run Siora Rosa is one Trieste's traditional buffets (bar-restaurants). Sit outside or in the wonderfully retro interior and tuck into boiled pork, sauerkraut and other Germanic and Hungarian offerings, or opt for something fishy like *baccalà* (salted cod) with polenta.

Information

Tourist Office (☎040 347 83 12; www.turismofvg.it; Via dell'Orologio 1; ⏰9am-6pm)

Getting There & Around

Trains run to Trieste from Venice (€13 to €19, two to three hours, at least hourly).

From the train station, bus 30 heads down to Piazza dell'Unità d'Italia and the seafront.

National and international buses operate from the **bus station** (☎040 42 50 20; www.autostazionetrieste.it; Via Fabio Severo 24). These include services to Croatia (Pula, Zagreb, Dubrovnik), Slovenia (Ljubljana) and further afield.

Bologna

POP 386,700

Bologna is one of Italy's great unsung destinations. Its medieval centre is an eye-catching ensemble of red-brick *palazzi,* Renaissance towers and 40km of arcaded porticoes, and there are enough sights to excite without exhausting. A university town since 1088 (Europe's oldest), it's also a prime foodie destination, home to the eponymous bolognese sauce *(ragù)* as well as *tortellini,* lasagne and *mortadella* (Bologna sausage).

Sights

★Basilica di San Petronio CHURCH
(www.basilicadisanpetronio.org; Piazza Galvani 5; photo pass €2; ⏰7.45am-6.30pm) FREE Bologna's hulking Gothic basilica is the world's 15th-largest church, measuring 132m by 66m by 47m. Work began on it in 1390, but it was never finished and still today its main facade remains incomplete. Inside, look out for the huge sundial that stretches 67.7m down the eastern aisle. Designed in 1656 by Gian Cassini and Domenico Guglielmi, this was instrumental in discovering the anomalies of the Julian calendar and led to the creation of the leap year.

Le Due Torri TOWER
(The Two Towers; Piazza di Porta Ravegnana) Standing sentinel over Piazza di Porta Ravegnana, Bologna's two leaning towers are the city's main symbol. The taller of the two, the 97.2m-high **Torre degli Asinelli** (€3; ⏰9am-7pm summer, to 5pm winter) is open to the public, although it's not advisable for vertigo-sufferers or owners of arthritic knees (there are 498 steps up a semi-exposed wooden staircase).

★Basilica di Santo Stefano CHURCH
(http://abbaziasstefano.wixsite.com/abbaziasstefano; Via Santo Stefano 24; ⏰8am-7pm) FREE Bologna's most unique religious site is this atmospheric labyrinth of interlocking ecclesiastical structures, whose architecture spans centuries of Bolognese history and incorporates Romanesque, Lombard and even ancient Roman elements. Originally there were seven churches – hence the basilica's nickname Sette Chiese – but only four remain intact today: Chiesa del Crocefisso, Chiesa della Trinità, Santo Sepolcro and Santi Vitale e Agricola.

Sleeping & Eating

Albergo delle Drapperie HOTEL €
(☎051 22 39 55; www.albergodrapperie.com; Via delle Drapperie 5; s €58-70, d €85-120, ste €115-150; ❄📶) Offering one of the best quality-to-price ratios in central Bologna, this hotel in the atmospheric Quadrilatero neighbourhood is snugly ensconced in the upper floors of a large building. Buzz in at ground level and climb the stairs to discover 19 attractive rooms with marble floors, wood-beamed ceilings, the occasional brick arch and colourful ceiling frescoes.

★Bologna nel Cuore B&B €€
(☎051 26 94 42; www.bolognanelcuore.it; Via Cesare Battisti 29; s €75-100, d €95-140, apt €125-130; P❄📶) This centrally located, immaculate and well-loved B&B features a pair of bright, high-ceilinged rooms with pretty tiled bathrooms and endless mod cons, plus two comfortable, spacious apartments with kitchen and laundry facilities. Owner and art historian Maria generously shares her knowledge of Bologna and serves breakfasts featuring jams made with fruit picked near her childhood home in the Dolomites.

★Osteria dell'Orsa ITALIAN €
(☎051 23 15 76; www.osteriadellorsa.com; Via Mentana 1; meals €10-20; ⏰noon-1am) If you were to make a list of the great wonders of Italy, hidden amid Venice's canals and Rome's Colosseum would be cheap, pretension-free

osterie (casual taverns) like Osteria dell'Orsa, where the food is serially sublime and the prices are giveaway cheap. So what if the waiter's wearing an AC Milan shirt and the wine is served in a water glass?

★ All'Osteria Bottega OSTERIA **€€**
(☎ 051 58 51 11; Via Santa Caterina 51; meals €35-45; ⌚12.30-2.30pm & 8-1am Tue-Sat) At this *osteria* truly worthy of the name, owners Daniele and Valeria lavish attention on every table between trips to the kitchen for plates of *culatello di Zibello* ham, tortellini in capon broth, pork shank in red wine reduction and other Slow Food delights. Desserts are homemade by Valeria, from the *ciambella* (Romagnola ring-shaped cake) to fresh fruit sorbets.

Information

Bologna Welcome (Tourist Office; ☎ 051 658 31 11; www.bolognawelcome.it; Piazza Maggiore 1e; ⌚9am-7pm Mon-Sat, 10am-5pm Sun) Also has an office at the airport.

Getting There & Around

AIR

European and domestic flights serve **Guglielmo Marconi Airport** (☎ 051 647 96 15; www.bologna-airport.it; Via Triumvirato 84), 8km northwest of the city.

From the airport, an **Aerobus shuttle** (€6, 25 minutes, every 11 to 30 minutes) connects with the train station.

BUS

Bologna has an efficient bus system, run by **TPER** (☎ 051 29 02 90; www.tper.it).

Lines 25 and 30 are among those that connect the train station with the city centre.

TRAIN

Bologna is a major rail hub. From the station on Piazza delle Medaglie d'Oro, there are regular high-speed trains to Milan (€34 to €84, one to two hours), Venice (€32, 1½ hours), Florence (€32, 40 minutes) and Rome (€84, two to 2½ hours).

Ravenna

POP 159,100

A rewarding and worthwhile day trip from Bologna, Ravenna is famous for its Early Christian mosaics. These Unesco-listed treasures have been impressing visitors since the 13th century, when Dante described them in his *Divine Comedy* (much of which was written here).

Sights

Ravenna's mosaics are spread over five sites in the centre: the Basilica di San Vitale, the Mausoleo di Galla Placidia, the Basilica di Sant'Appollinare Nuovo, the Museo Arcivescovile and the Battistero Neoniano. These are covered by a single ticket, available at any of the sites. The website www.ravennamosaici.it gives further information.

On the northern edge of the *centro storico*, the sombre exterior of the 6th-century **Basilica di San Vitale** (www.ravennamosaici.it; Via San Vitale; 5-site combo ticket €9.50; ⌚9am-7pm Mar-Oct, 10am-5pm Nov-Feb) hides a dazzling interior with mosaics depicting Old Testament scenes. In the same complex, the small **Mausoleo di Galla Placidia** (www.ravennamosaici.it; Via San Vitale; 5-site combo ticket €9.50 plus summer-only surcharge €2; ⌚9am-7pm Mar-Oct, 10am-5pm Nov-Feb) contains the city's oldest mosaics.

Adjoining Ravenna's unremarkable cathedral, the **Museo Arcivescovile** (www.ravennamosaici.it; Piazza Arcivescovado; 5-site combo ticket €9.50; ⌚9am-7pm Mar-Oct, 10am-5pm Nov-Feb) boasts an exquisite 6th-century ivory throne, while next door in the **Battistero Neoniano** (www.ravennamosaici.it; Piazza del Duomo; 5-site combo ticket €9.50; ⌚9am-7pm Mar-Oct, 10am-5pm Nov-Feb), the baptism of Christ is represented in the domed roof mosaic.

To the east, the **Basilica di Sant'Apollinare Nuovo** (www.ravennamosaici.it; Via di Roma 52; 5-site combo ticket €9.50; ⌚9am-7pm Apr-Sep, 9.30am-5.30pm Mar & Oct, 10am-5pm Nov-Feb) boasts, among other things, a superb mosaic depicting a procession of martyrs headed towards Christ and his apostles.

Five kilometres southeast of the city, the **Basilica di Sant'Apollinare in Classe** (Via Romea Sud 224; adult/reduced €5/2.50; ⌚8.30am-7.30pm Mon-Sat, 1-7.30pm Sun) is a must-see. Take bus 4 from the train station.

Eating

La Gardela TRATTORIA **€€**
(☎ 0544 21 71 47; www.ristorantelagardela.com; Via Ponte Marino 3; meals €25-30; ⌚noon-2.30pm & 7-10.30pm Fri-Wed) Economical prices, formidable home cooking and an attractive front terrace that's good for people-watching mean this bustling trattoria can be crowded, but in a pleasant, gregarious way. Professional waiters

glide by with plates of Italian classics: think risottos, pasta with *ragù,* and good grilled meats and fish. Fixed-price menus including water and coffee (but not wine) start at €15.

Information

Informazione e Accoglienza Turistica (IAT) - Centro (Tourist Information; 0544 3 54 04; www.turismo.ravenna.it; Piazza San Francesco 7; 8.30am-7pm, shorter hours in winter) Helpful office with maps and printed material; can help with booking accommodation.

Getting There & Around

Regional trains run to/from Bologna (€7.35,1½ hours, hourly) and destinations on the east coast.

TUSCANY & UMBRIA

Tuscany and its lesser-known neighbour, Umbria, are two of Italy's most beautiful regions. Tuscany's fabled landscape of rolling vine-covered hills dotted with cypress trees and stone villas has long been considered the embodiment of rural chic, while its historic cities and hilltop towns are home to a significant portfolio of the world's medieval and Renaissance art.

To the south, the predominantly rural region of Umbria, dubbed the 'green heart of Italy', harbours some of the country's best-preserved historic *borghi* (villages) and many important artistic, religious and architectural treasures.

Florence

POP 382,800

Visitors have been rhapsodising about Florence (Firenze) for centuries, and still today it looms large on Europe's 'must-sees' list. Tourists flock here to feast on world-class art and explore its historic streets, laden with grand palaces, jewel-box churches, trattorias, wine bars and elegant boutiques. Cradle of the Renaissance and home of Machiavelli, Michelangelo and the Medici, it's a magnetic, romantic and brilliantly absorbing place.

The city's golden age came under the Medici family between the 14th and 17th centuries. Later, it served as capital of the newly unified Italy from 1865 to 1870.

Piazza del Duomo

★Duomo CATHEDRAL

(Cattedrale di Santa Maria del Fiore; 055 230 28 85; www.ilgrandemuseodelduomo.it; Piazza del Duomo; 10am-5pm Mon-Wed & Fri, to 4.30pm Thu, to 4.45pm Sat, 1.30-4.45pm Sun) FREE Florence's Duomo is the city's most iconic landmark. Capped by Filippo Brunelleschi's red-tiled cupola, it's a staggering construction whose breathtaking pink, white and green marble facade and graceful *campanile* (bell tower) dominate the medieval cityscape. Sienese architect Arnolfo di Cambio began work on it in 1296, but construction took almost 150 years and it wasn't consecrated until 1436. In the echoing interior, look out for frescoes by Vasari and Zuccari and up to 44 stained-glass windows.

★Cupola del Brunelleschi LANDMARK

(Brunelleschi's Dome; 055 230 28 85; www.ilgrandemuseodelduomo.it; Piazza del Duomo; adult/reduced incl cupola, baptistry, campanile, crypt & museum €15/3; 8.30am-7pm Mon-Fri, to 5pm Sat, 1-4pm Sun) A Renaissance masterpiece, the Duomo's cupola – 91m high and 45.5m wide – was built between 1420 and 1436. Filippo Brunelleschi, taking inspiration from the Pantheon in Rome, designed a distinctive octagonal form of inner and outer concentric domes that rests on the drum of the cathedral rather than the roof itself. Over four million bricks were used, laid in consecutive rings according to a vertical herringbone pattern. Advance reservations, online or at the cathedral's Piazza di San Giovanni ticket office, are obligatory.

★Campanile TOWER

(Bell Tower; 055 230 28 85; www.ilgrandemuseodelduomo.it; Piazza del Duomo; adult/reduced incl campanile, baptistry, cupola, crypt & museum €15/3; 8.15am-8pm) The 414-step climb up the cathedral's 85m-tall *campanile,* begun by Giotto in 1334, rewards with staggering city views. The first tier of bas-reliefs around the base of its elaborate Gothic facade are copies of those carved by Pisano depicting the Creation of Man and *attività umane* (arts and industries). Those on the second tier depict the planets, cardinal virtues, the arts and the seven sacraments. The sculpted Prophets and Sibyls in the upper-storey niches are copies of works by Donatello and others.

ITALIAN ART & ARCHITECTURE

Italy is littered with architectural and artistic reminders of its convoluted history. **Etruscan** tombs and **Greek** temples tell of glories long past, **Roman** amphitheatres testify to ancient blood lust and architectural brilliance, and **Byzantine** mosaics reveal influences sweeping in from the East.

The **Renaissance** left an indelible mark, giving rise to some of Italy's greatest masterpieces: Filippo Brunelleschi's dome atop Florence's Duomo, Botticelli's *The Birth of Venus*, and Michelangelo's Sistine Chapel frescoes. Contemporaries Leonardo da Vinci and Raphael further brightened the scene.

Caravaggio revolutionised the late 16th-century art world with his controversial and highly influential painting style. He worked in Rome and the south, where **baroque** art and architecture flourished in the 17th century.

In the late 18th and early 19th centuries **neoclassicism** saw a return to sober classical lines. Its main Italian exponent was sculptor Antonio Canova.

In sharp contrast to backward-looking neoclassicism, early 20th-century **futurism** sought new ways to express the dynamism of the machine age, while Italian **rationalism** saw the development of a linear, muscular style of architecture.

Continuing in this modernist tradition are Italy's two contemporary **starchitects**: Renzo Piano, the visionary behind Rome's Auditorium, and Rome-born Massimiliano Fuksas.

Battistero di San Giovanni LANDMARK

(Baptistry; ☎055 230 28 85; www.ilgrandemuseodelduomo.it; Piazza di San Giovanni; adult/reduced incl baptistry, campanile, cupola, crypt & museum €15/3; ⏰8.15am-10.15am & 11.15am-7.30pm Mon-Fri, 8.15am-6.30pm Sat, 8.15am-1.30pm Sun) This 11th-century baptistry is a Romanesque, octagonal-striped structure of white-and-green marble with three sets of doors conceived as panels illustrating the story of humanity and the Redemption. Most celebrated are Lorenzo Ghiberti's gilded bronze doors at the eastern entrance, the Porta del Paradiso (Gate of Paradise). What you see today are copies – the originals are in the Grande Museo del Duomo. Buy tickets online or at the ticket office at Piazza di San Giovanni 7, opposite the main baptistry entrance.

Piazza della Signoria & Around

Piazza della Signoria PIAZZA

(Piazza della Signoria) Florentines flock to this piazza, the hub of local life since the 13th century, to meet friends and chat over early evening *aperitivi* at historic cafes. Presiding over everything is Palazzo Vecchio, Florence's city hall, and the 14th-century **Loggia dei Lanzi** FREE, an open-air gallery showcasing Renaissance sculptures, including Giambologna's *Rape of the Sabine Women* (c 1583), Benvenuto Cellini's bronze *Perseus* (1554) and Agnolo Gaddi's *Seven Virtues* (1384–89).

★Palazzo Vecchio MUSEUM

(☎055 276 85 58, 055 27 68 22; www.musefirenze.it; Piazza della Signoria; adult/reduced museum €10/8, tower €10/8, museum & tower €14/12, archaeological tour €4, combination ticket €18/16; ⏰museum 9am-11pm Fri-Wed, to 2pm Thu Apr-Sep, 9am-7pm Fri-Wed, to 2pm Thu Oct-Mar, tower 9am-9pm Fri-Wed, to 2pm Thu Apr-Sep, 10am-5pm Fri-Wed, to 2pm Thu Oct-Mar; 📶) This fortress palace, with its crenellations and 94m-high tower, was designed by Arnolfo di Cambio between 1298 and 1314 for the *signoria* (city government). It remains the seat of the city's power, home to the mayor's office and the municipal council. From the top of the **Torre d'Arnolfo** (tower), you can revel in unforgettable rooftop views. Inside, Michelangelo's *Genio della Vittoria* (Genius of Victory) sculpture graces the Salone dei Cinquecento, a magnificent painted hall created for the city's 15th-century ruling Consiglio dei Cinquecento (Council of 500).

★Galleria degli Uffizi GALLERY

(Uffizi Gallery; ☎055 29 48 83; www.uffizi.beniculturali.it; Piazzale degli Uffizi 6; adult/reduced €8/4, incl temporary exhibition €12.50/6.25; ⏰8.15am-6.50pm Tue-Sun) Home to the world's greatest collection of Italian Renaissance art, Florence's premier gallery occupies the vast

Florence

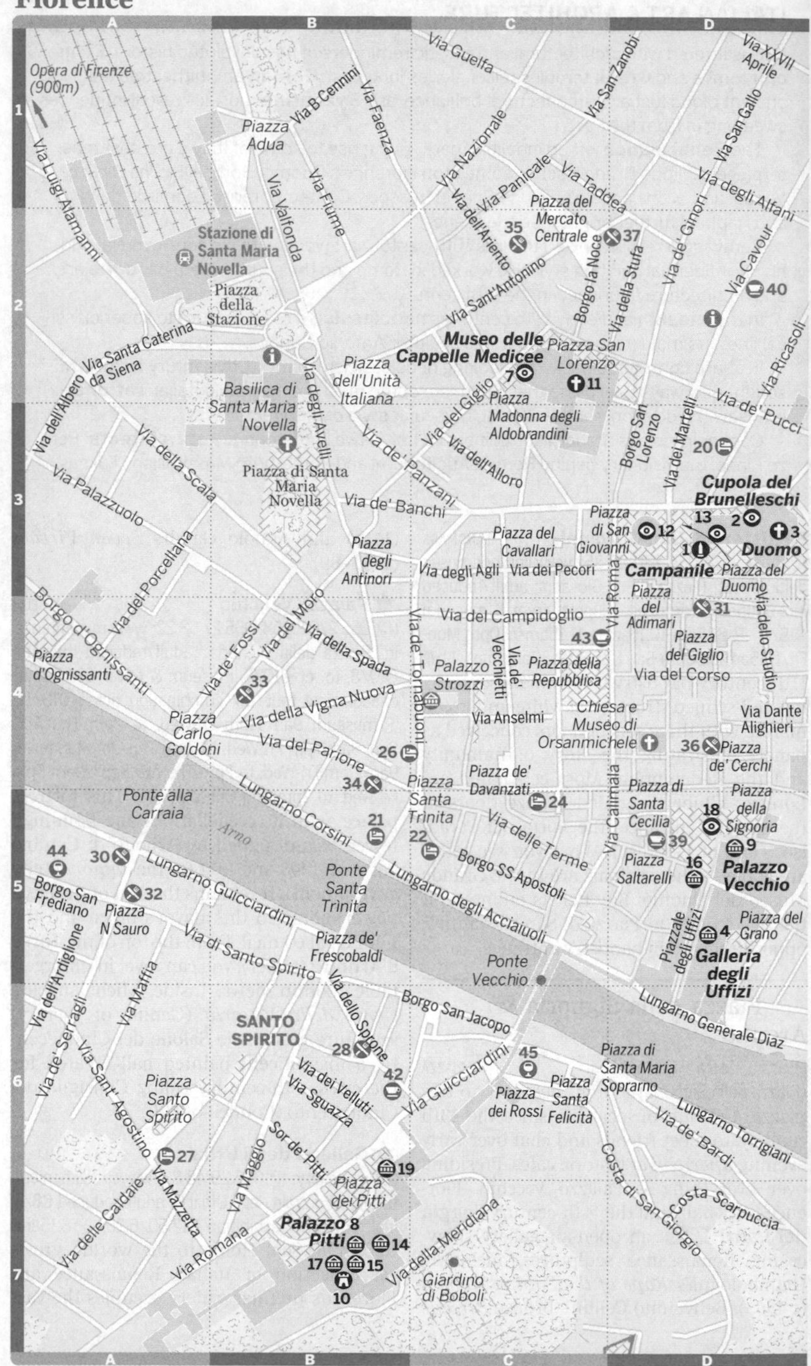

Opera di Firenze (900m)
Via Guelfa
Via XXVII Aprile
Via San Zanobi
Via San Gallo
Via B Cennini
Via Faenza
Piazza Adua
Via Luigi Alamanni
Via Nazionale
Via Valfonda
Via Fiume
Via Panicale
Via Taddea
Via degli Alfani
Piazza del Mercato Centrale
Via dell'Ariento
Via de' Ginori
Via Cavour
Stazione di Santa Maria Novella
Borgo la Noce
Via della Stufa
Via Sant'Antonino
Piazza della Stazione
Museo delle Cappelle Medicee
Piazza San Lorenzo
Via Santa Caterina da Siena
Via Ricasoli
Piazza dell'Unità Italiana
Basilica di Santa Maria Novella
Via degli Avelli
Via del Giglio
Piazza Madonna degli Aldobrandini
Via dell'Albero
Via de' Pucci
Borgo San Lorenzo
Via dei Martelli
Via della Scala
Via de' Panzani
Via dell'Alloro
Piazza di Santa Maria Novella
Via Palazzuolo
Via de' Banchi
Cupola del Brunelleschi
Piazza di San Giovanni
Duomo
Piazza del Cavallari
Via del Porcellana
Piazza degli Antinori
Via degli Agli
Via dei Pecori
Campanile
Piazza del Duomo
Borgo d'Ognissanti
Via del Moro
Via Roma
Piazza del Adimari
Via dello Studio
Via del Campidoglio
Via de' Tornabuoni
Via della Spada
Via de' Fossi
Piazza d'Ognissanti
Via de' Vecchietti
Palazzo Strozzi
Piazza della Repubblica
Piazza del Giglio
Via del Corso
Via della Vigna Nuova
Via Anselmi
Chiesa e Museo di Orsanmichele
Via Dante Alighieri
Piazza Carlo Goldoni
Via del Parione
Piazza de' Cerchi
Piazza de' Davanzati
Piazza Santa Trinita
Piazza di Santa Cecilia
Piazza della Signoria
Ponte alla Carraia
Lungarno Corsini
Via Calimala
Arno
Via delle Terme
Borgo SS Apostoli
Piazza Saltarelli
Palazzo Vecchio
Borgo San Frediano
Lungarno Guicciardini
Ponte Santa Trinita
Lungarno degli Acciaiuoli
Piazza N Sauro
Piazzale degli Uffizi
Piazza del Grano
Via dell'Ardiglione
Via di Santo Spirito
Piazza de' Frescobaldi
Ponte Vecchio
Galleria degli Uffizi
Via Maffia
Via dello Sprone
Borgo San Jacopo
Lungarno Generale Diaz
Via de' Serragli
Santo Spirito
Via Sant'Agostino
Via dei Velluti
Via Guicciardini
Piazza di Santa Maria Soprarno
Piazza Santo Spirito
Via Sguazza
Piazza dei Rossi
Piazza Santa Felicità
Lungarno Torrigiani
Via de' Bardi
Sdr de' Pitti
Via Maggio
Costa di San Giorgio
Piazza dei Pitti
Costa Scarpuccia
Via delle Caldaie
Via Mazzetta
Palazzo Pitti
Via Romana
Via della Meridiana
Giardino di Boboli

Florence

Top Sights

1 Campanile ... D3
2 Cupola del Brunelleschi ... D3
3 Duomo ... D3
4 Galleria degli Uffizi ... D5
5 Galleria dell'Accademia ... E1
6 Museo del Bargello ... E4
7 Museo delle Cappelle Medicee ... C2
8 Palazzo Pitti ... B7
9 Palazzo Vecchio ... D5

Sights

10 Appartamenti Reali ... B7
11 Basilica di San Lorenzo ... C2
12 Battistero di San Giovanni ... D3
13 Cripta Santa Reparata ... D3
14 Galleria d'Arte Moderna ... B7
15 Galleria Palatina ... B7
16 Loggia dei Lanzi ... D5
17 Museo della Moda e del Costume ... B7
18 Piazza della Signoria ... D5
19 Tesoro del Granduchi ... B6

Sleeping

20 Academy Hostel ... D3
21 Antica Torre di Via de' Tornabuoni 1 ... B5
22 Hotel Cestelli ... C5
23 Hotel Dalí ... E4
24 Hotel Davanzati ... C5
25 Hotel Morandi alla Crocetta ... F2
26 Hotel Scoti ... B4
27 Palazzo Guadagni Hotel ... A6

Eating

28 5 e Cinque ... B6
29 Carabé ... E2
30 Gelateria La Carraia ... A5
31 Grom ... D4
32 Il Santo Bevitore ... A5
33 L'Osteria di Giovanni ... B4
34 Mariano ... B4
35 Mercato Centrale ... C2
36 Osteria Il Buongustai ... D4
37 Trattoria Mario ... D2
38 Vivoli ... E5

Drinking & Nightlife

39 Caffè Rivoire ... D5
40 Ditta Al Cinema ... D2
41 Ditta Artigianale ... E5
42 Ditta Artigianale ... B6
43 Gilli ... C4
44 La Cité ... A5
45 Le Volpi e l'Uva ... C6

U-shaped Palazzo degli Uffizi, built between 1560 and 1580 to house government offices. The collection, bequeathed to the city by the

Medici family in 1743 on condition that it never leave Florence, contains some of Italy's best-known paintings, including Piero della Francesco's profile portaits of the Duke and Duchess of Urbino and rooms full of masterpieces by Sandro Botticelli.

★Museo del Bargello MUSEUM
(www.bargellomusei.beniculturali.it; Via del Proconsolo 4; adult/reduced €8/4; ⌚8.15am-1.50pm, closed 2nd & 4th Sun & 1st, 3rd & 5th Mon of month) It was behind the stark walls of Palazzo del Bargello, Florence's earliest public building redecorated in neo-Gothic style in 1845, that the *podestà* meted out justice from the 13th century until 1502. Today the building safeguards Italy's most comprehensive collection of Tuscan Renaissance sculpture with some of Michelangelo's best early works and several Donatellos. Michelangelo was just 21 when a cardinal commissioned him to create the drunken grape-adorned *Bacchus* (1496–97), on show at the Bargello.

San Lorenzo

★Museo delle Cappelle Medicee MAUSOLEUM
(Medici Chapels; www.firenzemusei.it; Piazza Madonna degli Aldobrandini 6; adult/reduced €8/4; ⌚8.15am-1.50pm, closed 1st, 3rd & 5th Mon, 2nd & 4th Sun of month) Nowhere is Medici conceit expressed so explicitly as in the Medici Chapels. Adorned with granite, marble, semi-precious stones and some of Michelangelo's most beautiful sculptures, it is the burial place of 49 dynasty members. Francesco I lies in the dark, imposing **Cappella dei Principi** (Princes' Chapel) alongside Ferdinando I and II and Cosimo I, II and III. Lorenzo il Magnifico is buried in the graceful **Sagrestia Nuova** (New Sacristy), which was Michelangelo's first architectural work.

San Marco

★Galleria dell'Accademia GALLERY
(www.firenzemusei.it; Via Ricasoli 60; adult/reduced €8/4, incl temporary exhibition €12.50/6.25; ⌚8.15am-6.50pm Tue-Sun) A queue marks the door to this gallery, built to house one of the Renaissance's most iconic masterpieces, Michelangelo's *David*. But the world's most famous statue is worth the wait. The subtle detail of the real thing – the veins in his sinewy arms, the leg muscles, the change in expression as you move around the statue – *is* impressive. Carved from a single block of marble, Michelangelo's most famous work was his most challenging – he didn't choose the marble himself and it was veined.

BEST OF THE UFFIZI

Cut to the quick of the gallery's collection and start by getting to grips with pre-Renaissance Tuscan art in **Room 2**, home to several shimmering alterpieces by Giotto et al. Then work your way on to **Room 8** and Piero della Francesca's iconic profile portrait of the Duke and Duchess of Urbino.

More familiar images await in the **Sala di Botticelli**, including the master's great Renaissance masterpiece, *La nascita di Venere* (The Birth of Venus). Continue on to **Room 15** for works by Leonardo da Vinci and then on to **Room 35** for Michelangelo's *Doni tondi* (The Holy Family).

Oltrarno

★Palazzo Pitti MUSEUM
(www.uffizi.beniculturali.it; Piazza dei Pitti; ⌚8.15am-6.50pm Tue-Sun) Commissioned by banker Luca Pitta and designed by Brunelleschi in 1457, this vast Renaissance palace was later bought by the Medici family. Over the centuries, it served as the residence of the city's rulers until the Savoys donated it to the state in 1919. Nowadays it houses an impressive silver museum, a couple of art museums and a series of rooms recreating life in the palace during House of Savoy times.

Festivals & Events

Scoppio del Carro FIREWORKS
(⌚Mar/Apr) A cart of fireworks is exploded in front of the cathedral in Piazza del Duomo at 11am on Easter Sunday.

Maggio Musicale Fiorentino PERFORMING ARTS
(www.operadifirenze.it; ⌚Apr-Jun) Italy's oldest arts festival features world-class performances of theatre, classical music, jazz, opera and dance. Events are staged at the Opera di Firenze (p471) and venues across town.

Festa di San Giovanni RELIGIOUS
(⌚24 Jun) Florence celebrates its patron saint, John, with a *calcio storico* (historic

football) match on Piazza di Santa Croce and fireworks over Piazzale Michelangelo.

Sleeping

★ Hotel Dalí HOTEL €
(055 234 07 06; www.hoteldali.com; Via dell'Oriuolo 17; d €90, s/d without bathroom €40/70, apt from €95; P) A warm welcome from hosts Marco and Samanta awaits at this lovely small hotel. A stone's throw from the *duomo,* it has 10 sunny rooms, some overlooking a leafy inner courtyard, decorated in a low-key modern way and equipped with kettles, coffee and tea. No breakfast, but – miraculous for downtown Florence – free parking in the rear courtyard.

★ Academy Hostel HOSTEL €
(055 239 86 65; www.academyhostel.eu; Via Ricasoli 9; dm €32-45, d €80-100; @) This classy 13-room hostel – definitely not a party hostel – sits on the 1st floor of Baron Ricasoli's 17th-century *palazzo*. The inviting lobby, with books to browse and computers to surf, was once a theatre and is a comfy spot to chill on the sofa over TV or a DVD. Dorms sport four, five or six beds, high moulded ceilings and brightly coloured lockers.

Hotel Cestelli HOTEL €
(055 21 42 13; www.hotelcestelli.com; Borgo SS Apostoli 25; d €100, s/d without bathroom €60/80; closed 2 weeks Jan & 10 days Aug;) Housed in a 12th-century *palazzo* a stiletto strut from fashionable Via de' Tornabuoni, this intimate eight-room hotel is a gem. Rooms reveal an understated style, tastefully combining polished antiques with spangly chandeliers, vintage art and silk screens. Owners Alessio and Asumi are a mine of local information and are happy to share their knowledge. No breakfast. Ask about low-season discounts for longer stays.

★ Hotel Scoti PENSION €€
(055 29 21 28; www.hotelscoti.com; Via de' Tornabuoni 7; d/tr/q €130/160/185; reception 8am-11.30pm;) Wedged between designer boutiques on Florence's smartest shopping strip, this hidden *pensione* is a fabulous mix of old-fashioned charm and value for money. Its 16 traditionally styled rooms are spread across the 2nd floor of a 16th-century *palazzo;* some have lovely rooftop views. Guests can borrow hairdryers, bottle openers, plug adaptors etc and the frescoed lounge (1780) is stunning. No breakfast.

★ Hotel Davanzati HOTEL €€
(055 28 66 66; www.hoteldavanzati.it; Via Porta Rossa 5; s/d/tr €143/215/281; @) Twenty-two steps lead up to this family-run hotel. A labyrinth of enchanting rooms, frescoes and modern comforts, it has bags of charisma – and that includes Florentine brothers Tommaso and Riccardo, and father Fabrizio, who run the show (Grandpa Marcello surveys proceedings). Rooms come with a mini iPad, meaning free wi-fi around town, direct messaging with the hotel and a handy digital city guide.

★ Palazzo Guadagni Hotel HOTEL €€
(055 265 83 76; www.palazzoguadagni.com; Piazza Santo Spirito 9; d €150-220, tr/q €265/310;) This romantic hotel overlooking Florence's liveliest summertime square is legendary – Zeffirelli shot scenes from *Tea with Mussolini* here. Housed in an artfully revamped Renaissance palace, it has 15 spacious if old-fashioned rooms and an impossibly romantic loggia terrace with wicker chairs and predictably dreamy views.

Hotel Morandi alla Crocetta BOUTIQUE HOTEL €€
(055 234 47 48; www.hotelmorandi.it; Via Laura 50; s €70-120, d €100-170, tr €130-210, q €150-250; P) This medieval convent-turned-hotel away from the madding crowd in San Marco is a stunner. Rooms are refined and traditional in look – think antique furnishings, wood beams and oil paintings – with a quiet, old-world ambience. Pick of the bunch is frescoed room No 29, the former chapel. Garage parking €25 per night.

★ Antica Torre di Via de' Tornabuoni 1 BOUTIQUE HOTEL €€€
(055 265 81 61; www.tornabuoni1.com; Via de' Tornabuoni 1; d €350;) Footsteps from

CUT THE QUEUES

- Book tickets for the Uffizi and Galleria dell'Accademia, as well as several other museums through **Firenze Musei** (Florence Museums; www.firenzemusei.it). Note that this entails a booking fee of €4 per museum.
- Alternatively, the **Firenze Card** (€72, valid for 72 hours) allows you to bypass both advance booking and queues. Check details at www.firenzecard.it.

the Arno, inside the beautiful 14th-century Palazzo Gianfigliazzi on Florence's smartest shopping strip, is this stylish hotel. Rooms and various suites are spacious and contemporary, but what completely steals the show is the stunning rooftop breakfast terrace – among the best in the city. Sip cappuccino and swoon over Florence graciously laid out at your feet.

Eating

★Mercato Centrale FOOD HALL €

(☎055 239 97 98; www.mercatocentrale.it; Piazza del Mercato Centrale 4; dishes €7-15; ⏲10am-midnight; 📶) Meander the maze of stalls rammed with fresh produce at Florence's oldest and largest food market, on the ground floor of a fantastic iron-and-glass structure designed by architect Giuseppe Mengoni in 1874. Head to the 1st floor's buzzing, thoroughly contemporary food hall with dedicated bookshop, cookery school and artisan stalls cooking steaks, burgers, tripe *panini,* vegetarian dishes, pizza, gelato, pastries and pasta.

★Trattoria Mario TUSCAN €

(☎055 21 85 50; www.trattoria-mario.com; Via Rosina 2; meals €25; ⏲noon-3.30pm Mon-Sat, closed 3 weeks Aug) Arrive by noon to ensure a stool around a shared table at this noisy, busy, brilliant trattoria – a legend that retains its soul (and allure with locals) despite being in every guidebook. Charming Fabio, whose grandfather opened the place in 1953, is front of house while big brother Romeo and nephew Francesco cook with speed in the kitchen. No advance reservations, no credit cards.

★Osteria Il Buongustai OSTERIA €

(☎055 29 13 04; Via dei Cerchi 15r; meals €15-20; ⏲8am-4pm Mon-Fri, to 11pm Sat) Run with breathtaking speed and grace by Laura and Lucia, this place is unmissable. Lunchtimes heave with locals who work nearby and savvy students who flock here to fill up on tasty Tuscan home cooking at a snip of other restaurant prices. The place is brilliantly no frills – expect to share a table and pay in cash; no credit cards.

★Mariano SANDWICHES €

(☎055 21 40 67; Via del Parione 19r; panini €3.50; ⏲8am-3pm & 5-7.30pm Mon-Fri, 8am-3pm Sat) Our favourite for its simplicity, around since 1973. From sunrise to sunset, this brick-vaulted, 13th-century cellar gently buzzes with Florentines propped at the counter sipping coffee or wine or eating salads and *panini.* Come here for a coffee-and-pastry breakfast, light lunch, *aperitivo* with cheese or salami tasting platter (€12), or *panino* to eat on the move.

★5 e Cinque VEGETARIAN €

(☎055 274 15 83; Piazza della Passera 1; meals €25; ⏲noon-3pm & 7.30-10pm Tue-Sun; 📶🌶) The hard work and passion of a photography and antique dealer is behind this highly creative, intimate eating space adored by many a savvy local. Cuisine is vegetarian with its roots in Genova's kitchen – '5 e Cinque' (meaning '5 and 5') is a chickpea sandwich from Livorno and the restaurant's *cecina* (traditional Ligurian flat bread made from chickpea flour) is legendary.

★Il Santo Bevitore TUSCAN €€

(☎055 21 12 64; www.ilsantobevitore.com; Via di Santo Spirito 64-66r; meals €40; ⏲12.30-2.30pm & 7.30-11.30pm, closed Sun lunch & Aug) Reserve or arrive right on 7.30pm to snag the last table at this ever-popular address, an ode to stylish dining where gastronomes eat by candlelight in a vaulted, whitewashed, bottle-lined interior. The menu is a creative reinvention of seasonal classics: risotto with monkfish, red turnip and fennel; *ribollita* with kale; chicken liver terrine with brioche and a Vin Santo reduction.

★Il Teatro del Sale TUSCAN €€

(☎055 200 14 92; www.teatrodelsale.com; Via dei Macci 111r; lunch/dinner/weekend brunch €15/35/20; ⏲11am-3pm & 7.30-11pm Tue-Sat, 11am-3pm Sun, closed Aug) Florentine chef Fabio Picchi is one of Florence's living treasures who steals the Sant' Ambrogio show with this eccentric, good-value members-only club (everyone welcome, membership €7) inside an old theatre. He cooks up weekend brunch, lunch and dinner, culminating at 9.30pm in a live performance of drama, music or comedy arranged by his wife, artistic director and comic actress Maria Cassi.

Trattoria Cibrèo TUSCAN €€

(www.cibreo.com; Via dei Macci 122r; meals €40; ⏲12.50-2.30pm & 6.50-11pm Tue-Sat, closed Aug) Dine here chez Fabio Picchi and you'll instantly understand why a queue gathers outside before it opens. Once inside, revel in top-notch Tuscan cuisine: perhaps *pappa al pomodoro* (a thick soupy mash of tomato, bread and basil) followed by *polpettine di pollo e ricotta* (chicken and ricotta meatballs). No reservations, no credit cards, no pasta and arrive early to snag a table.

★**L'Osteria di Giovanni** TUSCAN €€
(055 28 48 97; www.osteriadigiovanni.it; Via del Moro 22; meals €45; 7-10pm Mon-Fri, noon-3pm & 7-10pm Sat & Sun) Cuisine at this smart eatery is timelessly Tuscan. Imagine truffles, tender steaks and delicious pasta such as *pici al sugo di salsicccia e cavolo nero* (thick spaghetti with a sauce of sausage and black cabbage). Throw in a complimentary glass of *prosecco* as aperitif and sweet Vin Santo wine with a plate of almond-studded *cantuccini* to end your meal, and you'll be hooked.

Drinking & Nightlife

★**Le Volpi e l'Uva** WINE BAR
(055 239 81 32; www.levolpieluva.com; Piazza dei Rossi 1; 11am-9pm Mon-Sat) This unassuming wine bar hidden away by Chiesa di Santa Felicità remains as appealing as the day it opened over a decade ago. Its food and wine pairings are first class – taste and buy boutique wines by small producers from all over Italy, matched perfectly with cheeses, cold meats and the best *crostini* in town. Wine-tasting classes too.

★**Ditta Artigianale** CAFE, BAR
(055 274 15 41; www.dittaartigianale.it; Via de' Neri 32r; 8am-10pm Sun-Thu, 8am-midnight Fri, 9.30am-midnight Sat;) With industrial decor and welcoming laid-back vibe, this ingenious coffee roastery and gin bar is a perfect place to hang any time of day. The creation of three-times Italian barista champion Francesco Sanapo, it's famed for its first-class coffee and outstanding gin cocktails. If you're yearning a flat white, cold brew tonic or cappuccino made with almond, soy or coconut milk, come here.

Caffè Rivoire CAFE
(055 21 44 12; www.rivoire.it; Piazza della Signoria 4; 7am-midnight Tue-Sun summer, to 9pm winter) This golden oldie with an unbeatable people-watching terrace has produced some of the city's most exquisite chocolate since 1872. Black-jacketed barmen with ties set the formal tone. Save several euros by joining the local Florentine crowd standing at the bar rather than sitting down at a table.

Gilli CAFE
(055 21 38 96; www.gilli.it; Piazza della Repubblica 39r; 7.30am-1.30am) The most famous of the historic cafes on the city's old Roman forum, Gilli has been serving utterly delectable cakes, chocolates, fruit tartlets and *millefoglie* (sheets of puff pastry filled with rich vanilla or chocolate Chantilly cream) to die for since 1733 (it moved to this square in 1910 and sports a beautifully preserved art nouveau interior).

FLORENCE'S BEST GELATO

Vivoli (055 29 23 34; www.vivoli.it; Via dell'Isola delle Stinche 7; tubs €2-10; 7.30am-midnight Tue-Sat, 9am-midnight Sun, to 9pm winter) Select from the huge choice on offer and scoff it in the pretty piazza opposite.

Grom (055 21 61 58; www.grom.it; Via del Campanile 2; cones €2.60-4.60, tubs €2.60-5.50; 10am-10.30pm Sun-Thu, to 11.30pm Fri & Sat) Delectable flavours and organic seasonal ingredients.

Gelateria La Carraia (055 28 06 95; Piazza Nazario Sauro 25r; cones/tubs €1.50-6; 10.30am-midnight summer, 11am-10pm winter) Fantastic gelateria next to Ponte Carraia.

Carabé (055 28 94 76; www.parcocarabe.it; Via Ricasoli 60r; cones €2.50-4; 10am-midnight, closed mid-Dec–mid-Jan) Fill up on Sicilian ice cream as you wait to see *David*.

Entertainment

La Cité BAR
(055 21 03 87; www.lacitelibreria.info; Borgo San Frediano 20r; 2pm-2am Mon-Sat, 3pm-2am Sun;) A hip cafe-bookshop with an eclectic choice of vintage seating, La Cité makes a wonderful, intimate venue for book readings, after-work drinks and fantastic live music – jazz, swing, world music. Check its Facebook page for the week's events.

Opera di Firenze OPERA
(055 277 93 09; www.operadifirenze.it; Piazzale Vittorio Gui, Viale Fratelli Rosselli 15; box office 10am-6pm Tue-Fri, to 1pm Sat) Florence's strikingly modern opera house with glittering contemporary geometric facade sits on the green edge of city park Parco delle Cascine. Its three thoughtfully designed and multi-functional concert halls seat an audience of 5000 and play host to the springtime Maggio Musicale Fiorentino.

Information

24-Hour Pharmacy (☎055 21 67 61; Stazione di Santa Maria Novella; ⊙24hr) Nonstop pharmacy inside Florence's central train station; at least one member of staff usually speaks English.

Dr Stephen Kerr: Medical Service (☎335-836 16 82, 055 28 80 55; www.dr-kerr.com; Piazza Mercato Nuovo 1; ⊙3-5pm Mon-Fri, or by appointment 9am-3pm Mon-Fri) Resident British doctor.

Tourist Office (☎055 29 08 32; www.firenzeturismo.it; Via Cavour 1r; ⊙9am-1pm Mon-Fri) Tourist office not far from the historic centre.

Tourist Office (☎055 21 22 45; www.firenzeturismo.it; Piazza della Stazione 4; ⊙9am-6.30pm Mon-Sat, to 1.30pm Sun) Tourist office just across the street from Florence's central train station.

Getting There & Away

AIR

The main airport serving Tuscany is **Pisa International Airport** (p473).

The smaller **Florence Airport** (Aeroporto Amerigo Vespucci; ☎055 3 06 15, 055 306 18 30; www.aeroporto.firenze.it; Via del Termine 11) is 5km north of town.

BUS

The main bus station is just west of Piazza della Stazione.

Buses leave for Siena (€7.80, 1¼ hours, at least hourly) and San Gimignano via Poggibonsi (€6.80, 1¼ to two hours, hourly).

TRAIN

Florence's **Stazione di Santa Maria Novella** (Piazza della Stazione) is on the main Rome–Milan line. There are regular direct services to/from Pisa (€8, one hour), Rome (€65, 1½ to 3½ hours), Venice (€40 to €49, two hours) and Milan (€35 to €74, 1¾ hours).

Getting Around

TO/FROM THE AIRPORT

Volainbus (☎800 373760; www.fsbusitalia.it) The Volainbus shuttle runs between the bus station and Florence airport. Going to the airport, departures are roughly half-hourly between 6am and 8.30pm and then hourly until 11.30pm; from the airport between 5.30am and 8.30pm then hourly until 11.45pm. Journey time is 30 minutes and a single/return ticket costs €6/10.

PUBLIC TRANSPORT

City buses are operated by ATAF. Get tickets (€1.20 or €2 if bought on board) at the ticket office at Santa Maria Novella train station, at tobacconists and at news-stands. They are valid for 90 minutes on any bus.

Pisa

POP 89,160

A handsome university city, Pisa is best known as the home of an architectural project gone terribly wrong. However, the Leaning Tower is just one of a number of noteworthy sights in its compact medieval centre.

Pisa's golden age came in the 12th and 13th centuries when it was a maritime power to rival Genoa and Venice.

Sights

★Leaning Tower — TOWER

(Torre Pendente; ☎050 83 50 11; www.opapisa.it; Piazza dei Miracoli; €18; ⊙8am-8pm Apr-Sep, 9am-7pm Oct, to 6pm Mar, 10am-5pm Nov-Feb) One of Italy's signature sights, the Torre Pendente truly lives up to its name, leaning a startling 3.9 degrees off the vertical. The 56m-high tower, officially the Duomo's *campanile* (bell tower), took almost 200 years to build, but was already listing when it was unveiled in 1372. Over time, the tilt, caused by a layer of weak subsoil, steadily worsened until it was finally halted by a major stabilisation project in the 1990s.

★Duomo — CATHEDRAL

(☎050 83 50 11; www.opapisa.it; Piazza dei Miracoli; ⊙10am-8pm Apr-Sep, to 7pm Oct, to 6pm Nov-Mar) FREE Pisa's magnificent Romanesque Duomo was begun in 1064 and consecrated in 1118. Its striking tiered exterior, with cladding of green-and-cream marble bands, gives on to a vast columned interior capped by a gold wooden ceiling. The elliptical dome, the first of its kind in Europe at the time, was added in 1380.

Note that while admission is free, you'll need an entrance coupon from the ticket office or a ticket from one of the other Piazza dei Miracoli sights.

★Battistero — CHRISTIAN SITE

(Baptistry; ☎050 83 50 11; www.opapisa.it; Piazza dei Miracoli; €5, combination ticket with Camposanto or Museo delle Sinopie €7, Camposanto & Museo

€8; ⌚8am-8pm Apr-Sep, 9am-7pm Oct, to 6pm Mar, 10am-5pm Nov-Feb) Pisa's unusual round baptistry has one dome piled on top of another, each roofed half in lead, half in tiles, and topped by a gilt bronze John the Baptist (1395). Construction began in 1152, but it was remodelled and continued by Nicola and Giovanni Pisano more than a century later and finally completed in the 14th century. Inside, the hexagonal marble pulpit (1260) by Nicola Pisano is the highlight.

Sleeping & Eating

★ Hotel Pisa Tower HOTEL €€

(☎050 520 00 19; www.hotelpisatower.com; Via Andrea Pisano 23; d €115-125, tr €140-145, q €150-160; P ❄ ☎) Superb value for money, a superlative location, and spacious, high-ceilinged rooms – this polished three-star is one of Pisa's best deals. Chandeliers, marble floors and old framed prints adorn the classically attired interiors, while out back, a pristine lawn adds a soothing dash of green.

Hotel Bologna HOTEL €€

(☎050 50 21 20; www.hotelbologna.pisa.it; Via Giuseppe Mazzini 57; s €98-228; P ❄ ☎) Placed well away from the Piazza dei Miracoli mayhem, this elegant four-star mansion hotel is an oasis of peace and tranquillity. Its big, bright rooms have wooden floors and colour-coordinated furnishings – some are frescoed. Kudos for the small terrace and cypress-shaded garden out the back – delightful for lazy summertime breakfasts. Reception organises bike/scooter hire; courtyard parking for motorists costs €10 per night.

★ L'Ostellino SANDWICHES €

(Piazza Cavallotti 1; panini €3.50-7; ⌚noon-4.30pm Mon-Fri, to 6pm Sat & Sun) For a buster-size gourmet *panino* (sandwich) wrapped in crunchy waxed paper, this minuscule deli and *panineria* (sandwich shop) delivers. Take your pick from dozens of different combos written by hand on the blackboard (*lardo di colonnata* with figs or cave-aged pecorino with honey and walnuts are sweet favourites), await construction, then hit the green lawns of Piazza dei Miracoli to picnic with the crowds.

Osteria La Toscana OSTERIA €€

(☎050 96 90 52; Via San Frediano 10; meals €30; ⌚noon-3pm & 7-11pm Thu-Tue) This relaxed spot is one of several excellent eateries on Via San Frediano, a lively street off Piazza dei Cavalieri. Subdued lighting, bare brown walls and background jazz set the stage for ample pastas and delectable grilled meats served with a smile and quiet efficiency.

TOWER & COMBO TICKETS

Buy tickets for the Leaning Tower (€18) from one of two offices: the main **ticket office** (☎050 83 50 11; www.opapisa.it; Piazza dei Miracoli; ⌚8.30am-7.30pm summer, to 5.30pm winter) behind the tower or the smaller office inside **Museo delle Sinópie** (Piazza dei Miracoli; ⌚8am-8pm Apr-Sep, 9am-7pm Oct, to 6pm Mar, 10am-5pm Nov-Feb). To cut the long queue in high season, buy tickets online (note tickets can only be bought 20 days before visiting).

Ticket offices in Pisa also sell combination tickets covering admission to the Battistero (Baptistry), Museo delle Sinópie and Camposanto: buy a ticket covering one/two/three sights for €5/7/8.

Information

Tourist Office (☎050 55 01 00; www.turismo.pisa.it/en; Piazza dei Miracoli 7; ⌚9.30am-5.30pm) Provides city information and various services including bike hire and left luggage.

Getting There & Around

Pisa International Airport (Galileo Galilei Airport; ☎050 84 93 00; www.pisa-airport.com) is linked to the city centre by the PisaMover bus (€1.30, eight minutes, every 10 minutes).

Terravision buses link the airport with Florence (one way/return €5/10, 70 minutes, 18 daily).

Frequent trains run to Lucca (€3.50, 30 minutes), Florence (€8.40, one hour) and La Spezia (€7.50 to €15, one to 1½ hours) for the Cinque Terre.

Lucca

POP 89,000

Lucca is a love-at-first-sight type of place. Hidden behind monumental Renaissance walls, its historic centre is chock-full of handsome churches, alluring piazzas and excellent restaurants. Founded by the Etruscans, it became a city state in the 12th century and stayed that way for 600 years. Most of its streets and monuments date from this period.

Sights

City Wall HISTORIC SITE

Lucca's monumental *mura* (wall) was built around the old city in the 16th and 17th centuries and remains in almost perfect condition. It superceded two previous walls, the first built from travertine stone blocks as early as the 2nd century BC. Twelve metres high and 4.2km long, today's ramparts are crowned with a tree-lined footpath looking down on the *centro storico* and out towards the Apuane Alps. This path is a favourite location for the locals' daily *passeggiata* (traditional evening stroll).

★Cattedrale di San Martino CATHEDRAL

(☎0583 49 05 30; www.museocattedralelucca.it; Piazza San Martino; adult/reduced €3/2, incl Museo della Cattedrale & Chiesa e Battistero dei SS Giovanni & Reparata €9/5; ⊙9.30am-6pm Mon-Fri, to 6.45pm Sat, noon-6pm Sun summer, 9.30am-5pm Mon-Fri, to 6.45pm Sat, noon-6pm Sun winter) Lucca's predominantly Romanesque cathedral dates to the 11th century. Its stunning facade was constructed in the prevailing Lucca-Pisan style and designed to accommodate the pre-existing *campanile* (bell tower). The reliefs over the left doorway of the portico are believed to be by Nicola Pisano, while inside, treasures include the **Volto Santo** (literally, Holy Countenance) crucifix sculpture and a wonderful 15th-century tomb in the **sacristy**. The cathedral interior was rebuilt in the 14th and 15th centuries with a Gothic flourish.

Sleeping & Eating

★Piccolo Hotel Puccini HOTEL €

(☎0583 5 54 21; www.hotelpuccini.com; Via di Poggio 9; s/d/t €75/95/120; ❄📶) In a brilliant central location, this welcoming three-star hotel hides behind a discreet brick exterior. Its small guest rooms are attractive with wooden floors, vintage ceiling fans and colourful, contemporary design touches. Breakfast, optional at €3.50, is served at candlelit tables behind the small reception area. Rates are around 30% lower in winter.

★Da Felice PIZZA €

(☎0583 49 49 86; www.pizzeriadafelice.it; Via Buia 12; focaccias €1-3, pizza slices €1.30; ⊙11am-8.30pm Mon, 10am-8.30pm Tue-Sat) This buzzing spot behind Piazza San Michele is where the locals come for wood-fired pizza, *cecina* (salted chickpea pizza) and *castagnacci* (chestnut cakes). Eat in or take away, *castagnaccio* comes wrapped in crisp white paper, and, my, it's good married with a chilled bottle of Moretti beer.

★Ristorante Giglio TUSCAN €€

(☎0583 49 40 58; www.ristorantegiglio.com; Piazza del Giglio 2; meals €40; ⊙noon-2.30pm & 7.30-10pm Thu-Mon, 7.30-10pm Wed) Don't let the tacky plastic-covered pavement terrace deter. Splendidly at home in the frescoed 18th-century Palazzo Arnolfini, Giglio is stunning. Dine at white-tableclothed tables, sip a complimentary *prosecco,* watch the fire crackle in the marble fireplace and savour traditional Tuscan with a modern twist: think fresh artichoke salad served in an edible parmesan-cheese wafer 'bowl', or risotto simmered in Chianti.

Information

Tourist Office (☎0583 58 31 50; www.turismo.lucca.it; Piazzale Verdi; ⊙9am-7pm Apr-Sep, to 5pm Mar-Oct) Free hotel reservations, left-luggage service (two bags €1.50/4.50/7 per hour/half-day/day) and guided city tours in English departing at 2pm daily in summer and on Saturdays and Sundays in winter. The two-hour tour costs €10.

Getting There & Around

Regional trains run to/from Florence (€7.50, 1½ hours, every 30 to 90 minutes) and Pisa (€3.50, 30 minutes, half-hourly).

Siena

POP 53,900

Siena is one of Italy's most enchanting medieval towns. Its walled centre is a beautifully preserved warren of dark lanes punctuated with Gothic *palazzi,* and at its heart, Piazza del Campo (Il Campo), the sloping square that is the venue for the city's famous annual horse race, Il Palio.

In the Middle Ages, the city was a political and artistic force to be reckoned with, a worthy rival for its larger neighbour Florence.

Sights

★Piazza del Campo SQUARE

This sloping piazza, popularly known as Il Campo, has been Siena's civic and social centre since being staked out by the ruling Consiglio dei Nove in the mid-12th century. It was built on the site of a Roman marketplace, and its pie-piece paving design is divided into nine sectors to represent the number of members of that ruling council.

Palazzo Pubblico HISTORIC BUILDING
(Palazzo Comunale; Piazza del Campo) The restrained, 14th-century Palazzo Comunale serves as the grand centrepiece of the square in which it sits – notice how its concave facade mirrors the opposing convex curve. From the *palazzo* soars a graceful bell tower, the **Torre del Mangia** (☎0577 29 23 43; www.enjoysiena.it; admission €10; ⏲10am-6.15pm summer, to 3.15pm winter), 102m high and with 500-odd steps. The views from the top are magnificent.

★**Museo Civico** MUSEUM
(Civic Museum; ☎0577 29 22 32; Palazzo Pubblico, Piazza del Campo 1; adult/reduced €9/8; ⏲10am-6.15pm summer, to 5.15pm winter) Siena's most famous museum occupies rooms richly frescoed by artists of the Sienese school. Commissioned by the governing body of the city, rather than by the church, many – unusually – depict secular subjects. The highlight is Simone Martini's celebrated *Maestà* (Virgin Mary in Majesty; 1315) in the **Sala del Mappamondo** (Hall of the World Map). It features the Madonna beneath a canopy surrounded by saints and angels, and is Martini's first known work.

★**Duomo** CATHEDRAL
(Cattedrale di Santa Maria Assunta; ☎0577 28 63 00; www.operaduomo.siena.it; Piazza Duomo; summer/winter €4/free, when floor displayed €7; ⏲10.30am-7pm Mon-Sat, 1.30-6pm Sun summer, to 5.30pm winter) Siena's cathedral is one of Italy's most awe-inspiring churches. Construction started in 1215 and over the centuries many of Italy's top artists have contributed: Giovanni Pisano designed the intricate white, green and red marble facade; Nicola Pisano carved the elaborate pulpit; Pinturicchio painted some of the frescoes; Michelangelo, Donatello and Gian Lorenzo Bernini all produced sculptures. Buy tickets from the **duomo ticket office** (☎0577 28 63 00; ⏲10am-6.30pm summer, to 5pm winter).

★**Museale Santa Maria della Scala** MUSEUM
(☎0577 53 45 71, 0577 53 45 11; www.santamariadellascala.com; Piazza Duomo 1; adult/reduced €9/7; ⏲10am-5pm Mon, Wed & Thu, to 8pm Fri, to 7pm Sat & Sun, extended hours in summer) This former hospital, parts of which date from the 13th century, was built as a hospice for pilgrims travelling the Via Francigena pilgrimage trail. Its highlight is the upstairs Pellegrinaio (Pilgrim's Hall), with vivid 15th-century frescoes by Lorenzo Vecchietta, Priamo della Quercia and Domenico di Bartolo lauding the good works of the hospital and its patrons.

Festivals & Events

Palio PAGEANT, HORSE RACE
(⏲2 Jul & 16 Aug) Dating from the Middle Ages, this spectacular annual event includes a series of colourful pageants and a wild

WORTH A TRIP

SAN GIMIGNANO

This tiny hilltop town deep in the Tuscan countryside is a mecca for day trippers from Florence and Siena. Its nickname is the 'Medieval Manhattan' courtesy of the 14 11th-century towers that soar above its pristine *centro storico* (historic centre).

The **tourist office** (☎0577 94 00 08; www.sangimignano.com; ⏲10am-1pm & 3-7pm summer, 10am-1pm & 2-6pm winter) is on Piazza del Duomo. Next door, **Palazzo Comunale** (☎0577 99 03 12; www.sangimignanomusei.it; combined Civic Museums ticket adult/reduced €9/7; ⏲10am-7.30pm summer, 11am-5.30pm winter) houses San Gimignano's art gallery, the **Pinacoteca**, and tallest tower, the **Torre Grossa**.

Overlooking Piazza del Duomo, the **Collegiata** (Duomo or Basilica di Santa Maria Assunta; ☎0577 94 01 52; www.duomosangimignano.it; adult/reduced €4/2; ⏲10am-7pm Mon-Sat, 12.30-7pm Sun summer, 10am-4.30pm Mon-Sat, 12.30-4.30pm Sun winter), San Gimignano's Romanesque cathedral, boasts a series of superb 14th-century frescoes.

For a traditional Tuscan lunch, head to **Locanda Sant'Agostino** (☎0577 94 31 41; Piazza Sant'Agostino 15; meals €35, pizzas €8-10; ⏲noon-3pm & 7-10pm Thu-Tue).

Regular buses link San Gimignano with Florence (€6.80, 1¼ to two hours, hourly) via Poggibonsi. There are also services to/from Siena (€6, 1¼ hours, 10 daily Monday to Saturday).

WORTH A TRIP

ORVIETO

Strategically located on the main train line between Rome and Florence, this spectacularly sited hilltop town has one major drawcard: its extraordinary Gothic **Duomo** (☎0763 34 24 77; www.opsm.it; Piazza Duomo 26; €3; ⊙9.30am-7pm summer, shorter hours winter), built over 300 years from 1290. The facade is stunning, and the beautiful interior contains Luca Signorelli's awe-inspiring *Giudizio universale* (The Last Judgment) fresco cycle.

For information, the **tourist office** (☎0763 34 17 72; www.inorvieto.it; Piazza Duomo 24; ⊙8.15am-1.50pm & 4-7pm Mon-Fri, 10am-1pm & 3-6pm Sat & Sun) is opposite the cathedral. For a filling meal, search out the **Trattoria del Moro Aronne** (☎0763 34 27 63; www.trattoriadelmoro.info; Via San Leonardo 7; meals €25-30; ⊙noon-3pm & 7-10pm Wed-Mon).

Direct trains run to/from Florence (€16, 2¼ hours, hourly) and Rome (€8 to €17.50, 1¼ hours, hourly).

If you arrive by train, you'll need to take the **funicular** (tickets €1.30; ⊙every 10min 7.20am-8.30pm Mon-Sat, every 15min 8am-8.30pm Sun) up to the town centre.

horse race in Piazza del Campo. Ten of Siena's 17 *contrade* (town districts) compete for the coveted *palio* (silk banner). Each *contrada* has its own traditions, symbol and colours, plus its own church and *palio* museum.

Sleeping & Eating

★Hotel Alma Domus HOTEL €
(☎0577 4 41 77; www.hotelalmadomus.it; Via Camporegio 37; s €55, d €90-140; ❄@🛜) Your chance to sleep in a convent: Alma Domus is owned by the church and is still home to several Dominican nuns. The economy rooms, although supremely comfortable, are styled very simply. But the superior ones are positively sumptuous, with pristine bathrooms, pared-down furniture and bursts of magenta and lime. Many have mini-balconies with uninterrupted Duomo views. Families are welcome.

★Pensione Palazzo Ravizza BOUTIQUE HOTEL €€
(☎0577 28 04 62; www.palazzoravizza.it; Pian dei Mantellini 34; s €145-230, d €160-295, ste €250-315; P❄🛜) Heritage features and luxurious flourishes combine at this Renaissance-era *palazzo* to create an irresistible hotel. Frescoed ceilings, stone staircases and gilt mirrors meet elegant furnishings, wooden shutters and (from some bedrooms) captivating views. The greenery-framed rear garden is utterly delightful; settle down in a wicker chair here, gaze out towards the hills and you may never want to leave.

★Morbidi DELI €
(☎0577 28 02 68; www.morbidi.com; Via Banchi di Sopra 75; lunch/aperitivo buffet €12/from €7; ⊙8am-8pm Mon-Thu, to 10pm Fri & Sat) Possibly the classiest cheap feed in Siena: set in the stylish basement of Morbidi's deli, the lunch buffet on offer here is excellent. For a mere €12, you can join the well-dressed locals sampling antipasti, salads, risottos, pastas and a dessert of the day. Bottled water is supplied; wine and coffee cost extra. Buy your ticket upstairs before heading down.

★Enoteca I Terzi TUSCAN €€
(☎0577 4 43 29; www.enotecaiterzi.it; Via dei Termini 7; meals €35; ⊙11am-3pm & 6.30pm-1am Mon-Sat, shorter hours in winter) A favourite for many locals who head to this historic *enoteca* (wine bar) to linger over lunches, *aperitivi* and casual dinners featuring top-notch Tuscan *salumi* (cured meats), delicate handmade pasta and wonderful wines.

Osteria Nonna Gina TUSCAN €€
(☎0577 28 72 47; www.osterianonnagina.it; Pian dei Mantellini 2; meals €30; ⊙12.30-2.30pm & 7.30-10.30pm Tue-Sun) The atmosphere is pure Siena neighbourhood *osteria*: gingham tablecloths, postcards tacked to the rafters and pictures of Palio jockeys on the walls. The menu speaks of fine local traditions too: piles of local meat form the *antipasto Toscano* and the house red is a very decent Chianti, while the ingredients of the 'secret sauce' covering the plump, cheese-filled gnocchi will never be revealed.

Information

Tourist Office (☎0577 28 05 51; www.enjoysiena.it; Santa Maria della Scala, Piazza Duomo 1; ⊙9am-6pm summer, to 5pm winter)

Provides free Siena city maps, reserves accommodation, organises car and scooter hire, and sells train tickets (commission applies). Also takes bookings for a range of day tours.

Getting There & Away

Siena Mobilità (800 922984; www.sienamobilita.it), part of the **Tiemme** (0577 20 41 11; www.tiemmespa.it) network, links Siena with Florence (€7.80, 1¼ hours, at least hourly) and San Gimignano (€6, 1¼ hours, 10 daily Monday to Saturday), either direct or via Poggibonsi.

Sena (0861 199 19 00; www.sena.it) operates services to/from Rome Tiburtina (€20, three hours, up to 13 daily), Milan (€32, 4½ hours, three daily), Perugia (€18, 1¾ hours, one daily) and Venice (€27, 5¾ hours, two daily).

Ticket offices are in the basement under the bus station on Piazza Gramsci.

Perugia

POP 166,100

With its hilltop medieval centre and international student population, Perugia is Umbria's largest and most cosmopolitan city. In July, music fans inundate the city for the prestigious **Umbria Jazz festival** (www.umbriajazz.com), and in the third week of October the **Eurochocolate** (www.eurochocolate.com) festival lures chocoholics from across the globe.

Perugia has a dramatic and bloody past. In the Middle Ages, art and culture thrived – both Perugino and Raphael, his student, worked here – as powerful local dynasties fought for control of the city.

Sights

Cattedrale di San Lorenzo CATHEDRAL

(Piazza IV Novembre; 7.30am-12.30pm & 3.30-6.45pm Mon-Sat, 8am-12.45pm & 4-7.30pm Sun) Overlooking Piazza IV Novembre is Perugia's stark medieval cathedral. A church has stood here since the 900s, but the version you see today was begun in 1345 from designs created by Fra Bevignate. Building continued until 1587, although the main facade was never completed. Inside you'll find dramatic late Gothic architecture, an altarpiece by Signorelli and sculptures by Duccio. The steps in front of the facade are where seemingly all of Perugia congregates; they overlook the piazza's centrepiece, the delicate pink-and-white marble **Fontana Maggiore** (Great Fountain).

★Palazzo dei Priori PALACE

(Corso Vannucci 19) Flanking Corso Vannucci, this Gothic palace, constructed between the 13th and 14th centuries, is architecturally striking with its tripartite windows, ornamental portal and fortress-like crenellations. It was formerly the headquarters of the local magistracy, but now houses the city's main art gallery, the Galleria Nazionale dell'Umbria. Also of note is the **Nobile Collegio del Cambio** (Exchange Hall; www.collegiodelcambio.it; €4.50, incl Nobile Collegio della Mercanzia €5.50; 9am-12.30pm & 2.30-5.30pm Mon-Sat, 9am-1pm Sun), Perugia's medieval money exchange, with its Perugino frescoes.

Galleria Nazionale dell'Umbria GALLERY

(www.gallerianazionaleumbria.it; Palazzo dei Priori, Corso Vannucci 19; adult/reduced €8/4; 8.30am-7.30pm Tue-Sun, noon-7.30pm Mon Apr-Oct) Umbria's foremost art gallery is housed in Palazzo dei Priori on the city's main strip. Its collection, one of central Italy's richest, numbers almost 3000 works, ranging from Byzantine-inspired 13th-century paintings to Gothic works by Gentile da Fabriano and Renaissance masterpieces by hometown heroes Pinturicchio and Perugino.

Sleeping & Eating

★B&B San Fiorenzo B&B €

(393 3869987; www.sanfiorenzo.com; Via Alessi 45; d/qd €70/120;) Buried in Perugia's medieval maze of a centre is this charming 15th-century *palazzo*, where Luigi and Monica make you welcome in one of three unique rooms. A Florentine architect has carefully incorporated mod cons and marble bathrooms into spacious quarters with brick vaulting, lime-washed walls and antique furnishings, including an apartment with an 11th-century well shower and a 13th-century tower room.

Hotel Signa HOTEL €

(075 572 41 80; www.hotelsigna.it; Via del Grillo 9; s €34-59, d €49-99, tr €69-104, q €69-135;) Slip down an alley off Corso Cavour to reach Signa, one of Perugia's best budget picks. The petite rooms are simple, bright and well kept; many have balconies with cracking views of the city and countryside. Rooms at the cheaper end of the scale have shared bathrooms. Breakfast costs an extra €7. The owner, Mario, hands out maps and tips freely.

Pizzeria Mediterranea PIZZA €
(Piazza Piccinino 11/12; pizzas €4-12; ⏲12.30-2.30pm & 7.30-11.30pm; 👪) A classic pizzeria with a wood-fired oven and bustling atmosphere, this popular spot does the best pizzas in town. Served bubbling hot, they come with light, Neapolitan-style bases and flavoursome toppings. Expect queues at the weekend.

★**La Taverna** ITALIAN €€
(☎075 572 41 28; www.ristorantelataverna.com; Via delle Streghe 8; meals €30-40; ⏲12.30-3pm & 7.30-11pm; 📶) Way up there on the Perugia dining wish list, La Taverna consistently wins the praise of local foodies. Chef Claudio cooks market-fresh produce with flair and precision, while waiters treat you like one of the *famiglia*.

Information

Informazione e Accoglienza Turistica (IAT) (Tourist Information; ☎075 573 64 58; http://turismo.comune.perugia.it; Piazza Matteotti 18; ⏲9am-6pm) Housed in the 14th-century Loggia dei Lanari, Perugia's main tourist office has stacks of info on the city, maps (€0.50) and up-to-date bus and train timetables.

Getting There & Around

BUS

Perugia's bus station is on Piazza dei Partigiani, from where *scale mobili* (escalators) connect with Piazza Italia in the historic centre.

Sulga (☎800 099661; www.sulga.it) Buses run to/from Rome (€17, 2½ hours, up to five daily) and Fiumicino Airport (€22, 3¾ hours, four Monday to Saturday, two Sunday).

Umbria Mobilità (☎075 963 76 37; www.fsbusitalia.it) Operates buses to regional destinations, including Assisi (€4.20, 45 minutes, up to eight daily).

TRAIN

Direct trains connect with Florence (€14.55, 1½ to two hours, 10 daily).

To get to the centre from the train station, take the *minimetrò* (€1.50) to the Pincetto stop just below Piazza Matteotti. Alternatively, take the bus to Piazza Italia (€1.50, €2 on bus) .

Assisi

POP 28,300

The birthplace of St Francis (1182–1226), the medieval town of Assisi is a major destination for millions of pilgrims. The main sight is the Basilica di San Francesco, one of Italy's most visited churches, but the hilltop historic centre is also well worth a look.

Sights

★**Basilica di San Francesco** BASILICA
(www.sanfrancescoassisi.org; Piazza di San Francesco; ⏲upper church 8.30am-6.50pm, lower church & tomb 6am-6.50pm) FREE Visible for miles around, the Basilica di San Francesco is the crowning glory of Assisi's Unesco World Heritage ensemble. It's divided into an upper church, the **Basilica Superiore**, with a celebrated cycle of Giotto frescoes, and beneath, the lower, older **Basilica Inferiore**, where you'll find frescoes by Cimabue, Pietro Lorenzetti and Simone Martini. Also here, in the **Cripta di San Francesco**, is St Francis' elaborate and monumental tomb.

Basilica di Santa Chiara BASILICA
(www.assisisantachiara.it; Piazza Santa Chiara; ⏲6.30am-noon & 2-7pm summer, to 6pm winter) Built in a 13th-century Romanesque style, with steep ramparts and a striking pink-and-white facade, this church is dedicated to St Clare, a spiritual contemporary of St Francis and founder of the Sorelle Povere di Santa Chiara (Order of the Poor Ladies), now known as the Poor Clares. She is buried in the church's crypt, alongside the **Crocifisso di San Damiano**, a Byzantine cross before which St Francis was praying when he heard from God in 1205.

Sleeping & Eating

Hotel Alexander HOTEL €
(☎075 81 61 90; www.hotelalexanderassisi.it; Piazza Chiesa Nuova 6; s €50-75, d €75-108; ❄📶) On a small cobbled piazza by the Chiesa Nuova, Hotel Alexander offers nine spacious rooms and a communal terrace with wonderful rooftop views. The modern decor – pale wooden floors and earthy brown tones – contrasts well with the wood-beamed ceilings and carefully preserved antiquity all around.

★**Osteria Eat Out** UMBRIAN €€
(☎075 81 31 63; www.eatoutosteriagourmet.it; Via Eremo delle Carceri 1a; meals €40-50; ⏲7.30-10.30pm Mon-Fri, 7.30-10.30pm & 12.30-2.30pm Sat & Sun; 📶) With such astounding views and minimalist-chic interiors, you might expect the glass-fronted restaurant of the Nun Assisi hotel to prefer style over substance. Not so. Polished service and an exciting wine list are well matched with seasonal Umbrian cuisine flavoured with home-grown herbs. Dishes like *umbricelli* pasta with fresh truf-

fle and fillet of Chianina beef are big on flavour and easy on the eye.

Information

Informazione e Accoglienza Turistica (IAT) (Tourist Office; ☎075 813 86 80; www.visit-assisi.it; Piazza del Comune 22; ⏲9am-6pm Mon-Fri, to 7pm Sat, to 6pm Sun, shorter hours winter) Stop by here for maps, leaflets and info on accommodation.

Getting There & Away

It is better to travel to Assisi by bus rather than train.

Buses arrive at and depart from Piazza Matteotti in the *centro storico*.

Umbria Mobilità (☎075 963 76 37; www.fsbusitalia.it) Buses run to/from Perugia (€4.20, 45 minutes, up to eight daily).

SOUTHERN ITALY

A sun-bleached land of spectacular coastlines and rugged landscapes, southern Italy is a robust contrast to the more genteel north. Its stunning scenery, baroque towns and classical ruins exist alongside ugly urban sprawl and scruffy coastal development, sometimes in the space of just a few kilometres.

Yet for all its flaws, *il mezzogiorno* (the midday sun, as southern Italy is known) is an essential part of every Italian itinerary, offering charm, culinary good times and architectural treasures.

Naples

POP 974,000

A love-it-or-loathe-it sprawl of regal palaces, bombastic churches and chaotic streets, Naples (Napoli) is totally exhilarating. Founded by Greek colonists, it became a thriving Roman city and was later the Bourbon capital of the Kingdom of the Two Sicilies. In the 18th century it was one of Europe's great cities, something you'll readily believe as you marvel at its art-crammed museums and great baroque buildings.

THE ARTECARD

The **Campania Artecard** (www.campaniartecard.it) offers discounted museum admission and transport. It comes in various forms, of which the most useful are:

Napoli (€21, valid for three days) Gives free entry to three sights in Naples, then discounts on others, as well as free city transport.

Tutta la regione (€32/34, valid for three/seven days) Provides free entry to two/five sights (three-/seven-day card) across the region and discounts on others. Free public transport is covered by the three-day card, but not by the seven-day version.

Cards can be purchased online, at the dedicated artecard booth inside the tourist office at Stazione Centrale (p483), or at participating sites and museums.

Sights

★Museo Archeologico Nazionale MUSEUM

(☎848 80 02 88, from mobile 06 399 67050; www.museoarcheologiconapoli.it; Piazza Museo Nazionale 19; adult/reduced €12/6; ⏲9am-7.30pm Wed-Mon; Ⓜ Museo, Piazza Cavour) Naples' National Archaeological Museum serves up one of the world's finest collections of Graeco-Roman artefacts. Originally a cavalry barracks and later seat of the city's university, the museum was established by the Bourbon king Charles VII in the late 18th century to house the antiquities he inherited from his mother, Elisabetta Farnese, as well as treasures looted from Pompeii and Herculaneum. Star exhibits include the celebrated *Toro Farnese* (Farnese Bull) sculpture and a series of awe-inspiring mosaics from Pompeii's Casa del Fauno.

★Cappella Sansevero CHAPEL

(☎081 551 84 70; www.museosansevero.it; Via Francesco de Sanctis 19; adult/reduced €7/5; ⏲9.30am-6.30pm Wed-Mon; Ⓜ Dante) It's in this Masonic-inspired baroque chapel that you'll find Giuseppe Sanmartino's incredible sculpture, *Cristo velato* (Veiled Christ), its marble veil so realistic that it's tempting to try to lift it and view Christ underneath. It's one of several artistic wonders that include Francesco Queirolo's sculpture *Disinganno* (Disillusion), Antonio Corradini's *Pudicizia* (Modesty) and riotously colourful frescoes by Francesco Maria Russo, the latter untouched since their creation in 1749.

Central Naples

0 400 m
0 0.2 miles

A B C D

1

Museo Archeologico Nazionale
2
Museo
Palazzo Reale di Capodimonte (1.9km)
Via Foria
Via Maria Longo
Cerasiello B&B (350m); Casa D'Anna (500m)
Via Santissimi Apostoli
Piazza Cavour
Piazza Museo Nazionale
Via S Guiseppe dei Nudi
Via Santa Maria di Costantinopoli
Largo Regina Coeli
Via d Anticaglia
Via Pisanelli
Vico Giganti
Via Duomo
3
Via Tommasi
Via Broggia
Via San Paolo
Via dei Tribunali
Via della Zite
Via Francesco Saverio Correra
Via Enrico Pessina
Via della Sapienza
Via del Sole
Via Atri
Piazza San Gaetano
Vico Zuroli
Via Bellini

2

Piazza Luigi Miraglia
9
Vico Giuseppe Maffei
Via G Brombeis
Vico S Domenico Soriano
5
12
Via dei Tribunali
Via Nilo
Via Vicaria Vecchia
Piazza Bellini
Via Port'Alba
Cappella Sansevero
1
Piazza Museo Filangieri
11
Dante
Via San Biagio dei Librai
Via Montesanto
Piazza Dante
Via San Sebastiano
Palazzo dei Di Sangrio
Piazzetta del Nilo
Vico S Severino
Via d'Alagno
Via Tarsia
Via Benedetto Croce

3

Via Pellegrini
Duomo
Piazza Nicola Amore
Via B Capasso
Piazza del Gesù Nuovo
7
Funicolare di Montesanto (170m); Certosa e Museo di San Martino (1.5km)
Complesso Monumentale di Santa Chiara
Via Mezzocannone
Via G Paladino
Alibus (Stazione Central Stop) (850m); Terminal Metropark (1.1km); Stazione Centrale (1.2km); Circumvesuviana (1.2km)
Via S Anna dei Lombardi
Via Santa Chiara
Largo Giusso
Via Pasquale Scura
Via T Caravita
Largo Banchi Nuovi
Via Pignasecca
Via S Liborio
Via Formale
Corso Umberto I
Piazetta Orefici
Via Sedile di Porto
Via Nuova Marina

4

Eccelenze Campane (1.9km)
Piazza Carità
Via Donnalbina
Via Monteoliveto
Via G Simonelli
Via D. Cerriglio
Piazza Bovio
Vico P Galluppi
Via C Battisti
Via G C Cortese
Piazza Matteotti
Università
Via Concezione a Montecalvario
Via Bracco
Via A Diaz
Via Alside De Gasperi
Via Graziella
Tirrenia
Toledo
Via D Fiorentini
Via A Depretis

5

Calata Porta di Massa
Via Potracarrese a Montecalvario
Via S Tommaso d'Aquino
Via S Nicola alla Dogana
Via Cristoforo Colombo
Varco Immacolatella
Via F Gioia
Via Medina
Via S Bartolomeo
Via Speranzella
Via S Giacomo
4
Via Toledo
Piazza del Municipio
Via G Melisurgo
Piazza Francese
Via P E Imbriani
Bacino del Piliero
6
8
Via G Verdi
Municipio

6

Via Santa Brigida
Via Vittorio Emanuele III
Vico d'Aflitto
Molo Angioino
Funicolare Centrale
Castel Nuovo
Alibus For Airport
SNAV
Via San Carlo
Piazza Trieste e Trento
13
Alilauro
Parco Castello
Caremar
Via Chiaia
10
Muu Muuzzarella Lounge (600m); B&B Cappella Vecchia (700m)
Molo Beverello
Porto Immacolatella

7

Via A F Acton
Piazza del Plebiscito

A B C D

Central Naples

Top Sights

Sights

Sleeping

Eating

Drinking & Nightlife

Entertainment

★**Duomo** CATHEDRAL
(☎081 44 90 97; Via Duomo 149; cathedral/baptistry free/€2; ⊙cathedral 8.30am-1.30pm & 2.30-7.30pm Mon-Sat, 8am-1pm & 4.30-7.30pm Sun, baptistry 8.30am-12.30pm & 4-6.30pm Mon-Sat, 8.30am-1pm Sun; ▣E1, E2 to Via Duomo) Whether you go for Giovanni Lanfranco's fresco in the **Cappella di San Gennaro** (Chapel of St Janarius), the 4th-century mosaics in the baptistry, or the thrice-annual miracle of San Gennaro, do not miss Naples' cathedral. Kick-started by Charles I of Anjou in 1272 and consecrated in 1315, it was largely destroyed in a 1456 earthquake, with copious nips and tucks over the subsequent centuries.

★**Certosa e Museo di San Martino** MONASTERY, MUSEUM
(☎081 229 45 03; www.polomusealenapoli.beniculturali.it; Largo San Martino 5; adult/reduced €6/3; ⊙8.30am-7.30pm Thu-Tue; Ⓜ Vanvitelli, ▣Montesanto to Morghen) The high point (quite literally) of the Neapolitan baroque, this charterhouse turned museum was founded as a Carthusian monastery in the 14th century. Centred on one of the most beautiful cloisters in Italy, it has been decorated, adorned and altered over the centuries by some of Italy's finest talent, most importantly Giovanni Antonio Dosio in the 16th century and baroque master Cosimo Fanzago a century later. Nowadays, it's a superb repository of Neapolitan artistry.

★**Palazzo Reale di Capodimonte** MUSEUM
(☎081 740 91 30; www.museocapodimonte.beniculturali.it; Via Miano 2; adult/reduced €8/4; ⊙8.30am-7.30pm Thu-Tue; ▣R4, 178 to Via Capodimonte) Originally designed as a hunting lodge for Charles VII of Bourbon, this monumental palace was begun in 1738 and took more than a century to complete. It's now home to the **Museo Nazionale di Capodimonte**, southern Italy's largest and richest art gallery. Its vast collection – much of which Charles inherited from his mother, Elisabetta Farnese – was moved here in 1759 and ranges from exquisite 12th-century altarpieces to works by Botticelli, Caravaggio, Titian and Andy Warhol.

Festivals & Events

Festa di San Gennaro RELIGIOUS
The faithful flock to the Duomo to witness the miraculous liquefaction of San Gennaro's blood on the Saturday before the first Sunday in May. Repeat performances take place on 19 September and 16 December.

Sleeping

B&B Cappella Vecchia B&B €
(☎081 240 51 17; www.cappellavecchia11.it; Vico Santa Maria a Cappella Vecchia 11; s €50-80, d €75-110, tr €90-140; ❄@📶; ▣C24 to Piazza dei Martiri) Run by a super-helpful young couple, this B&B is a first-rate choice in the smart, fashionable Chiaia district. Rooms are simple and upbeat, with funky bathrooms, vibrant colours and Neapolitan themes. There's a spacious communal area for breakfast, and free internet available 24/7. Check the website for special offers.

Cerasiello B&B B&B €
(☎081 033 09 77, 338 926 44 53; www.cerasiello.it; Via Supportico Lopez 20; s €40-85, d €60-100, tr €75-110, q €90-125; ❄📶; Ⓜ Piazza Cavour, Museo) This gorgeous B&B consists of four rooms with private bathroom, an enchanting communal terrace and an ethno-chic look melding Neapolitan art with North African furnishings. The stylish kitchen offers a fabulous view of the Certosa di San Martino, a view shared by all rooms (or their bathroom) except Fuoco (Fire), which looks out at a beautiful church cupola.

Hostel of the Sun HOSTEL €
(☎081 420 63 93; www.hostelnapoli.com; Via G Melisurgo 15; dm €18-25, s €30-35, d €60-80; ❄@📶; Ⓜ Municipio) HOTS is an ultrafriendly hostel near the hydrofoil and ferry terminals. Located on the 7th floor (have €0.05 for the lift), it's a bright, sociable place with multicoloured dorms, a casual in-house bar (with cheap evening cocktails) and – a few floors down – a series of hotel-standard private rooms, many with en-suite bathrooms.

★**Hotel Piazza Bellini** BOUTIQUE HOTEL €€
(☎081 45 17 32; www.hotelpiazzabellini.com; Via Santa Maria di Costantinopoli 101; d €58-148; ❄@📶; Ⓜ Dante) Only steps from buzzing Piazza Bellini, this sharp, contemporary hotel occupies a 16th-century *palazzo,* its mint white spaces spiked with original maiolica tiles and the work of emerging artists. Rooms offer pared-back cool, with designer fittings, chic bathrooms and mirror frames drawn straight onto the wall. Rooms on the 5th and 6th floors feature panoramic terraces.

★**Casa D'Anna** GUESTHOUSE €€
(☎081 44 66 11; www.casadanna.it; Via dei Cristallini 138; s €80-114, d €113-163; ❄📶; Ⓜ Piazza Cavour, Museo) Everyone from artists to Parisian fashionistas adore this elegant guesthouse, lavished with antiques, books and original artwork. Its four guestrooms blend classic and contemporary design features of the highest quality, while the lush communal terrace is perfect for an alfresco tête-à-tête. Breakfast includes homemade baked treats and jams. There's a two-night minimum stay…though we doubt you'll be hurrying to leave.

★**La Ciliegina Lifestyle Hotel** BOUTIQUE HOTEL €€
(☎081 1971 8800; www.cilieginahotel.it; Via PE Imbriani 30; d €115-300, junior ste €144-400; ❄@📶; Ⓜ Municipio) An easy walk from the hydrofoil terminal, this chic, contemporary slumber spot is a hit with fashion-conscious urbanites. Spacious white rooms are splashed with blue and red accents, each with top-of-the-range Hästens beds, flatscreen TVs and marble-clad bathrooms with a water-jet Jacuzzi shower (one junior suite has a Jacuzzi tub).

Eating

★**Pizzeria Gino Sorbillo** PIZZA €
(☎081 44 66 43; www.sorbillo.it; Via dei Tribunali 32; pizzas from €3; ⌚noon-3.30pm & 7pm-11.30pm Mon-Thu, to midnight Fri & Sat; 📶; Ⓜ Dante) Day in, day out, this cult-status pizzeria is besieged by hungry hordes. While debate may rage over whether Gino Sorbillo's pizzas are the best in town, there's no doubt that his giant, wood-fired discs – made using organic flour and tomatoes – will have you licking fingertips and whiskers. Head in super early or prepare to queue.

★**Pintauro** PASTRIES €
(☎081 41 73 39; Via Toledo 275; sfogliatelle €2; ⌚9am-8pm, closed mid-Jul–early Sep; 🚌R2 to Via San Carlo, Ⓜ Municipio) Of Neapolitan *dolci* (sweets), the cream of the crop is the *sfogliatella,* a shell of flaky pastry stuffed with creamy, scented ricotta. This local institution has been selling *sfogliatelle* since the early 1800s, when its founder supposedly brought them to Naples from their culinary birthplace on the Amalfi Coast.

★**Muu Muuzzarella Lounge** NEAPOLITAN €
(☎081 40 53 70; www.muumuuzzarellalounge.it; Vico II Alabardieri 7; dishes €7-16; ⌚12.30pm-midnight Tue-Sun; 📶; 🚌C24 to Riviera di Chiaia) Pimped with milking-bucket lights and cow-hide patterned cushions, playful, contemporary Muu is all about super-fresh Campanian mozzarella, from cheese and charcuterie platters to creative dishes like buffalo bocconcini with creamy pesto and crunchy apple. Leave room for the chef's secret recipe white-chocolate cheesecake, best paired with a glass of Guappa (buffalo-milk liqueur).

★**La Taverna di Santa Chiara** NEAPOLITAN €€
(☎081 048 49 08; Via Santa Chiara 6; meals €25; ⌚1-2.30pm & 8-10.30pm, lunch to 3pm Fri-Sun, closed Tue lunch & Sun dinner; 📶; Ⓜ Dante) Gragnano pasta, Agerola pork, Benevento *latte nobile:* this intimate, two-level eatery is healthily obsessed with small, local producers and Slow Food ingredients. The result is a beautiful, seasonal journey across Campania. For an inspiring overview, order the *misto di salumi e formaggi* (an antipasto of cheese and cured meats), then tuck into lesser-known classics like *zuppa di soffritto* (spicy meat stew) with a glass of smooth house *vino.*

★ **Eccellenze Campane** NEAPOLITAN €€
(☎081 20 36 57; www.eccellenzecampane.it; Via Benedetto Brin 49; pizza from €6, meals around €30; ⏲complex 7am-11pm Sun-Fri, to 12.30am Sat, restaurants 12.30-3.30pm & 7.30-11pm Sun-Fri, to 12.30am Sat; 📶; 🚌192, 460, 472, 475) This is Naples' answer to Turin-based food emporium Eataly, an impressive, contemporary showcase for top-notch Campanian comestibles. The sprawling space is divided into various dining and shopping sections, offering everything from beautifully charred pizzas and light *fritture* (fried snacks) to finer-dining seafood, coveted Sal Da Riso pastries, craft beers and no shortage of take-home pantry treats. A must for gastronomes. Website in Italian.

★ **Ristorantino dell'Avvocato** NEAPOLITAN €€
(☎081 032 00 47; www.ilristorantinodellavvocato.it; Via Santa Lucia 115-117; meals €40-45; ⏲noon-3pm daily, also 7-11pm Tue-Sat; 📶; 🚌128 to Via Santa Lucia) This elegant yet welcoming restaurant has quickly won the respect of Neapolitan gastronomes. Apple of their eye is affable lawyer turned head chef Raffaele Cardillo, whose passion for Campania's culinary heritage merges with a knack for subtle, refreshing twists – think gnocchi with fresh mussels, clams, crumbed pistachio, lemon, ginger and garlic.

Drinking & Nightlife

Caffè Mexico CAFE
(Piazza Dante 86; ⏲5.30am-8.30pm Mon-Sat; Ⓜ Dante) Naples' best (and best-loved) coffee bar – even the local cops stop by for a quick pick-me-up – is a retro-tastic combo of old-school baristas, an orange espresso machine and velvety, full-flavoured *caffè*. The espresso is served *zuccherato* (sweetened), so request it *amaro* if you fancy a bitter hit.

Caffè Gambrinus CAFE
(☎081 41 75 82; www.grancaffegambrinus.com; Via Chiaia 1-2; ⏲7am-1am Sun-Thu, to 2am Fri & Sat; 🚌R2 to Via San Carlo, Ⓜ Municipio) Grand, chandeliered Gambrinus is Naples' oldest and most venerable cafe. Oscar Wilde knocked back a few here and Mussolini had some of the rooms shut to keep out left-wing intellectuals. The prices may be steep, but the *aperitivo* nibbles are decent and sipping a *spritz* or a luscious *cioccolata calda* (hot chocolate) in its belle époque rooms is something worth savouring.

Spazio Nea CAFE
(☎081 45 13 58; www.spazionea.it; Via Constantinopoli 53; ⏲9am-2am, to 3am Fri & Sat; 📶; Ⓜ Dante) Aptly skirting bohemian Piazza Bellini, this whitewashed gallery features its own cafe-bar speckled with books, flowers, cultured crowds and alfresco seating at the bottom of a baroque staircase. Eye up exhibitions of contemporary Italian and foreign art, then kick back with a *caffè* or a Cynar *spritz*. Check Nea's Facebook page for upcoming readings, live-music gigs or DJ sets.

☆ Entertainment

Teatro San Carlo OPERA, BALLET
(☎081 797 23 31; www.teatrosancarlo.it; Via San Carlo 98; ⏲box office 10am-5.30pm Mon-Sat, to 2pm Sun; 🚌R2 to Via San Carlo) One of Italy's top opera houses, the San Carlo stages opera, ballet and concerts. Bank on up to €40 for a place in the sixth tier, €75 to €110 for a seat in the stalls or – if you're under 30 and can prove it – €15 to €30 for a place in a side box. Ballet tickets range from €55 to €95, with €20 to €30 tickets for those under 30.

Information

Travellers should be careful about walking alone late at night near Stazione Centrale and Piazza Dante. Petty theft is also widespread so watchout for pickpockets (especially on the city's public transport) and scooter thieves.

Loreto Mare Hospital (Ospedale S. Maria di Loreto Nuovo; ☎081 254 21 11; www.aslnapoli1centro.it/818; Via A Vespucci 26; 🚌154) Central city hospital with an emergency department.

Police Station (Questura; ☎081 794 11 11; Via Medina 75; Ⓜ Università) To check if your car's been removed, call the municipal police on ☎081 787 06 37.

Tourist Information Office (☎081 26 87 79; Stazione Centrale; ⏲9am-8pm; Ⓜ Garibaldi) Tourist office inside Stazione Centrale (Central Station).

Tourist Information Office (☎081 551 27 01; www.inaples.it; Piazza del Gesù Nuovo 7; ⏲9am-5pm Mon-Sat, to 1pm Sun; Ⓜ Dante) Tourist office in the *centro storico*.

Tourist Information Office (☎081 40 23 94; www.inaples.it; Via San Carlo 9; ⏲9am-5pm Mon-Sat, to 1pm Sun; 🚌R2 to Via San Carlo, Ⓜ Municipio) Tourist office at Galleria Umberto I, directly opposite Teatro San Carlo.

Getting There & Away

AIR

Naples International Airport (Capodichino) (☎081 789 62 59; www.aeroportodinapoli.it) Capodichino airport, 7km northeast of the city centre, is southern Italy's main airport. It's served by a number of major airlines and low-cost carriers, including EasyJet, which operates flights to Naples from London, Paris, Berlin and several other European cities.

BOAT

Fast ferries and hydrofoils for Capri, Ischia, Procida and Sorrento depart from **Molo Beverello** in front of Castel Nuovo; hydrofoils also sail from Mergellina, 5km west.

Ferries for Sicily and Sardinia sail from **Molo Angioino** (right beside Molo Beverello) and neighbouring **Calata Porta di Massa**.

As a rough guide, bank on about €20 for the 50-minute jet crossing to Capri, and €12.50 for the 35-minute sail to Sorrento.

Tickets for shorter journeys can be bought at the ticket booths on Molo Beverello, Calata Porta di Massa or at Mergellina. For longer journeys try the offices of the ferry companies or a travel agent.

Hydrofoil and ferry companies include the following:

Alilauro (☎081 497 22 38; www.alilauro.it)

Caremar (☎081 1896 6690; www.caremar.it)

NLG (NLG; ☎081 552 07 63; www.navlib.it)

SNAV (☎081 428 55 55; www.snav.it)

Tirrenia (☎892 123; www.tirrenia.it)

BUS

Most national and international buses now leave from **Terminal Bus MetroPark** (☎800 65 00 06; Corso Arnaldo Lucci; Ⓜ Garibaldi), located on the southern side of Stazione Centrale. The bus station is home to **Biglietteria Vecchione** (☎331 88969217, 081 563 03 20; www.biglietteriavecchione.it; ⏲6.30am-9.30pm Mon-Fri, to 7.30pm Sat & Sun), a ticket agency selling national and international bus tickets.

TRAIN

Most trains arrive at or depart from **Stazione Centrale** (Piazza Garibaldi).

There are about 40 daily trains to Rome (€11 to €44, 1¼ to 2½ hours), many of which continue northwards.

From Piazza Garibaldi station (adjacent to Stazione Centrale), **Circumvesuviana** (☎800 21 13 88; www.eavsrl.it) operates half-hourly trains to Sorrento (€4.50, 65 minutes) via Ercolano (€2.50, 20 minutes) and Pompeii (€3.20, 40 minutes).

Getting Around

TO/FROM THE AIRPORT

Airport shuttle **Alibus** (☎800 63 95 25; www.anm.it) connects the airport to **Piazza Garibaldi** (Corso Novara) (Stazione Centrale) and **Molo Beverello** (€4, 45 minutes, every 20 minutes).

PUBLIC TRANSPORT

You can travel around Naples by bus, metro and funicular.

Tickets come in various forms, most usefully:

TIC Standard (Ticket Integrato Campania) Valid for 90 minutes, €1.50

TIC Daily €4.50

Note that these tickets are only valid for Naples city; they don't cover travel on the Circumvesuviana trains to Herculaneum, Pompeii and Sorrento.

Capri

POP 14,100

The most visited of the islands in the Bay of Naples, Capri deserves more than a quick day trip. Beyond the glamorous veneer of chichi cafes and designer boutiques is an island of rugged seascapes, desolate Roman ruins and a surprisingly unspoiled rural inland.

Ferries dock at Marina Grande, from where it's a short funicular ride up to Capri, the main town. A further bus ride takes you up to Anacapri.

Sights

Grotta Azzurra CAVE

(Blue Grotto; €14; ⏲9am-5pm) Capri's single most famous attraction is the Grotta Azzurra, a stunning sea cave illuminated by an other-worldly blue light. The easiest way to visit is to take a **tour** (☎081 837 56 46; www.motoscafisticapri.com; Private Pier 0, Marina Grande; €15) from Marina Grande; tickets include the return boat trip but the rowing boat into the cave and admission are paid separately. Allow a good hour.

Giardini di Augusto GARDENS

(Gardens of Augustus; €1; ⏲9am-7.30pm) Escape the crowds by seeking out these colourful gardens near the Certosa di San Giacomo. Founded by Emperor Augustus, they rise in a series of flowered terraces to a lookout point offering breathtaking views over to the **Isole Faraglioni**, a group of three limestone stacks that rise out of the sea.

WORTH A TRIP

POMPEII & HERCULANEUM

On 24 August AD 79, Mt Vesuvius erupted, submerging the thriving port of Pompeii in lapilli (burning fragments of pumice stone) and Herculaneum in mud. Both places were quite literally buried alive, leaving thousands of people dead. The Unesco-listed ruins of both provide remarkable models of working Roman cities, complete with streets, temples, houses, baths, forums, taverns, shops, and even a brothel.

Pompeii

A stark reminder of the malign forces that lie deep inside Vesuvius, the ruins of ancient **Pompeii** (081 857 53 47; www.pompeiisites.org; entrances at Porta Marina, Piazza Esedra & Piazza Anfiteatro; adult/reduced €13/7.50, incl Herculaneum €22/12; 9am-7.30pm Apr-Oct, to 5.30pm Nov-Mar) make for one of Europe's most compelling archaeological sites. The remains first came to light in 1594, when the architect Domenico Fontana stumbled across them while digging a canal, but systematic exploration didn't begin until 1748. Since then 44 of Pompeii's original 66 hectares have been excavated.

There's a huge amount to see at the site. Start with the **Terme Suburbane**, a public bathhouse decorated with erotic frescoes just outside **Porta Marina**, the most impressive of the city's original seven gates. Once inside the walls, continue down **Via Marina** to the grassy **foro** (forum). This was the ancient city's main piazza and is today flanked by limestone columns and what's left of the **basilica**, the 2nd-century-BC seat of the city's law courts and exchange. Opposite the basilica, the **Tempio di Apollo** is the oldest and most important of Pompeii's religious buildings, while at the forum's northern end the **Granai del Foro** (Forum Granary) stores hundreds of amphorae and a number of body casts. These were made in the 19th century by pouring plaster into the hollows left by disintegrated bodies. A short walk away, the **Lupanare** (Brothel) pulls in the crowds with its collection of red-light frescoes. To the south, the 2nd-century-BC **Teatro Grande** is a 5000-seat theatre carved into the lava mass on which Pompeii was originally built.

Other highlights include the **Anfiteatro**, the oldest known Roman amphitheatre in existence; the **Casa del Fauno**, Pompeii's largest private house, where many of the mosaics now in Naples' Museo Archeologico Nazionale originated; and the **Villa dei Misteri**, home to the Dionysiac frieze, the most important fresco still on site.

To get to Pompeii, take the Circumvesuviana train to Pompeii Scavi-Villa dei Misteri (€3.20, 40 minutes from Naples; €2.80, 30 minutes from Sorrento) near the main Porta Marina entrance.

Herculaneum

Smaller and less daunting than Pompeii, **Herculaneum** (081 857 53 47; www.pompeiisites.org; Corso Resina 187, Ercolano; adult/reduced €11/5.50, incl Pompeii €22/12; 8.30am-7.30pm Apr-Oct, to 5pm Nov-Mar; Circumvesuviana to Ercolano-Scavi) can reasonably be visited in a morning or afternoon.

A modest fishing port and resort for wealthy Romans, Herculaneum, like Pompeii, was destroyed by the Vesuvius eruption. But because it was much closer to the volcano, it drowned in a 16m-deep sea of mud and debris rather than in the lapilli and ash that rained down on Pompeii. This essentially fossilised the town, ensuring that even delicate items like furniture and clothing were well preserved. Excavations began after the town was rediscoverd in 1709 and continue to this day.

There are a number of fascinating houses to explore. Notable among them are the **Casa d'Argo**, a noble residence centred on a porticoed, palm-treed garden; the aristocratic **Casa di Nettuno e Anfitrite**, named after the extraordinary mosaic of Neptune in the nymphaeum (fountain and bath); and the **Casa dei Cervi** with its marble deer, murals, and beautiful still-life paintings.

Marking the sites' southernmost tip, the 1st-century-AD **Terme Suburbane** is a wonderfully preserved baths complex with deep pools, stucco friezes and bas-reliefs looking down on marble seats and floors.

To reach Herculaneum, take the Circumvesuviana train to Ercolano (€2.50, 20 minutes from Naples; €3.40, 45 minutes from Sorrento), from where it's a 500m walk from the station – follow signs downhill to the *scavi* (ruins).

★ **Villa Jovis** RUINS

(Jupiter's Villa; Via A Maiuri; €4; ⏲10am-7pm Tue-Sun summer, shorter hours rest of year, closed Jan–mid-Mar) A 45-minute walk east of Capri along Via Tiberio, Villa Jovis was the largest and most sumptuous of the island's 12 Roman villas and Tiberius' main Capri residence. A vast pleasure complex, now reduced to ruins, it famously pandered to the emperor's debauched tastes, and included imperial quarters and extensive bathing areas set in dense gardens and woodland.

★ **Seggiovia del Monte Solaro** CABLE CAR

(☎081 837 14 38; www.capriseggiovia.it; single/return €8/11; ⏲9.30am-5pm summer, to 3.30pm winter) A fast and painless way to reach Capri's highest peak, Anacapri's Seggiovia del Monte Solaro chairlift whisks you to the top of the mountain in a tranquil, beautiful ride of just 12 minutes. The views from the top are outstanding – on a clear day, you can see the entire Bay of Naples, the Amalfi Coast and the islands of Ischia and Procida.

Sleeping & Eating

★ **Hotel La Tosca** PENSION €€

(☎081 837 09 89; www.latoscahotel.com; Via Dalmazio Birago 5; s €50-105, d €75-165; ❄📶) Away from the glitz of the town centre, this charming one-star place is hidden down a quiet back lane overlooking the Certosa di San Giacomo. Rooms are airy and comfortable, with pine furniture, light tiles, striped fabrics and large bathrooms. Several also have private terraces or garden vistas. Breakfast is served on the terrace, with a view of the sea.

★ **Hotel Villa Eva** HOTEL €€

(☎081 837 15 49; www.villaeva.com; Via La Fabbrica 8; d €120-200, tr €150-220, apt per person €60-90; ⏲Apr-Oct; ❄@📶🏊) Nestled amid fruit and olive trees in the countryside near Anacapri, Villa Eva is an idyllic retreat, complete with swimming pool, lush gardens and sunny rooms and apartments. Whitewashed domes, terracotta floors, stained-glass windows and vintage fireplaces add character, while the location ensures peace and quiet.

★ **È Divino** ITALIAN €€

(☎081 837 83 64; www.edivinocapri.com/divino; Vico Sella Orta 10a; meals €30-35; ⏲8pm-1am daily Jun-Aug, 12.30-2.30pm & 7.30pm-midnight Tue-Sun rest of year; 📶) Look hard for the sign: this Slow Food restaurant is a well-kept secret. Step inside and you find yourself in what resembles a traditional sitting room; the only hints that this is a restaurant are the tantalising aromas and the distant tinkle of glasses. The menu changes daily, according to whatever is fresh from the garden or market.

La Rondinella ITALIAN €€

(☎081 837 12 23; www.ristorantelarondinella.com; Via Guiseppe Orlandi 295; meals €30; ⏲noon-2.30pm & 7-11.30pm Fri-Mon) La Rondinella has a relaxed, rural feel and remains one of Anacapri's better restaurants; apparently Graham Greene had a favourite corner table here. The menu features a number of Italian classics such as *saltimbocca alla romana* (veal slices with ham and sage).

ℹ Information

Tourist Office (☎081 837 06 34; www.capritourism.com; Banchina del Porto, Marina Grande; ⏲8.45am-1.30pm & 3.30-6pm Mon-Sat, 9am-1pm Sun summer, 8.30am-2.30pm Mon-Sat winter) Can provide a map of the island (€1) with town plans of Capri and Anacapri. For hotel listings and other useful information, ask for a free copy of *Capri è*.

ℹ Getting There & Around

There are year-round boats to Capri from Naples and Sorrento. Timetables and fare details are available online at www.capritourism.com.

From Naples Regular services depart from Molo Beverello. Tickets cost €20.50 for jetfoils, €12.80 for ferries.

From Sorrento Jetfoils cost €18.30, slower ferries €14.80.

On the island, buses run from Capri Town to/from Marina Grande, Anacapri and Marina Piccola. Single tickets cost €1.80 on all routes, including the funicular.

Sorrento

POP 16,700

Despite being a popular package-holiday destination, Sorrento manages to retain a laid-back southern Italian charm. There are very few sights to speak of, but there are wonderful views of Mt Vesuvius, and its small *centro storico* is an atmospheric place to explore. Sorrento's relative proximity to the Amalfi Coast, Pompeii and Capri also make it a good base for exploring the area.

Sights & Activities

Museo Correale MUSEUM

(☎081 878 18 46; www.museocorreale.it; Via Correale 50; €8; ⏰9.30am-6.30pm Tue-Sat, to 1.30pm Sun) East of the city centre, this museum is well worth a visit whether you're a clock collector, an archaeological egghead or into embroidery. In addition to the rich assortment of 17th- to 19th-century Neapolitan art and crafts, there are Japanese, Chinese and European ceramics, clocks, furniture and, on the ground floor, Greek and Roman artefacts.

Chiesa di San Francesco CHURCH

(Via San Francesco; ⏰8am-1pm & 2-8pm) Located next to the Villa Comunale Park, this is one of Sorrento's most beautiful churches. Surrounded by bougainvillea and birdsong, the evocative cloisters have an Arabic portico and interlaced arches supported by octagonal pillars. The church is most famous, however, for its summer program of concerts featuring world-class performers from the classical school. If this strikes a chord, check out the schedule at the tourist office. There are also regular art exhibitions.

Sleeping & Eating

★Ulisse HOTEL €

(☎081 877 47 53; www.ulissedeluxe.com; Via del Mare 22; dm €20-35, d €60-150; P ❄ ☎ ≋) Although it calls itself a hostel, the Ulisse is about as far from a backpackers' pad as a hiking boot from a stiletto. Most rooms are plush, spacious affairs with swish if rather bland fabrics, gleaming floors and large ensuite bathrooms. There are two single-sex dorms, and quads for sharers. Breakfast is included in some rates but costs €10 with others.

Casa Astarita B&B €€

(☎081 877 49 06; www.casastarita.com; Corso Italia 67; d €70-140, tr €95-165; ❄ ☎) Housed in an 18th-century *palazzo* on Sorrento's main strip, this charming B&B has a colourful, eclectic look with original vaulted ceilings, brightly painted doors and maiolica-tiled floors. Its six simple but well-equipped rooms surround a central parlour, where breakfast is served on a large rustic table.

★Da Emilia TRATTORIA €

(☎081 807 27 20; Via Marina Grande 62; meals €21-30; ⏰noon-3pm & 6-10.30pm Mar-Nov; 👪) Founded in 1947 and still run by the same family, this is a homely yet atmospheric joint overlooking the fishing boats in Marina Grande. There's a large informal dining room, complete with youthful photos of former patron Sophia Loren, a scruffily romantic terrace and a menu of straightforward, no-fail dishes like mussels with lemon, and spaghetti with clams.

Raki GELATO €

(www.rakisorrento.com; Via San Cesareo 48; cones & tubs from €2.50; ⏰11am-late) There are numerous gelaterie in Sorrento, but this place is a hit with its homemade preservative-free ice cream in a number of exciting flavours. Try ricotta, walnut and honey, or vanilla and ginger, which packs a surprisingly spicy punch.

OTHER SOUTHERN SPOTS WORTH A VISIT

Lecce Known as the Florence of the South; a lively university town famous for its ornate baroque architecture.

Matera A prehistoric town set on two rocky ravines, known as *sassi*, studded with primitive cave dwellings.

Aeolian Islands An archipelago of seven tiny islands off Sicily's northeastern coast. Lipari is the largest and the main hub, while Stromboli is the most dramatic, with its permanently spitting volcano.

Information

Main Tourist Office (☎081 807 40 33; www.sorrentotourism.com; Via Luigi de Maio 35; ⏰9am-6pm Mon-Fri winter, daily summer) In the Circolo dei Forestieri (Foreigners' Club). Ask for the useful publication *Surrentum*.

Getting There & Away

Circumvesuviana (☎800 21 13 88; www.eavsrl.it) trains run half-hourly between Sorrento and Naples (€4.50, 65 minutes) via Pompeii (€2.80, 30 minutes) and Ercolano (€3.40, 45 minutes from Sorrento).

Regular **SITA** (☎344 103 10 70; www.sitasudtrasporti.it) buses leave from the Circumvesuviana station for the Amalfi Coast, stopping at Positano (€2.20, 50 minutes) and Amalfi (€3.40, 1¾ hours).

From Marina Piccola, regular jetfoils (€18.30) and ferries (€14.80) sail to Capri (25 minutes, up to 16 daily).There are also summer sailings to Naples (€12.30, 35 minutes), Positano (€16, 40 minutes) and Amalfi (€17, 70 minutes).

Amalfi Coast

Stretching 50km along the southern side of the Sorrentine Peninsula, the Unesco-protected Amalfi Coast (Costiera Amalfitana) is a postcard-perfect vision of shimmering blue water fringed by vertiginous cliffs on which whitewashed villages and terraced lemon groves cling.

Getting There & Away

BOAT

Boat services generally run between April and October.

Alicost (089 87 14 83; www.alicost.it) Operates daily boats from Salerno (Molo Manfredi) to Amalfi (€8), Positano (€12) and Capri (€22.50).

Travelmar (089 87 29 50; www.travelmar.it) Has daily sailings from Salerno (Piazza Concordia) to Amalfi (€8) and Positano (€12).

BUS

SITA (344 103 10 70; www.sitasudtrasporti.it) buses run from Sorrento to Positano (€2.20, 50 minutes) and Amalfi (€3.40, 1¾ hours), and from Salerno to Amalfi (€2.80, 1¼ hours).

Positano

POP 3950

Approaching Positano by boat, you're greeted by an unforgettable view of colourful, steeply stacked houses clinging to near-vertical green slopes. In town, the main activities are hanging out on the small beach, drinking and dining on flower-laden terraces, and browsing the expensive boutiques.

The **tourist office** (089 87 50 67; www.aziendaturismopositano.it; Via Regina Giovanna 13; 8.30am-8pm Mon-Sat, to 2pm Sun May-Sep, reduced hrs rest of year) can provide information on walking in the densely wooded Lattari Mountains.

Sleeping & Eating

★Villa Nettuno HOTEL €
(089 87 54 01; www.villanettunopositano.it; Viale Pasitea 208; d €80-140; year-round;) Hidden behind a barrage of perfumed foliage, Villa Nettuno oozes charm. Go for one of the original rooms in the 300-year-old part of the building with heavy rustic decor and a communal terrace. Rooms in the renovated part of the villa lack the same character.

★La Fenice B&B €€
(089 87 55 13; www.lafenicepositano.com; Via Guglielmo Marconi 8; d €170; Easter-Oct;) With hand-painted Vietri tiles, white walls and high ceilings, the rooms here are simple but stylish; most have their own balcony or terrace. The views are stunning, but it feels very smartly homely and not super posh. As with everywhere in Positano, you'll need to be good at stomping up and down steps to stay here.

C'era Una Volta TRATTORIA, PIZZA €
(089 81 19 30; Via Marconi 127; meals €20-30; noon-3pm & 6.30-11pm) Up in the high part of town, this authentic trattoria is a good bet for honest, down-to-earth Italian grub. Alongside regional staples like *gnocchi alla sorrentina* (gnocchi served in a tomato and basil sauce), there's a decent selection of pizzas (to eat in or takeaway) and a full menu of pastas and fail-safe mains.

★Next2 RISTORANTE €€
(089 812 35 16; www.next2.it; Viale Pasitea 242; meals €50; 6.30-11.30pm) Understated elegance meets creative cuisine at this contemporary set-up. Local and organic ingredients are put to impressive use in beautifully presented dishes such as ravioli stuffed with aubergine and prawns or sea bass with tomatoes and lemon-scented peas. Desserts are wickedly delicious, and the alfresco sea-facing terrace is summer perfection.

Amalfi

POP 5150

Amalfi, the main hub on the coast, makes a convenient base for exploring the surrounding coastline. It's a pretty place with a tangle of narrow alleyways, stacked whitewashed houses and sun-drenched piazzas, but it can get very busy in summer as day-trippers pour in to peruse its loud souvenir shops and busy eateries.

The **tourist office** (089 87 11 07; www.amalfitouristoffice.it; Corso delle Repubbliche Marinare 27; 8.30am-1pm & 2-6pm Mon-Sat Apr-Oct, 8.30am-1pm Mon-Sat Nov-Mar) can provide information about sights, activities and transport.

Sights

★Cattedrale di Sant'Andrea CATHEDRAL
(☎089 87 10 59; Piazza del Duomo; ⏰7.30am-7.30pm) A melange of architectural styles, Amalfi's cathedral, one of the few relics of the town's past as an 11th-century maritime superpower, makes a striking impression at the top of its sweeping flight of stairs. Between 10am and 5pm entrance is through the adjacent **Chiostro del Paradiso** (☎089 87 13 24; adult/reduced €3/1; ⏰9am-7.45pm Jul-Aug, reduced hrs rest of year), a 13th-century cloister.

Grotta dello Smeraldo CAVE
(€5; ⏰9am-4pm) Four kilometres west of Amalfi, this grotto is named after the eerie emerald colour that emanates from the water. Stalactites hang down from the 24m-high ceiling, while stalagmites grow up to 10m tall. Buses regularly pass the car park above the cave entrance (from where you take a lift or stairs down to the rowing boats). Alternatively, **Coop Sant'Andrea** (☎089 87 31 90; www.coopsantandrea.com; Lungomare dei Cavalieri 1) runs boats from Amalfi (€10 return, plus cave admission). Allow 1½ hours for the return trip.

Sleeping & Eating

★Residenza del Duca HOTEL €€
(☎089 873 63 65; www.residencedelduca.it; Via Duca Mastalo II 3; r €70-175; ⏰Mar-Oct; ❄📶) This family-run hotel has just six rooms, all of them light, sunny, and prettily furnished with antiques, maiolica tiles and the odd chintzy cherub. The Jacuzzi showers are excellent. Call ahead if you are carrying heavy bags, as it's a seriously puff-you-out-climb up some steps to reach here and a luggage service is included in the price.

Hotel Lidomare HOTEL €€
(☎089 87 13 32; www.lidomare.it; Largo Duchi Piccolomini 9; s €65/145; ❄📶) Family run, this old-fashioned hotel has real character. The large, luminous rooms have an air of gentility, with their appealingly haphazard decor, vintage tiles and fine antiques. Some have Jacuzzi bath-tubs, others have sea views and a balcony, some have both. Rather unusually, breakfast is laid out on top of a grand piano.

Trattoria Il Mulino TRATTORIA, PIZZA €€
(☎089 87 22 23; Via delle Cartiere 36; pizzas €6-11, meals €30; ⏰11.30am-4pm & 6.30pm-midnight Tue-Sun) A TV-in-the-corner, kids-running-between-the-tables sort of place, this is about as authentic an eatery as you'll find in Amalfi. There are few surprises on the menu, just hearty, honest pastas, grilled meats and fish. For a taste of local seafood, try the *scialatielli alla pescatore* (ribbon pasta with prawns, mussels, tomato and parsley).

★Marina Grande SEAFOOD €€€
(☎089 87 11 29; www.ristorantemarinagrande.com; Viale Della Regioni 4; tasting menu lunch/dinner €28/60, meals €50; ⏰noon-3pm & 6.30-11pm Wed-Mon Mar-Oct) Run by the third generation of the same family, this beachfront restaurant serves fish so fresh it's almost flapping. It prides itself on its use of locally sourced organic produce, which, in Amalfi, means high-quality seafood. Reservations recommended.

WORTH A TRIP

RAVELLO

Elegant Ravello sits high in the clouds overlooking the coast. From Amalfi, it's a nerve-tingling half-hour bus ride (€1.60, up to three an hour), but once you've made it up, you can unwind in the ravishing gardens of **Villa Rufolo** (☎089 85 76 21; www.villarufolo.it; Piazza Duomo; adult/reduced €7/5; ⏰9am-9pm May-Sep, reduced hrs rest of year, tower museum 11am-4pm) and bask in awe-inspiring views at **Villa Cimbrone** (☎089 85 74 59; www.hotelvillacimbrone.com/gardens; Via Santa Chiara 26; adult/reduced €7/4; ⏰9am-sunset).

Sicily

Everything about the Mediterranean's largest island is extreme, from the beauty of its rugged landscape to its hybrid cuisine and flamboyant architecture. Over the centuries Sicily has seen off a catalogue of foreign invaders, from the Phoenicians and ancient Greeks to the Spanish Bourbons and WWII Allies. All have contributed to the island's complex and fascinating cultural landscape.

Getting There & Away

AIR

Flights from mainland Italian cities and European destinations serve Sicily's two main airports: Palermo's **Falcone-Borsellino** (☎800 541880, 091 702 02 73; www.gesap.it) and Catania's

Fontanarossa (☎095 723 91 11; www.aeroporto.catania.it).

BOAT

Regular car and passenger ferries cross to Sicily (Messina) from Villa San Giovanni in Calabria.

Ferries also sail from Genoa, Livorno, Civitavecchia, Naples, Salerno and Cagliari, as well as Malta and Tunisia.

Main operators:

Caronte & Tourist (☎090 36 46 01, 800 627414; www.carontetourist.it) To Messina from Salerno.

Grandi Navi Veloci (☎010 209 45 91; www.gnv.it) To Palermo from Civitavecchia, Genoa, Naples and Tunis.

Grimaldi (☎081 49 64 44; www.grimaldi-ferries.com) To Palermo from Livorno, Salerno and Tunis.

Tirrenia (☎892123; www.tirrenia.it) To Palermo from Naples and Cagliari.

BUS

SAIS Trasporti (☎091 617 11 41; www.saistrasporti.it) operates long-distance buses between Sicily and Italian mainland destinations including Rome and Naples.

TRAIN

Trenitalia (☎06 6847 5475, 892021; www.trenitalia.com) operates direct trains to Sicily from both Rome and Naples, along with direct night trains from Milan, Rome and Naples.

Palermo

POP 678,500

Still bearing the bruises of its WWII battering, Palermo is a compelling and chaotic city. It takes a little work, but once you've acclimatised to the congested and noisy streets you'll be rewarded with some of southern Italy's most imposing architecture, impressive art galleries, vibrant street markets and an array of tempting restaurants and cafes.

Sights

★Palazzo dei Normanni PALACE

(Palazzo Reale; ☎091 626 28 33; www.federicosecondo.org; Piazza Indipendenza 1; adult/reduced Fri-Mon €8.50/6.50, Tue-Thu €7/5, plus possible exhibition supplement; ⏲8.15am-5.40pm Mon-Sat, to 1pm Sun) Home to Sicily's regional parliament, this venerable palace dates to the 9th century. However, it owes its current look (and name) to a major Norman makeover, during which spectacular mosaics were added to its royal apartments and magnificent chapel, the Cappella Palatina. Visits to the apartments, which are off-limits from Tuesday to Thursday, take in the mosaic-lined **Sala dei Venti**, and **Sala di Ruggero II**, King Roger's 12th-century bedroom.

★Cappella Palatina CHAPEL

(Palatine Chapel; www.federicosecondo.org; Piazza Indipendenza; adult/reduced Fri-Mon €8.50/6.50, Tue-Thu €7/5, plus possible exhibition supplement; ⏲8.15am-5.40pm Mon-Sat, 8.15-9.45am & 11.15am-1pm Sun) Designed by Roger II in 1130, this extraordinary chapel is Palermo's top tourist attraction. Located on the mid-level of Palazzo dei Normanni's three-tiered loggia, its glittering gold mosaics are complemented by inlaid marble floors and a wooden *muqarnas* ceiling, the latter a masterpiece of Arabic-style honeycomb carving reflecting Norman Sicily's cultural complexity.

Note that queues are likely, and that you'll be refused entry if you're wearing shorts, a short skirt or a low-cut top.

★Mercato di Ballarò MARKET

(⏲7.30am-8pm Mon-Sat, to 1pm Sun) Snaking for several city blocks southeast of Palazzo dei Normanni is Palermo's busiest street market, which throbs with activity well into the early evening. It's a fascinating mix of noises, smells and street life, and the cheap-

BARI

Most travellers visit Puglia's regional capital to catch a ferry. And while there's not a lot to detain you, it's worth taking an hour or so to explore Bari Vecchia (Old Bari). Here, among the labyrinthine lanes, you'll find the **Basilica di San Nicola** (www.basilicasannicola.it; Piazza San Nicola; ⏲7am-8.30pm Mon-Sat, to 10pm Sun), the impressive home to the relics of St Nicholas (aka Santa Claus).

For lunch, **Terranima** (☎080 521 97 25; www.terranima.com; Via Putignani 213/215; meals €25-30; ⏲noon-3pm & 7-11pm) serves delicious Puglian food.

Regular trains run to Bari from Rome (€20 to €79, four to 6½ hours, six daily).

Ferries sail to Greece, Croatia, Montenegro and Albania from the port, accessible by bus 20/ from the train station.

est place for everything from Chinese padded bras to fresh produce, fish, meat, olives and cheese – smile nicely for *un assaggio* (a taste).

★ **Cattedrale di Palermo** CATHEDRAL

(☎091 33 43 73; www.cattedrale.palermo.it; Corso Vittorio Emanuele; cathedral free, tombs €1.50, treasury & crypt €2, roof €5, all-inclusive ticket adult/reduced €7/3; ⏰cathedral 7am-7pm Mon-Sat, 8am-1pm & 4-7pm Sun, royal tombs, treasury & roof 9am-5pm summer, 9am-1.30pm winter) A feast of geometric patterns, ziggurat crenellations, maiolica cupolas and blind arches, Palermo's cathedral has suffered aesthetically from multiple reworkings over the centuries, but remains a prime example of Sicily's unique Arab-Norman architectural style. The interior, while impressive in scale, is essentially a marble shell whose most interesting features are the **royal Norman tombs** (to the left as you enter), the **treasury** (home to Constance of Aragon's gem-encrusted 13th-century crown) and the panoramic views from the **roof**.

La Martorana CHURCH

(Chiesa di Santa Maria dell'Ammiraglio; Piazza Bellini 3; adult/reduced €2/1; ⏰9am-1pm & 3.30-5.30pm Mon-Sat, 9-10.30am Sun) On the southern side of Piazza Bellini, this luminously beautiful 12th-century church was endowed by King Roger's Syrian emir, George of Antioch, and was originally planned as a mosque. Delicate Fatimid pillars support a domed cupola depicting Christ enthroned amid his archangels. The interior is best appreciated in the morning, when sunlight illuminates magnificent Byzantine mosaics.

★ **Teatro Massimo** THEATRE

(☎tour reservations 091 605 32 67; www.teatromassimo.it; Piazza Giuseppe Verdi; guided tours adult/reduced €8/5; ⏰9.30am-6pm) Taking over 20 years to complete, Palermo's neoclassical opera house is the largest in Italy and the second-largest in Europe. The closing scene of *The Godfather: Part III,* with its visually arresting juxtaposition of high culture, crime, drama and death, was filmed here and the building's richly decorated interiors are nothing short of spectacular. Guided 30-minute tours are offered throughout the day in English, Italian, French, Spanish and German.

Sleeping

★ **Stanze al Genio Residenze** B&B €

(☎340 097 15 61; www.stanzealgeniobnb.it; Via Garibaldi 11; s/d €74/90; ❄📶) Speckled with Sicilian antiques, this B&B offers four gorgeous bedrooms, three with 19th-century ceiling frescoes. All four are spacious and thoughtfully appointed, with Murano lamps, old wooden wardrobes, the odd balcony railing turned bedhead, and top-quality, orthopaedic beds. That the property features beautiful maiolica tiles is no coincidence; the B&B is affiliated with the wonderful **Museo delle Maioliche** (Stanze al Genio; adult/reduced €7/5; ⏰by appointment) downstairs.

B&B Panormus B&B €

(☎091 617 58 26; www.bbpanormus.com; Via Roma 72; s €45-75, d €50-85, tr €75-120; ❄📶) Popular for its keen prices, charming host and convenient location between the train station and the Quattro Canti, this B&B offers five high-ceilinged rooms decorated in elegant Liberty style, each with double-glazed windows, flat-screen TV and a private bathroom down the passageway.

★ **BB22 Palace** B&B €€

(☎091 32 62 14; www.bb22.it; cnr Via Roma & Via Bandiera; d €120-180, whole apt €700-950) Occupying a flouncy *palazzo* in the heart of the city, BB22 Palace offers four chic, contemporary rooms, each with its own style. Top billing goes to the Stromboli room, complete with spa bath and a bedroom skylight offering a glimpse of its 15th-century neighbour. Peppered with artworks, coffee-table tomes and an honour bar, the communal lounge makes for an airy, chi-chi retreat.

Eating & Drinking

Touring Café CAFE €

(☎091 32 27 26; Via Roma 252; arancino €1.70; ⏰6.15am-11pm Mon-Fri, to midnight Sat & Sun) Don't let the gleaming Liberty-style mirrored bar and array of picture-perfect pastries distract you. You come here for the *arancine,* great fist-sized rice balls stuffed with *ragù,* spinach or butter, and fried to a perfect golden orange.

★ **Trattoria al Vecchio Club Rosanero** SICILIAN €

(☎091 251 12 34; Vicolo Caldomai 18; meals €15; ⏰1-3.30pm Mon-Sat & 8-11pm Thu-Sat; 📶) A veritable shrine to the city's football team (*rosa nero* refers to the team's colours, pink and black), cavernous Vecchio Club scores goals with its bargain-priced, flavour-packed grub. Fish and seafood are the real fortes here; if it's on the menu, order the *caponata e pesce spada* (caponata with swordfish), a sweet-and-sour victory. Head in early to avoid a wait.

Osteria Ballarò SICILIAN €€
(☎091 32 64 88; www.osteriaballaro.it; Via Calascibetta 25; meals €30-45; ⏰noon-3.15pm & 7-11.15pm) A slinky, buzzing restaurant-cum-wine bar, Osteria Ballarò marries an atmospheric setting with sterling, Slow Food island cooking. Bare stone columns, exposed brick walls and vaulted ceilings set an evocative scene for arresting *crudite di pesce* (local sashimi) and seafood *primi*, elegant local wines and memorable Sicilian *dolci* (sweets). Reservations recommended. Slow Food recommended.

★**Enoteca Buonivini** WINE BAR
(☎091 784 70 54; Via Dante 8; ⏰9.30am-1.30pm & 4pm-midnight Mon-Thu, to 1am Fri & Sat) Serious oenophiles flock to this bustling, urbane *enoteca* (wine bar), complete with bar seating, courtyard and a generous selection of wines by the glass. There's no shortage of interesting local drops, not to mention artisan cheese and charcuterie boards, beautiful pasta dishes and grilled meats. When you're done, scan the shelves for harder-to-find craft spirits (Australian gin, anyone?) and Sicilian gourmet pantry essentials.

ℹ Information

Hospital (Ospedale Civico; ☎091 666 11 11; www.arnascivico.it; Piazza Nicola Leotta; ⏰24hr) Emergency facilities.

Police (Questura; ☎091 21 01 11; Piazza della Vittoria 8) Main police station.

Municipal Tourist Office (☎091 740 80 21; http://turismo.comune.palermo.it; Piazza Bellini; ⏰8am-8pm Mon-Thu, to 6.30pm Fri, 9am-7pm Sat, 9.30am-6.30pm Sun) The main branch of Palermo's city-run information booths. Other locations include Teatro Politeama, Via Cavour, the Port of Palermo and Mondello, though these are only intermittently staffed, with unpredictable hours.

ℹ Getting There & Away

AIR

Falcone-Borsellino Airport (☎800 541880, 091 702 02 73; www.gesap.it) is at Punta Raisi, 35km northwest of Palermo on the A29 motorway. There are regular flights between Palermo and most mainland Italian cities.

BOAT

Numerous ferry companies operate from Palermo's port, just east of the New City. These include the following:

Grandi Navi Veloci (☎010 209 45 91, 091 6072 6162; www.gnv.it; Calata Marinai d'Italia)

Grimaldi Lines (☎091 611 36 91, 081 49 64 44; www.grimaldi-lines.com; Via del Mare)

Tirrenia (☎892123; www.tirrenia.it; Calata Marinai d'Italia)

BUS

The main **bus terminal** is on Piazzetta Cairoli, to the side of the train station. Other intercity buses depart from **Via Paolo Balsamo**, two blocks due east of the train station.

Main bus companies:

Cuffaro (☎091 616 15 10; www.cuffaro.info; Via Paolo Balsamo 13) Services to Agrigento (€9, two hours, three to eight daily).

Interbus (☎091 616 79 19; www.interbus.it; Piazzetta Cairoli Bus Terminal) To/from Syracuse (€13.50, 3½ hours, two to three daily).

SAIS Autolinee (☎800 211020, 091 616 60 28; www.saisautolinee.it; Piazzetta Cairoli Bus Station) To/from Catania (€12.50, 2¾ hours, nine to 12 daily) and Messina (€15, 2¾ hours, three to six daily).

TRAIN

Regular services leave from **Palermo Centrale train station** (Piazza Giulio Cesare; ⏰6am-9pm) to Messina (from €12.80, three to 3¾ hours, eight to 14 daily), Catania (from €13.50, 2¾ to 5½ hours, five to 10 daily) and Agrigento (€9, two hours, six to 10 daily). There are also Intercity trains to Reggio di Calabria, Naples and Rome.

ℹ Getting Around

TO/FROM THE AIRPORT

Prestia e Comandè (☎091 58 63 51; www.prestiaecomande.it; one way/return €6.30/11) Runs an efficient half-hourly bus service between 5am and 12.30pm that transfers passengers from the airport to the centre of Palermo, dropping people off outside the Teatro Politeama Garibaldi and Palermo Centrale train station. To find the bus, follow the signs past the downstairs taxi rank and around the corner to the right.

BUS

Walking is the best way to get around Palermo's centre, but if you want to take a bus, most stop outside or near the train station. Tickets cost €1.40 (€1.80 on board) and are valid for 90 minutes.

Taormina

POP 11,085

Spectacularly perched on a clifftop terrace overlooking the Ionian Sea and Mt Etna, this sophisticated town has attracted socialites, artists and writers ever since Greek times. Its pristine medieval core, proximity to beaches, grandstand coastal views and chic social scene make it a hugely popular summer holiday destination.

Sights & Activities

★Teatro Greco RUINS

(☎0942 2 32 20; Via Teatro Greco; adult/reduced €10/5; ⏲9am-1hr before sunset) Taormina's premier sight is this perfect horseshoe-shaped theatre, suspended between sea and sky, with Mt Etna looming on the southern horizon. Built in the 3rd century BC, it's the most dramatically situated Greek theatre in the world and the second largest in Sicily (after Syracuse). In summer, it's used to stage international arts and film festivals. In peak season, the site is best explored early in the morning to avoid the crowds.

Corso Umberto I STREET

Taormina's chief delight is wandering this pedestrian-friendly, boutique-lined thoroughfare. Start at the tourist office in **Palazzo Corvaja** (Piazza Santa Caterina), which dates back to the 10th century, before heading southwest for spectacular panoramic views from **Piazza IX Aprile**. Facing the square is the early-18th-century **Chiesa San Giuseppe** (⏲usually 8.30am-8pm). Continue west through **Torre dell'Orologio**, the 12th-century clock tower, into **Piazza del Duomo**, home to an ornate baroque fountain (1635) that sports Taormina's symbol, a two-legged centaur with the bust of an angel.

Villa Comunale PARK

(Parco Duchi di Cesarò; Via Bagnoli Croce; ⏲9am-midnight summer, 9am-sunset winter) To escape the crowds, wander down to these stunningly sited public gardens. Created by Englishwoman Florence Trevelyan in the late 19th century, they're a lush paradise of tropical plants and delicate flowers, punctuated by whimsical follies. You'll also find a children's play area.

Sleeping & Eating

Le 4 Fontane B&B €

(☎333 679 38 76; www.le4fontane.com; Corso Umberto I 231; s €40-70, d €60-110; ❄📶) An excellent budget B&B on the top floor of an old *palazzo,* Le 4 Fontane is run by a friendly couple and has three spacious, well-equipped rooms, two of which have views of Piazza del Duomo.

Isoco Guest House GUESTHOUSE €€

(☎0942 2 36 79; www.isoco.it; Via Salita Branco 2; r €130-220; ⏲Mar-Nov; P❄@📶) Each room at this welcoming, LGBT-friendly guesthouse is dedicated to an artist, from Botticelli to Keith Haring. While the older rooms are highly eclectic, the newer suites are chic and subdued, each with a modern kitchenette. Breakfast is served around a large table, while a pair of terraces offer stunning sea views and a hot tub. Multinight or prepaid stays earn the best rates.

★Osteria Nero D'Avola SICILIAN €€

(☎0942 62 88 74; Piazza San Domenico 2b; meals €40; ⏲12.30-3pm & 7-11pm Tue-Sun Sep-Jun, 7pm-midnight Jul & Aug) Not only does affable owner Turi Siligato fish, hunt and forage for his smart *osteria,* he'll probably greet you at your table, share anecdotes about the day's bounty and play a few tunes on the piano. Here, seasonality, local producers and passion underscore arresting dishes like the signature *cannolo di limone Interdonato* (thinly sliced Interdonato lemon with roe, tuna, tomato and chives).

Information

Tourist Office (☎0942 2 32 43; Palazzo Corvaja, Piazza Santa Caterina; ⏲8.30am-2.15pm & 3.30-6.45pm Mon-Fri year-round, also 8.30am-2.15pm & 3.30-6.45pm Sat & Sun summer) Has plenty of practical information, including transport timetables and a free map.

Getting There & Away

Bus is the easiest way to reach Taormina. The bus station is on Via Luigi Pirandello, 400m east of Porta Messina, the northeastern entrance to the old town. **Interbus** (www.interbus.it; Via Luigi Pirandello) services leave daily for Messina (€4.30, 55 minutes to 1¾ hours, up to six daily), Catania (€5.10, 1¼ hours, up to 16 daily) and Catania airport (€8.20, 1½ hours, up to 12 daily).

Syracuse

POP 122,500

A tumultuous past has left Syracuse (Siracusa) a beautiful baroque centre and some of Sicily's finest ancient ruins. Founded in 734 BC by Corinthian settlers, it became the dominant Greek city state on the Mediterranean and was known as the most beautiful city in the ancient world. A devastating earthquake in 1693 destroyed most of the city's buildings, paving the way for a city-wide baroque makeover.

Sights

★ Piazza del Duomo PIAZZA

Syracuse's showpiece square is a masterpiece of baroque town planning. A long, rectangular piazza flanked by flamboyant *palazzi*, it sits on what was once Syracuse's ancient acropolis (fortified citadel). Little remains of the original Greek building but if you look along the side of the Duomo, you'll see a number of thick Doric columns incorporated into the cathedral's structure.

★ Parco Archeologico della Neapolis ARCHAEOLOGICAL SITE

(☎0931 6 62 06; Viale Paradiso 14; adult/reduced €10/5, incl Museo Archeologico €13.50/7; ⏱9am-1hr before sunset Mon-Sat, 9am-1pm Sun) For the classicist, Syracuse's real attraction is this archaeological park, home to the pearly white 5th-century-BC **Teatro Greco**. Hewn out of the rocky hillside, this 16,000-capacity amphitheatre staged the last tragedies of Aeschylus (including *The Persians*), first performed here in his presence. In late spring it's brought to life with an annual season of classical theatre.

★ Museo Archeologico Paolo Orsi MUSEUM

(☎0931 48 95 11; www.regione.sicilia.it/beniculturali/museopaoloorsi; Viale Teocrito 66; adult/reduced €8/4, incl Parco Archeologico €13.50/7; ⏱9am-6pm Tue-Sat, to 1pm Sun) About 500m east of the archaeological park, this modern museum contains one of Sicily's largest and most interesting archaeological collections. Allow plenty of time to investigate the four sectors charting the area's prehistory, as well as Syracuse's development from foundation to the late Roman period.

Sleeping & Eating

B&B dei Viaggiatori, Viandanti e Sognatori B&B €

(☎0931 2 47 81; www.bedandbreakfastsicily.it; Via Roma 156; s €35-50, d €55-70, tr €75-85, q €100; ❄📶) Decorated with verve and boasting a prime Ortygia location, this relaxed B&B exudes an easy, boho vibe. It's a homely place, graced with books, antique furniture and imaginatively decorated rooms. The sunny roof terrace – complete with sweeping sea views – is a fine place for breakfast, whose offerings include biological bread and homemade marmalades.

★ Hotel Gutkowski HOTEL €€

(☎0931 46 58 61; www.guthotel.it; Lungomare Vittorini 26; d €90-140, tr €140; ❄@📶) Book well in advance for one of the sea-view rooms at this stylish, eclectic hotel on the Ortygia waterfront, at the edge of the Giudecca neighbourhood. Divided between two buildings, its rooms are simple yet chic, with pretty tiled floors, walls in teals, greys, blues and browns, and a sharply curated mix of vintage and industrial details.

Sicily PIZZA €

(☎392 9659949; www.sicilypizzeria.it; Via Cavour 67; pizzas €4.50-12; ⏱7pm-midnight Tue-Sun) Experimenting with pizzas is something you do at your peril in culinary-conservative Sicily. But that's what they do, and do well, at this funky retro-chic pizzeria. So if you're game for wood-fired pizzas topped with more-ish

WORTH A TRIP

PADUA

Were it just for Padua's medieval centre and lively university atmosphere, the city would be a rewarding day trip from Venice. But what makes a visit so special is the **Cappella degli Scrovegni** (Scrovegni Chapel; ☎049 201 00 20; www.cappelladegliscrovegni.it; Piazza Eremitani 8; adult/reduced €13/8, night ticket €8/6; ⏱9am-7pm), home to a remarkable cycle of Giotto frescoes. Considered one of the defining masterpieces of early Renaissance art, this extraordinary work consists of 38 colourful panels, painted between 1303 and 1305, depicting episodes from the life of Christ and the Virgin Mary. Note that visits to the chapel must be booked in advance.

To fuel your wanderings, lunch on hearty local fare at the **Osteria dei Fabbri** (☎049 65 03 36; Via dei Fabbri 13; meals €30; ⏱noon-3pm & 7-11pm, closed Sun dinner).

Trains leave for Padua (Padova) from Venice (€4 to €17, 25 minutes) every 20 minutes or so.

WORTH A TRIP

MT ETNA

The dark silhouette of Mt Etna (3329m) broods ominously over Sicily's east coast, more or less halfway between Taormina and Catania. One of Europe's highest and most volatile volcanoes, it erupts frequently, most recently in May 2016.

To get to Etna by public transport, take the AST bus from Catania (at 8.15am daily). This departs from in front of the train station (returning at 4.30pm; €6.60 return) and drops you at the Rifugio Sapienza (1923m), where you can pick up the **Funivia dell'Etna** (☎095 91 41 41; www.funiviaetna.com; return €30, incl bus & guide €63; ⏱9am-4.15pm Apr-Nov, to 3.45pm Dec-Mar) to 2500m. From there buses courier you up to the crater zone (2920m). If you want to walk, allow up to four hours for the round trip.

Gruppo Guide Alpine Etna Sud (☎389 3496086, 095 791 47 55; www.etnaguide.eu) is one of many outfits offering guided tours. Bank on around €85 for a full-day excursion.

Further Etna information is available from Catania's **tourist office** (☎095 742 55 73; www.comune.catania.it; Via Vittorio Emanuele 172; ⏱8am-7.15pm Mon-Sat, 8.30am-1.30pm Sun).

combos like sausage, cheese, Swiss chard, pine nuts, sun-dried tomatoes and raisins, this is the place for you.

★ **Bistrot Bella Vita** ITALIAN €€
(☎348 1939792; Via Gargallo 60; sweets €1.50, meals €25; ⏱cafe 8am-1am summer, to 11pm winter, restaurant noon-3pm & 6.30-11pm, closed Mon) Owned by affable Lombard expat Norma and her Sicilian pastry-chef husband Salvo, this casually elegant cafe-restaurant is one of Ortygia's latest stars. Stop by for good coffee (soy milk available) and made-from-scratch *cornetti, biscotti* and pastries (try the sour orange-and-almond tart). Or book a table in the intimate back dining room, where local, organic produce drives beautifully textured, technically impressive dishes.

ℹ Information

Tourist Office (☎0931 46 29 46; http://turismo.provsr.it; Via Roma 31; ⏱9am-12.30pm Mon-Fri) City maps and brochures.

ℹ Getting There & Around

Buses are a better bet than trains, serving a **terminal** (Corso Umberto I) close to the **train station** (Via Francesco Crispi).

Interbus (☎0931 6 67 10; www.interbus.it) runs services to/from Catania (€6.20, 1½ hours, 18 daily Monday to Friday, nine Saturday, seven Sunday) and its airport, and Palermo (€13.50, 3¼ to 3½ hours, two to three daily).

Up to 11 trains depart daily for Catania (from €7, one to 1½ hours) and Messina (from €10, 2½ to 3½ hours).

Sd'a Trasporti (www.siracusadamare.it; ticket/day pass/week pass €1/3/10) runs three lines of electric buses, the most useful of which is the red No 2 line, which links Ortygia with the train station and archaeological zone. Tickets, available on board, cost €1.

Agrigento

POP 59,600

Seen from a distance, Agrigento doesn't bode well, with rows of unsightly apartment blocks crowded onto the hillside. But behind the veneer, the city boasts a small but attractive medieval core and, down in the valley, one of Italy's greatest ancient sites, the Valley of the Temples (Valle dei Templi).

Founded around 581 BC by Greek settlers, the city was an important trading centre under the Romans and Byzantines.

For maps and information, ask at the **tourist office** (☎800 236837, 800 315555; www.livingagrigento.it; Piazzale Aldo Moro 1; ⏱8am-1pm & 2-7pm Mon-Fri, to 1pm Sat) in the Provincia building.

👁 Sights

★ **Valley of the Temples** ARCHAEOLOGICAL SITE
(Valle dei Templi; www.parcovalledeitempli.it; adult/reduced €10/5, incl Museo Archeologico €13.50/7; ⏱8.30am-7pm year-round, plus 7.30-10pm Mon-Fri, 7.30-11pm Sat & Sun mid-Jul–mid-Sep) Sicily's most enthralling archaeological site encompasses the ruined ancient city of Akragas, highlighted by the stunningly well-preserved **Tempio della Concordia** (Temple of Concordia), one of several ridge-top temples that once served as beacons for homecoming sailors. The 13-sq-km park, 3km south of Agrigento, is split into eastern and western zones. Ticket offices with car parks are at the park's southwestern corner (the main Porta V entrance) and at the northeastern corner near the Temple of Hera (Eastern Entrance).

ESSENTIAL FOOD & DRINK

Italian cuisine is highly regional in nature and wherever you go you'll find local specialities. That said, some staples are ubiquitous:

Pizza There are two varieties: Roman, with a thin crispy base; and Neapolitan, with a higher, more doughy base. The best are always prepared in a *forno a legna* (wood-fired oven).

Pasta Comes in hundreds of shapes and sizes and is served with everything from thick meat-based sauces to fresh seafood.

Gelato Classic flavours include *fragola* (strawberry), *pistacchio* (pistachio), *nocciola* (hazelnut) and *stracciatella* (milk with chocolate shavings).

Wine Ranges from big-name reds such as Piedmont's *Barolo* and Tuscany's *Brunello di Montalcino* to sweet Sicilian *Malvasia* and sparkling *prosecco* from the Veneto.

Caffè Italians take their coffee seriously, drinking cappuccino only in the morning, and espressos whenever, ideally standing at a bar.

Eat Like an Italian

A full Italian meal consists of an *antipasto*, a *primo* (first course; pasta or rice dish), *secondo* (main course; usually meat or fish) with an *insalata* (salad) or *contorno* (vegetable side dish), *dolce* (dessert) and coffee. Most Italians only eat a meal this large at Sunday lunch or on a special occasion, and when eating out it's fine to mix and match and order, say, a *primo* followed by an *insalata* or *contorno*.

Italians are late diners, often not eating until after 9pm.

Where to Eat & Drink

Trattorias are traditional, often family-run places serving local food and wine; *ristoranti* (restaurants) are more formal, with greater choice and smarter service; pizzerias, which usually open evenings only, often serve a full menu alongside pizzas.

At lunchtime bars and cafes sell *panini* (bread rolls), and many serve an evening *aperitivo* (aperitif) buffet. At an *enoteca* (wine bar) you can drink wine by the glass and snack on cheese and cured meats. Some also serve hot dishes. For a slice of pizza search out a *pizza al taglio* joint.

Sleeping & Eating

★PortAtenea B&B €

(☎349 093 74 92; www.portatenea.com; Via Atenea, cnr Via C Battisti; s €39-50, d €59-75, tr €79-95; ❄📶) This five-room B&B wins plaudits for its panoramic roof terrace overlooking the Valley of the Temples, and its super-convenient location at the entrance to the old town, five minutes' walk from the train and bus stations. Best of all is the generous advice about Agrigento offered by hosts Sandra and Filippo (witness Filippo's amazing Google Earth tour of nearby beaches!).

★Aguglia Persa SEAFOOD €€

(☎0922 40 13 37; Via Francesco Crispi 34; meals €25-40; ⏲noon-3.30pm & 7-11pm Wed-Mon) Set in a mansion with leafy courtyard just below the train station, this place is a welcome addition to Agrigento's fine-dining scene. Opened in 2015 by the owners of Porto Empedocle's renowned Salmoriglio restaurant, it specialises in fresh-caught seafood in dishes such as citrus-scented risotto with shrimp and wild mint, or marinated salmon with sage cream and fresh fruit.

Getting There & Away

The bus is the easiest way to get to Agrigento. The **intercity bus station** and ticket booth are on Piazza Rosselli, from where you can catch local bus 1, 2 or 3 to the Valley of the Temples (€1.20).

Cuffaro (☎091 616 15 10; www.cuffaro.info) runs buses to/from Palermo (€9, two hours, three to eight daily) and **SAIS Trasporti** (☎0922 2 60 59; www.saistrasporti.it) services go to Catania (€13.40, three hours, hourly).

SURVIVAL GUIDE

Directory A–Z

ACCOMMODATION

- The bulk of Italy's accommodation is made up of *alberghi* (hotels) and *pensioni* (small, often family run hotels). Other options are hostels, campgrounds, B&Bs, *agriturismi* (farm-stays), mountain *rifugi* (Alpine refuges), monasteries and villa/apartment rentals.
- High-season rates apply at Easter, in summer (mid-June to August), and over the Christmas to New Year period.
- Many places in coastal resorts close between November and March.

B&Bs

- Often great value, can range from rooms in family houses to self-catering studio apartments.
- Prices typically range from about €60 to €140 for a double room.
- Check www.bbitalia.it and www.bed-and-breakfast.it.

Camping

- Most Italian campgrounds are major complexes with on-site supermarkets, restaurants and sports facilities.
- In summer expect to pay up to €20 per person, and a further €25 for a tent pitch.
- Useful resources include www.campeggi.com, www.camping.it and www.italcamping.it.

Convents & Monasteries

Basic accommodation is often available in convents and monasteries. See www.monasterystays.com, a specialist online booking service.

Farm-Stays

- An *agriturismo* (farm-stay) is a good option for a country stay, although you'll usually need a car to get there.
- Accommodation varies from spartan billets on working farms to palatial suites at luxury retreats.
- For lists check out www.agriturist.it or www.agriturismo.com.

Hostels

- Official HI-affiliated *ostelli per la gioventù* (youth hostels) are run by the **Italian Youth Hostel Association** (AIG; Map p426; ☎06 487 11 52; www.aighostels.it; Via Nicotera 1, entrance Via Settembrini 4, Rome; ⊙8am-5.30pm Mon-Fri; 🚇Viale delle Milizie). A valid HI card is required for these; you can get a card in your home country or directly at hostels.
- There are also many excellent private hostels offering dorms and private rooms.
- Dorm rates are typically between €15 and €40, with breakfast usually included.

Hotels & Pensioni

- A *pensione* is a small, often family-run, hotel. In cities, they are often in converted apartments.
- Hotels and *pensioni* are rated from one to five stars. As a rule, a three-star room will come with an en-suite bathroom, air-con, hairdryer, minibar, safe and wi-fi.
- Many city-centre hotels offer discounts in August to lure clients from the crowded coast.

ACTIVITIES

Cycling Tourist offices can provide details on trails and guided rides. The best time is spring. Favourite areas include Tuscany, the flatlands of Emilia-Romagna, and the peaks around Lago Maggiore and Lago del Garda.

Hiking Thousands of kilometres of *sentieri* (marked trails) criss-cross the country. The hiking season is from June to September. The Italian Parks organisation (www.parks.it) lists walking trails in Italy's national parks.

Skiing Italy's ski season runs from December through to March. Prices are generally high,

COUNTRY FACTS

Area 301,230 sq km

Capital Rome

Currency Euro (€)

Emergency ☎112

Language Italian

Money ATMs widespread; credit cards widely accepted

Population 61 million

Telephone Country code ☎39, international access code ☎00

Visas Schengen rules apply

HOTEL TAX

Most Italian hotels apply a room occupancy tax *(tassa di soggiorno)*, which is charged on top of your regular hotel bill. The exact amount, which varies from city to city, depends on your type of accommodation, but as a rough guide reckon on €1 to €3 per person per night in a one-star hotel, €3 to €3.50 in a B&B, €3 to €4 in a three-star hotel etc.

Prices quoted in accommodation reviews do not include the tax.

SLEEPING PRICE RANGES

The following price ranges refer to a double room with private bathroom (breakfast included) in high season.

€ under €110 (under €120 in Rome & Venice)

€€ €110–€200 (€120–€250 in Rome, €120–€220 in Venice)

€€€ over €200 (over €250 in Rome, over €220 in Venice)

particularly in the top Alpine resorts – the Apennines are cheaper. A popular option is to buy a *settimana bianca* (literally 'white week') package deal, covering accommodation, food and ski passes.

FOOD

➡ On the bill expect to be charged for *pane e coperto* (bread and cover charge). This is standard and is added even if you don't ask for or eat the bread.

➡ Service (*servizio*) is generally included in restaurants – if it's not, a euro or two is fine in pizzerias, 10% in restaurants.

➡ Restaurants are nonsmoking.

GAY & LESBIAN TRAVELLERS

➡ Homosexuality is legal in Italy. It's well tolerated in major cities, but overt displays of affection could attract a negative response.

➡ Italy's main gay and lesbian organisation is **Arcigay** (☎ 051 095 72 00; www.arcigay.it; Via Don Minzoni 18, Cassero LGBT Center).

INTERNET ACCESS

➡ Most hotels, hostels, B&Bs and *pensioni* offer free wi-fi, as do many bars and cafes.

➡ Public wi-fi is available in many large cities, but you'll generally need an Italian mobile number to register for it.

MONEY

ATMs Known as *bancomat,* are widely available and most will accept cards tied into the Visa, MasterCard, Cirrus and Maestro systems.

Credit cards Good for payment in most hotels, restaurants, shops, supermarkets and toll-booths. Major cards such as Visa, MasterCard, Eurocard, Cirrus and Eurocheques are widely accepted. Amex is also recognised, though less common.

Tipping If *servizio* is not included, leave 10% in restaurants, a euro or two in pizzerias. It's not necessary in bars or cafes, but many people leave small change if drinking at the bar.

OPENING HOURS

Opening hours vary throughout the year. We've provided high-season opening hours; hours will generally decrease in the shoulder and low seasons. 'Summer' times generally refer to the period from April to September or October, while 'winter' times generally run from October or November to March.

Banks 8.30am–1.30pm and 2.45–3.45pm or 4.30pm Monday to Friday

Restaurants noon–2.30pm and 7.30–11pm or midnight

Cafes 7.30am–8pm

Bars and clubs 10pm–4am or 5am

Shops 9am–1pm and 4–8pm Monday to Saturday, some also open Sunday

PUBLIC HOLIDAYS

Most Italians take their annual holiday in August, with the busiest period occurring around 15 August, known locally as Ferragosto. As a result, many businesses and shops close for at least part of that month. Settimana Santa (Easter Holy Week) is another busy holiday period for Italians.

National public holidays:

Capodanno (New Year's Day) 1 January

Epifania (Epiphany) 6 January

Pasquetta (Easter Monday) March/April

Giorno della Liberazione (Liberation Day) 25 April

Festa del Lavoro (Labour Day) 1 May

Festa della Repubblica (Republic Day) 2 June

Ferragosto (Feast of the Assumption) 15 August

Festa di Ognisanti (All Saints' Day) 1 November

Festa dell'Immacolata Concezione (Feast of the Immaculate Conception) 8 December

Natale (Christmas Day) 25 December

Festa di Santo Stefano (Boxing Day) 26 December

EATING PRICE RANGES

The following price ranges refer to a meal of two courses (antipasto/*primo* and *secondo*), a glass of house wine, and *coperto* (cover charge) for one person.

€ under €25

€€ €25–€45

€€€ over €45

SAFE TRAVEL

Italy is generally a safe country, but petty theft is prevalent. Be on your guard against pickpockets in popular tourist centres such as Rome, Florence, Venice and Naples.

TELEPHONE

- Area codes must be dialled even when calling locally.
- To call Italy from abroad, dial ☎0039 and then the area code, including the first zero.
- To call abroad from Italy, dial ☎00, then the relevant country code followed by the telephone number.
- Italian mobile phone numbers are nine or 10 digits long and start with a three-digit prefix starting with a 3.

Mobile Phones

- Local SIM cards can be used in European, Australian and some unlocked US phones. Other phones must be set to roaming.
- You can get SIMs from **TIM** (Telecom Italia Mobile; ☎187; www.tim.it), **Wind** (☎155; www.wind.it) and **Vodafone** (☎190; www.vodafone.it) outlets. You'll need a passport or ID when you buy one.

VISAS

- Schengen visa rules apply for entry to Italy.
- Unless staying in a hotel/B&B/hostel etc, all foreign visitors are supposed to register with the local police within eight days of arrival.
- A *permesso di soggiorno* (permit to stay) is required by all non-EU nationals who stay in Italy longer than three months. Check details on www.poliziadistato.it.
- EU citizens do not require a *permesso di soggiorno*.

Getting There & Away

Italy is well served by international airlines and European low-cost carriers, and there are plenty of bus, train and ferry routes into the country.

Flights, tours and rail tickets can be booked online at lonelyplanet.com/bookings.

AIR

There are direct intercontinental flights to/from Rome and Milan. European flights also serve regional airports.

Italy's national carrier is **Alitalia** (☎89 20 10; www.alitalia.com).

Italy's principal airports:

Leonardo da Vinci (☎06 6 59 51; www.adr.it/fiumicino) Italy's main airport, in Rome; also known as Fiumicino.

Rome Ciampino (☎06 6 59 51; www.adr.it/ciampino) Rome's second airport.

Milan Malpensa(☎02 23 23 23; www.milanomalpensa-airport.com) Northern Italy's principal hub.

Venice Marco Polo (☎flight information 041 260 92 60; www.veniceairport.it) Venice's main airport.

Pisa International (Galileo Galilei Airport; ☎050 84 93 00; www.pisa-airport.com) Gateway for Florence and Tuscany.

MAIN INTERNATIONAL FERRY ROUTES

FROM	TO	COMPANY	HIGH SEASON FARE (€)	DURATION (HR)
Ancona	Igoumenitsa, Greece	Minoan, Superfast, Anek	64-109	16½-22
Ancona	Patra, Greece	Minoan, Superfast, Anek	64-109	22-29
Ancona	Split, Croatia	Jadrolinija, SNAV	42-58	10¾
Bari	Igoumenitsa, Greece	Superfast	67-96	8-12
Bari	Patra, Greece	Superfast	67-96	16
Bari	Dubrovnik, Croatia	Jadrolinija	48-58	10-12
Bari	Bar, Montenegro	Montenegro	50-55	9
Brindisi	Igoumenitsa, Greece	Grimaldi	55-101	8
Brindisi	Patra, Greece	Grimaldi	55-101	14
Genoa	Barcelona, Spain	GNV	42-87	19½
Genoa	Tunis, Tunisia	GNV	83-142	23½
Venice	Igoumenitsa, Greece	Superfast, Anek	69-99	14½-21

USEFUL WEBSITES

Lonely Planet (www.lonelyplanet.com/italy) Destination information, hotel bookings, traveller forum and more.

Trenitalia (www.trenitalia.com) Italian railways website.

Enit Italia (www.italia.it) Official Italian-government tourism website.

Naples Capodichino (☎081 789 62 59; www.aeroportodinapoli.it) Southern Italy's main airport.

Catania Fontanarossa (☎095 723 91 11; www.aeroporto.catania.it) Sicily's largest airport.

LAND

Bus

Eurolines (☎0861 199 19 00; www.eurolines.it) operates buses from European destinations to many Italian cities.

Train

Milan and Venice are Italy's main international rail hubs. International trains also run to/from Rome, Genoa, Turin, Verona, Bologna and Florence.

Main routes:

Milan To/from Paris, Geneva, Zürich and Vienna.

Rome To/from Munich and Vienna.

Venice To/from Paris, Munich and Vienna.

Voyages-sncf (☎0844 848 58 48; http://uk.voyages-sncf.com) can provide fare information on journeys from the UK to Italy, most of which require a change at Paris. Another excellent resource is www.seat61.com.

Eurail and Inter-Rail passes are valid in Italy.

ADMISSION PRICES

Admission to state-run museums, galleries, monuments and sites is free to under-18s. People aged between 18 and 25 are entitled to a discount. To get it, you'll need proof of your age, ideally a passport or ID card.

Admission is free to everyone on the first Sunday of each month.

SEA

- Ferries serve Italian ports from across the Mediterranean. Timetables are seasonal, so always check ahead.
- For routes, companies and online booking try www.traghettiweb.it.
- Holders of Eurail and Inter-Rail passes should check with the ferry company if they are entitled to a discount or free passage.
- Major ferry companies:

Anek Lines (☎071 207 22 75; www.anekitalia.com)

GNV (☎010 209 45 91; www.gnv.it)

Grimaldi Lines (☎0831 54 81 16; www.grimaldi-lines.com; Costa Morena Terminal)

Jadrolinija (☎Ancona 071 207 24 97, Bari 080 521 76 43; www.jadrolinija.hr)

Minoan Lines (☎071 20 17 08; www.minoan.it)

Montenegro Lines (☎Bar 382 3030 3469; www.montenegrolines.net)

SNAV (☎081 428 55 55; www.snav.it)

Superfast (☎Ancona 071 20 20 33, Bari 080 528 28 09; www.superfast.com)

Getting Around

BICYCLE

- Bikes can be taken on regional and certain international trains carrying the bike logo, but you'll need to pay a supplement (€3.50 on regional trains, €12 on international trains).
- Bikes can be carried free if dismantled and stored in a bike bag.
- Bikes generally incur a small supplement on ferries, typically €10 to €15.

BOAT

Craft *Navi* (large ferries) service Sicily and Sardinia, while *traghetti* (smaller ferries) and *aliscafi* (hydrofoils) service the smaller islands. Most ferries carry vehicles; hydrofoils do not.

Routes Main embarkation points for Sicily and Sardinia are Genoa, Livorno, Civitavecchia and Naples. Ferries for Sicily also leave from Villa San Giovanni and Reggio Calabria. Main arrival points in Sardinia are Cagliari, Arbatax, Olbia and Porto Torres; in Sicily they're Palermo, Catania, Trapani and Messina.

Timetables and tickets Direct Ferries (www.directferries.co.uk) allows you to search routes, compare prices and book tickets for ferry routes in Italy.

BUS

- ➡ Italy boasts an extensive and largely reliable bus network.
- ➡ Buses are not necessarily cheaper than trains, but in mountainous areas they are often the only choice.
- ➡ In larger cities, companies have ticket offices or operate through agencies, but in villages and small towns tickets are sold in bars or on the bus.
- ➡ Reservations are only necessary for high-season long-haul trips.

CAR & MOTORCYCLE

- ➡ Italy's roads are generally good, and there's an extensive network of toll autostrade (motorways).
- ➡ All EU driving licences are recognised in Italy. Holders of non-EU licences should get an International Driving Permit (IDP) through their national automobile association.
- ➡ Traffic restrictions apply in most city centres.
- ➡ To hire a car you'll require a driving licence (plus IDP if necessary) and credit card. Age restrictions vary, but generally you'll need to be 21 or over.
- ➡ If driving your own car, carry your vehicle registration certificate, driving licence and proof of third-party liability insurance cover.
- ➡ For further details, see the website of Italy's motoring organisation **Automobile Club d'Italia** (ACI; ☎803116, from a foreign mobile ☎800 116 800; www.aci.it).
- ➡ ACI provides 24-hour roadside assistance: call ☎803 116 from a landline or Italian mobile, ☎800 116 800 from a foreign mobile.

TRAIN

Italy has an extensive rail network. Most services are run by **Trenitalia** (☎892021; www.trenitalia.com) but **Italo** (☎89 20 20; www.italotreno.it) also operates high-speed trains.

There are several types of train:

Regionale/interregionale Slow local services.

InterCity (IC) Faster services between major cities.

Alta Velocità (AV) State-of-the-art, high-velocity trains: Frecciarossa, Frecciargento, Frecciabianca and Italo trains.

Tickets

- ➡ InterCity and Alta Velocità trains require prior reservation.
- ➡ If your ticket doesn't include a reservation with an assigned seat, you must validate it before boarding by inserting it into one of the machines dotted around stations.

The Netherlands

Includes ➡

Best Places to Eat

- Ron Gastrobar (p509)
- Bisschopsmolen (p524)
- Restaurant Allard (p515)
- Tante Nel (p519)
- Brick (p513)

Best Places to Stay

- Hoxton Amsterdam (p509)
- King Kong Hostel (p519)
- Mary K Hotel (p523)
- Pincoffs (p519)
- Collector (p509)

Why Go?

Old and new intertwine in the Netherlands. The legacies of great Dutch artists Rembrandt, Vermeer and Van Gogh, beautiful 17th-century canals, windmills, tulips and quaint brown cafes lit by flickering candles coexist with ground-breaking contemporary architecture, cutting-edge fashion, homewares, design and food scenes, phenomenal nightlife and a progressive mindset.

Much of the Netherlands is famously below sea level and the pancake-flat landscape offers idyllic cycling. Locals live on bicycles and you can too. Rental outlets are ubiquitous throughout the country, which is crisscrossed with dedicated cycling paths.

Allow plenty of time to revel in the magical, multifaceted capital Amsterdam, to venture further afield to charming canal-laced towns such as Leiden and Delft. Check out Dutch cities such as exquisite Maastricht, with its city walls, ancient churches and grand squares, and the pulsing port city of Rotterdam, currently undergoing an urban renaissance.

When to Go

Amsterdam

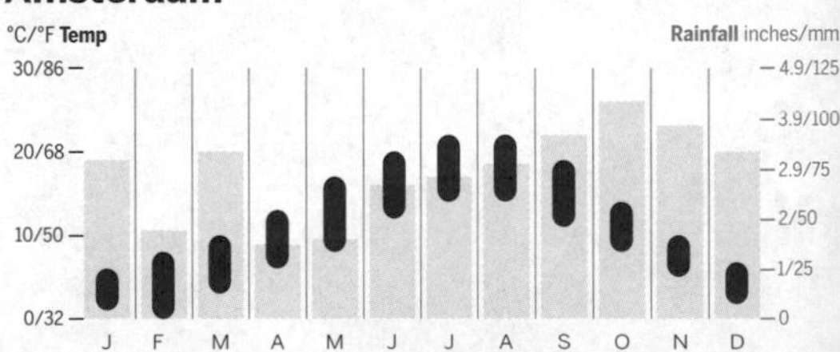

Mar–May Colour explodes as billions of bulbs bloom.

Jul Mild summer temps and long daylight hours keep you outside cycling and drinking.

Dec–Feb When the canals freeze, the Dutch passion for ice skating is on display nationwide.

AMSTERDAM

020 / POP 813,000

World Heritage–listed canals lined by gabled houses, candlelit cafes, whirring bicycles, lush parks, monumental museums, colourful markets, diverse dining, quirky shopping and legendary nightlife make the free-spirited Dutch capital one of Europe's great cities.

Amsterdam has been a liberal place since the Netherlands' Golden Age, when it was at the forefront of European art and trade. Centuries later, in the 1960s, it again led the pack – this time in the principles of tolerance, with broad-minded views on drugs and same-sex relationships taking centre stage.

Explore its many worlds-within-worlds, where nothing ever seems the same twice.

Sights

Amsterdam is compact and you can roam the city on foot but there's also an excellent public transport network.

City Centre

Crowned by the Royal Palace (p503), the square that puts the 'Dam' in Amsterdam anchors the city's oldest quarter, which is also home to its infamous Red Light District.

★**Royal Palace** PALACE

(Koninklijk Paleis; 020-620 40 60; www.paleisamsterdam.nl; Dam; adult/child €10/free; 10am-5pm; 4/9/16/24 Dam) Opened as a town hall in 1655, this building became a palace in the 19th century. The interiors gleam, especially the marble work – at its best in a floor inlaid with maps of the world in the great *burgerzaal* (citizens' hall), which occupies the heart of the building. Pick up a free audio tour at the desk after you enter; it will explain everything you see in vivid detail. King Willem-Alexander uses the palace only for ceremonies; check the website for periodic closures.

★**Begijnhof** SQUARE

(020-622 19 18; www.nicolaas-parochie.nl; off Gedempte Begijnensloot; 9am-5pm; 1/2/5 Spui) FREE This enclosed former convent dates from the early 14th century. It's a surreal oasis of peace, with tiny houses and postage-stamp gardens around a well-kept courtyard. The beguines were a Catholic order of unmarried or widowed women who cared for the elderly and lived a religious life without taking monastic vows. The last true beguine died in 1971.

Canal Ring

Amsterdam's Canal Ring was built during the 17th-century after the seafaring port grew beyond its medieval walls, and authorities devised a ground-breaking expansion plan.

Wandering here amid architectural treasures and their reflections on the narrow waters of the Prinsengracht, Keizersgracht and Herengracht can cause days to vanish.

★**Anne Frank Huis** MUSEUM

(020-556 71 05; www.annefrank.org; Prinsengracht 267; adult/child €9/4.50; 9am-10pm Apr-Oct, 9am-7pm Sun-Fri, to 9pm Sat Nov-Mar; 13/14/17 Westermarkt) The Anne Frank Huis draws almost one million visitors annually (prepurchase tickets online to minimise the queues). With its reconstruction of Anne's melancholy bedroom and her actual diary – sitting alone in its glass case, filled with sunnily optimistic writing tempered by quiet despair – it's a powerful experience.

ITINERARIES

One Week

Spend three days canal exploring, museum hopping and cafe crawling in **Amsterdam**. Work your way through the ancient towns of the **Randstad** and the contemporary vibe of **Rotterdam**, and save a day for the grandeur of **Maastricht**.

Two Weeks

Allow four days for Amsterdam's many delights, plus a day trip to the old towns of the north, and a day or two exploring some of the region's smaller towns. Then add a day each at beautiful **Delft**, regal **Den Haag** (The Hague), student-filled **Utrecht** and buzzing **Rotterdam**. Finish off with two days in historic **Maastricht**.

Netherlands Highlights

1. **Amsterdam** (p503) Cruising the canals while soaking up one of Europe's most enchanting old cities.

2. **Markthal Rotterdam** (p521) Marvelling at the architecture, a highlight of the Netherlands' hip-and-happening 'second city'.

3. **Fort Sint Pieter** (p524) Exploring the centuries-old tunnels below the resplendent city of Maastricht.

4. **Vermeer Centrum Delft** (p516) Learning about Vermeer's life and work in his evocative hometown.

5. **Den Haag** (p514) Discovering the beautiful tree-lined boulevards, classy museums and the palatial Binnenhof buildings.

6. **Keukenhof Gardens** (p514) Delving into the cache of mus in Leiden and dazzling tulip displays at its nearby garden

7. **Zaanse Schans** (p513) Watching windmills twirl and the millers at the delightful c air museum.

8. **Cycling** (p517) Following dikes along canals or touring tulip fields of the Randstad o world's best network of cycli routes.

Museumplein

Amsterdam's big three museums fan out around the grassy expanse of Museumplein, in the Old South neighbourhood.

★Van Gogh Museum MUSEUM

(☎020-570 52 00; www.vangoghmuseum.com; Museumplein 6; adult/child €17/free, audioguide €5; ⏱9am-7pm Sun-Thu, to 9pm Sat mid-Jul–Aug, to 6pm Sat-Thu Sep–mid-Jul, to 5pm Jan-Mar, to 10pm Fri; 📶; 🚋2/3/5/12 Van Baerlestraat) Framed by a gleaming new glass entrance hall, the world's largest Van Gogh collection offers a superb line-up of masterworks. Trace the artist's life from his tentative start through his giddy-coloured sunflower phase, and on to the black cloud that descended over him and his work. There are also paintings by contemporaries Gauguin, Toulouse-Lautrec, Monet and Bernard.

Queues can be huge; prebooked e-tickets and discount cards expedite the process with fast-track entry.

★Rijksmuseum MUSEUM

(National Museum; ☎020-674 70 00; www.rijksmuseum.nl; Museumstraat 1; adult/child €17.50/free; ⏱9am-5pm; 📶; 🚋2/5 Rijksmuseum) The Rijksmuseum is the Netherlands' premier art trove, splashing Rembrandts, Vermeers and 7500 other masterpieces over 1.5km of galleries. To avoid the biggest crowds, come after 3pm. Or prebook tickets online, which provides fast-track entry.

The Golden Age works are the highlight. Feast your eyes on still lifes, gentlemen in ruffled collars and landscapes bathed in pale yellow light. Rembrandt's *The Night Watch* (1642) takes pride of place.

★Stedelijk Museum MUSEUM

(☎020-573 29 11; www.stedelijk.nl; Museumplein 10; adult/child €18/free, audio guide €5; ⏱10am-6pm Sat-Thu, to 10pm Fri; 📶; 🚋2/3/5/12 Van Baerlestraat) Built in 1895 to a neo-Renaissance design by AM Weissman, the Stedelijk Museum is the permanent home of the National Museum of Modern Art. Amassed by post-war curator Willem Sandberg, the modern classics here are among the world's most admired. The permanent collection includes all the blue chips of 19th- and 20th-century painting – Monet, Picasso and Chagall among them – as well as sculptures by Rodin, abstracts by Mondrian and Kandinsky, and much, much more.

DON'T MISS

JORDAAN

A densely populated *volksbuurt* (district for the common people) until the mid-20th century, the intimate Jordaan is now one of Amsterdam's most desirable addresses. The neighbourhood is a pastiche of modest 17th- and 18th-century merchants' houses and humble workers' homes squashed in a grid of tiny lanes peppered with bite-sized cafes and shops. There's a handful of small-scale museums (houseboat museum, tulip museum) but the real pleasure here is simply losing yourself in its charming canal-side backstreets.

★Vondelpark PARK

(www.hetvondelpark.net; 🚋2/5 Hobbemastraat) The lush urban idyll of the Vondelpark is one of Amsterdam's most magical places – sprawling, English-style gardens with ponds, lawns, footbridges and winding footpaths. On a sunny day, an open-air party atmosphere ensues when tourists, lovers, cyclists, in-line skaters, pram-pushing parents, cartwheeling children, football-kicking teenagers, spliff-sharing friends and champagne-swilling picnickers all come out to play.

De Pijp

Immediately south of the Canal Ring, villagey De Pijp is Amsterdam's most spontaneous and creative quarter. Bohemian cafes, restaurants and bars spill out around its festive street market.

★Albert Cuypmarkt MARKET

(www.albertcuyp-markt.amsterdam; Albert Cuypstraat, btwn Ferdinand Bolstraat & Van Woustraat; ⏱9.30am-5pm Mon-Sat; 🚋16/24 Albert Cuypstraat) The best place to marvel at De Pijp's colourful scene is the Albert Cuypmarkt, Amsterdam's largest and busiest market. Vendors loudly tout their odd gadgets and their arrays of fruit, vegetables, herbs and spices. They sell clothes and other general goods too, often cheaper than anywhere else. Snack vendors tempt passers-by with herring sandwiches, egg rolls, doughnuts and caramel-syrup-filled *stroopwafels* (waffles). If you have room after all that, the surrounding area teems with cosy cafes and eateries.

Central Amsterdam

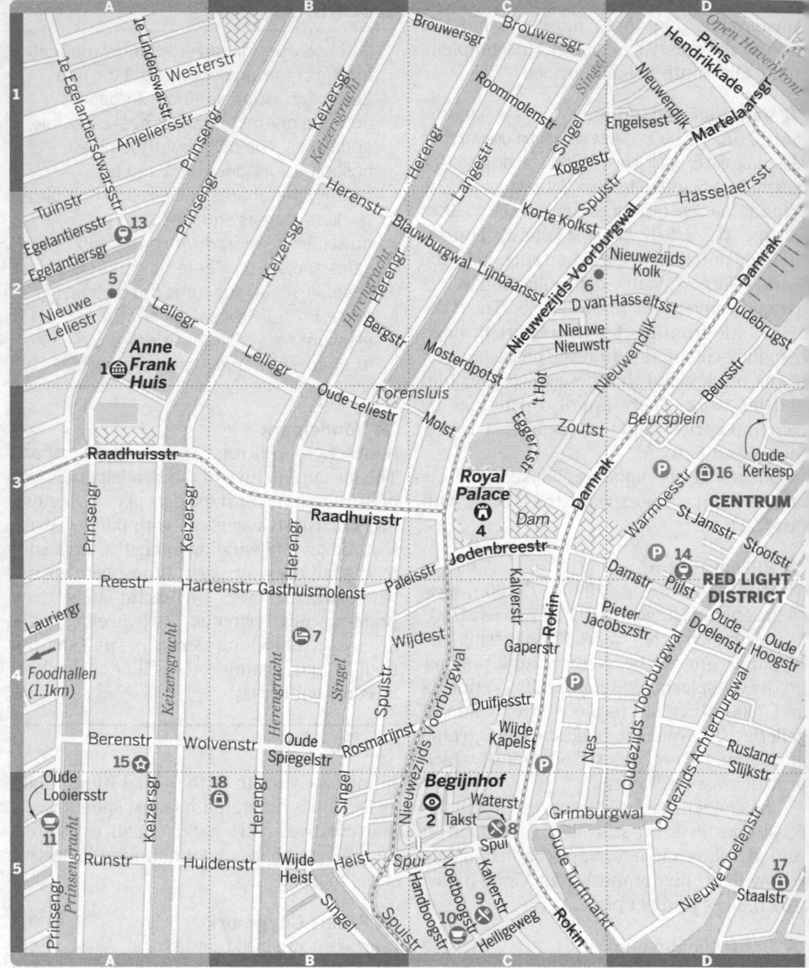

★**Heineken Experience** BREWERY
(☎020-523 92 22; www.heineken.com; Stadhouderskade 78; adult/child €18/14.50; ⏲10.30am-9pm daily Jul & Aug, to 7.30pm Mon-Thu, to 9pm Fri-Sun Sep-Jun; 🚋16/24 Stadhouderskade) On the site of the company's old brewery, the crowning glory of this self-guided 'Experience' (samples aside) is a multimedia exhibit where you 'become' a beer by getting shaken up, sprayed with water and subjected to heat. True beer connoisseurs will shudder, but it's a lot of fun. Admission includes a 15-minute shuttle boat ride to the Heineken Brand Store near Rembrandtplein. Prebooking tickets online saves you €2 on the entry fee and allows you to skip the ticket queues.

Nieuwmarkt & Plantage

The streets around the Rembrandt House are prime wandering territory, offering a vibrant mix of old Amsterdam, canals and quirky shops and cafes.

★**Museum het Rembrandthuis** MUSEUM
(Rembrandt House Museum; ☎020-520 04 00; www.rembrandthuis.nl; Jodenbreestraat 4; adult/

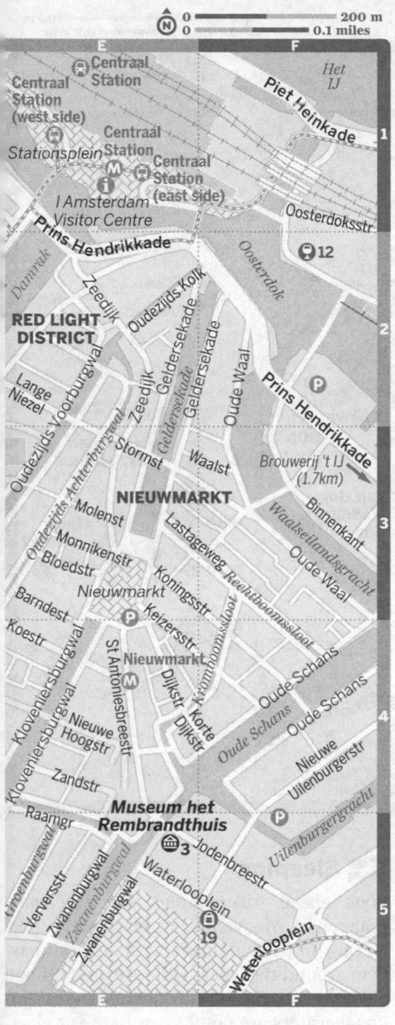

child €13/4; ⏲10am-6pm; 🚋9/14 Waterlooplein) You almost expect to find the master himself at the Museum het Rembrandthuis, where Rembrandt van Rijn ran the Netherlands' largest painting studio, only to lose the lot when profligacy set in, enemies swooped and bankruptcy came a-knocking. The museum has scores of etchings and sketches. Ask for the free audio guide at the entrance. You can buy advance tickets online, though it's not as vital here as at some of the other big museums.

Central Amsterdam

Top Sights

1	Anne Frank Huis	A2
2	Begijnhof	C5
3	Museum het Rembrandthuis	E5
4	Royal Palace	C3

Activities, Courses & Tours

5	Those Dam Boat Guys	A2
6	Yellow Bike	C2

Sleeping

7	Hoxton Amsterdam	B4

Eating

8	Gartine	C5
9	Vleminckx	C5

Drinking & Nightlife

10	Dampkring	C5
11	La Tertulia	A5
12	SkyLounge	F2
13	't Smalle	A2
14	Wynand Fockink	D3

Entertainment

15	Felix Meritis	A4

Shopping

16	Condomerie Het Gulden Vlies	D3
17	Droog	D5
18	Negen Straatjes	B5
19	Waterlooplein Flea Market	F5

Tours

Amsterdam's **canal boats** are a relaxing way to tour the town. Avoid steamed-up glass windows by choosing boats with open seating areas.

Those Dam Boat Guys BOATING
(☎06 1885 5219; www.thosedamboatguys.com; per person €25; ⏲1pm, 3pm & 5pm; 🚋13/14/17 Westermarkt) Here's your least-touristy canal-cruise option. The guys offer cheeky small tours (no more than 11 people) on electric boats. Feel free to bring food, beer, smoking material and whatever else you want for the 90-minute jaunt. Departure is from Cafe Wester (Nieuwe Leliestraat 2).

Yellow Bike CYCLING
(☎020-620 69 40; www.yellowbike.nl; Nieuwezijds Kolk 29; city/countryside tours from €22.50/32.50; 🚋1/2/5/13/17 Nieuwezijds Kolk) The original. Choose from city tours or the longer countryside tour through the pretty Waterland district to the north.

Southern Canal Ring

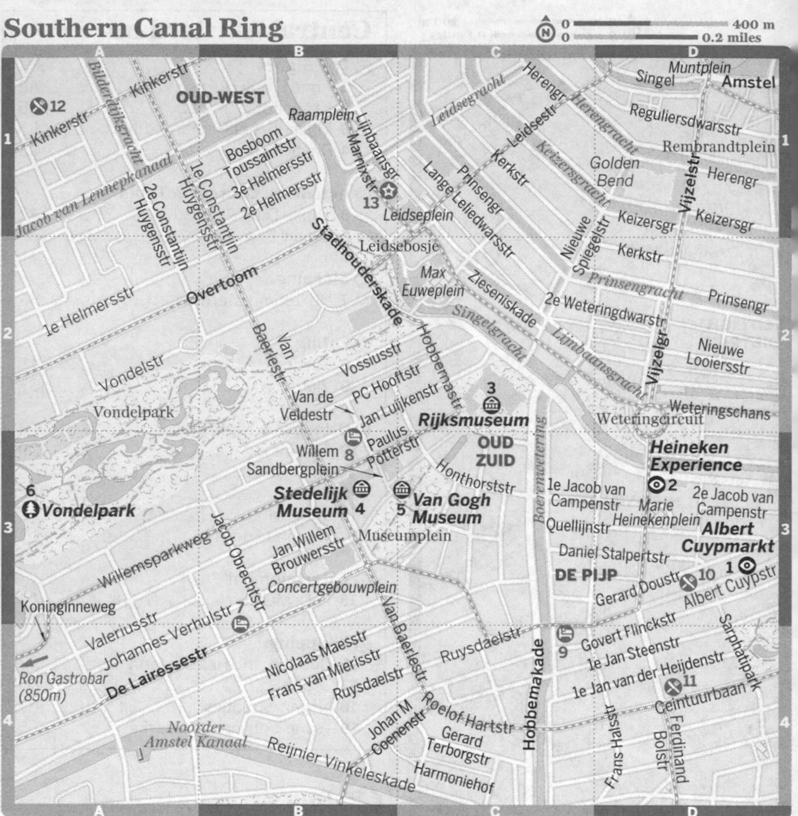

Southern Canal Ring

Top Sights

1	Albert Cuypmarkt	D3
2	Heineken Experience	D3
3	Rijksmuseum	C2
4	Stedelijk Museum	B3
5	Van Gogh Museum	C3
6	Vondelpark	A3

Sleeping

7	Collector	B3
8	Hotel Fita	B3
9	Sir Albert Hotel	C4

Eating

10	Butcher	D3
11	Dèsa	D4
12	Foodhallen	A1

Entertainment

13	Melkweg	B1

Sleeping

Book ahead for summer and weekends year-round. Many cheaper places cater specifically to party animals with general mayhem around the clock. Others exude refined old-world charm. Wi-fi is near universal but lifts/elevators are not.

Generator Amsterdam HOSTEL €
(☎020-708 56 00; www.generatorhostels.com; Mauritskade 57; dm/d/q €54/144/360; 9/14 9/10/14 Alexanderplein) Generator continues its push into the upscale hostel market: set in a century-old university building right by Oosterpark, this design-savvy property has 566 beds spread over 168 twin and quad rooms, all with en-suite bathrooms. Guests can socialise in the cafe with terrace overlooking the park, in a bar carved from the old lecture hall or in a basement speakeasy.

★Collector B&B €€

(☎020-673 67 79; www.the-collector.nl; De Lairessestraat 46; s/d from €90/125; @📶; 🚋5/16/24 Museumplein) This spotless B&B near the Concertgebouw is furnished with museum-style displays of clocks, wooden clogs and ice skates – things the owner, Karel, collects. Each of the three rooms has balcony access and a TV. Karel stocks the kitchen for guests to prepare breakfast at their leisure (the eggs come from his hens in the garden).

★Hotel Fita HOTEL €€

(☎020-679 09 76; www.fita.nl; Jan Luijkenstraat 37; s/d from €116/136; 📶; 🚋2/3/5/12 Van Baerlestraat) Family-owned Fita, on a quiet street off the Museumplein and PC Hooftstraat, has 15 handsome rooms with nicely appointed bathrooms; a bountiful free breakfast of eggs, pancakes, cheeses and breads; and a lift/elevator. The dynamic young owner keeps the property in mint condition (new furniture, new artwork, fresh paint), and service could not be more attentive.

★Hoxton Amsterdam DESIGN HOTEL €€€

(☎020-888 55 55; www.thehoxton.com; Herengracht 255; s/d from €159/199; ❄📶; 🚋13/14/17 Westermarkt) Part of a European-based chain known for high style at affordable prices, the Hoxton opened in 2015 to great hipster fanfare. The 111 rooms splash through five canal houses and come in sizes from 'shoebox' to 'roomy'. The breakfast snack, speedy wi-fi, free international calls and low-priced canteen items are nice touches.

★Sir Albert Hotel DESIGN HOTEL €€€

(☎020-305 30 20; www.sirhotels.com/albert; Albert Cuypstraat 2-6; d from €209; ❄@📶; 🚋16 Ruysdaelstraat) A 19th-century former diamond factory houses this glitzy design hotel. Its 90 creative rooms and suites have soaring ceilings and large windows, with custom-made linens and Illy espresso machines; iPads are available for guest use in the Persian-rug-floored study. Energetic staff are genuine and professional in equal measure.

Eating

Amsterdam abounds with eateries. Superb streets for hunting include Utrechtsestraat, near Rembrandtplein; Amstelveenseweg, along the Vondelpark's western edge; and any of the little streets throughout the western canals.

★Gartine CAFE €

(☎020-320 41 32; www.gartine.nl; Taksteeg 7; mains €7.25-11.50, high tea €17.50-24.75; ⌚10am-5pm Wed-Sun; 🖉; 🚋4/9/14/16/24 Spui/Rokin) Gartine is magical, from its covert location in an alley off busy Kalverstraat to its mismatched antique tableware and its sublime breakfast pastries, sandwiches and salads (made from produce grown in its garden plot). The sweet-and-savoury high tea is a scrumptious bonus.

★Foodhallen FOOD HALL €

(www.foodhallen.nl; Hannie Dankbaar Passage 3, De Hallen; dishes €5-15; ⌚11am-11.30pm Sun-Thu, to 1am Fri-Sat; 🚋17 Ten Katestraat) Inside De Hallen, this glorious international food hall has 21 stands surrounding an airy open-plan eating area. Some are offshoots of popular Amsterdam eateries, such as the **Butcher** (☎020-470 78 75; http://the-butcher.com; Albert Cuypstraat 129; burgers €7.50-11.50; ⌚11am-midnight; 🚋16/24 Albert Cuypstraat); also look out for Viet View Vietnamese street food, Jabugo Iberico Bar ham, Pink Flamingo pizza, Bulls & Dogs hot dogs, Rough Kitchen ribs and De Ballenbar *bitterballen* (croquettes).

★Vleminckx FAST FOOD €

(http://vleminckxdesausmeester.nl; Voetboogstraat 33; fries €2.30-4.50, sauces €0.70; ⌚noon-7pm Sun & Mon, 11am-7pm Tue, Wed, Fri & Sat, 11am-8pm Thu; 🚋1/2/5 Koningsplein) Vleminckx has been frying up *frites* (French fries) since 1887, and doing it at this hole-in-the-wall takeaway shack near the Spui for more than 50 years. The standard is smothered in mayonnaise, though you can also ask for ketchup, peanut sauce or a variety of spicy toppings.

★Ron Gastrobar DUTCH €€

(☎020-496 19 43; www.rongastrobar.nl; Sophialaan 55; dishes €15, desserts €9; ⌚noon-2.30pm & 5.30-10.30pm; 📶; 🚋2 Amstelveenseweg) Ron Blaauw ran his two-Michelin-star restaurant in these stunning designer premises before trading the stars in to transform the space into an egalitarian 'gastrobar', serving around 25 one-flat-price tapas-style dishes such as steak tartare with crispy veal brains, mushroom ravioli with sweet-potato foam, barbecue-smoked bone marrow, Dutch asparagus with lobster-and-champagne sauce, and wagyu burgers – with no minimum order restrictions.

Dèsa INDONESIAN €€

(020-671 09 79; www.restaurantdesa.com; Ceintuurbaan 103; mains €12.50-22, rijsttafel €18.50-35; 5-10.30pm; ; 3 Ferdinand Bolstraat) Named for the Indonesian word for 'village' (apt for this city, but especially this 'hood), Dèsa is wildly popular for its rijsttafel ('rice table') banquets. À la carte options include *serundeng* (spiced fried coconut), *ayam besengek* (chicken cooked in saffron and coconut milk), *sambal goreng telor* (stewed eggs in spicy Balinese sauce) and *pisang goreng* (fried banana) for dessert.

Drinking & Nightlife

In addition to the Medieval Centre and Red Light District, party hotspots include Rembrandtplein and Leidseplein, both awash with bars, clubs, *coffeeshops* (cafe authorised to sell cannabis) and pubs.

To truly experience the unique Dutch quality of *gezellig* (conviviality/cosiness), head to a history-steeped *bruin café* (brown cafe, ie pub, traditional drinking establishments named for the nicotine-stained walls). Many serve food.

★ Brouwerij 't IJ BREWERY

(www.brouwerijhetij.nl; Funenkade 7; brewery 2-8pm, English tour 3.30pm Fri-Sun; 10 Hoogte Kadijk) Beneath the creaking sails of the 1725-built De Gooyer windmill, Amsterdam's leading organic microbrewery produces delicious (and often very potent) standard, seasonal and limited-edition brews. Pop in for a beer in the tiled tasting room, lined by an amazing bottle collection, or on the plane tree–shaded terrace. A beer is included in the 30-minute brewery tour (€5).

★ 't Smalle BROWN CAFE

(www.t-smalle.nl; Egelantiersgracht 12; 10am-12.30am Sun-Thu, to 2am Fri & Sat; 13/14/17 Westermarkt) Dating back to 1786 as a *jenever* (Dutch gin) distillery and tasting house, and restored during the 1970s with antique porcelain beer pumps and lead-framed windows, locals' favourite 't Smalle is one of Amsterdam's charming *bruin cafés*. Dock your boat right by the pretty stone terrace, which is wonderfully convivial by day and impossibly romantic at night.

★ Wynand Fockink DISTILLERY

(www.wynand-fockink.nl; Pijlsteeg 31; 3-9pm; 4/9/16/24 Dam) This small tasting house (dating from 1679) serves scores of *jenever* (Dutch gin) and liqueurs in an arcade behind Grand Hotel Krasnapolsky. Although there are no seats or stools, it's an intimate place to knock back a shot glass or two of gin. Guides give an English-language tour of the distillery and tastings (six samples) on weekends at 3pm, 4.30pm, 6pm and 7.30pm (€17.50, reservations not required).

★ SkyLounge COCKTAIL BAR

(www.skyloungeamsterdam.com; Oosterdoksstraat 4; 11am-1am Sun-Tue, to 2am Wed & Thu, to 3am Fri & Sat; 1/2/4/5/9/14/16/24 Centraal Station) An unrivalled 360-degree panorama of Amsterdam extends from the glass-walled

COFFEESHOP DOS & DON'TS

➡ Do ask at the bar for the menu of cannabis-related goods on offer, usually packaged in small bags. You can also buy ready-made joints; most shops offer rolling papers, pipes or bongs to use.

➡ Don't light up anywhere besides a *coffeeshop* without checking that it's OK to do so.

➡ Don't use alcohol and tobacco products – these are not permitted in *coffeeshops*.

➡ Don't ask for hard (illegal) drugs.

RED LIGHT DISTRICT

Just southeast of Centraal Station, on and around the parallel neon-lit canals Oudezijds Voorburgwal and Oudezijds Achterburgwal, the warren of medieval alleyways making up Amsterdam's Red Light District (locally known as De Wallen), is a carnival of vice, seething with skimpily clad prostitutes in brothel windows, raucous bars, haze-filled 'coffeeshops', strip shows, sex shows, mind-boggling museums and shops selling everything from cartoonish condoms to S&M gear and herbal highs.

The area is generally safe, but keep your wits about you and don't photograph or film prostitutes in the windows – out of respect, and to avoid having your camera flung in a canal by their enforcers. Seriously.

SkyLounge on the 11th floor of the DoubleTree Amsterdam Centraal Station hotel – and just gets better when you head out to its vast, sofa-strewn SkyTerrace, with an outdoor bar. Deliberate over more than 500 different cocktails; DJs regularly hit the decks.

Coffeeshops

In the Netherlands, 'coffeeshops' are where one buys marijuana.

Dampkring COFFEE
(www.dampkring-coffeeshop-amsterdam.nl; Handboogstraat 29; 10am-1am; ; 1/2/5 Koningsplein) With an interior that resembles a larger-than-life lava lamp, Dampkring is a consistent Cannabis Cup winner, and known for having the most comprehensive menu in town (including details about smell, taste and effect). Its name references the ring of the earth's atmosphere where smaller items combust.

La Tertulia COFFEE
(020-623 85 03; www.coffeeshoptertulia.com; Prinsengracht 312; 11am-7pm Tue-Sat; 7/10/17 Elandsgracht) A backpackers' favourite, this mother-and-daughter-run *coffeeshop* has a greenhouse feel. You can sit outside by the Van Gogh–inspired murals, play some board games or contemplate the Jurassic-sized crystals by the counter. Bonus: Tertulia actually has good coffee, made with beans from a Dutch speciality roaster.

☆ Entertainment

Find out what's on at I Amsterdam (www.iamsterdam.com).

For tickets, including last-minute discounts, head to **Uitburo** (www.lastminuteticketshop.nl; online ticket sales from 10am on day of performance; 1/2/5/7/10 Leidseplein).

Melkweg LIVE MUSIC
(www.melkweg.nl; Lijnbaansgracht 234a; 6pm-1am; 1/2/5/7/10 Leidseplein) In a former dairy, the nonprofit 'Milky Way' is a dazzling galaxy of diverse music. One night it's electronica, the next reggae or punk, and next heavy metal. Roots, rock and mellow singer-songwriters all get stage time too. Check out the website for cutting-edge cinema, theatre and multimedia offerings.

Felix Meritis THEATRE
(626 23 21; www.felix.meritis.nl; Keizersgracht 324; box office 9am-7pm; ; 1/2/5 Spui) Amsterdam's centre for arts, culture and science puts on innovative modern theatre, music and dance, as well as talks on politics, diversity, art, technology and literature. Its adjoining cafe is exceptional for coffee or cocktails by the huge windows or outside overlooking the canal.

> **GAY AMSTERDAM**
>
> Amsterdam's gay scene is one of the largest in the world. Hubs include Warmoesstraat in the Red Light District and Reguliersdwarsstraat in the Southern Canal Ring. Gay Amsterdam (www.gayamsterdam.com) lists hotels, bars, clubs and more.

Shopping

The ultimate pleasure of shopping in Amsterdam is discovering some tiny shop selling something you'd find nowhere else. In the Western Canal Ring, the 'nine little streets' making up the **Negen Straatjes** (Nine Streets; www.de9straatjes.nl; 1/2/5 Spui) are dotted with them.

Markets of just about every description are scattered across the city, including Amsterdam's largest and busiest, De Pijp's Albert Cuypmarkt (p505).

★Droog DESIGN, HOMEWARES
(www.droog.com; Staalstraat 7; 9am-7pm; 4/9/14/16/24 Muntplein) Droog means 'dry' in Dutch, and this slick local design house's products are strong on dry wit. You'll find all kinds of smart items you never knew you needed, such as super-powerful suction cups. Also here is a gallery space, whimsical blue-and-white cafe, and fairy tale–inspired courtyard garden that Alice in Wonderland would love, as well as a top-floor apartment (double €278).

★Waterlooplein Flea Market MARKET
(www.waterlooplein.amsterdam; Waterlooplein; 9.30am-6pm Mon-Sat; 9/14 Waterlooplein) Covering the square once known as Vlooienburg (Flea Town), the Waterlooplein Flea Market draws bargain hunters seeking everything from antique knick-knacks to designer knock-offs. The street market started in 1880 when Jewish traders living in the neighbourhood began selling their wares here.

Food vendors waft falafel sandwiches, *frites* and other quick bites around the market's periphery.

I AMSTERDAM CARD

The **I Amsterdam Card** (www.iamsterdam.com; per 24/48/72hr €55/65/75) provides admission to more than 30 museums, a canal cruise and discounts at shops, entertainment venues and restaurants. Also includes a GVB transit pass. Available at VVV I Amsterdam Visitor Centres and some hotels.

★ **Condomerie Het Gulden Vlies** ADULT
(https://condomerie.com; Warmoesstraat 141; 11am-9pm Mon & Wed-Sat, 11am-6pm Tue, 1-6pm Sun; 4/9/14/16/24 Dam) Perfectly positioned for the Red Light District, this boutique sells condoms in every imaginable size, colour, flavour and design (horned devils, marijuana leaves, Delftware tiles…), along with lubricants and saucy gifts.

Information

I Amsterdam Visitor Centre (020-702 60 00; www.iamsterdam.com; Stationsplein 10; 9am-5pm Mon-Sat; 4/9/16/24 Centraal Station) Outside Centraal Station. Sells maps, attraction tickets, and transit passes.

Getting There & Away

AIR

Most major airlines serve Schiphol (p526), 18km southwest of the city centre.

BUS

Buses arrive at Amsterdam Duivendrecht train station, 7.5km southeast of the centre, which has an easy metro link to Centraal Station (about a 20-minute trip).

Eurolines' ticket office (www.eurolines.nl; Rokin 38a; 9am-5pm Mon-Sat; 4/9/14/16/24 Dam) is near the Dam.

TRAIN

Amsterdam's main train station is fabled **Centraal Station**, with extensive services to the rest of the country and major European cities.

For domestic destinations, visit the Dutch national train service, **NS** (www.ns.nl). **NS International** (www.nsinternational.nl) operates many international services.

Getting Around

TO/FROM THE AIRPORT

Taxi To Amsterdam from Schiphol airport takes 20 to 30 minutes and costs about €47.

Trains To Centraal Station depart every 10 minutes or so from 6am to 12.30am; the trip takes 17 minutes and costs €5.20.

BICYCLE

Amsterdam is cycling nirvana. The city has more bicycles (881,000) than residents (813,000). About 80,000 bicycles are stolen each year, so always lock up.

BOAT

Canal Bus (020-217 05 00; www.canal.nl; day pass adult/child €24/12; 10am-6pm; ; 1/2/5 Leidseplein) Offers a handy hop-on, hop-off service. Its 20 docks around the city are located near the big museums and landmarks.

PUBLIC TRANSPORT

Public transport in Amsterdam uses the OV-chipkaart. Rides cost €2.90 when bought on board. Unlimited-ride passes are available for one to seven days (€7.50 to €33) and are valid on trams, most buses and the metro.

TAXI

Amsterdam taxis are expensive, even over short journeys. Try **Taxicentrale Amsterdam** (TCA; 020-777 77 77; www.tcataxi.nl).

THE RANDSTAD

One of the most densely populated places on the planet, the Randstad stretches from Amsterdam to Rotterdam and is crammed with classic Dutch towns and cities such as Den Haag, Utrecht, Leiden and Delft. A cycling network links the towns amid tulip fields.

Haarlem

023 / POP 157,900

Just 15 minutes by train from Amsterdam, Haarlem's canals and cobblestone streets filled with gabled buildings, grand churches, terrific museums, cosy bars, fine cafes and antique shops draw scores of day trippers.

Sights

Haarlem's centre radiates out from the **Grote Markt**. The **Town Hall** (Grote Markt 2) is worth a look, as is the cathedral, **Grote Kerk van St Bavo** (www.bavo.nl; Oude Groenmarkt 22; adult/child €2.50/free; 10am-5pm Mon-Sat, noon-5pm Sun Jul & Aug, 10am-5pm Mon-Sat Sep-Jun).

★ **Frans Hals Museum** MUSEUM
(www.franshalsmuseum.nl; Groot Heiligland 62; adult/child €15.50/free; 11am-5pm Tue-Sat, from noon Sun;) A short stroll south of Grote Markt, the Frans Hals Museum is a must

WORTH A TRIP

ZAANSE SCHANS

The working, inhabited village Zaanse Schans functions as an open-air **windmill gallery** (www.dezaanseschans.nl; site free, per windmill adult/child €4/2; ⌚windmills 10am-5pm Apr-Nov, hours vary Dec-Mar) on the Zaan river. Popular with tourists, its mills are completely authentic and operated with enthusiasm and love. You can explore the windmills at will, seeing the vast moving parts first-hand.

The impressive **Zaans Museum** (☎075-616 28 62; www.zaansmuseum.nl; Schansend 7; adult/child €10/6; ⌚10am-5pm; 📶) shows how wind and water were harnessed.

Trains (€3.10, 17 minutes, four per hour) run from Amsterdam Centraal Station (direction Alkmaar) to Koog Zaandijk, from where it's a well-signposted 1.5km walk.

for anyone interested in the Dutch Masters. Located in the poorhouse where Hals spent his final years, the collection focuses on the 17th-century Haarlem School; its pride and joy are eight group portraits of the Civic Guard that reveal Hals' exceptional attention to mood and psychological tone. Look out for works by other greats such as Pieter Bruegel the Younger and Jacob van Ruisdael.

Eating & Drinking

Cafes and restaurants abound along Zijlstraat, Spaarne and especially Lange Veerstraat, as well as around the Grote Markt. The Saturday morning market here is one of the Netherlands' best; there's a smaller market on Monday.

★Brick MODERN EUROPEAN **€€**
(☎023-551 18 70; www.restaurantbrick.nl; Breestraat 24-26; mains lunch €6-10.50, dinner €15.50-21; ⌚6-9.30pm Mon-Thu, noon-4pm & 6-10pm Fri-Sun) You can watch Brick's chefs creating inspired dishes such as duck and hazelnut ravioli with black truffle and foie-gras sauce, not only from the street-level dining room but also the 1st-floor space, which has a glass floor directly above the open kitchen. There are pavement tables out front but in summer the best seats are on the roof terrace.

★Jopenkerk BREWERY
(www.jopenkerk.nl; Gedempte Voldersgracht 2; ⌚brewery & cafe 10am-1am, restaurant 5.30pm-late Tue-Sat) Haarlem's most atmospheric place to drink is this independent brewery inside a stained-glass-windowed 1910 church. Enjoy brews such as citrusy Hopen, fruity Lente Bier or chocolatey Koyt along with classic Dutch bar snacks (*bitterballen,* cheeses) beneath the gleaming copper vats. Or head to the mezzanine for dishes made from locally sourced, seasonal ingredients and Jopenkerk's beers, with pairings available.

Getting There & Away

Trains serve Haarlem's stunning art-nouveau station, a 10-minute walk north of the centre. Destinations include:

Amsterdam (€4.20, 15 minutes, four to eight per hour)

Den Haag (€8.30, 40 minutes, four to six per hour)

Rotterdam (€12.20, one hour, four to six per hour).

Leiden

☎071 / POP 122,500

Vibrant Leiden is renowned for being Rembrandt's birthplace, the home of the Netherlands' oldest university (and 23,000 students) and the place America's pilgrims raised money to lease the *Mayflower* that took them to the New World in 1620. Beautiful 17th-century buildings line its canals.

Sights

The best way to experience Leiden is by strolling the historic centre, especially along the Rapenburg canal.

★Hortus Botanicus Leiden GARDENS
(www.hortusleiden.nl; Rapenburg 73; adult/child €7.50/3; ⌚10am-6pm daily Apr-Oct, 10am-4pm Tue-Sun Nov-Mar) The lush Hortus Botanicus is one of Europe's oldest botanical gardens (1590; the oldest was created in Padua, Italy, in 1545), and is home to the Netherlands' oldest descendants of the Dutch tulips. It's a wonderful place to relax, with explosions of tropical colour and a fascinating (and steamy) greenhouse.

★Rijksmuseum van Oudheden MUSEUM
(National Museum of Antiquities; www.rmo.nl; Rapenburg 28; adult/child €12.50/4; ⌚11am-5pm Tue-Sun plus Mon during school holidays; 📶) This museum has a world-class collection of Greek, Roman

DON'T MISS

KEUKENHOF GARDENS

One of the Netherlands' top attractions is near Lisse, between Haarlem and Leiden. **Keukenhof** (www.keukenhof.nl; Stationsweg 166; adult/child €16/8, parking €6; 8am-7.30pm mid-Mar–mid-May, last entry 6pm;) is the world's largest bulb-flower garden, attracting nearly 800,000 visitors during a season almost as short-lived as the blooms on the millions of multicoloured tulips, daffodils and hyacinths.

Special buses link Keukenhof with Amsterdam's Schiphol airport and Leiden's Centraal Station in season; combination tickets covering entry and transport are available (adult/child €24/12.50). Pre-purchase tickets online to help avoid huge queues.

and Egyptian artefacts, the pride of which is the extraordinary **Temple of Taffeh**, a gift from former Egyptian president Anwar Sadat to the Netherlands for helping to save ancient Egyptian monuments from floods.

Pieterskerk CHURCH
(www.pieterskerk.com; Pieterskerkhof 1; admission €3; 11am-6pm) Crowned by its huge steeple, Pieterskerk is often under restoration – a good thing as it has been prone to collapse since it was built in the 14th century.

Museum De Lakenhal MUSEUM
(www.lakenhal.nl; Oude Singel 28-32) Leiden's foremost museum, the Lakenhal, displaying works by native son Rembrandt among others, has closed its doors between 2016 and 2019 while it undergoes a major renovation and expansion. Check online or with the tourist office for updates.

Sleeping & Eating

The city-centre canals and narrow old streets teem with choices. Saturday's market sprawls along Nieuwe Rijn.

Huys van Leyden BOUTIQUE HOTEL €€
(071-260 07 00; www.huysvanleyden.nl; Oude Singel 212; d from €109;) Steeped in history, this 1611 canal house has luxurious rooms and amenities including a sauna, roof terrace, and Nespresso machines in each of the five Golden-Age-meets-21st-century rooms richly decorated with shimmering fabrics and canopied beds. Its sister property, **De Barones van Leyden** (www.debaronesvanleyden.nl; Oude Herengracht 22; d from €109;), is, incredibly, even more opulent.

David's Burger BURGERS €€
(www.davidsburger.nl; Steenstraat 57; burgers €12.50-15.50; 4-11pm Tue-Sun) Cowhide covers the timber booths, and horseshoes and farm equipment hang on the walls at David's, serving Leiden's best, all-organic burgers such as the gaucho (beef with grilled pepper, courgette and chimichurri), spicy veggie (bean and chipotle-pepper patty with guacamole and cheese), lams (lamb with red-onion relish) and classic (beef with lettuce, tomato and pickles), plus corn on the cob.

★ **In den Doofpot** MODERN EUROPEAN €€€
(071-512 24 34; www.indendoofpot.nl; Turfmarkt 9; mains €22-35, 3-/4-course lunch menu €39/45, 4-/5-/6-/8-course dinner menu €55/65/70/80; noon-3pm & 5-10pm Mon-Fri, 5-10pm Sat) Given the sky-high calibre of chef Patrick Brugman's cooking, In den Doofpot's prices are a veritable steal. Pork belly with smoked eel, grilled lobster with truffle butter and micro-herb salad, organic Dutch beef fillet with Madeira sauce, potatoes and caramelised orange and other intense flavour combinations are all executed with artistic vision. Wines cost €8 per course.

Information

Tourist Office (071-516 60 00; www.visitleiden.nl; Stationsweg 26; 7am-7pm Mon-Fri, 10am-4pm Sat, 11am-3pm Sun) Across from the train station.

Getting There & Away

Buses leave from directly in front of Centraal Station.

Train destinations include:

Amsterdam (€9, 35 minutes, six per hour)

Den Haag (€3.50, 15 minutes, six per hour)

Schiphol Airport (€5.80, 15 minutes, six per hour)

Den Haag

070 / POP 518,600

Flanked by wide, leafy boulevards, Den Haag (The Hague) – officially known as 's-Gravenhage (Count's Hedge) – is the Dutch seat of government (although Amsterdam is the capital). Embassies and various international courts of justice give the city a worldly air.

Conversely, its seaside suburb of Scheveningen (pronounced as s'CHay-fuh-ninger) has a loud and lively kitsch, and a long stretch of beach. It sprawls about 5km northwest.

Sights

★Mauritshuis MUSEUM
(www.mauritshuis.nl; Plein 29; adult/child €14/free, combined ticket with Galerij Prins Willem V €17.50/2.50; ⌚1-6pm Mon, 10am-6pm Tue, Wed & Fri-Sun, 10am-8pm Thu) For a comprehensive introduction to Dutch and Flemish Art, visit the Mauritshuis, a jewel-box of a museum in an old palace and brand-new wing. Almost every work is a masterpiece, among them Vermeer's *Girl with a Pearl Earring*, Rembrandt's wistful self-portrait from the year of his death, 1669, and *The Anatomy Lesson of Dr Nicolaes Tulp*. A five-minute walk southwest, the recently restored **Galerij Prins Willem V** (Buitenhof 35; adult/child €5/2.50, combined ticket with Mauritshuis €17.50/2.50; ⌚noon-5pm Tue-Sun) contains 150 old masters (Steen, Rubens, Potter, et al).

★Binnenhof PALACE
The Binnenhof's central courtyard (once used for executions) is surrounded by parliamentary buildings. The splendid 17th-century North Wing is still home to the Upper Chamber of the **Dutch Parliament**. The Lower Chamber formerly met in the ballroom, in the 19th-century wing; it now meets in a modern building on the south side. A highlight of the complex is the restored 13th-century **Ridderzaal** (Knights' Hall).

To see the buildings you need to join a tour through visitor organisation **ProDemos** (☎070-757 02 00; www.prodemos.nl; Hofweg 1; 45min Ridderzaal tour €5, 90min Ridderzaal & House of Representative tour €8.50, 75min Ridderzaal & Senate tour €8.50, 90min Ridderzaal, House of Representative & Senate tour €10; ⌚office 10am-5pm Mon-Sat, tours by reservation).

Afterwards, stroll around the **Hofvijver**, where the reflections of the Binnenhof and the Mauritshuis have inspired countless snapshots.

★Escher in Het Paleis Museum MUSEUM
(www.escherinhetpaleis.nl; Lange Voorhout 74; adult/child €9.50/6.50; ⌚11am-5pm Tue-Sun) The Lange Voorhout Palace was once Queen Emma's winter residence. Now it's home to the work of Dutch graphic artist MC Escher. The permanent exhibition features notes, letters, drafts, photos and fully mature works covering Escher's entire career, from his early realism to the later phantasmagoria. There are some imaginative displays, including a virtual reality reconstruction of Escher's impossible buildings.

HOLLAND OR THE NETHERLANDS?

'Holland' is a popular synonym for the Netherlands, yet it only refers to the combined provinces of Noord (North) and Zuid (South) Holland. Amsterdam is Noord-Holland's largest city; Haarlem is the provincial capital. Rotterdam is Zuid-Holland's largest city; Den Haag is its provincial capital. The rest of the country is not Holland, even if locals themselves often make the mistake.

Sleeping & Eating

Expats on expense accounts support a diverse and thriving cafe culture. The cobbled streets and canals off Denneweg are an excellent place to start wandering.

Hotel Sebel HOTEL €€
(☎070-345 92 00; www.hotelsebel.nl; Prins Hendrikplein 20; s/d/tr from €89/99/139;) This 33-room hotel spreads out across three proud art-nouveau corner buildings. The cheapest rooms are minuscule but others have balconies, and studios have kitchenettes. Everything has been tastefully updated, including the minimalist lobby.

Bloem CAFE €
(www.bloemdenhaag.nl; Korte Houtstraat 6; dishes €3.50-9, high tea per person €20; ⌚11am-4pm Tue, to 6pm Wed-Sun) Across the Plein from the Binnenhof, this cute little cafe has white tables, chairs and flowers out front. Housemade tarts are superb; it also has great sandwiches and smoothies. Stop by for afternoon high tea.

★Restaurant Allard BISTRO €€
(☎070-744 79 00; www.restaurantallard.nl; Jagerstraat 6; mains €19-29, 2-/3-/4-course menus €35/42/49; ⌚5-11pm Tue-Sat) Tucked down a charming alleyway with outdoor tables, Allard is a diamond find for flavour-packed creations such as tuna tartare with sun-dried tomato crème, lamb fillet with honey and fig jus, truffle risotto with wild mushrooms, and grilled sea bass with spinach and potato gratin in a cosy, cellar-like space with exposed brick walls, low-lit chandeliers and black-and-white chessboard-tiled floors.

Shopping

Grote Markstraat is fittingly the street for large stores. Enticing boutiques line Hoogstraat, Noordeinde, Heulstraat and especially Prinsestraat.

Museumshop Den Haag GIFTS & SOUVENIRS
(www.museumshopdenhaag.com; Lange Voorhout 58b; ⌚noon-5pm Sun & Mon, 11am-5pm Tue-Sat) The Netherlands' first-ever independent museum shop is a one-stop-shop for books, prints, postcards, gifts and accessories of artworks and exhibitions from some of the country's most prestigious museums including Amsterdam's Rijksmuseum and Van Gogh Museum, as well as the Mauritshuis, and Escher in Het Paleis Museum.

Information

Tourist Office (VVV; ☎070-361 88 60; www.denhaag.com; Spui 68; ⌚noon-8pm Mon, 10am-8pm Tue-Fri, 10am-5pm Sat & Sun; 📶) On the ground floor of the public library in the landmark New Town Hall.

Getting There & Around

A day pass for local trams costs €6.50.

Most trains use Den Haag Centraal Station (CS), but some through trains only stop at Den Haag Hollands Spoor (HS) station just south of the centre.

Services include:

Amsterdam (€11.50, one hour, up to six per hour)
Rotterdam (€4.80, 25 minutes, up to six per hour) Also accessible by metro.
Schiphol airport (€8.30, 30 minutes, up to six per hour)

Delft

☎015 / POP 101,600

Compact and charming, Delft is synonymous with its blue-and-white-painted porcelain. It's *very* popular with day-trip visitors strolling its narrow canals, gazing at the remarkable old buildings and meditating on the career of Golden Age painter Johannes Vermeer, who was born here and lived here, so getting an early start helps beat the crowds.

Sights

The **town hall** and the **Waag** on the **Markt** are right out of the 17th century.

★Vermeer Centrum Delft MUSEUM
(www.vermeerdelft.nl; Voldersgracht 21; adult/child €9/5; ⌚10am-5pm) As the place where Johannes Vermeer was born, lived and worked, Delft is 'Vermeer Central' to many art-history and old-masters enthusiasts. Along with viewing life-sized images of Vermeer's oeuvre, you can tour a replica of Vermeer's studio, which reveals the way the artist approached the use of light and colour in his craft. A 'Vermeer's World' exhibit offers insight into his environment and upbringing, while temporary exhibits show how his work continues to inspire other artists.

★Oude Kerk CHURCH
(Old Church; www.oudeennieuwekerkdelft.nl; Heilige Geestkerkhof 25; adult/child incl Nieuwe Kerk €4/2.50, Nieuwe Kerk tower additional €4/2.50, combination ticket €7/4.50; ⌚9am-6pm Mon-Sat Apr-Oct, 11am-4pm Mon-Fri, 10am-5pm Sat Nov-Jan, 10am-5pm Mon-Sat Feb & Mar) The Gothic Oude Kerk, founded in 1246, is a surreal sight: its 75m-high tower leans nearly 2m from the vertical due to subsidence caused by its canal location, hence its nickname Scheve Jan ('Leaning Jan'). One of the tombs inside the church is Vermeer's.

★Nieuwe Kerk CHURCH
(New Church; www.oudeennieuwekerkdelft.nl; Markt 80; adult/child incl Oude Kerk €4/2.50, Nieuwe Kerk tower additional €4/2.50, combination ticket €7/4.50; ⌚9am-6pm Mon-Sat Apr-Oct, 11am-4pm Mon-Fri, 10am-5pm Sat Nov-Jan, 10am-5pm Mon-Sat Feb & Mar) Construction on Delft's Nieuwe Kerk began in 1381; it was finally completed in 1655. Amazing views extend from the 108.75m-high tower: after climbing its 376 narrow, spiralling steps you can see as far as Rotterdam and Den Haag on a clear day. It's the resting place of William of Orange (William the Silent), in a mausoleum designed by Hendrick de Keyser.

De Candelaer FACTORY
(☎015-213 1848; www.candelaer.nl; Kerkstraat 13; ⌚9.30am-5.30pm Mon-Fri, to 5pm Sat May-Sep, 10am-4pm Mon-Sat Oct-Apr) FREE The most central and modest Delftware outfit is de Candelaer, just off the Markt. It has five artists, a few of whom work most days. When it's quiet they'll give you a detailed tour of the manufacturing process.

THE NETHERLANDS BY BIKE

The Netherlands has more than 32,000km of dedicated bike paths *(fietspaden)*, which makes it one of the most bike-friendly places on the planet. You can crisscross the country on the motorways of cycling: the LF routes. Standing for *landelijke fietsroutes* (long-distance routes), but virtually always simply called LF, they cover approximately 4500km. All are well marked by distinctive green-and-white signs.

The best overall maps are the widely available Falk/VVV *Fietskaart met Knooppuntennetwerk* (cycling network) maps, an easy-to-use series of 22, with keys in English, that blanket the country in 1:50,000 scale, and cost €9. Every bike lane, path and other route is shown, along with distances.

Comprehensive cycling website Nederland Fietsland (www.nederlandfietsland.nl) has route planners and downloadable GPS tracks, and lists every bike-rental outlet in the country.

Bike Rentals

Bicycle hire is available all over the Netherlands at hotels, independent rental outlets and train stations. Prices average around €12 per 24 hours. You'll need to show ID and leave a deposit (usually €25 to €100).

On Trains

You may bring your bicycle onto any train outside peak hours (6.30am to 9am and 4.30pm to 6pm Monday to Friday) as long as there is room. Bicycles require a day pass (*dagkaart fiets*; €6.10).

Sleeping & Eating

Hotel de Plataan BOUTIQUE HOTEL **€€**
(015-212 60 46; www.hoteldeplataan.nl; Doelenplein 10; s/d from €110/120, themed d from €155; P) On a pretty canal-side square in the old town, this family-run gem has small but elegant standard rooms and wonderfully opulent theme rooms, including the 'Garden of Eden'; the Eastern-style 'Amber', with a Turkish massage shower; or the desert-island 'Tamarinde'. Modesty alert: many en suites are only partially screened from the room. Rates include breakfast and secure parking.

Stads-Koffyhuis CAFE **€**
(www.stads-koffyhuis.nl; Oude Delft 133; mains €8-15, sandwiches €6.50-9, pancakes €6.25-12.75; 9am-8pm Mon-Fri, 9am-6pm Sat, 11am-6pm Sun Jun-Sep, shorter hours Oct-May) The most coveted seats at this delightful cafe are on the terrace, aboard a barge moored out front. Tuck into award-winning bread rolls, with fillings such as aged artisan Gouda with apple sauce, mustard, fresh figs and walnuts, or house-speciality pancakes, while admiring possibly the best view of the Oude Kerk, just ahead at the end of the canal.

★ **Brasserie 't Crabbetje** SEAFOOD **€€**
(015-213 88 50; www.crabbetjedelft.nl; Verwersdijk 14; mains €18.50-34.50, 3-/4-course tasting menus €35.50/42.50; 5.30-10pm Wed-Sun;) Seafood is given the gourmet treatment at this cool, sophisticated restaurant. From scallops with leek and lobster reduction to skate wing with hazelnut crumb and beurre noisette (warm butter sauce), salmon carpaccio with smoked-eel croquette, and grilled lobster with tomato and truffle oil. Lavish seafood platters cost €41.50. Desserts are exquisite, too.

Spijshuis de Dis DUTCH **€€**
(015-213 17 82; www.spijshuisdedis.com; Beestenmarkt 36; soups €6-7.50, mains €17-24.50; 5-10pm Tue-Sat) Fresh fish and amazing soups served in bread bowls take centre stage at this romantic foodie haven, but meat eaters and vegetarians are well catered for too. Creative starters include smoked, marinated mackerel on sliced apple with horseradish. Don't skip the Dutch pudding served in a wooden shoe.

Drinking & Nightlife

Locus Publicus BROWN CAFE
(www.locuspublicus.nl; Brabantse Turfmarkt 67; 11am-1am Mon-Thu, 11am-2am Fri & Sat, noon-1am Sun) Cosy little Locus Publicus is filled with cheery locals quaffing their way through the 200-strong beer list including 13 on tap. There's great people-watching from the front terrace.

Information

Tourist Office (VVV; ☎015-215 40 51; www.delft.nl; Kerkstraat 3; ⏰10am-4pm Sun & Mon, 10am-5pm Tue-Sat Apr-Sep, noon-4pm Mon, 10am-4pm Tue-Sat, 11am-3pm Sun Oct-Mar) Sells excellent walking-tour brochures.

Getting There & Away

Delft's gleaming new train station opened in 2015. Services include:

Amsterdam (€13, one hour, four per hour)

Den Haag (€2.50, 15 minutes, six per hour)

Rotterdam (€3.30, 15 minutes, eight per hour)

Rotterdam

☎010 / POP 626,900

Futuristic architecture, a proliferation of art, and a surge of drinking, dining and nightlife venues make Rotterdam one of Europe's most exhilarating cities right now. The Netherlands' second-largest metropolis has a diverse, multiethnic community, an absorbing maritime tradition centred on Europe's busiest port and a wealth of top-class museums.

Rotterdam is a veritable open-air gallery of modern, postmodern and contemporary construction. It's a remarkable feat for a city largely razed to the ground by WWII bombers. Rebuilding has continued unabated ever since with ingenuity and vision.

Split by the vast Nieuwe Maas shipping channel, Rotterdam is crossed by a series of tunnels and bridges. On the north side of the water, the city centre is easily strolled.

Sights & Activities

Not only is Rotterdam an architectural gallery, its streets are also filled with art. Well over 60 sculptures are scattered all over town. For a full list and an interactive map of their locations, visit Sculpture International Rotterdam (www.sculptureinternationalrotterdam.nl).

★Museum Boijmans van Beuningen MUSEUM

(www.boijmans.nl; Museumpark 18-20; adult/child €15/7.50; ⏰11am-5pm Tue-Sun) Among Europe's finest museums, the Museum Boijmans van Beuningen has a permanent collection spanning all eras of Dutch and European art, including superb old masters. Among the highlights are *The Marriage Feast at Cana* by Hieronymus Bosch, the *Three Maries at the Open Sepulchre* by Van Eyck, the minutely detailed *Tower of Babel* by Pieter Brueghel the Elder, and *Portrait of Titus* and *Man in a Red Cap* by Rembrandt.

Overblaak Development NOTABLE BUILDING

(Overblaak) Designed by Piet Blom and built from 1978 to 1984, this mind-bending development facing the Markthal Rotterdam is marked by its pencil-shaped tower, **De Kolk**, and 'forest' of 45-degree-tilted, cube-shaped apartments on hexagonal pylons. One apartment, the **Kijk-Kubus Museum-House** (www.kubuswoning.nl; Overblaak 70; adult/child €2.50/1.50; ⏰11am-5pm), is open to the public; the **Stayokay Rotterdam** (☎010-436 57 63; www.stayokay.com; Overblaak 85-87; dm/d/tr from €21.50/59/93; 📶) youth hostel occupies the supersized cube at the southern end.

Euromast VIEWPOINT

(www.euromast.nl; Parkhaven 20; adult/child €9.75/6.25; ⏰9.30am-10pm Apr-Sep, 10am-10pm Oct-Mar) A 1960-built landmark, the 185m Euromast offers unparalleled 360-degree views of Rotterdam from its 100m-high observation deck, reached by elevator in 30 seconds.

Extra diversions include a brasserie serving lunch, high tea, high wine, dinner and Sunday brunch, as well as summertime abseiling (€55). Accommodation in the tower's two suites start from €385 each, including breakfast.

Erasmusbrug BRIDGE

A symbol of the city, this graceful bridge dubbed 'the Swan' was designed by architect Ben van Berkel in 1996 and spans 802m across the Maas river.

Maritiem Museum Rotterdam MUSEUM

(Maritime Museum; www.maritiemmuseum.nl; Leuvehaven 1; adult/child €11.50/7.50; ⏰10am-5pm Tue-Sat, 11am-5pm Sun, plus Mon during school holidays) This comprehensive, kid-friendly museum looks at the Netherlands' rich maritime traditions through an array of models that any youngster would love to take into the tub. There are great explanatory displays such as Mainport Live, giving a 'real time' view of the port's action in miniature, and a raft of fun temporary exhibitions.

★Urban Guides WALKING

(☎010-433 22 31; www.urbanguides.nl; Schiekade 205, Hofplein; ⏰office 10am-6pm Mon-Sat, noon-5pm Sun Apr-Oct, 10am-6pm Mon-Fri Nov-Mar) Based in the Schieblock, this hip young outfit of passionate Rotterdammers runs a fantastic selection of tours, from 2½ hour 'By Cycle' tours (per person €25) to architectural

DON'T MISS

DELFSHAVEN

Just 3km southwest of Rotterdam's centre, Delfshaven, once the official seaport for the city of Delft, survived the war and retains a village-like atmosphere. Take trams 4 or 8, or the metro to the Delfshaven station.

Oude Kerk (☎010-477 41 56; www.oudeofpelgrimvaderskerk.nl; Aelbrechtskolk 22; ⊙noon-4pm Sat & every 2nd Fri) The Pilgrims prayed for the last time at Delfshaven's 1417-founded Oude Kerk (aka Pilgrim Fathers Church) before leaving the Netherlands for America aboard the *Speedwell* on 22 July 1620. They could barely keep the leaky boat afloat and, in England, eventually transferred to the *Mayflower* – the rest is history. Models of their vaguely seaworthy boats are inside. It closes for events such as weddings and concerts.

Stadsbrouwerij De Pelgrim (www.pelgrimbier.nl; Aelbrechtskolk 12; ⊙noon-midnight Wed-Sat, to 10pm Sun) The heady scent of hops greets you at this vintage brewery abutting the Oude Kerk, with bubbling copper vats by the entrance. Here you can take a voyage through its wonderful seasonal and standard beers such as Rotterdams Stoombier and Mayflower Tripel in the bar, canal-side terrace or courtyard. A tasting flight of five beers costs €5. Ask and they'll usually let you peek at the tanks. There's a restaurant too.

Windmill (www.molendelfshaven.nl; Voorhaven 210) A reconstructed 18th-century windmill overlooks the water at Delfshaven. It still mills grain; the interior is closed to the public.

cycling tours (including an option led by architecture students), walking tours, building tours such as the **Van Nelle Fabriek** (Van Nelle Factory; www.vannellefabriek.com; Van Nelleweg 1), boat tours, exhibition tours and more. It also rents bikes (per day €10).

Sleeping

★King Kong Hostel HOSTEL **€**
(☎010-818 87 78; www.kingkonghostel.com; Witte de Withstraat 74; dm/d/q from €17.50/70/101; @ 📶) Outdoor benches made from salvaged timbers and garden hoses by Sander Bokkinga sit outside King Kong, a design haven on Rotterdam's coolest street. Artist-designed rooms and dorms are filled with vintage and industrial furniture; fab features include hammocks, lockers equipped with device-charging points, a gourmet self-catering kitchen, roof garden and barbecue area, and Netflix.

★Pincoffs BOUTIQUE HOTEL **€€**
(☎010-297 45 00; www.hotelpincoffs.nl; Stieltjesstraat 34; d/ste from €133/195; P ❄ 📶) A former customs house dating from 1879 encases this exquisite sanctum that blends recycled and vintage art and furniture with 21st-century style. Romantic rooms come with luxuries such as Egyptian cotton robes and towels. A wood-burning fireplace blazes in the bar, and there's a water-taxi stop outside the front door.

Hotel New York HISTORIC HOTEL **€€€**
(☎010-439 05 55; www.hotelnewyork.nl; Koninginnenhoofd 1; d €105-287.50; @ 📶) An art-nouveau showpiece, the Holland-America passenger-ship line's former HQ has sweeping vistas, superb dining options including an oyster bar, a barber shop and a water taxi ferrying guests across the Nieuwe Maas to the city centre. Rooms retain original, painstakingly restored fittings and decor; styles range from standard to timber-panelled suites in the old boardrooms with fireplaces.

Eating

Rotterdam's foodie scene is booming. Look out for new openings all over the city and especially in hotspots like **Station Hofplein** (www.stationhofplein.nl). The stunning Markthal Rotterdam (p521) has sit-down and takeaway eating options galore.

★Tante Nel FAST FOOD **€**
(www.tante-nel.com; Pannekoekstraat 53a; dishes €2.25-13.50; ⊙noon-10pm Tue-Sat, to 9pm Sun) New-generation Tante Nel is as tiny as a traditional *frites* (fries) stand but decked out with a stunning Dutch-design painted brick interior and marquee-style canopied terrace for savouring its organic, hand-cut fries (topped by nine different sauces), along with house-speciality milkshakes, beer, wine and 13 different gins.

Rotterdam

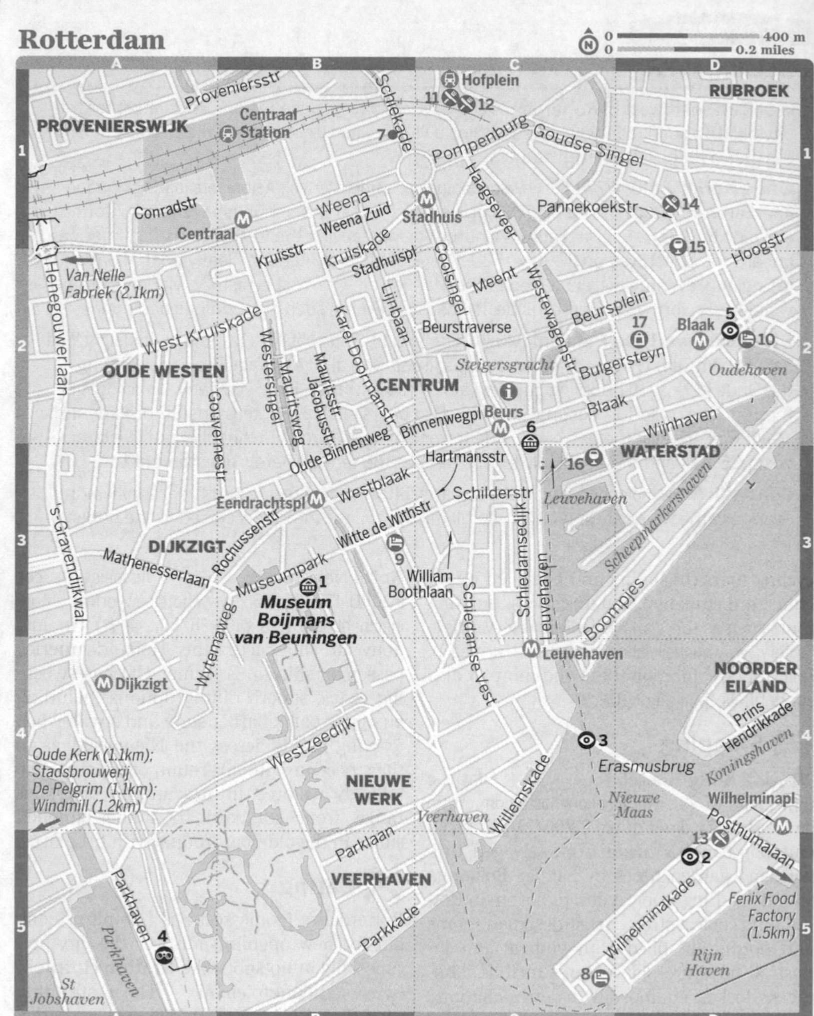

★ Fenix Food Factory MARKET €
(www.fenixfoodfactory.nl; Veerlaan 19d; ⏲10am-11pm Tue-Sat, noon-11pm Sun, individual stall hours vary) Almost everything in this vast former warehouse is made locally and sold by separate vendors making their mark on the food scene. They include Booij Kaasmakers (cheese), Cider Cider (cider), Jordy's Bakery (bread and baked goods), Stielman Koffiebranders (coffee roasters), Kaapse Brouwers (craft beer) and Rechtstreex (locally grown fruit and veggies).

HMB INTERNATIONAL €€
(☎010-760 06 20; www.hmb-restaurant.nl; Holland Amerika Kade 104; mains €20-22, 3-course lunch menu €37.50 Tue-Fri, 4-/5-/6-course dinner menu €57/67/77; ⏲noon-3pm & 5.30-10pm Tue-Fri, 5.30-10pm Sat, closed late Dec-early Jan) On the ground floor of the glitzy 'vertical city' **De Rotterdam** (www.derotterdam.nl), with dazzling views of the Erasmusbrug, chic HMB serves artistically presented contemporary cuisine (veal meatballs with truffled potatoes; foie gras with eel and apple) at impressively

Rotterdam

reasonable prices. Afterwards, head to the terrace of the building's 7th-floor cocktail bar.

★**FG Food Labs** GASTRONOMY €€€
(010-425 05 20; www.fgfoodlabs.nl; Katshoek 41; 3-course lunch menu Mon-Fri €42.50, snacks €6.50-27.50, 4-/5-/6-/7-/8-/9-course menus €32/40/48/56/64/72; noon-2pm & 6-10pm, closed early–mid-Jan) François Geurds' one-Michelin-star molecular gastronomy lab sits under timber and silvery pressed-tin ceilings within Station Hofplein. Dine on his evolving cuisine or even take a culinary electric-bike tour (€95) around Rotterdam starting from the lab and finishing with a three-course lunch at his flagship two-Michelin-star premises, **FG** (www.fgrestaurant.nl; Katshoek 37b).

Drinking & Nightlife

★**Bokaal** BAR
(www.bokaalrotterdam.nl; Nieuwemarkt 11; 11am-1am Sun-Thu, to 2am Fri & Sat) In a *bokaal* (trophy) location at the heart of the enclave around pedestrian Nieuwmarkt and Pannekoekstraat locally dubbed 'Soho Rotterdam', Bokaal's spectacularly designed bar has butcher-shop tiling, raw concrete floors, and an oak bar and huge all-day-sun terrace. Beer (craft and Trappist) is its speciality, with nine on tap, and more than 80 in bottles, along with charcuterie and cheese.

Vessel 11 PUB
(www.vessel11.nl; Wijnhaven 101; noon-10pm Tue-Thu, noon-2am Fri, 11am-2am Sat, 11am-10pm Sun) This fire-engine-red, 1951-built lighthouse vessel (with a working gas light and fog horn) is now a Brit-influenced pub which brews its own ale, hosts live gigs (mainly rock) and barbecues, and serves full English breakfasts and Sunday roasts. It also rents Rotterdam-designed HotTug hot-tub boats (per two hours for two/eight people €139/259) to pilot around the harbour while you soak.

Shopping

Brand-name shops line the bustling, open-air, semi-subterranean Beurstraverse, nicknamed *de Koopgoot* ('buying trench'). More alternative options congregate on and around Meent, as well as Nieuwemarkt, Pannekoekstraat, OudeBinnenweg and Nieuwe Binnenweg.

★**Markthal Rotterdam** FOOD & DRINKS
(www.markthalrotterdam.nl; Nieuwstraat; 10am-8pm Mon-Thu & Sat, to 9pm Fri, noon-6pm Sun) The Netherlands' inaugural indoor food market hit international headlines when it opened in 2014 due to its extraordinary inverted-U-shaped design, with glass-walled apartments arcing over the food hall's 40m-high fruit- and vegetable-muralled ceiling. There's a tantalising array of produce, prepared food and drinks; shops continue downstairs.

Information

Tourist Office (010-790 01 85; www.rotterdam.info; Coolsingel 114; 9am-5.30pm;) Main tourist office.

Getting There & Away

Completed in 2014, Rotterdam's Centraal Station is an architectural stunner. There are direct services to Brussels and Paris; from late 2017, Eurostar trains linking Amsterdam with London will stop here.

Major services:

Amsterdam regular (€15.10, 70 minutes, eight per hour)

Amsterdam high speed (€17.50, 40 minutes, four per hour)

Schiphol airport (€12.20–14.60, 20–50 minutes, eight per hour)

Utrecht (€10.30, 40 minutes, four per hour)

Getting Around

Rotterdam's trams, buses and metro are operated by **RET** (www.ret.nl). Most converge in front of Centraal Station, where there's an **information booth** (www.ret.nl; Stationsplein 20, Centraal Station; ⏲7am-10pm Mon-Fri, 9.30am-5.30pm Sat & Sun) that also sells tickets. Day passes are available for varying durations (one/two/three days €7.50/12.50/16.50). A single-ride ticket purchased from a bus driver or tram conductor costs €3.

Utrecht

☎030 / POP 338,500

One of the Netherlands' oldest cities, Utrecht retains a beautiful old-world city centre, ringed by unique 13th-century canal wharves below street level. Canal-side streets brim with shops, restaurants and cafes. Its spirited student community of 40,000 is the country's largest.

While the canals form Utrecht's restful core, elsewhere the city is busy reinventing itself, and part of the excitement is witnessing this ongoing transformation. Roads such as Catharijnebaan are being turned back into the canals they once were and the spectacular new train station adds a vital complement to the old town.

Sights

Focus your wanderings on the **Domplein** and south along the tree-lined **Oudegracht**.

★Domtoren HISTORIC BUILDING

(Cathedral Tower; www.domtoren.nl; Domplein 9; tower tour adult/child €9/5; ⏲11am-5pm Tue-Sat, noon-4pm Sun) A remnant of Utrecht's original 14th-century **cathedral** (Cathedral; www.domkerk.nl; Achter de Dom 1; donation requested; ⏲10am-4pm Mon-Fri, to 3.30pm Sat, 12.30-4pm Sun Jul-Sep, 11am-4pm Mon-Fri, to 3.30pm Sat, 12.30-4pm Sun Oct-Jun), this tower is 112m high, with 50 bells. It's worth the 465-step climb to the top for unbeatable city views; on a clear day you can see Amsterdam. Visit is by guided tour only, departing on the hour. Tickets can be purchased online or at the Tourist Office across the square.

★Centraal Museum MUSEUM

(☎030-236 23 62; www.centraalmuseum.nl; Agnietenstraat 1; adult/child €11/5, incl admission to Rietveld Schröderhuis plus €3 surcharge; ⏲11am-5pm Tue-Sun; 📶) Applied arts are at the heart of a wide-ranging collection that also features paintings by artists of the Utrecht School and a bit of De Stijl to boot. Here too is the world's most extensive Gerrit Rietveld collection, a dream for all minimalists. There's even a Viking longboat that was dug out of the local mud, plus a sumptuous 17th-century doll's house.

★Museum Catharijneconvent MUSEUM

(☎030-231 38 35; www.catharijneconvent.nl; Lange Nieuwestraat 38; adult/child €12.50/7; ⏲10am-5pm Tue-Fri, 11am-5pm Sat & Sun) Museum Catharijneconvent is the pick of Utrecht's museums, with the finest collection of medieval religious art in the Netherlands – virtually the history of Christianity, in fact – housed in a Gothic former convent and an 18th-century canalside house. Marvel at the many beautiful illuminated manuscripts, look for the odd Rembrandt and hope for one of the often salacious special exhibitions.

WORTH A TRIP

OTHER DUTCH DESTINATIONS WORTH A VISIT

Other Netherlands highlights worth considering for day trips or longer visits:

Alkmaar Although touristy, its cheese ceremony (Fridays from first Friday of April to the first Friday of September) dates from the 17th century.

Hoge Veluwe National Park Beautiful landscape of forests, dunes and marshes, with a bonus of a Van Gogh-rich art museum on site.

Kinderdijk & Dordrecht A good day trip by fast ferry from Rotterdam is to visit Kinderdijk's Unesco-listed windmills then Dordrecht's medieval canals.

Gouda The perfect little Dutch town.

Texel Largest of the Frisian Islands, with endless walks along dune-backed beaches and excellent local seafood.

Miffy Museum MUSEUM
(Nijntje Museum; ☎030-236 23 62; www.nijntjemuseum.nl; Agnietenstraat 2; adult/child €3.50/8.50; ⏲10am-5pm Tue-Sun) One of Utrecht's favourite sons, author and illustrator Dick Bruna is the creator of the beloved cartoon rabbit Miffy (Nijntje as she's known in Dutch) and she naturally takes pride of place at the artist's former studio, across the street from the Centraal Museum. The museum was renovated in 2015 to make it more toddler-friendly (ages two to six).

Sleeping

Strowis Hostel HOSTEL €
(☎030-238 02 80; www.strowis.nl; Boothstraat 8; dm from €20, s/d with bathroom €70/75, s/d/tr without bathroom €60/65/87.50; @ 📶) This 17th-century building is near the town centre and has been lovingly restored and converted into a hostel (with four- to 14-bed rooms). There's a fine rear garden that is a focus of activity. It's loose and lively and around the corner from its slacker sister, the ACU (p523).

★**Mary K Hotel** HOTEL €€
(☎030-230 48 88; www.marykhotel.com; Oudegracht 25; d from €125; 📶) A bevy of Utrecht artists decorated the rooms at this ideally situated canal house. Rooms come in three basic sizes (cosy, medium and large), but no two are alike. All make use of the original 18th-century features and you may find a timber beam running through your bathroom or a stuffed animal snoozing in the rafters.

Eating & Drinking

Gys CAFE €
(☎030-259 17 88; www.gysutrecht.nl; Voorstraat 77; dishes €5-10; ⏲10am-9.30pm; 📶) Everything's organic at this bright bistro, from the burgers (tofu or lamb) and sandwiches (smoked mackerel with beet mousse, tempeh with sweet potato, avocado and watercress) to the salads and eggplant schnitzel.

★**Lokaal Negen** FRENCH €€€
(☎030-231 13 18; www.lokaalnegen.nl; Trans 7; 3-/4-/5-course menus €35/39.50/45; ⏲5-10pm) Around the corner from the Domtoren, this long-standing option offers intimate dining in the living room of a sturdy old house with an interior garden. Instead of ordering, let yourself be pleasantly surprised by the multi-course set meals, each with an assortment of original starters.

ACU BAR
(www.acu.nl; Voorstraat 71; ⏲6-11pm Tue & Wed, 6pm-3am Thu, 8pm-4am Fri, 6pm-4am Sat, 2-11pm Sun) An anarcho-slacker reference point in Utrecht, ACU combines bar, music venue, lecture hall and more. Argue about whether Trotsky was too conservative while downing organic vegan food by the inimitable Kitchen Punx (6pm to 9pm Tuesday to Saturday).

Information

Tourist Office (VVV; ☎030-236 00 04; www.visit-utrecht.com; Domplein 9; ⏲11.45am-5pm Mon, 10am-5pm Tue-Sat, noon-5pm Sun, to 6pm mid-Jul–Aug) Sells Domtoren tickets. Another tourist info point is in the corridor between the train station and Hoog Catharijne shopping centre.

Getting There & Away

Utrecht's train station is a major connection point, including for Germany. Key services include the following:

Amsterdam (€7.50, 30 minutes, four per hour)
Cologne (€29-44, two hours, six direct services per day)
Maastricht (€23.60, two hours, two per hour)
Rotterdam (€10.30, 40 minutes, four per hour)

THE SOUTH

Actual hills rise on the Netherlands' southern edge, where Belgium and Germany are within range of a tossed wooden shoe. The star here is Maastricht.

Maastricht

☎043 / POP 123,000

In the far-flung south, the grand old city of Maastricht is well worth the journey from Amsterdam and the pearls of the Randstad, and you can easily continue to Belgium and Germany.

Among Maastricht's 1650 listed historic buildings, look for Spanish and Roman ruins, French and Belgian architectural twists, splendid food and the cosmopolitan flair that made Maastricht the location for the signing of the namesake treaty, which created the modern EU in 1992.

It's at its most exuberant during **carnaval** (February/March), from the Friday before Shrove Tuesday until late Wednesday.

Sights

Maastricht's delights are scattered along both banks of the Maas and reward walkers.

Ringed by grand cafes, museums and churches, the large **Vrijthof** square is a focal point. Intimate **Onze Lieve Vrouweplein** is a cafe-filled square named after its church, which still attracts pilgrims. The arched stone footbridge **Sint Servaasbrug** dates from the 13th-century and links Maastricht's centre with the Wyck district.

★ Sint Servaasbasiliek CHURCH
(www.sintservaas.nl; Keizer Karelplein 3; basilica free, treasury adult/child €4.50/free; 10am-6pm Jul & Aug, to 5pm Sep-Nov & Apr-Jun, 10am-5pm Mon-Sat, 12.30-5pm Sun Dec-Mar) Built around the shrine of St Servatius, the first bishop of Maastricht, the basilica presents an architectural pastiche dating from 1000. Its beautiful curved brick apse and towers dominate the Vrijthof. The **Treasury** is filled with medieval gold artwork. Be sure to duck around the back to the serene cloister garden.

★ Bonnefantenmuseum MUSEUM
(043-329 01 90; www.bonnefanten.nl; Ave Cèramique 250; adult/child €12/free; 11am-5pm Tue-Sun) Maastricht's star museum, in the Ceramique district east of the Maas, is easily recognisable by its rocket-shaped tower. Designed by the Italian Aldo Rossi, the distinctive E-shaped structure displays early European painting and sculpture on the 1st floor and contemporary works by Limburg artists on the next, linked by a dramatic sweep of stairs. The dome of the tower is reserved for large-scale installations.

Fort Sint Pieter FORTRESS
(043-325 21 21; www.maastrichtunderground.nl; Luikerweg 71; fort tour adult/child €6.40/5, combination tour €9.95/6.95; English tours 12.30pm) Looming atop a marlstone hill with commanding views of the Maas, the five-sided Fort Sint Pieter formed the city's southern defence and is linked to a network of underground tunnels. It's been fully restored to its original 1701 appearance. Visit is by guided tour only, which can be combined with a tunnel tour. Purchase tickets at the visitor centre below the fort. It's a 2km walk south of Maastricht, or take bus 7 and get off at 'Mergelweg'.

Sleeping

Botel Maastricht HOTEL €
(043-321 90 23; www.botelmaastricht.nl; Maasboulevard 95; dm €35, s/d with bathroom €63/70, without bathroom €57/64) Realise your dream of staying on a houseboat in one of the 34 compact cabins on this ship moored on the Maas' west bank. Most feature tiny but well-equipped bathrooms. Enjoy breakfast or a sunset drink on deck and admire the barges rolling down the river. Rates drop mid-week.

Kaboom Hotel HOTEL €€
(043-321 11 11; www.kaboomhotel.nl; Stationsplein 1; s/d from €63/126;) This just-unwrapped hotel bills itself as 'a touch rebellious', and its minimal decor strikes an irreverent tone without sacrificing such comforts as flat-screen TVs and hair dryers. It's right across the street from the station.

Eating & Drinking

Excellent restaurants are even more common than old fortifications in Maastricht.

★ Bisschopsmolen BAKERY €
(www.bisschopsmolen.nl; Stenebrug 3; vlaai €2.40, baguette sandwiches €6; 9am-6pm Tue-Sat, 10am-5pm Sun) A working 7th-century water wheel powers a vintage flour mill that supplies its adjoining bakery. Spelt loaves and *vlaai* (seasonal fruit pies) come direct from the ovens out back. You can dine on-site at the cafe, and, if it's not busy, self-tour the mill and see how flour's been made for aeons.

Café Sjiek DUTCH €€
(www.cafesjiek.nl; St Pieterstraat 13; mains lunch €12.50-19.50, dinner €14.50-26; kitchen 5-11pm Mon-Thu, noon-11pm Fri-Sun, bar to 2am;) Traditional local fare at this cosy spot ranges from *zuurvlees* (sour stew made with horsemeat) with apple sauce to hearty venison, fresh fish and Rommedoe cheese with pear syrup and rye bread. It doesn't take reservations and is always busy, but you can eat at the bar.

★ Take One BROWN CAFE
(www.takeonebiercafe.nl; Rechtstraat 28; 4pm-2am Thu-Mon) This narrow, eccentric 1930s tavern has well over 100 beers from the most obscure parts of the Benelux. It's run by a husband-and-wife team who help you select the beer most appropriate to your taste. The Bink Blonde is sweet, tangy and very good.

Information

Tourist Office (VVV; ☎043-325 21 21; www.vvvmaastricht.nl; Kleine Straat 1; ⊙10am-6pm Mon-Sat, 11am-5pm Sun May-Oct, 10am-6pm Mon-Fri, 10am-5pm Sat, 11am-5pm Sun Nov-Apr) In the 15th-century Dinghuis; cycling tours offered.

Getting There & Away

There is an hourly international train service to Liège (30 minutes), from where fast trains depart for Brussels, Paris and Cologne.

Domestic services include:

Amsterdam (€25.50, 2½ hours, two per hour)

Utrecht (€23.60, two hours, two per hour)

SURVIVAL GUIDE

Directory A–Z

ACCOMMODATION

Always book accommodation ahead, especially during high season. The tourist offices operate booking services.

Many Dutch hotels have steep, perilous stairs but no lifts/elevators, although most top-end and some midrange hotels are exceptions.

Stayokay (www.stayokay.com) is the Dutch hostelling association. A youth-hostel card costs €17.50; nonmembers pay an extra €2.50 per night and after six nights you become a member. The usual HI discounts apply.

DISCOUNT CARDS

Museumkaart (Museum Card; www.museumkaart.nl; adult/child €60/32.50, plus for 1st registration €5) Free and discounted entry to some 400 museums all over the country for one year. Purchase at participating museum ticket counters or from ticket shops.

INTERNET RESOURCES

Lonely Planet (www.lonelyplanet.com/the-netherlands)

Netherlands Tourism Board (www.holland.com)

Windmill Database (www.molendatabase.org)

TIPPING

Tipping is not essential as restaurants, hotels, bars etc include a service charge on their bills. A little extra is always welcomed though, and common; anything from rounding up to the nearest euro to adding on 10% of the bill.

SLEEPING PRICE RANGES

The following price ranges refer to a double room with bathroom in high season. Unless otherwise stated, breakfast is not included in the price.

€ less than €100

€€ €100–180

€€€ more than €180

LEGAL MATTERS

Drugs are actually illegal in the Netherlands. Possession of soft drugs up to 5g is tolerated but larger amounts can get you jailed. Hard drugs are treated as a serious crime.

Smoking is banned in all public places. In a uniquely Dutch solution, you can still smoke tobacco-free pot in *coffeeshops*.

MONEY

ATMs

ATMs proliferate outside banks, inside supermarkets and at train stations.

Credit Cards

Most hotels, restaurants and large stores accept major international cards. Some establishments, however, don't accept non-European credit cards – check first.

OPENING HOURS

Banks 9am–4pm Monday to Friday, some Saturday morning.

Cafes and Bars Open noon (exact hours vary); most close 1am Sunday to Thursday, 3am Friday and Saturday.

Museums Some closed Monday.

Restaurants Lunch 11am–2.30pm, dinner 6–10pm.

Shops 10am or noon to 6pm Tuesday to Friday, 10am to 5pm Saturday and Sunday, noon or 1pm to 5pm or 6pm Monday (if at all).

PUBLIC HOLIDAYS

Nieuwjaarsdag New Year's Day

Goede Vrijdag Good Friday

Eerste Paasdag Easter Sunday

Tweede Paasdag Easter Monday

Koningsdag (King's Day)27 April

Bevrijdingsdag (Liberation Day) 5 May

Hemelvaartsdag Ascension Day

Eerste Pinksterdag Whit Sunday (Pentecost)

Tweede Pinksterdag Whit Monday

Eerste Kerstdag (Christmas Day) 25 December

Tweede Kerstdag (Boxing Day) 26 December

ESSENTIAL FOOD & DRINK

Vlaamse frites Iconic French fries smothered in mayonnaise or myriad other sauces.

Cheese The Dutch consume almost 19kg of cheese per person per year, nearly two-thirds of which is Gouda. The tastiest hard, rich *oud* (old) varieties have strong, complex flavours.

Seafood Street stalls sell seafood snacks including raw, slightly salted *haring* (herring) cut into bite-sized pieces and served with onion and pickles.

Indonesian The most famous meal is arijsttafel (rice table): an array of spicy savoury dishes such as braised beef, pork satay and ribs served with rice.

Kroketten Croquettes are crumbed, deep-fried dough balls with various fillings, such as meat-filled *bitterballen*.

Beer Big names like Heineken are ubiquitous; small brewers like De Drie Ringen and Gulpener are the best.

Jenever Dutch gin is made from juniper berries and drunk chilled from a tulip-shaped shot glass. *Jonge* (young) *jenever* is smooth; strongly flavoured *oude* (old) *jenever* can be an acquired taste.

SAFE TRAVEL

The Netherlands is a safe country, but be sensible all the same and *always* lock your bike. Never buy drugs on the street: it's illegal. And don't light up joints just anywhere – stick to *coffeeshops*.

TELEPHONE

Country code ☎31

International access code ☎00

Getting There & Away

AIR

Huge **Schiphol International Airport** (AMS; www.schiphol.nl) is the Netherlands' main international airport. **Rotterdam The Hague Airport** (RTM; www.rotterdamthehagueairport.nl) and budget airline hub **Eindhoven Airport** (EIN; www.eindhovenairport.nl; Luchthavenweg 25) are small.

LAND

Bus

European bus network **Eurolines** (www.eurolines.com) serves 11 destinations across the Netherlands including the major cities.

Car & Motorcycle

Drivers need vehicle registration papers, third-party insurance and their domestic licence. The national auto club, **ANWB** (www.anwb.nl), has offices across the country and will provide info if you can show an auto-club card from your home country (eg AAA in the US or AA in the UK).

Train

International train connections are good. All Eurail and Inter-Rail passes are valid on the Dutch national train service, **NS** (Nederlandse Spoorwegen; www.ns.nl).

Many international services are operated by **NS International** (www.nsinternational.nl). In addition, **Thalys** (www.thalys.com) fast trains serve Brussels (where you can connect to the Eurostar) and Paris. From December 2017, direct Eurostar services will link Amsterdam, Schiphol airport and Rotterdam with London.

The high-speed line from Amsterdam (via Schiphol and Rotterdam) speeds travel times to Antwerp (1¼ hours), Brussels (two hours) and Paris (3¼ hours). German ICE high-speed trains run six direct services per day between Amsterdam and Cologne (2½ hours) via Utrecht. Many continue on to Frankfurt (four hours) via Frankfurt airport.

In peak periods, it's wise to reserve seats in advance. Buy tickets online at **SNCB Europe** (www.b-europe.com).

SEA

Several companies operate car/passenger ferries between the Netherlands and the UK:

Stena Line (www.stenaline.co.uk) Sails between Harwich and Hoek van Holland, 31km northwest of Rotterdam, linked to central Rotterdam by train (30 minutes).

P&O Ferries (www.poferries.com) Operates an overnight ferry every evening (11¾ hours) be-

EATING PRICE RANGES

The following price ranges refer to a main course:

€ less than €12

€€ €12–25

€€€ more than €25

tween Hull and Europoort, 39km west of central Rotterdam. Book bus tickets (40 minutes) to/from Rotterdam when you reserve your berth.

DFDS Seaways (www.dfdsseaways.co.uk) Sails between Newcastle and IJmuiden, 30km northwest of Amsterdam, linked to Amsterdam by bus; the 15-hour sailings depart every day.

Getting Around

BOAT

Ferries connect the mainland with the five Frisian Islands, including Texel. Other ferries span the Westerschelde in the south of Zeeland, providing a link between the southwestern expanse of the country and Belgium. These are popular with people using the Zeebrugge ferry terminal and run frequently year-round.

CAR & MOTORCYCLE

Hire

You must be at least 23 years of age to hire a car in the Netherlands.

Outside Amsterdam, car-hire companies can be in inconvenient locations if you're arriving by train.

Road Rules

Traffic travels on the right and the minimum driving age is 18 for vehicles and 16 for motorcycles. Seat belts are required and children under 12 must ride in the back if there's room. Trams always have the right of way and, if turning right, bikes have priority.

Speed limits are generally 50km/h in built-up areas, 80km/h in the country, 100km/h on major through-roads, and 130km/h on freeways (variations are clearly indicated). Hidden speeding cameras are everywhere and they will find you through your rental car company.

LOCAL TRANSPORT

National public transport info is available in English at **9292** (www.9292.nl), which has an excellent smartphone app.

COUNTRY FACTS

Area 41,543 sq km

Capital Amsterdam

Country Code 31

Currency Euro (€)

Emergency 112

Language Dutch, English widespread

Money ATMs common, cash preferred for small purchases

Visas Schengen rules apply

TIPS FOR BUYING TRAIN TICKETS

- Tickets can be bought at NS service counters or at ticketing machines. The ticket windows are easiest to use, though there is often a queue.
- Pay with cash, debit or credit card. Visa and Mastercard are accepted, though there is a €0.50 surcharge to use them, and they must have embedded chips (even then, international cards sometimes do not work).
- There is a €1 surcharge for buying a single-use disposable ticket.
- If you want to use a ticketing machine and pay cash, know that they accept coins only (no paper bills).
- There are basically two types of domestic train: Intercity (faster, with fewer stops) and Sprinter (slower, stops at each station).

Local transport tickets are smart cards called the OV-chipkaart (www.ov-chipkaart.nl).

- Either purchase a reusable OV-chipkaart in advance at a local transport-information office, or purchase a disposable one when you board a bus or tram.
- When you enter *and* exit a bus, tram or metro, hold the card against a reader at the doors or station gates. The system then calculates your fare and deducts it from the card.
- Fares for the reusable cards are much lower than the disposable ones (though you do have to pay an initial €7.50 fee; the card is valid for five years).
- You can also buy OV-chipkaarts for unlimited use for one or more days, and this often is the most convenient option. Local transport operators sell these.
- Stored-value OV-chipkaarts can be used on trains throughout the Netherlands.

TRAIN

The train network is run by NS (Nederlandse Spoorwegen; www.ns.nl). First-class sections are barely different from 2nd-class areas, but they are less crowded. Trains are fast and frequent and serve most places of interest. Distances are short. The high-speed line between Amsterdam, Schiphol and Rotterdam requires a small supplement (around €3). Most train stations have lockers operated by credit cards (average cost €6).

Portugal

Includes ➡

Best Places to Eat

- ➡ Ti-Natércia (p537)
- ➡ Mercado da Ribeira (p537)
- ➡ A Eira do Mel (p546)
- ➡ Cafe Santa Cruz (p551)
- ➡ Flor dos Congregados (p557)

Best Places to Stay

- ➡ Lisbon Destination Hostel (p534)
- ➡ Casa do Príncipe (p536)
- ➡ Moon Hill Hostel (p540)
- ➡ Canto de Luz (p556)
- ➡ 6 Only (p556)

Why Go?

With medieval castles, frozen-in-time villages, captivating cities and golden-sand bays, the Portuguese experience can mean many things. History, terrific food and wine, lyrical scenery and all-night partying are just the beginning.

Portugal's cinematically beautiful capital, Lisbon, and its soulful northern rival, Porto, are two of Europe's most charismatic cities. Both are a joy to stroll, with river views, rattling trams and tangled lanes hiding boutiques, new-wave bars and a seductive mix of restaurants, fado (traditional Portuguese melancholic song) clubs and open-air cafes.

Beyond the cities, Portugal's landscape unfolds in all its beauty. Stay in converted hilltop fortresses fronting age-old vineyards, hike amid granite peaks or explore medieval villages in the little-visited hinterland. More than 800km of coast shelters some of Europe's best beaches: gaze out over dramatic end-of-the-world cliffs, surf Atlantic breaks off dune-covered beaches or laze on sandy islands fronting the ocean.

When to Go

Lisbon

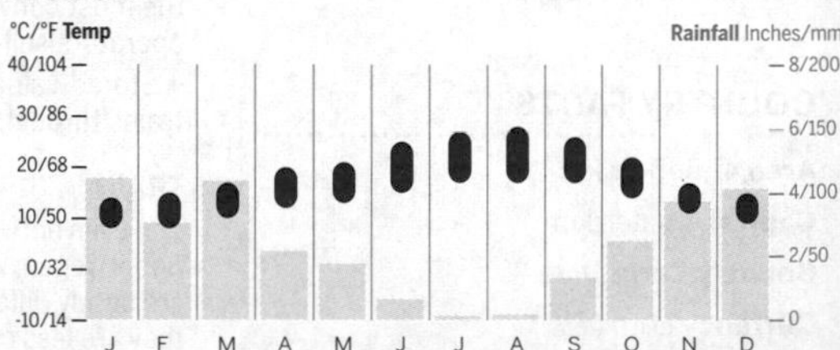

Apr & May Sunny days and wildflowers set the stage for hiking and outdoor activities.

Jun–Aug Lovely and lively, with a packed festival calendar and steamy beach days.

Late Sep & Oct Crisp mornings and sunny days; prices dip, crowds disperse.

Portugal Highlights

1 Alfama (p530) Following the sound of fado spilling from the lamplit lanes of this enchanting old-world neighbourhood in the heart of Lisbon.

2 Tavira (p543) Taking in the laid-back charms, before hitting some of the Algarve's prettiest beaches.

3 Coimbra (p550) Catching live music in a backstreet bar in this festive university town with a stunning medieval centre.

4 Sintra (p540) Exploring the wooded hills, studded with fairy tale–like palaces, villas and gardens.

5 Parque Nacional da Peneda-Gerês (p560) Conquering the park's ruggedly scenic trails.

6 Lagos (p544) Enjoying heady beach days in this surf-loving town with a vibrant drinking and dining scene.

7 Porto (p553) Exploring the Unesco World Heritage–listed city centre, sampling velvety ports at riverside wine lodges.

LISBON

POP 547,733

Spread across steep hillsides that overlook the Rio Tejo, Lisbon has captivated visitors for centuries. Windswept vistas at breathtaking heights reveal the city in all its beauty: Roman and Moorish ruins, white-domed cathedrals and grand plazas lined with sun-drenched cafes. The real delight of discovery, though, is delving into the narrow cobblestone lanes.

As bright-yellow trams clatter through curvy tree-lined streets, Lisboetas (residents of Lisbon) stroll through lamplit old quarters, much as they've done for centuries. Village-life gossip is exchanged over fresh bread and wine at tiny patio restaurants as fado singers perform in the background. In other parts of town, Lisbon reveals her youthful alter ego at stylish dining rooms and lounges, late-night street parties, riverside nightspots, and boutiques selling all things classic and cutting-edge.

Sights

Baixa & Alfama

Alfama is Lisbon's Moorish time capsule: a medina-like district of tangled alleys, hidden palm-shaded squares and narrow terracotta-roofed houses that tumble down to the glittering Tejo.

★Castelo de São Jorge CASTLE
(www.castelodesaojorge.pt; adult/student/child €8.50/5/free; ⌚9am-9pm Mar-Oct, to 6pm Nov-Feb) Towering dramatically above Lisbon, the mid-11th-century hilltop fortifications of Castelo de São Jorge sneak into almost every snapshot. Roam its snaking ramparts and pine-shaded courtyards for superlative views over the city's red rooftops to the river. Three guided tours daily (Portuguese, English and Spanish) at 1pm and 5pm are included in the admission price.

Sé de Lisboa CATHEDRAL
(Largo de Sé; ⌚9am-7pm Tue-Sat, to 5pm Mon & Sun) FREE One of Lisbon's icons is the fortress-like Sé de Lisboa, built in 1150 on the site of a mosque soon after Christians recaptured the city from the Moors.

It was sensitively restored in the 1930s. Despite the masses outside, the rib-vaulted interior, lit by a rose window, is calm. Stroll around the cathedral to spy leering gargoyles peeking above the orange trees.

Museu do Fado MUSEUM
(www.museudofado.pt; Largo do Chafariz de Dentro; adult/child €5/3; ⌚10am-6pm Tue-Sun) Fado (traditional Portuguese melancholic song) was born in the Alfama. Immerse yourself in its bittersweet symphonies at Museu do Fado. This engaging museum traces fado's history from its working-class roots to international stardom.

Belém

This quarter, 6km west of Rossio, whisks you back to Portugal's Age of Discoveries with its iconic sights. Besides heritage architecture, Belém bakes some of the country's best *pastéis de nata* (custard tarts).

To reach Belém, hop aboard tram 15 from Praça da Figueira or Praça do Comércio.

★Mosteiro dos Jerónimos MONASTERY
(www.mosteirojeronimos.pt; Praça do Império; adult/child €10/5, 1st Sun of month free; ⌚10am-6.30pm Tue-Sun, to 5.30pm Oct-May) Belém's undisputed heart-stealer is this Unesco-listed monastery. The *mosteiro* is the stuff of pure fantasy: a fusion of Diogo de Boitaca's creative vision and the spice and pepper dosh of Manuel I, who commissioned it to trumpet Vasco da Gama's discovery of a sea route to India in 1498.

Torre de Belém TOWER
(www.torrebelem.pt; adult/child €6/3, 1st Sun of month free; ⌚10am-6.30pm Tue-Sun, to 5.30pm Oct-Apr) Jutting out onto the Rio Tejo, this Unesco World Heritage–listed fortress epitomises the Age of Discoveries. You'll need to breathe in to climb the narrow spiral staircase to the tower, which affords sublime views over Belém and the river.

Museu Colecção Berardo MUSEUM
(www.museuberardo.pt; Praça do Império; ⌚10am-7pm) FREE Culture fiends get their contemporary-art fix for free at Museu Colecção Berardo, the star of the Centro Cultural de Belém. The ultrawhite, minimalist gallery displays millionaire José Berardo's eye-popping collection of abstract, surrealist and pop art, including Hockney, Lichtenstein, Warhol and Pollock originals.

Saldanha

★Museu Calouste Gulbenkian MUSEUM
(www.museu.gulbenkian.pt; Av de Berna 45; adult/child €5/free, Sun free; ⌚10am-6pm Wed-Mon) Famous for its outstanding quality and

breadth, the world-class Museu Calouste Gulbenkian showcases an epic collection of Western and Eastern art – from Egyptian treasures to Old Master and Impressionist paintings.

Centro de Arte Moderna MUSEUM
(Modern Art Centre; CAM; www.cam.gulbenkian.pt; Rua Dr Nicaulau de Bettencourt; adult/chilld €5/free, free Sun; ⏲10am-6pm Wed-Mon) Situated in a sculpture-dotted garden, the Centro de Arte Moderna reveals a stellar collection of 20th-century Portuguese and international art.

Santa Apolónia & Lapa

The museums listed here are west and east of the city centre, but are well worth visiting.

Museu Nacional do Azulejo MUSEUM
(www.museudoazulejo.pt; Rua Madre de Deus 4; adult/child €5/2.50, free 1st Sun of the month; ⏲10am-6pm Tue-Sun) Housed in a sublime 16th-century convent, Lisbon's Museu Nacional do Azulejo covers the entire *azulejo* (hand-painted tile) spectrum. Star exhibits feature a 36m-long panel depicting pre-earthquake Lisbon, a Manueline cloister with web-like vaulting and exquisite blue-and-white *azulejos*, and a gold-smothered baroque chapel.

★**Museu Nacional de Arte Antiga** MUSEUM
(Ancient Art Museum; www.museudearteantiga.pt; Rua das Janelas Verdes; adult/child €6/3, 1st Sun of month free; ⏲10am-6pm Tue-Sun) Set in a lemon-fronted, 17th-century palace, the Museu Nacional de Arte Antiga is Lapa's biggest draw. It presents a star-studded collection of European and Asian paintings and decorative arts.

LX Factory ARTS CENTRE
(www.lxfactory.com; Rua Rodrigues de Faria 103) Lisbon's hub of cutting-edge creativity hosts a dynamic menu of events from live concerts and film screenings to fashion shows and art exhibitions. There's a rustically cool cafe as well as a restaurant, bookshop and design-minded shops. Weekend nights see parties with a dance- and art-loving crowd.

Parque das Nações

The former Expo '98 site, this revitalised 2km-long waterfront area in the northeast equals a family fun day out, packed with public art, gardens and kid-friendly attractions.

Take the metro to **Oriente station** (Oriente Station; Av Dom João II) – a stunner designed by star Spanish architect Santiago Calatrava.

Oceanário AQUARIUM
(www.oceanario.pt; Doca dos Olivais; adult/child €14/9, incl temporary exhibition €17/11; ⏲10am-8pm, to 7pm winter) The closest you'll get to scuba diving without a wetsuit, Lisbon's Oceanário is mind-blowing. No amount of hyperbole, where 8000 marine creatures splash in 7 million litres of seawater, does it justice. Huge wrap-around tanks make you feel as if you are underwater, as you eyeball zebra sharks, honeycombed rays, gliding mantas and schools of neon fish.

Pavilhão do Conhecimento MUSEUM
(Pavilion of Knowledge; www.pavconhecimento.pt; Living Science Centre; adult/child €9/5; ⏲10am-6pm Tue-Fri, 11am-7pm Sat & Sun) Kids won't grumble about science at the interactive Pavilhão do Conhecimento, where they can experience the gravity on the moon (or lack thereof, rather) and get dizzy on a high-wire bicycle. Budding physicists have fun whipping up tornadoes and blowing massive soap bubbles, while tots run riot in the adult-free unfinished house.

HEAVENLY VIEWS

Lisbon's *miradouros* (lookouts) lift spirits with their heavenly views. Some have outdoor cafes for lingering.

Largo das Portas do Sol (Largo das Portas do Sol) Moorish gateway with stunning views over Alfama's rooftops.

Miradouro da Graça (Largo da Graça) Pine-fringed square that's perfect for sundowners.

Miradouro da Senhora do Monte (Rua da Senhora do Monte) The highest lookout, with memorable castle views.

Miradouro de São Pedro de Alcântara (Rua São Pedro de Alcântara; viewpoint 24hr, kiosk 10am-midnight Mon-Wed, to 2am Thu-Sun) Drinks and sweeping views on the edge of Bairro Alto.

Miradouro de Santa Catarina (Rua de Santa Catarina; ⏲24hr) FREE Youthful spot with guitar-playing rebels, artful graffiti and far-reaching views.

Central Lisbon

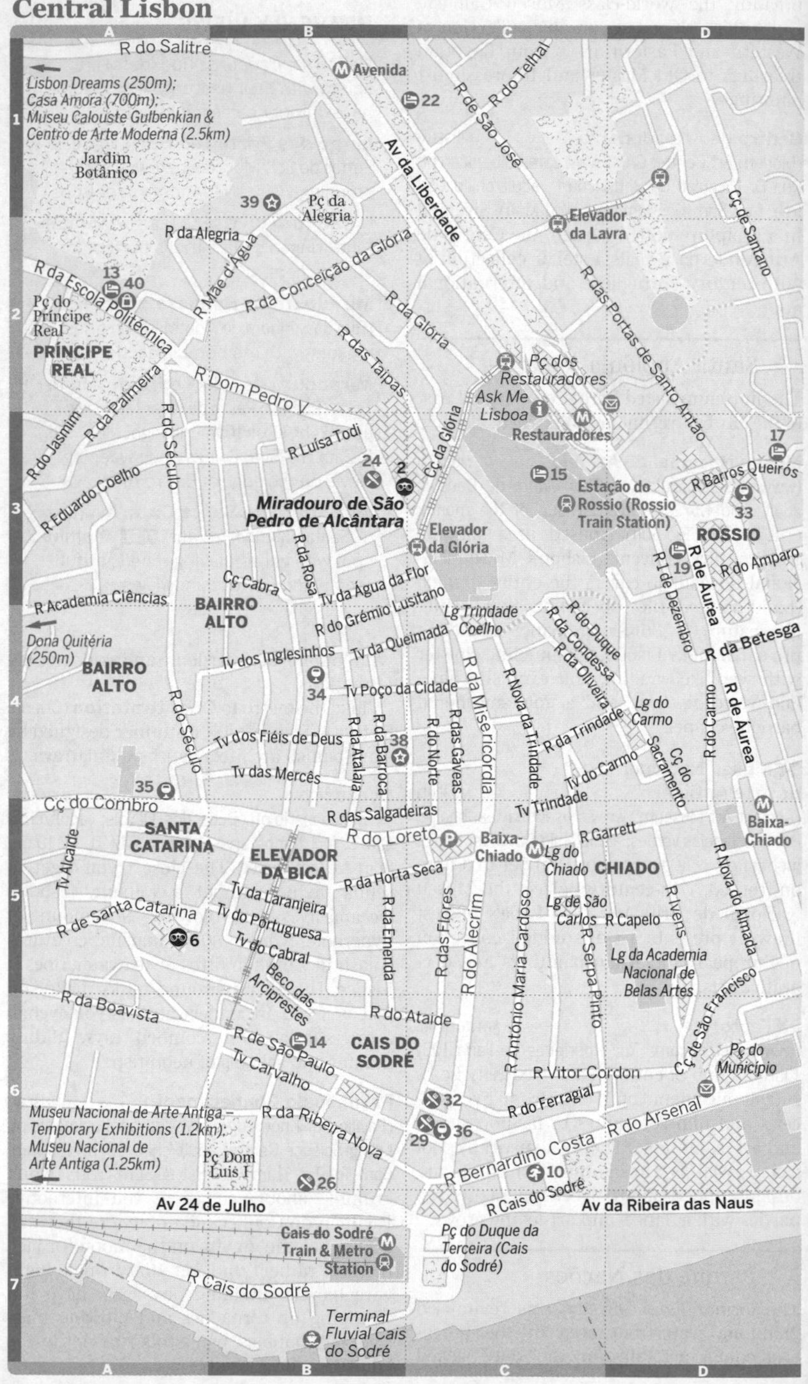

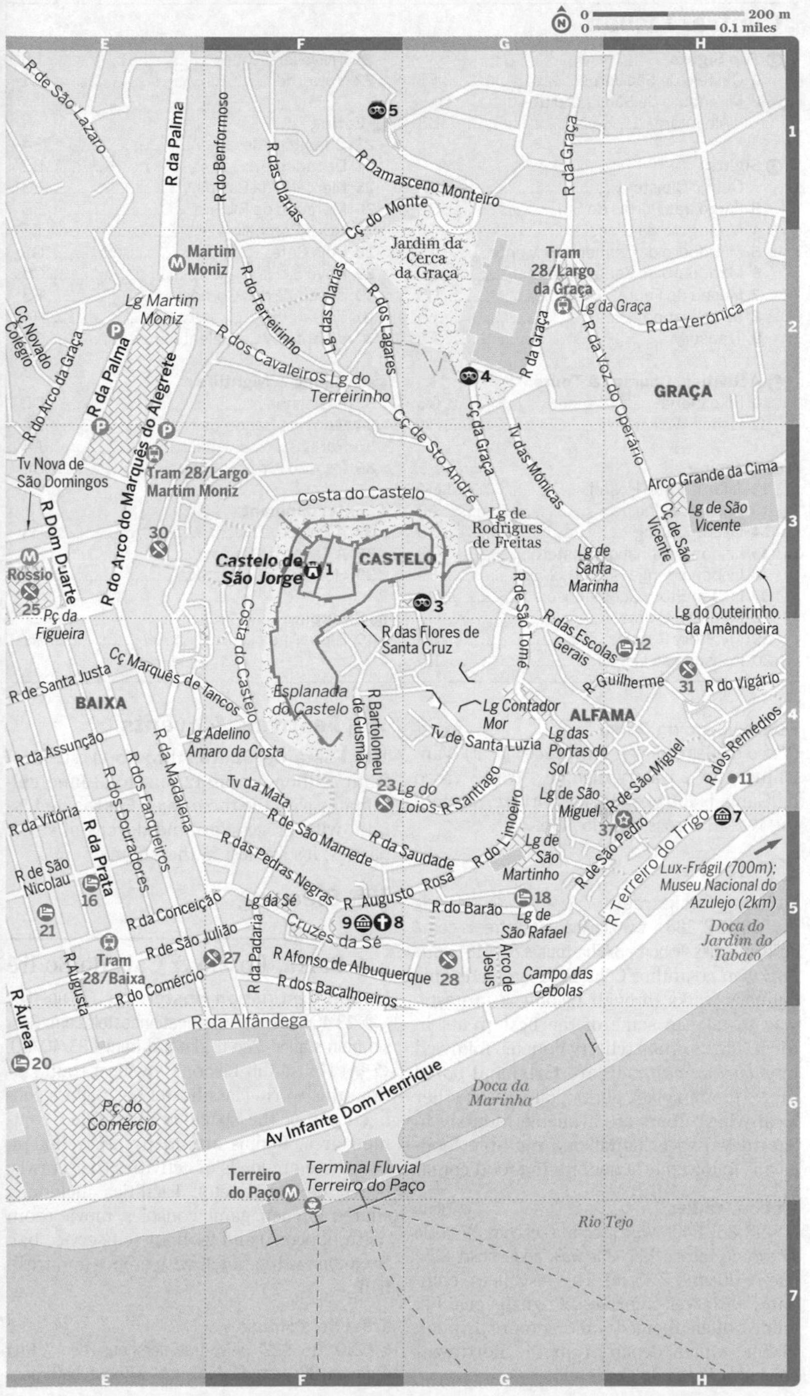
R de São Lazaro
R da Palma
R do Benformoso
R das Olarias
R Damasceno Monteiro
Cç do Monte
R da Graça
Jardim da Cerca da Graça
Martim Moniz
R do Terreirinho
Lg das Olarias
R dos Lagares
Tram 28/Largo da Graça
Lg da Graça
R da Verónica
Lg Martim Moniz
Cç Novado Colégio
R dos Cavaleiros
Lg do Terreirinho
R da Voz do Operário
GRAÇA
R do Arco da Graça
R do Arco do Marquês do Alegrete
Cç de Sto André
Cç da Graça
Tv das Mónicas
Tv Nova de São Domingos
Tram 28/Largo Martim Moniz
Costa do Castelo
Arco Grande da Cima
Lg de São Vicente
Cç de São Vicente
R Dom Duarte
Lg de Rodrigues de Freitas
Rossio
Castelo de São Jorge
CASTELO
Lg de Santa Marinha
Pç da Figueira
R de São Tomé
Lg do Outeirinho da Amêndoeira
R das Flores de Santa Cruz
R das Escolas Gerais
Cç Marquês de Tancos
R de Santa Justa
R Guilherme
R do Vigário
BAIXA
Esplanada do Castelo
R Bartolomeu de Gusmão
Lg Contador Mor
ALFAMA
Lg Adelino Amaro da Costa
Tv de Santa Luzia
Lg das Portas do Sol
R dos Remédios
R da Assunção
R dos Fanqueiros
R da Madalena
R dos Douradores
Tv da Mata
Lg do Loios
R Santiago
R do Limoeiro
Lg de São Miguel
R de São Miguel
R da Vitória
R da Prata
R de São Mamede
R da Saudade
Lg de São Martinho
R de São Pedro
R Terreiro do Trigo
R de São Nicolau
R das Pedras Negras
R Augusto Rosa
Lux-Frágil (700m); Museu Nacional do Azulejo (2km)
R da Conceição
Lg da Sé
R do Barão
Lg de São Rafael
Cruzes da Sé
Doca do Jardim do Tabaco
R de São Julião
R da Padaria
R Afonso de Albuquerque
Arco de Jesus
Campo das Cebolas
Tram 28/Baixa
R Augusta
R do Comércio
R dos Bacalhoeiros
R Áurea
R da Alfândega
Doca da Marinha
Pç do Comércio
Av Infante Dom Henrique
Terreiro do Paço
Terminal Fluvial Terreiro do Paço
Rio Tejo
PORTUGAL LISBON
200 m
0.1 miles

Central Lisbon

Top Sights
1 Castelo de São Jorge ... F3
2 Miradouro de São Pedro de Alcântara ... B3

Sights
Gothic Cloister ... (see 8)
3 Largo das Portas do Sol ... G3
4 Miradouro da Graça ... G2
5 Miradouro da Senhora do Monte ... F1
6 Miradouro de Santa Catarina ... A5
7 Museu do Fado ... H5
8 Sé de Lisboa ... F5
9 Treasury ... F5

Activities, Courses & Tours
10 Bike Iberia ... C6
11 Lisbon Walker ... H4

Sleeping
12 Alfama Patio Hostel ... H4
13 Casa do Príncipe ... A2
14 Lisbon Calling ... B6
15 Lisbon Destination Hostel ... C3
16 Lisbon Lounge Hostel ... E5
17 Lisbon Story Guesthouse ... D3
18 Memmo Alfama ... G5
19 My Story Rossio ... D3
20 Pousada de Lisboa ... E6
21 Travellers House ... E5
22 Valverde ... C1

Eating
23 Chapitô à Mesa ... F4
24 Decadente ... B3
25 Mercado da Baixa ... E3
26 Mercado da Ribeira ... B6
27 Nova Pombalina ... F5
28 Pois Café ... G5
29 Povo ... C6
30 Tasca Zé dos Cornos ... E3
31 Ti-Natércia ... H4
32 Vicente by Carnalentejana ... C6

Drinking & Nightlife
33 A Ginjinha ... D3
34 BA Wine Bar do Bairro Alto ... B4
35 Park ... A4
36 Pensão Amor ... C6

Entertainment
37 A Baîuca ... H5
38 A Tasco do Chico ... B4
39 Hot Clube de Portugal ... B1

Shopping
40 Embaixada ... A2

Ponte Vasco da Gama BRIDGE
(Vasco da Gama Bridge; www.lusoponte.pt) Vanishing into a watery distance, Ponte Vasco da Gama is Europe's longest bridge, stretching 17.2km across the Rio Tejo.

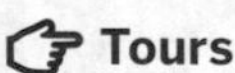

Tours

Culinary Backstreets FOOD & DRINK
(☎963 472 188; www.culinarybackstreets.com/culinary-walks/lisbon; 3/6hr tour €85/118) *Eat Portugal* co-author Célia Pedroso leads epic culinary walks through Lisbon, a fantastic way to take in some of the best treats in town. Try *ginjinha* (cherry liqueur) followed by *pastel de nata* (custard tarts) and *porco preto* (Iberian black pork), paired with killer local wines. Tours are available Monday to Saturday. Expect tantalising multiple foodgasms followed by a debilitating food coma.

Lisbon Walker WALKING
(☎218 861 840; www.lisbonwalker.com; Rua do Jardim do Tabaco 126; 3hr walk adult/child €15/free; ⏲10am & 2.30pm) This excellent company, with well-informed, English-speaking guides, offers themed walking tours through Lisbon, which depart from the northwest corner of Praça do Comércio.

Festivals & Events

The **Festa de Santo António** (Festival of Saint Anthony), from 12 June to 13 June, culminates with the three-week **Festas de Lisboa**, with processions and dozens of street parties; it's liveliest in the Alfama.

Sleeping

Baixa, Rossio & Cais do Sodré

Lisbon Destination Hostel HOSTEL €
(☎213 466 457; www.destinationhostels.com; Rossio train station, 2nd fl; dm/s/d from €23/40/80; @📶) Housed in Lisbon's loveliest train station, this world-class hostel has a glass ceiling lighting the spacious plant-filled common area. Rooms are crisp and well-kept, and there are loads of activities (bar crawls, beach day trips, etc). Facilities include a shared kitchen, game consoles, movie room (with popcorn) and 24-hour self-service bar. Breakfast is top-notch with crêpes and fresh fruit.

Travellers House HOSTEL €
(☎210 115 922; www.travellershouse.com; Rua Augusta 89; dm €28-30, s/d without bathroom

€40/70, d €80-90; ❄@📶) Travellers enthuse about this super-friendly hostel set in a converted 250-year-old house on Rua Augusta. As well as cosy dorms and a wealth of comfortable private rooms (some more minimalist than others), there's a retro lounge with beanbags, an internet corner and a communal kitchen. Newly installed CCTV and heaters keep everyone safe and warm.

Lisbon Lounge Hostel HOSTEL €
(☎213 462 061; www.lisbonloungehostel.com; Rua de São Nicolau 41; dm/d with shared bath from €22/64, d €84; ❄@📶) Lisbon Lounge Hostel has artfully designed dorms, and a slick lounge complete with faux moose head, plastic-bottle chandeliers and an old salon hood dryer. Three-course dinners, bike hire, walking tours and DJ nights are all part and parcel of these nicely chilled Baixa digs.

★**Lisbon Story Guesthouse** GUESTHOUSE €€
(☎218 879 392; www.lisbonstoryguesthouse.com; Largo de São Domingos 18; d €80-100, without bathroom €50-70, apt €120; @📶) 🍃 Overlooking Largo de São Domingos, Lisbon Story is a small, extremely welcoming guesthouse with nicely maintained, light-drenched rooms, all of which sport Portuguese themes (the Tejo, tram 28, fado etc) and working antique radios, record players and the like. The shoe-free lounge, with throw pillows and low tables, is a great place to chill.

My Story Rossio BOUTIQUE HOTEL €€
(☎213 400 380; www.mystoryhotels.com; Praça Dom Pedro IV 59; s/d from €127/137; ❄📶) This 2015 newcomer gets a gold star for its central location right on Rossio Sq. Carpeted hallways depicting Google Maps views of Lisbon lead to rooms (and bathrooms) that tend to be cramped (you'll be happier in a roomier superior), but travellers enjoy hi-tech mod cons such as TV/mirror hybrids, quirky themes (Fado, Amor, Lisboa) and value for money.

Pousada de Lisboa BOUTIQUE HOTEL €€€
(☎210 407 650; www.pestana.com/en/hotel/pousada-lisboa; Praça do Comércio 31; r from €210; ❄@📶≋) Location, location, location! Portugal's Pestana chain hit triple 7s with this 2015 newcomer's privileged position on Praça do Comércio. A €70-million renovation turned the former Ministry of Internal Affairs into a cosy *pousada* (upmarket inn) with museum-like qualities. Sculptures throughout represent epic moments in Portuguese history and, yes, you can sit on those 13th-century *liteiras* (litters).

Alfama

Alfama Patio Hostel HOSTEL €
(☎218 883 127; www.alfama.destinationhostels.com; Rua das Escolas Gerais 3; dm €18-24, s/d without bathroom from €30/45, d €60; @📶) In Alfama's heart, this beautifully run hostel offers custom-made, Cappadocia-inspired particle-board dorms with privacy curtains and lockable drawers. From the upper-floor rooms, you can practically file your fingernails across the top of the tram as it rattles past. A bevy of activities (fado, street art and surfing tours) and barbecues on the garden-like patio mean it's notably social.

★**Memmo Alfama** BOUTIQUE HOTEL €€€
(☎210 495 660; www.memmoalfama.com; Travessa Merceeiras 27; r €170-350; ❄📶≋) Slip down a narrow alley to reach these gorgeous boutique Alfama sleeps, a stunning conversion of a shoe-polish factory and former bakery. The rooms are an ode to whitewashed minimalism and staff are as sleek as the decor with their uniform-issued Chuck Taylor All-Stars and hipster aura. The view down to the Tejo from the roof terrace is phenomenal.

Chiado, Bairro Alto & Príncipe Real

Lisbon Calling HOSTEL €
(☎213 432 381; www.lisboncalling.net; Rua de São Paulo 126, 3rd fl; dm/d with shared bathroom €16/55, d €75; @📶) This fashionable, unsigned backpacker favourite near Santa Catarina features original frescoes, *azulejos* and hardwood floors – all lovingly restored

CYCLING THE TEJO

A **cycling/jogging path** courses along the Tejo for 7km, between Cais do Sodré and Belém. Complete with artful touches – including the poetry of Pessoa printed along parts of it – the path takes in ageing warehouses, weathered docks, and open-air restaurants and nightspots.

A handy place to rent bikes is a short stroll from Cais do Sodré: **Bike Iberia** (☎969 630 369; www.bikeiberia.com; Largo Corpo Santo 5; bike hire per hr/day from €5/14; ⏲9.30am-7pm).

by friendly Portuguese owners. The bright, spacious dorms and a brick-vaulted kitchen are easy on the eyes, but the private rooms – specifically room 1812 – will floor you: boutique-hotel-level dens of style and comfort that thunderously out-punch their price point.

★Casa do Príncipe B&B €€
(☎218 264 183; www.casadoprincipe.com; Praça do Príncipe Real 23; r €99-150; ❄📶) Perfectly located, exquisitely restored and priced to shock, this new nine-room B&B is housed inside what once was the same 19th-century neo-Moorish palace as **Embaixada** (www.embaixadalx.pt; Praça do Príncipe Real 26; ⏰noon-8pm, restaurants to 2am) next door. Original frescoes, *azulejos* and ornate moulded ceilings adorn the hardwood halls and spacious rooms, which are themed after the life of King Dom Pedro V. Indeed, you'll sleep like a king here yourself.

Avenida de Liberdade, Rato & Marquês de Pombal

★Casa Amora GUESTHOUSE €€
(☎919 300 317; www.casaamora.com; Rua João Penha 13; d €90-180, apt €120-220; ❄📶) Casa Amora has 11 beautifully designed guestrooms and studio apartments, with eye-catching art and iPod docks. There's a lovely garden patio where the first-rate breakfast is served. It's located in the peaceful neighbourhood of Amoreiras, a few steps from one of Lisbon's prettiest squares.

Lisbon Dreams GUESTHOUSE €€
(☎213 872 393; www.lisbondreamsguesthouse.com; Rua Rodrigo da Fonseca 29; s/d without bathroom €50/60, d €90; ❄@📶) On a quiet street lined with jacaranda trees, Lisbon Dreams offers excellent value for its bright, modern rooms with high ceilings and excellent mattresses. The green apples are a nice touch, and there are attractive common areas to unwind in. All bathrooms are shared except one, but are spotlessly clean.

Valverde BOUTIQUE HOTEL €€€
(☎210 940 300; www.valverdehotel.com; Av da Liberdade 164; d €200-325, ste €305-600; P❄@📶) Exquisite Valverde feels like a boutique town house (which of course it once was). Its facade is not showy, but once inside, an urban oasis of discerning design and personalised service is subtlety unveiled. The 25 rooms, reached by black-dominated, hushed hallways, are awash in cultured European art and unique mid-century modern pieces, and elicit style, form and function.

Eating

In addition to creative newcomers, you'll find inexpensive, traditional dining rooms home to classic Portuguese fare.

Baixa, Rossio & Cais do Sodré

★Mercado da Baixa MARKET €
(www.adbaixapombalina.pt; Praça da Figueira; ⏰10am-10pm Fri-Sun) This tented market/glorious food court on Praça da Figueira has been slinging cheese, wine, smoked sausages and other gourmet goodies since 1855. It takes place on the last weekend of each month and it is fantastic fun to stroll the stalls eating and drinking yourself into a gluttonous mess.

Povo PORTUGUESE €
(www.povolisboa.com; Rua Nova do Carvalho 32; small plates €7-11; ⏰6pm-2am Mon-Wed & Sun, to 4am Thu-Sat) On bar-lined Rua Nova do Carvalho, Povo serves tasty Portuguese comfort food in the form of *petiscos* (tapas/snacks). There's also outdoor seating, plus live performances a few times per week from in-house *fadista* Marta de Sousa (Thursdays are best; from 9.30pm).

Nova Pombalina PORTUGUESE €
(www.facebook.com/anovapombalina; Rua do Comércio 2; sandwiches €2.20-4; ⏰7am-7.30pm, closed Sun) The reason this bustling traditional restaurant is always packed around midday is its delicious *leitão* (suckling pig) sandwich, served on freshly baked bread in 60 seconds or less by the lightning-fast crew behind the counter.

Vicente by Carnalentejana PORTUGUESE €€
(☎218 237 126; www.restaurantecarnalentejana.com; Rua das Flores 6; mains €9-14; ⏰noon-11pm; 📶) This sexy newcomer dishes up succulent beef and pork dishes made with ultra-premium Carnalentejana DOP-certified meat from the Alentejo along with wines, cheeses, olive oils and other treats produced by the same artisan farmers. A former coal shop turned carnivore's den of decadence, the original low-slung stone walls, exposed air ducts and filament light bulbs are notably atmospheric.

Alfama

★ Ti-Natércia PORTUGUESE €

(☎218 862 133; Rua Escola Gerais 54; mains €5-12; ⏰7pm-midnight Mon-Fri, noon-3pm & 7pm-midnight Sat) A decade in and a legend in the making, 'Aunt' Natércia and her downright delicious Portuguese home cooking is a tough ticket: there are but a mere six tables and they fill up fast. She'll talk your ear off (and doesn't mince words!) while you devour her excellent take on the classics. Reservations essential (and cash only).

Pois Café CAFE €

(www.poiscafe.com; Rua de São João da Praça 93; mains €7-10; ⏰noon-11pm Mon, 10am-11pm Tue-Sun; 📶) Boasting a laid-back vibe under dominant stone arches, atmospheric Pois Café has creative salads, sandwiches and fresh juices, plus a handful of heartier daily specials (salmon quiche, sirloin steak). Its sofas invite lazy afternoons spent reading novels and sipping coffee, but you'll fight for space with the laptop brigade.

Chapitô à Mesa PORTUGUESE €€

(☎218 875 077; www.facebook.com/chapitoamesa; Rua Costa do Castelo 7; mains €18-21; ⏰noon-11pm Mon-Fri, 7.30-11pm Sat-Sun; 📶) Up a spiral iron staircase from this circus school's casual cafe, the decidedly creative menu of Chef Bertílio Gomes is served alongside views worth writing home about. His modern takes include classic dishes (*bacalhau à Brás*, stewed veal cheeks, suckling pig), plus daring ones (rooster testicles – goes swimmingly with a drop of Quinta da SilveiraReserva).

Tasca Zé dos Cornos PORTUGUESE €€

(☎218 869 641; www.facebook.com/ZeCornos; Beco Surradores 5; mains €10-15; ⏰8am-11pm Mon-Sat) This family-owned tavern welcomes regulars and first-timers with the same undivided attention. Lunchtime is particularly busy but the service is whirlwind quick and effective. Space is tight so sharing tables is the norm. The menu is typical Portuguese cuisine with emphasis on pork and *bacalhau* (dried salt cod) grilled on the spot, served in very generous portions.

Chiado, Bairro Alto & Príncipe Real

★ Mercado da Ribeira MARKET €

(www.timeoutmarket.com; Av 24 de Julho; ⏰10am-midnight Sun-Wed, to 2am Thu-Sat; 📶) Doing trade in fresh fruit and veg, fish and flowers since 1892, this oriental-dome-topped market hall is the word on everyone's lips since *Time Out* transformed half of it into a gourmet food court in 2014. Now it's like Lisbon in microcosm, with everything from Garrafeira Nacional wines to Conserveira de Lisboa fish, Arcádia chocolate and Santini gelato.

Dona Quitéria PORTUGUESE €

(☎213 951 521; Travessa de São José 1; small plates €5-12; ⏰7pm-midnight Tue-Sun) Locals do their best to keep this quaint corner *petiscaria* (small plates restaurant), a former grocery store from 1870, all to themselves – no such luck. Pleasant palate surprises such as tuna *pica-pau* instead of steak, or a pumpkin-laced cream-cheese mousse for dessert, put tasty creative spins on tradition. It's warm, welcoming and oh so tiny – so reserve ahead.

Decadente PORTUGUESE €€

(☎213 461 381; www.thedecadente.pt; Rua de São Pedro de Alcântara 81; mains €9-16; ⏰noon-11pm Sun-Wed, to midnight Thu-Sat; 📶) This beautifully designed restaurant inside a boutique hotel overlooking the stunning São Pedro de Alcântara lookout, with touches of industrial chic, geometric artwork and an enticing back patio, serves inventive dishes showcasing high-end Portuguese ingredients at excellent prices. The changing three-course lunch menu (€10) is first-rate. Start with creative cocktails in the front bar.

Belém

Antiga Confeitaria de Belém PASTRIES €

(☎213 637 423; www.pasteisdebelem.pt; Rua de Belém 84-92; pastries from €1.05; ⏰8am-11pm Oct-Jun, to midnight Jul-Sep) Since 1837 this patisserie has been transporting locals to sugar-coated nirvana with heavenly *pastéis de belém*. The crisp pastry nests are filled with custard cream, baked at 200°C for that perfect golden crust, then lightly dusted with cinnamon. Admire *azulejos* in the vaulted rooms or devour a still-warm tart at the counter and try to guess the secret ingredient.

Drinking & Nightlife

All-night street parties in Bairro Alto, sunset drinks from high-up terraces and sumptuous art deco cafes scattered about Chiado –

Lisbon has many enticing options for imbibers.

Lux-Frágil CLUB

(www.luxfragil.com; Av Infante Dom Henrique, Armazém A - Cais de Pedra, Santo Apolónia; ⏲11pm-6am Thu-Sat) Lisbon's ice-cool, must-see club, Lux hosts big-name DJs spinning electro and house. It's run by ex-Frágil maestro Marcel Reis and part-owned by John Malkovich. Grab a spot on the terrace to see the sun rise over the Tejo; or chill like a king on the throne-like giant interior chairs.

★ **Park** BAR

(www.facebook.com/00park; Calçada do Combro 58; cocktails €6.50-8; ⏲1pm-2am Tue-Sat, 1-8pm Sun; 📶) If only all multistorey car parks were like this... Take the elevator to the 5th floor, and head up and around to the top, which has been transformed into one of Lisbon's hippest rooftop bars, with sweeping views reaching right down to the Tejo and over the bell towers of Santa Catarina Church.

★ **Pensão Amor** BAR

(www.pensaoamor.pt; Rua do Alecrim 19; cocktails €5.50-13; ⏲noon-3am Mon-Wed, to 4am Thu-Sat, to 3am Sun) Set inside a former brothel, this cheeky bar pays homage to its passion-filled past with colourful wall murals, a library of erotic-tinged works, and a small stage where you can sometimes catch burlesque shows. The Museu Erótico de Lisboa (MEL) was on the way at time of research.

★ **A Ginjinha** BAR

(Largo de Saõ Domingos 8; ⏲9am-10pm) Hipsters, old men in flat caps, office workers and tourists all meet at this microscopic *ginjinha* (cherry liqueur) bar for that moment of cherry-licking, pip-spitting pleasure (€1.40 a shot).

★ **BA Wine Bar do Bairro Alto** WINE BAR

(☎213 461 182; bawinebar@gmail.com; Rua da Rosa 107; wines from €3, tapas from €12; ⏲6-11pm Tue-Sun; 📶) Reserve ahead unless you want to get shut out of Bairro Alto's best wine bar, where the genuinely welcoming staff will offer you three fantastic choices to taste based on your wine proclivities. The cheeses (from small artisanal producers) and charcuterie (melt-in-your-mouth black-pork *presuntos*) are not to be missed, either. You could spend the night here.

☆ Entertainment

For the latest goings-on, pick up the weekly *Time Out Lisboa* (www.timeout.pt) from bookstores, or the free monthly *Follow me Lisboa* from the tourist office.

Live Music

Hot Clube de Portugal JAZZ

(☎213 460 305; www.hcp.pt; Praça da Alegria 48; ⏲10pm-2am Tue-Sat) As hot as its name suggests, this small, poster-plastered cellar (and newly added garden) has staged top-drawer jazz acts since the 1940s. It's considered one of Europe's best.

A Baîuca FADO

(☎218 867 284; Rua de São Miguel 20; ⏲8pm-midnight Thu-Mon) On a good night, walking into A Baîuca is like gate-crashing a family party. It's a special place with *fado vadio*, where locals take a turn and spectators hiss if anyone dares to chat during the singing. There's a €25 minimum spend, which is as tough to swallow as the food, though the fado is spectacular. Reserve ahead.

A Tasco do Chico FADO

(☎961 339 696; www.facebook.com/atasca.dochico; Rua Diário de Notícias 39; ⏲noon-2am, to 3am Fri-Sat) This crowded dive (reserve ahead), full of soccer banners and spilling over with people of all ilk, is a fado free-for-all. It's not uncommon for taxi drivers to roll up, hum a few bars, and hop right back into their cabs, speeding off into the night. Portugal's most famous fado singer, Mariza, brought us here in 2005. It's still legit.

Sport

Lisbon's football teams are Benfica, Belenenses and Sporting. Euro 2004 led to the upgrading of the 65,000-seat **Estádio da Luz** (Estádio do Sport Lisboa e Benfica; ☎707 200 100; www.slbenfica.pt; Av General Norton de Matos) and the construction of the 54,000-seat **Estádio Nacional** (☎214 197 212; http://jamor.idesporto.pt; Av Pierre de Coubertin, Cruz Quebrada). State-of-the-art stadium **Estádio José de Alvalade** (www.sporting.pt; Rua Prof Fernando da Fonseca) seats 54,000 and is just north of the university. Take the metro to Campo Grande.

ℹ Information

EMERGENCY

Police Station (☎213 403 410; www.psp.pt; Rua da Atalaia 138) Police station in the heart of Bairro Alto, though non-Portuguese-speaking tourists are better off visiting the tourist police (Esquadra de Turismo; ☎213 421 623; www.psp.pt; Palácio Foz, Praça dos Restauradores; ⏲24hr) in non-emergency situations.

MEDICAL SERVICES

British Hospital (☎800 271 271; www.british-hospital.pt; Rua Tomás da Fonseca) English-speaking staff and English-speaking doctors.

Farmácia Estácio (Praça Dom Pedro IV 62; ⏲8.30am-8pm Mon-Fri, 10am-7pm Sat-Sun) A central pharmacy.

POST

Main Post Office (CTT; www.ctt.pt; Praça dos Restauradores 58; ⏲8am-10pm Mon-Fri, 9am-6pm Sat)

Post Office (CTT; www.ctt.pt; Praça do Município 6; ⏲8.30am-6.30pm) Central post office.

TOURIST INFORMATION

Ask Me Lisboa (☎213 463 314; www.askmelisboa.com; Praça dos Restauradores, Palácio Foz; ⏲9am-8pm) The largest and most helpful tourist office. Can book accommodation or reserve rental cars. There's also an office (☎218 450 660; www.askmelisboa.com; Aeroporto de Lisboa, Arrivals Hall; ⏲7.30am-9.30am Tue-Sat) in the arrivals hall at the airport.

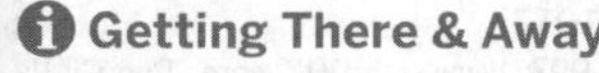

Getting There & Away

AIR

Around 6km north of the centre, **Aeroporto de Lisboa** (Lisbon Airport; ☎218 413 700; www.ana.pt; Alameda das Comunidades Portuguesas) operates direct flights to many European cities.

BUS

Lisbon's long-distance bus terminal is **Sete Rios** (Praça General Humberto Delgado, Rua das Laranjeiras), conveniently linked to both Jardim Zoológico metro station and Sete Rios train station. The big carriers, **Rede Expressos** (☎707 223 344; www.rede-expressos.pt) and **Eva** (☎707 223 344; www.eva-bus.com), run frequent services to almost every major town.

The other major terminal is **Gare do Oriente** (at Oriente metro and train station), concentrating on services to the north and to Spain. The biggest companies operating from here are **Renex** (☎218 956 836; www.renex.pt; Gare do Oriente) and the Spanish operator **Avanza** (☎912 722 832; www.avanzabus.com).

TRAIN

Santa Apolónia station is the terminus for northern and central Portugal. You can catch trains from Santa Apolónia to **Gare do Oriente train station**, which has departures to the Algarve and international destinations. **Cais do Sodré station** is for Belém, Cascais and Estoril. **Rossio station** is the terminal for trains to Sintra via Queluz.

For fares and schedules, visit www.cp.pt.

Getting Around

TO/FROM THE AIRPORT

The **AeroBus** (www.aerobus.pt; 1-way adult/child €3.50/2) runs every 20 minutes from 7am to 11pm, taking 30 to 45 minutes between the airport and Cais do Sodré.

A metro station on the red line gives convenient access to downtown. Change at Alameda (green line) to reach Rossio and Baixa. A **taxi** into town is about €15.

PUBLIC TRANSPORT

A 24-hour **Bilhete Carris/Metro** (€6.15) gives unlimited travel on all buses, trams, metros and funiculars. Pick it up from Carris kiosks and metro stations.

Bus, Tram & Funicular

Buses and trams run from 6am to 1am, with a few all-night services. Pick up a transport map from tourist offices or Carris kiosks. A single ticket costs more if you buy it on board (€2.85/1.80/3.60 for tram/bus/funicular), and much less (€1.40 per ride) if you buy a refillable **Viva Viagem** card (€0.50), available at Carris offices and in metro stations.

There are three funiculars: Elevador da Bica, Elevador da Glória and Elevador do Lavra.

Don't leave the city without riding tram 28 from Largo Martim Moniz through the narrow streets of the Alfama; tram 12 goes from Praça da Figueira out to Belém.

Ferry

Car, bicycle and passenger ferries leave frequently from the Cais do Sodré ferry terminal to Cacilhas (€1.20, 10 minutes). From Terreiro do Paço terminal, catamarans zip across to Montijo (€2.75, every 30 minutes) and Seixal (€2.35, every 30 minutes).

Metro

The **metro** (www.metro.transporteslisboa.pt; single/day ticket €1.40/6; ⏲6.30am-1am) is useful for hops across town and to the Parque das Nações. Buy tickets from metro ticket machines, which have English-language menus.

AROUND LISBON

Sintra

POP 26,000

Lord Byron called this hilltop town a 'glorious Eden' and, although best appreciated at dusk when the coach tours have left, it *is* a magnificent place. Less than an hour west of Lisbon, Sintra was the traditional summer retreat of Portugal's kings. Today, it's a fairytale setting of stunning palaces and manors surrounded by rolling green countryside.

Sights & Activities

Although the whole town resembles a historical theme park, there are several compulsory eye-catching sights.

★Quinta da Regaleira NOTABLE BUILDING, GARDENS

(www.regaleira.pt; Rua Barbosa du Bocage; adult/child €6/3; ⏲10am-8pm high season, shorter hours in low season) This magical villa and gardens is a neo-Manueline extravaganza, dreamed up by Italian opera-set designer Luigi Manini, under the orders of Brazilian coffee tycoon António Carvalho Monteiro, aka 'Monteiro dos Milhões' ('Moneybags Monteiro'). The villa is surprisingly cosy inside, despite its ferociously carved fireplaces, frescoes and Venetian-glass mosaics. Keep an eye out for mythological and Knights Templar symbols.

★Palácio Nacional de Sintra PALACE

(www.parquesdesintra.pt; Largo Rainha Dona Amélia; adult/child €10/8.50; ⏲9.30am-7pm, shorter hours in low season) The star of Sintra-Vila is this palace, with its iconic twin conical chimneys and lavish interior. The whimsical interior is a mix of Moorish and Manueline styles, with arabesque courtyards, barley-twist columns and 15th- and 16th-century geometric *azulejos* that figure among Portugal's oldest.

★Castelo dos Mouros CASTLE

(www.parquesdesintra.pt; adult/child €8/6.50; ⏲10am-6pm) Soaring 412m above sea level, this mist-enshrouded ruined castle looms high above the surrounding forest. When the clouds peel away, the vistas over Sintra's palace-dotted hill and dale, across to the glittering Atlantic are – like the climb – breathtaking.

The 10th-century Moorish castle's dizzying ramparts stretch across the mountain ridges and past moss-clad boulders the size of small buses.

★Palácio Nacional da Pena PALACE

(www.parquesdesintra.pt; combined ticket with Parque Nacional da Pena adult/child €14/12.50; ⏲10am-6pm) Rising from a thickly wooded peak and often enshrouded in swirling mist, Palácio Nacional da Pena is a wacky confection of onion domes, Moorish keyhole gates, writhing stone snakes and crenellated towers in pinks and lemons. It is considered the greatest expression of 19th-century romanticism in Portugal.

Sleeping & Eating

★Moon Hill Hostel HOSTEL €

(☎219 243 755; www.moonhillhostel.com; Rua Guilherme Gomes Fernandes 19; dm €19, d with/without bathroom €89/59; ❄@☁) 🍃 This design-forward, minimalist newcomer easily outshines the Sintra competition. Whether you book a boutique-hotel-level private room, with colourful reclaimed-wood headboards and wall-covering photos of enchanting Sintra forest scenes (go for 10 or 14 for Pena National Palace views, 12 or 13 for Moorish castle views), or a four-bed mixed dorm (lockers), you are sleeping in high style.

★Sintra 1012 B&B €€

(☎918 632 997; www.sintra1012.com; Rua Gil Vicente 10; d €60-120; ❄@☁) You'll probably need to go to war to book one of the four spacious and smart rooms in this highly recommended guesthouse run by a young Portuguese-American couple. Behind original medieval walls, it's a modern minimalist retreat which, in Roman times, was Sintra's first theatre. Today, it's all comfort and class right down to the basement studio, an astonishing deal (€60).

INcomum PORTUGUESE €€

(☎219 243 719; www.incomumbyluissantos.pt; Rua Dr Alfredo Costa 22; mains €14.50-15.50; ⏲noon-midnight; ☁) Chef Luis Santos is shaking up the scene in Sintra with his modern upgrades to Portuguese cuisine, served amid the muted greys and greens of his synchronic dining room. INcomum quickly established itself as the anti-traditional choice among serious foodies, first by dangling an unbeatable €9.50, three-course lunch carrot, then by letting the food seal the deal.

Information

Ask Me Sintra (Turismo; 219 231 157; www.askmelisboa.com/sintra; Praça da República 23; 9.30am-6pm) Near the centre of Sintra-Vila, Turismo de Lisboa's helpful multilingual office has expert insight on Sintra and the surrounding areas, as well as the interactive **'Myths & Legends' presentation** (€4.50). However, keep in mind this is a member-driven organisation, which only promotes those who pay. There's also a small train station (211 932 545; www.askmelisboa.com/sintra; Sintra train station; 10am-noon & 2.30-6pm) branch, often overrun by arriving visitors.

Getting There & Away

Train services (€2.20, 40 minutes, every 15 minutes) run between Sintra and Lisbon's Rossio station.

Getting Around

A handy bus for accessing the castle is the hop-on, hop-off **Scotturb bus 434** (219 230 381; www.scotturb.com; Av Dr Miguel Bombarda 59; 9am-6pm) (€5), which runs from the train station via Sintra-Vila to Castelo dos Mouros (10 minutes), Palácio da Pena (15 minutes), and back.

A taxi to Pena or Monserrate costs around €8 one way.

Cascais

POP 35,000

Cascais is a handsome seaside resort with elegant buildings, an atmospheric Old Town and a happy abundance of restaurants and bars.

Sights & Activities

Cascais' three sandy bays – **Praia da Conceição**, **Praia da Rainha** and **Praia da Ribeira** – are great for a sunbake or a tingly Atlantic dip, but attract crowds in summer.

The sea roars into the coast at **Boca do Inferno** (Hell's Mouth), 2km west of Cascais. Spectacular **Cabo da Roca**, Europe's westernmost point, is 16km from Cascais and Sintra, and is served by buses from both towns.

Casa das Histórias Paula Rego MUSEUM
(www.casadashistoriaspaularego.com; Av da República 300; adult/child €3/free; 10am-6pm Tue-Sun, to 7pm summer) The Casa das Histórias Paula Rego showcases the disturbing, highly evocative paintings of Portugal's finest living artist. Biannually changing exhibits span Rego's career, from early work with collage in the 1950s to the twisted fairy tale–like tableaux of the 1980s, and up to the disturbing realism of more recent years.

Museu Condes de Castro Guimarães MUSEUM
(www.cm-cascais.pt/equipamento/museu-condes-de-castro-guimaraes; Parque Marechal Camona; adult/child €3/free; 10am-5pm Tue-Sun) This whimsical early-19th-century mansion, complete with castle turrets and Arabic cloister, sits in the grounds of the **Parque Marechal Carmona** (www.cm-cascais.pt/equipamento/parque-marechal-carmona; A8.30am-6pm, to 8pm summer).

Sleeping & Eating

Perfect Spot Lisbon HOSTEL €
(924 058 643; www.perfectspot-lisbon.com; Av de Sintra 354; 3-/4-/7-day packages from €155/205/365; P) New parents Jon and Rita run this lovely hostel – perfect for families in addition to surfers and climbers – in a large home just a smidgen outside the tourist zone. Spacious rooms and dorms are themed with unique art, but the real coup is the closed-in garden, a supreme hang space with day beds and a BBQ lounge.

Villa Cascais BOUTIQUE HOTEL €€€
(214 863 410; www.thealbatrozcollection.com; Rua Fernandes Tomás 1; d from €145; @) If you like your hotels with a jolting dose of personality, the newly made-over, so-very-blue Villa Cascais (blue walls, blue couches and blue ceilings!) should sit quite well. Striking brass staircases lead to 11 beautiful and spacious rooms in three colours (two of which are not blue), each with discerning lounge furniture. Trendy, bright and beautiful!

★**Café Galeria House of Wonders** CAFE €€
(www.facebook.com/houseofwonders; Largo da Misericórdia 53; buffet 1/2 people €14.95/24.50, light meals €2.50-9.75; 10am-midnight;) This fantastically whimsical, Dutch-owned cafe is tucked away in the old quarter. Its astonishingly good Middle Eastern/Mediterranean vegetarian meze buffet downstairs includes a hot-dish add-on for €9.95 (aubergine moussaka, zucchini lasagne etc) amid a warm, welcoming ambience and artwork-filled interior. Don't miss it!

Information

Ask Me Cascais (Turismo; ☎ 912 034 214; www.visitcascais.com; Largo Cidade Vitória; ⏱ 9am-8pm summer, to 6pm winter) The official Cascais tourist information booth has a handy map and events guide (*What's in Cascais*), and is helpful to an extent.

Getting There & Around

Trains run frequently to Cascais via Estoril (€2.15, 40 minutes) from Cais do Sodré station in Lisbon.

THE ALGARVE

It's easy to see the allure of the Algarve: breathtaking cliffs, golden sands, scalloped bays and long sandy islands. Although overdevelopment has blighted parts of the coast, head inland and you'll land solidly in lovely Portuguese countryside once again. Algarve highlights include the riverside town of Tavira, party-loving Lagos and windswept Sagres. Faro is the regional capital.

Faro

POP 50,000

Faro is an attractive town with a palm-clad waterfront, well-maintained plazas and a small pedestrianised centre sprinkled with outdoor cafes. There are no beaches in Faro itself, though it's an easy jaunt by ferry to picturesque beaches nearby. A boat trip through the Parque Natural da Ria Formosa is another highlight.

Sights & Activities

★Parque Natural da Ria Formosa NATURE RESERVE

(www.icnf.pt) This sizeable system of lagoons and islands stretches for 60km along the Algarve coastline from west of Faro to Cacela Velha. It encloses a vast area of *sapal* (marsh), *salinas* (salt pans), creeks and dune islands. The marshes are an important area for migrating and nesting birds. You can see a huge variety of wading birds here, along with ducks, shorebirds, gulls and terns. This is the favoured nesting place of the little tern and the rare purple gallinule.

★Formosamar BOATING

(☎ 918 720 002; www.formosamar.com; Clube Naval, Faro Marina) This recommended outfit genuinely embraces and promotes environmentally responsible tourism. Among the excellent tours it provides are two-hour birdwatching trips around the Parque Natural da Ria Formosa (€25), dolphin watching (€45), cycling (€37), and a two-hour small-boat trip that penetrates some of the narrower lagoon channels (€25). All trips have a minimum number of participants (usually two or three).

Sleeping

★Casa d'Alagoa HOSTEL €

(☎ 289 813 252; www.farohostel.com; Praça Alexandre Herculano 27; dm not incl breakfast €22-30, d €80; wi-fi) Housed in a renovated mansion on a pretty square, this commendable budget option has all the elements of today's sophisticated hostel: it's funky, laid-back and cool (and clean!). There's a range of spacious dorms, a great lounge and an upstairs terrace, plus a communal kitchen…but hey, why do you need it when dinner is on offer? Bike rental also available.

Hotel Eva HOTEL €€

(☎ 800 8585 1234; www.hotel-eva-faro.h-rez.com; Avenida da República 1; d €88-105; P air-con wi-fi pool) Upmarket Eva has 134 spacious, pleasant rooms, with rates varying according to whether the view from the window is of sea, marina or city. There's a rooftop swimming pool for more marina gazing, and various meal plans are available for a fairly reasonable cost.

Eating

★Faz Gostos PORTUGUESE, FRENCH €€

(☎ 289 878 422; www.fazgostos.com; Rua do Castelo 13; mains €13-19.50; ⏱ noon-3pm & 7-11pm Mon-Fri, 7-11pm Sat; wi-fi) Elegantly housed in the old town, this restaurant offers high-class French-influenced Portuguese cuisine in a spacious, comfortably handsome dining area. There's plenty of game, fish and meat on offer with rich and seductive sauces, and a few set menus are available.

Gengibre e Canela VEGETARIAN €

(Travessa da Mota 10; buffet €7.50; ⏱ noon-3pm Mon-Sat, groups only evenings; wi-fi vegetarian) Give the taste buds a break from meat and fish dishes and veg out (literally) at this Zen-like restaurant. The buffet changes daily; there may be vegetable lasagne, vegetarian *feijoada* (bean casserole) and tofu dishes, but there's only the occasional curry. Wine and desserts are extra.

Information

Turismo (www.visitalgarve.pt; Rua da Misericórdia 8; ⌚9am-1pm & 2-6pm) Busy but efficient office with friendly staff.

Getting There & Away

Faro airport has both domestic and international flights.

From the **bus station**, just west of the centre, there are at least hourly express coaches to Lisbon (€20, five hours), plus several slower services, and frequent buses to other coastal towns.

The **train station** is a few minutes' walk west of the bus station. Five trains run daily to Lisbon's Sete Rios station (€21.20 to €22.20, 3¾ hours) and there are hourly services to all points along the Algarve coast.

Getting Around

Próximo (☎289 899 700; www.proximo.pt) city buses 14 and 16 run to the bus station (€2.22, 20 minutes, half-hourly June to August, slightly less frequently in low season). From here it's an easy stroll to the centre.

A taxi into town costs around €13.

Tavira

POP 15,100

Set on either side of the meandering Rio Gilão, Tavira is arguably the Algarve's most charming town, with a hilltop castle, an old Roman bridge and a smattering of Gothic churches. The pretty sands of Ilha da Tavira are a short boat ride away.

Sights & Activities

Núcleo Islâmico MUSEUM

(Praça da República 5; adult/child €2/1, with Palácio da Galeria €3/1.50; ⌚10am-12.30pm & 3-6pm mid-Jun–mid-Sep, 10am-4.30pm Tue-Sat mid-Sep–mid-Jun) Built around the globulous remains of an Islamic-era structure, this small 21st-century museum exhibits impressive Islamic pieces discovered in various excavations around the old town. There's a six-minute introductory video downstairs; one of the most important finds on display upstairs is the Tavira vase, an elaborate ceramic work with figures and animals around the rim. Multilingual handouts are available at reception.

The top floor of the museum is dedicated to temporary exhibitions with a local theme.

Igreja da Misericórdia CHURCH

(Largo da Misericórdia; ⌚9.30am-1pm & 2-6pm Mon-Sat) Built in the 1540s, this church is the Algarve's most important Renaissance monument, with a magnificent carved, arched doorway. Inside, the restrained Renaissance arches contrast with the cherub-heavy baroque altar; tiled panels depict the works of mercy. Behind is a museum with a rather effeminate St John, salvers, chalices, and a hall with an interesting 18th-century apple-wood ceiling and elegant furniture.

Sleeping & Eating

★**Pousada de Juventude Tavira** HOSTEL €

(☎281 326 731; www.pousadasjuventude.pt; Rua Dr Miguel Bombarda 36; dm €17, d €38-47; ⌚Jan-Nov; 📶) Forget the stereotypical youth hostel: this hip, modern spot is a comfortable haven for the budget traveller. It features a lovely living room decked out in a Moorish theme, spacious four-bed dorms, a fabulous kitchen and a laundry. Its ingenious design even allows for attractive hotel-style doubles. What's more, it's bang in the centre of town.

★**Casa Beleza do Sul** APARTMENT €€

(☎960 060 906; www.casabelezadosul.com; Rua Dr Parreira 43; apt €90-120; 📶) A gorgeous historical house in central Tavira is showcased to full advantage in this beautiful conversion. The result is a cute studio and three marvellous suites of rooms, all different, with original tiled floors and modern bathrooms. All have a kitchenette and there are numerous thoughtful touches that put this well above the ordinary. Minimum stays apply.

O Tonel PORTUGUESE €€

(☎963 427 612; Rua Dr Augo Silva Carvalho; mains €9.50-14; ⌚noon-3pm & 7-11pm Wed-Mon) Gourmet-style food for a decent price is the mantra at this brand-new restaurant where traditional dishes such as codfish *cataplana* (stew) and grilled meat and seafood dominate the menu. Dishes are served with hipster-esque imagination, though some may not appreciate their food served on slates and in jars.

Information

Turismo (☎281 322 511; www.visitalgarve.pt; Praça da República 5; ⌚9am-6pm daily Jul & Aug, 9am-6pm Mon-Wed, 9am-1pm & 2-6pm Thu-Sat Sep-Jun) Provides local and some regional information and has accommodation listings.

Getting There & Away

Some 15 trains run daily between Faro and Tavira (€3.15, 35 minutes).

Lagos

POP 22,000

In summer, the pretty fishing port of Lagos has a party vibe; its picturesque cobbled streets and pretty nearby beaches, including **Meia Praia** to the east and **Praia da Luz** to the west, are packed with revellers and sunseekers.

Activities

Blue Ocean DIVING

(964 665 667; www.blue-ocean-divers.de) For those who want to go diving or snorkelling. Offers a half-day discovery experience (€30), a full-day dive (€90) and a Divemaster PADI scuba course (€590). It also offers kayak safaris (half-/full day €30/45, children under 12 half price).

Dizzy Dolphins BOATING

(938 305 000; www.dizzydolphin.com) Run by a former BBC wildlife-documentary producer, this small outfit offers excellent 90-minute summer dolphin-spotting trips on a rigid inflatable.

Sleeping

Old Town Hostel HOSTEL €

(282 087 221; Rua da Barroca 70; dm €23;) If you're in town to party, this highly rated hostel is the place to sleep it all off during the day. Located in atmospheric Rua da Barroca, it has a kitchen, terrace and small common room, but the dorms are a little cramped and often full. The friendly staff is more than willing to show you the best bars.

★Hotel Mar Azul GUESTHOUSE €€

(282 770 230; www.hotelmarazul.eu; Rua 25 de Abril 13; s €50-60, d €60-85;) This little gem is one of Lagos' best-value spots. It's a central, well-run and delightfully welcoming place, with tidy, modern, compact rooms, some even boasting sea views. The simple breakfast is a mean €5 extra.

★Inn Seventies GUESTHOUSE €€

(967 177 590; www.innseventies.com; Rua Marquês de Pombal; d €90-129;) Though the entrance and stairwell don't give a great first impression, the rooms here are sexy suites with a vaguely 70s theme. They come well equipped with big TV, fridge and Nespresso machine, and there's a nice rooftop deck with views and plunge pool. The central location is fabulous and prices include the town's best buffet breakfast.

Eating

Café Gombá CAFE €

(282 762 188; Rua Cândido dos Reis 56; 8am-7pm Mon-Sat year round, Sun mid-Jun–mid-Sep) Although around since 1964, this traditional cafe-bakery with 21st-century decor looks more like it opened in 2014. Elderly locals hang out here for the best cakes, coffees and sandwiches in town, and it's correspondingly cheap.

★A Forja PORTUGUESE €€

(282 768 588; Rua dos Ferreiros 17; mains €8-17.50; noon-3pm & 6.30-10pm Sun-Fri) Like an Italian trattoria, this buzzing *adega tipica* (wine bar) pulls in the crowds – locals, tourists and expats – for its hearty, top-quality traditional food served in a bustling environment at great prices. Plates of the day are always reliable, as are the simply prepared fish dishes.

Information

Turismo (282 763 031; www.visitalgarve.pt; Praça Gil Eanes; 9am-7pm Jul & Aug, to 6pm Easter-Jun & Sep, to 5pm Oct-Easter) The very helpful staff offer excellent maps and leaflets.

Getting There & Away

Bus services depart frequently for other Algarve towns including Faro (€5.90, two hours 10 minutes, six daily), and around 10 times daily to Lisbon (€20, four hours). Lagos is the western terminus of the trans-Algarve line with hourly services to all coastal points east.

Silves

POP 11,000

The one-time capital of Moorish Algarve, Silves is a pretty town of jumbled orange rooftops scattered above the banks of the Rio Arade. It boasts one of the best-preserved castles in the Algarve, attractive redstone walls and winding, sleepy backstreets on a hillside.

Sights

★Castelo CASTLE
(☎282 440 837; adult/concession/under 10yr €2.80/1.40/free, joint ticket with Museu Municipal de Arqueologia €3.90; ⏲9am-8pm Jun-Aug, to 6.30pm Mar-May & Sep-Nov, to 5pm Dec-Feb) This russet-coloured, Lego-like castle – originally occupied in the Visigothic period – has great views over the town and surrounding countryside. What you see today dates mostly from the Moorish era, though the castle was heavily restored in the 20th century. Walking the parapets and admiring the vistas is the main attraction, but you can also gaze down on the excavated ruins of the Almohad-era palace. The whitewashed 12th-century water cisterns, 5m deep, now host temporary exhibitions.

Museu Municipal de Arqueologia MUSEUM
(☎282 444 838; Rua das Portas de Loulé; adult/under 10yr €2.10/free, joint ticket with Castelo €3.90; ⏲10am-6pm) Built tight against the defensive walls, this archaeological museum has a mix of interesting finds from the town and around. The modern building was constructed around an 18m-deep Moorish well with a spiral staircase heading into the depths that you can follow for a short stretch. Otherwise this is another Algarve museum that starts at the very prehistoric beginning but soon moves on to focus on the Almohad period of the 12th and 13th centuries.

Sleeping & Eating

Duas Quintas INN €€
(☎282 449 311; www.duasquintas.com; Santo Estevão; d/studios €105/130; P 📶 🏊) Set among orange groves and rolling hills, this utterly charming converted farmhouse has six pleasant rooms, a living space, terraces and a pool. Some of the furniture is antique and there are big discounts for staying a week or more. It's 6km northeast of Silves along the N124.

Pastelaria Rosa CAFE, DESSERTS €
(Largo do Município; pastries €1.50-3; ⏲7.30am-10pm Mon-Sat; 📶) On the ground floor of the town-hall building, this quaint, tile-lined place is Silves' oldest cafe and the best place to try Algarvian sweets. The table service is excellent and the extra you pay for the coffee and cakes here is worth it for the location and atmosphere. It's next to the tourist office.

★Restaurante O Barradas PORTUGUESE €€€
(☎282 443 308; www.obarradas.com; Palmeirinha; mains €8.50-25; ⏲6-10pm Thu-Tue; 👪) 🌿 The star choice for foodies is this delightful converted farmhouse run by Luís and his German wife, Andrea. They take pride in careful sourcing, and use organic fish, meat and fruit in season. Luís is a winemaker, so you can be assured of some fine wines. Follow the road to Lagoa and then to Palmeirinha; it's 3km from Silves.

Information

Centro de Interpretaçao do Património Islâmico (☎282 440 800; Largo do Município; ⏲9am-1pm & 2-5pm Mon-Fri)

Turismo (☎282 098 927; www.visitalgarve.pt; Parque das Merendas; ⏲9am-1pm & 2-6pm Tue-Sat)

Getting There & Away

Silves **train station** is 2km from town; trains from Lagos (€2.90, 35 minutes) stop nine times daily (from Faro, change at Tunes), to be met by local buses.

Sagres

POP 1900

The small, elongated village of Sagres has an end-of-the-world feel with its sea-carved cliffs and empty, wind-whipped fortress high above the ocean. This coast is ideal for surfing; hire windsurfing gear at sand-dune-fringed Praia do Martinhal.

Visit Europe's southwesternmost point, the **Cabo de São Vicente** (Cape St Vincent), 6km to the west. A solitary lighthouse stands on this barren cape.

Sights & Activities

Fortaleza de Sagres FORT
(☎282 620 140; adult/child €3/1.50; ⏲9.30am-6.30pm Apr, 9am-8pm May, Jun & Sep, 9am-8.30pm Jul & Aug, 9am-5pm Oct-Mar) Blank, hulking and forbidding, Sagres' fortress offers breathtaking views over the sheer cliffs, and all along the coast to Cabo de São Vicente. According to legend, this is where Prince Henry the Navigator established his navigation school and primed the early Portuguese explorers. It's quite a large site, so allow at least an hour to see everything.

Cabo de São Vicente LANDMARK
(⏲lighthouse complex 10am-6pm Tue-Sun Apr-Sep, to 5pm Oct-Mar) Five kilometres from Sagres,

Europe's southwesternmost point is a barren headland, the last piece of home that Portuguese sailors once saw as they launched into the unknown. It's a spectacular spot: at sunset you can almost hear the hissing as the sun hits the sea. A red **lighthouse** houses the small but excellent **Museu dos Faróis** (adult/child €1.50/1; ⏲10am-6pm Tue-Sun Apr-Sep, to 5pm Oct-Mar), showcasing Sagres' role in Portugal's maritime history.

★Walkin'Sagres WALKING

(☎925 545 515; www.walkinsagres.com) Multilingual Ana Carla offers recommended guided walks in the Sagres area, explaining the history and other details of the surrounds. The walks head through pine forests to the cape's cliffs, and vary from shorter 7.7km options (€25, three hours) to a longer 15km walk (€40, 4½ hours). There's also a weekend walk for parents with young children (€15, children free).

Sleeping & Eating

Mareta View Boutique B&B BOUTIQUE HOTEL €€

(☎282 620 000; www.maretaview.com; Beco D Henrique; s/d from €88.50/112.50; ❄@🛜) The Mareta View brings sleek – and classy – attitude to Sagres. White- and aquamarine-hued decor gives it a futuristic feel (the funky mood lighting in the rooms rivals the Cabo de São Vicente lighthouse beacon). It offers wonderful sea views, excellent breakfasts and a convenient location on the old plaza.

★A Eira do Mel PORTUGUESE €€€

(☎282 639 016; Estrada do Castelejo, Vila do Bispo; mains €16-22; ⏲noon-2.30pm & 7.30-10pm Tue-Sat) It's worth driving 10km north of Sagres to Vila do Bispo to enjoy José Pinheiro's creations at this much-lauded slow-food restaurant. The meat leans towards the Algarvian; the seafood has a more contemporary touch. Think rabbit in red-wine sauce (€16), octopus *cataplana* (seafood stew) with sweet potatoes (€35 for two people), curried Atlantic wild shrimps (€22) and *javali* (wild boar; €17). Mouth-watering.

Information

Turismo (☎282 624 873; www.cm-viladobispo.pt; Rua Comandante Matoso; ⏲9am-1pm & 2-6pm Tue-Sat, extended hours summer) Situated on a patch of green lawn, 100m east of Praça da República. Buses stop nearby.

Getting There & Away

The **bus stop** (Rua Comandante Matoso) is by the *turismo*. You can buy tickets on the bus.

Buses come from Lagos via Salema (€3.85, one hour, six daily). On weekends there are fewer services. It's only 10 minutes to Cabo de São Vicente (twice daily on weekdays only; €2).

CENTRAL PORTUGAL

The vast centre of Portugal is a rugged swathe of rolling hillsides, whitewashed villages, and olive groves and cork trees. Richly historic, it is scattered with prehistoric remains and medieval castles. It's also home to one of Portugal's most architecturally rich towns, Évora, as well as several spectacular walled villages. There are fine local wines and, for the more energetic, plenty of outdoor exploring in the dramatic Beiras region.

Évora

POP 49,000

Évora is an enchanting place to delve into the past. Inside the 14th-century walls, Évora's narrow, winding lanes lead to a striking medieval cathedral, a Roman temple and a picturesque town square. These old-fashioned good-looks are the backdrop to a lively student town surrounded by wineries and dramatic countryside.

Sights & Activities

Templo Romano RUINS

(Temple of Diana; Largo do Conde de Vila Flor) Once part of the Roman Forum, the remains of this temple, dating from the 2nd or early 3rd century, are a heady slice of drama right in town. It's among the best-preserved Roman monuments in Portugal, and probably on the Iberian Peninsula. Though it's commonly referred to as the Temple of Diana, there's no consensus about the deity to which it was dedicated, and some archaeologists believe it may have been dedicated to Julius Caesar.

Igreja de São Francisco CHURCH

(Praça 1 de Maio) Évora's best-known church is a tall and huge Manueline-Gothic structure, completed around 1510 and dedicated to St Francis. Legend has it that the Portuguese playwright Gil Vicente is buried here.

Sé CATHEDRAL
(Largo do Marquês de Marialva; €1.50, with cloister & towers €3.50, with museum €4.50; 9am-5pm) Guarded by a pair of rose granite towers, Évora's fortress-like medieval cathedral has fabulous cloisters and a museum jam-packed with ecclesiastical treasures. It was begun around 1186, during the reign of Sancho I, Afonso Henriques' son; there was probably a mosque here before. It was completed about 60 years later. The flags of Vasco da Gama's ships were blessed here in 1497.

Sleeping

Hostel Namaste HOSTEL €
(266 743 014; www.hostelnamasteevora.pt; Largo Doutor Manuel Alves Branco 12; dm/s/d €17/30/45;) Maria and Carla Sofia are the kind souls who run these welcoming digs in the historic Moorish quarter. Rooms are bright, spotlessly clean and decorated with splashes of art and colour, and there's a lounge, library, kitchen and bike hire. Breakfast costs €4.

★ **Albergaria do Calvario** BOUTIQUE HOTEL €€€
(266 745 930; www.albergariadocalvario.com; Travessa dos Lagares 3; r €116-133;) Unpretentiously elegant, discreetly attentive and comfortable, this beautifully designed guesthouse has an ambience that travellers adore. The staff leave no service stone unturned and breakfasts are among the region's best, with locally sourced organic produce, homemade cakes and egg dishes.

Eating & Drinking

Botequim da Mouraria PORTUGUESE €€
(266 746 775; Rua da Mouraria 16A; mains €14-17; 12.30-3pm & 7-10pm Mon-Fri, noon-3pm Sat) Poke around the old Moorish quarter to find some of Évora's finest food and wine – gastronomes believe this is Évora's culinary shrine. Owner Domingos will expertly guide you through the menu, which also features an excellent variety of wines from the Alentejo. There are no reservations and just nine stools at a counter. It is extremely popular, and lines are long. To have any chance of getting a seat, arrive before it opens.

Vinho e Noz PORTUGUESE €€
(266 747 310; Ramalho Orgigão 12; mains €11-13; noon-10pm Mon-Sat) This unpretentious place is run by a delightful family and offers professional service, a large wine list and good-quality cuisine. It's been going for over 30 years and is one of the best-value places in town.

Art Cafe CAFE
(Rua Serpa Pinto 6; 11am-midnight Tue-Sat, to 9pm Sun & Mon) Set in the cloisters of the old Palácio Barrocal, this bohemian cafe and drinking spot has outdoor tables, hipster wait staff and ambient electronic grooves. The outdoor tables are a fine spot to unwind with a sangria after a day exploring. Tasty veg-friendly snacks too (gazpacho, *tostas*, lasagne).

Information

Turismo (266 777 071; www.cm-evora.pt; Praça do Giraldo 73; 9am-7pm Apr-Oct, to 6pm Nov-Mar) This helpful, central tourist office offers a great town map.

Getting There & Away

Regular trains go direct to Lisbon (€12.20, 1½ hours, four daily) and indirectly, via Pinhal Novo, to Faro (€25.30, four to five hours, two daily) and Lagos (€26.30, 4½ to five hours, three daily). The train station is 600m south of the Jardim Público.

Peniche

POP 14,700

Popular for its nearby surfing beaches and also as a jumping-off point for Berlenga Grande, part of the beautiful Ilhas Berlengas nature reserve, the coastal city of Peniche remains a working port, giving it a slightly grittier and more 'lived-in' feel than its beach-resort neighbours. It has a walled historic centre and lovely beaches east of town.

From the bus station, it's a 10-minute walk west to the historic centre.

Sights

Baleal BEACH
About 5km to the northeast of Peniche is this scenic island-village, connected to the mainland village of Casais do Baleal by a narrow causeway (note: it's accessed through a car park). The fantastic sweep of sandy beach here offers some fine surfing. Surf schools dot the sands, as do several bar-restaurants.

Berlenga Grande ISLAND
Sitting about 10km offshore from Peniche, and part of the Berlenga archipelago, Berlenga Grande is a spectacular, rocky and remote island, with twisting, shocked-rock formations and gaping caverns.

Fortaleza FORT

(☎262 780 116; ⏲9am-12.30pm & 2-5.30pm Tue-Fri, from 10am Sat & Sun) FREE Dominating the south of the peninsula, Peniche's imposing 16th-century fortress was used in the 20th century as one of dictator Salazar's infamous jails for political prisoners.

Activities

Surfing

Surf camps offer week-long instruction as well as two-hour classes, plus board and wetsuit hire. Well-established names include **Baleal Surfcamp** (☎262 769 277; www.balealsurfcamp.com; Rua Amigos do Baleal 2; 1-/3-/5-day course €60/95/145) and **Peniche Surfcamp** (☎962 336 295; www.penichesurfcamp.com; Avenida do Mar 162, Casais do Baleal; ⏲1/2/10 surf classes €35/60/250).

Diving

There are good diving opportunities around Peniche, and especially around Berlenga. Expect to pay about €65 to €75 for two dives (less around Peniche) with **Acuasuboeste** (☎918 393 444; www.acuasuboeste.com; Porto de Pesca; diving intro course €80, two dives €65) or **Haliotis** (☎262 781 160; www.haliotis.pt; Casal da Ponte S/N, Atouguia da Baleia; single-/double-dive trip €35/75).

Sleeping & Eating

Peniche Hostel HOSTEL €

(☎969 008 689; www.penichehostel.com; Rua Arquitecto Paulino Montês 6; dm €18-20, d €50; @📶) This older-style little hostel run by friendly staff, only steps from the tourist office and a five-minute walk from the bus station, has colourfully decorated rooms with a hippie element. Front rooms have windows while some smaller, more claustrophobic rooms do not.

★**Casa das Marés** B&B €€

(☎Casa 1 262 769 200, Casa 2 262 769 255, Casa 3 262 769 371; www.casadasmares1.com; Praia do Baleal; d €80-89; 📶) At the picturesque, windswept tip of Baleal stands one of the area's most unique accommodation options. Three sisters inherited this imposing house from their parents and divided it into three parts – each of which now serves as its own little B&B. Breezy, inviting rooms all have great close-up sea views, and the sound of the breaking waves below is magical.

★**Nau dos Corvos** MODERN PORTUGUESE €€€

(☎262 783 168; www.naudoscorvos.com; Marginal Norte, Cabo Carvoeiro; mains €19.50-37; ⏲noon-3pm & 7-10.30pm) It's just you and the sea out here at Cabo Carvoeiro, 2.5km from the town centre at the tip of the peninsula. But as you gaze out at the Atlantic from the windy platform, it's nice to know that under your feet is an excellent, upmarket seafood restaurant (and Peniche's best). It boasts some of the best sunset views in Portugal.

Getting There & Away

Peniche's **bus station** (☎968 903 861; Rua Dr Ernesto Moreira) is served by **Rodotejo** (www.rodotejo.pt) and **Rede Expressos** (www.rede-expressos.pt). Destinations include Coimbra (€14.70, 2¾ hours, hourly), Leiria (€12.80, two hours, three to four daily), Lisbon (€9, 1½ hours, every one to two hours) and Óbidos (€3.20, 40 minutes, six to eight daily).

Óbidos

POP 3100

Surrounded by a classic crenellated wall, Óbidos' gorgeous historic centre is a labyrinth of cobblestoned streets and flower-bedecked, whitewashed houses livened up with dashes of vivid yellow and blue paint. It's a delightful place to pass an afternoon, but there are plenty of reasons to stay overnight, as there's excellent accommodation including a hilltop castle now converted into one of Portugal's most luxurious *pousadas* (upmarket hotels).

Sights

Castelo, Walls & Aqueduct HISTORIC SITE

FREE You can walk around the unprotected **muro** (wall) for uplifting views over the town and surrounding countryside. The walls date from Moorish times (later restored), but the **castelo** (castle) itself is one of Dom Dinis' 13th-century creations. It's a stern edifice, with lots of towers, battlements and big gates. Converted into a palace in the 16th century (some Manueline touches add levity), it's now a deluxe **pousada** (☎262 955 080; www.pousadas.pt; d/ste from €220/350; ❄📶).

The impressive 3km-long **aqueduct**, southeast of the main gate, dates from the 16th century.

Igreja de Santa Maria CHURCH
(Praça de Santa Maria; ⏲9.30am-12.30pm & 2.30-7pm summer, to 5pm winter) The town's elegant main church, near the northern end of Rua Direita, stands out for its interior, with a wonderful painted ceiling and walls done up in beautiful blue-and-white 17th-century *azulejos* (hand-painted tiles). Paintings by the renowned 17th-century painter Josefa de Óbidos are to the right of the altar. There's a fine 16th-century Renaissance tomb on the left, probably carved by French sculptor Nicolas Chanterène.

Sleeping & Eating

★Casa d'Óbidos HOTEL €€
(☎262 950 924; www.casadobidos.com; Quinta de São José; s/d €75/90, 2-/4-/6-person apt without breakfast €90/140/175; P 📶 🏊) In a whitewashed, 19th-century villa below town, this delightful option features spacious, breezy rooms with good new bathrooms and period furnishings, plus a tennis court, swimming pool and lovely grounds with sweeping views of Óbidos' bristling walls and towers. Breakfast is served at a common dining table. Trails lead through orchards up to town.

★Ja!mon Ja!mon PORTUGUESE €
(☎916 208 162; mains €5; ⏲10am-late Tue-Sun) Just outside Porta da Vila, before the tourist office, don't miss this cute little eatery. Six tables are crammed into a quaint room, a former *padeiria* (bakery), and fresh bread is baked in the wood-fired oven (along with other dishes). Each day brings a small selection of daily specials. We suggest just sitting back and letting the experience happen.

Information

Turismo (☎262 959 231; www.obidos.pt; ⏲9.30am-7.30pm summer, to 6pm winter) Outside Porta da Vila, near the bus stop, with helpful multilingual staff offering town brochures and maps in five languages.

Getting There & Away

There are direct buses Monday to Friday from Lisbon (€8.15, 65 minutes).

Nazaré

POP 10,500

Nazaré has a bustling coastal setting with narrow cobbled lanes running down to a wide, cliff-backed beach. The town centre is jammed with seafood restaurants and bars; expect huge crowds in July and August.

Sights & Activities

The **beaches** here are superb, although swimmers should be aware of dangerous currents. Climb or take the funicular to the clifftop **Sítio**, with its cluster of fishermen's cottages and great view.

Sleeping & Eating

Many townspeople rent out rooms; doubles start at €35. Ask around near the seafront at Avenida da República.

Information

Turismo (☎262 561 194; www.cm-nazare.pt; Avenida Vieira Giumarães, Edifício do Mercado Municipal; ⏲9.30am-1pm & 2.30-6pm Oct-Mar, 9.30am-12.30pm & 2.30-6.30pm Apr-Jun, 9am-9pm Jul & Aug) In the front offices of the food market. Helpful, multilingual staff.

Getting There & Away

Nazaré has numerous bus connections to Lisbon (€11, 1¾ hours).

Tomar

POP 16,000

Tomar is one of central Portugal's most appealing small towns. With its pedestrian-friendly historic centre, its pretty riverside park frequented by swans, herons and families of ducks, and its charming natural setting adjacent to the lush Mata Nacional dos Sete Montes (Seven Hills National Forest), it wins lots of points for aesthetics.

Sights

★Convento de Cristo MONASTERY
(www.conventocristo.pt; Rua Castelo dos Templários; adult/under 12yr €6/free, with Alcobaça & Batalha €15; ⏲9am-6.30pm Jun-Sep, 9am-5.30pm Oct-May) Wrapped in splendour and mystery, the Knights Templar held enormous power in Portugal from the 12th to 16th centuries, and largely bankrolled the Age of Discoveries. Their headquarters sit on wooded slopes above the town and are enclosed within 12th-century walls. The Convento de Cristo is a stony expression of magnificence, founded in 1160 by Gualdim Pais, Grand Master of the Templars. It has chapels, cloisters and choirs in diverging styles, added over the centuries by successive kings and Grand Masters.

Sleeping & Eating

★Hostel 2300 Thomar HOSTEL €
(☎249 324 256; www.hostel2300thomar.com; Rua Serpa Pinto 43; dm €18-20, d €40;) One of Portugal's funkiest hostels, this cleverly renovated mansion right in the heart of town celebrates Portugal, with each room brightly decorated in the country's theme: from the Lisbon tram to sardines. Airy dorms (and doubles), lockers, modern bathrooms and a cool and fun living space are enough to convert those after luxe experiences into a backpacker instead.

★Hotel dos Templários HOTEL €€
(☎249 310 100; www.hoteldostemplarios.pt; Largo Cândido dos Reis 1; s/d from €79/99, superior s/d from €99/132;) At the river's edge, just outside the historic centre, this spacious, efficient hotel offers excellent facilities including gym, sauna, and indoor and outdoor pools (the last adjacent to a small but stylish hotel bar). The rooms are large and very comfortable; most have balconies, some of which overlook the river. Service is five-star and the breakfast spread is great.

Restaurante Tabuleiro PORTUGUESE €€
(Rua Serpa Pinto 140; mains €8-12; noon-3pm & 7-10pm Mon-Sat;) Located just off Tomar's main square, this family-friendly local hangout features warm, attentive service, good traditional food and ridiculous (read: more-than-ample) portions. A great spot to experience local fare. The cod pie is a standout.

Information

Turismo (☎249 329 823; www.cm-tomar.pt; Avenida Dr Cândido Madureira; 9.30am-12.30pm & 2-6pm) Offers a good town map, an accommodation list and information about a historical trail.

Getting There & Away

Frequent trains run to Lisbon (€9.65 to €10.85, 1¾ to two hours).

Coimbra

POP POP 101,455

Coimbra is a dynamic, fashionable, yet comfortably lived-in city, with a student life centred on the magnificent 13th-century university. Aesthetically eclectic, there are elegant shopping streets, ancient stone walls and backstreet alleys with hidden *tascas* (taverns) and fado bars. Coimbra was the birth and burial place of Portugal's first king, and was the country's most important city when the Moors captured Lisbon. It's also home to a slightly different kind of *fado* music.

Sights

★Universidade de Coimbra UNIVERSITY
(☎239 242 744; www.uc.pt/en/informacaopara/visit/paco; adult/student €9/7, tower €1; 9am-7.30pm mid-Mar–Oct, 9.30am-1pm & 2-5.30pm Nov–mid-Mar) The city's high point, the university nucleus, consists of a series of remarkable 16th- to 18th-century buildings, all set within and around the vast Páteo das Escolas ('patio' or courtyard). These include the **Paço das Escolas (Royal Palace)**, **clock tower**, **Prisão Acadêmica (prison)**, **Capela de São Miguel (chapel)** and **Biblioteca Joanina** (João V Library; ☎239 859 818). Visitors to the library are admitted in small groups every 20 minutes. Buy your ticket at the university's visitor centre near the Porta Férrea. With the exception of the library, you can enter and explore on your own, or head off with a knowledgable university tour guide on one of three different tours (€12.50/15/20). These take place daily at 11am and 3pm.

★Museu Nacional de Machado de Castro MUSEUM
(☎239 853 070; www.museumachadocastro.pt; Largo Dr José Rodrigues; adult/child €6/free, cryptoportico only €3, with audio guide €7.50; 2-6pm Tue, 10am-7pm Wed-Sun Apr-Sep, 2-6pm Tue, 10am-6pm Wed-Sun Oct-Mar) This great museum is a highlight of central Portugal. It's built over the Roman forum, the remains of which can be seen and cover several levels. Part of the visit takes you down to the vaulted, spooky and immensely atmospheric galleries of the cryptoportico that allowed the forum to be level on such a hilly site. The artistic collection is wide-ranging and superb. The route starts with sculpture, from the architectural (column capitals) through Gothic religious sculpture and so on.

★Sé Velha CATHEDRAL
(Old Cathedral; ☎239 825 273; www.sevelha-coimbra.org; Largo da Sé Velha, Rua do Norte 4; €2.50; 10am-6pm Mon-Sat, 1-6pm Sun) Coimbra's stunning 12th-century cathedral is one of Portugal's finest examples of Romanesque architecture. The main portal and facade are exceptionally striking. Its crenellated exterior and narrow, slit-like lower windows serve

as reminders of the nation's embattled early days, when the Moors were still a threat. These buildings were designed to be useful as fortresses in times of trouble.

Sleeping

★ Serenata Hostel HOSTEL €
(☎239 853 130; www.serenatahostel.com; Largo da Sé Velha 21; dm/d without bathroom €15/38, d/ste/f with bathroom €49/55/79;) In the pretty heart of the (noisy-at-night) old town, this noble building with an intriguingly varied history has been converted to a fabulous hostel, chock-full of modern comforts and facilities while maintaining a period feel in keeping with this historic zone. Great lounge areas, a cute, secluded sun terrace, spacious dorms and a modern kitchen complete a very happy picture.

★ Casa Pombal GUESTHOUSE €€
(☎239 835 175; www.casapombal.com; Rua das Flores 18; s with/without bathroom €55/40, d with/without bathroom €65/54; @) In a lovely old-town location, this winning, Dutch-run guesthouse squeezes tons of charm into a small space. You can forgive the odd blip for the delicious breakfast (served in a gorgeous blue-tiled room) and the friendly staff who provide multilingual advice. Nine cosy wood-floored rooms (five with shared bathroom) are individually decorated in historical style; a couple boast magnificent views.

★ Quinta das Lágrimas HOTEL €€€
(☎239 802 380; www.quintadaslagrimas.pt; Rua António Augusto Gonçalves; r €160-260; P) This splendid historical palace is now one of Portugal's most enchanting upper-crust hotels. Choose between richly furnished rooms in the old palace, or Scandinavian-style minimalism in the modern annexe – complete with Jacuzzi. A few rooms look out on to the garden where Dona Inês de Castro reputedly met her tragic end. Discounts are sometimes available online, even in high season, and it's cheaper midweek.

Eating & Drinking

★ Tapas Nas Costas TAPAS €€
(☎239 157 425; www.tapasnascostas.pt; Rua Quebra Costas 19; tapas €3.50-6.60; noon-midnight Tue-Sat) *The* 'hotspot' about town at the time of research, this sophisticated tapas joint delivers delicious tapas. Decor is stylish, as are the gourmet-style goodies, such as *ovo com alheira de caça e grelos* (sausage with turnip greens and egg; €5.60). What are 'small-to-medium' sized servings for Portuguese are possibly 'normal' for anyone else, so share plates are a satisfying experience.

Restaurante Zé Neto PORTUGUESE €€
(☎239 826 786; Rua das Azeiteiras 8; mains €9-14; 9am-3pm & 7pm-midnight Mon-Sat) This marvellous family-run place specialises in homemade Portuguese standards, including *cabrito* (kid; half portions €6). Things have been modernised by the elderly owner's daughter, who is the chef (until recently her father used to tap out the menu on a vintage typewriter), but thankfully, it hasn't lost its flair for producing great meats.

★ Café Santa Cruz CAFE
(☎239 833 617; www.cafesantacruz.com; Praça 8 de Maio; 7.30am-midnight Mon-Sat) One of Portugal's most atmospheric cafes, where the elderly statesmen meet for their daily cuppas. Santa Cruz is set in a dramatically beautiful high-vaulted former chapel, with stained-glass windows and graceful stone arches. The terrace grants lovely views of Praça 8 de Maio. Don't miss the *crúzios*, award-winning, egg- and almond-based conventual cakes for which the cafe is famous.

★ Galeria Santa Clara BAR
(☎239 441 657; www.galeriasantaclara.com; Rua António Augusto Gonçalves 67; 1pm-2am Mon-Fri, to 3am Sat & Sun) Arty tearoom by day and chilled-out bar by night, this terrific place across the Mondego has good art on the walls, a series of sunny rooms and a fine terrace. It's got a great indoor-outdoor vibe and can feel like a party in a private house when things get going.

WORTH A TRIP

ROMAN RUINS

Conimbriga (ruins & museum adult/child €4.50/free; 10am-7pm), 16km south of Coimbra, is the site of the well-preserved ruins of a Roman town, including mosaic floors, elaborate baths and trickling fountains. It's a fascinating place to explore, with a **museum** that describes the once-flourishing and later abandoned town. Frequent buses run to Condeixa, 2km from the site; there are also two direct buses from Coimbra.

✪ Entertainment

Coimbra-style fado is more cerebral than the Lisbon variety, and its adherents are staunchly protective.

★ Fado ao Centro FADO

(☎910 679 838; www.fadoaocentro.com; Rua Quebra Costas 7; show incl drink €10) At the bottom of the old town, this friendly fado centre is a good place to introduce yourself to the genre. There's a performance every evening at 6pm. Shows include plenty of explanation, in Portuguese and English, about the history of Coimbra fado and the meaning of each song. It's tourist-oriented, but the performers enjoy it and do it well.

ℹ Information

Turismo Largo da Portagem (☎239 488 120; www.turismodecoimbra.pt; Largo da Portagem; ⏲9am-6pm Mon-Fri, 9am-1pm & 2-6pm Sat & Sun mid-Sep–mid-Jun, 9am-8pm Mon-Fri, 9am-6pm Sat & Sun mid-Jun–mid-Sep) By the bridge, in the centre of things.

ℹ Getting There & Away

BUS

From the rather grim **bus station** (Av Fernão de Magalhães), a 15-minute walk northwest of the centre, **Rede Expressos** (☎239 855 270; www.rede-expressos.pt) runs at least a dozen buses daily to Lisbon (€14.50, 2½ hours) and to Porto (€12, 1½ hours), with almost as many to Braga (€14, 2¾ hours) and to Faro (€27, six to nine hours).

TRAIN

Long-distance trains stop only at **Coimbra B** station, north of the city. Cross the platform for quick, free connections to more-central **Coimbra A** (called just 'Coimbra' on timetables).

Coimbra is linked by regular Alfa Pendular (AP) and *intercidade* (IC) trains to Lisbon (AP/IC €22.80/19.20, 1¾/two hours) and Porto (€16.70/13.20, one/1¼ hours); IC trains also stop at intermediate destinations north and south. Trains run roughly hourly to Figueira da Foz (€2.65, one hour) and Aveiro (€5.25, one hour).

Luso & the Buçaco Forest

This sylvan region harbours a lush forest of century-old trees surrounded by countryside that's dappled with heather, wildflowers and leafy ferns. There's even a fairy-tale **palace** (☎231 937 970; www.themahotels.pt; Mata Nacional do Buçaco; mains €11.50-15; ⏲8-10.30am, 1-3pm & 8-10pm; ✎) here, a 1907 neo-Manueline extravagance, where deep-pocketed visitors can dine or stay overnight. The palace lies amid the Mata Nacional do Buçaco, a forest criss-crossed with trails, dotted with crumbling chapels and graced with ponds, fountains and exotic trees. Buçaco was chosen as a retreat by 16th-century monks, and it surrounds the lovely spa town of Luso. From the centre, it's a 2km walk through forest up to the palace.

The **Maloclinic Spa** (www.maloclinictermasluso.com; Rua Álvaro Castelões; ⏲8am-1pm & 2-7pm daily high season, 9am-1pm & 2-6pm Mon-Sat low season) offers a range of soothing treatments.

🛏 Sleeping & Eating

Alegre Hotel BOUTIQUE HOTEL €

(☎231 930 256; www.alegrehotels.com; Rua Emídio Navarro 2, Luso; s/d €45/55; P 📶 🏊) This grand, atmospheric, pinkish-coloured 19th-century town house has large doubles with plush drapes, decorative plaster ceilings and polished period furniture. Its appeal is enhanced by an elegant entryway, formal parlour and pretty vine-draped garden with pool.

Palace Hotel do Buçaco HOTEL €€€

(☎231 937 970; www.themahotels.pt; Mata Nacional do Buçaco; s €148-199, d €169-225; P) This sumptuous royal palace was originally a hunting lodge (completed in 1907). It sits in the middle of the forest and offers a delightfully ostentatious place to stay. Common areas are stunning – particularly the tilework above the grand staircase – though some rooms feel a little musty and threadbare. Don't expect flatscreen TVs or period furniture, but do expect stunning marble bathrooms.

ℹ Information

Turismo (☎231 939 133; Rua Emídio Navarro 136, Luso; ⏲9.30am-1pm & 2.30-5.30pm) Has accommodation information, internet access, and town and forest maps, and is helpful.

ℹ Getting There & Away

Buses to/from Coimbra (around €4, 40 minutes) run four times daily each weekday and twice daily on Saturdays. Trains to/from Coimbra B station (€2.60, 25 minutes) run several times daily; it's a 15-minute walk to town from the station.

THE NORTH

Beneath the edge of Spanish Galicia, northern Portugal is a land of lush river valleys, sparkling coastline, granite peaks and virgin forests. This region is also gluttony for wine lovers: it's the home of the sprightly *vinho verde* wine (a young, slightly sparkling white or red wine) and ancient vineyards along the dramatic Rio Douro. Gateway to the north is Porto, a beguiling riverside city blending both medieval and modern attractions. Smaller towns and villages also offer cultural allure, from majestic Braga, the country's religious heart, to the seaside beauty Viana do Castelo.

Porto

POP 237,600

From across the Rio Douro at sunset, romantic Porto looks like a pop-up town – a colourful tumbledown dream with medieval relics, soaring bell towers, extravagant baroque churches and stately beaux-arts buildings piled on top of one another, illuminated by streaming shafts of sun. If you squint you might be able to make out the open windows, the narrow lanes and the staircases zigzagging to nowhere.

A lively walkable city with chatter in the air and a tangible sense of history, Porto's old-world riverfront district is a Unesco World Heritage site. Across the water twinkle the neon signs of Vila Nova de Gaia, the headquarters of the major port manufacturers.

Sights & Activities

Perfect for a languid stroll, the **Ribeira** district – Porto's riverfront nucleus – is a remarkable window into the city's history. Along the riverside promenade, *barcos rabelos* (the traditional boats used to ferry port wine down the Douro) bob beneath the shadow of the photogenic Ponte de Dom Luís I.

A few kilometres west of the city centre, the seaside suburb of **Foz do Douro** is a prime destination on hot summer weekends. It has a long beach promenade and a smattering of oceanfront bars and restaurants.

★Palácio da Bolsa HISTORIC BUILDING

(Stock Exchange; www.palaciodabolsa.com; Rua Ferreira Borges; tours adult/child €8/4.50; ⌚9am-6.30pm Apr-Oct, 9am-12.30pm & 2-5.30pm Nov-Mar) This splendid neoclassical monument (built from 1842 to 1910) honours Porto's past and present money merchants. Just past the entrance is the glass-domed **Pátio das Nações** (Hall of Nations), where the exchange once operated. But this pales in comparison with rooms deeper inside; to visit these, join one of the half-hour guided tours, which set off every 30 minutes.

★Sé CATHEDRAL

(Terreiro da Sé; cloisters adult/student €3/2; ⌚9am-12.30pm & 2.30-7pm Apr-Oct, to 6pm Nov-Mar) From Praça da Ribeira rises a tangle of medieval alleys and stairways that eventually reach the hulking, hilltop fortress of the cathedral. Founded in the 12th century, it was largely rebuilt a century later and then extensively altered during the 18th century. However, you can still make out the church's Romanesque origins in the barrel-vaulted nave. Inside, a rose window and a 14th-century Gothic cloister also remain from its early days.

★Igreja de São Francisco CHURCH

(Praça Infante Dom Henrique; adult/child €4/2; ⌚9am-8pm Jul-Sep, to 7pm Mar-Jun & Oct, to 6pm Nov-Feb) Sitting on Praça Infante Dom Henrique, Igreja de São Francisco looks from the outside to be an austerely Gothic church, but inside it hides one of Portugal's most dazzling displays of baroque finery. Hardly a centimetre escapes unsmothered, as otherworldly cherubs and sober monks are drowned by nearly 100kg of gold leaf. If you see only one church in Porto, make it this one.

★Jardim do Palácio de Cristal GARDENS

(Rua Dom Manuel II; ⌚8am-9pm Apr-Sep, to 7pm Oct-Mar) Sitting atop a bluff, this gorgeous botanical garden is one of Porto's best-loved escapes, with lawns interwoven with sun-dappled paths and dotted with fountains, sculptures, giant magnolias, camellias, and cypress and olive trees. It's actually a mosaic of small gardens that open up little by little as you wander – as do the stunning views of the city and Rio Douro.

★Serralves MUSEUM

(www.serralves.pt; Rua Dom João de Castro 210; adult/child museums & park €10/free, park only €5/free, 10am-1pm 1st Sun of the month free; ⌚10am-7pm Tue-Fri, to 8pm Sat & Sun May-Sep, reduced hours Oct-Mar) This fabulous cultural

Porto

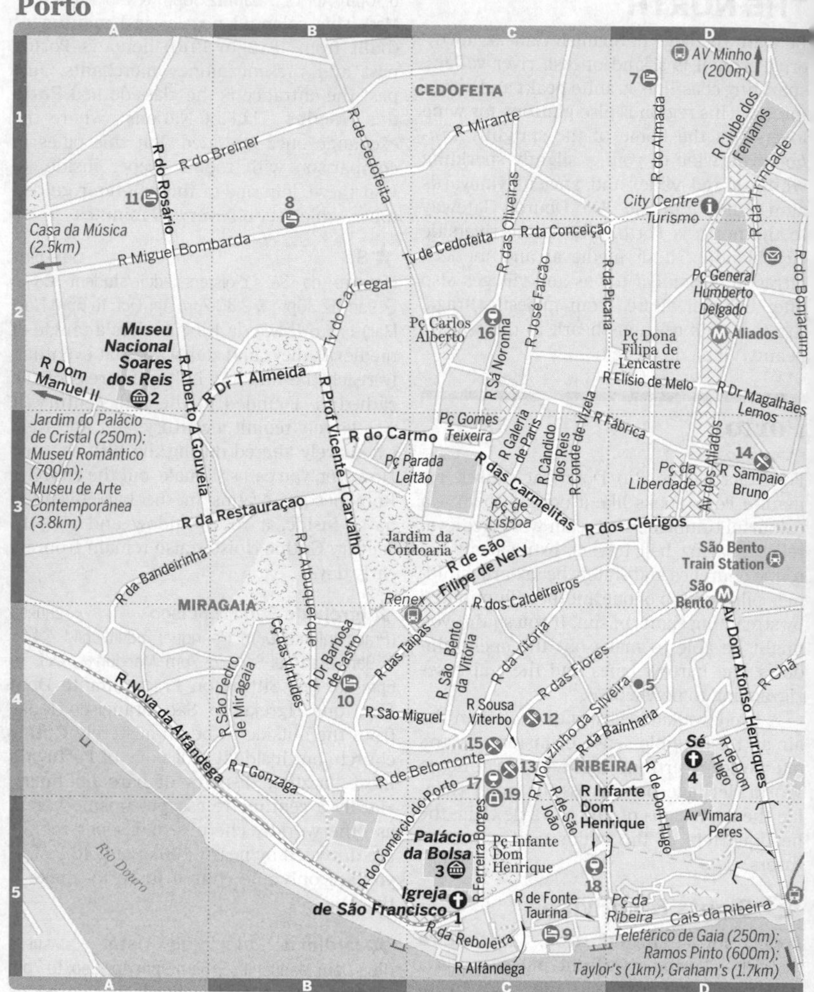

institution combines a museum, a mansion and extensive gardens. Cutting-edge exhibitions, along with a fine permanent collection featuring works from the late 1960s to the present, are showcased in the **Museu de Arte Contemporânea**, an arrestingly minimalist, whitewashed space designed by the eminent Porto-based architect Álvaro Siza Vieira. The delightful pink **Casa de Serralves** is a prime example of art deco, bearing the imprint of French architect Charles Siclis. One ticket gets you into both museums.

★ Museu Nacional Soares dos Reis — MUSEUM

(www.museusoaresdosreis.pt; Rua Dom Manuel II 44; adult/child €5/free,1st Sun of the month free; ⏲10am-6pm Tue-Sun) Porto's best art museum presents a stellar collection ranging from Neolithic carvings to Portugal's take on modernism, all housed in the formidable Palácio das Carrancas.

Teleférico de Gaia — CABLE CAR

(www.gaiacablecar.com; one-way/return €5/8; ⏲10am-8pm May-Sep, to 6pm Oct-Mar) Don't miss a ride on the Teleférico de Gaia, an

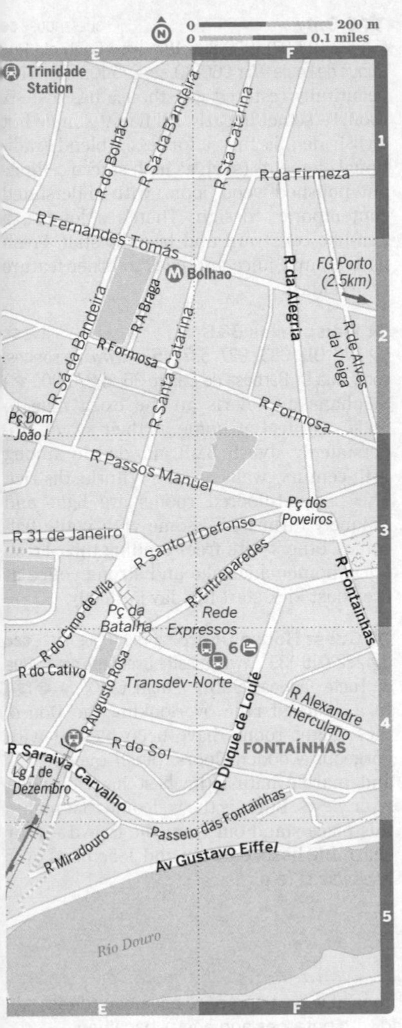

Porto

Top Sights

1 Igreja de São Francisco C5
2 Museu Nacional Soares dos Reis A2
3 Palácio da Bolsa C5
4 Sé D4

Activities, Courses & Tours

5 Other Side D4

Sleeping

6 6 Only F4
7 Canto de Luz D1
8 Gallery Hostel B2
9 Guest House Douro C5
10 Maison Nos B&B B4
11 ROSA ET AL Townhouse A1

Eating

12 Cantina 32 .... C4
13 DOP C4
14 Flor dos Congregados D3
15 Taberna do Largo C4

Drinking & Nightlife

16 Aduela C2
17 Prova C4
18 Vinologia C5

Shopping

19 Oliva & Co C4

aerial gondola that provides fine views over the Douro and Porto on its short, five-minute jaunt. It runs between the southern end of the Ponte Dom Luís I and the riverside.

★Taste Porto Food Tours TOURS

(☎967 258 750; www.tasteportofoodtours.com; food tour adult/child €59/39; ⊙food tours 10am, 10.30am & 4pm Tue-Sat) Loosen a belt notch for these superb half-day food tours, where you'll sample everything from Porto's best slow-roast-pork sandwich to éclairs, fine wines, cheese and coffee. Friendly, knowledgeable André and his team lead these indulgent 3½-hour walking tours, which take in viewpoints, historic back lanes and the Mercado do Bolhão en route to restaurants, grocery stores and cafes.

★Other Side TOURS

(☎916 500 170; www.theotherside.pt; Rua Souto 67; ⊙9am-8pm) Well-informed, congenial guides reveal their city on half-day walking tours of hidden Porto (€19), *petisco* (tapas) trails (€25), and e-bike tours of Porto and Foz (€29). They can also venture further afield with full-day trips to the Douro's vineyards (€85) and to Guimarães and Braga (€69).

Festivals & Events

Festa de São João RELIGIOUS

(St John's Festival) Porto's biggest party. For one night in June, on the 24th, the city erupts into music, competitions and riotous parties; this is also when merrymakers pound each other on the head with squeaky plastic mallets (you've been warned).

Serralves Em Festa CULTURAL
(www.serralvesemfesta.com; ⏲Jun) This huge (free) celebration runs for 40 hours nonstop over one weekend in early June. Parque de Serralves hosts the main events, with concerts, avant-garde theatre and kiddie activities. Other open-air events happen all over town.

Sleeping

★Gallery Hostel HOSTEL €
(☎224 964 313; www.gallery-hostel.com; Rua Miguel Bombarda 222; dm/d/tr/ste from €22/64/80/90; ❄📶) A true travellers' hub, this hostel-gallery has clean and cosy dorms and doubles, a sunny, glass-enclosed back patio, a grassy terrace, a cinema room, a shared kitchen and a bar-music room. Throw in its free walking tours, homemade dinners on request, port-wine tastings and concerts, and you'll see why it's booked up so often – reserve ahead.

★Canto de Luz B&B €€
(☎225 492 142; www.cantodeluz.com; Rua do Almada 539; r €70-95; 📶) *Ah oui,* this French-run guesthouse, just a five-minute walk from Trindade metro, is a delight. Rooms are light, spacious and make the leap between classic and contemporary, with vintage furnishings used to clever effect. Your kindly hosts André and Brigitte prepare delicious breakfasts, with fresh-squeezed juice, pastries and homemade preserves. There's also a pretty garden terrace.

★6 Only GUESTHOUSE €€
(☎222 013 971, 926 885 187; www.6only.pt; Rua Duque de Loulé 97; r €60-80, ste €75-100; 📶) This beautifully restored guesthouse has just six rooms – so get in early. All flaunt simple but stylish details that effortlessly blend traditional elements (such as high stucco ceilings and polished-wood floors) with understated contemporary design. There's a lounge, a Zen-like courtyard and friendly staff. Fresh pastries and juice and eggs to order feature at breakfast.

★Maison Nos B&B B&B €€
(☎222 011 683, 927 537 457; www.maisonnos.com; Rua Dr Barbosa de Castro 36; d €70-90; 📶) Stéphane and Baris go the extra mile to make you feel at home at their sweet, understatedly stylish B&B, nuzzled in among 14th-century walls in the Vitória district. The parquet-floored rooms are light and uniquely furnished – some with petite balconies, others with free-standing tubs. Fresh juice, homemade cake and strong coffee at breakfast kick-start the day perfectly.

★Guest House Douro BOUTIQUE HOTEL €€€
(☎222 015 135; www.guesthousedouro.com; Rua da Fonte Taurina 99-101; r from €140; ❄@📶) In a restored relic overlooking the Douro, these eight rooms have been blessed with gorgeous wooden floors, plush queen beds and marble baths; the best have dazzling river views. But it is the welcome that makes this place stand out from the crowd – your charming hosts Carmen and João bend over backwards to please.

ESSENTIAL FOOD & DRINK

Cod for all seasons The Portuguese have dozens of ways to prepare bacalhau (dried salt cod). Try bacalhau a brás (grated cod fried with potatoes and eggs), bacalhau espiritual (cod soufflé) or bacalhau com natas (baked cod with cream and grated cheese).

Drink Port and red wines from the Douro valley, alvarinho and vinho verde (crisp, semi-sparkling wine) from the Minho and great, little-known reds from the Alentejo and the Beiras (particularly the Dão region).

Field & fowl Porco preto (sweet 'black' pork), leitão (roast suckling pig), alheira (bread and meat sausage – formerly Kosher), cabrito assado (roast kid) and arroz de pato (duck risotto).

Pastries The *pastel de nata* (custard tart) is legendary, especially in Belém. Other delicacies: travesseiros (almond and egg pastries) and queijadas (mini-cheese pastries).

Seafood Char-grilled *lulas* (squid), *polvo* (octopus) or *sardinhas* (sardines). Other treats: *cataplana* (seafood and sausage cooked in a copper pot), *caldeirada* (hearty fish stew) and *açorda de mariscos* (bread stew with shrimp).

Eating

Taberna do Largo PORTUGUESE €

(222 082 154; Largo de São Domingos 69; petiscos €2-14; 5pm-midnight Tue-Thu, to 1am Fri, noon-1am Sat, noon-midnight Sun,) Lit by wine-bottle lights, this sweet grocery store, deli and tavern is run with passion by Joana and Sofia. Tour Portugal with your taste buds with their superb array of hand-picked wines, which go brilliantly with tasting platters of smoked tuna, Alentejo *salpicão* sausage, Azores São Jorge cheese, Beira *morcela* (blood sausage), *tremoços* (lupin beans) and more.

★ **Flor dos Congregados** PORTUGUESE €€

(222 002 822; www.flordoscongregados.pt; Travessa dos Congregados 11; mains €8-16; 7-10pm Mon, 10am-10pm Tue-Sat) Tucked away down a narrow alley, this softly lit, family-run restaurant brims with stone-walled, wood-beamed, art-slung nooks. The frequently changing blackboard menu goes with the seasons.

★ **Cantina 32** PORTUGUESE €€

(222 039 069; www.cantina32.com; Rua das Flores 32; petiscos €5-15; 12.30-2.30pm & 7.30-11pm;) Industrial-chic meets boho at this delightfully laid-back haunt, with its walls of polished concrete, mismatched crockery, verdant plants, and vintage knick-knacks ranging from a bicycle to an old typewriter. The menu is just as informal – *petiscos* such as *pica-pau* steak (bite-sized pieces of steak in a garlic and white-wine sauce), quail-egg croquettes, and cheesecake served in a flower pot reveal a pinch of creativity.

★ **DOP** GASTRONOMY €€€

(222 014 313; www.ruipaula.com; Largo de São Domingos 18; menus €20-56; 7-11pm Mon, 12.30-3pm & 7-11pm Tue-Sat;) Housed in the Palácio das Artes, DOP is one of Porto's most stylish addresses, with its high ceilings and slick, monochrome interior. Much-feted chef Rui Paula puts a creative, seasonal twist on outstanding ingredients, with dish after delicate, flavour-packed dish skipping from octopus carpaccio to cod with lobster rice. The three-course lunch is terrific value at €20.

Drinking & Nightlife

The bar-lined Rua Galeira de Paris and nearby streets are packed with revellers most nights. Down by the water, the open-air bar scene on Praça da Ribeira is great for drinks with a view.

DON'T MISS

TASTING PORT WINE

Sitting just across the Rio Douro from Porto, **Vila Nova da Gaia** is woven into the city's fabric by stunning bridges and a shared history of port-wine making. Since the mid-18th century, port-wine bottlers and exporters have maintained their lodges here.

Today, some 30 of these lodges clamber up the riverbank and most open their doors to the public for cellar tours and tastings. Among the best are **Taylor's** (223 772 956, 223 742 800; www.taylor.pt; Rua do Choupelo 250; tours incl tasting €12; 10am-6pm), **Graham's** (223 776 484; www.grahams-port.com; Rua do Agro 141; tours incl tasting €10-100; 9.30am-6pm) and **Ramos Pinto** (936 809 283; www.ramospinto.pt; Av Ramos Pinto 400; tours incl tasting €6; 10am-6pm May-Oct, reduced hours Nov-Apr).

★ **Prova** WINE BAR

(www.prova.com.pt; Rua Ferreira Borges 86; 4pm-2am Wed-Mon;) Diogo, the passionate owner, explains the finer nuances of Portuguese wine at this chic, stone-walled bar, where relaxed jazz plays. Stop by for a two-glass tasting (€5), or sample wines by the glass – including beefy Douros, full-bodied Dãos and crisp Alentejo whites. These marry well with sharing plates of local hams and cheeses (€14). Diogo's port tonics are legendary.

★ **Aduela** BAR

(Rua das Oliveiras 36; 3pm-2am Mon, 1pm-2am Tue-Sat, 2pm-midnight Sun) Retro and hip but not self-consciously so, chilled Aduela bathes in the nostalgic orange glow of its glass lights, which illuminate the green walls and mishmash of vintage furnishings. Once a sewing machine warehouse, today it's where friends gather to converse over wine and appetising *petiscos* (€3 to €8).

Vinologia WINE BAR

(www.vinologia.pt; Rua de São João 28-30; 11am-midnight) This cosy wine bar is an excellent place to sample the fine quaffs of Porto, with over 200 different ports on offer. If you fall in love with a certain wine, you can usually buy a whole bottle (or even send a case home).

✩ Entertainment

★ Casa da Música CONCERT VENUE

(House of Music; ☎220 120 220; www.casadamusica.com; Avenida da Boavista 604; ⏱box office 9.30am-7pm Mon-Sat, to 6pm Sun) Grand and minimalist, sophisticated yet populist, Porto's cultural behemoth boasts a shoebox-style concert hall at its heart, meticulously engineered to accommodate everything from jazz duets to Beethoven's Ninth.

FC Porto FOOTBALL

(www.fcporto.pt) The Estádio do Dragão is home to Primeira Liga heroes FC Porto. It's northeast of the centre, just off the VCI ring road (metro stop Estádio do Dragão).

ℹ Information

City Centre Turismo (☎223 393 472; www.visitporto.travel; Rua Clube dos Fenianos 25; ⏱9am-8pm May-Oct, to 7pm Nov-Apr) The main city *turismo* has a detailed city map, a transport map and the *Agenda do Porto* cultural calendar, among other printed materials.

Post Office (Praça General Humberto Delgado 320; ⏱8am-9pm Mon-Fri, 9am-6pm Sat) Across from the main tourist office.

Santo António Hospital (☎222 077 500; www.chporto.pt; Largo Prof Abel Salazar) Has English-speaking staff.

ℹ Getting There & Away

AIR

Porto's **airport** (OPO; ☎229 432 400; www.ana.pt) is connected by daily flights from Lisbon and London, and has direct links from other European cities, particularly with EasyJet and Ryanair.

BUS

Porto has many private bus companies leaving from different terminals; the main tourist office can help. In general, for Lisbon and the Algarve, the choice is **Renex** (www.renex.pt; Rua Campo Mártires de Pátria 37) or **Rede Expressos** (☎222 006 954; www.rede-expressos.pt; Rua Alexandre Herculano 366).

Three companies operate from or near Praceto Régulo Magauanha, off Rua Dr Alfredo Magalhães: **Transdev-Norte** (www.transdev.pt; Garagem Atlântico, Rua de Alexandre Herculano 366) goes to Braga (€6); **AV Minho** (www.avminho.pt) to Viana do Castelo (€8).

TRAIN

Porto is a northern Portugal rail hub. Most international trains, and all intercity links, start at Campanhã, 2km east of the centre.

At São Bento, you can book tickets to any other destination.

ℹ Getting Around

TO/FROM THE AIRPORT

The metro's 'violet' E line provides handy service to the airport. A one-way ride to the centre costs €1.85 and takes about 45 minutes. A daytime **taxi** costs €20 to €25 to/from the centre.

PUBLIC TRANSPORT

Save money on transport by purchasing a refillable **Andante Card** (€0.60), valid for transport on buses, metro, funicular and tram. You can buy them from STCP kiosks or newsagents. A 24-hour ticket for the entire public transport network, excluding trams, costs €7.

Bus

Central hubs of Porto's extensive bus system include Jardim da Cordoaria, Praça da Liberdade and São Bento station. Tickets purchased on the

WORTH A TRIP

THROUGH THE GRAPEVINES OF THE DOURO

Portugal's best-known river flows through the country's rural heartland. In the upper reaches, port-wine grapes are grown on steep terraced hills, punctuated by remote stone villages and, in spring, splashes of dazzling white almond blossom.

The Rio Douro is navigable right across Portugal. Highly recommended is the train journey from Porto to Pinhão (€11, 2½ hours, five daily), the last 70km clinging to the river's edge; trains continue to Pocinho (from Porto €13.30, 3¼ hours). **Porto Tours** (☎222 000 045; www.portotours.com; ⏱10am-7pm), situated next to Porto's cathedral, can arrange tours, including idyllic Douro cruises.

Cyclists and drivers can choose river-hugging roads along either bank, and can visit wineries along the way (check out www.dourovalley.eu for an extensive list of wineries open to visitors). You can also stay overnight in scenic wine lodges among the vineyards.

bus are one way €1.20/€1.85 with/without the Andante Card.

Funicular

The panoramic **Funicular dos Guindais** (one way €2.50; 8am-10pm May-Oct, to 8pm Nov-Apr) shuttles up and down a steep incline from Avenida Gustavo Eiffel to Rua Augusto Rosa.

Metro

Porto's **metro** (http://en.metrodoporto.pt) currently comprises six metropolitan lines that all converge at the Trinidade stop. Tickets cost €1.20 with an Andante Card. There are also various 24-hour passes (from €4.15) available.

Tram

Porto has three antique trams that trundle around town. The most useful line, 1E, travels along the Douro towards the Foz district. A single tram ticket costs €2.50, a day pass €8.

Viana do Castelo

POP 15,600

The jewel of the Costa Verde (Green Coast), Viana do Castelo has both an appealing medieval centre and lovely beaches just outside the city. In addition to its natural beauty, Viana do Castelo whips up some excellent seafood and hosts some magnificent traditional festivals, including the spectacular **Festa de Nossa Senhora da Agonia** in August.

Sights

The stately heart of town is **Praça da República**, with its delicate fountain and grandiose buildings, including the 16th-century **Misericórdia**, a former almshouse.

Monte de Santa Luzia HILL

There are two good reasons to visit Viana's 228m eucalyptus-clad hill. One is the wondrous view down the coast and up the Lima valley. The other is the fabulously over-the-top, 20th-century, neo-Byzantine **Templo do Sagrado Coração de Jesus** (Temple of the Sacred Heart of Jesus; 9am-6pm). You can get a little closer to heaven on its graffiti-covered roof, via a lift, followed by an elbow-scraping stairway – take the museum entrance on the ground floor.

Praia do Cabedelo BEACH

(ferry 9am-6pm) This is one of the Minho's best beaches: a 1km-long arch of blond, powdery sand that folds into grassy dunes backed by a grove of wind-blown pines. It's across the river from town, best reached on a five-minute **ferry trip** (one way/return adult €1.40/2.80, half-price/free under-12/under-six; to Praia do Cabedelo 9am-6pm) from the pier south of Largo 5 de Outubro.

Sleeping & Eating

★ Ó Meu Amor GUESTHOUSE €

(258 406 513; www.omeuamor.com; Rua do Poço 19; s/d without bathroom €25/45; @) Top choice in town right in the historic centre, this hideaway in a rambling town house full of nooks and crannies has nine adorable rooms with shared bathrooms. Guests can use the kitchen and cosy living room. Each room has a theme – such as the India and Africa rooms in the attic – and some have tiny balconies with rooftop and mountain views.

★ Margarida da Praça GUESTHOUSE €€

(258 809 630; www.margaridadapraca.com; Largo 5 de Outubro 58; s €60-75, d €78-88; @) Fantastically whimsical, this boutique inn offers thematic rooms in striking pinks, sea greens and whites, accented by stylish floral wallpaper, candelabra lanterns and lush duvets. The equally stylish lobby glows with candlelight in the evening.

O Pescador SEAFOOD €€

(258 826 039; Largo de São Domingos 35; mains €9.50-15.50; noon-3pm & 7-10pm Tue-Sat, noon-3pm Sun) A simple, friendly, family-run restaurant admired by locals for its good seafood, and tasty lunch specials (from €6.50).

Getting There & Away

Five to 10 trains go daily to Porto (€5 to €6.65, two hours), as well as express buses (€6.50, two hours).

Braga

POP 136,885

Portugal's third-largest city boasts a fine array of churches, their splendid baroque facades looming above the old plazas and narrow lanes of the historic centre. Lively cafes, trim little boutiques, and some good restaurants add to the appeal.

Sights

Sé CATHEDRAL

(www.se-braga.pt; Rua Dom Paio Mendes; 9am-7pm high season, 9am-6.30pm low season) Braga's extraordinary cathedral, the oldest in Portugal, was begun when the archdiocese was restored in 1070 and completed in the following century. It's a rambling complex made up of differing styles, and architecture buffs could spend half a day happily distinguishing the Romanesque bones from Manueline musculature and baroque frippery.

Museu dos Biscainhos MUSEUM
(Rua dos Biscainhos; adult/student €2/1, first Sun of the month free; 9.30am-12.45pm & 2-5.30pm Tue-Sun) An 18th-century aristocrat's palace is home to the enthusiastic municipal museum, with a nice collection of Roman relics and 17th- to 19th-century pottery and furnishings. The palace itself is the reason to come, with its polychrome, chestnut-panelled ceilings and 18th-century *azulejos* depicting hunting scenes. The ground floor is paved with deeply ribbed flagstones on which carriages would have once rattled through to the stables.

Sleeping

★Collector's Hostel HOSTEL €
(253 048 124; www.collectorshostel.com; Rua Francisco Sanches 42; dm €19-22, s/d €26/39) A lovely hostel, lovingly run by two well-travelled women who met in Paris (one of whom was born in the hostel's living room), restored the family house and all the furniture inside, and turned the three floors into a cosy hideaway where guests feel like they're in their grandparents' home, with a twist.

Tea 4 Nine GUESTHOUSE €€
(914 004 606; www.tea4nine.pt; Praça Conde Agrolongo 49; s/d €80/105) A swish new guesthouse with four stunning suites featuring clean-lined contemporary decor, pine floors and a full range of top-of-the-line amenities. Two face the square, two are out back, and three more sit in another building facing the square. Note that there's no elevator. The sweet downstairs bistro with a garden does great lunch menus and a Sunday brunch (€7.50).

Eating

Anjo Verde VEGETARIAN €
(Largo da Praça Velha 21; mains €7.50-8.60; noon-3pm & 7.30-10.30pm Mon-Sat;) Braga's vegetarian offering serves generous, elegantly presented plates in a lovely, airy dining room. Vegetarian lasagne, risotto and vegetable tarts are among the choices. Mains can be bland, but the spiced chocolate tart is a superstar.

Casa de Pasto das Carvalheiras FUSION €€
(253 046 244; Rua Dom Afonso Henriques 8; mains €4.50-14; noon-3pm & 7pm-midnight) This funky eatery with lots of colourful details and a long bar serves up flavourful fusion food served as *pratinhos* (small plates). The menus change weekly and feature dishes like salmon ceviche, *alheira* (a light garlicky sausage of poultry or game) rolls with turnip sprouts and black octopus polenta. Weekday lunch menus are a great deal (€8 or €12, depending on the number of dishes you order).

Information

Turismo (253 262 550; www.cm-braga.pt; Avenida da Liberdade 1; 9am-7pm Mon-Fri, 9am-12.30pm & 2-5.30pm Sat & Sun Jun-Sep, shorter hours in low season) Braga's helpful tourist office is in an art-deco-style building facing the fountain.

Getting There & Away

Trains run to/from Lisbon (€31, four hours, two to four daily), Coimbra (€19.80, 2¼ hours, five to seven daily) and Porto (€3.10, about one hour). Eight buses a day go to Viana do Castelo (€4.45, 1½ hours).

Parque Nacional da Peneda-Gerês

Spread across four impressive granite massifs, this vast park encompasses boulder-strewn peaks, precipitous valleys, gorse-clad moorlands and forests of oak and pine. It also shelters more than 100 granite villages that, in many ways, have changed little since Portugal's founding in the 12th century. For nature lovers, the stunning scenery here is unmatched in Portugal for camping, hiking and other outdoor adventures. The park's main centre is at **Vila do Gerês**, a sleepy, hot-springs village.

Activities

Hiking

There are trails and footpaths through the park, some between villages with accommodation. Leaflets detailing these are available from the park offices.

Day hikes around Vila do Gerês are popular. An adventurous option is the **old Roman road** from Mata do Albergaria (10km up-valley from Vila do Gerês), past the **Vilarinho das Furnas** reservoir to Campo do Gerês. More distant destinations include **Ermida** and **Cabril**, both with simple accommodation.

Cycling & Horse Riding

Mountain bikes can be hired in Campo do Gerês (15km northeast of Vila do Gerês) from **Equi Campo** (☎253 161 405; www.equicampo.com; ⏰9am-7pm Jun-Aug, 9am-7pm weekends Sep-May). Guides here also lead horse-riding trips, hikes and combination hiking/climbing/abseiling excursions.

Water Sports

Rio Caldo, 8km south of Vila do Gerês, is the base for water sports on the Caniçada Reservoir. English-run **AML** (☎253 391 779; www.aguamontanha.com; Lugar de Paredes) rents kayaks, pedal boats, rowing boats and small motorboats. It also organises kayaking trips along the Albufeira de Salamonde.

Sleeping & Eating

Vila do Gerês has plenty of *pensões* (guesthouses), but you may find vacancies are limited; many are block-booked by spa patients in summer.

Pousada do Gerês-Caniçada/São Bento POUSADA **€€€**
(☎210 407 650; www.pousadas.pt; Caniçada; s/d €180/190; P ❄ 📶 🏊) This lovely place has a spectacular setting. High above the Albufeira, it offers a splendid retreat at eagle's-nest heights. The rooms have wood-beamed ceilings and comfy furnishings; some have verandahs with magnificent views. There's a pool, gardens, a tennis court, and an excellent restaurant serving local delicacies (trout, roasted goat). To get here head south 3km from Rio Caldo along the N304, following signs to Caniçada.

Information

The head park office is **Adere-PG** (☎258 452 250; www.adere-pg.pt; Rua Dom Manuel I; ⏰9am-12.30pm & 2.30-6pm Mon-Fri) in Ponte de Barca. Obtain park information and reserve cottages and other park accommodation here.

Getting There & Away

Because of the lack of transport within the park, it's good to have your own wheels. You can rent cars in **Braga** (☎253 203 910; Rua Gabriel Pereira de Castro 28; ⏰9am-7pm Mon-Fri, 9am-12.30pm Sat).

SURVIVAL GUIDE

Directory A–Z

ACCOMMODATION

Portugal offers outstanding value by and large. Budget places provide some of Western Europe's cheapest digs, while you'll find atmospheric accommodation in converted castles, mansions and farmhouses.

Seasons

High season Mid-June to mid-September.

Mid-season May to mid-June and mid-September to October.

Low season November to April.

Ecotourism & Farmstays

Turismo de Habitação is a private network of historic, heritage or rustic properties, ranging from 17th-century manors to quaint farmhouses or self-catering cottages. Doubles run from €60 to €120.

Pousadas

These are government-run former castles, monasteries or palaces, often in spectacular locations. For details, contact tourist offices or Pousadas de Portugal.

Guesthouses

The most common types are the *residencial* and the *pensão:* usually simple, family-owned operations. Some have cheaper rooms with shared bathrooms. Double rooms with private bathroom typically run €40 to €60.

Hostels

Portugal has a growing number of cool backpacker digs, particularly in Lisbon. Nationwide, Portugal has over 30 pousadas da juventude within the Hostelling International (HI) system. The average price for a dorm room is about €20.

Camping

For detailed listings of campsites nationwide, pick up the Roteiro Campista, updated annually and sold at bookshops. Some of the swishest

SLEEPING PRICE RANGES

The following price ranges refer to a double room with bathroom in high season. Unless otherwise stated. breakfast is included in the price.

€ less than €60

€€ €60–€120

€€€ more than €120

places are run by **Orbitur** (☎226 061 360; www.orbitur.pt).

MONEY

ATMs are widely available, except in the smallest villages. Credit cards accepted in midrange and high-end establishments.

OPENING HOURS

Opening hours vary throughout the year. We provide high-season opening hours; hours will generally decrease in the shoulder and low seasons.

Banks 8.30am–3pm Monday to Friday

Bars 7pm–2am

Cafes 9am–7pm

Clubs 11pm–4am Thursday to Saturday

Restaurants noon–3pm and 7–10pm

Shopping malls 10am–10pm

Shops 9.30am–noon and 2–7pm Monday to Friday, 10am–1pm Saturday

PUBLIC HOLIDAYS

Banks, offices, department stores and some shops close on the public holidays listed here. On New Year's Day, Easter Sunday, Labour Day and Christmas Day, even *turismos* close.

New Year's Day 1 January

Carnaval Tuesday February/March – the day before Ash Wednesday

Good Friday March/April

Liberty Day 25 April

Labour Day 1 May

Corpus Christi May/June – ninth Thursday after Easter

Portugal Day 10 June – also known as Camões and Communities Day

Feast of the Assumption 15 August

Republic Day 5 October

All Saints' Day 1 November

Independence Day 1 December

Feast of the Immaculate Conception 8 December

Christmas Day 25 December

TELEPHONE

Portugal's country code is ☎351. There are no regional area codes. Mobile phone numbers within Portugal have nine digits and begin with ☎9.

For general information, dial ☎118, and for reverse-charge (collect) calls dial ☎120.

EATING PRICE RANGES

The following price ranges refer to a main course.

€ less than €10

€€ €10–20

€€€ more than €20

RESOURCES

Lonely Planet (www.lonelyplanet.com/portugal)

Portugal Tourism (www.visitportugal.com)

Getting There & Away

AIR

Most international flights arrive in Lisbon, though Porto and Faro also receive some. For more information, including live arrival and departure schedules, see www.ana.pt.

LAND

Bus

The major long-distance carriers that serve European destinations are Busabout (www.busabout.com) and Eurolines (www.eurolines.com); though these carriers serve Portugal, it is not currently included in the multicity travel passes of either company.

For some European routes, Eurolines is affiliated with the big Portuguese operators **Internorte** (☎707 200 512; www.internorte.pt) and **Eva Transportes** (☎289 899 760; www.eva-bus.com).

Train

The most popular train link from Spain is on the Sud Express, operated by Renfe, which has a nightly sleeper service between Madrid and Lisbon.

Two other Spain–Portugal crossings are at Valença do Minho and at Caia (Caya in Spain), near Elvas.

Getting Around

AIR

TAP Portugal has daily Lisbon–Porto and Lisbon–Faro flights (taking less than one hour) year round.

BUS

A host of small bus operators, most amalgamated into regional companies, run a dense network of services across the country. Among the largest companies are **Rede Expressos** (☎707 223 344; www.rede-expressos.pt), **Rodonorte** (☎259 340 710; www.rodonorte.pt) and the Algarve line **Eva** (p562).

Most bus-station ticket desks will give you a computer printout of fares, and services and schedules are usually posted at major stations.

Classes

Bus services are of four general types:

Alta Qualidade A fast deluxe category offered by some companies.

Carreiras Marked 'CR'; slow, stopping at every crossroad.

Expressos Comfortable, fast buses between major cities.

Rápidas Quick regional buses.

CAR & MOTORCYCLE

Automobile Associations

Automóvel Clube de Portugal (ACP; ☎213 180 100, 24hr emergency assistance 808 222 222; www.acp.pt) has a reciprocal arrangement with better-known foreign automobile clubs, including AA and RAC. It provides medical, legal and breakdown assistance. The 24-hour emergency help number is %707 509 510.

Hire

To hire a car in Portugal you must be at least 25 years old and have held your home licence for over a year. To hire a scooter of up to 50cc you must be over 18 years old and have a valid driving licence.

Road Rules

The various speed limits for cars and motorcycles are 50km/h within cities and public centres, 90km/h on normal roads and 120km/h on motorways.

The legal blood-alcohol limit is 0.5g/L, and there are fines of up to €2500 for drink-driving. It's also illegal in Portugal to drive while talking on a mobile phone.

TRAIN

Caminhos de Ferro Portugueses is the statewide train network and is generally efficient.

There are four main types of long-distance service. Note that international services are marked 'IN' on timetables.

Alfa Pendular Deluxe, marginally faster and much pricier service.

Interregional (IR) Reasonably fast trains.

Intercidade (IC) or Rápido Express trains.

Regional (marked R on timetables) Slow trains that stop everywhere.

Spain

Includes ➡

Best Places to Eat

- Casa Delfín (p594)
- La Cuchara de San Telmo (p603)
- Cinc Sentits (p595)
- El Poblet (p610)
- Adolfo (p584)

Best Places to Stay

- Un Patio en Santa Cruz (p619)
- Balcón de Córdoba (p622)
- Barceló Raval (p593)
- Hotel Costa Vella (p607)
- Hospedería La Gran Casa Mudéjar (p582)

Why Go?

Passionate, sophisticated and devoted to living the good life, Spain is at once a stereotype come to life and a country more diverse than you ever imagined.

Spanish landscapes stir the soul, from the jagged Pyrenees and wildly beautiful cliffs of the Atlantic northwest to charming Mediterranean coves, while astonishing architecture spans the ages at seemingly every turn. Spain's cities march to a beguiling beat with cutting-edge architecture and unrivalled nightlife, even as time-capsule villages serve as beautiful signposts to Old Spain. And then there's one of Europe's most celebrated (and varied) gastronomic scenes.

But, above all, Spain lives very much in the present. Perhaps you'll sense it along a crowded after-midnight street when all the world has come out to play. Or maybe that moment will come when a flamenco performer touches something deep in your soul. Whenever it happens, you'll find yourself nodding in recognition: *this* is Spain.

When to Go

Madrid

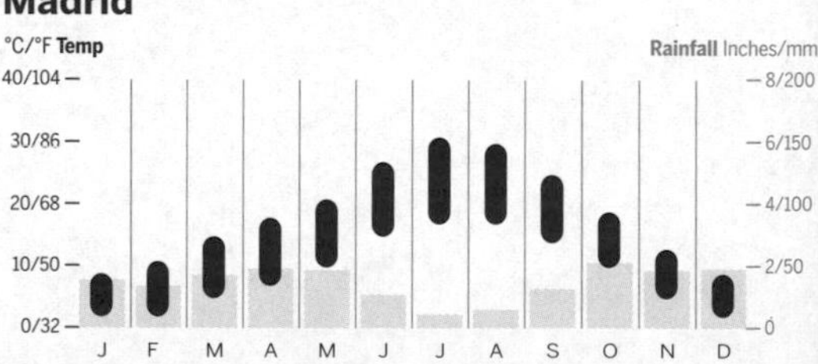

Mar–Apr Spring wildflowers, Semana Santa processions and mild southern temps.

May, Jun & Sep Balmy weather but without the crowds of high summer.

Jul–Aug Spaniards hit the coast in the summer heat, but quiet corners still abound.

MADRID

POP 3.3 MILLION

No city on earth is more alive than Madrid, a beguiling place whose sheer energy carries a simple message: this city really knows how to live. Explore the old streets of the centre, relax in the plazas, soak up the culture in Madrid's excellent art museums, and spend at least one night in the city's legendary nightlife scene.

Sights

★Museo del Prado MUSEUM

(Map p570; www.museodelprado.es; Paseo del Prado; adult/child €15/free, 6-8pm Mon-Sat & 5-7pm Sun free, audio guides €3.50, admission plus official guidebook €24; 10am-8pm Mon-Sat, 10am-7pm Sun; ; M Banco de España) Welcome to one of the world's premier art galleries. The more than 7000 paintings held in the Museo del Prado's collection (although only around 1500 are currently on display) are like a window onto the historical vagaries of the Spanish soul, at once grand and imperious in the royal paintings of Velázquez, darkly tumultuous in *Las pinturas negras* (The Black Paintings) of Goya, and outward looking with sophisticated works of art from all across Europe.

★Centro de Arte Reina Sofía MUSEUM

(Map p574; 91 774 10 00; www.museoreinasofia.es; Calle de Santa Isabel 52; adult/concession €8/free, 1.30-7pm Sun, 7-9pm Mon & Wed-Sat free; 10am-9pm Mon & Wed-Sat, 10am-7pm Sun; M Atocha) Home to Picasso's *Guernica*, arguably Spain's most famous artwork, the Centro de Arte Reina Sofía is Madrid's premier collection of contemporary art. In addition to plenty of paintings by Picasso, other major drawcards are works by Salvador Dalí (1904–89) and Joan Miró (1893–1983). The collection principally spans the 20th century up to the 1980s. The occasional non-Spaniard artist makes an appearance (including Francis Bacon's *Lying Figure;* 1966), but most of the collection is strictly peninsular.

★Plaza Mayor SQUARE

(Map p574; M Sol) Madrid's grand central square, a rare but expansive opening in the tightly packed streets of central Madrid, is one of the prettiest open spaces in Spain, a winning combination of imposing architecture, picaresque historical tales and vibrant street life coursing across its cobblestones. At once beautiful in its own right and a reference point for so many Madrid days, it also hosts the city's main tourist office, a Christmas market in December and arches leading to laneways leading out into the labyrinth.

★Museo Thyssen-Bornemisza MUSEUM

(Map p574; 902 760511; www.museothyssen.org; Paseo del Prado 8; adult/child €12/free, Mon free; 10am-7pm Tue-Sun, noon-4pm Mon; M Banco de España) The Thyssen is one of the most extraordinary private collections of predominantly European art in the world. Where the Prado or Reina Sofía enable you to study the body of work of a particular artist in depth, the Thyssen is the place to immerse yourself in a breathtaking breadth of artistic styles. Most of the big names are here, sometimes with just a single painting, but the Thyssen's gift to Madrid and the art-loving public is to have them all under one roof.

ITINERARIES

One Week

Marvel at the art nouveau–influenced Modernista architecture and seaside style of **Barcelona** before taking the train to **San Sebastián**. Head on to **Bilbao** for the Guggenheim Museum and end the trip living it up inthelegendary night-life scene of Madrid.

One Month

Fly into **Seville** and embark on a route exploring this and Andalucía's other magical cities, **Granada** and **Córdoba**. Take the train to **Madrid**, from where you can check out **Toledo**, **Salamanca** and **Segovia**. Make east for the coast and **Valencia**. Head up to the Basque Country to see the epoch-making Guggenheim Museum in **Bilbao** and feast on some of the world's best food in **San Sebastián**, then head east via the medieval villages of **Aragón** and the dramatic **Pyrenees** to Catalonia, spending time in **Tarragona** before reaching **Barcelona**. Take a plane or boat for some R and R on the beautiful **Balearic Islands** before catching a flight home.

Spain Highlights

1 Alhambra (p623) Exploring the exquisite Islamic palace complex in Granada.

2 La Sagrada Família (p589) Visiting Gaudí's singular work in progress in Barcelona, a cathedral that truly defies imagination.

3 Mezquita (p621) Wandering amid the horseshoe arches of Córdoba's great medieval mosque, close to perfection wrought in stone.

4 San Sebastián (p602) Eating your way through a food-lover's paradise with an idyllic setting.

5 Santiago de Compostela (p606) Joining the pilgrims in Galicia's magnificent cathedral city.

6 Seville (p616) Soaking up the scent of orange blossom, being carried away by the passion of flamenco and surrendering to the party atmosphere in this sunny southern city.

7 Menorca (p613) Discovering the impossibly beautiful beaches and coves of this less-developed Mediterranean island.

8 Madrid (p565) Spending your days in some of Europe's best art galleries and nights amid its best nightlife.

Bordeaux
FRANCE
Avignon
Nîmes
Montpellier
Toulouse
San Sebastián
Irún
NAVARRA
Vitoria
Golfe de Beauduc
PYRENEES
Perpignan
Pamplona
Jaca
ANDORRA LA VELLA
ANDORRA
Miranda de Ebro
Logroño
Figueres
Calahorra
Huesca
CATALONIA
Girona
Fornells
AP68
Soria
Lleida
Manresa
Tossa de Mar
Costa Brava
A9
Zaragoza
AP2
Barcelona
Sitges
Tarragona
ARAGÓN
A23
AP7
Guadalajara
Alcalá de Henares
Teruel
Ciutadella de Menorca
Menorca
Maó
Cuenca
A3
Inca
Mallorca
Artà
Sagunto
Manacor
Palma de Mallorca
Valencia
VALENCIA
Alginet
Balearic Islands
Manzanares
Albacete
AP7
Ibiza
Denia
Valdepeñas
Benidorm
Elche
Alicante
Cieza
MURCIA
Murcia
A7
Costa Blanca
MEDITERRANEAN SEA
A91
Cartagena
Guadix
Mojácar
Costa Cálida
Almería
Adra
Costa De Almería
ALGERIA
0 200 km
0 100 miles

MUSEO DEL PRADO ITINERARY: ICONS OF SPANISH ART

The collection of the **Museo del Prado** (p565) can be overwhelming in scope, and it's a good idea to come twice if you can – but if your time is limited, zero in on the museum's peerless collection of Spanish art.

Francisco José de Goya y Lucientes (Goya) is found on all three floors of the Prado, but we recommend starting at the southern end of the ground or lower level. In room 65, Goya's *El dos de mayo* and *El tres de mayo* rank among Madrid's most emblematic paintings; they bring to life the 1808 anti-French revolt and subsequent execution of insurgents in Madrid. Alongside, in rooms 67 and 68, are some of his darkest and most disturbing works, *Las pinturas negras*; they are so called in part because of the dark browns and black that dominate, but more for the distorted animalesque appearance of their characters.

There are more Goyas on the 1st floor in rooms 34 to 37. Among them are two more of Goya's best-known and most intriguing oils: *La maja vestida* and *La maja desnuda*. These portraits, in room 36, of an unknown woman, commonly believed to be the Duquesa de Alba (who may have been Goya's lover), are identical save for the lack of clothing in the latter. There are further Goyas on the top floor.

Having studied the works of Goya, turn your attention to Velázquez. Of all his works, *Las meninas* (room 12) is what most people come to see. Completed in 1656, it is more properly known as *La família de Felipe IV* (The Family of Felipe IV). The rooms surrounding *Las meninas* contain more fine works by Velázquez: watch in particular for his paintings of various members of royalty who seem to spring off the canvas – Felipe II, Felipe IV, Margarita de Austria (a younger version of whom features in *Las meninas*), El Príncipe Baltasar Carlos and Isabel de Francia – on horseback.

Further, Bartolomé Esteban Murillo (Room 17), José de Ribera (Room 9), the stark figures of Francisco de Zurbarán (Room 10a) and the vivid, almost surreal works of El Greco (Room 8b) should all be on your itinerary.

★**Palacio Real** PALACE

(Map p570; ☎91 454 88 00; www.patrimonionacional.es; Calle de Bailén; adult/concession €11/6, guide/audio guide €4/3, EU citizens free last 2hr Mon-Thu; ⏲10am-8pm Apr-Sep, 10am-6pm Oct-Mar; Ⓜ Ópera) Spain's lavish Palacio Real is a jewel box of a palace, although it's used only occasionally for royal ceremonies; the royal family moved to the modest Palacio de la Zarzuela years ago.

When the *alcázar* (fortress) burned down on Christmas Day 1734, Felipe V, the first of the Bourbon kings, decided to build a palace that would dwarf all its European counterparts. Felipe died before the palace was finished, which is perhaps why the Italianate baroque colossus has a mere 2800 rooms, just one-quarter of the original plan.

★**Parque del Buen Retiro** GARDENS

(Map p570; Plaza de la Independencia; ⏲6am-midnight May-Sep, to 10pm Oct-Apr; Ⓜ Retiro, Príncipe de Vergara, Ibiza, Atocha) The glorious gardens of El Retiro are as beautiful as any you'll find in a European city. Littered with marble monuments, landscaped lawns, the occasional elegant building (the Palacio de Cristal is especially worth seeking out) and abundant greenery, it's quiet and contemplative during the week but comes to life on weekends. Put simply, this is one of our favourite places in Madrid.

Museo Arqueológico Nacional MUSEUM

(Map p570; http://man.mcu.es; Calle de Serrano 13; €3, 2-8pm Sat & 9.30am-noon Sun free; ⏲9.30am-8pm Tue-Sat, 9.30am-3pm Sun; Ⓜ Serrano) The showpiece National Archaeology Museum contains a sweeping accumulation of artefacts behind its towering facade. Daringly redesigned within, the museum ranges across Spain's ancient history and the large collection includes stunning mosaics taken from Roman villas across Spain, intricate Muslim-era and Mudéjar handiwork, sculpted figures such as the *Dama de Ibiza* and *Dama de Elche*, examples of Romanesque and Gothic architectural styles and a partial copy of the prehistoric cave paintings of Altamira (Cantabria).

Festivals & Events

Fiesta de San Isidro CULTURAL

(www.esmadrid.com; ⏲May) Around 15 May, Madrid's patron saint is honoured with a week of nonstop processions, parties and bullfights. Free concerts are held throughout the city, and this week marks the start of the city's bullfighting season.

Sleeping

Plaza Mayor & Royal Madrid

★Central Palace Madrid HOTEL €€
(Map p574; ☎91 548 20 18; www.centralpalacemadrid.com; Plaza de Oriente 2; d with/without view €119/99; ❄📶; Ⓜ Ópera) Now here's something special. The views alone would be reason enough to come and definitely worth paying extra for – rooms with balconies look out over the Palacio Real and Plaza de Oriente. But the rooms themselves are lovely and light-filled, with tasteful, subtle faux-antique furnishings, comfortable beds, light wood floors and plenty of space.

La Latina

★Posada del León de Oro BOUTIQUE HOTEL €€
(Map p574; ☎91 119 14 94; www.posadadelleondeoro.com; Calle de la Cava Baja 12; r from €130; ❄📶; Ⓜ La Latina) This rehabilitated inn has muted colour schemes and generally large rooms. There's a *corrala* in its core, and thoroughly modern rooms (some on the small side) along one of Madrid's best-loved streets. The downstairs bar is terrific.

Sol, Santa Ana & Huertas

★Lapepa Chic B&B B&B €
(Map p574; ☎648 474742; www.lapepa-bnb.com; 7th fl, Plaza de las Cortes 4; s/d from €63/69; ❄📶; Ⓜ Banco de España) A short step off the Paseo del Prado and on a floor with an art nouveau interior, this fine little B&B has lovely rooms with a contemporary, clean-lined look so different from the dour *hostal* furnishings you'll find elsewhere – modern art or even a bedhead lined with flamenco shoes gives this place personality in bucketloads.

★Hotel Alicia BOUTIQUE HOTEL €€
(Map p574; ☎91 389 60 95; www.room-matehoteles.com; Calle del Prado 2; d €135-175, ste from €200; ❄📶; Ⓜ Sol, Sevilla, Antón Martín) One of the landmark properties of the designer Room Mate chain of hotels, Hotel Alicia overlooks Plaza de Santa Ana with beautiful, spacious rooms. The style (the work of designer Pascua Ortega) is a touch more muted than in other Room Mate hotels, but the supermodern look remains intact, the downstairs bar is oh-so-cool, and the service is young and switched on.

★Praktik Metropol BOUTIQUE HOTEL €€
(Map p574; ☎91 521 29 35; www.hotelpraktikmetropol.com; Calle de la Montera 47; s/d from €100/110; ❄📶; Ⓜ Gran Vía) You'd be hard-pressed to find better value anywhere in Europe than here in this recently overhauled hotel. The rooms have a fresh, contemporary look with white wood furnishings, and some (especially the corner rooms) have brilliant views down to Gran Vía and out over the city.

Malasaña & Chueca

★Hostal Main Street Madrid HOSTAL €
(Map p574; ☎91 548 18 78; www.mainstreetmadrid.com; 5th fl, Gran Vía 50; r from €68; ❄📶; Ⓜ Callao, Santo Domingo) Excellent service is what travellers rave about here, but the rooms – modern and cool in soothing greys – are also some of the best *hostal* rooms you'll find anywhere in central Madrid. It's an excellent package and not surprisingly it's often full, so book well in advance.

★Only You Hotel BOUTIQUE HOTEL €€
(Map p574; ☎91 005 22 22; www.onlyyouhotels.com; Calle de Barquillo 21; d €180-260; ❄@📶; Ⓜ Chueca) This stunning boutique hotel makes perfect use of a 19th-century Chueca mansion. The look is classy and contemporary and is the latest project by respected interior designer Lázaro Rosa-Violán. Nice touches include all-day à la carte breakfasts and a portable router that you can carry out into the city to stay connected.

★Hotel Orfila HOTEL €€€
(Map p570; ☎91 702 77 70; www.hotelorfila.com; Calle de Orfila 6; r from €230; P❄📶; Ⓜ Alonso Martínez) One of Madrid's best hotels, Hotel Orfila has all the luxuries of any five-star hotel – supremely comfortable rooms, for a start – but it's the personal service that elevates it into the upper echelon; regular guests get bathrobes embroidered with their own initials. An old-world elegance dominates the decor, and the quiet location and sheltered garden make it the perfect retreat at day's end.

Madrid

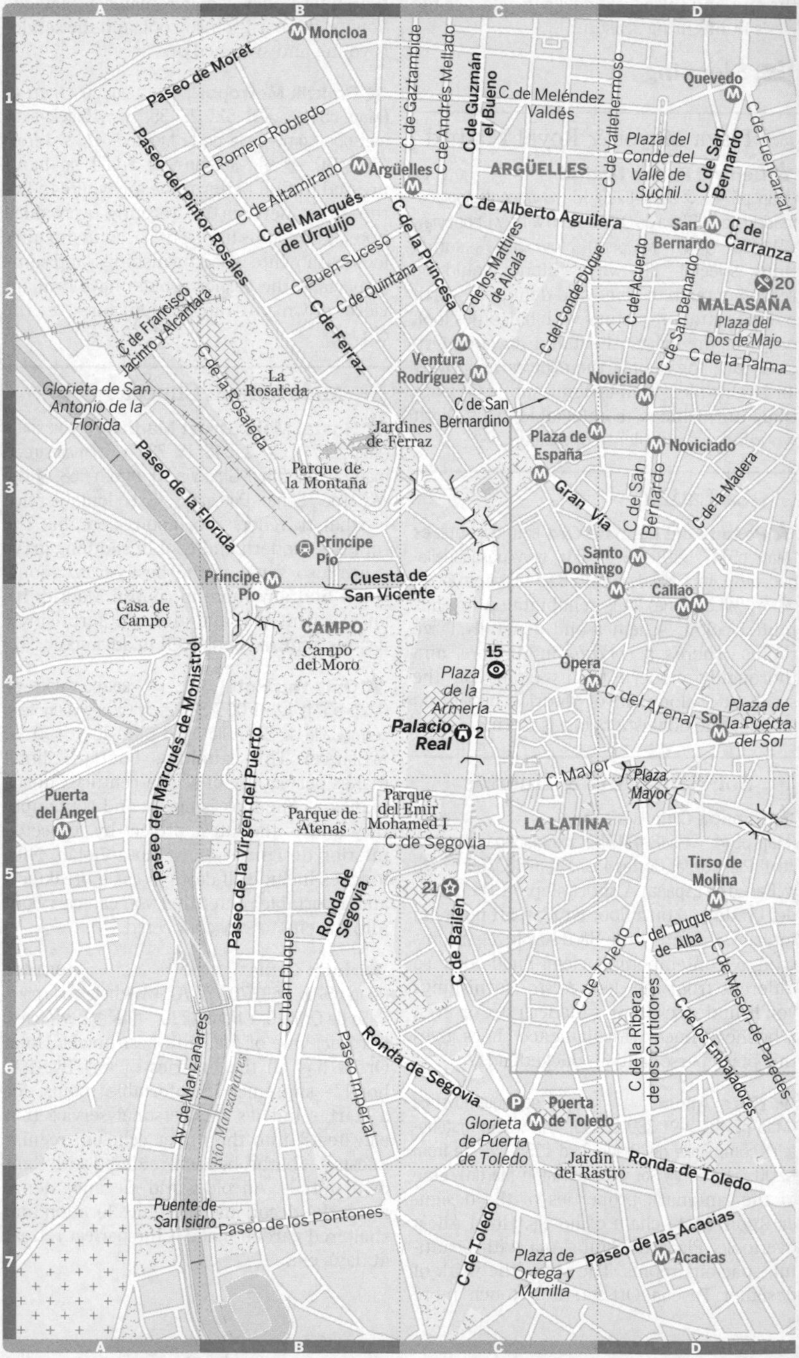

A B C D
1 2 3 4 5 6 7

Moncloa
Paseo de Moret
C Romero Robledo
Paseo del Pintor Rosales
C de Altamirano
Argüelles
C de Gaztambide
C de Andrés Mellado
C de Guzmán el Bueno
C de Meléndez Valdés
ARGÜELLES
C de Vallehermoso
Plaza del Conde del Valle de Suchil
Quevedo
C de San Bernardo
C de Fuencarral
C del Marqués de Urquijo
C de la Princesa
C de Alberto Aguilera
San Bernardo
C de Carranza
C Buen Suceso
C de Quintana
C de los Mattires de Alcalá
C del Conde Duque
C del Acuerdo
C de San Bernardo
20
MALASAÑA
Plaza del Dos de Majo
C de la Palma
C de Francisco Jacinto y Alcantara
C de la Rosaleda
C de Ferraz
Ventura Rodríguez
Noviciado
La Rosaleda
Glorieta de San Antonio de la Florida
C de San Bernardino
Jardines de Ferraz
Plaza de España
Noviciado
Paseo de la Florida
Parque de la Montaña
Gran Vía
C de San Bernardo
C de la Madera
Príncipe Pío
Santo Domingo
Príncipe Pío
Cuesta de San Vicente
Callao
Casa de Campo
CAMPO
Campo del Moro
15
Ópera
Plaza de la Armería
C del Arenal
Sol
Plaza de la Puerta del Sol
Palacio Real 2
Paseo del Marqués de Monistrol
Paseo de la Virgen del Puerto
C Mayor
Plaza Mayor
Puerta del Ángel
Parque del Emir Mohamed I
Parque de Atenas
LA LATINA
C de Segovia
Tirso de Molina
21
Ronda de Segovia
C Juan Duque
C de Bailén
C de Toledo
C del Duque de Alba
C de Mesón de Paredes
C de la Ribera de los Curtidores
C de los Embajadores
Av de Manzanares
Río Manzanares
Paseo Imperial
Ronda de Segovia
Puerta de Toledo
Glorieta de Puerta de Toledo
Jardín del Rastro
Ronda de Toledo
Puente de San Isidro
Paseo de los Pontones
C de Toledo
Paseo de las Acacias
Acacias
Plaza de Ortega y Munilla

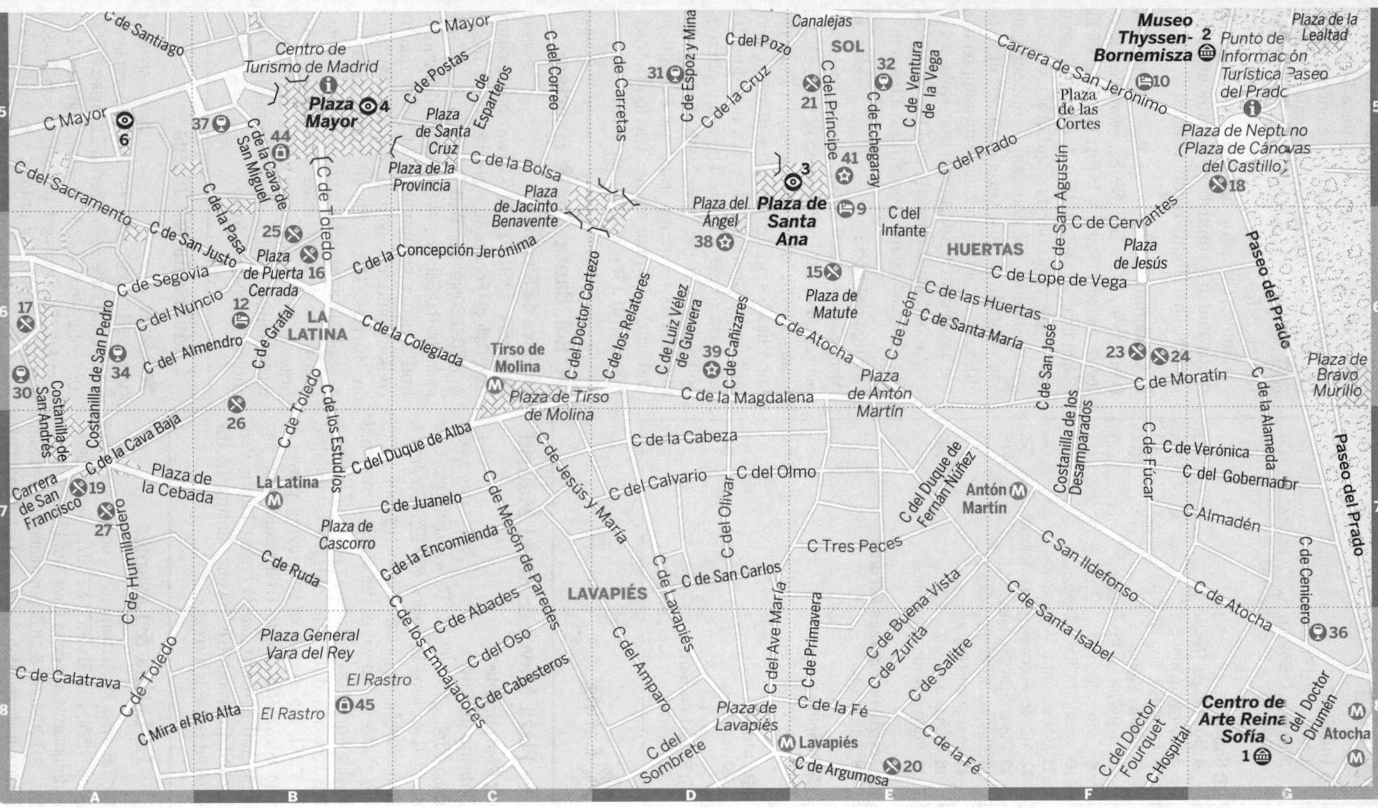
C de Santiago
C Mayor
Centro de Turismo de Madrid
Plaza Mayor
C de Postas
C de Esparteros
Plaza de Santa Cruz
Plaza de la Provincia
C del Correo
C de Carretas
C de Espoz y Mina
C del Pozo
C de la Cruz
Canalejas
SOL
C del Príncipe
C de Echegaray
C de Ventura de la Vega
Carrera de San Jerónimo
Museo Thyssen-Bornemisza
Punto de Información Turística Paseo del Prado
Plaza de la Lealtad
Plaza de las Cortes
Plaza de Neptuno (Plaza de Cánovas del Castillo)
C del Sacramento
C de la Cava de San Miguel
C de la Pasa
C de Toledo
C de la Bolsa
Plaza de Jacinto Benavente
Plaza del Ángel
Plaza de Santa Ana
C del Prado
C del Infante
C de San Agustín
C de Cervantes
HUERTAS
Plaza de Jesús
Paseo del Prado
C de San Justo
Plaza de Puerta Cerrada
C de la Concepción Jerónima
C de Segovia
C del Nuncio
LA LATINA
C de Grafal
C de la Colegiada
C del Doctor Cortezo
C de los Relatores
C de Luiz Vélez de Guevera
C de Cañizares
C de Atocha
Plaza de Matute
C de León
C de Lope de Vega
C de las Huertas
C de Santa María
C de San José
C de Moratín
C de la Alameda
Plaza de Bravo Murillo
Costanilla de San Pedro
C del Almendro
Tirso de Molina
Plaza de Tirso de Molina
C de la Magdalena
Plaza de Antón Martín
Costanilla de San Andrés
C de la Cava Baja
C de los Estudios
C del Duque de Alba
C de la Cabeza
C de Jesús y María
C del Calvario
C del Olmo
C del Olivar
C del Duque de Fernán Núñez
Antón Martín
Costanilla de los Desamparados
C de Fúcar
C de Verónica
C del Gobernador
Carrera de San Francisco
Plaza de la Cebada
La Latina
C de Juanelo
C de Mesón de Paredes
C Almadén
C de Humilladero
Plaza de Cascorro
C de la Encomienda
C Tres Peces
C San Ildefonso
C de Ruda
LAVAPIÉS
C de San Carlos
C de Lavapiés
C de Buena Vista
C de Atocha
C de Cenicero
C de Abades
C de los Embajadores
Plaza General Vara del Rey
C del Oso
C del Amparo
C del Ave María
C de Primavera
C de Zurita
C de Salitre
C de Santa Isabel
C de Calatrava
C de Toledo
El Rastro
C de Cabesteros
C Mira el Río Alta
Plaza de Lavapiés
C de la Fé
Centro de Arte Reina Sofía
C del Doctor Drumén
Atocha
C del Sombrete
Lavapiés
C de Argumosa
C del Doctor Fourquet
C Hospital

Madrid

Top Sights

1 Museo del Prado ... F5
2 Palacio Real ... C4
3 Parque del Buen Retiro ... G4

Sights

4 Bosque del Recuerdo ... G5
5 El Ángel Caído ... G5
6 Ermita de San Isidro ... H3
7 Fuente Egipcia ... G4
8 Jardín de los Planteles ... G5
9 La Rosaleda ... H5
10 Madrid's Oldest Tree ... G5
11 Monument to Alfonso XII ... G4
12 Museo Arqueológico Nacional ... G3
13 Palacio de Cristal ... H5
14 Palacio de Velázquez ... H5
15 Plaza de Oriente ... C4
16 Puerta de Dante ... H6
17 Puerta de los Jerónimos ... F5

Activities, Courses & Tours

18 Row Boats ... G4

Sleeping

19 Hotel Orfila ... F2

Eating

20 Albur ... D2

Entertainment

21 Corral de la Morería ... C5

Eating

Plaza Mayor & Royal Madrid

★Restaurante Sobrino de Botín CASTILIAN €€€

(Map p574; ☎91 366 42 17; www.botin.es; Calle de los Cuchilleros 17; mains €19-27; ⏲1-4pm & 8pm-midnight; Ⓜ La Latina, Sol) It's not every day that you can eat in the oldest restaurant in the world (the *Guinness Book of Records* has recognised it as the oldest – established in 1725). The secret of its staying power is fine *cochinillo asado* (roast suckling pig; €25) and *cordero asado* (roast lamb; €25) cooked in wood-fired ovens. Eating in the vaulted cellar is a treat.

La Latina & Lavapiés

★Taberna Matritum MODERN SPANISH €€

(Map p574; ☎91 365 82 37; www.tabernamatritum.es; Calle de la Cava Alta 17; mains €13-17; ⏲1.30-4pm & 8.30pm-midnight Wed-Sun, 8.30pm-midnight Mon & Tue; Ⓜ La Latina) This little gem is reason enough to detour from the more popular Calle de la Cava Baja next door. The seasonal menu here encompasses terrific tapas, salads and generally creative cooking – try the *cocido* croquettes or the winter *calçots* (large spring onions) from Catalonia. The wine list runs into the hundreds and it's sophisticated without being pretentious. Highly recommended.

El Estragón VEGETARIAN €€

(Map p574; ☎91 365 89 82; www.elestragonvegetariano.com; Plaza de la Paja 10; mains €8-15; ⏲1pm-1am; 🌶; Ⓜ La Latina) A delightful spot for crêpes, vegie burgers and other vegetarian specialities, El Estragón is undoubtedly one of Madrid's best vegetarian restaurants, although attentive vegans won't appreciate the use of butter. Apart from that, we're yet to hear a bad word about it, and the *menú del día* (daily set menu; from €12) is a bargain.

La Buga del Lobo SPANISH €€

(Map p574; ☎91 528 88 38; www.facebook.com/labugadellobo; Calle de Argumosa 11; mains €12-21; ⏲11am-2am Wed-Mon; Ⓜ Lavapiés) La Buga del Lobo has been one of the 'in' places in cool and gritty Lavapiés for years now and it's still hard to get a table. The atmosphere is bohemian and inclusive, with funky, swirling murals, contemporary art exhibitions and jazz or lounge music. The food's traditional with a few creative detours.

Sol, Santa Ana & Huertas

La Finca de Susana SPANISH €

(Map p574; ☎91 429 76 78; www.grupandilana.com; Calle del Principe 10; mains €8-14; ⏲1-3.45pm & 8.30-11.30pm Sun-Wed, 1-3.45pm & 8.15pm-midnight Thu-Sat; 📶; Ⓜ Sevilla) It's difficult to find a better combination of price, quality cooking and classy atmosphere anywhere in Huertas. The softly lit dining area has a sophisticated vibe and the sometimes-innovative, sometimes-traditional food draws a hip young crowd. The duck confit with plums, turnips and couscous is a fine choice. No reservations.

Malasaña & Chueca

★Bazaar MODERN SPANISH €

(Map p574; ☎91 523 39 05; www.restaurantbazaar.com; Calle de la Libertad 21; mains €6.50-10; ⏲1.15-4pm & 8.30-11.30pm Sun-Wed, 1.15-4pm & 8.15pm-midnight Thu-Sat; 📶; Ⓜ Chueca) Bazaar's popularity among the well-heeled Chueca set shows no sign of abating. Its pristine white interior design, with theatre-style lighting and wall-length windows, may draw a crowd that looks like it's stepped out of the pages of *¡Hola!* magazine, but the food is extremely well priced and innovative, and the atmosphere is casual.

★Yakitoro by Chicote JAPANESE, SPANISH **€€**
(Map p574; ☎91 737 14 41; www.yakitoro.com; Calle de la Reina 41; tapas €3-8; ⏲1pm-midnight; Ⓜ Banco de España) Based around the idea of a Japanese tavern, driven by a spirit of innovation and a desire to combine the best in Spanish and Japanese flavours, Yakitoro is a hit. Apart from salads, it's all built around brochettes cooked over a wood fire, with wonderful combinations of vegetable, seafood and meat.

Drinking & Nightlife

The essence of Madrid lives in its streets and plazas, and bar-hopping is a pastime enjoyed by young and old alike. If you're after the more traditional, with tiled walls and flamenco tunes, head to Huertas. For gay-friendly drinking holes, Chueca is the place. Malasaña caters to a grungy, funky crowd, while La Latina has friendly bars that guarantee atmosphere most nights of the week. In summer, the terrace bars that pop up all over the city are unbeatable.

The bulk of Madrid bars open to 2am Sunday to Thursday, and to 3am or 3.30am Friday and Saturday. As the bars wind down, the nightclubs *(discotecas)* that have brought such renown to Madrid start to open. Don't expect them to get going until after 1am at the earliest. Standard entry fee is €12, which usually includes the first drink, although megaclubs and swankier places charge a few euros more.

★Delic BAR
(Map p574; ☎91 364 54 50; www.delic.es; Costanilla de San Andrés 14; ⏲11am-2am Sun & Tue-Thu, 11am-2.30am Fri & Sat; Ⓜ La Latina) We could go on for hours about this long-standing cafe-bar, but we'll reduce it to its most basic elements: nursing an exceptionally good mojito (€8) or three on a warm summer's evening at Delic's outdoor tables on one of Madrid's prettiest plazas is one of life's great pleasures. Bliss.

★La Venencia BAR
(Map p574; ☎91 429 73 13; Calle de Echegaray 7; ⏲12.30-3.30pm & 7.30pm-1.30am; Ⓜ Sol, Sevilla) La Venencia is a *barrio* classic, with *manzanilla* (chamomile-coloured sherry) from Sanlúcar and sherry from Jeréz poured straight from the dusty wooden barrels, accompanied by a small selection of tapas with an Andalucian bent. Otherwise, there's no music, no flashy decorations; it's all about you, your *fino* (sherry) and your friends. As one reviewer put it, it's 'a classic among classics'.

MADRID'S BEST PLAZAS

A royal palace that once had aspirations to be the Spanish Versailles. Sophisticated cafes watched over by apartments that cost the equivalent of a royal salary. The **Teatro Real** (Map p574; ☎902 24 48 48; www.teatro-real.com; Plaza de Oriente; Ⓜ Ópera), Madrid's opera house and one of Spain's temples to high culture. Some of the finest sunset views in Madrid... Welcome to **Plaza de Oriente** (Map p570; Plaza de Oriente; Ⓜ Ópera), a living, breathing monument to imperial Madrid.

On the other hand, the intimate **Plaza de la Villa** (Map p574; Plaza de la Villa; Ⓜ Ópera) is one of Madrid's prettiest. Enclosed on three sides by wonderfully preserved examples of 17th-century *barroco madrileño* (Madrid-style baroque architecture – a pleasing amalgam of brick, exposed stone and wrought iron), it was the permanent seat of Madrid's city government from the Middle Ages until recent years, when Madrid's city council relocated to the grand Palacio de Cibeles on **Plaza de la Cibeles** (Map p574; Ⓜ Banco de España).

Plaza de Santa Ana (Map p574; Plaza de Santa Ana; Ⓜ Sevilla, Sol, Antón Martín) is a delightful confluence of elegant architecture and irresistible energy. It presides over the upper reaches of the Barrio de las Letras and this literary personality makes its presence felt with the statues of the 17th-century writer Calderón de la Barca and Federico García Lorca, and in the **Teatro Español** (Map p574; ☎91 360 14 84; www.teatroespanol.es; Calle del Príncipe 25; Ⓜ Sevilla, Sol, Antón Martín), formerly the Teatro del Príncipe, at the plaza's eastern end. Apart from anything else, the plaza is the starting point for many a long Huertas night.

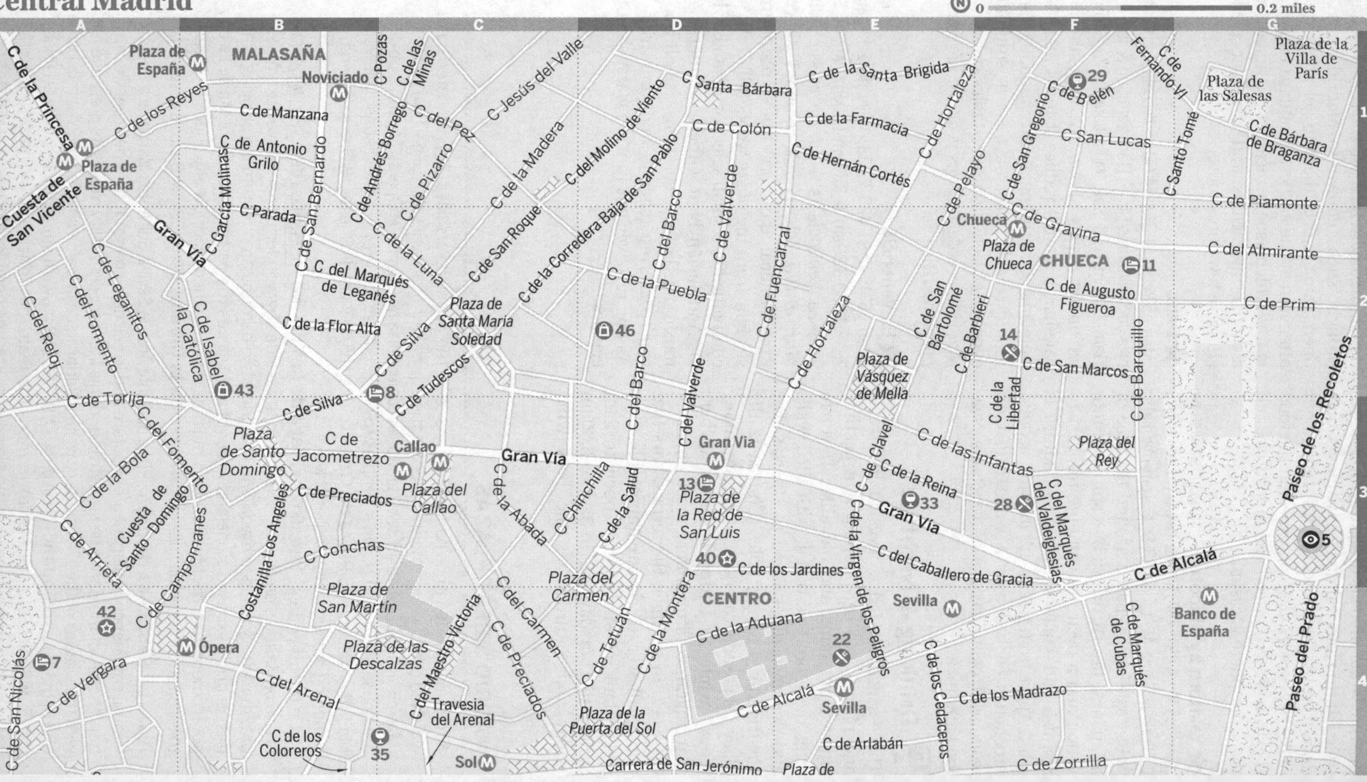
Central Madrid
0 400 m
0 0.2 miles
C de la Princesa
Plaza de España
MALASAÑA
Noviciado
C Pozas
C de las Minas
C Jesús del Valle
C Santa Bárbara
C de la Santa Brígida
C de Hortaleza
29
C de Belén
C de Fernando VI
Plaza de las Salesas
Plaza de la Villa de París
C de los Reyes
C de Manzana
C de Andrés Borrego
C del Pez
C de la Madera
C del Molino de Viento
C de Colón
C de la Farmacia
C de San Gregorio
C San Lucas
C Santo Tomé
C de Bárbara de Braganza
Plaza de España
Cuesta de San Vicente
C de Antonio Grilo
C García Molinas
C de San Bernardo
C de Pizarro
C de San Roque
C de la Corredera Baja de San Pablo
C del Barco
C de Valverde
C de Hernán Cortés
C de Pelayo
Chueca
C de Gravina
C de Piamonte
Gran Vía
C Parada
C de la Luna
C de Fuencarral
Plaza de Chueca
CHUECA
11
C del Almirante
C de Leganitos
C del Marqués de Leganés
C de la Puebla
C de Hortaleza
C de San Bartolomé
C de Barbieri
C de Augusto Figueroa
C de Prim
C del Reloj
C del Fomento
C de Isabel la Católica
C de la Flor Alta
C de Silva
Plaza de Santa María Soledad
46
Plaza de Vásquez de Mella
14
C de San Marcos
C de Barquillo
43
8
C de Tudescos
C del Barco
C del Valverde
C de la Libertad
Paseo de los Recoletos
C de Torija
C de Silva
Plaza de Santo Domingo
C de Jacometrezo
Callao
Gran Vía
Gran Vía
C de Clavel
C de las Infantas
Plaza del Rey
C del Fomento
C de la Bola
Cuesta de Santo Domingo
C de Preciados
Plaza del Callao
C de la Abada
C Chinchilla
C de la Salud
13
Plaza de la Red de San Luis
C de la Reina
33
Gran Vía
28
C del Marqués del Valdeiglesias
5
C de Arrieta
C de Campomanes
Costanilla Los Ángeles
C Conchas
40
C de los Jardines
C del Caballero de Gracia
C de Alcalá
Plaza del Carmen
Plaza de San Martín
CENTRO
Sevilla
Banco de España
42
C de la Virgen de los Peligros
C de la Aduana
C de Marqués de Cubas
Ópera
Plaza de las Descalzas
C del Maestro Victoria
C del Carmen
C de Tetuán
C de la Montera
22
7
C de Vergara
C del Arenal
C de los Cedaceros
C de los Madrazo
Paseo del Prado
C de San Nicolás
Travesía del Arenal
C de Preciados
Plaza de la Puerta del Sol
C de Alcalá
Sevilla
C de los Coloreros
35
Sol
C de Arlabán
Carrera de San Jerónimo
Plaza de
C de Zorrilla

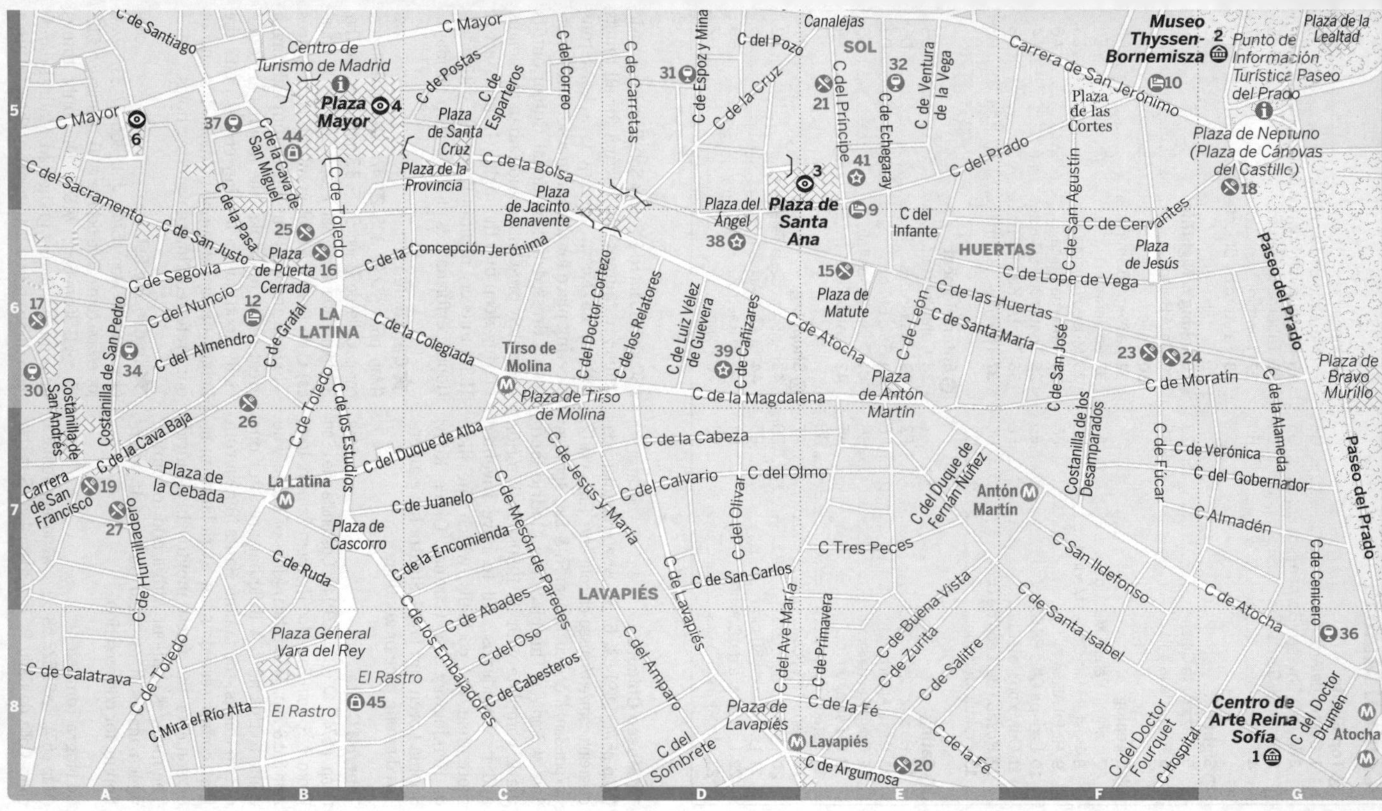
C de Santiago
C Mayor
Centro de Turismo de Madrid
Plaza Mayor
C de Postas
C de Esparteros
Plaza de Santa Cruz
Plaza de la Provincia
C del Correo
C de Carretas
C de Espoz y Mina
C de la Cruz
C del Pozo
Canalejas
SOL
C del Príncipe
C de Echegaray
C de Ventura de la Vega
Carrera de San Jerónimo
Museo Thyssen-Bornemisza
Punto de Información Turística Paseo del Prado
Plaza de la Lealtad
Plaza de las Cortes
Plaza de Neptuno (Plaza de Cánovas del Castillo)
C de la Cava de San Miguel
C de Toledo
C de la Bolsa
Plaza de Jacinto Benavente
Plaza del Ángel
Plaza de Santa Ana
C del Infante
C del Prado
C de San Agustín
C de Cervantes
Plaza de Jesús
HUERTAS
Paseo del Prado
C del Sacramento
C de San Justo
C de la Pasa
Plaza de Puerta Cerrada
C de la Concepción Jerónima
C de Segovia
C del Nuncio
C del Almendro
C de Grafal
LA LATINA
C de la Colegiada
Tirso de Molina
C del Doctor Cortezo
C de los Relatores
C de Luiz Vélez de Guevera
C de Cañizares
C de Atocha
Plaza de Matute
C de León
C de las Huertas
C de Santa María
C de Lope de Vega
C de San José
C de Moratín
Plaza de Bravo Murillo
Costanilla de San Pedro
Costanilla de San Andrés
C de la Cava Baja
Carrera de San Francisco
Plaza de la Cebada
C de Humilladero
La Latina
C de los Estudios
Plaza de Tirso de Molina
C de la Magdalena
Plaza de Antón Martín
Costanilla de los Desamparados
C de Fúcar
C de Verónica
C de la Alameda
C del Gobernador
C Almadén
C del Duque de Alba
C de la Cabeza
C de Jesús y María
C del Calvario
C del Olmo
C del Olivar
C del Duque de Fernán Núñez
Antón Martín
C de Juanelo
Plaza de Cascorro
C de la Encomienda
C de Mesón de Paredes
C Tres Peces
C San Ildefonso
C de Atocha
C de Cenicero
C de Ruda
LAVAPIÉS
C de San Carlos
C de Lavapiés
C de Santa Isabel
C de Abades
C del Oso
C de Cabesteros
C de los Embajadores
C del Amparo
C del Ave María
C de Primavera
C de Buena Vista
C de Zurita
C de Salitre
Plaza General Vara del Rey
El Rastro
C de Calatrava
C de Toledo
C Mira el Río Alta
Plaza de Lavapiés
C de la Fé
Lavapiés
C del Sombrete
C de Argumosa
C del Doctor Fourquet
C Hospital
Centro de Arte Reina Sofía
C del Doctor Drumén
Atocha
A
B
C
D
E
F
G
5
6
7
8

Central Madrid

Top Sights
- 1 Centro de Arte Reina Sofía ... G8
- 2 Museo Thyssen-Bornemisza ... G5
- 3 Plaza de Santa Ana ... E5
- 4 Plaza Mayor ... B5

Sights
- 5 Plaza de la Cibeles ... G3
- 6 Plaza de la Villa ... A5

Sleeping
- 7 Central Palace Madrid ... A4
- 8 Hostal Main Street Madrid ... B2
- 9 Hotel Alicia ... E6
- 10 Lapepa Chic B&B ... F5
- 11 Only You Hotel ... F2
- 12 Posada del León de Oro ... B6
- 13 Praktik Metropol ... D3

Eating
- 14 Bazaar ... F2
- 15 Casa Alberto ... E6
- 16 Casa Revuelta ... B6
- 17 El Estragón ... A6
- 18 Estado Puro ... G5
- 19 Juana La Loca ... A7
- 20 La Buga del Lobo ... E8
- 21 La Finca de Susana ... E5
- 22 La Terraza del Casino ... E4
- 23 Maceiras ... F6
- 24 Maceiras ... F6
- Mercado de San Miguel ... (see 37)
- 25 Restaurante Sobrino de Botín ... B6
- 26 Taberna Matritum ... B6
- 27 Txirimiri ... A7
- 28 Yakitoro by Chicote ... F3

Drinking & Nightlife
- 29 Café Belén ... F1
- 30 Delic ... A6
- 31 La Negra Tomasa ... D5
- 32 La Venencia ... E5
- 33 Museo Chicote ... E3
- 34 Taberna Chica ... A6
- 35 Teatro Joy Eslava ... C4
- 36 Teatro Kapital ... G8
- 37 The Sherry Corner ... B5

Entertainment
- 38 Café Central ... D6
- 39 Casa Patas ... D6
- 40 Sala El Sol ... D3
- 41 Teatro Español ... E5
- 42 Teatro Real ... A4

Shopping
- 43 Antigua Casa Talavera ... B2
- 44 El Arco Artesanía ... B5
- 45 El Rastro ... B8
- 46 Kling ... D2

★Museo Chicote COCKTAIL BAR
(Map p574; ☎91 532 67 37; www.grupomercado-delareina.com/en/museo-chicote-en/; Gran Vía 12; ⏰7pm-3am Mon-Thu, to 4am Fri & Sat, 4pm-1am Sun; Ⓜ Gran Vía) This place is a Madrid landmark, complete with its 1930s-era interior, and its founder is said to have invented more than 100 cocktails, which the likes of Hemingway, Ava Gardner, Grace Kelly, Sophia Loren and Frank Sinatra have all enjoyed at one time or another.

Taberna Chica BAR
(Map p574; ☎683 269114; Costanilla de San Pedro 7; ⏰8pm-2am Mon-Thu, 5pm-2am Fri, 1pm-2am Sat & Sun; Ⓜ La Latina) Most of those who come to this narrow little bar are after one of two things: the famous Santa Teresa rum that comes served in an extra-large mug, or some of the finest mojitos in Madrid. The music is chill-out with a nod to lounge, which makes it an ideal pit stop if you're hoping for conversation.

La Negra Tomasa BAR
(Map p574; ☎91 523 58 30; www.lanegratomasa.com; Calle de Cádiz 9; ⏰1.30pm-4am Sun-Thu, 1.30pm-5.30am Fri & Sat; Ⓜ Sol) Bar, live-music venue, restaurant and magnet for all things Cuban, La Negra Tomasa is a boisterous meeting place for the Havana set, with waitresses dressed in traditional Cuban outfits (definitely pre-Castro) and Cuban musicians playing deep into the night. Groups start at 11.30pm every night of the week, with additional performances at 3.30pm on Sundays.

★Café Belén BAR
(Map p574; ☎91 308 27 47; www.elcafebelen.com; Calle de Belén 5; ⏰3.30pm-3am Tue-Thu, 3.30pm-3.30am Fri & Sat, 7-10pm Sun; 📶; Ⓜ Chueca) Café Belén is cool in all the right places – lounge and chill-out music, dim lighting, a great range of drinks (the mojitos are especially good) and a low-key crowd that's the height of casual sophistication. It's one of our preferred Chueca watering holes.

★Teatro Joy Eslava CLUB
(Joy Madrid; Map p574; ☎91 366 37 33; www.joy-eslava.com; Calle del Arenal 11; admission €12-15; ⏰11.30pm-6am; Ⓜ Sol) The only things guaranteed at this grand old Madrid dance club (housed in a 19th-century theatre) are a

crowd and the fact that it'll be open (it claims to have operated every single day since 1981). The music and the crowd are a mixed bag, but queues are long and invariably include locals and tourists, and even the occasional *famoso* (celebrity).

Teatro Kapital CLUB
(Map p574; ☎91 420 29 06; www.grupo-kapital.com; Calle de Atocha 125; admission from €17; ⏲midnight-6am Thu-Sat; Ⓜ Atocha) One of the most famous megaclubs in Madrid, this seven-storey venue has something for everyone: from cocktail bars and dance music to karaoke, salsa, hip hop and chilled spaces; there's even a 'Kissing Room'.

☆ Entertainment

★Casa Patas FLAMENCO
(Map p574; ☎91 369 04 96; www.casapatas.com; Calle de Cañizares 10; admission incl drink €38; ⏲shows 10.30pm Mon-Thu, 8pm & 10.30pm Fri & Sat; Ⓜ Antón Martín, Tirso de Molina) One of the top flamenco stages in Madrid, this *tablao* (choreographed flamenco show) always offers flawless quality that serves as a good introduction to the art. It's not the friendliest place in town, especially if you're only here for the show, and you're likely to be crammed in a little, but no one complains about the standard of the performances.

★Café Central JAZZ
(Map p574; ☎91 369 41 43; www.cafecentralmadrid.com; Plaza del Ángel 10; admission €12-18; ⏲12.30pm-2.30am Mon-Thu, to 3.30am Fri, 11.30am-3.30am Sat, performances 9pm; Ⓜ Antón Martín, Sol) In 2011 the respected jazz magazine *Down Beat* included this art deco bar on its list of the world's best jazz clubs – the only place in Spain to earn the prestigious accolade (said by some to be the jazz equivalent of earning a Michelin star). With well over 1000 gigs under its belt, it rarely misses a beat.

★Corral de la Morería FLAMENCO
(Map p570; ☎91 365 84 46; www.corraldelamoreria.com; Calle de la Morería 17; admission incl drink from €49; ⏲7pm-12.15am, shows 8.30pm & 10.20pm; Ⓜ Ópera) This is one of the most prestigious flamenco stages in Madrid, with 50 years' experience as a leading venue and top performers most nights. The stage area has a rustic feel, and tables are pushed up close. Set menus from €47.

★Sala El Sol LIVE MUSIC
(Map p574; ☎91 532 64 90; www.elsolmad.com; Calle de los Jardines 3; admission incl drink €10, concert tickets €8-25; ⏲midnight-5.30am Tue-Sat Jul-Sep; Ⓜ Gran Vía) Madrid institutions don't come any more beloved than Sala El Sol. It opened in 1979, just in time for *la movida madrileña* (the Madrid scene), and quickly established itself as a leading stage for all the icons of the era, such as Nacha Pop and Alaska y los Pegamoides.

★Estadio Santiago Bernabéu STADIUM
(☎tickets 902 324324, tours 91 398 43 00/70; www.realmadrid.com; Av de Concha Espina 1; tours adult/child €24/18; ⏲tours 10am-7pm Mon-Sat, 10.30am-6.30pm Sun, except match days; Ⓜ Santiago Bernabéu) Football fans and budding Madridistas (Real Madrid supporters) will want to make a pilgrimage to the Estadio Santiago Bernabéu, a temple to all that's extravagant and successful in football. The self-guided tours take you into the stands, dressing rooms, trophy exhibit and out through the players' tunnel onto the pitch. Better still, attend a game alongside 80,000 delirious fans. For bigger games, tickets are hard to get. For less important matches, tickets can be purchased online, by phone or in person from the ticket office at gate 42 on Av de Concha Espina; for the last option, turn up early in the week before a scheduled game (eg a Monday morning for a Sunday game).

Shopping

Salamanca is the home of Spanish fashion. For offbeat boutiques, poke around La Latina and Lavapiés. Malasaña is the place for retro fashions, while nearby Chueca deals in more upmarket styles. For the best souvenirs, explore the Sol, Santa Ana and Huertas area.

★El Rastro MARKET
(Map p574; Calle de la Ribera de los Curtidores; ⏲8am-3pm Sun; Ⓜ La Latina) A Sunday morning at El Rastro is a Madrid institution. You could easily spend an entire morning inching your way down the hill and the maze of streets that host El Rastro flea market each week. Cheap clothes, luggage, old flamenco records, even older photos of Madrid, faux designer purses, grungy T-shirts, household goods and electronics are the main fare. For every 10 pieces of junk, there's a real gem (a lost masterpiece, an Underwood typewriter) waiting to be found.

★**Antigua Casa Talavera** CERAMICS
(Map p574; ☎91 547 34 17; www.antiguacasatalavera.com; Calle de Isabel la Católica 2; ⊙10am-1.30pm & 5-8pm Mon-Fri, 10am-1.30pm Sat; Ⓜ Santo Domingo) The extraordinary tiled facade of this wonderful old shop conceals an Aladdin's cave of ceramics from all over Spain. This is not the mass-produced stuff aimed at a tourist market, but comes from the small family potters of Andalucía and Toledo, ranging from the decorative (tiles) to the useful (plates, jugs and other kitchen items). The old couple who run the place are delightful.

Kling FASHION & ACCESSORIES
(Map p574; ☎91 522 51 45; www.kling.es; Calle de la Ballesta 6; ⊙11am-9pm Mon-Sat; Ⓜ Gran Vía) Like a classy version of Zara but with just a hint of attitude, Kling is housed in a reconceived former sex club (prostitutes still scout for clients outside) and is one of Madrid's best-kept secrets. It's ideal for fashion-conscious women who can't afford Salamanca's prices.

★**El Arco Artesanía** ARTS & CRAFTS
(Map p574; ☎913 65 26 80; www.artesaniaelarco.com; Plaza Mayor 9; ⊙11am-9pm Sun-Thu, to 11pm Fri & Sat; Ⓜ Sol, La Latina) This original shop in the southwestern corner of Plaza Mayor sells an outstanding array of homemade designer souvenirs, from stone, ceramic and glass work to jewellery and home fittings. The papier mâché figures are gorgeous, but there's so much else here to turn your head.

ℹ Information

SAFE TRAVEL

Madrid is a generally safe city, although you should, as in most European cities, be wary of pickpockets on transport and around major tourist sights. You're most likely to fall foul of pickpockets in the most heavily touristed parts of town, notably the Plaza Mayor and surrounding streets, the Puerta del Sol, El Rastro and around the Museo del Prado. Be wary of jostling on crowded buses and the metro and, as a general rule, dark, empty streets are to be avoided; luckily, Madrid's most lively nocturnal areas are generally busy with crowds having a good time.

To report thefts or other crime-related matters, your best bet is the **Servicio de Atención al Turista Extranjero** (Foreign Tourist Assistance Service; ☎91 548 80 08, 91 548 85 37; www.esmadrid.com/informacion-turistica/sate; Calle de Leganitos 19; ⊙9am-midnight; Ⓜ Plaza de España, Santo Domingo), where specially trained police officers work alongside representatives from the Tourism Ministry.

TOURIST INFORMATION

Centro de Turismo de Madrid (Map p574; ☎010, 91 578 78 10; www.esmadrid.com; Plaza Mayor 27; ⊙9.30am-8.30pm; Ⓜ Sol) The Madrid government's Centro de Turismo is terrific. Housed in the Real Casa de la Panadería on the north side of the Plaza Mayor, it allows free access to its outstanding website and city database, and offers free downloads of the metro map to your mobile; staff are helpful.

ℹ Getting There & Away

AIR

Adolfo Suárez Madrid-Barajas Airport (☎902 404704; www.aena.es; Ⓜ Aeropuerto T1, T2 & T3, Aeropuerto T4) The airport lies 15km northeast of the city and is Europe's sixth-busiest hub, with almost 50 million passengers passing through here every year. It has four terminals. Terminal 4 (T4) deals mainly with flights of Iberia and its partners (eg British Airways, American Airlines and Vueling), while the remainder leave from the conjoined T1, T2 and (rarely) T3.

BUS

Estación Sur de Autobuses (☎91 468 42 00; Calle de Méndez Álvaro 83; Ⓜ Méndez Álvaro) Just south of the M30 ring road, this is the city's principal bus station. It serves most destinations to the south and many in other parts of the country. Most bus companies have a ticket office here, even if their buses depart from elsewhere.

TRAIN

All trains are run by **Renfe** (☎902 320320; www.renfe.es/cercanias/madrid). High-speed AVE (Tren de Alta Velocidad Española) services connect Madrid with Alicante, Barcelona, Córdoba, Huesca, León, Málaga, Segovia, Seville, Tarragona, Toledo, Valencia, Valladolid, Zaragoza and some towns en route.

Estación de Chamartín (☎902 432343; Ⓜ Chamartín) North of the city centre, Estación de Chamartín has numerous long-distance rail services, especially those to/from northern Spain. This is also where long-haul international trains arrive from Paris and Lisbon.

Puerta de Atocha (www.renfe.es; Av de la Ciudad de Barcelona; Ⓜ Atocha Renfe) Madrid's main train station is at the southern end of the city centre. The bulk of trains for Spanish destinations depart from Atocha, especially those going south. For bookings, contact Renfe.

ℹ Getting Around

TO/FROM THE AIRPORT

Bus

The 24-hour Exprés Aeropuerto (Airport Express; bus 203; www.emtmadrid.es; €5, 40 minutes) runs between Puerta de Atocha train station and the airport. From 11.30pm until 6am, departures are from the Plaza de Cibeles, not the train station. Departures take place every 13 to 20 minutes from the station or at night-time every 35 minutes from Plaza de Cibeles.

Metro

The easiest way into town from the airport is line 8 of the metro (entrances in T2 and T4) to the Nuevos Ministerios transport interchange, which connects with lines 10 and 6. It operates from 6.05am to 1.30am. A one-way ticket to/from the airport costs €4.50. The journey to Nuevos Ministerios takes around 15 minutes, around 25 minutes from T4.

Taxi

There is a fixed rate of €30 for taxis from the airport to the city centre.

PUBLIC TRANSPORT

Madrid's modern metro (www.metromadrid.es) is a fast, efficient and safe way to navigate Madrid, and generally easier than getting to grips with bus routes. There are 11 colour-coded lines in central Madrid and colour maps showing the metro system are available from any metro station or online. The metro operates from 6.05am to 1.30am. Single-journey metro or bus tickets cost €1.50; Metrobús tickets valid for 10 rides on the metro or buses are €12.20.

TAXI

You can pick up a taxi at ranks throughout town or simply flag one down. From 7am to 9pm Monday to Friday, flag fall is €2.40 and you pay €1.05 per kilometre. The rest of the time flag fall is €2.90 and the per-kilometre charge is €1.20. Several supplementary charges, usually posted inside the taxi, apply; these include €3 from taxi ranks at train and bus stations.

CASTILLA Y LEÓN

Salamanca

POP 148,000

Whether floodlit by night or bathed in late afternoon sunlight, there's something magical about Salamanca. This is a city of rare architectural splendour, awash with golden sandstone overlaid with Latin inscriptions in ochre, and with an extraordinary virtuosity of plateresque and Renaissance styles. The monumental highlights are many, with the exceptional Plaza Mayor (illuminated to stunning effect at night) an unforgettable highlight. But this is also Castilla's liveliest city, home to a massive Spanish and international student population who throng the streets at night and provide the city with youth and vitality.

Sights

★Plaza Mayor SQUARE

Built between 1729 and 1755, Salamanca's exceptional grand square is widely considered to be Spain's most beautiful central plaza. The square is particularly memorable at night when illuminated (until midnight) to magical effect. Designed by Alberto Churriguera, it's a remarkably harmonious and controlled baroque display. The medallions placed around the square bear the busts of famous figures.

★Universidad Civil HISTORIC BUILDING

(☎923 29 44 00, ext 1150; www.salamanca.es; Calle de los Libreros; adult/concession €10/5, audio guide €2; ⏲10am-6.30pm Mon-Sat, to 1.30pm Sun) Founded initially as the Estudio General in 1218, the university reached the peak of its renown in the 15th and 16th centuries. The visual feast of the entrance facade is a tapestry in sandstone, bursting with images of mythical heroes, religious scenes and coats of arms. It's dominated by busts of Fernando and Isabel. Behind the facade, the highlight of an otherwise-modest collection of rooms lies upstairs: the extraordinary **university library**, the oldest one in Europe.

★Catedral Nueva CATHEDRAL

(☎923 21 74 76; www.catedralsalamanca.org; Plaza de Anaya; adult/child incl audio guide & admission to Catedral Vieja €4.75/3; ⏲10am-8pm Apr-Sep, 10am-5.15pm Oct-Mar) The tower of this late-Gothic cathedral lords over the city centre, its compelling churrigueresque (an ornate style of baroque architecture) dome visible from almost every angle. The interior is similarly impressive, with elaborate choir stalls, main chapel and retrochoir, much of it courtesy of the prolific José Churriguera. The ceilings are also exceptional, along with the Renaissance doorways – particularly the **Puerta del Nacimiento** on the western face, which stands out as one of several miracles worked in the city's native sandstone.

★Catedral Vieja CATHEDRAL

(☎923 28 10 45; www.catedralsalamanca.org; Plaza de Anaya; adult/child incl audio guide & admission to Catedral Nueva €4.75/3; ⏲10am-8pm Apr-Sep, 10am-5.15pm Oct-Mar) The Catedral Nueva's largely Romanesque predecessor, the Catedral Vieja is adorned with an exquisite

15th-century **altarpiece**, one of the finest outside Italy. Its 53 panels depict scenes from the lives of Christ and Mary and are topped by a haunting representation of the Final Judgement. The cloister was largely ruined in an earthquake in 1755, but the **Capilla de Anaya** houses an extravagant alabaster sepulchre and one of Europe's oldest organs, a Mudéjar work of art from the 16th century.

Sleeping

Hostal Concejo HOSTAL €
(923 21 47 37; www.hconcejo.com; Plaza de la Libertad 1; s €25-45, d €35-60; P ❄ wifi) A cut above the average *hostal*, the stylish Concejo has polished-wood floors, tasteful furnishings, light-filled rooms and a superb central location. Try to snag one of the corner rooms, such as room 104, which has a traditional, glassed-in balcony, complete with a table, chairs and people-watching views.

★ **Microtel Placentinos** BOUTIQUE HOTEL €€
(923 28 15 31; www.microtelplacentinos.com; Calle de Placentinos 9; s/d incl breakfast Sun-Thu €57/73, Fri & Sat €88/100; ❄ wifi) One of Salamanca's most charming boutique hotels, Microtel Placentinos is tucked away on a quiet street and has rooms with exposed stone walls and wooden beams. The service is faultless, and the overall atmosphere one of intimacy and discretion. All rooms have a hydromassage shower or tub and there's an outside whirlpool spa (open summer only).

★ **Salamanca Suite Studios** APARTMENT €€
(923 27 24 65; www.salamancasuitestudios.com; Plaza de la Libertad 4; r €59-110; ❄ wifi) This excellent place has smart and contemporary modern suites and apartments with kitchens; some have Nespresso coffee machines, and all have bucketloads of style with their white-and-turquoise colour schemes. The location is lovely and central and the service is discreet but attentive.

FIND THE FROG

The facade of the University of Salamanca is an ornate mass of sculptures and carvings, and hidden among this 16th-century plateresque creation is a tiny stone frog. Legend says that those who find the frog will have good luck in studies, life and love. If you don't want any help, look away now... It's sitting on a skull on the pillar that runs up the right-hand side of the facade.

Eating & Drinking

★ **La Cocina de Toño** TAPAS €€
(923 26 39 77; www.lacocinadetoño.es; Calle Gran Via 20; tapas from €1.60, menú €17, mains €18-23; noon-4.30pm & 8-11.30pm Tue-Sat, noon-4.30pm Sun; wifi) This place owes its loyal following to its creative *pinchos* (tapas-like snacks) and half-servings of dishes such as escalope of foie gras with roast apple and passionfruit gelatin. The restaurant serves more traditional fare as befits the decor, but the bar is one of Salamanca's gastronomic stars. Slightly removed from the old city, it draws a predominantly Spanish crowd.

Mesón Las Conchas CASTILIAN €€
(923 21 21 67; Rúa Mayor 16; mains €10-21; bar 8am-midnight, restaurant 1-4pm & 8pm-midnight;) Enjoy a choice of outdoor tables, an atmospheric bar or the upstairs, wood-beamed dining area. The bar caters mainly to locals who know their *embutidos* (cured meats). For sit-down meals, there's a good mix of roasts, *platos combinados* and *raciones* (full-size tapas). The restaurant serves a highly rated oven-baked turbot.

Doctor Cocktail COCKTAIL BAR
(923 26 31 51; Calle del Doctor Piñuela 5; 4pm-late) Excellent cocktails, friendly bar staff and a cool crowd make for a fine mix just north of the Plaza Mayor. Apart from the creative list of cocktails, it has 32 different kinds of gin to choose from and above-average tonic to go with it.

Information

Municipal & Regional Tourist Office (923 21 83 42; www.salamanca.es; Plaza Mayor 32; 9am-2pm & 4.30-8pm Mon-Fri, 10am-8pm Sat, 10am-2pm Sun Easter–mid-Oct, 9am-2pm & 4-6.30pm Mon-Fri, 10am-6.30pm Sat, 10am-2pm Sun mid-Oct–Easter) The municipal tourist office shares an office with the regional office, on Plaza Mayor. An audio guide to city sights can be accessed on your smartphone from www.audioguiasalamanca.es.

Getting There & Away

The bus and train stations are 10 and 15 minutes' walk, respectively, from Plaza Mayor.

BUS

There are buses to Madrid (regular/express €17/23, 2½ to 3½ hours, once or twice hourly) and Ávila (€9.25, 1½ hours, four daily).

WORTH A TRIP

BURGOS & LEÓN – A TALE OF TWO CATHEDRALS

Burgos and León are cathedral towns par excellence, and both are well connected by train and bus to Madrid.

Burgos

Catedral (947 20 47 12; www.catedraldeburgos.es; Plaza del Rey Fernando; adult/under 14yr incl audio guide €7/1.50, 4.30-6pm Tue free; 9.30am-7.30pm) This Unesco World Heritage–listed cathedral, once a former modest Romanesque church, is a masterpiece. Work began on a grander scale in 1221; remarkably, within 40 years most of the French Gothic structure had been completed. You can enter from Plaza de Santa María for free for access to the **Capilla del Santísimo Cristo**, with its much-revered 13th-century crucifix, and the **Capilla de Santa Tecla**, with its extraordinary ceiling. However, we recommend that you visit the cathedral in its entirety.

Hotel Norte y Londres (947 26 41 25; www.hotelnorteylondres.com; Plaza de Alonso Martínez 10; s €32-55, d €36-70; P @) Set in a former 16th-century palace and decorated with understated period charm, this fine, family-run hotel promises spacious rooms with antique furnishings and polished wooden floors. All rooms have pretty balconies; those on the 4th floor are more modern. The bathrooms are exceptionally large and the service friendly and efficient.

Cervecería Morito (947 26 75 55; Calle de Diego Porcelos 1; tapas/raciones from €3.50/5.00; 12.30-3.30pm & 7-11.30pm) Cervecería Morito is the undisputed king of Burgos tapas bars and as such it's always crowded. A typical order is *alpargata* (lashings of cured ham with bread, tomato and olive oil) or the *revueltos Capricho de Burgos* (scrambled eggs served with potatoes, blood sausage, red peppers, baby eels and mushrooms) – the latter is a meal in itself.

León

Catedral (987 87 57 70; www.catedraldeleon.org; Plaza de Regia; adult/concession/under 12yr €6/5/free; 9.30am-1.30pm & 4-8pm Mon-Fri, 9.30am-noon & 2-6pm Sat, 9.30-11am & 2-8pm Sun Jun-Sep, 9.30am-1.30pm & 4-7pm Mon-Sat, 9.30am-2pm Sun Oct-May) León's 13th-century cathedral, with its soaring towers, flying buttresses and breathtaking interior, is the city's spiritual heart. Whether spotlit by night or bathed in glorious northern sunshine, the cathedral, arguably Spain's premier Gothic masterpiece, exudes a glorious, almost luminous quality. The show-stopping facade has a radiant **rose window**, three richly sculpted doorways and two muscular towers. The main entrance is lorded over by a scene of the Last Supper, while an extraordinary gallery of *vidrieras* (stained-glass windows) awaits you inside.

Panteón Real (www.turismoleon.org; Plaza de San Isidoro; €5, 4-6.30pm Thu €1; 10am-1.30pm & 4-6.30pm Mon-Sat, 10am-2pm Sun) Attached to the **Real Basílica de San Isidoro** (987 87 61 61; Plaza de San Isidro; 7.30am-11pm), the stunning Panteón Real houses royal sarcophagi, which rest with quiet dignity beneath a canopy of some of the finest Romanesque frescos in Spain. Colourful motifs of biblical scenes drench the vaults and arches of this extraordinary hall, held aloft by marble columns with intricately carved capitals. The pantheon also houses a small **museum** where you can admire the shrine of San Isidoro, a mummified finger(!) of the saint and other treasures.

La Posada Regia (987 21 31 73; www.regialeon.com; Calle de Regidores 9-11; incl breakfast s €54-70, d €59-130;) This place has the feel of a *casa rural* (village or farmstead accommodation) despite being in the city centre. The secret is a 14th-century building, magnificently restored (with wooden beams, exposed brick and understated antique furniture), with individually styled rooms and supremely comfortable beds and bathrooms. As with anywhere in the Barrio Húmedo, weekend nights can be noisy.

TRAIN

Trains run to Madrid's Chamartín station (€12 to €24, two to three hours, 10 trains daily), Ávila (€12, 1¼ hours, seven trains) and Segovia (€9.50 to €32, 1¼ hours, two to four trains).

Segovia

POP 52,700

Unesco World Heritage–listed Segovia has a stunning monument to Roman grandeur and a castle said to have inspired Walt Disney, and is otherwise a city of warm terracotta and sandstone hues set amid the rolling hills of Castilla.

Sights

★Acueducto LANDMARK

(www.turismodesegovia.com) Segovia's most recognisable symbol is El Acueducto (Roman Aqueduct), an 894m-long engineering wonder that looks like an enormous comb plunged into Segovia. First raised here by the Romans in the 1st century AD, the aqueduct was built with not a drop of mortar to hold the more than 20,000 uneven granite blocks together. It's made up of 163 arches and, at its highest point in Plaza del Azoguejo, rises 28m high.

★Alcázar CASTLE

(☎921 46 07 59; www.alcazardesegovia.com; Plaza de la Reina Victoria Eugenia; adult/concession/child under 6yr €5.50/5/free, tower €2.50; ⏲10am-6.30pm Oct-Mar, to 7.30pm Apr-Sep; 👪) Rapunzel towers, turrets topped with slate witches' hats and a deep moat at its base make the Alcázar a prototype fairy-tale castle – so much so that its design inspired Walt Disney's vision of Sleeping Beauty's castle. Fortified since Roman days, the site takes its name from the Arabic *al-qasr* (fortress). It was rebuilt in the 13th and 14th centuries, but the whole lot burned down in 1862. What you see today is an evocative, over-the-top reconstruction of the original.

★Catedral CATHEDRAL

(☎921 46 22 05; www.turismodesegovia.com; Plaza Mayor; adult/concession €3/2, Sun morning free, tower tour €5; ⏲9.30am-6.30pm Apr-Oct, 9.30am-5.30pm Mon-Sat, 1.15-5.30pm Sun Nov-Mar, tower tours 10.30pm & 12.30pm year-round plus 4.30pm Apr-Oct, 4pm Nov-Mar) Started in 1525 on the site of a former chapel, Segovia's cathedral is a powerful expression of Gothic architecture that took almost 200 years to complete. The austere three-nave interior is anchored by an imposing choir stall and enlivened by 20-odd chapels, including the **Capilla del Cristo del Consuelo**, with its magnificent Romanesque doorway, and the **Capilla de la Piedad**, containing an important altarpiece by Juan de Juni. Join an hour-long guided tour to climb the tower for fabulous views.

Plaza Mayor SQUARE

The shady Plaza Mayor is the nerve centre of old Segovia, lined by an eclectic assortment of buildings, arcades and cafes and with an open pavilion in its centre. It's also the site of the cathedral and the regional tourist office.

Sleeping

Häb Urban Hostel HOSTAL €

(☎921 46 10 26; www.habhostel.com; Calle de Cervantes 16; r €48-75; ❄📶) This bright and welcoming *hostal* – think doubles with private bathrooms rather than dorms with bunk beds, despite the name – is modern and has a fine location just where the pedestrian street begins the climb up into the old town. Some rooms are on the small side, but the look is light and contemporary.

★Hospedería La Gran Casa Mudéjar HISTORIC HOTEL €€

(☎921 46 62 50; www.lacasamudejar.com; Calle de Isabel la Católica 8; r €45-95; ❄@📶) Spread over two buildings, this place has been magnificently renovated, blending genuine 15th-century Mudéjar carved wooden ceilings in some rooms with modern amenities. In the newer wing, top-floor rooms have fine mountain views out over the rooftops of Segovia's old Jewish quarter. Adding to the appeal is a small spa. The restaurant comes highly recommended.

Eating

★Restaurante El Fogón Sefardí JEWISH €€

(☎921 46 62 50; www.lacasamudejar.com; Calle de Isabel la Católica 8; tapas from €2.50, mains €14-25, set menus €18.50-24.50; ⏲1.30-4.30pm & 5.30-11.30pm) Located within the Hospedería La Gran Casa Mudéjar, this is one of the most original places in town. Sephardic Jewish cuisine is served either on the intimate patio or in the splendid dining hall with original 15th-century Mudéjar flourishes. The theme in the bar is equally diverse. Stop here for a taste of the award-winning tapas. Reservations recommended.

WORTH A TRIP

ÁVILA

Ávila's old city, 1½ hours from Madrid by train or bus, and about halfway between Segovia and Salamanca, is one of Spain's best-preserved medieval bastions, surrounded by imposing walls with eight monumental gates, 88 watchtowers and more than 2500 turrets. Ávila is also famed as the home town of the 16th-century mystic and religious reformer, Santa Teresa de Ávila.

Murallas (www.muralladeavila.com; adult/child under 12yr €5/free; ⏲10am-8pm Apr-Oct, to 6pm Nov-Mar; 👪) Ávila's splendid 12th-century walls stretch for 2.5km atop the remains of earlier Roman and Muslim battlements and rank among the world's best-preserved medieval defensive perimeters. Two sections of the walls can be climbed – a 300m stretch that can be accessed from just inside the **Puerta del Alcázar**, and a longer (1300m) stretch from **Puerta de los Leales** that runs the length of the old city's northern perimeter. The admission price includes a multilingual audio guide.

Catedral del Salvador (☎920 21 16 41; Plaza de la Catedral; admission incl audio guide €5; ⏲10am-7pm Mon-Fri, 10am-8pm Sat, noon-6.30pm Sun) Ávila's 12th-century cathedral is both a house of worship and an ingenious fortress: its stout granite apse forms the central bulwark in the historic city walls. The sombre, Gothic-style facade conceals a magnificent interior with an exquisite early 16th-century **altar frieze** showing the life of Jesus, plus Renaissance-era carved choir stalls and a **museum** with an El Greco painting and a splendid silver monstrance by Juan de Arfe. (Push the buttons to illuminate the altar and the choir stalls.)

Hotel El Rastro (☎920 35 22 25; www.elrastroavila.com; Calle Cepedas; s/d €35/55; ❄📶) This atmospheric hotel occupies a former 16th-century palace with original stone, exposed brickwork and a natural, earth-toned colour scheme exuding a calm, understated elegance. Each room has a different form, but most have high ceilings and plenty of space. Note that the owners also run a marginally cheaper *hostal* (budget hotel) of the same name around the corner.

★**Casa Duque** SPANISH €€€
(☎921 46 24 87; www.restauranteduque.es; Calle de Cervantes 12; mains €19.50-24, set menus €35-40; ⏲12.30-4.30pm & 8.30-11.30pm) Segovia's famed speciality *cochinillo asado* (roast suckling pig) has been served at this atmospheric *mesón* (tavern) since the 1890s. For the uninitiated, try the *menú de degustación* (€40), which includes *cochinillo*. Downstairs is the informal *cueva* (cave), where you can get tapas and full-bodied *cazuelas* (stews). Reservations recommended.

ℹ Information

Centro de Recepción de Visitantes (☎921 46 67 20; www.turismodesegovia.com; Plaza del Azoguejo 1; ⏲10am-8pm Mon-Sat, to 7pm Sun Apr-Sep, 10am-6.30pm Mon-Sat, to 5pm Sun Oct-Mar) Segovia's main tourist office runs at least two guided tours of the city's monumental core daily (€11 to €14 per person), usually departing at 10.30am and 4.30pm (although check as this schedule can change). Reserve ahead.

Regional Tourist Office (☎921 46 60 70; www.segoviaturismo.es; Plaza Mayor 10; ⏲9.30am-2pm & 5-8pm Mon-Sat, 9.30am-5pm Sun Jul–mid-Sep, 9.30am-2pm & 4-7pm Mon-Sat, 9.30am-5pm Sun mid-Sep–Jun)

ℹ Getting There & Away

BUS

The bus station is just off Paseo de Ezequiel González. Buses run half-hourly to Segovia from Madrid's Intercambiador de Moncloa bus stop (€7.90, 1½ hours). Buses depart to Ávila (€6.20, one hour, eight daily) and Salamanca (€14, three hours, four daily), among other destinations.

TRAIN

Up to five normal trains run daily from Madrid to Segovia (€8.25, two hours), leaving you at the main train station 2.5km from the aqueduct. The faster option is the 25 daily high-speed Avant (€13, 27 minutes) and Alvia (€24, 28 minutes) trains which deposit you at Segovia-Guiomar station, 5km from the aqueduct.

CASTILLA-LA MANCHA

Toledo

POP 85,600

Though one of Spain's smallest regional capitals, Toledo looms large in the nation's history and consciousness as a bulwark of the Spanish church and symbol of a flourishing multicultural medieval society where, tradition has it, Muslim, Christian and Jewish communities coexisted peacefully. The old town today is a treasure chest of churches, museums, synagogues and mosques set in a labyrinth of narrow streets, plazas and inner patios in a lofty setting high above the Río Tajo. Toledo's other forte is art, in particular the haunting canvases of El Greco, the impossible-to-classify painter with whom the city is synonymous. Crowded by day, Toledo changes dramatically after dark when the streets take on a moody, other-worldly air.

Sights

★Catedral CATHEDRAL

(www.catedralprimada.es; Plaza del Ayuntamiento; adult/child €12.50/free; 10am-6pm Mon-Sat, 2-6pm Sun) Toledo's illustrious main church ranks among the top 10 cathedrals in Spain. An impressive example of medieval Gothic architecture, its humongous interior is full of the classic characteristics of the style, rose windows, flying buttresses, ribbed vaults and pointed arches among them. Equally visit-worthy is the art. The cathedral's sacristy is a veritable art gallery of old masters, with works by Velázquez, Goya and – of course – El Greco.

★Alcázar FORTRESS

(Museo del Ejército; www.toledo-turismo.com; Calle Alféreces Provisionales; adult/child €5/free, Sun free; 10am-5pm Thu-Tue) At the highest point in the city looms the forbidding Alcázar. Rebuilt under Franco, it has been reopened as a vast **military museum**. The usual displays of uniforms and medals are here, but the best part is the exhaustive historical section, with an in-depth overview of the nation's history in Spanish and English.

★Sinagoga del Tránsito SYNAGOGUE, MUSEUM

(925 22 36 65; http://museosefardi.mcu.es; Calle Samuel Leví; adult/child €3/1.50, after 2pm Sat & all day Sun free; 9.30am-7.30pm Tue-Sat Mar-Oct, 9.30am-6pm Tue-Sat Nov-Feb, 10am-3pm Sun year-round) This magnificent synagogue was built in 1355 by special permission from Pedro I. The synagogue now houses the **Museo Sefardí**. The vast main prayer hall has been expertly restored and the Mudéjar decoration and intricately carved pine ceiling are striking. Exhibits provide an insight into the history of Jewish culture in Spain, and include archaeological finds, a memorial garden, costumes and ceremonial artefacts.

Sleeping & Eating

La Posada de Manolo BOUTIQUE HOTEL €

(925 28 22 50; www.laposadademanolo.com; Calle de Sixto Ramón Parro 8; s/d from €55/77;) This memorable hotel has themed each floor with furnishings and decor reflecting one of the three cultures of Toledo: Christian, Islamic and Jewish. There are stunning views of the old town and cathedral from the terrace.

★Hacienda del Cardenal HISTORIC HOTEL €€

(925 22 49 00; www.haciendadelcardenal.com; Paseo de Recaredo 24; r incl breakfast €95-135;) This wonderful 18th-century mansion has soft ochre-coloured walls, arches and columns. Some rooms are grand, others are spartan, and all come with dark furniture, plush fabrics and parquet floors. Several overlook the glorious terraced gardens.

La Abadía CASTILIAN, TAPAS €€

(www.abadiatoledo.com; Plaza de San Nicolás 3; raciones €7-15; bar 8am-midnight, restaurant 1-4pm & 8.30pm-midnight) In a former 16th-century palace, this atmospheric bar and restaurant has arches, niches and coloured bottles lined up as decoration, spread throughout a warren of brick-and-stone-clad rooms. The menu includes lightweight dishes and tapas, but the 'Menú de Montes de Toledo' (€20) is a fabulous collection of tastes from the nearby mountains.

★Adolfo MODERN EUROPEAN €€€

(925 22 73 21; www.adolforestaurante.com; Callejón Hombre de Palo 7; mains €25-28; 1-4pm & 8pm-midnight Mon-Sat, 1-4pm Sun) Toledo doffs its hat to fine dining at this temple of good food and market freshness. Run by notable La Mancha–born chef Adolfo Muñoz, the restaurant has been around for over 25 years, and in that time has morphed into one of Spain's best gourmet establishments. The king of Spain – no less – has sung the praises of Adolfo's partridge.

Information

Main Tourist Office (925 25 40 30; www.toledo-turismo.com; Plaza Consistorio 1; 10am-6pm) Within sight of the cathedral. There's another branch (9.30am-3pm) at the train station.

Getting There & Away

For most major destinations, you'll need to backtrack to Madrid.

BUS

Buses run from Madrid's Plaza Elíptica to Toledo's **bus station** (925 21 58 50; www.alsa.es; Avenida de Castilla La Mancha), and back, roughly every half-hour (€5.40, 45 minutes to 1½ hours), some going direct, some via villages.

TRAIN

High-speed trains run about hourly from Madrid's Puerta de Atocha station (one way/return €13/21, 33 minutes) to Toledo's pretty **train station** (902 24 02 02; www.renfe.es; Paseo de la Rosa).

CATALONIA

Barcelona

POP 1.6 MILLION

Barcelona is one of Europe's coolest cities. Despite two millennia of history, it's a forward-thinking place, always at the cutting edge of art, design and cuisine. Whether you explore its medieval palaces and plazas, admire the Modernista masterpieces of Antoni Gaudí and others, shop for designer fashions along its bustling boulevards, sample its exciting nightlife or just soak up the sun on the beaches, you'll find it hard not to fall in love with this vibrant city.

As much as Barcelona is a visual feast, it will also lead you into culinary temptation. Anything from traditional Catalan cooking to the latest in avant-garde new Spanish cuisine will have your appetite in overdrive.

Sights & Activities

La Rambla & El Raval

Spain's most famous boulevard, La Rambla is pure sensory overload. Stretching from Plaça de Catalunya to the waterfront, it's always a hive of activity, with buskers, hawkers, human statues and con artists (watch out!) mingling amid the sunlit cafes, flower stalls, historic buildings, markets, shops and a ceaseless parade of saunterers from all corners of the globe.

★Mercat de la Boqueria MARKET

(Map p590; 93 412 13 15; www.boqueria.info; La Rambla 91; 8am-8.30pm Mon-Sat; M Liceu) Mercat de la Boqueria is possibly La Rambla's most interesting building, not so much for its Modernista-influenced design (it was actually built over a long period, from 1840 to 1914, on the site of the former St Joseph Monastery), but for the action of the food market within.

Gran Teatre del Liceu ARCHITECTURE

(Map p590; 93 485 99 00; www.liceubarcelona.cat; La Rambla 51-59; tours 45/30min €9/6; 45min tours hourly from 2-6pm Mon-Fri, from 9.30am Sat, 30min tours 1.30pm; M Liceu) If you can't catch a night at the opera, you can still have a look around one of Europe's greatest opera houses, known to locals as the Liceu. Smaller than Milan's La Scala but bigger than Venice's La Fenice, it can seat up to 2300 people in its grand horseshoe auditorium.

Barri Gòtic

You could easily spend several days or even a week exploring the medieval streets of the Barri Gòtic, Barcelona's oldest quarter. In addition to major sights, its tangle of narrow lanes and tranquil plazas conceals some of the city's most atmospheric shops, restaurants, cafes and bars.

★La Catedral CATHEDRAL

(Map p590; 93 342 82 62; www.catedralbcn.org; Plaça de la Seu; free, 'donation entrance' €7, choir €3, roof €3; 8am-12.45pm & 5.15-7.30pm Mon-Fri, 8am-8pm Sat & Sun, entry by donation 1-5.30pm Mon,1-5pm Sat, 2-5pm Sun; M Jaume I) Barcelona's central place of worship presents a magnificent image. The richly decorated main facade, laced with gargoyles and the stone intricacies you would expect of northern European Gothic, sets it quite apart from other churches in Barcelona. The facade was actually added in 1870, although the rest of the building was built between 1298 and 1460. The other facades are sparse in decoration, and the octagonal, flat-roofed towers are a clear reminder that, even here, Catalan Gothic architectural principles prevailed.

Barcelona

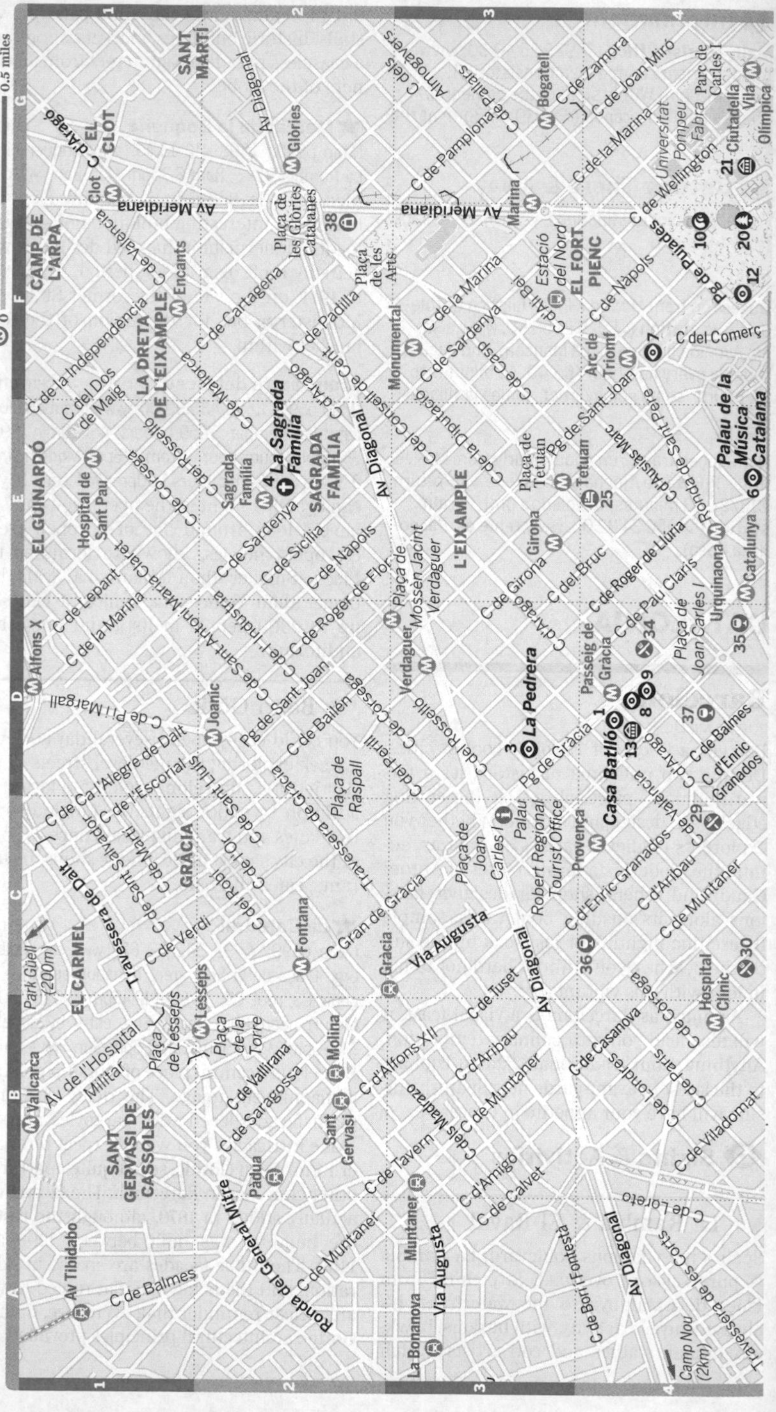

0 1 km
0 0.5 miles

A B C D E F G
1 2 3 4

Av Tibidabo
C de Balmes
Vallcarca
Av de l'Hospital Militar
Park Güell (200m)
EL CARMEL
Travessera de Dalt
SANT GERVASI DE CASSOLES
Plaça de Lesseps
Lesseps
Plaça de la Torre
Pàdua
Ronda del General Mitre
C de Saragossa
C de Vallirana
C de Muntaner
Sant Gervasi
Molina
C de Tavern
C dels Madrazo
C d'Alfons XII
La Bonanova
Muntaner
Via Augusta
C d'Amigó
C de Calvet
C de Muntaner
C d'Aribau
C de Tuset
C de Bori i Fontestà
Av Diagonal
Camp Nou (2km)
Travessera de les Corts
C de Loreto
C de Viladomat
C de Londres
C de París
C de Casanova
C de Còrsega
Hospital Clínic
30
C de Muntaner
C d'Aribau
C d'Enric Granados
36
Provença
C de Sant Salvador
C de Martí
C de Verdi
GRÀCIA
C de Ca l'Alegre de Dalt
C de l'Escorial
C del Robí
C de l'Or
C de Sant Lluís
Fontana
Gràcia
C Gran de Gràcia
Travessera de Gràcia
Plaça de Raspall
Via Augusta
Plaça de Joan Carles I
Palau Robert Regional Tourist Office
C del Perill
C de Còrsega
C del Rosselló
3 La Pedrera
Pg de Gràcia
1 Casa Batlló
13
8
9
34
C de València
C d'Aragó
C de Balmes
C d'Enric Granados
29
37
Plaça de Joan Carles I
35
Alfons X
C de Pi i Margall
Joanic
Pg de Sant Joan
C de Bailén
C de Sant Antoni Maria Claret
C de l'Indústria
C de Roger de Flor
C de Lepant
C de la Marina
EL GUINARDÓ
Hospital de Sant Pau
C del Dos de Maig
C de la Independència
C de Còrsega
C del Rosselló
C de Sardenya
C de Sicília
C de Nàpols
Sagrada Família
4 La Sagrada Família
SAGRADA FAMÍLIA
C d'Aragó
Av Diagonal
Verdaguer
Plaça de Mossèn Jacint Verdaguer
L'EIXAMPLE
C de Girona
Girona
C d'Aragó
C del Bruc
C de Roger de Llúria
C de Pau Claris
Passeig de Gràcia
Urquinaona
Catalunya
6 Palau de la Música Catalana
Plaça de Tetuan
Tetuan
25
Pg de Sant Joan
C d'Ausiàs Marc
Ronda de Sant Pere
C del Consell de Cent
C de la Diputació
C de Casp
C de Sardenya
C de la Marina
Monumental
Arc de Triomf
7
C del Comerç
C de Nàpols
C d'Alí Bei
Estació del Nord
EL FORT PIENC
Pg de Pujades
12
10
20
21
Ciutadella Vila Olímpica
Parc de Carles I
Universitat Pompeu Fabra
C de Wellington
C de la Marina
C de Joan Miró
C de Zamora
Bogatell
Marina
Av Meridiana
C de Pamplona
C de Pallars
C dels Almogàvers
Plaça de les Arts
38
C de Padilla
C de Mallorca
C de Cartagena
Encants
LA DRETA DE L'EIXAMPLE
C de València
CAMP DE L'ARPA
Clot
C d'Aragó
EL CLOT
SANT MARTÍ
Plaça de les Glòries Catalanes
Glòries
Av Diagonal

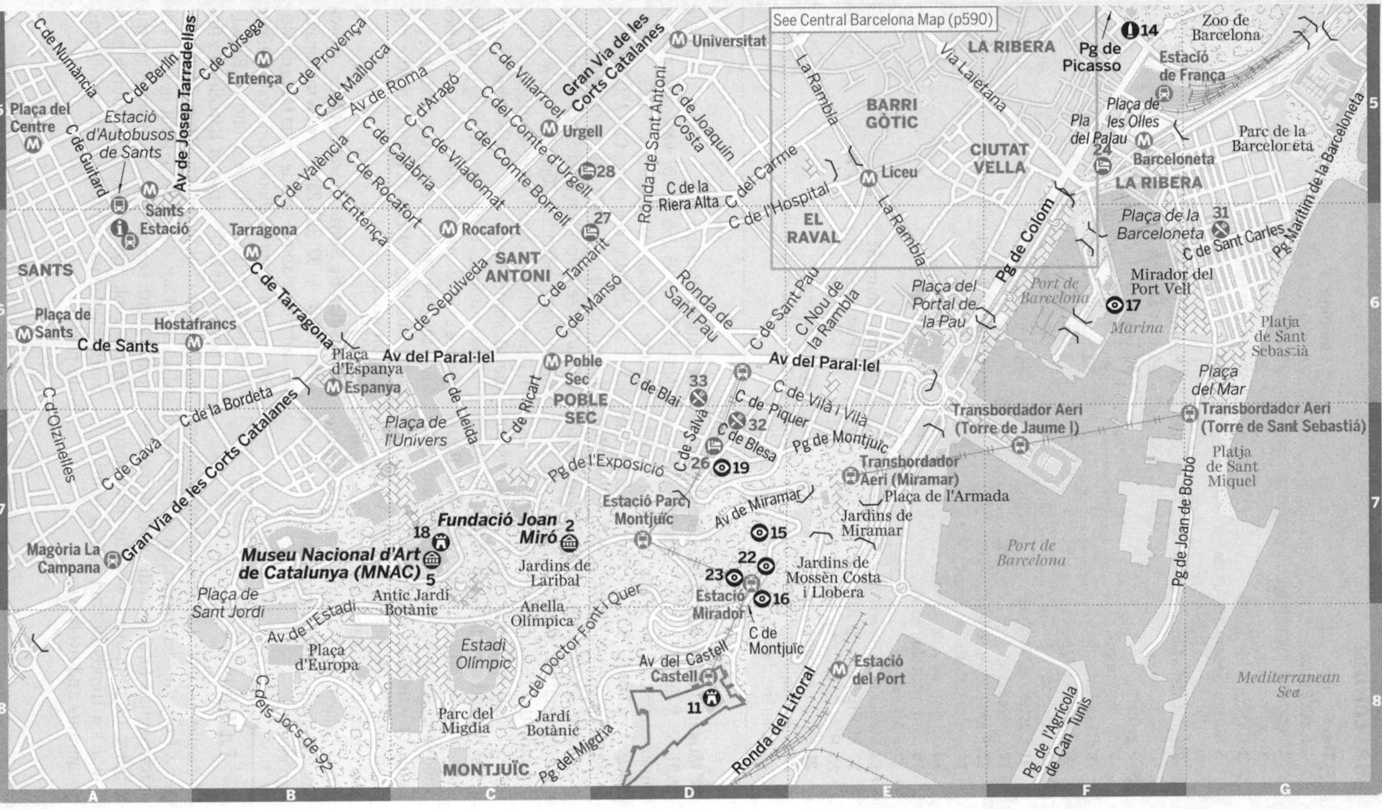

See Central Barcelona Map (p590)
C de Numància
Plaça del Centre
C de Guitard
Estació d'Autobusos de Sants
C de Berlín
Av de Josep Tarradellas
C de Còrsega
Entença
C de Provença
C de Mallorca
Av de Roma
C d'Aragó
C de València
C de Calàbria
C de Viladomat
C de Rocafort
C d'Entença
C de Villarroel
C del Comte d'Urgell
C del Comte Borrell
Urgell
Gran Via de les Corts Catalanes
Universitat
Ronda de Sant Antoni
C de Joaquín Costa
C de la Riera Alta
C del Carme
C de l'Hospital
EL RAVAL
La Rambla
BARRI GÒTIC
Liceu
CIUTAT VELLA
Via Laietana
LA RIBERA
Pg de Picasso
Zoo de Barcelona
Estació de França
Plaça de les Olles
Pla del Palau
Barceloneta
Parc de la Barceloneta
Plaça de la Barceloneta
C de Sant Carles
Pg Marítim de la Barceloneta
Sants Estació
Tarragona
Rocafort
SANTS
C de Tarragona
SANT ANTONI
C de Tamarit
C de Sepúlveda
C de Manso
Ronda de Sant Pau
C de Sant Pau
C Nou de la Rambla
Pg de Colom
Plaça del Portal de la Pau
Port de Barcelona
Mirador del Port Vell
Marina
Platja de Sant Sebastià
Plaça de Sants
Hostafrancs
C de Sants
Plaça d'Espanya
Espanya
Av del Paral·lel
Poble Sec
POBLE SEC
C de Lleida
C de Ricart
C de Blai
C de Salvà
C de Piquer
C de Blesa
C de Vila i Vilà
Pg de Montjuïc
Plaça del Mar
Transbordador Aeri (Torre de Jaume I)
Transbordador Aeri (Torre de Sant Sebastià)
Platja de Sant Miquel
Pg de Joan de Borbó
C d'Olzinelles
C de la Bordeta
C de Gavà
Gran Via de les Corts Catalanes
Plaça de l'Univers
Pg de l'Exposició
Transbordador Aeri (Miramar)
Plaça de l'Armada
Estació Parc Montjuïc
Av de Miramar
Jardins de Miramar
Fundació Joan Miró
Museu Nacional d'Art de Catalunya (MNAC)
Magòria La Campana
Jardins de Laribal
Jardins de Mossèn Costa i Llobera
Estació Mirador
Plaça de Sant Jordi
Antic Jardí Botànic
Av de l'Estadi
Anella Olímpica
C del Doctor Font i Quer
C de Montjuïc
Plaça d'Europa
Estadi Olímpic
Av del Castell
Castell
Estació del Port
Ronda del Litoral
Pg de l'Agrícola
de Can Tunis
Mediterranean Sea
C dels Jocs de 92
Parc del Migdia
Jardí Botànic
Pg del Migdia
MONTJUÏC

Barcelona

Top Sights

1 Casa Batlló ... D4
2 Fundació Joan Miró ... C7
3 La Pedrera ... D3
4 La Sagrada Família ... E2
5 Museu Nacional d'Art de Catalunya (MNAC) ... C7
6 Palau de la Música Catalana ... E4

Sights

7 Arc de Triomf ... F4
8 Casa Amatller ... D4
9 Casa Lleó Morera ... D4
10 Cascada ... F4
11 Castell de Montjuïc ... D8
12 Castell dels Tres Dragons ... F4
13 Fundació Antoni Tàpies ... D4
14 Homenatge a Picasso ... F5
15 Jardins de Joan Brossa ... D7
16 Jardins del Mirador ... D7
17 L'Aquàrium ... F6
18 Mirador del Palau Nacional ... C7
19 MUHBA Refugi 307 ... D7
20 Parc de la Ciutadella ... F4
21 Parlament de Catalunya ... G4
22 Plaça de la Sardana ... D7
23 Telefèric de Montjuïc ... D7

Sleeping

24 H10 Port Vell ... F5
25 Hostal Center Inn ... E4
26 Hotel Brummell ... D7
27 Hotel Market ... D6
28 Pars Tailor's Hostel ... C5

Eating

29 Cinc Sentits ... C4
30 Disfrutar ... C4
31 La Cova Fumada ... G6
32 Palo Cortao ... D7
33 Quimet i Quimet ... D6
Speakeasy ... (see 36)
34 Tapas 24 ... D4

Drinking & Nightlife

35 City Hall ... D4
36 Dry Martini ... C4
37 Monvínic ... D4

Entertainment

Palau de la Música Catalana ... (see 6)

Shopping

38 Els Encants Vells ... F2

★**Museu d'Història de Barcelona** MUSEUM
(MUHBA; Map p590; ☎93 256 21 00; www.museuhistoria.bcn.cat; Plaça del Rei; adult/concession/child €7/5/free, 3-8pm Sun & 1st Sun of month free; ⏲10am-7pm Tue-Sat, to 2pm Mon, to 8pm Sun; ; M Jaume I) One of Barcelona's most fascinating museums takes you back through the centuries to the very foundations of Roman Barcino. You'll stroll over ruins of the old streets, sewers, laundries and wine- and fish-making factories that flourished here following the town's founding by Emperor Augustus around 10 BC. Equally impressive is the building itself, which was once part of the Palau Reial Major (Grand Royal Palace) on Plaça del Rei, among the key locations of medieval princely power in Barcelona.

La Ribera

In medieval days, La Ribera was a stone's throw from the Mediterranean and the heart of Barcelona's foreign trade, with homes belonging to numerous wealthy merchants. Now it's a trendy district full of boutiques, restaurants and lively bars.

★**Museu Picasso** MUSEUM
(Map p590; ☎93 256 30 00; www.museupicasso.bcn.cat; Carrer de Montcada 15-23; adult/concession/child all collections €14/7.50/free, permanent collection €11/7/free, temporary exhibitions €4.50/3/free, 3-7pm Sun & 1st Sun of month free; ⏲9am-7pm Tue-Sun, to 9.30pm Thu; ; M Jaume I) The setting alone, in five contiguous medieval stone mansions, makes the Museu Picasso unique (and worth the probable queues). The pretty courtyards, galleries and staircases preserved in the first three of these buildings are as delightful as the collection inside.

★**Basílica de Santa Maria del Mar** CHURCH
(Map p590; ☎93 310 23 90; www.santamariadelmarbarcelona.org; Plaça de Santa Maria del Mar; €8; ⏲guided tours 1.15pm, 2pm, 3pm, 5.15pm; M Jaume I) At the southwest end of Passeig del Born stands the apse of Barcelona's finest Catalan Gothic church, Santa Maria del Mar (Our Lady of the Sea). Built in the 14th century with record-breaking alacrity for the time (it took just 54 years), the church is remarkable for its architectural harmony and simplicity.

★**Palau de la Música Catalana** ARCHITECTURE
(Map p586; ☎93 295 72 00; www.palaumusica.cat; Carrer de Palau de la Música 4-6; adult/concession/child €18/11/free; ⊙guided tours 10am-3.30pm, to 6pm Easter, Jul & Aug; Ⓜ Urquinaona) This concert hall is a high point of Barcelona's Modernista architecture, a symphony in tile, brick, sculpted stone and stained glass. Built by Domènech i Montaner between 1905 and 1908 for the Orfeo Català musical society, it was conceived as a temple for the Catalan Renaixença (Renaissance).

Parc de la Ciutadella PARK
(Map p586; Passeig de Picasso; ⊙8am-9pm May-Sep, to 7pm Oct-Apr; 👪; Ⓜ Arc de Triomf) Come for a stroll, a picnic, a boat ride on the lake or to inspect Catalonia's regional parliament, but don't miss a visit to this, the most central green lung in the city. Parc de la Ciutadella is perfect for winding down.

L'Eixample

Modernisme, the Catalan version of art nouveau, transformed Barcelona's cityscape in the early 20th century. Most Modernista works, including Antoni Gaudí's unfinished masterpiece, La Sagrada Família, were built in the elegant, if traffic-filled, L'Eixample (pronounced 'lay-sham-pluh'), a grid-plan district that was developed from the 1870s on.

★**La Sagrada Família** CHURCH
(Map p586; ☎93 208 04 14; www.sagradafamilia.cat; Carrer de Mallorca 401; adult/concession/under 11yr €15/13/free; ⊙9am-8pm Apr-Sep, to 6pm Oct-Mar; Ⓜ Sagrada Família) If you have time for only one sightseeing outing, this should be it. La Sagrada Família inspires awe by its sheer verticality, and in the manner of the medieval cathedrals it emulates, it's still under construction after more than 130 years. When completed, the highest tower will be more than half as high again as those that stand today.

★**La Pedrera** ARCHITECTURE
(Casa Milà; Map p586; ☎902 202138; www.lapedrera.com; Passeig de Gràcia 92; adult/concession/under 13yr/under 7yr €22/16.50/11/free; ⊙9am-6.30pm & 7pm-9pm Mon-Sun; Ⓜ Diagonal) This undulating beast is another madcap Gaudí masterpiece, built in 1905–10 as a combined apartment and office block. Formally called Casa Milà, after the businessman who commissioned it, it is better known as La Pedrera (the Quarry) because of its uneven grey stone facade, which ripples around the corner of Carrer de Provença.

DON'T MISS

LA SAGRADA FAMÍLIA HIGHLIGHTS

Roof The roof of **La Sagrada Família** is held up by a forest of extraordinary angled pillars. As the pillars soar towards the ceiling, they sprout a web of supporting branches, creating the effect of a forest canopy.

Nativity Facade The artistic pinnacle of the building. You can climb high up inside some of the four towers by a combination of lifts and narrow spiral staircases – a vertiginous experience.

Passion Facade The southwest Passion Facade, on the theme of Christ's last days and death, was built between 1954 and 1978 based on surviving drawings by Gaudí, with four towers and a large, sculpture-bedecked portal by Josep Subirachs.

Glory Facade The Glory Facade is under construction and will, like the others, be crowned by four towers – the total of 12 representing the Twelve Apostles.

Museu Gaudí The Museu Gaudí, below ground level, includes interesting material on Gaudí's life and other works, as well as models and photos of La Sagrada Família.

Exploring La Sagrada Família Booking tickets online avoids what can be very lengthy queues (La Sagrada Família gets around 2.8 million visitors a year). Although the church is essentially a building site, the completed sections and museum may be explored at leisure. Fifty-minute guided tours (€9) are offered. Alternatively, pick up an audio tour (€7), for which you need ID. Enter from Carrer de Sardenya or Carrer de la Marina. Once inside, €14 (which includes the audio tour) will get you into lifts that rise up inside towers in the Nativity and Passion facades.

Central Barcelona

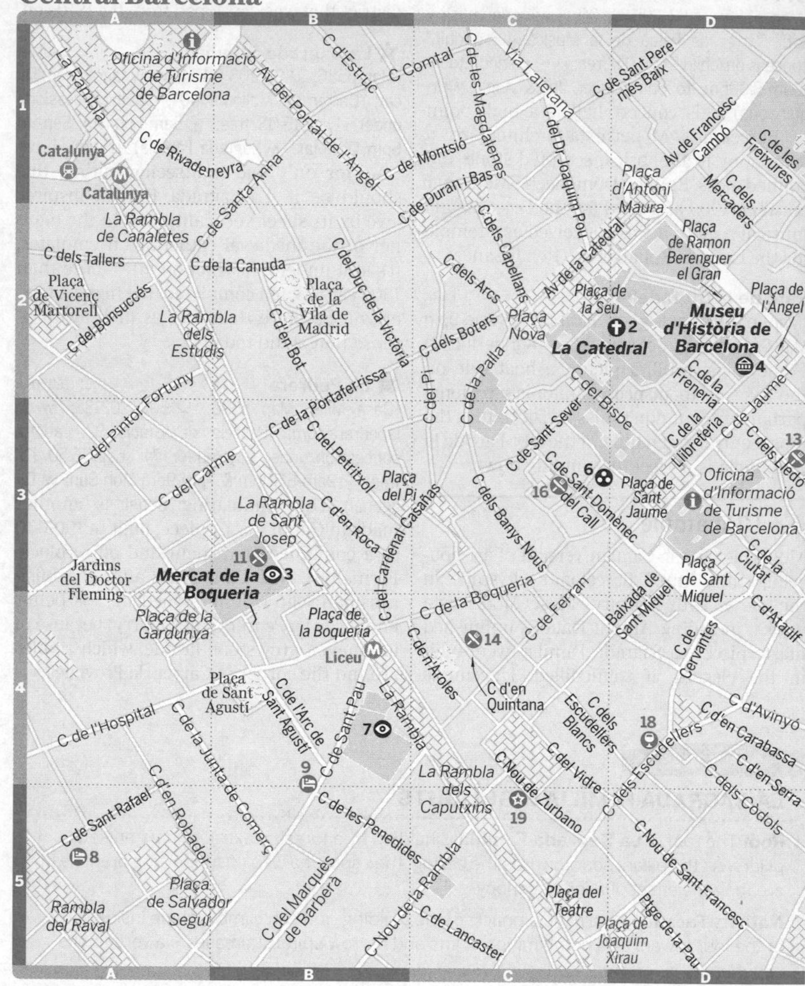

★Casa Batlló ARCHITECTURE

(Map p586; ☎93 216 03 06; www.casabatllo.es; Passeig de Gràcia 43; adult/concession/under 7yr €23.50/20.50/free; ⊙9am-9pm, last admission 8pm; Ⓜ Passeig de Gràcia) One of the strangest residential buildings in Europe, this is Gaudí at his hallucinatory best. The facade, sprinkled with bits of blue, mauve and green tiles and studded with wave-shaped window frames and balconies, rises to an uneven blue-tiled roof with a solitary tower.

Fundació Antoni Tàpies GALLERY

(Map p586; ☎93 487 03 15; www.fundaciotapies.org; Carrer d'Aragó 255; adult/concession €7/5.60; ⊙10am-7pm Tue-Sun; Ⓜ Passeig de Gràcia) The Fundació Antoni Tàpies is both a pioneering Modernista building (completed in 1885) and the major collection of leading 20th-century Catalan artist Antoni Tàpies. A man known for his esoteric work, Tàpies died in February 2012, aged 88; he left behind a powerful range of paintings and a foundation intended to promote contemporary artists.

Central Barcelona

Top Sights

1 Basílica de Santa Maria del Mar F2
2 La Catedral D2
3 Mercat de la Boqueria B3
4 Museu d'Història de Barcelona D2
5 Museu Picasso E2

Sights

6 Domus de Sant Honorat C3
7 Gran Teatre del Liceu B4

Sleeping

8 Barceló Raval A5
9 Hotel Peninsular B4
10 Serras Hotel E4

Eating

11 Bar Pinotxo B3
12 Bormuth F1
13 Cafè de l'Acadèmia D3
14 Can Culleretes C4
15 Casa Delfín F2
16 La Vinateria del Call C3

Drinking & Nightlife

17 El Born Bar F2
18 Marula Café D4

Entertainment

19 Jamboree C5

Shopping

20 Coquette F2
21 Custo Barcelona F2

★ Park Güell PARK

(☎93 409 18 31; www.parkguell.cat; Carrer d'Olot 7; adult/child €8/6; ⏲8am-9.30pm May-Aug, to 8pm Sep-Apr; 🚌24; Ⓜ Lesseps, Vallcarca) North of Gràcia and about 4km from Plaça de Catalunya, Park Güell is where Gaudí turned his hand to landscape gardening. It's a strange, enchanting place where his passion for natural forms really took flight – to the point where the artificial almost seems more natural than the natural.

Montjuïc

Southwest of the city centre, the hillside overlooking the port has some of the city's finest art collections, and also serves as a Central Park of sorts, a great place for a jog or stroll. The closest metro stops are Espanya, Poble Sec and Paral·lel. From Paral·lel a funicular railway runs up to Estació Parc Montjuïc, from where a cable car, the **Telefèric de Montjuïc** (Map p586; www.telefericdemontjuic.cat; Av de Miramar 30; adult/child one way €8/6.20; ⏲10am-9pm Jun-Sep, to 7pm Oct-May; 🚌55, 150), climbs to the Castell de Montjuïc. Bus 150 does a circle trip from Plaça d'Espanya to Castell de Montjuïc.

★ Museu Nacional d'Art de Catalunya (MNAC) MUSEUM

(Map p586; ☎93 622 03 76; www.museunacional.cat; Mirador del Palau Nacional; adult/student/child €12/8.40/free, after 3pm Sat & 1st Sun of month free; 10am-8pm Tue-Sat, to 3pm Sun May-Sep, to 6pm Tue-Sat Oct-Apr; ; M Espanya) From across the city, the bombastic neobaroque silhouette of the **Palau Nacional** (Map p586) can be seen on the slopes of Montjuïc. Built for the 1929 World Exhibition and restored in 2005, it houses a vast collection of mostly Catalan art spanning the early Middle Ages to the early 20th century. The high point is the collection of extraordinary Romanesque frescos.

★Fundació Joan Miró MUSEUM
(Map p586; 93 443 94 70; www.fmirobcn.org; Parc de Montjuïc; adult/child €12/free; 10am-8pm Tue-Wed & Fri, to 9pm Thu, to 3pm Sun Apr-Oct, shorter hours rest of the year; ; 55, 150, Paral·lel) Joan Miró, the city's best-known 20th-century artistic progeny, bequeathed this art foundation to his hometown in 1971. Its light-filled buildings, designed by close friend and architect Josep Lluís Sert (who also built Miró's Mallorca studios), are crammed with seminal works, from Miró's earliest timid sketches to paintings from his last years.

Castell de Montjuïc FORTRESS
(Map p586; 93 256 44 45; www.bcn.cat/castelldemontjuic; Carretera de Montjuïc 66; adult/child €5/free, after 3pm Sun free; 10am-8pm Apr-Oct, to 6pm Nov-Mar; 150, Telefèric de Montjuïc, Castell de Montjuïc) This forbidding *castell* (castle or fort) dominates the southeastern heights of Montjuïc and enjoys commanding views over the Mediterranean. It dates, in its present form, from the late 17th and 18th centuries. For most of its dark history, it has been used to watch over the city and as a political prison and killing ground.

La Barceloneta & the Waterfront

Barcelona's formerly industrial waterfront has been transformed in recent decades, with sparkling beaches, seaside bars and restaurants, elegant sculptures, yacht-filled marinas and long esplanades popular with walkers, runners and cyclists. Port Vell, at the foot of La Rambla, is where many visitors first lay eyes on Barcelona's slice of the Mediterranean. The pedestrian bridge of Rambla de Mar leads out to the Maremàgnum mall and one of Europe's biggest aquariums, **L'Aquàrium** (Map p586; 93 221 74 74; www.aquariumbcn.com; Moll d'Espanya; adult/child €20/15, dive €300; 9.30am-11pm Jul & Aug, to 9pm Sep-Jun; M Drassanes), next door.

East of there, where the old fishing quarter of La Barceloneta abuts the sea, you'll find open-air restaurants offering views out over the promenade and the artificial beaches beyond.

Festivals & Events

Festes de Santa Eulàlia CULTURAL
(http://lameva.barcelona.cat/santaeulalia; Feb) Around 12 February this big winter fest celebrates Barcelona's first patron saint with a week of cultural events, including parades of *gegants* (giants), open-air art installations, theatre, *correfocs* (fire runs) and *castells* (human castles).

Festes de la Mercè CULTURAL
(www.bcn.cat/merce; Sep) The city's biggest party involves four days of concerts, dancing, *castellers* (human-castle builders), a fireworks display synchronised with the Montjuïc fountains, dances of giants on the Saturday, and *correfocs* – a parade of firework-spitting dragons and devils – from all over Catalonia, on the Sunday. Held around 24 September.

Sleeping

Accommodation in Barcelona is more expensive than anywhere else in Spain except Madrid. La Rambla, the Barri Gòtic and El Raval can be noisy but are close to the action with a big selection of boxy hotels, glorious boutique options, hostels and fleapits. You'll find a few attractive boutique-style guesthouses and hostels in Poble Sec and up-and-coming Sant Antoni. L'Eixample has the greatest range of hotels in most classes, including some classic hotels and a long list of decent midrange places, though some are a bit far from the old city.

El Raval

Hotel Peninsular HOTEL €
(Map p590; 93 302 31 38; www.hotelpeninsular.net; Carrer de Sant Pau 34; s/d €50/70; ; M Liceu) An oasis on the edge of the slightly dicey Barri Xino, this former convent (which was connected by tunnel to the Església de Sant Agustí) has a plant-draped atrium extending its height and most of its length. The 60 rooms are simple, with tiled floors and whitewash, but mostly spacious and well kept. There are some great bargains to be had during quiet periods.

★**Barceló Raval** DESIGN HOTEL €€
(Map p590; ☎93 320 14 90; www.barceloraval.com; Rambla del Raval 17-21; r from €125; ❄📶; Ⓜ Liceu) Part of the city's plans to pull El Raval district up by the bootstraps, this oval-shaped designer hotel tower makes a 21st-century splash. The rooftop terrace offers fabulous views and the B-Lounge bar-restaurant is the toast of the town for meals and cocktails. Rooms have slick aesthetics (white with lime green or ruby-red splashes of colour), Nespresso machines and iPod docks.

Barri Gòtic

Serras Hotel BOUTIQUE HOTEL €€€
(Map p590; ☎93 169 18 68; www.hoteltheserrasbarcelona.com; Passeig de Colom 9; r from €302; ❄📶🏊; Ⓜ Barceloneta) A fresh and funky five-star that has every comfort – including a rooftop bar with a small dipping pool and a terrific view over the port – but never feels stuffy. Rooms at the front are brighter and have a better view (from the bathtub, in some cases) but rooms at the side are spared the traffic noise.

Poble Sec & Sant Antoni

Pars Tailor's Hostel HOSTEL €
(Map p586; ☎93 250 56 84; www.tailors-hostel.com; Carrer de Sepúlveda 146; dm €18-20; ❄📶; Ⓜ Urgell, Sant Antoni) Decorated like a mid-20th-century tailor's shop, this popular hostel has uncommon style, with old sewing machines, lovingly framed brassieres and vintage fixtures adorning the common areas. Aside from admiring the aesthetics, there's much afoot at Tailor's: you can shoot a round on the old billiards table, mingle with other guests in the comfy lounge, or join one of the many activities on offer.

★**Hotel Brummell** BOUTIQUE HOTEL €€
(Map p586; ☎93 125 86 22; www.hotelbrummell.com; Carrer Nou de la Rambla 174; d from €150; ❄📶🏊; Ⓜ Paral·lel) This stylish addition to Barcelona has been turning heads since its 2015 opening. It's a thoughtfully designed hotel with a creative soul and great atmosphere. The 20 rooms are bright with a cheerful, minimalist design, and the best of the bunch have sizeable terraces with views and even outdoor soaking tubs. The smallest (the Brummell Classic rooms) feel a little tight.

Hotel Market BOUTIQUE HOTEL €€
(Map p586; ☎93 325 12 05; www.andilanahotels.com; Carrer del Comte Borrell 68; r from €80; ❄@📶; Ⓜ Sant Antoni) Attractively located in a renovated building along a narrow lane just north of the grand old Sant Antoni market, this place has an air of simple chic, with wide plank floors, oversized armoires, bold art prints and nicely designed bathrooms (stone basins, rain showers). Some rooms have tiny (two-seat) balconies.

L'Eixample

Hostal Center Inn HOTEL €€
(Map p586; ☎93 265 25 60; www.centerinnbarcelona.com; Gran Via de les Corts Catalanes 688; s/d €75/85; ❄@📶; Ⓜ Tetuan) Simple rooms have quirky touches – wrought-iron bedsteads, Moroccan mosaic tables on the ample balconies, stripey Tim Burton wallpaper in one room, an antique escritoire in another. The bathrooms carry a vaguely Andalucian flavour. Get a back room if you can, as the Gran Via is noisy.

La Barceloneta & the Waterfront

H10 Port Vell BOUTIQUE HOTEL €€
(Map p586; ☎93 310 30 65; www.h10hotels.com; Pas de Sota Muralla 9; d from €188; ❄@📶🏊; Ⓜ Barceloneta) The location is excellent at this 58-room hotel within a short stroll of El Born and Barceloneta. Sleek, modern rooms have a trim, minimalist design with black and white bathrooms, and the best rooms (not all) have fine views over the marina. The rooftop terrace is the best feature, with sun loungers, a tiny plunge pool and cocktails by evening.

Eating

Barcelona is foodie heaven, fuelled by a combination of world-class chefs, imaginative recipes and magnificent ingredients fresh from farms and the sea. Catalan culinary masterminds like Ferran Adrià and Carles Abellan have reinvented haute cuisine, while classic old-world Catalan seafood and meat recipes continue to earn accolades in dining rooms and tapas bars across the city.

El Raval

★**Bar Pinotxo** TAPAS €€
(Map p590; www.pinotxobar.com; Mercat de la Boqueria; mains €8-17; ⏲7am-4pm Mon-Sat; Ⓜ Liceu) Bar Pinotxo is arguably La Boqueria's,

and even Barcelona's, best tapas bar. It sits among the half-dozen or so informal eateries within the market, and the popular owner, Juanito, might serve up chickpeas with pine nuts and raisins, a soft mix of potato and spinach sprinkled with salt, soft baby squid with cannellini beans, or a quivering cube of caramel-sweet pork belly.

Barri Gòtic

★La Vinateria del Call SPANISH €€
(Map p590; ☎93 302 60 92; www.lavinateriadelcall.com; Carrer de Sant Domènec del Call 9; raciones €7-12; ⊙7.30pm-1am; Ⓜ Jaume I) In a magical setting in the former Jewish quarter, this tiny jewel box of a restaurant serves up tasty Iberian dishes including Galician octopus, cider-cooked chorizo and the Catalan *escalivada* (roasted peppers, aubergine and onions) with anchovies. Portions are small and made for sharing, and there's a good and affordable selection of wines.

★Cafè de l'Acadèmia CATALAN €€
(Map p590; ☎93 319 82 53; Carrer dels Lledó 1; mains €15-20; ⊙1-3.30pm & 8-11.30pm Mon-Fri; ; Ⓜ Jaume I) Expect a mix of traditional Catalan dishes with the occasional creative twist. At lunchtime, local Ajuntament (town hall) office workers pounce on the *menú del día* (daily set menu; €15.70). In the evening it is rather more romantic, as low lighting emphasises the intimacy of the beamed ceiling and stone walls. On warm days you can also dine on the pretty square at the front.

Can Culleretes CATALAN €€
(Map p590; ☎93 317 30 22; www.culleretes.com; Carrer Quintana 5; mains €10-18; ⊙1.30-4pm & 9-11pm Tue-Sat, 1.30-4pm Sun; Ⓜ Liceu) Founded in 1786, Barcelona's oldest restaurant is still going strong, with tourists and locals flocking here to enjoy its rambling interior, old-fashioned tile-filled decor and enormous helpings of traditional Catalan food, including fresh seafood and sticky stews.

Poble Sec & Sant Antoni

★Palo Cortao TAPAS €€
(Map p586; ☎93 188 90 67; www.palocortao.es; Carrer de Nou de la Rambla 146; mains €10-15; ⊙8pm-1am Tue-Sun, 1-5pm Sat & Sun; Ⓜ Paral·lel) Palo Cortao has a solid reputation for its beautifully executed seafood and meat dishes, served at fair prices. Highlights include octopus with white bean hummus, skirt steak with foie Armagnac, and tuna tataki tempura. You can order half sizes of all plates – which will allow you to try more dishes.

★Quimet i Quimet TAPAS €€
(Map p586; ☎93 442 31 42; Carrer del Poeta Cabanyes 25; tapas €4-10, montaditos around €3; ⊙noon-4pm & 7-10.30pm Mon-Fri, noon-4pm Sat; Ⓜ Paral·lel) Quimet i Quimet is a family-run business that has been passed down from generation to generation. There's barely space to swing a *calamar* in this bottle-lined, standing-room-only place, but it is a treat for the palate, with *montaditos* (tapas on a slice of bread) made to order.

La Ribera

Bormuth TAPAS €
(Map p590; ☎93 310 21 86; Carrer del Rec 31; tapas €4-10; ⊙12.30pm-1.30am Sun-Thu, to 2.30am Fri & Sat; ; Ⓜ Jaume I) Located on the pedestrian Carrer del Rec, Bormuth has tapped into the vogue for old-school tapas with modern-day service and decor, and serves all the old favourites – *patatas bravas, ensaladilla* (Russian salad) and tortilla – along with some less predictable and superbly prepared numbers (try the chargrilled red pepper with black pudding).

★Casa Delfín CATALAN €€
(Map p590; ☎93 319 50 88; www.tallerdetapas.com; Passeig del Born 36; mains €10-15; ⊙8am-midnight Sun-Thu, to 1am Fri & Sat; ; Ⓜ Barceloneta) One of Barcelona's culinary delights, Casa Delfín is everything you dream of when you think of Catalan (and Mediterranean) cooking. Start with the tangy and sweet *calçots* (a cross between a leek and an onion; February and March only) or salt-strewn *padron* peppers, moving on to grilled sardines speckled with parsley, then tackle the meaty monkfish roasted in white wine and garlic.

L'Eixample

★Tapas 24 TAPAS €
(Map p586; ☎93 488 09 77; www.carlesabellan.com; Carrer de la Diputació 269; tapas €4-9.50; ⊙9am-midnight; ; Ⓜ Passeig de Gràcia) Carles Abellan, master of the now-defunct Comerç 24 in La Ribera, runs this basement tapas haven known for its gourmet versions of old faves. Specials include the *bikini* (toasted ham and cheese sandwich – here the ham is cured and the truffle makes all the difference)

and a thick black *arròs negre de sípia* (squid-ink black rice).

★Cinc Sentits INTERNATIONAL €€€
(Map p586; ☎93 323 94 90; www.cincsentits.com; Carrer d'Aribau 58; tasting menus €100-120; ⏲1.30-3pm & 8.30-10pm Tue-Sat; Ⓜ Passeig de Gràcia) Enter the realm of the 'Five Senses' to indulge in a jaw-dropping tasting menu consisting of a series of small, experimental dishes (there is no à la carte, although dishes can be tweaked to suit diners' requests). There is a lunch *menú* for €55.

★Disfrutar MODERN EUROPEAN €€€
(Map p586; ☎93 348 68 96; www.en.disfrutarbarcelona.com; Carrer de Villarroel 163; tasting menus €110-180; ⏲1-2.30pm & 8-9.30pm Tue-Sat; Ⓜ Hospital Clínic) In its first few months of life, Disfrutar rose stratospherically to become the city's finest restaurant – book now while it's still possible to get a table. Run by alumni of Ferran Adrià's game-changing El Bulli restaurant, it operates along similar lines.

La Barceloneta & the Waterfront

★La Cova Fumada TAPAS €
(Map p586; ☎93 221 40 61; Carrer del Baluard 56; tapas €4-8; ⏲9am-3.20pm Mon-Wed, 9am-3.20pm & 6-8.15pm Thu & Fri, 9am-1pm Sat; Ⓜ Barceloneta) There's no sign and the setting is decidedly downmarket, but this tiny, buzzing family-run tapas spot always packs in a crowd. The secret? Mouthwatering *pulpo* (octopus), *calamar, sardines* and 15 or so other small plates cooked to perfection in the small open kitchen. The *bombas* (potato croquettes served with *alioli*) and grilled *carxofes* (artichokes) are good, but everything is amazingly fresh.

Drinking & Nightlife

Barcelona is a night-lover's town, with an enticing spread of candlelit wine bars, old-school taverns, stylish lounges and kaleidoscopic nightclubs. Clubs mostly open from midnight until 6am, Thursday to Saturday. Entry can cost from nothing to over €20 (one drink usually included).

The best streets and plazas for bar-hopping include Plaça Reial and Carrer dels Escudellers in the Barri Gòtic, Carrer de Joaquín Costa in bohemian El Raval, Carrer Nou de la Rambla and Carrer del Parlament in hipster/bohemian Poble Sec and Sant Antoni, Passeig del Born in stylish La Ribera, and Carrer d'Aribau in L'Eixample.

Barcelona's vibrant gay and lesbian scene is concentrated in the 'Gaixample', an area in L'Eixample around Carrer del Consell de Cent, five or six blocks southwest of Passeig de Gràcia.

Barri Gòtic

Marula Café BAR
(Map p590; ☎93 318 76 90; www.marulacafe.com; Carrer dels Escudellers 49; ⏲11pm-6am Wed-Sun; Ⓜ Liceu) A fantastic find in the heart of the Barri Gòtic, Marula will transport you to the 1970s and the best in funk and soul. James Brown fans will think they've died and gone to heaven. It's not, however, a monothematic place and DJs slip in other tunes, from breakbeat to house. Samba and other Brazilian dance sounds also penetrate here.

La Ribera

El Born Bar BAR
(Map p590; ☎93 319 53 33; www.elbornbar.neositios.com; Passeig del Born 26; ⏲10am-2am Mon-Thu, to 3am Fri & Sat, noon-2.30am Sun; 📶; Ⓜ Jaume I) El Born Bar effortlessly attracts everyone from cool thirty-somethings from all over town to locals who pass judgement on Passeig del Born's passing parade. Its staying power depends on a good selection of beers, spirits, and *empanadas* and other snacks.

L'Eixample

★Dry Martini BAR
(Map p586; ☎93 217 50 80; www.drymartiniorg.com; Carrer d'Aribau 162-166; ⏲1pm-2.30am Mon-Thu, 6pm-3am Fri & Sat, 7pm-2.30am Sun; Ⓜ Diagonal) Waiters with a discreetly knowing smile will attend to your cocktail needs and make uncannily good suggestions, but the house drink, taken at the bar or in one of the plush green leather banquettes, is a safe bet. The gin and tonic comes in an enormous mug-sized glass – one will take you most of the night.

★Monvínic WINE BAR
(Map p586; ☎93 272 61 87; www.monvinic.com; Carrer de la Diputació 249; ⏲1-11pm Tue-Fri, 7-11pm Mon & Sat; Ⓜ Passeig de Gràcia) Apparently considered unmissable by El Bulli's sommelier, Monvínic is an ode, a rhapsody even, to wine loving. The interactive wine list sits on the bar for you to browse, on a digital tablet similar to an iPad, and boasts more than 3000 varieties.

DON'T MISS

SEEING AN FC BARCELONA MATCH

Football in Barcelona has the aura of religion and for much of the city's population, support of FC Barcelona is an article of faith. FC Barcelona is traditionally associated with the Catalans and even Catalan nationalism.

Tickets to FC Barcelona matches are available at **Camp Nou** (902 189900; www.fcbarcelona.com; Carrer d'Arístides Maillol; M Palau Reial), online (through FC Barcelona's official website), and through various city locations. Tourist offices sell them (the branch at Plaça de Catalunya is a centrally located option) as do FC Botiga stores. Tickets can cost anything from €39 to upwards of €250, depending on the seat and match. On match day the ticket windows (at gates 9 and 15) are open from 9.15am until kick-off.

Fans who can't get to a game will still enjoy the self-guided stadium tour **Camp Nou Experience** (902 189900; www.fcbarcelona.com; Gate 9, Avinguda de Joan XXIII; adult/child €25/20; 9.30am-7.30pm daily Apr-Sep, 10am-6.30pm Mon-Sat, to 2.30pm Sun Oct-Mar; M Palau Reial).

City Hall CLUB

(Map p586; 93 238 07 22; www.cityhallbarcelona.com; Rambla de Catalunya 2-4; cover €10-15, incl 1 drink; midnight-5am Wed & Thu, midnight-6am Fri & Sat, 11pm-5am Sun; M Catalunya) A long corridor leads to the dance floor of this venerable and popular club, located in a former theatre. House and other electric sounds dominate, with occasional funk nights. Check the website for details.

☆ Entertainment

★Palau de la Música Catalana CLASSICAL MUSIC

(Map p586; 93 295 72 00; www.palaumusica.cat; Carrer de Palau de la Música 4-6; tickets from €15; box office 9.30am-9pm Mon-Sat, 10am-3pm Sun; M Urquinaona) A feast for the eyes, this Modernista confection is also the city's most traditional venue for classical and choral music, although it has a wide-ranging program, including flamenco, pop and – particularly – jazz. Just being here for a performance is an experience. In the foyer, its tiled pillars all a-glitter, sip a pre-concert tipple.

Jamboree LIVE MUSIC

(Map p590; 93 319 17 89; www.masimas.com/jamboree; Plaça Reial 17; tickets €10-20; 8pm-6am; M Liceu) For over half a century, Jamboree has been bringing joy to the jivers of Barcelona, with high-calibre acts featuring jazz trios, blues, Afrobeats, Latin sounds and big-band sounds. Two concerts are held most nights (at 8pm and 10pm), after which Jamboree morphs into a DJ-spinning club at midnight. WTF jam sessions are held Mondays (entrance a mere €5).

Shopping

Most mainstream fashion stores are along a shopping 'axis' that runs from Plaça de Catalunya along Passeig de Gràcia, then left (west) along Avinguda Diagonal.

In La Ribera, El Born and Carrer del Rec are the places for cool designer boutiques that sell high-end fashion. There are plenty of shops scattered throughout the Barri Gòtic (stroll Carrer d'Avinyò). El Raval is a haven for vintage fashion (especially Carrer de la Riera Baixa) and all kinds of original and arty independent shops.

Coquette FASHION & ACCESSORIES

(Map p590; 93 310 35 35; www.coquettebcn.com; Carrer de Bonaire 5; 11am-3pm & 5-9pm Mon-Fri, 11.30am-9pm Sat; M Barceloneta) Elegant women's store with designers from around the globe, but particularly Spain.

Custo Barcelona FASHION & ACCESSORIES

(Map p590; 93 268 78 93; www.custo.com; Plaça de les Olles 7; 10am-9pm Mon-Sat, noon-8pm Sun; M Barceloneta) The psychedelic decor and casual atmosphere lend this avant-garde Barcelona fashion store a youthful edge. Custo presents daring new women's and men's collections each year on the New York catwalks. The dazzling colours and cut of everything from dinner jackets to hot pants are for the uninhibited. It has three other stores around town.

Els Encants Vells MARKET

(Fira de Bellcaire; Map p586; 93 246 30 30; www.encantsbcn.com; Plaça de les Glòries Catalanes; 9am-8pm Mon, Wed, Fri & Sat; M Glòries) In a gleaming open-sided complex near Plaça de les Glòries Catalanes, the 'Old Charms' flea market is the biggest of its kind in Barcelona. Over 500 vendors ply their wares beneath massive mirror-like panels. It's all here, from antique furniture through to secondhand clothes. A lot of it is junk, but occasionally you'll stumble across a *ganga* (bargain).

Information

Purse snatching and pickpocketing are major problems, especially around Plaça de Catalunya, La Rambla and Plaça Reial. Report thefts to the **Guàrdia Urbana** (Local Police; ☎092/93 256 24 30; www.bcn.cat/guardiaurbana; La Rambla 43; ⏲24hr; Ⓜ Liceu) on La Rambla. You're unlikely to recover your goods but you will need to make this formal *denuncia* (police report) for insurance purposes. Avoid walking around El Raval and the southern end of La Rambla late at night.

Oficina d'Informació de Turisme de Barcelona (Map p590; ☎93 285 38 34; www.barcelonaturisme.com; Plaça de Catalunya 17; ⏲9.30am-9.30pm; Ⓜ Catalunya) The main Barcelona tourist information office sells walking tours, bus tours, discount cards, transport passes and tickets to shows, and can help book accommodation. It's underground at the Plaça de Catalunya.

Palau Robert Regional Tourist Office (Map p586; ☎93 238 80 91; www.palaurobert.gencat.cat; Passeig de Gràcia 107; ⏲10am-8pm Mon-Sat, to 2.30pm Sun; Ⓜ Diagonal) A host of material on Catalonia, audiovisual resources, a bookshop and a branch of Turisme Juvenil de Catalunya (for youth travel).

Getting There & Away

AIR

El Prat Airport (☎902 404704; www.aena.es) Barcelona's El Prat airport lies 17km southwest of Plaça de Catalunya at El Prat de Llobregat. The airport has two main terminal buildings: the new T1 terminal and the older T2, itself divided into three terminal areas (A, B and C).

BOAT

Barcelona has ferry connections to the Balearic Islands and Italy. Boats depart from the port just south of the old city.

Trasmediterranea (☎902 454645; www.trasmediterranea.es; Ⓜ Drassanes) Passenger and vehicular ferries operated by Trasmediterranea to/from the Balearic Islands dock around the Moll de Barcelona wharf in Port Vell. Information and tickets are available at the terminal buildings along Moll de Sant Bertran and on Moll de Barcelona or from travel agents.

BUS

Long-distance buses leave from Estació del Nord. A plethora of companies service different parts of Spain; many come under the umbrella of **Alsa** (☎902 422242; www.alsa.es). For other companies, ask at the bus station. There are frequent services to Madrid, Valencia and Zaragoza (20 or more a day) and several daily departures to distant destinations such as Burgos, Santiago de Compostela and Seville.

Eurolines (www.eurolines.com), in conjunction with local carriers all over Europe, is the main international carrier. Its website provides links to national operators; it runs services across Europe and to Morocco from **Estació del Nord** (Map p586; ☎902 26 06 06; www.barcelonanord.cat; Carrer d'Ali Bei 80; Ⓜ Arc de Triomf), and from **Estació d'Autobusos de Sants** (Map p586; ☎93 339 73 29; www.adif.es; Carrer de Viriat; Ⓜ Estació Sants), next to Estació Sants Barcelona.

TRAIN

The main station is **Estació Sants** (www.adif.es; Plaça dels Països Catalans; Ⓜ Estació Sants), 2.5km west of La Rambla. About 30 daily high-speed trains to Madrid via Zaragoza take as little as 2½ hours; prices vary from €50 to over €200 (book well ahead for lowest fares). Other daily trains run to Valencia (€12 to €45, three to 4½ hours, up to 19 daily), Pamplona, San Sebastián, Bilbao, Santiago de Compostela, Seville and Málaga. Direct overnight trains from Paris, Geneva, Milan and Zürich also arrive at Estació Sants.

Getting Around

TO/FROM THE AIRPORT

The frequent Aerobús (www.aerobusbcn.com) runs every five or 10 minutes between both airport terminals and Plaça de Catalunya (€5.50, 35 minutes), from 5.30am to 1am. The L9 Sud line of the Barcelona metro also serves both terminals (€4.50) but you need a couple of changes to reach central areas. Taxis cost around €30.

WORTH A TRIP

ANDORRA

This mini-country wedged between France and Spain offers by far the best ski slopes and resort facilities in all the Pyrenees. Once the snows melt, there's an abundance of great walking, ranging from easy strolls to demanding day hikes in the principality's higher, more remote reaches. Strike out above the tight valleys and you can walk for hours, almost alone.

The only way to reach Andorra is by road from Spain or France. If driving, fill up in Andorra; fuel is substantially cheaper there. There are buses to/from Barcelona's Estació del Nord, Estació Sants and airport, Lleida, La Seu d'Urgell and Toulouse (France). All bus services arrive at and leave from Andorra la Vella.

WORTH A TRIP

GIRONA

A tight huddle of ancient arcaded houses, grand churches, climbing cobbled streets and medieval baths, all enclosed by defensive walls and a lazy river, constitutes a powerful reason for visiting northern Catalonia's largest city, Girona (Castilian: Gerona). From Girona station there are at least 15 trains per day to Figueres (€4.10 to €5.45, 30 to 40 minutes) and 30 to Barcelona (from €9.30, 40 minutes to 1¼ hours).

Catedral (www.catedraldegirona.org; Plaça de la Catedral; adult/student incl Basílica de Sant Feliu €7/5, Sun free; ⏲10am-6.30pm Apr-Oct, 10am-5.30pm Sep-Mar) Towering over a flight of 86 steps rising from Plaça de la Catedral, this edifice is far more ancient than its billowing baroque facade suggests. Built over an old Roman forum, parts of the cathedral's foundations date from the 5th century. Today, Gothic styling – built over the Romanesque church during the 14th century – dominates, though a fine, double-columned Romanesque **cloister** dates from the 12th century. It's a surprisingly formidable sight to explore, but an audio guide is included in the price.

Museu d'Història dels Jueus de Girona (www.girona.cat/call; Carrer de la Força 8; adult/child €4/free; ⏲10am-6pm Mon-Sat, to 2pm Sun Sep-Jun, to 8pm Jul & Aug) Until 1492 Girona was home to Catalonia's second most important medieval Jewish community (after Barcelona), and one of the finest Jewish quarters in the country. The Call was centred on the narrow Carrer de la Força for 600 years, until relentless persecution forced the Jews out of Spain. This excellent museum shows genuine pride in Girona's Jewish heritage without shying away from the less salubrious aspects, such as persecution by the Inquisition and forced conversions.

Bells Oficis (☎972 22 81 70; www.bellsoficis.com; Carrer dels Germans Busquets 2; r incl breakfast €42-93; ❄📶) A lovingly restored, 19th-century flat just by the Rambla in the heart of Girona makes a stylish and ultra-welcoming place to stop. It's the former home of Catalan artist Jaume Busquets i Mollera, and retains period details in each of the five individually styled rooms. Some rooms share bathrooms, while those with en suite have no bathroom door. The largest room has ample room for four people.

Nu (☎972 22 52 30; www.nurestaurant.cat; Carrer d'Abeuradors 4; mains €16-18; ⏲1.15-3.45pm & 8.15-10.45pm Tue-Sat, 1.15-3.45pm Mon; 📶) Sleek and confident, this handsome contemporary old-town spot has innovative, top-notch plates prepared in view by the friendly team. Flavour combinations keep things interesting: sample tuna tataki with red fruit glaze, tandoori pork cheeks with mango, and orange flower crème brûlée. Great value for this quality.

PUBLIC TRANSPORT

Barcelona's metro system spreads its tentacles around the city in such a way that most places of interest are within a 10-minute walk of a station. Buses and suburban trains are needed only for a few destinations. A single metro, bus or suburban train ride costs €2.15, but a T-10 ticket, valid for 10 rides, costs €10.30.

TAXI

Taxis charge €2.10 to €2.30 flagfall plus meter charges of €1.10 to €1.40 per kilometre (the higher rates are for nights and weekends). You can flag a taxi down in the street or call one:

Fonotaxi (☎93 300 11 00; www.fonotaxi.net)

Radio Taxi 033 (☎93 303 30 33; www.radiotaxi033.com)

The call-out charge is between €3.40 and €4.50.

Tarragona

POP 132,200

In this effervescent port city, Roman history collides with beaches, nightlife and a food scene that perfumes the air with freshly grilled seafood. The biggest lure is the wealth of remains from one of Spain's most important Roman cities, including mosaic-packed museums and a seaside amphitheatre. A roll-call of excellent places to eat gives you good reason to linger in the knot of lanes in the medieval centre, flanked by a broad cathedral with Gothic flourishes.

👁 Sights

★Catedral de Tarragona CATHEDRAL

(www.catedraldetarragona.com; Plaça de la Seu; adult/child €5/3; ⏲10am-7pm Mon-Sat mid-Mar–

Oct, 10am-5pm Mon-Fri, 10am-7pm Sat Nov–mid-Mar) Sitting grandly atop town, Tarragona's cathedral has both Romanesque and Gothic features, as typified by the main facade. The cloister has Gothic vaulting and Romanesque carved capitals, one of which shows rats conducting a cat's funeral…until the cat comes back to life! It's a lesson about passions seemingly lying dormant until they reveal themselves. Chambers off the cloister incorporate the **Museu Diocesà**, with its large collection extending from Roman hairpins to some lovely 12th- to 14th-century polychrome woodcarvings of a breastfeeding Virgin.

Passeig Arqueològic Muralles WALLS
(www.tarragonaturisme.cat; adult/child €3.30/free; sites 9am-9pm Tue-Sat, 10am-3pm Sun Easter-Sep, 10am-7pm Tue-Sat, 10am-3pm Sun Oct-Easter) A peaceful walk takes you around part of the perimeter of the old town between two lines of city walls. The inner ones are mainly Roman and date back to the 3rd century BC, while the outer ones were put up by the British in 1709 during the War of the Spanish Succession. The earliest stretches are a mighty 4m thick. Prepare to be awed by the vast gateways built by the Iberians and clamber up onto the battlements from the doorway to the right of the entrance for all-encompassing views of the city.

★Museu Nacional Arqueològic de Tarragona MUSEUM
(www.mnat.cat; Plaça del Rei 5; adult/child €4.50/free; 9.30am-6pm Tue-Sat, to 8.30pm Jun-Sep, 10am-2pm Sun) This excellent museum does justice to the cultural and material wealth of Roman Tarraco. The mosaic collection traces the changing trends – from simple black-and-white designs to complex full-colour creations; a highlight is the large, almost complete *Mosaic de Peixos de la Pineda*, showing fish and sea creatures. Explanation in the museum is in Catalan and Spanish, but there is a multilingual audio guide included in the price.

Amfiteatre Romà RUINS
(www.tarragonaturisme.cat; Parc de l'Anfiteatre; adult/child €3.30/free; 9am-9pm Tue-Sat, 10am-3pm Sun Easter-Sep, 10am-7pm Tue-Sat, 10am-3pm Sun Oct-Easter) Near the beach is this well-preserved amphitheatre, where gladiators hacked away at each other, or wild animals. In its arena are the remains of 6th- and 12th-century churches built to commemorate the martyrdom of the Christian bishop Fructuosus and two deacons, believed to have been burnt alive here in AD 259. Much of the amphitheatre was picked to bits, with the stone used to build the port, so what you see now is a partial reconstruction.

Sleeping & Eating

Look for tapas bars and inexpensive cafes on the Plaça de la Font. The quintessential Tarragona seafood experience can be had in Serrallo, the town's fishing port, where a dozen bars and restaurants sell the day's catch.

Tarragona Hostel HOSTEL €
(877 05 58 96; www.tarragonahostel.com; Carrer de la Unió; dm/d €12/30;) All the backpacker essentials are well executed at this dead-centre hostel with chirpy staff. Choose from eight-bed dorms or a double room, and avail yourself of free wi-fi, a comfy common room, shared kitchen and laundry facilities (€4).

Hotel Plaça de la Font HOTEL €€
(977 24 61 34; www.hotelpdelafont.com; Plaça de la Font 26; s/d €60/75;) Comfortable modern rooms, decorated in individual styles with photos of Tarragona monuments, fill this cheerful hotel on popular Plaça de la Font. Rooms at the front are pretty well soundproofed from the sociable murmur below and have tiny balconies for people-watching. Breakfast is an extra €6.

Barquet SEAFOOD €€
(977 24 00 23; www.restaurantbarquet.com; Carrer del Gasometre 16; mains €12-20; 1-3.30pm & 9-10.30pm Tue-Sat, 1-3.30pm Mon) This popular neighbourhood restaurant is a short downhill stroll from the centre. It's deservedly famous for its excellent rice dishes bursting with maritime flavour, and also has great *raciones* (large plates) of seafood. Don't be fooled by the nautical warehouse interior, fish dishes and jewel-like desserts are executed with finesse.

AQ MEDITERRANEAN, FUSION €€
(977 21 59 54; www.aq-restaurant.com; Carrer de les Coques 7; mains €11-22; 1.30-3.30pm & 8.30-11pm Tue-Sat) The crisp interior design of this stone-walled restaurant promises fine dining, and AQ amply delivers. Its impeccably crafted fusion dishes – taking inspiration from Catalan, Italian and Asian cuisines – are playfully executed. Treat your taste buds to Iberico pork burgers, squid carbonara or chop suey lobster. The three-course lunch *menú* (€19.80) is excellent value.

DALÍ'S CATALONIA

The only name that could come into your head when you set eyes on the red castle-like building in central Figueres, topped with giant eggs and stylised Oscar-like statues and studded with plaster-covered croissants, is Salvador Dalí. With its entrance watched over by medieval suits of armour balancing baguettes on their heads, the **Teatre-Museu Dalí** (www.salvador-dali.org; Plaça de Gala i Salvador Dalí 5; adult/child under 9yr incl Museu de l'Empordà €14/free; ⏲9am-8pm Tue-Sun Jul-Sep, 10.30am-6pm Tue-Sun Oct-Jun, closed Mon) is an entirely appropriate final resting place for the master of surrealism. 'Theatre-museum' is an apt label for this trip through the incredibly fertile imagination of one of the great showmen of the 20th century. It's full of surprises, tricks and illusions, and contains a substantial portion of Dalí's life's work.

Port Lligat, a 1.25km walk from Cadaqués, is a tiny settlement around a lovely cove, with fishing boats pulled up on its beach. The **Casa Museu Dalí** (☎972 25 10 15; www.salvador-dali.org; adult/under 8yr €11/free; ⏲10.30am-6pm Tue-Sun, closed mid-Jan–mid-Feb) started life as a fisherman's hut, but was steadily enlarged by Dalí and his wife Gala during their residence here from 1930 to 1982 (apart from a dozen or so years abroad around the Spanish Civil War). It provides a fascinating insight into the lives of the (excuse the pun) surreal couple. We probably don't need to tell you that it's the house with a lot of little white chimneypots and two egg-shaped towers, overlooking the western end of the beach. You must book ahead.

Information

Tourist Office (☎977 25 07 95; www.tarragonaturisme.es; Carrer Major 39; ⏲10am-2pm & 3-5pm Mon-Fri, 10am-7pm Sat, 10am-2pm Sun) Good place for booking guided tours of the city. Opens extended hours in high season.

Getting There & Away

BUS

The **bus station** (www.alsa.es; Plaça Imperial Tarraco) is 1.5km northwest of the old town along Rambla Nova. Destinations include Barcelona (€8.80, 1½ hours, up to 16 daily) and Valencia (€19 to €22, three to 4½ hours, six daily).

TRAIN

Tarragona station is a 10-minute walk from the old town while fast AVE trains stop at Camp de Tarragona station, 10km north. Departures from Tarragona station include trains to Barcelona (€7 to €21, one to 1½ hours, about half-hourly) and Valencia (€14 to €38, 2½ hours, 17 daily).

ARAGÓN, BASQUE COUNTRY & NAVARRA

Zaragoza

POP 679,600

Zaragoza (Saragossa), on the banks of the mighty Río Ebro, is a vibrant, elegant and fascinating city. Its residents, who form over half of Aragón's population, enjoy a lifestyle that revolves around some superb tapas bars, great shopping and a vigorous nightlife. But Zaragoza is much more than just a good-time city: its host of historical sights spans all the great civilisations that have left their mark on the Spanish soul. This is also a good place to get acquainted with the artistic genius of Francisco de Goya, who was born a short horse-ride away in 1746.

Sights

★Basílica de Nuestra Señora del Pilar CHURCH

(www.basilicadelpilar.es; Plaza del Pilar; ⏲6.45am-8.30pm Mon-Sat, to 9.30pm Sun) FREE Brace yourself for this great baroque cavern of Catholicism. The faithful believe that it was here on 2 January AD 40 that Santiago saw the Virgin Mary descend atop a marble *pilar* (pillar). A chapel was built around the remaining pillar, followed by a series of ever-more-grandiose churches, culminating in the enormous basilica. A **lift** (admission €3; ⏲10am-2pm & 4-8pm Apr-Oct, to 6pm Nov-Mar) whisks you most of the way up the north tower from where you climb to a superb viewpoint over the domes and city.

★Aljafería PALACE

(☎976 28 96 83; www.turismodezaragoza.es; Calle de los Diputados; €5, Sun free; ⏲10am-2pm & 4-6.30pm Mon-Sat, 10am-2pm Sun) The Aljafería is Spain's finest Islamic-era edifice outside Andalucía. Built as a pleasure palace for

Zaragoza's Islamic rulers in the 11th century, it underwent its first alterations in 1118 when the city passed into Christian hands. In the 1490s, the Catholic Monarchs, Fernando and Isabel, tacked on their own palace, whereafter the Aljafería fell into decay. Twentieth-century restorations brought the building back to life, and in 1987 Aragón's regional parliament was established here. Tours take place throughout the day (multilingual in July and August).

La Seo CATHEDRAL
(Catedral de San Salvador; ☎976 29 12 31; www.turismodezaragoza.es; Plaza de la Seo; adult/child €4/free; ⊙10am-2pm & 4-6.30pm Tue-Fri, 10am-12.30pm & 4-6.30pm Sat, 10am-noon & 4-6.30pm Sun) Dominating the eastern end of Plaza del Pilar, La Seo was built between the 12th and 17th centuries and displays a fabulous spread of architectural styles from Romanesque to baroque. The cathedral stands on the site of Islamic Zaragoza's main mosque (which in turn stood upon the temple of the Roman forum). The admission price includes entry to La Seo's **Museo de Tapices** (☎976 29 12 38), a collection of 14th- to 17th-century Flemish and French tapestries considered the best of its kind in the world.

Museo del Foro de Caesaraugusta MUSEUM
(☎976 72 12 21; www.turismodezaragoza.es; Plaza de la Seo 2; adult/child €4/free; ⊙10am-2pm & 5-9pm Tue-Sat, 10am-2.30pm Sun) The trapezoidal building on Plaza de la Seo is the entrance to an excellent reconstruction of part of Roman Caesaraugusta's forum, now well below ground level. The remains of porticoes, shops, a great *cloaca* (sewer) system, and a limited collection of artefacts from the 1st century AD are on display. An multilingual 15-minute audiovisual show breathes life into it all.

★Museo Goya – Colección Ibercaja MUSEUM
(☎976 39 73 28; www.museogoya.ibercaja.es; Calle de Espoz y Mina 23; with/without audio guide €6/4; ⊙10am-2pm & 4-8pm Mon-Sat, 10am-2pm Sun) Outside of Madrid's Museo del Prado, this excellent museum contains what is arguably the best exposé of the work of one of Spain's most revered artists. The place is exceedingly well laid-out with each of its three floors carrying a different theme.

★Museo del Teatro de Caesaraugusta MUSEUM
(☎976 72 60 75; www.turismodezaragoza.es; Calle de San Jorge 12; adult/child €4/free; ⊙10am-2pm & 5-9pm Tue-Sat, 10am-2.30pm Sun) The finest in the quartet of Zaragoza's Roman museums was discovered during the excavation of a building site in 1972. The crumbling but precious theatre once seated 6000 spectators, and great efforts have been made to help visitors reconstruct the edifice's former splendour, including evening projections of a virtual performance (May to October) and an entertaining audiovisual production. The theatre is visible from the surrounding streets and an on-site cafe. The all-round aesthetics are fabulous.

Sleeping

Hotel Río Arga HOTEL €
(☎976 39 90 65; www.hotelrioarga.es; Calle Contamina 20; s/d €40/45; P ❄ 📶) Río Arga offers comfortable, spacious rooms with easy-on-the-eye decor and large bathrooms with tubs. The private parking is a real boon given this central city location. Breakfast costs €3.75.

★Hotel Sauce BOUTIQUE HOTEL €€
(☎976 20 50 50; www.hotelsauce.com; Calle de Espoz y Mina 33; s from €45, d €51-66; ❄ 📶) This chic, small hotel with a great central location has a hip feel thanks largely to its white wicker, painted furniture, stripy fabrics and tasteful watercolours on the walls. The superior rooms are well worth the few euros extra. There's a thoroughly pleasant 24-hour coffee shop/cafe on the ground floor with a cake display case that's rarely left empty.

Catalonia El Pilar HOTEL €€
(☎976 20 58 58; www.hoteles-catalonia.com; Calle de la Manifestación 16; r from €78; ❄ @ 📶) Ten out of ten for the facade, a magnificent Modernista construction that has been artfully renovated to house this eminently comfortable contemporary hotel. Inside, rooms are spacious and decorated in restful muted earth tones with elegant marble-clad bathrooms. Some of the beds are king-size.

Eating & Drinking

Head to the tangle of lanes in El Tubo, north of Plaza de España, for one of Spain's richest gatherings of tapas bars.

Calle del Temple, southwest of Plaza del Pilar, is the spiritual home of Zaragoza's roaring nightlife. This is where the city's students head out to party, with more bars lined up cheek to jowl than anywhere else in Aragón.

★Restaurante Méli Mélo TAPAS €
(☎976294695; www.restaurantemelimelozaragoza.com; Calle Mayor 45; tapas €2.50-6; ⊙1-4pm &

8pm-midnight Mon-Sat, 1-4pm Sun) Typically, *pintxos* are Basque-style tapas presented on small slices of bread, but in Méli Mélo they are stacked up so high they look like mini-skyscrapers topped with creative arrangements of cured hams, breaded cod, octopus and aubergine. Come here at 8pm before the rush and you'll see a veritable Manhattan of *pintxos* lined up on the bar all ready for tasting.

Los Xarmientos ARAGONESE €€
(☎976 29 90 48; www.facebook.com/xarmientos; Calle de Espoz y Mina 25; mains €12-19; ⏲1.30-4.30pm & 8-11.30pm Wed-Sat, 1-4pm Tue & Sun) Aragonese meat dishes are a speciality at this artfully designed restaurant. It styles itself as a *parrilla*, meaning the dishes are cooked on a barbecue-style grill. It's a fine place to sample the local *ternasco* (lamb), Aragon's most emblematic dish, served here with a jacket potato on the side.

ℹ Information

Municipal Tourist Office (☎976 20 12 00; www.zaragozaturismo.es; Plaza del Pilar; ⏲9am-9pm mid-Jun–mid-Oct, 10am-8pm mid-Oct–mid-Jun; 📶) Has branch offices around town, including the train station.

Oficina de Turismo de Aragón (☎976 28 21 81; www.turismodearagon.com; Plaza de España 1; ⏲9am-2pm & 5-8pm Mon-Fri, from 10am Sat & Sun; 📶) Has plenty of brochures on the region.

ℹ Getting There & Away

BUS

Dozens of bus lines fan out across Spain from the bus station attached to the Estación Intermodal Delicias train station, 3km northwest of the centre. **ALSA** (☎902 42 22 42; www.alsa.es) runs to/from Madrid (€17 to €23, 3¾ hours, 17 daily buses) and Barcelona (€16 to €22, 3¾ hours, 15 buses). **Alosa** (☎902 490690; http://alosa.avanzabus.com) runs half-hourly buses to/from Huesca (€7.80, 1¼ hours) and seven daily buses to Jaca (€16, 2½ hours).

TRAIN

Zaragoza's futuristic **Estación Intermodal Delicias** (☎902 404 704; www.renfe.com; Calle Rioja 33; ⏲5.30am-midnight) is connected by almost hourly high-speed AVE services to Madrid (€21 to €65, 1½ hours) and Barcelona (€18 to €100, 1¾ hours). Other destinations include Huesca (from €7, one hour, seven trains daily), Jaca (€15, 3¼ hours, two trains) and Teruel (€20, 2½ hours, four trains).

Around Aragón

Aragón is a beautiful and fascinating region to explore if you have a few days to do so. In the south, little visited **Teruel** is home to some stunning Mudéjar architecture. Nearby, **Albarracín** is one of Spain's prettiest villages.

In the north, the **Parque Nacional de Ordesa y Monte Perdido** is the most spectacular stretch of the Spanish Pyrenees, with dramatic mountain scenery and superb hiking; the pretty village of **Torla** is the main gateway (though it gets overrun with visitors in July and August). En route to the mountains are several towns and villages with enchanting medieval quarters or fascinating medieval monuments, such as **Aínsa**, **Jaca** and **Huesca**.

In Aragón's northwest, **Sos del Rey Católico** is another gorgeous stone village draped along a ridge.

San Sebastián

POP 186,100

With Michelin stars apparently falling from the heavens onto its restaurants, not to mention a *pintxo* (tapas) culture almost unmatched anywhere else in Spain, stylish San Sebastián (Donostia in Basque) frequently tops lists of the world's best places to eat. Charming and well-mannered by day, cool and happening by night, the city has an idyllic location on the shell-shaped Bahía de la Concha, with crystalline waters, a flawless beach and green hills on all sides.

👁 Sights & Activities

★Playa de la Concha BEACH
(Paseo de la Concha) Fulfilling almost every idea of how a perfect city beach should be formed, Playa de la Concha (and its westerly extension, Playa de Ondarreta), is easily among the best city beaches in Europe. Throughout the long summer months a fiesta atmosphere prevails, with thousands of tanned and toned bodies spread across the sands. The swimming is almost always safe.

Monte Igueldo VIEWPOINT
(www.monteigueldo.es; ⏲10am-10pm Jun-Sep, shorter hours rest of year) The views from the summit of Monte Igueldo, just west of town, will make you feel like a circling hawk staring down over the vast panorama of the Bahía de la Concha and the surrounding

coastline and mountains. The best way to get there is via the old-world **funicular railway** (Plaza del Funicular; return adult/child €3.15/2.35; ⌚10am-9pm Jun-Aug, shorter hours rest of year) to the **Parque de Atracciones** (☎943 21 35 25; Paseo de Igeldo; adult/child €3.15/2.35; ⌚11am-2pm & 4-8.30pm Mon-Fri, to 9pm Sat & Sun Jul-Sep, shorter hours rest of year), a slightly tacky theme park at the top of the hill.

San Telmo Museoa MUSEUM
(☎943 48 15 80; www.santelmomuseoa.com; Plaza Zuloaga 1; adult/student/child €6/3/free; ⌚10am-8pm Tue-Sun) Although it's one of the newest museums in the Basque Country, the San Telmo Museoa has actually been around since the 1920s. It was closed for many years, but after major renovation work it reopened in 2011. The displays range from historical artefacts to the squiggly lines of modern art, with all pieces reflecting Basque culture and society.

Sleeping

Pensión Altair PENSIÓN €
(☎943 29 31 33; www.pension-altair.com; Calle Padre Larroca 3; s/d €55/75; ❄@🛜) This *pensión* is in a beautifully restored town house, with unusual church-worthy arched windows and modern, minimalist rooms that are a world away from the fusty decor of the old-town *pensiones*. Interior rooms lack the grandiose windows but are much larger.

Pensión Amaiur BOUTIQUE HOTEL €€
(☎943 42 96 54; www.pensionamaiur.com; Calle de 31 de Agosto 44; d with/without bathroom €60/75; @🛜) A top-notch guesthouse in a prime old-town location, Amaiur has bright floral wallpapers and bathrooms tiled in Andalucían blue and white. The best rooms are those that overlook the main street, where you can sit on a little balcony and be completely enveloped in blushing red flowers. Some rooms share bathrooms.

Hotel de Londres y de Inglaterra HISTORIC HOTEL €€
(☎943 44 07 70; www.hlondres.com; Calle de Zubieta 2; d from €124; P❄🛜) Sitting pretty on the beachfront, Hotel de Londres y de Inglaterra (Hotel of London and England) is as proper as it sounds. Queen Isabel II set the tone for this hotel well over a century ago, and things have stayed pretty regal ever since. The place exudes elegance; some rooms have stunning views over Playa de la Concha.

Eating & Drinking

As if 16 Michelin stars weren't enough, San Sebastián is overflowing with bars weighed down under mountains of *pintxos* (Basque tapas, typically towering creations pinned in place on pieces of bread by large toothpicks) that almost every Spaniard will tell you (sometimes grudgingly) are the best in country.

Do what the locals do – crawl the city centre's bars. *Pintxo* etiquette is simple. Ask for a plate and point out what *pintxos* you want. Keep the toothpicks and go back for as many as you'd like. Accompany with *txakoli*, a cloudy white wine poured like cider to create a little fizz. When you're ready to pay, hand over the plate with all the toothpicks and tell bar staff how many drinks you've had. It's an honour system that has stood the test of time. Expect to pay €2.50 to €3.50 per *pintxo*.

★**La Fábrica** BASQUE €€
(☎943 98 05 81; www.restaurantelafabrica.es; Calle del Puerto 17; mains €15-20, menús from €28; ⌚12.30-4pm & 7.30-11.30pm Mon-Fri, 1-4pm & 8-11pm Sat-Sun) The red-brick interior walls and white tablecloths lend an air of class to this restaurant, whose modern takes on Basque classics have been making waves with San Sebastián locals over the last couple of years. At just €25, the multi-dish tasting *menú* is about the best-value deal in the city. Advance reservations are essential.

★**La Cuchara de San Telmo** BASQUE €€
(☎043 44 16 55; www.lacucharadesantelmo.com; Calle de 31 de Agosto 28; pintxos from €2.50; ⌚7.30-11pm Tue, noon-3.30pm & 7.30-11pm Wed-Sun) This unfussy, hard-to-find bar offers miniature *nueva cocina vasca* (Basque nouvelle cuisine) from a supremely creative kitchen. Unlike many San Sebastián bars, this one doesn't have any *pintxos* (Basque

SAN SEBASTIÁN SPLURGE

With three shining Michelin stars, acclaimed chef Juan Mari Arzak takes some beating when it comes to *nueva cocina vasca* (Basque nouvelle cuisine) and his restaurant is considered one of the best places to eat in the world. **Arzak** (☎943 27 84 65; www.arzak.info; Avenida Alcalde Jose Elosegui 273; meals around €195; ⌚Tue-Sat, closed Nov & late Jun) is now assisted by his daughter Elena and they never cease to innovate. Reservations, well in advance, are obligatory.

tapas) laid out on the bar top; instead you must order from the blackboard menu behind the counter.

Astelena BASQUE €€

(☎943 42 58 67; www.restauranteastelena.com; Calle de Iñigo 1; pintxos from €2.50; ⏰1-4.30pm & 8-11pm Tue & Thu-Sat, 1-4.30pm Wed) The *pintxos* (Basque tapas) draped across the counter in this bar, tucked into the corner of Plaza de la Constitución, stand out. Many of them are a fusion of Basque and Asian inspirations, but the best of all are the foie-gras-based treats. The great positioning means that prices are slightly elevated.

Restaurante Kokotxa MODERN SPANISH €€€

(☎943 42 19 04; www.restaurantekokotxa.com; Calle del Campanario 11; mains €25-35, menús from €60; ⏰1.30-3.30pm & 8.45-11pm Tue-Sat) This Michelin-star restaurant is hidden away down an overlooked alley in the old town, but the food rewards those who search. Most people opt for the *menú de mercado* (€60) and enjoy the flavours of the traders from the busy city market. It's closed for parts of February, June and October.

Information

Oficina de Turismo (☎943 48 11 66; www.sansebastianturismo.com; Alameda del Boulevard 8; ⏰9am-8pm Mon-Sat, 10am-7pm Sun Jul-Sep, shorter hours rest of year) Friendly office with comprehensive information on the city and the Basque Country in general.

Getting There & Away

BUS

Services leave for Bilbao (from €6.50, 1½ hours, frequent), Bilbao Airport (€17, 1¼ hours, hourly), Biarritz (France; €5 to €7, one hour, six daily), Madrid (€36, six hours, nine daily) and Pamplona (€8, one to two hours, 12 daily).

TRAIN

Euskotren (www.euskotren.eus) runs local trains half-hourly from Amara station, about 1km south of San Sebastián centre, to Hendaye (Hendaya; €2.45, 40 minutes), just across the border in France, from where there are frequent trains to Paris and other French destinations. San Sebastián's Renfe station, opposite the bus station on the east side of the Río Urumea, has six departures daily to Madrid (from €16, 5½ to eight hours) and two to Barcelona (from €19, six hours).

Bilbao

POP 346,600

The commercial hub of the Basque Country, Bilbao (Bilbo in Basque) is best known for the magnificent Guggenheim Museum. An architectural masterpiece by Frank Gehry, the museum was the catalyst of a turnaround that saw Bilbao transformed from an industrial port city into a vibrant cultural centre (without losing its down-to-earth soul). After visiting this must-see temple to modern art, spend time exploring Bilbao's Casco Viejo (Old Quarter), a grid of elegant streets dotted with shops, cafes, *pintxo* bars and several small but worthy museums.

Sights

★Museo Guggenheim Bilbao GALLERY

(☎944 35 90 16; www.guggenheim-bilbao.es; Avenida Abandoibarra 2; adult/student/child from €13/7.50/free, depends on exhibits; ⏰10am-8pm, closed Mon Sep-Jun) Shimmering titanium Museo Guggenheim Bilbao is one of modern architecture's most iconic buildings. It has almost single-handedly lifted Bilbao out of its post-industrial depression and into the 21st century – and with sensation. It boosted the city's already inspired regeneration, stimulated further development and placed Bilbao firmly in the international art and tourism spotlight. Inside, the often excellent temporary exhibitions are usually the chief attraction – but it's the building itself that is the star of the show.

★Museo de Bellas Artes GALLERY

(☎944 39 60 60; www.museobilbao.com; Plaza del Museo 2; adult/student/child €9/7/free, Wed free; ⏰10am-8pm Wed-Mon) The Museo de Bellas Artes houses a compelling collection that includes everything from Gothic sculptures to 20th-century pop art. There are three main subcollections: classical art, with works by Murillo, Zurbarán, El Greco, Goya and van Dyck; contemporary art, featuring works by Paul Gauguin, Francis Bacon and Anthony Caro; and Basque art, with works of the great sculptors Jorge Oteiza and Eduardo Chillida, and strong paintings by the likes of Ignacio Zuloaga and Juan de Echevarría.

Casco Viejo OLD TOWN

The compact Casco Viejo, Bilbao's atmospheric old quarter, is full of charming streets, boisterous bars and plenty of quirky and independent shops. At the heart of the Casco are

Bilbao's original seven streets, Las Siete Calles, which date from the 1400s. The 14th-century Gothic **Catedral de Santiago** (www.bilbaoturismo.net; Plaza de Santiago; ⏲10am-1pm & 5-7.30pm Tue-Sat, 10am-1pm Sun & holidays) has a splendid Renaissance portico and pretty little cloister.

Euskal Museoa MUSEUM
(Museo Vasco; ☎944 15 54 23; www.euskal-museoa.org/es/hasiera; Plaza Miguel Unamuno 4; adult/child €3/free, Thu free; ⏲10am-7pm Mon & Wed-Fri, 10am-1.30pm & 4-7pm Sat, 10am-2pm Sun) This is probably the most complete museum of Basque culture and history in all of Spain. The story begins in prehistory; from this murky period the displays bound rapidly up to the modern age, in the process explaining just how long the Basques have called this corner of the world home. Explanatory matter is in Spanish and Basque only, however.

Sleeping & Eating

The Bilbao tourism authority has a useful **reservations department** (☎902 87 72 98; www.bilbaoreservas.com; ⏲10am-9pm) for accommodation.

Pintxos (Basque tapas) are as good in Bilbao as they are in San Sebastián, and slightly cheaper (from around €2.50). Plaza Nueva, on the edge of the Casco Viejo, offers especially rich pickings, as do Calle de Perro and Calle Jardines.

Casual Bilbao Gurea PENSION €
(☎944 16 32 99; www.casualhoteles.com; Calle de Bidebarrieta 14; s/d from €45/55; 📶) The family-run Gurea has arty, modern rooms with wooden floors and large bathrooms (most of which have bathtubs) and exceptionally friendly staff. Add it all up and you get what is easily one of the best deals in the old town.

Hostal Begoña GUESTHOUSE €
(☎944 23 01 34; www.hostalbegona.com; Calle de la Amistad 2; s/d from €50/65; P @ 📶) Friendly Begoña has guestrooms with modern artwork, wrought-iron beds and colourful tiled bathrooms. The cosy common areas have plenty of books and information about local culture and attractions. It's a great place to meet other travellers, too.

Miró Hotel DESIGN HOTEL €€
(☎946 61 18 80; www.mirohotelbilbao.com; Alameda Mazarredo 77; d from €137; ❄ @ 📶) This hip hotel, facing the Museo Guggenheim Bilbao, is the passion project of fashion designer Antonio Miró. It's filled with modern photography and art, quirky books, and minimalist decor – a perfect fit with arty Bilbao.

★**La Viña del Ensanche** PINTXOS €
(☎944 15 56 15; www.lavinadelensanche.com; Calle de la Diputación 10; pintxos from €1.35, menú €30; ⏲8.30am-11.30pm Mon-Fri, noon-1am Sat) Hundreds of bottles of wine line the walls of this outstanding octogenarian *pintxos* (Basque tapas) bar. This could very well be the best place to eat *pintxos* in the entire city. If you can't decide what to sample, opt for the €30 tasting menu.

★**Agape Restaurante** BASQUE €€
(☎944 16 05 06; www.restauranteagape.com; Calle de Hernani 13; menú del día €12.90, menús €21-36; ⏲1-4pm Sun-Wed, 1-4pm & 8.30-11.30pm Thu-Sat; 📶) With a solid reputation among locals for good-value meals that don't sacrifice quality, this is a great place for a slice of real Bilbao

PAMPLONA & SANFERMINES

Immortalised by Ernest Hemingway in *The Sun Also Rises*, the pre-Pyrenean city of Pamplona (Iruña in Basque) is home of the wild Sanfermines festival, but is also an extremely walkable city that's managed to mix the charm of old plazas and buildings with modern shops and a lively nightlife.

The Sanfermines festival is held from 6 to 14 July, when Pamplona is overrun with thrill-seekers, curious onlookers and, yes, bulls. The Encierro (Running of the Bulls) begins at 8am daily, when bulls are let loose from the Coralillos Santo Domingo. The 825m run through the streets to the bullring lasts just three minutes.

Since records began in 1924, 16 people have died during Pamplona's bullrun. Many of those who run are full of bravado (and/or drink) and have little idea of what they're doing. For dedicated *encierro* news, check out www.sanfermin.com.

Animal rights groups oppose bullrunning as a cruel tradition, and the participating bulls will almost certainly all be killed in the afternoon bullfight. PETA (www.peta.org.uk) organises eye-catching protests in Pamplona at every Sanfermines.

culinary life. It's away from the standard tourist circuit, but worth the short walk.

Information

Main Tourist Office (944 79 57 60; www.bilbaoturismo.net; Plaza Circular 1; 9am-9pm;)

Getting There & Away

BUS

Bilbao's main bus station, **Termibus** (944 39 50 77; www.termibus.es; Gurtubay 1, San Mamés), is west of the centre. Services operate to San Sebastián (from €6.50, 1½ hours, frequent), Madrid (from €31, four to five hours, 15 buses daily), Barcelona (€47, eight hours, four daily), Pamplona (€15, 2½ hours, seven buses), Santander (from €6.60, 1½ hours, frequent) and Santiago de Compostela (from €20, nine hours, four buses).

TRAIN

Two Renfe trains run daily to Madrid (€15 to €50, 5¼ hours) and Barcelona (€20 to €85, seven hours) from the Abando station. Slow **FEVE** (www.renfe.com/viajeros/feve) trains from Concordia station next door head west to Santander (€8.90, three hours, three daily), where you can connect for places further west in Cantabria, Asturias and Galicia.

CANTABRIA, ASTURIAS & GALICIA

With a landscape reminiscent of parts of the British Isles, 'Green Spain' offers great walks and scenery in mountainous national and regional parks, seafood feasts in sophisticated towns or quaint fishing villages, and a spectacular coastline strung with oodles of beautiful beaches washed by the chilly waters of the north Atlantic.

Santillana del Mar

Thirty kilometres west of the Cantabrian capital, Santander, Santillana del Mar is a bijou medieval village and the obvious overnight base for visiting nearby Altamira. Buses run three or more times a day from Santander to Santillana del Mar.

Spain's finest prehistoric art, in the **Cueva de Altamira**, 2.5km southwest of Santillana, was discovered in 1879. It took more than 20 years, after further discoveries of cave art in France, before scientists accepted that these wonderful paintings of bison, horses and other animals really were the handiwork of primitive people many thousands of years ago. A replica cave here in the **Museo de Altamira** (942 81 88 15; http://museodealtamira.mcu.es; Avenida Marcelino Sanz de Sautuola; adult/child €3/free, Sun & from 2.30pm Sat free; 9.30am-8pm Tue-Sat May-Oct, to 6pm Tue-Sat Nov-Apr, to 3pm Sun & holidays year-round;) now enables everyone to appreciate the inspired, 13,000 to 35,000-year-old paintings – advance bookings advisable.

Santiago de Compostela

POP 80,000

The supposed burial place of St James (Santiago), this unique cathedral city and goal of pilgrims for nearly 1200 years is a bewitching place. The hundreds of thousands who walk here every year along the Camino de Santiago are often struck mute with wonder on entering the city's medieval centre. Fortunately, they usually regain their verbal capacities over a celebratory nocturnal foray into the city's lively bar scene.

Sights & Activities

★Catedral de Santiago de Compostela CATHEDRAL

(www.catedraldesantiago.es; Praza do Obradoiro; 7am-8.30pm) The grand heart of Santiago, the cathedral soars above the city centre in a splendid jumble of spires and sculpture. Built piecemeal over several centuries, its beauty is a mix of the original Romanesque structure (constructed between 1075 and 1211) and later Gothic and baroque flourishes. The tomb of Santiago beneath the main altar is a magnet for all who come to the cathedral. The artistic high point is the Pórtico de la Gloria inside the west entrance, featuring 200 masterly Romanesque sculptures.

★Cathedral Rooftop Tour TOURS

(902 557812; www.catedraldesantiago.es; adult/senior, pilgrim, unemployed & student/child €12/10/free, combined ticket with Museo da Catedral €15/12/free; tours hourly 10am-1pm & 4-6pm or 7pm;) For unforgettable bird's-eye views of the cathedral interior from its upper storeys, and of the city from the cathedral roof, take the rooftop tour, which starts in the visitor reception centre beneath the Obradoiro facade. The tours are popular, so book beforehand, or book online. One of the afternoon tours is usually given in English; the rest are in Spanish.

★ **Praza do Obradoiro** PLAZA

The grand square in front of the cathedral's west facade earned its name (Workshop Sq) from the stonemasons' workshops set up here while the cathedral was being built. It's free of both traffic and cafes, and has a unique, magical atmosphere.

★ **Museo da Catedral** MUSEUM

(Colección Permanente; www.catedraldesantiago.es; Praza do Obradoiro; adult/senior, pilgrim, unemployed & student/child €6/4/free; ⏲9am-8pm Apr-Oct, 10am-8pm Nov-Mar) The Museo da Catedral spreads over four floors and includes the cathedral's large, 16th-century, Gothic/plateresque cloister. You'll see a sizeable section of Maestro Mateo's original carved stone choir (destroyed in 1604 but recently pieced back together), an impressive collection of religious art (including the *botafumeiros,* in the 2nd-floor library), the lavishly decorated 18th-century *sala capitular* (chapter house), a room of tapestries woven from designs by Goya, and, off the cloister, the Panteón de Reyes, with tombs of kings of medieval León.

★ **Museo das Peregrinacións e de Santiago** MUSEUM

(http://museoperegrinacions.xunta.gal; Praza das Praterías; adult/pilgrim & student/senior & child €2.40/1.20/free, Sat afternoon & Sun free; ⏲9.30am-8.30pm Tue-Fri, 11am-7pm Sat, 10.15am-2.45pm Sun) Installed in a newly converted premises on Praza das Praterías, the brightly displayed Museum of Pilgrimages & Santiago gives fascinating insights into the phenomenon of Santiago (man and city) down the centuries. Much of the explanatory material is in English as well as Spanish and Galician. There are also great close-up views of some of the cathedral's towers from the 3rd-floor windows.

Sleeping

The Last Stamp HOSTEL €

(El Último Sello; ☎981 563 525; www.thelaststamp.es; Rúa Preguntoiro 10; dm €18-20; ⏲closed late Dec-late Feb; ⊖@☰) A purpose-designed hostel, the Last Stamp occupies a 300-year-old, five-storey house (with lift) in the heart of the old town. The cleverly designed dorms feature semi-private modules with ultra-solid bunks, good mattresses and individual reading lights. Some rooms enjoy cathedral views. Bathrooms and kitchen are good and big – and Camino-themed murals add a bit of fun.

WORTH A TRIP

PICOS DE EUROPA

These jagged mountains straddling corners of Asturias, Cantabria and Castilla y León amount to some of the finest walking country in Spain. They comprise three limestone massifs (the highest peak rises to 2648m). The 671-sq-km **Parque Nacional de los Picos de Europa** covers all three massifs and is Spain's second-biggest national park.

There are numerous places to stay and eat all around the mountains, with Cangas de Onís (Asturias) and Potes (Cantabria) the main centres for accommodation and information. Getting here and around by public transport can be slow going but the Picos are accessible by bus from Oviedo and Santander (the former is easier).

The official websites, www.mapama.gob.es and www.parquenacionalpicoseuropa.es, are mostly in Spanish, but www.picosdeeuropa.com and www.liebanaypicosdeeuropa.com are useful for the Asturias and Cantabria sides respectively.

★ **Hotel Costa Vella** BOUTIQUE HOTEL €€

(☎981 569 530; www.costavella.com; Rúa da Porta da Pena 17; s/d €59/81; ⊖❄☰) Tranquil, thoughtfully designed rooms (some with typically Galician *galerías* – glassed-in balconies), a friendly welcome, super-helpful management and staff, and a lovely garden **cafe** (breakfast €6; ⏲8am-11pm; ☰) make this family-run hotel in an old stone house a wonderful option – and the €6 breakfast is substantial.

★ **Parador Hostal dos Reis Católicos** HISTORIC HOTEL €€€

(☎981 582 200; www.parador.es; Praza do Obradoiro 1; r incl breakfast €166-294, ste from €347; P⊖❄@☰) Opened in 1509 as a pilgrims' hostel, and with a claim to be the world's oldest hotel, this palatial *parador* occupies a wonderful building that is one of Santiago's major monuments in its own right, just steps from the cathedral. Even standard rooms are regal, with canopied beds, wooden floors, original art and generously sized bathrooms with bathtubs and big glass showers.

If you're not staying, stop in for a look round and coffee and cakes at the elegant cafe, or dine at one of the two restaurants.

Eating

★ Abastos 2.0 GALICIAN €€
(☎654 015937; www.abastosdouspuntocero.es; Rúa das Ameas 3; dishes €3-12, menú €21; ⊙noon-3.30pm & 8-11pm Mon-Sat) This highly original and incredibly popular marketside eatery offers new dishes concocted daily from the market's offerings. Go for small individual items, or plates to share, or a six-item *menú* that adds up to a meal for €21. The seafood is generally fantastic, but whatever you order you're likely to love the great tastes and delicate presentation – if you can get a seat!

★ O Curro da Parra GALICIAN €€
(www.ocurrodaparra.com; Rúa do Curro da Parra 7; mains €10-18, tapas & starters €6-13; ⊙1.30-3.30pm & 8.30-11.30pm Tue-Sun) With a neat little stone-walled dining room upstairs and a narrow tapas and wine bar below, always-busy Curro da Parra serves a broad range of tasty, thoughtfully created, market-fresh fare. You might go for crunchy prawn-and-soft-cheese rolls with passion-fruit sauce, or the free-range chicken skewers with mayonnaise-style *grebiche* sauce – or just ask about the fish and seafood of the day.

La Bodeguilla de San Roque SPANISH €€
(☎981 564 379; www.bodeguilladesanroque.com; Rúa de San Roque 13; raciones & mains €5-16; ⊙9am-11.30am Mon-Fri, from 10.30am Sat & Sun) A busy two-storey restaurant-cum-wine-bar just northeast of the old town, the Bodeguilla serves an eclectic range of excellent dishes ranging from salads to casseroles of shrimp, mushroom and seaweed, Galician beef sirloin in port, or plates of cheeses, sausages or ham.

Information

Turismo de Santiago (☎981 555 129; www.santiagoturismo.com; Rúa do Vilar 63; ⊙9am-9pm Apr-Oct, 9am-7pm Mon-Fri, 9am-2pm & 4-7pm Sat & Sun Nov-Mar) The efficient main municipal tourist office.

Getting There & Around

AIR

Santiago has direct flights to/from some 20 European and Spanish cities, many of them operated by budget airlines EasyJet, Ryanair and Vueling.

BUS

The **bus station** (☎981 542 416; www.alsa.es; Praza de Camilo Díaz Baliño; 📶) is 1.5km northeast of the city centre. There are services to León (€30, six hours, one daily), Madrid (€46, eight to 10 hours, four daily), Porto (Portugal; €33, 3¼ hours, one daily), Santander (€50, nine to 10 hours, two daily) and many places around Galicia.

TRAIN

From the **train station** (www.renfe.es; Rúa do Hórreo), plentiful trains run up and down the Galician coast as far as A Coruña and Vigo. High-speed AVE service to/from Madrid is due to start during 2018: in the meantime there are three daily trains (from €17, 5¼ hours).

Around Galicia

Galicia's dramatic coastline is one of Spain's best-kept secrets, with wild and precipitous cliffs, long inlets running far inland, splendid beaches and isolated fishing villages. The lively port city of **A Coruña** has a lovely city beach and fabulous seafood (a recurring Galician theme). It's also a gateway to the stirring landscapes of the **Costa da Morte** and **Rías Altas**; the latter's highlight among many is probably **Cabo Ortegal**. Inland Galicia is also worth exploring, especially the old town of **Lugo**, surrounded by what many consider the world's best preserved Roman walls.

VALENCIA

POP 786,200

Spain's third-largest city is a magnificent place, content for Madrid and Barcelona to grab the headlines while it gets on with being a wonderfully liveable city with thriving cultural, eating and nightlife scenes. The star attraction is the strikingly futuristic buildings of the Ciudad de las Artes y las Ciencias, designed by local-boy-made-good Santiago Calatrava. Valencia also has a fistful of fabulous Modernista architecture, great museums and a large, characterful old quarter. Surrounded by fertile fruit-and-veg farmland, the city is famous as the home of rice dishes like paella, but its buzzy dining scene offers plenty more besides.

Sights & Activities

★ Ciudad de las Artes y las Ciencias NOTABLE BUILDING
(City of Arts & Sciences; ☎902 100031; www.cac.es; 👪) The aesthetically stunning City of Arts & Sciences occupies a massive 35-hectare swath of the old Turia riverbed. It's mostly the work of world-famous, locally born architect Santiago Calatrava. He's a controversial

figure for many Valencians, who complain about the expense, and various design flaws that have necessitated major repairs here. Nevertheless, if your taxes weren't involved, it's awe-inspiring stuff, and pleasingly family-oriented.

Oceanogràfic AQUARIUM
(☎902 100031; www.oceanografic.org; Camino de las Moreras; adult/child €29.10/22, audio guide €3.70, combined ticket with Hemisfèric & Museo de las Ciencias €37.40/28.40; ⏲10am-5pm Sun-Fri, 10am-7pm Sat, 10am-midnight Jul & Aug; 👪) Spain's most famous aquarium is the southernmost building of the City of Arts & Sciences. It's an impressive display; the complex is divided into a series of climate zones, reached overground or underground from the central hub building. The sharks, complete with tunnel, are an obvious favourite, while a series of beautiful tanks present species from temperate, Mediterranean, Red Sea and tropical waters. Less happily, the aquarium also keeps captive dolphins and belugas: research suggests that this is detrimental to their welfare.

★**Catedral** CATHEDRAL
(☎963 91 81 27; www.catedraldevalencia.es; Plaza de la Virgen; adult/child incl audio guide €7/5.50; ⏲10am-6.30pm Mon-Sat, 2-5.30pm Sun, to 5.30pm Nov-Mar, closed Sun Nov-Feb; 📶) Valencia's cathedral was built over the mosque after the 1238 reconquest. Its low, wide, brick-vaulted triple nave is mostly Gothic, with neoclassical side chapels. Highlights are rich Italianate frescos above the altarpiece, a pair of Goyas in the **Capilla de San Francisco de Borja**, and...ta-dah...in the flamboyant Gothic **Capilla del Santo Cáliz**, what's claimed to be the **Holy Grail** from which Christ sipped during the Last Supper. It's a Roman-era agate cup, later modified, so at least the date is right.

★**La Lonja** HISTORIC BUILDING
(☎962 08 41 53; www.valencia.es; Calle de la Lonja; adult/child €2/1, Sun free; ⏲9.30am-7pm Mon-Sat, 9.30am-3pm Sun) This splendid building, a Unesco World Heritage site, was originally Valencia's silk and commodity exchange, built in the late 15th century when Valencia was booming. It's one of Spain's finest examples of a civil Gothic building. Two main structures flank a citrus-studded courtyard: the magnificent Sala de Contratación, a cathedral of commerce with soaring twisted pillars, and the Consulado del Mar, where a maritime tribunal sat. The top floor boasts a stunning coffered ceiling brought here from another building.

★**Mercado Central** MARKET
(☎963 82 91 00; www.mercadocentralvalencia.es; Plaza del Mercado; ⏲7.30am-3pm Mon-Sat) Valencia's vast Modernista covered market, constructed in 1928, is a swirl of smells, movement and colour. Spectacular seafood counters display cephalopods galore and numerous fish species, while the fruit and vegetables, many produced locally in Valencia's *huerta* (area of market gardens), are of special quality. A tapas bar lets you sip a wine and enjoy the atmosphere.

★**Museo de Bellas Artes** GALLERY
(San Pío V; ☎963 87 03 00; www.museobellasartesvalencia.gva.es; Calle de San Pío V 9; ⏲10am-8pm Tue-Sun) FREE Bright and spacious, this gallery ranks among Spain's best. Highlights include a collection of magnificent late-medieval altarpieces, and works by several Spanish masters, including some great Goya portraits, a haunting Velázquez selfie, an El Greco *John the Baptist*, Murillos, Riberas and works by the Ribaltas, father and son. Downstairs, an excellent series of rooms focuses on the great, versatile Valencian painter Joaquín Sorolla (1863–1923), who, at his best, seemed to capture the spirit of an age through sensitive portraiture.

Beaches

Valencia's town beaches are 3km east of the centre. **Playa de las Arenas** runs north into **Playa de la Malvarrosa** and **Playa de la Patacona**, forming a wide strip of sand some 4km long. It's bordered by the **Paseo Marítimo** promenade and a string of restaurants and cafes. One block back, lively bars and discos thump out the beat in summer.

Sleeping

★**Russafa Youth Hostel** HOSTEL €
(☎963 28 94 60; www.russafayouthhostel.com; Calle Padre Perera 5; dm/d €18/40; @📶) You'll feel instantly at home in this super-welcoming, cute hostel set over various floors of a venerable building in the heart of vibrant Russafa. It's all beds, rather than bunks, and with a maximum of three to a room, there's no crowding. Sweet rooms and spotless bathrooms make for a mighty easy stay.

★**Hostal Antigua Morellana** HOSTAL €€
(☎963 91 57 73; www.hostalam.com; Calle En Bou 2; s/d €50/60; ❄📶) This friendly, family-run, 18-room spot occupies a renovated 18th-century *posada* (where wealthier merchants bringing their produce to the nearby food market would spend the night), and has cosy, good-sized rooms, most with balconies. It's kept extremely shipshape by the rightly house-proud owners and there are loads of great features including memory-foam mattresses and hairdryers. Higher floors have more natural light. Good value.

★**Caro Hotel** HOTEL €€€
(☎963 05 90 00; www.carohotel.com; Calle Almirante 14; r €156-330; P❄📶) Housed in a sumptuous 19th-century mansion, this hotel sits atop two millennia of Valencian history, with restoration revealing a hefty hunk of the Arab wall, Roman column bases and Gothic arches. Each room is furnished in soothing dark shades, and has a great king-sized bed and varnished cement floors. Bathrooms are tops. For special occasions, reserve the 1st-floor grand suite, once the ballroom.

Eating

The number of restaurants has to be seen to be believed! In the centre there are numerous traditional options, as well as trendy tapas choices. The main eating zones are the Barrio del Carmen, L'Eixample and, above all, the vibrant tapas-packed streets of Russafa.

★**Navarro** VALENCIAN €€
(☎963 52 96 23; www.restaurantenavarro.com; Calle del Arzobispo Mayoral 5; rices €11-18, set menu €22; ⏲1.30-4pm daily, 8.30-11pm Sat; 📶) A byword in the city for decades for its quality rice dishes, Navarro is run by the grandkids of the original founders and it offers plenty of choice, outdoor seating and a set menu, including one of the rices as a main.

★**Refugio** FUSION €€
(☎690 61 70 18; www.refugiorestaurante.com; Calle Alta 42; mains €14-22, set menu €12-15; ⏲2-4pm & 9pm-midnight; 📶) Named for the civil-war hideout opposite and simply decorated in whitewashed brick, Refugio preserves some of the Carmen *barrio's* former revolutionary spirit. Excellent Med-fusion cuisine is presented in lunchtime menus of surprising quality: there are some stellar plates on show, though the vegie options aren't always quite as flavoursome. Evening dining is high quality and innovative.

★**Delicat** TAPAS €€
(☎963 92 33 57; Calle Conde Almodóvar 4; lunch menú €14.50, mains €10-15; ⏲1.45-3.30pm & 8.45pm-12.30am Tue-Sat, 1.45-3.45pm Sun; 📶) At this particularly friendly, intimate option, Catina, up front, and her partner, Paco, on full view in the kitchen, offer an unbeatable-value, five-course menu of samplers for lunch and a range of truly innovative tapas plates, designed for sharing, anytime. There's a range of influences at play; the decor isn't lavish but the food is memorable.

★**El Poblet** GASTRONOMY €€€
(☎961 11 11 06; www.elpobletrestaurante.com; Calle de Correos 8; menus €58-118; ⏲1.30-3.30pm Tue, 1.30-3.30pm & 8.30-10.30pm Wed-Sat & Mon; 📶) Run by noted chef Luis Vallis Rozalén, this upstairs restaurant offers elegance and fine gastronomic dining at prices that are very competitive for this quality. Modern French and Spanish influences combine to create sumptuous degustation menus. Some of the imaginative presentation has to be seen to be believed, and staff are genuinely welcoming and helpful.

Drinking & Nightlife

Russafa has the best bar scene, with a huge range of everything from family-friendly cultural cafes to quirky bars, and also a couple of big clubs. The Barrio del Carmen is also famous nightlife territory. In summer the port area and Malvarrosa beach leap to life.

Radio City CLUB
(☎963 91 41 51; www.radiocityvalencia.es; Calle de Santa Teresa 19; ⏲10.30pm-3.30am, from 8.30pm Thu & Fri) Almost as much mini cultural centre as club, Radio City, which gets packed from around 1am, pulls in the punters with activities such as language exchange, and DJs or live music every night. There's everything from flamenco (Tuesday) to reggae and funk, and the crowd is eclectic and engaged.

L'Umbracle Terraza/Mya BAR, CLUB
(www.umbracleterraza.com; Avenida del Professor López Piñero 5; admission €10; ⏲midnight-7.30am Thu-Sat) At the southern end of the Umbracle walkway within the Ciudad de las Artes y las Ciencias, this is a cool, sophisticated spot to spend a hot summer night. Catch the evening breeze under the stars on the

terrace (from 6pm Thursday to Sunday May to October), then drop below to Mya, a top-of-the-line club with an awesome sound system. Admission covers both venues.

La Fustería BAR
(☎633 100428; www.lafusteriaruzafa.com; Calle de Cádiz 28; ⏱7-11.30pm Mon-Thu, 7pm-2.30am Fri & Sat; 📶) This former carpentry workshop is now a likeable jumbled bar and restaurant with mismatched furniture and exposed brick walls. It's a great venue for an after-dinner drink, with an amiable mix of folk, and regular events – flamenco when we were last there – out the back.

ℹ Information

Tourist Kiosk (☎963 52 49 08; www.turisvalencia.es; Plaza del Ayuntamiento; ⏱9am-7pm Mon-Sat, 10am-2pm Sun)

Regional Tourist Office (☎963 98 64 22; www.comunitatvalenciana.com; Calle de la Paz 48; ⏱10am-6pm Mon-Fri, 10am-2pm Sat & Sun) A fount of information about the Valencia region.

ℹ Getting There & Away

AIR

Valencia's **airport** (VLC; ☎902 40 47 04; www.aena.es) is 10km west of the city centre along the A3, towards Madrid. Budget flights serve major European destinations including London, Paris and Berlin.

BOAT

Trasmediterranea (☎902 45 46 45; www.trasmediterranea.es) operates car and passenger ferries to Ibiza, Mallorca and Menorca. **Baleària** (☎902 16 01 80, from overseas 966 42 87 00; www.balearia.com) goes to Mallorca and Ibiza.

BUS

Valencia's **bus station** (☎963 46 62 66; Avenida Menéndez Pidal) is beside the riverbed. Bus 8 connects it to Plaza del Ayuntamiento.

Avanza (www.avanzabus.com) Operates 10 daily buses to/from Madrid (€27 to €36, 4¼ hours).

ALSA (www.alsa.es) Has nine daily buses to/from Barcelona (€26 to €36, four to 5¼ hours) and services to Andalucian cities including Granada, Málaga and Seville.

TRAIN

Thirteen daily high-speed AVE trains to Madrid (€22 to €72, 1¾ hours), eight fast Euromed trains to Barcelona (€16 to €45, 3¼ hours), and one AVE to Seville (€37 to €56, four hours), go from Valencia Joaquín Sorolla station, 800m south of the old town. A few slower but not necessarily cheaper trains to the same and other destinations go from Estación del Norte, 500m away. The two stations are linked by free shuttle bus.

WORTH A TRIP

LAS FALLAS

In mid-March, Valencia hosts one of Europe's wildest street parties: **Las Fallas de San José** (www.fallas.com; ⏱Mar). From 15 to 19 March the city is engulfed by an anarchic swirl of fireworks, music, festive bonfires and all-night partying. On the final night, hundreds of giant effigies *(fallas)*, many of them representing political and social personages, are torched.

If you're not in Valencia then, see the *ninots* (figurines placed at the base of the *fallas*) that have been saved from the flames by popular vote (one per year) at the **Museo Fallero** (☎963 52 54 78; www.valencia.es; Plaza Monteolivete 4; adult/child €2/free, Sun free; ⏱9.30am-7pm Mon-Sat, 9.30am-3pm Sun).

ℹ Getting Around

Valencia has an integrated bus, tram and metro network. Rides are €1.50; one-/two-/three-day travel cards cost €4/6.70/9.70. Metro lines 3 and 5 connect the airport, central Valencia and the port. The tram is a pleasant way to get to the beach and port. Pick it up at Pont de Fusta or where it intersects with the metro at Benimaclet.

BALEARIC ISLANDS

The Balearic Islands (Illes Balears in Catalan) adorn the glittering Mediterranean waters off Spain's eastern coastline. Beach tourism destinations par excellence, each of the islands has a quite distinct identity and they have managed to retain much of their individual character and beauty. All boast beaches second to none in the Med, but each offers reasons for exploring inland too.

Check out websites like www.illesbalears.es and www.platgesdebalears.com.

ℹ Getting There & Away

AIR

In summer, charter and regular flights converge on Palma de Mallorca and Ibiza from all over Europe.

BOAT

The major ferry companies are **Trasmediterranea** (p597) and **Baleària** (☎902 16 01 80;

www.balearia.com). Compare prices and look for deals at Direct Ferries (www.directferries.com).

The main ferry routes to the mainland, most operating only from Easter to late October, include the following:

Ibiza (Ibiza City) To/from Barcelona and Valencia (Trasmediterranea, Baleària) and Denia (Baleària)

Ibiza (Sant Antoni) To/from Denia and Valencia (Baleària)

Mallorca (Palma de Mallorca) To/from Barcelona and Valencia (Trasmediterranea, Baleària) and Denia (Baleària)

Mallorca (Port d'Alcúdia) To/from Barcelona (Baleària)

Menorca (Maó) To/from Barcelona (Trasmediterranea, Baleària) and Valencia (Trasmediterranea)

The main interisland ferry routes include the following:

Ibiza (Ibiza City) To/from Palma de Mallorca (Trasmediterranea, Baleària)

Mallorca (Palma de Mallorca) To/from Ibiza City (Trasmediterranea, Baleària) and Maó (Trasmediterrnea)

Mallorca (Port d'Alcúdia) To/from Ciutadella (Trasmediterranea, Baleària)

Menorca (Ciutadella) To/from Port d'Alcúdia (Trasmediterranea, Baleària)

Menorca (Maó) To/from Palma de Mallorca (Trasmediterranea)

Mallorca

The sunny, warm hues of the medieval heart of Palma de Mallorca, the archipelago's capital, make a great introduction to the islands. Getting beyond the beach developments and out to some of the more secluded bays, and into the mountains and pretty inland towns, is the key to enjoying the island if you have time to venture beyond Palma. The northwest coast, dominated by the limestone Serra de Tramuntana mountain range, is a beautiful region of olive groves, pine forests and ochre villages, with a spectacularly rugged coastline. Most of Mallorca's best beaches are on the north and east coasts, and although many have been swallowed up by tourist developments, you can still find the occasional deserted cove.

Palma de Mallorca

Palma de Mallorca is a graceful and historic Mediterranean city with some world-class attractions and equally impressive culinary, art and nightlife scenes.

Sights

★Catedral de Mallorca CATHEDRAL

(La Seu; www.catedraldemallorca.org; Carrer del Palau Reial 9; adult/child €7/free; 10am-6.15pm Mon-Fri Jun-Sep, to 5.15pm Apr, May & Oct, to 3.15pm Nov-Mar, 10am-2.15pm Sat year-round) Palma's vast cathedral ('La Seu' in Catalan) is the city's major architectural landmark. Aside from its sheer scale and undoubted beauty, its stunning interior features, designed by Antoni Gaudí and renowned contemporary artist Miquel Barceló, make this unlike any cathedral elsewhere in the world. The awesome structure is predominantly Gothic, apart from the main facade, which is startling, quite beautiful and completely mongrel.

★Palau de l'Almudaina PALACE

(www.patrimonionacional.es; Carrer del Palau Reial; adult/child €7/4, audio guide/guided tour €3/4; 10am-8pm Apr-Sep, to 6pm Oct-Mar) Originally an Islamic fort, this mighty construction opposite the cathedral was converted into a residence for the Mallorcan monarchs at the end of the 13th century. The King of Spain resides here still, at least symbolically. The royal family are rarely in residence, except for the occasional ceremony, as they prefer to spend summer in the Palau Marivent (in Cala Major). At other times you can wander through a series of cavernous stone-walled rooms that have been lavishly decorated.

★Palau March MUSEUM

(971 71 11 22; www.fundacionbmarch.es; Carrer del Palau Reial 18; adult/child €4.50/free; 10am-6.30pm Mon-Fri Apr-Oct, to 2pm Nov-Mar, to 2pm Sat year-round) This house, palatial by any definition, was one of several residences of the phenomenally wealthy March family. Sculptures by 20th-century greats including Henry Moore, Auguste Rodin, Barbara Hepworth and Eduardo Chillida grace the outdoor terrace. Within lie many more artistic treasures from such luminaries of Spanish art as Salvador Dalí and Barcelona's Josep Maria Sert and Xavier Corberó. Not to be missed are the meticulously crafted figures of an 18th-century Neapolitan *belén* (nativity scene).

★Es Baluard GALLERY

(Museu d'Art Modern i Contemporani; 971 90 82 00; www.esbaluard.org; Plaça de Porta de Santa Catalina 10; adult/temporary exhibitions/child €6/4/free; 10am-8pm Tue-Sat, to 3pm Sun;) Built with flair and innovation into the shell of the Renaissance-era seaward walls, this contemporary art gallery is one of the finest

WORTH A TRIP

MENORCA

Renowned for its pristine beaches and archaeological sites, tranquil Menorca was declared a Biosphere Reserve by Unesco in 1993. **Maó** absorbs most of the tourist traffic. North of Maó, a drive across a lunar landscape leads to the lighthouse at **Cap de Faváritx**. South of the cape stretch some fine remote sandy bays and beaches reachable only on foot, including **Cala Presili** and **Platja d'en Tortuga**.

Ciutadella, with its smaller harbour and historic buildings, has a more Spanish feel to it and is the more attractive of the island's two main towns. A narrow country road leads south of Ciutadella (follow the 'Platges' sign from the *ronda*, or ring road) and then forks twice to reach some of the island's loveliest beaches: (from west to east) **Arenal de Son Saura**, **Cala es Talaier, Cala en Turqueta** and **Cala Macarella**. As with most beaches, you'll need your own transport.

In the centre of the island, the 357m-high **Monte Toro** has great views; on a clear day you can see Mallorca. On the northern coast, the picturesque town of **Fornells** is on a large bay popular with windsurfers.

The ports in both Maó and Ciutadella are lined with bars and restaurants.

on the island. Its temporary exhibitions are worth viewing, but the permanent collection – works by Miró, Barceló and Picasso – give the gallery its cachet. Entry on Fridays is by donation, and anyone turning up on a bike, on any day, is charged just €2.

★Museu Fundación Juan March GALLERY
(☎91 435 42 40; www.march.es; Carrer de Sant Miquel 11; ⏲10am-6.30pm Mon-Fri, 10.30am-2pm Sat) FREE The 17th-century Can Gallard del Canya, a 17th-century mansion overlaid with minor Modernist touches, now houses a small but significant collection of painting and sculpture. The permanent exhibits – some 80 pieces held by the Fundación Juan March – constitute a veritable who's who of modern Spanish art, including Miró, Picasso, fellow cubist Juan Gris, Dalí, and the sculptors Eduardo Chillida and Julio González.

Sleeping

★Misión de San Miguel BOUTIQUE HOTEL €€
(☎971 21 48 48; www.urhotels.com; Carrer de Can Maçanet 1A; d/ste €140/175; P ✱ @ ☜) This boutique hotel, with its 32 stylish designer rooms gathered discreetly around a quiet inner courtyard, is a real bargain. Good-quality mattresses and rain shower heads are typical of a place where the little things are always done well, although some rooms open onto public areas and can be a tad noisy. Service is friendly and professional.

★Hotel Tres BOUTIQUE HOTEL €€€
(☎971 71 73 33; www.hoteltres.com; Carrer dels Apuntadors 3; s/d/ste €187/258/300; ✱ @ ☜ ≋) Hotel Tres swings joyously between 16th-century town palace and fresh-faced Scandinavian design. Centred on a courtyard with a single palm, the rooms are cool and minimalist, with cowhide benches, anatomy-inspired prints, and nice details like rollaway desks and Durance aromatherapy cosmetics. Head up to the roof terrace at sunset for a steam and dip as the cathedral begins to twinkle.

Eating

★Can Cera Gastro-Bar MEDITERRANEAN €€
(☎971 71 50 12; www.cancerahotel.com; Carrer del Convent de Sant Francesc 8; tapas €9-22; ⏲12.30-11pm) This restaurant spills onto a lovely inner patio at the Can Cera hotel, housed in a *palau* (palace) that dates originally to the 13th century. Dine by lantern light on tapas-sized dishes such as *frito mallorquín* (seafood fried with potato and herbs), Cantabrian anchovies, and pork ribs with honey and mustard. The vertical garden attracts plenty of attention from passers-by.

★Toque INTERNATIONAL €€
(☎971 28 70 68; www.restaurante-toque.com; Carrer Federico García Lorca 6; mains €17-19, 3-course lunch menú €14.50; ⏲1-4pm & 7-11pm Tue-Sat; 👪) A father-and-son team run this individual little place with real pride and warmth. The food is Belgian-meets-Med (perhaps cauliflower cream with *butifarrón* sausage, raisins and pine nuts, or pork cheeks with peach) and has generated a loyal following among *palmeros*. Wines are well chosen and modestly priced, and the €14.50 lunch *menú* is a dead-set bargain.

★Marc Fosh MODERN EUROPEAN €€€
(☎971 72 01 14; www.marcfosh.com; Carrer de la Missió 7A; menús lunch €28-40, dinner €68-89; ⏲1-4.30pm & 7.30pm-midnight) The flagship of Michelin-starred Fosh's burgeoning flotilla of Palma restaurants, this stylish gastronomic destination introduces novel twists to time-honoured Mediterranean dishes and ingredients, all within the converted refectory of a 17th-century convent. The weekly lunch *menú,* three/five courses for €28/40, is a very reasonable way to enjoy dishes such as foie gras and duck terrine, or truffled pasta with burrata.

ℹ Information

Consell de Mallorca Tourist Office (☎971 17 39 90; www.infomallorca.net; Plaça de la Reina 2; ⏲8.30am-8pm Mon-Fri, to 3pm Sat; 📶)

Around Palma de Mallorca

Mallorca's northwestern coast is a world away from the high-rise tourism on the other side of the island. Dominated by the dramatic, razorback Serra de Tramuntana, it's a beautiful region of olive groves, pine forests and small villages with shuttered stone buildings. There are a couple of highlights for drivers: the hair-raising road down to the small port of **Sa Calobra**, and the amazing trip along the peninsula at the island's northern tip, **Cap Formentor**.

Sóller is a good place to base yourself for hiking and the nearby village of **Fornalutx** is one of the prettiest on Mallorca.

From Sóller, it's a 10km walk to the beautiful hilltop village of **Deià**, where Robert Graves, poet and author of *I Claudius,* lived for most of his life. From the village, you can scramble down to the small shingle beach of **Cala de Deià**. The pretty streets of **Valldemossa**, further southwest down the coast, are crowned by a fine monastery.

Further east, **Pollença** and **Artà** are attractive inland towns. Nice beaches include those at **Cala Sant Vicenç**, **Platja des Coll Baix** hidden on Cap des Pinar, **Cala Agulla** and others near Cala Ratjada, **Cala Mondragó** and **Cala Llombards**.

Buses and/or trains cover much of the island, but hiring a car (in any town or resort) is best for exploring the remoter beaches, hill towns and mountains.

Ibiza

Ibiza (Eivissa in Catalan) is an island of extremes. Its formidable party reputation is completely justified, with some of the world's greatest clubs attracting hedonists from the world over. The interior and northeast of the island, however, are another world. Peaceful country drives, hilly green territory, a sprinkling of mostly laid-back beaches and coves, and some wonderful inland accommodation and eateries are light years from the throbbing all-night dance parties that dominate the west.

Ibiza City

👁 Sights

Ibiza City's port and nightlife area **Sa Penya** is crammed with funky and trashy clothing boutiques and arty-crafty market stalls. From here, you can wander up into **D'Alt Vila**, the atmospheric old walled town.

★Ramparts HISTORIC SITE
Encircling D'Alt Vila, Ibiza's colossal protective walls reach over 25m in height and include seven bastions. Evocatively floodlit at night, these fortifications were constructed to safeguard Ibiza's residents against the threat of pirate attack. You can walk the entire perimeter of these impressive Renaissance-era ramparts, designed to withstand heavy artillery. Along the way, enjoy great views over the Port Area and south to Formentera.

Catedral CATHEDRAL
(Plaça de la Catedral; ⏲9.30am-1.30pm & 4-8pm) FREE Ibiza's cathedral, which sits close to the highest ground in D'Alt Vila, elegantly combines several styles: the original 14th-century structure is Catalan Gothic, the sacristy was added in 1592, and a major baroque renovation took place in the 18th century. Inside, the **Museu Diocesà** (€1.50; ⏲9.30am-1.30pm Tue-Sun, closed Dec-Feb) contains some impressive religious art.

🛏 Sleeping

Many of Ibiza City's hotels and *hostales* are closed in winter and heavily booked between April and October. Make sure you book ahead.

Hostal Parque HOSTAL €€

(☎971 30 13 58; www.hostalparque.com; Plaça des Parc 4; s €61-83, d €83-143, tr €132; ❄📶) Overlooking palm-dotted Plaça des Parc, this *hostal's* rooms have been spruced up with boutique touches such as wood floors, contemporary art and ultramodern bathrooms. There's a price hike for *ático* (penthouse) rooms, but their roof terraces with D'Alt Vila views are something else. Street-facing rooms might be a tad noisy for light sleepers.

★Urban Spaces DESIGN HOTEL €€€

(☎871 51 71 74; Carrer de la Vía Púnica 32; ste €200-270; ❄📶) Ira Francis-Smith is the brains behind this design hotel with an alternative edge. Some of the world's most prolific street artists (N4T4, INKIE, JEROM, et al) have pooled their creativity in the roomy, mural-splashed suites, with clever backlighting, proper workstations and balconies with terrific views. Extras such as yoga on the roof terrace and clubber-friendly breakfasts until 1pm are sure-fire people-pleasers.

Eating

★S'Escalinata MEDITERRANEAN, CAFE €

(☎971 30 61 93; www.sescalinata.es; Carrer Portal Nou 10; snacks/meals from €5/9; ⏲10.30am-3.30am Apr-Oct; 📶) Enjoying an incredibly picturesque location inside D'Alt Vila, this casual cafe-restaurant's low tables and cushioned seating (on the steps of a steep stone staircase) create a relaxed vibe. Healthy breakfasts, tapas, *bocadillos* (filled rolls) and a satisfying dinner menu are offered. It's open late into the night, doubling as a bar with good house sangria and cocktails.

S'Ametller IBIZAN €€€

(☎971 31 17 80; www.restaurantsametller.com; Carrer de Pere Francès 12; menús €24-38; ⏲8pm-11pm Mon-Sat Jun-Sep, 1-4pm Mon-Sat, 8pm-11pm Wed-Sat Oct-May) The 'Almond Tree' specialises in local, market-fresh cooking. The daily *menú* is inventive and superb value. For dessert, choose the house *flaó*, a mint-flavoured variant of cheesecake and a Balearic Islands speciality. S'Ametller also offers cookery courses – including one that imparts the secrets of that *flaó*.

Drinking & Nightlife

Sa Penya is the nightlife centre. Dozens of bars keep the port area jumping. Alternatively, various bars at Platja d'en Bossa combine sounds, sand, sea and sangria.

CLUBBING IN IBIZA

Ibiza's clubs are the stuff of legend. From late May to the end of September, the west of the island is one big, nonstop dance party from sunset to sunrise and back again. Space, Amnesia and Pacha were Nos 1, 3 and 4 in *DJ Mag*'s top 100 clubs for 2016.

The major clubs operate nightly from around midnight to 6am from mid-May or June to early October. Theme nights, fancy-dress parties and foam parties are regular features.

Entertainment Ibiza-style doesn't come cheaply. Admission can cost anything from €15 to €75 (mixed drinks and cocktails then go for around €10 to €15).

Pacha (www.pachaibiza.com; Avinguda 8 d'Agost; admission from €20, drinks from €10; ⏲11pm-6am daily May-Sep, 11pm-6am Sat Oct-Apr) Going strong since 1973, Pacha is Ibiza's original and most classy nightclub. Built around the shell of a farmhouse, it boasts an amazing main dance floor, the Funky Room (for soul and disco sounds), a huge VIP section and myriad other places to groove or chill, including a fab open-air terrace and a Global Room for hip hop and R & B.

Amnesia (www.amnesia.es; Carretera Ibiza a Sant Antoni Km 5; €35-70; ⏲midnight-6am end May-Oct) Amnesia is arguably Ibiza's most influential club, its decks welcoming such DJ royalty as Sven Väth, Paul Van Dyk, Paul Oakenfold and Avicii. There's a warehouse-like main room and a terrace topped by a graceful atrium. Big nights include techno-fest Cocoon; Cream; foam-filled Espuma, which always draws a big local crowd; and La Troya, the biggest gay night on the island.

Ushuaïa (www.ushuaiabeachhotel.com; Platja d'en Bossa 10; €40-75; ⏲3pm or 5pm-midnight; 📶) Queen of daytime clubbing, ice-cool Ushuaïa is an open-air megaclub. The party starts early with superstar DJs such as David Guetta, Luciano and Sven Väth, and poolside lounging by a lagoon with Bali beds. Check out the Sky Lounge for sparkling sea views, or stay the night in the minimalist-cool hotel (there are even swim-up rooms!).

Much cheaper than a taxi, the **Discobus** (www.discobus.es; per person €3; ⏲ midnight-6am Jun-Sep) does an all-night whirl of the major clubs, bars and hotels in Ibiza City, Platja d'en Bossa, Sant Rafel, Es Canar, Santa Eulària and Sant Antoni.

★ Bar 1805 BAR
(☎ 651 625972; www.bar1805ibiza.com; Carrer Santa Lucía 7; ⏲ 8pm-3.30am May-Oct; 📶) Tucked away on a Sa Penya backstreet, this terrific boho bar has the best cocktails in town. There's lots of absinthe action on the list – try a Green Beast (served in a punch bowl) or the house margarita (with mescal instead of tequila), which packs a mean Mexican punch.

Bora Bora Beach Club BAR
(www.boraboraibiza.net; Carrer d'es Fumarell 1, Platja d'en Bossa; ⏲ noon-6am May-Sep) This is *the* place – a long beachside bar where sun and fun worshippers work off hangovers and prepare new ones. Entry's free and the ambience is chilled, with low-key club sounds wafting over the sand.

Around Ibiza City

Ibiza has numerous unspoiled and relatively undeveloped beaches. On the east coast, north of Santa Eulària d'es Riu, are the small and serene **Cala Llenya** and **Cala Mastella**. A bit further north, **Cala Boix** is the only black-sand beach on the island, and a few kilometres further is the lovely, clothing-optional **Aigües Blanques**.

On the north coast near Portinatx, **Cala d'en Serra** is one of Ibiza's most beautiful cove beaches, and near Sant Miquel de Balansat is the spectacular **Benirrás** beach.

In the southwest, **Cala d'Hort** is a long arc of sand in a spectacular setting overlooking the 380m-high limestone islet Es Vedrá.

The best thing about rowdy **Sant Antoni**, the island's second-biggest town, north of Ibiza City, is heading to the small rock-and-sand strip on the north shore to join hundreds of others for sunset drinks at a string of chilled bars, among them the island's most famous bar, **Café del Mar** (www.cafedelmarmusic.com; Carrer Vara de Rey 27; ⏲ 4pm-midnight May–mid-Oct).

Check out rural accommodation at www.ibizaruralvillas.com. For more standard accommodation, start at www.ibizahotelsguide.com.

Local buses (www.ibizabus.com) run to most destinations between May and October.

ANDALUCÍA

So many of the most powerful images of Spain emanate from Andalucía that it can be difficult not to feel a sense of déjà vu It's almost as if you've already been there in your dreams: the flashing fire of a flamenco dancer, the scent of orange blossom, a festive summer fair, magical nights in the shadow of the Alhambra. In the bright light of day, the picture is no less magical.

Seville

POP 703,000

It takes a stony heart not to be captivated by stylish but ancient, proud yet fun-loving Seville – home to two of Spain's most colourful festivals, fascinating and distinctive *barrios* (neighbourhoods) such as the flower-decked Santa Cruz, great historic monuments, and a population that lives life to the fullest. Being out among the celebratory, happy crowds in the tapas bars and streets on a warm spring night in Seville is an unforgettable experience. But try to avoid July and August, when it's so hot that most locals flee to the coast!

Sights

★ Alcázar FORTRESS
(☎ tours 954 50 23 24; www.alcazarsevilla.org; adult/child €9.50/free; ⏲ 9.30am-7pm Apr-Sep, to 5pm Oct-Mar) If heaven really *does* exist, then let's hope it looks a little bit like the inside of Seville's Alcázar. Built primarily in the 14th century during the so-called 'dark ages' in Europe, the fortress' intricate architecture is anything but dark. Indeed, compared to our modern-day shopping malls, the Alcázar marks one of history's architectural high points. Unesco agreed, making it a World Heritage site in 1987.

Catedral & Giralda CATHEDRAL
(www.catedraldesevilla.es; adult/child €9/free; ⏲ 11am-3.30pm Mon, 11am-5pm Tue-Sat, 2.30-6pm Sun) Seville's immense cathedral, one of the largest Christian churches in the world, is awe-inspiring in its scale and sheer majesty. It stands on the site of the great 12th-century Almohad mosque, with the mosque's minaret (the Giralda) still towering beside it.

Museo de Bellas Artes GALLERY
(Fine Arts Museum; ☎ 955 54 29 31; www.museodebellasartesdesevilla.es; Plaza del Museo 9; EU citizens/other free/€1.50; ⏲ 10am-8.30pm Tue-Sat, to 5pm Sun) Housed in the beautiful former

Seville

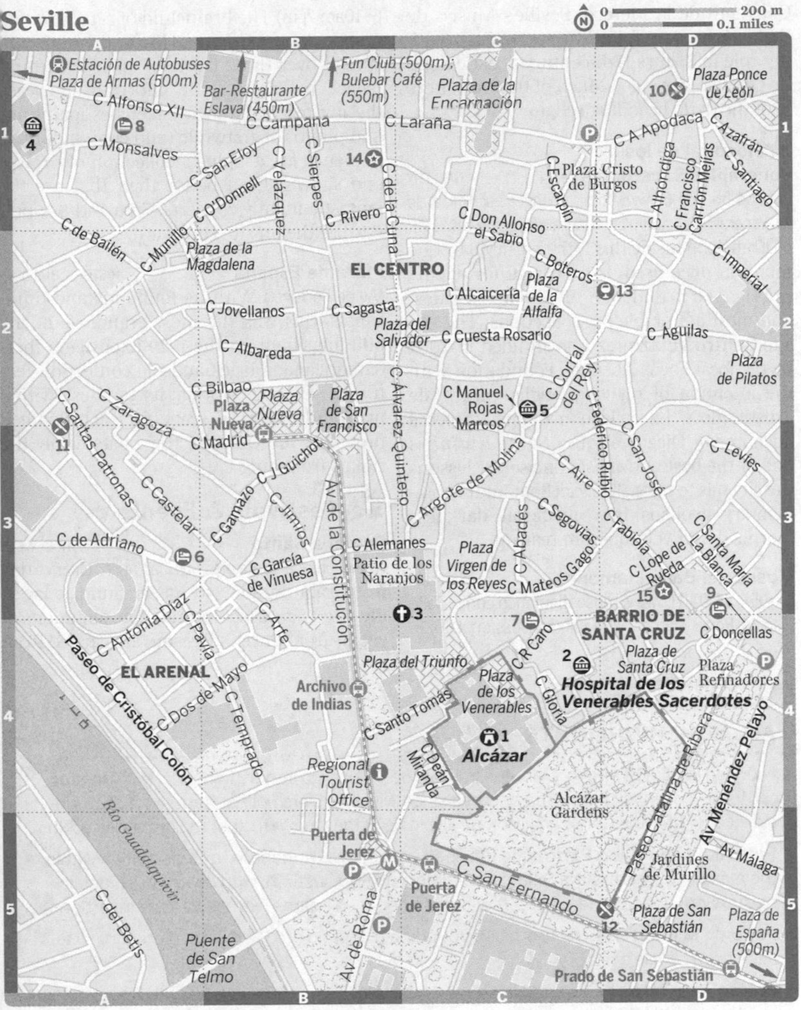

Seville

Top Sights

1 Alcázar C4
2 Hospital de los Venerables Sacerdotes C4

Sights

3 Catedral & Giralda C3
4 Museo de Bellas Artes A1
5 Museo del Baile Flamenco C2

Sleeping

6 Hotel Adriano A3
7 Hotel Casa 1800 .... C4
8 Oasis Backpackers' Hostel A1
9 Un Patio en Santa Cruz D3

Eating

10 El Rinconcillo D1
11 La Brunilda A3
12 Restaurante Oriza D5

Drinking & Nightlife

13 El Garlochi D2

Entertainment

14 Casa de la Memoria B1
15 La Casa del Flamenco D3

Convento de la Merced, Seville's Museo de Bellas Artes does full justice to Seville's leading role in Spain's 17th-century artistic Siglo de Oro (Golden Age). Much of the work here is of the dark, brooding religious type.

★Hospital de los Venerables Sacerdotes GALLERY
(☎954 56 26 96; www.focus.abengoa.es; Plaza de los Venerables 8; adult/child incl audio guide €8/3.75; ⏰10am-4pm) Inside this 17th-century baroque mansion once used as a hospice for ageing priests, you'll find one of Seville's greatest and most admirable art collections. The on-site **Centro Velázquez** was founded in 2007 by the local Focus-Abengoa Foundation with the intention of reviving Seville's erstwhile artistic glory. Its collection of masterpieces anchored by Diego Veláquez' *Santa Rufina* is one of the best and most concise art lessons the city has to offer. The excellent audio commentary explains how medieval darkness morphed into Velázquezian realism.

Museo del Baile Flamenco MUSEUM
(☎954 34 03 11; www.museoflamenco.com; Calle Manuel Rojas Marcos 3; adult/concession €10/8; ⏰10am-7pm) The brainchild of *sevillana* flamenco dancer Cristina Hoyos, this museum spread over three floors of an 18th-century palace makes a noble effort to showcase the mysterious art with sketches, paintings and photos of erstwhile (and contemporary) flamenco greats, plus a collection of dresses and shawls. Even better than that are the fantastic nightly concerts (7pm and 8.45pm; €20) in the on-site courtyard.

Plaza de España HISTORIC BUILDING
(Av de Portugal) With its fountains and mini-canals, this was the most grandiose of the buildings built for the 1929 Exposición Iberoamericana, a brick-and-tile confection featuring Seville tilework at its gaudiest, with a map and historical scene for each Spanish province. You can hire row boats to ply the canals from only €5.

Festivals & Events

Semana Santa HOLY WEEK
(www.semana-santa.org; ⏰Mar/Apr) Every day from Palm Sunday to Easter Sunday, large, life-sized *pasos* (sculptural representations of events from Christ's Passion) are carried from

DON'T MISS

ALCÁZAR HIGHLIGHTS

Founded in AD 913 as a fort for Muslim Córdoba's local governors in Seville, the **Alcázar** (p616) has been revamped many times since. Muslim rulers built at least two palaces inside it and after the Christians took Seville in 1248 they made further major modifications.

Patio del León (Lion Patio) The garrison yard of an 11th-century Islamic palace within the Alcázar. Off here is the Sala de la Justicia (Hall of Justice), with beautiful Mudéjar plasterwork and an *artesonado* (ceiling of interlaced beams with decorative insertions).

Patio de la Montería The rooms surrounding this patio are filled with interesting artefacts from Seville's history.

Cuarto Real Alto The Cuarto Real Alto (Upper Royal Quarters; used by the Spanish royal family on visits to Seville) are open for tours several times a day. The 14th-century Salón de Audiencias is still the monarch's reception room.

Palacio de Don Pedro Built by the Castilian king Pedro I ('the Cruel') in the 1360s, this is the single most stunning building in Seville. At its heart is the wonderful Patio de las Doncellas (Patio of the Maidens), surrounded by beautiful arches, plasterwork and tiling. The Alcoba Real (Royal Quarters), on the patio's northern side, has stunningly beautiful ceilings. The little Patio de las Muñecas (Patio of the Dolls), the heart of the palace's private quarters, features delicate Granada-style decoration. The Salón de Embajadores (Hall of Ambassadors), at the western end of the Patio de las Doncellas, was the throne room. Its fabulous wooden dome of multiple star patterns, symbolising the universe, was added in 1427.

Salones de Carlos V Reached via a staircase at the southeastern corner of the Patio de las Doncellas, these are the much-remodelled rooms of Alfonso X's 13th-century Gothic palace.

Gardens From the Salones de Carlos V you can go out and wander in the Alcázar's large and sleepy gardens, some with pools and fountains.

Seville's churches through the streets to the cathedral, accompanied by processions that may take more than an hour to pass. The processions are organised by more than 50 different *hermandades* or *cofradías* (brotherhoods, some of which include women).

Feria de Abril SPRING FAIR
(www.turismosevilla.org; ⏲Apr) The April fair, held in the second half of the month (sometimes edging into May), is the jolly counterpart to the sombre Semana Santa. The biggest and most colourful of all Andalucía's ferias (fairs) is less invasive (and also less inclusive) than the Easter celebration. It takes place on El Real de la Feria, in the Los Remedios area west of the Río Guadalquivir.

Sleeping

Oasis Backpackers' Hostel HOSTEL €
(☎955 26 26 96; www.oasissevilla.com; Calle Almirante Ulloa 1; dm/d incl breakfast from €13/44; ❄@📶🏊) It's not often you get to backpack in a palace. A veritable oasis in the busy city-centre district, this place is a friendly welcoming hostel set in a palatial 19th-century mansion with some private room options, a cafe-bar and a rooftop deck with a small pool.

★ **Hotel Adriano** HOTEL €€
(☎954 29 38 00; www.adrianohotel.com; Calle Adriano 12; s/d €65/75; P❄📶) A solid Arenal option with great staff, rooms with attractive *sevillano* features and one of the best coffee shops in Seville out front.

Un Patio en Santa Cruz HOTEL €€
(☎954 53 94 13; www.patiosantacruz.com; Calle Doncellas 15; s €65-85, d €65-120; ❄📶) Feeling more like an art gallery than a hotel, this place has starched white walls coated in loud works of art, strange sculptures and preserved plants. The rooms are immensely comfortable, staff are friendly, and there's a cool rooftop terrace with mosaic Moroccan tables. It's easily one of the hippest and best-value hotels in town.

★ **Hotel Casa 1800** LUXURY HOTEL €€€
(☎954 56 18 00; www.hotelcasa1800sevilla.com; Calle Rodrigo Caro 6; r from €195; ❄@📶) Reigning as number one in Seville's 'favourite hotel' charts is this positively regal Santa Cruz pile where the word *casa* (house) is taken seriously. This really is your home away from home (albeit a posh one), with charming staff catering for your every need. Historic highlights include a complimentary afternoon-tea buffet, plus a quartet of penthouse garden suites with Giralda views.

Eating

★ **Bar-Restaurante Eslava** FUSION, ANDALUCIAN €€
(☎954 90 65 68; www.espacioeslava.com; Calle Eslava 3; medias raciones €9-13; ⏲1.30-4pm & 9-11.30pm Tue-Sat, 12.30-4pm Sun) A legend in its own dinnertime, Eslava shirks the traditional tilework and bullfighting posters of tapas-bar lore and delivers where it matters: fine food backed up with equally fine service.

★ **La Brunilda** TAPAS €€
(☎954 22 04 81; www.labrunildatapas.com; Calle Galera 5; tapas €4-7.50; ⏲1-4pm & 8.30-11.30pm Tue-Sat, 1-4pm Sun) Seville's crown as Andalucía's tapas capital is regularly attacked by well-armed rivals from the provinces, meaning it constantly has to reinvent itself and offer up fresh competition. Enter La Brunilda, a newish font of fusion tapas sandwiched into an inconspicuous backstreet in the Arenal quarter where everything – including the food, staff and clientele – is pretty.

El Rinconcillo TAPAS €€
(☎954 22 31 83; www.elrinconcillo.es; Calle Gerona 40; tapas/raciones €3/12; ⏲1pm-1.30am) Some say the Rinconcillo is resting on its laurels. Maybe so; but, with more than 345 years of history, there is a lot to rest on. Seville's oldest bar first opened in 1670, when the Inquisition was raging and tapas were still just tops you screwed on bottles.

Restaurante Oriza CONTEMPORARY SPANISH €€€
(☎954 22 72 54; www.restauranteoriza.com; Calle San Fernando 41; mains €22-32; ⏲noon-11.30pm Mon-Sat, noon-5pm Sun) Say Basque and you've got a byword for fine dining these days, so it's not surprising that Basque-run Oriza is regarded as one of the city's standout restaurants. Situated close to the Prado de San Sebastián bus station, this could be your first (and best) culinary treat in Seville. There's an equally posh tapas spot on the ground floor.

Drinking & Nightlife

Drinking and partying really get going around midnight on Friday and Saturday (daily when it's hot). Classic drinking areas include Plaza de la Alfalfa (cocktail and dive bars), the Barrio de Santa Cruz and the Alameda de Hércules. The latter is the hub for young *sevillanos* and the city's gay nightlife. In summer, dozens of open-air late-night bars (*terrazas de verano*) spring up along both banks of the river.

El Garlochi BAR

(Calle Boteros 4; ⌚9pm-3am) Dedicated entirely to the iconography, smells and sounds of Semana Santa, the ultracamp El Garlochi is a true marvel. Taste the rather revolting sounding cocktail Sangre de Cristo (Blood of Christ) or the Agua de Sevilla, both heavily laced with vodka, whisky and grenadine, and pray they open more bars like this.

Bulebar Café BAR

(☎954 90 19 54; www.facebook.com/BulebarCafe; Alameda de Hércules 83; ⌚9am-2am) This place gets pretty *caliente* (hot) at night but is pleasantly chilled in the early evening, with friendly staff. Don't write off its spirit-reviving alfresco breakfasts that pitch early birds with up-all-nighters. It's in the ubercool Alameda de Hércules.

☆ Entertainment

Seville is arguably Spain's flamenco capital and there are many opportunities to experience live performances.

★Casa de la Memoria FLAMENCO

(☎954 56 06 70; www.casadelamemoria.es; Calle Cuna 6; admission €18; ⌚shows 7.30pm & 9pm) Neither a *tablao* (choreographed flamenco show) nor a private *peña* (club, usually of flamenco aficionados), this cultural centre offers what are, without doubt, the most intimate and authentic nightly flamenco shows in Seville. It's accommodated in the old stables of the Palacio de la Condesa de Lebrija.

It's perennially popular and space is limited to 100, so reserve tickets a day or so in advance by calling or visiting the venue.

La Casa del Flamenco FLAMENCO

(☎954 50 05 95; www.lacasadelflamencosevilla.com; Calle Ximénez de Enciso, 28; adult/child €18/10; ⌚shows 8.30pm) This beautiful patio in an old Sephardic Jewish mansion in Santa Cruz is home to La Casa del Flamenco and the performances on a stage hemmed in by seating on three sides are mesmerising.

Fun Club LIVE MUSIC

(☎958 25 02 49; www.funclubsevilla.com; Alameda de Hércules 86; admission €5; ⌚midnight-late Thu-Sun, from 9.30pm live-band nights) Positively ancient by live music club standards, the emblematic Fun Club has been entertaining the nocturnal Alameda de Hércules crowd since the late 1980s. Its speciality is live bands This is ground zero for Seville's alternative music scene.

ℹ Information

Regional Tourist Office (☎954 22 14 04; www.turismosevilla.org; Avenida de la Constitución 21; ⌚9am-7pm Mon-Fri, 10am-2pm & 3-7pm Sat, 10am-2pm Sun, closed holidays) The Constitución office is well informed but often very busy. There is also a branch at the airport (☎954 44 91 28; Aeropuerto San Pablo; ⌚9am-8.30pm Mon-Fri, 10am-6pm Sat, 10am-2pm Sun, closed holidays).

ℹ Getting There & Away

AIR

Seville's **airport** (SVQ; ☎954 44 90 00; www.aena.es; A4, Km 532) has a fair range of international and domestic flights.

BUS

Buses to Córdoba (€12, two hours, seven daily), Granada (€23 to €29, three hours, nine daily), Málaga (€19 to €24, 2½ to four hours, six daily), Madrid (€22, 6½ hours, eight daily) and Lisbon (€45 to €50, 7½ hours, two daily) go from the **Estación de Autobuses Plaza de Armas** (☎902 45 05 50; www.autobusesplazadearmas.es; Avenida del Cristo de la Expiración).

TRAIN

Estación Santa Justa (☎902 43 23 43; www.renfe.es; Avenida Kansas City) is 1.5km northeast of the centre. Up to 20 AVE and other high-speed trains whiz daily to/from Madrid (€29 to €125, 2½ to 2¾ hours). Other destinations include Córdoba (€12 to €30, 45 minutes to 1¼ hours, more than 30 trains daily), Granada (€30, 3½ hours, four daily), Málaga (€24 to €44, two to 2¾ hours, 11 daily) and Barcelona (€19 to €117, 5½ to 11½ hours, five daily).

Córdoba

POP 326,600

A little over a millennium ago Córdoba was the capital of Islamic Spain and Western Europe's biggest, most cultured city, where Muslims, Jews and Christians coexisted peaceably. Its past glories place it among Andalucía's top draws today. The centrepiece is the mesmerising, multiarched Mezquita. Surrounding it is an intricate web of winding streets, geranium-sprouting flower boxes and cool intimate patios that are at their most beguiling in late spring.

Sights

★Mezquita MOSQUE, CATHEDRAL

(Mosque; ☎957 47 05 12; www.catedraldecordoba.es; Calle Cardenal Herrero; adult/child €10/5, 8.30-9.30am Mon-Sat Mar-Oct free; ⏲8.30-9.30am & 10am-7pm Mon-Sat, 8.30-11.30am & 3-7pm Sun Mar-Oct, 10am-6pm Mon-Sat, 8.30-11.30am & 3-6pm Sat & Sun Nov-Feb) It's impossible to overemphasise the beauty of Córdoba's great mosque, with its remarkably serene (despite tourist crowds) and spacious interior. One of the world's greatest works of Islamic architecture, the Mezquita hints, with all its lustrous decoration, at a refined age when Muslims, Jews and Christians lived side by side and enriched their city with a heady interaction of diverse, vibrant cultures.

★Alcázar de los Reyes Cristianos FORTRESS

(Fortress of the Christian Monarchs; ☎957 42 01 51; www.alcazardelosreyescristianos.cordoba.es; Campo Santo de Los Mártires; admission 8.30am-2.30pm €4.50, other times incl water, light & sound show adult/child €7/free; ⏲8.30am-8.45pm Tue-Fri, to 4.30pm Sat, to 2.30pm Sun Sep-Jun, to 3pm Tue-Sun Jul-Aug; 👪) Built under Castilian rule in the 13th and 14th centuries on the remains of a Moorish predecessor, this fort-cum-palace hosted both Fernando and Isabel, who made their first acquaintance with Columbus here in 1486. One hall displays some remarkable Roman mosaics, dug up from the Plaza de la Corredera in the 1950s. The Alcázar's terraced gardens – full of fish ponds, fountains, orange trees and flowers – are a delight to stroll around.

★Museo Arqueológico MUSEUM

(☎957 35 55 17; www.museosdeandalucia.es; Plaza de Jerónimo Páez 7; EU citizen/other free/€1.50; ⏲9am-8pm Tue-Sat, to 3pm Sun mid-Sep–mid-Jun, 9am-3.30pm Tue-Sun mid-Jun–mid-Sep) The excellent Archaeological Museum traces Córdoba's many changes in size, appearance and lifestyle from pre-Roman to early Reconquista times, with some fine sculpture, an impressive coin collection, and interesting exhibits on domestic life and religion. In the basement you can walk through the excavated remains of the city's Roman theatre.

★Centro Flamenco Fosforito MUSEUM

(Posada del Potro; ☎957 47 68 29; www.centroflamencofosforito.cordoba.es; Plaza del Potro; ⏲8.30am-7.30pm Tue-Fri, 8.30am-2.30pm Sat & Sun) FREE Possibly the best flamenco museum in Andalucía, the Fosforito centre has exhibits, film and information panels in English and Spanish telling you the history of the guitar and all the flamenco greats. Touch-screen videos demonstrate the important techniques of flamenco song, guitar, dance and percussion – you can test your skill at beating out the *compás* (rhythm) of different *palos* (song forms). Regular live flamenco performances are held here, too.

★Madinat al-Zahra ARCHAEOLOGICAL SITE

(Medina Azahara; ☎957 10 49 33; www.museosdeandalucia.es; Carretera Palma del Río Km 5.5; EU citizen/other free/€1.50; ⏲9am-7.30pm Tue-Sat Apr–mid-Jun, to 3.30pm mid-Jun–mid-Sep, to 6pm mid-Sep–Mar, 9am-3pm Sun year-round; P) Eight kilometres west of Córdoba stands what's left of Madinat al-Zahra, the sumptuous palace-city built by Caliph Abd ar-Rahman III in the 10th century. The complex spills down a hillside with the caliph's palace (the area you visit today) on the highest levels overlooking what were gardens and open fields. The residential areas (still unexcavated) were

DON'T MISS

MEZQUITA HIGHLIGHTS

Emir Abd ar-Rahman I founded the **Mezquita** in AD 785. Three later extensions nearly quintupled its original size and brought it to the form you see today – except for one major alteration: a 16th-century cathedral plonked right in the middle.

Torre del Alminar You can climb inside the 54m-tall bell tower (originally the Mezquita's minaret) for fine panoramas.

Patio de los Naranjos This lovely courtyard, with its orange and palm trees and fountains, was the site of ritual ablutions before prayer in the mosque.

Prayer Hall Divided into 19 'naves' by lines of two-tier arches striped in red brick and white stone. Their simplicity and number give a sense of endlessness to the Mezquita.

Mihrab & Maksura The arches of the *maksura* (the area where the caliphs and their retinues would have prayed) are the mosque's most intricate and sophisticated, forming a forest of interwoven horseshoe shapes. The portal of the mihrab itself is a sublime crescent arch in glittering gold mosaic.

The Cathedral 16th-century construction in the Mezquita's heart.

JEWISH CÓRDOBA

Jews were among the most dynamic and prominent citizens of Islamic Córdoba. The medieval *judería* (Jewish quarter), extending northwest from the Mezquita almost to Avenida del Gran Capitán, is today a maze of narrow streets and whitewashed buildings with flowery window boxes. The **Sinagoga** (957 74 90 15; www.turismodecordoba.org; Calle de los Judíos 20; EU citizen/other free/€0.30; 9am-3.30pm Tue-Sun mid-Jun–mid-Sep, to 8pm Tue-Sat mid-Sep–mid-Jun), built in 1315, is one of the few surviivng testaments to the Jewish presence in Andalucía. Across the street is the **Casa de Sefarad** (957 42 14 04; www.casadesefarad.es; cnr Calles de los Judíos & Averroes; €4; 10am-6pm Mon-Sat, 11am-6pm Sun), an interesting museum on the Sephardic (Iberian Peninsula Jewish) tradition.

set away to each side. A fascinating modern museum has been installed below the site.

Sleeping

Option Be Hostel HOSTEL €
(661 420733; www.bedandbe.com; Calle Leiva Aguilar 1; dm €15-25, d €20-40;) Contemporary-design hostel in the old city, with mostly private bathrooms and a delightful communal terrace, kitchen and lounge area, run by the Bed and Be team.

Casa de los Azulejos HOTEL €€
(957 47 00 00; www.casadelosazulejos.com; Calle Fernando Colón 5; incl breakfast s €78, d €89-134;) Mexican and Andalucian styles converge in this stylish nine-room hotel, where the patio is all banana trees, ferns and potted palms bathed in sunlight. Colonial-style rooms feature tall antique doors, big beds, walls in lilac and sky blue, and floors adorned with the beautiful old *azulejos* (tiles) that give the place its name.

★**Balcón de Córdoba** BOUTIQUE HOTEL €€€
(957 49 84 78; www.balcondecordoba.com; Calle Encarnación 8; r incl breakfast €165-260;) Offering top-end boutique luxury, the 10-room Balcón is a riveting place with a charming *cordobés* patio, slick rooms, antique doorways, and ancient stone relics dotted around as if it were a wing of the nearby archaeological museum. Service doesn't miss a beat and the rooms have tasteful, soothing, contemporary decor with a little art but no clutter.

Eating

★**Garum 2.1** ANDALUCIAN €€
(957 48 76 73; Calle de San Fernando 122; tapas €3-7, raciones €7-17; noon-midnight, to 2am Fri & Sat) Garum serves up traditional meaty, fishy and vegie ingredients in all sorts of creative, tasty new concoctions. We recommend the *presa ibérica con herencia del maestro* (Iberian pork with potatoes, fried eggs and ham). Service is helpful and friendly.

★**La Boca** FUSION €€
(957 47 61 40; www.facebook.com/restaurante.laboca; Calle de San Fernando 39; mains €10-18; noon-midnight Wed-Mon, to 5pm Tue) Trendy for a reason, this cutting-edge eatery whips up exciting global variations from traditional ingredients, then presents them in eye-catching ways: Iberian pork cheeks with red curry and basmati? Battered cod chunks with almonds and garlic? It's very well done, though portions are not for giant appetites. Reservations advisable at weekends.

★**Bodegas Campos** ANDALUCIAN €€
(957 49 75 00; www.bodegascampos.com; Calle de Lineros 32; mains & raciones €12-25; 1.30-4.30pm daily, 8-11.30pm Mon-Sat) This atmospheric warren of rooms and patios is popular with smartly dressed *cordobeses*. The restaurant and more informal *taberna* (tavern) serve up delicious dishes, putting a slight creative twist on traditional Andalucian fare – the likes of cod-and-cuttlefish ravioli or pork sirloin in grape sauce. Campos also produces its own house Montilla.

Information

Centro de Visitantes (Visitors Centre; 902 201774, 957 35 51 79; www.turismodecordoba.org; Plaza del Triunfo; 9am-2.30pm & 5pm-7.30pm Mon-Fri, 9.30am-3pm Sat & Sun) The main tourist-information centre, with an exhibit on Córdoba's history, and some Roman and Visigothic remains downstairs.

Getting There & Away

BUS

The **bus station** (957 40 40 40; www.estacionautobusescordoba.es; Avenida Vía Augusta) is 2km northwest of the Mezquita, behind the train station. Destinations include Seville

(€12, two hours, seven buses daily), Granada (€15 to €17, 2¾ hours, eight daily) and Málaga (€12 to €15, 2½ to three hours, four daily).

TRAIN

Córdoba's **train station** (☎902 24 05 05; www.renfe.com; Glorieta de las Tres Culturas) is on the high-speed AVE line between Madrid and Seville/Málaga. Rail destinations include Seville (€12 to €30, 45 minutes to 1¼ hours, more than 30 trains daily), Madrid (€25 to €105, 1¾ hours, 29 daily), Málaga (€17 to €41, one hour, 17 daily) and Barcelona (€18 to €120, five to 10 hours, six or more daily). Trips to Granada (€18 to €36, two to 2¾ hours, four or more daily) include changing to a train or bus at Antequera.

Granada

ELEV 690M / POP 258,000

Granada's eight centuries as a Muslim city are symbolised in its keynote emblem, the remarkable Alhambra, one of the most graceful achievements of Islamic architecture. Granada is chock-full of history, the arts and life, with tapas bars filled to bursting and flamenco dives resounding to the heart-wrenching tones of the south. Today, Islam is more present here than for many centuries in the shops, tearooms and mosque of a growing North African community around the maze of the Albayzín.

Sights

★Alhambra PALACE

(☎902 441221; www.granadatur.com/la-alhambra; adult/under 12yr €14/free, Generalife only €7; ⏰8.30am-8pm mid-Mar–mid-Oct, to 6pm mid-Oct–mid-Mar, night visits 10-11.30pm Tue-Sat mid-Mar–mid-Oct, 8-9.30pm Fri & Sat mid-Oct–mid-Mar) The Alhambra is Granada's – and Europe's – love letter to Moorish culture, a place where fountains trickle, leaves rustle, and ancient spirits seem to mysteriously linger. Part palace, part fort, part World Heritage site, part lesson in medieval architecture, the Alhambra has long enchanted a never-ending line of expectant visitors. As a historic monument, it is unlikely it will ever be surpassed – at least not in the lifetime of anyone reading this.

★Capilla Real HISTORIC BUILDING

(☎958 22 78 48; www.capillarealgranada.com; Calle Oficios; €4; ⏰10.15am-1.30pm & 3.30-6.30pm Mon-Sat, 11am-1.30pm & 2.30-5.30pm Sun) Here they lie, Spain's notorious Catholic Monarchs, entombed in a chapel adjoining Granada's cathedral; far more peaceful in death than their tumultuous lives would have suggested. Isabel and Fernando commissioned the elaborate Isabelline-Gothic-style mausoleum that was to house them, but it was not completed until 1521, hence their temporary interment in the Alhambra's Convento de San Francisco.

Albayzín

On the hill facing the Alhambra across the Darro valley, the Albayzín is an open-air museum in which you can lose yourself for most of a day. The cobbled streets are lined with gorgeous *cármenes* (large mansions with walled gardens). It survived as the Muslim quarter for several decades after the Christian conquest in 1492.

Calle Caldereria Nueva STREET

Linking the upper and lower parts of the Albayzín, Calle Caldereria Nueva is a narrow

DON'T MISS

ALHAMBRA HIGHLIGHTS

It was Granada's Nasrid emirs of the 13th and 14th centuries who turned a relatively modest fortress-palace into the fairytale **Alhambra** we see today.

Palacios Nazaríes The central palace complex is the pinnacle of the Alhambra's design, a harmonious synthesis of space, light, shade, water and greenery that sought to conjure the gardens of paradise for the rulers who dwelt here.

Patio de los Leones (Courtyard of the Lions) Glorious, recently restored patio in the Palacios Nazaríes with a famous fountain and exceptional rooms around the perimeter.

Palacio de Carlos V Renaissance-era circle-in-square ground plan. Inside, the Museo de la Alhambra displays Alhambra artefacts.

Generalife These gardens are a soothing arrangement of pathways, patios, pools, fountains, trees, topiary and, in season, flowers of every imaginable hue.

Alcazaba The Alhambra's main fortifications.

Granada

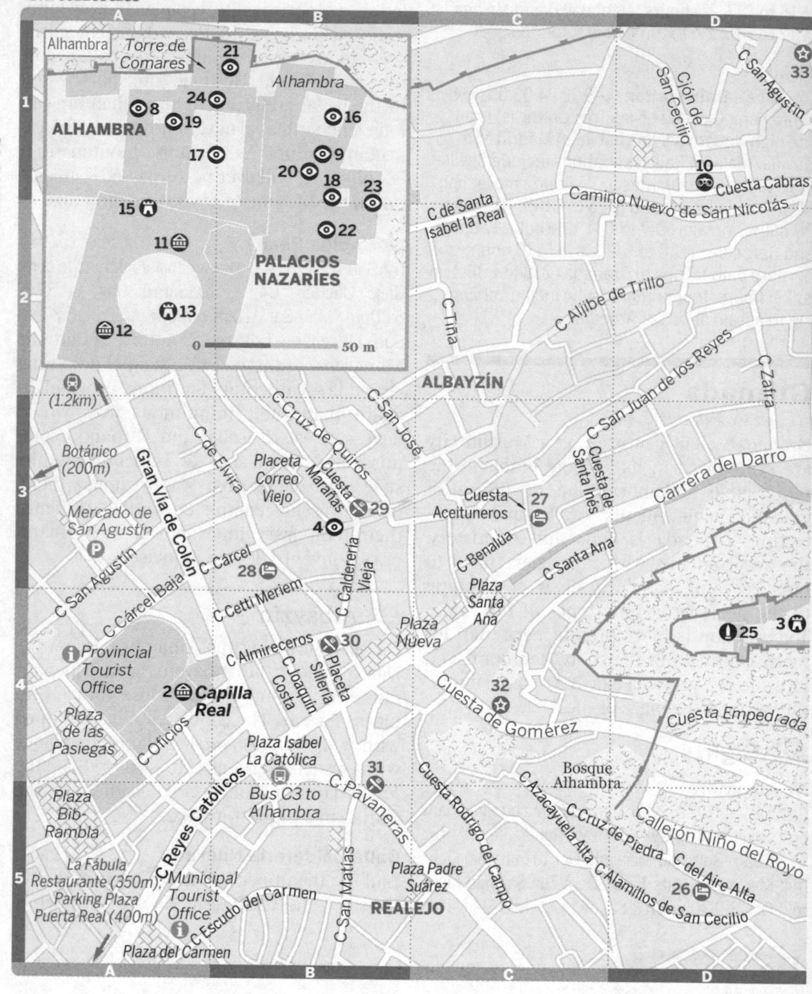

street famous for its *teterías* (teahouses), but also a good place to shop for slippers, hookahs, jewellery and North African pottery from an eclectic cache of shops redolent of a Moroccan souk.

Mirador San Nicolás VIEWPOINT

(Callejón de San Cecilio) Callejón de San Cecilio leads to the Mirador San Nicolás, a lookout with unbeatable views of the Alhambra and Sierra Nevada. Come back here for sunset (you can't miss the trail then!). At any time of day take care: skilful, well-organised wallet-lifters and bag-snatchers operate here. Don't be put off – it is still a terrific atmosphere, with buskers and local students intermingling with camera-toting tourists.

Colegiata del Salvador CHURCH

(☎958 27 86 44; www.granadatur.com; Plaza del Salvador; €0.75; ⏰10am-1pm & 4.30-6.30pm) Plaza del Salvador, near the top of the Albayzín, is dominated by the Colegiata del Salvador, a 16th-century church on the site of the Albayzín's former main mosque, the patio of which still survives at the church's western end.

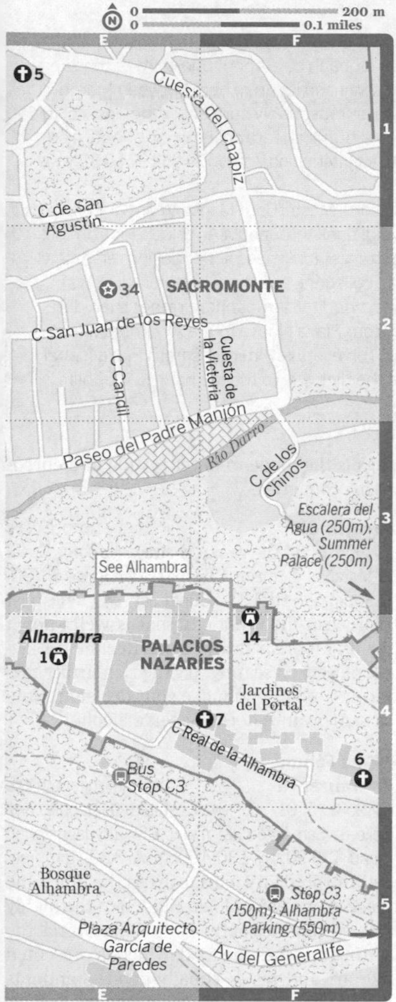

Granada

Sleeping

Hotel Posada del Toro HOTEL €

(958 22 73 33; www.posadadeltoro.com; Calle de Elvira 25; d incl breakfast from €50;) A lovely small hotel with rooms set around a tranquil central patio. Walls are coloured like Italian gelato in pistachio, peach and cream flavours. The rooms are similarly tasteful with parquet floors, Alhambra-style stucco, rustic-style furniture and small but perfectly equipped bathrooms with double sinks and hydromassage showers. A bargain – especially considering its central location.

★Carmen de la Alcubilla del Caracol HISTORIC HOTEL €€

(958 21 55 51; www.alcubilladelcaracol.com; Calle del Aire Alta 12; s/d €110/130; mid-Jul–31-Aug;) This much-sought-after small hotel inhabits a traditional *carmen* on the slopes of the Alhambra. It feels more like a B&B than a hotel thanks to the attentiveness of its Granada-loving host, Manuel. The seven rooms are furnished luxuriously, but not ostentatiously.

ALHAMBRA TICKETS

Up to 6600 tickets to the Alhambra are available for each day. About one-third of these are sold at the entrance on the day, but they sell out early and if you're here between March and October you need to start queuing by 7am to be reasonably sure of getting one. Fortunately, it's also possible to buy tickets up to three months ahead, online or by phone, from **Alhambra Advance Booking** (902 88 80 01, for international calls +34 958 92 60 31; www.alhambra-tickets.es), for €1.40 extra per ticket.

For internet or phone bookings you need a Visa card, MasterCard Maestro card or Eurocard. Tickets can be collected from ATMs of La Caixa bank throughout Andalucía, or from ticket machines or ticket windows at the Alhambra entrance. You'll need your booking reference number and your payment card (or ID document if collecting at Alhambra ticket windows).

The Palacios Nazaríes are open for night visits, good for atmosphere rather than detail.

It's a pleasant (if uphill) walk of just over 1km from Plaza Nueva to the Alhambra's main entrance. Alternatively, buses C3 and C4 (€1.20) run every few minutes from Plaza Isabel La Católica. By car, follow 'Alhambra' signs from the highway to the car park, just uphill from the ticket office.

Hotel Casa del Capitel Nazarí HISTORIC HOTEL €€
(958 21 52 60; www.hotelcasacapitel.com; Cuesta Aceituneros 6; s/d €68/85;) Another slice of Albayzín magic in a 1503 Renaissance palace that's as much architectural history lesson as midrange hotel. Rooms have Moroccan inflections and the courtyard hosts art exhibits. It's just off Plaza Nueva.

Eating

Granada is a bastion of that fantastic practice of free tapas with every drink, and some have an international flavour. The labyrinthine Albayzín holds a wealth of eateries tucked away in the narrow streets. Calle Caldereria Nueva is a fascinating muddle of *teterías* (tearooms) and Arabic-influenced takeaways.

Bodegas Castañeda TAPAS €
(958 21 54 64; Calle Almireceros; tapas €2-3, raciones €6-9; 11.30am-4.30pm & 7.30pm-1.30am) A relic much loved by locals and tourists alike, the buzzing Castañeda is the Granada tapas bar to trump all others. Don't expect any fancy new stuff here, but do expect lightning-fast service, booze from big casks mounted on the walls, and eating as a contact sport.

★**Carmela Restaurante** TAPAS €€
(958 22 57 94; www.restaurantecarmela.com; Calle Colcha 13; tapas €5-10; 8am-midnight) Long a bastion of traditional tapas, Granada has taken a leaf out of Seville's book and come up with something a little more out-of-the-box at this streamlined restaurant, guarded by the statue of Jewish philosopher Yehuba ibn Tibon at the jaws of the Realejo quarter. The best of Carmela's creative offerings is the made-to-order tortilla and cured-ham croquettes.

Arrayanes MOROCCAN €€
(958 22 84 01; www.rest-arrayanes.com; Cuesta Marañas 4; mains €15; 1.30-4.30pm & 7.30-11.30pm Sun-Fri, 1.30-4.30pm Sat;) The best Moroccan food in a city that is well known for its Moorish throwbacks. Recline on lavish patterned seating, try the rich, fruity tagine casseroles and make your decision. Note that Arrayanes does not serve alcohol.

★**La Fábula Restaurante** MODERN EUROPEAN €€€
(958 25 01 50; www.restaurantelafabula.com; Calle de San Antón 28; mains €24-28, degustation menu €75-90; 1.30-4.30pm & 8.30-11pm Tue-Sat) In Fábula it's hard to avoid the pun – the place is pretty fabulous. Hidden in the highly refined confines of the Hotel Villa Oniria, the setting matches the food, which is presented like art and tastes equally good. Standouts are the venison with chestnuts and quince, or the baby eels with basil in venere rice.

Drinking & Entertainment

The best street for drinking is the rather scruffy Calle de Elvira, but other chilled bars line the Río Darro at the base of the Albayzín and Calle Navas in Realejo.

Botánico BAR
(958 27 15 98; www.botanicocafe.es; Calle Málaga 3; 10am-1am Mon-Fri, noon-1am Sat & Sun) A haven for cool dudes with designer beards, students finishing off their Lorca dissertations, and anyone else with arty inclinations, Botánico is a casual snack restaurant by day,

a cafe at *merienda* time (5pm to 7pm), and a bar and club come dusk, with DJs or live music emphasising jazz and blues.

The bright colour scheme screams 'orange', while the name comes from the peaceful botanical garden across the road.

Peña La Platería FLAMENCO
(958 21 06 50; www.laplateria.org.es; Placeta de Toqueros 7) Buried in the Albayzín warren, Peña La Platería claims to be the oldest flamenco aficionados' club in Spain, founded in 1949. Unlike other more private clubs, it regularly opens it doors to nonmembers for performances on Thursday nights (and sometimes Saturdays) at 10.15pm. Tapas and drinks are available. Reservations recommended.

Jardines de Zoraya FLAMENCO
(958 20 60 66; www.jardinesdezoraya.com; Calle Panaderos 32; tickets with drink/dinner €20/43; shows 8pm & 10.30pm) A little larger than some of Andalucía's new flamenco cultural centres, and hosted in a restaurant that serves food and drink, the Jardines de Zoraya appears, on first impression, to be a touristy *tablao* (choreographed flamenco show). But reasonable entry prices, top-notch performers and a highly atmospheric patio make the Abayzín venue a worthwhile stop for any aficionado.

Casa del Arte Flamenco FLAMENCO
(958 56 57 67; www.casadelarteflamenco.com; Cuesta de Gomérez 11; tickets €18; shows 7.30pm & 9pm) A small newish flamenco venue that is neither *tablao* (choreographed flamenco show) nor *peña* (private club), but something in between. The performers are invariably top-notch, while the atmosphere depends largely on the tourist-local make-up of the audience.

Information

Municipal Tourist Office (958 24 82 80; www.granadatur.com; Plaza del Carmen; 9.30am-7pm Mon-Sat, 9.30am-2pm Sun) New digs in the Town Hall.

Provincial Tourist Office (958 24 71 28; www.granadatur.com; Cárcel Baja 3; 9am-8pm Mon-Fri, 10am-7pm Sat, 10am-3pm Sun) Information on all of Granada province.

Getting There & Away

BUS

Granada's **bus station** (902 42 22 42; www.alsa.es; Carretera de Jaén; 6.30am-1.30am) is 3km northwest of the city centre. Destinations include Córdoba (€15 to €17, 2¾ hours, eight buses daily), Seville (€23 to €29, three hours, seven daily), Málaga (€11 to €14, 13/4 hours, 15 daily) and Madrid (€19 to €45, five hours, 13 daily).

TRAIN

The **train station** (958 24 02 02; Avenida de Andaluces) is 1.5km west of the centre. Services run to Seville (€30, 3¼ hours, four daily), Almería (€20, 2½ hours, four daily), Madrid (€27 to €77, four hours, five daily) and Barcelona (€35 to €117, eight hours, two daily). Due to line construction work west of Granada, all these except Almería include a bus transfer as far as Antequera until at least 2018.

Málaga

POP 568,500

Málaga is a world apart from the adjoining, overdeveloped Costa del Sol: an exuberant, historic port city that has rapidly emerged as a city of culture, its so-called 'mile of art' being compared to Madrid, and its dynamism and fine dining to Barcelona.

The tastefully restored historic centre is a delight, with a Gothic cathedral surrounded by narrow pedestrian streets flanked by traditional and modern bars, and shops that range from idiosyncratic and family owned to urban-chic and contemporary. The city's terrific bars and nightlife, the last word in Málaga *joie de vivre,* stay open very late.

Sights

★Museo Picasso Málaga MUSEUM
(902 443377; www.museopicassomalaga.org; Calle San Agustín 8; €7, incl temporary exhibition €10; 10am-8pm Jul-Aug, to 7pm Mar-Jun & Sep-Oct, to 6pm Nov-Feb;) The Museo Picasso has an enviable collection of 204 works, 155 donated and 49 loaned to the museum by Christine Ruiz-Picasso (wife of Paul, Picasso's eldest son) and Bernard Ruiz-Picasso (his grandson), and includes some wonderful paintings of the family, including the heartfelt *Paulo con gorro blanco* (Paulo with a White Cap), a portrait of Picasso's eldest son painted in the 1920s.

Don't miss the Phoenician, Roman, Islamic and Renaissance archaeological remains in the museum's basement, discovered during construction works.

★Catedral de Málaga CATHEDRAL
(952 21 59 17; www.malagaturismo.com; Calle Molina Lario; cathedral & museum €5, tower €6; 10am-6pm Mon-Sat) Málaga's cathedral was

ANDALUCÍA'S QUIETEST BEACHES

The coast east of Almería in eastern Andalucía is perhaps the last section of Spain's Mediterranean coast where you can (sometimes) have a beach to yourself. This is Spain's sunniest region – even in March it can be warm enough to strip off and take in the rays. The best thing about it is the wonderful coastline and semidesert scenery of the **Cabo de Gata** promontory. All along the 50km coast from El Cabo de Gata village to Agua Amarga, some of the most beautiful beaches on the Mediterranean, from long sandy strands to tiny rock-girt coves, alternate with precipitous cliffs and scattered villages. The main base is laid-back **San José**, with excellent beaches nearby, such as Playa de los Genoveses, Playa de Mónsul and the four isolated little beaches of the Calas de Barronal. The former gold-mining village of **Rodalquilar**, a few kilometres inland, is a bit of a boho-chic hideaway.

started in the 16th century on the site of the former mosque. Of the mosque, only the **Patio de los Naranjos** survives, a small courtyard of fragrant orange trees.

Inside, the fabulous domed ceiling soars 40m into the air, while the vast colonnaded nave houses an enormous cedar-wood choir. Aisles give access to 15 chapels with gorgeous 18th-century retables and religious art. Climb the tower (200 steps) to enjoy stunning panoramic views of the city skyline and coast.

★Alcazaba CASTLE

(☎630 932987; www.malagaturismo.com; Calle Alcazabilla; €2.20, incl Castillo de Gibralfaro €3.40; ⌚9.30am-8pm Tue-Sun) No time to visit Granada's Alhambra? Then Málaga's Alcazaba can provide a taster. The entrance is next to the **Roman amphitheatre**, from where a meandering path climbs amid lush greenery: crimson bougainvillea, lofty palms, fragrant jasmine bushes and rows of orange trees. Extensively restored, this palace-fortress dates from the 11th-century Moorish period; the caliphal horseshoe arches, courtyards and bubbling fountains are evocative of this influential period in Málaga's history.

★Centre Pompidou Málaga MUSEUM

(☎951 92 62 00; www.centrepompidou.es; Pasaje Doctor Carrillo Casaux, Muelle Uno; €7, incl temporary exhibition €9; ⌚9.30am-8pm Wed-Mon; 📶) Opened in 2015 in the port, this offshoot of the Paris Pompidou Centre is housed in a low-slung modern building crowned by a playful multicoloured cube. The permanent exhibition includes the extraordinary *Ghost*, by Kader Attia, depicting rows of Muslim women bowed in prayer and created from domestic aluminium foil, plus works by such modern masters as Frida Kahlo, Francis Bacon and Antoni Tàpies. There are also audiovisual installations, talking 'heads' and temporary exhibitions.

Castillo de Gibralfaro CASTLE

(☎952 22 72 30; www.malagaturismo.com; Camino Gibralfaro; €2.20, incl Alcazaba €3.40; ⌚9am-9pm Apr-Sep) One remnant of Málaga's Islamic past is the craggy ramparts of the Castillo de Gibralfaro, spectacularly located high on the hill overlooking the city. Built by Abd ar-Rahman I, the 8th-century Cordoban emir, and later rebuilt in the 14th century when Málaga was the main port for the emirate of Granada, the castle originally acted as a lighthouse and military barracks.

Nothing much is original in the castle's interior, but the airy walkway around the ramparts affords the best views over Málaga.

Museo Automovilístico Málaga MUSEUM

(☎951 13 70 01; www.museoautomovilmalaga.com; Avenida Sor Teresa Prat 15; adult/child €7.50/free; ⌚10am-7pm Tue-Sun; 📶) Petrol heads and fashionistas will love this museum, housed in a former tobacco factory, which combines the history of the automobile with 20th-century fashion from style gurus such as Chanel, Yves Saint Laurent and Dior. Around 85 cars have been immaculately restored, including a Bugatti, a Bentley and a fabulous flower-power-painted Rolls. From Málaga Centre Alameda Principal, take bus 3, 15 or 16 and get off at Avenida La Paloma (€1.35, 10 minutes).

Sleeping

★Dulces Dreams HOSTEL €

(☎951 35 78 69; www.dulcesdreamshostel.com; Plaza de los Mártires 6; r incl breakfast €45-60; ❄📶) Run by an enthusiastic young team, the rooms at Dulces (sweet) Dreams are appropriately named after desserts; 'Cupcake' is a good choice with its terrace overlooking the imposing red-brick church across the way. This is an older building so there's no lift and the rooms vary in size, but they are bright and whimsically decorated using recycled materials as far as possible.

El Riad Andaluz GUESTHOUSE €

(☎952 21 36 40; www.elriadandaluz.com; Calle Hinestrosa 24; s/d/tr €45/55/75; ❄@📶) This French-run guesthouse, in the historic part of town, has eight rooms set around the kind of atmospheric patio that's known as a *riad* in Morocco. The decoration is Moroccan but each room is different, including colourful tiled bathrooms. Breakfast is available.

Eating & Drinking

Málaga has a staggering number of tapas bars and restaurants, particularly around the historic centre (over 400 at last count). One of the city's biggest pleasures is a slow crawl round its numerous tapas bars and old bodegas (cellars). The best bar-hop areas are from Plaza de la Merced in the northeast to Calle Carretería in the northwest, plus Plaza Mitjana and Plaza de Uncibay.

★El Mesón de Cervantes TAPAS, ARGENTINIAN €€

(☎952 21 62 74; www.elmesondecervantes.com; Calle Álamos 11; mains €13-16; ⏲7pm-midnight Wed-Mon) Cervantes started as a humble tapas bar run by expat Argentinian Gabriel Spatz (the original bar is still operating around the corner), but has expanded into plush spacious digs with an open kitchen, fantastic family-style service and incredible meat dishes.

★Óleo FUSION €€

(☎952 21 90 62; www.oleorestaurante.es; Edificio CAC, Calle Alemania; mains €12-16; ⏲10am-midnight Mon-Sat; 📶) Located at the city's contemporary art museum with white-on-white minimalist decor, Óleo provides diners with the unusual choice of Mediterranean or Asian food with some subtle combinations such as duck breast with a side of seaweed with hoisin, as well as more purist Asian and gourmet palate-ticklers such as candied, roasted piglet.

Los Patios de Beatas WINE BAR

(☎952 21 03 50; www.lospatiosdebeatas.com; Calle Beatas 43; ⏲1-5pm & 8pm-midnight Mon-Sat, 1-6pm Sun; 📶) Two 18th-century mansions have metamorphosed into this sumptuous space where you can sample fine wines from a selection reputed to be the most extensive in town. Stained-glass windows and beautiful resin tables inset with mosaics and shells add to the overall art-infused atmosphere. Innovative tapas and *raciones* (full-plate servings) are also served.

Entertainment

Kelipe FLAMENCO

(☎692 829885; www.kelipe.net; Muro de Puerta Nueva 10; €24-35; ⏲9.30pm show Thu-Sat) Málaga's substantial flamenco heritage has its nexus to the northwest of Plaza de la Merced. This flamenco centre puts on authentic performances Thursday to Saturday at 9.30pm; €24 entry includes two drinks – reserve ahead.

Information

Municipal Tourist Office (☎951 92 60 20; www.malagaturismo.com; Plaza de la Marina; ⏲9am-8pm Mar-Sep, to 6pm Oct-Feb) Offers a range of city maps and booklets. It also operates information kiosks at the Alcazaba entrance (Calle Alcazabilla), at the main train station (Explanada de la Estación), on Plaza de la Merced and on the eastern beaches (El Palo and La Malagueta).

JAMÓN – A PRIMER

Unlike Italian prosciutto, Spanish *jamón* is a bold, deep red and well marbled with buttery fat. Like wines and olive oil, Spanish *jamón* is subject to a strict series of classifications. *Jamón serrano* refers to *jamón* from white-coated pigs introduced to Spain in the 1950s. Originally it was salted and semidried by the cold, dry winds of the Spanish sierras (mountain ranges), hence the name; most now goes through a similar process of curing and drying in a climate-controlled shed for around a year. *Jamón serrano* accounts for approximately 90% of cured ham in Spain.

Jamón ibérico – more expensive and generally regarded as the elite of Spanish hams – comes from a black-coated pig indigenous to the Iberian Peninsula and a descendant of the wild boar. If the pig gains at least 50% of its body weight during the acorn-eating season, it can be classified as *jamón ibérico de bellota*, the most sought-after designation for *jamón*.

WORTH A TRIP

ANDALUCÍA BEYOND THE CITIES

The Andalucian countryside, with its white villages, rugged mountains, winding country roads and appealing small towns, is every bit as magical as the region's famed cities – and packs in huge variety.

On the south flank of the Sierra Nevada (mainland Spain's highest mountain range), the jumble of valleys known as **Las Alpujarras** juxtaposes arid mountainsides and deep ravines with oasis-like, Berber-style villages set amid orchards and woodlands. There's great walking, a unique ambience derived from the area's Moorish past, and plenty of good accommodation in and around scenic villages like **Capileira**, **Ferreirola**, **Trevélez** and **Cádiar**, one to two hours' drive south from Granada.

Further afield, 200km northeast from Granada, the **Parque Natural Sierras de Cazorla, Segura y Las Villas** is 2099 sq km of craggy mountains, remote hilltop castles and deep green river valleys with some of the most abundant and visible wildlife in Spain – including three types of deer, ibex, wild boar, mouflon (a wild sheep), griffon vultures and golden eagles. The picturesque medieval town of **Cazorla** is a great base, and en route you shouldn't miss the gorgeous towns of **Úbeda** and **Baeza**, World Heritage–listed for their outstanding Renaissance architecture.

If you're starting from Seville, it's about an hour's drive west to the vast wetlands of the **Parque Nacional de Doñana**, Western Europe's biggest roadless region, where flocks of flamingos tinge the sky pink, huge herds of deer and boar roam the woodlands, and the iberian lynx fights for survival. Four-hour minibus safaris into the park go from **El Rocío**, **Sanlúcar de Barrameda** and **El Acebuche** visitors centre.

Along back roads between Seville and Málaga, hung from the skies between the spectacular clifftop towns of **Arcos de la Frontera** and **Ronda**, the gorgeously green limestone gorges and crags of the **Sierra de Grazalema** are crisscrossed by beautiful, marked trails between charming white villages such as **Grazalema**, **Benaoján** and **Zahara de la Sierra**.

All these areas have plenty of good accommodation including many charming country guesthouses or small hotels. They can be reached by bus with a bit of effort: a car is the ideal way to get to and around them.

Getting There & Around

AIR

Málaga's **airport** (AGP; ☎ 952 04 88 38; www.aena.es), 9km southwest of the city centre, is the main international gateway to Andalucía, served by top global carriers as well as budget airlines. Buses (€3, 15 minutes) and trains (€1.80, 12 minutes) run every 20 or 30 minutes between airport and city centre.

BUS

Málaga's **bus station** (☎ 952 35 00 61; www.estabus.emtsam.es; Paseo de los Tilos) is 1km southwest of the city centre. Destinations include Seville (€19 to €24, 2¾ hours, six buses daily), Granada (€11 to €14, 1½ to two hours, 18 buses), Córdoba (€12, 2¼ to four hours, five buses) and Ronda (€11, two to three hours, 13 buses).

TRAIN

The main station, **Málaga María Zambrano Train Station** (☎ 902 43 23 43; www.renfe.es; Explanada de la Estación; ⏰ 5am-12.45am), is around the corner from the bus station. The superfast AVE service runs to Madrid (€32 to €134, 2¾ hours, 13 daily). Trains also go to Córdoba (€17 to €41, one hour, 19 daily) and Seville (€24 to €44, two to 2¾ hours, 11 daily).

EXTREMADURA

Cáceres

POP 95,600

Few visitors make it to the region of Extremadura, bordering Portugal, but those who do are rewarded with some true gems of old Spain, especially Roman Mérida and the 16th-century towns of Trujillo and Cáceres. The Ciudad Monumental, Cáceres' old centre, is truly extraordinary. Narrow cobbled streets twist and climb among ancient stone walls lined with palaces and mansions, while the skyline is decorated with turrets, spires, gargoyles and enormous storks' nests. Protected by defensive walls, it has survived almost intact from its 16th-century heyday.

Sights

★ Palacio de los Golfines de Abajo HISTORIC BUILDING
(☎927 21 80 51; www.palaciogolfinesdeabajo.com; Plaza de los Golfines; tours adult/senior/child €2.50/1.50/free; ⏱tours hourly 10am-1pm & 5-7pm Tue-Sat, 10am-1pm Sun May-Sep, 4.30-6.30pm Tue-Sat Oct-Apr) The sumptuous home of Cáceres' prominent Golfín family has been beautifully restored. Built piecemeal between the 14th and 20th centuries, it's crammed with historical treasures: original 17th-century tapestries and armoury murals, a 19th-century bust of Alfonso XII, a signed 1485 troops request from the Reyes Católicos (Catholic Monarchs) to their Golfín stewards. But it's the detailed, theatrical tours (Spanish, English, French or Portuguese), through four richly decorated lounges, an extravagant chapel and a fascinating documents room, that make it a standout.

★ Museo de Cáceres MUSEUM
(☎927 01 08 77; www.museodecaceres.gobex.es; Plaza de las Veletas; EU citizens/other free/€1.20; ⏱9am-3.30pm & 5-8.30pm Tue-Sat, 10.15am-2.30pm Sun mid-Apr–Sep, 9am-7pm Tue-Sat, 10am-3.30pm Sun Oct–mid-Apr) The excellent Museo de Cáceres, spread across 12 buildings in a 16th-century mansion built over an evocative 12th-century *aljibe* (cistern), is the only surviving element of Cáceres' Moorish castle. The impressive archaeological section includes an elegant stone boar dated to the 4th to 2nd centuries BC, while the equally appealing fine-arts display (behind the main museum; open only in the mornings) showcases works by such greats as Picasso, Miró, Tàpies and El Greco.

Sleeping & Eating

★ Hotel Casa Don Fernando BOUTIQUE HOTEL €€
(☎927 21 42 79, 927 62 71 76; www.casadonfernando.com; Plaza Mayor 30; s €55-75, d €63-85; P❄📶) Cáceres' smartest midrange choice sits on Plaza Mayor right opposite the Arco de la Estrella. Boutique-style rooms, spread over four floors, are tastefully modern, with gleaming bathrooms through glass doors. Pricier 'superiors' enjoy the best plaza views (though weekend nights can be noisy), and attic-style top-floor rooms are good for families. Service hits that perfect professional-yet-friendly note.

★ La Cacharrería TAPAS €€
(☎927 03 07 23; lacacharreria@live.com; Calle de Orellana 1; tapas €4.50, raciones €10-14.50; ⏱restaurant 12.30-4pm & 8.30-midnight Thu-Mon, cafe 4pm-1.30am Thu-Sat, 4-11pm Sun; 🌿) Local flavours and ingredients combine in exquisite, international-inspired concoctions at this packed-out, minimalist-design tapas bar tucked into an old-town house. *Solomillo* (tenderloin) in Torta del Casar cheese arrives in martini glasses. Delicious guacamole, hummus, falafel and 'salsiki' are a godsend for vegetarians. No advance reservations: get here by 1.45pm or 8.30pm.

Information

Oficina de Turismo Regional (☎927 25 55 97; www.turismocaceres.org; Palacio Carvajal, Calle Amargura 1; ⏱8am-8.45pm Mon-Fri, 10am-1.45pm & 5-7.45pm Sat, 10am-1.45pm Sun) Covers Cáceres city and province; very helpful.

Getting There & Away

BUS

The **bus station** (☎927 23 25 50; www.estacionautobuses.es; Calle Túnez 1; ⏱6.30am-10.30pm) has services to Madrid (€25, four hours, seven daily), Seville (€20, 3¾ hours, six daily), Salamanca (€16, three hours, seven daily) and Trujillo (€3.66, 40 minutes, six daily).

TRAIN

Trains run to Madrid (€28 to €33, four hours, five daily), Mérida (€6.10, one hour, six daily) and Seville (€27, 4¾ hours, 6.50am).

SURVIVAL GUIDE

Directory A–Z

ACCOMMODATION

Budget options range from backpacker hostels to family-style *pensiones* and slightly better-heeled *hostales*. At the upper end of this category you'll find rooms with air-conditioning and private bathrooms. Midrange *hostales* and hotels are more comfortable and most offer standard hotel services. Business hotels, trendy boutique hotels and luxury hotels are usually in the top-end category.

Camping

Spain has around 1000 officially graded *campings* (camping grounds) and they vary greatly in service, location, cleanliness and style. They're officially rated as 1st class (1ªC), 2nd class (2ªC)

SLEEPING PRICE RANGES

The following price brackets refer to a double room with private bathroom:

€ less than €65

€€ €65–€140

€€€ more than €140

The price ranges for Madrid and Barcelona are inevitably higher:

€ less than €75

€€ €75–€200

€€€ more than €200

or 3rd class (3ªC). Camping grounds usually charge per person, per tent and per vehicle – typically €5 to €10 for each. Many camping grounds close from around October to Easter.

Campings Online (www.campingsonline.com/espana) Booking service.

Guía Camping (www.guiacampingfecc.com) Online version of the annual *Guía Camping* (€14), which is available in bookshops around the country.

Hotels, Hostales & Pensiones

Most accommodation options fall into the categories of hotels (one to five stars; full amenities, everything from classic luxury to designer to boutique to family-run), *hostales* (high-end guesthouses with private bathroom; one to three stars) or *pensiones* (guesthouses, usually with shared bathroom; one to three stars). The **paradores** (☎ in Spain 902 54 79 79; www.parador.es) are a state-funded chain of luxury hotels often in historical monuments (castles, monasteries...) and/or stunning locations.

Hostels

Spain has a good supply of international backpacker hostels, often with private rooms as well as dorms, in addition to the 250 or so hostels of the **Red Española de Albergues Juveniles** (www.reaj.com), Spain's Hostelling International (HI) organisation. The latter can be heavily booked with school groups and may have curfews.

Typical dorm rates are between €15 and €25. A good resource is Hostel World (www.hostelworld.com).

Seasons & Reservations

Most of the year is high season in Barcelona and Madrid. July and August can be dead in the cities, but are high season along the coasts. Spring, early summer and autumn are high season in some inland areas. Reserving a room is always recommended in high season.

ACTIVITIES

Hiking

- Top walking areas include the Pyrenees, Picos de Europa, Las Alpujarras (Andalucía) and the Galician coast.
- Best season is June to September in most areas, but April to June and September–October in most of Andalucía.
- Region-specific walking guides are published by Cicerone Press (www.cicerone.co.uk).
- GR (*Gran Recorrido;* long distance) trails are indicated with red-and-white markers; PR (*Pequeño Recorrido*; short distance) trails have yellow-and-white markers.
- Good hiking maps are published by Prames (www.prames.com), Editorial Alpina (www.editorialalpina.com) and the Institut Cartogràfic de Catalunya (www.icgc.cat).
- The Camino de Santiago pilgrim route to Santiago de Compostela has many variations starting from all over Spain (and other countries). Most popular is the Camino Francés, running 783km from Roncesvalles, on Spain's border with France. Good websites: Caminolinks (www.santiago-compostela.net/caminos), Mundicamino (www.mundicamino.com), Camino de Santiago (www.caminodesantiago.me).

Skiing

Skiing is cheaper but less varied than in much of the rest of Europe. The season runs from December to mid-April. The best resorts are in the Pyrenees, especially in northwest Catalonia and in Aragón. The Sierra Nevada in Andalucía offers the most southerly skiing in Western Europe.

Surfing, Windsurfing & Kitesurfing

The Basque Country has good surf spots, including San Sebastián, Zarautz and the legendary left at Mundaka. Tarifa in Andalucía, with its long beaches and ceaseless wind, is generally considered to be the kitesurfing and windsurfing capital of Europe.

GAY & LESBIAN TRAVELLERS

Homosexuality is legal in Spain. Same-sex marriages were legalised in 2005. Madrid, Barcelona, Sitges, Torremolinos and Ibiza have particularly active and lively gay scenes. Gay Iberia (www.gayiberia.com) has gay guides to the main destinations.

INTERNET ACCESS

- Wi-fi is available at most hotels and in some cafes, restaurants and airports; generally (but not always) free.

INTERNET RESOURCES

Fiestas.net (www.fiestas.net) Festivals around the country.

Lonely Planet (www.lonelyplanet.com/spain) Destination information, hotel bookings, traveller forums and more.

Renfe (Red Nacional de los Ferrocarriles Españoles; www.renfe.com) Spain's rail network.

Turespaña (www.spain.info) Spanish tourist office's site.

Oh Hello, Spain (www.ohhellospain.blogspot.co.uk) English-language blog, aimed at youngish travellers.

MONEY

- Many credit and debit cards can be used for withdrawing money from *cajeros automáticos* (ATMs) and for making purchases. The most widely accepted cards are Visa and MasterCard.
- Most banks will exchange major foreign currencies and offer the best rates. Ask about commissions and take your passport.
- Exchange offices, indicated by the word *cambio* (exchange), offer longer opening hours than banks, but worse exchange rates and higher commissions.
- Value-added tax (VAT) is known as IVA *(impuesto sobre el valor añadido)*. Non-EU residents are entitled to a refund of the 21% IVA on purchases costing more than €90.16 from any shop if they are taking them out of the EU within three months.
- Menu prices include a service charge. Most people leave some small change. Taxi drivers don't have to be tipped but a little rounding up won't go amiss.

OPENING HOURS

Banks 8.30am to 2pm Monday to Friday; some also open 4pm to 7pm Thursday and 9am and 1pm Saturday

Central post offices 8.30am to 9.30pm Monday to Friday, 8.30am to 2pm Saturday

Nightclubs midnight or 1am to 5am or 6am

Restaurants lunch 1pm to 4pm, dinner 8.30pm to midnight or later

Shops 10am to 2pm and 4.30pm to 7.30pm or 5pm to 8pm Monday to Saturday; big supermarkets and department stores generally open from 9am or 10am to 9pm or 10pm Monday to Saturday

PUBLIC HOLIDAYS

The two main periods when Spaniards go on holiday are Semana Santa (the week leading up to Easter Sunday) and July or August. At these times accommodation can be scarce and transport heavily booked.

Everywhere in Spain has 14 official holidays a year, some observed nationwide, others just locally. The following are commonly observed nationwide:

Año Nuevo (New Year's Day) 1 January

Epifanía (Epiphany) or **Día de los Reyes Magos** (Three Kings' Day) **6 January**

Jueves Santo (Holy Thursday) March/April (not observed in Catalonia)

Viernes Santo (Good Friday) March/April

Fiesta del Trabajo (Labour Day) 1 May

La Asunción (Feast of the Assumption) 15 August

Fiesta Nacional de España (National Day) 12 October

Todos los Santos (All Saints' Day) 1 November

Día de la Constitución (Constitution Day) 6 December

La Inmaculada Concepción (Feast of the Immaculate Conception) 8 December

Navidad (Christmas) 25 December

The following are observed in many regions and localities:

Lunes de Pascua (Easter Monday) March/April

Día de San José (St Joseph's Day) 19 March

Día de San Juan Bautista (Feast of St John the Baptist) 24 June

Día de Santiago Apóstol (Feast of St James the Apostle) 25 July

SAFE TRAVEL

Most visitors to Spain never feel remotely threatened, but you should be aware of the possibility of petty theft (which may of course not seem so petty if your passport, cash, credit card and phone go missing). Stay alert and you can avoid most thievery techniques. Barcelona, Madrid and Seville are the worst offenders, as are popular beaches in summer (never leave belongings unattended).

TELEPHONE

The once widespread, but now fast disappearing, blue payphones accept coins, *tarjetas telefónicas* (phonecards) issued by the national phone company Telefónica and, in some

COUNTRY FACTS

Area 505,370 sq km

Capital Madrid

Country Code ☎34

Currency Euro (€)

Emergency ☎112

Languages Spanish (Castilian), Catalan, Basque, Galician (Gallego)

Money ATMs everywhere

Population 48 million

Visas Schengen rules apply

ESSENTIAL FOOD & DRINK

Paella This signature rice dish comes in infinite varieties, although Valencia is its true home.

Cured meats Wafer-thin slices of *chorizo, lomo, salchichón* and *jamón serrano* appear on most Spanish tables.

Tapas These bite-sized morsels range from uncomplicated Spanish staples to pure gastronomic innovation.

Olive oil Spain is the world's largest producer of olive oil.

Wine Spain has the largest area of wine cultivation in the world. La Rioja and Ribera del Duero are the best-known wine-growing regions.

Seafood Plentiful everywhere and best in Galicia at Spain's northwest corner.

cases, various credit cards. Calling from your smartphone, tablet or computer using an internet-based service such as Skype or FaceTime is generally the cheapest and easiest option.

Mobile Phones

Local SIM cards are widely available and can be used in unblocked European and Australian mobile phones but are not compatible with many North American or Japanese systems. The Spanish mobile-phone companies (Telefónica's MoviStar, Orange and Vodafone) offer *prepagado* (prepaid) accounts for mobiles. The SIM card costs from €10, to which you add some prepaid phone time.

Phone Codes

Spain has no area codes. All numbers are nine digits and you just dial that nine-digit number.

Numbers starting with ☎900 are national toll-free numbers, while those starting ☎901 to ☎905 come with varying costs; most can only be dialled from within Spain.

TOURIST INFORMATION

Most towns and large villages of any interest have a helpful *oficina de turismo* (tourist office) where you can get maps and brochures.

Turespaña (www.spain.info) is the country's national tourism body.

VISAS

Spain is one of 26 member countries of the Schengen Convention and Schengen visa rules apply.

Citizens or residents of EU & Schengen countries No visa required.

Citizens or residents of Australia, Canada, Israel, Japan, NZ and the USA No visa required for tourist visits of up to 90 days.

Other countries Check with a Spanish embassy or consulate.

To work or study in Spain A special visa may be required – contact a Spanish embassy or consulate before travel.

ℹ Getting There & Away

Flights, cars and tours can be booked online at lonelyplanet.com/bookings.

ENTERING THE COUNTRY

Immigration and customs checks usually involve a minimum of fuss, although there are exceptions. Your vehicle could be searched on arrival from Morocco; they're looking for controlled substances. Expect long delays at these borders, especially in summer.

The tiny principality of Andorra is not in the EU, so border controls (and rigorous customs checks for contraband) remain in place.

AIR

Flights from all over Europe (including numerous budget airlines), plus direct flights from North and South America, Africa, the Middle East and Asia, serve main Spanish airports. All of Spain's airports share the user-friendly website and flight information telephone number of **Aena** (☎91 321 10 00, 902 404 704; www.aena.es), the national airports authority. Each airport's page on the website has details on practical information (such as parking and public transport) and a list of (and links to) airlines using that airport.

Madrid's Aeropuerto de Barajas is Europe's sixth-busiest airport. Other major airports include Barcelona's Aeroport del Prat and the airports of Palma de Mallorca, Málaga, Alicante, Ibiza, Valencia, Seville, Bilbao, Menorca and Santiago de Compostela.

LAND

Spain shares land borders with France, Portugal and Andorra.

Bus

Aside from the main cross-border routes, numerous smaller services criss-cross Spain's borders with France and Portugal. Regular buses connect Andorra with Barcelona (including winter ski buses and direct services to the airport) and other destinations in Spain (including Madrid) and France.

Eurolines (www.eurolines.com) is the main operator of international bus services to Spain from most of Western Europe and Morocco. Services from France include Nice to Madrid, and Paris to Barcelona.

EATING PRICE RANGES

The following price brackets refer to a standard main dish:

€ less than €10

€€ €10–€20

€€€ more than €20

Avanza (www.avanzabus.com) runs three buses daily each way between Lisbon and Madrid (€41, 8½ hours).

Train

France to Barcelona A high-speed service runs from Paris' Gare de Lyon (from €59, 6½ hours, two daily) via Nimes, Montpellier, Perpignan, Figueres and Girona. High-speed services also run from Toulouse (from €35, 3¼ hours), Lyon (from €44, five hours) and Marseille (from €39, five hours).

France to Madrid You can take a high-speed train to Barcelona and change there to a Spanish high-speed AVE (total fare from €144, 9¾ hours). Or take a high-speed train from Paris-Montparnasse to Hendaye, walk across the border to Irún and board a Spanish train there (total fare from €68, 15 hours). High-speed service runs from Marseille to Madrid (from €59, 7¾ hours).

Lisbon to Madrid (seat/sleeper from €24/34, 10 hours, 9.30pm) via Salamanca and Ávila.

Lisbon to Irún (seat/sleeper from €28/38, 13 hours, 9.30pm)

Porto to Vigo (€15, 2½ hours, two daily)

SEA

Trasmediterranea (www.trasmediterranea.es) Many Mediterranean ferry services are run by the Spanish company Trasmediterranea.

Brittany Ferries (www.brittany-ferries.co.uk) Services between Spain and the UK.

Grandi Navi Veloci (www1.gnv.it) High-speed luxury ferries between Barcelona and Genoa.

Grimaldi Lines (www.grimaldi-lines.com) Barcelona to Civitavecchia (near Rome), Savona (near Genoa) and Porto Torres (northwest Sardinia).

Getting Around

Students and seniors are eligible for discounts of 30% to 50% on most types of transport within Spain.

AIR

Air Europa (www.aireuropa.com) Madrid to Ibiza, Palma de Mallorca, Málaga, Bilbao, Barcelona and Vigo as well as other routes between Spanish cities.

Iberia (www.iberia.com) Spain's national airline has an extensive domestic network.

Ryanair (www.ryanair.com) Extensive Spanish network including to Santiago de Compostela and Ibiza from Barcelona, Madrid, Málaga and Seville, and to Barcelona from Seville and Málaga.

Volotea (www.volotea.com) Budget airline with domestic routes taking in Alicante, Bilbao, Ibiza, Málaga, Maó, Oviedo, Palma de Mallorca, Santander, Valencia and Zaragoza (but not Madrid or Barcelona).

Vueling (www.vueling.com) Spanish low-cost company with loads of domestic flights, especially from Barcelona.

BOAT

Regular ferries connect the Spanish mainland with the Balearic Islands.

BUS

Spain's bus network is operated by countless independent companies and reaches into the most remote towns and villages. Many towns and cities have one main bus station where most buses arrive and depart.

It is not necessary, and often not possible, to make advance reservations for local bus journeys. It is, however, a good idea to turn up at least 30 minutes before the bus leaves to guarantee a seat. For longer trips, you can and should buy your ticket in advance.

ALSA Countrywide bus network.

CONNECTIONS

Spanish airports are among Europe's best connected, while the typical overland route leads many travellers from France over or round the Pyrenees into Spain. Numerous roads and the Madrid–Lisbon rail line connect Spain with Portugal.

The most obvious sea journeys lead across the Strait of Gibraltar to Morocco. The most common routes connect Algeciras or Tarifa with Tangier, from where there's plenty of transport deeper into Morocco. Car ferries also connect Barcelona with Italian ports, and the northern ports of Santander and Bilbao with the UK.

There are two main rail lines to Spain from Paris: a high-speed route to Barcelona (with direct trains taking 6½ hours), and another to Madrid and the north via the Basque Country, requiring a change of trains at the border.

Avanza Buses from Madrid to Extremadura, western Castilla y León and Valencia.

Socibus Services between Madrid and western Andalucía including Seville.

CAR & MOTORCYCLE

Spain's roads vary enormously but are generally good. Fastest are the *autopistas;* on some, you have to pay hefty tolls.

Every vehicle should display a nationality plate of its country of registration and you must always carry proof of ownership of a private vehicle. Third-party motor insurance is required throughout Europe. A warning triangle and a reflective jacket (to be used in case of breakdown) are compulsory.

Driving Licences

All EU member states' driving licences are recognised. Other foreign licences should be accompanied by an International Driving Permit (although in practice local licences are usually accepted). These are available from automobile clubs in your country and valid for 12 months.

Hire

To rent a car in Spain you have to have a licence, be aged 21 or over and have a credit or debit card. Rates vary widely: the best deals tend to be in major tourist areas, including airports. Prices are especially competitive in the Balearic Islands.

Road Rules

- The blood-alcohol limit is 0.05%.
- The legal driving age for cars is 18. The legal driving age for motorcycles and scooters is

FERRIES TO SPAIN

A useful website for comparing routes and finding links to the relevant ferry companies is www.ferrylines.com.

From Algeria

ROUTE	DURATION	FREQUENCY
Ghazaouet to Almería	9hr	2-3 weekly

From Italy

ROUTE	DURATION	FREQUENCY
Genoa to Barcelona	18hr	1-2 weekly
Civitavecchia (near Rome) to Barcelona	20hr	6 weekly
Porto Torres (Sardinia) to Barcelona	12hr	5 weekly
Savona (near Genoa) to Barcelona	20hr	2 weekly

From Morocco

ROUTE	DURATION	FREQUENCY
Tangier to Algeciras	1-2hr	15 or more daily
Tangier to Barcelona	27-33hr	2-3 weekly
Tangier to Tarifa	35–60min	13 or more daily
Nador to Almería	6hr	2-3 daily

From the UK

ROUTE	DURATION	FREQUENCY
Plymouth to Santander	21hr	weekly Apr-Oct
Portsmouth to Santander	24hr	1-2 weekly
Portsmouth to Bilbao	24hr	2-3 weekly

16 (80cc and over) or 14 (50cc and under). A licence is required.

➡ Motorcyclists must use headlights at all times and wear a helmet if riding a bike of 125cc or more.

➡ Drive on the right.

➡ In built-up areas, the speed limit is 50km/h (and in some cases, such as inner-city Barcelona, 30km/h), which increases to 100km/h on major roads and up to 120km/h on *autovías* and *autopistas* (toll-free and tolled dual-lane highways, respectively). Cars towing caravans are restricted to a maximum speed of 80km/h.

TRAIN

The national railway company is **Renfe** (✆902 243 402; www.renfe.com). Trains are mostly modern and comfortable, and late arrivals are the exception. The high-speed network is in constant expansion.

Passes are valid for all long-distance Renfe trains; Inter-Rail users pay supplements on Talgo, InterCity and AVE trains. All pass-holders making reservations pay a small fee.

Among Spain's numerous types of train:

Altaria, Alvia and Avant Long- and medium-distance intermediate-speed services.

AVE (Tren de Alta Velocidad Española) High-speed trains that link Madrid with Alicante, Barcelona, Córdoba, Cuenca, Huesca, León, Lleida, Málaga, Segovia, Seville, Tarragona, Valencia, Valladolid and Zaragoza. There are also Barcelona–Seville, Barcelona–Málaga and Valencia–Seville services. In coming years Madrid–Granada, Madrid–Cádiz and Madrid–Bilbao should come on line.

Cercanías For short hops and services to outlying suburbs and satellite towns of Madrid, Barcelona and 12 other cities.

Euromed Similar to AVE trains, they connect Barcelona with Valencia and Alicante.

Regionales Trains operating within one region, usually stopping at all stations.

Talgo Slower long-distance trains.

Trenhotel Overnight trains with sleeper berths, operating to Galicia from Madrid and Barcelona.

Classes & Costs

➡ Fares vary enormously depending on the service (faster trains cost considerably more) and, for many long-distance trains, on the time and day of travel and how far ahead you book (the earlier the better).

➡ Long-distance trains have 2nd and 1st classes, known as *turista* and *preferente*, respectively. The latter is 20% to 40% more expensive.

➡ Children aged between four and 14 years are entitled to a 40% discount; those aged under four travel for free (but on long- and medium-distance trains only if they share a seat with a fare-paying passenger). Buying a return ticket gives a 20% discount on most long- and medium-distance trains. Students and people up to 25 years of age with a Euro<26 or GO 25 card are entitled to 20% off most ticket prices.

Reservations

Reservations are recommended for long-distance trips, and you can make them in train stations, **Renfe** offices and travel agencies, as well as online. In a growing number of stations, you can pick up prebooked tickets from machines scattered about the station concourse.

Switzerland

Includes ➡

Best Places to Eat

- Chez Vrony (p648)
- Volkshaus Basel (p658)
- Restaurant 1903 (p653)
- Buvette des Bains (p641)
- Alpenrose (p656)

Best Places to Stay

- Esther's Guest House (p654)
- Gletschergarten (p653)
- Guesthouse Castagnola (p661)
- Il Fuorn (p660)
- Backpackers Villa Sonnenhof (p651)

Why Go?

What giddy romance Zermatt, St Moritz and other glitterati-encrusted names evoke. This is Sonderfall Schweiz ('special-case Switzerland'), a privileged neutral country set apart from others, proudly idiosyncratic, insular and unique. It's blessed with gargantuan cultural diversity: its four official languages alone speak volumes.

The Swiss don't do half measures: Zürich, their most gregarious urban centre, has cutting-edge art, legendary nightlife and one of the world's highest living standards. The national passion for sharing the great outdoors provides access (by public transport, no less!) to some of the world's most inspiring panoramic experiences.

So don't depend just on your postcard images of Bern's and Lucerne's chocolate-box architecture, the majestic Matterhorn or those pristine lakes – Switzerland is a place so outrageously beautiful it simply must be seen to be believed.

When to Go

Bern

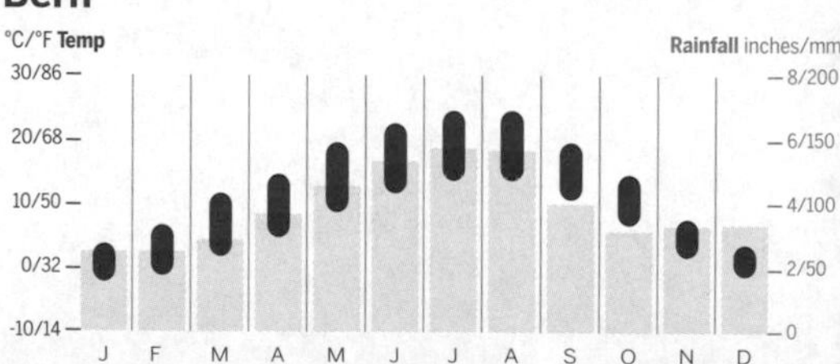

Dec–early Apr Carve through powder and eat fondue at an Alpine resort.

Jun–Sep Hike in the shadow of the mesmerising Matterhorn and be wowed by its perfection.

Aug Celebrate Swiss National Day on 1 August and witness Swiss national pride in full force.

Switzerland Highlights

❶ **Zürich** (p654) Discovering this zesty city via a daytime stroll along the city's sublime lake followed by a rollicking night out.

❷ **Zermatt** (p646) Marvelling at the iconic Matterhorn and wandering around this car-free Alpine village.

❸ **Bern** (p648) and **Lucerne** (p649) Enjoying the charm of these famous beauties: think medieval Old Town appeal, folkloric fountains and art.

❹ **Jungfraujoch** (p653) Being wowed by the Eiger's monstrous north face on a ride to the 'top of Europe', 3471m Jungfraujoch.

❺ **Geneva** (p639) Boarding a boat in this sophisticated city for a serene Lake Geneva cruise to medieval **Lausanne** (p644).

❻ **Bernina Express** (p647) Riding one of Switzerland's legendary scenic trains, such as the Bernina Express.

❼ **Lugano** (p660) Going Italian at Lugano, with its lovely, temperate lake setting.

GENEVA

POP 198,072

The whole world seems to be in Geneva, Switzerland's second city. The UN, the International Red Cross, the World Health Organization – 200-odd governmental and nongovernmental international organisations fill the city's plush hotels with big-name guests, who feast on an extraordinary choice of cuisine and help prop up the overload of banks, jewellers and chocolate shops for which Geneva is known.

Sights & Activities

The city centre is so compact it's easy to see many of the main sights on foot. Begin your explorations on the southern side of Lake Geneva and visit the **Jardin Anglais** (Quai du Général-Guisan) to see the **Horloge Fleurie** (Flower Clock). Crafted from 6500 flowers, the clock has ticked since 1955 and sports the world's longest second hand (2.5m).

★Jet d'Eau FOUNTAIN

(Quai Gustave-Ador) When landing by plane, this lakeside fountain is the first dramatic glimpse you get of Geneva. The 140m-tall structure shoots up water with incredible force – 200km/h, 1360 horsepower – to create the sky-high plume, kissed by a rainbow on sunny days. At any one time, 7 tonnes of water is in the air, much of which sprays spectators on the pier beneath. Two or three times a year it is illuminated pink, blue or another colour to mark a humanitarian occasion.

★Cathédrale St-Pierre CATHEDRAL

(www.cathedrale-geneve.ch; Cour St-Pierre; towers adult/child Sfr5/2; ⏲9.30am-6.30pm Mon-Sat, noon-6.30pm Sun Jun-Sep, 10am-5.30pm Mon-Sat, noon-5.30pm Sun Oct-May) Begun in the 11th

century, Geneva's cathedral is predominantly Gothic with an 18th-century neoclassical facade. Between 1536 and 1564 Protestant John Calvin preached here; see his seat in the north aisle. Inside the cathedral, 96 steps spiral up to the **northern tower and attic** – offering a fascinating glimpse at the cathedral's architectural construction. From here, another 60 steps climb into the **southern tower**, revealing close-up views of the bells and panoramic city vistas up top.

★CERN RESEARCH CENTRE

(☎022 767 84 84; www.cern.ch; Meyrin; ⏲guided tours in English 11am & 1pm Mon-Sat) FREE Founded in 1954, the European Organisation for Nuclear Research, 8km west of Geneva, is a laboratory for research into particle physics. It accelerates protons down a 27km circular tube (the Large Hadron Collider, the world's biggest machine) and the resulting collisions create new matter. Two exhibitions shed light on its work and two-hour guided tours in English delve deeper; reserve online up to 15 days ahead and bring photo ID. From the train station take tram 18 (Sfr3, 20 minutes).

Musée International de la Croix-Rouge et du Croissant-Rouge MUSEUM

(International Red Cross & Red Crescent Museum; ☎022 748 95 11; www.redcrossmuseum.ch; Av de la Paix 17; adult/child Sfr15/7; ⏲10am-6pm Tue-Sun Apr-Oct, to 5pm Nov-Mar) Compelling multimedia exhibits at Geneva's fascinating International Red Cross and Red Crescent Museum trawl through atrocities perpetuated by humanity. The litany of war and nastiness, documented in films, photos, sculptures and soundtracks, is set against the noble aims of the organisation created by Geneva businessmen and philanthropists Henri Dunant and Henri Dufour in 1864. Excellent temporary exhibitions command an additional entrance fee.

Take bus 8 from Gare de Cornavin to the Appia stop.

★Patek Philippe Museum MUSEUM

(☎022 807 09 10; www.patekmuseum.com; Rue des Vieux-Grenadiers 7; adult/child Sfr10/free; ⏲2-6pm Tue-Fri, 10am-6pm Sat) This elegant museum by one of Switzerland's leading luxury watchmakers displays exquisite timepieces and enamels from the 16th century to the present.

Sleeping

When checking in, ask for your free Public Transport Card, covering unlimited bus travel for the duration of your hotel stay.

★Hôtel Bel'Esperance HOTEL €€

(☎022 818 37 37; www.hotel-bel-esperance.ch; Rue de la Vallée 1; s/d/tr/q from Sfr150/170/210/250; ⏲reception 7am-10pm; @ 📶) This two-star hotel is extraordinary value. Rooms are quiet and cared for, those on the 1st floor share a kitchen, and there are fridges for guests to store picnic supplies – or sausages – in! Ride the lift to the 5th floor to flop on its wonderful flower-filled rooftop terrace, complete with barbecue.

Hôtel N'vY HOTEL €€

(☎022 544 66 66; www.hotelnvygeneva.com; Rue de Richemont 18; r weekend/weekday from Sfr175/260; ❄@📶) Contemporary flair abounds at this modish four-star northeast of the train station, from the purple-lit bar downstairs to in-room amenities like international power outlets, Bluetooth connectiv-

ITINERARIES

One Week

Starting in vibrant **Zürich**, shop famous Bahnhofstrasse, then eat, drink and be merry. Next, head to the **Jungfrau region** to explore some kick-ass Alpine scenery, whether it be by hiking or skiing. Take a pit stop in beautiful **Lucerne** before finishing up in Switzerland's delightful capital, **Bern**.

Two Weeks

As above, then head west for a French flavour in **Geneva** or lakeside **Lausanne**. Stop in **Gruyères** to dip into a cheesy fondue and overdose on meringues drowned in thick double cream. Zip to **Zermatt** or across to **St Moritz** to frolic in snow or green meadows, then loop east to taste the Italian side of Switzerland at lakeside **Lugano**.

LOCAL KNOWLEDGE

GENEVA'S TOP PICNIC SPOTS

With mountains of fine views to pick from, Geneva is prime picnicking terrain for those reluctant to pay too much to eat. Shop for supplies at downtown *boulangeries* (bakeries) and delis, or at the takeaway food hall in the **Globus** (www.globus.ch/fr/store/116/globus-geneve; Rue du Rhône 48; ⏲9am-7pm Mon-Wed, to 9pm Thu, to 7.30pm Fri, to 6pm Sat; food hall 7.30am-10pm Mon-Fri, 8.30am-10pm Sat) department store, and head for one of these classic picnic spots:

➡ In the contemplative shade of Henry Moore's voluptuous sculpture *Reclining Figure: Arch Leg* (1973) in the park opposite the Musée d'Art et d'Histoire.

➡ Behind the cathedral on **Terrasse Agrippa d'Abigné**, a tree-shaded park with benches, sandpit and see-saw for kids, and a fine rooftop and cathedral view.

➡ On a bench on **Quai du Mont-Blanc** with Mont Blanc view (sunny days only).

➡ On the world's longest bench (126m long) on chestnut-tree-lined Promenade de la Treille in the **Parc des Bastions**.

ity and chromotherapy lighting. Among the five room categories, all but the standards come with big-screen TV, espresso machine and parquet wood floor. Upper-floor executive rooms have views of Lake Geneva and the Alps.

Hôtel Beau-Rivage HISTORIC HOTEL €€€
(☎022 716 66 66; www.beau-rivage.ch; Quai du Mont-Blanc 13; d weekend/weekday from Sfr550/670; P❄@🛜) Run by the Mayer family for five generations, this grand hotel with its evocative setting at the meeting of the Rhône and Lake Geneva is a 19th-century jewel dripping in opulence.

Eating

Eateries crowd Place du Bourg-de-Four, Geneva's oldest square, in the lovely Old Town. Otherwise, head down the hill towards the river and Place du Molard, packed with tables and chairs for much of the year. In Pâquis, there's a tasty line-up of more affordable restaurants on Place de la Navigation.

★**Buvette des Bains** CAFETERIA €
(☎022 738 16 16; www.bains-des-paquis.ch; Quai du Mont-Blanc 30, Bains des Pâquis; mains Sfr14-23; ⏲7am-10.30pm) Meet Genevans at this earthy beach bar – rough and hip around the edges – at the Bains des Pâquis lakeside pool and sauna complex. Grab breakfast, a salad or the *plat du jour* (dish of the day), or dip into a *fondue au crémant* (Champagne fondue).

Cottage Café MEDITERRANEAN €
(☎022 731 60 16; www.cottagecafe.ch; Rue Adhémar-Fabri 7; tapas & mezze Sfr9-16; ⏲7.30am-midnight Mon-Fri, 9am-midnight Sat) Hovering near the waterfront, this quaint cottage hides in a park guarded by two stone lions and a mausoleum (Geneva's Brunswick Monument, no less). On clear days, views of Mont Blanc from its garden are swoon-worthy, and lunching or lounging inside is akin to hanging out in your grandma's book-lined living room.

★**Le Relais d'Entrecôte** STEAK €€
(☎022 310 60 04; www.relaisentrecote.fr; Rue Pierre Fatio 6; steak, salad & chips Sfr42; ⏲noon-2.30pm & 7-11pm) Key vocabulary at this timeless classic where everyone eats the same dish is *à point* (medium), *bien cuit* (well done) and *saignant* (rare). It doesn't even bother with menus, just sit down, say how you like your steak cooked and wait for it to arrive – two handsome servings pre-empted by a green salad and accompanied by perfectly crisp, skinny fries.

★**Brasserie des Halles de l'Île** EUROPEAN €€
(☎022 311 08 88; www.brasseriedeshallesdelile.ch; Pl de l'Île 1; weekday lunch specials Sfr18.90, dinner mains Sfr20-35; ⏲10.30am-midnight Sun & Mon, to 1am Tue & Wed, to 2am Thu-Sat) At home in Geneva's old market hall on an island, this industrial-style venue cooks up a buzzing cocktail of after-work aperitifs with music, after-dark DJs and seasonal fare of fresh veggies and regional products – look for

Geneva

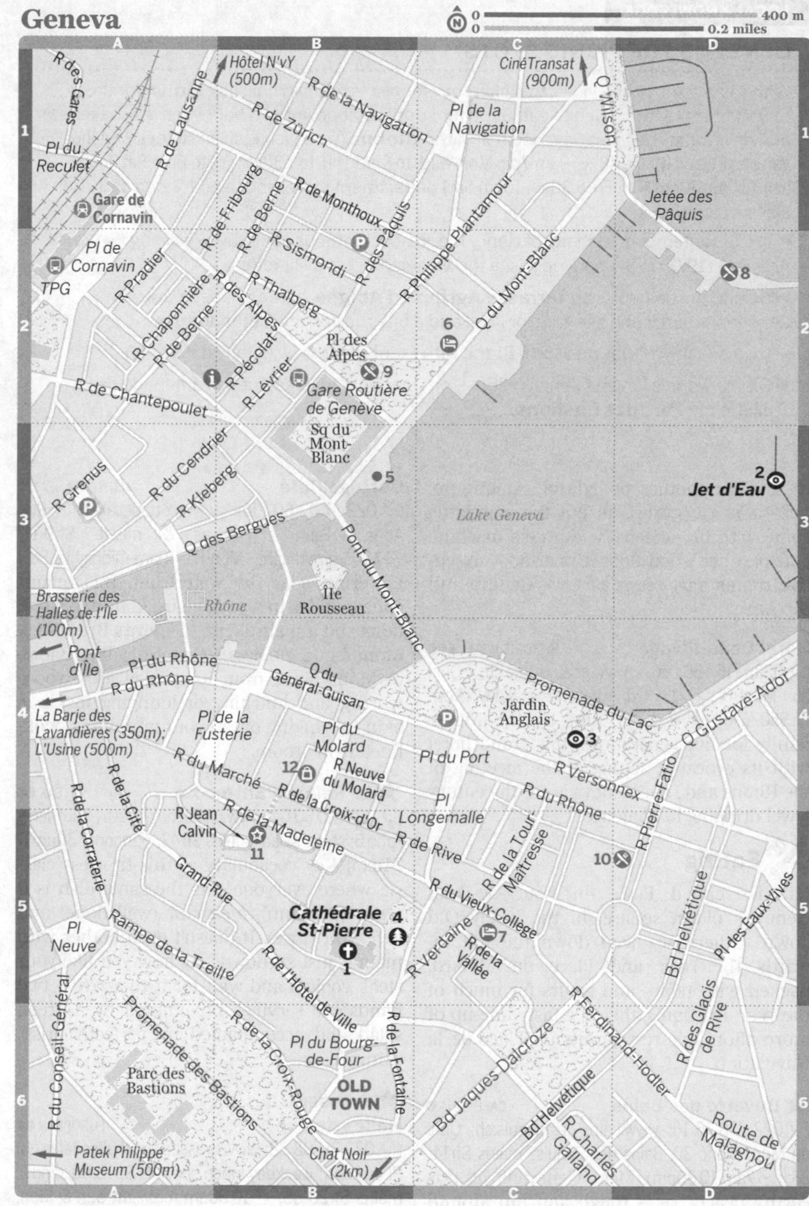

the Appellation d'Origine Contrôllée (AOC) products flagged on the menu. Arrive early to snag the best seat in the house – a superb terrace hanging over the water.

Drinking & Entertainment

Pâquis, the district in-between the train station and lake, is particularly well endowed with bars. For a dose of Bohemia, head to Carouge on tram 12. This shady quarter of

Geneva

Top Sights
1 Cathédrale St-Pierre B5
2 Jet d'Eau D3

Sights
3 Jardin Anglais C4
4 Terrasse Agrippa d'Abigné B5

Activities, Courses & Tours
5 CGN B3

Sleeping
6 Hôtel Beau-Rivage C2
7 Hôtel Bel'Esperance C5

Eating
8 Buvette des Bains D2
9 Cottage Café B2
10 Le Relais d'Entrecôte D5

Entertainment
11 Alhambra B5

Shopping
12 Globus B4

17th-century houses and narrow streets has galleries, funky shops and hip nightlife.

In warm weather, waterfront bars pop up along the banks of the Rhône and Lake Geneva. In July and August, catch free movies under the stars at **CinéTransat** (www.cinetransat.ch; ⌚ lounge chair rental from 7pm, films start at sunset).

★ Chat Noir BAR
(☎ 022 307 10 40; www.chatnoir.ch; Rue Vauthier 13; ⌚ 6pm-4am Tue-Thu, to 5am Fri & Sat) One of the busiest night spots in Carouge, the Black Cat is packed most nights thanks to its all-rounder vibe: arrive after work for an aperitif with a selection of tapas to nibble on, and stay until dawn for dancing, live music and DJ sets.

La Barje des Lavandières BAR
(www.labarje.ch; Promenade des Lavandières; ⌚ 11am-midnight Mon-Fri, noon-midnight Sat, noon-11pm Sun May-Sep) This summertime address is not a barge at all, but rather a vintage caravan with tin roof and candy-striped facade, parked on the grassy banks of the Rhône near the Bâtiment des Forces Motrices. The beer and music are plentiful, outside concerts and art performances pull huge crowds, and proceeds go towards helping young people in difficulty.

L'Usine PERFORMING ARTS
(www.usine.ch; Pl des Volontaires 4) At the gritty heart of Geneva's alternative culture scene, this nonprofit collection of 18 arts-related initiatives is housed beside the Rhône in a former gold-processing factory. On any given night, expect to see cutting-edge theatre at **TU** (www.theatredelusine.ch), live music at **Le Zoo** (www.lezoo.ch) or up-and-coming VJ artists at **Kalvingrad** (www.kalvingrad.com).

Alhambra LIVE MUSIC
(☎ 078 966 07 97; www.alhambra-geneve.ch; Rue de la Rôtisserie 10) Reopened in 2015 after extensive renovations, this gorgeous historic theatre with its cut-glass chandeliers, embossed silver ceilings and scarlet chairs makes a classy venue for live concerts ranging from Brazilian 'electrotropical' to African drumming, disco to salsa, and Afro-Caribbean to R&B.

Shopping

Designer shopping is wedged between Rue du Rhône and Rue de Rive; the latter has lots of chain stores. Grand-Rue in the Old Town and Carouge boast artsy boutiques.

Information

Tourist Office (☎ 022 909 70 00; www.geneve.com; Rue du Mont-Blanc 18; ⌚ 10am-6pm Mon, 9am-6pm Tue-Sat, 10am-4pm Sun) Helpful, well-stocked office just downhill from the train station.

Getting There & Away

AIR

Geneva Airport (p663), 4km northwest of the town centre, is served by a wide variety of Swiss and international airlines.

BOAT

CGN (Compagnie Générale de Navigation; ☎ 0900 929 929; www.cgn.ch; Quai du Mont-Blanc) runs steamers from Jardin Anglais and Pâquis to other Lake Geneva villages. Many only sail May to September, including those to/from Lausanne (Sfr66, 3½ hours). Eurail and Swiss passes are valid on CGN boats.

BUS

Buses to neighbouring France depart from **Gare Routière de Genève** (☎ 0900 320 230, 022 732 02 30; www.coach-station.com; Pl Dorcière).

TRAIN

More-or-less-hourly trains run from Geneva's central station, **Gare de Cornavin** (Pl de Cornavin), to Swiss cities including Lausanne

(Sfr23, 35 to 50 minutes), Bern (Sfr51, 1¾ hours) and Zürich (Sfr89, 2¾ hours).

International daily rail connections from Geneva include Paris by TGV (3¼ hours) and Milan (four hours).

Getting Around

TO/FROM THE AIRPORT

Getting from the airport is easy with regular trains into Gare de Cornavin (Sfr3, seven minutes). Slower bus 10 (Sfr3, 30 minutes) does the same 4km trip. Grab a free public transport ticket from the machine inside the airport's luggage hall. A metered taxi costs Sfr35 to Sfr50.

BICYCLE

Pick up a bike at **Genèveroule** (☎022 740 13 43; www.geneveroule.ch; Pl de Montbrillant 17; 4hr free, then per hour Sfr2; ⏲8am-9pm May-Oct, to 6pm Nov-Apr) just outside the train station.

PUBLIC TRANSPORT

Buses, trams, trains and boats operated by **TPG** (www.tpg.ch; Rue de Montbrillant; ⏲7am-7pm Mon-Fri, 9am-6pm Sat) serve the city, and ticket dispensers are found at all stops. A one-hour ticket costs Sfr3; a day pass offering unlimited rides costs Sfr10 (Sfr8 if purchased after 9am).

LAKE GENEVA REGION

Lausanne

POP 135,629

In a fabulous location overlooking Lake Geneva, Lausanne is an enchanting beauty with several distinct personalities: the former fishing village of Ouchy, with its lakeside bustle; the Vieille Ville (Old Town), with charming cobblestone streets and covered staircases; and Flon, a warehouse district of bars and boutiques.

Sights & Activities

★Musée Olympique MUSEUM

(Olympic Museum; ☎021 621 65 11; www.olympic.org/museum; Quai d'Ouchy 1; adult/child Sfr18/10; ⏲9am-6pm daily May–mid-Oct, 10am-6pm Tue-Sun mid-Oct–Apr) Musée Olympique is easily Lausanne's most lavish museum and an essential stop for sports buffs (and kids). Thoroughly revamped in 2014, the state-of-the-art installations recount the Olympic story from its inception to the present day through video, interactive displays, memorabilia and temporary themed exhibitions. Other attractions include tiered landscaped gardens, site-specific sculptural works and a fabulous cafe with champion lake views from its terrace.

★Cathédrale de Notre Dame CATHEDRAL

(Pl de la Cathédrale; ⏲9am-7pm Apr-Sep, to 5.30pm Oct-Mar) Lausanne's Gothic cathedral, Switzerland's finest, stands proudly at the heart of the Old Town. Raised in the 12th and 13th centuries on the site of earlier, humbler churches, it lacks the lightness of French Gothic buildings but is remarkable nonetheless. Pope Gregory X, in the presence of Rudolph of Habsburg (the Holy Roman Emperor) and an impressive following of European cardinals and bishops, consecrated the church in 1275.

Place de la Palud SQUARE

In the heart of the Old Town, this 9th-century medieval market square – pretty as a picture – was originally bogland. For five centuries it has been home to the city government, now housed in the 17th-century **Hôtel de Ville** (town hall). A fountain pierces one end of the square, presided over by a brightly painted column topped by the allegorical figure of Justice, clutching scales and dressed in blue.

Sleeping

Hotel guests get a Lausanne Transport Card providing unlimited use of public transport for the duration of their stay.

Lhotel BOUTIQUE HOTEL €

(☎021 331 39 39; www.lhotel.ch; Pl de l'Europe 6; r from Sfr130; ❄📶) This smart small hotel is ideally placed for the city's lively Flon district nightlife. Rooms are simple and startlingly white, and come with iPads; breakfast costs Sfr14. There's a fab rooftop terrace and your stay gives you access to the spa at the five-star Lausanne Palace & Spa nearby for Sfr55.

★Hôtel Beau-Rivage Palace HISTORIC HOTEL €€€

(☎021 613 33 33; www.brp.ch; Pl du Port 17-19; r from Sfr510; ❄@📶🏊) Easily the most stunningly located hotel in town, this luxury lakeside address is sumptuous. A beautifully maintained early 19th-century mansion set in immaculate grounds, it tempts with magnificent lake and Alp views, a grand spa, and a number of bars and upmarket restaurants (including a superb gastronomic temple headed by Anne-Sophie Pic, the only French female chef with three Michelin stars).

DON'T MISS

MONTREUX

This tidy lakeside town boasts Switzerland's most extraordinary castle.

Originally constructed on the shores of Lake Geneva in the 11th century, **Château de Chillon** (☎021 966 89 10; www.chillon.ch; Av de Chillon 21; adult/child Sfr12.50/6; ⊙9am-7pm Apr-Sep, 9.30am-6pm Mar & Oct, 10am-5pm Nov-Feb, last entry 1hr before close) was brought to the world's attention by Lord Byron and the world has been filing past ever since. Spend at least a couple of hours exploring its numerous courtyards, towers, dungeons and halls filled with arms, period furniture and artwork.

The castle is a lovely 45-minute lakefront walk from Montreux. Alternatively, take bus 201 (10 minutes) or a CGN steamer (15 minutes).

Crowds throng to the legendary (and not all-jazz) **Montreux Jazz Festival** (www.montreuxjazz.com; ⊙Jul) for a fortnight in early July. Free concerts take place every day, but big-name gigs cost Sfr75 to Sfr250. Lovers of Freddie Mercury should hightail it to the **Queen Studio Experience** (www.mercuryphoenixtrust.com/studioexperience; Rue du Théâtre 9, Casino Barrière de Montreux; ⊙10.30am-10pm) FREE and also to the **Freddie Mercury statue** on Place du Marché.

There are frequent trains to Lausanne (Sfr13, 20 to 35 minutes) and other lakeside points. Make the scenic journey to Interlaken via the **GoldenPass Line** (www.goldenpass.ch; 2nd class one way Sfr54, three hours, daily; rail passes valid).

Eating & Drinking

★Holy Cow BURGERS €
(www.holycow.ch; Rue Cheneau-de-Bourg 17; burger with chips & drink Sfr16-25; ⊙11am-11pm;) A Lausanne success story, with branches in Geneva, Zürich and France, burgers (beef, chicken or veggie) feature local ingredients, creative toppings and witty names. Grab a beer, sit at a shared wooden table, and wait for your burger and fab fries to arrive in a straw basket. A second outlet can be found at Rue des Terreaux 10.

Café Romand SWISS €
(☎021 312 63 75; www.cafe-romand.ch; Pl St François 2; mains Sfr18-41; ⊙9am-midnight Mon-Sat) Tucked away in an unpromising-looking arcade, this Lausanne legend dating to 1951 is a welcome blast from the past. Locals pour into the broad, somewhat sombre dining area filled with timber tables to revel in fondue, *cervelle au beurre noir* (brains in black butter), tripe, *pied de porc* (pork trotters) and other feisty traditional dishes.

★Great Escape PUB
(☎021 312 31 94; www.the-great.ch; Rue Madeleine 18; ⊙11.30am-late Mon-Fri, from 10am Sat, from noon Sun) Everyone knows the Great Escape, a busy student pub with pub grub (great burgers) and an enviable terrace with a view over Place de la Riponne. From the aforementioned square, walk up staircase Escaliers de l'Université and turn right.

Information

Tourist Office (☎021 613 73 73; www.lausanne-tourisme.ch; Pl de la Gare 9; ⊙9am-7pm) Conveniently located in Lausanne's train station. Other branches are at Lausanne's **cathedral** (Pl de la Cathédrale; ⊙9.30am-6.30pm Mon-Sat, 1-5.30pm Sun Jun-Aug, shorter hours Sep-May) and lakeside in **Ouchy** (☎021 613 73 21; Pl de la Navigation 6; ⊙9am-7pm Apr-Sep, to 6pm Oct-Mar).

Getting There & Away

BOAT

The **CGN** (Compagnie Générale de Navigation; www.cgn.ch) steamer service runs from early April to mid-September to/from Geneva (Sfr45, 3½ hours) via Nyon. Other services lace the lake, including to Montreux (Sfr27, 1½ hours, up to six daily).

TRAIN

There are frequent trains to/from Geneva (Sfr23, 35 to 50 minutes) and Bern (Sfr34, 70 minutes).

Getting Around

Lausanne spans several steep hillsides, so prepare for some good walks.

Buses and trolley buses service most destinations; the vital m2 Métro line (single trip/day pass Sfr2.30/9.30) connects the lake (Ouchy) with the train station (Gare), cathedral area and Flon.

A DAY AT CHARLIE CHAPLIN'S MANSION

Opened in 2016, the engaging **Chaplin's World** (www.chaplinsworld.com; Route de Fenil 2, Corsier-sur-Vevey; adult/child Sfr23/17; ⏲10am-6pm) museum celebrates the life and work of iconic London-born film star Charlie Chaplin. Split between the neoclassical Manoir de Ban – the Corsier-sur-Vevey mansion where Chaplin spent his last quarter century – and a purpose-built interactive studio, the exhibits include multimedia displays, excerpts from Chaplin's films, recreations of film sets, family photos and other evocative memorabilia, right down to Chaplin's trademark hat and cane. A tour of the mansion's splendid gardens rounds out the visit.

From Lausanne, catch a train to Vevey (15 minutes), then bus 212 to the museum (11 minutes, total cost Sfr11.20).

Gruyères

POP 2153

Cheese and featherweight meringues drowned in thick cream are what this dreamy village is all about. Named after the emblematic *gru* (crane) brandished by the medieval Counts of Gruyères, it is a riot of 15th- to 17th-century houses tumbling down a hillock. Its heart is cobbled, a castle is its crowning glory and hard AOC Gruyère (the village is Gruyères, but the 's' is dropped for the cheese) has been made for centuries in its surrounding Alpine pastures. Fondue-serving cafes line the main square.

Sights

Château de Gruyères CASTLE

(☎026 921 21 02; www.chateau-gruyeres.ch; Rue du Château 8; adult/child Sfr12/4; ⏲9am-6pm Apr-Oct, 10am-5pm Nov-Mar) This bewitching turreted castle, home to 19 different Counts of Gruyères, who controlled the Sarine Valley from the 11th to 16th centuries, was rebuilt after a fire in 1493. Inside you can view period furniture, tapestries and modern 'fantasy art', plus watch a 20-minute multimedia film about Gruyères' history. Don't miss the short footpath that weaves its way around the castle. Combined tickets covering the château and other area attractions are available.

La Maison du Gruyère FARM

(☎026 921 84 00; www.lamaisondugruyere.ch; Place de la Gare 3; adult/child Sfr7/6; ⏲9am-6.30pm Jun-Sep, to 6pm Oct-May) The secret behind Gruyère cheese is revealed in Pringy, directly opposite Gruyères train station (1.5km below town). Cheesemaking takes place three to four times daily between 9am and 11am and 12.30pm to 2.30pm. A combined ticket for both the dairy and Château de Gruyères costs Sfr16 (no child combo).

Getting There & Away

Gruyères is served by hourly trains from Montreux (Sfr20.40, 1¼ hours, via Montbovon). The village is a 10-minute walk uphill from the station (or take the free shuttle bus).

VALAIS

This is Matterhorn country, an intoxicating land that seduces the toughest of critics with its endless panoramic vistas and breathtaking views. Switzerland's 10 highest mountains rise to the sky here, while snow fiends ski and board in one of Europe's top resorts, Zermatt.

Zermatt

POP 5759

Since the mid-19th century, Zermatt has starred among Switzerland's glitziest resorts. Today, it attracts intrepid mountaineers and hikers, skiers who cruise at a snail's pace, spellbound by the scenery, and style-conscious darlings flashing designer togs in the lounge bars. But all are smitten with the **Matterhorn** (4478m), the Alps' most famous peak and an unfathomable monolith synonymous with Switzerland that you simply can't quite stop looking at.

Sights & Activities

Zermatt is **skiing** heaven, with mostly long, scenic red runs, plus a smattering of blues for ski virgins and knuckle-whitening blacks for experts. The main skiing areas in winter are **Rothorn**, **Stockhorn** and **Klein Matterhorn** – 350km of ski runs in all, with a link from Klein Matterhorn to the Italian resort of Cervinia and a **freestyle park** with half-pipe for snowboarders. **Summer skiing** (20km of runs) and **boarding** (gravity park at Plateau Rosa on the Theodul glacier) is Europe's most extensive. One-/two-day summer ski passes are Sfr84/125.

Zermatt is also excellent for **hiking**, with 400km of summer trails through some of the most incredible scenery in the Alps – the tourist office has trail maps. For Matterhorn close-ups, nothing beats the highly dramatic **Matterhorn Glacier Trail** (two hours, 6.5km) from Trockener Steg to Schwarzsee; 23 information panels en route tell you everything you could possibly need to know about glaciers and glacial life.

★**Gornergratbahn** RAILWAY
(www.gornergrat.ch; Bahnhofplatz 7; adult/child round trip Sfr94/47; ⏲7am-7.15pm) Europe's highest cogwheel railway has climbed through picture-postcard scenery to **Gornergrat** (3089m) – a 30-minute journey – since 1898. On the way up, sit on the right-hand side of the little red train to gawp at the Matterhorn. Tickets allow you to get on and off en route; there are restaurants at Riffelalp (2211m) and Riffelberg (2582m). In summer an extra train runs once a week at sunrise and sunset – the most spectacular trips of all.

★**Matterhorn Glacier Paradise** CABLE CAR
(www.matterhornparadise.ch; adult/child return Sfr100/50; ⏲8.30am-4.20pm) Views from Zermatt's cable cars are all remarkable, but the Matterhorn Glacier Paradise is the icing on the cake. Ride Europe's highest-altitude cable car to 3883m and gawp at 14 glaciers and 38 mountain peaks over 4000m from the **Panoramic Platform** (only open in good weather). Don't miss the **Glacier Palace**, an ice palace complete with glittering ice sculptures and an ice slide to swoosh down bum first. End with some exhilarating **snow tubing** outside in the snowy surrounds.

Sleeping & Eating

Most places close May to mid- (or late) June and again from October to mid-November.

★**Hotel Bahnhof** HOTEL €
(☎027 967 24 06; www.hotelbahnhof.com; Bahnhofstrasse; dm Sfr35-50, s/d from Sfr80/120; ⏲closed May–mid-Jun & mid-Oct–Nov; 📶) Opposite the train station, these five-star budget digs have comfy beds, spotless bathrooms and family-perfect rooms for four. Dorms (Sfr5 liner obligatory) are cosy and there's a stylish lounge with armchairs to flop in and books to read. No breakfast, but feel free to prepare your own in the snazzy, open-plan kitchen.

SWITZERLAND'S SCENIC TRAINS

Swiss trains, buses and boats are more than a means of getting from A to B. Stunning views invariably make the journey itself the destination. Switzerland boasts the following routes among its classic sightseeing journeys.

You're able to choose just one leg of the trip. Also, scheduled services often ply the same routes for standard fares; these are cheaper than the named trains, which often have cars with extra-large windows and require reservations.

Glacier Express (www.glacierexpress.ch) Hop aboard this red train with floor-to-ceiling windows for the famous eight-hour journey between St Moritz and Zermatt. Scenic highlights include the climb through Alpine meadows to Oberalp Pass (2033m) – the journey's high point between Disentis/Mustér and Andermatt – and the crossing of the iconic 65m-high Landwasser Viaduct between St Moritz and Chur.

Bernina Express (www.rhb.ch) This unforgettable four-hour train ride cuts 145km through the Engadine's glaciated realms, linking Chur, St Moritz and Tirano, Italy. Between May and October, continue 2½ hours by bus from Tirano to Lugano along Italy's Lake Como and Ticino's palm-fringed Lake Lugano.

Jungfrau Region (www.jungfrau.ch) You can spend days ogling stunning Alpine scenery from the trains, cable cars and more here.

GoldenPass Line (www.goldenpass.ch) Travels between Lucerne and Montreux. The journey is in three legs, and you must change trains twice. Regular trains, without panoramic windows, work the whole route hourly.

Centovalli Express (www.centovalli.ch) An underappreciated gem of a line (two hours) that snakes along fantastic river gorges in Switzerland and Italy, from Locarno to Domodossola. Trains run through the day and it is easy to connect to Brig and beyond from Domodossola in Italy.

★ **Snowboat Bar & Yacht Club** INTERNATIONAL €

(☎027 967 43 33; www.zermattsnowboat.com; Vispastrasse 20; mains Sfr22-39; ⏲noon-midnight) This hybrid eating-drinking riverside address, with marigold-yellow deckchairs sprawled across its rooftop sun terrace, is a blessing. When fondue tires, head here for barbecue-sizzled burgers (not just beef, but crab and veggie burgers too), super-power creative salads (the Omega 3 buster is a favourite) and great cocktails. The vibe? 100% friendly, fun and funky.

★ **Chez Vrony** SWISS €€

(☎027 967 25 52; www.chezvrony.ch; Findeln; breakfast Sfr15-28, mains Sfr25-45; ⏲9.15am-5pm Dec-Apr & mid-Jun–mid-Oct) Ride the Sunnegga Express funicular (one-way/round trip Sfr 16/24) to 2288m, then ski down blue piste 6 or summer-hike 15 minutes to Zermatt's tastiest slope-side address in the Findeln hamlet. Keep snug in a blanket or lounge on a sheepskin-cushioned chaise longue and revel in the effortless romance of this century-old farmhouse with potted edelweiss, first-class Matterhorn views and exceptional organic cuisine.

ℹ Getting There & Around

CAR

Zermatt is car-free. Motorists have to park in **Täsch** (☎027 967 12 14; www.matterhorn terminal.ch; per 24hr Sfr15.50) and ride the Zermatt Shuttle train (adult/child Sfr8.40/4.20, 12 minutes, every 20 minutes from 6am to 9.40pm) the last 5km to Zermatt.

TRAIN

Trains depart regularly from Brig – a major rail hub (Sfr38, 1½ hours), stopping at Visp en route. Zermatt is also the starting point of the popular Glacier Express to Graubünden.

BERN

POP 131,554

One of the planet's most underrated capitals, Bern is a fabulous find. With the genteel old soul of a Renaissance man and the heart of a high-flying 21st-century gal, the riverside city is both medieval and modern. The 15th-century Old Town is gorgeous enough to sweep you off your feet and make you forget the century (it's definitely worthy of its 1983 Unesco World Heritage Site status).

Sights

Bern's flag-bedecked **medieval centre** is an attraction in its own right, with 6km of covered arcades and cellar shops and bars descending from the streets. After a devastating fire in 1405, the wooden city was rebuilt in today's sandstone. The city's 11 **decorative fountains** (1545) depict historical and folkloric characters. Most are along Marktgasse as it becomes Kramgasse and Gerechtigkeitsgasse, but the most famous lies in Kornhausplatz: the **Kindlifresserbrunnen** (Ogre Fountain) of a giant snacking...on children.

★ **Zytglogge** TOWER

(Marktgasse) Bern's most famous Old Town sight, this ornate clock tower once formed part of the city's western gate (1191–1256). Crowds congregate to watch its revolving figures twirl at four minutes before the hour, after which the chimes begin. Tours enter the tower to see the clock mechanism from May to October; contact the tourist office for details. The clock tower supposedly helped Albert Einstein hone his special theory of relativity, developed while working as a patent clerk in Bern.

Münster CATHEDRAL

(www.bernermuenster.ch; Münsterplatz 1; tower adult/child Sfr5/2; ⏲10am-5pm Mon-Sat, 11.30am-5pm Sun Apr–mid-Oct, noon-4pm Mon-Fri, 10am-5pm Sat, 11.30am-4pm Sun mid-Oct–Mar) Bern's 15th-century Gothic cathedral boasts Switzerland's loftiest spire (100m); climb the 344-step spiral staircase for vertiginous views. Coming down, stop by the **Upper Bells** (1356), rung at 11am, noon and 3pm daily, and the three 10-tonne **Lower Bells** (Switzerland's largest). Don't miss the main portal's **Last Judgement**, which portrays Bern's mayor going to heaven, while his Zürich counterpart is shown into hell. Afterwards, wander through the adjacent **Münsterplattform**, a bijou clifftop park with a sunny pavilion cafe.

★ **Zentrum Paul Klee** MUSEUM

(☎031 359 01 01; www.zpk.org; Monument im Fruchtland 3; adult/child Sfr20/7; ⏲10am-5pm Tue-Sun) Bern's answer to the Guggenheim, Renzo Piano's architecturally bold 150m-long wave-like edifice houses an exhibition space that showcases rotating works from Paul Klee's prodigious and often playful career. Interactive computer displays and audioguides help interpret the Swiss-born artist's work.

Next door, the fun-packed **Kindermuseum Creaviva** (☎031 359 01 61; www.creaviva-zpk.org; ⏰10am-5pm Tue-Sun; 👪) FREE lets kids experiment with hands-on art exhibits or create original artwork with the atelier's materials during the weekend **Five Franc Studio** (www.creaviva-zpk.org/5-franc-studio; Sfr5; ⏰10am-4.30pm Sat & Sun; 👪).

Bus 12 runs from Bubenbergplatz direct to the museum.

Sleeping

Hotel Landhaus HOTEL €
(☎031 348 03 05; www.landhausbern.ch; Altenbergstrasse 4; dm Sfr38, s Sfr115-130, d Sfr160-180, s/d without bathroom from Sfr85/120; P@令) Fronted by the river and Old Town spires, this well-run boho hotel offers a mix of stylish six-bed dorms, family rooms and doubles. Its buzzing ground-floor cafe and terrace attracts a cheery crowd. Breakfast (included with private rooms) costs Sfr10 extra for dorm-dwellers.

Hotel Schweizerhof LUXURY HOTEL €€€
(☎031 326 80 80; www.schweizerhof-bern.ch; Bahnhofplatz 11; s Sfr359-640, d Sfr449-790; P❄@令) This classy five-star offers lavish accommodation with excellent amenities and service. A hop, skip and a jump from the train station, it's geared for both business and pleasure.

Eating & Drinking

Look for interesting cafes and bistros scattered amid the arcades on Old Town streets including Zeughausgasse, Rathausgasse, Marktgasse and Kramgasse.

Altes Tramdepot SWISS €€
(☎031 368 14 15; www.altestramdepot.ch; Grosser Muristalden 6, Am Bärengraben; mains Sfr18-44; ⏰11am-12.30am Mon-Fri, from 10am Sat & Sun) At this cavernous microbrewery, Swiss specialities compete against wok-cooked stir-fries for your affection, and the microbrews go down a treat: sample three different varieties for Sfr10.90, four for Sfr14.60, or five for Sfr18.20.

Café des Pyrénées BAR
(☎031 311 30 63; Kornhausplatz 17; ⏰9am-11.30pm Mon-Wed, to 12.30am Thu-Sat, noon-9pm Sun) This bohemian corner joint, under new ownership as of 2016, remains a beloved Bern institution for its traditional Parisian cafe-bar vibe. Its central location near the tram tracks makes for good people-watching.

Information

Tourist Office (☎031 328 12 12; www.bern.com; Bahnhoftplatz 10a; ⏰9am-7pm Mon-Sat, to 6pm Sun) Street-level floor of the train station. City tours, free hotel bookings, internet access. There's also a branch near the bear park (Grosser Muristalden 6, Bärengraben; ⏰9am-6pm Jun-Sep, 10am-4pm Mar-May & Oct, 11am-4pm Nov-Feb).

Getting There & Around

Frequent trains connect to most Swiss cities, including Geneva (Sfr51, 1¾ hours), Basel (Sfr41, 55 minutes) and Zürich (Sfr51, 55 minutes to 1½ hours).

Buses and trams are operated by **BernMobil** (www.bernmobil.ch); many depart from stops near Bahnhofplatz.

CENTRAL SWITZERLAND & BERNESE OBERLAND

These two regions should come with a health warning – caution: may cause breathlessness as the sun rises and sets over Lake Lucerne, trembling before the north face of Eiger and uncontrollable bouts of euphoria at the foot of Jungfrau.

Lucerne

POP 81,295

Recipe for a gorgeous Swiss city: take a cobalt lake ringed by mountains of myth, add a medieval Old Town and sprinkle with covered bridges, sunny plazas, candy-coloured houses and waterfront promenades. Bright, beautiful Lucerne has been Little Miss Popular since the likes of Goethe, Queen Victoria and Wagner savoured her views in the 19th century.

Sights

Your first port of call should be the medieval **Old Town**, with its ancient rampart walls and towers. Wander the cobblestone lanes and squares, pondering 15th-century buildings with painted facades and the two much-photographed covered bridges over the Reuss.

★**Kapellbrücke** BRIDGE
(Chapel Bridge) You haven't really been to Lucerne until you have strolled the creaky 14th-century Kapellbrücke, spanning the Reuss River in the Old Town. The octagonal

WORTH A TRIP

MOUNTAIN DAY TRIPS FROM LUCERNE

Among the several (heavily marketed) day trips from Lucerne, consider the one to 2132m-high **Mt Pilatus** (www.pilatus.com). From May to October, you can reach the peak on a classic 'golden round-trip'. Board the lake steamer from Lucerne to Alpnachstad, then rise with the world's steepest cog railway to Mt Pilatus. From the summit, cable cars bring you down to Kriens via Fräkmüntegg and Krienseregg, where bus 1 takes you back to Lucerne. The return trip costs Sfr106 (less with valid Swiss, Eurail or InterRail passes).

water tower is original, but its gabled roof is a modern reconstruction, rebuilt after a disastrous fire in 1993. As you cross the bridge, note Heinrich Wägmann's 17th-century triangular roof panels, showing important events from Swiss history and mythology. The icon is at its most photogenic when bathed in soft golden light at dusk.

★Museum Sammlung Rosengart MUSEUM

(041 220 16 60; www.rosengart.ch; Pilatusstrasse 10; adult/child Sfr18/10; 10am-6pm) Lucerne's blockbuster cultural attraction is the Sammlung Rosengart, occupying a graceful neoclassical pile in the heart of town. It showcases the outstanding stash of Angela Rosengart, a Swiss art dealer and close friend of Picasso. Alongside works by the great Spanish master are paintings and sketches by Klee, Cézanne, Renoir, Chagall, Kandinsky, Miró, Matisse, Modigliani and Monet, among others. Complementing this collection are some 200 photographs by David Douglas Duncan documenting the last 17 years of Picasso's life.

★Lion Monument MONUMENT

(Löwendenkmal; Denkmalstrasse) By far the most touching of the 19th-century sights that lured so many British to Lucerne is the Lion Monument. Lukas Ahorn carved this 10m-long sculpture of a dying lion into the rock face in 1820 to commemorate Swiss soldiers who died defending King Louis XVI during the French Revolution. Mark Twain once called it the 'saddest and most moving piece of rock in the world'. For *Narnia* fans it often evokes Aslan at the stone table.

Verkehrshaus MUSEUM

(Swiss Museum of Transport; 0900 333 456; www.verkehrshaus.ch; Lidostrasse 5; adult/child Sfr30/15; 10am-6pm Apr-Oct, to 5pm Nov-Mar;) A great kid-pleaser, the fascinating interactive Verkehrshaus is deservedly Switzerland's most popular museum. Alongside rockets, steam locomotives, aeroplanes, vintage cars and dugout canoes are hands-on activities such as pedalo boats, flight simulators, broadcasting studios and a walkable 1:20,000-scale map of Switzerland.

The museum also shelters a **planetarium** (adult/child Sfr15/9), Switzerland's largest **3D cinema** (www.filmtheater.ch; adult/child Sfr18/14), and the **Swiss Chocolate Adventure** (adult/child Sfr15/9), a 20-minute ride that whirls visitors through multimedia exhibits on the origins, history, production and distribution of chocolate, from Ghana to Switzerland and beyond.

Spreuerbrücke BRIDGE

(Spreuer Bridge; btwn Kasernenplatz & Mühlenplatz) Downriver from Kapellbrücke, this 1408 structure is darker and smaller but entirely original. Lore has it that this was the only bridge where Lucerne's medieval villagers were allowed to throw *Spreu* (chaff) into the river. Here, the roof panels consist of artist Caspar Meglinger's movie-storyboard-style sequence of paintings, *The Dance of Death*, showing how the plague affected all levels of society.

Sleeping

Backpackers Lucerne HOSTEL €

(041 360 04 20; www.backpackerslucerne.ch; Alpenquai 42; dm/tr Sfr33/111, tw Sfr78-84; reception 7.30-10am & 4-11pm; @) Just opposite the lake, a 15-minute walk southeast of the station, this is a soulful place to crash, with art-slung walls, bubbly staff and immaculate dorms with balconies. There's no breakfast, but guests have access to a well-equipped kitchen.

Hotel Waldstätterhof HOTEL €€

(041 227 12 71; www.hotel-waldstaetterhof.ch; Zentralstrasse 4; s Sfr190, d Sfr270-300, ste Sfr340-380; P) Opposite the train station, this hotel with faux-Gothic exterior offers smart, modern rooms with hardwood-style floors and high ceilings, plus excellent service.

The Hotel HOTEL €€€
(☎041 226 86 86; www.the-hotel.ch; Sempacherstrasse 14; r Sfr255-395, ste Sfr555-595; ❄@📶) This shamelessly hip hotel, bearing the imprint of architect Jean Nouvel, is all streamlined chic, with refined suites featuring stills from movie classics on the ceilings. Downstairs, the hotel boasts one of Lucerne's trendiest restaurants, and the gorgeous green park across the street is a cool place to idle.

Eating & Drinking

★**Grottino 1313** ITALIAN €€
(☎041 610 13 13; www.grottino1313.ch; Industriestrasse 7; lunch menus Sfr20-38, dinner menu Sfr64; ⏰11am-2pm & 6-11.30pm Mon-Fri, 6-11.30pm Sat & Sun) Offering a welcome escape from Lucerne's tourist throngs, this relaxed yet stylish eatery serves ever-changing 'surprise' menus featuring starters like chestnut soup with figs, creative pasta dishes, meats cooked over an open fire and scrumptious desserts. The gravel-strewn, herb-fringed front patio is lovely on a summer afternoon, while the candlelit interior exudes sheer cosiness on a chilly evening.

★**Wirtshaus Galliker** SWISS €€
(☎041 240 10 02; Schützenstrasse 1; mains Sfr21-51; ⏰11.30am-2pm & 6-8.30pm Tue-Sat) Passionately run by the Galliker family for over four generations, this old-style, wood-panelled tavern attracts a lively bunch of regulars. Motherly waitresses dish up Lucerne soul food (rösti, *chögalipaschtetli* and the like) that is batten-the-hatches filling.

Rathaus Bräuerei BREWERY
(☎041 410 52 57; Unter den Egg 2; ⏰11.30am-midnight Mon-Sat, to 11pm Sun) Sip home-brewed beer under the vaulted arches of this buzzy tavern near Kapellbrücke, or nab a pavement table and watch the river flow.

Information

Lake Lucerne Region Visitors Card (Vierwaldstättersee Gästekarte; www.luzern.com/en/festivals-events/visitors-card) Stamped by your hotel, this free card entitles visitors to discounts on various museums, sporting facilities, cable cars and lake cruises in Lucerne and the surrounding area.

Tourist Office (☎041 227 17 17; www.luzern.com; Zentralstrasse 5; ⏰8.30am-7pm Mon-Fri, 9am-7pm Sat, 9am-5pm Sun May-Oct, shorter hours Nov-Apr) Reached from Zentralstrasse or platform 3 of the Hauptbahnhof. Offers city walking tours (Sfr18). Call for hotel reservations.

Getting There & Around

Frequent trains serve Interlaken Ost (Sfr33, 1¾ hours), Bern (Sfr36 to Sfr40, one hour), Lugano (Sfr61, two hours) and Zürich (Sfr26, 45 minutes to one hour).

SGV (www.lakelucerne.ch) operates extensive boat services on Lake Lucerne (including some paddle steamers). Rail passes are good for free or discounted travel.

Interlaken

POP 5692

Once Interlaken made the Victorians swoon with its dreamy mountain vistas, viewed from the chandelier-lit confines of its grand hotels. Today, it makes daredevils scream with its adrenalin-loaded adventures. Straddling the glittering Lakes Thun and Brienz (thus the name), and dazzled by the pearly whites of Eiger, Mönch and Jungfrau, Interlaken boasts exceptional scenery.

Sights & Activities

Switzerland is the world's second-biggest adventure-sports centre and Interlaken is its busiest hub. Sample prices are Sfr120 for rafting or canyoning, Sfr140 for hydrospeeding, Sfr130 to Sfr180 for bungee or canyon jumping, Sfr170 for tandem paragliding, Sfr180 for ice climbing, Sfr220 for hang-gliding and Sfr430 for skydiving. A half-day mountain-bike tour will set you back around Sfr25.

Harder Kulm MOUNTAIN
(www.jungfrau.ch/harderkulm; adult/child Sfr16/8) For far-reaching views to the 4000m giants, take the eight-minute **funicular ride** (adult/child return Sfr32/16) to 1322m Harder Kulm. Many hiking paths begin here, and the vertigo-free can enjoy the panorama from the **Zweiseensteg** (Two Lake Bridge) jutting out above the valley. The wildlife park near the valley station is home to Alpine critters, including marmots and ibex.

Sleeping

★**Backpackers Villa Sonnenhof** HOSTEL €
(☎033 826 71 71; www.villa.ch; Alpenstrasse 16; dm Sfr39.50-47, d Sfr110-148; P📶) Repeatedly voted one of Europe's best hostels, Sonnenhof is a slick, ecofriendly combination of ultramodern chalet and elegant art-nouveau villa. Dorms are immaculate, and some have balconies with Jungfrau views. There's also a relaxed lounge, a well-equipped kitchen, a kids' playroom and a vast backyard for mountain gazing. Special family rates are available.

★ Victoria-Jungfrau Grand Hotel & Spa LUXURY HOTEL €€€
(☎033 828 28 28; www.victoria-jungfrau.ch; Höheweg 41; d Sfr479-749, junior ste from Sfr539, ste from Sfr950; P @ ☎ ≋) The reverent hush and impeccable service here (as well as the prices) evoke an era when only royalty and the seriously wealthy travelled. A perfect melding of well-preserved art-nouveau features and modern luxury make this Interlaken's answer to Raffles – with plum views of Jungfrau, three first-class restaurants and a gorgeous spa to boot.

Eating & Drinking

Höheweg, east of Interlaken Ost train station, is lined with ethnic eateries with reasonable prices.

Sandwich Bar SANDWICHES €
(www.sandwichbar.ch; Rosenstrasse 5; sandwiches Sfr6-9.50; ⌚7.30am-7pm Mon-Fri, 8am-5pm Sat) Choose your bread and get creative with fillings like air-dried ham with sun-dried tomatoes and brie with walnuts. Or try the soups, salads, toasties and locally made ice cream.

Information

Tourist Office (☎033 826 53 00; www.interlakentourism.ch; Marktgasse 1; ⌚8am-7pm Mon-Fri, to 5pm Sat, 10am-4pm Sun Jul & Aug, shorter hours Sep-Jun) Relocated next to the post office in 2017, Interlaken's well-stocked, well-staffed tourist office also provides hotel booking services.

Getting There & Away

There are two train stations. Interlaken West is slightly closer to the centre and is a stop for trains to Bern (Sfr29, 50 minutes). Interlaken Ost (East) is the rail hub for all lines, including the scenic ones up into the Jungfrau region and the lovely GoldenPass Line to Lucerne (Sfr33, 1¾ hours).

Jungfrau Region

If the Bernese Oberland is Switzerland's Alpine heart, the Jungfrau region is where yours will skip a beat. Presided over by glacier-encrusted monoliths Eiger, Mönch and Jungfrau (Ogre, Monk and Virgin), the scenery stirs the soul and strains the neck muscles. It's a magnet for skiers and snowboarders with its 214km of pistes, 44 lifts and much more; a one-day ski pass for either Grindelwald-Wengen or Mürren-Schilthorn costs adult/child Sfr63/32.

Come summer, hundreds of kilometres of walking trails allow you to capture the landscape from many angles, but it never looks less than astonishing.

Getting There & Around

Hourly trains (www.jungfrau.ch) depart for the Jungfrau region from Interlaken Ost station. Sit in the front half of the train for Lauterbrunnen (Sfr7.60) or the back half for Grindelwald (Sfr11.40).

From Grindelwald, trains ascend to Kleine Scheidegg (Sfr31), where you can transfer for Jungfraujoch. From Lauterbrunnen, trains ascend to Wengen (Sfr6.80) and continue to Kleine Scheidegg (Sfr24) for Jungfraujoch.

You can reach Mürren two ways from Lauterbrunnen: with a bus and cable car via Stechelberg (Sfr16.40) or with a cable car and train via Grütschalp (Sfr11.40). Do a circle trip for the full experience. Gimmelwald is reached by cable car from Stechelberg and Mürren.

Many cable cars close for servicing in April and November.

Grindelwald

POP 3740

Grindelwald's charms were discovered by skiers and hikers in the late 19th century, making it one of Switzerland's oldest resorts and the Jungfrau's largest. It has lost none of its appeal over the decades, with archetypal Alpine chalets and verdant pastures set against the chiselled features of the Eiger north face.

Activities

The **Grindelwald-First** skiing area has a mix of cruisy red and challenging black runs stretching from Oberjoch at 2486m to the village at 1050m, plus 15.5km of well-groomed cross-country ski trails. In the summer it caters to hikers with 90km of trails at about 1200m, 48km of which are open year-round.

★ Kleine Scheidegg Walk HIKING
One of the region's most stunning day hikes is this 15km trek from Grindelwald Grund to Wengen via Kleine Scheidegg, which heads up through wildflower-freckled meadows to skirt below the Eiger's north face and reach Kleine Scheidegg, granting arresting views of the 'Big Three'. Allow around 5½ to six hours. The best map is the SAW 1:50,000 *Interlaken* (Sfr22.50).

JUNGFRAU REGION HIKING 101

There are hundreds of hikes along the hundreds of kilometres of trails in the Jungfrau region; all include some of the world's most stunning scenery. Every skill and fortitude level is accommodated and options abound. Here are two to get you started:

Grütschalp to Mürren Ride the cable car up from Lauterbrunnen and follow the trail along the railway tracks. The walk to Mürren takes about an hour and is mostly level. There are unbeatable views, Alpine woods and babbling glacier-fed streams.

Männlichen to Kleine Scheidegg Reach the Männlichen lift station by cable car from Wengen or Grindelwald. Now follow the well-marked, spectacular path down to Kleine Scheidegg. It takes about 90 minutes and you have nothing but Alps in front of you.

Grindelwald Sports ADVENTURE SPORTS
(☎033 854 12 80; www.grindelwaldsports.ch; Dorfstrasse 103; ⏲8.30am-7pm) Opposite the tourist office, this outfit arranges mountain climbing, ski and snowboard instruction, canyon jumping and glacier bungee jumping at the Gletscherschlucht. It also houses a cosy cafe and sells walking guides.

Sleeping

Mountain Hostel HOSTEL €
(☎033 854 38 38; www.mountainhostel.ch; Grundstrasse 58; dm Sfr35-39, d Sfr98, q Sfr156; P 📶) In a bright blue building halfway between Grindelwald Grund train station and the Männlichen cable-car station, this is an ideal base for sports junkies, with well-kept dorms and a helpful crew. There's a beer garden, ski storage, TV lounge and mountain and e-bike rental.

★ **Gletschergarten** HISTORIC HOTEL €€
(☎033 853 17 21; www.hotel-gletschergarten.ch; Obere Gletscherstrasse 1; s Sfr130-170, d Sfr230-320; P 📶) The sweet Breitenstein family make you feel at home in their rustic timber chalet, brimming with heirlooms from landscape paintings to snapshots of Elsbeth's grandfather who had 12 children (those were the days...). Decked out in pine and flowery fabrics, the rooms have balconies facing Unterer Gletscher at the front and Wetterhorn (best for sunset) at the back.

Wengen

POP 1300

Photogenically poised on a mountain ledge, Wengen has celestial views of the glacier-capped giant peaks' silent majesty as well as the shimmering waterfalls spilling into the Lauterbrunnen Valley below.

The village is car-free and can only be reached by train. It's a fabulous hub for **hiking** for much of the year as well as **skiing** in winter.

From Wengen's train station, loop back under the tracks and head three minutes downhill to **Hotel Bären** (☎033 855 14 19; www.baeren-wengen.ch; s Sfr190-280, d Sfr220-310, f Sfr340-470, all incl half-board; 📶), a snug log chalet with bright, cosy rooms; the affable Brunner family serves a hearty breakfast and delicious seasonal cuisine in the attached restaurant. For superb regional fare in an even dreamier setting, check out the leafy mountain-facing terrace or the pine-clad, candlelit dining room at **Restaurant 1903** (☎033 855 34 22; www.hotel-schoenegg.ch; mains Sfr35-58; ⏲6.30-10pm, closed May & mid-Oct–mid-Dec), a 250m walk uphill from the station.

Jungfraujoch

Jungfraujoch (3471m) is a once-in-a-lifetime trip and there's good reason why two million people a year visit Europe's highest train station. Clear good weather is essential; check www.jungfrau.ch for current conditions, and don't forget warm clothing, sunglasses and sunscreen.

From Interlaken Ost, the journey time is two to 2½ hours each way (Sfr210.80 return, discounts with rail passes). The last train back sets off at 6.43pm in summer and 4.43pm in winter. From May to October there's a cheaper Good Morning Ticket costing Sfr145 if you take one of the first two trains from Interlaken Ost (6.35am or 7.05am) and leave the summit by 1pm.

Gimmelwald

POP 130

Decades ago some anonymous backpacker scribbled these words in the guestbook at the Mountain Hostel: 'If heaven isn't what

it's cracked up to be, send me back to Gimmelwald'. Enough said. When the sun is out in Gimmelwald, this pipsqueak of a village will simply take your breath away. Sit outside and listen to the distant roar of avalanches on the sheer mountain faces arrayed before you.

The charming, spotless **Esther's Guest House** (☎033 855 54 88; www.esthersguesthouse.ch; Kirchstatt; s Sfr60-90, d Sfr120-180, apt Sfr240-250; 📶) is run with love and care. For an extra Sfr16, you'll be served a delicious breakfast of homemade bread, cheese and yoghurt.

Mürren

POP 450

Arrive on a clear evening when the sun hangs low on the horizon, and you'll think you've died and gone to heaven. Car-free Mürren *is* storybook Switzerland.

Sleeping options near the train station include **Eiger Guesthouse** (☎033 856 54 60; www.eigerguesthouse.com; s Sfr95-140, d Sfr120-200, q Sfr180-250; 📶), with its downstairs pub serving tasty food, and **Hotel Eiger** (☎033 856 54 54; www.hoteleiger.com; s Sfr183-228, d Sfr275-370, ste Sfr420-1250; 📶🏊), a huge wooden chalet with swimming pool and picture-windows perfectly framing the Eiger, Mönch and Jungfrau.

Schilthorn

There's a tremendous 360-degree panorama available from the 2970m Schilthorn. On a clear day, you can see over 200 peaks, from Titlis to Mont Blanc and across to the German Black Forest. Note that this was the site of Blofeld's HQ in the under-appreciated 1969 James Bond film *On Her Majesty's Secret Service*. The **Bond World 007** (www.schilthorn.ch; Schilthorn; free with cable-car ticket; ⏲8am-6pm) interactive exhibition gives you the chance to pose for photos secret-agent style and relive movie moments in a helicopter and bobsled.

From Interlaken Ost, take a Sfr129.60 excursion to Schilthorn via Lauterbrunnen, Grütschalp and Mürren, returning via Stechelberg to Interlaken. A return from Lauterbrunnen costs Sfr102 via Grütschalp and Mürren, or Sfr111 via the Stechelberg cable car. A return from Mürren is Sfr80. Ask about discounts for early-morning trips. There are discounts with rail passes.

ZÜRICH

POP 396,955

Culturally vibrant, efficiently run and attractively set at the meeting of river and lake, Zürich is regularly recognised as one of the world's most liveable cities. Long known as a savvy, hard-working financial centre, Switzerland's largest and wealthiest metropolis has also emerged in the 21st century as one of central Europe's hippest destinations, with an artsy, post-industrial edge that is epitomised in its exuberant summer Street Parade.

Sights & Activities

The cobbled streets of the pedestrian Old Town line both sides of the river, while the bank vaults beneath Bahnhofstrasse, the city's most elegant shopping street, are said to be crammed with gold. On Sunday all of Zürich strolls around the lake – on a clear day you'll glimpse the Alps in the distance.

★Fraumünster CATHEDRAL

(www.fraumuenster.ch/en; Münsterhof; Sfr5 incl audioguide; ⏲10am-6pm Mar-Oct, to 5pm Nov-Feb) The 13th-century cathedral is renowned for its stunning stained-glass windows, designed by the Russian-Jewish master Marc Chagall (1887–1985), who executed the series of five windows in the choir stalls in 1971 and the rose window in the southern transept in 1978. The rose window in the northern transept was created by Augusto Giacometti in 1945. Admission includes a multilingual audioguide.

★Kunsthaus MUSEUM

(☎044 253 84 84; www.kunsthaus.ch; Heimplatz 1; adult/child Sfr16/free, Wed free; ⏲10am-8pm Wed & Thu, to 6pm Tue & Fri-Sun) Zürich's impressive fine-arts gallery boasts a rich collection of largely European art. It stretches from the Middle Ages through a mix of Old Masters to Alberto Giacometti stick figures, Monet and Van Gogh masterpieces, Rodin sculptures, and other 19th- and 20th-century art. Swiss Rail and Museum Passes don't provide free admission but the ZürichCard does.

Schweizerisches Landesmuseum MUSEUM

(Swiss National Museum; ☎058 466 65 11; www.nationalmuseum.ch/e/zuerich; Museumstrasse 2; adult/child Sfr10/free; ⏲10am-5pm Tue, Wed & Fri-Sun, to 7pm Thu) Inside a purpose-built cross between a mansion and a castle sprawls this

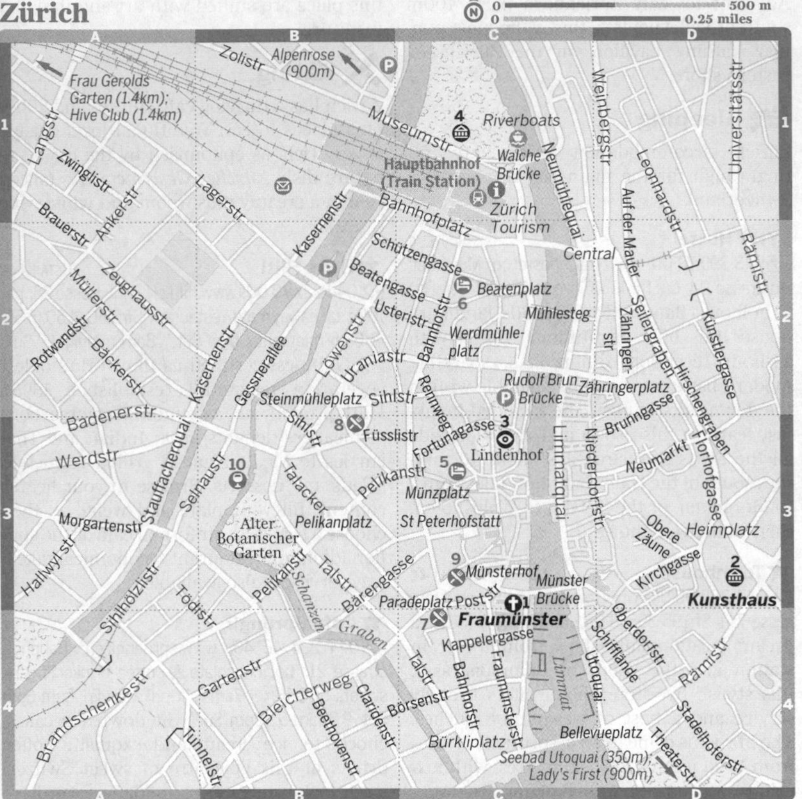

Zürich

Top Sights
1 Fraumünster C3
2 Kunsthaus D3

Sights
3 Lindenhof C3
4 Schweizerisches Landesmuseum C1

Sleeping
5 Hotel Widder C3
6 Townhouse C2

Eating
7 Café Sprüngli C4
8 Haus Hiltl B3
9 Zeughauskeller C3

Drinking & Nightlife
10 Rimini Bar B3

eclectic and imaginatively presented museum. The permanent collection offers an extensive tour through Swiss history, with exhibits ranging from elaborately carved and painted sleds to household and religious artefacts to a series of reconstructed historical rooms spanning six centuries. In August 2016 the museum celebrated a major expansion with the opening of its new archaeology section in a brand-new wing.

Lindenhof SQUARE

Spectacular views across the Limmat to the Grossmünster from a tree-shaded hilltop park, smack in the heart of the Aldstadt (Old Town). Bring a picnic and watch the boules players while you eat.

Seebad Utoquai SWIMMING

(☎044 251 61 51; www.bad-utoquai.ch; Utoquai 49; adult/child Sfr8/4; ⏰7am-8pm mid-May–late Sep)

Adjacent to leafy Zürichhorn park, 400m south of Bellevueplatz, this is the most popular bathing pavilion on the Zürichsee's eastern shore.

Sleeping

Zürich accommodation prices are fittingly high for the main city of expensive Switzerland.

SYHA Hostel HOSTEL €

(043 399 78 00; www.youthhostel.ch; Mutschellenstrasse 114; dm Sfr43-46, s/d Sfr120/144;) A bulbous, Band-Aid-pink 1960s landmark houses this busy, institutional hostel with 24-hour reception, dining hall, sparkling modern bathrooms and dependable wi-fi in the downstairs lounge. The included breakfast features miso soup and rice alongside all the Swiss standards. It's about 20 minutes south of the Hauptbahnhof. Take tram 7 to Morgental, or the S-Bahn to Wollishofen, then walk five minutes.

★**Townhouse** BOUTIQUE HOTEL €€

(044 200 95 95; www.townhouse.ch; Schützengasse 7; s Sfr195-395, d Sfr225-425;) With a dream location only steps from the train station and the shops of Bahnhofstrasse, this stylish five-storey hotel offers friendly service and a host of welcoming touches. The 21 rooms come in an assortment of sizes from 15 sq metres to 35 sq metres, with luxurious wallpapers, wall hangings, parquet floors, retro furniture, DVD players and iPod docking stations.

Lady's First HOTEL €€

(044 380 80 10; www.ladysfirst.ch; Mainaustrasse 24; r Sfr180-338;) Despite the name, discerning guests of all genders are welcome at this attractive hotel near the opera house and lake – though the attached wellness centre with its rooftop terrace is open to women only. The immaculate, generally spacious rooms abound in aesthetic touches such as traditional parquet flooring and designer furnishings.

Hotel Widder HOTEL €€€

(044 224 25 26; www.widderhotel.ch; Rennweg 7; s/d from Sfr523/625;) A supremely stylish hotel in the equally grand district of Augustiner, the Widder is a pleasing fusion of modernity and traditional charm. Rooms and public areas across the eight individually decorated town houses that make up this place are stuffed with art and designer furniture.

Eating

Zürich has a thriving cafe culture and 2000-plus places to eat. Traditional local cuisine is very rich, as epitomised by the city's signature dish, *Zürcher Geschnetzeltes* (sliced veal in a creamy mushroom and white wine sauce).

★**Haus Hiltl** VEGETARIAN €

(044 227 70 00; www.hiltl.ch; Sihlstrasse 28; per 100g takeaway/cafe/restaurant Sfr3.50/4.50/5.50; 6am-midnight Mon-Sat, 8am-midnight Sun;) Guinness-certified as the world's oldest vegetarian restaurant (established 1898), Hiltl proffers an astounding smorgasbord of meatless delights, from Indian and Thai curries to Mediterranean grilled veggies to salads and desserts. Browse to your heart's content, fill your plate and weigh it, then choose a seat in the informal cafe or the spiffier adjoining restaurant (economical takeaway service is also available).

★**Café Sprüngli** SWEETS €

(044 224 46 46; www.spruengli.ch; Bahnhofstrasse 21; hot chocolate & coffee drinks Sfr5-14, sweets Sfr8-16; 7am-6.30pm Mon-Fri, 8am-6pm Sat, 9.30am-5.30pm Sun) Sit down for cakes, chocolate, ice cream and exquisite coffee drinks at this epicentre of sweet Switzerland, in business since 1836. You can have a light lunch too, but whatever you do, don't fail to check out the heavenly chocolate shop around the corner on Paradeplatz.

★**Alpenrose** SWISS €€

(044 431 11 66; www.restaurantalpenrose.ch; Fabrikstrasse 12; lunch menus Sfr21-25, dinner mains Sfr22-38; 9am-11.30pm Tue-Fri, 5-11.30pm Sat & Sun) With its tall stencilled windows, warm wood panelling and stucco ceiling ornamentation, the Alpenrose exudes cosy old world charm, and the cuisine here lives up to the promise. Hearty Swiss classics such as herb-stuffed trout with homemade *Spätzli* (egg noodles) and buttered carrots are exquisitely prepared and presented, accompanied by a good wine list and a nice selection of desserts.

Zeughauskeller SWISS €€

(044 220 15 15; www.zeughauskeller.ch; Bahnhofstrasse 28a; mains Sfr19-37; 11.30am-11pm;) The menu (in eight languages) at this

huge, atmospheric beer hall with ample sidewalk seating offers more than a dozen varieties of sausage, along with numerous other Swiss specialities, including some vegetarian options.

Drinking & Entertainment

Options abound across town, but the bulk of the more animated drinking dens are in Züri-West, especially along Langstrasse in Kreis 4 and Hardstrasse in Kreis 5.

★Frau Gerolds Garten BAR
(www.fraugerold.ch; Geroldstrasse 23/23a; ⏲bar-restaurant 11am-midnight Mon-Sat, noon-10pm Sun Apr-Sep, 6pm-midnight Mon-Sat Oct-Mar, market & shops 11am-7pm Mon-Fri, to 6pm Sat year-round; 🚸) Hmm, where to start? The wine bar? The margarita bar? The gin bar? Whichever poison you choose, this wildly popular focal point of Zürich's summer drinking scene is pure unadulterated fun and one of the best grown-up playgrounds in Europe.

Strewn with shipping containers, overhung with multicoloured fairy lights and sandwiched between cheery flower beds and a screeching railyard, its outdoor seating options range from picnic tables to pillow-strewn terraces to a 2nd-floor sundeck. In winter, the restaurant moves indoors to a funky pavilion and great fondue warms the soul.

★Rimini Bar BAR
(www.rimini.ch; Badweg 10; ⏲7.15pm-midnight Sun-Thu, 6.45pm-midnight Fri, 2pm-midnight Sat Apr-Oct) Secluded behind a fence along the Sihl River, this bar at the Männerbad public baths is one of Zürich's most inviting open-air drinking spots. Its vast wood deck is adorned with red-orange party lights, picnic tables and throw cushions for lounging, accompanied by the sound of water from the adjacent pools. Open in good weather only.

Hive Club CLUB
(☎044 271 12 10; www.hiveclub.ch; Geroldstrasse 5; ⏲11pm-4am Thu, to 7am Fri, to 9am Sat) Electronic music creates the buzz at this artsy, alternative club adjacent to Frau Gerolds Garten in Kreis 5. Enter through an alley strung with multicoloured umbrellas, giant animal heads, mushrooms and watering cans. Big-name DJs keep things going into the wee hours three nights a week.

Rote Fabrik LIVE MUSIC
(☎music 044 485 58 68, theatre 044 485 58 28; www.rotefabrik.ch; Seestrasse 395) With a fabulous lakeside location, this multifaceted performing-arts centre stages rock, jazz and hip-hop concerts, original-language films, theatre and dance performances. There's also a bar and a restaurant. Take bus 161 or 165 from Bürkliplatz.

ℹ Information

Zürich Tourism (☎044 215 40 00, hotel reservations 044 215 40 40; www.zuerich.com; train station; ⏲8am-8.30pm Mon-Sat, 8.30am to 6.30pm Sun May-Oct, 8.30am-7pm Mon-Sat, 9am-6pm Sun Nov-Apr)

ℹ Getting There & Away

AIR

Zürich Airport (ZRH; ☎043 816 22 11; www.zurich-airport.com), 9km north of the centre, is Switzerland's main airport.

TRAIN

Direct trains run to Stuttgart (Sfr63, three hours), Munich (Sfr96, 4¼ hours), Innsbruck (Sfr76, 3½ hours) and other international destinations.

There are regular direct departures to most major Swiss towns, such as Lucerne (Sfr26, 45 to 50 minutes), Bern (Sfr51, one to 1¼ hours) and Basel (Sfr34, 55 minutes to 1¼ hours).

ℹ Getting Around

TO/FROM THE AIRPORT

Up to nine trains an hour run in each direction between the airport and the main train station (Sfr6.80, nine to 13 minutes).

BICYCLE

Züri Rollt (☎044 415 67 67; www.schweizrollt.ch) allows visitors to borrow or rent bikes from a handful of locations, including Velostation Nord across the road from the north side of the Hauptbahnhof. Bring ID and leave Sfr20 as a deposit. Rental is free if you bring the bike back on the same day and Sfr10 a day if you keep it overnight.

PUBLIC TRANSPORT

The comprehensive, unified bus, tram and S-Bahn public transit system **ZVV** (☎0848 988 988; www.zvv.ch) includes boats plying the Limmat River. Short trips under five stops are Sfr2.60; typical trips are Sfr4.30. A 24-hour pass for the city centre is Sfr8.60.

NORTHERN SWITZERLAND

With businesslike Basel at its heart, this region also prides itself on having the country's finest Roman ruins (at Augusta Raurica) and a gaggle of proud castles and pretty medieval villages scattered across the rolling countryside of Aargau Canton.

Basel

POP 169,916

Tucked up against the French and German borders in Switzerland's northwest corner, Basel straddles the majestic Rhine. The town is home to art galleries, 30-odd museums and avant-garde architecture, and it boasts an enchanting Old Town centre.

Sights & Activities

Old Town AREA

(Altstadt) Begin exploring Basel's delightful medieval Old Town in **Marktplatz**, dominated by the astonishingly vivid red facade of the 16th-century **Rathaus** (Town Hall). From here, climb 400m west along Spalenberg through the former artisans' district to the 600-year-old **Spalentor** city gate, one of only three to survive the walls' demolition in 1866. Along the way, linger in captivating lanes such as Spalenberg, Heuberg and Leonhardsberg, lined by impeccably maintained, centuries-old houses.

★ **Fondation Beyeler** MUSEUM

(☎061 645 97 00; www.fondationbeyeler.ch; Baselstrasse 101, Riehen; adult/child Sfr25/6; ⊙10am-6pm Thu-Tue, to 8pm Wed) This astounding private-turned-public collection, assembled by former art dealers Hildy and Ernst Beyeler, is housed in a long, low, light-filled, open-plan building designed by Italian architect Renzo Piano. The varied exhibits juxtapose 19th- and 20th-century works by Picasso and Rothko against sculptures by Miró and Max Ernst and tribal figures from Oceania. Take tram 6 to Riehen from Barfüsserplatz or Marktplatz. Admission is reduced to Sfr20 Wednesday after 5pm and all day Monday.

Sleeping

Hotels are often full during Basel's trade fairs and conventions; book ahead. Guests receive a pass for free travel on public transport.

★ **SYHA Basel St Alban Youth Hostel** HOSTEL €

(☎061 272 05 72; www.youthhostel.ch; St Alban-Kirchrain 10; dm Sfr41 46.50, s/d Sfr120/132; 📶) Designed by Basel-based architects Buchner & Bründler, this swank modern hostel in a very pleasant neighbourhood is flanked by tree-shaded squares and a rushing creek. It's only a stone's throw from the Rhine, and 15 minutes on foot from the SBB Bahnhof (or take tram 2 to Kunstmuseum and walk five minutes downhill).

★ **Hotel Krafft** HOTEL €€

(☎061 690 91 30; www.krafftbasel.ch; Rheingasse 12; s Sfr99-162, d Sfr158-284; 📶) Design-savvy urbanites will love this renovated historic hotel. Sculptural modern chandeliers dangle in the creaky-floored dining room overlooking the Rhine, and minimalist Japanese-style tea bars adorn each landing of the spiral stairs.

Eating & Drinking

Head to the Marktplatz for a daily market and several stands selling excellent quick bites, such as local sausages and sandwiches.

★ **Volkshaus Basel** BRASSERIE, BAR €€

(☎061 690 93 10; www.volkshaus-basel.ch; Rebgasse 12-14; mains Sfr29-54; ⊙restaurant noon-2pm & 6-10pm Mon-Sat, bar 10am-midnight Mon-Wed, to 1am Thu-Sat) This stylish Herzog & de Meuron–designed venue is part resto-bar, part gallery and part performance space. For relaxed dining, head for the atmospheric beer garden, in a cobblestoned courtyard decorated with columns, vine-clad walls and light-draped rows of trees. The menu ranges from brasserie classics *(steak-frites)* to more innovative offerings (house-pickled wild salmon with mustard, dill and beetroot).

Information

Basel Tourismus (☎061 268 68 68; www.basel.com) SBB Bahnhof (Centralbahnstrasse 10; ⊙8-6pm Mon-Fri, 9am-5pm Sat, 9am-3pm Sun); Stadtcasino (Steinenberg 14; ⊙9am-6.30pm Mon-Fri, to 5pm Sat, 10am-3pm Sun) The Stadtcasino branch organises two-hour city walking tours (adult/child Sfr18/9) in English and German (or French upon request) starting at 2.30pm Monday to Saturday May through October, and on Saturdays the rest of the year.

WORTH A TRIP

LIECHTENSTEIN

If Liechtenstein (population 37,937) didn't exist, someone would have invented it. A tiny German-speaking mountain principality (160 sq km) governed by an iron-willed monarch in the heart of 21st-century Europe, it certainly has novelty value. Only 25km long by 12km wide (at its broadest point) – just larger than Manhattan – Liechtenstein is mostly visited by people who want a glimpse of the castle and a spurious passport stamp. Stay a little longer and you can escape into its pint-sized Alpine wilderness.

Vaduz

Vaduz is a postage-stamp-size city with a postcard-perfect backdrop. Crouching at the foot of forested mountains, hugging the banks of the Rhine and crowned by a turreted castle, the city has a visually stunning location.

The centre itself is curiously modern and sterile, yet just a few minutes' walk brings you to traces of the quaint village that existed just 50 years ago and quiet vineyards where the Alps seem that bit closer.

Vaduz Castle is closed to the public but is worth the climb for the vistas.

Information

Liechtenstein's international phone prefix is ☎423.

The **Liechtenstein Center** (www.tourismus.li) offers brochures, souvenir passport stamps (Sfr3) and the **Philatelie Liechtenstein**, which will interest stamp collectors.

Getting There & Around

The nearest train stations are in the Swiss border towns of Buchs and Sargans. From each of these towns there are frequent buses to Vaduz (Sfr4.80/9.60 from Buchs/Sargans). Buses traverse the country. Single fares (buy tickets on the bus) are Sfr3/4/6/8 for one/two/three/four zones. Swiss Passes are valid on all main routes.

Getting There & Away

AIR

The **EuroAirport** (MLH or BSL; ☎+33 3 89 90 31 11; www.euroairport.com), 5km northwest of town in France, is the main airport for Basel. It is a hub for easyJet and there are flights to major European cities.

TRAIN

Basel is a major European rail hub. The main station has TGVs to Paris (three hours) and fast ICEs to major cities in Germany.

Services within Switzerland include frequent trains to Bern (Sfr41, one hour) and Zürich (Sfr34, one hour).

Getting Around

Bus 50 links the airport and Basel's main train station (Sfr4.40, 20 minutes). Trams 8 and 11 link the station to Marktplatz. Tram and bus tickets cost Sfr2.30 for short trips (maximum four stops), Sfr3.80 for longer trips within Basel and Sfr9.90 for a day pass.

TICINO

Switzerland meets Italy: in Ticino the summer air is rich and hot, and the peacock-proud posers propel their scooters in and out of traffic. Italian weather, Italian style. Not to mention the Italian ice cream, Italian pizza, Italian architecture and Italian language.

Locarno

POP 15,968

Italianate architecture and the northern end of Lago Maggiore, plus more hours of sunshine than anywhere else in Switzerland (2300 hours, to be precise), give this laid-back town a summer resort atmosphere.

Locarno is on the northeastern corner of Lago Maggiore, which mostly lies in Italy's Lombardy region. **Navigazione Lago Maggiore** (www.navigazionelaghi.it) operates boats across the entire lake.

SWISS NATIONAL PARK

The Engadine's pride and joy is the Swiss National Park, easily accessed from Scuol, Zernez and S-chanf. Spanning 172 sq km, Switzerland's only national park is a nature-gone-wild swath of dolomitic peaks, shimmering glaciers, larch woodlands, pastures, waterfalls and high moors strung with topaz-blue lakes. This was the first national park to be established in the Alps, on 1 August 1914, and more than 100 years later it remains true to its original conservation ethos, with the aims to protect, research and inform.

Given that nature has been left to its own devices for a century, the park is a glimpse of the Alps before the dawn of tourism. There are some 80km of well-marked hiking trails, where, with a little luck and a decent pair of binoculars, ibex, chamois, marmots, deer, bearded vultures and golden eagles can be sighted. The **Swiss National Park Centre** (☎081 851 41 41; www.nationalpark.ch; exhibition adult/child Sfr7/3; ⊙8.30am-6pm Jun-Oct, 9am-noon & 2-5pm Nov-May) should be your first port of call for information on activities and accommodation. It sells an excellent 1:50,000 park map (Sfr14, or Sfr20 with guidebook), which covers 21 walks through the park.

You can easily head off on your own, but you might get more out of one of the informative guided hikes (Sfr25) run by the centre from late June to mid-October. These include wildlife-spotting treks to the Val Trupchun and high-alpine hikes to the Offenpass and Lakes of Macun. Most are in German, but many guides speak a little English. Book ahead by phone or at the park office in Zernez.

Entry to the park and its car parks is free. Conservation is paramount here, so stick to footpaths and respect regulations prohibiting camping, littering, lighting fires, cycling, picking flowers and disturbing the animals.

For an overnight stay in the heart of the park, look no further than **Il Fuorn** (☎081 856 12 26; www.ilfuorn.ch; s/d Sfr120/196, without bathroom Sfr95/150, half-board extra Sfr35; ⊙closed Nov, 2nd half Jan & Easter–late Apr), an idyllically sited guesthouse that serves fresh trout and game at its excellent on-site restaurant.

Sights & Activities

Piazza Grande AREA

Locarno's Italianate Old Town fans out from Piazza Grande, a photogenic ensemble of arcades and Lombard-style houses. A craft and fresh-produce market takes over the square every Thursday.

★Santuario della Madonna del Sasso CHURCH

(www.madonnadelsasso.org; ⊙7.30am-6pm) Overlooking the town, this sanctuary was built after the Virgin Mary supposedly appeared in a vision to a monk, Bartolomeo d'Ivrea, in 1480. There's a highly adorned church and several rather rough, near-life-size statue groups (including one of the Last Supper) in niches on the stairway. The best-known painting in the church is *La Fuga in Egitto* (Flight to Egypt), painted in 1522 by Bramantino.

A **funicular** (one way/return adult Sfr4.80/7.20, child Sfr2.20/3.60; ⊙8am-10pm May, Jun & Sep, to midnight Jul & Aug, to 9pm Apr & Oct, to 7.30pm Nov-Mar) runs every 15 minutes from the town centre past the sanctuary to Orselina, but a more scenic, pilgrim-style approach is the 20-minute walk up the chapel-lined Via Crucis (take Via al Sasso off Via Cappuccini).

Getting There & Away

Locarno is well linked to Ticino and the rest of Switzerland via Bellinzona, or take the scenic **Centovalli Express** (www.centovalli.ch) to Brig via Domodossola in Italy.

Lugano

POP 63,583

Ticino's lush, mountain-rimmed lake isn't its only liquid asset. Lugano is also the country's third-most-important banking centre. Suits aside, it's a vivacious city, with bars and pavement cafes huddling in the spaghetti maze of steep cobblestone streets that untangle at the edge of the lake and along the flowery promenade.

Sights & Activities

The **Centro Storico** (Old Town) is a 10-minute walk downhill from the train station; take the stairs or the funicular (Sfr1.30).

Wander through the mostly porticoed lanes woven around the busy main square, **Piazza della Riforma** (which is even more lively when the Tuesday- and Friday-morning markets are held).

Cattedrale di San Lorenzo CATHEDRAL
(St Lawrence Cathedral; Via San Lorenzo; ⌚6.30am-6pm) Freshly renovated in 2016, Lugano's early 16th-century cathedral conceals some fine frescoes and ornate baroque statues behind its Renaissance facade. Out front are far-reaching views over the Old Town's jumble of terracotta rooftops to the lake and mountains.

Società Navigazione del Lago di Lugano BOATING
(☎091 971 52 23; www.lakelugano.ch; Riva Vela; ⌚Apr-Oct) A relaxed way to see the lake's highlights is on one of these cruises, including one-hour bay tours (Sfr27.40) and three-hour morning cruises to Ponte Tresa at the lake's western end (Sfr45.60). Visit the website for timetables.

Sleeping & Eating

Many hotels close for part of the winter.

Hotel & Hostel Montarina HOTEL, HOSTEL €
(☎091 966 72 72; www.montarina.ch; Via Montarina 1; dm/s/d Sfr29/105/140; P 🛜 🏊) Occupying a pastel-pink villa dating to 1860, this hotel/hostel duo extends a heartfelt welcome. Mosaic floors, high ceilings and wrought-iron balustrades are lingering traces of old-world grandeur. There's a shared kitchen-lounge, toys to amuse the kids, a swimming pool set in palm-dotted gardens and even a tiny vineyard. Breakfast costs an extra Sfr15.

★**Guesthouse Castagnola** GUESTHOUSE €€
(☎078 632 67 47; www.gh-castagnola.com; Salita degli Olivi 2; apt Sfr125-180; P 🛜) Kristina and Maurizio bend over backwards to please at their B&B, lodged in a beautifully restored 16th-century townhouse. Exposed stone, natural fabrics and earthy colours dominate in three rooms kitted out with Nespresso coffee machines and flat-screen TVs. There's also a family-friendly apartment with washing machine and full kitchen.

Bottegone del Vino ITALIAN €€
(☎091 922 76 89; Via Magatti 3; mains Sfr20-42; ⌚11.30am-midnight Mon-Sat) Favoured by Lugano's downtown banking brigade, this place has a season-driven menu, with ever-changing lunch and dinner options scrawled on the blackboard daily. Expect specialities such as ravioli stuffed with fine Tuscan Chianina beef, accompanied by a wide selection of local wines. Knowledgeable waiters fuss around the tables and are only too happy to suggest the perfect Ticino tipple.

Getting There & Away

Lugano is on the main line connecting Milan to Zürich and Lucerne. Services from Lugano include Milan (Sfr27, 1¼ hours), Zürich (Sfr68, 2½ hours) and Lucerne (Sfr61, two hours).

GRAUBÜNDEN

St Moritz

POP 5067

Switzerland's original winter wonderland and the cradle of Alpine tourism, St Moritz (San Murezzan in Romansch) has been luring royals, celebrities and moneyed wannabes since 1864. With its shimmering aquamarine lake, emerald forests and aloof mountains, the town looks a million dollars.

Activities

With 350km of slopes, ultramodern lifts and spirit-soaring views, **skiing** in St Moritz is second to none, especially for confident intermediates. The general ski pass covers all the slopes.

If cross-country skiing is more your scene, you can glide across sunny plains and through snowy woods on 220km of groomed trails. In summer, the region has excellent hiking trails.

Schweizer Skischule SKIING
(☎081 830 01 01; www.skischool.ch; Via Stredas 14; ⌚8am-noon & 2-6pm Mon-Sat, 8-9am & 4-6pm Sun) The first Swiss ski school was founded in St Moritz in 1929. Today, you can arrange skiing or snowboarding lessons for Sfr120/85 per day for adults/children.

Sleeping & Eating

Jugendherberge St Moritz HOSTEL €
(081 836 61 11; www.youthhostel.ch/st.moritz; Via Surpunt 60; dm/s/d/q Sfr41/136/161/216;) On the edge of the forest, this hostel has clean, quiet four-bed dorms and doubles. There's a children's toy room, bike hire and laundrette. Bus 3 offers door-to-door connections with the town centre (five minutes) and train station (10 minutes).

Chesa Spuondas HOTEL €€
(081 833 65 88; www.chesaspuondas.ch; Via Somplaz 47; s/d/f incl half board Sfr155/280/290; P) This family hotel nestles amid meadows at the foot of forest and mountains, 3km southwest of the town centre. Rooms are in keeping with the Jugendstil villa, with high ceilings, parquet floors and the odd antique. Kids are the centre of attention here, with dedicated meal times, activities, play areas and the children's ski school a 10-minute walk away.

Chesa Veglia ITALIAN €€€
(081 837 28 00; www.badruttspalace.com; Via Veglia 2; pizza Sfr25-39, mains Sfr45-60; noon-11.30pm) This slate-roofed, chalk-white chalet restaurant dates from 1658. The softly lit interior is all warm pine and creaking wood floors, while the terrace affords lake and mountain views. Go for pizza or regional specialities such as *Bündner Gerstensuppe* (creamy barley soup) and venison medallions with *Spätzli* (egg noodles).

Getting There & Away

Regular hourly trains make the scenic run to/from the rail hub of Chur (Sfr42, two hours).

St Moritz is also an end point on the much-hyped **Glacier Express** (www.glacierexpress.ch; one way adult/child Sfr153/76.50), which takes in some spellbinding Alpine scenery on its eight-hour run to Zermatt.

The **Bernina Express** (www.berninaexpress.ch; one way Chur-Tirano Sfr64; mid-May–early Dec) provides seasonal links to Lugano from St Moritz, which include the stunning Unesco-recognised train line over the Bernina Pass to Tirano, Italy.

SURVIVAL GUIDE

Directory A–Z

ACCOMMODATION

Switzerland sports traditional and creative accommodation in every price range. Many budget hotels have cheaper rooms with shared toilet and shower facilities. From there, truly, the sky is the limit. Breakfast buffets can be extensive and tasty but are not always included in room rates. Rates in cities and towns stay constant most of the year. In mountain resorts prices are seasonal (and can fall by 50% or more outside high season).

Low season Mid-September to mid-December, mid-April to mid-June

Mid-season January to mid-February, mid-June to early July, September

High season July to August, Christmas, mid-February to Easter

DISCOUNT CARDS

Swiss Museum Pass (www.museumspass.ch; adult/family Sfr166/288) Regular or long-term visitors to Switzerland may want to buy this pass, which covers entry to 500 museums countrywide.

Visitors' Cards Many resorts and cities have a visitors' card (*Gästekarte*), which provides benefits such as reduced prices for museums, pools, public transit or cable cars, plus free local public transport. Cards are issued by your accommodation.

ESSENTIAL FOOD & DRINK

Fondue Switzerland's best-known dish, in which melted Emmental and Gruyère cheese are combined with white wine in a large pot and eaten with small bread chunks.

Raclette Another popular artery-hardener of melted cheese served with potatoes.

Rösti German Switzerland's national dish of fried shredded potatoes is served with everything.

Veal Highly rated throughout the country; in Zürich, veal is thinly sliced and served in a cream sauce *(Zürcher Geschnetzeltes)*.

Bündnerfleisch Dried beef, smoked and thinly sliced.

Chocolate Good at any time of day and available seemingly everywhere.

SLEEPING PRICE RANGES

The following price ranges refer to a double room with a private bathroom, except in hostels or where otherwise specified. Quoted rates are for high season and include breakfast, unless otherwise noted:

€ less than Sfr170

€€ Sfr170–Sfr350

€€€ more than Sfr350

ELECTRICITY

Electrical current in Switzerland is 230V, 50Hz. Swiss sockets are recessed, three-holed, hexagonally shaped and incompatible with many plugs from abroad. They usually, however, take the standard European two-pronged plug.

INTERNET ACCESS

Free wi-fi hot spots can be found at airports, dozens of Swiss train stations and in many hotels and cafes. Public wi-fi (provided by Swisscom) costs Sfr5 per day.

INTERNET RESOURCES

MySwitzerland (www.myswitzerland.com)
Swiss Info (www.swissinfo.ch)

MONEY

➡ Swiss francs are divided into 100 centimes (*Rappen* in German-speaking Switzerland). There are notes for 10, 20, 50, 100, 200 and 1000 francs, and coins for five, 10, 20 and 50 centimes, as well as for one, two and five francs. Euros are accepted by many tourism businesses.

➡ Exchange money at large train stations.

➡ Tipping is not necessary, given that hotels, restaurants, bars and even some taxis are legally required to include a 15% service charge in bills. You can round-up the bill after a meal for good service, as locals do.

OPENING HOURS

We list high-season opening hours for sights and attractions; hours tend to decrease during low season. Most businesses shut completely on Sunday.

Banks 8.30am–4.30pm Monday to Friday
Restaurants noon–2.30pm and 6–9.30pm; most close one or two days per week
Shops 10am–6pm Monday to Friday, to 4pm Saturday
Museums 10am–5pm, many close Monday and open late Thursday

PUBLIC HOLIDAYS

New Year's Day 1 January
Easter Sunday & Monday March/April
Ascension Day 40th day after Easter
Whit Sunday & Monday (Pentecost) 7th week after Easter
National Day 1 August
Christmas Day 25 December
St Stephen's Day 26 December

TELEPHONE

➡ The country code for Switzerland is ☎41. When calling Switzerland from abroad, drop the initial zero from the number; hence to call Bern, dial ☎41 31 (preceded by the overseas access code of the country you're dialling from).

➡ The international access code from Switzerland is ☎00. To call Britain (country code ☎44), start by dialling ☎00 44.

➡ Most mobile phones brought from overseas will function in Switzerland. Prepaid local SIM cards are available from network operators Salt (www.salt.ch), Sunrise (www.sunrise.ch) and Swisscom Mobile (www.swisscom.ch/mobile).

VISAS

For up-to-date details on visa requirements, go to www.sem.admin.ch.

Visas are not required for passport holders from the UK, the EU, Ireland, the USA, Canada, Australia, New Zealand, Norway and Iceland.

Getting There & Away

AIR

The main international airports:

Geneva Airport (GVA; Aéroport International de Genève; www.gva.ch) Geneva's airport is 4km northwest of the town centre.

Zürich Airport (ZRH; ☎043 816 22 11; www.zurich-airport.com) The airport is 9km north of the centre, with flights to most European capitals as well as some in Africa, Asia and North America.

LAND

Bus

Eurolines (www.eurolines.com) has buses with connections across Western Europe.

Train

Switzerland is a hub of train connections to the rest of the Continent. Zürich is the busiest international terminus, with service to all neighbouring countries. Destinations include Münich (4¼ hours), and Vienna (eight hours), from where there are extensive onward connections to cities in Eastern Europe.

COUNTRY FACTS

Area 41,285 sq km

Capital Bern

Country Code ☎41

Currency Swiss franc (Sfr)

Emergency Ambulance ☎144, fire ☎118, police ☎117

Languages French, German, Italian, Romansch

Money ATMs readily available

Population 8.18 million

Visas Schengen rules apply

➡ Numerous TGV trains daily connect Paris to Geneva (3¼ hours), Lausanne (3¾ hours), Basel (three hours) and Zürich (four hours).

➡ Nearly all connections from Italy pass through Milan before branching off to Zürich, Lucerne, Bern or Lausanne.

➡ Most connections from Germany pass through Zürich or Basel.

➡ **Swiss Federal Railways** (www.sbb.ch) accepts internet bookings but does not post tickets outside of Switzerland.

Getting Around

Swiss public transport is an efficient, fully integrated and comprehensive system, which incorporates trains, buses, boats and funiculars.

Marketed as the Swiss Travel System, the network has a useful website (www.swisstravelsystem.ch). Excellent free maps covering the country are available at train stations and tourist offices.

PASSES & DISCOUNTS

Convenient discount passes make the Swiss transport system even more appealing. For extensive travel within Switzerland, the following national travel passes generally offer better savings than Eurail or InterRail passes.

Swiss Travel Pass This entitles the holder to unlimited travel on almost every train, boat and bus service in the country, and on trams and buses in 41 towns, plus free entry to 500-odd museums. Reductions of 25% to 50% apply on funiculars, cable cars and private railways. Different passes are available, valid between three (Sfr216) and 15 (Sfr458) consecutive days.

Swiss Travel Pass Flex This pass allows unlimited travel for a certain number of days within a one-month period – from three (Sfr248) to 15 (Sfr502) days.

Half-Fare Card As the name suggests, you pay only half the fare on trains with this card (Sfr120 for one month), plus you get some discounts on local-network buses, trams and cable cars.

BICYCLE

➡ **Rent-a-Bike** (www.rentabike.ch) allows you to rent bikes at 80 train stations in Switzerland. For a Sfr10 surcharge you can collect from one station and return to another.

➡ **Suisseroule** (Schweizrollt; www.schweizrollt.ch) lets you borrow a bike for free or cheaply in places like Geneva, Bern and Zürich. Bike stations are usually next to the train station or central square.

➡ Local tourist offices often have good cycling information.

BOAT

Ferries and steamers link towns and cities on many lakes, including Geneva, Lucerne, Lugano and Zürich.

BUS

➡ Yellow **post buses** (www.postbus.ch) supplement the rail network, linking towns to difficult-to-access mountain regions.

➡ Services are regular, and departures (usually next to train stations) are linked to train schedules.

➡ Swiss national travel passes are valid.

➡ Purchase tickets on board; some scenic routes over the Alps (eg the Lugano–St Moritz run) require reservations.

CAR & MOTORCYCLE

➡ Headlights must be on at all times, and dipped (set to low-beam) in tunnels.

➡ The speed limit is 50km/h in towns, 80km/h on main roads outside towns, 100km/h on single-lane freeways and 120km/h on dual-lane freeways.

EATING PRICE RANGES

Price indicators refer to the average cost of a main meal.

$ less than Sfr25

$$ Sfr25–Sfr50

$$$ more than Sfr50

ℹ TRANSPORT CONNECTIONS

Landlocked between France, Germany, Austria, Liechtenstein and Italy, Switzerland is well linked, especially by train. Formalities are minimal when entering Switzerland by air, rail or road thanks to the Schengen Agreement. Fast, well-maintained roads run from Switzerland through to all bordering countries; the Alps present a natural barrier, meaning main roads generally head through tunnels to enter Switzerland. Switzerland can be reached by steamer from several lakes: from Germany, arrive via Lake Constance and from France via Lake Geneva. You can also cruise down the Rhine to Basel.

- Some minor Alpine passes are closed from November to May – check with the local tourist offices before setting off.

TRAIN

The Swiss rail network combines state-run and private operations. The **Swiss Federal Railway** (www.sbb.ch) is abbreviated to SBB in German, CFF in French and FFS in Italian.

- All major train stations are connected to each other by hourly departures, at least between 6am and midnight.
- Second-class seats are perfectly acceptable, but cars are often close to full. First-class carriages are more comfortable and spacious and have fewer passengers.
- Ticket vending machines accept most major credit cards from around the world.
- The SBB smartphone app is an excellent resource and can be used to store your tickets electronically.
- Check the SBB website for cheap Supersaver tickets on major routes.
- Most stations have 24-hour lockers, usually accessible from 6am to midnight.
- Seat reservations (Sfr5) are advisable for longer journeys, particularly in the high season.

Survival Guide

Directory A–Z

Accommodation

Where you stay in Western Europe may be one of the highlights of your trip, with options as diverse as the region itself. Wherever you go, book ahead during peak holiday periods.

Hotels Range from simple to extravagant, historic to cutting edge.

B&Bs and Guesthouses Get a local perspective by staying in private homes.

Hostels Shared-facility options spanning Hostelling International (HI) premises though to designer flashpacker pads exist all over Western Europe.

Camping Magnificent scenery forms a backdrop to basic grounds though to luxury sites.

Resorts From spa and golf complexes and to beachfront havens, resorts offer easy living.

B&Bs & Guesthouses

In Britain and Ireland, B&Bs – where you get bed and breakfast in a private home – can be real bargains. Elsewhere, similar private accommodation – though often without breakfast – may go under the name of pension, guesthouse, *gasthaus*, *zimmerfrei*, *chambre d'hôte* and so on. Although the majority of guesthouses are simple affairs, there are plenty of luxurious ones around.

Check that accommodation is centrally located and not in a dull, distant suburb.

Camping

Camping is immensely popular in Western Europe and provides the cheapest form of accommodation.

➡ There's usually a charge per tent or site, per person and per vehicle.

➡ National tourist offices often provide booklets or brochures listing camping grounds throughout their countries.

➡ In large cities, most camping grounds will be some distance from the centre of town, so it's best suited to those with their own transport. If you're on foot, the money you save by camping can quickly be eaten up by the cost of commuting to and from a town centre.

➡ Many camping grounds rent bungalows or cottages accommodating two to eight people.

➡ Camping other than at designated camping grounds is difficult; you usually need permission from the local authorities (the police or local council office) or from the owner of the land.

➡ In some countries, such as Austria, France and Germany, free camping (aka wild camping) is illegal on all but private land; in Greece it's illegal altogether. Free camping is permissible anywhere in Scotland but not the rest of Britain.

Hostels

Hostels offer the cheapest secure roof over your head in Western Europe, and you generally don't have to be a youngster to use them.

HOSTELLING INTERNATIONAL

Most hostels are part of the national Youth Hostel Association (YHA), which is affiliated with **Hostelling International** (HI; www.hihostels.com).

➡ The HI website has links to all the national organisations and you can use it to book beds or rooms in advance.

➡ You can join YHA or HI in advance or at the hostels. Members usually pay about 10% less on rates.

➡ At a hostel, you get a bed in a dorm or a private room plus the use of communal facilities, which often include

BOOK YOUR STAY ONLINE

For more accommodation reviews by Lonely Planet authors, check out http://lonelyplanet.com/hotels/. You'll find independent reviews, as well as recommendations on the best places to stay. Best of all, you can book online.

a kitchen where you can prepare your own meals.

- Hostels vary widely in character, but increased competition from other forms of accommodation – particularly the emergence of privately owned hostels – have prompted many places to improve their facilities and cut back on rules and regulations.
- The trend is moving toward smaller dormitories with just four to six beds. Single and double rooms with private bathrooms are common and it's not unusual for families to stay at hostels.
- Some more institutional hostels regularly host school groups, which means they can be booked out or can be noisy.

PRIVATE HOSTELS

There are many private hostelling organisations in Western Europe and hundreds of unaffiliated backpacker hostels. Private hostels have fewer rules (eg no curfew, no daytime lockout), more self-catering facilities and a much lower number of large, noisy school groups. They often also have a much more sociable, party-friendly vibe.

However, whereas HI hostels must meet minimum safety and cleanliness standards, private hostels do not, which means that facilities vary greatly. Dorms in some private hostels can be mixed gender. Most private hostels now have small dorm rooms of three to eight beds, and private singles and doubles.

Hotels

From fabulous five-star icons to workaday cheapies, the range of hotels in Western Europe is immense. You'll often find inexpensive hotels clustered around bus and train station areas, which are always good places to start hunting; but these can be charmless and scruffy. Look for moderately priced places closer to the interesting parts of town.

Check whether breakfast is included (often it's not). Wi-fi is almost always free.

Rental Accommodation

Rentals can be both advantageous and fun for families travelling together or for those staying in one place for a few nights. You can have your own chic Left Bank apartment in Paris or a villa in Tuscany with a pool – and often at cheaper rates than hotels. All rentals should be equipped with kitchens (or at least a kitchenette), which can save on the food bill and allow you to browse the neighbourhood markets and shops, eating like the locals do. Some are a little more upmarket with laundry facilities and parking.

Booking websites abound; alternatively, check with local tourist offices. Beware direct-rental scams: unless you book through a reputable agency, your property might not actually exist. Scammers often compile fake apartment advertisements at too-good-to-be-true prices. Never send payment to an untraceable account via a money transfer.

Resorts

From Irish mansions amid rambling grounds to grand Swiss spa hotels, golf resorts and beach properties with water sports and activities galore, Western Europe has many fabled resorts, where travellers try to avoid ever checking out. Ask about deals and all-inclusive packages.

Activities

Western Europe offers infinite opportunities to get active in its great outdoors. Its varied geography and climate means it offers the full range of pursuits: from swimming, surfing, windsurfing, paddleboarding and boating on its coastline, to skiing, snowboarding and mountaineering in its peaks, and fishing, hiking and cycling almost everywhere.

Boating

Europe's many lakes, rivers and diverse coastlines offer an incredible variety of boating options. You can houseboat in France, kayak in Switzerland, charter a yacht in Greece, row on a peaceful Alpine lake, join a cruise along the Rhine, Main and Danube rivers from Amsterdam to Vienna (and beyond), rent a sailing boat on the French Riviera, go white-water rafting in Austria, or pilot a canal boat along the extraordinary canal network of Britain (or Ireland, or France) – the possibilities are endless.

Cycling

Along with hiking, cycling is ideal for getting up close to the scenery. It's also a superb way to get around many cities and towns.

Popular cycling areas include the Belgian Ardennes, the west of Ireland, much of the Netherlands (the world's most bike-friendly nation), the coasts of Sardinia and Puglia in Italy, anywhere in the Alps (for those fit enough), and the south of France.

Check with your airline about taking bikes in the cargo hold. Alternatively, places to hire a bicycle are myriad. Bikes can be carried on most European trains (some outside peak hours).

Hiking

Keen hikers can spend a lifetime exploring Western Europe's trails. Popular routes feature places to stay, often with jaw-dropping views.

Highlights include:

The Alps Spanning Switzerland, Austria, Germany and Italy, with bell-wearing dairy cows and trails organised with Swiss precision.

Pyrenees Follow trails through hills in both France and Spain.

Corsica and Sardinia Sun-drenched beauty, with a Mediterranean view around every corner.

Northern Portugal A glass of port awaits after a day on the trail.

Connemara Prime hillwalking on the west coast of Ireland.

Scotland Vast tracts of wilderness.

In the UK, **Ramblers** (www.ramblers.org.uk) is a nonprofit organisation that promotes long-distance walking and can help you with maps and information. The British-based **Ramblers Holidays** (www.ramblersholidays.co.uk) offers hiking-oriented trips in Europe and elsewhere. For shorter day hikes, local tourist offices are excellent resources.

Every country in Western Europe has national parks and other scenic areas or attractions. Guided hikes are often available.

Skiing & Snowboarding

In winter Europeans take to the pistes, flocking to hundreds of resorts in the Alps and Pyrenees for downhill skiing and snowboarding. Cross-country skiing is also very popular in some areas, such as around Switzerland's St Moritz.

Equipment hire (or even purchase) can be relatively cheap, and the hassle of bringing your own skis may not be worth it. **Intersport Rent** (www.intersportrent.com) has numerous outlets.

The ski season generally lasts from early December to late March, though at higher altitudes it may extend an extra month either side. Snow conditions can vary greatly from one year to the next and from region to region, but January and February tend to be the best (and busiest) months. For comprehensive reports on ski conditions, try **OnTheSnow** (www.onthesnow.com).

Surfing & Windsurfing

Surfing hotspots include Ireland's west coast, France (especially around Biarritz), Spain (especially around San Sebastián) and Portugal. Gear rental and lessons are readily available.

Windsurfing is a European passion, practised most places there's water and sand (which also says something about the breezy nature of Western European beaches and lakes). It's easy to rent sailboards in many tourist centres, and courses are usually available for beginners.

Children

Europe is the home of Little Red Riding Hood, Cinderella, King Arthur, Tintin et al, and is a great place to travel with kids. Successful travel with young children requires some careful planning and effort. Don't try to overdo things; even for adults, packing too much sightseeing into your schedule can be counterproductive.

- Most car-hire firms in Western Europe have children's safety seats for hire at a nominal cost, but it's essential that you book in advance.
- High chairs and cots (cribs) are available in many restaurants and hotels but numbers are often limited.
- Disposable nappies (diapers) are widely available.
- Babysitters are best sourced through your hotel.
- Attitudes to breastfeeding in public vary; ask locally for advice.

Customs Regulations

- Duty-free goods are not sold to those travelling from one EU country to another.
- For goods purchased at airports or on ferries *outside* the EU, the usual allowances apply for tobacco (200 cigarettes, 50 cigars or 250g of loose tobacco) – although some countries have reduced this – and alcohol (1L of spirits or 2L of liquor with less than 22% alcohol by volume; 4L of wine).
- The total value of other duty-free goods (perfume, electronic devices etc) cannot exceed €430 for air and sea travellers or €300 for other travellers.

Discount Cards

Camping Card International

Camping Card International (http://campingcardinternational.com) is a camping-ground ID can be used instead of a passport when checking into a camping ground and includes third-party insurance. Many camping grounds offer a small discount (usually 5% to 10%) if you sign in with one.

Senior Cards

Museums and various other sights and attractions (including public swimming pools and spas), as well as transport companies, frequently offer discounts to retired people, old-age pensioners and/or those aged over 60. Make sure you bring proof of age.

Student & Youth Cards

The **International Student Travel Confederation** (ISTC; www.istc.org) issues three cards for students, teachers and under-30s, offering thousands of worldwide discounts on transport, museum entry, youth hostels and even some restaurants.

ISIC (International Student Identity Card)

ITIC (International Teacher Identity Card)

IYTC (International Youth Travel Card).

Issuing offices include **STA Travel** (www.statravel.com). Most places, however, will also accept regular student identity cards from your home country.

The **European Youth Card** (www.eyca.org) has scores of discounts for under-30s. You don't need to be an EU citizen.

Electricity

Most of Europe runs on 220V/50Hz AC (as opposed to, say, North America, where the electricity is 120V/60Hz AC). Chargers for phones, iPods and laptops *usually* can handle any type of electricity. If in doubt, read the fine print.

CONTINTENAL EUROPE

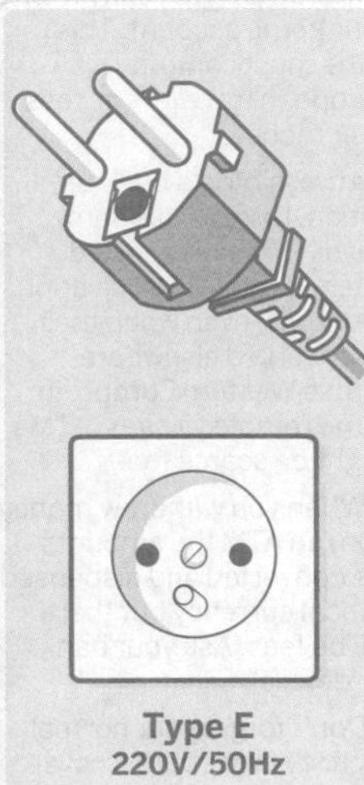

Type E
220V/50Hz

BRITAIN & IRELAND

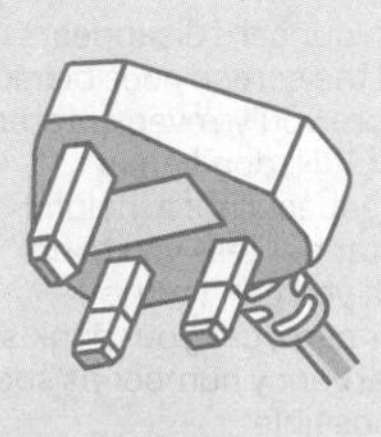

Type G
230V/50Hz

Embassies & Consulates

As a tourist, it is crucial that you understand what your own embassy (the embassy of the country of which you are a citizen) can and cannot do. Generally speaking, embassies won't be much help in emergencies if the trouble you're in is even remotely your fault.

Remember that you are bound by the laws of the country that you are in. Your embassy will show little sympathy if you end up in jail after committing a crime locally, even if such actions are legal in your own country.

In genuine emergencies you might get some assistance, but only if other channels have been exhausted. For example, if you need to get home urgently, the embassy would expect you to have insurance. If you have all your money and documents stolen, the embassy might assist with getting a new passport, but a loan for onward travel is almost always out of the question.

Locations

Embassies and consulates are located in Western European capitals and major cities. You can find locations online at the following websites:

Australia (www.dfat.gov.au)

Canada (www.international.gc.ca)

New Zealand (www.mfat.govt.nz)

United Kingdom (www.gov.uk/fco)

United States (https://travel.state.gov)

Gay & Lesbian Travellers

In cosmopolitan centres in Western Europe you'll find very liberal attitudes toward homosexuality. Belgium, France, the Republic of Ireland, Luxembourg, the Netherlands, Portugal, Spain and the UK (except Northern Ireland) have legalised same-sex marriages. Many other countries allow civil partnerships that grant all or most of the rights of marriage.

London, Paris, Berlin, Madrid, Lisbon and Amsterdam have thriving gay communities and pride events. The Greek islands of Mykonos and Lesvos are popular gay beach destinations.

Useful organisations:

Damron (http://damron.com) The USA's leading gay publisher offers guides to world cities.

Spartacus International Gay Guide (www.spartacusworld.com) A male-only directory of gay entertainment venues and hotels in Europe and the rest of the world.

Health

It is unlikely that you will encounter unusual health problems in Western Europe, and if you do, standards of care are world-class. It's vital to have health insurance for your trip.

Recommended Vaccinations

No jabs are necessary for Western Europe. However, the World Health Organization (WHO) recommends that all travellers be covered for diphtheria, tetanus, measles, mumps, rubella and polio, regardless of their destination. Since most vaccines don't produce immunity until at least two weeks after they're given, visit a doctor at least six weeks before departure.

Insurance

It's foolhardy to travel without insurance to cover theft, loss and medical problems.

➡ Before you buy insurance, see what your existing insurance covers, be it medical, home owner's or renter's. You may find that some aspects of travel in Western Europe are covered.

➡ If you need to purchase coverage, there's a wide variety of policies, so check the small print.

➡ Strongly consider a policy that covers you for the worst possible scenario.

Worldwide travel insurance is available at lonelyplanet.com/travel-insurance. You can buy, extend and claim online any time – even if you're already on the road.

Internet Access

The number of internet cafes is plummeting. You'll occasionally still find them in tourist areas and around big train stations. Libraries are another option. Tourist offices can provide advice. Hotels will usually print documents (such as boarding passes) for guests.

➡ Wi-fi (called WLAN in Germany) access is better the further north in Western Europe you go.

➡ Wi-fi is invariably free in hostels and hotels.

➡ Many cities and towns have free hotspots (sometimes time-limited); check with local tourist offices.

➡ An increasing number of airlines, trains, buses and taxis offer on-board wi-fi.

Legal Matters

Most Western European police are friendly and helpful, especially if you have been a victim of a crime. You are required by law to prove your identity if asked by police, so always carry your passport, or an identity card if you're an EU citizen.

Illegal Drugs

Narcotics are sometimes openly available in Europe, but that doesn't mean they're legal.

➡ The Netherlands is famed for its liberal attitudes, with 'coffeeshops' openly selling cannabis. However, it's a case of the police turning a blind eye. Possession of cannabis is decriminalised but not legalised (except for medicinal use). Don't take this relaxed attitude as an invitation to buy harder drugs; if you get caught, you'll be punished.

➡ Austria, Belgium, Italy and Switzerland have all decriminalised marijuana use; possession of small amounts will incur a fine but won't result in a criminal record.

➡ In Spain, cannabis has been decriminalised and is legal to use in private areas but not public spaces.

➡ In Portugal, the possession of *all* drugs has been decriminalised, however, selling is illegal.

Money

ATMs

➡ Most countries in Western Europe have international ATMs allowing you to withdraw cash directly from your home account. This is the most common way European travellers access their money.

➡ Always have a back-up option, however, as some travellers have reported glitches with ATMs in various countries, even when their card worked elsewhere across Western Europe. In some remote villages, ATMs might be scarce too.

➡ When you withdraw money from an ATM the amounts are converted and dispensed in local currency but there will be fees. Ask your bank for details.

➡ Don't forget your normal security procedures: cover the keypad when entering your PIN and make sure there are no unusual devices (which might copy your card's information) attached to the machine.

➡ If your card disappears and the screen goes blank before you've even entered your PIN, don't enter it – especially if a 'helpful' bystander tells you to do so. If you can't retrieve your card, call your bank's emergency number as soon as possible.

Cash

Nothing beats cash for convenience...or risk. If you lose it, it's gone forever and very few travel insurers will come to your rescue. Those that do will limit the amount to somewhere around €300 or £200.

If flying into Western Europe from elsewhere, you'll find ATMs and currency

EURO

The euro is the official currency used in 19 of the 28 EU states: Austria, Belgium, Cyprus, Estonia, Finland, France, Germany, Greece, the Republic of Ireland, Italy, Latvia, Lithuania, Luxembourg, Malta, the Netherlands, Portugal, Slovakia, Slovenia and Spain. Denmark, the UK, Switzerland and Sweden have held out against adopting the euro for political reasons.

The euro is divided into 100 cents and has the same value in all EU member countries. There are seven euro notes (€5, €10, €20, €50, €100, €200 and €500) and eight euro coins (€1 and €2, then €0.01, €0.02, €0.05, €0.10, €0.20 and €0.50). One side is standard for all euro coins and the other side bears a national emblem of participating countries. Some countries, such as the Netherlands, don't use €0.01 and €0.02 coins.

exchanges in the arrivals area of the airport. There is no reason to get local currency before arriving in Western Europe, especially as exchange rates in your home country are likely to be abysmal.

MINIMISING ATM CHARGES

When you withdraw cash from an ATM overseas there are several ways you can get hit. Firstly, most banks add a hidden 2.75% loading to what's called the 'Visa/MasterCard wholesale' or 'interbank' exchange rate. In short, they're giving you a worse exchange rate than strictly necessary. Additionally, some banks charge their customers a cash withdrawal fee (usually 2% with a minimum €2 or more). If you're really unlucky, the bank at the foreign end might charge you as well. Triple whammy. If you use a credit card in ATMs you'll also pay interest – usually quite high – on the cash withdrawn.

If your bank levies fees, then making larger, less frequent withdrawals is better. It's also worth seeing if your bank has reciprocal agreements with banks where you are going that minimise ATM fees.

Credit Cards

➡ Credit cards are often necessary for major purchases such as air or rail tickets, and offer a lifeline in certain emergencies.

➡ Visa and MasterCard are much more widely accepted in Europe than Amex and Diners Club.

➡ There are regional differences in the general acceptability of credit cards. In the UK, for example, you can usually flash your plastic in the most humble of budget restaurants; in Germany some restaurants don't take credit cards. Cards are not widely accepted off the beaten track.

➡ As with ATM cards, banks have loaded up credit cards with hidden charges for foreign purchases. Cash withdrawals on a credit card are almost always a much worse idea than using an ATM card due to the fees and high interest rates. Plus, purchases in different currencies are likely to draw various conversion surcharges that are simply there to add to the bank's profit. These can run up to 5% or more. Check before leaving home.

International Transfers

In an emergency, it's quicker and easier to have money wired via **Western Union** (www.westernunion.com) or **MoneyGram** (www.moneygram.com) but it can be quite costly.

Money Exchange

➡ In general, US dollars and UK pounds are the easiest currencies to exchange in Western Europe.

➡ Get rid of Scottish and Northern Ireland banknotes before leaving the UK; nobody outside it will touch them.

➡ Most airports, central train stations, big hotels and many border posts have banking facilities outside regular business hours, at times on a 24-hour basis.

➡ Post offices in Western Europe often perform banking tasks, tend to be open longer hours and outnumber banks in remote places.

➡ The best exchange rates are usually at banks. *Bureaux de change* usually – but not always – offer worse rates or charge higher commissions. Hotels are almost always the worst places to change money.

Taxes & Refunds

Sales tax applies to many goods and services in Western Europe (although the amount – 10% to 25% – is already built into the price of the item). When non-EU residents spend more than a certain amount (about €75) they can usually reclaim that tax when leaving the country.

Making a tax-back claim is straightforward:

➡ Make sure the shop offers duty-free sales (often a sign will be displayed reading 'Tax-Free Shopping').

➡ When making your purchase ask the shop attendant for a tax-refund voucher, filled in with the correct amount and the date.

➡ The voucher can be used to claim a refund directly at international airports (beware, however, of very long lines), or be stamped at ferry ports or border crossings and mailed back for a refund.

EU residents aren't eligible for this scheme. Even an American citizen living in London is not entitled to a rebate on items bought in Paris. Conversely, an EU-passport holder living in New York is.

Travel Money Cards

In recent years prepaid cards – also called travel money cards, prepaid currency cards or cash passport cards – have become a popular way of carrying money.

These enable you to load a card with as much foreign currency as you want to spend. You then use it to withdraw cash at ATMs – the money comes off the card and not out of your account – or to make direct purchases in the same way you would with a Visa or MasterCard. You can reload it via telephone or online.

One source of travel money cards is **Travelex** (www.travelex.com).

Advantages of a prepaid card:

- You avoid foreign-exchange fees as the money you put on the card is converted into foreign currency at the moment you load it.
- You can control your outlay by only loading as much as you want to spend.
- Security: if it's stolen your losses are limited to the balance on the card as it's not directly linked to your bank account.
- Lower ATM-withdrawal fees.
- Americans and others who carry credit cards without embedded chips (or whose chip-and-PIN cards don't work in Europe) can use these cards (which have chips and PINs) for the many European purchases that require such cards. Train ticket-vending machines in the Netherlands are an example.

Against these you'll need to weigh the costs:

- Fees are charged for buying the card and then every time you load it. ATM withdrawal fees also apply.
- You might also be charged a fee if you don't use the card for a certain period of time or to redeem any unused currency.
- If the card has an expiry date, you'll forfeit any money loaded on to the card after that date.

Safe Travel

On the whole, you should experience few problems travelling in Western Europe – even alone – as the region is well developed and relatively safe. But do exercise common sense.

- Work out how friends and relatives can contact you in case of an emergency and keep in touch.
- Scanning your passport, driving licence and credit and ATM cards and storing them securely online gives you access from anywhere. If things are stolen or lost, replacement is much easier when you have the vital details available.
- Train stations in many Western European cities can be sketchy late at night.

Scams

Be aware of shopkeepers in touristy places who may shortchange you. The same applies to taxi drivers.

Never buy tickets other than from official vendors – they may turn out to be counterfeit.

Theft

Watch out for theft in Western Europe, including theft by other travellers. The most important things to secure are your passport, documents (such as a driving licence), tickets and money, in that order.

- Protect yourself from 'snatch thieves' who go for cameras and shoulder bags. They sometimes operate from motorcycles or scooters and expertly slash the strap before you have a chance to react. A small day pack is better, but watch your rear.
- At cafes and bars; loop the strap of your bag around your leg while seated. A jacket or bag left on the back of a chair is an invitation for theft.
- Pickpockets come up with endlessly creative diversions to distract you: tying friendship bracelets on your wrist, peddling trinkets, pretending to 'find' a gold ring on the ground that they've conveniently placed there, posing as beggars or charity workers, or as tourists wanting you to take their photograph...ignore them.
- Beware of gangs of kids – whether dishevelled or well dressed – demanding attention, who may be trying to pickpocket you or overtly rob you.
- Pickpockets are most active in dense crowds, especially in busy train stations and on public transport during peak hours.

Smoking

Cigarette-smoking bans have been progressively introduced across Europe. Although outdoor seating has long been a tradition at European cafes, it's gained new popularity given that most Western European countries have banned smoking in public places, including restaurants and bars. Almost all hotel rooms are now non-smoking.

Telephone

Hotel phones notoriously have outrageous rates and hidden charges. Public phone booths have almost completely disappeared.

Mobile Phones

Travellers can easily purchase prepaid mobile phones (from £20/€30) or SIM cards (from £5/€10). GSM phones can be used throughout Western Europe. Mobile shops are everywhere.

You can bring your mobile phone from home and buy a local SIM card to enjoy cheap local calling rates if it is both unlocked and compatible with European GSM networks. Check first.

A great option is a **Toggle** (www.togglemobile.co.uk) multicountry SIM card. It allows you to have up to nine numbers in countries across much of Europe, allowing calls, text and data at local rates, plus you receive free incoming calls in some 20 countries. Purchase SIMs online or at certain phone

shops; topping up online is easy.

If you plan to use your mobile phone from home:

- Check international roaming rates in advance; often they are very expensive.
- Check roaming fees for data/internet usage; smartphone users can get socked with huge fees. You may be able to buy a data package to limit your costs.

Time

Greenwich Mean Time/UTC Britain, Ireland, Portugal, Canary Islands (Spain)

Central European Time (GMT/UTC plus one hour) Austria, Belgium, France, Germany, Italy, Luxembourg, the Netherlands, Spain (except Canary Islands), Switzerland

Eastern European Time (GMT/UTC plus two hours) Greece

Daylight Saving Time/Summer Time Last Sunday in March to the last Sunday in October

Tourist Information

Tourist offices in Western Europe are common and almost universally helpful. They can help find accommodation, issue maps, advise on sights, activities, nightlife and entertainment while you're visiting, and help with more obscure queries such as where to find laundry facilities.

Official tourism authority websites:

Austria Austria.info (www.austria.info)

Belgium Visit Belgium (www.visitbelgium.com)

Britain Visit Britain (www.visitbritain.com)

France France.fr (uk.france.fr)

Germany Germany.travel (www.germany.travel)

Greece Visit Greece (www.visitgreece.gr)

Ireland Discover Ireland (www.discoverireland.ie)

Italy Italia (http://www.italia.it)

Luxembourg Visit Luxembourg (www.visitluxembourg.com)

The Netherlands Holland.com (www.holland.com)

Northern Ireland Discover Northern Ireland (www.discovernorthernireland.com)

Portugal Visit Portugal (www.visitportugal.com)

Spain Spain.info (www.spain.info)

Switzerland MySwitzerland.com (www.myswitzerland.com)

Visas

The Schengen Agreement (no passport controls at borders between member countries) applies to most areas; the UK and Ireland are exceptions.

Citizens of Australia, Canada, Japan, New Zealand and the USA don't need visas for tourist visits to the UK, Ireland or any Schengen country. With a valid passport you should be able to visit Western European countries for up to 90 days in a six-month period, provided you have some sort of onward or return ticket and/or 'sufficient means of support' (ie money).

Nationals of other countries (eg China and India) will need a Schengen visa, which is good for a maximum stay of 90 days in a six-month period. For those who do require visas, it's important to remember that these will have a 'use-by' date, and you'll be refused entry after that period has elapsed. It may not be checked when entering these countries overland, but major problems can arise if it is requested during your stay or on departure and you can't produce it.

Schengen Visa Rules

As per the Schengen Agreement, there are no passport controls at borders between the following countries:

- Austria
- Belgium
- Czech Republic
- Denmark
- Estonia
- Finland
- France
- Germany
- Greece
- Hungary
- Iceland
- Italy
- Latvia
- Liechtenstein
- Lithuania
- Luxembourg
- Malta
- The Netherlands
- Norway
- Poland
- Portugal
- Slovakia
- Slovenia
- Spain
- Sweden
- Switzerland

New EU members Bulgaria, Croatia, Cyprus and Romania are required to join the Schengen zone (expected by 2020).

Note that Ireland and the UK are outside the Schengen zone; they are part of the separate Common Travel Area border controls (along with the Bailiwick of Guernsey, Bailiwick of Jersey and Isle of Man).

Weights & Measures

The metric system is used throughout Western Europe. In the UK, however, nonmetric equivalents are common (distances continue to be given in miles and beer is sold in pints, not litres).

Transport

GETTING THERE & AWAY

The beginning of your Western European adventure is deciding how to travel here, and in these days of cutthroat competition among airlines there are plenty of opportunities to find cheap tickets to a variety of gateway cities.

Flights, cars and tours can be booked online at lonelyplanet.com/bookings.

Air

Western Europe is well served by just about every major airline in the world.

Major cities have at least one airport.

Key intercontinental hubs include Amsterdam (Schiphol Airport), Frankfurt (Frankfurt Airport), London (Heathrow), Paris (Charles de Gaulle) and Rome (Leonardo da Vinci aka Flumicino).

Land

You can easily get to Western Europe from the rest of Europe by road, bus or train. The further away you're coming from, however, the more complicated it can be.

Train

It's possible to get to Western Europe by train from central and eastern Asia, but count on spending at least eight days doing it.

Four different train lines wind their way to Moscow: the Trans-Siberian (9259km from Vladivostok), the Trans-Mongolian (7621km from Beijing) and the Trans-Manchurian (8986km from Beijing) all use the same tracks across Siberia but have different routes east of Lake Baikal, while the Trans-Kazakhstan (another Trans-Siberian line) runs between Moscow and Urumqi in northwestern China. Prices vary enormously depending on where you buy the ticket and what's included – advertised 2nd-class fares cost €720/£555 from Beijing to Moscow.

There are many travel options between Western Europe and Moscow as well as other Eastern European countries. Poland, the Czech Republic and Hungary have myriad rail links.

There are also rail links between Germany and Denmark with connections to other Scandinavian countries.

Sea

Ferries

Numerous ferries cross the Mediterranean between Africa and Western Europe. Options include Spain–Morocco, France–Morocco, France–Tunisia and Italy–Tunisia. There are also ferries between Greece and Israel via Cyprus. Ferries also serve Germany from all the Scandinavian countries.

Ferry Lines (www.ferrylines.com) is a useful resource for researching ferry routes and operators.

Passenger Ships

Cruise ships have occasional transatlantic crossings.

Cunard's *Queen Mary 2* (www.cunard.com) sails between New York, USA and Southampton, England several times a year; the trip takes seven days one-way. Prices start from €2158 for two people in a standard double cabin. Deals abound.

GETTING AROUND

Air

Discount airlines are revolutionising the way people cover long distances within Europe. However, trains can sometimes work out to be quicker, taking you directly between city centres rather than farther-flung airports, and are better for the environment.

Dozens of tiny airports across Europe now have airline services. For instance, a trip to Italy doesn't mean choosing between Milan and Rome, but rather scores of airports up and down the 'boot'.

It's possible to put together a practical itinerary that might bounce from London to the south of Spain to Italy to Amsterdam in a two-week period, all at an affordable price and avoiding endless train rides.

Airlines in Western Europe

Although many people first think of budget airlines when they consider a cheap ticket in Western Europe, you should compare all carriers, including established ones like British Airways and Lufthansa, which serve major airports close to main destinations. Deals crop up frequently.

Various websites compare fares across a range of airlines within Europe, including the following:

- www.cheapoair.com
- www.kayak.com
- www.skyscanner.net

Scores of smaller low-cost airlines serve Western Europe along with major budget airlines including the following:

Air Berlin (www.airberlin.com) Hubs in Germany; service across Europe.

easyJet (www.easyjet.com) Flies to major airports across Europe.

Eurowings (www.eurowings.com) Hubs in Germany; service across Europe.

Ryanair (www.ryanair.com) Flies to scores of destinations across Europe, but confirm your destination airport is not a deserted airfield out in the sticks.

Vueling (www.vueling.com) Serves a broad swath of Europe from its Spanish hubs.

> **DISCOUNT AIRLINES**
>
> With cheap fares come many caveats.
>
> - Some of the bare-bones airlines are just that – expect nonreclining seats and nonexistent legroom.
> - Baggage allowances are often minimal and extra baggage charges can be costly.
> - At some small airports, customer service may be nonexistent.
> - Convenience can be deceptive. If you really want to go to Carcassonne in the south of France, then getting a bargain-priced ticket from London will be a dream come true. But if you want to go to Frankfurt in Germany and buy a ticket to 'Frankfurt-Hahn', you will find yourself at a tiny airport 120km west of Frankfurt and almost two hours away by bus.
> - Beware of discount airline websites showing nonstop flights that are actually connections.

Bicycle

A tour of Western Europe by bike may seem daunting but it can be a fantastic way to travel.

Cycling UK (www.cyclinguk.org) Offers members an information service on all matters associated with cycling, including cycling conditions, detailed routes, itineraries and maps.

Bike Tours (www.biketours.com) Has details of self-guided tours.

Wearing a helmet is not always compulsory but is advised. A seasoned cyclist can average about 80km a day, but this depends on the terrain and how much you are carrying.

The key to a successful cycling trip is to travel light. What you carry should be determined by your destination and the type of trip you're taking. Even for the most basic trip, it's worth carrying the tools necessary for repairing a puncture. Bicycle shops are found everywhere, but you still might want to pack the following if you don't want to rely on others:

- Allen keys
- Spanners
- Spare brake and gear cables
- Spare spokes
- Strong adhesive tape

Hire

It's easy to hire bicycles in Western Europe and you can often negotiate good deals. Rental periods vary. Local tourist offices, hostels and hotels will have information on rental outlets. Occasionally you can drop off the bicycle at a different location so you don't have to double back on your route.

Urban bike-share schemes, where you check out a bike from one stand and return it to another after brief use, have taken off in cities and towns across Western Europe.

Purchase

For major cycling tours it's best to have a bike you're familiar with, so consider bringing your own rather than buying one on arrival. If you can't be bothered with the hassle of transporting it, there are plenty of places to buy bikes in Western Europe (shops sell them new and secondhand).

Transporting a Bicycle

Check with the airline for details of taking your bicycle with you on the plane before you buy your ticket as each one has a different policy.

Within Western Europe, bikes can often be taken on to a train with you (usually outside peak hours), subject to a small supplementary fee.

Boat

The main areas of ferry service for Western Europe travellers are between Ireland and the UK; Ireland and France; the UK and the Continent (especially France, but also Belgium, the Netherlands and Spain); and Italy and Greece.

Multiple ferry companies compete on the main ferry routes, and the resulting service is comprehensive but complicated.

- A ferry company can have a host of different prices for the same route, depending on the time of day or year, the validity of the ticket or the length of your vehicle.
- It's worth planning (and booking) ahead where possible as there may be special reductions on off-peak crossings and advance-purchase tickets.
- Most ferry companies adjust prices according to the level of demand (so-called 'fluid' or 'dynamic' pricing), so it may pay to offer alternative travel dates.
- Vehicle tickets generally include the driver and a full complement of passengers.
- You're usually denied access to your vehicle during the voyage.
- Rail-pass holders are entitled to discounts or free travel on some lines.
- Compare fares and routes using **Ferrysavers** (www.ferrysavers.com).

Bus

Buses are invariably cheaper but slower and much less comfortable than trains, and not as quick (or sometimes as cheap) as airlines. There are many services, however, and it's possible to travel extensive distances for less than €100.

Eurolines (www.eurolines.com) A consortium of bus companies operates under the name Eurolines. Its various affiliates offer many national and regional bus passes.

FlixBus (www.flixbus.com) New, rapidly expanding international bus company linking 900 destinations in 20 countries. On-board facilities include free wi-fi and plentiful power sockets.

Campervan

A popular way to tour Europe is to buy or rent a campervan. Campervans usually feature a fixed high-top or elevating roof and two to five bunk beds. Apart from the essential gas cooker, professional conversions may include a sink, a fridge and built-in cupboards. Prices and facilities vary considerably and it's certainly worth getting advice from a mechanic to see if you are being offered a fair price. Getting a mechanical check (costing from £40) is also a good idea.

London is the usual embarkation point. Good British websites to check for campervan purchases and rentals include the following.

Auto Trader (www.autotrader.co.uk)

Loot (http://loot.com)

Worldwide Motorhome Hire (www.worldwide-motorhome-hire.com)

Car

Travelling with your own vehicle allows increased flexibility and the option to get off the beaten track. Unfortunately, cars can be problematic in city centres when you have to negotiate one-way streets or find somewhere to park amid a confusing concrete jungle and a welter of expensive parking options.

Remember to never leave valuables in the vehicle.

Driving Licences

Proof of ownership of a private vehicle should always be carried (a Vehicle Registration Document for British-registered cars). An EU driving licence is acceptable for driving throughout Europe.

Many non-European driving licences are valid in Europe.

An International Driving Permit (IDP) is technically required in addition to a current driving licence for foreign drivers in some Western European countries (in practice, it's rare you'll be asked for it). Your national auto club can advise if you'll need one for the itinerary you

CLIMATE CHANGE & TRAVEL

Every form of transport that relies on carbon-based fuel generates CO_2, the main cause of human-induced climate change. Modern travel is dependent on aeroplanes, which might use less fuel per kilometre per person than most cars but travel much greater distances. The altitude at which aircraft emit gases (including CO_2) and particles also contributes to their climate change impact. Many websites offer 'carbon calculators' that allow people to estimate the carbon emissions generated by their journey and, for those who wish to do so, to offset the impact of the greenhouse gases emitted with contributions to portfolios of climate-friendly initiatives throughout the world. Lonely Planet offsets the carbon footprint of all staff and author travel.

plan to take and can sell you this multilingual document.

Fuel

Fuel prices can vary enormously from country to country (though it's always more expensive than in North America or Australia) and may bear little relation to the general cost of living. For fuel prices across the EU, visit **AA Ireland** (www.theaa.ie/aa/motoring-advice/petrol-prices.aspx).

Unleaded petrol and diesel are available across Western Europe. To reduce pollution, cities including Paris and London are planning to ban diesel vehicles from 2020.

Hire

Renting a vehicle is straightforward.

➡ All major international rental companies operate in Western Europe and will give you reliable service and a good standard of vehicle.

➡ Usually you will have the option of returning the car to a different outlet at the end of the rental period.

➡ Rates vary widely, but expect to pay between €25 and €70 per day, not including insurance. Prebook for the lowest rates – if you walk into an office and ask for a car on the spot, you will pay much more.

➡ For really good deals, prepay for your rental. Fly/drive combinations and other programs are worth looking into.

➡ It's imperative to understand exactly what is included in your rental agreement (collision waiver, unlimited mileage etc). Make sure you are covered with an adequate insurance policy.

➡ Check whether mileage is unlimited or whether you'll be charged for additional kilometres beyond a particular threshold – extra mileage can quickly add up.

➡ Less than 4% of European cars have automatic transmissions. If you don't want to drive a manual (stick-shift), you'll need to book much further ahead, and expect to pay more than double for the car.

➡ The minimum age to rent a vehicle is usually 21 or even 23, and you'll need a credit card.

➡ If you get a ticket from one of Europe's thousands of hidden speeding cameras, they will track you down through your rental company.

RENTAL BROKERS

Rental brokers (clearing houses) can be a lot cheaper than the major car-rental firms. Good companies to try include the following.

Auto Europe (www.autoeurope.com)

AutosAbroad (www.autosabroad.com)

Car Rentals.co.uk (www.carrentals.co.uk)

Holiday Autos Car Hire (www.holidayautos.com)

Kemwel (www.kemwel.com)

Insurance

Third-party motor insurance is compulsory in Europe if you are driving your own car (rental cars usually come with insurance). Most UK motor-insurance policies automatically provide this for EU countries. Get your insurer to issue a Green Card (which may cost extra), which is an internationally recognised proof of insurance, and check that it lists all the countries you intend to visit.

It's a good investment to take out a European motoring-assistance policy, such as the **AA** (www.theaa.com) Five Star Service or the **RAC** (www.rac.co.uk) European Motoring Assistance. Expect to pay about £85 for 14 days' cover, with a 10% discount for association members.

Non-Europeans might find it cheaper to arrange international coverage with their national motoring organisation before leaving home. Ask your motoring organisation for details about free services offered by affiliated organisations around Western Europe.

Every vehicle travelling across an international border should display a sticker (or number/licence plate) showing its country of registration. Car-rental/hire agencies usually ensure cars are properly equipped; if in doubt, ask.

Purchase

Britain is probably the best place to buy a vehicle as secondhand prices are good and, whether buying privately or from a dealer, if you're an English speaker the absence of language difficulties will help you establish what you are getting and what guarantees you can expect in the event of a breakdown.

Bear in mind that you will be getting a car with the steering wheel on the right-hand side in Britain, whereas in Continental Europe the steering wheel is on the left.

If you're driving a right-hand-drive car, by law you'll need adjust your headlamps to avoid blinding oncoming traffic.

Leasing

Leasing a vehicle involves fewer hassles and can work out much cheaper than hiring for longer than 17 days. This program is limited to certain new cars, including **Renault** (www.renault-eurodrive.com) and **Peugeot** (www.peugeot-openeurope.com), but you save money because short-term leasing is exempt from VAT and inclusive insurance plans are cheaper than daily insurance rates.

Leasing is also open to people as young as 18 years old. To lease a vehicle your permanent address must be outside the EU. The maximum lease is five-and-a-half months; it's possible to pick up the vehicle in one country

and return it in another. Leases include all on-road taxes as well as theft and collision insurance.

Road Conditions

Conditions and types of roads vary across Western Europe, but it is possible to make some generalisations.

➡ The fastest routes are four- or six-lane dual carriageways/highways, ie two or three lanes either side (motorway, autobahn, autoroute, autostrada etc).

➡ Motorways and other primary routes are great for speed and comfort but driving can be dull, with little or no interesting scenery.

➡ Some fast routes incur expensive tolls (eg in Italy, France and Spain) or have a general tax for usage (Switzerland and Austria), but there will usually be an alternative route you can take.

➡ Motorways and other primary routes are almost always in good condition.

➡ Road surfaces on minor routes are not perfect in some countries (eg Greece), although normally they will be more than adequate.

➡ Minor roads are narrower and progress is generally much slower. To compensate, you can expect much better scenery and plenty of interesting villages along the way.

Road Rules

➡ Automobile associations can supply members with country-by-country information about motoring regulations.

➡ With the exception of Britain and Ireland, driving is on the right-hand side of the road.

➡ Take care with speed limits, as they vary from country to country.

➡ You may be surprised at the apparent disregard of traffic regulations in some places (particularly in Italy and Greece), but as a visitor it is always best to be cautious.

➡ In many countries, driving infringements are subject to an on-the-spot fine; always ask for a receipt.

➡ European drink-driving laws are particularly strict. The blood-alcohol concentration (BAC) limit when driving is generally 0.05% but in certain cases it can be as low as 0%. The European Transport Safety Council (http://etsc.eu) lists the limits for each country.

➡ Some countries require compulsory in-car equipment, such as a portable breathalyser, warning triangle and fluorescent vest. These are supplied by rental companies, but you'll need to have them if you're driving your own vehicle.

➡ In Austria and Switzerland, motorists must buy a motorway tax sticker (*vignette* in German and French; *contrassegno* in Italian) to display on the windscreen. Buy *vignettes* in advance from motoring organisations or (in cash) at petrol stations, Austrian post offices and tobacconists at borders before crossing into the country.

Hitching

Hitching is never entirely safe in any country and we don't recommend it. Travellers who decide to hitch should understand they are taking a small but potentially serious risk. Key points to remember:

➡ Hitch in pairs; it will be safer.

➡ Solo women should never hitch.

➡ Don't hitch from city centres; take public transport to suburban exit routes.

➡ Hitching is usually illegal on motorways – stand on the slip roads or approach drivers at petrol stations and truck stops.

➡ Look presentable and cheerful, and make a cardboard sign indicating your intended destination in the local language.

➡ Never hitch where drivers can't stop in good time or without causing an obstruction.

➡ At dusk, give up and think about finding somewhere to stay.

➡ It is sometimes possible to arrange a lift in advance: scan student noticeboards in colleges or contact car-sharing agencies. Such agencies are particularly popular in Germany – visit www.blablacar.de.

Motorcycle

With its good-quality winding roads, stunning scenery and an active motorcycling scene, Western Europe is made for motorcycle touring.

➡ The weather is not always reliable, so make sure your wet-weather gear is up to scratch.

➡ Helmets are compulsory for riders and passengers everywhere in Western Europe.

➡ On ferries, motorcyclists can sometimes be squeezed on board without a reservation, although booking ahead is advisable during peak travelling periods.

➡ Take note of local customs about parking motorcycles on footpaths. Although this is illegal in some countries, the police often turn a blind eye as long as the vehicle doesn't obstruct pedestrians. Don't try this in Britain – excuses to traffic wardens will fall on deaf ears.

➡ If you're thinking of touring Europe on a motorcycle, contact the **British Motorcyclists Federation** (www.bmf.co.uk) for help and advice.

- Motorcycle and moped rental is easy in countries such as Italy, Spain and Greece and in the south of France. In tourist areas just ask around for nearby rental agencies.

Local Transport

Most Western European cities have excellent public-transport systems, which comprise some combination of metros (subways), trains, trams and buses. Service is usually comprehensive. Major airports generally have fast-train or metro links to the city centre.

Taxi

Taxis in Western Europe are metered and rates are generally high. There might also be supplements (depending on the country) for things such as luggage, the time of day, the location at which you boarded and for extra passengers.

Good public transport networks make the use of taxis almost unnecessary, but if you need one in a hurry they can usually be found idling near train stations or outside big hotels. Spain, Greece and Portugal have lower fares, which makes taking a taxi more viable.

Don't underestimate the local knowledge that can be gleaned from taxi drivers. They can often tell you about the liveliest places in town and know all about events happening during your stay.

Tours

A huge variety of tours – whether standard or tailor-made – are available.

Many people have had memorable trips on tours organised by cultural institutions such as the USA's **Smithsonian Institution** (www.smithsonianjourneys.org), which runs tours led by experts in fields such as art.

Boat

One of the biggest advantages of a liveaboard cruise is only having to unpack once.

CroisiEurope (www.croisieuroperivercruises.com) Cruises along Europe's great rivers and canals.

Viking Cruises (www.vikingcruises.com) European river cruises and Mediterranean ocean cruises.

Bus

Bus tours vary enormously in price and corresponding comfort of nightly accommodation, from camping and hostels through to luxury hotels.

Globus Journeys (www.globusjourneys.com) runs budget bus tours for all ages covering Western Europe's most famous attractions.

Contiki (www.contiki.com) caters specifically for travellers aged 18 to 35. Expect a party atmosphere.

Insight Vacations (www.insightvacations.com) operates tours at the high end of the market, attracting an older clientele.

Cycling

Western Europe covers a vast area so multicountry cycling tours are rare; most tours stick to a particular country or region. The website www.biketours.com lists hundreds of options throughout Western Europe.

Train

Escorted rail tours of Western Europe are another way to discover the region. The excellent website **Man in Seat 61** (www.seat61.com) recommends several options.

Great Rail (www.greatrail.com) offers a range of guided itineraries.

Train

Trains are an ideal way of getting around: they are comfortable, frequent and generally on time. The Channel Tunnel makes it possible to get from Britain to continental Europe using **Eurostar** (www.eurostar.com).

These days, Western Europe's fast, modern trains are like much-more-comfortable versions of planes. Dining cars have mostly been replaced by snack bars or trolleys, although most people buy food before boarding.

Information

Every national railway has a website with a vast amount of schedule and fare information.

- Major national railway companies' smartphone apps are excellent for checking schedules. Many can be used to store tickets bought online. Instead of having to print electronic tickets, the conductor can scan your phone's screen.
- **DB Bahn** (www.bahn.de) provides excellent schedule and fare information in English for trains across Europe.
- **Man In Seat Sixty-One** (www.seat61.com) has invaluable train descriptions and comprehensive practical details of journeys to the far reaches of the continent.
- If you plan to travel extensively by train, the **European Rail Timetable** (www.europeantimetable.eu), issued by Thomas Cook for 140 years and now produced independently, gives a condensed listing of train schedules that indicate where extra fees apply or where reservations are necessary. The timetable is updated monthly and is available online and at selected European bookshops.

Tickets

Normal international tickets are valid for two months and you can make as many stops as you like en route. Used this way, a ticket from Paris to Vienna, for example, can

serve as a mini-rail pass, as long as you stay on the route shown on the ticket.

High-Speed Trains

High-speed networks (300km/h or more) continue to expand and have given the airlines major competition on many routes.

Sample travel times:

ROUTE	DURATION
Amsterdam–Paris	3¼hr
Barcelona–Madrid	2½hr
Brussels–Cologne	1¾hr
London–Paris	2¼hr
Milan–Rome	3hr
Nuremberg–Munich	1¼hr
Paris–Frankfurt	4hr
Paris–Marseille	3hr
Zürich–Milan	3¾hr

Major high-speed trains that cross borders include the following:

Eurostar (www.eurostar.com) Links beautiful St Pancras station in London to Brussels and Paris in about two hours; direct services also include London to Marseille via Lyon and Avignon. From late 2017, direct Eurostar services will link London with Amsterdam via Brussels, Antwerp, Rotterdam and Schiphol Airport.

ICE (www.bahn.de) The fast trains of the German railways span the country and extend to Paris, Brussels, Amsterdam, Vienna and Switzerland.

TGV (www.sncf.com) The legendary fast trains of France reach Belgium, Luxembourg, Germany, Switzerland and Italy.

Thalys (www.thalys.com) Links Paris with Brussels, Amsterdam and Cologne.

Other Trains

NIGHT TRAINS

The romantic image of the European night train is disappearing with the popularity of budget airlines and budget constraints.

Night trains still in service include the following:

Caledonian Sleeper (www.scotrail.co.uk) Links London overnight with Scotland (as far north as Inverness and Aberdeen).

Thello (www.thello.com) Runs services between France and Italy.

Trenhotel (www.renfe.com) Services include Madrid–Lisbon.

ÖBB Nightjet (www.oebb.at) Routes include Vienna–Rome, Hamburg–Zürich and Munich–Milan.

EXPRESS TRAINS

Slower but still reasonably fast trains that cross borders are often called EuroCity (EC) or InterCity (IC). Reaching speeds of up to 200km/h or more, they are comfortable and frequent. A good example is Austria's RailJet service, which reaches Munich and Zurich.

Reservations

At weekends and during holidays and summer, it's a good idea to reserve seats on trains (which costs about €3 to €5). Standing at the end of the car for five hours is not what holiday dreams are made of, especially if you're travelling with kids or have reduced mobility. Some discounted tickets bought online may include an assigned seat on a train, but most regular tickets are good for any train on the route.

You can usually reserve ahead of time using a ticket machine at stations or at a ticket window. On many high-speed trains – such as France's TGVs – reservations are mandatory.

Pass-holders should note that reservations are a good idea for the same reasons. Just because your pricey pass lets you hop-on/hop-off at will, there's no guarantee that you'll have a seat.

Train Passes

Think carefully about purchasing a rail pass. Check the national railways' websites and determine what it would cost to do your trip by buying the tickets separately. More often than not, you'll find that

DISCOUNT TRAIN TICKETS ONLINE

Many railways offer cheap ticket deals through their websites. It's always worth checking online for sales including advance-purchase reductions, one-off promotions and special circular-route tickets.

How you actually receive the discount train tickets you've purchased online varies. Common methods include the following:

- The ticket is sent to the passenger either as an email or as a stored graphic on an app from the train company (increasingly widespread).
- A reservation number is issued with the reservation which you use at a station ticket-vending machine (some UK lines).
- The credit card you used to purchase the tickets can be used to retrieve them at a station ticket-vending machine (in some cases, nonlocal credit-card holders must retrieve their tickets at a ticket window).
- If nonlocal credit cards aren't accepted online and you can't buy the discounted fares at the station (the Netherlands), purchase them online from **SNCB Europe** (www.b-europe.com) instead.

you'll spend less than if you buy a Eurail pass.

Shop around as pass prices can vary between different outlets. Once purchased, take care of your pass as it cannot be replaced or refunded if lost or stolen. Passes get reductions on the Eurostar through the Channel Tunnel and on certain ferry routes (eg between France and Ireland). In the USA, **Rail Europe** (www.raileurope.com) sells a variety of rail passes, as does its UK equivalent **Voyages-sncf.com** (http://uk.voyages-sncf.com); note that individual train tickets tend to be more expensive than what you'll pay buying from railways online or in stations.

EURAIL & HIGH-SPEED TRAINS

Eurail likes to promote the 'hop-on/hop-off any train' aspect of their passes. But when it comes to the most desirable high-speed trains this is not always the case. Many require a seat reservation and the catch is that these are not always available to pass holders on all trains.

In addition, some of the high-speed services require a fairly hefty surcharge from pass users. For example, Thalys trains from Brussels to Amsterdam incur a 1st-/2nd-class surcharge of €25/15; German ICE trains from Paris to Munich incur a surcharge of €30/13; Spanish AVE trains from Barcelona to Lyon have a surcharge of €20/18.

On some high-speed routes it may work out cheaper to buy a separate ticket rather than use your pass, especially if you can find a discount fare.

EURAIL

There are so many different **Eurail** (www.eurail.com) passes to choose from and such a wide variety of areas and time periods covered that you need to have a good idea of your itinerary before purchasing one. These passes can only be bought by residents of non-European countries and are supposed to be purchased before arriving in Europe but they can be delivered to a European address. There are two options: one for adults, one for people aged under 26. The Adult Pass is valid in both 1st- and 2nd-class coaches; a 1st-class Youth Pass is valid in both 1st- and 2nd-class coaches but the 2nd-class Youth Pass is only for 2nd-class coaches.

Eurail passes are valid for unlimited travel on national railways and some private lines in the Western European countries of Austria, Belgium, France, Germany, Greece, Ireland, Italy, Luxembourg, the Netherlands, Portugal, Spain and Switzerland (including Liechtenstein), plus several more neighbouring ones. They are also valid on some ferries between Italy and Greece. Reductions are given on some other ferry routes and on river/lake steamer services in various countries and on the Eurostar to/from the UK.

The UK is *not* covered by Eurail – it has its own Britrail pass.

Pass types include the following:

Eurail Global All the European countries (despite the much grander-sounding name) for a set number of consecutive days.

Eurail Saver Two to five people travelling together as a group for the entire trip can save about 15% on various pass types.

Eurail Selectpass Buyers choose which neighbouring countries it covers and for how long. Options are myriad and can offer significant savings over the other passes if, for example, you are only going to three or four countries. Use the Eurail website to calculate these.

INTERRAIL

The **InterRail** (www.interrail.eu) pass is available to European residents of more than six months' standing (passport identification is required), as well as citizens of Russia and Turkey. Terms and conditions vary slightly from country to country, but in the country of origin there is a discount of around 30% to 50% on the normal fares. The pass covers 30 countries.

InterRail passes are generally cheaper than Eurail, but most high-speed trains require that you also buy a seat reservation and pay a supplement of €3 to €40 depending on the route.

InterRail passes are also available for individual countries. Compare these to passes offered by the national railways.

NATIONAL RAIL PASSES

If you're intending to travel extensively within one country, check what national rail passes are available as these can sometimes save you a lot of money. In a large country such as Germany where you might be covering long distances, a pass can make sense, whereas in a small country such as the Netherlands it won't.

Language

This chapter offers basic vocabulary to help you get around Western Europe. If you read our coloured pronunciation guides as if they were English, you'll be understood.

Note that, in our pronunciation guides, the stressed syllables are indicated with italics. The abbreviations 'm' and 'f' indicate masculine and feminine gender respectively.

DUTCH

Dutch is spoken in The Netherlands and the northern part of Belgium (Flanders).

Vowels in Dutch can be long or short. Note that ew is pronounced as 'ee' with rounded lips, oh as the 'o' in 'note', uh as the 'a' in 'ago', and kh as the 'ch' in the Scottish *loch* (harsh and throaty).

Hello.	*Dag.*	dakh
Goodbye.	*Dag.*	dakh
Please.	*Alstublieft.*	al·stew·*bleeft*
Thank you.	*Dank u.*	dangk ew
Excuse me.	*Pardon.*	par·*don*
Sorry.	*Sorry.*	*so*·ree
Yes./No.	*Ja./Nee.*	yaa/ney
Help!	*Help!*	help
Cheers!	*Proost!*	prohst

Do you speak English?
Spreekt u Engels? — spreykt ew *eng*·uhls

I don't understand.
Ik begrijp het niet. — ik buh·*khreyp* huht neet

WANT MORE?

For in-depth language information and handy phrases, check out Lonely Planet's *Western Europe Phrasebook*. You'll find it at **shop.lonelyplanet.com**, or you can buy Lonely Planet's iPhone phrasebooks at the Apple App Store.

How much is it?
Hoeveel kost het? — hoo·*veyl* kost huht

Where's ...?
Waar is ...? — waar is ...

Can you show me (on the map)?
Kunt u het aanwijzen (op de kaart)? — kunt ew huht *aan*·wey·zuhn (op duh kaart)

I'm lost.
Ik ben de weg kwijt. — ik ben duh wekh kweyt

I'm ill.
Ik ben ziek. — ik ben zeek

Where are the toilets?
Waar zijn de toiletten? — waar zeyn duh twa·*le*·tuhn

FRENCH

French is spoken in France, Switzerland, Luxembourg and the southern part of Belgium (Wallonia).

French has nasal vowels (pronounced as if you're trying to force the sound through your nose), which are indicated in our guides with o or u followed by an almost inaudible nasal consonant sound m, n or ng. Note also that air is pronounced as in 'fair', ew as ee with rounded lips, r is a throaty sound, and zh is pronounced as the 's' in 'pleasure'. Syllables in French words are, for the most part, equally stressed.

Hello.	*Bonjour.*	bon·zhoor
Goodbye.	*Au revoir.*	o·rer·vwa
Please.	*S'il vous plaît.*	seel voo play
Thank you.	*Merci.*	mair·see
Excuse me.	*Excusez-moi.*	ek·skew·zay·mwa
Sorry.	*Pardon.*	par·don
Yes./No.	*Oui./Non.*	wee/non
Help!	*Au secours!*	o skoor
Cheers!	*Santé!*	son·tay

Do you speak English?
Parlez-vous anglais? par·lay·voo ong·glay

I don't understand.
Je ne comprends pas. zher ner kom·pron pa

How much is it?
C'est combien? say kom·byun

Where's ...?
Où est ...? oo ay ...

Can you show me (on the map)?
Pouvez-vous m'indiquer (sur la carte)? poo·vay·voo mun·dee·kay (sewr la kart)

I'm lost.
Je suis perdu/ perdue. (m/f) zher swee pair·dew

I'm ill.
Je suis malade. zher swee ma·lad

Where are the toilets?
Où sont les toilettes? oo son ley twa·let

GERMAN

The language of Germany, Austria and Liechtenstein also has official status, and is spoken in Switzerland, Luxembourg and Belgium.

Vowels in German can be short or long. Note that air is pronounced as in 'fair', aw as in 'saw', eu as the 'u' in 'nurse', ew as ee with rounded lips, ow as in 'now', kh as the 'ch' in the Scottish *loch* (pronounced at the back of the throat), and r is also a throaty sound.

Hello.		
(in general)	*Guten Tag.*	*goo*·ten taak
(Austria)	*Servus.*	*zer*·vus
(Switzerland)	*Grüezi.*	*grew*·e·tsi
Goodbye.	*Auf Wiedersehen.*	owf *vee*·der·zey·en
Please.	*Bitte.*	*bi*·te
Thank you.	*Danke.*	*dang*·ke
Excuse me.	*Entschuldigung.*	ent·*shul*·di·gung
Sorry.	*Entschuldigung.*	ent·*shul*·di·gung
Yes./No.	*Ja./Nein.*	yaa/nain
Help!	*Hilfe!*	*hil*·fe
Cheers!	*Prost!*	prawst

Do you speak English?
Sprechen Sie Englisch? *shpre*·khen zee *eng*·lish

I don't understand.
Ich verstehe nicht. ikh fer·*shtey*·e nikht

How much is it?
Wie viel kostet das? vee feel *kos*·tet das

Where's ...?
Wo ist ...? vaw ist ...

Can you show me (on the map)?
Können Sie es mir (auf der Karte) zeigen? *keu*·nen zee es meer (owf dair *kar*·te) *tsai*·gen

I'm lost.
Ich habe mich verirrt. ikh *haa*·be mikh fer·*irt*

I'm ill.
Ich bin krank. ikh bin krangk

Where are the toilets?
Wo ist die Toilette? vo ist dee to·a·*le*·te

GREEK

Greek is the language of mainland Greece and its islands (as well as a co-official language of Cyprus).

Note that dh is pronounced as the 'th' in 'that', and that gh and kh are both throaty sounds, similar to the 'ch' in the Scottish *loch*.

Hello.	Γεια σου.	yia su
Goodbye.	Αντίο.	a·*di*·o
Please.	Παρακαλώ.	pa·ra·ka·*lo*
Thank you.	Ευχαριστώ.	ef·kha·ri·*sto*
Excuse me.	Με συγχωρείτε.	me sing·kho·*ri*·te
Sorry.	Συγνώμη.	si·*ghno*·mi
Yes./No.	Ναι./Οχι.	ne/*o*·hi
Help!	Βοήθεια!	vo·*i*·thia
Cheers!	Στην υγειά μας!	stin i·*yia* mas

Do you speak English?
Μιλάς Αγγλικά; mi·*las* ang·gli·*ka*

I don't understand.
Δεν καταλαβαίνω. dhen ka·ta·la·*ve*·no

How much is it?
Πόσο κάνει; *po*·so *ka*·ni

Where's ...?
Που είναι ...; pu *i*·ne ...

Can you show me (on the map)?
Μπορείς να μου δείξεις (στο χάρτη); bo·*ris* na mu *dhik*·sis (sto *khar*·ti)

I'm lost.
Εχω χαθεί. e·kho kha·*thi*

I'm ill.
Ειμαι άρρωστος/ άρρωστη. (m/f) i·*me* *a*·ro·stos/ *a*·ro·sti

Where are the toilets?
Που είναι η τουαλέτα; pu *i*·ne i tu·a·*le*·ta

ITALIAN

The language of Italy also has official status – and is spoken – in Switzerland.

Italian vowel are generally shorter than those in English. The consonants sometimes have a stronger, more emphatic pronunciation – if the word is written with a double consonant, pronounce them stronger. Note that r is rolled and stronger than in English.

Hello.	*Buongiorno.*	bwon·*jor*·no
Goodbye.	*Arrivederci.*	a·ree·ve·*der*·chee
Please.	*Per favore.*	per fa·*vo*·re
Thank you.	*Grazie.*	*gra*·tsye
Excuse me.	*Mi scusi.*	mee *skoo*·zee
Sorry.	*Mi dispiace.*	mee dees·*pya*·che
Yes./No.	*Sì./No.*	see/no
Help!	*Aiuto!*	ai·*yoo*·to
Cheers!	*Salute!*	sa·*loo*·te

Do you speak English?
Parla inglese? par·la een·*gle*·ze

I don't understand.
Non capisco. non ka·*pee*·sko

How much is it?
Quant'è? kwan·*te*

Where's ... ?
Dov'è ... ? do·*ve* ...

Can you show me (on the map)?
Può mostrarmi (sulla pianta)? pwo mos·*trar*·mee (*soo*·la *pyan*·ta)

I'm lost.
Mi sono perso/a. (m/f) mee *so*·no *per*·so/a

I'm ill.
Mi sento male. mee *sen*·to *ma*·le

Where are the toilets?
Dove sono i gabinetti? *do*·ve *so*·no ee ga·bee·*ne*·tee

PORTUGUESE

Most vowel sounds in Portugal's language have a nasal version (ie pronounced as if you're trying to force the sound through your nose), which is indicated in our pronunciation guides with ng after the vowel. Note also that oh is pronounced as the 'o' in 'note', ow as in 'how', and rr is a throaty sound.

Hello.	*Olá.*	o·*laa*
Goodbye.	*Adeus.*	a·de·*oosh*
Please.	*Por favor.*	poor fa·*vor*
Thank you.	*Obrigado.* (m) *Obrigada.* (f)	o·bree·*gaa*·doo o·bree·*gaa*·da
Excuse me.	*Faz favor.*	faash fa·*vor*
Sorry.	*Desculpe.*	desh·*kool*·pe
Yes./No.	*Sim./Não.*	seeng/nowng
Help!	*Socorro!*	soo·*ko*·rroo
Cheers!	*Saúde!*	sa·oo·de

Do you speak English?
Fala inglês? *faa*·la eeng·*glesh*

I don't understand.
Não entendo. nowng eng·*teng*·doo

How much is it?
Quanto custa? *kwang*·too *koosh*·ta

Where's ...?
Onde é ...? *ong*·de e ...

Can you show me (on the map)?
Pode-me mostrar (no mapa)? *po*·de·me moosh·*traar* (noo *maa*·pa)

I'm lost.
Estou perdido/perdida. (m/f) shtoh per·*dee*·doo/per·*dee*·da

I'm ill.
Estou doente. shtoh doo·*eng*·te

Where are the toilets?
Onde é a casa de banho? *ong*·de e a *kaa*·za de *ba*·nyoo

SPANISH

Spanish is the main language of Spain. Spanish vowels are generally pronounced short. Note that r is rolled and stronger than in English, and v is pronounced as a soft 'b'.

Hello.	*Hola.*	o·la
Goodbye.	*Adiós.*	a·*dyos*
Please.	*Por favor.*	por fa·*vor*
Thank you.	*Gracias.*	*gra*·thyas
Excuse me.	*Perdón.*	per·*don*
Sorry.	*Lo siento.*	lo *syen*·to
Yes./No.	*Sí./No.*	see/no
Cheers!	*¡Salud!*	sa·*loo*
Help!	*¡Socorro!*	so·*ko*·ro

Do you speak English?
¿Habla/Hablas inglés? (pol/inf) *a*·bla/*a*·blas een·*gles*

I don't understand.
Yo no entiendo. yo no en·*tyen*·do

How much is it?
¿Cuánto cuesta? *kwan*·to *kwes*·ta

Where's ...?
¿Dónde está ...? *don*·de es·*ta* ...

Can you show me (on the map)?
¿Me lo puede indicar (en el mapa)? me lo *pwe*·de een·dee·*kar* (en el *ma*·pa)

I'm lost.
Estoy perdido/a. (m/f) es·*toy* per·*dee*·do/a

I'm ill.
Estoy enfermo/a. (m/f) es·*toy* en·*fer*·mo/a

Where are the toilets?
¿Dónde están los servicios? *don*·de es·*tan* los ser·*vee*·thyos

Behind the Scenes

SEND US YOUR FEEDBACK

We love to hear from travellers – your comments keep us on our toes and help make our books better. Our well-travelled team reads every word on what you loved or loathed about this book. Although we cannot reply individually to your submissions, we always guarantee that your feedback goes straight to the appropriate authors, in time for the next edition. Each person who sends us information is thanked in the next edition – the most useful submissions are rewarded with a selection of digital PDF chapters.

Visit **lonelyplanet.com/contact** to submit your updates and suggestions or to ask for help. Our award-winning website also features inspirational travel stories, news and discussions.

Note: We may edit, reproduce and incorporate your comments in Lonely Planet products such as guidebooks, websites and digital products, so let us know if you don't want your comments reproduced or your name acknowledged. For a copy of our privacy policy visit lonelyplanet.com/privacy.

OUR READERS

Many thanks to the travellers who used the last edition and wrote to us with helpful hints, useful advice and interesting anecdotes: Adrienne Nielsen, Max Dickinson, Stella Italiano, Yeonghoon Kim

WRITER THANKS

Catherine Le Nevez

Merci mille fois first and foremost to Julian, and to everyone throughout Western Europe who has provided insights and inspiration over the years. Huge thanks also to Destination Editor Daniel Fahey and everyone at LP. As ever, a heartfelt *merci encore* to my parents, brother, belle-sœur and neveu for sustaining my love of Western Europe.

ACKNOWLEDGEMENTS

Climate map data adapted from Peel MC, Finlayson BL & McMahon TA (2007) 'Updated World Map of the Köppen-Geiger Climate Classification', *Hydrology and Earth System Sciences*, 11, 163344.

Cover photograph: Hand of Constantine the Great statue, Capitoline Museums, Rome. Stefano Politi Markovina / AWL ©

THIS BOOK

This 13th edition of Lonely Planet's *Western Europe* guidebook was curated by Oliver Berry, Gregor Clark, Marc Di Duca, Duncan Garwood, Catherine Le Nevez, Korina Miller, John Noble, Andrea Schulte-Peevers, Andy Symington, Donna Wheeler, Neil Wilson and Karla Zimmerman. This guidebook was produced by the following:

Destination Editors Daniel Fahey, Gemma Graham, Lauren Keith, James Smart, Tom Stainer, Anna Tyler

Product Editors Anne Mason, Jenna Myers

Senior Cartographer Mark Griffiths

Book Designer Mazzy Prinsep

Assisting Editors Janet Austin, Sarah Bailey, Michelle Bennett, Kate Chapman, Katie Connolly, Melanie Dankel, Bruce Evans, Carly Hall, Trent Holden, Kate James, Amy Karafin, Kellie Langdon, Sam Forge, Jodie Martire, Anne Mulvaney, Rosie Nicholson, Lauren O'Connell, Kristin Odijk, Charlotte Orr, Sarah Reid, Gabbi Stefanos, Saralinda Turner, Fionnuala Twomey

Assisting Cartographer Valentina Kremenchutskaya

Cover Researcher Naomi Parker

Thanks to Cheree Broughton, Jennifer Carey, David Carroll, Kate Chapman, Neill Coen, Daniel Corbett, Joel Cotterell, Shona Gray, Jane Grisman, Andi Jones, Ivan Kovanovic, Catherine Naghten, Claire Naylor, Karyn Noble, Martine Power, Rachel Rawling, Kirsten Rawlings, Kathryn Rowan, Ellie Simpson, Tony Wheeler, Dora Whitaker

Index

Map Pages **000**
Photo Pages **000**

C

Map Pages **000**
Photo Pages **000**

D

E

Map Pages **000**
Photo Pages **000**

S

Map Pages **000**
Photo Pages **000**

T

U

V

W

Y

Z

Map Legend

Sights

- Beach
- Bird Sanctuary
- Buddhist
- Castle/Palace
- Christian
- Confucian
- Hindu
- Islamic
- Jain
- Jewish
- Monument
- Museum/Gallery/Historic Building
- Ruin
- Shinto
- Sikh
- Taoist
- Winery/Vineyard
- Zoo/Wildlife Sanctuary
- Other Sight

Activities, Courses & Tours

- Bodysurfing
- Diving
- Canoeing/Kayaking
- Course/Tour
- Sento Hot Baths/Onsen
- Skiing
- Snorkelling
- Surfing
- Swimming/Pool
- Walking
- Windsurfing
- Other Activity

Sleeping

- Sleeping
- Camping

Eating

- Eating

Drinking & Nightlife

- Drinking & Nightlife
- Cafe

Entertainment

- Entertainment

Shopping

- Shopping

Information

- Bank
- Embassy/Consulate
- Hospital/Medical
- Internet
- Police
- Post Office
- Telephone
- Toilet
- Tourist Information
- Other Information

Geographic

- Beach
- Gate
- Hut/Shelter
- Lighthouse
- Lookout
- Mountain/Volcano
- Oasis
- Park
- Pass
- Picnic Area
- Waterfall

Population

- Capital (National)
- Capital (State/Province)
- City/Large Town
- Town/Village

Transport

- Airport
- Border crossing
- Bus
- Cable car/Funicular
- Cycling
- Ferry
- Metro station
- Monorail
- Parking
- Petrol station
- S-Bahn/Subway station
- Taxi
- T-bane/Tunnelbana station
- Train station/Railway
- Tram
- Tube station
- U-Bahn/Underground station
- Other Transport

Note: Not all symbols displayed above appear on the maps in this book

Routes

- Tollway
- Freeway
- Primary
- Secondary
- Tertiary
- Lane
- Unsealed road
- Road under construction
- Plaza/Mall
- Steps
- Tunnel
- Pedestrian overpass
- Walking Tour
- Walking Tour detour
- Path/Walking Trail

Boundaries

- International
- State/Province
- Disputed
- Regional/Suburb
- Marine Park
- Cliff
- Wall

Hydrography

- River, Creek
- Intermittent River
- Canal
- Water
- Dry/Salt/Intermittent Lake
- Reef

Areas

- Airport/Runway
- Beach/Desert
- Cemetery (Christian)
- Cemetery (Other)
- Glacier
- Mudflat
- Park/Forest
- Sight (Building)
- Sportsground
- Swamp/Mangrove

Donna Wheeler

Austria Donna has written guidebooks for Lonely Planet for ten years, including the Italy, Norway, Belgium, Africa, Tunisia, Algeria, France, Austria and Melbourne titles. She is the author of Paris Precincts, a curated photographic guide to the city's best bars, restaurants and shops and is reporter for Italian contemporary art publisher My Art Guides. Donna's work on contemporary art, architecture and design, food, wine, wilderness areas and cultural history also can be found in a variety of other publications. She became a travel writer after various careers as a commissioning editor, creative director, digital producer and content strategist.

Neil Wilson

Britain & Ireland Neil was born in Scotland and has lived there most of his life. Based in Perthshire, he has been a full-time writer since 1988, working on more than 80 guidebooks for various publishers, including the Lonely Planet guides to Scotland, England, Ireland and Prague. An outdoors enthusiast since childhood, Neil is an active hill-walker, mountain-biker, sailor, snowboarder, fly-fisher and rock-climber, and has climbed and tramped in four continents, including ascents of Jebel Toubkal in Morocco, Mount Kinabalu in Borneo, the Old Man of Hoy in Scotland's Orkney Islands and the Northwest Face of Half Dome in California's Yosemite Valley.

Karla Zimmerman

The Netherlands Karla lives in Chicago, where she eat doughnuts, yells at the Cubs, and writes stuff for books, magazines, and websites when she's not doing the first two things. She has contributed to 40-plus guidebooks and travel anthologies covering destinations in Europe, Asia, Africa, North America, and the Caribbean – all of which are a long way from the early days, when she wrote about gravel for a construction magazine and got to trek to places like Fredonia, Kansas. To learn more, follow her on Instagram and Twitter (@karlazimmerman).

Contributing Writers & Researchers

Kate Armstrong (Portugal)
Jean-Bernard Carrillet (France)
Kerry Christiani (France)
Fionn Davenport (Britain & Ireland)
Belinda Dixon (Britain)
Peter Dragicevich (Britain)
Damian Harper (Britain & Ireland)
Anita Isalska (France)
Anja Mutić (Portugal)
Hugh McNaughtan (Britain & France)
Isabella Noble (Britain)
Christopher Pitts (France)
Daniel Robinson (France)
Regis St Louis (Portugal & France)
Ryan Ver Berkmoes (Ireland)
Nicola Williams (France)

Catherine Le Nevez

Austria, Britain, France, Ireland & The Netherlands Catherine's wanderlust kicked in when she roadtripped across Europe from her Parisian base aged four, and she's been hitting the road at every opportunity since, travelling to around 60 countries and completing her Doctorate of Creative Arts in Writing, Masters in Professional Writing, and postgrad qualifications in Editing and Publishing along the way. Over the past dozen-plus years she's written scores of Lonely Planet guides and articles covering Paris, France, Europe and far beyond. Her work has also appeared in numerous online and print publications. Topping Catherine's list of travel tips is to travel without any expectations.

Korina Miller

Greece Korina first ventured to Greece as a backpacking teenager, sleeping on ferry decks and hiking in the mountains. Since then, she's found herself drawn back to soak up the timelessness of the old towns and drink coffee with locals in seaside *kafeneio*. Korina grew up on Vancouver Island and has been exploring the globe independently since she was 16, visiting or living in 36 countries and picking up a degree in Communications and Canadian Studies and an MA in Migration Studies en route. Korina has written nearly 40 titles for Lonely Planet and also works as a children's writing coach.

John Noble

Spain John has been travelling since his teens and doing so as a Lonely Planet writer since the 1980s. The number of LP titles he's written or co-written is well into three figures, covering a somewhat random selection of countries scattered across the globe, predominantly ones where Spanish, Russian or English are spoken (usually alongside numerous local languages). He still gets as excited as ever about heading out on the road to unfamiliar experiences, people and destinations, especially remote, off-the-beaten-track ones. Above all, he loves mountains, from the English Lake District to the Himalaya. See his pics on Instagram: @johnnoble11.

Josephine Quintero

Spain Josephine first got her taste of not-so-serious travel when she slung a guitar on her back and travelled in Europe in the early 70s. She eventually reached Greece and caught a ferry to Israel where she embraced kibbutz life and the Mexican-American she was to subsequently wed. Josephine primarily covers Spain and Italy for Lonely Planet.

Andrea Schulte-Peevers

Germany Born and raised in Germany and educated in London and at UCLA, Andrea has travelled the distance to the moon and back in her visits to some 75 countries. She has earned her living as a professional travel writer for over two decades and authored or contributed to nearly 100 Lonely Planet titles as well as to newspapers, magazines and websites around the world. She also works as a travel consultant, translator and editor. Andrea's destination expertise is especially strong when it comes to Germany, Dubai and the UAE, Crete and the Caribbean Islands. She makes her home in Berlin.

Andy Symington

Belgium & Luxembourg, Britain & Portugal Andy has written or worked on over a hundred books and other updates for Lonely Planet (especially in Europe and Latin America) and other publishing companies, and has published articles on numerous subjects for a variety of newspapers, magazines, and websites. He part-owns and operates a rock bar, has written a novel and is currently working on several fiction and non-fiction writing projects. Andy, from Australia, moved to Northern Spain many years ago. When he's not off with a backpack in some far-flung corner of the world, he can probably be found watching the tragically poor local football side or tasting local wines after a long walk in the nearby mountains.

OUR STORY

A beat-up old car, a few dollars in the pocket and a sense of adventure. In 1972 that's all Tony and Maureen Wheeler needed for the trip of a lifetime – across Europe and Asia overland to Australia. It took several months, and at the end – broke but inspired – they sat at their kitchen table writing and stapling together their first travel guide, *Across Asia on the Cheap*. Within a week they'd sold 1500 copies. Lonely Planet was born.

Today, Lonely Planet has offices in Franklin, London, Melbourne, Oakland, Dublin, Beijing and Delhi, with more than 600 staff and writers. We share Tony's belief that 'a great guidebook should do three things: inform, educate and amuse'.

OUR WRITERS

Oliver Berry

Britain & France Oliver is a writer and photographer from Cornwall. He has worked for Lonely Planet for more than a decade, covering destinations from Cornwall to the Cook Islands, and has worked on more than 30 guidebooks. He is also a regular contributor to many newspapers and magazines, including *Lonely Planet Traveller*. His writing has won several awards, including The Guardian Young Travel Writer of the Year and the TNT Magazine People's Choice Award. His latest work is published at www.oliverberry.com.

Gregor Clark

France, Switzerland & Liechtenstein Gregor is a US based writer whose love of foreign languages and curiosity about what's around the next bend have taken him to dozens of countries on five continents. Chronic wanderlust has also led him to visit all 50 states and most Canadian provinces on countless road trips through his native North America. Since 2000, Gregor has regularly contributed to Lonely Planet guides, with a focus on Europe and the Americas.

Marc Di Duca

Britain, Germany & Portugal A travel author for the last decade, Marc has worked for Lonely Planet in Siberia, Slovakia, Bavaria, England, Ukraine, Austria, Poland, Croatia, Portugal, Madeira and on the Trans-Siberian Railway, as well as writing and updating tens of other guides for other publishers. When not on the road, Marc lives between Sandwich, Kent and Mariánské Lázně in the Czech Republic with his wife and two sons.

Duncan Garwood

Italy From facing fast bowlers in Barbados to sidestepping hungry pigs in Goa, Duncan's travels have thrown up many unique experiences. These days he largely dedicates himself to Italy, his adopted homeland where he's been living since 1997. From his base in the Castelli Romani hills outside Rome, he's clocked up endless kilometres exploring the country's well-known destinations and far-flung reaches, working on guides to Rome, Sardinia, Sicily, Piedmont, and Naples & the Amalfi Coast. Other LP titles include *Italy's Best Trips*, the *Food Lover's Guide to the World*, and *Pocket Bilbao & San Sebastian*. He also writes on Italy for newspapers, websites and magazines.

OVER PAGE MORE WRITERS

Published by Lonely Planet Global Limited
CRN 554153
13th edition – October 2017
ISBN 978 1 78657 147 2

10 9 8 7 6 5 4 3 2 1
Printed in China